3rd ed. 2012 available
& use this volume

Routledge Dictionary of Economics

Second edition

The most informative dictionary of economics available, the *Routledge Dictionary of Economics* avoids the tendency to indulge in long-winded definitions of the major concepts and provides students with a lucid, comprehensive and accurate guide to the discipline. Employing the key feature of further reading with many of the terms, the book uses the subject classification system defined by the *Journal of Economic Literature* and *The Economic Journal*.

There have been sweeping developments in economics in the decade since the appearance of the first edition of the dictionary and the new version reflects this by including a wealth of material on additional topics, including:

- economic anthropology
- Blairism
- endogenous growth theory
- French Circuit School
- output floor regulation
- predator–prey models.

The dictionary has been compiled for the needs of students and teachers of economics, finance, accountancy and business studies and should prove to be an invaluable resource.

Donald Rutherford is Lecturer in Economics and Associate Dean of the Faculty of Social Sciences at the University of Edinburgh.

Routledge Dictionary of Economics

Second edition

Donald Rutherford

London and New York

First published in 1992 as the *Dictionary of Economics*
Second edition published 2002
by Routledge
11 New Fetter Lane, London EC4P 4EE

Simultaneously published in the USA and Canada
by Routledge
29 West 35th Street, New York, NY 10001

Routledge is an imprint of the Taylor & Francis Group

Typeset in Times by Taylor & Francis Books Ltd
Printed and bound in Great Britain by MPG Books Ltd, Bodmin

British Library Cataloguing in Publication Data
A catalogue record for this book is available from the British
Library

Library of Congress Cataloging-in-Publication Data
A catalog record for this book has been requested

ISBN 0–415–25090–0 (hbk)
ISBN 0–415–25091–9 (pbk)

Contents

Preface to the first edition

Economics, the Queen of the Social Sciences, has now established itself as a major subject in dialogue with the physical sciences, law and the arts. There are few aspects of human behaviour that do not have an economic dimension and little of current affairs can be understood without a knowledge of economic principles. It is, therefore, not surprising that it is a major discipline in schools, colleges and universities throughout the world, studied by millions and the topic of conversation of millions more.

The *Routledge Dictionary of Economics* has as its concerns as many issues as the subject Economics now covers. The breadth can be appreciated by considering the subject classifications used by the *Journal of Economic Literature* (USA) and *The Economic Journal* (UK). The related specialties of economic history, commercial law, and econometric and statistical techniques are all within its ambit. However, to prevent a subject dictionary becoming encyclopedic, a lexicographer can follow the useful conventions of taking from sister disciplines only what is regularly used in mainstream economic literature. For example, from law, it is customary to emphasize competition, fiscal and banking law more than constitutional or criminal law. This interpretation of economics in the broad sense makes a dictionary of this kind more of a dictionary *for* economists, rather than a dictionary *of* economics with terms peculiar to the subject.

Even if a dictionary takes a broad view of its subject matter, it is usually addressed to a particular audience, such as first-year undergraduates. This is an approach that I have wanted to avoid, as there is a substantial heterogeneity of economics courses and students often need to research some areas of the subject in more depth than others. Also, it can be patronizing to the general reader to regard all of his or her knowledge to date as rudimentary. Even the reader of the daily newspapers who never looks at an economics textbook will encounter the most complex of ideas, chaos theory for example.

To produce a dictionary of this kind, I started with an assortment of basic textbooks and many current newspapers and journals. I soon discovered that about a thousand concepts are common to all the textbooks, for example notions of cost, economic systems and banking. From general textbooks I moved to a perusal of specialist books on the diverse divisions of the subject. The areas of economics encompassed obviously have to reflect current concerns; many environmental concepts are included and the 'male' character of many economics works has been partially avoided by including biographies of several leading female economists. Newspapers and journals provide a modern guide to current economic discourse. There is no foreseeable end to the creation of economic neologisms – major events such as the deregulation of financial markets and the political developments in Eastern Europe, which have changed the nature of many economies, have produced an expansion of new terms. Some terminology is ephemeral but many words that start as slang, such as 'yuppy', have a surprising longevity. I have taken the optimistic view that numerous catchwords and catchphrases will render linguistic service for many years.

The entries in this *Dictionary* are sequenced alphabetically letter by letter: for example, *discounted share price* precedes *discount house*, which precede *discounting*. The standard form for each item included begins with a headword followed by one or more single letter and number codes to indicate the branch or branches of economics that most frequently use that term. As it is important to ensure that all entries are immediately comprehensible and independent of the others, the text of each entry begins with a short definition before any discussion is included. Where related entries can profitably be read in conjunction, reference is made to them. Standard diagrams are included in the entries that require them. For the longer or more difficult entries, references to other works that either indicate the original use of that idea or provide a modern discussion of it are given.

A dictionary is a solace for the perplexed, a guide for the scholar and a map of a new terrain for the general reader. I hope that this *Routledge Dictionary of Economics* is all of these.

Preface to the second edition

Ten years have elapsed since the first edition of this *Dictionary*. The vocabulary of economics in the broadest sense has considerably grown. Many neologisms have sprung from continued changes in national economies, not least the innovations in financial markets and growing concerns about the environment. Institutional changes, for example, the coming of the World Trade Organisation, and new interests in economic thought, not least through the further awards of Nobel Prizes for Economics, have inspired new entries. Inevitably some terms in the first edition have not been as durable as others and recommended reading needed revision.

Extensive reading of economics journals and monographs, as well as newspapers, has produced over a thousand new entries. The organisation of the *Dictionary* has also been changed. The newer version of the subject classification employed by the *Journal of Economic Literature* and *The Economic Journal* has been applied to previous and new entries. There is now a separate listing of abbreviations and acronyms, together with tables for currencies and stock market indexes.

Without the resources of major libraries this new edition could not have been undertaken. I am grateful for having access to Edinburgh University Library, Cambridge University Library, and to the Economics Library and Bodleian Library of Oxford University. Colleagues and friends have been very supportive. In particular I would like to mention Graham Richardson, Stuart Sayer, John Gordon and Gillian Gordon.

Abbreviations

AARCH	augmented autoregressive conditional heteroscedasticity
AC	advanced country
ACAS	Advisory, Conciliation and Arbitration Service
ACH	automated clearinghouse
ACM	Andean Common Market; Arab Common Market
ACP	African, Caribbean and Pacific
ACRS	Accelerated Cost Recovery System
ACT	advanced corporation tax
AD	anti-dumping
AD–AS	aggregate demand–aggregate supply
ADB	Asian Development Bank
ADR	American Depository Receipt
AEA	American Economic Association
AESOP	all-employee share ownership plan (UK)
AFBD	Association of Futures Brokers and Dealers (London)
AfDB	African Development Bank
AFDC	Aid to Families with Dependent Children
AFL–CIO	American Federation of Labor and Congress of Industrial Organizations
AG	Aktiengesellschaft
AGM	Annual General Meeting
AGNP	augmented gross national product
AIBD	Association of International Bond Dealers
AIM	Alternative Investment Market (London)
ALC	Australian Loan Council
ALM	asset-liability management
AMEX	American Stock Exchange
AMU	Arab Maghreb Union
ANOVA	analysis of variance
AOSIS	Alliance of Small Island States
APACS	Association for Payment Clearing Services

APB	Accounting Principles Board (UK)
APC	average propensity to consume
APCIMS	Association of Private Client Investment Managers and Stock-brokers
APR	average percentage rate (of interest)
ARCH	autoregressive conditional heteroscedasticity
Ariel	Automated Real-time Investment Exchange
ARIMA	autoregressive integrated moving average
ARM	adjustable rate mortgage
ARMA	autoregressive moving average
ASEAN	Association of South East Asian Nations
ATM	automated teller machine; air transport movement
ATP	Aid and Trade Provisions
ATS	automatic transfer from a savings account; automatic transfer service account
BACS	Banks Automated Clearing System (UK)
BAT	best available technology
BCEAO	Banque Centrale des Etats de l'Afrique de l'Ouest (Central Bank of West African States)
b/d	barrels per day
BDI	Bundesverrand der deutschen Industrie
BDR	British Depository Receipt
BEA	Bureau of Economic Analysis (USA)
BERD	La banque européenne pour la reconstruction et la développement (European Bank for Reconstruction and Development)
BIDS	British Institute of Dealers in Securities
BIS	Bank for International Settlements
BNB	basic needs budget
BOF	Balance for Official Financing
BOY	beginning of the year (or of an accounting period)
bp	base points (of an interest rate)
BP	balance of payments
BRITE	Basic research in industrial technologies for Europe
C	aggregate consumption
C-20	Committee of Twenty
CA	confluence analysis; chartered accountant
CAC	Central Arbitration Committee; Consumer Advisory Council (USA)
CACM	Central American Common Market
CAP	Common Agricultural Policy
CAPM	capital asset pricing model
CAR	compounded annual rate (of interest)
CARICOM	Caribbean Community

CARIFTA	Caribbean Free Trade Area
CAT	Charges, Access, Terms
CATS	Computer-assisted Trading System
CBD	central business district (of a city)
CBI	Caribbean Basin Initiative; Confederation of British Industry
CBO	Congressional Budget Office (USA)
CBOE	Chicago Board Options Exchange
CC	Competition Commission (UK)
CCC	Commodity Credit Corporation (USA); Competition and Credit Control (UK)
CCT	compensating common tariff; compulsory competitive tendering
CD	Certificate of Deposit
CDB	Caribbean Development Bank
CEA	Council of Economic Advisers
CEAO	Communauté Economique de l'Afrique de l'Ouest
CEC	Commission of the European Communities
CENIS	Centre for International Studies
CEMAC	Communauté Economique et Monetaire en Afrique Centrale (Central African Economic and Monetary Community)
CEO	Chief Executive Officer
CEPAL	Commisión Economica para América Latina
CEPGL	Communité économique des Pays des Grands Lacs
CES	constant elasticity of substitution
CET	common external tariff
CETA	Comprehensive Employment and Training Act
CEV	constant elasticity of variance
CFA	Communauté Financière Africaine; chartered financial analyst
CFF	compensatory financial facility
CFTC	Commodity Futures Trading Commission
CGE	computable general equilibrium
CGT	capital gains tax
CHAPS	Clearing House Automatic Payments System (UK)
CHIPS	Clearing House Interbank Payments System (New York)
c.i.f.	cost, insurance, freight
CIR	Commission on Industrial Relations (UK)
CIS	cash incentive scheme
CITES	Convention on International Trade in Endangered Species
CMB	Cash Management Bill
CMEA	Council for Mutual Economic Aid
CMO	collateralized mortgage obligation
CMSA	Consolidated Metropolitan Statistical Area
CO	Certification Officer
COB	Commission des Opérations de Bourse (the Stock Exchange Commission of France)
COLA	cost of living adjustment

Comex	Commodity Exchange of New York
CONSOB	Commissione nazionale per la società e la borsa (the Stock Exchange Commission of Italy, founded 1974)
CPE	centrally planned economy
CPI	consumer price index
CPP	current purchasing power
CPR	common pool resources
CPS	Centre for Policy Studies; current population survey
CS	cross-section data
CSO	Central Statistical Office
CSR	Comprehensive Spending Review
CTD	certificate of tax deposit
CTN	confectioner, tobacconist and newsagent
CTT	capital transfer tax
CVD	countervailing duty
C'vr	cover
CW	comparable worth
d	penny; denarius
DAC	Development Aid Committee (of the OECD)
DC	developed country
DCE	domestic credit expansion
DCF	discounted cash flow
DEA	Department of Economics (UK); econometric model
DIDMCA	Depository Institutions Deregulation and Monetary Control Act
div net	dividend net
DLO	direct labour organization
DME	decentralized market economy
DPP	direct product profitability
DRC	direct resource cost
DRY	disposable real income
DTB	Deutsche Terminboerse
DTC	Design-to-cost
DTP	desktop publishing
DTR	double-taxation relief
DUP	directly unproductive profit seeking
DW	Durbin–Watson
EA	Environmental Agency (UK)
EAGGF	European Agricultural Guidance and Guarantee Fund
EAT	Employment Appeal Tribunal
EBIT	earnings before interest and taxes
EBITDA	earnings before interest, tax, depreciation and amortization
EBRD	European Bank for Reconstruction and Development

ECA	Economic Commission for Africa; European Co-operation Administration
ECB	European Central Bank
ECOWAS	European Community of West African States
ecu	European currency unit
EEA	exchange equalization account
EEC	European Economic Community
EFA	expedited funds availability
EFF	extended fund facility
EFT	electronic funds transfer
EFTA	European Free Trade Association
EGARCH	exponential generalized autoregressive conditional heteroscedasticity
EIB	European Investment Bank
EMCF	European Monetary Co-operation Fund
EMS	European Monetary System
EMU	European Monetary Union
EMV	expected monetary value
EOC	Equal Opportunities Commission
EONIA	Euro overnight index average
EP	export promotion
EPA	Environmental Protection Agency
ERA	effective rate of assistance; exchange rate agreement
ERDF	European Regional Development Fund
ERM	Exchange Rate Mechanism
ERP	European Recovery Program ('Marshall Aid')
ESA	European System of Accounts
ESOP	Employee Stock Ownership Plan
ETAS	Economic Trends Annual Survey (UK)
EU	expected utility; European Union
EUA	European Unit of Account
EURIBOR	EuroInterBank offered rate
Exim	Export–Import Bank
FAO	Food and Agricultural Organization
FAS	free alongside ship
FCC	Federal Communications Commission (USA)
FCO	Federal Cartel Office (USA)
FDI	foreign direct investment
FDIC	Federal Deposit Insurance Corporation
Fed	Federal Reserve System
FES	Family Expenditure Survey (UK)
FIBS	financial information and budgeting systems
FIFG	Financial Instrument for Fisheries Guidance (EU)
FIFO	first in, first out

FIGARCH	fractionally integrated generalized autoregressive conditional heteroscedasticity
Fimbra	Financial Intermediaries, Managers and Brokers Regulatory Association (London)
FIML	full information maximum likelihood
FOB	free on board
FOMC	Federal Open Market Committee
FPE	factor price equalization
FRN	floating rate note
FSA	Financial Services Act; Food Standards Agency (UK)
FSB	Federation of Small Businesses (UK)
FSBR	Financial Statement and Budget Report (UK)
FSLIC	Federal Savings and Loan Insurance Corporation
FTC	Federal Trade Corporation; Federal Trade Commission Act
FTO	foreign trade organization
FTSE 100	Financial Times Stock Exchange 100 Share Index
FTZ	free trade zone
FY	fiscal year (USA)
G3	Group of Three (Germany, Japan, USA)
G7	Group of Seven (Canada, France, Germany, Italy, Japan, UK, USA)
G8	Group of Eight (G7 plus Russia)
GAB	General Agreement to Borrow
GAO	General Accounting Office (USA)
GAR	guaranteed annuity rate
GARCH	generalized autoregressive conditional heteroscedasticity
GATS	General Agreement on Trade in Services
GATT	General Agreement on Tariffs and Trade
GDP	gross domestic product
GE	general equilibrium
GHS	General Household Survey
Ginny Mae	General National Mortgage Association (USA)
GLAM	grey, leisured, affluent, married
GLS	generalized least squares
GmbH	Gesellschaft mit beschkranter Haftung (German or Swiss private company)
GNMA	Government National Mortgage Association (US)
GNP	gross national product
GSP	generalized system of preferences; gross social product; gross state product
GSPS	generalized system of preference schemes
HA	housing association
HICP	harmonized index of consumer prices

HIPC	heavily indebted poor countries
HLT	high-leveraged takeover
HOBS	home and office banking systems
HR	human resources
HRM	human resource management
i	rate of interest
I	net investment
IAS	International Accounting Standard
IATA	International Air Travel Association
IBEC	International Bank for European Co-operation
IBEL	interest-bearing eligible liability
IBF	International Banking Facility
IBRD	International Bank for Reconstruction and Development
ICC	income–consumption curve; Interstate Commerce Commission (USA)
ICCH	International Commodities Clearing House
ICFC	International and Commercial Finance Corporation
ICOR	incremental capital–output ratio
ICSID	International Centre for Settlement of Investment Disputes
ICU	International Clearing Union
IDA	International Development Association
IDB	Inter-American Development Bank; inter-dealer broker
IEA	Institute of Economic Affairs (UK); International Energy Agency
IET	interest equalization tax
IFC	International Finance Corporation
IFS	Institute for Fiscal Studies (UK)
IGARCH	integrated generalized autoregressive conditional heteroscedasticity
IIB	International Investment Bank
IIF	Institute for International Finance
ILO	International Labour Office
ILS	indirect least squares
IMF	International Monetary Fund
IMM	International Monetary Market
IMO	International Miners' Organization
IMRO	Investment Managers Regulatory Organization (London)
INSEE	Institut National de la Statistique et des Etudes Economiques
IO	industrial organization
IOB	Insurance Ombudsman Bureau
IP	intellectual property
IPC	integrated pollution control
IPE	International Petroleum Exchange
IPMA	International Primary Markets Association

IPO	initial public offering
IPR	intellectual property rights
IR	individually rational
IRA	individual retirement account (USA)
IRC	Industrial Reorganization Corporation (UK)
IRR	internal rate of return
IRS	Internal Revenue Service (USA)
IS	investment saving; import substitution
ISCO-88	International Standard Classification of Occupations
ISE	International Stock Exchange
ISRO	International Securities Regulatory Organization
IT	information technology
ITA	International Trade Administration (USA)
ITC	International Trade Commission
ITO	International Trade Organization
ITS	Intermarket Trading System
k	a thousand
K	capital stock
L	liquidity; a measure of the US money supply
LAFTA	Latin American Free Trade Association
LBO	leveraged buyout
lc	local currency
LCH	life-cycle hypothesis
LDC	less developed country
LDMA	London Discount Market Association
LEA	Local Enterprise Agency
LFA	less favoured area
LFPR	labour force participation rate
LGS	liquid assets and government securities
LIBOR	London Inter-Bank Offered Rate
LIFFE	London International Financial Futures Exchange
LIFO	last in, first out
LIML	limited information maximum likelihood
LLC	limited liability company (USA)
LMBO	leveraged management buyout
LPM	linear probability model
LRE	likelihood ratio statistic
LSE	London Stock Exchange; London School of Economics
Ltd	private limited company (UK)
Ltip	long-term incentive package
LTOM	London Traded Options Market
LTU	long-term unemployed

LTV	labour theory of value
M	money supply; imports
M&A	merger and acquisition
MA	moving average
MABP	monetarist approach to the balance of payments
MAP	market anti-inflation plan
MBO	management by objectives; management buyout
MCA	marginal cost of abatement; Monetary Compensation Amount
MCT	mainstream corporation tax
MDP	multidisciplinary practice (of lawyers, accountants, etc.)
MERCOSUR	Mercado Comun del Sur
MES	minimum efficient scale
MEW	measure of economic welfare
MFA	Multi-Fibre Arrangement
MFC	most favoured customer
MFN	most favoured nation
MFR	minimum funding requirement
MIGA	Multilateral Investment Guarantee Agency
MIRAS	Mortgage Interest Relief at Source (UK)
MITI	Ministry of International Trade and Industry (Japan)
ML	maximum likelihood
MLE	maximum likelihood estimator
MLH	minimum list heading
MLM	multi-level marketing
MLR	minimum lending rate
MMC	money market certificate
MMDA	money market deposit account
MMMF	money market mutual fund
MNC	multinational corporation
MPA	marginal principle of allocation
MPC	marginal propensity to consume; Monetary Policy Committee, UK
MPD	marginal private damage
MPM	marginal propensity to import
MPP	marginal physical product
MPS	marginal propensity to save; (Soviet) Material Product System
MRP	marginal revenue product
MRR	minimum reserve requirements
MRS	minimum rate of substitution
MSA	Metropolitan Statistical Area
MSD	marginal social damage
MTFS	Medium-term Financial Strategy
N	The quantity of employment

NAFA	net acquisition of financial assets
NAFTA	North American Free Trade Area
NAIC	National Association of Insurance Commissioners (USA)
NAIRU	non-accelerating inflation of unemployment
NAMU	North American Monetary Union
NARCH	non-linear autoregressive conditional heteroscedasticity
NASDAQ	National Association of Securities Dealers Automated Quotation System (USA)
NASDIM	National Association of Securities Dealers and Investment Managers
NAV	net asset value
NBER	National Bureau of Economic Research (USA)
NBPI	National Board for Prices and Incomes (UK)
NDP	net domestic product
NEB	National Enterprise Board (UK)
NEDC	National Economic Development Council (UK)
NEDO	National Economic Development Office (UK)
NEP	New Economic Policy (Soviet Union)
NEW	net economic welfare
NIBM	non-interest-bearing M1
NIC	newly industrialized country
NIE	new institutional economics
NIEO	New International Economic Order
NIESR	National Institute of Economic and Social Research (UK)
NIF	note issuance facility
NIMBY	'not in my backyard'
NIPA	National Income and Product Accounts (USA)
NOW	negotiable order of withdrawal
NPE	non-profit enterprise
NPV	net present value
NRV	net realizable value
NSA	non-sterling area
NTB	non-tariff barrier
NV	Naamlose venootschap (Dutch public company)
NYMEX	New York Mercantile Exchange
NYSE	New York Stock Exchange
OASDHI	Old Age, Survivors, Disability and Health Insurance (USA)
OB	organizational behaviour
OBRA	Omnibus Budget Reconciliation Act (USA)
OCD	other checkable deposits
ODA	official development assistance; Overseas Development Administration
OECD	Organization for Economic Co-operation and Development
OEEC	Organization for European Economic Co-operation

OF—	Office of a UK regulator (e.g. OFGAS, of gas)
OFT	Office of Fair Trading (UK)
OID	original issue discount
OLG	overlapping generations model
OLS	ordinary least squares
OM	Options Model
OMA	orderly market agreement
OMB	Office of Management and Budget
OMO	open market operation
ONS	Office for National Statistics (UK)
OPCS	Office of Population Censuses and Surveys (UK)
OPEC	Organization of Petroleum Exporting Countries
OSA	overseas sterling area
OTCM	over-the-counter market
PAF	percentage annual fixed (rate of interest)
PAYE	pay as you earn (UK)
PCC	price–consumption curve
PCT	primary care trust (UK)
PDI	personal disposable income
PDV	present discounted value
P/E	price–earnings ratio
PEP	personal equity plan (UK)
PESC	Public Expenditure Survey Committee (UK)
PFI	private finance initiative (UK)
PIBOR	Paris Inter-Bank Offered Rate
PIK	payment in kind
PIN	personal identification number; Philippine Investment Note
plc	public limited company (formerly Co. Ltd) (UK)
PPB	planning, programming, budgeting
PPF	production possibility frontier
PPI	producer price index
PPP	purchasing power parity; public–private partnership
PQLI	physical quality of life index
PRF	population regression function
PRP	performance-related pay; profit-related pay
PRT	petroleum revenue tax
PSA	public service agreement (UK)
PSBR	public sector borrowing requirement
PSDR	public sector debt repayment
PSE	public service employment
PSL	private sector liquidity (UK)
PSNB	public sector net borrowing
PTA	preferential trading arrangement; preferential trade agreement

QALY	quality-adjusted life years
QARCH	quadratic autoregressive conditional heteroscedasticity
QR	quantitative restrictions
QTARCH	qualitative threshold autoregressive conditional heteroscedasticity
r	coefficient of correlation
RBC	real business cycle
RD	reserve deposits (of a bank)
R&D	research and development
RDA	Regional Development Agency (England)
RD and D	research, development and demonstration
RE	rational expectations
REP	regional employment premium
REPO	repurchase agreement
RER	real exchange rate
ROCE	return on capital employed
ROI	return on investment
ROW	rest of the world
RPB	recognized professional body
RPI	retail price index (UK)
RPM	resale price maintenance
RRR	real rate of return
RSA	regional selective assistance
RSG	rate support grant
RTB	right to buy
RTC	Resolution Trust Corporation (USA)
RTM	rent to mortgage
RUF	revolving underwriting facility
SA	Société anonyme (French, Belgian, Luxemburgese or Swiss public company)
SACU	South African Customs Union
SADCC	South African Development Co-ordination Committee
Sarl	Société à responsabilité limité (French private limited company)
SAYE	save as you earn (UK scheme)
SBA	Small Business Administration (USA)
SCOPE	System Committee on Paperless Entry
SCP	structure–conduct–performance
SDR	special drawing rights
SEAQ	Stock Exchange Automated Quotation System (UK)
SEC	Securities and Exchange Commission (UK)
SEM	special employment measures
SEPON	Stock Exchange Pool Nominees (UK)
SERPS	State Earnings-related Pension Scheme

SETS	Stock Exchange Electronic Trading Service (UK)
SFA	Securities and Futures Authority (UK)
SIB	Securities and Investments Board (UK)
SIBOR	Singapore Inter-Bank Offered Rate
SIC	Standard Industrial Classification
SIMEX	Singapore International Monetary Exchange
SIP	state implementation plan (US pollution control)
SITC	Standard International Trade Classification
SLM	segmented labour market
SME	small and medium-sized enterprise
SMSA	Standard Metropolitan Statistical Area
SNA	System of National Accounts (United Nations)
SNB	Swiss National Bank (Switzerland's central bank)
SNIG	sustained non-inflationary growth
SOE	state-owned enterprise; small open economy
S&P 500	Standard & Poor 500
SRD	Statutory Reserve Deposit
SRF	sample regression function
SRO	self-regulatory organization
SSAP	Statement of Standard Accounting Practice
SWIFT	Society for Worldwide Interbank Financial Telecommunications
SWING	sterling warrant into gilt-edged stock
SWOT	strengths, weaknesses, opportunities, threats (business appraisal technique)
TAA	trade adjustment assistance
TAPS	Transatlantic Payment System
TARCH	threshold autoregressive conditional heteroscedasticity
Taurus	Transfer and Automatic Registration of Unregistered Stock
TDP	tradable discharge permit
TFR	total fertility rate
TIBOR	Tokyo Inter-Bank Offered Rate
TINA	'there is no alternative'
TIP	tax-based incomes policy
TNC	transnational corporation
TOT	terms of trade
TQM	total quality management
TVA	Tennessee Valley Authority; taxe sur la valeur ajoutée (the French value-added tax)
TWER	trade-weighted exchange rate
UBR	uniform business rate
UDEAC	Union Douanière et Economique des Etats de l'Afrique Centrale (Central African Customs and Economic Union)

UEMOA	Union économique et monétaire de l'Afrique de l'Ouest (West African Economic and Monetary Union)
UNCTAD	United Nations Conference on Trade and Development
UNDP	United Nations Development Programme
UNFCCC	United Nations Framework Convention on Climate Change
UNIDO	United Nations Industrial Development Organization
UPF	utility possibility frontier; Uniform Presentation Framework (Australia)
USM	Unlisted Securities Market
UTV	utility theory of value
UVI	unit value index
VAN	value-added network
VaR	value at risk
VAR	vector autoregression
VAT	value-added tax
VECM	vector error correction model
VER	voluntary export restraint
VIE	voluntary import expansion
WIPO	World Intellectual Property Organization
X	exports
XD	ex-dividend
xr	ex rights
Y	income – often real disposable income
Y'ld Gr's	yield gross
ZBB	zero-base budgeting
ZIRP	zero interest rate policy
ZPG	zero population growth

A

AAA (G1)
The top credit rating of the securities issued by corporations and companies, as judged by the US rating agency Standard & Poor. This rating is based on the view that default is likely to be minimal.

See also: BB; BBB; C; D; DDD; Prime-1

abatement (Q2) *see* marginal cost of abatement

ability to pay (H2)
1 The principle of taxation that persons with equal incomes and equal capacity to pay a tax should be taxed the same. This alternative to a BENEFIT TAX was suggested as early as the MERCANTILIST period because it appears to be a 'just' approach. John Stuart MILL argued that equality in taxation meant equality of sacrifice: this is ambiguous as the sacrifice may be in absolute, proportional or marginal terms. As sacrifice means loss of utility, the theory can only work if different persons' UTILITIES can be compared.
2 An employer's stance in wage bargaining of making offers according to a firm's financial state.

abortive benefits (H2)
Social benefits which fail to achieve their purpose. There is no net increase in a recipient's income as the benefits are outweighed by income taxation. Proposals for a NEGATIVE INCOME TAX, which would merge benefits and taxation into a single system, attempt to ensure that benefits raise net income.

above the line (H5, M3)
1 A type of expenditure and revenue of a government. For UK budgets from 1947 to 1963, it referred to spending out of current tax revenue.
2 A firm's expenditure on direct advertising.
3 The items in the summary UK balance of payments which are within the current and capital balances.

See also: below the line

Abramovitz, Moses, 1912– (B3)
Educated at Harvard and Columbia Universities. He was on the staff of the National Bureau of Economic Research from 1938 to 1942 and Director of Business Cycles Study from 1946 to 1948; principal economist of the War Production Board in 1942 before serving in the US Army; and professor at Columbia University, 1940–2 and 1946–8, and of Stanford University, 1948–77. After early work on price theory, he turned to a study of inventories and business cycles. Later he examined determinants of long swings in growth, considering changes in the supply of factors of production and the influence of an initial level of productivity on subsequent economic progress.

References

Abramovitz, M. (1950) *Inventories and Business Cycles*, New York: National Bureau of Economic Research.

Abramovitz, M. (ed.) (1958) *Capital Formation and Economic Growth*, Princeton, NJ: Princeton University Press.

absenteeism (J2)

A form of industrial unrest often used instead of a STRIKE. Workers dissatisfied with their conditions take days off work without pay. Some industries have been noted for this practice, e.g. the UK coal-mining industry. It is a form of expressing a grievance available to non-unionized workers.

See also: exit-voice

absolute advantage (F1)

An early theory of trade which states that one country enters into trade with another because it has a greater productivity than that country in a particular industry or industries, e.g. its cotton industry is more productive than the foreign cotton industry. SMITH advanced this as the reason for trade because a nation, like a household, should specialize.

See also: comparative advantage

absolute concentration (L1) *see* aggregate concentration

absolute income hypothesis (E2)

A theory of the CONSUMPTION FUNCTION stating that consumption is a function of current personal disposable income. This was KEYNES's original view, later refined by TOBIN and Smithies. The consumption function is non-linear because the MARGINAL PROPENSITY TO CONSUME declines as national income increases. Keynes asserted that 'men are disposed, as a rule and on average, to increase their consumption as their income increases, but not by as much as the increase in their income'. The early approach was superseded by the RELATIVE INCOME, PERMANENT INCOME and LIFE-CYCLE HYPOTHESES.

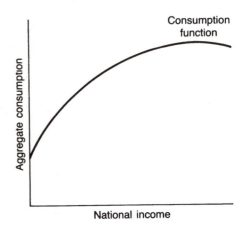

Consumption function

Aggregate consumption

National income

absolute poor (I3)

People with income below what is needed to maintain a minimum standard of nutrition.

See also: poverty, subsistence

absolute scarcity (Q3)

The limited non-renewable nature of some resources, notably metals and fossil fuels.

absolute surplus value (N5) *see* surplus value

absolute tax incidence (H2)

The burden of a particular tax compared with a situation in which there are no taxes or governmental expenditures.

See also: tax incidence

absorption approach (F4)

A method of analysing a country's BALANCE OF PAYMENTS by comparing its total output with its 'absorption', i.e. its domestic expenditure on goods and services. There will only be an improvement in a country's balance of payments if its total output is greater than its absorption of its own output. By the use of PRICE ELASTICITIES and a MULTIPLIER, it is possible to examine the effects on output and absorption of the DEVALUATION of a currency.

References

Kyle, J.F. (1976) *The Balance of Payments in a Monetary Economy*, Princeton, NJ: Princeton University Press.

absorptive capacity (E2)

1 The physical limit to the amount of investment because PRODUCTIVITY declines as the rate of investment increases.

2 The extent to which a country can increase investment without depressing returns to that investment.

References

Adler, J. (1965) *Absorptive Capacity: the Concept and its Determinants*, Washington, DC: Brookings Institution.

abstinence (D3)

A justification for the payment of interest, first advanced by Nassau SENIOR. An individual who abstains from current consumption is rewarded with interest for adding to the capital stock. Abstinence explains the supply of savings: that supply, together with the demand for capital, forms a theory of the interest rate.

References

Senior, N.W. (1836) *An Outline of the Science of Political Economy*. Reprinted New York: Augustus M. Kelly, 1965.

abstract labour (J0)

Labour which is abstracted from expenditures of human labour power. MARX regarded abstract labour as the creator of exchange values.

See also: concrete labour

abundance (Q2)

The opposite of SCARCITY. Abundant goods and services cost nothing to produce and are made freely available. Principal examples are some natural resources but increasingly as population has grown their scarcity has been discovered.

Accelerated Cost Recovery System (H2)

US federal tax allowance introduced in 1981 and subsequently modified. Most capital goods were assumed to have a life of three, five or ten years; as many were more durable, this system was a means of cutting corporate taxation. An example of SUPPLY-SIDE ECONOMICS.

accelerated depreciation (H2)

An initial depreciation allowance greater than the annual wear and tear of a fixed capital asset. For an asset with an expected life of ten years, under the straight-line method of depreciation the value of the asset would be deemed to depreciate by 10 per cent per year. But under accelerated depreciation, the value of the asset could perhaps be depreciated by 20 per cent in the first year. Governments have used this fiscal device to encourage private sector investment.

acceleration clause (G0)

A clause in many mortgage agreements making the PRINCIPAL and interest immediately payable on the occurrence of an event such as failure to make payments on time or to keep a covenant.

accelerator principle (E2)

A major theory of investment which asserts that the amount of net investment in a given time period will be equal to a coefficient approximating to the amount of capital needed to produce another unit of output multiplied by the change in income. An early writer using this principle was Aftalion in *Les Crises periodiques de surproduction* (1913); later Lundberg, HARROD, SAMUELSON, HICKS and Goodwin included it in their investment equations. The basic principle, expressed in an equation where I is net investment in year t, a is the accelerator coefficient and ΔY is the annual change in income, has been modified to take into account different reaction times to a change in income and the existence of EXCESS CAPACITY:

$$I = \alpha \Delta Y_{t-1}$$

where ΔY_{t-1} is the change in income in the previous year;

$$I = \alpha \Delta Y_t - \beta K_t$$

where β is the proportion of the capital stock which is excess capacity and K is the capital stock in year t.

In combination with the MULTIPLIER, CEILINGS and FLOORS, the accelerator plays an important role in the explanation of BUSINESS CYCLES, and is prominent in HARROD–DOMAR models.

References

Hicks, J.R. (1950) *A Contribution to the Theory of the Trade Cycle*, Oxford: Clarendon Press (reprinted 1978).

Knox, A. D. (1952) 'The acceleration principle and the theory of investment: a survey', *Economica, New Series* 19: 269–97.

Lundberg, E. (1937) *Studies in the Theory of Economic Expansion*, Oxford: Basil Blackwell (reprinted 1955).

accepting house (G2)

A UK merchant bank which, by approving a commercial bill of exchange, created a short-term marketable asset. In the past such accepting was the major activity of many of these banks but now they have diversified into other activities, including corporate finance and portfolio management. In 1981, the Bank of England ended their special status as endorsers of bills: the Bank of England now regards other COMMERCIAL PAPER as eligible for purchase.

access differential (J3)

A difference in access to goods and services and to their producers. This addition to monetary rewards was used in the SOVIET-TYPE ECONOMY, so higher ranking officials could use shops, schools and clinics not open to the rest of society.

accession tax (D0, P2)

A tax on the gifts and bequests received by heirs.

access–space trade-off model (R1)

In URBAN ECONOMICS this theory sought to demonstrate that a household's choice of location and amount of land depends on the trade-off between cheaper rent and a longer trip to work.

References

Alonso, W. (1964) *Location and Land Use: toward a general theory of land rent*, Cambridge, MA: Harvard University Press.

accommodating credit (F3)

A form of automatic credit, especially in international trade, consisting of the seller (exporter) financing the purchase by a buyer (importer).

account (G2, M4)

1 A financial statement expressed in words and sums of money.

2 A standard time period used on the STOCK EXCHANGE for settling payments and delivering securities, referring to a fortnight (or three weeks if there is a public holiday). During an account, stocks and shares can be bought and sold without any cash settlement.

account days (G2)

The days on which London STOCK EXCHANGE transactions have to be settled, usually the second Monday after the end of an account.

See also: rolling settlement

accounting (M4)

The recording of the economic activities of firms and national economies. As early as 1494, double-entry bookkeeping, the basis of modern accounting, was explained in Pacioli's 'The Method of Venice', although civilizations as early as the Babylonian practised intricate accounting. In the nineteenth century, the development of joint stock companies and corporations necessitated auditing, greatly expanding the role of the accountant. Accounting has moved from FINANCIAL ACCOUNTING (the historical recording of past activities) to MANAGEMENT ACCOUNTING (the frequent presentation of information to managers to help them in current decision making).

References

Bull, R.J. (1984) *Accounting in Business*, 5th edn, London: Butterworth.

Chatfield, M. (1977) *A History of Accounting Thought*, rev. edn, Huntington, NY: Robert E. Krieger.

accounting balance of payments (F4)
A record of all the financial transactions between the residents of one country and the residents of foreign countries in a given time period (usually a quarter or a whole year).

accounting costs (M4)
All the costs of producing a good or service recorded in the accounts of a firm. These include most economic costs but are likely to omit the cost of the owner's time and the OPPORTUNITY COST of the financial capital used in the firm.

accounting cycle (M4)
The period from the start to finish of an operational sequence. Accountants typically consider periods of a month, three months, six months or a year.

accounting identity (E0, M4)
A balance with each side of an equation equal to the other because of the accounting definitions used. In economics this identity is usually contrasted with equilibrium conditions. Thus, in basic macroeconomics, the accounting equations $Y = C + I$ and $Y = C + S$ entail that $I = S$, but planned saving and investment may diverge (Y is national income, C is aggregate consumption, I is net investment and S is aggregate saving).

accounting profit (M2, M4)
The excess of total revenue over the costs and expenses of a productive activity in a given time period. Contrast with ECONOMIC PROFIT

accretion of a discount (G1)
The accumulation of capital gains on DISCOUNT BONDS anticipating payment of the bond at par when the bond matures.

accrual accounting (M4)
Accounts based on transactions when they occur, as opposed to when the cash is received or paid; not CASH FLOW ACCOUNTING.

accrual interest rate (G0)
The rate at which interest accrues on a loan as distinct from the rate at which it is

actually paid. This accrual rate can be the current market rate or the original rate when the loan was made.

accrued expense (M4)
An expense incurred in a particular time period but not yet paid.

accrued income (M4)
Income earned in a particular time period but not yet received in cash.

accumulation (E2)
The increase in assets which creates CAPITAL. Individual persons and businesses do this for their own gain; governments accumulate with the future welfare of a country in view. SMITH and MARX were early analysts of this process.

acid-test ratio (M2, M4)
The ratio of liquid assets such as cash, accounts receivable and short-term marketable securities to current liabilities. Also known as quick assets ratio.

active fiscal policy (H3, H5)
Frequently used discretionary fiscal policy. Using this, a government makes many changes in its spending and taxation, instead of relying on automatic stabilizers, to achieve a desired level of aggregate demand.

activist (E6)
An economic policy adviser who believes in the use of discretionary monetary and fiscal instruments for fine-tuning the economy.

activity analysis (C6) *see* linear programming

activity rate (J2)
Official UK term for the LABOUR FORCE PARTICIPATION RATE. If the female population is 100 million and the female labour force is 55 million, the female activity rate will be 55 per cent.

activity ratio (M2, M4)
1 An accounting measure of the amount of activity of a firm: (standard hours for actual output/standard hours for bud-

geted output) × 100.

2 Net sales divided by total assets or net fixed assets.

3 Accounts receivable divided by daily credit sales.

actual budget (H6)

The national taxation and expenditure accounts of a government. They can be in balance, in surplus or in deficit; often contrasted with a FULL-EMPLOYMENT BUDGET.

actual deficit (H6) *see* primary deficit

acyclical (E3)

Not subject to fluctuations caused by various types of business cycle. Planned economies with little openness to the international economy, such as the former USSR, hoped to avoid the cyclical instability which they claimed to be an inherent feature of CAPITALISM.

Adam Smith Institute (E6)

Free market economic policy research think-tank based in London, UK, and founded in 1977 by a group of like-minded graduates of St Andrews University, Scotland. It has published reports on economic policies since 1979.

adaptive expectations (E0)

The expected value of an economic variable at a future date measured by the weighted average of all previous values of the variable. The concept was first applied to the study of investment behaviour and the CONSUMPTION FUNCTION and then later to inflation. This approach to expectations, first advanced by Cagan, although easy for economic model-builders, ignores the fact that forecasters often take into account more information than the past behaviour of the variable being studied.

References

Cagan, P. (1956) 'The monetary dynamics of hyperinflation', in M. Friedman (ed.) *Studies in the Quantity Theory of Money*, Chicago: University of Chicago Press.

adding-up controversy (D3)

A dispute concerning 'solutions' to the problem of ensuring that the total amount of income going to factors of production is equal to the national income. From P.H. Wicksteed's *An Essay in the Coordination of the Laws of Distribution* (1894) onwards, many attempts to solve the problem have been limited to the special case of a long-run perfectly competitive equilibrium.

See also: Euler's theorem; perfect competition

additional facilities (F3)

Extra credit arrangements of the INTERNATIONAL MONETARY FUND to ease the balance of payments difficulties of member countries. These include:

- 1963 Compensatory Financing Facility to provide compensation for a shortfall in export earnings;
- 1969 Buffer Stock Financing Facility;
- 1974–5 Oil Facility;
- 1974 Extended Fund Facility;
- 1974 Supplementary Financing Facility;
- 1986 Structural Adjustment Facility.

additionality (H2)

The imposition of an extra obligation. This is also a financing principle of the EUROPEAN UNION in that some grants it makes have to be matched by a grant from a member state set as a fixed proportion of the EU grant.

additional-worker hypothesis (J2)

The assertion that unemployment will encourage more labour force participation amongst SECONDARY WORKERS thus increasing the size of the labour force. This often occurs when there is a shift from heavy to light industry. If those made redundant in the heavy industries are males but the jobs available in the light industries are predominantly suitable for females, then male unemployment will coincide with women joining the labour force.

See also: discouraged worker hypothesis; labour force participation rate

References

Cann, G.G. (1967) 'Unemployment and the labor force participation of secondary workers', *Industrial and Labor Relations Review* 20: 275–97.

adjustable peg (F3)

A FIXED EXCHANGE RATE which can occasionally be altered according to certain rules. The best example is the BRETTON WOODS AGREEMENT which permitted revaluations and devaluations of up to 10 per cent without the permission of the INTERNATIONAL MONETARY FUND. An adjustable peg has the disadvantage of requiring the costly accumulation of foreign exchange reserves and can be unstable as every rumour about a currency change may provoke speculation necessitating an adjustment. A currency can be pegged to another single currency (often the US dollar) or to a basket of currencies such as a SPECIAL DRAWING RIGHT or a basket chosen to reflect the trade structure of the country.

See also: Bretton Woods Agreement

adjustable rate mortgage (G3)

A MORTGAGE bearing an interest rate that fluctuates according to market interest rates. These are popular with savings institutions as they have less INTEREST RISK, and with individuals and households because they offer lower initial interest rates.

adjusted claim (G0) *see* note issuance facility

adjustment cost (D0)

The cost to an economic agent, e.g. a firm or a household, of a change in the value of a variable crucial to its decisions. If, for example, a firm were to change its capital stock by embarking on an investment programme, it would incur the adjustment costs of research, planning, installation of equipment and training of workers.

adjustment gap (Q1)

The ratio of international to domestic food prices. The greater the amount of farm support, the greater the gap. In the 1980s, the ratio for the EUROPEAN COMMUNITY was about one-third.

adjustment speed (D0)

The time it takes a price to adjust to EXCESS DEMAND or EXCESS SUPPLY in a particular market. This is crucial to the study of money wage rates, product prices, interest rates and nominal exchange rates.

administered inflation (E3)

INFLATION brought about by firms increasing the profit mark-up on their products; a form of COST-PUSH INFLATION.

See also: mark-up pricing

administered pricing (D4, M2)

The practice of setting prices according to a formula, irrespective of the short-run forces of demand and supply. This is possible because of the market power of monopolistic and oligopolistic firms. As it is expensive to change prices (e.g. new catalogues have to be printed) and as there is always the possibility of adverse consumer reaction, there is a tendency for prices to be more rigid when administered. As part of an anti-inflation programme, especially in wartime, governments will administer major prices, the prices of goods and services prominent in most consumers' budgets; in these circumstances the rules for increasing prices are strictly laid down. Most administered prices are calculated by adding a profit margin to AVERAGE COST.

See also: mark-up pricing

References

Means, G.C. (1935) 'Industrial prices and their relative inflexibility', *Senate Document No. 13*, Washington, DC: US Government Printing Office.

administration lag (H0) *see* implementation lag

administrative cost (H2, M2)

1 The personnel and equipment costs of collecting taxes (public finance).
2 Costs incurred to manage an enterprise (managerial economics).

See also: transaction cost

administrative costs of regulation (H1, L5)
All the costs of employing officials and running the offices of regulatory agencies. These are contrasted with COMPLIANCE COSTS.

ad valorem tax (H2)
An INDIRECT TAX levied as a percentage of the value of a transaction. SALES TAXES, EXCISE DUTIES and VALUE-ADDED TAXES are major examples. In calculating such taxes, either the final price of the good or service or the value added at a particular stage of production is the basis. This tax reduces the amount of revenue that a firm obtains from the sale of a good or a service.

See also: unit tax

advance (G0)
A bank loan or an overdraft which has a term of less than three years, usually less than one year. When a bank creates money, it does so by allowing advances to its customers, i.e. permitting them to draw on the extra bank deposits created for them. An overdraft is a permission to 'overdraw' up to a certain amount for a specified period, but a loan results in an immediate crediting of the borrower's account.

advance corporation tax (H2)
An interim settlement of UK corporation tax. If a company makes a qualifying distribution of earnings, e.g. by distributing a dividend, during its accounting period, it pays a proportion of the amount of the dividend as an advanced payment of tax which will later be deducted from its tax liability for that period. The proportion levied varies from year to year but has often been about 30 per cent.

advanced organic economy (P0)
An ECONOMY which reaches a considerable level of real income by using agricultural products, especially wood, for energy and raw materials. A pre-industrial economy.

References

Wrigley, E.A. (1988) *Continuity, Chance and Change*, ch. 2, Cambridge: Cambridge University Press.

adverse selection (D0, G2)
A problem of insurance arising when the insurer does not know whether or not an insured person is at risk, with the consequence that the same premium is charged, irrespective of whether that individual is likely to claim. This can occur, for example, if applicants for life insurance do not disclose all their health details.

See also: asymmetric information

adverse supply shock (E0)
A change in a factor price, e.g. of energy or labour, which reduces AGGREGATE SUPPLY at each price level. In the short term, the macroeconomic consequences of a shock are an increase in the price level and a fall in output.

advertising (M3)
A communication activity used to influence potential buyers, voters or others who can help the advertiser to reach defined goals. For firms, it is a selling cost incurred with the hope of increasing sales. Advertising increases the amount of information available in a market but also helps to create monopoly situations as it can be a BARRIER TO ENTRY. The theory of MONOPO-LISTIC COMPETITION was the first major economic theory to incorporate considerations of advertising. By advertising, OLIGOPOLISTS can create wants and markets, escaping the strictures of CONSUMER SOVEREIGNTY. The annual amount of a firm's advertising expenditure is often determined by an arbitrary ratio of advertising expenditure to sales revenue with the frequent effect of redistributing demand among the firms of an industry and adding to their costs, not of enlarging total expenditure on a particular good or service. Although large advertising expenditures are associated with MARKET ECONOMIES, advertising has a role in COMMAND ECONOMIES, particularly to

increase consumer demand for products new to the market or in EXCESS SUPPLY.

References

Carter, M., Casson, M. and Suneja, V. (1998) *The economics of marketing*, Cheltenham, UK, and Northampton, MA: Edward Elgar.

Reekie, W.D. (1981) *The Economics of Advertising*, London: Macmillan.

Schinalensee, R. (1972) *The Economics of Advertising*, Amsterdam: North-Holland.

Advisory, Conciliation and Arbitration Service (J5)

The central UK body, set up in 1974 under the TRADE UNION AND LABOUR RELATIONS ACT, to promote an improvement in industrial relations, to encourage an extension of collective bargaining and its reform through advice, conciliation, enquiries and arbitration, and to run the CENTRAL ARBITRATION COMMITTEE. An important aspect of its activities has been the publication of codes of practice in industrial relations.

affinity card (G2)

A CREDIT CARD linked with a charity that receives donations in proportion to the amount spent by the user of that card.

affirmative action (J7)

A series of actions taken by an employer or public authority to advance the opportunities of disadvantaged groups, especially ethnic minorities, to increase their representation, particularly in employment and other activities.

See also: reverse discrimination

AFL–CIO (J5)

American Federation of Labor and Congress of Industrial Organizations: a merger of two rival labour federations of the USA in 1955 which brought back the breakaway industrial unions that had separated from their colleagues in craft unions. Some US labour unions are not affiliated to the AFL–CIO.

See also: craft union; general union; industrial union

African–American economists (B2)

The earliest black economists in the USA include William Edward Burghardt Du Bois (1868–1963), Sadie Tanner Mossell Alexander (1898–1989), George Edmund Haynes (1880–1960) and William Henry Dean Jr (1910–52). Their work has included the study of MIGRATION, DISCRIMINATION and LOCATION THEORY.

African Development Bank (G2)

A bank operating from 1966: it finances investment projects in Africa and raises capital throughout the world. By 1985, it had fifty African and twenty-five non-African countries as members, including the UK, the USA, Germany and Japan.

See also: development bank

after-hours dealings (G2)

Dealings in stocks and shares after the London STOCK EXCHANGE closes for the day. Such BARGAINS are recorded as the next day's business. In the past these dealings were at less attractive prices to both buyer and seller because of the greater risk of trading when market opinion was unknown; now, long hours of electronic dealing have removed this price differential.

See also: twenty-four-hour trading

aftermarket (G2)

The trading in securities immediately after they have been issued.

age–earnings profile (J3)

A graph plotting earnings against age. Such profiles are frequently used in HUMAN CAPITAL analysis to show the financially beneficial effects of education. More education usually raises the profile to a new plateau; rules for salary structures and seniority can also affect the profile's shape. The frequently used method of constructing a profile from cross-section data provides a poor estimate if age differentials in earnings change. LONGITUDINAL DATA provide a more accurate picture of life-time earnings.

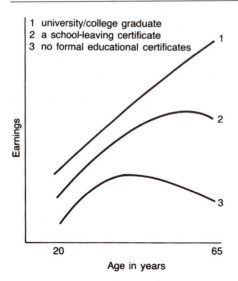

1 university/college graduate
2 a school-leaving certificate
3 no formal educational certificates

Earnings (vertical axis)

20   65

Age in years

ageing population (J1)

1 population with an increasing proportion of its population in older age groups, often because a large group born in a period of high birth rate is maturing.

2 A population with a rising MEDIAN age. In developed countries, a decline in the birth rate since the 1960s has added to this demographic effect. A slower growth in GROSS NATIONAL PRODUCT of a nation can encourage emigration of the young, with the consequence that the remaining population 'ages'. A typical pattern of consumption and saving is associated with each age group and hence, when a population 'ages', it changes its demand for particular goods and services in the private and public sectors; also, innovation may be affected and the size of the MULTIPLIER for the whole economy may change.

See also: grey society; life-cycle hypothesis

References

Clark, R.L. and Spengler, J.J. (1980) *The Economics of Individual and Population Ageing*, Cambridge and New York: Cambridge University Press.

Clark, R.L., Kreps, J. and Spengler, J.I. (1978) 'Economics of ageing: a survey', *Journal of Economic Literature* 16 (September): 919–62.

Lee, R.D., Arthur, W.B. and Rodgers, O. (eds) (1989) *Economics of Changing Age Distributions in Developed Countries*, Oxford: Oxford University Press.

ageism (J7)

Treating people who have reached a particular age, the customary age of retirement in that society or even younger, as of little value so that they are excluded from employment and many other activities. This form of DISCRIMINATION is being fought by senior citizens' lobbies in the USA and elsewhere. Increasing shortages of young workers in developed countries in the late twentieth century have diminished some of this discrimination. Also, firms which have waived age rules have discovered that many older workers have lower ABSENTEEISM, and higher numeracy and literacy than younger workers.

agency broker (G2)

A stockbroker who buys and sells shares of companies from MARKET-MAKERS. It is argued that agency brokers have the advantage of being able to find better prices than an individual market-maker can offer and of providing more confidentiality.

agency cost (D0)

A cost arising from a contractual relationship between a principal and an agent. These costs include the expenses of drawing up and enforcing a contract, as well as TRANSACTION COSTS, MORAL HAZARD costs and INFORMATION COSTS. Agency costs are major determinants of how firms are organized and how their staff are remunerated.

agency pass-through (G2)

A MORTGAGE PASS-THROUGH SECURITY guaranteed by a US agency such as the Government National Mortgage Association so that there is no default on the principal and interest payments.

agency relationship (D0) *see* agency theory

agency shop (J5)

A voluntary UNION SHOP, extensively present

in the US public sector, in which employees pay the equivalent of union dues in
return for that union acting as a bargaining agent. It is used to evade the ban on
CLOSED SHOPS in RIGHT-TO-WORK STATES.

agency theory (L2)
A theory of the firm which explores the
relationships between PROPERTY RIGHTS and
financial structures. The central concept
used is the 'agency relationship', i.e. the
contractual relationship between a principal person(s) and those who render services
as agents, e.g. between the stockholders of
a corporation and the managers they
appoint to run that firm. The costs of the
agency include the costs to the principal of
monitoring the agreement and any loss if
the agent's decisions fail to maximize his
or her welfare; the agent often incurs the
costs of putting up a bond as a guarantee
of not harming the principal. This theory
can be applied to many other aspects of
co-operative behaviour.

References
Jensen, M.C. and Meckling, W.H. (1976)
    'Theory of the firm: managerial beha-
    vior, agency costs and ownership struc-
    ture', *Journal of Financial Economics* 3:
    305–60.

agent bank (G2)
A bank which arranges with a consortium
of banks a credit facility for a borrower.

agent de change (G2) *see* specialist

agglomeration diseconomy (R1)
An external DISECONOMY OF SCALE caused by
the growth of a town or city. For example,
the population growth of a city often
results in increased pollution and congestion.

agglomeration economy (R1)
An external ECONOMY OF SCALE brought
about by the massing of a population in
one place. As the population of a town or
city increases, a more complex infrastructure is possible and a greater DIVISION OF
LABOUR achieved than in a smaller settlement. The larger the settlement, the more

likely it is to have a full range of transport,
shopping, cultural and health facilities.

aggregate concentration (L1)
The CONCENTRATION of the economic activity of a nation or an industry in the hands
of a few giant firms. Also called absolute
concentration.

See also: concentration   ratio;   relative
concentration

aggregate demand (D1, E2, H6)
The total amount of national planned
expenditure by firms, households, governments and other sectors at each price or
income level.

aggregate output (E2)
An output measure of the NATIONAL INCOME
calculated by summing the amount of VA-
LUE ADDED contributed by each industry.
This aggregate is measured at FACTOR COST.

aggregate supply (E2)
1 The total output which all the producers of an economy are willing to
  supply at each price level.
2 Total output as a function of the
  amount of labour.

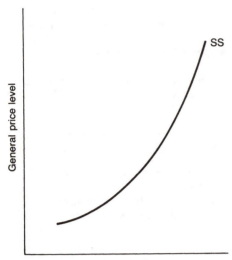

Real GNP

aggregation problem (C3)

The choice of a suitable procedure for reducing numerous and detailed data to aggregate variables for use in an econometric equation. In particular, microeconomic parameters have to be expressed in macroeconomic parameters. The difficult task is to eliminate bias so that stable macroparameters are produced for use in forecasting models. Sometimes aggregation is based on weighted averages of the microparameters.

References

Fisher, W. D. (1969) *Clustering and Aggregation in Economics*, Baltimore, MD: Johns Hopkins University Press.

Gupta, K.L. (1969) *Aggregation in Economics*, Rotterdam: Rotterdam University Press.

agio theory of interest (E4)

An explanation for interest being paid. Interest is paid to allow money or goods to be obtained now because they are desired more in the present than in the future. 'Agio' literally means ease or convenience.

agreement corporation (G2)

A state chartered US banking corporation engaged in international banking under an agreement with the FEDERAL RESERVE Board of Governors to limit its activities to those permissible under the EDGE ACT.

agribusiness (Q1)

A large organization which processes or distributes agricultural products. It benefits from ECONOMIES OF SCALE and is managed as an industrial firm, separating personnel, marketing, finance and production functions.

References

Davis, J.H. and Goldberg, R.A. (1957) *A Concept of Agribusiness*, Cambridge, MA: Harvard University Press; London: Barley & Swinfen.

Agricultural Adjustment Act 1933 (Q1)

The basis of US federal support to farmers which has provided price support to maintain farm incomes. It created the COMMODITY CREDIT CORPORATION to execute its policy.

agricultural household (N0)

A farm with a labour force provided by residents of a household. This economic institution, analysed as both a firm and a household, was the basic economic unit of Ancient Greece and is extensive today in less developed countries.

See also: Ancient Greeks; villa economy

agricultural policy (Q1)

Price and income support schemes designed mainly to stabilize or increase farmers' incomes. Although consumers of food suffer through having to pay higher prices under most agricultural policies, it is unlikely that developed countries with highly productive agricultural sectors will allow a market in unsubsidized agricultural products as governments seek the votes of farmers to be re-elected. As the GENERAL AGREEMENT ON TARIFFS AND TRADE has become increasingly concerned with world trade in agricultural products, national agricultural policies may be harmonized more in the future.

See also: Agricultural Adjustment Act 1933, Common Agricultural Policy, Uruguay Round

References
Moyer, H.W. and Josling, T.E. (1990) *Agricultural Policy Reform. Politics and Process in the EC and USA*, Hemel Hempstead: Harvester Wheatsheaf.

aid (H5, O0) *see* foreign aid

Aid and Trade Provisions (H5, O0)
UK governmental assistance to exporters to make their contractual terms more attractive. Some of the 'aid' goes to the richer developing countries instead of the poorest. This government financial help is paid as a subsidy to companies and not directly to its ultimate beneficiaries.

Aid to Families with Dependent Children (I3)
The US federal welfare programme, originally 'Aid to Dependent Children', inaugurated under Title IV of the 1935 Social Security Act. It enabled states to provide financial assistance to needy dependent children: the states had the tasks of planning and supervising the use of these federal grants. When it began in 1936, there were about half a million recipients; by 1987 the average number of monthly recipients was 11 million. Originally intended to enable female heads of households to stay at home to rear their children, in 1967, the scheme was amended to encourage mothers to join the labour force: this was done by reducing the implicit tax rate on earnings from 100 per cent to 67 per cent.

Akerlof, George Arthur, 1940– (B3)
Born in New Haven, Connecticut, and educated at Yale University and the Massachusetts Institute of Technology. A professor at the University of California, Berkeley, from 1968 to 1978, at the London School of Economics from 1978 to 1980 and again at Berkeley from 1980. Won the NOBEL PRIZE FOR ECONOMICS, with STIGLITZ and SPENCE, in 2001. He became famous in 1970 for raising the problem of asymmetric information in an article on the market for 'lemons'. Also he has made important contributions to monetary economics, the study of unemployment and wages and the economics of the family. From 1974 he has been a senior fellow of the Brookings Institution.

aleatory contract (K0)
An agreement under which the liabilities and benefits depend on chance. This is the basis of much gambling.

alienated work (J2)
Wage labour; work which is subject to the will of another. This kind of work is a non-fulfilling means to an end, often because it is work performed out of personal economic necessity. SMITH's notion of labour as 'toil and trouble' explains much of alienation. As professional jobs are often deeply satisfying they rarely involve alienation.

alienation (J0)
Workers' estrangement from their work which they do not control, from their products which are appropriated, from other men who are capitalists, and from the human species as man becomes a mere animal, according to MARX. Adam SMITH noted that increasing the subdivision of labour would unfortunately affect workers as repetitive simple work dulls the brain and causes a variety of occupational health problems.

Allais, Maurice, 1911– (B3)
Educated at the Ecole Polytechnique and the Ecole Supérieure des Mines before serving in the army from 1943 to 1948. Director of the Bureau of Mines Documentation and Statistics, Paris and professor of economic analysis at Ecole Supérieure des Mines from 1944. Inspired by WALRAS, PARETO and FISHER, he undertook the synthesis of real and monetary phenomena and the relationship between economics and other social sciences in his *In Quest of an Economic Discipline*, Part 1, *Pure Economics* (1943) and subsequent five volumes. Later he studied the theory of choice under uncertainty (which included the use of surveys to investigate CARDINAL UTILITY) and comparative interna-

tional studies of real income. Awarded the NOBEL PRIZE FOR ECONOMICS in 1988.

alleviation (O2)

A DEVELOPMENT strategy of softening POVERTY, not eliminating it; for example, by giving every child primary education and every mother health care.

allocative efficiency (M2)

The selection of factor inputs which minimises the cost of producing goods and services to satisfy given wants, subject to resource and technological constraints. This allocation includes efficiency of both production and distribution. Setting out the conditions for efficiency, including the appropriate set of prices, has been the concern of WELFARE ECONOMICS. Recognition of the existence of INDIVISIBILITIES and EXTERNALITIES has necessitated departures from the approach of NEOCLASSICAL ECONOMICS.

See also: Pareto optimality

allotment letter (G2)

A letter confirming the purchase of newly issued shares.

all-pay auction (D0)

A public sale which takes the form of RENT SEEKING. The prize is always awarded to the competitor exerting the highest effort. This means that in an auction setting, each bidder has an incentive to bid just above the highest bidder, providing there is a positive pay-off.

alpha stock (G2)

One of the most actively traded stocks of the London STOCK EXCHANGE which is always quoted on the STOCK EXCHANGE AUTOMATED QUOTATION SYSTEM. There are usually ten or more market-makers for each of such shares. In 1990, the ISE had about 110 such stocks.

See also: beta stock; delta stock; gamma stock

alternative economic strategy (E6) *see* New Cambridge Economics

altruism (D0, L3, P0)

Seeking the good of others. This alternative to SELF-INTEREST can be a major motive for economic activity. Many schemes of idealistic socialism rest on this principle. Adam SMITH used the concept of the INVISIBLE HAND to show that unconscious altruism can occur in an economy based on the principle of self-interest.

See also: non-profit enterprise; utopia

References

Collard, D.A. (1978) *Altruism and Economy*, Oxford: Martin Robertson; New York: Oxford University Press.

ambient standard (Q2)

A standard for air quality set in the USA by the ENVIRONMENTAL PROTECTION AGENCY.

See also: primary standard; secondary standard

American Depository Receipt (G2)

A share certificate or bearer security entitling the holder to shares of a non-US company which have been deposited in a bank located outside the USA. This US financial instrument, originally devised in 1927, is now traded on both US and UK stock exchanges.

American Economic Association (A1)

The leading US professional association of academic and other economists, founded in 1885 and based at Evanston, Illinois (now at Nashville, Tennessee). From its earliest years it has sought to promote economic research, particularly by publishing its prestigious *American Economic Review*, a core journal of economics, from 1911 and *Journal of Economic Literature* from 1963. The AEA currently has over 25,000 members.

References

Coats, A.W. (1985) 'The American Economic Association and the economics profession', *Journal of Economic Literature* 23: 1697–1727.

American Federation of Labor (J5) *see* AFL–CIO

American option (G1)
An OPTION that can be activated before its expiry date.

American Stock Exchange (G2)
Previously the New York Curb Market and then the New York Curb Exchange, tracing its ancestry back to trading conducted in the streets of lower Manhattan in 1793. It acquired its current name in 1953 and was incorporated in 1971; by 1987 it had 661 regular members with 60 per cent of its business with private clients and 40 per cent with institutional investors. It ended fixed commissions on dealings in 1975 and from 1985 has been linked to the Toronto Stock Exchange.

See also: New York Stock Exchange

America Works (I3)
US private company founded in 1984. It seeks to get people off welfare into employment. This privatization of welfare to work programmes is based upon contracts between the company and a state or city. A bounty is paid to the company for each person placed in a job for at least seven months. Job search and interview skills are taught and the worker's performance is monitored for four months.

amortization (G0)
Gradually extinguishing a liability or debt by allocating the cost of it to a number of time periods. Major examples are the DEPRECIATION of an asset and the repayment of a loan by regular instalments to cover the amount advanced and the interest.

analysis of variance (C1)
The decomposition of the variance in a dependent variable into the variance explained by the regression and the residual variance.

See also: linear regression

anarchism (B0, P0)
The political doctrine which asserts that economic and social life should not be subject to any governmental control. The leading early exponents of this view were Pierre Proudhon (1809–65) and Mikhail Bakunin (1815–76). In practice, anarchism has been applied to industrial organization in the form of workers' syndicates, but experiments of this nature in France and Spain in the early twentieth century were short lived. Although anarchists share with socialists a dislike of capitalism, with LAISSEZ-FAIRE economists a mistrust of the state and with members of the co-operative movement a belief that firms should be managed by labour, they are more extreme, especially in wanting the abolition of private property and being prepared to risk the abandonment of systems of law and order.

References
Ritter, A. (1980) *Anarchism: A Theoretical Analysis*, Cambridge: Cambridge University Press.

anchor tenant (R0)
The leading commercial tenant of an office block which influences its design and has its logo on the façade in return for leasing a large portion of the building, thereby making the return on the property developer's investment more secure. Sometimes the anchor tenant is given a marketable share in the equity of the building.

Ancient Greeks (B1)
One of the earliest groups of writers on economic problems who, despite living in an underdeveloped economy mainly agrarian in character, discussed value, money, comparative property systems, the division of labour, exchange controls and public finance.

See also: Aristotle; Plato; villa economy; Xenophon

References
Finley, M.I. (1985) *The Ancient Economy*, 2nd edn, London: Hogarth.
Gordon, B. (1975) *Economic Analysis before Adam Smith*, London: Macmillan.
Laistner, M.L.W. (1923) *Greek Economics*, London: Dent; New York: Dutton.

Lowry, S.T. (1979) 'Recent literature on Ancient Greek economic thought', *Journal of Economic Literature* 17(March): 65–86.

Andean Common Market (F0)
An association of Bolivia, Chile, Colombia, Ecuador and Peru set up in 1969 to co-ordinate responses to overseas investors and to organize a common market.

Anderson, James, 1739–1808 (B3)
Scottish farmer and agricultural economist who was probably the first to expound a clear theory of DIFFERENTIAL RENT in his *An Inquiry into the Nature of the Corn Laws* (Edinburgh, 1777), regarding rent as a payment for using land superior in fertility. This was to inspire MALTHUS and RICARDO. His other major work of economic interest was *Observations on the National Industry of Scotland* (1775). In addition, he proposed schemes for developing the Scottish Highlands and edited *The Bee*, a weekly journal with articles on literature and current affairs, from 1790 to 1794. As his professional papers are reputed to have been used by his widow to scorch chickens, research on his work is difficult.

See also: differential theory of rent

References
Mullet, C.F. (1968) 'A village Aristotle and the harmony of interests: James Anderson of Monks Hill', *Journal of British Studies* 8: 94–118.

angel (M2)
An investor in a stage production or new business venture. The risk and returns to this kind of investment can be very high. In London, for example, there are several hundred 'angelic' investors in the theatre.

Anglo-Saxon capitalism (P1)
An economic system based on private enterprise, highly flexible labour practices, disproportionately large remuneration for top executives, a fast responsiveness of firms to economic conditions, a major role for financial markets in determining the industrial structure and rapid growth based on rapid diffusion of technology. Both the US and UK economies attempt to follow these principles.

animal spirits (E2)
KEYNES's description of the whimsical investment attitudes of entrepreneurs, sometimes optimistic, sometimes pessimistic; an approach much emphasized by Joan ROBINSON.

announcement burden of a tax (H2)
The loss of PRODUCER'S and CONSUMER'S SURPLUSES as a consequence of a tax change. The announcement has the effect of adjusting taxpayers' behaviour, e.g. in supplying labour.

References
Pigou, A.C. (1928) *A Study in Public Finance*, Part 11, ch. 5, London: Macmillan.

announcement effect (E6)
The immediate effect on households and firms of a government's publication of a change in monetary or fiscal policy. Unlike the other effects of policy changes, there is no time lag. The first effects are felt in financial markets as security prices can be adjusted immediately.

annualized-hours system (J2, J3)
A form of labour contract under which a worker agrees to work for a year of working weeks; an alternative to the standard working week. The annual number of hours is calculated by aggregating the previous weekly hours, less leave. It is a useful system for avoiding substantial overtime and other premium payments. Continuous-process industries were among the first to use this system.

annual percentage rate (of interest) (E4, G0)
Actual annual cost of borrowing. The Truth in Lending Act (USA, 1968) and the Consumer Credit Act (UK, 1974) have required all lenders to state the true cost of borrowing. This annual rate, expressed as a percentage, is calculated by using the formula

$$\text{APR} = 100 \left(\frac{1 + \text{total charge for credit}}{\text{amount of credit}} \right) 1/t$$

where t is the number of years of the loan.

annuity (G0)
An amount of money paid annually or at other regular intervals. Major examples include life assurance premiums, pensions, rent payments and instalment payments. An annuity certain has a fixed term, unlike a perpetuity whose payments continue indefinitely (e.g. an unredeemable government stock). An annuity contingent depends on an uncertain event, e.g. the death of a person. The purchase price, or present value V, of an annuity depends on the rate of interest used in the calculation

$$V = A \frac{1 - (1 + i)^{-n}}{i}$$

where i is the rate of interest (expressed as a decimal) and n is the number of periods that the annuity is paid.

antagonistic growth (O4)
1 Tensions, often of a social nature, in the growth process because of the trade-offs between growth, stability and equity.
2 The deliberate creation of disequilibria to bring about new economic activities, e.g. an infrastructure deficiency which stimulates the growth of a transport industry.

anthropogenic climate impact (Q0)
A climate change brought about by humans, rather than by Nature.

anticipatory pricing (D4, L1)
The practice of including expected cost increases in the make-up of prices. Firms adopting this policy hope that it will stabilize their prices as prices will not have to fluctuate with every change in costs. This type of pricing reduces the MENU COSTS OF INFLATION.

anti-competitive practices (L4)
Corporate behaviour in a market which attempts to increase a firm's market power, e.g. licensing agreements, special selling conditions and other measures less serious than monopolization or cartelization.

See also: antitrust; competition policy

Anti-injunction Act (J5) *see* Norris–La Guardia Act

antitrust (L4)
US policy to prevent monopolistic practices in interstate commerce. It started with the Sherman Act 1890; the states have similar legislation applicable to production industries. Although national competition policies are common in OECD countries, few are as tough, with criminal sanctions, as the US antitrust legislation administered by the Department of Justice and the Federal Trade Commission. The chief federal antitrust statutes are: SHERMAN ACT 1890; CLAYTON ACT 1914; FEDERAL TRADE COMMISSION ACT 1914; ROBINSON PATMAN ACT 1936 and CELLER KEFAUVER ANTIMERGER ACT 1950.

References
Blair, R.D. and Kaserman, D.L. (1985) *Antitrust Economics*, Homewood, IL: Richard D. Irwin.
Kwoka, J.E. and White, L.J. (eds) (1999) *The antitrust revolution. Economics, competition and policy*, 3rd edn, New York and Oxford: Oxford University Press.
Neale, A.D. and Goyder, D.G. (1980) *The Antitrust Laws of the USA*, 3rd edn, Cambridge: Cambridge University Press.
Shepherd, W.G. (2000) 'In perspective: the role of economics at the Antitrust Division since 1974', *Review of Industrial Organization* 16: 107–11.
Viscusi, W.K., Vernon, J.M. and Harrington, J.E. (1995) *Economics of regulation and antitrust*, 2nd edn, Cambridge, MA, and London: MIT Press.

apprenticeship (J2)
A period of training in a firm which enables a trainee to learn a craft under the supervision of a skilled worker. The

length of the apprenticeship varies from trade to trade and country to country. Adam SMITH noted that in ancient times the period was commonly seven years, even in universities for studying for a Master of Arts degree. Apprenticeships have long provided technological education and transmitted sophisticated manual skills from one generation to another. But critics have viewed them as a union restrictive practice for they have been used to limit the number in a trade, and hence to increase average earnings. Recurrent skilled labour shortages in engineering have been attributed to the system.

appropriate technology (O3)
Labour-intensive small-scale methods of production using renewable energy. A technology advocated for Third World countries.

See also: Schumacher

References

Dunn, P. (1978) *Appropriate Technology: Technology with a Human Face*, London: Macmillan.
Jequier, N. (ed.) (1976) *Appropriate Technology: Problems and Promises*, Paris: Development Centre of the Organization for Economic Co-operation and Development.

Appropriation Bill (H5)
A US federal legislative bill authorising expenditure for a particular purpose, e.g. defence, which has to be passed by both the US House of Representatives and the Senate. Annually all the bills are expected to be reconciled by a Reconciliation Bill by the end of June; if reconciliation is impossible, a continuing resolution is passed which permits departments to continue at their current expenditure levels.

approximate equilibrium (D5)
A DISEQUILIBRIUM price, usually manifest in the existence of EXCESS DEMAND. This is close to an EQUILIBRIUM PRICE.

Aquinas, St Thomas, 1225–74 (B3)
The leading medieval economic and social thinker and theologian, the most prominent of the Schoolmen. His interpretation of the teaching of ARISTOTLE and the early Christian Fathers is set out in his massive *Summa Theologica*. He expounded the doctrine of the JUST PRICE, permitted the charging of interest (when there was a risk that the lender would not be paid on time) and supported the institutions of private property and trade (if the public good is promoted).

References

Baldwin, J.W. (1959) *The Mediaeval Theories of the Just Price*, Philadelphia: American Philosophical Society.
Gordon, B. (1975) *Economic Analysis before Adam Smith*, London: Macmillan.
Worland, S.T. (1967) *Scholasticism and Welfare Economics*, Notre Dame, IN: University of Notre Dame Press.

Arab Common Market (F0)
A COMMON MARKET set up in 1964 with the aims of free movement of labour and capital, free trade and unimpeded transport access among the member countries which, originally, were Jordan, Kuwait, Morocco, Syria and the United Arab Republic (Egypt and Syria).

Arab Maghreb Union (F0)
An economic union of Morocco, Algeria, Tunisia, Mauritania and Libya set up in 1989. Progress towards free mobility of labour and capital and the creation of a common or single currency has been slow.

arb (G1)
Arbitrageur, especially a speculator in the stocks of companies likely to be taken over by others.

arbitrage (F0, G0)
An investment strategy taking the form of a simultaneous purchase of an item in one market and sale of it in another with the expectation of a positive return. Profits can often be made from small differences in price. This is common in currency and commodity markets and is a force producing price equalization, after allowing for transport and transaction costs and risk.

In the case of a currency market, arbitrage continues until the cross exchange rates are consistent. For example, if initially US\$1 = DM4, DM1 = 2 guilders and US\$1 = 6 guilders, the correct cross-rate should be DM1 = 1.5 guilders. The arbitrageurs sell spot and buy forward if they believe that the value of a currency is falling: they benefit from the difference between two prices, with the forward contract protecting them from a fall in the exchange rate.

arbitration (J5)
Settlement of a dispute by referral to a third party, used in industrial relations and in many commercial disagreements. The arbitrator may be a court of law, an independent arbitrator chosen by the parties in dispute or a permanent government body, e.g. the ADVISORY, CONCILIATION AND ARBITRATION SERVICE (UK). As arbitration is either voluntary or imposed, it can be binding, compulsory, mandatory or unilateral. Landlord and tenant, shipping and building contracts often use this method of resolving conflicts. Private arbitration, which may be instituted in advance by a contractual term, is cheaper and quicker than resort to litigation.

See also: pendulum arbitration

arc elasticity (C1, D0, D1)
The elasticity of demand over a portion of a demand curve or the elasticity of supply over a section of a supply curve. It is calculated from the midpoint between old and new prices and quantities on the curve, using the ratio of the percentage change in quantity to the percentage change in price, i.e.

$$\text{elasticity} = \frac{\Delta Q/(Q_1 + Q_2)}{\Delta P/(P_1 + P_2)}$$

where P_1 and Q_1 are the price and quantity originally and P_2 and Q_2 are the price and quantity after the change. It provides an average of POINT ELASTICITIES.

Aristotle, 384–22 BC (B3)
One of the earliest writers on economics who anticipated many later debates on value, money and economic systems. In the *Nichomachean Ethics*, Book V, he discussed the nature of value in the context of a discussion of justice; in *Topica*, he anticipated subsequent ideas of value based on utility. He supported the idea of private property on the grounds that it leads to increased production and clearly saw that money has the important functions of serving as a unit of account, a medium of exchange and a store of value.

References

Gordon, B. (1975) *Economic Analysis before Adam Smith*, London: Macmillan.
Soudek, J. (1952) 'Aristotle's theory of exchange: an inquiry into the origin of economic analysis', *Proceedings of the American Philosophical Society* 96: 45–75.

arithmetic mean (C1)
The sum of a set of values divided by the number of values in that set.

See also: geometric mean; harmonic mean

arithmetic progression (C6)
A series of numbers increasing by a constant increment called a common difference, e.g. 2, 4, 6, 8. MALTHUS asserted that the means of subsistence increases arithmetically.

See also: geometric progression

ARMA (C5)
Autoregressive moving-average model. This model of a stationary random process, i.e. a process whose mean is constant over time, recognizes that a combination of moving-average and autoregressive models is necessary.

References

Box, G.E.P. and Jenkins, G.M. (1970) *Time Series Analysis: Forecasting and Control*, San Francisco: Holden-Day.

Armington assumption (F1)
The supposition that internationally traded

products are differentiated according to country of origin.

References

Armington, Paul S. (1969) 'A theory of demand for products distinguished by place of production', *IMF Staff Papers* 16(March): 159–78.

Arrow–Debreu model (D5)

An economic theory concerned with establishing the existence of an equilibrium for an integrated model of production, exchange and consumption. The two theorems produced by the authors were that (1) a competitive equilibrium exists if every individual has initially some positive quantity of every commodity available for sale and (2) there are individuals capable of supplying a positive amount of at least one type of labour with positive usefulness in the production of desired commodities.

See also: general equilibrium

References

Arrow, K.J. and Debreu, G. (1954) 'The existence of an equilibrium for a competitive economy', *Econometrica* 22: 265–90.

Arrow–Debreu security (G1)

A financial instrument, or combination of securities, with a fixed payment of one unit only according to a specified contingency.

Arrow, Kenneth Joseph, 1921– (B3)

US economist, educated at City College, New York, and Columbia University; professor at Stanford University from 1953 to 1968, and from 1979, with an interlude at Harvard from 1968 to 1979. His study of social choice led him to formulate the IMPOSSIBILITY THEOREM, his most famous contribution to economics. Also, he and DEBREU proved in an *Econometrica* article of 1954 that a multimarket equilibrium under perfect competition required the existence of forward markets for all goods and services. His work on risk aversion and on growth theory (particularly LEARNING-BY-DOING) is also notable.

In 1972, he shared the NOBEL PRIZE FOR ECONOMICS with HICKS. The range of his contribution to economic theory and his interest in the functioning of a GENERAL EQUILIBRIUM system are evident in his *Collected Papers*. He shows how he developed the ideas in Hicks's *Value and Capital* to explain what it means to be better off. His analysis of VOTING PROCEDURES advanced the study of social choice. Also, he has written much on the economics of information.

See also: social choice theory

References

Leading works include the following:
Arrow, K.J. (1966) *Social Choice and Individual Values*, New York: Wiley.
—— (1984–5) *Collected Papers of Kenneth J. Arrow*, Vols I–V, Oxford: Basil Blackwell.
Arrow, K.J. and Hahm, F. (1971) *General Competitive Analysis*, San Francisco: Holden-Day; Edinburgh: Oliver & Boyd.
Feiwel, G.R. (ed.) (1987) *Arrow and the Ascent of Modern Economic Theory*, Basingstoke and London: Macmillan.

artificial barrier to entry (L1)

A BARRIER TO ENTRY of firms into a market or industry erected by a government or the existing firms and not by natural market forces. Governments may insist on licensing new entrants; firms may refuse to provide access to existing technology.

artificial currency (F3)

A currency unit used either as a common unit of account for international transactions or as an international reserve asset. Principal examples of these are SPECIAL DRAWING RIGHTS, EUROPEAN CURRENCY UNITS, EUROPEAN UNITS OF ACCOUNT and, in general, baskets of currencies. Such currencies are very useful for international accounting in times of volatile exchange rates.

See also: gold franc

A share (G1, G2)

1 A Chinese stock market share payable

in the Chinese currency, the renminbi.

2 Usually a non-voting share of the equity capital of a UK company. These shares have been created to enable the founders of a company to retain control. A shares trade at lower prices than B shares as they are useless to other companies attempting to gain control of the company. Gradually these shares have been accorded voting rights as the London Stock Exchange regards them as unfair.

Asian Development Bank (G2)

Bank founded in 1966 with capital provided by Asian countries, the USA, Canada, the UK and West Germany on the recommendation of the United Nations Economic Commission for Asia and the Far East. It covers half of the world's population. It is based in Manilla, the Philippines, and is dominated by the Japanese, the largest contributor of its capital. Its conservative lending policy has chiefly favoured loans for specific projects, e.g. to build ports, roads and bridges, rather than sectoral lending to restructure troubled economies. It has increased its lending to the private sector and has a joint venture with commercial banks, the Asian Finance and Investment Corporation (AFIC).

Asian option (G1)

A DERIVATIVE settled in cash whose pay-off is related to the average price of the underlying asset in a certain time period. Also known as an average option.

Asiatic mode of production (P0)

The most primitive form of production, according to MARX, in which self-sufficient agricultural communities are despotically governed. The state, through taxation, appropriates the economic surplus of the agricultural sector to finance the building of the country's infrastructure. The concept was developed in the 1950s and 1960s to examine more aspects of state forma-tion and the formation of classes in primitive communities.

References

Krader, L. (1975) *The Asiatic Mode of Production*, Assen, The Netherlands: Van Gorcum.

Marx, K. (1964) *Pre-capitalist Economic Formations*, ed. E. Hobsbawm, London: Lawrence & Wishart.

O'Leary, B. (1989) *The Asiatic Mode of Production: Oriental Despotism, Historical Materialism and Indian History*, Oxford: Basil Blackwell.

ask price (G0)

The selling price of a SECURITY set by a financial institution.

See also: bid price

asset (D0, G0)

1 A resource with a market value.
2 A unit of wealth capable of earning an income.
3 A large enough estate to discharge the burden on an heir or executor.

Real (or tangible) assets include land and machinery; intangible assets include goodwill and patents; financial assets include cash and stock market securities.

See also: national wealth; wealth

asset card (G1)

A DEBIT CARD.

asset motive (E4)

A motive for holding money. To avoid risky investments, people are prepared to sacrifice high returns by keeping their portfolios in a liquid or near-liquid form.

See also: speculative demand for money

asset specificity (G0)

The unique character of a durable asset, e.g. a machine, a skilled worker or a production site, which means that it has a low return in other uses. For many specific assets the cost of employing them is in the nature of a SUNK COST.

See also: economic rent; transfer earnings

asset stripping (M2)
The sale of parts of a company which, in many cases, has recently been taken over by another company. Large holding companies have been built up in the past this way as each stripping provides resources for another company acquisition. By selling off parts of a company previously undervalued, finance for further acquisitions is obtained.

asset sweating (M2)
Raising bank finance on the security of the property owned by a company. Sweating can also be effected by SECURITIZATION of the property.

assistance-in-kind (H2)
A grant expressed in goods and services; an alternative to a cash gift.

assisted area (R5)
A region or smaller area of a country eligible for grants and SOFT LOANS under the regional policy of a national government or the EUROPEAN UNION. The criteria for assistance to a region include its rate of unemployment, the decay of its infrastructure and its participation in a larger plan to achieve interregional balance.

Association of International Bond Dealers (G2)
An association of 850 dealing firms mainly outside the UK. Under new rules in force from 1987, interdealer brokers are only able to deal with reporting dealers. Every evening there is electronic reporting of closing bids, offered quotations and that day's highest and lowest prices for each bond in which the association trades. In January 1992 became the International Securities Market Association.

Association of South East Asian Nations (F0)
The trading association of Brunei, Indonesia, Malaysia, the Philippines, Singapore and Thailand founded in 1967. Its principal task has been to arrange preferential import tariff rates on trade between its members.

Although 19,000 products are given preference, they have little impact on freeing trade as the major items (about 95 per cent of trade) are excluded from the list. ASEAN hopes by the year 2000 to free most of the intra-association trade and be more than an association representing this area in international negotiations. Industrial JOINT VENTURES with non-Asian countries, a new insurance company and improved transportation arrangements are likely to promote further economic integration. It was agreed in 1987 that goods at present enjoying preferential tariffs should have the preference increased to 50 per cent of the tariff and goods enjoying preference for the first time should have 25 per cent of the tariff.

asymmetric information (D0, L1)
Information possessed by one side of a market only. If, for example, buyers but not sellers have relevant information, they will be at an advantage. In labour markets, employers usually know more about the present and future financial state of their firms than trade unions and thereby have a bargaining advantage in wage negotiations. This view of information has also been incorporated into models of industrial organization and of the valuation of PUBLIC GOODS.

See also: lemons market

atomistic competition (L1)
Similar to PERFECT COMPETITION in that there are a large number of buyers and sellers, each with no significant influence on the market, behaving like atoms – very small but with a joint importance. This view of competition is based on an individualistic view of economic activity.

at the money (G1)
The state of an OPTION where its UNDERLIER equals its STRIKE PRICE.

at-will employment contract (J5)
A labour contract under which an employer can lawfully dismiss or retain an

employee whether the reason is good or not.

auction (D0, D4)

A type of selling in which a system of bidding determines the price and the successful buyer. WALRAS showed the crucial role of auction models in his discussion of *tâtonnement*, using the idea of crying out prices to describe the movement of a market to equilibrium with supply equal to demand.

See also: Dutch auction; English auction; first price auction; second price auction; hybrid auction

References

Engelbrecht-Wiggans, R., Shubik, M. and Stark, R. M. (eds) (1983) *Auctions, Bidding and Contracting: Uses and Theory*, New York: New York University Press.

McAfee, R.F. and McMillan, J. (1987) 'Auctions and bidding', *Journal of Economic Literature* 25(June): 699–738.

Smith, C.M. (1989) *Auctions: The Social Construction of Value*, Hemel Hempstead: Harvester Wheatsheaf.

audit market (M4)

The accounting firms and their clients concerned with the checking of company accounts to ensure that legal requirements are met and that financial transactions are accurately recorded. A free audit market is proposed for the EUROPEAN UNION so that the same auditors could examine the accounts of all of a firm's European subsidiaries.

augmented GNP (E2)

GROSS NATIONAL PRODUCT plus the value of public goods and services of all kinds, whether marketed or not. This measure takes into account the criteria for a good environment by measuring 'goods' net of 'bads'.

See also: measure of economic welfare; public good

Australian Industries Preservation Acts 1906–50 (L4)

Commonwealth of Australia statutes modelled on the SHERMAN ACT of the USA: these have created a COMPETITION POLICY for Australia. The difficulty of successfully prosecuting firms under them has caused antitrust actions to be more a concern of the individual Australian states.

Australian Loan Council (H5)

An agency of federal government, founded in 1928, to raise loans for state governments and for public utilities.

Austrian School (B1, B2)

A prominent school of economics which has provided an opposing view to much of mainstream economics since it was founded by Carl MENGER in the 1870s. At its inception, the school shared with JEVONS and WALRAS an interest in expounding a subjective theory of value based on MARGINAL UTILITY but it did not use a mathematical approach as it sought to deal with essences and not quantities. The 'Austrians' opposed the popular contemporary GERMAN HISTORICAL SCHOOL partly because they took the view that economic laws are based on simple elements such as needs and satisfaction expressed as invariable sequences not influenced by time and space.

MENGER's leadership of the school was taken over by BOEHM-BAWERK and WIESER. Boehm-Bawerk extended the analysis of consumer valuation to explain costs, prices, interest rates and economic growth. However, he is chiefly known for his time analysis of capital as a ROUNDABOUT METHOD OF PRODUCTION and his interest rate theory. Wieser used his broad knowledge as an economist, sociologist and historian to examine all social phenomena with an attitude to economic POLICY which transcended both laissez-faire and interventionist approaches. His idea that the chief importance of prices is to provide information on all economic conditions was to inspire both MISES and HAYEK; his concept of entrepreneurial leadership was followed by SCHUMPETER in the latter's theory of development. Both Mises and Schumpeter were members of Boehm-Bawerk's celebrated seminar.

After the collapse of the Austro-Hungarian Empire at the end of the First World War, the members of the school dispersed to the UK, USA and Germany. Prominent new members of it included HABERLER and MACHLUP. In the late twentieth century HAYEK and Ludwig LACHMANN were leaders. Later Austrians have attempted to use the basic concepts of radical subjectivism, human purpose and a spontaneous market order to contribute to modern debates about expectations, competition and economic welfare. Their policy concerns have included the relationship between MONETARY POLICY and the TRADE CYCLE, FREE BANKING and criticism of socialism.

References

Grassl, W. and Smith, B. (1986) *Austrian Economics*, London: Croom Helm.
Hicks, J.R. and Weber, W. (eds) (1973) *Carl Menger and the Austrian School of Economics*, Oxford: Oxford University Press.
Lachmann, L. (1976) 'From Mises to Shackle: an essay on Austrian economics and the Kaleidic Society', *Journal of Economic Literature* 14: 54–62.
Littlechild, S. (1990) *Austrian Economics*, 3 vols, Aldershot: Edward Elgar.

autarky (P0)

1 Self-sufficiency.

2 A completely closed economy which does not engage in international trade. Although many economies have wanted such independence from the rest of the world to increase employment, their enthusiasm has been tempered by an examination of the other effects of protection.

See also: utopia

authoritative contracting (J2, J3) *see* employment contract

autocorrelation (C1)

The state of an econometric relation such that some or all of the explanatory variables are highly correlated with each other. Poor specification of the relationship between variables in the regression equation is often the cause.

auto-economy (G0)

That part of an economy, according to HICKS, which finances itself from its own stock of liquid assets.

References

Hicks, J. (1974) *The Crisis in Keynesian Economics*, ch. 2, Oxford: Basil Blackwell.

autogestion (J5)

A French approach to WORKERS' PARTICIPATION in the running of enterprises, proposed after the 1968 uprisings in France. This philosophy of management holds that enterprises should be less hierarchical, with all employees participating directly in decision making, especially about work organization, promotion and other employment rules, technology and methods of production. This democratization would include a new framework for discussions between enterprises.

See also: syndicalism

References

Chauvey, D. (1970) *Autogestion*, Paris: Editions du Seuil.

automated clearing house (G2)

An organization for the electronic matching of cheques drawn on different banks so that interbank indebtedness can be settled.

See also: CHAPS; CHIPS

Automated Real-time Investment Exchange (G1)

A computerized arrangement for dealing in shares set up by MERCHANT BANKS in the City of London in 1974 to bypass the INTERNATIONAL STOCK EXCHANGE and thus save brokers' commission. It never attracted a high proportion of the London trading volume.

automated teller machine (G2)

A cash-dispensing machine of a bank or other deposit-taking institution. The machine allows customers continuous access to their bank deposits. Other services provided by automated teller machines include the production of bank statements.

automatic neural network modelling (C8)

A method of data analysis using the analogy of the neural networks in the brain. A 'training set' of data based on input–output relationships for different cases is used to compute patterns. Automation of these procedures reduces the complexity of network construction. This analytical approach is used in financial econometrics.

automatic stabilizer (E3, H3)

A built-in feature of tax structures and public expenditure programmes. It reduces fluctuations in an economy, making it respond more easily to shocks. Prominent examples of stabilizers include PROGRESSIVE TAXES (which prevent post-tax income rising at the same rate as pre-tax income) and unemployment insurance (which prevents personal income from falling below a predefined 'floor'). The GOLD STANDARD was a major type of automatic stabilizer. All these stabilizers have the characteristic of preventing the rise or fall of national income, and consequently employment, being as great as it would be in the absence of a government with an ACTIVE FISCAL POLICY. It is the experience of most countries that as these stabilizers are insufficient in themselves to remove fluctuations they need to be combined with discretionary changes in taxation and public expenditure.

See also: fine-tuning

autonomous consumption (E2)

Consumption unrelated to the level of income. At zero income, in the short run, there can be autonomous consumption to maintain physical existence. It is financed by borrowing and the liquidation of assets.

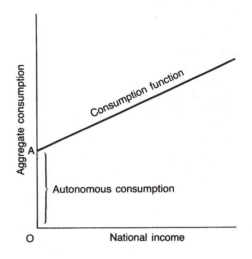

autonomous expenditure (E2)

Expenditure independent of the level of income, often because of its necessary character.

autonomous investment (E2)

Investment independent of the level of income. It can be affected by changes in interest rates and in the 'ANIMAL SPIRITS' of entrepreneurs. It is shown by a parallel shift in the aggregate demand schedule.

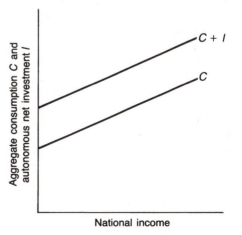

25

Autumn Statement (H5)

UK statement on public expenditure produced separately from the March budget until the budget date was changed to November in 1994.

availability thesis (F1)

The proposition that a high proportion of international trade is an exchange between goods which are only available in one or a few countries. ELASTICITY OF SUPPLY in one country and inelasticity of supply in another give rise to trade. Some new products are only available in some countries, partly because of the nature of their patent protection.

References

Kravis, I.B. (1956) 'Availability and other influences on the commodity composition of international trade', *Journal of Political Economy* 64: 143–55.

average (C1)

A value showing the central tendency of a set of data and often used to compare that set with others; for example, the average age of the Finnish population is compared with the average age of the Romanian population.

See also: mean; median; mode

average deviation (C1) *see* mean deviation

average incremental cost (D0)

Change in total cost divided by change in output; an approximation to MARGINAL COST necessary because marginal cost refers to such small quantity changes that in practice it is difficult to measure it. In the 1978 guidelines for UK NATIONALIZED INDUSTRIES it was used as a measurable alternative to marginal cost. Because it is a rough approximation, it fails to give precise guidance for the expansion of integrated systems.

References

HMSO (1978) *White Paper on Nationalised Industries*, Cmnd 7131.

average option (G1) *see* Asian option

average propensity to consume (E2)

The ratio of a consumer's total consumption to his or her total income. For low-income groups the average propensity to consume is unity, or close to unity, as there is no surplus over expenditure available for saving. As income rises and basic consumer goods have been purchased, this propensity declines; also it varies over the life cycle (see LIFE-CYCLE HYPOTHESIS). If a graph of the CONSUMPTION FUNCTION passes through the origin, the average propensity to consume (C/Y) equals the MARGINAL PROPENSITY TO CONSUME ($\Delta C/\Delta Y$) at all levels of income and is unity; a consumption function with a constant slope has the same MARGINAL PROPENSITY TO CONSUME at all income levels.

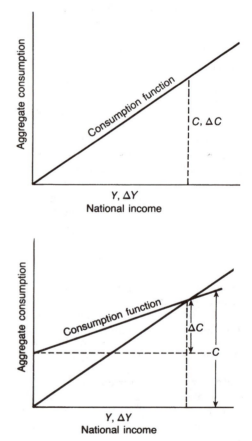

average propensity to save (E2)

Total savings as a proportion of total income. This proportion is likely to be negative at low levels of income as poor households often need to borrow to finance basic consumption; at higher income levels, households can afford to save because their consumption needs have been met. The average propensity to save for a national economy will depend on its income distribution and average level of income.

See also: savings; savings ratio

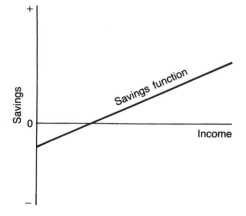

average tax rate (H2)

The fraction of a person's total income which is paid in taxes. A person with a gross income of £50,000 per year, paying £10,000 in tax, will have an average tax rate of 20 per cent. This tax rate is usually contrasted with the MARGINAL TAX RATE and is calculated for some or all of the taxes paid by a person.

average total cost (D0)

Total costs of a firm divided by its output. Sub-components of average total cost are average fixed cost (fixed cost divided by output) and average variable cost (total variable cost divided by output). The average total cost curve will fall if there are ECONOMIES OF SCALE and rise if there are DISECONOMIES. In the short run, such curves are typically U-shaped; in the long run, L-shaped.

Averch–Johnson effect (L5)

The misallocation in resources resulting from regulatory agencies relating price levels to a 'fair' rate of return. Averch and Johnson asserted that REGULATION of this kind would fail to minimize SOCIAL COST: a firm would not equate marginal rates of factor substitution to the ratio of factor costs. Firms would have an incentive to move into other regulated markets where they would be able to operate at a loss and drive out the lowest cost producers.

References

Averch, H.A. and Johnson, L.L. (1962) 'Behavior of the firm under regulatory constraint', *American Economic Review* 52: 1052–69.

axioms of preference (D1)

The assumptions necessary for consumer rationality. They are completeness (that a consumer can order all available combinations preferred), transitivity (if A is preferred to B and B to C, then A is preferred to C), selection (the consumer chooses the most preferred state), non-satiation (the consumer prefers more to less of a good) and continuity (there is a boundary in the form of an INDIFFERENCE CURVE separating preferred from non-preferred combinations of goods).

Ayres, Clarence Edwin, 1891–1972 (B3)
A leading US INSTITUTIONALIST economist
who was educated at Brown and Chicago
Universities. He taught philosophy at Chicago, Amherst and Reed Universities from
1917 to 1930 and was Professor of Economics, University of Texas, from 1930 to
1968. VEBLEN and the philosopher John
Dewey (1859–1952) were major influences
upon him. His powerful analysis of economic progress asserted that the technology essential to industrialization is constantly
in conflict with established institutions
which approve of ceremony to protect
vested interests. Ayres's work has made a
great impact on development economics.

References

Breit, W. and Culbertson, W.P., Jr (1976)
*Science and Ceremony: The Institutional
Economics of C.E. Ayres*, Austin, TX:
University of Texas Press.

B

baby-boom period (J1)
The 1970s when persons who were born in the high-birth-rate period following the Second World War became adults.

baby-bust generation (J1)
The 1990s and later when there were fewer young adults.

backtesting (C1, G1)
A simulation of actual trading in SECURITIES using past data.

backwardation (G1)
1 The charge made on a stock exchange for carrying the settlement of a BARGAIN into the next accounting period.
2 In commodity markets, it is the amount by which a SPOT PRICE and the cost of carrying a commodity over time exceeds the forward price. The opposite is CONTANGO.

backward-bending labour supply curve (J3)
A curve plotting the supply of labour against wage rates which becomes negatively sloped at higher wage rates as proportionately less labour is supplied. This phenomenon is caused by the relative size of the INCOME and SUBSTITUTION EFFECTS of the wage rate change. As an increase in the wage rate also represents an increase in the price of leisure, this price effect can be divided into a substitution effect (the effect on the number of hours of leisure chosen of an increase in its price) and an income effect (the effect of an increased wage rate that a given income is reached with fewer hours of work – in the figure, beyond point A higher real wage discourages workers from supplying more hours of work). A negative income effect greater than zero or a positive substitution effect will produce the backward bend in the labour supply curve.

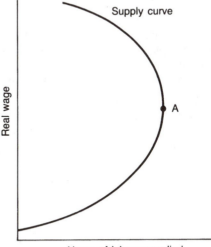

References

Buchanan, J.M. (1971) 'The back-bending supply curve of labour: an example of doctrinal retrogression', *History of Political Economy* 3: 383–90.

backward linkage (L0) *see* linkage

backward shifting (H2) *see* shifting of taxes

backwash effect (R5)
The unfavourable effect of economic growth in a region on other regions in the same national economy. The growing region attracts capital and labour from other regions, bringing about a concentration in economic activity and regional economic differentials. This effect has been noted in the context of the study of the CORE and PERIPHERY of a country.

See also: spread effect

bad (D6)
An output from economic activity which does not benefit consumers. Most bads are external costs associated with production, e.g. pollution and other health hazards. Bads must be taken into account when measuring the welfare conferred by a particular level of the national income.

See also: economic welfare; externality; good; illth; measure of economic welfare

bad equilibrium (E0)
A balance in an ECONOMY at a low level of activity, e.g. low per capita income, a structural imbalance in the balance of payment and unequal income distribution.

badge engineering (L6)
Production of a range of automobile/car models with similar characteristics to create a number of distinct brands.

Bagehot, Walter, 1826–77 (B3)
Nineteenth-century economic and political journalist who was the most famous editor of *The Economist* (1861–77) and inventor of the TREASURY BILL, still used by the UK Treasury as a source of short-term finance. After his début as an economics writer with a review of John Stuart MILL's *Principles of Political Economy* (first published in 1848) he quickly showed his ability to distil economic truth from a mass of evidence. In *Lombard Street* (1873) he acutely analysed the UK banking system and money market showing the crucial role of the Bank of England and the importance of confidence as the basis of credit.

References

Bagehot, W. (1965–78) *The Collected Works of Walter Bagehot*, ed. N. St John-Stevas, London: The Economist.

Bailey, Samuel, 1791–1870 (B3)
A major opponent of the Ricardian theory of value, mainly known for his *A Critical Dissertation on the Nature, Measures and Causes of Value: Chiefly in Reference to the Writings of Mr Ricardo and his Followers* (1825) in which he equated value with 'esteem' and emphasized its essentially relative nature. In his attack on intrinsic and labour theories of value, he stressed the importance of the forces of supply and demand as determinants of relative value. His entire career was spent on the Sheffield Town Trust (a quasi-governmental agency), although he stood for election to parliament in 1832 and 1835.

References

Bailey, S. (1825, reprinted 1931) *Critical Dissertation on the Nature, Measures, and Causes of Value: Chiefly in Reference to the Writings of Mr Ricardo and his Followers*, London: Series of Scarce Tracts in Economic and Political Science, No. 7.

Rauner, R.M. (1961) *Samuel Bailey and the Classical Theory of Value*, London: G. Bell.

Seligman, E.R.A. (1905) 'On some neglected British economists', *Economic Journal* 13: 335–63, 511–35.

Bain, Joe Staten, 1912– (B3)
An American economist educated at the University of California at Los Angeles and Harvard, and a professor of economics for thirty years at Berkeley, California, until his retirement in 1975. He is particularly famous for his study of BARRIERS TO ENTRY as a cause of MONOPOLY POWER. Also, he has provided a detailed examination of the relationship between CONCENTRATION RATIOS and profitability.

References

Bain, J.S. (1956) *Barriers to Entry*, Cambridge, MA: Harvard University Press.

—— (1972) *Essays on Price Theory and Industrial Organisation*, Boston: Little, Brown.

Baker plan (F3)

US plan for easing the Third World debt problem, proposed by US Secretary for the Treasury James Baker at the annual meeting of the WORLD BANK and the INTERNATIONAL MONETARY FUND in Seoul, South Korea, October 1985. It proposed that once the debtor countries put together 'supply-side packages' (trade liberalization and more reliance on the price mechanism to allocate resources) and serviced their debts on time, money would be available in the form of loans from the World Bank, the IMF and commercial banks. It was not enthusiastically received among debtor countries (except for Mexico which reached a preliminary agreement in July 1986 to obtain US$7 billion of money as a loan). The plan has been criticized because it tries to solve a debt problem by creating more debt; gives time for procrastination and fails to deal with the root problem – that the rate of growth of Third World exports has been slower than the rate of interest on dollar loans since 1981.

It was proposed in 1986 that the World Bank would lend a net US$20 billion over three years to a selected group of fifteen countries with a combined foreign debt of US$430 billion; it was difficult to persuade the commercial banks, who are lending less to these countries, to match the generosity of the World Bank.

See also: world debt problem

balanced budget (H6)

A government budget which equates revenue with expenditure. This prudent approach to fiscal policy long advocated by conservative finance ministers has frequently been attacked by KEYNESIANS who regard it as an inflexible rule which ignores the levels of aggregate demand and unemployment. A government surplus will increase public sector saving; a government deficit will require borrowing. However, unbalanced budgets could result in CROWDING OUT or long-term insolvency of a country (if the national debt is financed at a rate of interest in excess of the country's rate of growth) or inflation (if a country increases its money supply to finance its borrowing).

Balanced Budget and Emergency Deficit Control Act 1985 (H6) *see* Gramm–Rudman–Hollings Act

balanced budget multiplier (E2, E6)

A measure of the expansion or contraction of NATIONAL INCOME which occurs despite an equal change in the revenue and expenditure of a government. An expansion in national income is possible where the PROPENSITY TO CONSUME of a government is greater than the private sector's. If the government taxed £100 million of personal income at 30 per cent, it would receive revenue of £30 million which, if spent in its entirety, would be a greater addition to total demand than if the tax was not raised but was left with persons who habitually saved 20 per cent of their incomes.

balanced growth (O4)

1 Growth of different sectors of an economy at the same rate. This has been advocated by many development economists as a strategy. Ragnar Nurske propounded the view that growth should take the form of the co-ordinated and simultaneous application of capital to a wide range of industries so that the national economy would not be a mixture of expanding, declining and stationary sectors.

2 Steady state growth such that the real variables of the economy, including output and employment, grow at the same positive rates.

References

Rosenstein-Rodan, P.N. (1943) 'Problems of industrialization of Eastern and south-eastern Europe', *Economic Journal* 53: 202–11.

Balance for Official Financing (F4)

The current balance of the BALANCE OF PAYMENTS + capital transfers + investment transactions + BALANCING ITEM.

balance of payments (F4)

1 Credits and debits in international transactions.

2 The record of the transactions between the residents of one country and the rest of the world in a given time period. The balance of payments is divided into a current account which records trade in goods and services and a capital account. In accounting terms the balance of payments always 'balances', as a surplus or deficit has to be offset by loans granted or received, but the balance does not indicate whether there is an equilibrium between a domestic economy and rest of the world demand. A balance of payments may be in deficit in the 'STOCK' sense of a country switching from cash balances into stocks of commodities, or in the 'FLOW' sense of a country spending more than its income, a more serious type of deficit. There have been changes in the presentation of the UK balance of payments accounts. Before 1970, the equation used was

visible + invisible
balance   = current balance + balance of long-term capital
= basic balance + balancing item + balance of monetary movements
= 0

From 1970 to 1980, it was

visible + invisible
balance   = current balance + balance of private and other autonomous capital flows + balancing item
= total currency flow + allocation of special drawing rights – gold subscription to the IMF + total official financing
= 0

After 1980, it has been

visible + invisible
balance   = current balance + total investment and other capital transactions + balancing item + allocation of special drawing rights – gold subscription to the IMF
= total official financing + methods of financing
= 0

The US balance of payments consists of:

exports of goods and services + transfer of goods and services under US military grants net –
imports of goods and services –
US military grants of goods and services net –
unilateral transfers (excluding military grants) net –
US assets abroad net (increase/capital outflow) +
foreign assets in the USA net (increase/capital inflow) +
allocations of special drawing rights +
balances of the above subaccounts.

See also: accounting balance of payments; balance of payments equilibrium; fundamental equilibrium; market balance of payments

References
Central Statistical Office (annual) *UK Balance of Payments*, London: HMSO.

Stern, R.M. (1973) *The Balance of Payments*, London: Macmillan.

Thirlwall, A.P. (1986) *Balance of Payments Theory and the United Kingdom Experience*, London: Macmillan.

balance of payments equilibrium (F4)
A balance within the overall ACCOUNTING BALANCE OF PAYMENTS. The equilibria most frequently examined are in the current account, in the visible trade account or in the current and long-term capital accounts combined. The balance chosen for examination depends on the purpose of the analysis. If the performance of industry is being considered, then the balance of trade will be examined, but the capital accounts merit attention if a foreign exchange market is under scrutiny.

balance of trade (F4) *see* trade balance

balance sheet (M4)
A statement of the assets and liabilities of a firm or other organization which possesses property. The assets show what the firm owns, and what the firm owes is indicated by its liabilities. For a bank, the management of its balance sheet from day to day is a central part of its business tasks.

balancing item (F4)
Part of the BALANCE FOR OFFICIAL FINANCING which takes into account statistical discrepancies.

Baldwin envelope (F1)
As defined by Baldwin: 'The consumption possibility frontier for a large country constructed as the envelope formed by moving the foreign offer curve along the country's transformation curve.'

References

Baldwin, R.E. (1948) 'Equilibrium in international trade: a diagrammatic analysis', *Quarterly Journal of Economics* 67: 748–62.

balloon payment (G0)
An additional and large charge levied at the end of a lease or loan.

bancor (F3)
An international currency proposed by KEYNES at BRETTON WOODS as part of his INTERNATIONAL CLEARING UNION scheme. It was hoped that this new currency would be the medium for settling intercountry indebtedness. As Keynes's recommendation was not accepted, the US dollar assumed the role designed for bancor.

bandit problem (C9)
A learning problem. Repeatedly a choice is made from a fixed number of options in order to maximize the total reward over a particular time period. The one-armed bandit is a familiar slot machine game.

References

Berry, D.A. and Fristedt, B. (1985) *Bandit Problems: Sequential Allocation of Experiments*, London: Chapman and Hall.

bank advance (G2) *see* advance

bank capital (G2)
Assets of a bank which constitute its ultimate means of meeting the demands of its creditors. It consists of both the stockholders' equity in a bank and funds obtained by selling bonds and notes with a maturity of more than seven years on average. This capital is necessary to reduce the demands made on DEPOSIT INSURANCE organizations, e.g. the FEDERAL DEPOSIT INSURANCE CORPORATION, and on uninsured deposit holders. As definitions of this capital (e.g. whether to include both stock and equity) vary from country to country, in January 1987 the Bank of England and the US banking authorities created a common system for measuring the capital strength of UK and US banks. The system introduced the concept of PRIMARY CAPITAL and assigned a weight to each asset or off-balance-sheet item so that a risk–asset ratio could be calculated.

See also: risk–asset system

bank charges (G2)
The charges that retail banks make to their customers for bank advances or for various transactions, including the transfer

of funds, the purchase of foreign currency and accounting facilities. These tend to be greatest in countries with high inflation and consequently high and variable nominal interest rates, and also where there are many regulations restricting the types of financial mediation. As both the UK and the US economies have had these characteristics, there has been great scope in their banking sectors for a reduction in charges.

See also: Islamic banking

Bank Charter Act 1844 (E5, N2)
UK statute which was the last major nineteenth-century attempt to regulate the UK banking system by the creation of new rules for the operation of the Bank of England, particularly through control of the note issue. The Bank was divided into an Issue Department responsible for the note issue and a Banking Department engaged in other bank activities. The Bank's note issue was limited to a 'fiduciary issue' of £14 million (backed by government securities) and the remainder was backed by gold which rose and fell in amount according to international transactions. The Act also regulated the seventy-two country banks which had rights of note issue: not until 1921 did the Bank have a monopoly of note issue in England and Wales (Scotland retained its separate banking system with a number of banks having the power to issue banknotes after the Act of Union in 1707). The rigidity of the Act necessitated its suspension during several trade depressions. However, it did represent a triumph for the thinking of the CURRENCY SCHOOL.

bank deposits (G2)
The liabilities of banks which constitute the major part of the money supply of modern national economies. They are liabilities because a bank can transfer its deposits by cheque to other banks who then have a claim on it. Such deposits are created by an individual or firm giving an asset to a bank, e.g. coin and banknotes, or a promise to repay a loan at a future date.

See also: current account; demand deposit; NOW account; sight deposit

bank efficiency (G2)
A measure of a bank's effectiveness in using the money available to it. This can be assessed by the 'mark-up' between interest rates, i.e. either the ninety-day bank time deposit day rate minus the PRIME RATE OF INTEREST, or the bank demand deposit rate minus the bank prime rate. Mark-ups are similar within one country but differ between countries.

banker's turn (G2)
The margin between the rate of interest a bank pays to depositors and the rate it receives for money lent out.

See also: endowment effect

Bank for International Settlements (F3)
Founded in Basle, Switzerland, in 1930 by Belgium, Germany, Italy, Japan and the UK. Since 1945 it has continued to arrange currency swaps between European central banks. It is also the agent for the EUROPEAN MONETARY CO-OPERATION FUND and other European institutions.

bank holding company (G2)
A company which owns one or more banks and, often, firms engaged in non-banking activities. The development of such companies in the USA in the twentieth century made the expansion of banking possible, despite the existence of UNIT BANKING.

Bank Holding Company Act 1956 (E5, G2)
US federal statute which defined a bank holding company as one which directly or indirectly owns or holds power to vote 25 per cent or more of the shares of two or more major banks. Previously, bank holding companies were only mildly controlled by the BANKING ACT 1933 if they were member banks of the Federal Reserve System. In 1966, the Act was amended to apply ANTITRUST law to the chartering and acquisitions of these companies. The 1956 Act prohibited the companies from participation in non-banking activities; amend-

ments to the Act in 1970 permitted the Board of Governors of the Federal Reserve System to authorize many non-banking activities, which have included leasing, insurance, mortgage banking, community development and data processing.

banking (G2)

Money changing originally; after the Church permitted the charging of interest, primarily money lending. Banks began producing money by issuing banknotes and then expanded credit by creating bank deposits, which became the major part of the broadly defined money supply. The power to create credit made banks key institutions in modern economies, influencing the level of economic activity.

In the twentieth century banks increased in size through mergers and joint operations (e.g. in the UK through mergers in the 1920s and 1960s, and in the USA through the growth of bank holding companies), through internationalization of their operations and by an extension of the range of their services. In a sense, every major commercial bank of today aims to be a financial conglomerate supplying every form of credit, financial advice and service.

See also: branch banking; domestic banking system; fractional reserve banking; free banking; investment banking; Islamic banking; laser banking; merchant bank; offshore banking; unit banking; usury

References

Lewis, M.K. and Davis, K.T. (1987) *Domestic and International Banking*, Deddington: Philip Allan.

Banking Act 1933 (E5, G2) *see* Glass–Steagall Act

Banking Act 1979 (E5, G2)

The aims of this UK statute were to regulate deposit-taking business under the control of the Bank of England. It defined 'deposit-taking business' as the receiving of deposits of money and then lending to others, or as being financed out of the capital or interest received by way of deposit. The Act also set up a Deposit Protection Board to manage a deposit protection fund.

See also: Financial Services Act

Banking Act 1987 (E5, G2)

This UK statute extended the amount of regulation of deposit-taking business under the BANKING ACT 1979, gave the Bank of England exclusive powers to authorize the business of deposit taking and to revoke such powers, instructed the Bank of England to establish a Board of Banking Supervision and regulated financial advertisements.

Banking School (N2)

A group of UK economists, led by Thomas Tooke and John Stuart MILL, who argued that there could never be an excess note issue as notes were only issued to cover real transactions. Also, they wanted the Bank of England to have higher reserves and the growing importance of bank deposits to be incorporated into monetary theory.

See also: Bank Charter Act 1844; Currency School; Free Banking School; real bills doctrine

bank margin (G2)

The operating margin of a bank.

banknote (G2)

Paper CURRENCY issued by a bank. Although the first known notes were issued by Chinese banks in the eleventh century, it was not until the eighteenth and nineteenth centuries that they substantially replaced coinage and BILLS OF EXCHANGE. In London, banknotes originally took the form of receipts for bullion stored with goldsmiths and then became a form of bank advance when banks discovered their power to create money. When countries were on the GOLD STANDARD, it was possible to convert banknotes into bullion; since 1931 notes have been FIAT MONEY. In most countries the only note issue today is that of the CENTRAL BANK (the limited power of

Scottish banks to issue notes is exceptional).

See also: Bradbury

Bank of Canada (E5)
The central bank of Canada founded in 1934 and taken into government ownership in 1938. It has the task of formulating and executing monetary policy.

Bank of England (E5)
The UK's CENTRAL BANK which received its first charter in 1694. Although originally a privately owned bank, it administered the national debt from 1752. In a series of statutes culminating in the BANK CHARTER ACT 1844, it was increasingly subjected to government regulation, particularly in its note-issuing powers. After the collapse of the GOLD STANDARD in 1931, it operated EXCHANGE CONTROLS from 1939 to 1979 and from 1945 was more and more involved in supervising the UK banking sector. It was nationalized in 1946. It conducts MONETARY POLICY through OPEN MARKET OPERATIONS and by influencing market interest rates. The note issue is now entirely FIDUCIARY, but the monetary assets backing the note issue are used for the bank's daily interventions in government security and money markets. Also, the bank holds accounts for about 130 overseas central banks, the INTERNATIONAL MONETARY FUND and some private and public sector clients. It acts, too, as the registrar of government stocks of the UK, several Commonwealth countries and UK local authorities.

See also: bank rate; Competition and Credit Control; corset; minimum lending rate

References

Geddes, P. (1987) *Inside the Bank of England*, London: Boxtree.
Sayers, R.S. (1976) *The Bank of England, 1891–1944*, Cambridge: Cambridge University Press.

Bank of Italy (BOI) (E5)
The central bank of Italy founded in 1883 through the merger of four note-issuing banks. It was granted its independence from the Italian government in 1993.

Bank of Japan (BOJ) (E5)
The central bank of Japan controlled by the Policy Board whose members are chosen by the Cabinet and approved by the Diet.

bank rate (E5)
The lowest rate charged by the Bank of England prior to September 1971 for discounting high-quality short-term BILLS presented by financial institutions to preserve their liquidity. It was replaced by the MINIMUM LENDING RATE.

bank run (G2) *see* run on a bank

bankruptcy (K2)
A legal action which leads to the control of the property of an insolvent debtor for the benefit of creditors. After the court has appointed a receiver, the debtor can make an offer to his or her creditors.

bank settlement system (G2).
An electronic means of transferring deposits between banks to settle their mutual indebtedness. In the USA, Fed Wire is the Federal Reserve's system, Bank Wire is a system for domestic payments and CHIPS is a system for payments between New York banks. Japan has the Zenyin system for interbank transfers. The UK has CHAPS for the clearing banks, as well as BACS.

bank underwriting (G2)
The underwriting by banks, especially the subsidiaries of US bank holding companies, of the DEBT SECURITIES of low-credit-rated firms. This practice has enhanced the credit of many small firms.

Banque de France (E5)
The central bank of France founded in 1800 by Napoleon I and nationalized in 1946. It was granted independence to formulate monetary policy in 1994.

Baran, Paul, 1910–64 (B3)
Leading US Marxist economist of Russian descent who was educated at the Univer-

sities of Berlin and Harvard. During 1940–7, he worked in the US Office of Strategic Services, and was Professor of Economics at Stanford University from 1948 to 1964. His exposition of Marxist economics included theories of MONOPOLY CAPITAL and DEPENDENCY.

References

Baran, P. (1957) *The Political Economy of Growth*, New York: Monthly Review Press.

Baran, P. and Sweezy, P.M. (1966) *Monopoly Capital: An Essay on the American Economic and Social Order*, New York: Monthly Review Press.

barbell (G1)
A stock market investment strategy of investing in bonds with mainly very short- or long-term maturities.

Barber boom (E3, N1)
The 1971–4 period in the UK when Anthony Barber as Chancellor of the Exchequer over-stimulated the economy with inevitable inflationary consequences. In the property market, in particular, there was appreciable inflation, e.g. between 1970 and 1973 commercial property prices almost tripled.

Barbon, Nicholas, *c.*1640–98 (B3)
Born in London and then a student of medicine in Leyden, and Utrecht. He established the first fire insurance office in London 1681, was elected Member of Parliament for Bramber in 1690 and 1695; founder of a LAND BANK in 1698. In *A Discourse of Trade* (1690), his principal work, he discusses trade, value and money and distances himself from MERCANTILISTS who considered the TRADE BALANCE to be the central concern of economic policy.

bargain (D4, G2)
1 A good or service supplied at a lower than expected price.
2 A sale or purchase of stocks or shares on the London STOCK EXCHANGE at the price agreed, not necessarily at a low price as would be the case outside that stock exchange.

bargaining (D7, J5)
Negotiation between parties with opposing interests. They hope to reach an agreement in the form of a compromise or a victory for one of them. If there is a failure to agree, conflict might ensue. From earliest times, bargaining has been a major activity of markets as it can reconcile the opposing interests of buyers for low prices and of sellers for high prices. As a method of co-ordinating an economy bargaining is the alternative to PLANNING, although even under central planning the managers of different enterprises bargain with government officials to bring about the allocation of goods and services. In the labour market, the advent of trade unions has transformed individual bargaining into COLLECTIVE BARGAINING.

See also: arbitration; game theory; Nash bargaining

bargaining theory of wages (J3)
An attempt to show how wages are determined by modelling the wage negotiating process. HICKS was a pioneer with his wage bargaining model. In Hicks's diagram, OZ is the wage rate an employer would have paid if unconstrained by a trade union and OA is the highest wage union negotiators can obtain from the employer. The union, as shown by the downward-sloping resistance curve, will begin by asking a high

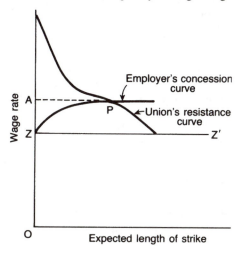

wage rate knowing little of the employer's position; the employer will gradually increase his or her offer to avoid a costly strike.

References

Hicks, J.R. (1963) *The Theory of Wages*, ch. 7, London: Macmillan; New York: St Martin's Press.

bargaining unit (J5)

The group of US workers represented by a labour union. The rules for the boundaries of the unit have been devised by the NATIONAL LABOR RELATIONS BOARD under the provision of the WAGNER and TAFT-HARTLEY ACTS with a view to making them homogeneous units which reflect local needs and further COLLECTIVE BARGAINING.

Barings Bank collapse (G2)

The failure of the long-established UK MERCHANT BANK in February 1995 caused by overtrading in Singapore by Nick Leeson, its senior Singapore trader. This gambling in FUTURES and OPTIONS of the Nikkei 225 index of the Japanese stock market resulted in a loss of $1.3 billion when the stock market began to fall and MARGIN CALLS could not be covered. The losses absorbed all the EQUITY of the bank. The ING Group acquired the bank. In a previous Barings crisis in 1890 the BANK OF ENGLAND rescued the bank by raising £17 million.

Barnett formula (H7)

A method of calculating UK public expenditure for the component countries of the UK introduced by Joel Barnett, Chief Secretary to the Treasury, in 1978. It was intended to bring about convergence in per capita spending but when it failed to do so was criticized for being too generous to Scotland.

barometric firm leadership (L1)

The leadership of an oligopolistic firm which first makes price changes to act as a 'barometer' to test the market. Often a small firm is chosen for this role, as used

to happen when UK clearing banks changed their bank charges.

barrier option (G1)

An OPTION with a pay-off depending on the underlying asset reaching or exceeding a predetermined price. A double barrier option has two trigger prices.

barrier to entry (L1)

A principal method of creating or preserving a monopoly position. Such barriers can be legal (governments only permit certain qualified persons to enter the market), technological (only large-scale production is possible, as is the case with steel mills and the mass production of consumer durables), financial (a large amount of capital is required to set up a business) or based on customers' loyalty (through PRODUCT DIFFERENTIATION). In the labour market, trade unions and professional associations (e.g. medical associations) limit the number of entrants to an occupation to preserve the income and employment of their members.

See also: artificial barrier to entry; barrier to exit

References

Bain, J.S. (1956) *Barriers to New Competition*, Cambridge, MA: Harvard University Press.

barrier to exit (L1)

The costs or forgone profits of a firm which will occur if it leaves an industry. Barriers to exit are less common than barriers to entry, excepting where a government, to prevent increased unemployment, keeps in existence a large organization threatened with financial collapse; specialized assets may also deter a firm from leaving an industry.

See also: barrier to entry

References

Caves, R.E. and Porter, M.E. (1977) 'From entry barriers to mobility barriers: conjectural decisions and contrived deterrence to new competition', *Quarterly Journal of Economics* 91: 241–62.

barter (D4, F1)

The most primitive form of exchange in which commodities are directly exchanged for each other. An exchange is possible when two persons mutually desire each other's production. Barter is more cumbersome than using money as a medium of exchange because the bartering parties usually have to search for each other without the advantage of an intermediary. Nevertheless, in modern times countries short of foreign exchange, e.g. the former USSR, have used this form of trade. If trade bartering is used, there can be a balance at a point of time or over a few years, e.g. in this way Finland and the former USSR balanced their bilateral trade over a five-year period.

See also: countertrade

barter economy (P0)

One of the earliest forms of an economy in which goods are directly changed for other goods without using money as a medium of exchange. Prices are expressed in relative terms, e.g. X amount of A = Y amount of B. Transactions can be expensive as high search costs can be incurred in the pursuit of trading partners. However, to avoid taxation and create employment, in some areas of, for example, Canada and the UK, the exchange of services has replaced the usual market.

base capital (G2)

The capital of a securities house required to protect it against a fall in its profitability.

base currency (F3)

The CURRENCY used to quantify a RISK.

base rate (E5, G2)

The rate of interest that a UK clearing bank uses as the basis of its structure of interest rates for lending and receiving deposits. Lending rates are above, and rates on deposits below, base rate. Only large and creditworthy institutions borrow

close to the base rate. Base rates came into force in 1971. Despite the abolition of their interest rate cartel, few clearing banks have base rates out of line with their competitors.

basic commodity (D0)

A good which directly or indirectly enters into the production of all commodities. A concept introduced by SRAFFA.

References

Sraffa, P. (1960) *Production of Commodities by Means of Commodities: Prelude to a Critique of Economic Theory*, Cambridge: Cambridge University Press.

basic income (I3)

An unconditional income sufficient for basic needs. Earnings beyond this allowance would be progressively taxed eventually reaching the income level at which the person would be a net contributor to the scheme. The disabled and the elderly would get more than the basic income. A government using this approach would ensure that all citizens received a share of the NATIONAL INCOME.

See also: negative income tax

basic industry (L0)

An industry which exports its products to other regions, thus being a major determinant of its own regional prosperity.

See also: non-basic industry

References

Alexander, J. (1954) 'The basic-non-basic concept of urban economic functions', *Economic Geography* 30: 246–61.

basic needs budget (I3)

A method of calculating POVERTY rates which assumes that families with limited incomes survive by consuming inferior goods. The cost of this bundle of goods can rise at a different rate from the basket used to calculate a price index.

See also: subsistence

basic relief (H2)

Income tax relief for all taxpayers

irrespective of their marital and other personal characteristics.

basic wage (J3)
The common and fundamental element in all Australian wages to which MARGINS are added to produce a differentiated wage structure. The basic wage is not merely a national wage but a general component of all wages which can in itself be altered. An increase in the basic wage will be awarded only if the economy has the economic capacity to pay for it.

See also: over-award payment

basing point pricing (L2)
A system of uniform pricing which includes a transport charge for delivery from an arbitrarily chosen geographical base. In the USA, it was first used to sell steel at Pittsburgh prices plus freight charges from Pittsburgh to consumers (hence the name 'Pittsburgh-Plus' for the system). The system has also been used in Europe, including the UK cement industry. ANTITRUST and COMPETITION POLICIES have long condemned this departure from price competition. This practice distorts the location choices of firms as they are charged less than actual freight charges in some places but in others have to pay for phantom journeys.

See also: Robinson–Patman Act 1936

basis point (G0)
The smallest measure of the yield on a bond or a note. This point is 0.01 per cent of a yield.

Basle Concordat on Banking Supervision (G2)
An international pact, drawn up in 1975 by the BANK FOR INTERNATIONAL SETTLEMENTS, to supervise banking activities.

bastard Keynesianism (E6)
This expression was invented by JOAN ROBINSON to describe the imposition of NEOCLASSICAL thinking on the theories of KEYNES. She complained that the concept of EFFECTIVE DEMAND had been abandoned

and that there was less concern for the meaning of capital than for its measurement. In particular, she was angry that modern theorists had distorted Keynes by stating that, given a level of savings, the government ensures that there is enough investment, a view little different from the classical assertion that savings determine investment, ignoring the effect of DISTRIBUTION on consumption and investment. HICKS with his IS-LM analysis, PATINKIN and her US opponents in the CAMBRIDGE CONTROVERSIES were included in the ranks of the illegitimate.

References

Robinson, J. (1979) 'What has become of the Keynesian revolution?', in *Collected Economic Papers*, Vol. V, pp. 168–77, Oxford: Basil Blackwell.

batch production (L6)
The production of a limited quantity of a particular product, rather than continuous mass production.

Bauer, Peter Thomas, 1915– (B3)
A prominent development economist born in Budapest, Hungary, and professor at the London School of Economics 1960–83. He was created a life peer on retirement. After early field work in Malaysia and West Africa, he progressed to a general study of economic development, emphasizing the superiority of markets as a method of allocation: he has long been a trenchant critic of many forms of economic aid and central economic planning and is therefore opposed to barriers to trade, investment and migration.

References

Bauer, P.T. (1948) *The Rubber Industry*, Cambridge, MA: Harvard University Press.
—— (1954) *West African Trade*, Cambridge: Cambridge University Press.
—— (1957) *Economic Analysis and Policy in Underdeveloped Countries*, Durham, NC: Duke University Press.
—— (1971) *Dissent on Development Studies and Debates in Development Eco-*

nomics, London: Weidenfeld & Nicolson.

—— (1984) *Reality and Rhetoric: Studies in the Economics of Development*, London: Weidenfeld & Nicolson; Cambridge, MA: Harvard University Press.

Baumol, William Jack, 1922– (B3)

US economist, educated at City College, New York, and London University and a professor at Princeton University from 1954 to 1971. He is famous for his economic analysis of management science, particularly his research conclusion that businesses set out to maximize their sales subject to minimum profit targets. Also, his 'unbalanced growth' model demonstrates that the different opportunities for technical progress in the various sectors of an economy lead to chronic problems in the financing of cities, medical care, educational systems and the performing arts. Recently he has been concerned with the environmental implications of welfare economics and CONTESTABLE MARKETS.

References

Baumol, W.J. (1966) *Performing Arts, the Economic Dilemma: a Study of Problems Common to Theatre, Opera, Music and Dance*, New York: Twentieth Century Fund.

—— (1977) *Economic Theory and Operations Analysis*, 4th edn, Englewood Cliffs, NJ: Prentice Hall.

Baumol, W.J. and Oates, W.E. (1975) *The Theory of Environmental Policy*, Englewood Cliffs, NJ; London: Prentice Hall.

Baumol, W.J., Willig, R.D. and Panzar, L.S. (1982) *Contestable Markets and the Theory of Industry Structure*, New York: Harcourt Brace Jovanovich.

Bayesian econometrics (C5)

This is founded on Bayes's theorem, or the principle of inverse probability: that the information in given data can be used to infer the random processes generating them. Both sample and a priori information are used.

References

Jeffreys, H. (1957) *Scientific Inference*, 2nd edn, Cambridge: Cambridge University Press.

Bayesian equilibrium (C7)

A NASH EQUILIBRIUM in which the players in a game with incomplete information value their expected utility using subjective probabilities; the local best response at each information set.

References

Harsanyi, J. (1967–8) 'Games with incomplete information played by Bayesian players, I–III', *Management Science* 14: 159–82, 320–34, 486–502.

Bayesian method (C1)

A method of revising the probability of an event occurring by taking into account experimental evidence. The usefulness of this approach depends on the size of the sample used in an experiment. Bayes's theorem of 1763 originally stated that the probability of q conditional on H (prior information) and p (some further event) varies as the probability of q on H times the probability of p, given q and H.

References

Cyert, R.M. (1987) *Bayesian Analyses and Uncertainty in Economic Theory*, London: Chapman and Hall.

Bayes, Thomas, 1702–61 (B3)

Born in London. A Presbyterian minister in Holborn, London and Tunbridge Wells, Kent; admitted to the Royal Society in 1742. He used an inductive approach to establish a mathematical basis for probability in his posthumous 'Essay towards Solving a Problem in the Doctrine of Chances', *Transactions of the Royal Society of London* (1763). This inspired an approach to the calculation of probabilities and the foundation of a new branch of ECONOMETRICS.

BB (G2)

STANDARD & POOR credit rating of securities which designates them as speculative.

See also: AAA; BBB; C; D; DDD

BBB (G2)

STANDARD & POOR credit rating of securities which states that they are of medium grade.

See also: AAA; BB; QD; DDD

BDI (J5)

Bundesverrand der deutchen Industrie. A major employers' association in Germany founded in 1949 by an amalgamation of thirty-nine national industrial federations. BDI now has separate sections for the sectors of the economy.

bear (G1)

A market speculator who, believing that prices will fall, sells securities (for example) now and purchases them later to effect delivery of them. A profit is made by the difference between the selling and buying prices. This reversal of the normal sequence of transactions is possible on stock exchanges as securities do not have to be immediately delivered. Also, there is speculation of this nature in currency and commodity markets where there is a choice between spot and future transactions. If the bear already possesses what is being sold, he or she is 'protected' or 'covered'; if not, he or she is selling short.

See also: bull; stag

bearer bond (G1)

A bond owned by the person currently holding it. As no endorsement is needed to transfer such bonds, there is no central register of the owners of any particular bearer bond issue. The EUROBOND is a major example of bearer bonds.

bearer security (G1) *see* bearer bond; bearer share

bearer share (G1)

A company share owned by the person holding it at a particular time.

Becker, Gary Stanley, 1930– (B3)

US economist, educated at Princeton and Chicago, who was a professor at Columbia University from 1960 to 1970 and then at Chicago from 1970. Famous for his analy-sis of racial and sexual DISCRIMINATION in labour markets using the utility functions of employers and employees to demonstrate a 'taste for discrimination'; the formalisation of the study of HUMAN CAPITAL by an examination of the investment-like nature of schooling and on-the-job training; the analysis of crime as an occupation with expected benefits and expected costs (if caught); and a new economics of the family as a multi-person production unit practising division of labour amongst its members. His work has extended economic study into areas previously the preserve of sociologists, psychologists and anthropologists. He was awarded the Nobel Prize for Economics in 1992.

References

Becker, G.S. (1968) 'Crime and punishment: an economic approach', *Journal of Political Economy* 76: 169–217.

—— (1971) *Economies of Discrimination*, 2nd edn, Chicago: University of Chicago Press.

—— (1975) *Human Capital: A Theoretical and Empirical Analysis, with Special Reference to Education*, New York: Columbia University Press.

—— (1977) *The Economic Approach to Human Behaviour*, Chicago and London: University of Chicago Press.

—— (1981) *Treatise on the Family*, Cambridge, MA: Harvard University Press.

Shackleton, J.R. (1981) 'Gary S. Becker: the economist as empire-builder', in J.R. Shackleton and G. Locksley (eds) *Twelve Contemporary Economists*, London and Basingstoke: Macmillan.

bed and breakfast (G1, L8)

1 A sale and purchase of securities within twenty-four hours to accumulate tax-deductible losses.

2 Tourist accommodation for one night with a breakfast included in the TARIFF.

beggar-my-neighbour policy (F1)

A PROTECTIONIST foreign trade policy which attempts to improve the domestic economy at the expense of foreign countries. This policy was at the heart of much of

MERCANTILIST thinking and was later practised in the 1930s by many countries. First predominantly agricultural economies adopted it; later it was adopted by the UK, USA, France, the Netherlands and Switzerland. After 1945, currency devaluations have embodied this principle. A policy of this type has always been criticized because of its self-defeating character: domestic industries can ignore foreign competition so become more inefficient and export industries facing retaliation have a reduced output and consequentially higher unit costs which make them even more uncompetitive in world markets.

See also: General Agreement on Tariffs and Trade; Smoot–Hawley Tariff Act 1930

behavioural economics (D1, L2)
The varied approaches to the study of economic behaviour, including decision making in firms and other organizations, a psychological approach to the study of consumers and a multidisciplinary 'technological economics' with some of the assumptions of the POST-KEYNESIANS. This school of economics, mainly concerned with microeconomic issues, also considers macroeconomic matters such as inflation and unemployment. The specialist journals of this branch of economics are the *Journal of Behavioral Economics* and the *Journal of Economic Behavior and Economics*.

See also: economics and psychology; evolutionary theory of the firm

References

Earl, P.E. (ed.) (1988) *Behavioral Economics*, 2 vols, Aldershot: Edward Elgar.
Gilad, B. and Kaish, S. (eds) (1986) *Handbook of Behavioral Economics*, Vols A and B, Greenwich, CT: JAI Press.
Loasby, B. (1976) *Choice, Complexity and Ignorance: An Inquiry into Economic Theory and the Practice of Decision-Making*, Cambridge: Cambridge University Press.

behavioural finance (G1)
The study of financial markets making use of the ideas of INVESTOR SENTIMENT and

LIMITED ARBITRAGE. Research of this kind examines irrationality in markets.

References

Shleifer, A. (2000) *Inefficient markets*, Oxford: Oxford University Press.

behaviour line (D0)
An INDIFFERENCE CURVE.

Beige Book (E6)
A report of US regional economic conditions published by the FEDERAL RESERVE eight times a year. It is based on anecdotal evidence collected by each of the twelve Federal District Banks. The economic state of different industries and of the labour market is described.

Bellman's equation (C8)
This asserts that the value of a state in a probability distribution equals the expected value of successor states. This equation is used in dynamic programming to establish the greatest return over the long run.

bell-wether of the economy (E3)
A sector that indicates the future of a whole national ECONOMY. The advertising industry is often in this role as changes in advertising expenditure precede an upturn or downturn in the economy.

bell-wether stock (G1)
A stock exchange security regarded as representative of the state of the stock market as a whole. It is usually the stock of one of the largest companies.

below the line (F4, H6, M3)
1 In the UK budgets of 1947–63 receipts and expenditure relating to borrowed funds or the servicing of the national debt.
2 For a firm, expenditure on sales promotion other than on direct advertising.
3 In the UK balance of payments, official financing.

See also: above the line

benefit approach to taxation (H2)
The levying of taxation so that the burden

of taxation matches the amount of PUBLIC GOODS received by each taxpayer. The principle was first enunciated by Thomas Hobbes (1588–1679), Hugo Grotius (1583–1645) and John Locke (1632–1704). In essence taxpayers and a government exchange taxes for services. Since public goods are collectively provided and taxes are individually paid, a taxation system on this basis will always be criticized. For example, it would be difficult to allocate charges for the maintenance of external defence to individuals in proportion to their consumption. Until governments know more of the preferences of taxpayers it will be impossible to apply the principle exactly.

benefit tax (H2)

A tax linked to a service provided by government, e.g. a bridge toll, or a leisure centre admission charge. The principle followed is 'he who benefits should pay'.

See also: ability to pay; user charge

Benelux (F0)

Customs union of Belgium, the Netherlands and Luxembourg. In 1943, the three countries signed a monetary convention for controlling payments between them after the Second World War. In 1944, they agreed to a customs union to come into force in 1948: this abolished tariffs within Benelux and set a COMMON EXTERNAL TARIFF. The aims of Benelux include the free movement of goods and factors of production, the co-ordination of economic, financial and social policies to attain a satisfactory employment level and the highest standard of living, and a joint trade policy.

Bentham, Jeremy, 1748–1832 (B3)

Legal philosopher and writer on many economic, constitutional and prison reform issues; founder of the UK utilitarian school of philosophy. Educated at Westminster School, Queen's College, Oxford (which he hated, leading him to inspire the opening of University College London in 1828), and Lincoln's Inn, London, where

he read for the English Bar. He is most famous for his exposition of UTILITARIANISM, the principle that there should be a 'felicific calculus', to see if a course of action promotes the greatest happiness for the greatest number. This inspired JEVONS in his subjective value theory of exchange. John Stuart MILL, who was much under Bentham's influence in his youth, rebelled against the cold rationality of utilitarianism.

Bentham studied political economy from 1786 to 1804, between the ages of 38 and 56, when he was at his intellectual peak. A reading of SMITH's *The Wealth of Nations* was decisive for his economic thinking, although he had an earlier interest in unemployment, With an atomistic view of social life, it was not surprising that he used induction as his principal approach and only resorted to mathematics as a convenient method of expression. His first work on economics, *Defence of Usury* (1787), was inspired by a rumour that the legal maximum for interest was to fall from 5 per cent to 4 per cent: Bentham recommended that there should be free determination of interest rates. Although the work did not advance a theory of the rate of interest, it was nevertheless widely praised in the UK, France and the USA.

He was against artificial attempts to increase trade, e.g. by having colonies, because he believed that trade is limited by capital. His *Manual of Political Economy* (1793–5) dealt with international trade. He took to public finance in *Supply without Burthen* (1795) in which he combined a minimal view of the state with a new proposal to raise the small amount of taxation still necessary – the public auction of all properties in vacant possession because no relatives were alive to inherit. Further, in *A Plan for Augmentation of the Revenue* (1794–5), he proposed a reduction in the national debt by the use of government-run lotteries and government dealings in life annuities. His *Proposal for the Circulation of a New Species of Paper Currency* (1795–6) argued that a government monopoly on the issue of paper currency is a cheaper form of government borrowing than the issue of interest-bearing bills. *Circulating Annuities* (1800) also suggested a new type of paper currency, and in *True Alarm* (1801) he contributed to the raging BULLIONIST CONTROVERSY of the period by tracing the effects of excessive country bank issues on prices, as well as enunciating a theory of value based on utility. *Of the Balance of Trade* (1801) attacked MERCANTILISM, *Defence of a Maximum* (1801) advocated price controls for grain and *Institute of Political Economy* (1801–4) set out his views on the role and limits of government policy, as well as discussing whether political economy is an art or a science.

References

Dinwoody, J. (1989) *Bentham*, Oxford: Oxford University Press.

Stark, W. (1955) *Jeremy Bentham's Economic Writings*, London: Allen & Unwin.

Bergson, Abram, 1914– (B3)

US economist educated at Johns Hopkins and Harvard Universities. After wartime experience from 1942 to 1945 as chief of the Russian Economic Subdivision of the US Office of Strategic Services, he returned to academic life and has been a professor at Harvard since 1956. In 1938, he created the new welfare economics by asserting that a social welfare function can be established by attaching weights to each individual's welfare function: this rejected the earlier CARDINAL UTILITY approach. Also, he introduced the distinction between 'efficiency' and 'equity', applying it to an analysis of the individual income effects of economic change. He has applied his welfare analysis to many areas of economics, including MARKET SOCIALISM and monopoly. Also, he became a leading US authority on the Soviet economy.

References

Bergson, A. (1964) *Economics of Soviet Planning*, New Haven, CT: Yale University Press.

—— (1966) *Essays in Normative Economics*, Cambridge, MA: Harvard University Press.

—— (1982) *Welfare Planning and Employment: Selected Essays in Economic Theory*, Cambridge, MA: MIT Press.

Bergson social welfare function (D6)

The welfare of a community in a given time period expressed as a function of the amounts of consumer goods produced, the amounts of labour and non-labour factor inputs and the production unit for which the work is performed. BERGSON, in his approach, intended to challenge the view that a community's welfare is the sum of individuals' welfare.

References

Bergson, A. (1938) 'A reformulation of certain aspects of welfare economics', *Quarterly Journal of Economics* 52: 310–34.

Bernoulli hypothesis (D0)

The hypothesis, named after Daniel Bernoulli (1700–82), that in a gamble an individual will participate according to the personal UTILITIES he or she attaches to the probabilities. This approach is prominent in the economics of RISK and UNCERTAINTY.

References

Pearson, K. (1978) *The History of Statistics in the 17th and 18th Centuries*, New York: Macmillan.

Bertrand duopoly model (L1)

A development of COURNOT'S DUOPOLY MODEL which uses price adjustments to bring about an equilibrium. At equilibrium, neither firm would benefit from charging a different price so the price becomes zero.

best available technology (O3)

A technique of production which reduces pollution levels by using the cleanest available method.

beta (G1)

The ratio of a change in the return on a security to a change in the returns on all securities of a particular stock market. Beta is unity if the changes in the individual share and in the whole of the market are the same. Betas are positive if the individual and market returns move in the same direction, and negative if they move in opposite directions.

See also: alpha; Sharpe

beta stock (G1)

Five hundred or so stocks and shares which are the most actively traded on the STOCK EXCHANGE AUTOMATED QUOTATION system after alpha stocks.

See also: alpha stock; delta stock; gamma stock

Beveridge, William Henry, 1879–1963 (B3)

In many senses, the founder of the UK WELFARE STATE. After an education at Balliol College, Oxford, he was a law Fellow at University College, Oxford from 1902 to 1909, as well as Sub-warden of Toynbee Hall, London, from 1903 to 1905, where he investigated casual labour and unemployment in the London docks. As Director of Labour Exchanges at the UK Board of Trade in 1909–15 he created a national system of employment exchanges. In 1919 as Permanent Secretary of the Ministry of Food he devised a national food rationing scheme. From 1919 to 1937 as Director of the London School of Economics he expanded the range of its activities, attracting scholars such as HAYEK and HICKS, as well as encouraging empirical studies. Subsequently he was master of University College, Oxford, from 1937 to 1944, and chairman of the committee which drew up the Beveridge Report on social security in 1942, which was expanded into the celebrated *Full Employment in a Free Society* (1944), a report which laid the intellectual foundations for many post-war UK welfare policies.

References

Harris, J. (1977) *William Beveridge: a Biography*, Oxford: Clarendon Press.

Williams, K. and Williams, J. (eds) (1987) *A Beveridge Reader*, London: Unwin Hyman.

bid (D0)

An offer of a price as in an AUCTION or in a TENDER.

See also: designated competitive bidding; general competitive bidding; limited general competitive bidding

bidding technique (C8)

Estimation of consumers' valuation of benefits using questionnaires.

See also: contingent valuation

bid price (G1)

The selling price for UNIT TRUST units or shares of companies.

bid rent (Q2)

The amount of money a household will offer a landowner for space to provide a particular level of UTILITY.

References

Wheaton, W. (1977) 'A bid rent approach to housing demand', *Journal of Urban Economics* 4: 200–17.

bid vehicle (Q2)

A proposed means of payment based on surveys to make a CONTINGENT VALUATION, e.g. the amount of cash charged to obtain a permit to hunt wildlife.

Big Bang (G1)

The DEREGULATION of the London Stock Exchange on 27 October 1986 which involved the ending of minimum dealing commissions and the distinction between dealers and jobbers. Under the fierce gale of competition, smaller firms found it difficult to survive and even the larger firms withdrew from market-making by 1990. Firms anxious to be ahead of their rivals offered grossly inflated salaries to prospective staff and the best of existing staff, making the volume of consequent redundancies greater.

The seeds of the recent changes were sown in the early 1970s when UK COMPETI-

TION POLICY was extended to cover the provision of services as well as goods. The present changes were forced on the London Stock Exchange when, to avoid investigation under the restrictive trade practices legislation, it agreed in 1983 to abolish minimum commissions within three years. The abolition of UK EXCHANGE CONTROLS in 1979 made internationalization of the London market inevitable. The first stage of these changes was on 1 March 1986 when financial institutions such as banks and insurance companies were allowed to acquire holdings in firms of stockbrokers and stockjobbers. In the USA the equivalent set of changes took place on 1 May 1975 and the consequences of those were the formation of many new financial conglomerates.

Three years of preparation enabled London to adjust quickly to the new regime. The high volume of trading in the early months made it easier for firms to adjust to lower commissions and to cope with the huge costs of setting up new dealing systems. Instead of the old practice of charging clients on the basis of price plus commission, the majority of deals are quoted at prices net of commission. The next step will be to use the London system to enable brokers throughout the world to quote prices to each other. In the period 1986–9, the volume of stocks traded in London fell by a third and the number of jobs fell by 35,000, but much of this decline was the consequence of the BLACK MONDAY stock market crash.

See also: Mayday

References

Thomas, W.A. (1986) *The Big Bang*, Deddington: Philip Allan.
—— (1989) *The Securities Market*, London: Philip Allan.

'Big Board' (G1)

The nickname for the New York Stock Exchange situated at 11 Wall Street and established in 1792. It dominates world securities markets by conducting 60 per cent of world trading and 85 per cent of US trades.

BigMac index (F3)

A measure of the purchasing power of different currencies using the prices of hamburgers sold by the international food chain McDonald's. This was devised by *The Economist* of London and has been calculated since 1986. This index, based on the theory of PURCHASING POWER PARITY, is calculated by dividing the price of a hamburger in the local currency by its price in US dollars. This ratio, the implied PPP, is compared with the actual exchange rate to determine the extent of a currency's over- or undervaluation relative to the US dollar. The BigMac was chosen for comparative purposes as it is a popular fast food item produced everywhere to the same recipe.

big push (O4)

A theory of simultaneous economic development in several sectors. Rosenstein-Rodan asserted that for economic development to succeed there should be, as a minimum, several large investment projects in different industries in order to secure INCREASING RETURNS TO SCALE from INDIVISIBILITIES in production. It was hoped that the scale of such development would reduce divergences between private and social products. However, the lack of resources of many Third World countries made it unlikely that so ambitious a scheme would be implemented.

References

Rosenstein-Rodan, P. (1943) 'Problems of industrialization in Eastern and south-eastern Europe', *Economic Journal* 53: 202–11.

bilateral aid (F4, O1)

Aid flowing between a particular donor country and a particular recipient; often TIED AID.

See also: foreign aid; multilateral aid

bilateral monopoly (L1)

A market consisting of a MONOPOLIST and a

MONOPSONIST. In many national economies there are examples of this form of monopoly in the public sector, e.g. when a state education employer faces a single teachers' UNION in the labour market. To analyse bilateral monopoly, as is the case with DUOPOLY, the interaction of both sides, buyer and seller, has to be considered.

bill (G1, M2)
1 A short-term monetary asset.
2 An invoice stating the amount owed for the supply of goods or services.

See also: bill of exchange; commercial bill; trade bill; treasury bill

bill of exchange (F1, G1)
A short-term financial instrument, usually with a life of ninety days, which is used to finance foreign trade; in the nineteenth century it was widely used for short-term domestic borrowing. The Bills of Exchange Act (UK) 1882 defined it as 'an unconditional order in writing, addressed by one person to another, signed by the person giving it, requiring the person to whom it is addressed to pay on demand or at a fixed or determinable future time a sum certain in money to or to the order of a specified person, or to bearer'.

bimetallism (E5, N2)
The use of two metals, usually gold and silver, in a fixed ratio as the standard of value and ultimate means of payment. This currency system met with the approval of Adam SMITH. The arguments for bimetallism were that each metal would be more stable in value if connected with the other, that the low production levels of gold caused falling prices and trade recession, and that fixed exchange rates between countries on a pure gold standard and those on a pure silver standard would be possible. The system was practised in the nineteenth century in the USA and in Europe in the Latin Union (a monetary alliance of France, Belgium, Switzerland, Italy, Greece and Romania formed in 1865 and abandoned in 1873 as a consequence of the large amount of Nevada silver and

Germany's conversion from a silver to a gold standard).

bimodal frequency curve (C1)
A FREQUENCY CURVE with two maxima.

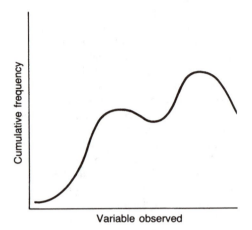

Variable observed

binary economy (P0)
An ECONOMY with many personal incomes arising from both labour and capital. This occurs because of widespread ownership of financial capital. Despite economies becoming capital intensive, this form of organization enables a high proportion of a population to share in rising incomes. Wider dispersion of wealth could promote social justice, democracy, efficiency and economic growth.

References
Ashford, R. (1996) 'Louis Kelso's binary economy', *Journal of Socio-Economics* 25: 1–53.
Kelso, L.O. and Adler, M.J. (1958) *The Capitalist Manifesto*, New York: Random House.

binomial charge (D4)
A TWO-PART TARIFF consisting of a fixed payment that allows a consumer access to the service and variable payments related to the use made of the service, e.g. a telephone rental and telephone call charges.

See also: price discrimination

bioeconomics (P0, Q0, Q2)
1 The application of sociobiology to eco-

nomics, first suggested by BECKER in 1979. It is argued that competitiveness and self-interest, not selfishness and collectivism, when built into human genes produce an effective economic system of the capitalist type.

2 A study of economic behaviour in its natural environment. Herbert Spencer, 1820–1903, an inspiration for Charles Darwin, 1809–82, produced an evolutionary account of society. MARSHALL stated that in the early stages of tackling an economic problem a mechanical approach should be used but later a biological form of analysis. This branch of economics has flourished because of an increased awareness of environmental economics.

3 The economics of renewable natural resources.

See also: altruism; economic man; homo economicus; homo sovieticus

References

Georgescu-Roegen, Nicholas (1971) *The Entropy Law and the Economic Process*, Cambridge, MA: Harvard University Press.

Hodgson, G.M. (ed.) (1995) *Economics and Biology*, Aldershot: Edward Elgar.

blackboard trading (G1)

A method of trading in small quantities which involves buyers writing their bids on one side of the blackboard and sellers their offers on the other side. When a deal is agreed, it is recorded on the sales panel as a binding future contract. The Chicago Mercantile Exchange deals this way in agricultural commodities. Under heavy trading, this method is abandoned.

black chip (G1)

A SECURITY issued by a black-dominated company quoted on the Johannesburg Stock Exchange.

black economy (P0)

The unofficial, and often illegal, part of a national ECONOMY. In it are tax evaders and illegal producers of goods and services.

Companies participating in this sector falsify their accounts by omissions or inaccurate entries. Rich and poor, capitalist and socialist, economies all have black sectors. These sectors are prominent in India, Portugal, Italy, as well as the USA and the UK. The large black economy in Italy could amount to 25 per cent of GROSS DOMESTIC PRODUCT. Methods of measuring the black economy include a comparison of national income with national expenditure (a method flawed through errors in both of these aggregates) and the use of household expenditure surveys to calculate undisclosed incomes through discrepancies between household income and spending. Also, changes in the ratio of cash transactions to total transactions indicate that many prefer the less detectable form of trading central to the black economy. If tax authorities succeeded in discovering these activities, they would risk stopping this form of work altogether.

References

Heertje, A., Allen, M. and Cohen, A. (1982) *The Black Economy*, London: Pan.

Smithies, E. (1984) *The Black Economy in England since 1914*, Atlantic Highlands, NJ: Humanities Press; Dublin: Gill & Macmillan.

blackfield site (Q3)

Land virtually destroyed by heavy industrial use.

black gold (Q4)

1 Coal (originally).
2 Oil when it became a more important source of energy than coal.

black knight (G3)

A company which makes a hostile takeover bid for another firm.

blackleg (J5)

A worker who reduces the effectiveness of a STRIKE by continuing to work during a period of an industrial dispute. Police protection has often been needed for such dissenters.

black market (D4)

An unauthorized market with transactions contrary to governmental regulations. Markets of this kind are often found when there are price or EXCHANGE CONTROLS or the restriction of trading to a list of authorized dealers. Soviet-type economies were characterized by these markets.

Black Monday (G1)

Stock market crash in New York and London of 19 October 1987. In London the FTSE index dropped by 500 points.

See also: Brady Commission

References

Bose, M. (1988) *The Crash*, London: Mandarin Paperback.

Black–Scholes option pricing model (D4, G1)

A formula for calculating the value of a call or put EUROPEAN OPTION. This form of pricing takes into account the stock price, exercise price, risk-free interest rate, time to expiry and the standard deviation of the stock return.

References

Black, F. and Scholes. M. (1972) 'The Valuation of Option Pricing Contracts and a Test of Market Efficiency', *Journal of Financial Economics* 27: 339–418.
—— (1973) 'The pricing of options and corporate liabilities', *Journal of Political Economy* 81: 637–57.

Blairism (E6)

The creed of the UK government led by Tony Blair from May 1997. It continued the public expenditure, education, privatization and trade union policies of the previous Conservative governments but also adopted a socialist 'tax and spend' policy with increased spending delayed until the NATIONAL DEBT was reduced. Other aspects of this doctrine are the excessive targeting of most government-funded activities, economic regulation and government centralization characteristic of previous socialist regimes. Also called New Labour and the Third Way.

See also: Thatcherism

Blaug, Mark, 1927– (B3)

Leading historian of economic thought, education economist and biographer of the economics profession. Born in the Netherlands and educated at Columbia University. After working as a statistician at the US Department of Labor, he was assistant professor of economics at Yale University (1954–62) before becoming Professor of the Economics of Education at the University of London Institute of Education; since 1984 he has held chairs in England at Buckingham and Exeter and in the Netherlands at Rotterdam. He has written extensively on both human capital theory and labour forecasting and moved from an early interest in the Poor Laws and Ricardian economics to wide-ranging writing and editing of major works on the history of economic thought.

See also: Ricardian theory of value

References

Blaug, M. (1958) *Ricardian Economics: A Historical Study*, New Haven, CT: Yale University Press.
—— (1970) *An Introduction to the Economics of Education*, London: Allen Lane.
—— (1997) *Economic Theory in Retrospect*, 5th edn, Cambridge: Cambridge University Press.
—— (1999) *Who's Who in Economics*, 3nd edn, Brighton: Wheatsheaf.

bliss point (D6)

An optimal combination of PRIVATE and PUBLIC GOODS. This combination is derived from a SOCIAL WELFARE FUNCTION. In the figure W_1, W_2 and W_3 are different social welfare functions, BB is a grand utility maximization frontier, P is the bliss point, U_x and U_y are ordinal preference functions and $W = W(U_x, U_y)$ is a social welfare function. At the bliss point P, social welfare is at a maximum because BB touches the highest welfare function contour.

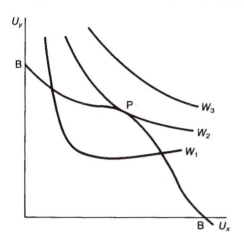

References

Bator, F.M. (1957) 'The simple analysis of welfare maximization', *American Economic Review* 47: 22–59.

bloc grant (H7)

The revenue transferred by the US federal government to a state or local government so that the lower level government has sufficient revenues to provide a service, e.g. education, at the standard desired by central government.

blocked development (O1)

Economic DEVELOPMENT deliberately impeded by other more developed countries. It has been asserted that dominant countries of the world have blocked the development of Third World countries, permitting them only 'PERIPHERAL CAPITALISM'.

References

Amin, S. (1976) *Unequal Development: An Essay on the Social Formations of Peripheral Capitalism*, Hassocks: Harvester Press; New York: Monthly Review Press.

block of shares (G1)

Any block of more than 10,000 shares, according to the New York Stock Exchange Rule 390. With few exceptions, this rule requires that listed stocks must be traded on the floor of the exchange, even if sold in 'blocks'.

block trade (G1) *see* put-through

Blue Book (C8, E6, J5)

1 The annually published national income and expenditure accounts of the UK.
2 The document setting out the terms and conditions of a firm agreed through COLLECTIVE BARGAINING or unilaterally imposed by an employer, e.g. the Ford Agreement.

blue chip (G1)

A stock issue by a company or corporation with a high standing because of its earnings record. Such shares are chosen as a basis for the Financial Times, Dow Jones and other share indices. The term is taken from the game of poker as the highest value chips used are blue.

blue-collar worker (J2)

US expression for a person engaged in manual employment; usually contrasted with a WHITE-COLLAR worker. DE-INDUSTRIALIZATION and the increasing education of the labour force has reduced the number of these workers and, also, labour union membership.

blue economy (P0)

The official economy, known to and recorded by government. The term is derived in the UK from the term BLUE BOOK, the annual summary of the national income accounts.

See also: black economy; informal economy; unofficial economy

blue return (H2)

A self-assessment business income tax system, recommended by the SHOUP MISSION to Japan of 1949, for collecting taxes from small and medium-sized firms. This system was intended to encourage smaller businesses to maintain minimal accounting systems.

blue-sky laws (G1, K2)

US Securities Act 1933 and other US statutes which regulate and supervise the US securities industry so that financiers do not attempt to sell something which they do not possess, e.g. part of the sky, to another person, or to devise other fraudulent investment schemes.

See also: bubble; Securities and Exchange Commission

bogey (G1)
The return to or income from an investment which is used as the benchmark to judge the performance of a fund manager. Movements in a stock market index are often used as a bogey.

Böhm–Bawerk, Eugen von, 1851–1914 (B3)
Leading economist of the AUSTRIAN SCHOOL and disciple of Carl MENGER. He read law at Vienna University and then economics at Heidelberg, Leipzig and Jena Universities; his student contemporary was WIESER. From 1889 to 1893 he was a civil servant working on income tax and currency reform. On three occasions (1893, 1896–7 and 1900–4) he was the Minister of Finance of Austria; in 1902 University of Vienna appointed him to a chair. In his economic writings, he began with a theory of value based on MARGINAL UTILITY and then proceeded to a theory of interest and capital. His lengthy exposition of the ROUNDABOUT METHOD OF PRODUCTION, possible through the use of capital, is central to his work. Production more capitalistic in nature has on average a longer period of production. He refused to relate the payment of interest to either productivity or exploitation, asserting that interest is paid because present goods have a higher subjective value than future goods.

References

Böhm-Bawerk, E. von (1959) *Capital and Interest*, 3 vols, trans. G.D. Huncke and H.F. Sennholz, South Holland, IL: Libertarian Press.
Kuenne, R.E. (1971) *Eugen von Böhm-Bawerk*, New York and London: Columbia University Press.

Boisguilbert, Pierre Le Pesant de, 1646–1714 (B3)
Born at Sainte-Croix Saint Ouen de Rouen,

studied law at Paris and later became a lieutenant of police. He is credited with introducing the principle of LAISSEZ-FAIRE. His main work was *Dissertation de la nature des richesses, de l'argent et des tributes, où l'on découvre la fausse idée qui régne dans le monde à l'égard de ces trois articles* (1707).

bond (G1, M2)
1 A promise under seal to pay money.
2 A fixed interest security issued by a government, corporation or company.

See also: deep discount bond; government bond; junk bond; straight bond

bond fund (G1)
A fund established to receive the proceeds of a bond issue and to make subsequent disbursements. Such funds are often set up by local authorities.

bonding cost (M2)
The cost to an agent of putting up a BOND as a guarantee to meet losses. Bonding is common amongst travel agents and insurance underwriters.

bond market (G1)
A market which raises long-term capital for governments and firms through bonds bearing a fixed rate of interest, as well as arranging the trading of issued bonds.

bond rating agency (G1)
A financial markets specialist which rates the creditworthiness of the principal issuers of bonds – governments, municipalities and corporations. Standard & Poor and Moody's are the leading US agencies of this kind.

See also: AAA; BB; BBB; D; DDD; Prime-1

bonus issue (G1)
An issue to present shareholders of extra shares in proportion to existing holdings. If issued without charge, known as a SCRIP ISSUE.

book value (M4)
The value of an asset as recorded in the

books or accounts of a firm or other organization. Often this valuation is made at the time that assets are originally purchased with the consequence that changes in value caused by inflation are ignored.

See also: inflation accounting

boom (E3)
A peak in economic activity, the upper turning point in the business cycle. Booms are characterized by high output, low unemployment, speculative investment and many short strikes.

See also: recession

boom and bust (E3)
The characteristic of a cyclical economy. Despite the overall stability of the UK economy, for example, in the late 1990s there were fluctuations in some sectors, especially agriculture and manufacturing.

See also: cycles; stop–go

boomernomics (G1)
US investment practice of investing in equities related to the expenditure carried out by the people born in the late 1940s after the ending of the war with Japan brought men home to marry in the USA.

bootblack economy (P0)
A derogatory term for a national ECONOMY dominated by LABOUR-INTENSIVE service industries. Bootblacking is manual and non-exportable, unlike the products of modern, technologically advanced and internationally oriented service industries, e.g. banking and accounting.

See also: services

bootstrap (G1)
A self-fulfilling expectation: for example, the belief that investment is pointless because the economy is slowing down with the consequence that the economy does go into recession.

border trade (F1)
Importing and exporting across a border which is often INTRA-INDUSTRY TRADE. If the border is long, the products exported over one part of a border will also be imported over another. This happens, for example, with building materials over the USA–Canada border.

borrower's curse (G0)
Having excessive optimism about a project that is loan financed.

borrower's risk (G1)
The hazard of not knowing whether the expected returns to a project will materialize.

bottleneck (D2)
A shortage in the supply of a FACTOR OF PRODUCTION which, if not remedied, can add to inflationary pressures; hence an economy with full employment suffers many bottlenecks. Also, lack of an appropriate INFRASTRUCTURE has often been a major bottleneck impeding the development of less developed countries.

bottom fisher (G1)
An investor who buys stock market securities whose prices have recently slumped in the belief the market has reached its lower turning point.

See also: bull

bottom-line accounting (M2)
Accounting which is especially concerned with the net profit or earnings that appears at the bottom of a profit and loss account.

bottom-up linkage model (R0)
An interregional model of a national economy which aggregates the values of regional variables. The quality of these models in many countries is affected by shortages of regional data.

References

Ballard, K.P., Gustely, R.D. and Wendling, R. (1980) *NRIES. Structure, Performance and Applications of a Bottom-up Interregional Econometric Model*, Washington, DC: Bureau of Economic Analysis.

bought deal (G1)
The purchase of a stock issue or a portfolio of investments by one or more financial institutions for resale in whole or part. Offloading parts of an acquired portfolio has become easier as there are now so many types of financial instrument. As these deals cut dealing costs, they provide a popular method for INVESTMENT TRUSTS to acquire securities.

Boulding, Kenneth Ewart, 1910–92 (B3)
A polymath economist born in the UK who made diverse contributions to many areas of US economics. He was educated at Oxford, Chicago and Harvard Universities. His career, which began as an assistant lecturer at Edinburgh University, was spent chiefly at Michigan from 1949 to 1977 and subsequently at Colorado. His writing began with an article in the *Economic Journal* in 1932 on displacement cost and resulted in the production of over 300 articles and twelve books. His major textbook, *Economic Analysis*, blended together KEYNESIANISM and NEOCLASSICAL ECONOMICS. In 1950, in *A Reconstruction of Economics*, he urged a theoretical switch from flows to stocks, from incomes to assets, and from the prices of labour and capital to their national income shares. His close examination of equilibrium linked price and ecological equilibria. His study of social organization contrasted the exchange system and its threat system of war with the integrative system of a grants economy.

See also: grants economics

References

Boulding, K.E. (1945) *Economics of Peace*, New York: Prentice Hall.
—— (1950) *A Reconstruction of Economics*, New York: Wiley.
—— (1966) *Economic Analysis*, 4th edn, New York: Wiley.
—— (1978) *Ecodynamics*, Beverly Hills, CA, and London: Sage.
—— (1981) *A Preface to Grant Economics: The Economy of Love and Fear*, New York: Praeger.
Kernan, C.E. (1974) *Creative Tension: The Life and Thought of Kenneth Boulding*, New York: Basic Books.

Boulwareism (J5)
A substitute for collective BARGAINING, named after Lemuel Boulware, the Vice-President for Industrial Relations at General Electric. It consisted of a company making a unilateral offer based on research into a union's demands. It was held by the US Supreme Court in 1969 that this was not US collective bargaining in 'good faith' as intended by the TAFT–HARTLEY ACT.

boundary constraint (C1)
The limit to the value of a variable, e.g. zero or positive.

See also: Tobit model

bounded rationality (D0)
A theory of decision making taking into account the capacities of the human mind, which has become a central theme of BEHAVIOURAL ECONOMICS. It asserts that the rational choice of a decision-maker is subject to cognitive limits because human beings lack knowledge and have only a limited ability to forecast the future.

See also: cognitive dissonance; economics and psychology; Simon

References

Cyert, R.M. and March, J.G. (1975) *A Behavioral Theory of the Firm*, 2nd edn, Englewood Cliffs, NJ: Prentice Hall.
Simon, H.A. (1982) *Models of Bounded Rationality*, 2 vols, Cambridge, MA: MIT Press.

bourgeoisie (D6, N3)
The capitalist middle class created by the Industrial Revolution at the beginning of the nineteenth century and regarded as exploitative by MARX. The bourgeoisie was accused of wrongly appropriating surplus value from the product of the PROLETARIAT.

bourse (G1)
Stock market of a European country. The term is derived from the Bruges commod-

ity exchange founded in 1360 in front of the home of Chevalier van de Buerse.

Box–Jenkins (C1)

A methodological approach to the study of TIME SERIES which has improved short-term economic forecasting by following the method of identification of economic relationships and then estimation of them and diagnostic checking.

References

Box, G.E.P. and Jenkins, G.M. (1970) *Time Series Analysis: Forecasting and Control*, San Francisco: Holden-Day.

boycott (J5)

1 Stopping trade by refusing to deal with a particular country or supplier. This form of protest, first used against Ireland's landlords in the nineteenth century, was employed against South Africa when apartheid was in force, and in many trade disputes.

2 An action by a TRADE (LABOR) UNION which prevents a firm from distributing its goods in an attempt to force it to concede the union's demands. However, industrial relations legislation and ANTI-TRUST law in the USA have increasingly made this illegal.

See also: economic sanctions

bracket creep (H2)

The movement of income tax payers into higher tax brackets as the inevitable consequence of the growth of money incomes with the income bands for each rate of income tax remaining the same. The results of this are higher marginal and average tax rates. The TAX REFORM ACT 1986 (USA) attempted to eliminate this creep by indexing tax brackets and reducing the number of tax brackets.

See also: indexation;
Rooker–Wise Amendment

Bradbury (E5)

UK Treasury note of £1 or 10 shillings issued in 1914 to 1928 after the withdrawal of gold coins. These were named after

John Bradbury, Permanent Secretary to the Treasury, and were also known as Treasury notes or UK currency notes. The Bank of England's dislike of small denomination notes necessitated issue by the Treasury. The smallest Bank of England note until 1928 was a £5 note; in that year, £1 and 10 shilling notes were included in the Bank of England issue.

See also: banknote

Brady Commission (G1, K2)

US presidential commission which reported in 1988 on the Wall Street stock market crash of October 1987. Its principal recommendations were that one institution, preferably the FEDERAL RESERVE SYSTEM, should have the task of co-ordinating financial regulation; that clearing systems should be unified as a means of reducing financial risk; that there should be better information, including the trade, time of trade and ultimate customer in each major market; that there should be a harmonization of rules on margins; and that 'circuit breakers' should be co-ordinated across markets.

See also: circuit breaker mechanism

brain drain (F2)

International migration of highly qualified persons, especially surgeons, physicians, scientists, information technology specialists and engineers, from low-income countries to more prosperous economies, especially the USA. Differences in salaries and research facilities, as well as an oversupply of specialized graduates in less developed countries, have occasioned this, resulting in an increase in the HUMAN CAPITAL stock of advanced countries. Some countries have proposed the repayment of state financed education as a deterrent to emigration.

See also: immigration; migration

branch banking (G2)

A system of banking which permits a banking institution to operate at many locations. This eighteenth-century Scottish invention was slow to be copied by other countries: the USA only began to adopt it in 1933. Branch banking reduces the risk arising from an overcommitment to the financial needs to a single area. Major UK clearing banks expanded in the past through establishing large branch networks. In the USA in the late twentieth century, branches sprang up in response to the liberalization of state banking laws, the growth of suburbs, the movement of industry to peripheral locations and the difficulty of reaching banks situated in congested city centres. The Interstate Banking and Branch Efficiency Act 1994 permitted branch banking across US state boundaries.

branch economy (F4, P0)
A national or regional economy substantially controlled elsewhere because many of its businesses are foreign-owned subsidiaries. The Scottish economy has acquired a branch status through the use of regional policies which encourage inward investment; in many less developed countries MULTINATIONAL CORPORATIONS have substantially transferred economic power abroad.

branding (L1, M3)
PRODUCT DIFFERENTIATION that establishes individuality for a particular product. A producer hopes thereby to gain a measure of MONOPOLY POWER through reducing the amount of substitution between its products and those of its competitors.

See also: monopolistic competition

brand loyalty (D1, M3)
A consumer's continued purchasing of the same differentiated good for a considerable period of time. As firms benefit from a stable regular demand, they will make it an objective of their advertising to achieve this goal. Brand loyalty lowers the ELASTICITY OF DEMAND for a good and gives firms a measure of MONOPOLY POWER.

See also: monopolistic competition

brand stretching (M3)
Applying the name of an established

brand to other products. This is extensively practised by tobacco companies.

Brandt Commission (F3, O0)
The Independent Commission on International Development chaired first by Willy Brandt, previous Chancellor of West Germany, and then by Julius Nyerere, ex-President of Tanzania. Its first report, *North-South: a Programme for Survival* (1980), failed to produce any action; its second report, *Common Crisis: North-South Cooperation for World Recovery* (1983), responded to the THIRD WORLD debt problem by recommending the AMORTIZATION of old debts.

breakeven analysis (C1, D4)
A graphical representation of the relationship between total costs and total revenue with breakeven taking place where total cost is equal to total revenue (i.e. average cost is equal to average revenue).

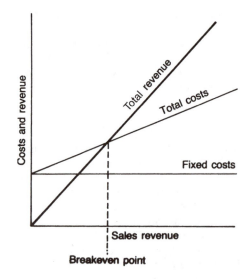

breakeven level of income (M2)
The level of income at which all income is consumed and no debts are incurred.

breakeven pricing (C1, D4)
A firm's policy of setting prices equal to average total costs with the consequence

that neither SUPERNORMAL PROFITS nor losses are made. This was the original pricing policy laid down for UK NATIONALIZED INDUSTRIES.

breakthrough (O3)
A major technological change consisting of a new method of production, a new product or a new market.

See also: innovation

Bretton Woods Agreement (F3)
An agreement signed in Bretton Woods, New Hampshire, USA, in 1944 that created the INTERNATIONAL MONETARY FUND. It set rules for exchange rate behaviour and created a pool of COMMON CURRENCIES, thereby making the IMF the world's 'lender of last resort'. This agreement was a compromise between KEYNES's proposals for an INTERNATIONAL CLEARING UNION and Harry White's plan for an International Stabilization Fund. Par values for exchange rates were fixed in terms of gold. A country had to intervene if its exchange rate was 1 per cent above or below par. An adjustment of more than 10 per cent was permitted if the IMF thought there was a fundamental disequilibrium (a condition vaguely defined) in a country's BALANCE OF PAYMENTS. Temporary borrowings from the IMF were possible to support a currency. This GOLD EXCHANGE STANDARD of Bretton Woods was abandoned on 15 August 1971.

Critics of Bretton Woods noted that the agreement did not provide a mechanism for changing inappropriate national exchange rate policies, that it failed to make national monetary and exchange rate policies compatible, and that it discouraged frequent changes in exchange rate parities. In practice, it was a DOLLAR STANDARD as most countries fixed their currencies against the US dollar. Its demise was hastened by the problems created by the Vietnam War for the US economy.

References

Dormael, A. van (1978) *Bretton Woods: Birth of a Monetary System*, London: Macmillan.

bridefare (I3)
A welfare programme in Wisconsin, USA, enacted in 1994 that increased welfare benefits to teenage mothers who got married. Originally this amounted to $91 extra for a single mother with one child on top of benefit of $440 per month.

bridge financing (G2) *see* bridging

bridging (G2)
Short-term lending needed by a borrower prior to the receipt of permanent finance. This financing is a popular way of effecting a major purchase such as a house, or of adjusting an investment portfolio. It is often necessary as purchases are financed by the delayed proceeds from the sale of another asset.

Bridlington rules (J5)
TRADE UNION recruitment rules agreed by the UK Trades Union Congress in 1939 at its Bridlington Conference to prevent trade unions competing with each other for potential members in the same occupational group.

Britannia (E5)
UK gold coin issued since 1987 in denominations of £10, £25, £50 and £100.

British depository receipt (G1)
A means of purchasing US Treasury BONDS in New York and settling in London which was introduced in 1984.

See also: American depository receipt

broad money (E4)
M2 or M3.

brokered deposit (G1, G2)
A deposit obtained by stockbrokers for a bank in order to increase its liquidity. As such deposits seek the highest yield, they are highly volatile and consequently unreliable as liquid assets.

broker loan rate (G1)
US money market rate, usually 1–1½ per cent below the US prime rate, charged on the debit balances of margin traders; often

regarded as an indicator of future changes in the PRIME RATE OF INTEREST.

Brookings Institution (E6)
An independent centre founded in 1927 in Washington, DC, for research into economics, government, foreign policy and other social sciences. It is famous for its forecasting model of the US economy and for its influential studies of major economies, including those of Japan and the UK. Taxation, international economics, growth and stabilization have been major research concerns.

References

Fromm, G. and Klein, I. R. (1975) *The Brookings Model: Perspectives and Recent Developments*, Amsterdam: North-Holland.

brownfield (Q3)
Land previously used for industrial purposes which requires reclamation before new building can be undertaken.

See also: blackfield site; greenfield

brown good (D2, L6)
A consumer durable used for leisure purposes, e.g. a television set or a compact disc player.

Brundtland Report (Q0)
The 1987 report of the World Commission on Environment and Development which recommended that THIRD WORLD development projects should take into account environmental issues such as the destruction of forests and excessive farming which ruins agricultural land for a long time.

References

World Commission on Environment and Development (1987) *Our Common Future*, Oxford: Oxford University Press.

B share (G1)
1 Chinese stock market share denominated in Chinese currency but payable in foreign currency and designated for foreign investors.
2 An ordinary share of a UK company with voting rights.

See also: A share

bubble (D4, G1)
1 An unsustainable rise in an asset price.
2 A speculative venture. Famous bubbles include the Dutch tulip mania of 1625–37 and the South Sea Bubble in England of 1720. Unless there are an infinite number of traders, a bubble is irrational in nature.

References

Blanchard, O. I. and Watson, M.W. (1982) 'Bubbles, rational expectations and financial markets', in P. Wachtel (ed.) *Crises in the Economic and Financial Structure*, Lexington, MA: Lexington Books.
Carswell, J. (1960) *The South Sea Bubble*, London: Cresset Press.
Kindleberger, C. (1978) *Manias, Panics and Crashes*, New York: Basic Books; London: Macmillan.

bubble economy (P1)
1 An economy engaged mainly in marketing currencies and securities rather than in material production.
2 An unstable economy likely to be deflated after a burst of growth. The precarious nature of the NEW ECONOMY with different technologies is a modern example.

bubble policy (Q2)
A policy which allows an emitter of pollutants to discharge more at one source if there is an equivalent reduction at other sources. An example would be a firm with two plants A and B being permitted to increase its emissions at A if it reduces them at B.

Buchanan, James McGill, 1919– (B3)
US economist, educated at the Universities of Tennessee and Chicago and professor of economics from 1956 at various universities in Virginia; appointed University Distinguished Professor and General Director of the Center for the Study of Public Choice, Virginia Polytechnic Institute, in 1969. He is famous for founding PUBLIC CHOICE THEORY: this unites

the theories of market exchange and of the functioning of political markets. Inspired by a year in Italy (1955), where he read nineteenth-century European classics of PUBLIC FINANCE, he developed the concept of a democratic government receiving taxes from consenting citizens in return for governmental services by establishing constitutional rules to maintain majority consensus. His wide-ranging critique of public sector economics relies on the notion that costs are basically subjective; also he departs from the doctrine of the MARGINAL COST PRICING of public utilities. His analysis of choice is extended to cover the behaviour of politicians, legislators and bureaucrats.

Although a leader of the school of public choice economics, he recognized the early contribution of WICKSELL who discussed the distribution of the costs of proposed public expenditure. As Frank KNIGHT and Henry SIMONS were his mentors when he was a postgraduate student at Chicago, it is not surprising that his work has been loyal to the principles of capitalism and individualism. In 1986, he was awarded the NOBEL PRIZE FOR ECONOMICS for his work on public choice theory.

References

Buchanan, J.M. (1966) *Public Finance in a Democratic Process: Fiscal Institutions and Individual Choice*, Chapel Hill, NC: University of North Carolina.
—— (1972) *Theory of Public Choice: Political Applications of Economics*, Ann Arbor, MI: University of Michigan Press.
Buchanan, J.M. and Tullock, G. (1962) *The Calculus of Consent*, Ann Arbor, MI: University of Michigan Press.
Reisman, D. (1990) *The Political Economy of James Buchanan*, Basingstoke: Macmillan.

bucket shop (L2, L8)
An agency selling goods, services or securities at a discount. The main examples of these are vendors of unsold newly issued shares, and travel agents selling low-priced air tickets of airlines operating their scheduled flights with many unoccupied seats.

Buddhist economics (O4)
An approach to ECONOMIC GROWTH which takes into account spiritual development and does not squander NATURAL RESOURCES so that all have a 'right livelihood'.

References

Buiter, W. (1989) *Principles of Budgetary and Financial Policy*, Hemel Hempstead: Harvester Wheatsheaf.
Schumacher, E.F. (1973) *Small is Beautiful: a Study of Economics as if People Mattered*, ch. 4, London: Blond & Briggs.

budgetary policy (H2)
The principles underlying the revenue and expenditure accounts of a governmental or other organization. The accounts used in a budget will reflect the responsibilities of that organization and its relationships with others, e.g. a state budget will show its financial relationship with the federal government of that country. In those accounts will be stated the sources of revenue and objects of expenditure, a reflection of the taxing and other fund raising carried out and the spending programmes chosen by that government or firm. It is usual to divide budgets into current and capital budgets. An overall budgetary policy can be summarized by whether it is balanced, in surplus or in deficit. Until Keynesian policy ideas influenced governments, government budget deficits were regarded as a sign of financial recklessness; now budget deficits are regarded as a fiscal policy option available to most governments.

See also: fiscal policy

References

Report of the President's Commission on Budget Concepts, Washington, DC: US Government Printing Office, 1967.

budget constraint (D0)

A line showing the maximum amount of goods, in different combinations, which a consumer can obtain from his or her income. It is drawn in combination with INDIFFERENCE CURVES to indicate the maximum utility which can be obtained from a particular level of real income. In the figure, if AB is the budget line and I_1, I_2 and I_3 are indifference curves, then M is the combination of quantities of goods X and Y at which this consumer maximizes utility. The slope of this budget line shows the relative prices of the two goods; a shift of the line away from the origin indicates an increase in real income.

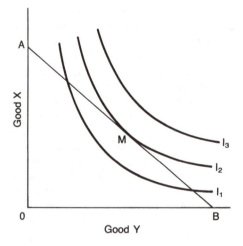

budget cutting (H5)

Proposals to reduce planned public expenditure. In the USA, this has been a prominent feature of recent SUPPLY-SIDE ECONOMICS and has taken the form of attempts to reduce federal outlays for civil purposes. A major cut proposed has been in social transfer payments, on the grounds that such payments discourage the supply of labour.

budget incidence (H2, H5)

The total effect on a household of the taxation and expenditure policies of a government.

See also: tax incidence

budget line (D0) *see* budget constraint

Budget Resolution (H5)

The statement passed by the US Senate and House of Representatives which details spending outlays and authorizes the future expenditure of moneys for specific purposes.

budget year (H5)

The fiscal year chosen by national finance ministries and treasuries. In the UK the year runs from 5 April to 4 April of the next year; in the USA from 1 October to 30 September of the following year.

buffer stock (E4, F3)

1 An accumulation of a commodity for the purpose of stabilizing its world price. The stock built up provides a means of intervention, particularly in the markets for metals, oil and agricultural produce. Buffer stock managers buy in the commodity in times of falling prices and sell when prices are rising. But there are limits to the efficacy of buffer stocks – for example, the major price fall of tin in 1985 was so cataclysmic that the managers were unable to prevent it. Governments have financed many of these stocks to maintain the incomes and employment of primary producers.

2 A cash balance which can absorb unexpected variations in expenditure and income.

References

Laidler, D. (1984) 'The buffer stock notion in monetary economics', *Economic Journal (Supplement)* 94: 17–34.

building and loan association (G2)

US co-operative association whose stockholders offer mortgage loans for the purchase or building of houses.

See also: building society; savings and loan association

Building Societies Act 1986 (G2, K2)
UK statute which liberalized the operating rules for building societies and aligned them with other financial institutions. The societies were allowed to lend to non-members, hold and develop land as a commercial asset and invest in companies and other corporate bodies. Also diversification into banking, insurance, investment, trusteeship and executorship, and land management services was allowed. Liquid assets were limited to a third of a society's assets. Instead of being required to have 90 per cent of their loans secured by property, building societies were permitted to reduce that proportion to 75 per cent by 1992, enabling them to have broader investment portfolios. A new Building Societies Commission regulates the building societies.

Building Societies Association (G2)
UK association of building societies which jointly represents their interests. When it fixed common mortgage interest rates, it was a powerful CARTEL.

building society (G2)
A UK financial institution primarily concerned with raising, through members' deposits, a stock or fund for making advances to them secured on land and buildings for residential use, according to the BUILDING SOCIETIES ACT 1986. As they stand between those who save and those who ultimately borrow money, they act as financial intermediaries. All of them were founded as local non-profit-making institutions, the earliest dating from the 1840s. Through mergers some societies acquired a power rivalling that of the major banks and, like the latter, offering a wide range of financial services. In 1900, there were 2,286 building societies; in 1990, 105; in 2000, 67. The recent decline in their numbers occurred through mergers with

banks or insurance companies. The 1986 Act freed them from many restrictions, changing their character from organizations with social aims to competitive firms with a commercial orientation.

See also: thrift

built-in stabilizer (E6) *see* automatic stabilizer

bulge-bracket firm (G2)
A top investment bank of the USA, one of the leading oligopolists of the US securities industry. The separation of commercial from investment banking under the GLASS-STEAGALL ACT protects their privileged position.

bull (F3, G1)
A speculator who, expecting prices of shares, commodities or currencies to rise, will buy now and sell after prices have risen, thereby making a capital gain. The opposite is a BEAR.

bulldog bond (G1)
A bond denominated in sterling by a company whose accounts are in another currency.

bulldog issue (G1)
A long-term sterling bond issue, mostly purchased by UK INSTITUTIONAL INVESTORS.

bullet strategy (G1)
An investment rule to concentrate the securities in a portfolio at one point of the YIELD CURVE.

bullion (E4)
Gold or silver ingots or bars used as bank reserves and as private stores of wealth.

See also: gold bullion standard

Bullionist controversy (N2)
A major debate in classical monetary theory from 1797 to 1825 which was occasioned by the suspension of cash payments, i.e. the inconvertibility of the pound sterling, during the Napoleonic Wars. The Bullionists, named after the supporters of the Bullion Committee's report of 1810 to the House of Com-

mons, included RICARDO: they recommended a restoration of convertibility as soon as practicable. During the period of suspension, the Bank of England was accused of over-issuing banknotes and creating much of the wartime inflation. However, Henry THORNTON, a commercial banker, in his brilliant *Paper Credit*, took a broader view of money and the banking system.

See also: Currency School

Bullock Committee (J5, L2)

UK governmental committee on workers' participation in the management of companies which reported in 1977. The committee, headed by the historian Lord Bullock and consisting of trade unionists, employers and industrial relations experts, was asked to devise a scheme based on the assumption that there is a need for a radical expansion of industrial democracy through trade union representation. The trade unionists and academic experts in the majority recommended that UK companies with more than 2,000 employees should reconstitute their boards of directors according to a '$2x + y$' principle of equal numbers of employee and shareholder representatives ($2x$) and co-opted directors (y). This was intended to be an extension of COLLECTIVE BARGAINING into the boardroom. The minority report recommended two-tier (supervisory and executive) boards following the European example of West Germany. The report's recommendations were not embodied in legislation.

References

Committee of Inquiry on Industrial Democracy (1977) *Report*, London: HMSO, Cmnd 6706.

bunch map (C1)

A set of lines from the origin of a graph with each line measuring a coefficient between two variables. These maps have been used to check for the presence of MULTICOLLINEARITIES in data.

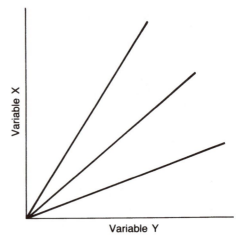

Variable X / Variable Y

Bundesbank (E5)

Germany's CENTRAL BANK which replaced the Reichsbank in 1957. Its principal duty has been to safeguard the value of the currency by regulating the quantities of money in circulation and of credit in the economy. Although expected to support the government's general economic policy, it is independent of instructions from the government. The bank's president chairs fortnightly meetings of the Bank Council on which bank directors and presidents from the federal states sit; the council fixes interest rates and credit policy. Also, the Bundesbank decides on the size of the note issue, is custodian of the nation's gold and foreign currency reserves and is in charge of official dealings in foreign exchange markets. The Bundesbank's contribution to low German inflation in the past has been praised, but critics have accused the bank of setting money market interest rates which were too high on several occasions, risking recession in the economy.

References

Frowen, S.F. and Pringle, R. (eds) (1998) *Inside the Bundesbank*, New York: St Martin's Press; London: Macmillan.

bundled deal (D0) *see* interlinked transaction

bundling (D0)

The sale of two or more goods or services in a package deal. A seller is able to increase sales of less popular items by combining them with those in great demand.

See also: mixed bundling; pure bundling

References

Adams, W.J. and Yellen, J.L. (1976) 'Commodity bundling and the burden of monopoly', *Quarterly Journal of Economics* 90: 475–98.

bunny bond (G1)

A fixed interest security entitling the holder to an interest payment in cash or to more units of the asset.

buoyant tax (H2)

A tax with a rising yield because of increases in the extent of the TAX BASE, e.g. through rises in income or property values.

Bureau of Economic Analysis (H1)

The branch of the US Department of Commerce responsible for assembling and publishing US national income accounts.

See also: National Income and Product Accounts

Bureau of the Budget (H1)

A US federal bureau created within the US Treasury by the Accounting Act 1921 to provide operational control over expenditure programmes. In 1939 it was transferred to the President's Office, at which time it changed its function increasingly to ensuring managerial efficiency.

See also: Office of Management and Budget

Burns, Arthur Frank, 1904–87 (B3)

An Austro-Hungarian who emigrated to the USA in 1914; educated at Columbia University and professor at Rutgers University from 1927 to 1958. Principally renowned for his BUSINESS CYCLE research at the NATIONAL BUREAU OF ECONOMIC RESEARCH, Washington, DC, in 1930–44 and chairman of the Board of Governors of the US FEDERAL RESERVE SYSTEM from 1970 to 1978, where he practised his conservative monetary beliefs. As US Ambassador to West Germany in 1981–5 he negotiated the German Treaty of 1982 to obtain more German logistic support for US troops. His final years were spent in research at the American Enterprise Institute. In his important exposition of business cycle theory (with Wesley Mitchell) he compiled a list of economic indicators which became the basis of business cycle forecasting in the USA after 1945. He calculated 'reference cycles' as the single indicator of turning points in cycles. A noted anti-Keynesian in economic policy matters.

References

Burns, A.F. (1946) *Economic Research and the Keynesian Thinking of Our Times*, Washington, DC: National Bureau of Economic Research.
—— (1954) *Frontiers of Economic Knowledge*, Princeton, NJ: Princeton University Press.
—— (1969) *The Business Cycles in a Changing World*, New York: National Bureau of Economic Research.
Burns, A.F. and Mitchell, W.C. (1946) *Measuring Business Cycles*, Washington, DC: National Bureau of Economic Research.
Mullineux, A. (1990) *Business Cycles and Financial Crises*, Hemel Hempstead: Harvester Wheatsheaf.

business cycle (E3)

'A type of fluctuation found in the aggregate economic activity of nations that organize their work mainly in business enterprises: a cycle consists of expansions occurring at about the same time in many economic activities, followed by similarly general recessions, contractions, and revivals which merge into the expansion phase of the next cycle; this sequence of changes is recurrent but not periodic; in duration business cycles vary from more than one year to ten or twelve years' (Mitchell).

Previously these were known as periodic 'commercial crises'. The NATIONAL BUREAU OF ECONOMIC RESEARCH has studied these

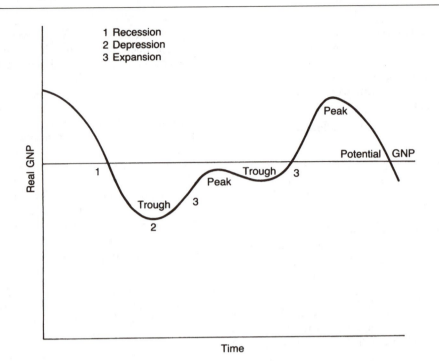

cycles since 1920. HABERLER, in an extensive survey of business cycle research, noted the many possible causes of cycles, including credit changes, overinvestment, costs of production, underconsumption, mass psychology, variations in harvests – the interaction of the MULTIPLIER and the ACCELERATOR and international influences. More recently, the cycle of elections in democratic countries has been associated with fluctuations in national economies. (See figure.)

See also: accelerator principle; Juglar cycle; Kitchin cycle; Kondratieff cycle; Kuznets cycle; political business cycle

References

Bowers, D.A. (1985) *An Introduction to Business Cycles and Forecasting*, Reading, MA, and Wokingham: Addison-Wesley.

Burns, A.F. and Mitchell, W.C. (1946) *Measuring Business Cycles*, New York: National Bureau of Economic Research.

Haberler, G. (1958) *Prosperity and Depression. A Theoretical Analysis of Cyclical Movements*, 3rd edn, London: Allen & Unwin.

Mitchell, W.C. (1927) *Business Cycles: The Problem and its Setting*, New York: National Bureau of Economic Research; London: Pitman.

Business Expansion Scheme (G2)
UK investment scheme introduced in 1981 to encourage small businesses, especially by giving them access to the finance provided by the UNLISTED SECURITIES MARKET. Tax incentives are available to investors in these businesses.

business organization (M1)
A particular legal arrangement for owning a firm. The principal types of business are the sole trader, the partnership and the company/corporation. These forms have different liabilities for debt and varying numbers of owners. There is limited liability for the shareholders of companies and corporations have limited liability, but sole traders and members of partnerships are unlimited.

See also: limited partnership

business studies (M0)
The multidisciplinary analysis of the problems of business, using economic, accounting, psychological, legal and statistical methods. It blossomed as a subject as a consequence of the establishment of business schools, especially the Wharton School of Finance and Commerce in Philadelphia in 1881 and the Henley Administrative Staff College (UK) in 1947. These postgraduate schools, the chief practitioners of business studies, have reduced many managerial inefficiencies which used to be regarded as the principal cause of DISECONOMIES OF SCALE. The distinctive discipline developed by the subject has been ORGANIZATION THEORY.

Butskellism (E6)
The similar economic policies pursued by Hugh Gaitskell and R.A. Butler as Chancellors of the Exchequer in the early 1950s.

The techniques of DEMAND MANAGEMENT that they employed were based on a mixture of planning and market freedom. This form of macroeconomic policy was criticised for entailing too many monetary and fiscal changes.

See also: mixed economy

butterfly effect (C0, E0, F0)
The large differences in the values of dependent economic variables as a consequence of minuscule differences in inputted economic variables. This type of effect makes it difficult for policy-makers to be sure of the effects of their decisions. Foreign exchange markets often display butterfly effects.

See also: chaos theory

buyers' market (D4)
A market in which buyers have a dominant influence on price because of excess supply. Contrast with SELLERS' MARKET.

C

C (E2, G2)

1 Total consumer expenditure of a national economy. This is shown as a function of national income in the CONSUMPTION FUNCTION.

2 The lowest quality of security, according to Standard & Poor, as such securities have no interest paid on them.

See also: AAA; BB; BBB; D; DDD

cable (F4)

Transactions between the dollar and sterling in foreign exchange trading.

cabotage (L9)

1 Coastal and commercial navigation between ports.

2 Permission for an air carrier of a foreign country to pick up passengers or freight in another country for transport to a third country.

cab rank rule (J4)

The customary regulation that UK barristers must accept a brief appropriately priced if it is within their competence.

cadastral survey (H2)

A survey of the ownership, extent and value of land usually undertaken for taxation purposes.

Cadbury code of corporate governance (G3)

The recommendations of the Committee on the Financial Aspects of Corporate Governance chaired by Sir Adrian Cad-bury. The final report, issued in December 1992, recommended at least three non-executive directors on boards of directors, checks on the power of any individual with 'unfettered powers of decision' and an audit committee of non-executives.

Cairn's Group (F0)

The group of major agricultural exporting countries founded in 1986 and based in Australia. It consists of Argentina, Australia, Brazil, Canada, Chile, Colombia, Fiji, Hungary, Indonesia, Malaysia, New Zealand, the Philippines, Thailand and Uruguay. It seeks to liberalize trade in agricultural products, especially through reductions in agricultural export subsidies and barriers to consumer markets: these entail changes in national agricultural policies. The group also acts as the representative of these countries in GENERAL AGREEMENT ON TARIFFS AND TRADE talks.

call (G1)

An order to pay a further instalment of cash for the purchase of shares.

call centre (L2)

Business premises where workers dealing with incoming and outgoing telephone calls undertake market research, sell products or answer customer enquiries. These centres have been criticized for the low rates of pay offered and for strict working conditions. By 2001 there were in the UK about 7,000 call centres of all sizes employing in total about 400,000 workers. A centre with fewer than twenty staff is called a 'pocket centre'.

call money (E4, G2)

Money lent within the City of London by CLEARING BANKS to DISCOUNT HOUSES for short periods, sometimes only overnight, and immediately payable on demand. This is ranked after cash and deposits with the Bank of England as the most liquid asset of the UK clearing banks as it can be recalled at any time.

call option (G1)

The right to buy a stock exchange security at the current price within a specified period, normally three months.

Cambridge Circus (B2)

Several young economists who debated with KEYNES in the early 1930s the development of his ideas in *A Treatise of Money* (1930) into the theories central to *The General Theory of Employment, Interest and Money*. The group included Joan ROBINSON, Roy HARROD, Richard KAHN, James MEADE and Piero SRAFFA.

References

Keynes, J.M. (1985) *Collected Works*, Vols XIII and XXIX, London: Macmillan.

Cambridge controversies (D3, E0)

Disputes between economists in Cambridge, England (ROBINSON and KALDOR), and Cambridge, Massachusetts (SOLOW and SAMUELSON), about the nature of CAPITAL. In particular, the English contestants attacked the neoclassical assumptions of their transatlantic opponents by questioning the existence of the aggregate PRODUCTION FUNCTION. Also, they debated the theory of profits and capital, the determination of savings and the interest rate, aggregate capital and the re-switching of techniques.

References

Blaug, M. (1975) *The Cambridge Revolution: Success or Failure?*, rev. edn, London: Institute of Economic Affairs.
Harcourt, G.C. (1972) *Some Cambridge*

Controversies in the Theory of Capital, Cambridge: Cambridge University Press.

Cambridge Economic Policy Group (B2, H3)

A group of Cambridge economists led by Wynne Godley who recommended an expansionary fiscal policy and import controls in order to alleviate UK unemployment after 1974. They opposed the use of DEMAND MANAGEMENT and INCOMES POLICIES as central instruments for determining the level of AGGREGATE DEMAND.

See also: New Cambridge economics

Cambridge School (B1, B2)

Successive generations of economists at Cambridge University, particularly after the establishment of the separate Economics Tripos in 1903. The school was founded by MARSHALL and was made famous in the 1930s by KEYNES, its intellectual leader. After 1945 its prominent leaders included KALDOR, Joan ROBINSON, SRAFFA and Wynne Godley. A succession of ideas has occupied the school in the post-war period: in the 1950s, the refinement of Keynesian ideas; in the 1960s, 'the CAMBRIDGE CONTROVERSIES' about CAPITAL; and, more recently, an examination of the nature of markets to show that MARKET CLEARING is so poor that DISEQUILIBRIUM is a major economic problem.

See also: New Cambridge economics

Canal Age (N7)

The period 1757–1830 in UK history when a network of 4,250 miles (6,800 km) of navigable rivers and canals was created to transport agricultural produce and the manufactures of the Industrial Revolution. It was succeeded by a railway age.

canons of taxation (H2)

Adam SMITH's criteria for taxes: equality (based on a person's ability to pay), certainty (the time for payment, manner of payment and quantity to be paid should be clear), convenience (payable at the time the taxpayer is in receipt of income) and economy in collection.

References

Smith, A. (1776) *The Wealth of Nations*, ed. R.H. Campbell and A.S. Skinner, Book V, ch. II, Part II, Oxford: Clarendon Press, 1976.

Cantillon effect (E4)

The differential impact of an increase in the money supply. As different recipients of extra cash have different uses for it, there will be a change in the relative demand for, and relative prices of, goods and services. The rate of interest will fall if the recipients of the extra money save and invest.

Cantillon, Richard, *c.1680–c.1734* (B3)

Irish-born banker and economist who spent much of his life in France where he made a large personal fortune after the collapse of John LAW's Mississippi Company. His writings on economics, other than the *Essai sur la Nature du Commerce en Général*, appear to have perished with him when his house in Albemarle Street, London, was burnt down. His remarkable *Essai* showed his keen reading of several economists, including PETTY, and his immense practical knowledge of banking. In many senses he anticipated QUESNAY and other PHYSIOCRATS by setting out a model of the economy with villages, market towns and cities engaged in mutual exchanges. Also, he powerfully explained the role of the ENTREPRENEUR in economic activity, with a more plausible explanation than Smith's INVISIBLE HAND postulate. His analysis of exchange rates, open market operations and the bank credit multiplier gives his work a modern focus.

References

Cantillon, R. (1755) *Essai sur la Nature du Commerce en Général*, English trans. H. Higgs, London: Macmillan, for the Royal Economic Society, 1931.
Murphy, A.E. (1986) *Richard Cantillon: Entrepreneur and Economist*, Oxford: Clarendon Press.

cap (E4, G1)

The maximum interest rate paid on a floating rate security by its issuer. The seller gives funds to cover interest payments over a specified rate. Also applies to an adjustable rate mortgage.

See also: collar; floor

capacity (D2, E4)

1 The maximum output that a firm or a national economy can produce from its existing supply of factors of production. A firm can increase its capacity by enlarging its labour force or its capital stock.
2 The maximum amount of money which a financial institution can lend.

See also: capital utilization

capacity charge (D4, M2)

A component of the price of the goods or services of public enterprises which is expected to cover the costs of fixed capital.

capacity ratio (J2) *see* volume ratio

capacity utilization (D0, E0)

The ratio of the actual output of a firm, industry or national economy to its maximum output at a point in time. This ratio will fluctuate cyclically. A high degree of utilization will be a signal for more net investment.

See also: accelerator principle; trade cycle

capital (D0, E0)

1 Durable goods capable of producing a stream of goods or services over a period of time.
2 A factor of production distinct from land, the entrepreneur and the labour currently being used.
3 A sum of money which is invested in a business enterprise.
4 Accumulated expenditures giving rise to higher subsequent incomes, as in HUMAN CAPITAL.
5 Wealth.
6 Stored-up labour; exchange value which is becoming wealth, according to Marx.

See also: Cambridge controversies; capital theory

capital account (F4)

A balance of payments account which

records the flow of capital assets between one country and the rest of the world. World interest rates will have a major influence on a country's capital account, as capital mobility is stimulated by differences in the rates of return to financial assets in different countries.

capital accumulation (E2)
Increasing the capital stock by undertaking investment in excess of REPLACEMENT INVESTMENT. This accumulation has been viewed as the expansion of the productive potential of the economy and as the adjustment of the amount of capital to the equilibrium level necessary to achieve an optimal allocation of scarce resources. Adam SMITH attributed this investment to a person's desire for betterment; MARX to the innate greed of capitalists. Today, the principal motivation is to achieve a desired rate of economic growth.

capital adequacy (G0)
Sufficient capital to protect depositors and counter-parties from the risks present in a bank's balance sheet and off-balance sheet activities. Rules have been devised to ensure adequacy, especially by the Basle Committee on Banking Supervision. The committee issued the Capital Accord 1988 (revised 1999, 2000). This included a minimum capital 8 per cent of liabilities, with higher requirements for each of the five classes of asset according to risk. Subsequently the committee experimented with internal models to calculate market risks of capital and ordered more disclosure of information. Other capital adequacy tests are based on measuring liquidity, solvency, market and settlements risks.

capital asset pricing model (G1)
A model which demonstrates that the reward for holding a risky security which is part of a well-diversified portfolio is based on its BETA risk. It is assumed that the securities market is in a state of frictionless PERFECT COMPETITION, that investors invest for the same length of time and have identical expectations concerning the probable returns from securities invested then, and that investors can borrow or lend unlimited amounts of money at a risk-free rate of interest. The publication of beta statistics for many shares has often enabled investors to increase the overall return to their portfolios. Criticisms of the model are directed chiefly at its assumptions.

References

Levy, H. and Sarnat, M. (eds) (1977) *Financial Decision Making under Uncertainty*, New York: Academic Press.

Merton, R.C. (1973) 'An intertemporal capital asset pricing model', *Econometrica* 41: 867–87.

capital-augmenting technical progress (O3)
Technical progress which increases output even though the rate of investment remains the same as measured in machine hours.

capital budgeting (M2)
Appraising the financial implications of investment plans using techniques such as calculating DISCOUNTED CASH FLOW, NET PRESENT VALUE, PAYBACK METHOD and RATES OF RETURN. As major investments are risky and irreversible, capital budgeting is a crucial managerial activity of firms.

capital consumption (M2)
DEPRECIATION. Given that fixed assets have only a limited life-span, it is necessary to add to the annual costs of an enterprise or a national economy an estimate of the amount notionally spent on the wear and tear of such assets. Capital consumption is deducted from the gross national product to obtain the net national product, or NATIONAL INCOME.

capital controls (F2)
Barriers to the flow of capital between countries erected in order to calm financial markets and provide short-term protection for a country with a balance of payments deficit. The UK suddenly abandoned its controls in 1979; in the

European Union controls have been progressively abandoned.

capital deepening (E2, O4)
Investment which produces an increase in a CAPITAL–LABOUR RATIO because the capital stock grows at a faster rate than the labour force.

See also: capital widening

capital flight (F2)
A capital outflow from a particular country. This is broadly defined as all purchases of foreign assets (other than to increase official reserves), together with the errors and omissions item of a BALANCE OF PAYMENTS; narrowly, it can be regarded as short-term capital outflows (hot money) plus errors and omissions.

capital gains tax (H2)
A tax based on the increase in capital value of an asset between its purchase and its sale. This tax discourages investors from adjusting their portfolios and reduces business for stockbrokers. The country with the highest rate of tax is Australia (48.5 per cent) followed by the UK and the USA.

capital income tax (H2)
A tax levied on the returns from investments or capital. Often such a tax is levied at a higher rate than taxes on employment incomes.

capital intensive (D2)
A form of production using much physical capital per unit of labour input. The degree of factor intensity is usually measured by the slope of an ISOQUANT.

See also: capital deepening; labour intensive

capitalism (P1)
1 A socioeconomic system of production using ROUNDABOUT METHODS OF PRODUCTION.
2 An ECONOMY based on private enterprise.
3 The use of markets not planning to allocate economic resources.

4 Production motivated by the profit motive.

The PHYSIOCRATS and classical economists such as SMITH regarded capitalism as the natural form of economic organization based upon man's propensity to truck and barter and likely to be the most successful in increasing ECONOMIC WELFARE. MARX criticized many definitions of capitalism for being timeless, ignoring the different historical forms it takes, and for the institution of private property, which prevents the reconciliation of individual and general interests, causing the alienation of workers. Marxists have classified capitalism into different stages, namely agricultural capitalism, merchant capitalism, industrial capitalism and state capitalism.

See also: creative destruction; fundamenal contradiction of capitalism; industrial capitalism; late capitalism; lemonade-stand capitalism; merchant capitalism; monopoly capitalism; peripheral capitalism; personal capitalism; popular capitalism; socialism; state capitalism; state monopoly capitalism

References
Dobb, M. (1946) *Studies in the Development of Capitalism*, London: Routledge.
Graham, D. and Clarke, P. (1986) *The New Enlightenment: The New Birth of Liberalism*, London: Macmillan.
Hirschman, A. O. (1982) 'Rival interpretations of market society: civilizing, destructive, or feeble', *Journal of Economic Literature* 20 (December): 1463–84.
Tribe, K. (1981) *Genealogies of Capitalism*, London: Macmillan.
Wallerstein, I. (1979) *The Capitalist World-Economy*, Cambridge: Cambridge University Press.

capitalist class (J5) *see* bourgeoisie

capitalist imperialism (L2, O0)
The exercise of power by major capitalist countries over less developed countries, often through the medium of MULTINATIONAL CORPORATIONS. Marxists have argued

that the declining rate of profit on home production forced capitalists to expand overseas.

References

Owen, R. and Sutcliffe, B. (eds) (1972) *Studies in the Theory of Imperialism*, London: Longman.

capitalization (G1)

The conversion of an interest payment or a liquid asset into permanent capital. A company can capitalize its cash reserves by the issue of shares (a free, BONUS or SCRIP ISSUE). A debtor, even a nation, can capitalize interest payments by adding them to the original sum borrowed.

See also: securitization

capitalization effect of a tax (H2)

The reduced value of an asset resulting from the imposition of a tax on the income from the asset; for example, a tax on the imputed income from owner-occupied housing depresses the value of houses.

capital–labour ratio (D2)

The amount of physical capital employed by each worker usually measured by dividing the value of the capital stock by the size of the labour force. These ratios are central to theories of growth and of COMPARATIVE ADVANTAGE.

See also: capital deepening; capital intensive; capital widening

capital market (G1)

A market which issues securities to raise long-term capital.

See also: primary market; secondary market

capital mobility (F2)

The flow of financial capital between one employment and another. It was assumed by RICARDO and other practitioners of CLASSICAL ECONOMICS that capital would flow between places and industries until rates of profit were equalized.

See also: mobility of labour; multinational corporation

capital–output ratio (D2)

The amount of capital divided by the amount of output produced by it. This measure of CAPITAL INTENSITY underlies the ACCELERATOR PRINCIPLE.

capital re-switching (D2)

A return to more CAPITAL-INTENSIVE methods of production because a technique has become more profitable through an increase in the marginal product of capital or a fall in the rate of interest.

See also: Cambridge controversies

capital reversing (E2)

A challenge to the NEOCLASSICAL view that input substitution responds to the relative scarcity of factors of production. Instead of relative prices, changes in the quantity of capital lead to capital reversing. Also known as reverse capital deepening because a lower rate of profit can be associated with a lower capital–labour ratio.

capital tax (H2)

A tax based on the value of assets. Such taxes, which are very costly to collect because of valuation problems, rarely constitute a large proportion of a country's total tax revenue but are imposed for the distributional reason of increasing the relative tax burden of the rich. In practice, governments often reduce the effective rate of capital taxes by a variety of allowances, e.g. to allow for depreciation, life insurance and pensions.

See also: wealth tax

capital theory (D2, E2)

A theory which links the theories of production, growth, value and distribution to explain why capital produces a return which keeps capital intact but yields interest (or profit) which is permanent. Over the past 200 years the notion of capital has varied greatly: to many of the CLASSICAL ECONOMISTS it was to a large extent the raw materials and the WAGES FUND; later it was viewed as a physical INTERMEDIATE good. To MARX capital was a social mode of production; to the AUSTRIAN SCHOOL time was crucial to the concept; to FISHER capital was a stock which produced a stream of income with its value determined by relative preference for future rather than present goods. Important debates include the relationship between the RATE OF INTEREST and the value of capital, as well as discussion of the notion of aggregate capital. As there are many important sub-species of capital, including HUMAN CAPITAL and EQUITY capital, specialist theories of capital are also propounded. Capital theory expanded its concerns in the 1960s within the context of growth theory. A major issue discussed then was the method of measuring aggregate or social capital to achieve a value independent of distribution and prices. Joan ROBINSON suggested using labour time as a measure; Champernowne introduced a CHAIN INDEX METHOD.

See also: Cambridge controversies

References

Harcourt, G.C. (1972) *Some Cambridge Controversies in the Theory of Capital*, Cambridge: Cambridge University Press.

Kregel, J.A. (1976) *Theory of Capital*, London: Macmillan.

capital transfer tax (H2)
UK tax introduced in 1975 on transfers of wealth payable by the donor or recipient during life or at death. Estate duty, in force from 1894 to 1975, was the predecessor of this tax.

capital utilization (D2, E2)
1 The proportion of fixed capital (buildings and machinery) in use. If machinery is worked for only half of a time period, the capital utilization rate is 50 per cent.
2 Actual output as a percentage of potential output at a reference date.

See also: capacity utilization

capital value (E2, M2)
A valuation of an asset broadly measured either by discounting the total future income expected from the asset or by capitalizing the expected income.

See also: discounting; net present value

capital widening (E2)
An increase in the real capital stock leaving the CAPITAL-LABOUR RATIO unchanged as the capital stock and the labour force grow at the same rate.

See also: capital deepening

capitation tax (H2) *see* poll tax

capping an interest rate (G1)
Separating the part of interest payments in excess of real interest payments and then capitalizing it by adding it to the long-term debt.

captive insurance (G2)
An insurance company whose business is mainly supplied and controlled by its owners. The principal beneficiaries are those originally insured.

capture theory (K2, L4) *see* regulatory capture

carbon sequestration (Q2)
Storing carbon dioxide by planting trees or pumping into underground reservoirs: an approach to reducing global warming.

carbon sink (Q2)
An area with trees and plants which has been created to absorb carbon dioxide. This has been proposed to reduce global warming.

carbon tax (H2, Q2)
A tax related to the carbon content of coal, natural gas or oil, which is imposed to improve the natural environment. The tax can take the form of a fixed amount per ton of carbon embodied in each fuel or be an AD VALOREM TAX. The level of the tax is related to the emission reduction target chosen.

See also: effluent fee; environmental tax; marketable discharge permit

cardinal utility (D0)
The satisfaction obtained from consump-

tion, or engaging in an economic activity, which is directly measurable in monetary or other units. The cardinalist argues that it is possible to compare, e.g. in UTILS, the relative amount of satisfaction from consuming different quantities of the same or other goods. Thus, the law of DIMINISHING MARGINAL UTILITY could be described as follows: a woman obtains 10 utils from the first glass of champagne, 8 utils from the second, 6 utils from the third .... Proxy measures of utility, e.g. the amount of money which a person is prepared to give up to obtain x amount of a good, have all been considered too indirect.

See also: ordinal utility; revealed preferences; utility

References

Majumdar, T. (1961) *The Measurement of Utility*, London and New York: Macmillan.

carer (I3)

An unpaid family worker who provides nursing and domestic care to young, infirm or elderly relatives. Moral obligation is the basis for undertaking this work.

Caribbean Basin Initiative (F0)

An arrangement agreed in 1984 to give exports of countries of the Caribbean region tariff-free access to the USA.

Caribbean Community (F0)

A common market with agricultural and industrial integration founded in 1973 in succession to the Caribbean Free Trade Area (1968–73). The members are Anguilla, Antigua, Barbados, Belize, Dominica, Grenada, Guyana, Jamaica, Montserrat, St Kitts-Nevis, St Lucia, St Vincent, Trinidad and Tobago.

Caribbean Development Bank (G2)

DEVELOPMENT BANK founded in 1970 consisting of seventeen member countries from the Caribbean region as well as Canada and the UK.

caring society (D6, P0) *see* altruism; welfare state

carry-back, carry-forward system (H2)

A tax system which permits businesses to carry net operating losses back or forward against past or future gains in income or capital appreciation.

carrying capacity (J1)

The ability of a particular area to sustain a population at a specified level of subsistence, usually specified as the number of persons per unit of land.

cartalist (E4)

A person believing that the value of a currency depends on the power of the issuing authority and not on its intrinsic value or its convertibility into gold.

See also: Banking School; fiat money; metallist

carte à mémoire (G2)

French for SMART CARD.

cartel (L1)

An association of producers who agree to fix common prices and output quotas in an oligopolistic market. As the aim of a cartel is to prevent competition, there is a tendency for the producers to strive to maintain existing market shares, with the consequence that a firm can only increase its output if total market demand rises. The device of a cartel has long been used as a method of restricting competition: Adam SMITH acknowledged the existence of cartels in the eighteenth century: 'People of the same trade seldom meet together, even for merriment and diversion, but the conversation ends in a conspiracy against the public or in some contrivance to raise prices.' Firms afraid of the effects of recession are eager to join such associations, e.g. in the 1880s in the USA and in Germany in the interwar period. Increasingly tough legislation in the USA and Western Europe has outlawed many cartels. The ORGANIZATION OF PETROLEUM EXPORTING COUNTRIES has some of the characteristics of a cartel.

See also: competition policy

cash (E4)

The most LIQUID of ASSETS, consisting of coin and banknotes; often defined as a zero-interest asset, although Goodhart and others have suggested that interest could be paid by running a national lottery on the serial numbers of the notes. Commercial banks also regard deposits at the 'central' bank as cash.

References

Goodhart, C.A.X. (1986) 'How can non-interest bearing assets co-exist with safe interest-bearing assets?', *British Review of Economic Issues* 8: 1–12.

cash accounting (M4)

The recording of income and expenses when cash is actually received or spent. This method is often used to calculate income tax.

See also: accrual accounting

cash budgeting (M2)

Predicting the cash flows of a business.

See also: cash flow; cash flow accounting

cash crop (Q1)

Agricultural produce marketed for cash, rather than retained for the use of the farmer's household.

See also: agricultural household

cash–deposits ratio (G2)

The ratio of a bank's holdings of cash to its total deposits, sometimes used as a measure of control over the banking system to guarantee its liquidity. In the second half of the twentieth century, LIQUID ASSET ratios came to be the preferred method of controlling the total volume of bank deposits.

cash dispenser (G2)

A machine provided by a bank or other deposit-taking institution, often at its premises, to dispense cash through the insertion of a card to account-holders of that bank or a bank in association with it. Usage of dispensers varies from country to country. In the UK and France they are particularly popular: by 1985, there were 6,886 in the UK and 7,172 in France but only 2,000 in West Germany.

See also: automated teller machine; debit card; smart card

cash economy (G2, P0)

Part of a national ECONOMY using cash to make all payments. This occurs either because of a shortage of banking facilities or because of a desire to evade tax. In modern economies, much of the BLACK or INFORMAL ECONOMY is of this nature.

cash flow (M2)

1 The net amount of money received by a firm over a given period.
2 Retained profits and funds set aside for depreciation. This flow permits a firm to finance its own investment.

cash flow accounting (M4)

Accounting based on the transactions which are recorded when payment is actually made. Contrast with ACCRUAL ACCOUNTING.

cash-in-advance constraint (E4)

A good has the status of money through being involved in most types of exchange, so purchases within a period are constrained by the amount of money available at the beginning of that period. Also known as the finance or effective demand constraint.

References

Kohn, M. (1981) 'In defense of the finance constraint', *Economic Inquiry* 19: 177–95.

cashless society (G2, P0)

A modern economy which uses CREDIT CARDS and direct debiting of bank accounts to make payments, instead of notes and coins.

See also: debit card

cash limit (H5)

A method of controlling government spending in the UK which replaced a constant-prices system. From 1974 to 1976, cash limits were used for several public sector building programmes and from 1976 for about 60 per cent of central government expenditures. Originally, the government calculated the real value of current programmes and then added an amount to compensate for some or all of inflationary increases. From 1981, the system was simplified by expressing public expenditure targets entirely in cash terms.

cash management account (G2)
A bank deposit of US commercial banks, a CHECKING ACCOUNT that pays a return linked to investments. Originally designed by Merrill Lynch (with the processing done by Bank One, Columbus, Ohio) in 1977 to evade the strictures of REGULATION Q.

See also: NOW account

Cash Management Bill (E5, G1)
US treasury bill with very short maturity that is sold occasionally by the US Treasury to boost the Treasury's cash balance.

cash nexus (E4, P0)
Human relationships based on monetary transactions. Thomas Carlyle in *Chartism* wrote: 'Cash payment had not then grown to be the universal sole nexus of man to man'.

See also: dismal science

cash positive (M3)
A surplus in cash but not necessarily profits; a positive CASH FLOW.

cash price–earnings ratio (G1)
A modified version of a PRICE–EARNINGS RATIO, with earnings measured as post-tax earnings + non-cash provisions (e.g. depreciation). This ratio removes some of the effects of conservative accounting, making international comparisons more meaningful. But as depreciation reflects the CAPITAL INTENSITY of an industry, the cash price–earnings ratio will undervalue service industry shares.

cash ratio (G2) *see* cash–deposits ratio

cash transfer (H2)
An income or grant by a government to a person or firm in the private sector, e.g. a pension, an educational bursary, a training grant, which is made to implement a government's redistribution policy. Unlike the alternative, IN-KIND TRANSFER, the recipient has more freedom to determine consumption.

Cassel, Karl Gustav, 1866–1945 (B3)
After studying mathematics at Uppsala University, Sweden, he became a professor of economics at Stockholm University in 1902. He was a founder of modern Swedish economics, especially noted for *Theory of Social Economy* (originally published in 1918) and monetary writings. He rejected both labour and MARGINAL UTILITY theories of value in favour of a price theory which he also applied to his study of the RATE OF INTEREST. He relied on the QUANTITY THEORY OF MONEY in his monetary economics and was anti-Keynesian. His pupils included OHLIN and MYRDAL.

References

Mitchell, W.C. (1969) *Types of Economic Theory*, Vol. 2, ch. 16, New York: Augustus M. Kelley.

casualization (J2)
The process of changing employment from regular and permanent to occasional and part-time forms. This is done to increase the flexibility of a labour force.

catallactics (D4)
The study of all market phenomena, i.e. of actions conducted on the basis of monetary calculation.

References

von Mises, L. (1949) *Human Action*, 3rd edn, New Haven, CT: Yale University Press.

catalytic policy mix (E6)
A mixture of major and subsidiary policies: the latter are used as a catalyst to avert the undesired effects of a major policy.

catastrophe theory (C1)
The applied mathematical study of discon-

tinuities which states how many stable equilibria exist given a choice of control variables but does not indicate which of them will be in a particular system. A 'catastrophe' occurs when transition from one equilibrium to another produces instability in the system.

References

Poston, T. and Stewart, I. (1978) *Catastrophe Theory and its Applications*, London and San Francisco: Pitman.

Saunders, P.T. (1980) *An Introduction to Catastrophe Theory*, Cambridge: Cambridge University Press.

catching-up hypothesis (N1, O4)

1 The view that in the post-1945 period the countries which had lost a great deal of their capital stock in the Second World War, and had to renew it, experienced higher growth and productivity through having modern plant and machinery.

2 More generally, the way the national income of any low-productivity country is raised. Thus, gross investment (including replacement investment) has been regarded as a more important determinant of economic growth than net investment.

References

Abramovitz, M. (1986) 'Catching up, forging ahead, and falling behind', *Journal of Economic History* 46: 385–406.

categorical grant (H2)

A grant from a central or federal government to a lower level of government to be spent on only a particular category of expenditure. Such grants can be based on a formula (e.g. reflecting the size and age distribution of the population) or on a project (e.g. introducing a new educational curriculum). They usually require matching funds by state or local government.

cats and dogs (G1)

Speculative stocks and shares with a poor history of sales and earnings.

CAT standard (L5)

The standard a product has to meet in Charges, Access and Terms. This approach to quality management was introduced in the UK in the 1990s.

ceiling (E3)

A peak in economic activity; the maximum level of production in a BUSINESS CYCLE or TRADE CYCLE after which there is a downturn in output, employment and prices. The peak is often associated with FULL EMPLOYMENT of the factors of production: shortages of skilled labour and BOTTLENECKS in production bring about a decline from peak activity.

See also: crisis; floor

ceiling price (D4, L5)

Maximum price set under a system of price control. If, as is often the case, this price (OC in the figure) is less than the market equilibrium price OE, there will be excess demand MN and some need for rationing to allocate goods.

Celler–Kefauver Antimerger Act 1950 (L4)

This US federal statute, amending the SHERMAN and CLAYTON Acts, limited the expansion of firms by merger by making it illegal for major firms to acquire their competitors' assets or stock if the effect is a substantial reduction in competition or a contribution to the creation of a monopoly.

Celtic tiger (P0)

Ireland, because of its exceptional economic and employment growth among OECD countries. GDP growth averaged over 9 per cent annually in the 1994–8 period and unemployment fell by nine percentage points. There was labour force and labour productivity growth. Merchandise trade grew to 25 per cent of GDP and the fiscal surplus to 1.75 per cent of GDP. Although European Union funds and foreign inward investment contributed to economic growth, there was no overriding policy plan which drove the economy forward.

Census of Manufactures (L6)

A regularly published statistical account of the economic activities of the firms of the manufacturing sector of a national ECONOMY. In the USA, this census was first conducted in 1809 and has been published every five years since 1967.

Census of Retail Trade (L8)

A survey of the economic activities of retailing ESTABLISHMENTS and FIRMS. In the USA, it was first published in 1929; since 1967 there has been a census every five years.

Center for International Studies (F0)

Founded in 1951 at the Massachusetts Institute of Technology.

Central Arbitration Committee (J5)

UK body established in 1975 with the concerns of SEXUAL DISCRIMINATION, COLLECTIVE BARGAINING agreements and pay structures, as well as making awards if employers refuse to disclose information for collective bargaining purposes.

central bank (E5)

The bank of any country which ultimately guarantees the LIQUIDITY of the banking system as a whole. It is usually owned by the government (in the USA, the Federal Reserve System is owned by the member banks). By setting interest rates for discounting the short-term BILLS of the banking system and by OPEN MARKET OPERATIONS, a central bank is able to exert a powerful influence over the size of the money supply. Other methods of control over the banking and financial systems include the prescribing of RESERVE ASSETS ratios, the issuing of directives and the examination of the accounts of banks and other financial institutions.

Although the oldest central bank is Sweden's Riksbank (founded in 1668), the Bank of England was the first central bank to specialize as a central bank, i.e. largely to abandon its private functions and to concentrate on issuing banknotes, acting as the government's bank in managing the national debt and controlling the money supply and the exchange value of the pound sterling. In the nineteenth century, England's example influenced France, the Netherlands, Austria, Norway, Denmark, Belgium, Spain, Germany and Japan to set up their own national banks. The USA's Federal Reserve System of twelve district banks was set up in 1913.

See also: Bank of England; Bundesbank; Federal Reserve System

References

Blinder, A.S. (1998) *Central banking in theory and practice*, Cambridge, MA, and London: MIT Press.
Goodhart, C.A.E. (1987) 'Why do banks need a central bank?', *Oxford Economic Papers* 39: 75–89.

central bank independence (E5)

The conduct of MONETARY POLICY by a CENTRAL BANK, independent of governmental control through its Treasury. This has long been true of the USA with its FEDERAL RESERVE SYSTEM, and of the UK since 1997.

See also: Monetary Policy Committee

central limit theorem (C1)

An attempt to explain why so many distributions of independent variables are close to the NORMAL DISTRIBUTION.

centrally planned economy (P2)

1 An ECONOMY whose investment and production is co-ordinated by a central governmental body.

2 A COMMAND ECONOMY. Inspired by the celebrated Soviet five-year plans of the 1930s, many countries in Eastern Europe and in the Third World used this alternative to the MARKET ECONOMY but found it impossibly inefficient, with the result that in the late 1980s it was largely abandoned. In this type of economy information is regularly collected to form the basis of a forecast of economic activity and to construct proposals for the future development of production. There is an annual issue of targets for subordinate state enterprises. Some economies of this type tried to reform their planning procedures, e.g. Hungary with its major economic reform of 1 January 1968.

See also: indicative planning; market socialism

References

Dembinski, P. (1990) *The Logic of the Planned Economy: The Seeds of the Collapse*, trans. K. Cook, Oxford: Clarendon Press.

central occupation (J2)

The main occupation which characterizes an industry and is essential to its working, e.g. doctors and nurses in medical services, farmworkers in agriculture.

central place theory (B1)

An account of the way a continuous hierarchy of economic activities determines the optimal locations of cities. It takes into account THRESHOLD POPULATION size and the IDEAL LIMIT of consumers' travel to trading enterprises. The central place is the settlement in a region complementing it, offering goods and producing services for consumers at dispersed points. This key settlement is often located at the geographical periphery because of factors such as marketing and traffic

References

Christaller, W. (1966) *The Central Places of Southern Germany*, Englewood Cliffs, NJ: Prentice Hall.

Losch, A. (1954) *The Economics of Location*, New Haven, CT: Yale University Press.

Centre for Policy Studies (E6)

An independent London-based economics research institute founded in 1975 with the aims of research and education in economic and social affairs. It is noted for applying market solutions to economic problems.

centre–periphery system (F0, P0)

A system of international economic relations consisting of active world industrial centres and a passive periphery. The periphery produces and exports raw materials to the centre; the centre receives a disproportionate share of income and is slow to transmit technical knowledge to the periphery – it does so mainly in exporting industries.

certainty equivalent (D0)

The amount of money definitely available that will give a decision-maker the same utility as that from a more risky course of action.

certificate of deposit (G2)

A marketable bank deposit receipt which has the advantage of allowing the holder to gain the higher rate of interest associated with fixed or long-term deposits. Certificates of deposit (CDs) were introduced in the USA in 1961 and grew in volume after 1973 when REGULATION Q no longer insisted that there had to be a ceiling to the rate of interest. Dollar CDs have had to be registered securities from 1983 onwards. The Eurodollar CD was introduced in London in 1966 and the sterling CD in 1968. Companies, and even banks, depositing surplus funds short term and obtaining CDs both increase their investment income and maintain their liquidity.

Certification Officer (J5)
UK official whose post was established in 1975 with the particular remit of certifying that trade unions are independent; also concerned with the political funds of trade unions.

ceteris paribus (D0)
Latin expression meaning 'other things being equal'. A term popular from the mid-nineteenth century, especially in PARTIAL EQUILIBRIUM ANALYSIS when the relationship between two variables is investigated, all other variables which might be influential being assumed to have unchanging values. This is a useful concept in MICROECONOMICS as a DEMAND CURVE shows the relationship between price and quantity demanded with income, tastes and the prices of other goods held constant.

chaebol (L0, M1)
Korean group of giant companies controlled by a family-owned holding company.

See also: zaibatsu

chain bank (G2)
A bank linked to others through common stockholding. Banks of this kind were present in Chicago as early as 1893.

chain index method (D2)
A measure proposed by Champernowne to enable a conventional production function to be built which is compatible with MARGINAL PRODUCTIVITY THEORY. All alternative production techniques are arranged in a 'chain' for some predetermined rates of profit.

References
Champernowne, D.G. (1953) 'The production function and the theory of capital:

a comment', *Review of Economic Studies* 21: 112–35.

chain migration (F2, J1)
A sequential process of migration with one phase of migration linked to subsequent phases of migration. A major example is when the first cohort of migrants induces subsequent flows of migrants consisting of their relatives and friends who have been persuaded to move because of the information sent back by the 'pioneers'.

Chamberlin, Edward Hastings, 1899–1967 (B3)
Educated at the Universities of Iowa, Michigan and Harvard where his PhD, supervised by Allyn YOUNG, formulated the theory of MONOPOLISTIC COMPETITION, his principal achievement. Although Joan ROBINSON produced a theory of IMPERFECT COMPETITION in the same period, Chamberlin was always keen to differentiate his theory from hers.

References
Chamberlin, E.H. (1933) *Theory of Monopolistic Competition*, Cambridge, MA: Harvard University Press.
Kuenne, R.E. (ed.) (1967) *Monopolistic Competition Theory: Studies in Impact: Essays in Honor of Edward H. Chamberlin*, New York: Wiley.
Robinson, R. (1971) *Edward H. Chamberlin*, New York: Columbia University Press.

Chancellor of the Exchequer (H1)
UK finance minister who is the ministerial head of the Treasury. The Chancellor is responsible for proposing changes in public expenditure and taxation, the conduct of monetary policy nationally (apart from the independent setting of interest rates) and internationally and all currency matters

See also: Monetary Policy Committee

change in demand or supply (D0)

An increase or decrease (e.g. of income) which causes a shift in the demand or SUPPLY CURVE. A shift in the DEMAND CURVE from DD to D′D′ raises prices for each quantity, e.g. from OP to OP′ at OQ. An increase in supply from SS to S′S′ leads to more being supplied at each price level, e.g. from OQ to OQ′ at OP. This is not caused by a price change, which would result in a movement along the particular curve, but by a change in the CETERIS PARIBUS conditions.

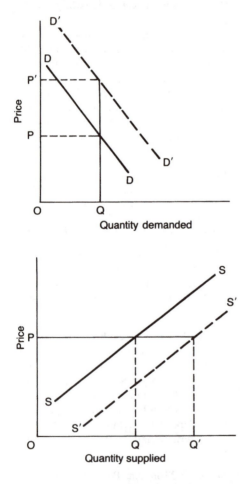

change point analysis (C5)

An attempt to determine whether and when a change has occurred. Changes are detected by cumulative sum charts and by calculating the number of BOOTSTRAPS. A 90 per cent or 95 per cent confidence is needed to establish a change.

chaos theory (D0, G1)

An analysis of random movements applied to the price data of stock and currency markets, as well as to meteorology. Chaotic behaviour appears random in that changes in prices or other economic variables show no regular periodicity and are not part of a structure detectable by statistical tests. However, more sophisticated tests offer a chance of identifying underlying non-linear mathematical structures.

See also: butterfly effect

References

Baumol, W.J. and Benhabib, J. (1989) 'Chaos: significance, mechanism and economic applications', *Journal of Economic Perspectives* 3: 77–105.
Gleick, J. (1988) *Chaos Making a New Science*, London: Heinemann.
Grauwe, P. de and Vansauten, K. (1990) 'Deterministic chaos in the foreign exchange market', Paper 370, London: Centre for Economic Policy Research.
Savit, R. (1988) 'When random is not random: an introduction to chaos in market prices', *Journal of Futures Markets* 8: 271

Chapter 17 (E5)

The authority for the BUNDESBANK to provide temporary liquidity to financial markets using the funds deposited with it.

characteristics theory of consumer demand (D1)

Consumer theory based on the assertion that consumers demand the characteristics of goods rather than the goods themselves. For example, instead of there being a demand for housing, there is a demand to live in a house with certain amenities located in a pleasant area. Kelvin Lancaster proposed this alternative to traditional utility-based consumer theory.

References

Lancaster, K. (1971) *Consumer Demand. A*

New Approach, New York: Columbia University Press.

charge (D0, G2)
1 The price of a service.
2 A right over property given to a creditor in return for a loan.

See also: bank charges; binomial charge; capacity charge; emission charge; user charge

charge card (G2)
A plastic card issued by a financial institution, such as a bank or a retailer, which allows the holder to charge the sum due for the purchase of goods or services to an account. This reduces the need to hold cash for transactions purposes and provides the holder with credit until the account is payable. Major examples of such cards include those issued by American Express and the Diners' Club.

See also: credit card; debit card

chartered company (M1)
A UK company established by a Royal Charter. Several, in particular the East India Company and the Hudson's Bay Company, were set up in Elizabethan England in the early seventeenth century.

chartism (G2, N0)
1 A technique of market analysis which predicts prices by extrapolating future price movements from a chart of previous price fluctuations. This has been applied to the study of stock and foreign exchange markets. It is argued that prices represent all influences on demand and supply, including information. Recurrent patterns, e.g. a 'head and shoulders' shape, are used to predict changes in trends.
2 A political movement in England and Scotland of the 1830s and 1840s for the reform of the franchise, named after a charter presented to parliament.

References

Edwards, R.D. and Magee, J. (1966) *Tech-nical Analysis of Stock Trends*, 5th edn, Boston: John Magee.

chart point (F3, G1)
A significant point on a graph of price movements, especially of a currency, which usually prompts intervention in that market.

cheap money (E4)
A policy of keeping interest rates low to encourage capital accumulation and economic development. In the UK, this policy was launched by the War Loan Conversion of June 1932 and continued until 1951: under it the bank rate was only 2 per cent. In the USA, this policy was used to ease the cost of servicing the national debt during the Second World War and in the immediate post-war years. Also some Latin American countries followed it. A policy of this kind has its problems. Real interest rates can become negative, generating an excess demand for credit, with the consequence that finance has to be rationed rather than allocated by interest rates.

check (G2) *see* cheque

checking account (G2)
A US commercial bank deposit available for immediate use by the writing of a check (cheque). These deposits are part of the M1 money supply: until 1980 they did not bear interest. In the UK, they are known as CURRENT ACCOUNTS.

See also: Depository Institutions Deregulation and Monetary Control Act 1980; NOW account

check-off provision (J3)
A clause in an employment contract requiring an employer to deduct TRADE UNION subscriptions from workers' pay. This arrangement lowers the cost of trade union administration and stabilizes trade union membership as many persons will remain in the union through inertia.

Chenery, Hollis Burnley, 1918– (B3)
A prominent US development economist.

A graduate in mathematics, engineering and economics from Arizona, Oklahoma, Virginia and Harvard Universities. Professor at Harvard from 1965 to 1970 and from 1983; economic adviser to the president of the WORLD BANK in 1970–2 and the bank's vice-president in charge of development policies in 1972–82. His quantitative approach to DEVELOPMENT ECONOMICS views self-sustaining economic growth as a function of industrialization, which is itself associated with a switch from agricultural to industrial products in the commodity structure of a country's exports. In 1959, he published a widely used INPUT-OUTPUT text. He collaborated with ARROW and others in 1961 to produce the CONSTANT ELASTICITY OF SUBSTITUTION PRODUCTION FUNCTION which substantially replaced the popular COBB–DOUGLAS PRODUCTION FUNCTION.

References

Arrow, K.J., Chenery, H.B., Minhas, B.S. and Solow, R.M. (1961) 'Capital-labour substitution and economic efficiency', *Review of Economics and Statistics* 43: 225–50.
Chenery, H.B. and Clark, P. (1959) *Inter-industry Economics*, New York: Wiley.

cheque (G2)
A written instruction for transferring a bank deposit from one person to another. In the nineteenth century, the cheque gradually replaced banknotes and BILLS OF EXCHANGE as a means of settling claims. Today, cheque cards have made the cheque even more acceptable. The usage of the cheque for monetary transactions varies from country to country, being especially popular for non-cash transactions in France.

See also: debit card; eftpos

cheque card (G2)
A plastic card issued by a bank to an account-holder to guarantee a cheque up to a specified amount.

See also: credit card; debit card; smart card

Chicago Board Options Exchange (G1)
The world's largest options market, trading over half of the US options contracts. It was created by the Chicago Board of Trade in 1973 and is subject to SECURITIES AND EXCHANGE COMMISSION regulations. Originally it dealt in call options; put options were introduced in 1977. The majority of options traded are based on the Standard & Poor 100 stock index.

Chicago School (B2)
A group of liberal US economists which first acquired its identity in the 1930s under the leadership of Frank KNIGHT, Jacob VINER and Henry C. SIMONS. Prominent in this group since 1950 have been Milton FRIEDMAN, George STIGLER, Ronald COASE, James BUCHANAN and Gary BECKER: they share an all-embracing belief in the power of MARKET FORCES to solve most economic problems and the desirability of minimizing the role of the state. They also believe that man is a rational agent constantly attempting to maximise his advantages. Recent crusades of the school have included its advocacy of a monetary policy based on rules, not discretion, and of unrestricted capitalism.

References

Friedman, M. and Friedman, R.D. (1962) *Capitalism and Freedom*, Chicago: University of Chicago Press.
Patinkin, D. (1981) *Essay on and in the Chicago Tradition*, Durham, NC: Duke University Press.
Reder, M.W. (1982) 'Chicago economics: permanence and change', *Journal of Economic Literature* 20: 1–38.
Simon, H.C. (1948) *Economic Policy for a Free Society*, Chicago: Chicago University Press.
Stigler, G.J. (ed.) (1988) *Chicago Studies in Political Economy*, Chicago: University of Chicago Press.

chief executive officer (M1)
The person appointed by the board of directors of a company, corporation or other organization to ensure that its decisions are implemented in its day-to-day

operations and to co-ordinate the different functions of the organization. The CEO sometimes is also a director or president or chairman/woman.

Child, Sir Francis, 1684?–1740 (B3)

In 1721 he became head of the family banking firm Francis Child & Co.; elected Member of Parliament for Middlesex in 1727 and 1734, Lord Mayor of London in 1731. He introduced promissory bank-notes in 1729, thereby abandoning the GOLDSMITH BANKING SYSTEM.

Chinese modernization drive (N1)

The successor to the CULTURAL REVOLUTION. From 1978 it attempted to achieve rapid growth of production through a ten-year plan with ambitious targets, e.g. the doubling of coal and steel output.

References

Riskin., C. (1987) *China's Political Economy*, Oxford: Oxford University Press.

'Chinese Wall' (G2)

The separation of the corporate finance department from the investment and trading departments of an INVESTMENT BANK (USA) or MERCHANT BANK (UK).

chi-squared distribution (C1)

The distribution of chi-squared statistics where chi is the sum of the squares of the deviations of observations from their sample mean divided by the square of the standard deviation of the population from which the sample is taken. There are different chi-squared distributions corresponding to different DEGREES OF FREEDOM.

choice variable (C1)

An independent variable in an OBJECTIVE FUNCTION which an economic agent attempts to maximize or minimize. Also known as a decision variable or policy variable.

choke price (Q0)

The price of a natural resource at which quantity demanded is zero.

Choquet expected utility (D0)

A valuation of the EXPECTED UTILITY of an action over a set of potentially relevant probability models. The minimum of possible expected utilities is maximized.

Christian socialism (P2)

The intellectual and practical endeavour to apply Christian social principles to an industrial and competitive society. It is particularly associated in England with Frederick Denison Maurice (1805–72) and Charles Kingsley (1819–75) who preached the merits of co-operation, promoted associations for working men and founded in 1854 a working men's college. In the twentieth century, the FABIAN SOCIETY and GUILD SOCIALISM continued the tradition; many in the UK Labour Party have attempted to marry Christian ideals to socialism. In France SAINT-SIMON (1760–1825) recommended a new Christianity which would encourage producer associations; later in the nineteenth century there were strong Roman Catholic movements to provide a theology of socialism. In the USA Washington Gladden (1836–1918) fought to make the Congregational Church accept its social responsibilities and inspired the Social Gospel movement. Richard Ely (1854–1943), a founder of the AMERICAN ECONOMIC ASSOCIATION, expressed his Christianity in his advocacy of the public control of resources and the encouragement of trade unions. The Society of Christian Socialists was founded in 1889. The earliest inspirations for Christian socialism were the New Testament, with its injunction 'Love Thy neighbour as Thyself', and the experiment of the early Church of holding all things in common. In the Middle Ages, AQUINAS and others recommended a JUST PRICE.

References

Cort, J.C. (1988) *Christian Socialism: an informal history*, Mary Knoll, NY: Orbis.

Norman, Edward (1987) *The Victorian Christian Socialists*, Cambridge: Cambridge University Press.

Churitsuroren (J5)

National Federation of Independent Unions: this Japanese national federation of trade unions was merged with Domei in 1987 to form Rengo.

churning (G1)

1 Cancelling an existing insurance policy and purchasing a new one as a replacement.
2 Frequent changes in a portfolio of securities. Commission-hungry life insurance agents and stockbrokers often propose a rapid turnover of this kind.

circuit breaker mechanism (G1)

A price limit or trading halt used in major US stock markets. If the market drives the Standard & Poor 500 index twenty points in either direction, the trading session will be terminated. This intervention in price determination prevents fluctuations from creating excessively high prices or a price collapse such as happened in the market crash of October 1987.

See also: Brady Commission

circular flow (E1)

The circulation of expenditures and in- comes throughout an economy, describing the relationship between households, firms, the government, the capital market and the rest of the world. (See the figure.)

circular migration (J1)

Temporary or repetitive population movement. This can be COMMUTING or repeated movements from one's residence to a distant place within one year.

circulating capital (D0, M2)

WORKING CAPITAL which is used to finance the current expenditure of a business, especially its wage bill and purchase of raw materials and energy, together with stocks of goods. SMITH distinguished this form of capital from fixed capital, i.e. buildings, machinery, land improvements and HUMAN CAPITAL.

Civil Rights Act 1964 (J7)

US federal statute which outlawed many forms of racial and sexual discrimination. Under Title II, racial discrimination in public accommodation was forbidden; under Title VI, racial discrimination in fed-

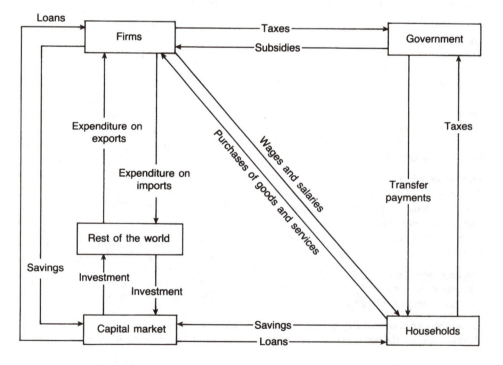

erally assisted programmes was proscribed; Title VII made sexual and racial discrimination in employment illegal.

See also: discrimination

Clark, Colin Grant, 1905–89 (B3)
UK-born pioneer of NATIONAL INCOME accounting, educated at Oxford University. He was a lecturer at Cambridge University in 1931–7 before emigrating to Queensland, Australia, where in 1938–52 he was a financial adviser and Under-Secretary of State for Labour and Industry; subsequently Director of the Institute for Research in Agricultural Economics of Oxford University from 1953 to 1969. His foundational work on national income accounting included the major advance of making one of the first calculations of the MULTIPLIER. In 1940, he broadened his interests to consider the nature of economic development; also well known for his writings on population and land use.

References
Clark, C. (1932) *The National Income, 1924–31*, London: Macmillan.
—— (1940) *Conditions of Economic Progress*, London: Macmillan.
—— (1962) *Growthmanship: a Study in the Methodology of Investment*, 2nd edn, London: Institute of Economic Affairs.
—— (1977) *Population, Growth and Land Use*, rev. edn, London: Macmillan.

Clark, John Bates, 1847–1938 (B3)
US economist famous for the theory of MARGINAL PRODUCTIVITY. He was educated at Brown University, Amherst College and the University of Heidelberg. For most of his academic career, from 1895 to 1923, he was a professor at Columbia University. His major achievement, in *Distribution of Wealth* (1899), was to expand MARGINALISM into the concept of marginal productivity in order to tackle problems of production and distribution. In *Philosophy of Wealth* (1885) he used CLASSICAL ECONOMICS as the foundation of his own economic theory; in *Capital and its Earnings* (1888) he became

one of the founders of modern capital theory.

References
Clark, A.H. and Clark, J.M. (1938) *John Bates Clark: A Memorial*, New York: Columbia University Press.

classical classical fallacy (J3)
The view that CIRCULATING CAPITAL by creating a wage fund improves wages and increases the demand for labour but FIXED CAPITAL does not. SAMUELSON asserted that this view makes the mistake of identifying the wage fund with the whole of circulating capital and ignores the contribution of fixed capital to the growth of REAL WAGES.

References
Samuelson, P.A. (1994) 'The Classical Classical Fallacy', *Journal of Economic Literature*, 32: 620–39.

classical dichotomy (B1, E4)
The view attributed to classical economists that real variables are determined by other real variables alone and monetary variables by only other monetary variables. Output and employment thus are determined by the real wage but the money supply can change the general price level without affecting relative prices. PATINKIN used this term to describe this theoretical stance. KEYNES was much concerned when advancing from his *Treatise on Money* to his *General Theory* to demolish this dualism. But with the advent of the New Classical School there has been revival of this view.

classical econometrics (C1)
ECONOMETRICS that seeks to formulate economic models to test hypotheses about appropriate data.

See also: Bayesian econometrics

classical economics (B1)
The dominant school of UK economics from 1752 to 1870. David HUME in his attack on MERCANTILISM anticipated a new approach to economics but it was Adam SMITH in *The Wealth of Nations* (1776) who

is credited as being the virtual founder: all subsequent writers of the school used Smith as a starting point. The school was grand in its aims, providing theories of value, growth, distribution, international trade, public finance and money. All the major figures – SMITH, RICARDO, MALTHUS and John Stuart MILL – wrote comprehensive texts, in most cases entitled 'Principles'. Their economic liberalism was manifest in their limited view of the role of the state and in their attack on the CORN LAWS, which were incompatible with free trade, economic growth and international specialization. Ricardo inspired MARX; more recently Smith has been regarded as an apostle of the NEW RIGHT.

References

Coats, A.W. (ed.) (1971) *The Classical Economists and Economic Policy*, London: Methuen.

Hollander, S. (1987) *Classical Economics*, Oxford: Basil Blackwell.

O'Brien, D.P. (1975) *The Classical Economists*, Oxford: Clarendon Press.

classical model (E1)

A formal macroeconomic model of the economy which assumes that factor and product prices are completely flexible so that there are no rigidities to prevent market clearing. This economy will have FULL EMPLOYMENT of its resources when it is in equilibrium. KEYNES associated this view of the economy particularly with the French economist Jean Baptiste SAY, although it is possible to find other classical economists, including James MILL, who use similar assumptions.

classical savings theory (D3) *see* class savings theory

class savings theory (D3)

The supposition that in a two-class society consisting of capitalists and workers only capitalists save and workers consume all of their incomes. This is an integral part of Cambridge growth theories.

References

Kaldor, N. (1956) 'Alternative theories of distribution', *Review of Economic Studies* 23: 83–100.

Clayton Act 1914 (L4)

The important amendment to the US SHERMAN ACT 1890 which extended federal ANTITRUST law. It forbad PRICE DISCRIMINATION, tying arrangements and exclusive dealing, and the acquisition of another corporation's stock if it was likely to reduce competition or lead to the creation of a monopoly; it also allowed triple damages to those suffering breaches of the antitrust law. It exempted labour unions and agricultural associations from antitrust actions.

See also: Celler–Kefauver Antimerger Act; Robinson–Patman Act

Clean Air Act Amendments 1970 (Q2)

US federal statute which required the ENVIRONMENTAL PROTECTION AGENCY (EPA) to set air quality standards for specified pollutants and to issue control technology guidelines for stationary emission sources. The EPA, which attempts to control all sources of pollution, sought a 90 per cent reduction in hydrocarbon and carbon monoxide emissions by 1975.

clean float (F3)

An EXCHANGE RATE regime in which market forces freely determine the value of currencies as there is no intervention by governments and central banks.

See also: dirty float; fixed exchange rate; floating exchange rate

clean opinion (M4)

An auditor's unqualified acceptance of a set of financial statements. If there is no opinion expressed the auditor issues a disclaimer of opinion.

clear income (H2)

Taxable income in excess of the amount of personal and other allowances permitted by a government's revenue service.

clearing (D0, G2)
1 The matching of demand and supply in a particular market.
2 The exchange between banks of the cheques drawn upon them.

clearing bank (G2)
A UK COMMERCIAL BANK which accepts deposits from the public and gets its name from being a member of the clearing house which 'clears' cheques by settling inter-bank indebtedness. There are separate sets of clearing banks for England and Wales, Scotland and Northern Ireland. The Scottish and Northern Irish banks also have the right to issue banknotes. A bank of this kind is distinguished from other financial intermediaries in that its reserves are the monetary liabilities of the government sector, i. e. bills, bonds and deposits with the central bank.

clearing house (G2)
The financial institution which settles the mutual indebtedness of commercial banks by clearing cheques. A bank with a net debt after the clearing to another bank will settle by drawing a cheque on its deposits with the central bank

Clearing House Interbank Payments System (G2)
New York automated clearing facility for transferring dollars between major US banks, branches of foreign banks and some subsidiaries of out-of-state banks. CHIPS, for short.

clearing market (D0)
A free market with flexible prices which quickly establishes an equilibrium between demand and supply, eliminating any excess demand or supply. Financial markets provide excellent examples.

See also: disequilibrium economics; equilibrium

climacteric (N0)
A critical period in the history of a country of a national economy, e.g. the UK in the late nineteenth century.

climate levy (Q4)
A UK indirect tax levied as a percentage of the energy bills of firms with the hope of reducing their contribution to global warming.

cliometrics (N0)
The quantitative study of history originally carried out in the USA in studies of the profitability of slavery and the role of railroads. This elaborate econometric analysis has been applied to the study of economic growth.

See also: Fogel; North

References
McCloskey, D.N. (1978) 'The achievement of the cliometric school', *Journal of Economic History* 38: 13–28.

clipping (E5)
Debasing a coinage made of precious metals by cutting off part of the edge of coins. This problem for monetary authorities was solved first by milling the edges and later by the introduction of TOKEN MONEY AND BANKNOTES which had no intrinsic value to be removed.

See also: Gresham's law

closed economy (F1, P0)
An ECONOMY which does not engage in international trade. There are no economies of this type in the world today but countries such as Japan were closed to foreigners for centuries. The concept is important theoretically to construct simple macroeconomic models uncomplicated by international trade.

See also: autarky; open economy

closed-end credit (G2)
A form of CREDIT granted on condition that the PRINCIPAL and charges for the loan are repaid over a specified time period.

closed-end fund (G1)
A MUTUAL FUND bought at a discount. Sales and purchases can only be made between investors thus maintaining a stable pool of investment money. The price is determined

by demand and supply, not being decided by the fund managers who would base the price on net assessment value. These funds can be illiquid if few potential buyers exist and their prices can be more volatile than mutual funds.

closed pension fund (G2)

An accumulation of assets which can be used only for the payment of retirement incomes according to the set rules of a pension fund.

closed population (J1)

A population with no emigration or immigration. The size of this population will depend entirely on birth and death rates.

closed shop (J5)

An arrangement between a TRADE (LABOR) UNION and a management to restrict employment in a particular place of work or occupation to members of that union. A pre-entry closed shop is based on the rule that only trade union members can apply for work; in a post-entry closed shop a worker must become a member before or on joining the firm. The Trade Union and Labour Relations Act 1974 (UK) passed during the period of office of a Labour government made possible universal enforcement of the closed shop. The subsequent aim of Conservative governments was to remove the pre-entry closed shop (Industrial Relations Act 1971 and Employment Act 1980); the European Court in 1981 ordered the UK government to end the rail closed shop. The strongest argument in its favour is the equitable view that, as all employees benefit from a union's bargaining, all should pay union dues. Some employers have argued that a closed shop promotes harmonious industrial relations. In the USA, the post-entry closed shop is called a 'UNION SHOP'. Even in countries such as France where the closed shop is illegal, shops of this kind still exist in the docks and in printing.

closely held corporation (L2)

A private corporation owned by only a few private stockholders, often members of the same family. Many US states have specific legislation for this type of firm.

club good (H4)

A good available to a group of individuals and hence is a mixture of PRIVATE and PUBLIC GOODS. Non-members can be excluded but a member's consumption is not diminished by another member's. Examples of club goods include many forms of entertainment, e.g. the cinema and sporting facilities.

Club of Rome (O4)

A group of leading economists and scientists which studied the effects of economic growth from 1968 onwards. Their study of poverty, environmental issues, urbanization, unemployment, inflation and the nature of growth led them to set out the conditions for a global equilibrium in their famous *Limits to Growth* report.

References

Meadows, D.H., Meadow, D.L., Randers, J. and Behrens, W.W. III (1972) *The Limits to Growth: a Report for the Club of Rome's Project on the Predicament of Mankind*, London: Earth Island.

cluster analysis (C8)

A method of organizing data into meaningful structures. Biologists and statisticians have used different methods to achieve this goal. There is tree clustering to organise data into successively larger clusters, two-joining when clusters in two variables are simultaneously examined, and k-means clustering to see how distinctive each cluster is.

References

Tryon, R.C. (1970) *Cluster Analysis*. New York: McGraw-Hill.

Coase, Ronald Harry 1910– (B3)

Born in Willesden, England, and a graduate in commerce from the London School of Economics. After holding academic posts in Dundee, Liverpool and the London School of Economics he emigrated to the USA in 1951 to hold chairs in Buffalo and Virginia before settling in Chicago in

1964–79. His principal contributions to economic theory have been his analysis of the nature of the FIRM, which he asserted seeks to reduce the costs of participating in a market by internalizing activities, and of SOCIAL COST, building on PIGOU to analyse the problem of pollution to take into account PROPERTY RIGHTS so that the aim of environmental regulation is to maximize the value of production. His many applied studies include an examination of broadcasting, monopoly pricing and anti-trust enforcement. He was awarded the NOBEL PRIZE FOR ECONOMICS in 1991.

References

Coase, R.H. (1988) *The Firm, the Market and the Law*, Chicago and London: University of Chicago Press.

—— (1994) *Essays on Economics and Economists*, Chicago and London: University of Chicago Press.

Coase theorem (D6, Q2)

The proposition that the value and composition of the national income is unaffected by the precise pattern of liability for pollution which the perpetrators and victims have determined. Thus EXTERNALITIES do not lead to a misallocation of resources provided that there are no TRANSACTION COSTS, and PROPERTY RIGHTS are clearly defined. Private and social costs will be equal under PERFECT COMPETITION.

References

Coase, R.H. (1960) 'The problem of social cost', *Journal of Law and Economics* 3: 1–44.

Cobb–Douglas production function (C5, D2)

An equation showing physical output as the product of labour and capital inputs. This function predicted rewards to labour and capital that were close to the observed shares of manufacturing income in national income. The Cobb–Douglas approach was dominant in the analysis of economic growth from 1945 to 1961.

cobweb (C5, D2)

A dynamic model of the relationship

between demand and supply in a particular market. Central to the model is the assumption that there is a time lag between planning and completing production. A familiar application, not surprisingly, is agricultural production (particularly hog/pig production) which often has a twelve-month production period. It is assumed that (1) supply depends solely on the expected price for the product, (2) actual market price adjusts to demand so as to eliminate EXCESS DEMAND instantaneously, (3) expected price is equal to the previous equilibrium price, with the length of delay determined by the production lag, (4) there are no INVENTORIES and (5) neither buyers nor sellers have an incentive to speculate. Whether or not there is movement to equilibrium in the model depends on the relative ELASTICITIES of the demand and supply curves. If the elasticity of demand exceeds that of supply, there will be a movement to the original equilibrium price and output; if elasticity of supply is greater then there will be continuing DISEQUILIBRIUM until the elasticities change (see the figures).

References

Nerlove, M. (1958) 'Adaptive expectations and cobweb phenomena', *Quarterly Journal of Economics* 72: 227–40.

coconut model (E1)

A model of a tropical island in which there is a taboo against eating the coconuts one has picked so there has to be a trade of nuts for nuts before consumption can occur. The ability to trade depends on the number of potential trading partners. There is no mechanism to ensure forecasts of the time to complete a trade. This model reflects the modern reality of producers consuming little of what they produce.

See also: Robinson Crusoe economy

References

Diamond, P.A. (1982) 'Aggregate demand in search equilibrium', *Journal of Political Economy* 90: 881–94.

coefficient of correlation (C1)

Referred to as *r* by statisticians and used as a measure of the interrelatedness of two variables. This coefficient is measured by the formula

$$\frac{\sum (x\,y)}{\sqrt{(\sum x^2 \sum y^2)}}$$

A perfect negative relationship has the value −1; a perfect positive relationship +1. Values in between these extremes will depend on how strong the relationship between *x* and *y* is.

coefficient of determination (C1)

A ratio of the explained variation to the total variation of values from a regression line, usually referred to as *r'*. It is measured by the formula

$$\frac{\sum \{[Y(\text{estimated}) - Y(\text{mean})]^2\}}{\sum \{[Y(\text{actual}) - Y(\text{mean})]^2\}}$$

This ratio can range from 0 to 1, being 0 if all the variation is unexplained and 1 if all the variation is explained.

See also: linear correlation

coefficient of multiple correlation (C1)

A statistic which measures the extent to which changes in a dependent variable are explained by the joint variation in the independent variables chosen to explain it. It is the square root of the COEFFICIENT OF MULTIPLE DETERMINATION.

coefficient of multiple determination (C1)

For two independent variables this coefficient, $R_{1.23}$ is equal to $1 - s_{1.23}^2 / s_1^2$, where $s_{1.23}$ is the standard error of an estimate of variable X, on independent variables X_2, and X_3, and s is the standard deviation of X_1.

coefficient of variation (C1)

The ratio of a STANDARD DEVIATION to an ARITHMETIC MEAN of a set of values, usually expressed as a percentage. This is a better measure of the dispersion of a set of values than the standard deviation as it can be used for different measures with different magnitudes and can cope with two measures expressed in different units, e.g. monetary and physical.

cognitive consonance (D0)

The state of a cognitive system when ideas and beliefs are in harmony.

cognitive dissonance (D0)

The coexistence of discordant cognitions. As a consequence of this dissonance, people will avoid situations and information likely to increase such discomfort. This theory of Festinger's, about an unpleasant state of tension, has been applied by economists to the explanation of work behaviour, home ownership and discrimination.

See also: economics and psychology

References

Akerlof, G. and Dickens, W.T. (1982) 'The economic consequences of cognitive dissonance', *American Economic Review* 72: 307–19.

Festinger, L. (1957) *A Theory of Cognitive Dissonance*, Evanston, IL: Row, Peterson.

Cohesion Fund (O0)

EUROPEAN UNION fund created in 1993 by the MAASTRICHT TREATY to provide money for environmental and trans-European network projects in member states whose gross domestic product is less than 90 per cent of the EU average. The fund can contribute up to 85 per cent of the public expenditure on a project.

coinage (E4)

Pieces of metal of a standard size and weight stamped by a sovereign power to give them the status of money. Coins were first used as money by the Lydians (Greek inhabitants of what is now West Turkey) in the seventh century BC. The first coins were made of electrum, a natural alloy of gold and silver. Silver, bronze and copper were later used in Ancient Greece and the Roman Empire. Copper coins, used for small transactions, were issued with a monetary value in excess of the value of metal used, establishing the principle of token money, which is the nature of coinage today. The first problems of coinage, clipping and forgery, were solved by a change in production method from hammering to milling to ensure a standard size. The second problem, the inconvenience of transporting it to carry out large financial transactions, was remedied by the use of banknotes.

coincident indicators (E3)

Measures of economic activity used by economic forecasters to track cyclical movements in the ECONOMY. The main ones used are employment in non-agricultural enterprises, personal income less transfer payments. and indices of total industrial production and manufacturing and trade sales.

See also: economic indicators

Colbertism (H2, L5, N4, N6)

Government intervention in industry, named after the French MERCANTILIST Jean Baptiste Colbert (1619–83) who successfully reformed the French economy after 1649. In France, the home of Colbertism, the government's ability to subsidize industry and follow protectionist policies has been limited since entry to the European Economic Community in 1958.

See also: dirigisme

collaborative production (L2)

A form of workplace organization which decentralizes production. This reaction to TAYLORISM can take many forms, including TEAM WORK and QUALITY CIRCLES.

collar (E4, G2)

A combination of a CAP and a FLOOR to give an interest rate a fixed range.

collateralized mortgage obligation (G1)

A bond based on a portfolio of mortgages with interest and capital repayments paid by the original mortgagors.

collecting bank (G2)

Any bank, other than the payer bank, handling a bank item, e.g. a cheque, for collection.

collective bargaining (J5)

Negotiations between a TRADE (LABOR) UNION and a single employer or EMPLOYERS' ASSOCIATION over pay, working conditions and other employment matters. It can only be genuine if the parties are free to initiate discussions and reach a settlement: under INCOMES POLICIES, and in countries where trade unions have little independence from the state, this is not possible. It is usually bilateral, but sometimes other interested parties are at the bargaining table, e.g. in some US teachers' negotiations where parents are represented. It can take place at different levels – national, industrial, the firm or workplace. The level at which the major decisions are made distinguishes one country's system sharply from another. In Japan, the enterprise level is very important; in Germany, the industrial level. In the USA, the parties produce a legally enforceable contract; in the UK, a framework for individual employment contracts.

Collective bargaining makes possible the collective provision of workplace 'public goods', e.g. safety, conditions, lighting, heating, speed of the production line, grievance procedures, pension plans. It permits the individual to express his or her own preferences without the danger of being sacked. Also it helps to change the social relations of the workplace, bridging the gap between labour and capital, by making possible the enforcement of labour contracts.

See also: exit-voice

References

Bean, R. (1985) *Comparative Industrial Relations: an Introduction to Cross-national Perspectives*, London: Croom Helm.

Clegg, H.A. (1976) *Trade Unionism under Collective Bargaining. A Theory Based on Comparisons of Six Countries*, Oxford: Basil Blackwell.

Coddington, A. (1968) *Theories of the Bargaining Process*, London: Allen & Unwin.

Kochan, T.A. (1980) *Collective Bargaining and Industrial Relations*, Homewood, IL: Irwin.

—— (1986) *The Transformation of American Industrial Relations*, New York: Basic Books.

Sisson, K. (1987) *The Management of Collective Bargaining. An International Comparison*, Oxford: Basil Blackwell.

collective good (H4)

A PUBLIC GOOD allocated by political decisions, not by the market.

collectivization of agriculture (N5)

The reorganization of a country's agriculture into state farms thereby depriving peasants of landownership and management. Collectivization in the USSR was introduced in 1929 but was not implemented in a major and systematic way until the 1930s: it was accompanied by much resistance and a famine which killed millions. Subsequently, other countries following the principles of Marxist-Leninism have attempted draconian changes of this kind, e.g. Mao's China and Ethiopia.

collectivized investment (G1)

A MUTUAL FUND or UNIT TRUST.

Collor Plan (E6)

A plan to stabilize the Brazilian economy. Collor I was launched in 1990, Collor II in 1991. The plans included wage and price freezes to combat inflation rising at 1,800 per cent; they were named after Fernando Collor, President of Brazil.

collusion (L2)

Joint action, usually by OLIGOPOLISTS, to control prices and market shares. It is illegal in most capitalist countries, e.g. in the USA under ANTITRUST legislation. As Adam SMITH, the apostle of competition, observed in his *Wealth of Nations* (Book 1, ch. X, Part II), 'People of the same trade seldom meet together, even for merriment and diversion, but the conversation ends in a conspiracy against the public, or in some contrivance to raise prices.'

Combination Acts (J5)

UK legislation of 1799 and 1800 which, like the Common Law, outlawed TRADE UNION membership and activities amounting to conspiracy. The repeal of these Acts in 1824 made possible the organization of labour in England.

com-dev company (L3)

Commercial development company whose activities often include commercial real estate and commercial software.

COMET (E1)

An econometric model of European economies whose name is an abbreviation of 'COmmon market MEdium Term model'. It was created in 1970 and based on eight national models for West Germany, France, Italy, the Netherlands, Belgium, the UK, Ireland and Denmark. It is dynamic, giving predictions over time paths of five to ten years. It models the real sector of these economies: monetary and financial elements, represented by interest rates, are exogenous. The interdependence of the economies are chiefly described by trade flows. One of the applications of the model has been to develop the methodology of EUROPEAN UNION economic policy.

See also: linkage model

References

Barten, A.P., d'Alcantara, G. and Carrin, G.J. (1976) 'COMET: a medium-term macroeconomic model for the European Economic Community', *European Economic Review* 7: 63–115.

command and control regulation (Q2)
Administrative and statutory rules concerning pollution control. Sources of pollution are narrowly defined, specific control devices prescribed and emissions standards applied. Critics of this approach to POLLUTION CONTROL assert that it ignores both the extent of pollution damage and the costs of regulation.

command economy (P3)
An ECONOMY in which the orders of a central planning authority to lower level economic organizations have the force of law. Lower level organizations are instructed to follow particular practices and to use stated prices, inputs and output targets. The first modern economy of this type was devised by Lenin who was inspired by the German military organization of the First World War. Until the mid-1980s, the planning mechanism of the Soviet-type economy had command characteristics.

See also: perestroika

commanding heights (I2, L0)
1 The basic industries of an economy, especially energy, transport and telecommunications. It is argued that as a high proportion of their output consists

of INTERMEDIATE GOODS, these industries if controlled would contribute substantially to the control of the ECONOMY as a whole.
2 Education and training which are basic to the performance and growth of industry.

See also: nationalized industry

commercial bank (G2)
A bank providing a wide range of banking services, including receiving deposits from the public and the making of loans. As a consequence of more competition in the financial sector, these banks have diversified into insurance, mortgage finance and a wide range of business finance, previously the concern of investment/merchant banks alone.

See also: clearing bank; retail bank; wholesale bank

References

Ballarin, E. (1987) *Commercial Banks amid the Financial Revolution: Developing a Competitive Strategy*, London: Harper & Row; Cambridge, MA: Ballinger.

commercial bill (G1)
A short-term BILL OF EXCHANGE by which the person who draws it promises to pay the drawee the sum specified on a particular future date, one, two, three or six months hence. This method of finance was extensively used in the UK in the early nineteenth century before banks were prepared to make short-term advances in the form of overdrafts to their customers. It is still a popular form of short-term finance. When a bill of this kind is accepted by an ACCEPTING HOUSE, becoming a bank bill, it is possible for the drawee to obtain immediate payment at a discount (fixed according to the ruling short-term money market interest rate).

See also: treasury bill

commercial paper (G1, M2)
A form of short-term company borrowing,

usually for thirty days. These unsecured IOUs permit companies to borrow directly from investors, bypassing banks and bond markets. Banks, however, are used as agents to place the paper; sometimes investment banks underwrite the IOUs investing themselves. This type of financing, long used in the USA, was introduced into the UK in 1986; also used in many other countries, including France, Australia, Hong Kong and Singapore.

See also: IOU money

commercial policy (F1)

The international trading policy of a national government with respect to import duties/quotas and export subsidies. These policies have been a central issue in economics since the MERCANTILISTS first debated the merits of TARIFFS.

See also: General Agreement on Tariffs and Trade

Committee of Twenty (F3)

A committee of twenty leading members of the INTERNATIONAL MONETARY FUND, officially known as the 'Committee on the Reform of the International Monetary System', with the task of considering the possibility of reviving a BRETTON WOODS type of PEGGED EXCHANGE RATE regime and the supply of international reserve assets. The floating of several exchange rates prevented it from reaching its central objective. It finally reported in June 1974.

commodification (E4)

The transformation of money into a COMMODITY. This has occurred because COMMERCIAL BANKS now resemble industrial conglomerates with a range of financial products. MARX had previously stated that the nature of exchange under CAPITALISM is to change money into a unique commodity exchangeable with all commodities.

commodity (D0)

1 Something, usually physical, which can be bought and sold and is directly measurable. The concept is used extensively in both MARXIAN ECONOMICS and

GENERAL EQUILIBRIUM analysis since HICKS. MARX argued that through the exchange process goods lose their use value, becoming 'citizens of the world' and merely the vehicle for merchants to earn SURPLUS VALUE. SRAFFA regarded a commodity as a good or service produced by a unique combination of factor inputs.

2 A raw material or primary product.

commodity agreement (F1)

An international agreement between producing and consuming countries to stabilize prices and organize quotas for major metals and foodstuffs.

The UNITED NATIONS CONFERENCE ON TRADE AND DEVELOPMENT recommended eighteen agreements in 1977 but only achieved them for sugar, cocoa, tin, rubber and coffee.

Commodity Credit Corporation (Q1)

US federal body set up by the AGRICULTURAL ADJUSTMENT ACT 1933 to provide a price support system for US farmers. It lends to farmers who pledge their crops as collateral. Farmers can deliver their crops to the CCC in lieu of repaying the loan and any accumulated interest. These crops can be resold by the CCC if their market price is greater than the 'loan rate', i.e. the price on which the loan was based.

Commodity Exchange of New York (G1)

The major US metals exchange in 1870. Most of its trading is in FUTURES.

commodity fetishism (D2)

Marxian term for a fantastic attitude towards production, i.e. regarding a social relationship between men as a relation between things divorced from their use value.

See also: commodity

Commodity Futures Trading Commission (G2, H1)

US federal commission set up in 1974 and operational since 1975 to regulate the eleven US futures exchanges, its members and brokerage houses. It covers a wide range of futures trading, including trading in agricultural commodities, currencies, metals and securities. It aims to ensure fair trading and financial integrity, e.g. by requiring customer funds to be kept in separate bank accounts.

commodity reserve currency (F3)
A currency with a value based on a 'basket' of commodities representative of average consumption. This currency tends to be stable over time, as happened under the GOLD STANDARD, and can take a variety of forms reflecting the technical characteristics of commodities at a particular time and the desired level of stability. However, it has been argued that few commodities are suitable for inclusion in the 'basket', e.g. on account of storage difficulties, but using commodity futures could eliminate many of these problems.

References

Friedman, M. (1953) *Essays in Positive Economics*, pp. 204–50, Chicago: University of Chicago Press.

commodity stabilization schemes (F1)
International agreements designed to introduce order into international primary commodity markets, usually with the aim of helping less developed countries. A typical scheme would draw up a price stabilization plan to prevent the agricultural incomes of these countries falling below their present levels.

See also: buffer stock; commodity agreement; price stabilization; primary commodity prices

commodity tax (H2)
A tax on a good, usually taking the form of a SALES TAX or an EXCISE DUTY.

commodity terms of trade (F1) *see* net barter terms of trade

commodity trade structure (F1)
The composition of a country's imports and exports classified by major product groups. The structure is some indication of the stage of economic development of the country, e.g. Third World countries tend to have a preponderance of PRIMARY PRODUCTS amongst their exports. The commodity structure is examined to test hypotheses about international trade, e.g. the HECKSCHER–OHLIN TRADE THEOREM.

common access resources (Q0)
Jointly owned natural resources, e.g. a piece of agricultural land open to all adjoining a town. The major departure from the principle of common access occurred in Great Britain from the thirteenth century onwards when common land was enclosed into private holdings.

Common Agricultural Policy (Q1)
The major economic policy of the EUROPEAN COMMUNITY costing over 40 per cent of the community's budget. The principles of the policy were formulated at the Stresa Conference of 1958 and embodied in Articles 38 to 47 of the TREATY OF ROME. It has been more protectionist than several of the national agricultural policies that it replaced. The policy, started in the first Mansholt Plan of 1960, intended to control the 'agriculture' of the member countries in the widest sense of farming and all related industries, including fertilizer producers, machinery and food processing. Implementation of the policy was slow, e.g. the target price for cereals, the central agricultural commodity of the European Community, was not agreed until December 1964. The European Agricultural Guidance and Guarantee Fund was set up to finance refunds on exports to third countries, intervention measures to stabilize markets and common measures, including structural modifications.

The policy has used a 'single price system' of target prices throughout the European Community for fixing intervention prices and frontier crossing point c.i.f. prices. These prices are expressed in council regulations. Price support has been intended both to support farmers' incomes and to make the European Community self-sufficient in agricultural produce. But it has been very costly as overproduction has led to at least 60 per cent of the agricultural budget being spent on disposing of surpluses. Temporary bans on production and the giving of surpluses to charities are used from time to time. Mansholt in *Agriculture 1980* (published 1968) set out a ten-year plan for restructuring European agriculture, including the retiring of farmers and the concentration of agricultural production into larger and more efficient units. The plan achieved little as it met with national resistance, especially for threatening the existence of small family farms. This policy has reduced European Community imports from the rest of the world and insulated community domestic prices for agricultural produce from world price fluctuations, destabilizing the prices and incomes of the farmers of other countries. Within the European Community, the policy has redistributed income from consumers and taxpayers to producers and discriminated against industry. In countries such as the UK, higher food costs have met with much criticism; in developing countries, many farmers have gone out of business through being excluded by so large a market as the European Community. The URUGUAY ROUND of the GENERAL AGREEMENT ON TARIFFS AND TRADE negotiations attempted to reduce the protectionism of the CAP.

common cost (D0)
The cost of an input simultaneously used in the production of several goods and services of a firm.

See also: joint cost

common currency (F3)
A currency available for transactions by several countries which still retain their own currencies; not a SINGLE CURRENCY. It was suggested that the ECU could take on this role.

See also: hard ecu

common external tariff (F1)
The tariff protecting a free-trade area, e.g.

the EUROPEAN COMMUNITY. Some countries outside the area may be permitted to have privileged access, e.g. those Third World countries allowed by the LOMÉ CONVENTION to export to European Community countries preferentially.

See also: customs union

common market (F0)
A CUSTOMS UNION within which there is free movement of labour and capital, no tariffs between its member countries and a COMMON EXTERNAL TARIFF to exclude other countries' produce. A common market in many respects behaves like a national ECONOMY as all firms of the same industry are in competition across national boundaries and can draw upon the same pool of labour and financial capital. The absence of tariffs within this market enables production to be allocated according to the principle of COMPARATIVE ADVANTAGE. The EUROPEAN UNION is a major modern example.

See also: single market

common ownership (P0)
1 Property rights conferred upon a group, e.g. the use of land by residents of a village.
2 Ownership by the state or one of its agencies, e.g. a NATIONALIZED INDUSTRY.

common pool resources (Q0)
Natural or human-made resources which provide social and economic benefits for a community or communities. These include forests, wetlands and water accumulations. It is difficult to exclude individual users from these common resources but it is easy for an individual to exploit the resource to the detriment of the community. Use has to be co-ordinated to prevent over- exploitation.

See also: public good

common property resources (Q0)
Land or other natural resources which are not owned by an individual because no property rights have been defined or a

corporate body has made them freely available to all.

common resource problem (Q0)

The difficulty of assigning to a particular user the cost of using a resource available to several users.

Commons, John Rogers, 1862–1945 (B3)

US economist who was born in Hollandsburg, Ohio, and a founder of INSTITUTIONAL economics. Although educated as a graduate student at Johns Hopkins University, he was never able to finish a college or university degree course. He held academic posts at Wesleyan University and Syracuse University. Much of his life was spent in empirical work in Wisconsin, constructing an index of wholesale prices, investigating labour unions and investigating the economic concepts present in legal reasoning. He took as the foundation of economics volitional theories of value and cost, rather than those based on UTILITY or a COMMODITY. He used US Supreme Court cases to establish the working rules which guide and restrain individuals in transactions, the key units of economics. 'Value' and 'economy' were treated as the transactions of millions of people engaged in valuing and economizing. His legal researches also led him to analyse the nature of bargaining power.

See also: Ayres; Galbraith; Veblen

References

Commons, J.R. (1893) *The Distribution of Wealth*, New York: Macmillan.
—— (1905) *Trade Unions and Labor Problems*, Boston: Ginn.
—— (1924) *The Legal Foundations of Capitalism*, New York: Macmillan.
—— (1934) *Institutional Economics: Its Place in Political Economy*, New York: Macmillan.
—— (1934) *Myself*, New York: Macmillan.
Harter, L.G. (1962) *John R. Commons: His Assault on Laissez-Faire*, Corvallis, OR: Oregon State University Press.
Rutherford, M.H. (1983) 'J.R. Commons' institutional economics', *Journal of Economic Issues* 17: 721–44.

common stock (G1)

The EQUITY capital of a US corporation. The owner of common stock is entitled to vote in general meetings, to receive declared dividends and to obtain a share in the net assets of the corporation on its dissolution. This stock does not usually have a PAR VALUE.

Commonwealth Grants Commission (H7)

An independent Australian statutory body founded in 1933 with the original aim of dealing with states in need of special assistance. Now it makes special grants to the states to enable services to conform to minimum standards. Most of these grants are unconditional, i.e. not EARMARKED.

See also: federal finance; unconditional grant

communal economy (P0)

An ECONOMY consisting of communes as basic units of production. Usually, income is equally distributed among commune members and there is no outside ownership of capital. As communes tend to be self-sufficient, production is primarily for members' consumption. Modern technology is often deplored and strict rules govern the conduct of the commune members. Many examples of these idealistic communities exist, including Robert OWEN's experiment at New Lanark, Scotland, in the nineteenth century, the Israeli kibbutz and, in the USA, the Shakers and the Hutterites.

See also: autarky

Communauté Economique de L'Afrique de l'Ouest (F0)

A CUSTOMS UNION with joint sectoral policies created in 1974 and consisting of the Ivory Coast, Mali, Mauritania, Niger, Senegal and Upper Volta as members.

commune (P0)

An association of persons jointly owning a

productive enterprise and managing it themselves. The most famous examples are the Paris Commune of 1871, the Israeli kibbutz and Robert OWEN's communities in the early nineteenth century in England and the USA.

See also: common ownership

communism (P2)

A society with common ownership of capital and income distribution according to need. Under Marxist-Leninism it is strictly defined as the final stage of socialism when the state has withered away, everyone is equal as members of a universal proletariat, and there is no DIVISION OF LABOUR. MARX's vision was exceedingly vague because his concern was to analyse contemporary capitalism rather than future socialism. The nearest to communism has been in small idealistic communities; larger societies are unlikely to consent to such levelling. The term was often applied loosely to the centrally planned state capitalist countries of the COMECON and China.

See also: command economy; socialism

References

Daniels, R.V. (ed.) (1965) *Marxism and Communism: Essential Readings*, Syracuse, NY: Singer.

communitarianism (P4)

An economic philosophy sometimes called the THIRD WAY that is opposed to the doctrine of INDIVIDUALISM and the praise of ECONOMIC MAN. A collectivist successor to socialism that opposes libertarianism.

community (P0)

A collectivity: a household, a neighbourhood, village, city, state, transnational interest group, in ascending order of size.

See also: communitarianism

community charge (H2, H7)

A form of UK local taxation often called the 'poll tax' and levied on most adults over 18 years old. It was introduced in Scotland in 1989 and in England and Wales gradually from 1990. It replaced the existing RATES system and was combined with a UNIFORM BUSINESS RATE. A principal aim of this charge was to encourage the adult population to bring pressure upon their local governments to moderate their expenditure: by increasing the number paying local taxation it was hoped there would be more opposition to local government overspending. Critics opposed its high collection cost and regressive nature (only giving rebates to the very poor). Also it was argued that a community charge should only be used to finance PUBLIC GOODS. In 1991, it was decided to replace it with a modified property tax, the COUNCIL TAX.

References

HMSO (1986) *Paying for Local Government*, Cmnd 9714.

Mason, D. (1985) *Revising the Rating System*, London: Adam Smith Institute.

community programme (J2)

UK employment measure to help the long-term unemployed by providing them with jobs of benefit to the community, e.g. rehabilitating wasteland. These are offered on a temporary basis and are often disliked for being low paid.

See also: workfare

commuting (R4)

Daily journeys of workers between their homes and places of work. When a transport network makes places distant from a centre of production more accessible, house building occurs in outlying areas, causing land and property prices to rise. Other effects of commuting include increased traffic congestion and the difficulty of financing city services used by, but not paid for, commuting workers.

See also: circular migration; fiscal mobility

company (M1)

A legal entity or corporate body brought into existence by registration under the UK Companies Acts (1844 and subsequently).

A company is owned by shareholders whose legal personalities are distinct from the corporate body, and it has a range of activities defined under its Articles of Association. For the past hundred years this has been a dominant form of business organization in capitalist economies. The existence of companies is compatible with SOCIALISM, provided that the state sets the economic and social aims of each company.

See also: corporation; firm

company town (R1)

A town run by one firm, e.g. a place run by a mining company which provides all jobs, services and housing. These towns have been criticized for permitting unscrupulous firms to perpetrate many forms of exploitation, including the monopoly sale of poor-quality goods at inflated prices.

company union (J5)

A TRADE (LABOR) UNION dependent on the company which approves it. Only the employees of that company are permitted to be members. In the nineteenth and twentieth centuries, especially in the USA, organized labour objected to these fake unions.

See also: enterprise union; sweetheart contract; truck

comparable worth (J3)

The relative value of a worker's labour based on productivity rather than personal characteristics. A principle adopted in Australia in 1972 and introduced in three uniform steps by June 1975 to counter SEXUAL DISCRIMINATION.

See also: Equal Pay Acts 1963 and 1970

References

McGavin, P.A. (1983) 'Equal pay for women: a reassessment of the Australian experience', *Australian Economic Papers* 22: 48–59.

comparative advantage (F1)

The principle justifying individuals or nations specializing in those economic activities which they perform relatively better. From its first enunciation in 1815 by TORRENS, this principle has stated that a country's pattern of production and international trade and specialization are determined by its relative efficiency in producing goods. This approach advances Smith's doctrine of ABSOLUTE ADVANTAGE, which was a simple extension of his DIVISION OF LABOUR principle. Torrens and RICARDO argued that even if country A were more productive in every agricultural and industrial activity than country B, trade would still take place if internal production cost ratios were different from country to country. Although this advanced international trade theory, it was later criticized for assuming constant costs, ignoring transport costs and for not determining the ratio at which exchange would take place. John Stuart MILL, with his LAW OF RECIPROCAL DEMAND, completed the theory by establishing the actual exchange rate resulting from trade.

Ricardo's example of trade in cloth and wine between England and Portugal states that to produce a given amount of each commodity the following amounts of labour are required in each country:

	England	Portugal
Cloth	100 men	90 men
Wine	120 men	80 men

Thus, England can produce cloth relatively more cheaply than wine and Portugal can produce wine more cheaply than cloth. The countries will both gain by increased specialization in the production of the good for which they have a comparative advantage, even though Portugal has an absolute advantage in the production of both commodities.

See also: Heckscher–Ohlin trade theorem; Leontief paradox; Rybczynski theorem; terms of trade

comparative costs (F1) *see* comparative advantage

comparative statics (E1)

A technique of economic analysis comparing one equilibrium position with a later one which is the product of changes in the values of PARAMETERS and EXOGENOUS VARIABLES. KEYNES used this method; ROBERTSON and HARROD preferred dynamic methods which, unlike comparative statics, have the advantage of showing how an earlier equilibrium is transformed into a later one.

compassionate conservatism (I3)

A political creed advocating the shrinking of the WELFARE STATE by using faith-based organizations to provide welfare services. This in the USA entailed the dismantling of the GREAT SOCIETY project of President Lyndon B. Johnson. President George W. Bush in his election campaign of 1999–2000 often referred to this philosophy of conservatism.

References

Olasky, M.N. (2000) *Compassionate Conservatism*, New York: Simon & Schuster.

compensated demand curve (D1)

A demand curve constructed so that a consumer's initial level of UTILITY is constant because of an adjustment to his or her money income. This curve eliminates

the INCOME EFFECT of price changes so that only the SUBSTITUTION EFFECT is in force.

compensating common tariff (F1)

A TARIFF which keeps the rest of the world as well off after the formation of a CUSTOMS UNION as it was previously.

compensating wage differential (J3)

A differential in wages or salaries created to compensate for a poor job attribute, e.g. a health hazard or variability of earnings. Firms grant these differentials to enable them to retain staff in undesirable jobs and to recruit new workers.

compensation principle (D6)

The rule that redistribution leads to an improvement in economic welfare if those who gain an increase in real income and welfare are able to compensate the losers and still be better off. This major principle of modern WELFARE ECONOMICS was devised by KALDOR and HICKS to deal with the problem of making interpersonal comparisons of UTILITY; it has often been applied in COST–BENEFIT ANALYSIS.

References

Mishan, E.J. (1981) *Introduction to Normative Economics*, New York: Oxford University Press.

compensatory finance (H5)

Expenditures by a government to offset LEAKAGES from the CIRCULAR FLOW of income. Thus, the impact of taxes, savings and imports which reduce the value of the MULTIPLIER for a national economy can be reduced by a government increasing its public expenditure and boosting exports through subsidizing export industries.

compensatory financial facility (F3)

An INTERNATIONAL MONETARY FUND arrangement in force since 1963 to help with the fluctuations in commodity prices which cause a shortfall in the value of exports. Repayments are made to the International Monetary Fund over a three- to five-year period.

See also: additional facilities

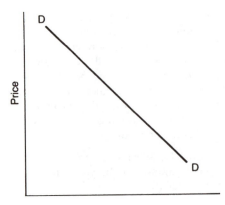

competition (L1)

The state of a market in which several suppliers of goods or services struggle with each other to acquire the custom of buyers. The principal types of competition are perfect, duopolistic, monopolistic and oligopolistic. Adam SMITH and MARSHALL analysed perfect competition; COURNOT presented a model of DUOPOLY; CHAMBERLIN propounded a theory of MONOPOLISTIC COMPETITION. Competition has often been criticized by socialists and idealists for bringing about an unfair distribution of incomes and discouraging co-operation.

Competition and Credit Control (E5)

UK discussion paper proposing new techniques of monetary policy to combine effective control over credit conditions with competition and innovation. Its recommendations included: (1) the requirement that all banks hold not less than 12½ per cent of their sterling deposit liabilities in specified reserve assets, which included cash at the Bank of England, money at call, treasury and local authority bills and UK government securities with less than one year to run; (2) the placing of SPECIAL DEPOSITS, variable in amount, by the banks with the Bank of England; and (3) the withdrawal of Bank of England support for the UK GILTS MARKET. These proposals were implemented in the 1970s.

References

'Competition and Credit Control', *Bank of England Quarterly Bulletin* 11: 189–93, 1971.

Competition Commission (L4)

The UK regulatory body inaugurated in 1999 to replace the MONOPOLIES AND MERGERS COMMISSION. It conducts inquiries referred to it on monopolies, mergers and the economic regulation of utility companies and handles appeals against the decisions of the Director-General of Fair Trading.

competition policy (L4)

The set of statutory measures of a country, or of the EUROPEAN COMMUNITY, which attempt to control dominant monopolies, RESTRICTIVE PRACTICES and ANTI-COMPETITIVE PRACTICES, to monitor mergers and to protect consumers.

In the UK, this policy was gradually developed from 1948. The Monopolies and Restrictive Practices (Inquiry and Control) Act 1948 permitted the Board of Trade to refer to the newly constituted Monopolies and Restrictive Practices Commission 'monopoly situations' where one-third of the supply of goods was supplied by one firm, or two or more interconnected firms, in order to ascertain whether that situation was against the 'public interest', which was regarded as the promotion of efficiency, the suitable pricing of goods for domestic and foreign markets and technical progress. The commission's report on 'Collective discrimination' recommended the separate and judicial investigation of restrictive practices. The Restrictive Trade Practices Act 1956 set up a register of permitted restrictive agreements and a Restrictive Practices Court to ascertain whether it was right to regard an agreement as against the public interest. The legislation was also extended in 1964 by the Resale Prices Act to cover individual enforcement of RESALE PRICE MAINTENANCE. References to the renamed Monopolies and Mergers Commission were possible under the Monopolies and Mergers Act 1965 where a monopoly situation was strengthened or the value of assets taken over was in excess of £5 million. The investigation of firms supplying services was another concern of the 1965 Act. Further legislation on restrictive practices in the 1968 Restrictive Trade Practices Act brought INFORMATION AGREEMENTS within the ambit of the Restrictive Practices Court. The Fair Trading Act 1973 set up the office of Director-General of Fair Trading with wide powers to investigate and refer to the Monopolies and Mergers Commission. The monopoly situations which could be investigated included those with only a quarter of the market, not only nationally, but also in local areas; the concept of 'public interest' was clarified by relating it to 'competition'. The Competition Act 1980 transferred the investigation of prices to the Director-General of Fair Trading and gave the latter the task of investigating ANTI-COMPETITIVE PRACTICES; under the Act, various public bodies, e.g. bus and water authorities, could be referred to the Monopolies and Mergers Commission for a consideration of their efficiency and costs, the service provided and possible abuse of a monopoly situation. The 1984 Act consolidated the legislation. The Competition Act 1998 introduced new rules to prohibit agreements, business practices and conduct that would damage competition with fines up to 10 per cent of a business's turnover.

The EUROPEAN ECONOMIC COMMUNITY from its inception regarded the promotion of competition as a major policy goal. The TREATY OF ROME in Articles 3, 7, 37 and 85–94 deals with many aspects of the promotion of competition. State monopolies, restrictive agreements, abuses of dominant positions in markets, the control of public enterprises by national governments and state aid to industries by national governments are all covered by the policy.

In the USA, since 1890 the federal government has pursued an active competition policy, known as ANTITRUST.

References

Cini, M. and McGowan, L. (1998) *Competition Policy in the European Union.* New York: St Martin's Press.
Wilks, S. (1999) *In the public interest: Competition Policy and the Monopolies and Mergers Commission,* Manchester: Manchester University Press.

Competitive Equality Banking Act 1987 (G2, K2)

US federal statute which establishes that transactions between member banks of the FEDERAL RESERVE and their subsidiaries and holding company affiliates be on the same terms as those offered to unaffiliated companies. A bank was broadly defined

to include institutions receiving deposits, having deposit insurance and being engaged in commercial lending.

competitive fringe (L1)

The smaller firms coexisting with a few large firms in an oligopolistic industry: these firms have no influence over the market, especially in the setting of prices.

competitiveness index (F3)

An index to determine average annual increase in GDP per capita based on seven types of variable: openness, government policies, finance, infrastructure, technology, management, labour and civil institutions. It is compiled by the World Economic Forum of Geneva, Switzerland.

competitive process (L1)

A process consisting of two opposing tendencies: the transfer mechanism which reallocates the market shares of the less efficient firms to the more efficient and the INNOVATION mechanism which enables firms lagging behind their competitors to introduce new products or processes to reassert their position in a market.

References

Downie, J. (1958) *The Competitive Process,* London: Duckworth.

competitive tendering (M2) *see* compulsory competitive tendering

competitive trading (D4)

The traditional method of exchange in a market consisting of buyers and sellers using their relative market strengths to reach an agreed single market price.

See also: barter; countertrade

complement (D0)

A good consumed in conjunction with another, e.g. petroleum with a car. Whether two goods are complements of each other can be discovered by measuring the CROSS PRICE ELASTICITY OF DEMAND between them. If the cross-elasticity is negative, then the good is a complement.

See also: substitute

complexity theory (D0)

A study of agents interacting simultaneously in a multiple cause and effect feedback. It looks at the emergence of a new phase of a system and a large range of potentials instead of forecasting on the basis of a simple cause and effect chain. The Santa Fe Institute of New Mexico, founded in 1984, pioneered this form of analysis.

References

Arthur, W.B., Durlauf, S.D. and Lane, D.A. (1997) 'The economy as an evolving complex system', *Proceedings of the Evolutionary Path of the Global Economy Workshop, Santa Fa, New Mexico, September*, Boulder, CO: Westview Press.

compliance cost (D0)

The cost of complying with a government regulation, including taxation. Such costs are incurred by the private sector and by governmental organizations below the level of central/federal government. The costs of compliance include accountants' fees and the OPPORTUNITY COST of the time spent filling in forms.

composite commodity (D0)

A collection of goods representing purchasing power in general, or money as it is a medium of exchange. This composite is only possible if the prices of other goods remain constant. HICKS introduced the concept.

See also: *ceteris paribus*

References

Hicks, J.R. (1939) *Value and Capital*, ch. 2, Oxford: Oxford University Press.

composite insurance company (G2)

An insurance company transacting a wide range of life and non-life insurance business.

compound interest (E4)

Cumulative interest paid on both the original amount lent and subsequent interest which is added to the PRINCIPAL. If the total accumulation period is long, the total

sum becomes immense compared with the original sum. Not surprisingly, Keynes asserted that 'there is no more powerful force than compound interest'.

Comprehensive Employment and Training Act 1973 (J2)

US federal statute consolidating previous, mainly youth, training programmes which hoped to give every youth and adult an opportunity to work. It decentralized planning procedures and its implementation, including ON-THE-JOB TRAINING. The Job Corps set up under Title IV was a residential programme to provide remedial work and skills training for severely disadvantaged youths.

Comptroller of the Currency (G2, H1)

US office set up under the NATIONAL BANKING ACT 1863 originally to deal with currency and monetary matters, but the task of chartering and monitoring national banks also given to it has become its principal concern.

compulsory competitive tendering (H7, M1)

The rule that UK local authorities put out major services, e.g. street cleaning, to TENDER instead of providing them by their own departments. In many cases, the contract is awarded to the original local authority service.

compulsory savings (E2) *see* forced savings

Computer-assisted Trading System (G2)

Toronto-based securities trading system, the first of its type to receive orders from abroad electronically and to direct them immediately to its trading floor.

See also: Stock Exchange Automated Quotation System

concentration (L1)

The extent to which an industry is dominated by a few firms. This can be measured by examining the proportion of production, sales, value added or employment attributable to the largest firm or firms. MONOPOLY, DUOPOLY and OLIGOPOLY are the most concentrated of market forms; PERFECT COMPETITION is the least. UK industry is more concentrated than that of the USA or other West European countries, partly because of its smaller domestic market, which necessitates few firms per industry if ECONOMIES OF SCALE are to be achieved, and partly because of the weakness of the UK policy on mergers.

See also: aggregate concentration; concentration ratio; Gini coefficient; Herfindahl–Hirschman index; Lerner index; Lorenz curve; relative concentration

concentration economy (D0)
An ECONOMY OF SCALE arising from the concentration of industry in a particular area.

See also: agglomeration economy

concentration ratio (L1)
1 An absolute ratio (sometimes called a leading firms ratio) which shows the percentage of sales, output, assets, value added or employment which can be ascribed to the largest firms of the industry, usually the top four or five. These ratios are more accurate if they are adjusted for imports and exports.
2 A relative ratio based on a size distribution of firms showing, for example, what proportion of firms has what proportion of output; LORENZ CURVES and GINI COEFFICIENTS are used for this purpose.

See also: aggregate concentration; Herfindahl–Hirschman index; Lerner index; *N*-firm concentration ratio

concrete labour (D2, J0)
The labour required to produce a particular product, e.g. a piece of furniture. Labour in this qualitative sense creates use values.

See also: abstract labour

conditionality (F3)
Lending to a debtor on condition that the loan is used for a specific purpose so that

there is less risk of default in servicing the loan. It is argued that the INTERNATIONAL MONETARY FUND and WORLD BANK in making this stipulation make 'conditionality' a PUBLIC GOOD.

Condorcet criterion (D0)
A voting procedure by which the candidate is chosen on the basis of defeating all the others by obtaining the majority of the votes in pairwise elections.

Confederation of British Industry (L0)
The major representative body for private and public sector firms of UK industry. The CBI was created in 1965 as a result of the merging together of the Federation of British Industries (founded in 1916), the British Employers' Federation and the National Association of British Manufacturers.

confidence interval (C1)
The range within which, to a certain percentage, one is confident that a sample statistic lies. Thus, with a 95 per cent confidence interval, if we sample 1,000 voters to ascertain their current opinion of the government we can be confident that only fifty are unrepresentative of the population as a whole. Confidence intervals are stated for MEANS, STANDARD DEVIATIONS, proportions and differences.

See also: confidence level

confidence level (C1)
A confidence limit, or CRITICAL VALUE, expressed as a percentage.

conflicting claims approach to inflation (E3)
Attributing INFLATION to the total wage claims of workers exceeding the total income available.

References
Rowthorn, R.E. (1977) 'Conflict, inflation and money', *Cambridge Journal of Economics* 1: 215–39.

confluence analysis (C1)
A general statistical method used in econometrics created by FRISCH and others

from the 1930s onwards. It attempts to discover the different linear relationships between several observable variables, taking into account measurement errors.

References

Frisch, R. (1934) *Statistical Confluence Analysis by Means of Complete Regression Systems*, Oslo: Universitetets økonomiske institutt.

conglomerate (M1)

A large firm, particularly in the USA, with many subsidiary firms producing unrelated goods and services so as to reduce risk. Famous US conglomerates include ITT, LTV, Litton, Textro and Gulf and Western. Their past growth was based on a simple mathematical truth that if a company with a high PRICE-EARNINGS RATIO takes over one with a lower price–earnings ratio, the acquiring company's earnings per share will automatically rise, helping to finance further acquisitions. Their recent growth has been hampered by the opposition of the US Department of Justice and periods of falling stock market prices.

conglomerate merger (L1)

A MERGER between two firms with different products or activities. These mergers are motivated by the desire to use underutilized resources, particularly management and marketing. Although it is hoped that the merger will create a financially strong firm, rather than a firm with an increased market share, experience has shown that many mergers of this kind have not been financially successful.

Congressional Budget and Impound-ment Control Act 1974 (H6)

Major US federal statute which reformed the US budget process by changing the fiscal year from 1 July to 1 October to give Congress more time to consider the budget, created new budget committees, introduced a first budget resolution to establish ceilings on expenditure, revenue and debt and made anti-impoundment provisions to stop the president from seizing money

voted to particular programmes: previously the president could refuse to spend moneys for purposes which had been the subject of appropriation bills despite Congressional approval.

See also: Gramm–Rudman–Hollings Act

consideration (G1, K0)

1 The value of a stock exchange transaction expressed in a particular currency.
2 The advantage or detriment which establishes a particular contract under common law jurisdictions such as England and Wales, the USA and some Commonwealth countries.

consol (G1)

A consolidated fund stock ('Consolidated Annuity') of the UK government issued as an unredeemable fixed interest security. They were introduced in 1751 as a means of replacing a variety of government bonds of different MATURITIES and interest rates with a single government stock. The yield on consols has often been used as a measure of the long-term rate of interest. The consols currently traded in the UK have nominal interest rates of 2½ per cent and 4 per cent.

Consolidated Fund (H1)

The fund of the UK central government into which all direct and indirect tax revenues and other receipts are paid. Prior to its establishment in 1787, separate funds existed for each type of government revenue.

See also: funding

Consolidated Fund standing services (H6)

An item of the UK budget covering expenditures which do not require annual approval by parliament, e.g. interest on the NATIONAL DEBT and the salaries of judges.

Consolidated Metropolitan Statistical Area (J1, R1)

A large metropolitan complex of the USA

including PRIMARY METROPOLITAN STATISTICAL AREAS.

consolidation loan (G2)

A loan offered by a financial institution to replace several outstanding loans of a debtor. The replacement loan will be less costly to service each month and will be over a longer period. Persons with burdensome credit card debts can use loans of this kind, often secured on residential property.

consortium bank (G2)

A bank jointly owned by a number of other banks for the purposes of giving small banks representation in a financial centre. These consortia deal with specific types of financing, especially massive loans for infrastructure investment.

conspicuous consumption (E2)

Expenditure on expensive goods to impress others with one's wealth and status rather than to satisfy basic needs. VEBLEN was the first to analyse ostentation of this nature.

constant capital (D2, E2)

The MARXIAN term for raw materials and machinery. This form of capital transfers only its own value, originally created by labour, to the finished product.

See also: organic composition of capital; variable capital

constant elasticity of substitution production function (C5, D2)

A production function in which the elasticity of input substitution is constant at 1 or some other value. This production function succeeded the COBB–DOUGLAS PRODUCTION FUNCTION.

References

Arrow, K.J., Chenery, H.B., Minhas, B.S. and Solow, R.M. (1961) 'Capital-labour substitution and economic efficiency', *Review of Economics and Statistics* 43: 225–50.

constant prices (D0, E3)

A measure of an economic variable deflated to allow for price changes; for example, the NATIONAL INCOME at constant prices would show national income for a number of years at the prices of one year.

constant returns to scale (D0) *see* returns to scale

constrained market pricing (D4, L5)

Prices in little need of regulation because they are constrained by competition. This concept is used by US regulatory agencies, such as the INTERSTATE COMMERCE COMMISSION, in its pricing policies. Prices not constrained by competition have to be between a floor price equal to marginal cost and a ceiling price equal to the STANDALONE COST.

Consumer Advisory Council (L4)

A subordinate organization of the US FEDERAL RESERVE Board of Governors established in 1976 to advise the board on the discharge of its duties under the Consumer Credit Protection Act. It has thirty members.

consumer credit (G2)

Credit granted by banks, finance houses and other financial institutions usually to purchase CONSUMER DURABLES. The volume of this credit can be controlled by altering its price, i.e. by changing interest rates or the minimum size of initial deposits.

Consumer Credit Act 1974 (G2, K2)

UK statute which set up a system of consumer protection administered by the Director-General of Fair Trading. Agreements for credit under £5,000 were regulated, businesses conducting consumer credit or consumer hire were licensed, credit advertisements were controlled and consumers were allowed a cooling-off period in which agreements could be cancelled.

consumer durable (D0)

A consumer GOOD not immediately consumed but the producer of a stream of services over a period of years. Vehicles, electrical goods and other durable household articles are major examples. Unlike the services of houses, there is no inclusion of the benefits of consumer durable ownership and allowance for their depreciation in NATIONAL INCOME accounts. Despite consumer durables resembling the fixed capital used by firms, they are classified as part of consumption. However, as their purchase often requires CONSUMER CREDIT, like fixed capital, they are subject to a fluctuating demand sensitive to monetary policy.

See also: brown good; white good

consumer equilibrium (D1)

That choice of expenditures, using a given income, which will maximize a consumer's UTILITY. Formally it is expressed in the statement that each ratio of marginal utility from a particular good relative to its price is equal to every other such ratio throughout the consumer's purchases (if it is not, it will be possible to redistribute one's expenditures to increase total utility). This equilibrium is based on the LAW OF DIMINISHING MARGINAL UTILITY:

$$\frac{\text{marginal utility of good A}}{\text{price of A}} = \frac{\text{marginal utility of good B}}{\text{price of B}}$$

$$= \text{marginal utility}$$

$$= \frac{\text{good } n}{\text{price of } n}$$

Consumer Expenditure Survey (C8)

US survey of the current expenditure of US residents which began in 1979. It is used to revise the CONSUMER PRICE INDEX and is conducted by the Bureau of the Census for the Bureau of Labor Statistics. Information is collected from a panel which is interviewed five times every three months, and from records kept by participating households over a specified fortnight.

consumerism (D1)

1 Concerted action to make firms pursue the interests of consumers, even at the cost of shareholders' incomes. Action can take the form of lobbying parliaments for legislation, protest marches and legal suits. In response to these campaigns, many Western countries since the 1960s have introduced elaborate consumer protection legislation to ensure that consumers get a fair deal before, during and after buying a good or service. In the USA, for example, the FEDERAL TRADE COMMISSION supervises advertising, the Fair Packaging and Labeling Act 1965 prevents inadequate product information on packages and labels, the Consumer Credit Protecting Act 1968 requires a simple statement of the details of loans, the Fair Credit Reporting Act 1970 allows consumers access to their credit reports, and a variety of safety acts protect the users of cars, toys and other products. In the UK, the CONSUMER CREDIT ACT 1974 provides protection for consumers. However, there are still opponents of consumer protection who argue that regulation is an expensive and bureaucratic procedure unduly restricting the behaviour of firms. Also, some consumers may be prepared to endure lower quality to make some purchases fall within their budgets.

2 Advocacy of materialism, of purchasing more and more goods and services rather than being frugal.

See also: consumer sovereignty

References

Evans, J. (1980) *Consumerism in the United States*, New York: Praeger.

Swagler, R. (1994) 'Evolution and Applications of the Term Consumerism: Theme and Variations', *Journal of Consumer Affairs* 28: 347–60.

Swann, D. (1979) *Competition and Consumer Protection*, Harmondsworth: Penguin.

consumer price index (E3)

US price index which shows the average change in the prices of a representative basket of goods and services purchased for daily living by US households. Data are collected on the prices of food, clothing, housing, fuels and services, etc., from eighty-five areas. Market prices, including indirect taxes, are used and each item is weighted according to its importance in consumers' budgets. The US Bureau of Labor Statistics began the compilation of this index in 1919. Two versions of it are published: the CPI-U and the CPI-W.

See also: Consumer Expenditure Survey; retail price index

consumer protection legislation (D1, K2)

Measures to enforce minimum standards in the provision of goods and services, to provide advisory services for consumers and, in the case of public corporations (UK), to establish users' councils to handle complaints. The principal measures protecting the UK consumer are the Sale of Goods Act 1979, the Trade Descriptions Acts 1968 and 1972 and the Consumer Credit Act 1974. In the USA, the Food and Drug Administration and the Consumer Product Safety Council energetically protect the consumer.

See also: consumerism

consumer society (D1, P0)

A society which devotes a high proportion of its income to luxury goods and undertakes little saving. Only MARKET ECONOMIES have been prosperous enough to choose this lifestyle.

See also: conspicuous consumption

consumer sovereignty (D1, M3)

The decisive power of consumers to determine the amount and pattern of production by freely choosing goods and services in accordance with their preferences. Adam SMITH in his rejection of MERCANTILISM turned the goal of economic activity to satisfying the consumer rather than producers. NEOCLASSICAL ECONOMICS built many of its theories on the notion of CONSUMER EQUILIBRIUM. Given the growth of

large corporations with huge advertising budgets, GALBRAITH and others have challenged this view of the influence of consumers. Also, the increase in the role of government and the importance of MERIT GOODS have reduced the power of individual consumers in modern economies.

See also: countervailing power

consumer's surplus (D1)

The area, shaded in the figure, under an individual consumer's demand curve which shows the difference between what a consumer is willing to pay and what actually is paid. It will be greater for richer consumers as they have a higher demand; hence, when the price structure is designed to reflect consumer incomes, higher income groups pay more for a good service, e.g. employed persons are charged more than unemployed. This major concept, introduced into economics by DUPUIT and refined by MARSHALL and HICKS, has become a major tool of COST-BENEFIT ANALYSIS.

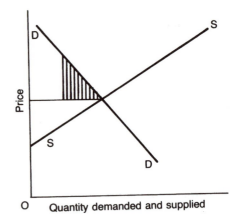

See also: producer's surplus

References

Bergson, A. (1975) 'A note on consumer's surplus', *Journal of Economic Literature* 13: 38–44.

Deaton, A. and Muellbauer, J. (1980) *Economics and Consumer Behavior*, New York and Cambridge: Cambridge University Press.

consumption externality (D6)

The effect of one person's consumption on the production and consumption of others. A modern example is the effect of cigarette smoking on the health of non-smokers who are forced to be 'passive smokers' and are compelled to pay for the consequences of smoking on the health of smokers through higher medical insurance premiums or higher taxes.

See also: externality

consumption function (E2)

The relationship which shows aggregate consumption as a function of income (measured absolutely, relatively or permanently at current or constant prices) and possibly wealth or the rate of interest. As consumption is the major part of national expenditure, the consumption function is central to models of income determination. KEYNES in his *General Theory* inspired much of later work, which has included the ABSOLUTE INCOME, RELATIVE INCOME, PERMANENT INCOME and LIFE-CYCLE approaches.

consumption tax (H2)

A tax levied on actual expenditures with the hope that it will encourage saving. In wartime when it has been necessary to curb consumption, taxes of this kind have been levied as an alternative to rationing.

See also: expenditure tax

contango (G1)

1 A charge a stockbroker used to make for carrying over a sale or purchase of a security to the next accounting period.
2 In commodity markets it refers to spot prices being lower than futures prices.

See also: backwardation

contemporaneous externality (D6, Q0)

An economic activity affecting another type of production in the same time period, e.g. bee-keeping helps fruit farming.

See also: sequential externality

contestable markets thesis (L1)

BAUMOL's view that competition can be maintained by the state ensuring that an industry's barriers to entry are kept low. Under such circumstances, free entry and exit will maintain the market in a competitive state. This thesis is compatible with recent UK COMPETITION POLICY.

References

Baumol, W.J., Panzar, L.C. and Willig, R.D. (1982) *Contestable Markets and the Theory of Industry Structure*, New York: Harcourt Brace Jovanovich.

contingency claims contracting (J3) *see* employment contract

contingency table (C1)

A table whose columns and rows are observed frequencies so that the expected frequency of a particular hypothesis can be investigated. These tables can be extended to more than two dimensions.

contingent commodity (D0)

A new commodity resulting from the occurrence of a particular event.

contingent fee (D4)

A fee paid only on the successful outcome of an activity, e.g. a fee for a lawyer's services which is a percentage of the damages awarded to a plaintiff. In the USA this fee system is alleged to encourage vexatious litigation.

contingent market (D4, G1)

A market, particularly an insurance market, which transfers risk from those facing it to those who are prepared to undertake it. An example of this is when a ship owner faced with the risk of the loss of a ship can transfer the risk to LLOYD'S insurers. If the insurance market is in equilibrium, the insurance premium should settle at the rate which equates the marginal cost of insurance to the marginal benefit of losing an undesired risk.

contingent valuation (D0, Q0)

Valuation of commodities not traded in markets, e.g. clean air, landscapes and wildlife. The valuation is based upon the responses of individuals to questions about what their actions would be if a particular hypothetical situation were to occur. When the average of responses has been calculated with weighting if necessary, people's valuation of a PUBLIC GOOD is ascertained. A proxy measure already used is the travel cost a person will incur to benefit from that environment.

References

Brookshire, D., Ives, B. and Schulze, W. (1976) 'The valuation of aesthetic preferences', *Journal of Environmental Economics and Management* 3: 325–46.

continuity thesis (B1)

The view that there is a continuum between the allocation theory of classical and neoclassical economists with the consequence that there was no marginal revolution in the 1870s. Thus it is asserted that MARSHALL was not overturning CLASSICAL ECONOMICS but using the sharper tools of mathematics to clarify Ricardian economics as stated by John Stuart MILL.

See also: marginalists

References

Shove, G.F. (1942) 'The place of Marshall's *Principles* in the development of economic theory', *Economic Journal* 52: 294–329.

continuous double auction (D4)

Bids are submitted by both buyers and sellers, then ranked from highest to lowest and a trade is effected when there is a match. A DUTCH AUCTION is a continuous descending auction.

continuous variable (C6)

A variable, expressed in symbolic form, e.g. x or y, which can assume any value between two given values.

See also: discrete variable

contract compliance (H0, J7)

Obeying the terms and conditions of governmental contracts awarded to private sector firms. This approach has often been used, especially in the USA, as a means of advancing employment policies, e.g. the employment of women, blacks and disabled persons.

See also: Fair Wages Resolution

contract curve (D0)

1 A curve connecting the points of tangency of two individuals' respective INDIFFERENCE CURVES such that the MARGINAL RATE OF SUBSTITUTION for them is the same.
2 AN ISOQUANT showing where the marginal rate of technical substitution is the same for the production of two different goods.

See also: Edgeworth box

contracting (D0, K0)

Forming an agreement to supply a factor of production or a product.

See also: employment contract; tendering

contracting out (L2, L3)

Partial PRIVATIZATION of a public service often through employing subcontractors to undertake a specific function such as cleaning, laundering or accounting.

contractionary national income gap (E1) *see* deflationary gap

contractual savings (E2, G2)

Savings made under a contract that specifies regular payments into a fund over a minimum time period. The advantage to pension funds and life assurance companies of savings of this type is that they make possible long-term institutional investments, e.g. in real estate.

contracyclical policy (E3) *see* countercyclical policy

contrarian investment strategy (G1)

A stock market practice of buying stocks and shares that have been losing value and selling stocks short which have been improving. This approach is based on the view that a stock market overreacts to the information it receives. Price–earnings and book–market ratios are used to identify stocks suitable for the pursuit of this strategy.

References

Chan, K.C. (1988) 'On the contrarian investment strategy', *Journal of Business* 61: 147–63.

contribution standard (D3)

A principle of income distribution that asserts that the productivity of different kinds of resources should determine income distribution. This principle is derived from the MARGINAL PRODUCTIVITY THEORY of distribution and is criticized on the grounds that it is very difficult to apply as a factor of production's own productivity is often inseparable from others.

See also: equality standard

controlled market (D4, L5)

A market regulated by a central or local government. There can be control over pricing, over the quantities which can be sold or in the range of people allowed to buy and sell. Many European countries in the past gave the police the power to regulate markets; today the principal organizations regulating prices have been set up under national price or agricultural policies. In practice, it is difficult to have complete control over a market as the prices set are unlikely to be permanently in equilibrium, thus giving buyers and sellers an incentive to evade the controls.

See also: black market; prices policy

convergence criteria (F3)

The five macroeconomic rules set out in the Treaty of Maastricht for member countries of the European Union to enter the single currency, the euro: the public deficit to be no more than 3 per cent of GDP; average inflation rate over 1997 not to exceed 1.5 per cent of the three best-performing member states; gross government debt to be less than 60 per cent of GDP; the national currency to fluctuate within the margins set by the Exchange Rate Mechanism for at least two years, avoiding devaluation and severe tensions;

long-term interest rates to be no more than 2 per cent of the three member countries with the greatest price stability.

convergence hypothesis (P0)

The supposition that different types of economy are becoming similar. This view emerged in the 1960s because SOVIET-TYPE ECONOMIES modified their planning methods by making more use of the price system and MARKET ECONOMIES became more corporate and sympathetic towards PUBLIC ENTERPRISE. It was argued that all economies were becoming mixed economies. Although economic reforms using prices have become increasingly popular in Eastern Europe, PRIVATIZATION has caused market economies to revert more to their original form which was more capitalist than mixed.

conversion (G1)

Replacing one kind of stock market security with another. Major types of conversion occur when an equity replaces a debenture, or a dated government bond is replaced by an undated one.

convertible currency (F3)

A currency exchangeable for gold or a major currency. After the Second World War, the UK pound did not return to full convertibility until 1958; in the late twentieth century, East European currencies were the last major currencies to remain inconvertible.

See also: Bullionist controversy

cookie jar accounting (L1)

Setting aside reserves in the years of a company's prosperity to be used in a recession so that income available for shareholders is stabilized.

See also: Swedish budget

co-operative (L2)

A group of producers or consumers who join together to share the rewards of production including profits from retailing. The oldest consumers' co-operative was founded in Rochdale, Lancashire, in

1844; many producer co-operatives were founded in the USA and the UK in the last quarter of the nineteenth century. Unfair business competition, especially the withholding of supplies, destroyed many of the US co-operatives, but some of the UK co-operatives founded then still survive in printing, clothing and footwear manufacture. Self-management of Yugoslav enterprises and the large workers' co-operatives at Mondragon (in the Basque region of Spain) attracted much attention. All these enterprises have had to face the problems of underinvestment (as producer members often prefer present wages to future profits), low PRODUCTIVITY and a lack of managerial experience. But poor performance has not been universal, as Mondragon shows.

See also: industrial democracy; workers' participation

References

Ireland, N.J. and Law, P.J. (1982) *The Economics of Labour-Managed Enterprises*, London: Croom Helm.

Vanek, J. (1970) *The General Theory of Labour-Managed Market Economies*, Ithaca, NY: Cornell University Press.

co-operative federalism (H7)

A federal state with much intergovernmental co-operation between federal and state governments. In particular, the different layers of government jointly participate in many programmes.

See also: dual federalism; fiscal federalism

core (D0)

A set of possible equilibrium prices. As originally devised by EDGEWORTH in *Mathematical Psychics* (1881), it corresponds to all PARETO-EFFICIENT positions in a two-person, two-good economy which show improvement after trade. This concept has been applied to the study of co-operative games and is shown by the CONTRACT CURVE in the EDGEWORTH BOX diagram. The core coincides with a set of price equilibria

under PERFECT COMPETITION, i.e. GENERAL EQUILIBRIUM.

core economy (P0)

A major economy, usually a MARKET ECONOMY, which plays a leading role in world trade.

core firm (L1)

A giant corporation that dominates a market.

core inflation rate (E3)

The underlying trend in INFLATION which depends solely on past labour and capital costs and firms' EXPECTATIONS of changes in these costs. This rate changes only if expectations based on extrapolating from past costs change. To bring the core inflation rate of a major economy, such as the USA's, down to zero could require a steady fall in national output for several years. This rate is usually estimated by excluding volatile food and energy prices from the CONSUMER PRICE INDEX.

See also: headline rate

References

Eckstein, O. (1981) *Core Inflation*, Englewood Cliffs, NJ, and London: Prentice Hall.

core region (R1)

A dominant or leading region of a country which often includes the capital city. The accumulation of physical and HUMAN CAPITAL is encouraged there by the AGGLOMERATION and CONCENTRATION ECONOMIES possible in such a large population.

corner solution (C1)

An answer to an OPTIMIZATION PROBLEM in which one of the variables in a TRADE-OFF is zero at an optimum.

Corn Laws (N4, N5)

The series of English laws dating from the reign of Edward IV which protected English agriculture by imposing tariffs on the import of corn to maintain its price; also export bounties (subsidies) were granted to farmers. CLASSICAL ECONOMISTS such as SMITH objected to this interference with

FREE TRADE; RICARDO viewed it as an encouragement to production which would expand agriculture, a form of production subject to the LAW OF DIMINISHING RETURNS, and bring about a decline in the rate of profit and a STATIONARY STATE in the economy. The growing manufacturing interest also opposed these laws as PROTECTION kept up food prices and wages. The laws were repealed by the government led by Sir Robert Peel in 1846.

References

Kadish, A. (ed.) (1996) *The Corn Laws: The formation of popular economics in Britain*, London: Pickering.

corn model (E2)

RICARDO's simple model of an economy with one commodity, corn, which is both the single input and single output of that country. Corn provides subsistence for workers who produce an annual output of corn. Thus a single commodity is both the intermediate and final product.

See also: Sraffa

cornucopia (D1, P0)

An abundance of consumer goods possible only in a high-income capitalist country, e.g. the USA.

corporate finance (G3)

Specialist financial services to corporations and other large organizations. Advice is given on raising new capital and on acquisitions.

corporate governance (G3)

The set of rules which are used to control and run a firm or other organization. The powers of different managers, the formulae for calculating remuneration and grievance procedures are part of governance.

See also: Cadbury code; Greenbury code; Myners Committee

corporate income tax (H2)

A separate tax on firms which has the advantage of being easier to collect than an income tax applied to both persons and firms. As it is a tax on a special kind of

factor income, pure corporate profits, it does not affect output in the short or long run.

corporate morality (M0)

The maintenance of high ethical standards by businesses. This requires honesty in the accounting and other statements of corporate activity, high-quality safe products, participation in community programmes, care for the environment, an awareness of the long-term interests of the economy in its investment policy and prompt payment of taxation in order to contribute sufficiently to public expenditure.

corporate state (P0)

A state considerably influenced by relatively few large firms and trade unions which jointly, with the collaboration of the government, make the major economic decisions on which the running of an economy is based. Italian fascism of the interwar period took this form; UK governments of the 1960s and 1970s, according to their critics, adopted such a political philosophy. As the proportion of output produced by a few major companies increases in the USA and other Western countries, CORPORATISM becomes a more important issue.

See also: minimal state; state monopoly capitalism

corporate veil (L2)

The disguises of firms to prevent government and shareholders knowing all of their activities, including the extent of their income. Shareholders' ignorance of a company's actual behaviour leads them to underestimate the true value of a company, e.g. they ignore the effect of current corporate saving on prospective PRICE-EARNINGS RATIOS and hence the stock market valuation of the company. Governments collect less in corporate taxation because of their ignorance of firms' total earnings.

corporation (M1)

A privately or publicly owned firm whose

powers and activities are defined in the statute or articles which set it up. It is the major way of organizing a large firm in many countries and hence is responsible for most industrial and commercial output of several national economies. As most large corporations, whether in the public or private sectors, are to a large extent controlled by their managers, many have asked to whom they are ultimately responsible.

See also: managerial models of the firm; multinational corporation; public enterprise; transnational corporation

corporation income tax (H2)
A major tax used by the US federal government for raising revenue. To avoid its constitutionality being challenged in the courts, it was levied as an excise on the privilege of doing business as a corporation. Until 1941, it raised more revenue than the INDIVIDUAL INCOME TAX. The tax is paid in two instalments in the first six months of the year following the tax year in which a corporation's income arises.

corporation tax (H2)
A direct tax on the profits, after interest and depreciation, of companies. Separate income taxation for individuals and companies enables different rates to be charged. The yield from the corporation tax varies from country to country as a consequence of different tax rates and differences in corporate profitability.

corporatism (L2, P0)
Control of an economy by giving major economic decision making to corporations, industrial ministries and, in some economies, leading TRADE (LABOR) UNIONS. This was said to be the character of the UK economy in the 1960s and 1970s and has long been true of France.

See also: corporate state; indicative planning

corrective subsidy (D6, H2)
A SUBSIDY given to a firm as an incentive for internalizing an EXTERNALITY; a pay-

ment to cover the social costs borne by a firm.

See also: Pigovian subsidy

corrective tax (H2)
An INDIRECT TAX used to counter EXTERNAL-ITIES thereby bringing about a PARETO equilibrium.

See also: effluent fee

correlation (C1)
The extent of interdependence between two variables. Unlike regression, this calculation is not used to predict the value of one variable from the other.

See also: autocorrelation; coefficient of correlation; Durbin–Watson statistic; multiple correlation; non-linear correlation; rank correlation; Spearman's rank correlation formula

correspondent bank (G2)
A bank accepting deposits from another bank located in another area to provide local services for it. Many banks internationally have this arrangement to be able to make payments in different currencies. In the USA, the UNIT BANKING system necessitated correspondent banking as a means of transferring funds between different localities.

corridor (E0)
A range above and below the equilibrium path of an economy. Within the corridor, normal market forces bring the economy back to the equilibrium path.

corruption (K4)
The use of public office for private gain by the political establishment, bureaucrats or legislators. Its different forms include accepting bribes to change decisions, fraud, LAUNDERING MONEY and BLACK MARKET operations. Corruption increases TRANSACTION COSTS and the final cost of many goods and services, especially where a government licence is needed. Although it can discourage foreign investors, it does make some economic systems work faster.

References

Elliott, K.A. (ed.) (1997) *Corruption and the Global Economy*, Washington, DC: Institute for International Economics.

Treisman, D. (2000) 'The causes of corruption: a cross-national study', *Journal of Public Economics* 76: 399–457.

'corset' (E5)

The method of Bank of England control over commercial banks' liabilities in force from December 1973 to June 1980. A limit was placed on the amount of banks' sterling deposits and foreign currency deposits lent in sterling: if the limit was exceeded, a special deposit, bearing no interest, had to be lodged at the Bank of England. Banks objected to the way in which it encouraged companies to lend directly to each other rather than using banks as intermediaries. The removal of the corset led to an upsurge in the money supply.

See also: disintermediation

cost–benefit analysis (C1, D6, R1)

The evaluation of an investment project with a long-term perspective from the viewpoint of the economy as a whole (although it is sometimes used in the private sector) by comparing the effects of undertaking the project with not doing so. This form of analysis was designed to provide a means for evaluating public works and development projects in cases where the value of them could be measured empirically. It can be traced back to DUPUIT's *De la mesure de l'utilité des travaux publics* (1844), but it was first applied as a technique for assessing projects under the US Flood Control Act 1936. The theoretical justification for many cost–benefit procedures was slight until HICKS published an article in 1943 on CONSUMERS' SURPLUSES. A calculation of the NET PRESENT VALUE of expected costs and expected benefits makes it possible to use the decision rule that a project will only be undertaken if the benefits exceed the costs. The maximization of net social benefits came to be regarded as the appropriate criterion for selecting a project. The benefits and costs can be real (tangible or intangible) or pecuniary. Tangible benefits can often be equated with increased output; intangible benefits with prestige and the creation of something beautiful; and pecuniary benefits with a change in the relative remuneration of an industry or an occupation.

See also: compensation principle

References

Hicks, J.R. (1943) 'The four consumers' surpluses', *Review of Economic Studies* II: 31–41.

Pearce, D.W. (1983) *Cost-Benefit Analysis*, 2nd edn, London: Macmillan.

cost-effectiveness analysis (H5)

An analysis of the costs of alternative programmes designed to meet a single objective. The programme which costs least will be the most cost effective. This form of analysis was first developed when Robert McNamara was US Secretary of Defense in the 1960s.

See also: planning programming; budgeting

cost gradient (M2)

The increase in costs resulting from an enterprise being less than optimum size.

costing margin (D4, M2)

An addition to average direct costs to cover indirect costs and provide a normal level of net profit under FULL-COST PRICING. This rule is most likely to be used in a mature oligopolistic industry not faced with potential competition.

References

Andrews, P.W.S. (1949) *Manufacturing Business*, London: Macmillan.

cost, insurance and freight (F3)

The full-cost valuation of imports paid by purchasers. International trade statistics usually measure imports 'c.i.f.' so that all the charges of international trade are included in balance of payments accounts.

cost leader (L1)
The lowest cost producer of an industry. This leadership is usually established by ECONOMIES OF SCALE, exclusive rights over new technology or preferential access to raw materials. A cost advantage has often been the basis of monopoly power.

cost of living adjustment (J3)
A provision in a US labour contract providing for automatic wage increases in line with rises in the CONSUMER PRICE INDEX. Usually abbreviated to COLA.

cost of living index (J3)
Now termed in the UK the RETAIL PRICE INDEX. It shows changes in the cost of purchasing a bundle of goods and services representative of the average consumer. The Ministry of Labour and now its successor, the Department for Education and Employment, had to maintain this index as it is of crucial importance to wage bargaining.

See also: consumer price index

cost-push inflation (E3)
Inflation caused by an autonomous increase in costs in the absence of an increase in demand. The principal cost increases are wage increases forced by powerful trade unions, imported raw material costs pushed up by international producers' cartels and the profit MARK-UPS of oligopolistic firms.

cost ratio (M2)
The ratio to sales of factory costs, administrative costs, research and development costs, capital expenditure, selling costs or distribution costs.

cost-utility analysis (I1)
A method of evaluating health programmes by calculating the cost per effect produced of a medical procedure or treatment. Effects are converted into preferences or utilities. It makes use of QUALITY-ADJUSTED LIFE YEARS.

cottage industry (L0)
An industry whose production takes place in workers' homes. Handloom weaving before the INDUSTRIAL REVOLUTION was organized in this way; now, NETWORKING and TELECOMMUTING are home based.

See also: domestic system; home production; homework; networking economy; proto-industrialization

Council for Mutual Economic Aid (F0)
The intergovernmental council 'Comecon' of the USSR, Bulgaria, Czechoslovakia, Hungary, Poland and Romania established in 1949, which promoted mutual international trade and the co-ordination of national economic plans. (Albania joined in 1949, East Germany in 1950, Mongolia in 1962 and Vietnam in 1978; Romania weakened its ties in 1973 by making separate agreements with the European Community; Yugoslavia became an associate member in 1964; China and North Korea enjoyed observer status from 1964.) It was established by Stalin to provide a socialist 'market' to oppose the world-wide capitalist market – hence Comecon was called 'the Russian MARSHALL PLAN'. To Comecon were added the INTERNATIONAL BANK FOR ECONOMIC CO-OPERATION and the INTERNATIONAL INVESTMENT BANK as alternatives to the INTERNATIONAL MONETARY FUND. Initially, Comecon agreed on general goals for trade and technical assistance which led to the joint organization of scientific research, technical assistance in the building of industrial plants and the development of mineral resources. In 1954, a step was made towards economic integration by the co-ordination of five-year plans and in 1955 production priorities for member states were established. Multilateral trade agreements were recommended, as was the co-ordination of energy policies. Although in 1961 'Basic Principles' for the long-term plans of member countries were drawn up, Soviet proposals the following year for a single plan and a single planning authority were rejected as being an encroachment on national sovereignty. The International Bank for Economic Co-operation was chartered in 1963 to arrange multilateral

payments and short-term credits and the International Investment Bank was created in 1970 to finance specific projects which were part of co-ordinated five-year plans. In 1970, medium- and long-term co-operation up to 1980 was agreed; to implement this, central economic planning machinery was set up in Moscow. In 1987, direct links within Comecon between productive enterprises and research institutes of the USSR and Eastern Europe in the form of joint ventures were set up. To avoid currency negotiations, dividends could be paid in goods. The political convulsions of 1989 in Eastern Europe provoked some members of Comecon to call for a more market-oriented approach to their economic decision making. Comecon was dissolved in 1991.

References

Schiavone, G. (1981) *The Institutions of Comecon*, London: Macmillan.

council housing (R2)
UK housing owned by local governments. Less of the UK housing stock is now publicly owned as a result of the Conservative government policy in the 1980s of allowing council house tenants to purchase the houses which they had for a long time rented at less than market rates. Economists have been concerned that much of this housing has been let at less than market rents and by the impact on geographical labour mobility of access to housing being dependent on continued residence in the same locality.

Council of Economic Advisers (H1)
The team of three in the USA which advises the president on the state of the economy. This council was set up under the EMPLOYMENT ACT 1946. A principal task of the council is to assist the president in preparing his annual Economic Report to the Congress, a report formulating broad guidelines for stabilization policy and other aspects of the government's economic programme. The academics chosen as members of the council usually have

political views close to those of the administration.

References

Feldstein, M. (1992) 'The Council of Economic Advisers and Economic Advising in the United States', *Economic Journal* 102: 1223–34.

council tax (H2)
UK local property tax introduced in 1991 as a replacement of the COMMUNITY CHARGE. Poorest households are exempted from it; other households are assessed on the assumption that two adults live in the household (a single person would have a rebate of 25 per cent). The value of each property is placed within one of seven bands, which are defined differently for England, Scotland and Wales.

countercyclical policy (E3)
Government policy to reduce fluctuations in government spending which has to be such as to restore the economy to an equilibrium path, the trend line through cyclical fluctuations. Since 1933 Sweden has been the best-known user of such policies but in the 1950s, when DEMAND MANAGEMENT was believed to be a possible art, many Western economies used monetary, fiscal and other policies to reduce fluctuations in the gross domestic product and in employment. In less developed countries it is more difficult to have successful countercyclical measures: fluctuations in climate and in export demand (which are of central importance to primary producers) cannot be controlled by governments. Also, poverty itself is more a product of long-run factor shortages than deficiency in home demand, and taxation and expenditure affect a smaller percentage of the population.

See also: investment reserve system; Swedish budget

References

Baumol, W.J. (1961) 'Pitfalls in contracyclical policy: some tools and results',

Review of Economics and Statistics 43: 21–6.

counterparty capital (G2)

The capital required by a securities house to cover the risk that a party being dealt with in the settlement system has little or no credit to meet a payment due.

counterpurchase (F3)

COUNTERTRADE not entirely BARTER as the exporter requires part payment in cash.

countertrade (F3)

BARTER or parallel sales and purchases; a method of trade between East and West which has been used to minimize the need for East European countries to use hard currencies.

References

Hammond, G.T. (1990) *Countertrade: Offsets and Barter in International Political Economy*, London: Pinter.

Korth, C.M. (ed.) (1987) *International Countertrade*, New York: Quorum.

countervailing duty (F1)

A selective TARIFF on imports to counter government subsidies in the exporting nation. This is used to reduce some trade distortions.

countervailing power (J5, L1, M3, P0)

The power of an opposing group, e.g. of a trade union facing a large firm, or of a consumer facing a monopolist or oligopolist. The best examples of it occur under BILATERAL MONOPOLY. GALBRAITH regarded such power as a means of stabilizing and making fairer the capitalist system.

See also: consumer sovereignty

References

Galbraith, J.K. (1952) *American Capitalism: The Concept of Countervailing Power*, London: Hamish Hamilton; Boston: Houghton Mifflin.

country fund (G2)

A fund of stocks and shares invested in the securities of only one country. These funds provide a means of investing in countries whose stock exchanges allow only limited access by foreigners. As such funds are less liquid than OPEN-ENDED FUNDS which can invest globally, they often sell at a discount to their net asset value.

coupon (E4, G1)

1 Originally the warrant which had to be presented to obtain interest on a bond.

2 The nominal rate of interest, e.g. £5 per £100 of nominal stock. It is to be distinguished from the bond's YIELD, which will be higher than the coupon if the market price of the bond is lower than its nominal price, and vice versa.

Cournot, Antoine Augustin, 1801–77 (B3)

French mathematician and philosopher who was a major founder of MATHEMATICAL ECONOMICS. His important work, which was to inspire MARSHALL considerably, formulated the law of demand (with demand curves constructed for the first time in economics), rigorously expounded theories of DUOPOLY, BILATERAL MONOPOLY and OLIGOPOLY, and examined the incidence of INDIRECT TAXES and costs. As a French civil servant and academic he also wrote on probability and epistemology. His principal work on economics was *Recherches sur les Principes Mathématiques de la Théorie des Richesses* (1838), republished in English as *Researches into the Mathematical Principles of the Theory of Wealth* (New York, 1960).

References

Theocharis, R.D. (1983) *Early Developments in Mathematical Economics*, 2nd edn, ch. 9, London: Macmillan.

Cournot's duopoly model (D4, L1)

A market model of two springs and two proprietors, each of whom independently seeks to maximize their income. As proprietor A has no direct influence on the sales of water from proprietor B's spring, A can only adjust the price but B is forced to accept A's price. If A's sales are D_1, and B's sales are D_2, the final and stable equilibrium occurs where

$$f(D_1 + D_2) + D_1 f'(D_1 + D_2) = 0$$

$$f(D_1 + D_2) + D_2 f'(D_1 + D_2) = 0$$

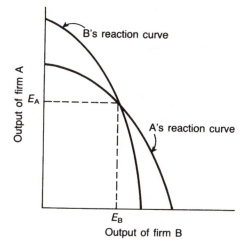

Output of firm A

E_A

B's reaction curve

A's reaction curve

E_B

Output of firm B

See also: duopoly

References

Cournot, A. (1897) *Researches into the Mathematical Principles of the Theory of Wealth*, trans. N.T. Bacon, ch. 7, New York: Macmillan.

cover (G1)
Earnings available to shareholders divided by the total amount of dividend paid. Thus, if cover is 3.2, the dividend is covered more than three times so it is unlikely that the dividend will have to be cut in the next year and the company has sufficient retained earnings to be able to expand. However, a company with a high cover for a number of years appears to be cautious and neglecting growth opportunities.

cowboy (M1)
A small-scale business, often in the construction industry, which dishonestly performs a contract and then rides away before non-performance of the contract is discovered.

cowboy economy (M0)
An economy, like the US economy, which behaves as if natural resources are infinite in supply and that Nature can absorb any amount of refuse. BOULDING coined this term to describe the 'Wild West' philosophy still prevalent in modern USA.

See also: spaceman economy

Cowles Commission (B2, C0)
US econometric research centre founded in Colorado Springs in 1932 and then moving to Chicago University in 1939 to avoid the Colorado state income tax which affected its publisher benefactor. It was noted in its early days for the distinctive econometric methodology of HAAVELMO and his followers which concentrated on the problems of simultaneity, identification and estimation.

See also: econometrics

References

Haavelmo, T. (1944) 'The probability approach in econometrics', *Econometrica* (Supplement) 12: 1–115.
Hildreth, C. (1986) *The Cowles Commission in Chicago, 1935–55*, Berlin: Springer Verlag.

CPI-U (E3)
A version of the US CONSUMER PRICE INDEX for all urban consumers covering about 80 per cent of the US population.

CPI-W (E3)
A version of the US CONSUMER PRICE INDEX for all urban wage earners and clerical workers covering about 32 per cent of the US population.

craft union (J5)
A TRADE (LABOR) UNION drawing all of its membership from a 'trade', i.e. a few closely related occupations, e.g. in engineering or printing. Many of the first unions in the UK and the USA were of this nature. Craft unionism has been blamed for much DEMARCATION, a practice which raises labour costs by insisting on a rigid subdivision of labour. Unskilled

workers, before forming general unions, resented the craft unions for maintaining a labour elite.

See also: general union; industrial union

crashometrics (G1)

The quantitative analysis of crashes in security or currency markets. This exercise provides a means of estimating the exposure of a portfolio to a market crash.

crawling peg (F3)

An exchange rate adjustment method which gradually changes the par value of an exchange rate by small amounts. This is less disruptive than DEVALUATION or revaluation as it does not encourage speculation.

creative accounting (M4)

The manipulation of the accounts of a firm or other enterprise to produce a more favourable picture of its financial state. Profits are made to appear higher to induce a rise in the company's share price; costs are inflated to justify product price increases. A variety of methods can be used, e.g. changing the method of allocating expenses, changing the valuation of assets and using more convenient exchange rates than those ruling at the time of the transaction. Some of these practices are within the rules of company law; others are so questionable as to amount to deception. UK local authorities in the 1980s used many devices to increase their spending, including selling their principal buildings and leasing them back, barter (e.g. exchanging council land for a new building), rescheduling debts and capitalizing current expenditure (e.g. including house repairs in their capital programme).

References

Griffiths, I. (1986) *Creative Accounting: How to Make Your Profits What You Want Them to Be*, London: Sedgeworth & Jackson.

creative destruction (O3, P1)

SCHUMPETER's description of the evolutionary process inherent in CAPITALISM consisting of entrepreneurs employing new products and new processes to supplant the old.

References

Schumpeter, J.A. (1976) *Capitalism, Socialism and Democracy*, 5th edn, New York: Harper; London: Allen & Unwin.

creative federalism (H7)

A co-operative partnership between the federal, state and local governments of the USA which led to many new programmes. President Lyndon B. Johnson used this term to describe US federalism in the 1960s.

See also: co-operative federalism; dual federalism; fiscal federalism

credit (G2)

1 A loan, or an agreement to lend money, to be repaid at a later date.
2 Bank lending (in macroeconomics) as credit is chiefly analysed within the context of the money supply.
3 All the sources of finance available to firms (including TRADE CREDIT) and to households.

In the past two decades there has been a great increase in the amount of credit given to households on the basis either of collateral (a house in the case of a building society mortgage) or of CREDIT SCORING for hire purchase expenditure on CONSUMER DURABLES. The creation of new credit instruments, e.g. the credit card, has resulted in an expansion in the total volume of credit.

References

Beckman, T.N. and Foster, R.S. (1969) *Credits and Collections: Management and Theory*, 8th edn, New York: McGraw-Hill.

credit card (G2)

A means of purchasing consumer goods and services by presenting a card issued by a bank, financial institution or retailer permitting the buyer to settle in part or in full the amount payable. Major examples of these include Visa and Mastercard. Such cards, in use in the USA since 1950 and in the UK since 1966, have contributed to the large increase in consumer debt. As the banks financing these cards advance the amount due to retailers and collect from the cardholders later, they bring about a short-term increase in the money supply. Like the development of other modern financial arrangements, credit cards have made it more difficult for central banks to control the money supply.

See also: affinity card; charge card; debit card; smart card

credit crunch (E5)

A shortage of bank loans and other forms of credit which brings about the curtailment of a business's activities or even its collapse. Credit can be limited by its price, by the type of borrower or by the state of the lender's balance sheet relative to the criteria used by a regulatory body (this often happened in the USA under REGULATION Q). The crunch comes under regulation because the lenders cannot use their own funds.

References

Wojnilower, A.M. (1980) 'The central role of credit crunches as recent financial history', *Brookings Papers on Economic Activity* 2: 277–326.

credit enhancement (G1)

A technique for improving the creditworthiness of a security or asset-backed debt. The collateral can be larger than the debt, or losses can be underwritten.

credit money (E4)

Banknotes and bank deposits which have been created by banks. This MEDIUM OF EXCHANGE has gradually displaced coinage made of precious metals.

credit multiplier (E4) *see* money multiplier

credit rating (G0, H0)

Measuring the creditworthiness of a government or corporation. For a govern-

ment, a scale from the lowest (0) to the best (100) using the information supplied by leading international banks is used; for corporations, the most famous rating is conducted by STANDARD & POOR.

credit rationing (E5)

Restricting the total amount which can be borrowed or excluding types of borrower so that a central bank can control the total volume of bank deposits. The aim of this rationing is to reduce the risk of borrowers defaulting or to prevent increases in interest rates. In the UK this was traditionally done by the BANK RATE, which provided the basis for all other interest rates. However, in the UK as elsewhere a greater variety of controls have been employed. The recent growth of new money markets, where interest rates are largely determined separately within each market, has weakened the power of central banks to exercise complete control.

See also: 'corset'; special deposit

credit reserves (F3)

Gold and foreign currency reserves of central banks which are used to settle intercountry indebtedness. Increasingly, major currencies, such as those of the USA, Germany, Japan, Switzerland and the UK, have been held in preference to gold.

credit scoring (G2)

Assessments of applicants for credit using a points system. A score is awarded for each of the applicant's characteristics, e.g. home ownership, employment and payment record for previous credit. Credit is granted if the total score is above the acceptance level.

credit spread (G1)

That part of the yield to maturity attributable to credit risk. Treasury bonds have no credit risk but financial instruments with less liquidity do.

credit tranche facility (F3)

An INTERNATIONAL MONETARY FUND lending facility to help a member country deal with a short-term balance of payments problem, similar to a COMPENSATORY FINANCIAL FACILITY. The loan has to be repaid over a three- to five-year period.

credit union (G2)
A friendly society whose members save to provide small loans to other members in need of financial assistance at an interest rate lower than the market rate. The group forming a credit union usually resides in the same area, or works for the same employer or belongs to another association, e.g. a church. In the depressed areas of the UK in the 1980s credit unions became popular alternatives to the main financial institutions. By 1990, 310 were formed in the UK with over 40,000 members; the USA has more than 60 million persons in credit unions; in Germany they appeared as early as the 1860s.

crisis (E3)
In Marxian economics, a phase of the TRADE CYCLE which is the upper turning point where an economy turns down from a boom to a recession. Marx believed that such crises were inevitable under CAPITALISM and would occur every ten years. A crisis could occur for two reasons. The preceding increase in employment pushes up wages and reduces the rate of profit below the normal level, cutting back capital accumulation. Also, producers who are slow to innovate have higher costs and may go bankrupt and cause a collapse of firms throughout the economy. Crises, according to Marxists, are inevitable under capitalism because of its continual capital accumulation without the co-ordination of investment decision making which planning would achieve.

References

Sweezy, P.M. (1942) *The Theory of Capitalist Development: Principles of Marxian Political Economy*, chs 8–10, New York: Oxford University Press; London: D. Dobson.

crisis management (H1, L2, Q2)
Working out strategies to deal with possible disasters, e.g. floods, interference with the quality of a product or an act of war. The police, fire and ambulance services have to consider worst case scenarios but firms also need contingency planning. They can maintain EXCESS CAPACITY and keep large inventories, e.g. to guard against a disruption in the supply of crucial components, as well as contracting to retain the services of other firms as back-up.

critical economy (E3, P0)
An atypical ECONOMY subject to disruptions and shocks.

critical value (C1)
The lower or upper value of a CONFIDENCE INTERVAL.

cross price elasticity of demand (C1, D0)
The responsiveness of the quantity demanded of one good to a change in the price of another good. It can be measured, for example, as the ratio of the percentage change in quantity demanded of good A to the percentage change in the price of good B. If A and B are substitutes the cross price elasticity is positive; it is negative if A and B are complements. The concept has been used extensively by analysts of market concentration and ANTITRUST lawyers as it indicates whether the dissimilar output from different firms is supplied to one or several markets.

See also: elasticity

cross-section data (C8)
Data referring to different groups at the same point in time, e.g. wages of workers in different countries at a particular date. Economic analysis based on time series data faces the problem of the effects of the passage of time on exogenous variables; cross-sectional analysis eliminates this difficulty.

cross-subsidization (L1, L3)
The financing of an unprofitable part of an enterprise by a more profitable part. A public enterprise, instead of following the

rule of attributing costs properly to each division to make each part of that enterprise individually financially accountable, could allow the profitable divisions to finance loss-making divisions. In the private sector, cross-subsidization occurs within firms if some of their products are sold at less than incremental cost. To ensure maximum efficiency, firms should avoid this practice as far as possible.

cross-trading (D4)
A method of disposing of all the goods a seller offers in a market by selling the same good at different prices throughout a trading day, with prices falling towards the end of the day.

crowding hypothesis (J2, J7)
The view that DISCRIMINATION occurs because some workers are crowded into the few occupations lacking barriers to entry. Women's wages, for example, have been depressed by an excess supply to the few jobs traditionally available for women. Both John Stuart MILL and EDGEWORTH used this model of discrimination.

See also: occupational segregation

crowding in (E2)
Public expenditure which stimulates private sector investment.

See also: crowding out

crowding out (E2)
An alleged effect on private sector demand of an increase in public expenditure. It was argued, especially by MONETARISTS, that KEYNESIAN--style budget deficits will raise borrowing with the effect of increasing interest rates which will lead to a reduction in private sector investment and expenditure on consumer durables. The stimulative effect of increased government expenditure will be cancelled out by expenditure reductions in the private sector. The reduction in business investment, in the long term, will further reduce the ability of the private sector to spend. The size of this effect depends strongly on the

ELASTICITY of IS-LM CURVES. In the figure, although an increase in government expenditure raises the IS curve from IS_1 to IS_2, because of the INELASTICITY of the LM curve the rate of interest rises from r_1 to r_2, without an increase in national income. Crowding out may also occur because increased government spending changes private sector expectations about the future of the economy, thereby reducing the amount of investment carried out.

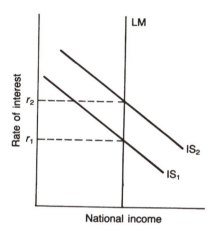

References
Carlson, K.M. and Spencer, R.M. (1975) 'Crowding out and its critics', *Federal Reserve Bank of St Louis Review* 57: 2–17.
Friedman, B.M. (1978) 'Crowding out or crowding in? Economic consequences of financing government deficits', *Brookings Papers on Economic Activity* 9: 593–641.

crude population rate (J1)
The ratio of births, deaths, or other demographic events, to the average total population of a country at the midpoint of a specified period, usually a year. These rates are called 'crude' because the population used in the denominator is not adjusted to give the measure theoretical significance, e.g. a crude birth rate per total population is less useful in a demographic model than a birth rate per women of child-bearing age.

C share (G1)

A Chinese stock market share owned only by state-owned enterprises. It is denominated and payable in either Chinese or foreign currency.

cultivated capital (E0, Q0)

A hybrid form of CAPITAL combining human-made and NATURAL CAPITAL, e.g. food, wood and natural fibres.

cultural economics (Z1)

The analysis of the demand for and production of literature, music, opera, drama, painting and sculpture. The peculiarities of the labour market for these performers and producers are analysed and the role of public subsidies considered.

References

Baumol, W.J. and Bowen, W.G. (1966) *The Economic Dilemma*, New York: The Twentieth Century Fund.

Peacock, A. and Rizzo, I. (1994) *Cultural Economics and Cultural Policies*, Dordrecht: Kluwer Academic.

Ruskin, J. (1857) *The Political Economy of Art*, London: Smith, Elder.

Cultural Revolution (N0)

A change in the organization of the Chinese society and economy in the late 1960s and 1970s. This revolution challenged the DIVISION OF LABOUR previously practised, especially by breaking down the division between the town and countryside. Revolutionary factory committees were set up to implement changes. These included using five-year plans only as general guidelines, requiring administrators to work two or three days per week in manual work and setting up of work teams involved in matters as diverse as production planning, assigning production tasks, establishing safety regulations and managing welfare funds. Mass action was used to unify the working class.

References

Bettelheim, C. (1974) *Cultural Revolution and Industrial Organization in China. Changes in Management and the Division of Labour*, trans. A. Ehrenfeld, New York and London: Monthly Review Press.

cum dividend (G2)

A stock exchange security with the entitlement to receive an imminent dividend.

cumulative multistage cascade system (H2)

A sales tax on the gross value of a commodity at each stage of production. It does not allow a rebate of taxes paid at earlier stages of production. This tax was in force in West Germany until the end of 1967, in Luxemburg until the end of 1969 and in the Netherlands until the end of 1968.

cumulative preference share (G1) *see* preference share

cumulative security (G1)

A stock exchange security which accumulates unpaid interest or preference dividends so that the holder does not suffer from a year of poor profitability. In return for this greater security of income, many cumulative PREFERENCE SHARES are without voting rights.

currencies of the world (F3) *see* Appendix A

currency (F3)

The official money currently circulating in a country and available for immediate use as a medium of exchange. It can take the form of coins, BANKNOTES and, in a broader sense, BANK DEPOSITS. Currencies are called by various names, the most popular being dollar, franc and kroner. The value of a currency is regarded as an overall indicator of world opinion about that country's economy. Apart from the use of prudent fiscal and monetary policies to boost confidence in a currency, there are other ways of making a currency attractive. A central bank can produce beautiful banknotes, offer CONVERTIBILITY into another currency or raise its interest rates to encourage foreign holdings of that currency. A few small countries – Luxemburg,

Panama and Liechtenstein – do not have their own currencies.

See also: coinage

currency appreciation (F3)

A rise in the international value of a currency. If, for example, more French francs are exchanged than previously for the same amount of US dollars, the dollar has appreciated.

currency basket (F3)

A combination of currencies to produce a common unit, e.g. the ECU. The values of these currencies are weighted, e.g. by shares in world trade or the gross national products of the countries participating.

currency cocktail (F3)

A mixture of contributing currencies, e.g. the ECU or SDR.

currency depreciation (F3)

A fall in the international value of a currency as less of another currency is exchanged for one unit of one's own. Residents of one country using the currency in other countries will have their purchasing power per unit of the currency reduced. Depreciation can occur very rapidly in foreign exchange markets in reaction to bad news about the state of the economy issuing the currency.

currency devaluation (F3)

A fall in a FIXED EXCHANGE RATE which reduces the value of a currency in terms of other currencies. The pound, for example, was devalued in 1949 from US$4.03 to US$2.80 and in 1967 from US$2.80 to US$2.40. The aim of devaluation is to improve the balance of payments CURRENT ACCOUNT. The change in the exchange rate by raising import prices and lowering export prices will reduce imports and increase exports, if there is a price-elastic demand for both and the possibility of diverting production to exports and substitutes for imports by reducing domestic expenditure.

See also: J-curve; Marshall–Lerner condition

currency market (F3) *see* foreign exchange market

currency reform (F3)

Replacing an existing currency which has lost its value with a new currency. Germany after the First and Second World Wars provides good examples of this. On an appointed day, holdings of the old currency are replaced by the new at a particular exchange rate. The intention of such reform is to restore confidence in the money used by a state. In some extreme cases where a currency has been severely devalued, it has changed its name, e.g. in Peru the sol de oro became the inti.

currency revaluation (F3)

A deliberate increase in the price of a currency with a fixed exchange rate. This is undertaken to reduce a balance of payments surplus. Revaluation is often urged by countries in deficit to enable them to compete more easily in international markets. As a consequence of a revaluation, a CENTRAL BANK suffers losses from the fall in value of its foreign exchange holdings: taxpayers ultimately bear these losses as central banks are usually owned by governments.

currency risk (F3)

The possibility of suffering a financial loss through holding a currency which falls in value. Supporters of the EURO argue that one of the principal arguments for monetary union is the reduction in this type of risk.

currency run (G2)

A great increase in the public's demand for cash because of the belief that other forms of finance, including CREDIT CARDS, will be ineffective. At the time of the beginning of the new millennium, 1 January 2000, many believed that only coins and banknotes were reliable at a time when widespread computer failures were possible.

Currency School (B1, N2)
A group of UK economists who, following RICARDO, believed that the note issue should be convertible and strictly determined by the amount of gold possessed by the Bank of England. The leaders of the school, Robert TORRENS and Samuel LOYD (later Lord Overstone), convinced Prime Minister Sir Robert Peel of their theory – hence the BANK CHARTER ACT 1844 which was to provide the framework for many of the operations of UK banking until 1980.

References
Felter, F.W. (1965) *Development of British Monetary Orthodoxy, 1719–1875*, Cambridge, MA: Harvard University Press.

currency stabilization scheme (F3)
An international arrangement by which a group of states agrees to link the exchange rate values of their currencies to gold, a leading currency (e.g. the US dollar) or an artificial currency. The first scheme in the post-1945 period was BRETTON WOODS; the major one in force at the beginning of the twenty-first century is the EUROPEAN MONETARY SYSTEM.

currency swap (F3)
A capital market exchange of a loan in one currency for a loan in another, e.g. a fixed interest dollar loan for a floating interest loan in Swiss francs.

current account (F4, G2)
1 A bank account of a UK CLEARING BANK immediately available for making payments. In the past, bank accounts of this type never earned interest; some now do. In the USA they are known as CHECKING ACCOUNTS or SIGHT DEPOSITS.
2 A sub-account of a nation's BALANCE OF PAYMENTS accounts consisting of visible and invisible trade plus private and official current transfers; capital flows are in the separate capital account.

See also: NOW account

current assets (M2)
The assets of a firm convertible into cash within a period of twelve months. They consist of stock in trade, work in progress, debts owed to the firm, readily realizable investments, bills receivable, prepayments, cash at the bank and in hand.

See also: current liabilities

current cost accounting (M4)
A form of accounting which includes adjustments for the effects of inflation. The UK's Statement of Standard Accounting Practice 1980 required several adjustments to be made: to DEPRECIATION for fixed assets which had risen in price, to sales figures for the higher cost of replacing stocks and to monetary working capital.

See also: inflation accounting; Sandilands Report

current deposit (G2)
A bank deposit of a UK bank which is payable on demand, now termed a SIGHT DEPOSIT.

See also: demand deposit; time deposit

current liabilities (M2)
The debts of a firm payable within the current accounting period, usually twelve months, which include sums owed by creditors and bills payable. These are liquid if payable within a month; otherwise, 'deferred'.

See also: current assets

current operating profit (M2)
The current value of output sold over a period, less the current cost of related inputs.

current population survey (J2)
A survey of US households undertaken by the US Census Bureau. Its monthly surveys are used to provide data on employment, unemployment, wages and hours statistics. Also it provides annual figures on school enrolments, living arrangements, annual incomes, poverty status and other important socioeconomic variables.

current prices (C1)
A measurement of an income variable at the prices of the period for which data

were collected; for example, consumption at current prices would show for years X, Y and Z the actual cost of purchasing such goods and services at the prices ruling in years X, Y and Z respectively.

current purchasing power (M2, M4)
The historic value of an asset adjusted by changes in a retail price index.

See also: inflation accounting

current ratio (M2)
The ratio of CURRENT ASSETS to CURRENT LIABILITIES of a firm. Also known as a working capital ratio or 2:1 ratio following the rule of thumb that assets should be twice liabilities, unless the seasonal or speculative nature of the firm requires more working capital. This is the principal measure of the LIQUIDITY of a firm.

customize (L2)
To modify the standard design of a CONSUMER DURABLE by minor changes in its appearance or functions to allow its owner to express his or her personality, e.g. replacing small car/automobile wheels by larger ones.

customs union (F0)
A group of countries with a COMMON EXTERNAL TARIFF but with free trade amongst themselves and free movement of labour and capital. The EUROPEAN COMMUNITY is a major example of such an arrangement. Many theories about customs unions are based not only on how free trade based on COMPARATIVE ADVANTAGE is beneficial but also on LOCATION THEORY to understand the changes within the customs union, e.g. the movement of capital and population towards GROWTH POLES creating a dynamic effect of a union.

cycles (E4)
Regular fluctuations in a national economy from a peak through a downswing to a trough and then an upswing back to the peak. Few national economies are without this instability.

See also: boom and bust; business cycle; Juglar cycle; Kitchin cycle; Kondratieff cycle; Kuznets cycle; stop–go

cyclical trade (F1)
A type of INTRA-INDUSTRY TRADE, particularly in agricultural products which are traded north to south between the two hemispheres in one harvest and south to north in the other part of the year.

cyclical unemployment (J6)
Recurrent unemployment occurring at particular phases of the business cycle, starting with the downturn from a boom. This unemployment is caused by a deficiency of AGGREGATE DEMAND and is associated with a fall in the number of job vacancies.

cyclical variations (C1)
Movements in a TIME SERIES brought about by the BUSINESS or TRADE CYCLE. These components of changes in the values of a variable can be removed from raw data by first removing seasonal variations by making a SEASONAL ADJUSTMENT and then dividing the adjusted data by corresponding trend values.

D

D (G1)

A SECURITY of questionable value according to the rating agency Standard & Poor.

See also: AAA; BBB; BB; Q DDR

daisy-chain scheme (H2, M2)

A commercial scheme for passing a commodity through a chain of company subsidiaries to avoid taxation.

Dalton improving tax reform (H2)

An income transfer from a household of high social rank to a lower ranking household that does not change the ranking of households. This MARGINAL TAX change yields a marginal improvement in social welfare.

References

Dalton, H. (1920) 'The measurement of the inequality of income', *Economic Journal* 30: 348–61.

data (C8)

Measured observations obtained from officially or privately collected statistics: the raw material of empirical economics.

data-mining (C1)

Persistent and repeated attempts to find significant relationships between variables. However, the excessive zeal of the researcher may produce a false relationship. This misuse of ECONOMETRICS gives undue prominence to insignificant economic relationships.

David Hume Institute (H0)

An economic research institute founded in 1985 and now based in Edinburgh, Scotland, with Sir Alan Peacock as its first executive director. It has examined the economics of regulation, broadcasting, small firms and banking.

Davignon Plan (L5)

The plan of the European Coal and Steel Community in 1980 to restructure the European steel industry; named after the EUROPEAN COMMUNITY's Industry Commissioner, Viscount Etienne Davignon. State aid was offered (mainly for environmental improvements or research and development) provided that there was a cut in steel-making capacity. Minimum prices were set together with production quotas to cover 85 per cent of the European Community's output. The plan succeeded in scrapping production quotas by the end of 1987 and using MARKET FORCES to complete the adjustment process.

Davos man (F0)

A businessman, banker, official or intellectual who is a literate and numerate graduate with a belief in individualism, market economics and democracy. These men, from any culture, control governments and their economic capabilities. The World

Economic Forum is held annually in Davos, Switzerland.

dawn raid (G1)
A method of acquiring the shares of a company popular in London in the early 1980s. A company was taken over by rapid purchase of shares at the beginning of the working day. Since shares were acquired at different prices, the International Stock Exchange Council has now regulated this technique.

days of grace (G0)
The extra days after a debt, e.g. an insurance premium, is due in which the debtor is allowed to pay.

day trade (G1)
The purchase and sale of a stock market security in a margin account within the same day. Also known as daylight trade.

See also: bed and breakfast

DDD (G1)
Standard & Poor's credit rating of a security which reflects that servicing of it is in default or in arrears.

See also: AAA; BBB; BB; C; D

dead cat bounce (G1)
A short lived rise in the price of a stock that had dropped considerably.

deadweight loss (D6)
A loss of CONSUMER'S SURPLUS by buyers not matched by a corresponding PRODUCER'S

SURPLUS. This concept is crucial to much of WELFARE ECONOMICS, e.g. the analysis of the effects of a monopoly, of taxes and of tariffs. The size of the deadweight loss depends on the ELASTICITY of demand or supply.

Deane, Phyllis Mary, 1918– (B3)
Educated at Glasgow University. Research officer at the National Institute for Economic and Social Research from 1941 to 1945, at the Colonial Office from 1946 to 1949 and at the Department of Applied Economics, Cambridge University, from 1950 to 1951. Fellow of Newnham College, Cambridge, from 1961 to 1983 and professor of economic history from 1981 to 1982. She has produced several works on colonial national income accounting and the celebrated *The First Industry Revolution* (Cambridge University Press, 1965) and *The Evolution of Economic Ideas* (Cambridge University Press, 1978), one of the finest introductions to the history of economic thought.

debasing a currency (F3)
An action taken by a monetary authority to reduce the value of the money it issues, e.g. by diminishing the intrinsic value of the currency or by over-issuing banknotes. This is mainly done to finance government expenditure and to extract a high level of SEIGNORAGE.

debenture (G1)
A company or corporation security, usually taking the form of a fixed interest loan, secured on the assets of a company.

debit card (G2)
A card which makes possible the immediate debiting of a bank account at the time of purchasing goods or services; an 'electronic cheque book'. In the late 1980s major UK clearing banks, for example, made arrangements with retailers to introduce this system which makes possible transactions without the use of CASH, CHEQUES or CREDIT CARDS. Credit is only given to debit cardholders with permission to overdraw.

MP monopoly profits
DW deadweight loss
MR marginal revenue
LAC long-run average cost
LMC long-run marginal cost

Debreu, Gerard, 1921– (B3)

A French émigré to the USA in 1948, educated in mathematics in Paris and subsequently professor at Chicago, Yale and Berkeley (since 1960) Universities. With Arrow in 1954, he used topological methods to prove the existence of GENERAL EQUILIBRIUM. His *Theory of Value: an Axiomatic Analysis* (1959, 1971) produced a more sophisticated exposition of competitive price theory, using set theory and topology. In 1983 he was awarded the NOBEL PRIZE FOR ECONOMICS. His work is theoretical rather than empirical in nature.

References

Debreu, G. (1983) *Mathematical Economics: Twenty Papers of Gerard Debreu*, Cambridge: Cambridge University Press.

debt (G0, M2)

The liabilities of a firm, a government or a household. A company's debt often takes the form of fixed interest DEBENTURES, cumulative non-voting preference shares and short-term bank loans. A government has BILLS as short-term debt and long-term debt issued as BONDS. A household's debts include bank loans and liabilities incurred to purchase property and consumer durables.

debt contract (G0)

An agreement to lend money.

debt–equity swap (F3, G2)

The exchange of a fixed interest debt for an equity shareholding. Countries with large debts to Western banks have been offered this solution to their indebtedness. Previously, swaps took the form of banks giving loans to companies wanting to make an investment in a debtor country. Fixed interest debt has also grown in Third World countries because of their lack of developed stock markets.

See also: securitization

debt finance (G2)

Short- or long-term fixed interest finance that does not involve the transfer of ownership but usually requires collateral.

Whatever the financial success or failure of an enterprise the commitment to servicing the debt remains. It is contrasted with EQUITY finance.

debt illusion (H0)

Voters' lack of awareness of the cost of public sector expenditure being financed by borrowing rather than taxation. They cannot perceive correctly the present value of future benefits in the public sector because of imperfect information, with the consequence that a larger amount of public expenditure is approved.

See also: fiscal illusion; renter illusion

debt-led growth (O4)

Economic development financed by borrowing, usually from foreign countries. This turned out to be a disastrous policy in the 1970s leading to the THIRD WORLD DEBT PROBLEM.

debt neutrality (G0)

Non-responsiveness of a portfolio of investments to changes in the mixture of taxes and borrowing used by a government to finance the public sector's real spending programme on goods and services.

debt policy (H7)

The course of action taken to manage a country's NATIONAL DEBT. The official approach often adopted is to maintain market conditions so as to maximize the present and future demand for government debt, but such a policy stance may be in conflict with credit/interest rate policy.

debt ratio (G0) *see* gearing

debt restructuring (G0)

Changing the MATURITIES of the debts of a government or a firm so that it is easier to service them. Restructuring often takes the form of lengthening the maturity of debt. It is allowed by creditors who would otherwise have little prospect of receiving interest and repayment of the PRINCIPAL.

debt security (G0)

A loan made by an investor to an issuer

who agrees to repay the debt at a specified date and to pay interest. These securities are issued by both governments and corporations and can be linked to an EQUITY issued by a financial intermediary.

debt service indicator (G0)
A measure of the ability of a borrower to meet capital and interest payments on a debt. Indicators used include the debt service ratio (interest and capital repayments due divided by export earnings), the cash flow ratio (current account surplus minus interest payments divided by export earnings), and the solvency ratio (the percentage of a country's export earnings which it would have to devote to debt servicing to keep its total debt–export ratio on a declining trend).

debt sustainability (F4)
The calculation of the projected earnings from exports relative to the cost of servicing the external debt of a country.

See also: debt trap

debt trap (G0)
The consequence for a government, or an individual, of borrowing at a rate of interest greater than the rate of growth of its income causing its current expenditure on items other than debt servicing to be increasingly reduced.

decelerator (H3)
A fiscal change, e.g. a cut in public expenditure or an increase in taxation, which counteracts the expansionary effects of the investment ACCELERATOR.

decentralized market economy (P0)
An ECONOMY in which economic agents below the level of central government take major investment, production and pricing decisions. Allocation is according to market conditions rather than planning targets.

See also: centrally planned economy; economic devolution

decile (C1)
The value obtained from a set of data

arranged in order of magnitude by dividing it into ten equal parts. The first, or lowest, decile is sometimes used as a benchmark for calculating LOW PAY.

See also: lower quartile; median; percentile; upper quartile

decimalization (E5)
A change in the currency of a country so that the basic unit is divisible into ten parts. The French franc and US dollar have been divided into a hundred cents since the eighteenth century and the Australian dollar since 1966. In the UK in 1971 the pound, previously divisible into twenty shillings or 240 pence, was made equivalent to 100 new pence. It is feared that this type of currency change leads to consumers losing their PRICE PERCEPTION and unwittingly accepting price increases. However, the quotation of prices in old and new forms reduces this disguised inflation.

decision cycle (D0, E6)
The recurrent round of economic decisions made by national governments and other economic agents. Exchange rate decisions have to be made several times a day; many commodity prices and interest rates are changed weekly; tax changes, wages and product prices mainly annually. Major investment decisions are made infrequently.

decision variable (C6) *see* choice variable

deconcentration (L1, L4)
1 Dispersal of an industry over a wider area.
2 The break-up of an industry dominated by a few firms. This has occurred under ANTITRUST legislation.

decreasing returns (D2) *see* returns to scale

dedicated budget (H6)
A budget which permits the use of funds for specified types of public expenditure only because of strict legislation. Much US federal budgeting has this inflexibility

so further Congressional approval is needed to make some public spending changes.

See also: earmarking; ringfencing

deemed tax (H2)
US corporate tax concession equal to the amount of total income already paid to a foreign government. If a US corporation has paid $10 million tax abroad on a pre-tax income of $20 million when it remits $5 million in dividends to the USA its deemed tax will be $10 million × 0.5.

deep discount bond (G1)
A bond paying little or no interest which is sold below its redemption value. Investors make a capital gain by holding it to the date of redemption and, in many cases, reduce their total tax burden as income taxation is often more punitive than capital gains taxation.

deep integration (F1)
An association of national economies going beyond FREE TRADE to a harmonizing of national economic regulations. Increasingly the EUROPEAN UNION has pursued this course to realize its original objectives.

de *facto* population (J1)
A population count based on where people were on census night. This is a popular form of census, especially in developing countries.

See also: *de jure* population

deficiency payment (H2, Q1)
A form of governmental subsidy to farmers equal to the difference between the market price of an agricultural commodity and the price set under an agricultural policy. The purpose of the payment is to achieve a desired level of farmers' incomes.

See also: intervention price

deficit financing (F4, H6)
1 Government spending not fully financed by government revenue usually undertaken to reduce unemployment and to stimulate the growth of output.

This type of financing, also known as 'pump priming', has often taken the form of PUBLIC WORKS. KEYNES recommended that the government's current expenditure budget should be in balance but that its capital budget could go into deficit in times when aggregate demand needed to be stimulated.

2 The financing of a BALANCE OF PAYMENTS deficit.

See also: functional financing

deflation (E3, E6)
1 A reduction in AGGREGATE DEMAND. A deflationary policy of extra taxation and lower public expenditure is chosen by governments to correct balance of payments deficits and to lower the price level.
2 A fall in the average price level.
3 The elimination of price increases from an index of production or consumption. Economic statisticians are frequently engaged in 'deflating' time series to separate real from nominal changes.

deflationary gap (E6)
The excess of AGGREGATE SUPPLY over AGGREGATE DEMAND of a national economy. This overall situation of an economy at less than FULL EMPLOYMENT has often encouraged KEYNESIAN policies of deficit spending.

degrees of freedom (C1)
The number of observations in a sample minus the number of population PARAMETERS to be estimated by the sample.

de-industrialization (L6)
The decline of a country's manufacturing industry absolutely or relatively. This fall in manufacturing activity is most noticeable in employment, but a slower rate of growth, or even a fall, in output and a fall in the world share of trade in manufactures also measure this change. Most OECD countries have experienced de-industrialization in the past twenty years as economic activity has switched from manufacturing to service industries. Marxist economists

are especially concerned with this because of their view that what is productive is the creation of goods, not of services.

References

Blackaby, F. (1979) *De-Industrialisation*, London: Heinemann Educational.

Bluestone, B. and Harrison, B. (1982) *The Deindustrialization of America: Plant Closings, Community Abandonment, and the Dismantling of Basic Industry*, New York: Basic Books.

Rodwin, L. and Sazanami, H. (eds) (1989) *Deindustrialization and Regional Economic Transformation: The Experience of the United States*, Boston and London: Unwin Hyman.

Saeger, S.S. (1997) 'Globalization and the Deindustrialization: Myth and Reality in the OECD', *Weltwirtschaftliches Archiv* 133: 579–608.

de jure population (J1)

The population permanently resident in a particular area.

See also: *de facto* population

delinking (F1)

The breaking off of trading and other relationships between Third World countries and Western countries. It is argued that the benefits of such a course of action include an increased freedom to shape the development of that country, as well as less chance of economic exploitation by foreign investors.

See also: dependency theory

Delors Plan (F0)

The plan of the European Community Committee for the Study of Economic and Monetary Union of 1989 chaired by Jacques Delors, the President of the EUROPEAN COMMUNITY. The European Community set up the committee to propose a progression from the SINGLE EUROPEAN ACT 1986 to a SINGLE CURRENCY and a common MONETARY POLICY throughout the European Community. It was proposed that there should be three stages in the movement to the committee's goals. The first stage would

be the greater convergence of economic performance through co-ordination of budgetary and monetary policies, possibly with a European Reserve Fund with reserves drawn from each participating central bank. The second stage would provide a medium-term framework for key economic objectives so that stable economic growth could be achieved. Finally precise rules of a non-binding nature would be created for annual budgets and the finance of government activity, and a European System of Central Banks for the formulation of a common monetary policy would be set up. It was later agreed to let the EURO replace national currencies in 2002.

See also: Eurofed; European Monetary System; European Monetary Union; Werner Report

References

Committee for the Study of Economic and Monetary Union (1989) *Report on Economic and Monetary Union in the European Community*, Luxemburg: Office for Official Publications of the European Communities.

Delphi method (M2)

A method of business forecasting used by many large US corporations consisting of panels of experts expressing their views of the future and then revising them in the light of their colleagues' views so that bias and extreme opinions can be eliminated

See also: alpha stock; beta stock; gamma stock

delta stock (G1)

The least traded stocks and shares which are not quoted on the STOCK EXCHANGE AUTOMATED QUOTATION SYSTEM.

demand (D0)

1 The amount of factors of production, or of their products, desired at a particular price. This is shown graphically in a DEMAND CURVE.

2 Total expenditure on a good or service.

demandable debt instruments (G0)
Banknotes, current/checking bank accounts.

demand curve (D0)
A graph relating the quantity demanded of a good, service or factor of production to different prices of it. Although John STUART MILL first had the idea of such schedules, it was COURNOT and the MARGINALISTS who introduced them to economics. As the curve shows the relationship between only two variables, the CETERIS PARIBUS assumption has to be made. Much controversy has arisen about the nature of the MARSHALLIAN DEMAND CURVE, particularly the circumstances under which there can be a movement along the demand curve without affecting the assumption that real income is constant. The normal demand curve is assumed to be downward sloping because of the psychological belief underlying the LAW OF DIMINISHING MARGINAL UTILITY.

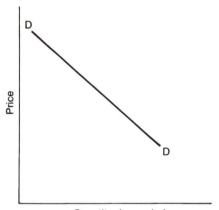

Quantity demanded

See also: Giffen paradox; price–consumption curve

demand deposit (G2)
Funds held at a bank with a notice period of less than seven days. They can take many forms, including CHECKING ACCOUNTS, certified cashier's and officer's cheques, travellers' cheques, LETTERS OF CREDIT sold

for cash, withheld taxes, withheld insurance and TIME DEPOSITS whose notice of withdrawal has expired.

See also: NOW account

demand for money (E4)
The demand for cash or a bank deposit, not for an asset such as a stock certificate or bond. KEYNES, by distinguishing the TRANSACTIONS, PRECAUTIONARY and SPECULATIVE DEMANDS FOR MONEY revolutionized monetary theory. It is a broader theory about the motivation for holding money than the QUANTITY THEORY OF MONEY that money is held solely for transactions purposes. The demand for money by a representative individual can be considered in terms of MARGINAL UTILITY as being the result of balancing the imputed yield from holding it (the convenience and security of a cash holding) against the cost in terms of interest income forgone. Discussions of MONETARISTS' views have led to many econometric studies of demand for money functions which have shown them to be less stable than originally asserted.

References
Fisher, D. (1989) *Money Demand and Monetary Policy*, Hemel Hempstead: Harvester Wheatsheaf.

demand management (E5, H3)
Discretionary changes in national MONETARY and FISCAL POLICIES attempting to change the level of AGGREGATE DEMAND. Under the influence of KEYNESIANISM such policies were very popular in the 1950s and 1960s. However, some critics of demand management have asserted that frequent changes destabilized the economy.

See also: fine-tuning

demand-pull inflation (E3)
INFLATION originating in EXCESS DEMAND. KEYNES introduced this approach to inflation in his *How to Pay for the War* (1940). The notion of an 'INFLATIONARY GAP', i.e. an excess of AGGREGATE DEMAND over AGGREGATE SUPPLY at FULL EMPLOYMENT, was used

to explain this phenomenon instead of the view inherent in the QUANTITY THEORY OF MONEY that inflation was caused by an increase in the money supply. The fullest form of demand-pull inflation is when excess demand occurs in both factor and product markets.

See also: demand-shift inflation

demand-shift inflation (E3)
INFLATION brought about by a structural change in an economy which permanently raises demand. This is a consequence of increases in wages and in the prices of capital goods in expanding sectors being communicated to other sectors. It is a mixed form of inflation as changes in both demand and cost bring about the ultimate increase in product prices.

demarcation (J2, J5)
Reserving work activities for a particular occupation. Thus, for example, in an engineering plant where there is demarcation, tasks will be assigned separately to mechanical, electrical and electronics engineers. CRAFT UNIONS, anxious to protect the work available for their members, have been keen to follow this practice, especially in the UK. The inflexibility in the use of labour brought about by this practice has lowered productivity and increased labour costs.

See also: job control unionism

dematerialization (G1)
Paperless settlement of stock exchange transactions.

See also: paperless entry; Taurus

demerger (L1) *see* unbundling

demerit good (H0) *see* merit bad

demographic accounting (J1)
The tabulation of the population according to its characteristics and its states (at birth, death and place) at various dates.

References

Stone, R. (1971) *Demographic Accounting and Model-building*, Paris: OECD.

demographic transition (J1)
A model showing a society's population changes through four stages (see the figure). Stage 1 is the traditional society with little population growth, a stable population with a high birth rate counteracted by an equally high death rate. Stage 2 shows rapid population growth because improved health care has pushed down the death rate but the birth rate is still high.

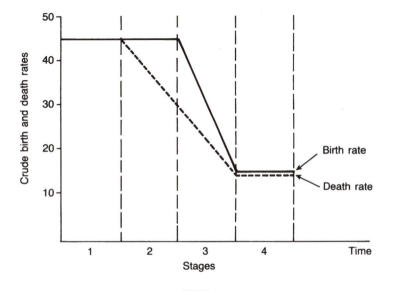

Stage 3 has a population decline caused by couples desiring fewer children. Stage 4 is a mature society with a stable population brought about by higher incomes and better education, where couples have about two children each. Many Third World countries are still in the second stage; most of the OECD countries are in stage 4.

References

Caldwell, J.C. (1976) 'Toward a restatement of demographic transition theory', *Population and Development Review* 2: 321–66.
Notestein, E.W. (1945) 'Population: the long view', in T.W. Schultz (ed.) *Food for the World*, Chicago: University of Chicago Press.

demography (J1)

The study of the size and composition of human populations, particularly their births, deaths and migration. Both historical recording and projections of future populations are calculated to provide the basis for economic and social planning.

See also: population census; Malthus; Petty

References

Pressat, R. (1972) *Demographic Analysis. Methods, Results, Applications*, London: Edward Arnold; Chicago: Aldine Atherton.

demometrics (J1)

The measurement of the relationship between socioeconomic variables and demographic variables, e.g. between income levels and interregional migration.

denationalized money (E4)

Money issued by a variety of private and foreign banks and not by a national government. This money is less likely to be debased. This diminution of the role of the state enables banks to benefit from SEIGNORAGE.

See also: debasing a currency; free banking

References

Hayek, F.A. (1990) *Denationalisation of Money - the Argument Refined*, 3rd edn, London: Institute of Economic Affair.

Denison residual (O4)

Advances in knowledge and associated causes of economic growth. Denison discovered this important growth determinant in his study of the USA and eight West European countries for the period 1950–62.

References

Denison, E.F. (1967) *Why Growth Rates Differ*, ch. 20, Washington, DC: Brookings Institution.

Denison's law (E2)

This states that the private sector saving of companies and households is a constant proportion of national income. This relationship held for twenty-five years but it is now being disputed.

References

Denison, E. F. (1958) 'A Note on Private Saving', *Review of Economics and Statistics*, 40: 261–7.

department (M1, P1)

1 Part of an economy or economic organization.
2 A branch of capitalist production, according to MARX. He divided the economy into three departments: Department I, the means of production, i.e. energy, machines and tools, raw materials and buildings; Department II, consumer goods which reconstitute both the labour force and capitalists, contributing to their well-being; Department III, luxury goods, weapons, which renew neither constant nor variable capital.

dependency culture (D6, H2)

A society, or major part of it, permanently dependent on TRANSFER INCOMES because the extensive provision of welfare benefits has inhibited work and individual effort. Several governments, including those of the USA and the UK, fear that benefits fix the poor in a perpetual state of relative deprivation. It is also argued that excessive international AID can have the same effect on whole countries.

dependency ratio (I3, J1)

The proportion of a population which has to be supported by recipients of FACTOR INCOMES. It is commonly measured as

$$\frac{\text{children under the age of 15} + \text{adults over 64}}{\text{number of adults in the labour force}} \times 100 \text{ per cent}$$

The value of this ratio is large when persistently high birth rates have increased the proportion of children in a population, or much international emigration has left an old population.

See also: grey society

dependency theory (O1)

Exploitation theory applied to small countries. A small country exporting agricultural commodities finds that the control of its economy, especially its trade, shipping, insurance, banking and port facilities, passes to foreigners who are often associated with a local wealthy elite. The economy suffers from the repatriation of profits and imports, both of which are detrimental to domestic industries. The deterioration in local industry reduces industrial employment and pushes indigenous workers into the subsistence sector. In order to counteract the losses created by dependency, these theorists recommend fast independent growth and the granting of priority to basic needs. Critics argue that the theory at best is applicable only to some tropical colonies in the 1900–50 era, that it exaggerates the extent of profit repatriation and that it fails to establish a single optimal set of prices.

References

Frank, A.G. (1978) *Dependent Accumulation and Underdevelopment*, London: Macmillan.

Smith, T. (1995) 'The underdevelopment of development literature: the case of dependency theory', in S. Haggard (ed.) *The International Political Economy and the Developing Countries*, Vol. 1, pp. 300–41, Aldershot: Edward Elgar.

dependent economy (F0, P0)

An economy closely linked with another, either through economic treaties (see COMECON) or through dependence on a narrow range of exported goods. Many Third World countries are dependent on a single export, e.g. Mauritius on sugar and Zaire on copper.

See also: branch economy

depletable externality (D0)

An EXTERNALITY which by affecting one person affects others less, e.g. horse manure used in gardening.

See also: pollution control

deposit account (G2)

An interest-bearing bank account (UK) which cannot be withdrawn without due notice (in most cases, at least seven days). In the USA, such accounts are known as savings accounts or time deposits.

deposit base (E4, G2)

Narrow money.

See also: M0; M1

deposit insurance (G2)

Insurance used to protect deposits held in banks and other financial institutions. In the USA, the major scheme has been the FEDERAL DEPOSIT INSURANCE CORPORATION which from 1933 insured the deposits of the member banks of the FEDERAL RESERVE SYSTEM and of non-member banks choosing to join. Instability in the banking system of the USA in the 1990s put deposit insurance under a great strain. Critics argued that insurance made banks more reckless in their lending policies, causing the financial difficulties which insurance sought to avoid.

See also: Banking Act 1979; Resolution Trust Corporation

Depository Institutions Deregulation and Monetary Control Act 1980 (G2, K2)

US federal statute which increased fair competition in US banking by imposing universal reserve requirements of 3 per cent for the first $25 million of deposits and 12 per cent of further deposits on COMMERCIAL BANKS, mutual savings banks, SAVINGS BANKS, SAVINGS AND LOAN ASSOCIATIONS and CREDIT UNIONS. The FEDERAL RESERVE SYSTEM was empowered to demand supplementary reserves of 4 per cent of deposits for a maximum of ninety days and allowed to charge for its services. NOW ACCOUNTS were legalized and many interest rate ceilings phased out.

See also: Hunt Commission

deposit-taking business (G2)

A COMMERCIAL BANK, or other financial institution, licensed to conduct financial business according to the rules of a CENTRAL BANK, e.g. the Bank of England.

See also: Banking Act 1979

depreciation (F3, M4)

1 The decline in value of an asset measured by various accounting rules of thumb. Under the straight-line method, the annual amount of depreciation is equal to a fraction of the capital expenditure (the value of an asset divided by its life). Other methods include the 'declining balance' approach which makes depreciation equal to a fraction of the written-down value of the asset, and the 'sum of digits' approach under which a fraction of the capital expenditure declines linearly over time. True economic depreciation, the replacement cost of physical wear and tear, is difficult to calculate as capital markets are often imperfect.

2 The fall in value of a currency under a FLOATING EXCHANGE RATE regime.

See also: currency appreciation

depression (E3)

A fall in national output continuing for a few years. Over the past 200 years, there have been several depressions, especially in the nineteenth century, in the economies of Western countries. The term is often used loosely to refer to a period of extensive unemployment and business failures. The start of the 1930s is usually cited as the major recent example of a depression in the strict sense.

See also: Great Depression; recession

References

Bernanke, B.S. (2000) *Essays on the Great Depression*, Princeton, NJ: Princeton University Press.

Hall, T.E. and Ferguson, J.D. (1998) *The Great Depression: An international disaster of perverse economic policies*, Ann Arbor: University of Michigan Press.

deprival value (M4)

A measure of the value of an asset to its owner; the lower of the replacement cost or ECONOMIC VALUE.

See also: Sandilands Report

deregulation (K2, L5)

Abolition of governmental regulations, especially for prices and the operations of publicly owned organizations, with the aims of lowering prices through more competition, and of stimulating the growth of small businesses. Examples of deregulation include the securities markets of New York and London, US airlines and UK buses. Deregulation of stock markets occurred in the USA in 1975, in the UK in 1986 and in Japan gradually in the mid-1980s. In banking the USA amended its regulatory bank legislation in the DEPOSITORY INSTITUTIONS DEREGULATION AND MONETARY CONTROL ACT OF 1980 and the GARN–ST GERMAIN DEPOSITORY INSTITUTIONS ACT OF 1982, to remove ceilings on interest rates and to allow THRIFTS to diversify their financial activities, e.g. credit cards and commercial and industrial loans.

Critics of deregulation argue that safety suffers, industries are destabilized and there is less provision for underused services thought desirable for social reasons.

Some large bank failures in the 1980s were partly attributed to the removal of regulatory safeguards.

See also: economic devolution

References

Kahn, A.E. (1988) *The Economics of Regulation*, Cambridge, MA: MIT Press.

Majone, G. (1990) *Deregulation or Re-regulation? Regulatory Reform in Europe and the United States*, London: Pinter.

derivative (C6, G1)

1 A sophisticated financial product, e.g. SWAP, WARRANT, OPTION or FUTURE available in security, commodity and currency markets. The product is derived from a simple transaction in a SPOT MARKET.

2 A function $f(x)$ of x which shows the slope of a graph of the function x. For the function x to be at a maximum or a minimum, it is necessary that this derivative be zero. Major derivatives in economics include MARGINAL COST, MARGINAL REVENUE, the MARGINAL PROPENSITY TO CONSUME, the MARGINAL PROPENSITY TO IMPORT and the MARGINAL PRODUCT OF LABOUR.

derived demand (D0)

The demand for a factor of production derived from the demand for its product, e.g. there is a demand for labour in the construction industry because of a demand for houses. Demand for a product and the derived demand for a factor will change by the same proportion if the input–output ratio is constant, which is unlikely in a period of technological change.

deserving poor (I3)

Those with low incomes through no fault of their own, e.g. the victims of a trade DEPRESSION. The distinction between the deserving and undeserving poor has been used to deprive the latter of welfare benefits.

See also: Poor Laws; poverty

designated competitive bidding (M2)

A restricted form of offer in which firms wishing to participate are screened for their expertise and location.

destructive competition (L1)

Fierce competition, often in the form of price wars, which drives many firms out of an industry and weakens those that remain.

See also: creative destruction

devalorization (D0)

The process that reduces the value of CAPITAL through a fall in the price of intermediate or final goods, or as a result of bankruptcy.

devaluation (F3) *see* currency devaluation

development (O1, O4)

1 The movement of an economy from agricultural activities using simple technology to the production of industrial products and a range of services using modern technology. (Even in the seventeenth century PETTY regarded development as the growth of service industries.)

2 The cumulative growth of per capita income, accompanied by structural and institutional changes. Although per capita income is a crude measure unless problems of measuring the GROSS DOMESTIC PRODUCT and its distribution are taken into account, this is often the best proxy measure. Post-1945 development policies have often failed to help the poorest 40 per cent of the world's population. Although many aid programmes have an urban bias, they have widely achieved lower rates of infant mortality, more hospital beds, an increased supply of piped water and the building of many all-season roads.

See also: industrialization

References

Kitching, G. (1989) *Development and Underdevelopment in Historical Perspective.*

Populism, Nationalism and Industrialization, rev. edn, London: Routledge.

Lipton, M. (1977) *Why Poor People Stay Poor*, London: Temple Smith.

Little, I.M.D. (1982) *Economic Development: Theory, Policy and International Relations*, New York: Basic Books.

Myrdal, G. (1956) *Development and Underdevelopment*, Cairo: National Bank of Egypt.

development bank (G2, O1)

A bank specializing in the provision of finance for development projects in developing countries and depressed regions. Major international development banks use both capital subscribed by donor countries and capital borrowed from international capital markets to support particular projects and programmes, often over the medium term. The principal international development banks include the INTERNATIONAL BANK FOR RECONSTRUCTION AND DEVELOPMENT, the INTERNATIONAL FINANCE CORPORATION, the INTER-AMERICAN DEVELOPMENT BANK, the ASIAN DEVELOPMENT BANK, the AFRICAN DEVELOPMENT BANK, the CARIBBEAN DEVELOPMENT BANK, the EUROPEAN INVESTMENT BANK, the EUROPEAN BANK FOR RECONSTRUCTION AND DEVELOPMENT and the INTERNATIONAL INVESTMENT BANK.

development economics (O1)

Growth theory applied to the economic problems of developing countries. In a sense, it started with SMITH's *The Wealth of Nations* which was concerned with an analysis of the causes of economic growth, but it boomed as a subject in the period of decolonialization of the 1950s. When development economists began devising growth policies for less developed countries, they were inspired by Soviet economic management of the 1930s, wartime economic management and the MARSHALL PLAN for recovery in Western Europe. Criticism of the industrialization bias of early development plans, and their consequent environmental effects, made INTERMEDIATE TECHNOLOGY increasingly popular as a development strategy.

References

Hirschman, A.O. (1981) 'The rise and decline of development economics', in A.O. Hirschman (ed.) *Essays in Trespassing*, New York: Cambridge University Press.

Meier, G.M. (1989) *Leading Issues in Economic Development*, 5th edn, New York and Oxford: Oxford University Press.

Myint, H. (1980) *The Economics of Developing Countries*, London: Hutchinson.

development planning (O2)

The use of CENTRAL PLANNING in Third World countries as a route to economic development. The earliest plans were carried out before and after the Second World War in British, French, Belgian and Portuguese colonies. These plans included a crash investment programme, especially in the public sector, and a commitment to rapid industrialization.

development policy (O2) *see* aid; development

diamond model (F1)

A theory of competitive advantage based on four different determinants within a domestic economy: factor conditions, domestic demand conditions, the presence of related and supporting industries, and strategy, structure and rivalry of firms within the industry.

References

Porter, M.E. (1990) *The Competitive Advantage of Nations*, London: Macmillan.

difference equation (C6)

An equation relating a variable measured at one time to variables measured at previous times. This mathematical device is much used in DYNAMIC ECONOMICS, e.g. in the case of a COBWEB the quantity supplied in year $t + 1$ is a function of the price in year 1. Difference equations can be linear or non-linear, homogeneous or non-homogeneous, of first or second order.

References

Goldberg, S. (1958) *Introduction to Difference Equations*, New York: Wiley.

differential tax incidence (H2)

The burden of one tax compared with another.

See also: tax incidence

differential theory of rent (D3)

The theory of ANDERSON, RICARDO and others which asserted that the rent on land subject to DIMINISHING RETURNS arose from differences in fertility or location with no rent being paid on the least fertile or most distant land. As the margin of cultivation is extended, the total amount of rent paid increases.

differentiated good (D0, M3)

A good appearing different from its market rivals by being sold under a brand name and packaged differently. Recognition of this marketing device made a great contribution to the formation of the theory of MONOPOLISTIC COMPETITION.

See also: branding; brand loyalty; product differentiation

differentiated marketing (M3)

A marketing strategy with separate marketing programmes for each product of a firm.

differentiated product (D0, L1) *see* product differentiation

differentiation (C6, L1)

1 A major business strategy to acquire some MONOPOLY POWER by the differentiation of products, or of their marketing and distribution to the consumer.
2 A mathematical method of calculating the derivative of a function; this is much used in NEOCLASSICAL ECONOMICS.

See also: branding; monopolistic competition; product differentiation

diffusion index (C1, E3)

A measure used to identify BUSINESS CYCLES. The standard diffusion index is calculated by giving a value to each component

series. The value is 0 per cent for a decrease, 50 per cent if there is no change in the overall number rising or falling, or 100 per cent if there is an increase over a given time period. In the USA, *Business Cycle Indicators*, published from 1961, has measured diffusion for twenty-one economic indicators.

diffusion rate (O3)

The proportion of output of an industry using a particular technique by a stated date, e.g. the percentage of the steel industry using technique X by 2000. This is a major measure of technical progress and of INNOVATION. High rates of diffusion are encouraged by the possibility of cost reduction and by energetic advisory and information services.

Dillon Round (F1)

The fifth round of tariff reductions, organized under the GENERAL AGREEMENT ON TARIFFS AND TRADE, of 1960–1. Under it, the USA agreed to a 20 per cent reduction in tariffs on 20 per cent of its dutiable imports. As the concessions were concentrated on manufactures, the round had little effect on the exports of less developed countries whose industrialization was at a low level. It was of far more importance for bilateral deals between the USA and industrialized countries.

diminishing marginal rate of substitution (D1)

This rule of consumer behaviour states that at the same level of utility a consumer will sacrifice decreasing amounts of good Y to obtain extra units of good X. This is usually expressed as an INDIFFERENCE CURVE.

References

Hicks, J.R. (1939) *Value and Capital*, ch. 1, Oxford: Clarendon Press.

diminishing marginal utility law (D1)

This states that the amount of satisfaction derived from the consumption of successive units of the same good or service will decline. The law is used to explain the downward-sloping nature of the normal DEMAND CURVE, to resolve the so-called WATER AND DIAMONDS PARADOX and to justify redistribution from the rich to the poor. Although BENTHAM, SENIOR and JEVONS are noted for their clear exposition of this law, hints of it appeared in earlier economic writings.

diminishing returns law (D2)

The decline in output which occurs as successive units of a variable factor of production are applied to a fixed factor. The most familiar example was the application of increasing amounts of labour to a fixed amount of land with the consequence that the MARGINAL PRODUCT of labour declined. This view of agricultural production was central to much of CLASSICAL ECONOMICS, including RICARDO's model of the economy. The US economist Henry Charles Carey (1793–1879) was one of the few economic writers of the nineteenth century to argue that in a developing economy cultivation can proceed from the least to the most fertile land bringing about increasing returns.

See also: returns to scale

References

Carey, H.C. (1848) *The Past, The Present and The Future*, Philadelphia: Carey & Hart.

Dinks (J1)

Double income, no kids: US professional couple with a high joint income and no dependants.

direct and indirect taxation (H2)

Two broad categories of taxation differentiated according to administrative arrangements, incidence, or the characteristics of taxpayers. Income taxes, for example, are paid directly to revenue authorities, can directly reduce taxpayers' real incomes and be directly related to taxpayers' characteristics. But an indirect tax, such as a sales tax, is indirectly paid by an individual through purchasing goods and services, is not directly related to the personal circum-

stances of a taxpayer and can have its incidence shifted to the producer. Direct taxation is regarded as more equitable but it is more difficult and expensive to collect.

See also: tax incidence

direct cost (D0)

1 A production cost directly attributable to the cost of producing one unit of a particular output.
2 Variable cost.

See also: indirect cost

direct factor content (M0)

The amounts of FACTORS OF PRODUCTION used only in the last stage of production.

direct foreign investment (F2)

1 Investment in productive facilities by a foreign company, e.g. the purchase or building of factories.
2 The purchase of stocks and shares which give a foreign company control over existing real assets.

See also: multinational corporation; portfolio investment

direct–indirect taxes ratio (H2)

A measure of the TAX STRUCTURE which compares the yields from the various types of tax to see their relative importance as sources of revenue.

direct labour organization (L3)

A department of a UK local authority carrying out building, street cleansing or other activities itself rather than contracting them out to private sector firms. They were severely criticised for their low productivity. In the 1980s, the UK government began the replacement of direct labour organizations by private firms through COMPETITIVE TENDERING in an attempt to reduce the cost of local government services.

directly unproductive profit-seeking activities (L3)

Activities yielding pecuniary returns but not producing goods or services. A major example is the evasion of tariffs.

References

Buchanan, J.M., Tellison, R.D. and Tullock, G. (eds) (1980) *Toward a Theory of the Rent Seeking Society*, College Station, TX: Texas A & M University Press.

direct product profitability (M4)

A measure of a retailer's net profit after all labour, equipment and storage costs attributable to that product have been deducted. This is a more precise cost accounting technique than the previously popular method of calculating gross profit margins before deducting the average costs of handling and storage of each product. The knowledge gained from applying the direct product profitability method enables a retailer to have a more optimal product mix and a better use of shop space.

direct sale (M3)

A sale to a customer without the use of agents and the payment of their commission. This is a cheaper way of selling, especially for services such as insurance.

direct tax (H2) *see* direct and indirect taxation

direct utility function (D0)

A consumer's utility related to the quantities of goods consumed.

See also: indirect utility function

dirigisme (L5)

State intervention in society and direction of the economy as practised in France from the seventeenth century.

See also: Colbertism; mercantilism

dirty float (F3)

An exchange rate regime which, for the most part, is dominated by market forces but occasionally has interference by governments and central banks to prevent an excessive fluctuation in the value of a currency.

See also: floating exchange rate

disappointment aversion (D0, G1)

Being willing to suffer more pain from a loss than receiving pleasure from gaining the same amount. This aversion causes many people to prefer the high probability of a small loss in a lottery to the low probability of a high loss through investing in EQUITIES.

References

Gul, F. (1991) 'A theory of disappointment aversion', *Econometrica* 59: 667–86.

discomfort index (E3, J6)

OKUN defined this as the sum of the unemployment rate plus the rate of inflation.

disconnective taxation (H2)

Taxation unconnected to any spending. The opposite of a BENEFIT TAX.

discount bond (G1)

A BOND valued at less than its nominal value because of its high risk or its low COUPON.

discounted cash flow (M4)

A method of investment appraisal which discounts the future benefits and costs of an investment to discover its present value. The method can be used to evaluate whether an investment project is worthwhile either by following the rule that the present value of benefits must exceed the present value of costs, or by considering whether the INTERNAL RATE OF RETURN is acceptable compared with that on other investment projects.

discounted share price (G1)

A share price which takes into account expectations of future changes in earnings per share. As stock markets are constantly responding to information about particular companies' prospects, the announcement of a fall or rise in company profits can often have little impact on a share price.

discount house (G2)

A financial institution of the City of London, which borrows MONEY AT CALL from banks and other institutions and invests it in TREASURY BILLS, high-quality

COMMERCIAL BILLS and CERTIFICATES OF DEPOSIT. The twelve discount houses, forming the money market, act as a buffer between the commercial banks and the BANK OF ENGLAND. Banks short of cash will recall money lent to the money market which then has to discount bills to balance its books. The Bank of England as LENDER OF LAST RESORT is always prepared to lend to discount houses, by discounting bills, in order to preserve the liquidity of the banking system as a whole.

Curiously, many of these discount houses are now owned by clearing banks who could easily abolish them by abandoning an agreement not to compete in the money market which has existed since the 1930s: the banks prefer this unusual buffer between themselves and the Bank of England.

discounting (D0, M4)
A method used to value at the same date economic flows or stocks which have originated at different dates. A typical use of discounting is to convert the expected future incomes from an asset to present values using a DISCOUNT RATE.

See also: discounted cash flow

discount market (G1)
The money market specializing in transactions in short-term financial assets.

See also: short-term money market

discount market loans (G1) *see* overnight money

discount rate (D0, E4)
1 The rate of interest charged by a CENTRAL BANK to lower level financial institutions (usually COMMERCIAL BANKS) for discounting their bills, i.e. lending them money, often when acting as the LENDER OF LAST RESORT.
2 The rate used for discounting future values to the present. In COST-BENEFIT ANALYSIS there is a distinction between a private and a social rate of discount. A private rate of discount reflects the time preference of private consumers; a so-

cial rate is based on the government's view, which can be more long-sighted as it attempts, in most cases, to take into account the welfare of future generations.

discount window (E5)
US term for lending to depository institutions by each of the twelve district FEDERAL RESERVE BANKS. From 1913 to 1916, this was the only lending a FEDERAL RESERVE BANK could undertake. It is either adjustment credit to meet a temporary need for funds or extended credit to help banks subject to seasonal fluctuations, or accommodation to cope with special circumstances, e.g. the effects of a change in the financial system. Other lending is by discounting eligible paper, e.g. a commercial or agricultural loan made by the bank to a customer. Before 1980, such lending was only made to Federal Reserve member banks; now, under the DEPOSITORY INSTITUTIONS DE-REGULATION AND MONETARY CONTROL ACT 1980, it is open to all depository institutions except bankers' banks which maintain transaction accounts or non-personal time deposits. Discount window loans are usually only a small proportion of bank reserves, e.g. less than 3 per cent in 1985. This lending can be used in MONETARY POLICY instead of OPEN MARKET OPERATIONS.

References

Mengle, D.L. (1986) 'The discount window', *Federal Reserve Bank of Richmond Economic Review* 72(3): 2–10.

discouraged workers hypothesis (J2, J6)
The view that workers give up job search activity because high unemployment rates and a lack of hiring by businesses make it unlikely that they will succeed in gaining employment. Lack of search loses them the status of being unemployed and so they drop out of the LABOUR FORCE.

See also: additional worker hypothesis

discrete variable (C6)
A variable which can take only some of the values between two given values, e.g.

the number of countries in the world can be 50, 100 or 200 but not 1.8.

See also: continuous variable

discriminating auction (D4)
A form of sale with discrimination based on price. The bids are ranked from the highest. Each bidder pays what has been bid until the good or service auctioned is sold out.

discriminating monopoly (L1) *see* price discrimination

discrimination (J7)
1 Unfair and unfavourable treatment of a group of workers or other persons.
2 Setting different wages for workers with the same productivity but different personal characteristics, i.e. sex, age or race, or refusing to hire them.

Different schools of economics have chosen different approaches to the issue: NEOCLASSICAL economists such as BECKER examined how a taste for discrimination affects the demand for each group, while others have placed discrimination in the context of wider concerns such as class conflict.

See also: ageism; horizontal discrimination; racial discrimination; sexual discrimination; vertical discrimination

References

Becker, G.S. (1971) *The Economics of Discrimination*, Chicago: University of Chicago Press.
Marshall, R. (1974) 'The economics of racial discrimination: a survey', *Journal of Economic Literature* 12: 849–71.
Reich, M. (1981) *Racial Inequality*, Princeton, NJ: Princeton University Press.

diseconomy of scale (D2)
A rise in average costs as a consequence of an increase in output. This is visible in the positively sloped part of the AVERAGE COST curve. Early writers on the subject attributed such diseconomies to the managerial problem of co-ordinating the activities of large enterprises. Later writers noted other sources of diseconomies, including mate-

rial fatigue, increases in the marginal cost of attracting more customers and rising factor prices – how many of these 'causes' are valid depends on how strictly a diseconomy is defined.

See also: economy of scale

disembedded economy (P0)
An ECONOMY in which economic relationships dominate the social relationships of kinship and polity. This phenomenon, observed by the GERMAN HISTORICAL SCHOOL, is followed today by an emphasis on markets.

disembodied technical progress (O3)
An increase in PRODUCTIVITY which occurs without the installation of new capital goods. Examples include organizational changes or LEARNING-BY-DOING.

See also: embodied technical progress

disequilibrium (D0, E3)
1 An economic system in a state of EXCESS DEMAND or EXCESS SUPPLY.
2 The state of an economic system whose key variables continue to fluctuate around an EQUILIBRIUM or an equilibrium growth path. Expectations of economic agents or lags in the system can cause this.

disequilibrium economics (D0, E0)
The analysis of non-clearing markets or national economies with less than FULL EMPLOYMENT. In macroeconomics, the DYNAMIC MULTIPLIER shows how disequilibrium occurs in the economy as a whole; in the MULTIPLIER–ACCELERATOR MODEL changes in the national income are studied. KEYNESIAN ECONOMICS is believed to be essentially a theory of disequilibrium rather than a theory of GENERAL EQUILIBRIUM as NEO-KEYNESIANS would assert.

References

Barro, R.J., Howitt, P.W and Grossman, H.I. (1979) 'Macroeconomics: an appraisal of the non-market clearing paradigm', *American Economic Review* 69: 54–69.
Hey, J.D. (1981) *Economics in Disequilibrium*, Oxford: Basil Blackwell.
Muellbauer, J. and Portes, R. (1979)

'Macroeconomics when markets do not clear', in W. Branson (ed.) *Macroeconomic Theory and Policy*, ch. 16, New York: Harper & Row.

Samuelson, P. (1939) 'Interactions between multiplier analysis and the principle of acceleration', *Review of Economic Statistics* 21(May): 75–8.

disequilibrium growth theory (O4)

A dynamic theory with KEYNESIAN foundations accounting for the course of change of a national economy. This growth process can be initiated by disequilibrium in a factor or product market or through the non-equality of aggregate demand and aggregate supply.

References

Ito, I. (1980) 'Disequilibrium growth theory', *Journal of Economic Theory* 23: 380–409.

disequilibrium money (E4)

The mismatch between the demand for and supply of money brought about by lags that prevent SUPPLY-SIDE SHOCKS from affecting the demand for money. These shocks in money and credit markets lead to asset prices overshooting their equilibrium level.

disequilibrium price (D4)

A price that fails to equate demand with supply. In the figure, P_e is the equilibrium price. Above P_e prices will be determined by the demand curve; below it, by the supply curve.

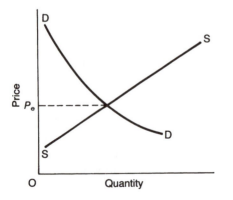

disguised unemployment (J6)

That part of the LABOUR FORCE consisting of employed workers with a low productivity making little contribution to the GROSS DOMESTIC PRODUCT. A low level of investment per worker, or the reluctance of labour to move to more productive and higher paid work in the more modern sectors of an economy, can cause this unemployment. Countries or regions with large agricultural sectors, e.g. less developed countries and southern regions of the EUROPEAN UNION, often have a great deal of this sort of unemployment.

disincentive effect (H2, H3)

The discouraging effect of a tax on the supply of effort or the number of persons available for work. The best example is an income tax with a high marginal rate. This can result in a BACKWARD-BENDING LABOUR SUPPLY CURVE.

See also: incentive effect

disinflation (E3)

The reduction of inflation to a very low level. A major way of attempting to reach this goal is to lower AGGREGATE DEMAND by the use of MONETARY and FISCAL POLICIES.

disinflation cost (E3, E5)

The loss of output resulting from a MONETARY POLICY seeking to reduce inflation by a reduction in aggregate demand, often through increasing interest rates.

disintermediation (G2, M2)

Bypassing the banking system by direct borrowing and lending between companies/corporations or other users and suppliers of finance. When the BANK OF ENGLAND introduced the 'corset' as a means of reducing bank lending, disintermediation enabled companies to continue to borrow short term when refused credit by their bankers.

'dismal science' (A1)

The summary dismissal of ECONOMICS made by Thomas Carlyle (1795–1881). He argued that as utilitarianism had been mechanically applied and as humans were increasingly connected only by cash payments, fundamental spiritual values were being neglected.

See also: cash nexus

References

Rutherford, D. (1996–7) 'Dismal Carlyle and the "Dismal Science"', *The Carlyle Society Papers* New Series, No. 8: 24–36.

disposable income (D3, H2)

1 PERSONAL INCOME plus TRANSFER INCOME net of all taxes levied on incomes.
2 The amounts of money a person can spend or save in a given time period.

See also: final income

dissaving (E2)

1 The spending of accumulated savings.
2 A net increase in borrowing.

distortion (D6)

The failure to reach a welfare optimum because the social marginal cost of producing goods is less or more than the social marginal benefit of consuming that good. WELFARE ECONOMICS is much concerned with distortions when analysing taxation and monopoly.

distortionary tax (H2)

A biased tax causing inefficiencies. Many specific taxes, e.g. those levied on the products of one industry but not on those of another, can change the post-tax allocation of demand.

distribution (D3, L8)

1 The division of the NATIONAL INCOME among the FACTORS OF PRODUCTION in the form of WAGES, PROFITS, INTEREST and RENT. TURGOT, in his *Réflections sur la formation et la distribution des richesses* (1766), was probably the first economic writer to examine the distribution as a separate issue. Despite John Stuart MILL's attempt to separate the laws of production from the laws of distribution, there has always been an intimate relationship between distribution and other economic theories. Socialist economists have made the study of distribu-

tion a major concern.
2 The distribution of one type of income between persons or between groups.
3 The last stage of production in which goods or services reach final consumers.

See also: labour's share of national income; post-Keynesians

distributional/social weights (C1)

The increased weighting of one social or income group in COST-BENEFIT ANALYSIS. This gives a group more significance: for example, if the LOWER QUARTILE of an income distribution is given a weight of 4 but the UPPER QUARTILE only 1 then costs and benefits affecting the lowest income group will be regarded as four times as important as those of the top group.

disturbance term (C1)

A variable, positive or negative in value, or ERROR term which indicates the extent to which the dependent variable of a regression equation falls short of the central value of the independent variables. In the equation $I = a(Y - Y_1) + u$, I is net investment, Y is this year's income, Y_1 is last year's income and u is the disturbance term showing the extent to which I is more or less than the central value of $a(Y - Y_1)$. This term reflects the random element in economic relationships.

disutility (D0)

A negative satisfaction, e.g. pain, tiredness, unhappiness. Study and work supposedly create disutility, justifying higher earnings to better educated and more productive workers. Consumption of a good or service, according to the law of DIMINISHING MARGINAL UTILITY, can continue to the point where UTILITY turns into disutility, e.g. a few glasses of claret can give a person utility, a few litres severe disutility. A BAD produces disutility.

See also: labour disutility theory

divergence indicator (F3)

The margin by which a currency in the EXCHANGE RATE MECHANISM can diverge from its central or PAR VALUE. This is ± 2.25 per cent except for the later entrants to the mechanism, e.g. Italy and the UK, which can diverge by 6 per cent in either direction to make adjustment to a fixed exchange rate easier.

divergence threshold (F3)

The crucial value of the DIVERGENCE INDICATOR for a currency of the EXCHANGE RATE MECHANISM. At this value, either a change in the domestic economic policies of the country concerned or a change in the PAR VALUE of its currency is required.

diversification (D2, G1, L0)

1 The production of a range of products by a firm.
2 The establishment of several industries in a region or a country.
3 The spreading of investments over a range of assets with different degrees of risk.

Ultimately diversification is always concerned with minimizing the risk of a loss of income.

See also: conglomerate

diversification cone (F1)

Combinations of factor endowments which produce the same set of goods at the same factor prices in the HECKSCHER–OHLIN TRADE THEOREM.

diversification discount (M2)

The discount arising from a firm having several divisions each with the authority to make investments. The discount occurs owing to the lack of co-operation between divisions.

divestment (L1)

The disposal of part of the assets of a firm; the opposite of a MERGER. An appraisal of the activities of a diversified firm often results in divestment as a means of rationalizing its interests.

dividend (G1)

The variable return to equity shares, decided by the board of directors of a company or corporation according to its policy on net profit distribution. For PREFERENCE SHARES, the dividend is at a fixed rate determined when they were issued, unless there is a right to participate in residual profits.

dividend discount model (G1)

The fair pricing of an asset measured as the present value of expected cash flows from it. In the case of a COMMON STOCK or EQUITY it is the expected dividend payments and the expected price of the stock at a future date.

References

William, J.B. (1938) *The Theory of Investment Value*, Cambridge, MA: Harvard University Press.

dividend net (G2)

The rate of dividend paid in the last year, less income tax paid at the standard rate.

dividend yield (G1)

The yearly return on each £100 or $100 invested:

$$\text{yield } (\%) = \frac{\text{nominal value of a share} \times \text{dividend } (\%)}{\text{market price} \times 100} \times 100$$

Divisia money index (E4)

A combination of different measures of money weighted by the amount of interest paid on each. The higher the interest rate, the less the monetary instrument is 'money' in the narrow sense of being CASH. The growth of interest-bearing CURRENT ACCOUNTS has rendered the index less useful.

See also: money supply

References

Barnett, W.A., Fisher, D. and Serletis, A. (1992) 'Consumer theory and the demand for money', *Journal of Economic Literature* 30: 2086–119.

division of labour (D2)

Specialization of productive activity either by persons in different occupational groups undertaking particular tasks or by dividing a task into its component operations. Although writers as early as XENO-PHON had mentioned the principle, SMITH, with his famous example of pin making, made it a central explanation of the growth process, He noted that such specialization would save time as there would not have to be frequent changes from one activity to another, that workers would become more dextrous and that the analysis of jobs would make possible the introduction of machinery. However, he was aware that workers would become dull through repetitive tasks – a Smithian point often misinterpreted by Marxists: division of labour in itself can produce ALIENATION amongst workers, whether or not they own the capital they use.

division of thought (D2)

Specialization in the processing of information and acting upon that data. Such specialists will undertake either strategic planning or executive operations.

References

Arrow, K.J. (1979) 'The division of labour in the economy, the polity and society', in G.P. O'Driscoll (ed.) *Adam Smith and Modern Political Economy: Bicentennial Essays on The Wealth of Nations*, Ames, IA: Iowa State University Press.

do-able (O2)

A development strategy emphasizing projects and methods wanted by local populations as they are more likely to be maintained in the long term.

Dobb, Maurice Herbert, 1900–76 (B3)

UK Marxist economist, educated at Cambridge and the London School of Economics, and a fellow of Trinity College, Cambridge, from 1924 to 1967 and Reader in Economics from 1959. Throughout his academic career his Communist Party ideological stance informed his views and his writings. As a defender of Soviet-style economic planning, he participated in major debates with MISES and HAYEK. His analysis of capitalism defended the Marxian interpretation of economic history,

provoking a long-running controversy amongst Marxists. He had a deep interest in the history of economic thought, collaborating with SRAFFA in the editing of RI-CARDO's works and suggesting that economic theory descended from QUESNAY through RICARDO and MARX to LEONTIEF and SRAFFA. Current policy issues also concerned him: he was able to make use of a Ricardo–Marx two-sector model to make policy recommendations for less developed economies.

References

Dobb, M.H. (1946) *Studies in the Development of Capitalism*, London: Routledge.
—— (1966) *Soviet Economic Development since 1917*, London: Routledge.
—— (1978) 'Maurice Dobb Memorial Issue', *Cambridge Journal of Economics* 2: 2.

dogs of the Dow (G1)

An approach to investment based on using dividend data. At the beginning of the year, US stocks listed by Dow are ranked by dividend yield from the highest to the lowest and then an equal amount is invested in each of the top ten stocks. The following year the procedure is repeated and the stocks whose rank has fallen below the top ten are sold.

dole bludger (J6)

An Australian unemployed person who does not seek work but enjoys a life of leisure financed by social security benefits. Abolition of unemployment benefit was intended to force such persons into retraining or job search.

See also: job-seeker's allowance; New Deal

dollar (F3)

The name of the USA's currency since 1785. Other countries, including Hong Kong, Canada and Australia, have followed the US lead. The term is derived from the Bohemian thaler introduced in 1517. 'Yen' (Japanese) and 'yuan' (Chinese) both mean dollar.

See also: currencies

dollarization (F3)

1 The use of the US dollar for domestic monetary transactions outside the USA because the local currency is depreciating rapidly through high inflation. In 1904 Panama abandoned its own currency for the dollar, as did Ecuador in 2000 and El Salvador in 2001.

2 The abandonment of a national currency in favour of the US dollar. In countries such as Ecuador a rapid decline in the value of its currency, the sucre, required this drastic economic reform.

See also: dual exchange rate

dollar overhang (F3)

US dollars held outside the USA in the 1960s in excess of the gold backing for them.

See also: monetary overhang

dollar standard (F3)

The basis of value for INTERNATIONAL MONETARY FUND currencies, the US dollar, under the BRETTON WOODS system (1968–73), a successor to the GOLD STANDARD. Unlike linking currencies to gold, this standard did not require dollar holdings as a backing for other currencies, thus making it a less potent system of international money.

domain (C6)

The set of values a variable can take.

See also: continuous variable; discrete variable

Domar, Evsey David, 1914– (B3)

A founder of modern economic growth theory. Educated at the Universities of California (Los Angeles), Michigan and Harvard. Early in his career he was an economist with the FEDERAL RESERVE Board of Governors and then at the COWLES COMMISSION, and professor at the Massachusetts Institute of Technology from 1958 to 1972. He is best known for reviving economic growth theory in the HARROD–DOMAR MODEL; his other works include

studies of taxation and comparative economic systems.

References

Domar, E.V. (1957) *Essays in the Theory of Economic Growth*, New York: Oxford University Press.

Domei (J5)

Japanese Federation of Labour. This labour union national federation merged with Churitsuroren to form Rengo in 1987. Domei had 2.09 million members in 1987.

domestic absorption (E2)

A nation's total use of its own output of goods and services in consumption and investment.

See also: absorption approach

domestic banking system (G2)

The interconnected banking institutions of a particular country. These receive deposits from the public, lend at home and abroad and effect the transfer of funds. As the ultimate guarantor of the LIQUIDITY of a banking system, a national CENTRAL BANK operates and, to a large extent, attempts to control all WHOLESALE and RETAIL BANKS.

The greater sophistication attributed to the banking systems of Western countries is a product of their long period of relative freedom to develop a variety of financial instruments, unlike the MONO-BANKS of Soviet-type economies whose role was limited through subservience to a system of central planning.

The Second World War created an excessive volume of public sector debt which made possible a post-war expansion in bank advances to meet the demands of private sector borrowers. Other changes have been a widening of the range and activities of COMMERCIAL BANKS, including new techniques and financial products, particularly in the UK and the USA. In the USA in the 1960s, for example, there was a switch from asset management to liability management and later a shift from fixed rates to variable rates for lending. To assess a domestic banking system a commonly used indicator is the trend in the prices of the stocks and shares of issued bank securities as these reflect investors' confidence.

See also: banking; derivative

References

Lewis, M.K. and Davis, K.T. (1981) *Domestic and International Banking*, Cambridge, MA: MIT Press; Hemel Hempstead: Philip Alan.

domestic credit expansion (E5)

Growth of the money supply, adjusted by the deficit or surplus on the BALANCE OF PAYMENTS current and capital accounts. It consists of the PUBLIC SECTOR BORROWING REQUIREMENT less net sales of public sector debt to the non-bank private sector and bank lending to the private and overseas sectors. The reasoning behind this measure is that a balance of payments deficit leads to a reduction in the expansion of the domestic money stock through excess spending overseas. Conversely, a money supply expands with a balance of payments surplus, increasing foreign currency reserves. This measure was intended to produce a monetary aggregate suitable for open economies. It was first used in the UK in 1968 when it was monetary target popular with the INTERNATIONAL MONETARY FUND.

See also: monetarism; money supply

domestic labour (J4)

1 Unpaid work within households often undertaken by women.
2 Hired servants engaged in cleaning, cooking and other household tasks.

domestic resource cost (D2)

The OPPORTUNITY COST of using a FACTOR OF PRODUCTION to produce one unit of output, divided by the international value added by producing that unit. This is used as an alternative measure to the EFFECTIVE RATE OF PROTECTION.

domestic system (D2)

A primitive form of production in which MERCHANT CAPITALISTS advance capital to self-employed craftworkers and artisans who, using their own simple tools, make a product. Before the Industrial Revolution in Great Britain, the textile industry was organized in this way.

See also: advanced organic economy; Asiatic mode of production; cottage industry; homework

dominant firm (L1)

A firm making most of the sales of an industry and often a price leader. There are many firms of this type in oligopolistic industries.

See also: competitive fringe

dominant strategy (L1)

The pursuit of objectives by a firm which ignores the possible actions or reactions of its rivals.

Donovan Commission (UK) (J5)

The Royal Commission on Trade Unions and Employers' Associations of 1965–68 chaired by Lord Donovan. It concluded that the UK had two systems of industrial relations: a formal system with industry-wide collective agreements on pay, hours of work and other employment conditions; and an informal system at the factory level setting earnings supplements to national wage rates and causing WAGE DRIFT and unofficial strikes to enforce workers' demands. This dual system was partly the consequence of FULL EMPLOYMENT in the UK in the 1950s and 1960s. To remedy these faults in the INDUSTRIAL RELATIONS system, the Donovan Commission recommended the limitation of industry-wide agreements to matters which could be regulated effectively at the industry level and the introduction of factory agreements to replace informal understandings.

See also: shop steward

References

Royal Commission on Trade Unions and

Employers' Associations 1965–8 (1968) *Report*, London: HMSO, Cmnd 3623.

dose–response function (I1, Q0)

The relationship between a dose of pollution and the physical consequences, including mortality, morbidity, crop yields and material deterioration.

References

Lave, L. and Seskin, E. (1967) *Air Pollution and Human Health*, Baltimore, MD: Johns Hopkins University Press.

Ridker, R. (1967) *Economic Costs of Air Pollution*, New York: Praeger.

dot com company (L2)

A firm which markets its goods and services from its website on the Internet.

double counting (M4)

Recording something twice with the consequence that the total resulting from aggregating individual items is incorrectly too large. In NATIONAL INCOME accounting, double counting is a crucial problem to be avoided. It is essential, for example, to ensure that TRANSFER INCOMES are not added to FACTOR INCOMES as transfer incomes are derived from factor incomes.

double discounting (M4)

A calculation which twice takes into account inflation thus producing too small a net present value. Double discounting is only approved when it is used to correct for both inflation and time preference.

double factorial terms of trade (F1)

NET BARTER TERMS OF TRADE multiplied by the ratio of the productivity change index for one country's export industries and the productivity change index for a foreign country's export industries. This measure of the TERMS OF TRADE indicates the exchange rate between domestic and foreign factor services.

See also: single factorial terms of trade

double switching (D0) *see* reswitching

double taxation of savings (H2)

Taxing both the income out of which savings are made and the income from the savings when they are invested. Many income tax systems have this feature.

double-taxation relief (H2)

A tax credit allowed against the tax payable by a resident of a country on account of income already having been taxed abroad, e.g. if a US citizen has already been taxed in France, then that will be taken into account when calculating that person's liability for paying US taxation.

This relief is only possible if there is a tax treaty between the two countries concerned or between states in a country, such as the USA, with a federal constitution. In the USA where the rate of INDIVIDUAL INCOME TAX can vary from state to state, a person who resides in one state and works in another can gain relief by being given tax credits by one state.

See also: deemed tax

Douglas Amendment 1965 (G2)

An amendment to the BANK HOLDING COMPANY ACT (USA) prohibiting bank holding companies from acquiring banks in other states.

Douglas, Paul Howard, 1892–1976 (B3)

A US economist who was taught, and much influenced, by John Bates CLARK at Columbia University. For most of his academic career, i.e. 1920–4 and 1927–48, he was a professor at Chicago. As US Senator for Illinois in 1948–66, he fought for family allowances, old-age pensions and pro-union legislation.

In 1928, he used MARGINAL PRODUCTIVITY THEORY as the foundations of the COBB–DOUGLAS PRODUCTION FUNCTION, the leading approach on the subject until 1961. His early work on wages included a seminal study of LABOUR FORCE PARTICIPATION relating wages to participation within major US cities and attempting to vindicate MARGINAL PRODUCTIVITY THEORY.

References

Douglas, P.H. (1934) *Theory of Wages*, New York: Macmillan.

Douglas, P.H. and Cobb, C.W. (1928) 'A theory of production', *American Economic Review (Supplement)* 18: 139–65.

Dow Jones Industrial Average (G2)

The leading US index of stock market prices, which is an unweighted arithmetic average of the thirty industrial shares most widely quoted in the USA. Averages are also published every trading day for transportation and utilities stocks, as well as a composite index combining the movements in the three indices.

See also: Standard & Poor 500

downsizing (J6)

Reducing the size of a labour force by making workers redundant. A term particularly applied to the staff reductions made by securities houses after 1987.

See also: Big Bang

downstream dumping (F1)

Exporting goods with artificially low prices because intermediate goods have been purchased below cost.

downstream firm (L2)

A firm engaged in a later stage of production or retailing.

droit de suite (K2, M3)

A directive approved by the European Parliament and European Commission in June 2001 that the authors of works of art should benefit from the resale of their artistic work; not to be fully implemented until 2010. The fees charged will be according to five bands of selling prices with the lowest band giving the artist 4 per cent of the value of the sale and the highest 0.4 per cent.

drug economy (P0)

The part of a national ECONOMY financed by the proceeds from the sale of illegal drugs. It is so large in some economies, including the USA, that it is sufficient to keep consumer spending buoyant whatever macroeconomic policy is being followed. In the USA, examination of large and suspicious cash deposits at banks, possible evidence of drug dealing, are required under the Money Laundering Act 1986 and the Anti-Drug Abuse Act 1988. In the UK, a court can order the confiscation of the assets of drug-traffickers.

See also: laundering money

dual-decision hypothesis (E6)

Clower's reinterpretation of KEYNES's unemployment equilibrium by distinguishing 'notional' demand, the demand of households at prices reflecting a FULL- EMPLOYMENT equilibrium from 'effective' demand, the demand of households whose actual incomes have fallen through unemployment. Adjustment to unemployment equilibrium takes place through incomes and not through relative prices. This hypothesis recognizes that in a market system a household cannot buy and sell what it pleases if there is excess supply in the economy, and attempts to reconcile WALRAS'S LAW with KEYNES's *General Theory*.

References

Clower, R.W. (ed.) (1969) *Monetary Theory*, ch. 19, Harmondsworth: Penguin.

dual economy (P0)

A national economy consisting of a rich modern sector and a poor traditional sector. Originally this term was used to describe many colonial economies after the Second World War.

References

Boeke, J.H. (1953) *Economics and Economic Policy of Dual Societies, as Exemplified by Indonesia*, New York: Institute of Pacific Relations.

dual exchange rate (F3)

The two values of a currency determined separately for different sets of monetary transactions. A fixed exchange rate can be used for normal commercial transactions and a floating rate for capital account transactions. Mexico has followed this system.

See also: multiple exchange rate

dual federalism (H7)

A loose form of federalism in which the federal and state levels act separately but in parallel. This traditional view of the US Constitution implies that federal government is mainly concerned with interstate commerce with production being the concern of the states.

See also: co-operative federalism; fiscal federalism; new federalism

dual labour market (J4)

A labour market divided into a primary sector with better jobs and a secondary sector with inferior jobs. The primary sector consists of large firms offering training and high remuneration but the secondary sector has many small marginal firms offering small rewards and prospects to their workers. The primary sector firms use INTERNAL LABOUR MARKETS but in the secondary sector there is heavy reliance on the EXTERNAL LABOUR MARKET. Students of sexual and racial DISCRIMINATION frequently use this concept, pointing out that women and blacks are often trapped in the secondary market.

dual pricing (D4, F3)

The practice of quoting prices in two currencies. This occurs as part of the transition to a new currency or because of lack of confidence in the national currency. This occurred in many eastern European countries and in EUROPEAN UNION countries after the introduction of the EURO.

dummy variable (C1)

A variable in an econometric equation only taking the values 0 or 1. It is used to refer to being in one state or another, e.g. married or not married, living in one century or another. A shift dummy reflects an EXOGENOUS shift; a slope dummy, a change in the slope of a function.

dumping (F1)

The sale of goods by a firm or government at a price below their cost of production with the aim of increasing a market share

or avoiding the costs of storing unsold goods. Although in some countries the practice is encouraged, and made possible by means of government subsidization, there is much opposition to dumping, e.g. the GENERAL AGREEMENT ON TARIFFS AND TRADE has an International Dumping Code and the USA passed the Anti-Dumping Act in 1921. In some cases, dumping can only be prevented by retaliatory acts such as the imposition of duties or the severing of trading relationships.

References

Jackson, J.H. and Vermulst, E.A. (eds) (1990) *Antidumping Law and Practice. A Comparative Study*, Hemel Hempstead: Harvester Wheatsheaf.

Dunlop, John Thomas, 1914– (B3)

A leading US expositor of labour economics educated at the University of California at Berkeley. Apart from governmental posts, including being US Secretary of Labor from 1975 to 1976, he has held a succession of academic posts at Harvard University from 1936. His chief research interests have been wage determination and labour management relations in many national economies, including those of the USA, Eastern Europe and the Third World. His detailed work on the relationship between MARKET STRUCTURES and wage setting contributed to the analytical linking of INDUSTRIAL ORGANIZATION and labour economics.

References

Dunlop, J.T. (1944) *Wage Determination under Trade Unions*, New York: Macmillan.
—— (1957) *The Theory of Wage Determination*, New York: Macmillan.
Dunlop, J.T., Kerr, C., Harbison, F.H. and Myers, C.A. (1960) *Industrialism and Industrial Man*, Cambridge, MA: Harvard University Press.

duopoly (L1)

An industry with two firms. Each duopolist's output and prices will depend on the market actions of the other. COURNOT'S analysis of 1838 considered two firms making an identical product, each aiming to maximize its profits on the assumption that the other firm kept its output constant. He proved that equilibrium would be reached with equal division of the market and the charging of the same price, a price lower than a monopolist's price but higher than under PERFECT COMPETITION.

See also: Bertrand duopoly model; Cournot duopoly model; spatial duopoly model; Stackelberg duopoly model

Du Pont formula (G2)

An analysis of the determinants of the difference between an actual rate of return on investment and the budgeted return where return on investment = return on sales × asset turnover.

Dupuit, Arsène Jules Etienne Juvénal, 1804–66 (B3)

French engineer educated at l'Ecole Polytechnique des Ponts et Chaussées. In his work on public utilities, especially the construction of bridges and public works, he pioneered the use of COST–BENEFIT ANALYSIS. He was one of the earliest MARGINALISTS, introducing a DEMAND CURVE related to MARGINAL UTILITY and suggesting the notion of CONSUMER'S SURPLUS. His contributions to economics are chiefly contained in two articles, 'De la mesure de l'utilité des travaux publics' (1884) and 'De l'influence des péages sur l'utilité des voies de communication' (1849) in the *Annales desponts et chaussées*. JEVONS and MARSHALL recognized him as their forerunner.

References

Ekelund, R.B. Jr (1968) 'Jules Dupuit and the early theory of marginal cost pricing', *Journal of Political Economy* 76: 462–71.

Durbin–Watson statistic (C1)

A test for the presence of autocorrelated disturbances. This statistic (DW) is calculated as the ratio of the sum of the squares of the differences between regression residuals in the present period and in the previous time period to the sum of the squares of the residuals in the present period. These disturbances are usually absent if the DW statistic has a value of about 2.

See also: autocorrelation; disturbance term

Dutch auction (D4)

A method of selling which consists of an auctioneer inviting a bid much higher than what is regarded as likely to be acceptable to the buyers. The starting price is gradually reduced until a buyer shouts 'mine' and accepts the item at that price. In Holland, an automated method is used for such auctions: the buyers face a 'clock' with prices on its face and a pointer moves gradually counterclockwise from the higher to the lower prices.

See also: auction

Dutch book (D7)

A principle for dynamic decision-making situations that leads to a sequence of bets finishing in an inescapable loss, as in the case of a bookmaker always gaining from gambling on the outcome of horse races.

Dutch disease (L0)

The harmful consequences for a national economy of discovering natural resources, especially the decline in traditional industries brought about by the rapid growth and prosperity of a new industry. New dominant industries can afford to pay wages far in excess of other industries, so the latter raise their wage levels to unaffordable levels causing unemployment. The successful new industry has high exports, creating a foreign exchange surplus and raising the country's exchange rate, with the consequence that other industries of the economy become internationally uncompetitive. This was noticeable in the Netherlands after the discovery of North Sea gas. There rising prosperity brought about higher levels of welfare benefits which persisted after the downturn in the economy, causing immense difficulties for the financing of public expenditure. Many other economies have experienced this phenomenon, e.g. Jamaica with its bauxite industry, Venezuela with its petroleum industry.

References

Corden, W.M. and Neary, L.P. (1982) 'Booming sector and de-industrialization in a small open economy', *Economic Journal* 92: 825–48.

Wijnbergen, S. van (1984) 'The Dutch disease: a disease after all?', *Economic Journal* 94: 41–55.

dynamically inconsistent policy (E6)

A policy based on decisions which later cease to be optimal.

dynamic economics (E1)

The study of the movement of an economy from a particular state at a particular date to another state later usually using lagged variables. Although classical economists such as Adam SMITH and John Stuart MILL were concerned to study the nature of economic progress, it was particularly ROBERTSON, HARROD, HICKS and the STOCKHOLM SCHOOL in the 1930s who began the creation of formal dynamic models of ECONOMIC GROWTH and change. The inclusion of time in the study distinguishes this approach from static models of economic systems. In dynamic models, at least one variable is measured at a different time from the others; subscripts are attached to each variable to indicate the date(s) to which they refer.

See also: comparative statics; static model

References

Simonovits, A. (2000) *Mathematical methods in dynamic economics*, New York: St Martin's Press; London: Macmillan.

dynamic gains from trade (F1)

The effects of a trade policy on ECONOMIC GROWTH. Important determinants of these gains are the accumulation of physical capital, the transmission of technology and improvements in the quality of macroeconomic policy.

dystopia (P0)

A disagreeable state, the opposite of a UTOPIA. It is likely to have low incomes, high crime and other social problems, and few economic prospects.

E

early retirement scheme (J2, J6)
A modern proposal to reduce unemployment, or make space in a firm for younger workers, by lowering, or making more flexible, the statutory retiring age. The principal aim of these schemes, to redistribute jobs from older to younger workers, can be frustrated if the rising productivity of the firm's labour force reduces its total demand for labour.

earmarked gold (E5)
Gold held at US FEDERAL RESERVE BANKS for foreign and international accounts; it is not part of the US gold stock.

earmarking (H5)
The allocation of public revenue exclusively to the execution of a particular function of government, e.g. using the proceeds of television licences in the UK to finance the British Broadcasting Corporation. Some governments have rejected this approach because of the inflexibility it introduces into public finances, arguing that different types of public expenditure grow at different rates from various tax revenues. Nevertheless, the principle is often followed in social expenditure and is a method of controlling it.

See also: dedicated budget; ringfencing; trust fund

earnings (D3, J3, M2)
1 Total pre-tax pay of employees, consist-ing of basic wages or salaries and all other premium and bonus elements.
2 The INCOME of a business available for distribution to shareholders.
3 The share of the proceeds of production going to a FACTOR OF PRODUCTION.

earnings per share (G2)
Pre-tax earnings divided by the number of shares entitled to a variable dividend. This ratio, when used as an indicator of the long-term growth potential of a company, should be compared with other indicators of a firm's performance, including its market share and its research and development expenditure. Earnings per share are usually larger than dividend per share as few companies distribute all of their profits.

earnings ratio (G2)
Net profit (excluding preference dividends) divided by equity capital.

earnings yield (G2)
Earnings (per cent) × par value/market price; for example, for a company with a dividend of 25 per cent earned on a share with a par value of £1 with a market price of 125p, the earnings yield is 25 × 100/125 = 20 per cent.

East Asian economic crisis (E3, G1, N1, P0)
The crisis of 1997–8 in the financial sector of five Asian countries: Indonesia, South

Korea, Malaysia, the Philippines and Thailand. In 1996 there was a capital inflow into these countries of $73 billion but in 1997 an outflow of $30 billion. With financial deregulation came careless lending by international banks to these Asian countries. When the extent of indebtedness was known, the creditors panicked. There was a fall in exchange rates, an ineffective rescue effort by the IMF and subsequently a banking crisis and a severe fall in effective demand.

easy money policy (E5)
A relaxed monetary policy permitting high rates of growth of the money supply to keep interest rates low. This has been advocated as a means of keeping aggregate demand high and unemployment low. The UK and the USA used the policy in the years immediately following the Second World War.

See also: cheap money

easy rider (H3, J5) *see* free rider

ecfare (D6)
ROBERTSON's abbreviated expression for ECONOMIC WELFARE.

eclectic Keynesians (B2) *see* new Keynesian

eclectic theory (F2)
A theory drawn from various sources to explain FOREIGN DIRECT INVESTMENT. Location theory is employed to explain why production occurs at several locations; INTERNALIZATION THEORY explains why the internal market is preferred to the external; ownership advantages, especially of product brands and PATENTS explain why a firm produces overseas rather than license its technology. This theory has been used to explain the expansion of multinational banking and of hotel chains.

ecodevelopment valuation (D4, Q0)
Valuation of an environment according to relative scarcity and minimal dislocation.

ecological capital (Q0)
The changing stock of plant, animal species, the physical environment and the weather.

ecological footprint (Q0)
The amount of land an individual needs to support his or her present consumption. This concept was anticipated by Richard CANTILLON's land and labour theory of value.

e-commerce (L8)
Trade in goods and services effected by e-mail (electronic mail).

econometrics (C1, C2, C3)
The measurement of economic relationships using statistical techniques, and the testing of economic theories. Econometrics has become the basis for economic forecasting.

It was inseparable from mathematics and statistics as an academic discipline until the foundation of the Econometrics Society in 1931. Although a quantitative approach to economics goes back to PETTY, in the twentieth century it owes its origins to Henry Moore's attempt in 1911 to provide statistical evidence for MARGINAL PRODUCTIVITY theory. Gradually it changed its emphasis from searching for constant economic laws to probabilistic models.

The major techniques most frequently used are MULTIPLE REGRESSION, TWO-STAGE LEAST SQUARES and a multitude of tests to prevent problems such as AUTOCORRELATION. After 1945, the growth of macroeconomics and the more sophisticated study of consumer behaviour inspired a great volume of econometric work. The data used are either TIME SERIES provided by official governmental statistical organizations or CROSS-SECTION DATA collated through surveys.

See also: Cowles Commission

References
Griliches, Z. (1983) *Handbook of Econometrics*, Amsterdam: North-Holland.
Haavelmo, T. (1944) 'The probability approach in econometrics', *Econometrica (Supplement)* 12: 1–115.

Marchi, N. de and Gilbert, C. (eds) (1989) *History and Methodology of Econometrics*, Oxford: Clarendon Press.

Pagan, A. (1987) 'Three econometric methodologies: a critical appraisal', *Journal of Economic Surveys* 1: 3–24.

Pagan, A.R. and Wickens, M.R. (1989) 'A survey of some recent econometric methods', *Economic Journal* 99: 962–1025.

Walters, A.A. (1968) *An Introduction to Econometrics*, London: Macmillan.

economic agent (D0, M0)

A person or firm with the power to make decisions about output, investment, prices, etc.

Economic and Social Council (F0)

United Nations council elected by the General Assembly of the UN to co-ordinate its economic and social work. Its commission's remit includes population, human rights, the status of women, drugs and regional problems. It has fifty-four members.

economic anthropology (A1)

The study of socioeconomic organizations. In succession to the classical political economy of QUESNAY, SMITH, RICARDO and MARX that traced the economic consequences of human nature, it has examined economic behaviour. VEBLEN used an anthropological approach in his distinctive INSTITUTIONAL ECONOMICS. Increasingly economic anthropologists have studied non-market economic institutions.

References

Gregory, C.A. (1982) *Gifts and Commodities*, London: Academic Press.

North, Douglass C. (1990) *Institutions, Institutional Change and Economic Performance*, Cambridge: Cambridge University Press.

economic base multiplier (R0) *see* regional multiplier

economic calculation (D2, P2)

Valuations based on present and expected future conditions used to allocate scarce capital resources among competing uses. The purpose of the calculation is to achieve economic efficiency. MISES argued that markets are essential to this process and used this concept to attack socialism.

References

Horwitz, S. (1998) 'Monetary calculation and Mises "Critique of Planning"', *History of Political Economy* 30: 427–50.

economic climate (E6)

The persisting state of an economy apparent in its general trends over a specified time period.

See also: economic weather

Economic Community of the countries of the Great Lakes (F0)

An economic association of Zaire, Rwanda and Burundi set up in 1979 to establish trade agreements.

Economic Community of West African States (F0)

An economic association with free movement of labour and a proposed COMMON EXTERNAL TARIFF set up in 1975. The member countries are Benin, Gambia, Ghana, Guinea, Guinea-Bissau, Ivory Coast, Liberia, Mali, Mauritania, Niger, Nigeria, Senegal, Sierra Leone, Togo and Upper Volta.

economic cost (D0) *see* opportunity cost

economic crime (K4)

A crime undertaken for financial gain. Its specific nature depends on the rules of a particular economic system. In the former USSR frequent use was made of this concept. It covers both the theft of state property and the illicit making of profits; in the UK, it refers to fraud and INSIDER DEALING.

See also: economics of crime

economic development (O1) *see* development

economic devolution (D0, P0)

1 The transfer of all economic decision making to individual households and businesses.

2 The principal characteristic of a MINIMAL STATE.

economic efficiency (D0)
The simultaneous achievement of both TECHNICAL and ALLOCATIVE EFFICIENCY. Farrell also described it as product or global efficiency.

References

Farrell, M.J. (1957) 'The measurement of productive efficiency', *Journal of the Royal Statistical Society. Series A* 120: 253–81.

economic forecasting (C5)
Predictions of the values of particular economic variables, often on the basis of extrapolation of past trends, modified by other information and using the techniques of econometrics. National economic forecasting is an essential element of DEMAND MANAGEMENT, as well as a first stage in national and corporate PLANNING. The forecasts drawn up by private institutes and newspapers provide different views of the future to the government's.

See also: linkage models; Treasury model

References

Clements, M.P. and Hendry, D.F. (1998) *Forecasting economic time series*, Cambridge, New York and Melbourne: Cambridge University Press.
Fildes, R. (ed.) (1995) *World Index of Economic Forecasts*, 4th edn, Aldershot: Gower Press.
Kacapyr, E. (1996) *Economic forecasting: the state of the art*, Armonk, NY, and London: Sharpe.

economic geography (R1)
Economic analysis of the location of economic activity, together with the study of land use and urban areas. Although von Thünen was, in a sense, the father of LOCATION THEORY, it was not until the 1950s that much detailed work was done in this branch of geography.

See also: land economy

References

Hanink, D.M. (1997) *Principles and applications of economic geography: Econ-*

omy, policy, environment, New York and Chichester: Wiley.
Lloyd, P.E. and Dicken, P. (1977) *Location in Space: A Theoretical Approach to Economic Geography*, New York: Harper & Row.

economic good (D0)
A scarce good, yielding UTILITY, which must be allocated either by rationing or by the price mechanism; not a FREE GOOD.

economic growth (O4)
The growth in the total, or per capita, output of an economy, often measured by an increase in real GROSS NATIONAL PRODUCT, and caused by an increase in the supply of FACTORS OF PRODUCTION or their PRODUCTIVITY.

This approach was central to Smith's *Wealth of Nations* and to much of CLASSICAL ECONOMICS. HARROD and DOMAR in 1948 were major founders of modern growth theory. Growth theorists have wedded their work to DEVELOPMENT ECONOMICS and to a study of ECONOMIC PLANNING. Ecologists and others concerned about the scarcity of natural resources have advocated zero economic growth rates as appropriate for the twenty-first century. A writer as early as John Stuart MILL (in his *Principles of Political Economy*, Book IV, ch. 6) extolled the benefits of the STATIONARY STATE.

References

Mishan, E.J. (1977) *The Economic Growth Debate. An Assessment*, London: Allen & Unwin.
Rostow, W.W. (1990) *Theorists of Economic Growth from David Hume to the Present*, New York: Oxford University Press.

economic incidence (H2) *see* tax incidence

economic indicators (C8, E3)
Statistics used in economic forecasting to analyse the state of an ECONOMY. Overall indicators of economic activity include indices of industrial production, manufacturing output, engineering orders, retail sales volume, registered unemployment

and unfilled vacancies. Indicators of output show the growth of production of principal industries; indicators of external trade include indices of export and import volume, the visible and current balances and the terms of trade plus the size of the official reserves; financial indicators include changes in various measures of the MONEY SUPPLY. Inflation indicators include those for retail prices, basic materials and wholesale prices of manufactured products.

See also: coincident indicators

economic institution (P0)
1 An organization which is a component of an economy.
2 A system of PROPERTY RIGHTS.
3 A norm of economic behaviour.
4 A decision-making unit.
5 A type of contract, e.g. a form of insurance to cover a particular sort of risk.

References
Wiles, P.J.D. (1977) *Economic Institutions Compared*, Oxford: Basil Blackwell.

economic integration (F0)
The joining together of economic activities, especially the trade of several countries. This can take different forms, including FREE-TRADE AREAS, CUSTOMS UNIONS, COMMON MARKETS and federations of national economies. Different forms of integration can be distinguished by the extent to which individual national governments retain independence in decision making.

See also: European Monetary System

economic journals (A1)
The learned academic periodicals, mostly published quarterly, containing articles and book reviews, which, by presenting the research findings of the economics profession, give the clearest indication of the present state of the subject. Some of them, e.g. the *American Economic Review*, attempt to cover all branches of economics, but increasingly journals specializing

in a particular branch of the discipline have been founded. Many economists only publish articles and avoid publishing books because of the great status the journals have attained in the economics profession. Recently many of these periodicals have added assessments of computer software to their book reviews. The leading academic journals of economics include *American Economic Review, Bank of England Quarterly Review, Economica, Economic Journal, Journal of Industrial Economics, Journal of Political Economy, Manchester School of Economic and Social Studies, National Institute Economic Review, Oxford Economic Papers, Quarterly Journal of Economics, Review of Economic Studies, Review of Economics and Statistics*.

See also: financial journalism

economic justice (D6)
Distributive justice based on fully informed and voluntary transactions. Since Aristotle's *Nicomachean Ethics* many economic writings have asserted the importance of ensuring that exchange is fair to both parties and that the fruit of production should be distributed to factors of production according to their relative inputs.

See also: Rawlsian justice

economic life (M4)
The period during which an asset is expected to yield a return. For the purposes of calculating DEPRECIATION, assets are assumed to have a standard life. Houses are given a notional life of 80 years, coal mines 100 years and machines 8, 16 or 25 years.

economic man (D0)
A person, motivated by self-interest, who attempts in consumption, work and leisure to maximize his total utility. Much of CLASSICAL and NEOCLASSICAL economics makes this assumption about human nature. To behave as an economic man, it is

necessary to engage in many mathematical calculations.

See also: *homo economicus*; *homo sovieticus*

economic methodology (B4)
The different approaches to the task of formulating economic theories and models. Economists have inevitably been influenced by parallel debates in science, especially Popper's assertion of the falsification principle, Kulin's emphasis on paradigms and Lakatos' stress on scientific research programmes. Nevertheless, throughout the development of economics particular works on, and demonstrations of, economic methodology have been prominent. In the classical period, RICARDO demonstrated the power of simple economic model building when setting out the effects of protectionism on wages, profits, rent and economic growth. John Stuart MILL praised but did not practise the a priori abstract approach to formulating economic theories, and SENIOR considered the crucial difference between normative and positive issues. In the 1930s, ROBBINS clearly set economics apart from other social science disciplines by making the study of 'ends and means which have alternative uses' central to the subject. With the growth of mathematical economics and econometrics in the twentieth century, it was inevitable that the formalization and empirical testing of theories became the major ways in which economists went about their work: writers such as SAMUELSON guided economics in this direction. However, the empirical thrust of much of present-day economics is balanced by the wrestlings of welfare economists who have sought to put value judgements on a sounder basis.

See also: economics as rhetoric

References
Backhouse, R.E. (ed.) (1994) *New directions in economic methodology*, London and New York: Routledge.
Blaug, M. (1980) *The Methodology of*

Economics, or How Economists Explain, Cambridge and New York: Cambridge University Press.
Keynes, J.N. (1891) *The Scope and Method of Political Economy*, London: Macmillan.
Kulin, T.S. (1970) *The Structure of Scientific Revolutions*, Chicago: University of Chicago Press.
Popper, K. (1959) *The Logic of Scientific Discovery*, New York: Harper Torch Books.
Robbins, L. (1949) *An Essay on the Nature and Significance of Economic Science*, London: Macmillan.
Samuelson, P.A. (1947) *Foundations of Economic Analysis*, Cambridge, MA: Harvard University Press.

economic methods (D2, P2)
1 In a specialized sense, the use of the market or the price mechanism as part of PERESTROIKA.
2 Production techniques at least cost.

References
Aganbegyan, A. (1988) *The Challenge to Economics of Perestroika*, London: Hutchinson.

economic model (D0, E1)
A simplified picture of economic reality showing the interrelationships between a few economic variables. CANTILLON, QUESNAY and RICARDO were the first economists to formalize their economic theories in this way. With the increasing use of mathematics and ECONOMETRICS by economists, economic models have become more complex.

economic paradigm (B4)
A major principle central to a school of economics as it provides a fundamental analytical tool of economic theorizing. MARGINALISM and NEOCLASSICAL ECONOMICS, for example, have been able to demonstrate the powerful applications of the marginal concept backed up by calculus. In periods when there has been great dissatisfaction with the state of economics, a cry for a new paradigm has often heard: in the 1930s the concepts of KEYNES in his

General Theory provided one for a generation of macroeconomists.

See also: economic methodology

References

Latsis, S.J. (ed.) (1976) *Method and Appraisal in Economics*, Cambridge and New York: Cambridge University Press.

economic planning (D2, L1, O2, P2)
The allocation of economic resources and the determination of production on the basis of a plan; the alternative to allocation by markets. The Soviet plans of the 1930s were the first major attempts to organize entire national economies according to this method. In the post-war period, French INDICATIVE PLANNING also attracted much attention. Governments also use planning for aspects of their economies, particularly for regional development and major investment. Since planning essentially commits a government to a future course of action, it can lead to many inflexibilities, including a slow reaction to change, especially in the foreign trade sector. As planners rely greatly on economic FORECASTING the difficulties of modelling complex economies can make the quality of their plans suffer. Also planning necessitates much bureaucracy, which is both costly and often opposed to entrepreneurship. Increasingly planning in countries such as Hungary allowed the reintroduction of market mechanisms for small-scale production. At the beginning of the twenty-first century there is little enthusiasm for the revival of large-scale national planning.

See also: centrally planned economy; development

References

Cave, M. and Hare, P.G. (1981) *Alternative Approaches to Economic Planning*, London: Macmillan.

economic profit (D3, M4)
The surplus of revenue over all costs, including the OPPORTUNITY COSTS of employing all inputs.

See also: accounting profit

economic programming (P1)
The co-ordination of the independent production decisions of independent companies in late capitalist economies.

economic refugee (F2, J1)
A person migrating from one country to another to improve economic prospects but often posing as a person fleeing from political persecution. An increasing European phenomenon after the fall of communism and conflict in the Balkans.

economic rent (D3, R2)
1 Part of the earnings of a factor of production in excess of its TRANSFER EARNINGS arising from its scarcity. (See the figure.)
2 A factor's earnings over its OPPORTUNITY COST, according to PARETO.
3 The full market rate for housing services.

As land was regarded in CLASSICAL ECONOMICS as the only fixed factor of production, it alone earned rent. However, as any factor of production can be fixed in supply, 'rent' can be earned by any factor of production. Popular examples of factors with an INELASTICITY of supply abound. Labour can earn economic rent: especially persons with rare talents such as opera singers and top sports players

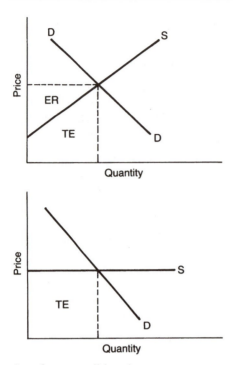

See also: council housing; rent

economics (A1, A2)

'The study of the general methods by which men co-operate to meet their material needs' (Sir William Beveridge); 'the study of mankind in the ordinary business of life' (A. Marshall); 'a science which studies human behaviour as a relationship between ends and scarce means which have alternative uses' (L. Robbins); 'Economics investigates the arrangements between agents each tending to his own maximum utility' (F.Y. Edgeworth); 'Wants, Efforts, Satisfaction – this is the circle of Political Economy' (Frederic Bastiat); 'Not a gay science ... what we might call ... the dismal science' (Thomas Carlyle).

First discussed by the Ancient Greeks, and the subject of general textbooks since the eighteenth century, economics has changed its focus as the concerns and techniques of its practitioners have developed. Originally the word meant 'household management' as the household was the basic economic unit of the time, including both farming and manufacturing activ-

ities. But the Greeks also, to their credit, raised the basic issues of VALUE, the nature of MONEY and the DIVISION OF LABOUR.

The word 'économistes' was first used by the French PHYSIOCRATS in the 1760s and in that century CANTILLON and SMITH produced the first comprehensive treatises on the subject. Smith, and his classical disciples, produced theories of growth, value, distribution and taxation. CANTILLON, the PHYSIOCRATS and RICARDO introduced model building into economics. Although methodological debates were present in the subject as early as John Stuart MILL and SENIOR, particularly in the standard debate about deduction and induction, it was DUPUIT, the MARGINALISTS and EDGEWORTH who first encouraged a mathematical treatment of economic theory.

The hints of earlier writers have provided the foundations for present-day economists. Issues of welfare, raised by MARSHALL and his follower PIGOU, led to a formal study of WELFARE ECONOMICS. The concern for measurement, first proposed by PETTY, has inspired the econometric testing of economic theories. The wider discussion of economics as 'POLITICAL ECONOMY' has linked economics to ideological positions in current policy debates, and later KEYNES produced a general theory of the economy which determined the postwar agenda for macroeconomic theory. The increased size of the economics profession (in the UK there were only sixteen professional economists in 1908) has inevitably led to subdivision of the subject, especially in more empirical areas.

economic sanctions (F1)

Trade and financial penalties and barriers to trade imposed upon a country in order to induce it to change its basic political system or policies. Occasions when this strategy has been used include the 1930s when Italy invaded Abyssinia, the 1960s when Southern Rhodesia (now Zimbabwe) refused to adopt a system of majority rule, the 1980s to force South Africa to treat all racial groups equally and the 1990s to end Iraq's occupation of Kuwait.

The use of sanctions has long been available as an ultimate economic weapon (e.g. the Continental System of Napoleon at the beginning of the nineteenth century), but it has always been difficult to enforce sanctions universally. In the form of a trade embargo, sanctions stimulate domestic industry to produce import substitutes, but this movement of an economy towards AUTARKY causes losses in ECONOMIC WELFARE as production cannot be concentrated in the most efficient industries. Article 41 of the Charter of the United Nations mentions sanctions as a permissible form of international action.

References

Carter, B.E. (1989) *International Economic Sanctions*, Cambridge: Cambridge University Press.

Curtin, T. and Murray, D. (1965) *Economic Sanctions and Rhodesia*, London: Institute of Economic Affairs.

Hufbauer, G. and Schott, J. (1985) *Economic Sanctions Reconsidered*, Washington, DC: Institute for International Economics.

economics and psychology (D1)

Psychological theory has been used in economics to improve the modelling of the motivation of economic agents, to understand how human beings behave when faced with UNCERTAINTY and to learn about the formulation of preferences. Psychology has contributed to many areas of economics, including the examination of entrepreneurship, unemployment, poverty, taxation and marketing.

See also: bounded rationality; cognitive consonance; cognitive dissonance

References

Earl, P.E. (1988) *Psychological Economics: Development, Tensions, Prospects*, Boston: Kluwer.

—— (1990) 'Economics and psychology: a survey', *Economic Journal* 100: 718–55.

MacFadyen, A.J. and MacFadyen, H.W. (eds) (1986) *Economic Psychology: Intersections in Theory and Application*, Amsterdam: North-Holland.

economics as rhetoric (B4)

A disciplined form of conversation that rejects modern quantitative economics which has prediction as its goal, in favour of a literary approach which examines the nature of economists' various arguments, recognizing the metaphors used and questioning the objectivity of the subject.

See also: economic methodology

References

Klamer, A., McCloskey, D.N. and Solow, R.M. (eds) (1989) *The Consequences of Economic Rhetoric*, Cambridge: Cambridge University Press.

McCloskey, D.N. (1983) 'The rhetoric of economics', *Journal of Economic Literature* 21 (June): 481–517.

—— (1986) *The Rhetoric of Economics*, Brighton: Wheatsheaf.

economics of crime (K4)

1 A branch of NEOCLASSICAL ECONOMICS which analyses the decision making of criminals in terms of a comparison of the marginal benefit of succeeding and the MARGINAL COST of being detected and sentenced. This celebrated analysis of BECKER'S is mainly applicable to the study of property offences.

2 A study of the effects of allocating resources to law enforcement and crime prevention. The poor quality of crime statistics, partly caused by varying rates of reporting offences, makes empirical work difficult.

References

Anderson, R.W. (1976) *The Economics of Crime*, London and Basingstoke: Macmillan.

Andreano, R. and Siegfried, J.J. (1980) *The Economics of Crime*, Cambridge, MA: Schenkman.

Becker, G.S. (1968) 'Crime and punishment: an economic approach', *Journal of Political Economy* 76: 169–217.

Fiorentini, G. and Peltzman, S. (eds)

(1995) *The economics of organised crime*, Cambridge, New York and Melbourne: Cambridge University Press.

economics of information (D8)

A branch of economics that recognizes the imperfection of information, the costs of obtaining it and its asymmetric character because of the actions of firms and individuals. The sources of information, including that which is spontaneously generated by the market, are considered. Information economics has many implications for financial markets.

References

Stigler, G.J. (1961) 'The economics of information', *Journal of Political Economy* 69: 213–25.
Stiglitz, J.E. (2000) 'The contribution of the economics of information to twentieth century economics', *Quarterly Journal of Economics* 115 November): 1441–78.

economics of law (K0)

1 The economic analysis of legal issues, especially PROPERTY RIGHTS, negligence, contract and crime, as well as the more obviously related areas of regulation, competition and monopoly.
2 The application of price theory and statistical methods to the study of legislation, legal decisions and courts of law. COMMONS was one of the first economists to use legal materials to further economic analysis. COASE pioneered the rigorous application of economics to a legal problem – in his case the law of nuisance. STIGLER and others brought the illumination of economics into dark areas of REGULATION. Posner demonstrated that most branches of the law can benefit by the use of economic concepts. The valuation of costs and benefits and the application of the notion of OPPORTUNITY COST to many legal problems are the principal ways in which economists have shown themselves to be invaluable colleagues of lawyers.

Such is the importance of this modern branch of economics that several journals specialize in blending economic and legal analysis, notably *Journal of Law and Economics*, *Journal of Legal Studies*, *International Review of Law and Economics* and *Journal of Law, Economics and Organization*.

See also: economics of crime

References

Hirsch, W.Z. (1999) *Law and economics: An introductory analysis*, 3rd edn, San Diego and London: Academic Press.
Ogus, A.I. and Veljanovski, C.G. (eds) (1984) *Readings in the Economics of Law and Regulation*, Oxford: Clarendon Press.
Polinsky, A. (1989) *An Introduction to Law and Economics*, Boston: Little, Brown.
Posner, R.A. (1986) *Economic Analysis of Law*, 3rd edn, Boston: Little, Brown.
'Symposium on law and economics', *Columbia Law Review* 85: 899–1116, 1985.
Veljanovski, C. (1990) *The Economics of Law. An Introductory Text*, London: Institute of Economic Affairs.

economics of religion (L3)

A study of non-market behaviour within communities of believers. Matters covered include the influence of religious belief on economic behaviour, the use of theology to criticize economic policy, and the application of microeconomic theory to the study of individual and collective religious behaviour.

References

Azzi, C. and Ehrenber, F.G. (1975) 'Household allocation of time and church attendance', *Journal of Political Economy* 83: 27–56.
Iannaccone, L.R. (1998) 'Introduction to the economics of religion', *Journal of Economic Literature* 36: 1465–96.

economics of the arts (Z1) *see* cultural economics

economic specificity (A1, J5)

An economic commitment to a firm or person. Cases include a firm's hiring of a worker, a worker's choice of a particular firm as a training establishment, and bank credit to a particular firm. Specificity increases RISK.

economic summits (E6, F0)
Meetings of the GROUP OF SEVEN which attempt to co-ordinate the economic policies of the major world economies. These have taken place annually since the oil-price shock of 1973–4:

- Rambouillet (November 1975) approved of intervention to maintain the orderliness of financial markets (Canada was absent).
- Puerto Rico (June 1976) made the reduction of unemployment and inflation central goals.
- London (May 1977) announced growth targets for the Group of Three.
- Bonn (July 1978) extended growth targets to all of Group of Seven, using West Germany as the initiator of growth.
- Tokyo (June 1979) fixed ceilings for oil imports.
- Venice (June 1980) changed the emphasis of economic policy to the lowering of inflation rates.
- Ottawa (July 1981) announced the goals of cutting public sector debt and reducing the rate of growth in the money supply.
- Versailles (June 1982) ordered a study of intervention to stabilize exchange rates.
- Williamsburg (May 1983) ordered a study of the international monetary system.
- London (June 1984) tackled the world debt problem by announcing arrangements for debt rescheduling.
- Bonn (May 1985) continued to support strict fiscal and monetary policies.
- Tokyo (May 1986) agreed on more economic co-operation and ordered a study of appropriate economic indicators.
- Venice (June 1987) announced continued support for the LOUVRE ACCORD; also

Japan agreed to reflate its economy.
- Toronto (1988) provided a framework for the rescheduling of Third World debt.
- Paris (1989) was principally concerned with the global environment and international traffic in drugs.
- Houston (1990) discussed the aftermath of the collapse of communism in Eastern Europe, set up a study of appropriate methods to revive the Soviet economy and agreed to phase out subsidies to farmers.
- London (1991) agreed to co-operate on keeping interest rates low, encouraging greater personal savings and reducing emissions which contribute to 'global warming'.
- Munich (1992) failed to produce agreements to stimulate the world economy but urged the completion of the URUGUAY ROUND of GATT and the cutting of government budget deficits to lower interest rates.
- Tokyo (1993) asked the USA, Canada and European countries to cut their fiscal deficits and Japan to bolster domestic demand. Unemployment was to be cut through non-inflationary growth.
- Naples (1994) agreed to take steps to reduce high unemployment levels. Leaders were pleased with the reduction in inflation.
- Halifax (1995) urged the reform of the IMF and the World Bank to provide emergency financing to cope with Mexico-type liquidity crises.
- Lyons (1996) agreed to write off 80 per cent of the debts of poor countries in six years.
- Denver (1997) admitted Russia as an associate member and urged the continuance of democracy in Hong Kong; the USA resisted European demands for a reduction in greenhouse gas emissions.
- Birmingham (1998) agreed to strengthen financial architecture to avoid new financial crises but no agreement on extending debt relief to developing countries.

- Cologne (1999) produced an aid package for Kosovo and the Balkans and considered restructuring Russia's external debt.
- Okinawa (2000) considered the elimination of poverty in developing countries and financial assistance to provide information technology for them.
- Genoa (2001) provided a global fund to combat AIDS, recommended a New Deal for Africa and called for new world trade talks.

economic system (P0)
The system of ownership, institutions and allocation mechanisms of an ECONOMY. Ownership is the principal criterion for distinguishing various forms of SOCIALISM from CAPITALISM. Institutions indicate the degree of freedom from central control, particularly the nature of trade unions, productive enterprises and banks. Methods of allocation contrast planned with market economics. University and college courses on comparative or alternative systems contrast different types of economy.

See also: economic institution; economy

economic transition (P0)
The change from one type of ECONOMIC SYSTEM, usually from a centrally planned to a market economy. The principal recent aspects of this transformation in Eastern Europe have included PRIVATIZATION of state industries, liberalization of capital and labour markets, the founding of stock exchanges and the strengthening of private property rights.

economic underpinning (P0)
The economic activities which finance a society. Previously this support was mainly agricultural and industrial; now it is increasingly based on information.

economic union (F0)
This uniting of national economies consists of four elements. A SINGLE MARKET, COMPETITION POLICY, common policies on structural change and regional development, and macroeconomic policy co-ordi-nation by the imposition of binding rules for budgetary policies, especially by stating upper limits for budget deficits and by defining an overall FISCAL STANCE. A union of this kind has been proposed for the EUROPEAN UNION.

See also: Delors Plan

economic value (D0, M4) *see* replacement cost

economic weather (E6)
The short-term conditions under which an economy operates over periods as short as a week, a month or a quarter of a year.

See also: economic climate

economic welfare (D6)
The total satisfaction residents of a country receive from the consumption of available goods and services. Increasingly there have been attempts to move beyond NATIONAL INCOME measures as a proxy estimate of economic welfare to the use of a wider range of social and economic indicators so that EXTERNALITIES and the subtleties of human tastes can be taken into account. Total welfare conferred by the production of goods and services must be viewed alongside welfare losses, e.g. more income is judged within the context of the amount of leisure enjoyed by workers. A high-welfare country usually has a high proportion of the population owning the major types of consumer durable, e.g. washing machines and television sets; a low-welfare country has poor housing, much pollution and long working hours.

Dissatisfaction with an economy has several indirect indicators, including the incidence of alcoholism, the rate of suicide, infant mortality rates, life expectancy, disease and disability rates.

See also: measure of economic welfare; social welfare

economism (D0)
A taste for material success. To Marxists, economism amounts to pursuing intermediate economic goals instead of ulti-

mate political goals. In modern economies, workers with low economism often end up in the SECONDARY LABOUR MARKET where there is little training and small chance of economic advancement

economy (P0)

1 The market order.
2 A set of exchanges.
3 The entirety of the economic activities of one nation using the same currency.
4 Frugal use of resources in order to minimize costs.

See also: advanced organic economy; auto-economy; barter economy; black economy; blue economy; bootblack economy; branch economy; cash economy; centrally planned economy; closed economy; command economy; core economy; communal economy; cowboy economy; decentralized market economy; dependent economy; drug economy; dual economy; enclave economy; estate economy; financial economy; first best economy; formal economy; hansom cab economy; informal economy; market economy; mature economy; mesoeconomy; mineral-based economy; moonlight economy; networking economy; one-crop economy; open economy; parallel market economy; permanent arms economy; pink economy; primitive economy; protean economy; psychological economy; pure credit economy; revenue economy; second economy; self-sufficient economy; shadow economy; share economy; shortage economy; socialist economy; Soviet-type economy; spaceman economy; steady state economy; underground economy; villa economy; warehouse economy

economy of scale (D2)

A reduction in long-run AVERAGE COST as a result of an expansion in output leading to increasing RETURNS TO SCALE. To measure a purely scale effect, it is necessary to make some strict assumptions: that, as output changes, there is no change in techniques used, factor prices are constant and the same degree of vertical integration holds as output changes. Scale economies may

arise in many aspects of a firm's operations – its financing, marketing and production. An excellent example of a scale economy is the spreading of a fixed cost over a larger output, e.g. typesetting costs spread over an increased print run. In the figure, there are economies of scale up to output OP but diseconomies at higher outputs.

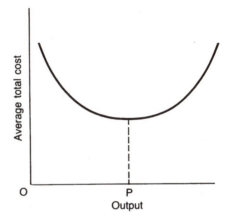

See also: diseconomy of scale; economy of scope; external economy of scale; internal economy of scale

References

Gold, B. (1981) 'Changing perspectives on size, scale and returns: an interpretive survey', *Journal of Economic Literature* 19(March): 5–33.

economy of scope (D2)

A reduction in AVERAGE COST brought about by the joint production of two or more goods or services by a single firm, rather than by several firms. The similarities of the products permit the use of the same factor inputs for different products, e.g. marketing, basic research. In the transport industry the use of the same fixed capital for both passenger and freight vehicles provides a good example of this economy.

References

Panzar, L.C. and Willig, R.D. (1981) 'Economics of scope', *American Economic*

Review Papers and Proceedings 71(May): 268–72.

economy of size (D2, M2)

A reduction in AVERAGE COST resulting from the growth in size of a firm, e.g. the managerial economics arising from the multiplant nature of a large firm or from its superior type of marketing organization.

economyth (A1)

A false economic generalization following a wrong paradigm and based on poor, or no, empirical research.

ecu (E4)

The European Currency Unit, a composite basket of currencies consisting of the currencies of EUROPEAN COMMUNITY countries. In 1990, the Deutschmark comprised about 30 per cent, the French franc about 19 per cent, sterling about 12 per cent and the Italian lira about 10 per cent of this basket.

It is increasingly used in commercial banking transactions because its greater stability makes it more suitable for fixing contractual terms than a national currency. Employees of the European Commission are paid in ecus and even Bank of England treasury bills are denominated in them. It was replaced by the EURO in 1999 on a 1:1 basis.

See also: hard ecu

Edge Act Corporation (G2, M1)

A type of US financial corporation in existence since 1919 which can receive deposits from foreign governments and other non-US residents and from US citizens whose deposits are transmitted abroad. It can also hold foreign securities and engage in foreign exchange activities. These corporations can be either banking corporations mainly concerned with accepting deposits or corporations principally involved in investing in foreign non-banking firms. The advantages of being a corporation of this kind are that they can operate across state boundaries, in the case

of international transactions, and that their investments can be wider than those of FEDERAL RESERVE member banks, e.g. in foreign finance.

See also: McFadden Branch Banking Act

Edgeworth box (D0, F1)

This depicts the trading relationships between two persons or two countries using INDIFFERENCE CURVES and a CONTRACT CURVE which joins the points of tangency where each indifference curve of X touches an indifference curve of Y. In the figure, I_{X1}–I_{X7} and I_{Y1}–I_{Y7} are indifference curves of consumer X and consumer Y respectively. CC is the contract curve. The MARGINAL RATES OF SUBSTITUTIONS are equalized for each consumer.

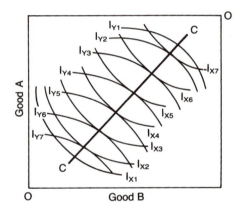

Edgeworth, Francis Ysidro, 1845–1926 (B3)

Irish-born economist and statistician who received a classical education at Trinity College, Dublin, and Oxford University. He began his academic employment as a lecturer in logic in 1880 and afterwards the Tooke Chair of Political Economy at King's College, London, in 1890; then Drummond Professor of Political Economy at Oxford from 1891 to 1922. A natural mathematical ability enabled him to write the very influential *Mathematical Psychics* (1881), much admired by MARSHALL: in it he applied mathematics to UTILITARIANISM, analysed the nature of con-

tract in a free market and invented INDIF-
FERENCE CURVES and CONTRACT CURVES, still
much used in international and labour
economics. In many articles he made
major contributions to the theories of
index numbers and probability theory.
Also, he was the first editor of the
Economic Journal from 1891 to 1926.

References

Creedy, J. (1986) *Edgeworth and the Devel-
opment of Neoclassical Economics*, Ox-
ford: Basil Blackwell.
Edgeworth, F.Y. (1925) *Papers Relating to
Political Economy* (2002), Oxford: OUP.
O'Brien, D.P. and Presley, J.R. (eds) (1981)
*Pioneers of Modern Economics in Brit-
ain*, ch. 3, London: Macmillan.

effective demand (E0)

The value of AGGREGATE DEMAND equal to
aggregate supply. KEYNES introduced this
concept in his *General Theory*.

See also: effectual demand

References

Amadeo, E.J. (1989) *Keynes's Principle of
Effective Demand*, Aldershot: Edward
Elgar.
Keynes, J.M. (1936) *The General Theory of
Employment, Interest and Money*, Book
1, ch. 3, London: Macmillan.

effective exchange rate (F3)

An index of a currency's international
value in terms of a basket of currencies,
weighted by the relative importance of
each foreign country in the trade of the
currency concerned. For sterling, the basket of currencies included the US dollar,
the Japanese yen and the Deutschmark,
and the weights reflected the UK's trade
with the USA, Japan and Germany.

effective rate of assistance (F1)

VALUE ADDED to a country's production as a
result of PROTECTION as a proportion of the
value added by producers under FREE
TRADE. This is calculated by the formula
$(A - B)/B$, where A is the domestic price
of a good, including a tariff, minus the
subsidized cost of inputs per unit of out-

put, and B is the world price of a good
minus the unsubsidized cost of inputs per
unit of output.

effective rate of protection (F1)

This measures the extra value added, as a
result of TARIFFS, as a proportion of the
free trade value added. The most commonly used formula is $t_e = t_1 - kt_2/(1 - k)$,
where t_e is the effective rate of tariff
protection, t_1 is the tariff rate on output,
t_2 is the tariff rate on input and k is the
proportion of total price accounted for by
inputs.

effective tax rate (H2)

The average rate of tax levied on gross
personal income. This rate for companies
refers to taxation as a proportion of VALUE
ADDED.

effectual demand (E0)

The notion stated by MALTHUS in his
Principles of Political Economy of a level
of demand in a national economy able to
bring about FULL EMPLOYMENT of land and
labour. He used this idea to challenge the
complacent view that there could not be a
general GLUT. Effectual demand, Malthus
asserted, could be increased by landlords
employing menial servants, more distribution of wealth to the middle classes and
PUBLIC WORKS employment for the poor.
KEYNES saw Malthus as one of his precur-
sors in the formulation of macroeconomic
ideas.

See also: effective demand

References

Eltis, W.A. (1980) 'Malthus's theory of
effective demand and growth', *Oxford
Economic Papers* 32: 19–56.
Rutherford, R.P. (1987) 'Malthus and
Keynes', *Oxford Economic Papers* 39:
175–89.

efficiency wage (J3)

'A wage measured with reference to the
exertion of ability and efficiency required
of the worker' (Marshall). He asserted that
there would be a tendency towards efficiency wages or earnings in the same

district. Many firms attempt to base their wage structure on a productivity principle.

See also: local labour market

References

Marshall, A. (1920) *Principle of Economics*, 8th edn, Book V1, ch. 3, London: Macmillan.

efficient estimator (C1)
The statistic of two sampling distributions with the same mean but the smaller variance.

efficient job mobility (J6)
Movement of workers to different jobs in response to a changing pattern of demand which results in the elimination of labour shortages.

See also: labour mobility

efficient market (D4)
A market in which prices reflect all available information. In a weak version of this market prices reflect past prices; in a stronger version, prices reflect fully all publicly available information. Profits in an efficient market cannot be made by studying historical prices as the traders have that data already. This concept is crucial to the macroeconomic theory of the RATIONAL EXPECTATIONS School. The efficient market hypothesis applied to the stock market is the RANDOM WALK hypothesis.

References

Mandelbrot, B. (1966) 'Forecasts of future prices, unbiased markets and martingale models', *Security Prices: A Supplement Journal of Business* 39: 242–55.
Samuelson, P. (1965) 'Proof that properly anticipated prices fluctuate randomly', *Industrial Management Review* 6: 41–9.

effluent fee (Q2)
A charge to a polluter giving the right to discharge into the air or a watercourse a noxious emission. Although this approach to pollution control has been criticized as a 'licence to pollute', it does encourage firms to minimize the discharge of pollutants. Ideally, the fee should be fixed such that the revenue from it is equal to the marginal costs of pollution. An early example of the use of these fees has been in Germany's Ruhr Valley; they have also been charged in the USA, France and the Netherlands.

See also: pollution control; pollution tax

eftpos (G2)
Electronic funds transfer at point of sale, i.e. automatic debiting of customers' bank or credit card accounts. This is the major method of introducing the cashless society but unlikely to replace the present variety of payment methods.

See also: debit card

egalitarianism (D3)
1 Advocating universal suffrage.
2 EQUALITY OF OPPORTUNITY because there are no barriers to entering any occupation with or without the financial means being offered to facilitate entry.
3 An absence of income differentials.

See also: Bentham

eigenprices (D0)
The economically rational prices of an economy derived from the actual state of an economy, as shown in an INPUT–OUTPUT table. Each eigenprice is a full-cost price, reflecting the input–output coefficients for the production of that good. Eigenprices make output and factor prices consistent, taking into account the final yield of an economy and the principle of full-cost pricing. Actual prices are irrational if they diverge from eigenprices. Eigenprices are 'ideal' because factors of production are rewarded according to their marginal revenue products.

References

Seton, F. (1985) *Cost, Use and Value. The Evaluation of Performance, Structure and Prices across Time, Space and Economic Systems*, Oxford: Clarendon Press.

elasticity (D0)
The responsiveness of the value of an economic variable to a change in the value

of another which is related to it. The most common use of the concept is PRICE ELASTICITY OF DEMAND. This concept, one of the most durable tools of the economist, is used extensively in price theory, international economics and industrial economics.

See also: cross price elasticity of demand; elasticity of supply; income elasticity of demand

elasticity of a factor of production (D0)
The proportionate change in output caused by a proportionate increase in the input of one factor of production, holding the other factors constant.

elasticity of demand (D0)
The responsiveness of quantity demanded of a good or service to a change in its price or in a consumer's income.

elasticity of expectations (D0)
HICKS defined this as the ratio of the proportional change in the expected future values of X to the proportional change in its current value. If this is equal to unity, expected values and current values change in the same direction and by the same proportion, e.g. if present prices double then it is expected that future prices will double also.

elasticity of substitution (D0)
The ease with which one factor of production can be substituted for another. If the elasticity of substitution is greater than unity for a FACTOR OF PRODUCTION, then an increase in its supply will increase its relative share of the national income. HICKS introduced this concept in his *Theory of Wages* (1926) to show the effect of a change in the supply of one factor, assuming two factors only and constant returns to scale, on the marginal productivity of the other. The concept has been extensively used in the study of PRODUCTION FUNCTIONS and the analysis of the effects of INVENTIONS.

References

Bronfenbrenner, M. (1960) 'A note on relative shares and the elasticity of substitution', *Journal of Political Economy* 68: 284–7.

elasticity of supply (D0)
The responsiveness of the quantity supplied to a change in the price of that factor, good or service. In the short term,

supply can be increased only by using existing factors of production more intensively (e.g. by overtime working); in the long term supply can be increased by increasing factor supply (e.g. recruiting and training more workers, increasing the capital stock). Supply elasticities increase as the time period lengthens, as demonstrated (in the figures) by the changing slope of the supply curves (S).

elephant (G1)
US term for an INSTITUTIONAL INVESTOR.

eligible liability (E5, G2)
Sterling deposit liabilities (excluding deposits with an original maturity of over two years) + sterling resources obtained by switching foreign currencies into sterling. From 1971 to 1981 in the UK, commercial banks had to maintain 12½ per cent of their eligible liabilities in the form of reserve assets.

embargo (F1)
Prohibition of trade or an activity such as the publication of a book.

embodied technical progress (O4)
Technical improvements embodied in the capital stock. Net or replacement investment can increase the amount of embodied technical progress as in both cases the equipment available and chosen for purchase will usually employ the latest technology.

See also: disembodied technical progress; innovation

emission charge (Q2)
A fee related to the quantity of a pollutant discharged, e.g. a noxious liquid, and imposed on the firm causing pollution.

emission fee (Q2)
A payment giving a firm the right to pollute. If the fee is too low, then it does little to prevent pollution levels from rising; if too high, it may require expensive monitoring and prevent the production of any output at all.

emission reductions banking (Q2)
An environmental control policy allowing

a source of pollution which reduces its emissions more than legally required to 'bank' the right to pollute more in the future. Thus over a period of time the flow of emissions is on average at the legal limit.

empirics (C8)
Empirical findings acquired through observation and experiment.

employee ratios (J2)
Measures of the characteristics of a LABOUR FORCE which include:

1 capital employed per employee, a CAPITAL–LABOUR RATIO;
2 sales per employee, a measure of the PRODUCTIVITY of sales staff;
3 profit per employee, a measure of labour utilization;
4 average wage per employee, a measure of labour costs.

Employee Stock Ownership Plan (J3)
An arrangement for a company to set up an employee trust to allow employees to acquire the shares of the company. These schemes have flourished in the USA and the UK. In the USA, the National Center for Employee Ownership (NCEO) estimated in 1986 that 8,000 US firms had such schemes by then, covering 10 million to 11 million workers, i.e. 8 per cent of the total national workforce. The company makes regular tax-deductible contributions to the Employee Stock Ownership Plan. Ownership exercises a strong psychological effect on workers: someone earning £18,000 per annum would accumulate £32,000 in ten years' time. It is mainly a scheme for the more successful firms. In the UK, the Companies Act of 1989 helped to accelerate the growth of these schemes by allowing companies more freedom to purchase their own shares. In developing countries, there is scope for such schemes as a means of redistributing wealth from rich elites to the poor. The usefulness of the schemes is judged by the extent to which employees become more profit conscious, management–worker communications are im-

proved and the recruitment and retention of staff are facilitated.

See also: industrial democracy; workers' participation

employer–employee bargaining (J5)

Negotiations between an employer, or employers' association, with a worker or a TRADE (LABOR) UNION concerning pay and working conditions. It can take the forms of individual or COLLECTIVE BARGAINING.

employers' association (J5)

A federation of firms of one industry which jointly engages in COLLECTIVE BAR-GAINING with the TRADE UNIONS representing their workers. As employers usually apply negotiated wages to all of their workers, irrespective of their union membership, collective bargaining covers a larger part of the labour force than that part which is unionized. These associations often represent their industries on other matters, e.g. proposed legislation.

employment (D0, J2)

The engagement of a factor of production in a productive activity with the result that it receives a factor income. Employment gives people wages or salaries, and rewards capital with interest or profits. Increased LABOUR FORCE PARTICIPATION makes more persons available for employment; economic growth makes possible actual employment growth. Even in advanced economics with an employed labour force static in size, technological change effects many sectoral shifts in the composition of employment.

Employment Act 1946 (E6)

Federal statute of the USA which set out major economic goals for the USA, including the FULL EMPLOYMENT of labour and other resources. Under the Act, the COUN-CIL OF ECONOMIC ADVISERS was established. The Act sought to promote 'maximum employment' rather than FULL EMPLOYMENT; it did not guarantee a high level of employment by pledging the use of federal resources to job creation programmes.

Employment Act 1980 (J5)

UK statute providing for the financing of secret ballots on trade union matters such as strike action, the election of union officials and the amendment of trade union rules. The protection of trade union members was increased by making it unlawful unreasonably to refuse trade union membership or to terminate it and to require trade unions to make compensation if a member's complaint was well founded. The Act also narrowed the range of SECONDARY ACTION exempt from actions in tort to those actions relating to the breaking of a contract of employment.

Employment Act 1982 (J5)

This UK statute extended industrial relations legislation by declaring contracts for the supply of goods and services void if only members of a specified trade union can carry out the work or if a trade union has to be recognized. Also, there was a requirement that only union officials could authorize trade union acts. Damages could be recovered from trade unions, employers' associations, their trustees, members and officials, except for protected property, e.g. a political fund. The limit for damages was set at £250,000 for the largest unions with 100,000 or more members.

Employment Act 1988 (J5)

This UK statute amended labour legislation by stating various rights of union members, including a right to a ballot before industrial action, a right of access to the courts, a right to inspect a union's accounting records and a right to require an employer to stop deductions of union subscriptions. Also, the Act stated that trade union funds cannot be used to pay fines imposed by a court and that industrial action to enforce membership of a CLOSED SHOP is a tort.

Employment Appeal Tribunal (J5)

UK body established in 1975 to hear appeals from industrial tribunals, particularly concerning discrimination and unfair dismissal.

employment contract (J2, J3)

The terms on which a person is hired by a firm. Williamson distinguishes four types: recurrent spot contracting (by which an employee is hired from day to day); contingency claims contracting (being hired depends upon the occurrence of an event, e.g. ball-boys are needed at Wimbledon on a fine day); authoritative contracting (a master–slave contract, a modern example might be military conscription); and INTERNAL LABOUR MARKET contracting (a flexible form of hiring to the senior posts of an organization determined by managerial rules).

See also: implicit contract theory; invisible handshake

References

Williamson, O.E., Wachter, M.L. and Harris, J.E. (1975) 'Understanding the employment relation: the analysis of idiosyncratic exchange', *Bell Journal of Economics* 6: 250–78.

employment function (J2)

The desired level of employment as a function of the demand for output.

References

Ball, R.J. and St Cyr, E.B.A. (1966) 'Short term employment functions in British manufacturing industry', *Review of Economic Studies* 33: 179–207.

Employment Institute (L3)

London-based institute founded in 1985 and originally headed by Richard Layard and Sir Richard O'Brien. It has enjoyed widespread political support for its neo-Keynesian approach to the problems of UK unemployment. It has advocated some general reflation, special measures for the long-term unemployed and infrastructure investment.

employment multiplier (E0)

The first version of a formal MULTIPLIER, suggested by KAHN in 1930. It shows the ratio of secondary to primary employment. Primary employment consists of the jobs in an industry where the original investment occurs and in associated industries, e.g. those producing and transporting raw materials. Secondary employment is the consequential employment in the production of consumption goods to meet the increased expenditure of the recipients of wages and profits in the primary industries. Employment effects of government expenditure are variable as the value of the employment multiplier changes with the type of expenditure. Expenditure directly on personnel has a greater multiplier effect than consumption and capital spending.

References

Kahn, R.F. (1931) 'The relation of home investment to unemployment', *Economic Journal* 41: 173–98.

employment rate (E0, J2)

The proportion of the LABOUR FORCE employed. This alternative to the unemployment rate is used to estimate the level of demand in a national economy.

See also: activity rate; labour force participation rate

Employment Relations Act 1999 (J5)

Its provisions, based on the White Paper *Fairness at Work* (1998), concern recognition and derecognition of trade unions for collective bargaining purposes, the blacklisting of workers with membership of a union, an extension of the right to claim for unfair dismissal, and a right for workers to be accompanied in some disciplinary and grievance proceedings.

empty nester (J1)

A married person in late middle age whose children have moved elsewhere leaving an 'empty nest'.

See also: Third Age

enclave economy (P0)

1 An isolated economy without forward and backward economic linkages within it, e.g. an agrarian economy which imports its tractors and fertilizers and exports its products. In such economies,

an economic activity does not have any spin-offs in terms of services and processing and so there is an absence of the dynamic effects of intersectoral growth.
2 A sub-economy of an advanced economy, e.g. in the USA, ethnic groups have formed distinct sub-economies with, for example, Cubans or Mexicans comprising both the owners and workers.

end of geography (F3, G1)
A way of referring to global financial integration.

References
O'Brien, R. (1992) *Global Financial Integration. The End of Geography*, London: Chatham House.

endogenizing the exogenous (E1)
The inclusion in an economic model of something previously regarded as given. Classical economists, for example, regarded FULL EMPLOYMENT as given, whereas KEYNES included it as a variable in his model of the national economy. Expectations were often regarded as given but now many economic models include them.

See also: endogenous variable; exogenous variable

endogenous growth theory (O4)
An explanation of ECONOMIC GROWTH as the product of the structural features of an ECONOMY. An early theory was HARROD'S warranted rate of growth that made the growth rate depend on the savings ratio and output–capital ratio, both structural features. Later versions of this theory had foundations in microeconomics and emphasized the contribution of accumulated HUMAN CAPITAL to increased productivity.

See also: post-neoclassical endogenous growth theory

endogenous variable (D0, E1)
An economic variable whose values are determined by the other variables of an economic model.

See also: exogenous variable

endowment (A1)
1 An original asset, especially land; inherent ability.
2 Something of value bestowed upon another.

endowment effect (G2)
An increase in a bank's profitability as a result of a rise in interest rates.

endowment insurance (G2)
A form of insurance which provides for a fixed sum of money to be paid on a specified date, or at death.

endowment mortgage (G3)
A mortgage linked to an insurance policy that provides at the end of its term a sum to redeem the mortgage. The mortgagor pays both interest on the amount borrowed and insurance premiums. In times of falling property prices the problem of NEGATIVE EQUITY makes this form of house purchase unattractive.

Engel, Ernst, 1821–96 (B3)
German statistician who was educated at the Ecole des Mines, Paris. Director of the statistical bureaux of Saxony from 1850 to 1858 and of Prussia from 1861 to 1862. In 1857 he propounded Engel's law, one of the first major empirical findings of lasting importance.

Engel coefficient (D2)
Expenditure on food, beverages and tobacco as a proportion of final private consumption expenditure.

Engels, Friedrich, 1820–95 (B3)
The principal intellectual collaborator of MARX from 1844. Although his family owned textile mills in the Rhineland and Manchester, he was a social critic from the age of 18. He never attended university but came under the influence of the Young Hegelians in Berlin; his practical knowledge of business was to temper Marxian theory. His interest in economics began with an essay *Outlines of a Critique of Political Economy* (1844). His analysis of industrialization and his prophecy of a proletarian revolution impressed Marx.

They jointly wrote *Die Heilige Familie* (The Holy Family) (1845), *Die Deutsche Ideologie* (The German Ideology) (1845–6) and *Manifest der Kommunistischen Partei* (The Communist Manifesto) (1848). Engels is also noted for his *Umrisse zu einer Kritik der Nationalökonomie* (Outlines of a Critique of Political Economy) (1844) and *Die Lage der arbeitenden Klasse in England* (The Condition of the Working Class in England) (1945), as well as his posthumous editing of the second and third volumes of Marx's *Das Kapital*. His frequent financial help to the Marx family maintained his great friend in his chosen career. Living in retirement for twenty-six years, he was able to reconstruct the remainder of Marx's *Das Kapital* from mounds of notes.

References

Carver, T. (1983) *Marx and Engels: The Intellectual Relationship*, Brighton: Wheatsheaf.

Henderson, W.O. (1976) *The Life of Friedrich Engels*, 2 vols, London and Portland, OR: Frank Cass.

Engel's law (E2)

The assertion that, as income rises, the proportion spent on food falls. Formally, this can be stated as the INCOME ELASTICITY OF DEMAND for food is less than unity.

engine of growth (O4)

1 The mechanism, often said to be international trade, which starts an economy's expansion. This view has been contrasted with the view that trade is a 'handmaiden'. A concept attributed to ROBERTSON.

2 A major economy of the world, e.g. the USA, which is so large that its expansion generates a demand for imports which stimulates many other national economies.

English auction (D4)

A method of selling an item which begins with the first bid being requested by the auctioneer and ends when the bids reach an uncontested peak. The item is sold to the highest bidder, provided that the bid is not less than the seller's reserve price. The earliest auctions in the Roman Empire were probably like this since 'auction' is derived from the Latin word *auctus* meaning 'increase'.

See also: auction

English disease (J5)

The consequences of poor industrial relations and industrial organization manifest in strikes, low productivity and low growth.

enterprise culture (P0)

An ECONOMY with little REGULATION and every encouragement to ENTREPRENEURS.

enterpriser (M1) *see* entrepreneur

enterprise union (J5)

A Japanese TRADE UNION covering all the workers below supervisor level within an enterprise or within an establishment of that enterprise. The union has its headquarters on company premises and is often run by company employees on secondment from their usual employment. This is the most important level of unionism in Japan as most of workers' contributions are spent at this level and vital wage bargaining is done. Often an enterprise union is given the task of allocating between types of worker the gross addition to the enterprise's wage bill. Although there were 72,605 unions by 1989, this does not imply a weak union movement as there is joint action through their national federations, the major ones having been RENGO, SOHYO, DOMEI, SHINSANBESU. Since 1948, statistics on Japanese unions have been produced by the Basic Survey on Trade Unions.

See also: company union; local union

enterprise zone (R5)

A local UK or US area, often a decaying inner city, selected for special government help in the form of exemption from property taxation and from many governmental regulations. The purpose of these zones is to encourage the location of new industries and new jobs by reducing the factor cost of doing so. The creation of such zones leads to conflict between local authorities and businesses within and without these areas as the latter can suffer a loss of industry.

See also: regional policy

entrepôt (F1)
A commercial centre or warehouse engaged in the distribution of goods throughout the world.

entrepreneur (M1)
The fourth FACTOR OF PRODUCTION, after land, labour and capital, which organizes production and undertakes the risk of an enterprise. In JOINT STOCK COMPANIES, the risk bearing is undertaken by the shareholders; in small businesses, usually by the manager–proprietor. The idea of entrepreneurship was introduced into economics by CANTILLON, literally to mean the 'undertaker', i.e. a person who buys at a fixed price and sells at an uncertain price. Subsequently different economists debated alternative definitions, which include riskbearer, organizer of production, innovator and decision-maker in circumstances which give people unequal access to information. New entrepreneurs are often well-educated persons with managerial experience having small firms in areas with wealthy local markets.

References

Casson, M.C. (1982) *The Entrepreneur: An Economic Theory*, Oxford: Robertson.
Gilder, G. (1984) *The Spirit of Enterprise*, New York: Simon & Schuster; Harmondsworth: Viking, Penguin.
Knight, F.H. (1921) *Risk, Uncertainty and Profit*, Chicago: Chicago University Press.
Schumpeter, J.A. (1934) *The Theory of Economic Development*, Cambridge, MA: Harvard University Press; London: H. Milford.

envelope curve (D0)
A curve enclosing a whole family of curves, each of which contributes at least one point to the envelope. The main use of envelope curves is in relating long-run to short-run cost curves. In the figure $SATC_1$–$SATC_4$ are short-run average total cost curves; LRAC is the long-run average total cost curve.

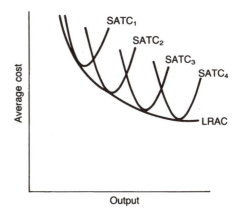

environmental accounting (M4)
Accounting for the private and social costs of environmental events in NATIONAL INCOME accounting, FINANCIAL ACCOUNTING and MANAGEMENT ACCOUNTING.

environmental determinism (Q0)
The doctrine that economic and social activities are determined by the physical environment, particularly the climate. Development economists ascribe to this determinism the lower incidence of development in some areas of the world and the international DIVISION OF LABOUR.

environmental issues (Q0)
World population growth, the demand for exhaustible resources, the loss of topsoil and forests, and pollution are the principal matters discussed.

Environmental Protection Agency (Q2)
Washington-based US federal agency established in 1970 for research into the environment and the control of pollution. It reinforces the efforts of other federal agencies and co-ordinates the anti-pollution enforcement work of state and local governments. It is concerned with air, water,

radiation, solid waste, pesticides and toxic substances.

environmental tax (Q2)

A tax on a polluter related to the external costs of private production.

See also: effluent fee

EPA (C5, F0)

A world econometric model of the Japanese Economic Planning Agency which includes nine country models (of the seven major OECD countries, Australia and South Korea) and six trading regions.

See also: linkage models

References

Amano, A., Maruyama, A. and Yoshitomi, M. (eds) (1982) *EPA World Economic Model*, Vols 1 and 2, Tokyo: Economic Planning Agency.

epidemic model (O3)

An explanation of the diffusion of technology using the analogy of the spread of infectious disease. The rate of diffusion is regarded as a function of the product of (1) the share of the population with a particular innovation and (2) the number of the fixed population without it. The model attempts to explain why a diffusion rate follows a sigmoid S-shaped time path with low initial rates, a quickening of diffusion, then a fall back to low rates as the potential for diffusion diminishes.

References

Romer, P. (1990) 'Endogenous technological change', *Journal of Political Economy* (October 1990 Supplement) 99: S71–102.

equality (D6)

The achievement of the same amount of ECONOMIC WELFARE per head or the same economic opportunities for each individual. As the creed of EGALITARIANISM, it denies differences in innate abilities and argues that superior abilities are merely the product of training.

See also: human capital

equality of opportunity (D6, J7)

1 Access by minority groups and the disadvantaged to education and everything necessary for full participation in society.
2 An absence of DISCRIMINATION so that people are judged only by the personal attributes relevant to a particular task or activity. Individuals are responsible for outcomes.

References

Roemer, J.E. (1998) *Equality of opportunity*, Cambridge, MA: Harvard University Press.

equality standard (D6)

An idealistic approach to income distribution giving equal shares to all by equalizing per capita incomes. Critics of this approach assert that human nature is not so altruistic as to tolerate a system of reward which ignores differences in individual persons' contributions to output. Also a fall in labour productivity is a likely consequence of using this policy.

See also: altruism; contribution standard; egalitarianism; needs standard

equalizing wage differential (J3)

A wage differential which compensates a worker for a non-pecuniary aspect of a job, e.g. the degree of risk or the dirtiness of working conditions. These differentials discourage labour mobility to more pleasant occupations. CANTILLON and SMITH were both aware of this reason for wage differentials.

Equal Opportunities Commission (J7)

UK institution set up in 1976 to deal with complaints about SEXUAL DISCRIMINATION. Initially the bulk of complaints concerned job adverts specifying applicants of a particular sex; subsequently the issues covered have included a wider range of grievances. It publishes annual statistics on sexual wage differentials.

Equal Pay Act 1963 (USA) (J3, J7)

US federal statute which sought to equalize male and female pay for workers in interstate commerce. Employment discrimination against women and ethnic minorities was dealt with under Title VII of the Civil Rights Act 1964.

Equal Pay Act 1970 (UK) (J3, J7)
UK legislation that enforced the principle of equal pay for equal work: this was to apply to all collectively bargained agreements and STATUTORY MINIMUM WAGE RATES by 1975. Despite the Act, there is still a divergence between male and female earnings, reflecting OCCUPATIONAL SEGREGATION of women, differences in hours worked and promotion policies of firms.

Equal Pay Directive (J3, J7)
A directive issued by the EUROPEAN COMMISSION in 1975 to counter discrimination in pay, especially on the grounds of sex.

equal product curve (D0) *see* isoquant

equilibrium (D0, E0)
A state of balance such that a set of selected interrelated variables has no inherent tendency to change. In economics, a major example is the balance of the forces equating demand and supply. SMITH in his discussion of prices used the idea of market prices fluctuating around the NATURAL PRICE which can be considered a central price. The SUBSISTENCE THEORY OF WAGES regarded expansions and contractions of a population as equilibrating forces making the subsistence wage rate the long-run equilibrium wage. An equilibrium can exist for an economy as a whole, for a sector of it, for a particular market or for an institution, such as a firm. Although the term is applied principally to static models, there can be an equilibrium in dynamic models when variables proceed along an equilibrium-type path. Equilibria can be stable or unstable, temporary or permanent: some of them do not exist. The Marshallian and Keynesian cross-diagrams are the most famous diagrammatical representations of equilibrium (E, equilibrium).

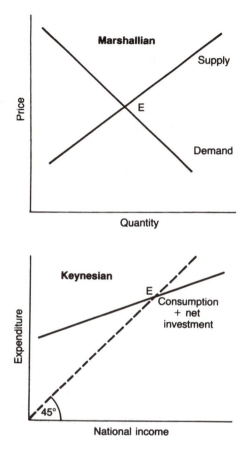

See also: general equilibrium; temporary equilibrium

References

Amendola, M. and Gaffard, J.-L. (1998) *Out of equilibrium*, Oxford and New York: Clarendon Press.
Caravale, G. (ed.) (1997) *Equilibrium and economic theory*, London and New York: Routledge.
Fisher, F.M. (1983) *Disequilibrium Foundations of Equilibrium Economics*, Cambridge: Cambridge University Press.
Samuelson, P.A. (1965) *Foundations of Economic Analysis*, 2nd edn, New York: Athenaeum.

equilibrium GNP (E0)
The level of real national income at which AGGREGATE DEMAND equals AGGREGATE SUPPLY, i.e. desired expenditure equals the

quantity of goods and services supplied in that economy.

equilibrium price (D0)
The price which equates demand and supply in a market in a particular time period.

equilibrium velocity (E4)
The VELOCITY OF CIRCULATION that maintains interest rates on deposits at their long-run equilibrium (i.e. average) rates.

equipment trust bond (G2)
A financial arrangement for leasing equipment. The holder of the bond owns the equipment and then leases it to the firm which has issued the bond via a trustee. The trustee pays the interest and principal to the bondholder, receiving rental payments from the issuer of the bond.

equity (G1)
1 ORDINARY SHARES.
2 COMMON STOCK.
3 The portion of a company's capital which does not earn a fixed rate of interest. Equity holders usually receive dividends varying with the profitability of the company/corporation and its profit distribution policy. The issue of equity shares enables a company to expand its capital and to spread business risk.
4 Fairness.

See also: horizontal equity; Rawlsian justice; vertical equity

equity comovement (G1)
The extent to which the prices of equities on different stock exchanges change by the same amount and in the same direction. The removal of exchange controls has increased the possibility of comovement.

equity joint venture (M1)
A business jointly owned and run by a private firm and a governmental organization. As it is financed partly by equity capital, the return to the private investor is a variable dividend. This arrangement was used by capitalist firms to invest in CEN-TRALLY PLANNED ECONOMIES. To the participating government there is the advantage of not having to pay fixed interest charges. Many East European countries turned to this organizational form after 1989 as a means of reconstructing their economies.

See also: European Bank for Reconstruction and Development; joint venture

equity-linked mortgage (G2, R2)
A method of purchasing commercial or residential property. The lender offers to pay, for example, half the current interest rate on the mortgage in return for acquiring half the equity in the property (or another proportion). This device makes it possible for borrowers to obtain finance for large property purchases and for lenders to benefit from the capital appreciation of properties.

equity premium (G1)
The excess of the average real return to stock market securities over the interest rate on treasury bills. In the USA this has been about 6 per cent for 100 years.

References
Kocherlakota, N.R. (1996) 'The equity premium: it's still a puzzle', *Journal of Economic Literature* 34: 42–71.
Mehra, R. and Prescott, E.C. (1985) 'The equity premium: a puzzle', *Journal of Monetary Economics* 15: 145–61.

equity release scheme (G2)
A loan obtained by a house owner through taking out a mortgage on the property to buy a high-yield bond in order to provide an income. Falling house prices caused some owners to lose their homes.

equity-style management (G2)
The choice by a portfolio manager between large or small growth or value of a client's investments where growth is measured by earnings growth and value is the ratio of price to book value of a share. A popular strategy is to choose growth at a reasonable price.

equity taxation (G2)

Taxation based on the fairness principle that each person should suffer an equal sacrifice. 'Sacrifice', however, is an ambiguous term as it can refer to equality in absolute terms or at the margin.

See also: ability to pay

equity warrant (G2)

An option to buy an ORDINARY SHARE or COMMON STOCK at a fixed price in the future. It is issued in the form of a bond with a low COUPON. In the case of EUROBONDS, the warrant is issued attached to a bond denominated in a particular currency. However, the warrant is often detached and traded separately. The popularity of this cheap method of stock market speculation is reflected in the rapid increase in warrant prices.

equivalent variation (D6)

The minimum amount a person who gains from a change has to be given to forgo the change.

ergonomics (J2)

The scientific study of the physical methods of work with the aim of minimizing effort and maximizing output. Inspired by the study of the practical problems of using military equipment in the Second World War, it became a recognized discipline in 1949. Much work has been done on the appropriate ways of displaying information, on the study of machine controls and on the relationship between a worker and the physical environment.

References

Singleton, W.T. (ed.) (1982) *The Body at Work*, Cambridge: Cambridge University Press.

error (C1)

The difference between observed and true values brought about by chance rather than systematically.

See also: probable error; standard error of estimate; Type I error; Type II error

error-correction model (C5)

An econometric method of adjusting a policy instrument to keep a target variable close to its desired value used as early as 1954 by PHILLIPS.

References

Salmon, M. (1982) 'Error correction mechanisms', *Economic Journal* 92: 615–29.

escalator clause (M2)

A clause in a contract designed to revise payments due under that contract in line with changes in a specified price index. In times of considerable inflation, these clauses are popular in labour and building contracts, as well as in tax schedules and social security benefits tables.

See also: cost of living adjustment

establishment (M1)

A place of business, a factory or a plant which is part or the whole of a firm.

estate economy (P4)

An underdeveloped economy with much of its agriculture organized into large estates, usually foreign owned. Malaysia with its rubber plantations, Ceylon with its tea plantations and Argentina with its cattle ranches had this character. Although wages of the estate workers were low by international standards, they were high enough to induce the movement of workers from subsistence agriculture. These estates were the basis of development in several ex-colonial countries.

e-tail company (L8)

A company which retails its goods and services using e-mail.

ethical unit trust (G2)

UK equivalent of a SOCIAL CONSCIENCE FUND.

Euler's theorem (D3)

The rule that if FACTORS OF PRODUCTION are paid according to their MARGINAL PRODUCTS, the total product will be distributed completely if and only if there are constant RETURNS TO SCALE. The theorem is of importance when considering the application of the MARGINAL PRODUCTIVITY OF WAGES since if there are DIMINISHING RETURNS and workers are paid according to their marginal products, the total wage bill will be less than the total product. Conversely, if there are increasing returns to scale and workers' wages equal their marginal products, the total wage bill will be more than the value of their output.

euro (F3)

The common currency of the EUROPEAN UNION adopted by all member states excepting Denmark, Sweden and the UK. It came into force on 1 January 1999 in parallel with the currencies of participating states. Euro coins and notes were issued from 1 January 2002 and became the sole currency in circulation in the states of the eurozone by 28 February 2002. Soon after its inception it experienced a slump in its value.

Eurobank (G2)

A bank able to receive TIME DEPOSITS and make loans in currencies other than that of the country in which it is located.

Eurobond (G1)

A long-term bond marketed internationally by an international syndicate of banks in countries other than the country with the currency in which the bond is denominated, e.g. a bond in French francs can be marketed anywhere outside France. The advantage of this type of financial instrument is that it escapes national financial regulations.

Eurobond market (G1)

An international market, founded in the early 1960s, as a PRIMARY and SECONDARY MARKET in BEARER BONDS issued outside the country of that particular currency. The anonymity of this market has attracted investors who wish to remain discreet about their holdings. Previously able to avoid any regulation, it is now under the ASSOCIATION OF INTERNATIONAL BOND DEALERS in the UK. It has become a leading world securities market.

Eurocheque (F3, G2)

A CHEQUE that can be written in any one of a number of CURRENCIES.

Euroclear (G2)

An international agency for clearing bank cheques between ten European countries.

See also: Cedal

Eurocurrency market (G2)

The international market dealing in bank deposits in the major currencies, including the US dollar, yen, Deutschmark, Swiss franc, French franc, guilder and ecu, which has been in existence since the 1950s. Its early growth was stimulated by REGULATION Q which encouraged the expatriation of US dollars in search of higher interest rates.

Eurodollar (F3)

Dollars on deposit with banks outside the USA, some of them the European branches of US banks. Originally, the attraction of such deposits was that they could evade the RESERVE REQUIREMENTS needed for domestic deposits and any restrictions on maximum interest rates (REGULATION Q). As a consequence of US balance of payments deficits, dollars are supplied for the reserves of the central banks other than the FEDERAL RESERVE SYSTEM. Increases in Eurodollar deposits are encouraged by the investment facilities and interest rates of the Eurobanks. There is also a small creation of Eurodollars by the Eurobanks themselves.

Eurodollar market (F3, G2)

A WHOLESALE MONEY MARKET dealing in expatriate US dollars, outside the control of national banking authorities. However, increasingly the BANK OF ENGLAND, the BUNDESBANK and the US FEDERAL RESERVE BANKS have introduced controls on the foreign banks within their jurisdiction. Despite these controls, the banks operating in this market are more competitive than other commercial banks because their operating costs are lower as a consequence of the insistence on minimum deposits of at least £50,000.

Euroequity (G2)

An EQUITY of one country which is issued

or sold in another, e.g. the sale of Fiat shares in Germany.

Eurofed (E5) *see* European Central Bank

Eurofranc (G2)
A franc deposit in a non-French bank in Europe but outside France.

euro interbank offered rate (F3)
The interest rate at which euro interbank term deposits of the eurozone are offered by one prime bank to another.

Euroland (P4)
The member states of the European Union in the EUROPEAN MONETARY UNION using the euro as their currency.

Euromarket (G1)
A financial market trading in financial instruments that are denominated in currencies other than that of the country where that market is located, e.g. London trading in bonds denominated in French francs.

Euromoney deposit (G2)
A bank deposit in another currency, e.g. US dollars, French francs, Swiss francs and yen.

Euronext (G1)
The stock exchange formed by the merger of the exchanges of Amsterdam, Brussels and Paris in September 2000. This cross-border exchange began with trading in over 1,600 securities.

Euro overnight index average (F3)
The effective overnight interest rate of the panel banks in the euro interbank market.

European Bank for Reconstruction and Development (G2)
The development bank founded in 1991 and based in London which lends to the East European countries in order to ease their transition from centrally planned to market economies. Its capital was raised from EUROPEAN COMMUNITY institutions and forty-one countries. Its lending policy is to make 40 per cent of its loans for infra-

structure investment and 60 per cent for private sector commercial investment.

European Central Bank (E5)
Established in June 1998 and located at Frankfurt, Germany. It conducts monetary policy for all the twelve European countries using the EURO as their only currency. It has a six-member Executive Board, a Governing Council consisting of the members of the Executive Board and the governors of the central banks using the single currency, and a General Council which includes governors of central banks of the European Union not using the single currency (they are not allowed to vote).

European Communities (F0)
The three organizations consisting of the European Coal and Steel Community, established in 1952, the EUROPEAN ECONOMIC COMMUNITY, established in 1958, and the European Atomic Energy Community, also established in 1958. The original member states of each of the three communities were France, West Germany, Italy, Belgium, the Netherlands and Luxemburg. In 1967 the original institutional structures of the three communities were merged to create the common executive, judicial and legislative institutions of the EUROPEAN COMMUNITY.

European Community (F0)
The name given to the EUROPEAN COMMUNITIES since 1967. The original six member states (France, West Germany, Italy, Belgium, the Netherlands and Luxemburg) were joined, in 1973, by the UK, Ireland and Denmark, followed by Greece in 1982, and Spain and Portugal in 1986. The signatory countries of the European Community hoped to promote a greater equality of incomes between nations and regions, to raise the rate of economic growth, to help Third World countries and to establish a major economic power, rivalling the USA and the USSR. By 1987, the European Community had a population of 323 million inhabitants, making it

the largest market in the industrialized world (USA, 244 million; Japan, 122 million), but Japanese per capita income was then 48 per cent higher and US per capita income 40 per cent higher than in the European Community. The industrial strength of the European Community lies especially in its chemical, transport equipment and industrial machinery industries.

See also: European Economic Community; European Union

References

El-Agraa, A.M. (1990) *The Economics of the European Community*, 3rd edn, New York and London: Philip Allan.

European Co-operation Administration (F0, H1)

The US agency which administered MARSHALL AID to Europe, 1948–52.

European Currency Unit (E5) *see* ecu

European Economic Community (F0)

A CUSTOMS UNION of Western Europe, also known as the Common Market. It was founded by the Treaty of Rome in 1958 when France, West Germany, Italy, Belgium, the Netherlands and Luxemburg agreed to enter into a customs union with a common external tariff, mobility of labour and capital between the nation states, and a COMMON AGRICULTURAL POLICY. In 1967 its institutional structures were merged with those of the European Coal and Steel Community and the European Atomic Energy Community to form the common institutions of the EUROPEAN COMMUNITY.

European Free Trade Association (F0)

Founded in 1959 as the alternative European trade organization to the EUROPEAN ECONOMIC COMMUNITY with Austria, Denmark, Norway, Portugal, Sweden, Switzerland and the UK. Its members are now Austria, Finland, Iceland, Liechtenstein, Norway and Sweden (Denmark, Portugal and the UK left on joining the European Economic Community). At its inception, EFTA aimed to expand economic activity,

full employment and productivity in its area, to trade on the basis of fair competition and to remove tariffs between members by 1 January 1970. Although it reduced TARIFFS in 1961 and quotas among members during 1961–6, it was not originally intended to be a CUSTOMS UNION, i.e. with a COMMON EXTERNAL TARIFF. After 1973, a series of agreements between EFTA and the European Economic Community reduced tariffs between the member countries: by 1977 duties on most industrial goods between EFTA and the European Economic Community had been abolished.

European Investment Bank (F3, G2)

The major lending institution of the EUROPEAN COMMUNITY founded in 1958 to provide loans to assist 'the balanced and smooth development of the Common Market' with an initial capital of $1,000 million. It provides loans for three types of project: the modernization of less developed regions, the conversion of undertakings to new types of production and employment, and the financing of projects of interest to several member countries. In its first fifteen years, 60 per cent of its lending went to Italy, in particular to assist the development of the Italian south.

European monetary co-operation (F3)

A series of plans and agreements leading to the launching of the EUROPEAN MONETARY SYSTEM in 1979. It began with the Barre Plan and the Hague Summit of 1969 and was followed in 1971 by the WERNER REPORT and the European Council of Ministers' resolution. These initiatives resulted in an agreement between EUROPEAN COMMUNITY central banks in 1970 to provide a short-term monetary support system, a central banks' medium-term financial assistance scheme in 1972, the 'snake in the tunnel' short-term financing facility in European currencies of April 1972 to February 1973, the joint floating of European currencies, and the 'snake outside the tunnel', March 1973 to March 1979. Prior to 1979, there were unsuccessful attempts towards European monetary union in the Tindemans Report of 1976 and the Jenkins Initiative of 1977.

European Monetary Co-operation Funds (F3)

Part of the EUROPEAN MONETARY SYSTEM that finances imbalances in payments between the countries participating.

European Monetary System (F3)

The West European system for aligning exchange rates and bringing about a convergence in monetary policies. It came into being when West Germany, France, Denmark, the Netherlands, Italy, Belgium and Ireland decided in 1979 to change their exchange rates only within a joint consultation procedure. The principal components of the system are the ECU, the EXCHANGE RATE MECHANISM and credit mechanisms. Major currency alignments have taken place in September and November 1979, March and September 1981, February and June 1982, March 1983, July 1985, April 1986 and January 1987. The size of realignments has tended to increase over time: by the 1980s they were as great as 10 per cent per realignment. Under the system, Ireland and Italy, the highest inflation countries, have suffered deteriorating competitiveness and other countries, particularly Belgium and Denmark, have improved. The system is a hybrid of a fixed rate system and a managed float.

Prior to 1992 it created a zone of exchange rate stability in Europe and contributed to the convergence of the economic policies of the members. Speculation forced the pound and the lira out of the EMS in September 1992. Further speculation in August 1993 required the widening of the permitted fluctuation margin to 15 per cent for six of the remaining currencies.

See also: European monetary co-operation

References

Coffey, P. (1984) *The European Monetary System – Past, Present and Future*, Amsterdam, Dordrecht and Lancaster: Nijhoff.

de Grauwe, P. and Papadenos, L. (1990) *The European Monetary System in the 1990s*, Harlow: Longman.

European Monetary Union (F3)

The integration of the monetary policies and currencies of member states under a new EUROPEAN CENTRAL BANK using a single currency. This union was envisaged by the WERNER REPORT and designed by the DELORS PLAN which set out three stages towards integration. The first stage started in 1990 with the abolition of restrictions on capital movements in the EEC; the second stage amended the Treaty of Rome under the Maastricht Treaty 1992 to create the European Monetary Institute 1994 to provide for central bank co-operation and monetary policy co-ordination (the Institute was dissolved after the creation of the European Central Bank 1998) and there was an irrevocable fixing of exchange rates of the participating currencies by 1 January 1999; the third stage from 1999 led to the abolition of national currencies of 12 countries with the euro in circulation from 1 January 2002.

European option (G1)

An OPTION that can only be exercised on its expiry date.

European Recovery Program (O2) *see* Marshall Plan

European Regional Development Fund (R5)

A EUROPEAN COMMUNITY fund offering regional assistance, particularly for infrastructure projects, in member countries.

European Social Charter (I3, J0)

A treaty of the Council of Europe signed in 1961. It sought to protect social and economic human rights. Most of its articles concern employment conditions but it also grants social and medical assistance to resourceless people, the right to social security and the protection of mothers and children, and migrant workers. By June 2001 the Social Charter had been ratified by eighteen countries including Iceland and Turkey; the UK agreed to implement it in 1997.

European system of accounts (E0)

A classification of household expenditures by categories of use. It is a coherent framework for the presentation of the national income accounts of the member countries of the EUROPEAN COMMUNITY. The principal accounts are:

1 Domestic accounts

> Goods and services accounts
> Production account
> Generation of income account
> Distribution of income account
> Use of income account
> Capital account
> Financial account.

2 Rest of the world accounts

> Current transactions account
> Capital account
> Financial account.

References

European System of Integrated Economic Accounts ESA, 2nd edn, Luxemburg: Statistical Office of the European Communities, 1980.

European Union (F0)

A combination of the EUROPEAN COMMUNITY, co-ordination of foreign and security policies, and co-ordination of justice and interior affairs established by the Maastricht Treaty and effective from 1 November 1993. The Council of the EU consists of the appropriate ministers from each member state for the matter under discussion.

European Unit of Account (E4)

A basket of the currencies of the member countries of the EUROPEAN ECONOMIC COMMUNITY. Each currency is weighted according to its standing and amount in circulation.

See also: ecu

Eurosystem (E5)

This consists of the EUROPEAN CENTRAL BANK

and the central banks of the fifteen member states.

eurozone (F3)

The countries of the EUROPEAN UNION which accepted the euro as their common currency.

event study (C5, G0)

The analysis of the statistical significance of the occurrence of a particular type of event, e.g. a stock repurchase or financial restructuring, for the market value of a company in a financial market.

evolutionary game theory (C7)

An application of evolutionary methods to game theory. Through learning and evolution it is possible to reach an equilibrium lacking in rationality. A trial and error process establishes which strategy works best. A search for new microfoundations to evolutionary dynamics has been undertaken to enable the theory to be applicable to human society.

References

Samuelson, L. (1997) *Evolutionary Games and Equilibrium Selection*, London and Cambridge, MA: MIT Press.
Weibull, J.W. (1995) *Evolutionary Game Theory*, London and Cambridge, MA: MIT Press.

evolutionary theory of the firm (L1, L5)

A study of the determinants of the 'destiny' of firms which rejects the view that firms are maximizers and asserts that firms' actions have evolved from their own traditions. Innovatory change is only accepted in a crisis; it is not part of a long-term growth plan. MARSHALL, with his biological analogies for the growth of the firm, was a founder of this theoretical approach. The viable firm, according to ALCHIAN, has profits greater than are needed to maintain current activities; therefore under conditions of UNCERTAINTY, managers cannot predict the outcome of their decisions, so luck is quite important.

See also: Penrose

References

Alchian, A. (1950) 'Uncertainty, evolution and economic theory', *Journal of Political Economy* 58: 211–21.

Nelson, R.R. and Winter, S.G. (1982) *An Evolutionary Theory of Economic Change*, Cambridge, MA: Belknap Press of Harvard University Press.

ex ante, ex post (E0)

A widely used distinction in macroeconomics, coined by MYRDAL, to distinguish what is planned (i.e. *ex ante*) from what actually happens (i.e. *ex post*). These alternative concepts are often used in discussions of investment and welfare. If, for example, *ex post* investment is less than what was planned, then the expectations of the investor have not been realized.

References

Myrdal, G. (1939) *Monetary Equilibrium*, London: William Hodge.

ex ante variables (E0)

Measures of what is planned or intended, e.g. intended investment. These have been used since the STOCKHOLM SCHOOL and Keynesians started modern macroeconomics; increasingly *ex ante* measures have been used to estimate EXPECTATIONS. In practice, surveys of business enterprises are used to ascertain intended levels of production, investment and employment.

See also: *ex post* variables

excess burden of a tax (H2)

The DEADWEIGHT LOSS from a tax. This has two meanings:

1 The deadweight loss suffered by taxpayers in excess of what the government collects.

2 The amount a taxpayer would sacrifice in excess of the taxes being collected in exchange or the removal of all taxes.

See also: tax incidence

excess capacity (D0)

1 In competitive theory, a level of output below that level of output which minimizes average total cost.

2 More generally, any output level less than the maximum amount technically possible.

See also: X-efficiency

excess capacity theorem (L1)

The theoretical outcome of MONOPOLISTIC COMPETITION which holds that profit-maximizing firms choose a level of production that is lower and with higher average costs than under PERFECT COMPETITION. In the figure, ATC is AVERAGE TOTAL COST, MC is MARGINAL COST, D is demand, AR is AVERAGE REVENUE, MR is MARGINAL REVENUE, OP is the profit-maximizing price, OQ_2 is the profit-maximizing output and Q_1Q_2 is the excess capacity.

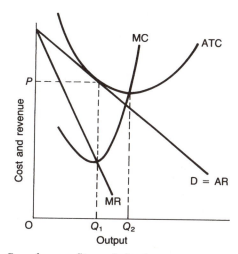

See also: profit maximization

excess demand (D0)

The amount by which demand exceeds supply at a given price. As excess demand can be positive or negative, it is a useful way of stating the relationship between demand and supply. When a market is in equilibrium, excess demand is zero. The rate of excess demand can be measured as (demand − supply)/supply. Markets subject to maximum price control are usually characterized by long-term positive excess demand which necessitates rationing and encourages the growth of BLACK MARKETS;

East European countries have provided many examples of this.

excess supply (D0)
Supply less demand at a given price. It can be regarded as negative excess demand.

exchange (D0)
1 The mutual transfer of goods, money or something of value between two or more parties.
2 The sale of one currency to obtain another.
3 A place for the sale of currencies, securities or commodities.

See also: trade

exchange controls (F3)
Limitations on the free movement of a national CURRENCY probably first advocated by PLATO. These usually take the form of restrictions on the purchases of foreign currency and on the export of capital. The UK had such controls from 1939 until 1979 when, helped by North Sea oil revenues, sterling needed no such support. France used exchange controls in 1981 to defend the franc; the Italian lira

long needed the support of controls. When exchange controls are in force, BLACK MARKETS in currency are tolerated by most governments as a means of delaying the formal announcement of change in the official rate.

See also: dual exchange rate

exchange cross-rate (F3)
The value of one of the world's leading CURRENCIES against another. The leading ten currencies usually quoted have been the US dollar, sterling, Deutschmark, yen, French franc, Swiss franc, Belgian franc, Dutch guilder, Italian lira and Canadian dollar. These are published daily in leading financial newspapers. This rate can be regarded as the exchange rate between currencies B and C when the exchange rates between A and B and A and C are known already; this cross-rate should be consistent with the other exchange rates.

exchange efficiency (D6)
An exchange of goods which makes at least one person better off, without anyone being worse off according to PARETO.

Exchange Equalization Account (E5)
The account of the BANK OF ENGLAND holding UK foreign exchange reserves. After the UK abandoned the GOLD STANDARD from 1932, the establishment of this account was necessary to provide a mechanism for supporting sterling through the sale and purchase of gold and foreign currencies: the account sells foreign currency to buy pounds when there is a desire to stabilize or improve the sterling exchange rate.

exchange rate (F3)
The price of a currency in terms of another, e.g. how many US dollars can be bought for one pound sterling. Such rates vary because of changes in the relative demand for different countries' goods and services and because national MONETARY and FISCAL POLICIES are inconsistent with each other. Differences in tax rates and in interest rates cause capital flows that affect

a country's balance of payments and, consequently, its exchange rate. An overvalued exchange rate leads to a CURRENT ACCOUNT balance of payments deficit and bearish speculative capital movements; an undervalued exchange rate creates a current account surplus and an influx of capital. Volatile exchange rates and volatile interest rates coincide.

References

Isard, P. (1978) *Exchange Rate Determination: A Survey of Popular Views and Recent Models*, Princeton, NJ: International Finance Section, Department of Economics, Princeton University.

Stein, J.L. *et al.* (1997) *Fundamental determinants of exchange rates*, 2nd edn, Oxford and New York: Clarendon Press.

Witteveen, H.J. (1982) *The Problem of Exchange Rates*, New York: Group of Thirty.

exchange rate agreement (F3)

A foreign exchange hedging technique requiring only the net amount owed at the end of a banking day to be paid. Otherwise, purchases and sales of a foreign currency at different times require several transactions; this kind of agreement requires only one.

Exchange Rate Mechanism (F3)

A crucial element of the EUROPEAN MONETARY SYSTEM which links the values of participating European currencies and limits the extent of their fluctuations to 2.25 per cent against the rest in the system, unless a wider band has been specially negotiated, e.g. Spain's and the UK's 6 per cent. Also it produces indicators of currency divergence against the ecu, makes available short-term credit to support intervention in foreign exchange markets on behalf of currencies which diverge too far and, in extreme cases, realigns currencies at new EXCHANGE CROSS-RATES. The ERM reduces speculative gains from changes in exchange rate movements and concentrates the minds of investors on the interest rate offered for deposits in a particular

currency, unless there are frequent realignments.

References

Giavazzi, F. and Spaventa, L. (1990) *The 'New' EMS*, Paper No. 369, London: Centre for Economic Policy Research.

exchange rate premium (F3)

The difference between the forward exchange rate and the expected future spot exchange rate.

exchange rate regime (F3)

The system chosen by national governments for the mutual determination of their exchange rates. The main choice is concerned with the extent to which there are fixed parities between different currencies, e.g. under the BRETTON WOODS system and under the EUROPEAN MONETARY SYSTEM or FLOATING EXCHANGE RATES.

exchange rate target zone (F3)

A softer version of a fixed exchange rate regime which permits wide bands for each currency participating provided that the countries concerned take corrective action when the values of their currencies come close to their limits.

See also: European Monetary System

References

Williamson, J. (1985) *The Exchange Rate System*, Washington, DC: Institute for International Economics.

exchange risk (F3)

The risk of an exchange rate changing and thereby lowering the value of one's holding of another currency. A MULTINATIONAL CORPORATION, for example, constantly faces the risk when doing business in another country that the foreign currency it acquires there will fall in value.

exchange standpoint epistemology (D4)

An approach to studying economics favouring market and market policy measures.

Exchequer (E5)

The UK government's account held at the

Bank of England. Holding this account is one of the activities of the Bank of England as a CENTRAL BANK.

Exchequer White (E5)
The daily internal Bank of England statement which shows its cash needs by detailing flows into and out of the bank, chiefly as a consequence of the government's receipt of tax payments and disbursement of governmental expenditures. If the bank is short, it will buy bills; if there is excess cash in the banking system, it will sell them.

excise duty (H2)
An indirect tax levied on a specific good, especially petrol, alcohol or tobacco. Duties of this kind have been an important source of government revenue in some countries, e.g. the USA, for longer than INCOME TAXES. Given the INELASTICITY of demand for these goods, they provide a reliable source of revenue. Also, the duties have been imposed as TARIFFS to protect domestic industries from the competition of imports.

See also: direct and indirect taxation

excise tax (H2) *see* excise duty

exclusion principle (D0)
A major characteristic of a PRIVATE GOOD: one person's consumption excludes others' consumption, e.g. my consumption of a piece of fruit excludes your consumption of it. PUBLIC GOODS are non-exclusive, e.g. my consumption of the benefit of the nation's armed services does not reduce your consumption.

exclusive dealing (L4)
A RESTRICTIVE PRACTICE in a market whereby distributors agree not to trade with firms which are not party to an agreement. In return for loyalty a rebate on purchases is often given.

ex dividend (G2)
An ORDINARY SHARE which does not bear the entitlement to receive the dividend

recently announced and payable at that time.

executive leasing (G2)
The offering of management services by experienced mid-career managers for short periods, usually for less than a year. Leasing is attractive to companies when a particular type of skill is needed either to cope with an unusual task, e.g. organizing a merger, or during an interregnum until a permanent executive is appointed.

executive stock option (J3, M1)
Part of the remuneration of a manager granting the right to purchase stocks/ shares at a preferential price. This form of incentive rewards executives who increase the market value of a company.

exercise price (G1) *see* put price

exit–voice (D0)
A distinction used to classify the physical or verbal methods individuals use to reveal their preferences. 'Voice' can take the form of voting (as in democratic politics) or complaints (as under grievance procedures); 'exit' is movement away from a less desired situation, e.g. a particular employment, region or country. 'Exit–voice' can be applied to collective or individual choice.

See also: Tiebout hypothesis

References
Hirschman, A.O. (1970) *Exit, Voice and Loyalty: Responses to Decline in Firms, Organizations and States*, Cambridge MA: Harvard University Press.

exogenous expectations (E0)
EXPECTATIONS that are given and are thus excluded from an economic model or theory. Few economists would now take this view of expectations.

exogenous growth model (O4)
A process of ECONOMIC GROWTH driven by an outside factor, especially technical change or foreign trade.

exogenous variable (C1, C6)
An economic variable whose values are not determined by the other variables of an economic model.

See also: endogenous variable

expectations (D0, E0)
The views of households or firms or governments about the future. They are based either on the simple view that the future will be like the past or on a more sophisticated view that the future will be partly like the past and partly different because of responses to previous forecasting errors. This is now the dominant theme of much of macroeconomics. The study of expectations has become much more elaborate than it was in the hands of MYRDAL and KEYNES.

See also: adaptive expectations; *ex ante* variables; exogenous expectations; extrapolative expectations; Keynes expectations; rational expectations; regressive expectations

expected monetary value (E4)
The product of the probability of the ith outcome and the value of the ith outcome:

$$EMV = \sum_{i=1}^{n} p_i.X_i$$

expected utility (D0)
The product of the probability of the ith outcome and the utility of the ith outcome:

$$EU = \sum_{i=1}^{n} p_i.U_i$$

See also: Bernoulli hypothesis; prospect theory

References
Savage, L.J. (1954) *Foundations of Statistics*, New York: Wiley.

expedited funds availability (G2)
The prompt availability of check deposits by US commercial banks.

expenditure function (E2)
An equation used to describe the consumption possibilities for a consumer at a given set of prices.

expenditure tax (H2)
A tax based on the amount actually spent by a consumer. Proponents of such taxation argue that the tax might be easier to collect than capital or income taxes and that the growth of personal savings (which would escape the tax) is encouraged. There have been many supporters of this type of taxation, including John Stuart MILL, MARSHALL, Irving FISHER, KALDOR and the MEADE Committee.

See also: double taxation of savings

References
Kaldor, N. (1955) *An Expenditure Tax*, London: Allen & Unwin.

expense preference (M1)
A manager's weighted preference for a particular type of cost. As managers often prefer an expansion of staff (as a means of being in charge of a larger establishment), they will prefer extra expenditure on staff to other forms of expenditure.

expense ratio (M2) *see* cost ratio

expensive easy money (E4, G2)
OKUN regarded this as credit extensively available, and therefore easy, but offered at higher interest rates and thus expensive.

experience good (D0)
A GOOD usually purchased frequently by a consumer who acquires information about it through the repeat purchases.

See also: search good

experimental economics (C9)
The study of simulated markets in order to test microeconomic theory. This attempt to give economic theory firm foundations has always been methodologically controversial.

References

Hey, J. (1991) *Experiments in Economics*, Oxford: Blackwell.

Kagel, J. and Roth, A. (eds) (1995) *The Handbook of Experimental Economics*, Princeton, NJ: Princeton University Press.

expert system (M1)

Computer software that reproduces the expertise of a specialist by providing a set of rules and a knowledge base so that a user is asked a set of questions before the computer program gives advice. The many applications of these systems include controlling production plants and insurance underwriting.

explicit contract (D0)

An agreement whose terms are stated clearly by the parties. This is usually in writing and legally enforceable.

See also: implicit contract theory

explicit cost (D0)

Actual money expenditure incurred to obtain a factor of production or a good or service.

See also: implicit cost

exploitation (J7, Q2)

1 Using or misusing a natural resource. Extraction of minerals constitutes use; misuse arises from causing long-term damage to the environment.
2 Treating labour unjustly by either paying it less than its MARGINAL PRODUCT or extracting SURPLUS VALUE from it.

export (F3)

The sale to a resident of another country of a domestically produced good or service. Unless an economy is self-sufficient, it will be necessary for it to export in order to be able to pay for the imports demanded by its residents. The volume of a country's exports has many determinants, including the exchange rate, marketing methods, delivery times, product design and government subsidization, especially the guarantee of export finance so that firms will not be discouraged from exporting by the risk of buyers' defaulting. Exports net of imports are included in the GROSS DOMESTIC PRODUCT.

See also: import

Export Import Bank (G2)

Washington bank set up in 1934 as an agency of the US federal government to facilitate and finance exports, e.g. by issuing guarantees, direct loans and insurance programmes to minimize buyers' default.

export promotion (F3)

A set of measures, usually taken by a national government, to subsidize the marketing overseas of domestically produced goods and to guarantee foreign payments for them.

export requirement (F2)

A rule imposed by a host government on foreign investors to export a minimum percentage of their output. This is a policy response to the practice of a MULTINATIONAL company of diverting to other markets the output of a domestic producer it has taken over to the detriment of the host country's pattern of trade.

export subsidy (F1, H2)

A reduction in the cost of exports brought about by a government grant. There can be reductions in the costs of labour, of capital or of export financing, as well as more favourable tax treatment. SMITH referred to such subsidies as 'bounties'.

ex post variables (E0)

Variables which show actual economic outcomes, e.g. the amount of fixed investment which has been undertaken. In the 1930s there was much discussion in macroeconomics of how *ex ante* savings and investment that were different in amount became equal *ex post*. One possibility was for there to be saving at each round of income generated from an *ex ante* investment excess over *ex ante* saving.

See also: *ex ante* variables

extended equilibrium (D5)
An expansion of the concept of GENERAL EQUILIBRIUM to include the natural environment.

extended fund facility (F3)
A type of INTERNATIONAL MONETARY FUND loan introduced in 1974 which is granted to a country which agrees to an economic adjustment programme over a three-year period. Repayment begins four and a half years after the loan is granted and is extended over a six-year period. The facility was used to the extent of about $100 million annually in the 1970s, and by the mid-1980s had risen to over $2 billion per year. It can be used in conjunction with a SUPPLEMENTARY FINANCING FACILITY.

external account (F4, G2)
1 The BALANCE OF PAYMENTS accounts of a nation.
2 A bank account of a person who is not a resident of the country.

external balance (F4)
The state of a country's BALANCE OF PAYMENTS such that it is neither in deficit nor in surplus. In accounting terms, the balance of payments always balances because of the principles of double-entry bookkeeping. However, in economic terms, for a country to have an external balance there must be an equality between the flows of payments and receipts between that country and the rest of the world in a given time period.

See also: internal balance

References
Meade, J.E. (1951) *The Theory of International Economic Policy*, Vol. I, *The Balance of Payments*, ch. 10, London and New York: Oxford University Press.
Swan, T.W. (1963) 'Longer run problems of the balance of payments', in H.W. Arndt and W.M. Corden (eds) *The Australian Economy*, Melbourne: F. W. Cheshire.

external credit rating (F4, G2)
1 The rating accorded to a bank of its exposure to risk.

2 The reliability of a country in servicing its external debt to banks and other countries.

external debt (F4, H6)
The debt a country owes to foreign banks and governments which accumulates through its persistent BALANCE OF PAYMENTS deficits. An attempt to achieve economic growth in a short time period is often the cause of such indebtedness. In extreme cases of foreign indebtedness, national governments will attempt to reschedule their debts and, in a crisis, apply to the INTERNATIONAL MONETARY FUND for loans.

See also: internal debt

external economy of scale (D0)
A reduction in the AVERAGE COSTS of a firm as a result of the expansion of the whole industry of which it is part. A major example of these economies occurs in the case of the training of labour: the general expansion of an industry requires more skilled labour to provide a pool of suitable labour for other firms.

See also: internal economy of scale

externality (D0, Q0)
The benefit or cost to society or another person of a private action (e.g. production or consumption); a third-party effect. Since PIGOU's discussion of the distinction between SOCIAL AND PRIVATE COST, it has been a central concept of WELFARE ECONOMICS. 'Internalizing an externality', in the case of an external cost, can be achieved by a government levying taxes equal to the difference between a private cost and a social cost.

external labour market (J4)
A market consisting of competing employers and competing workers. Workers can and will enter firms at different pay and status levels but often with lower remuneration than in oligopolistic firms with INTERNAL LABOUR MARKETS. Much of the external labour market is coterminous with the SECONDARY LABOUR MARKET.

external shock (E6)

A large unanticipated change in world economic conditions which impacts upon a particular national economy. Shocks can take many forms, including a shift in the TERMS OF TRADE, a slowdown in the growth of world export demand and an increase in the interest rates set by world financial markets. However, the major shocks of the 1970s, particularly the increase in the price of oil, had an uneven impact on the prosperity of particular nations with producing countries welcoming the shocks and consumers having to make major adjustments.

See also: structural adjustment policy; supply-side shocks

extralegal property (P0)

Assets, especially houses, which lack a legal title because of the absence of a system of PROPERTY RIGHTS in that country. Often this occurs in developing countries with the consequence that the *de facto* owners cannot use their property as collateral for loans. In many countries, in-cluding the USA, property was held in this way by occupation rather than established title. Also known as informal ownership.

extrapolative expectations (D0, E0)

EXPECTATIONS based on the past level of an economic variable and whether that variable is increasing or decreasing in value.

References

Metzler, L.A. (1941) 'The nature and stability of inventory cycles', *Review of Economics and Statistics* 23: 113–29.

extreme value theory (C8)

An account of the probabilities associated with extreme and rare events. It is used in financial economics to model the maxima and minima of a series. Inferences have to be made about the levels of a process for which there is no data. The MARKOV CHAIN MODEL has been used to examine extremes.

extremum (C1, C6)

An extreme value, i.e. a maximum or a minimum.

See also: optimization problem

F

Fabian Society (P2)

Founded in 1883 by Edith Nesbit and Hubert Bland to promote socialism. It contributed to the ideological development of the UK Labour Party and had as its earliest members Beatrice and Sidney Webb and George Bernard Shaw. In its many pamphlets on economic and related issues it has advocated gradualist, rather than revolutionary, socialism.

factor-augmenting technical progress (O2)

Technical progress arising from an increase in factor PRODUCTIVITY in the absence of an increase in the stock of capital or the size of the labour force.

factor cost (D0)

1 The cost of employing a FACTOR OF PRODUCTION.
2 A method of valuing the NATIONAL INCOME. This valuation at factor cost excludes indirect taxes, is net of subsidies and indicates what factors of production are actually received.

factor endowment (Q0)

1 Quantities of land, labour, capital and entrepreneurs owned by a particular country. This uses a stock approach to consider the total WEALTH of a country. The crudest measures of the size of a country would be in terms of its land area, population and labour force; more elaborate estimates of its wealth would include a calculation of the amount of HUMAN CAPITAL it has and the replacement cost value of its physical capital.
2 The ratio of one factor to another. This indicates the extent to which the country's production is predominantly CAPITAL INTENSIVE or LABOUR INTENSIVE. HECKSCHER and OHLIN made factor endowment central to their international trade theory by examining the extent to which a country's trade is a reflection of the scarcity or abundance of particular factors of production.

See also: stock and flow concepts

factorial terms of trade (F1)

The NET BARTER TERMS OF TRADE multiplied by the PRODUCTIVITY change in a country's export industries (single factorial terms) or by the ratio of the index of productivity change of the country's export industries to the corresponding index for the foreign export industries producing its imports (double factorial terms). This modification of the net barter terms of trade is made to show the welfare effects of the terms of trade, because an increase in productivity, for example, which worsens a country's terms of trade indicates that it is sharing its productivity gain with another country.

See also: terms of trade

factor income (D3)

Part of the national product distributed to a particular factor of production. The factor labour receives wages and salaries, the factor land receives rent, and capital earns interest and profits.

factoring (G2)
The sale at a discount of debts due to a firm. The factor purchasing these rights is entitled to collect the amount due. Factoring can be used to increase the short-term funds available to a business enterprise or to finance exporting.

See also: bill of exchange

factor market (D4)
A market for a FACTOR OF PRODUCTION. The most prominent of these markets are the labour market and the capital market. In such markets the buyers are firms and the sellers are households – a reversal of the roles of firms and households in PRODUCT MARKETS. The principal task of such markets is to arrive at a MARKET CLEARING PRICE. Factor markets are linked to product markets because the demand for a factor of production is derived from the demand for its product.

factor of production (D0)
An input to a productive process producing a good or service. Before the eighteenth century it was common to classify all factors as either land or labour; later, CAPITAL and the ENTREPRENEUR were considered as separate factors of production. In many modern economics models, only labour and capital are included as factors of production.

factor price equalization theorem (F1)
This asserts that free trade in final goods brings about the equalization of factor prices, especially of labour and capital, throughout the world.

References

Lerner, A.P. (1952) 'Factor prices and international trade', *Economica* 19: 1–15.

factor productivity (D2)
Output per unit of a factor input, e.g. output per person employed. To measure the PRODUCTIVITY of one factor of production requires holding other factors' inputs constant – a difficult task, especially in the case of CAPITAL.

factor tax (H2)
A tax levied on a particular income-earning FACTOR OF PRODUCTION. Taxes on capital, taxes on residential and commercial property and taxes on employment are important examples.

fad (D1, G0)
1 A speculative BUBBLE.
2 A demand arising from a passing fashion which causes the price of a good or service to be temporarily much higher than its intrinsic value.

fair division problem (C7)
The division of a set of goods among a set of players to obtain an equitable distribution such that no other distribution would improve the welfare of one player without reducing the welfare of another.

fair price (D4)
1 A benchmark export price used to ascertain whether there has been DUMPING. It reflects full costs, including transport costs.
2 A product price which achieves a minimum return for labour and capital.
3 A competitive price fixed by a market and not by administrators.
4 A price in a market where neither producers nor consumers have excessive power.

See also: just price

fair trading (F1, M3)
1 Genuine free trade in which there are no attempts to have hidden subsidies to export industries and protection of domestic industries to prevent imports, e.g. by imposing rigorous quality controls. Without fair trading in the EU, the Single Market will be impossible.
2 Selling under a system of free competition.

See also: dumping

fair value (G1)

In stock market trading, a suggested formula for fair value is

$$FV = S + [I - (1 - D)]$$

where FV is fair value, S is the STANDARD AND POOR 500 stock index, I is the interest to a stockbroker to borrow in order to buy all the stocks in the index, and D is the amount of dividends from all the stocks in the index owned. Fair value is thus the adjusted value of the S&P index and was devised by Hans Stoll of Vanderbilt University.

Fair Wages Resolution (J3)

A resolution of the UK House of Commons, first passed in 1891 (and followed by many local authorities), which stipulated that government contractors should not employ workers under terms and conditions less favourable than those negotiated under collective bargaining for that trade or industry. In recent years many of the cases which raised wages concerned cleaning firms. The Conservative government, consistent with its belief that the setting of minimum wages under wages councils contributed to unemployment, successfully repealed the resolution in 1983.

falling knife (G1)

A stock exchange security experiencing a rapid fall in price.

See also: dead cat bounce

falling rate of profit (D3, O1)

The tendency of the rate of profit to fall. SMITH attributed this to a competition of capitals leading to an increase in the WAGE FUND and in real wages with the consequence that profit rates declined. RICARDO noted an inverse relationship between wages and profits so that when population expanded and food prices and wages rose profits fell. MARX predicted that falling profits in a domestic market would encourage capitalists to seek higher profits through investment abroad. Thomas De Quincey (1785–1859) in his *Logic of Political Economy* (1944) argued that the tendency of the rate of profit is to fluctuate.

false trading (D4)

Making exchanges at non-equilibrium prices in an attempt to find the MARKET CLEARING PRICE.

Family Expenditure Survey (C8, D1)

UK sample survey of the characteristics of households, including earnings, education, unemployment and consumption. This survey, published annually by the UK Department of Employment, reports on:

- Household characteristics
- Expenditure
- Income
- Regional characteristics
- Regional expenditure
- Regional income.

Farm Credit System (H2, Q1)

US federation of thirty-seven banks consisting of 387 lending associations owned by the farmers who borrow from them; established by US Congress in 1916–33. There are three banks in each of the twelve districts of the FEDERAL RESERVE SYSTEM and another bank specializing in the sale of bonds to Wall Street institutions.

The purpose of the system is to provide credit to farmers and ranchers during their 'growing season'. Before the establishment of the Farm Credit System, it was hard for farmers to borrow because money was very scarce in most rural areas. The federal government's guarantee of the farm credit system's bonds gives the banks of the farm credit system 'agency status' on Wall Street. The excessive borrowing by farmers when farm land values were high in the early 1970s and 1980s led to the creation of large farm debts.

References

Gifford Hoag, W. (1976) *The Farm Credit*

System, Danville, IL: Interstate Printers and Publishers.

fast-track trade procedure (F1)

A procedure of the US Congress to legislate for trade agreements at the request of the president, who promised to keep to the agreed procedure.

fat cat (M1, J3)

An executive with large total remuneration.

featherbedding (J2)

Work practices advocating low labour productivity methods to maintain employment. These include payment for time when no work is performed.

See also: demarcation

Federal Cartel Office (L4)

US agency engaged in monitoring mergers, thus making a major contribution to the running of US ANTITRUST policy.

Federal Deposit Insurance Corporation (G2)

US regulatory body founded in 1933 to insure depositors against bank failures and to take on the role of chartering national COMMERCIAL BANKS. It is largely financed by assessments on the deposits held by insured national and state banks. When an insured bank fails, each depositor can claim up to $100,000 from the FDIC. To protect depositors, the FDIC can also facilitate bank mergers through loans and the purchase of assets from insured banks. Its three directors include the COMPTROLLER OF THE CURRENCY. Critics of the principle of deposit insurance assert that it encourages banks to have imprudent lending policies.

federal finance (H7)

Public finance arrangements between central and state governments in a country with a federal constitution, e.g. the USA, Germany, Canada, Australia and Switzerland. There can be REVENUE SHARING of money raised from taxation or different types of taxation at each level of government. Federal finance systems vary in (1) the degree of fiscal autonomy of lower levels of government, (2) the extent to which a federal government imposes limits on the power of lower levels of government to borrow and (3) the degree of independence of a federal budget from those of sub-federal governments.

See also: US federal finance

References

Hughes, G.A. (1987) 'Fiscal federalism in the UK', *Oxford Review of Economic Policy* 3: 1–23.

Pechman, J.A. (1977) *Federal Tax Policy*, 3rd edn, Washington, DC: Brookings Institution.

federal funds (E5)

The reserve deposits of banks and other financial institutions of the USA held in a FEDERAL RESERVE BANK. Since these deposits earn no interest, banks want to minimize the size of their holdings and increase their investment in assets, e.g. loans, which will increase their profitability.

federal funds market (G1)

US money market in which commercial banks sell short-term financial assets.

federal funds rate (E5)

The rate at which the member banks of the FEDERAL RESERVE SYSTEM trade reserves with each other. Banks with more reserves than required lend their surplus to other banks with a deficiency. Although this rate is determined by the demand for and supply of excess reserves in the banking system, the Federal Reserve can influence it.

See also: prime rate of interest

Federal Home Loan Board (G2)

US independent federal agency established in 1932 to provide a credit reserve for member savings institutions specializing in home mortgage lending, i.e. savings and loan associations, co-operative banks, homestead associations and insurance companies.

See also: Federal Savings and Loan Insurance Corporation

Federal Open Market Committee (E5)
A committee of the US FEDERAL RESERVE SYSTEM which sets the policy for the use of the principal instrument of US monetary policy, OPEN MARKET OPERATIONS. The New York Federal Reserve Bank executes the policy. The committee consists of seven of the board's governors plus five of the presidents of the regional Federal Reserve Banks, one of whom is always the President of the Federal Reserve Bank of New York. It was given its statutory authority under the BANKING ACT 1933 but it had existed as an informal investment committee of the Federal Reserve Banks from 1922. During and after the Second World War until 1952, the committee had a policy of maintaining interest rates at low levels, whilst in the 1970s, a policy of attempting to achieve target rates of growth for monetary aggregates.

Federal Reserve Bank (E5) *see* Federal Reserve System

Federal Reserve Note (E5)
US financial instrument issued by the Federal Reserve Banks which is legal tender and used to be backed by gold or silver. It is the major form of US currency.

Federal Reserve System (E5)
The US banking system established in 1913 to execute the functions of a CENTRAL BANK for the USA. The original aims of the system were to give the country an elastic currency, to provide facilities for DISCOUNTING COMMERCIAL PAPER and to improve the supervision of banking. Heading the system is a Board of Governors in control of twelve district reserve banks with banking responsibility for a region of the USA. District 1 is the Federal Reserve Bank of Boston, District 2 is the Federal Reserve Bank of New York and District 12 the Federal Reserve Bank of San Francisco. Member banks are below the reserve banks in this pyramid of authority with the Board of Governors as its apex. There are also a FEDERAL OPEN MARKET COMMITTEE and a Federal Advisory

Council. The seven governors are appointed by the US president, with US Senate approval, and serve for fourteen years: they appoint the directors of the twelve district banks, fix RESERVE and MARGIN requirements and determine DISCOUNT RATES and major banking regulations. The principal tasks of the district banks are to supervise member banks in their respective regions, to provide cheque collection services, to supply coin and currency, to lend to member banks at the discount rate and to act as the fiscal agent of the US Treasury, collecting taxes, marketing and redeeming US Treasury securities and paying interest on them. Fewer than 60 per cent of US commercial banks have membership of the Federal Reserve: if they do, they have the advantages of cheaper banking services but the disadvantage of losing profits through having to meet tougher reserve requirements.

The changing monetary policies of the Federal Reserve reflect the dominant economic policy thinking of the decades of its history. The Roosevelt and Truman Administrations of the 1930s and 1940s gave it the task of maintaining FULL EMPLOYMENT and pegging interest rates at a low level. The Reagan Administration of the 1980s asked it to consider MONETARY AGGREGATES as its principal targets.

References

Beckhart, B.H. (1972) *Federal Reserve System*, New York: American Institute of Banking.
Moore, C.H. (1990) *The Federal Reserve System: A History of the First 75 Years*, Jefferson, NC: McFarland.

Federal Savings and Loan Insurance Corporation (G2)
Founded in 1934 to insure shareholders in federal savings and loan associations (THRIFTS). Its overseer is the FEDERAL HOME LOAN BANK BOARD. It insures savings up to $100,000 in amount and is financed by the premiums paid by insured financial institutions and by interest received on its own investments. It is also authorized to

borrow from the US Treasury. By 1987 it had run out of funds to reimburse depositors and needed to be recapitalized by the savings bank industry. The higher deposit insurance premiums charged by the Federal Saving and Loan Insurance Corporation caused many thrifts to change to the FEDERAL DEPOSIT INSURANCE CORPORATION scheme.

See also: Resolution Trust Corporation

Federal Trade Commission (L5)
US federal commission established in 1914 to maintain competitive enterprise in the USA and formulate competition policy. It seeks to prevent general trade restraints and price discrimination and to ensure accurate credit cost disclosure. The commission enforces its judgements through voluntary co-operation with the offending parties or through litigation.

See also: antitrust

Federal Trade Commission Act 1914 (L5)
This federal statute of the USA both established the FEDERAL TRADE COMMISSION as an independent agency and gave it authority to investigate and declare illegal 'unfair' and 'predatory' competitive practices.

Fed funds (E5) *see* federal funds

Feldstein, Martin, 1939– (B3)
US economist who is an authority on public finance and welfare policies. He was educated at Harvard and Oxford Universities, returning to the former to be professor of economics from 1967. His quantitative work on fiscal programmes has shown their effect on employment and investment and interaction with macroeconomic policy. He became president of the influential NATIONAL BUREAU FOR ECONOMIC RESEARCH in 1977.

felicific calculus (D0)
BENTHAM's method of judging the worth of an action by calculating the likely pleasure or pain which would result.

See also: utilitarianism

female economists (B1, B2)
In the period of CLASSICAL ECONOMICS Jane MARCET, author of *Conversations on Political Economy* (1816), Harriet MARTINEAU, author of the bestselling *Illustrations of Political Economy* (issued monthly in 1832–4), and Harriet Taylor, later to be the wife of John Stuart MILL, were well known. University courses were opened to women in the late nineteenth century and Mary PALEY, who married Alfred MARSHALL, was one of the first to teach economics at Cambridge. In the twentieth century the important works of Rosa LUXEMBURG, Joan ROBINSON, Barbara WOOTTON, Anna SCHWARTZ, Edith PENROSE, Margaret REID, Phyllis DEANE and Anne O. KRUEGER have killed the myth that economics is an exclusively male subject.

feminist economics (D1)
The economic analysis of women's issues, especially the economics of the family, participation in the labour market and welfare benefits. It is usually assumed that women are oppressed according to INTERPERSONAL UTILITY COMPARISONS and ought to be compensated. The concepts of scarcity, selfishness and competition are the main ideas that feminist economists seek to challenge.

See also: female economists

feudalism (N4)
The hierarchical medieval system of power and production in European countries with the monarch at the top and serfs tied to the land at the bottom. More recently the term has been loosely used to describe private agricultural estates in Latin America and Japanese industrial companies, with varying degrees of justification.

References

Strayer, J.R. (1965) *Feudalism*, New York: Van Nostrand Reinhold.

FF curve (F4)
A curve showing the combinations of national income and the rate of interest

for which the trade balance is zero. It is usually positively sloped but with full international capital mobility it becomes horizontal.

See also: Mundell–Fleming model

National income Y

fiat money (E5)
Anything declared to be acceptable as MONEY by a CENTRAL BANK or finance ministry in charge of the currency. It is this declaration, rather than the intrinsic value of the money as a good (as is the case with gold and silver coinage), which gives it value. Fiat money mostly takes the form of banknotes.

See also: token money

fiduciary issue (E5)
An inconvertible issue of banknotes not backed by gold: as the name suggests, these notes are issued in faith. In the nineteenth century when banknotes constituted a larger proportion of the MONEY SUPPLY than now, controlling the size of the fiduciary issue was important; this is no longer so.

See also: Bank Charter Act 1844; fiat money

filière concept (D2, L0)
A French term for vertical lines of production intimately linked together. When applied to industrial planning, it means that

planning for a particular sector extends to planning both for the industry concerned and for the industries linked to it.

See also: linkage

filtering (R2)
The downgrading of residential property, either by splitting it into smaller units affordable to lower income groups or by the movement of more prosperous residents to outer suburbs. Urban economists use this to explain the creation of inner city slums. Chicago is a major example of this process.

final demand (R2)
The demand for goods and services by the ultimate consumers, domestic and foreign households.

final good (D0)
A good directly used by its ultimate consumer, unlike an INTERMEDIATE GOOD. The distinction between final and intermediate goods is crucial to the construction of an INPUT–OUTPUT table.

final income (E2)
The amount of disposable income available to a household for expenditure and saving. It is measured as gross earnings minus taxation and social security contributions plus housing benefits and transfers.

final offer arbitration (J5) *see* pendulum arbitration

final salary pension (J3)
A retirement income calculated according to a formula based on a person's final employment salary and years of service.

finance constraint (E4) *see* cash-in-advance constraint

financial accounting (M4)
The recording of the business transactions of a firm in a manner ordered by the legislation of the country of domicile of that firm. The main elements of it are the construction of a balance sheet to measure the assets and liabilities of a firm on a

particular day, and the construction of a profit and loss account to show revenue, expenditure and profit over a period of time, usually three, six or twelve months.

See also: accounting; management accounting

financial architecture (F3)

The framework and set of measures, including EXCHANGE RATE REGIMES, in which national ECONOMIES conduct their activities. This architecture is constructed with a view to avoiding currency crises. The WORLD BANK has devised codes on corporate governance, financial standards and accounting.

financial asset (G1)

A piece of paper entitling its holder to interest or dividends. In the past the major types of financial asset were stocks and shares of governments and companies. Recent innovations in financial markets have produced more sophisticated versions of these, including a variety of types of equity.

financial capital (G1)

The money invested in a business to establish and extend it. In the case of a company or corporation it can take various forms, including fixed interest DEBENTURES, PREFERENCE SHARES and ORDINARY SHARES.

financial centre (G2)

A cluster of different financial institutions at one geographical location. The growth of population and business encouraged banking, insurance and other types of financing. The large amounts of capital required to conduct these institutions have inevitably led to mergers within the financial sector of the same or related types of institution, as well as the disproportionate growth of cities such as New York, London and Tokyo as financial centres.

financial conglomerate (G2)

A bank or other depository institution offering a wide range of lending and credit facilities. UK BUILDING SOCIETIES and US THRIFTS have increasingly followed the practice of COMMERCIAL BANKS by diversifying into new areas of financial services, aiming to offer customers a wide range of financial products and services. By becoming conglomerates they have become exposed to risks of a kind they have not been used to, and this, together with the increased number of participants in so many financial markets, has threatened profit margins.

References

Benston, G. (ed.) (1983) *Financial Services*, Englewood Cliffs, NJ: Prentice Hall.

financial contagion (G2)

The spread of the consequences of shocks affecting only a few financial institutions to the rest of the financial sector and the wider economy.

References

Allan, F. and Gale, D. (2000) 'Financial contagion', *Journal of Political Economy* 108: 1–33.

financial crisis (G1, G2)

The simultaneous collapse of related financial institutions brought about by the attempts of investors, speculators, lenders and depositors to liquidate their assets. This liquidation occurs because of a change from optimistic to pessimistic EXPECTATIONS. An exogenous event such as a major war or a natural disaster can destabilize markets and create a crisis. A speculative investment boom with the promotion of many dubious schemes and OVERTRADING are also common causes of crises. These crises can occur within one economy or in several which are interlinked, as happened in 1929. The role of a CENTRAL BANK in restoring liquidity and general business confidence is crucial.

See also: bubble

References

Altman, E.I. and Sametz, A.W. (eds) (1977) *Financial Crises: Institutions and Markets in a Fragile Environment*, New York: Wiley.

Bordo, M. (1991) *Financial Crises*, Aldershot: Edward Elgar.

Galbraith, J.K. (1955) *The Great Crash*, Boston, MA: Houghton Mifflin.

Kindleberger, C.P. (1978) *Manias, Panics and Crashes*, London: Macmillan; New York: Basic Books.

Kindleberger, C.P. and Laffargue, J.P. (eds) (1982) *Financial Crises: Theory, History and Policy*, Cambridge: Cambridge University Press.

financial deepening (G2)

An increase in the ratio of financial assets to REAL ASSETS. This will depend on the number and range of financial institutions and household savings.

financial economy (P1)

An ECONOMY using a variety of financial assets and services, other than money, for the purposes of exchange and storing value; a 'post-money' economy.

References

Podolski, T.M. (1986) *Financial Innovation and the Money Supply*, Oxford: Basil Blackwell.

'financial engineering' (G2, G3)

1 The making of major deals, especially mergers and underwriting, rather than daily trading in major financial centres such as Wall Street, New York. As a consequence the structure of ownership of industries is radically changed.

2 The use of financial instruments to solve problems. Risk management, trading, investment management and structured finance are all within its ambit.

financial intermediary (G2)

An institution collecting deposits and making loans. Apart from the prominent example of banks, there are many financial intermediaries today including building societies (savings and loans institutions), insurance companies and hire-purchase finance houses. The creation of many new types of institution has made the task of monetary control more difficult for central banks and finance ministries.

financial investment (G1)

The purchase of financial assets, e.g. stocks and shares. As most of the financial assets traded represent claims to past investment in fixed capital and inventories, financial investment is different from 'INVESTMENT'.

financial journalism (G0)

The specialized reporting of financial and economic news. It had its origins in the reporting of prices in Antwerp and Venice in the sixteenth century and in *Lloyd's List*, founded in 1734. Newspaper articles on financial matters probably began in Great Britain, as London was the first major financial centre. Thomas Massa Alsager became the first financial editor of *The Times* in 1817, although the *Weekly Register* of Baltimore was a pioneer of US business journalism from 1811. Early reports concentrated on stock movements and banking liquidity but, with the participation of major economic writers in journalism, the financial press broadened its interests to an examination of home and foreign economies. *The Economist* was founded in 1843 by James Wilson (a former Financial Secretary to the Treasury), *The Statist* in 1873 by Sir Robert Giffen, *Financial News* in 1884 and the *Financial Times* in 1888 (the last two merging in 1945).

Many leading economists, including KEYNES, SAMUELSON and GALBRAITH have regularly contributed to the press. This is one of the most demanding forms of journalism as a great deal of technical expertise is required, as well as personal integrity to resist the demands of many businesses and interest groups wanting favourable coverage.

References

Parsons, W. (1989) *The Power of the Press*, Aldershot: Edward Elgar.

financial leverage ratio (G2, G3)

Total debt as a proportion of total assets; also known as gearing. This is an indication of the extent to which a firm has to meet interest payments. If a firm suffering a downturn in its gross profits has high leverage, it could face insolvency.

See also: leverage; leveraged management buyout

financial liberalization (G2)
The removal of government regulations, as happened in the USA in the 1980s, to permit the prices and availability of finance to be market determined. Principal forms of liberalization include deregulation of interest rate fixing and barriers to capital flows between countries and industries.

financial panic (G2)
A lack of confidence in a banking system causing depositors to reclaim their deposits, thereby bringing about the collapse they fear. In a centralized banking system, a collapse in part of the system can be overcome by a CENTRAL BANK helping to restore liquidity.

See also: bubble; financial crisis; run on a bank

financial policy (G3)
For a firm, this will include its attitude towards raising capital, distributing dividends, structuring its debt and investing its surplus funds.

financial regime (G2)
The set of laws, government guidelines and policies which set the boundaries to the activities of financial institutions.

Financial Reporting Council (M4)
UK council set up in 1990 to replace the Accounting Standards Committee. With its subsidiaries, the Accounting Standards Board and Review Panel, it can make regulations on the form of company accounts to standardize the treatment of, for example, goodwill and off-balance-sheet finance.

financial repression (G2)
The limitation of banking and other financial sector activity by regulations such as RESERVE REQUIREMENTS, interest rate ceilings, rules about the composition of bank balance sheets, foreign exchange regulations and burdensome taxation of the financial sector.

See also: deregulation

Financial Services Act 1986 (G2, K2)
This UK statute set out the regulation of investment business in the UK and also regulated the business of insurance companies and friendly societies. (THE BANK OF ENGLAND, LLOYD'S and CLEARING HOUSES are exempt from its provisions.) It made provision for the Secretary of State to recognize 'SELF-REGULATING ORGANIZATIONS' to regulate the carrying on of investment business by enforcing rules on their members and to recognize 'professional bodies' to regulate professions. The Act controls the promotion and advertising of investment schemes and can ban persons as unfit to conduct investment business.

References

Anderson, R.W. (1986) 'Regulation of futures trading in the United States and United Kingdom', *Oxford Review of Economic Policy* 2: 41–57.

Financial Statement and Budget Report (H6)
An annual report of the UK Treasury on the UK's recent economic performance and forecasts for the next year. The major sections of the report detail output and expenditure aggregates, movements in the retail price index, the growth of money, gross domestic product at market prices, the current account balance of payments and the public sector borrowing requirement. This report is colloquially referred to as the 'Red Book'.

financial supermarket (G2) *see* financial conglomerate

financial system (G2)
Interrelated institutions engaged in collecting savings and distributing them to borrowers, making possible the separation of the ownership of wealth from the control of physical capital. The more developed an

economy is, the greater its range of financial instruments; for example, since 1960 the US and UK financial systems have produced a large range of new instruments, e.g. derivatives, in order to meet the different needs of savers and borrowers. New financial facilities contribute to economic growth.

See also: disintermediation

References

Drake, P.J. (1980) *Money, Finance and Development*, Oxford: Robertson.

Financial Times Actuaries All-Share Index (G1)

A London stock market price index designed by actuaries and compiled by the *Financial Times*, which began in 1962. The purpose of this index is to indicate the level of the whole UK equity market by including over 700 shares, more than 80 per cent of market capitalization.

Financial Times Industrial Ordinary Share Index (G1)

A price index of thirty leading industrial shares traded on the INTERNATIONAL STOCK EXCHANGE of London which was first published in 1935. This valuation of stock market shares is made at the beginning of each trading day, hourly throughout and at the end of the day.

Financial Times Stock Exchange 100 Share Index (G1)

A price index of the shares of the 100 largest companies traded on the INTERNATIONAL STOCK EXCHANGE of London. It was introduced in 1984 as a means of basing futures contracts on the UK equity market. Popularly known as 'Footsie'.

fine-tuning (E6)

The frequent use of monetary and fiscal policies to avoid prolonged recessions and inflation by keeping a national ECONOMY steadily on course. The over-ambitious attempts of the US Administration to achieve precise goals prompted Walter Heller to describe such a policy as 'fine-tuning'. As a policy it ran into difficulties

partly because those using it believed that disturbances were caused by AGGREGATE DEMAND and not by supply shocks. The problems of ignoring supply shocks became vividly clear after the oil-price increases of 1974.

firm (L2)

1 The basic unit for organizing production which performs the crucial role of linking product, factor and money markets.

2 An administrative organization utilizing a pool of resources.

3 A business organization under a single management with one or more ESTABLISHMENTS.

A firm can be classified according to the number of persons owning it or according to the extent of the liability of its owners for the firm's debts. A sole trader is the single owner with unlimited liability; a partnership has joint ownership but unlimited liability; companies and corporations are owned by many shareholders with limited liability.

See also: limited partnership

References

Putterman, L. and Kroszner, R.S. (eds) (1996) *The Economic Nature of the Firm: A Reader*, Cambridge and New York: Cambridge University Press.

firm consumption (L2)

The proportion of a firm's production it consumes itself, e.g. the electricity a power station consumes to run its own operations.

See also: intermediate good

firm-specific asset (L2)

Tangible and intangible property of use only to a particular firm. These assets enhance the uniqueness of a firm and its competitiveness but affect its ability to borrow as specific assets cannot be redeployed so are unsuitable as collateral for loans.

See also: specific training

first best economy (P0)
An abstract model of a real economy in which resources are allocated according to the rules of PARETO OPTIMALITY.

first-degree price discrimination (D4)
Selling different units of output at different prices so that each price is the maximum amount of money a consumer will pay.

See also: price discrimination

First Development Decade (O1)
A name given to the 1960s by President John F. Kennedy when he launched the USA's Peace Corps.

first economy (P2)
A socialist economy following the dictates of the national plan. It consists of governmental agencies, state-owned firms, co-operatives and other officially registered institutions.

See also: second economy

First Industrial Revolution (N1)
The bunching of innovations, introduction of steam power and establishment of factories chiefly in Great Britain from 1760 to 1830.

See also: industrial revolution

References

Ashton, T.S. (1948) *The industrial revolution, 1760–1830*, London: Oxford University Press.

first-in, first-out (M4)
A method of valuing physical stocks which, by assuming the oldest stocks will be used first, values at historic cost. The method has largely been abandoned in favour of the LAST-IN, LAST-OUT principle. The FIFO method has the effect of including in profits the effects of stock appreciation, thus giving an unrealistic picture of a firm's financial state.

first-price auction (D4)
A method of selling whereby the buyers submit sealed written bids with the item going to the highest bidder. This method is used weekly by the US Treasury when it issues its short-term securities, and also by Scottish solicitors for the sale of houses.

See also: auction

First Welfare Theorem (D6)
The assertion that every competitive equilibrium is PARETO-efficient in that markets clear, consumers maximize utility and firms maximize profits. EXTERNALITIES are absent and the price mechanism is superior to other forms of co-ordination of demand and supply.

First World (P1)
Developed free market ECONOMIES which were early to industrialize and, until the emergence of large oil revenues in developing countries, had the highest per capita incomes.

See also: Second World; Third World

fiscal approximation (H2)
Bringing the tax rates of different countries into line, e.g. the different rates of value-added tax in the EUROPEAN COMMUNITY, as a preparation for the SINGLE MARKET of 1992.

See also: tax harmonization

fiscal crisis (H2, H3)
A shortage in the tax revenues needed to finance a desired level of public expenditure. Marxists and others have asserted that there is a built-in tendency for modern fiscal systems to head for crisis as the increasing demands for EGALITARIANISM and more public services are not matched by a desire to pay more taxation. A concern for the disincentive and allocative effects of higher rates of tax makes it difficult to raise extra tax revenue, making a fiscal crisis incurable.

fiscal dividend (H2)
Tax reductions and/or increases in government expenditures.

fiscal drag (H3)
1 The reduction in personal disposable income resulting from tax rates not

being adjusted for INFLATION.

2 The increase of tax revenue at a faster rate than public expenditure.

The spending power of taxpayers is 'dragged' down by an increase in average tax rates: for example, if pre-tax incomes rise by 10 per cent and personal allowances are not increased then many taxpayers will be pushed into higher tax bands. The ROOKER–WISE AMENDMENT of 1975 attempted to reduce much of fiscal drag in the UK; in the USA, the Tax Reform Act of 1980 indexed the US individual income tax for the same reason. Fiscal drag can be remedied by a FISCAL DIVIDEND.

References

Council of Economic Advisers (1962) 'Automatic stabilizers and fiscal drag', in *Annual Report of the Council of Economic Advisers*, Washington, DC: US Government Printing Office.

fiscal federalism (H7)

The system of sharing tax revenues and public expenditure commitments between a central government and state governments. By making grants to lower levels of government, a national government can determine the standard of provision of public services, especially education. Different levels of government can be financed by different types of tax, e.g. an income tax for the national level but sales and property taxes for the state and local levels, or by the different governments of a country sharing in the revenues from the same range of taxes.

See also: federal finance

References

Barnett, R.R. and Meadows, J. (1989) *The Political Economy of Fiscal Federalism*, Aldershot: Edward Elgar.

Oates, W.E. (1972) *Fiscal Federalism*, New York: Harcourt Brace Jovanovich.

fiscal illusion (H3)

An unawareness of actual fiscal policy because of the poor definitions used of 'taxes', 'spending' and 'deficits'. By not making explicit the financing of every government programme, the size of a fiscal stimulus cannot be properly measured. Illusion can only be cured by identifying for each fiscal instrument its direct effect on the economy and its indirect effects through the changing of household budget constraints.

fiscal incidence (H6) *see* budget incidence

fiscal indicators (H3)

Measures of the fiscal effects of a government which include national and regional expenditures and net lending.

fiscalist (H3)

An economic policy-maker preferring FISCAL to MONETARY POLICIES. Many Keynesians tend to favour a fiscal approach on the grounds that it can be used to pursue a greater range of policy aims than monetary policy.

fiscal military state (P0)

A state in which wealthy corporations and individuals together with the armed forces have dominant political power.

See also: military–industrial complex

fiscal mobility (H3)

The geographical movement of taxpayers from high-tax to low-tax areas. The extent of this movement depends on several factors including the availability of housing and employment and the non-tax attractions of different places.

See also: Tiebout hypothesis

fiscal neutrality (H3)

The nature of a government's public finance policy which does not favour one group of persons, type of consumption or behaviour over another. The extent of neutrality is apparent from a study of a country's tax and benefit structure. As a policy, neutrality is recommended because its non-interventionist character gives greater freedom to individuals. A way of implementing it is by abolishing most tax allowances.

See also: neutral budget; tax structure

fiscal policy (H3)
The taxation and expenditure policy of a government. Prior to KEYNES, public finance economists were chiefly interested in TAX INCIDENCE; subsequently, they accorded fiscal policy a more active role, making it a major part of STABILIZATION POLICY in the 1950s and 1960s. The extent to which fiscal policy can be employed depends on what a government can observe of economic behaviour (thus it cannot tax the black economy), on behavioural responses to fiscal changes and on time lags.

See also: fine-tuning; fiscal neutrality

fiscal rectitude (H3)
A strict fiscal policy of cutting public expenditure and reducing the amount of government borrowing, usually with the aim of keeping a national budget in balance or surplus for several years. This policy has often been recommended by the INTERNATIONAL MONETARY FUND to correct balance of payments deficits.

fiscal stance (H3)
1 The combination of taxation and expenditure chosen by a government.
2 The effect of the public sector on the level of aggregate demand, often measured by the size of a government's deficit. This is only valid if there has been no change in economic conditions.

See also: public finance

fiscal union (H2)
A group of separate countries, or states within them, subject to the same taxing and spending authority. These unions provide mutual insurance and ECONOMIES OF SCALE in the provision of PUBLIC GOODS. There is a greater chance of redistribution the greater the geographical scope of the union, but a large union is likely to create more taxpayer discontent as it is difficult to aggregate the preferences of a great range of people.

See also: harmonization

fiscal year (H3)
The twelve-month period chosen by a government or a business organization for accounting purposes. In 1974 the starting date for the US government's fiscal year was changed from 1 July to 1 October, partly to enable US Congressional appropriations to be made by the start of the fiscal year.

Fisher effect (E5)
An effect of MONETARY POLICY that causes nominal interest rates to rise to a level which reflects price changes.

Fisher equation of exchange (E5)
A famous statement of the QUANTITY THEORY OF MONEY as $MV = PT$. M is the stock of money, P the general price level, V the velocity of circulation and T the volume of transactions.

Fisher, Irving, 1867–1947 (B3)
The celebrated US economist who made major contributions to capital, interest and monetary theory. During his long career as student and professor at Yale University (1892–1935), he published many influential works. His doctoral thesis, *Mathematical Investigations in the Theory of Value and Price* (1892) advanced general equilibrium theory; his *The Nature of Capital and Income* (1906) and *The Rate of Interest* (1907) introduced the important distinctions between real and nominal interest rates and between stocks and flows. Many works on monetary economics, including *The Purchasing Power of Money* (1911) and *Booms and Depressions* (1932) showed a progression from an exposition of the QUANTITY THEORY OF MONEY to a concern with stabilization policies. His contribution to economic statistics in *The Making of Index Numbers* (1927) is well known. His other writings on nutrition, prohibition and pacifism made him known to a wider public. He also earned a great deal from inventing a visible card index system widely used by businesses.

References

Schumpeter, J.A. (1948) *Ten Great Economists from Marx to Keynes*, Oxford: Oxford University Press.

five-star mutual fund (G2)

A US fund achieving the best return to capital employed relative to the return on a treasury bill for a given amount of risk (based on a comparison with other funds' performance) in a particular time period. With hundreds of funds achieving this rating, this form of assessment has begun to be questioned.

five-year plan (P3)

A medium-term national economic plan, first used in the USSR in 1928 and subsequently followed by many developing countries including India and China. These plans set targets for the economy as a whole and for particular sectors. Early plans used principally physical output targets but subsequent plans have set more goals, sometimes in conflict with each other. The broad framework of the five-year plan is supplemented by an annual operational plan setting detailed goals for individual enterprises.

See also: central planning; development

fix (G1)

Twice daily fixing of the price of gold by the London gold market.

fixed capital (E2)

Investment in buildings and equipment. Demand for fixed capital is determined within the framework of a firm's plan, including its sale projections and the cost of finance.

See also: gross domestic fixed capital formation

fixed cost (D0)

A cost to an enterprise which is incurred even when that enterprise's output is zero. These costs occur in the short run. The principal examples of them are equipment costs and the costs of FACTORS OF PRODUCTION which a firm has contracted to pay

for a minimum period of time, e.g. managerial staff. In the long term, all costs become variable as fixed capital can be changed and contracts revised.

See also: average total cost; circulating capital; human capital; quasi-fixed factor; variable cost

fixed exchange rate (F3)

An exchange rate whose value is tied to gold or a major currency or basket of currencies. The GOLD STANDARD was not used after the Second World War, being replaced by a DOLLAR STANDARD under BRETTON WOODS until 1971. Later in Europe a fixed exchange rate regime tied several currencies to other European currencies under the EXCHANGE RATE MECHANISM of the EUROPEAN MONETARY SYSTEM. Currencies with a fixed parity are permitted to vary only within a narrow range above and below par value. Fixed exchange rates promote stability in international trade but carry the cost of holding greater reserves of foreign currencies and other reserve assets. A revaluation or devaluation of a fixed exchange rate creates considerable problems of adjustment in the national economy concerned.

fixprice (D0)

A price determined exogenously outside the model of a market. KEYNESIAN ECONOMICS with its assumptions of a floor to the rate of interest and to money wages employs this method. In an economy with much oligopolistic industry, firms fix their prices independently of market forces and can be in a state of DISEQUILIBRIUM for a considerable time by increasing or decreasing their stocks. Some would argue that there was a fixprice economy as early as 1890.

See also: flexprice

References

Hicks, J.R. (1965) *Capital and Growth*, ch. 7, Oxford: Clarendon Press.

flat grant (H2) *see* grant in aid

flat pay-off (C7)

A situation when there are few financial

penalties for departing from an optimum position.

flat rate tax (H2)

1 An INCOME TAX levied at the same rate for every level of income. The justification for a tax of this kind is its simplicity and lack of the disincentive effects inherent in some forms of tax progression. However, a flat rate tax is likely to be an unfair burden on low-income groups if its rate is high.

2 In 2000 Russia introduced a 13 per cent income tax flat rate in place of a sliding scale of 12 per cent to 39 per cent.

See also: progressive tax

flat tax (H2) *see* flat rate tax

flawed marketplace (D4)

1 A competitive market which generates multiple prices for the same thing.

2 A market requiring social action to protect resources, people, capital and human values.

flexible exchange rate (F3) *see* floating exchange rate

flexible firm (L2)

A firm with a core of permanent employees and a periphery of temporary workers whose labour force fluctuates in size according to the demand for its products. In Japan, many industries have this type of organization through the extensive use of subcontractors who themselves have the flexibility which comes from employing temporary workers.

flexible working-time schemes (J2)

Non-standard distributions of working hours with several starting and finishing times. These proliferate in the service sector and have been important in the recruitment of women with domestic responsibilities and others who want to combine labour market activity with equally demanding pursuits.

flex mex (Q2)

Methods rich countries employ to attempt to achieve reduction targets for green-house gas emissions. These methods include investing in reductions in other countries, especially by joint implementation, EMISSION REDUCTIONS BANKING and clean development mechanisms.

flexprice (D0)

A price freely fluctuating in order to equate demand with supply, e.g. a price determined at an AUCTION. Such a view of prices is central to MARSHALLIAN economics.

See also: fixprice

References

Hicks, J.R. (1965) *Capital and Growth*, ch. 7, Oxford: Clarendon Press.

flight from money (E4)

A reduction in the DEMAND FOR MONEY because of an expectation of rising prices or a fall in nominal interest rates.

flip-flop arbitration (J5) *see* pendulum arbitration

floating exchange rate (F3)

A market-determined exchange rate which can change continuously as it is not pegged to another currency or to gold by a CENTRAL BANK. Canada, after the Korean War, floated the Canadian dollar in 1950–62 and again in 1970 after the Vietnam War; Lebanon from 1950 and Japan and some West European countries from August to December 1971 also floated their currencies. In practice, an exchange rate can be stabilized by speculation or central bank intervention, the latter being 'a dirty float'. Although lower reserves of gold and hard currencies are needed under a floating exchange rate regime, this regime has disadvantages, including a greater amount of uncertainty amongst exporters.

References

MacDonald, R. (1988) *Floating Exchange Rates: Theories and Evidence*, London: Unwin Hyman.

floating rate note (G1)

A long-term SECURITY whose rate of interest is linked to short-term interest rates.

Some of these notes are perpetuals with no maturity date. Changes in the US and UK rules concerning the definition of banks' PRIMARY CAPITAL has substantially reduced the demand for these notes, although their yields, which are higher than those for commercial paper and certificates of deposit, will continue to make them attractive to many money market investors.

floor (E3, E4)
1 The trough of a business cycle or trade cycle after which production, employment and prices rise.
2 The minimum rate of interest which an issuer of a floating rate security is required to pay.

See also: cap; ceiling; collar

flooring (G2) *see* floor planning

floor planning (G2)
Inventory financing by US commercial banks, e.g. to contribute to the purchase by dealers in CONSUMER DURABLES of the goods they have on display.

floor price (D4, K2)
A minimum controlled price, e.g. a MINIMUM WAGE or agricultural product prices. Minimum wage laws are enforced by inspectorates; agricultural prices are prevented from falling below pre-set minima by government purchases of excess production. If P_1 is the floor price and P_e is the equilibrium price the government can

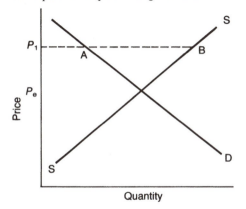

Quantity

satisfy both producers and consumers by purchasing quantity AB.

flotation (G1)
The market debut of a company when its shares are offered to the public for the first time. The motives for a flotation include the desire of the original owners to reduce their financial stake in that company as well as the wish to obtain more finance.

flow (E0) *see* stock and flow concepts

flow of funds account (E1)
A component of a system of NATIONAL INCOME accounts showing financial transactions between the major sectors of the economy. The transactions analysed are purchases and sales, and transfers such as taxes and dividends. The sectors used are different types of business, non-profit organizations, central and local government, banks, savings institutions, insurance, other finance and the rest of the world.

References

Bain, A.D. (1973) 'Flow of funds analysis: a survey', *Economic Journal* 83: 1055–93.
National Bureau of Economic Research (1962) *The Flow of Funds Approach to Social Accounting: Appraisal, Analysis and Applications. Studies in Income and Wealth*, Vol. 261, Princeton, NJ: Princeton University Press.

flypaper effect (H7)
The effect of giving grants, particularly under a system of FEDERAL FINANCE, to governments and not individuals. The grants 'stick' to their use as expenditure and cannot be used to reduce taxation as could happen if individuals directly received these grants.

See also: dedicated budget; earmarking; ringfencing

Fogel, Robert William, 1926– (B3)
Educated at Columbia and Johns Hopkins Universities, he taught at Rochester, Chicago and Harvard Universities before being appointed Charles R. Wargreen Professor of American Institutions at Chicago in 1981. His renowned works on economic

history include *Railroads and American Growth: Essays in Econometric History* (1964), which asserted that railways made only a small contribution to the growth of the US gross national product, and *Time on the Cross: the Economics of American Slavery* (1974, with Stanley Engerman), which stated that slavery was economically efficient although morally repugnant. In 1993 he shared with NORTH the NOBEL PRIZE FOR ECONOMICS.

Food and Agriculture Organization (Q1)

Rome-based United Nations agency founded in 1945. It aims (1) to raise nutrition levels, (2) to improve the efficiency of the production and distribution of all agricultural products and (3) to improve the condition of rural populations. FAO provides an information service, technical assistance and the promotion of national and international action, including international COMMODITY AGREEMENTS.

food chain (Q1)

The linked stages of production of food from the original farmer to the ultimate consumer.

football pool (D1)

A method of gambling on the outcome of a number of football matches on the same day. The fixed stakes of the punters are accumulated in a fund out of which dividends are paid to those who have successfully predicted the outcome of matches, with most points going to a prediction of teams which score the same number of goals as each other. The balance of the weekly fund is acquired by the pools promoter.

football transfer system (J4)

The method of selling professional footballers from one club to another. The fee is paid to bind the player to play exclusively for the new club. Both the transferring club and the transferred player financially benefit. The fee is proportional to the previous performance of the player with the expectation that excellence will continue. Since 1978 in the UK a player can negotiate a move to a new club on the expiry of a one- to five-year contract.

References

Carmichael, F., Forrest, D. and Simmons, R. (1999) 'The labour market in Association Football: who gets transferred and for how much', *Bulletin of Economic Research* 51: 125–50.
Sloane, P. (1971) 'The economics of professional football: the football club as a utility maximiser', *Scottish Journal of Political Economy* 18: 121–46.

footloose industry (L0)

An INDUSTRY locatable anywhere without incurring extra locational costs. Heavy industries, e.g. steel and shipbuilding, are not footloose; new industries using microchip technology can locate in many places without increasing their costs, although proximity to large markets and the availability of regional subsidies will guide them to particular locations.

See also: locked-in industry

footloose knowledge (O3)

Technical knowledge not specific to any production process and which is interchangeable between industries.

See also: locked-in knowledge

Footsie (G1)

Slang for FINANCIAL TIMES STOCK EXCHANGE 100 SHARE INDEX.

forced labour (H2)

Taxation of employment earnings causing a person to work longer hours than is necessary to obtain a given income. NOZICK advances this argument in his discussion of redistribution.

References

Nozick, R. (1974) *Anarchy, State and Utopia*, ch. 7, Oxford: Basil Blackwell; New York: Basic Books.

forced saving (E2, H3)

1 Involuntary saving arising in an economy when it is at FULL EMPLOYMENT and has an excess supply of loans. That

excess supply pushes down the market rate of interest and stimulates an increased demand for investment finance, bringing about general inflation. As a consequence of a rise in prices, those with fixed incomes can consume less and so savings are 'forced' out of them: this extra saving finances the extra investment. This view was widely held by members of the Classical School, including BENTHAM, THORNTON, MALTHUS and John Stuart MILL; in the twentieth century, ROBERTSON and PIGOU were also adherents of this doctrine. A crucial part of KEYNES's transition in thinking, which resulted in his *General Theory of Employment, Interest and Money*, was to reject this doctrine.

2 Compulsory saving as part of a tough fiscal policy. KEYNES recommended this as a method of financing the Second World War. He argued that this taxation of current incomes was needed to match current consumption and domestic production and imports as a means of preventing inflation. This 'deferred pay' would accumulate at compound interest in friendly societies and the Post Office Savings Bank. The scheme was adopted. Forced savings were gradually repaid as post-war credits after 1945 in line with the improvement of the national economy.

References

Corry, B.A. (1962) *Money, Saving and Investment in English Economics 1800–1850*, ch. 3, London: Macmillan; New York: St Martin's Press.

Hayek, F. von (1932) 'A note on the development of the doctrine of forced saving', *Quarterly Journal of Economics* 47: 123–33.

Keynes, J.M. (1940) *How to Pay for the War* (reprinted in his *Collected Works*, Vol. 9, pp. 367–439, London: Macmillan).

Machlup, F. (1943) 'Forced or induced saving: an exploration into synonyms and homonyms', *Review of Economics and Statistics* 25: 26–39.

Fordism (L6, P1)

A late, and successful, stage of CAPITALISM characterized by large-scale production, semi-skilled labour, easy credit and mass consumption. This concept is based upon the production methods of the Ford Motor Company, particularly its use of assembly lines for automobile production.

foreign aid (H2, O0)

Grants, loans on favourable terms or the supply of services by governments or charitable bodies to less developed countries. In its favour, it has been argued that aid creates the notion of an international human community, reduces political tension within countries by encouraging balanced development and increases the priority of development within less developed countries. A shortage of domestic savings and balance of payments problems in the early stage of expansion, when imports exceed exports, will retain the need for aid. As it is difficult to decide the basis for selecting aid recipients, it has been suggested that poverty, a good record in economic and social policies or a good performance in raising the share of savings and taxes in the national income should be used as alternative criteria.

Aid is given for many purposes including relief (often consumer goods are sent to alleviate a short-term supply deficiency, e.g. famine relief to Ethiopia), reconstruction (as in the rebuilding of an economy after a war, e.g. the MARSHALL PLAN), stabilization (especially short-term help with a country's balance of payments until adjustments are made to its economy) and long-term development to raise the level of per capita incomes permanently. Critics of aid programmes point out that aid can have the defects of creating economic or political dependence, introducing inappropriate technology or spending disproportionately on urban populations.

See also: bilateral aid; multilateral aid; tied aid

References

Casson, R. (1986) *Does Aid Work?*, Oxford: Oxford University Press.

Mosley, P. (1986) *Overseas Aid: Its Defence and Reform*, Hemel Hempstead, Harvester Wheatsheaf.

foreign direct investment (F2)

Investment in the businesses of another country which often takes the form of the setting up of local production facilities or the purchase of existing businesses. It is to be contrasted with PORTFOLIO INVESTMENT, which is the acquisition of securities. FDI has been much criticized, in the case of MULTINATIONAL CORPORATIONS, as a form of neo-colonialism. In its favour it can be said that it increases the level of investment in countries which otherwise would be undercapitalized and, as dividends vary with the prosperity of an industry (and a high proportion is reinvested in the local economy), it can be less burdensome than the servicing of fixed interest borrowing. For political reasons in the past, a disproportionate amount of direct investment in Third World countries went to Brazil, Mexico and South Africa, as well as to the EUROPEAN COMMUNITY to escape the COMMON EXTERNAL TARIFF. Some advanced economies fear the takeover of their industries by stronger, foreign economies, e.g. the USA is anxious about Japanese investment in many parts of the US economy.

foreign exchange (E5)

The CURRENCIES or short-term monetary claims of foreign countries.

References

Douch, N. (1989) *The Economics of Foreign Exchange*, Cambridge: Woodhead Faulkner.

foreign exchange market (G1)

A market where currencies are exchanged for each other. Both spot and forward trading are used. In 1991, the top banking centres measured as a percentage share of Reuters currency quotations were: London 17 per cent, New York 15 per cent, Singapore 11 per cent, Hong Kong 11 per cent, Zurich 7 per cent, Tokyo 6 per cent, Paris 5 per cent and Frankfurt 4 per cent. As the most important influence on these markets is company cash flows, this in a sense makes MULTINATIONAL CORPORATIONS mini-banks through their CORPORATE FINANCE activities. Central banks intervene to achieve a desired exchange rate for their own currencies. If they force their exchange rates down, speculators will leave the market. A stable exchange rate at the desired level usually requires active use of MONETARY and FISCAL POLICIES.

See also: forward market; spot market

foreign trade multiplier (E6, F1)

The ratio of a change in income to the change in exports and domestic investment which have generated that extra income. It is measured for an open economy without taxation as $1/(1 - \text{MPC} + \text{MPM})$, where MPC is the MARGINAL PROPENSITY TO CONSUME and MPM is the MARGINAL PROPENSITY TO IMPORT. The multiplier is crucial to explanations of the path to BALANCE OF PAYMENTS equilibrium and to the transmission of cyclical fluctuations throughout the world.

See also: multiplier

foreign trade organization (F1, P3)

A state agency of a COMECON country which exported and imported on behalf of state enterprises of a particular sector of a national economy. From the 1920s, it was a major organization of the Soviet economy. However, with Hungary as an example, enterprises in Comecon countries increasingly allowed the choice of trading directly or through foreign trade organizations.

See also: state trading organization

foreign trade zone (F1)

A tariff-free area, often around a port or an airport, which, by allowing the duty-free import and export of goods, can make manufactures flourish.

forex (E5)

Foreign exchange, or forward foreign exchange.

forex trading (G1)

Foreign exchange trading which is a major determinant of exchange rates. This volatile trading, sensitive to political events and movements in ECONOMIC INDICATORS, is conducted in financial centres throughout the world. HEDGING is continuously practised to reduce currency fluctuations. The growth of MULTINATIONAL CORPORATIONS has greatly increased the volume of business in foreign exchange markets.

forfaiting (F3)

A method of financing exporting. The exporter's bank assumes the risk of the buyer not paying by advancing the value of the exports to the exporter and discounting a BILL OF EXCHANGE or PROMISSORY NOTE in a secondary financial market where the market rate of interest is charged for the period until the buyer has paid in full. This originated as a method of financing West German exports to Eastern Europe but now is used to finance both exports and specific capital projects; only a minuscule amount of world trade is financed in this way.

See also: export promotion

forfait system (H2)

A system of taxation which uses indirect indicators of income, e.g. a sole proprietor's lifestyle or average profit margins, to assess a person for payment of a lump-sum tax. This system is used in France to assess taxes on the incomes of farmers, unincorporated businesses and the professions. It has many applications in less developed countries.

formal economy (P0)

1 The range of economic activities which are officially recorded.
2 That part of an economy in which labour is predominantly supplied by employees of firms and public enterprises.

See also: blue economy; underground economy

formal indexation (H2)

Automatic adjustments to income tax allowances in line with rises in retail prices at regular intervals. The nature of this mechanism for protection against inflation is decided by legislative enactments.

See also: bracket creep; Rooker–Wise Amendment

forms of integration (P0)

Karl POLANYI's description of various economies in terms of redistribution, reciprocity and exchange.

References

Polanyi, K. (1957) *The Great Transformation*, Boston: Beacon Press.

Fortune 500 (L0)

The annual listing by Fortune, the US business magazine, of the 500 largest world corporations ranked by revenue.

forward integration (L1)

The expansion through merger of the productive activities of manufacturers into wholesaling and distribution. This was made possible by advances in transport and information systems and resulted in greater production ECONOMIES OF SCALE as manufacturers' markets expanded.

See also: vertical integration

forward linkage (L0) *see* linkage

forward market (G1)

A market in currencies, commodities or securities which fixes prices for future delivery. The forward rates determined are linked to SPOT RATES by SPECULATION and HEDGING.

fountain pen money (E5)

Money created by a banker who uses a pen to approve a loan. This increases the bank deposit of the borrower and adds to total bank credit.

Fourier, Charles, 1772–1837 (B3)
Born at Besançon, France, the son of a
linen draper. After an education at a Jesuit
school he studied law at the local university before being forced to become a
draper as a condition of an inheritance.
His experience in a cavalry regiment in
1794–5 gave him a lifelong horror of social
turmoil. He collected ideas on the nature
of society to create a total science based
on gratifying and harmonizing all human
passions. His ideal community, the Pha-
lanstery, was tried near Paris but failed
through lack of finance. He opposed the
principle of the division of labour as he
believed everyone has a passion for variety
and pointed out the oppression of women.
His leading work was *The Theory of the
Four Movements* (1808).

See also: Owen, Saint-Simon

References

Beecher, J. (1986) *Charles Fourier. The Visionary and His World*, Berkeley, CA, and
London: University of California Press.

Fourth World (O0)
The poorest least developed countries of
the world, about twenty-five in all.

See also: First World; Second World;
Third World

fractal Brownian motion (C6)
A mathematical model used to generate
random numbers, originally noticed by
Robert Brown in 1827 when studying
botanical processes. 'Fractal' means that
it is independent of scale. It has been used
to analyse optimal production processes
and the movement of share prices.

fractional reserve banking (G2)
A banking system using HIGH-POWERED
MONEY as only a fraction of its total assets
rather than ONE HUNDRED PER CENT RESERVE
BANKING. According to the country and
phase of banking evolution, cash, and
assets which can be quickly converted into
cash without capital loss, can be as little as
a third or a quarter of the total volume of
commercial banks' deposits. This system

has made possible a major increase in
credit in many countries in the past
hundred years.

fragmentation (D2)
Division of a production process into
component parts so that production can
occur at several domestic or foreign locations.

See also: division of labour

framing effects (D8)
The effects of representing or framing
problems of choice, including deciding on
a reference point.

References

Machina, M.J. (1987) 'Choice under uncertainty: problems solved and unsolved',
Journal of Economic Perspectives 1:
121–54.

franchise (M3)
A legal privilege allowing a firm under
licence to sell another firm's products and
use its trade name. In return for the use of
a famous name and much free marketing
promotion, an initial payment and often a
royalty of 5–10 per cent of gross sales are
requested. As it is a condition of some
franchises that supplies be obtained from
the franchising company, competition law
in the USA and Western Europe has tried
to prevent such agreements. The arrangement is widespread in the fast food trade.

franchise financing (F3)
The financing of public works such as
bridges, airports and power stations by
foreign private investment. Examples include the Anglo-French Channel Tunnel
and various public works in Turkey, Malaysia and Jordan. A typical implementation of the method would be the creation
of a JOINT EQUITY VENTURE COMPANY owned
by the contractor, the operator and the
customer utility. Borrowing from banks
and credit agencies for the financing of
construction is on the security of revenue
from the project. When the loan is repaid,
the host government owns the new, public
work.

franchise gap (G1)

A band around the value of a currency in which it can be bought and sold.

See also: Common Agricultural Policy

fraud (K4, M4)

1 Deceitful accounting.

2 Misappropriation of funds.

See also: creative accounting; long fraud

free alongside ship (F1)

A type of exporter's price quotation, including delivery to a designated vehicle of the importer who then pays for subsequent transportation.

free banking (G2)

A LAISSEZ-FAIRE monetary system in which banks compete freely without state control and have the power to issue their own banknotes. However, even the most ardent supporters of this freedom would admit that some restrictions are necessary to guarantee the liquidity of the banking system and price stability. In the USA, free-banking laws were passed in the early nineteenth century, beginning with Michigan in 1837 and New York and Georgia in 1838. Anyone could set up banks subject to the minimum capital requirements prescribed by each state, and their note issues had to be backed by bonds deposited with a state auditor and redeemable on demand. There was free banking in Scotland from 1810 to 1845.

References

Dowd, K. (1989) *The State and the Monetary System*, Hemel Hempstead: Philip Allan.

Glasner, D. (1989) *Free Banking and Monetary Reform*, Cambridge: Cambridge University Press.

Rockoff, H. (1975) *The Free Banking Era: A Reconsideration*, New York: Arno Press.

Free Banking School (B1)

A group of early nineteenth-century English writers on monetary matters who argued that England should follow the Scottish principle of having several banks with note-issuing power, thus ending the monopoly of the Bank of England.

See also: Banking School

References

White, L.H. (1984) *Free Banking in Britain: Theory, Experience and Debate, 1800–45*, Cambridge: Cambridge University Press.

free cash flow (D3, M4)

A firm's intake of cash in excess of what is required to fund all profitable activities. Managers try to invest it in risky projects; shareholders ask for a distribution of it.

free depreciation (M4)

The amount of depreciation of an asset permitted by a taxation authority before actual wear and tear has taken place. All, or part, of the value of an asset is written off at the beginning of its life as a form of investment grant to a firm. In general, depreciation allowances are generous if the notional life of the asset for tax purposes is longer than its true life.

free good (D0)

A good with a zero price. This is possible because its supply is either abundant or rationed. A free good is the opposite of an ECONOMIC GOOD.

free list (F1)

Those goods that can be imported into a country without being subject to tariffs and licences.

free market (D4)

A market in which buyers and sellers are free to contract on whatever terms they wish without governmental interference.

free on board (F1)

A measure of the value of trade excluding insurance and transport costs. Exports are usually valued this way as it is assumed that importers will pay such costs.

freeport (F1)

An enclave in which imported goods are processed and then re-exported. This production arrangement has been a great success in many places, including Hamburg, South Korea and the Caribbean, but less so in the UK in which six freeport schemes were launched in 1984. Freeports were popular as far back as the Middle Ages, when they were known as 'staples'.

See also: in-bond manufacturing

free rider (D1, J5)
An individual who does not pay for the goods or services he or she consumes. Free riders include non-residents using the public services of a city and non-unionized workers who gain wage increases achieved under COLLECTIVE BARGAINING, without paying dues to a union to represent them. In the case of public goods the free-rider problem has resulted in the finance of such goods by general taxation; under trade unionism, the existence of free riders has led to demands for a UNION or CLOSED SHOP.

free trade (F1)
International trade, unhindered by TARIFFS, other restrictions on imports and export subsidies. This freedom was strongly recommended by the CLASSICAL ECONOMISTS on the basis of ABSOLUTE ADVANTAGE, in the case of SMITH, or COMPARATIVE ADVANTAGE in the cases of RICARDO and TORRENS. Today, it is recommended as a means of achieving international specialization of production and maximization of world economic welfare. In practice, completely free trade is rare. There are always particular interest groups and industries within a country demanding PROTECTION, with varying degrees of success. Even within a CUSTOMS UNION there can be disguised protection, e.g. within the EUROPEAN COMMUNITY through the imposition of quality and other controls. In the post-1945 period, the GENERAL AGREEMENT ON TARIFFS AND TRADE has attempted to prevent a return to the extensive protectionism characteristic of the 1930s. In the 1980s there was some support for protectionism, especially in the USA and in NEWLY INDUSTRIALIZED COUNTRIES. Free trade has always been

most strenuously advocated by major countries with trade surpluses, e.g. the UK in the nineteenth century and the USA in the 1950s and 1960s.

See also: Corn laws; protection; Smoot–Hawley Tariff Act 1930

References
Bhagwati, J. (1988) *Protectionism*, Cambridge, MA: MIT Press.
Corden, W.M. (1974) *Trade Policy and Economic Welfare*, Oxford: Clarendon Press.

free-trade area (F1)
A group of independent nations with free trade among them, but not necessarily with a joint trading policy for the rest of the world.

See also: European Free Trade Association

Free Trade Area of the Americas (F1)
An ambitious proposal to extend NAFTA to encompass all American countries from the Bering Strait to Cape Horn. The area would cover thirty-four countries with a population of 800 million and, in 2000, a joint GDP of $11 trillion.

freezing assets/an account (K2)
Making the owner of an asset or a depositor unable to use or transfer the amounts deposited with a financial institution because of a court or other order against the order. The assets become ILLIQUID.

French Circuit School (B1, B2)
Writers who have studied the economic process as a monetary circuit. QUESNAY'S *Tableau Economique* is an early example of this approach; WICKSELL and SCHUMPETER favoured this too. From the 1960s there has been a resurgence of interest in this approach, especially in publications such as *Monnaie et Production*. POST-KEYNESIANS have also taken up this type of analysis.

frequency curve (C1)
A curve constructed from a FREQUENCY DISTRIBUTION which can be obtained from a

FREQUENCY POLYGON. The different shapes of these curves include SYMMETRICAL, SKEWED, J-SHAPED, REVERSE J-SHAPED, U-SHAPED, BIMODAL and MULTIMODAL.

frequency distribution (C1)

An arrangement of RAW DATA into classes which are then tabulated: for example, the prices of houses can be classified as $100,000–$149,999, $150,000–$199,999, etc., and presented in two columns of house prices and the number of houses in each price range.

frequency polygon (C1)

A graph of the frequency of classes of a distribution often constructed by joining the midpoints of the tops of the rectangles in a HISTOGRAM.

See also: frequency curve

frequency table (C1) *see* frequency distribution

frictional unemployment (J6)

Short-period unemployment brought about by workers changing jobs. This minimum level of unemployment, which coexists with job vacancies, occurs even when an economy is at FULL EMPLOYMENT and is a feature of all types of national ECONOMY. Frictional unemployment is often measured by the number of people unemployed for less than a short period, e.g. eight weeks. Labour market policies can reduce this type of unemployment by making job information more available and accurate and by subsidizing search costs.

Friedman, Milton, 1912– (B3)

US economic prophet of CAPITALISM and MONETARISM and leading libertarian economist. After an education at Rutgers, Chicago and Columbia Universities, he was professor at Chicago from 1948 to 1979. His pronounced LIBERTARIAN ECONOMICS led to his appointments as adviser to Barry Goldwater (unsuccessful US presidential candidate in 1964) and President Richard Nixon. He was awarded the NOBEL PRIZE FOR ECONOMICS in 1976.

Friedman's long advocacy of monetarism has consisted of a powerful revival of the QUANTITY THEORY OF MONEY, reasserting that changes in the MONEY SUPPLY explain changes in the levels of prices and economic activity. He is also noted for his contributions to economic methodology (1953), his PERMANENT INCOME approach to the CONSUMPTION FUNCTION and his explanation of STAGFLATION (1968) which modified the PHILLIPS CURVE (by the inclusion of EXPECTATIONS) and introduced the concept of the NATURAL RATE OF UNEMPLOYMENT. Although much of Friedman's economics is anti-Keynesian in character, like KEYNES he ignores many micro-issues in favour of a heavy reliance on economic aggregative analysis. His distinctive approach to ECONOMIC METHODOLOGY is to argue that the fruitfulness of an economic theory must be judged by predictions that are empirically corroborated. Using FISHER's theory of capital, Friedman was able in his study of the CONSUMPTION FUNCTION to use the concept of permanent income, allowing expectations of future income to be a determinant of current expenditure. He reinstated the quantity theory of money by turning it into a theory of the demand for money as the k of the Cambridge equation $M = kPY$, with k, according to Friedman, a variable, not a constant. He was able to extend the Keynesian liquidity preference theory into a more modern portfolio approach. In his monetary history with Schwartz, he attributed the Great Depression to the FEDERAL RESERVE SYSTEM's reducing the US money stock in the period 1929–33 by one-third. In the stock market crashes of October 1987, many monetary authorities were anxious to avoid the same mistake.

References

De Marchi, N. and Hirsch, A. (1988) *Milton Friedman*, Brighton: Harvester Wheatsheaf.

Friedman, M. (1953) *Essays in Positive Economics*, Chicago: Phoenix Books.

—— (1956) *Studies in the Quantity Theory*

of Money, Chicago: University of Chicago Press .

—— (1957) *A Theory of the Consumption Function: A Study by the National Bureau of Economic Research, New York*, Princeton, NJ: Princeton University Press.

—— (1982) *Capitalism and Freedom*, Chicago and London: University of Chicago Press.

Friedman, M. and Schwartz, A.F. (1963) *Monetary History of the United States, 1867–1960*, Princeton, NJ: Princeton University Press.

—— (1982) *Monetary Trends in the United States and the United Kingdom: Their Relation to Income, Prices and Interest Rates 1867–1975*, Chicago: University of Chicago Press.

Thygessen, N. (1975) 'The scientific contributions of Milton Friedman', *Scandinavian Journal of Economics* 79: 56–98.

fringe banking crisis (G2) *see* secondary banking crisis

fringe benefits (J3)

Benefits in kind which constitute part of the remuneration of many employees, especially managers. These additions to wages and salaries can be provided either collectively, e.g. sports and leisure facilities, or individually, e.g. a company car, a low-interest mortgage, free health insurance, etc. In the USA they amounted to 17 per cent of the compensation of blue-collar workers in 1951 and 30 per cent (in some large corporations, 50 per cent) in 1981. Their incidence is higher for unionized than for non-unionized workers and are usually worth more to higher income groups because many fringe benefits are not subject to taxation.

See also: labour cost

Frisch, Ragnar Anton Kittil, 1895–1973 (B3)

A Norwegian economist who did much to establish ECONOMETRICS as a separate academic subject. After training under his father as a goldsmith and an education in Oslo and France, he was professor of economics in Oslo from 1931 to 1965. He

founded the Econometric Society in 1930 and was awarded the first NOBEL PRIZE FOR ECONOMICS (with TINBERGEN) in 1969. His advice to the Norwegian Labour Party in the 1930s and 1950s, to adopt central planning for key industries, applied his econometric ideas; his fiscal advice was similar to KEYNES'S. His early work on demand theory rigorously derived a consistent theory from basic axioms. Later he devoted much attention to the creation of a logical national accounting system, to economic planning and to the application of decision modelling to economic policy making. He was a pioneer in the development of dynamic economic theory.

References

Arrow, K.J. (1960) 'The work of Ragnar Frisch, econometrician', *Econometrica* 28: 175–92.

front-end loading (G2)

The inclusion of administrative charges into the first payment by a customer. This can apply to a unit trust price, an insurance premium or interest on a loan.

fronting loan (G2, G3)

A loan from a parent corporation to a local foreign subsidiary using the 'front' of an international bank to channel the loan. There is more chance of repayment to an international bank in times of political turmoil as many countries are reluctant to upset major financial institutions.

frostbelt (L0) *see* snowbelt

F test (C1)

The ratio of the VARIANCES of two independent samples of the variance of one population which has a NORMAL DISTRIBUTION. This SIGNIFICANCE TEST is used to test joint hypotheses with two or more regression PARAMETERS.

full-cost pricing (D4)

A theory of pricing first advanced in Oxford studies in 1938 by Hall and Hitch as a challenge to MARGINALISM. Prices, according to their observation of businessmen's behaviour, were calculated on the basis of average variable cost plus a gross profit margin (which would finance fixed costs) or average total cost with a net profit margin. Many questioned the view that such a rigid pricing policy would be followed if there were great changes in demand either making possible higher prices and greater profits or necessitating price cuts so that at least variable costs would be covered. Out of the theory came the assertion that oligopolists have a KINKED DEMAND CURVE.

References

Hall, R.L and Hitch, C.L. (1939) 'Price theory and business behaviour', *Oxford Economic Papers* 2: 12–45.

full employment (E0, G2)

The maximum use of a FACTOR OF PRODUCTION, especially labour. In the labour market, full employment occurs when unemployment has fallen to an irreducible minimum, approximately the level of FRICTIONAL UNEMPLOYMENT. In the USA, the EMPLOYMENT ACT 1946 made government responsible for economic stability and growth; in the UK, BEVERIDGE's *Full Employment in a Free Society* (1944) introduced the same goal explicitly. Many governments have only paid lip service to it as a goal, letting control of inflation take precedence. Many would argue that it is a dangerous goal, unsettling the labour market and bringing about lower PRODUCTIVITY as a strong desire to maintain employment can overheat an economy.

See also: natural rate of unemployment

References

Ginsburg, H. (1983) *Full Employment and Public Policy: The United States and Sweden*, Lexington, MA: Lexington Books; Toronto: D.C. Heath.

full-employment budget (H6)

The budget of a central government adjusted by deducting expenditure relating to unemployment and by adding the extra tax revenues the unemployed would contribute if in employment. This permits the calculation of the underlying FISCAL STANCE. Such budget balances are regularly published in the USA.

See also: structural deficit

full insurance (G2)

Coverage of all the perceived RISK of a client.

full-set industrial structure (L1)

A complete range of all industrial sectors at a high level of development. Japan achieved this range and level, unlike the more specialized countries of Europe.

See also: autarky

functional financing (H5)

A framework for public finance policies proposed by Lerner which would require the government to use every policy instrument available to contribute to the prevention of inflation and deflation and the promotion of the general interest, rather than following traditional goals of governments such as balancing the budget.

References

Lerner, A.P. (1943) 'Functional finance and the Federal debt', *Social Research* 10 (February): 38–51.

functional income distribution (D3)

The distribution of the NATIONAL INCOME between the factors of production, usually land, labour and capital. Statistics on this indicate, for example, the proportion of the national income going to wages and salaries.

See also: labour's share of national income

fundamental contradiction of capitalism (F1)

The conflict in industrial development between the need for national planning and the fragmentary nature of the individual plans of each capitalist. MARX asserted that this contradiction leads to CRISES.

fundamental equilibrium (F4)

For a BALANCE OF PAYMENTS this occurs

when the current and capital accounts are both in balance and the economy is internally balanced at a full-employment level. A departure from equilibrium can result in an underuse of resources, inflation and inefficiency.

See also: external balance; internal balance

fundamentals (E6)
The key economic statistics used to judge the state of an ECONOMY. At the simplest level, these are the inflation, growth and unemployment rates. A deeper analysis includes the rates of savings and productivity, external debt and current balance of payments.

fundamental value (G1)
That price of a security in a LIQUID MARKET equal to the present value of its future earnings.

See also: efficient market

funding (H6)
Conversion of short-term debt to long-term debt. Before governments had control over CENTRAL BANKS, funding was seen as a means of protecting a treasury against a short-term collapse of confidence in government securities leading to heavy sales of TREASURY BILLS and GOVERNMENT BONDS. Funding can also be practised by a firm, e.g. it can raise cash to pay off short-term liabilities such as bank loans by issuing shares, thereby lengthening its debt.

funding gap (H6, M2)
A shortage of revenue to meet the expenditure demands on a fund. This problem is often encountered in the public sector since a variety of forces, e.g. demographic changes, can lead to expanding programmes; also, for ideological and other reasons there may be a reluctance to increase taxes. ECONOMIES in recession often

have a gap of this kind as a fall in incomes reduces tax revenues and a rise in unemployment increases welfare expenditures.

See also: budgetary policy; Gramm–Rudman-Hollings Act

fungible asset (D0)
An asset which loses its identity through use. WORKING CAPITAL, unlike FIXED CAPITAL, is fungible.

future (D0, G1)
An agreed contract for the sale or purchase of an ASSET, CURRENCY or COMMODITY at a future date.

See also: option; spot price

future goods (D0)
The product of INVESTMENT. By the sacrifice of present consumption, it is possible to devote resources to capital goods which by a ROUNDABOUT METHOD OF PRODUCTION create a greater volume of future goods than the present goods not available for consumption today.

See also: Böhm-Bawerk

futures market (G1)
A currency, commodity or security market which permits present dealing for future delivery. Centres for futures trading include Chicago, London, New York, Paris and Toronto. The 'products' include commodities, currencies and STOCK MARKET PRICE INDICES. Trading is done 'on the margin', i.e. only a small percentage of the value of the contract has to be paid by the buyer or seller, but further MARGIN CALLS are made if there is an adverse market movement against the contracting party. Falls in the value of futures contracts in the autumn of 1987 prompted further calls to be made. In the 1980s there was a considerable increase in futures markets for financial assets.

G

gains from trade (F1)

The increase in output or welfare received by a country, or the world as a whole, through international trade making possible specialization of production. The theory of COMPARATIVE ADVANTAGE demonstrates how this is possible.

See also: absolute advantage

Galbraith, John Kenneth, 1908– (B3)

A Canadian–American liberal economist who has achieved astounding publishing success in his books on capitalism, the Great Depression, the affluent society and the industrial state. With a training in agriculture in Ontario and in agricultural economics at Berkeley, California, he has taught at Harvard University since 1949. His early work on industrial price rigidities and on price controls made use of his wartime experience as head of the Price Section of the US Office of Price Administration. In 1952, *American Capitalism* launched his career as a best-selling economic guru. His works contain strikingly novel analyses, e.g. of consumers' COUNTERVAILING POWER to large oligopolists, of the contrast between private affluence and public squalor and of the managerial nature of modern capitalism. Outside the university, he was a leading adviser to President John F. Kennedy and his ambassador to India. Much of his writing has the broad sweep of an eighteenth-century economist who has espoused the mixed economy: this approach is not without its critics as modern economists are often irritated by his avoidance of the empirical testing of his theories. But it is greatly to his credit that one of his most thorough books is his late survey of economic thought in 1987.

References

Galbraith, J.K. (1938) *Modern Competition and Business Policy*, Boston, MA: Houghton Mifflin; London: Hamish Hamilton.
—— (1952) *American Capitalism: the Concept of Countervailing Power*, London: Hamish Hamilton.
—— (1952) *A Theory of Price Control*, Cambridge, MA: Harvard University Press.
—— (1954) *The Great Crash 1929*, Boston: Houghton Mifflin; London: Hamish Hamilton.
—— (1958) *The Affluent Society*, London: Hamish Hamilton.
—— (1967) *The New Industrial State*, Boston: Houghton Mifflin; London: Hamish Hamilton.
—— (1973) *Economics and the Public Purpose*, Boston: Houghton Mifflin; London: Hamish Hamilton.
—— (1987) *A History of Economics: The Past as Present*, London: Hamish Hamilton.
Reisman, D.A. (1980) *Galbraith and Market Capitalism*, New York: New York University Press.

galloping inflation (E3) *see* hyperinflation

game theory (C7)
The study of the 'behaviour of independent decision makers whose fortunes are linked in an interplay of collusion, conflict and compromise' (Shubik). The theory is central to much formulation and testing of models in economics as it studies multilateral decision making. The earliest exponents of the art were COURNOT, EDGEWORTH, BÖHM-BAWERK and ZEUTHEN. Much of the theory recognizes UNCERTAINTY; recently it has taken into account ignorance of rules, incomplete information and indefinite time horizons. Important solution concepts utilized are the NASH EQUILIBRIUM, the CORE, the Neumann–Morgenstern stable set and the SHAPLEY value. Major applications include BILATERAL MONOPOLY, DUOPOLY, planning processes, WELFARE ECONOMICS and the study of markets and monetary institutions.

References
Neumann, J. von and Morgenstern, O. (1983) *Theory of Games and Economic Behaviour*, Princeton, NJ: Princeton University Press.
Schotter, A. and Schwodiauer, G. (1980) 'Economics and the theory of games: a survey', *Journal of Economic Literature* 18: 479–527.
Shubik, M. (1983) *Game Theory in the Social Sciences: Concepts and Solutions*, Cambridge, MA, and London: MIT Press.

gamma stock (G1)
The least active stock or share quoted on the STOCK EXCHANGE AUTOMATED QUOTATION SYSTEM.

See also: alpha stock; beta stock; delta stock

Gandhian economics (B2, P4)
A spiritual approach to economics involving self-reliance in a local environment, honesty, equality, surrender of private property for the sake of all, and a distinction between 'stranger-defined work' and 'self-defined work'. This type of economics tries to increase the level of minimum consumption, lower the prices of necessaries and raise the prices of luxuries. The goal is to replace riches in material goods with the wealth of being surrounded by caring people.

See also: altruism; Schumacher

References
Gandhi, M.K. (1957) *Economic and Industrial Life and Relations*, Ahmedbad: Navjivan Publishing.
Narayan, S. (1970) *Relevance of Gandhian Economics*, Ahmedbad: Navjivan Publishing.

Gang of Four (O0)
The Republic of Korea, Taiwan, Hong Kong and Singapore.

See also: newly industrialized country

gang system economy (P4)
A slave ECONOMY practising the subdivision of labour. This was a principal characteristic of the sugar colonies of the Caribbean.

gap analysis (G1)
The amount of assets with variable rates financed by fixed rate liabilities. This is used in the analysis of the relationship between the interest rates and maturities of assets and liabilities.

Garn St Germain Depository Institutions Act 1982 (G2, K2)
The sequel to the DEPOSITORY INSTITUTIONS DEREGULATION AND MONETARY CONTROL ACT 1980 which continued the deregulation of the US banking industry, particularly through the removal of interest rate ceilings.

Gastarbeiter (F2)
German word for GUESTWORKER.

gazumping (R2)
Breaking an agreement to sell a house because another prospective buyer has offered a higher price in the period between an oral promise to sell and the exchange of contracts. A sharp practice prevalent in England in the 1970s and 1980s.

GDP deflator (E0)
The ratio of the GROSS DOMESTIC PRODUCT at current prices to gross domestic product at constant prices multiplied by 100. It is the weighted average of the detailed price indices used to deflate the gross domestic product: the weights used reflect the importance of each category of output in the gross domestic product.

gearing (G0)
The ratio of a bank or other company's total borrowings of a fixed term or perpetual nature to its shareholders' funds and minority interests.

gender discrimination (J7) *see* sexual discrimination

gender division of labour (J2)
The traditional assignment of particular occupations or tasks with men continuing to have a wide range of job opportunities, and women restricted to a narrow range.

General Accounting Office (H1)
An independent US agency, outside the Executive Office, directly responsible to the US Congress for seeing that the funds voted by Congress are spent as enacted in legislation.

General Agreement on Tariffs and Trade (F1)
A multilateral trade agreement signed in 1947. It covers all major trading countries with the exceptions of the Soviet republics and China. It was originally intended to be part of the International Trade Organization, a body intended to police international transactions, and, together with the INTERNATIONAL MONETARY FUND and the WORLD BANK, constituted a new international economic system. As the INTERNATIONAL TRADE ORGANIZATION was never established, the General Agreement on Tariffs and Trade remains as a treaty. Under Article 1, each contracting party to the agreement pledged to offer most favoured nation treatment to the others; Article 3 challenged trade discrimination by requiring contracting parties to charge

only domestic taxation on imports from treaty partners; Articles 11 to 15 stated that quantitative restrictions on imports were permitted, after consultation, for balance of payments reasons. Trade has gradually been liberalized in a number of rounds of negotiations.

Most disputes between members have been solved, with the exception of the problem of the subsidization of agricultural products. But it can be argued that the continued existence of VOLUNTARY EXPORT RESTRAINTS and deals such as market sharing have retained PROTECTION in a modern guise.

See also: Dillon Round; Kennedy Round; Tokyo Round; Uruguay Round; World Trade Organization

References
Hoekman, B.M. and Kostecki, M.M. (1995) *The political economy of the world trading system: from GATT to WTO*, Oxford and New York: Oxford University Press.
Oxley, A. (1990) *The Challenge of Free Trade*, Hemel Hempstead: Harvester Wheatsheaf.

General Agreement to Borrow (E5, F3)
The credit line set up by the GROUP OF TEN for the INTERNATIONAL MONETARY FUND in 1962 to provide loans to the group's members. The facility was enlarged in January 1983 when other IMF members were permitted to contribute to it and make use of it in emergencies.

general competitive bidding (M2)
A method of selecting a contractor for a large investment. Typically an outline of a construction project is announced. Anyone can participate in the bidding and the bidder offering the lowest price wins the contract. Also known as the 'open bidding system'.

general equilibrium (D5)
The state of an economy in which all its markets for consumer goods, capital goods, labour services, financial assets and money are in equilibrium and the

economy is in overall balance. The leading MARGINALIST WALRAS was the first economist to set out the conditions for general equilibrium. Today, the basic questions about a general equilibrium always include whether the solution proposed exists, whether it is unique and whether it is stable. General equilibrium analysis has the advantage of being flexible enough to be able to incorporate many goals and resources in a model. It is contrasted with MARSHALL'S PARTIAL EQUILIBRIUM ANALYSIS and is a half-way house between microeconomics and macroeconomics.

See also: Arrow–Debreu model

References

Allingham, M. (1975) *General Equilibrium*, New York: Wiley; London: Macmillan.
Kornai, J. (1971) *Anti-Equilibrium and the Tasks of Research*, Amsterdam: North-Holland.
Weintraub, E.R. (1974) *General Equilibrium Theory*, London and Basingstoke: Macmillan.

general fund (H6, M2)
Part of a budget providing finance for a variety of purposes.

See also: dedicated budget

general government net worth (H6)
The fixed capital stock of central or local government less its net financial liabilities. This BALANCE SHEET approach to the study of government finance has been suggested as a framework for assessing a government's ability to sustain its economic policies. It also has the useful function of making governments distinguish productive investments from debt servicing.

General Household Survey (C8, H1)
A sample survey used in the UK to collect data on the labour force and on household expenditure.

generalized least squares (C1)
An improved method of estimating relationships between economic variables. Each observation is weighted by the reciprocal of the STANDARD DEVIATION of the

disturbance concerned before applying the LEAST SQUARES METHOD.

generalized medium (E4)
Something generally acceptable for the purpose of making many transactions. MONEY performs this in modern economies as it can be used to effect exchanges in numerous markets and measure the value of millions of different types of goods and services.

See also: medium of account; medium of exchange; money

generalized system of preferences (F1)
A proposal made at the 1964 meeting of UNITED NATIONS CONFERENCE ON TRADE AND DEVELOPMENT, and accepted in 1968, that developed countries grant preferential tariff treatment for imports of manufactures and semi-manufactured products from developing countries. Those granting preferential treatment include the USA, the EUROPEAN COMMUNITY, Canada, Australia and Japan.

See also: most favoured nation

general market equilibrium (D5)
The EQUILIBRIUM of a market with several interdependent commodities traded with, for each commodity, the quantity demanded being equal to the quantity supplied.

See also: isolated market equilibrium

References

Dorfman, R., Samuelson, P.A. and Solow, R.M. (1958) *Linear Programming and Economic Analysis*, ch. 13, New York: McGraw-Hill.

general sales tax (H2)
An INDIRECT TAX levied on the sales of most consumer goods and services, usually expressed as a percentage of the value of the purchases.

See also: expenditure tax

general strike (J5)
Simultaneous STRIKES in most major industries of a country: famous examples include that in the UK in 1926 and several

in Poland and Sweden in the 1980s. These strikes often start in a major sector and become general through sympathetic action.

General Theory (E0) *see* Keynes's *General Theory*

general training (J2)
Training of members of a labour force in skills of use to many employers, e.g. word processing. There is a case for education of this kind to be provided by an educational institution, or financed by an industry as a whole, to avoid an employer gaining no return to the investment made in a worker's training because the worker moves to another job.

See also: human capital; specific training

general union (J5)
A TRADE (LABOR) UNION which organizes workers from different occupations and industries, e.g. the Teamsters (USA), the Transport and General Workers' Union (UK). General unions are often so large as to dominate a national trade union movement.

See also: craft union; industrial union

generational accounting (H6)
The construction of accounts showing the taxes paid less transfer payments received over a person's lifetime in order to execute long-term fiscal planning and analysis. Lifetime net fiscal burdens are calculated by summing the net taxation of all generations living at a point in time. In most major OECD countries, often in central banks or treasuries, these accounts are produced. This analysis examines the fiscal burden on future generations created by current policies to see if they are sustainable and achieving a balance in the fiscal burden between generations. At the end of the 1990s the USA, Germany and Japan had serious generational imbalances.

References

Kotlikoff, L.J. (1992) *Generational accounting*, New York: Free Press.

generative city (R1)
A city whose existence and growth are a major cause of the growth of a region. The best example in most countries is the capital city.

See also: parasitic city

gentrification (R2)
Improvement of older working-class inner city housing by rich professionals, e.g. in San Francisco and south London.

geographical trade structure (F1)
Analysis of a nation's international trade showing the countries of origin of its imports and the countries of destination for its exports. This structure reflects international trading agreements and the extent of economic interdependence among countries. In the UK, for example, membership of the EUROPEAN COMMUNITY from 1972 has brought about a switch from trade with the Commonwealth to trade with major European economies, especially Germany.

See also: commodity trade structure

geometric mean (C1)
The nth root of a set of numbers which have been multiplied together, e.g. the geometric mean of 2, 4, 8 is the third root of 64, i.e. 4.

See also: arithmetic mean; harmonic mean

geometric progression (C6)
A series of numbers which increases by a constant, or common, ratio, e.g. 2, 4, 8, 16, where 2 is the common ratio. MALTHUS asserted that population grows according to this progression.

See also: arithmetic progression

George, Henry, 1839–97 (B3)
US economist and politician famous for advocating that all taxation should be raised from a single tax on land, an idea which had its origins in the writings of the PHYSIO-CRATS and the classical DIFFERENTIAL THEORY OF RENT. He regarded increases in land

values in the nineteenth century as a major cause of inequality and injustice in society. His famous work, *Progress and Poverty* (1879), which was very popular in the USA in the 1880s and 1890s, is still closely studied in the many Henry George Schools of Economics which provide expositions of the master's ideas throughout the world. The Henry George Foundation of America, founded in 1926 and based at Columbia, Maryland, still researches into land value taxation and site value taxation.

German capitalism (P1)
An economic system noted for high wages, high international competitiveness and a promotion of social cohesion through strong trade unions, labour–management co-operation and high levels of spending on health care and welfare.

German Historical School (B1, B2)
Successive generations of German economists in the nineteenth and early twentieth centuries who took a holistic approach to economics, attempting to examine all economic phenomena, using material from social history. Their researches included fiscal policy, administration, industrial organization, cities, bank credit, government and private enterprise. The earliest writers of this school were Bruno HILDEBRAND (1812–78), Wilhelm ROSCHER (1817–94) and Karl KNIES (1821–98), the leader was Gustav von SCHMOLLER (1838–1917) and the later writers were Arthur Spiethoff (1873–1957), Werner SOMBART (1863–1941) and Max Weber (1864–1920).

References

Pearson, H. (1999) 'Was there really a German Historical School of Economics?', *History of Political Economy* 31: 547–62.

Shionoya, Y. (ed.) (2001): *The German Historical School: the historical and ethical approach to economics*, London and New York: Routledge.

Gerschenkron effect (C1, N0, F2)
The effect of the choice of a particular base year on an index of industrial output.

In a largely agrarian society, the base year chosen will determine the rate of growth exhibited by that index. This was originally applied to the Soviet economy by the Austro-American economic historian Alexander Gerschenkron (1904–78).

References

Gerschenkron, A. (1947) 'The Soviet indices of industrial production', *Review of Economics and Statistics* 29: 217–26.

gestation period (E2)
The time it takes for production or a capital project to be completed. CLASSICAL ECONOMISTS, e.g. RICARDO, asserted that the average period was twelve months, as in agriculture where there is only one harvest per year.

Gibrat's law (L2, R1)
The relationship between size and rate of growth of an entity such as a firm or a city.

See also: Zipf's law

References

Sutton, J. (1997) 'Gibrat's legacy', *Journal of Economic Literature* 35: 40–59.

Giffen good (D0)
A good increasingly demanded as its price rises. GIFFEN noted this exception to the normal demand curve inverse relationship between price and quantity demanded of a good in the case of an essential foodstuff.

Giffen paradox (D0)
An exception to the normal inverse relationship between price and quantity demanded made famous by GIFFEN. He noticed in the case of bread consumption that the quantity demanded rose when the price did, an exception to the general law of demand. If a poor family spends its income on bread and meat, a rise in the price of bread would make it impossible for it to afford a discrete amount of meat, with the consequence that there would be an excess of income after maintaining the same level of bread consumption which would be used to purchase more bread – hence an increased consumption of bread

despite a rise in its price. INCOME AND SUBSTITUTION EFFECTS analysis is used to explain this paradox: the income effect outweighs the substitution effect and there is a change in the sign of the income effect from positive to negative.

In the figure, I_1 and I_2 are the indifference curves of a particular consumer faced with the choice between goods F and G. There is a fall in the price of good G (more of it can be obtained for a fixed amount of F) expressed by a shift in the budget line from AC to AD, but there is also a fall in the quantity demanded of it from Or to Oq as the income effect yz is more than the substitution effect xz.

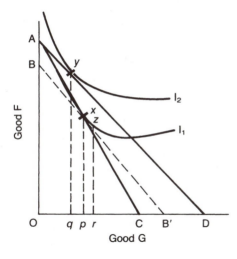

Good G

References

Boland, L.A. (1977) 'Giffen goods, market prices and testability', *Australian Economic Papers* 16: 72–85.
Stigler, G.J. (1947) 'Notes on the history of the Giffen paradox', *Journal of Political Economy* 55: 152–6.

Giffen, Sir Robert, 1837–1910 (B3)

Born in Strathaven, Scotland. After careers in law and journalism (he was assistant editor of *The Economist* from 1868 to 1876 and city editor of the *Daily News* from 1873 to 1876), he became a civil servant working at the Board of Trade as Chief of the Statistical Depart-

ment and then Assistant Secretary until he retired in 1897. A founder of the Royal Economic Society and famous for the GIFFEN PARADOX.

References

Giffen, R. (1904) *Economic Inquiries and Studies*, London: G. Bell.
Mason, R.S. (1989) *Robert Giffen and the Giffen Paradox*, Hemel Hempstead: Philip Allan.

gifts tax (H2)

A tax on the transfer of personal capital to someone else, often a close relative. The tax is imposed to prevent persons from avoiding inheritance taxes by transferring ownership before death; small gifts of a single year are usually exempted.

gilt-edged security (E5) *see* gilts

gilts (E5, G1)

UK government security with a guarantee that interest will be paid and capital repaid on its redemption day (if any). The term arose because of the high value of these bonds.

Gini coefficient (C1, D3)

A measure of income distribution, devised by the Italian demographer and statistician Corrado Gini (1884–1965). It is the ratio of the area between a LORENZ curve and the line of absolute equality (shaded in the figure) to the area of the entire triangle below that line (ABC). It has also

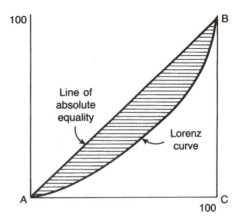

been applied to the measurement of INDUSTRIAL CONCENTRATION.

Ginny Mae (G3) *see* Government National Mortgage Association

giro (G3)
A system for transferring bank deposits long used in most European countries and offered as a service by the UK Post Office from 1968 and by UK CLEARING BANKS shortly afterwards. Instead of a transfer being effected by a cheque, the holder of a giro account instructs the bank concerned to make a change in its ledgers to pay another giro account-holder a particular amount of money.

GLAM (J1)
Grey, leisured, affluent, married: the key socioeconomic group of the late twentieth century, aged between 45 and 59 years.

Glass–Steagall Act 1933 (G2, K2)
Banking Act 1933 (USA) which separated INVESTMENT BANKING from deposit-taking banking with the aim of discouraging speculation and conflicts of interest, e.g. between underwriting new share issues and normal COMMERCIAL BANK lending. It banned the payment of interest on demand deposits and allowed the Federal Reserve System to set RESERVE REQUIREMENTS. Since 1980, there have been US calls for the repeal of the Act so that US banks can have as wide a range of financial products as European banks. Japan's version of Glass–Steagall (Article 65 of its Securities and Exchange Law) was also much criticized.

References

Benston, G.I. (1990) *The Separation of Commercial and Investment Banking. The Glass-Steagall Act Revisited and Reconsidered*, London: Macmillan.

gliding rate (F3) *see* sliding parity

global depository receipt (G1)
A bank certificate referring to domestic shares sold internationally through the foreign branches of a bank.

See also: American Depository Receipt

global deregulation (F3)
The abolition of exchange controls, tax barriers, fixed dealing commissions and limitations on overseas investment together with the creation of new financial instruments which foreigners can use. More and more countries are heading down the path of deregulation. Since 1979, the UK, Japan, Germany and many other countries have abolished their exchange controls. Japan, long reluctant to allow foreigners to invest in the country, has allowed more foreign access to its financial markets. Also, the New York and London Stock Exchanges have undertaken massive deregulation.

See also: Big Bang; Mayday

globalization (F0)
The expansion of domestic markets and activities into a world-wide system. As long ago as the Roman Empire trade was encouraged internationally. In the seventeenth century companies trading to the East Indies from Western Europe not only exported and imported but established factories in distant countries. From the late nineteenth century major industrial and banking companies set up foreign subsidiaries. Today globalization does mean that increasingly economic activity takes place within world-wide markets, often electronically. BRANDING has produced more homogenization of tastes and reduced the scope for local production. With globalization national governments become less important: large corporations and world markets dictate the distribution of production and of incomes. Critics point out the threat to democracy posed by the establishment of institutions not subject to national governments.

See also: multinational corporation

References

Turner, A. (2001) *Just capital: the liberal economy*, London: Macmillan.

global monetarism (F3)

A proposed regime of fixed exchange rates with a collective MONETARY POLICY for participant countries. The aim of this form of MONETARISM is to stabilize the average price of traded goods.

glut (E3)

Excess supply of all or most goods and services. CLASSICAL ECONOMISTS regarded a glut as a general economic depression, characterized by failing output, employment and prices – it was only temporary as price changes were expected to restore the economy to a full-employment equilibrium.

See also: effectual demand; Malthus; Mill, John Stuart; Say's law

gnomes of Zurich (E3)

A description of the Swiss bankers alleged to be speculating against sterling in the 1960s used by Harold Wilson, then prime minister of the UK.

goal equilibrium (D0)

An EQUILIBRIUM that attempts to achieve a particular aim, e.g. the maximization of consumers' utility.

See also: non-goal equilibrium

goal system (H2)

A method of raising tax revenue which requires each tax office to achieve a quota of tax revenue.

See also: tax farming

goal variable (E6)

A policy objective forming part of the objective utility function of a policy-maker, e.g. price stability, a balance of payments equilibrium.

See also: instrument variable; target variable

going concern (M1)

A commercial organization, usually a firm, expected to continue to operate for the foreseeable future because of its stable financial condition.

going rate (J3)

A wage rate regarded as the acceptable pay at a particular time for an occupational group. Often it is the pay set by a major employer or bargaining group.

See also: key rate; wage round

goldbug (G0)

Someone in favour of a return to the GOLD STANDARD.

gold bullion standard (F3)

A fixed exchange rate system which existed in its purest form from 1880 to 1914. National currencies were valued in terms of weight units of gold, and exchange rates were fixed through the medium of gold. If international transactions were not in balance then internal adjustment was needed in the debtor country. Currencies on the gold standard were convertible into each other merely with the cost of shipping gold from one country to another. The key player of the system was the CENTRAL BANK of each country as it had the tasks of contracting the internal money supply – in the case of a balance of payments deficit to produce a credit contraction, and the reverse in the case of a balance of payments surplus. Both domestically and internationally, gold was ideal because of its unique qualities as a standard of value and as a medium of exchange. It applied the ONE-PRICE LAW throughout the world, permitting gold to flow according to the price specie-flow mechanism. But too little co-operation between the central banks (many of whom were reluctant to follow the harsh rules of the system) weakened the automatic effects of the gold standard. The gold standard was in force in the UK from 1717 to 1931 (apart from the Napoleonic Wars and the First World War). Before the First World War the BANK OF ENGLAND, as the CENTRAL BANK of the creditor country of the world, operated according to the rules, but the USA did not do so when it had a similar task after 1918: it had a great inflow of gold, but it did not allow domestic prices to rise. When debtor countries introduced EXCHANGE CONTROLS and entered into trade wars, the gold standard was at an end.

See also: commodity reserve currency; dollar standard; gold exchange standard

References

Bordo, M.D. and Schwartz, A.J. (eds) (1984) *A Retrospective on the Classical Gold Standard 1821–1931*, Chicago: University of Chicago Press.

gold coinage (E5)
Coins now used chiefly for investment or collecting purposes. Leading examples include the BRITANNIA, the KRUGERRAND and the MAPLE LEAF.

gold demonetization (F3)
Ceasing to use gold as the basis for valuing a currency. The major example of this was when the US dollar replaced gold after the collapse of the BRETTON WOODS system as the peg for many currencies.

See also: dollar standard

golden age (O4)
A period of steady growth with continuous full employment. In this age, the WARRANTED RATE OF GROWTH is equal to the NATURAL RATE OF GROWTH.

References

Robinson, J. (1962) *Essays in the Theory of Economic Growth*, London: Macmillan.

golden handcuffs (J3)
A gratuity or deferred benefit given to an employee to discourage him or her from moving to another employer.

golden handshake (J3)
A gratuity given to an employee on retiring from a firm.

golden hello (J3)
A gratuity of a substantial amount offered to a potential employee to induce him or her to join a firm.

golden parachute (J3)
A financial arrangement made by a company director to secure future income, e.g. a consultancy in the event of a company takeover.

golden rate (J3)
An excessive rate of pay for overtime which is several times the normal rate for working contracted hours.

golden rule (O4)
Equating the rate of profit with the rate of growth. In the theory of ECONOMIC GROWTH, it is the optimal growth path for an economy such that the maximum level of consumption per head of a population is sustained.

References

Phelps, E.S. (1961) 'The golden rule of accumulation: a fable for growthmen', *American Economic Review* 51: 638–43.

golden share (G1, M1)
A voting share in a company, especially one which has been privatized, which can prevent the company from being taken over and gives the holder the power to insist that the company be run in a prescribed way. The UK government retained such shares when it privatized NATIONALIZED INDUSTRIES.

See also: privatization

Golden Triangle (R1)
1 Thailand, Laos and Burma: the most important opium-producing region in the world.
2 The megalopolis of North West Europe.
3 The business centre of Pittsburgh, Pennsylvania.

gold exchange standard (F3)
The linking of a currency to a currency which is on the gold standard so that it acquires a stability making it useful as a reserve currency. This substitute for the gold standard was in force in the 1920s (in

the UK from 1925 to 1932) and in effect in the 1960s.

See also: dollar standard; gold bullion standard

gold franc (F3)
An ARTIFICIAL CURRENCY used by the International Telecommunications Union (Geneva) to express telecommunications charges of different countries in the same 'currency'. In 1865, the Telegraph Convention adopted the French franc as the monetary unit to be used in calculating international tariffs as it was a major hard currency. In 1928, to avoid the problem of fluctuations in the value of the franc, a standardized 'gold franc' equal to 10/31 of a gram of gold was the basic unit chosen. In 1947, many countries were dissatisfied with the system but the proposal to devalue the gold franc was rejected as it meant a reduction in international telegraph and telephone rates. Lacking an alternative, the system continued. However, the gold franc was never a reserve currency (accounts are settled in national currencies) but merely a unit of account: thus it has only one of the functions of money. Since the floating of currencies in 1971, the conversion of gold francs into national currencies has produced divergent results. Also, gold francs of different values are used for different types of transactions, e.g. the value for shipping tolls is different from that for telegrams. In 1987, the value of the gold franc was fixed with 3.0061 gold francs equal to 1 special drawing right.

goldilocks economy (N0, P0)
The US economy in the late 1990s when it enjoyed high growth without inflationary pressures. It was noted for its low rate of household saving and rising trade deficit.

See also: soft landing

gold market (G1)
The market with official and private dealings in gold coin and bullion. In March 1968, US monetary authorities persuaded European authorities to separate private and monetary gold markets, creating a two-tier market. The USA wanted South Africa to sell all its gold to the private market so that the price would come down to $30 or $32 to shake central banks' confidence in gold. However, world inflation made gold a popular private holding and so its price approached $70 by mid-1972; by September 2001 the price had exceeded over $290. The London Gold Market was run by five firms since 1919, namely N.M. Rothschild, Samuel Montagu, Mocatta and Goldsmid, Sharps, Pixley and Westpac (formerly Johnson Matthey Bankers). Internationalization of financial markets brought about proposals to admit foreign traders. There is now the London Bullion Market Association with seven clearers.

gold plating (K2)
The practice of the UK Civil Service of converting EUROPEAN UNION directives into longer and more onerous legislation and statutory instruments.

gold reserves (E5)
Gold holdings of a CENTRAL BANK used only for transactions with other central banks. The amount of gold reserves in the world at any time is equal to the amount produced less the private demand for jewellery, dentistry and hoarding, together with past accumulations.

See also: gold bullion standard

gold shortage (N2)
The world shortage of gold in 1900–72. In this period, US wholesale prices rose 300 per cent, a much greater rise than in the monetary gold price (up only 75 per cent). The shortage was brought about to a large extent by the small margin between the production cost and the selling price of gold, a disincentive to producers. An increase in the price of gold pushed up US Treasury holdings from $7 billion in 1934 to $20 billion in 1939, but the shortage continued, exacerbated by the Second

World War and the post-war demand for gold.

goldsmith banking system (G2)

The seventeenth-century beginnings of modern commercial banking in the City of London. Goldsmiths who accepted personal and business gold holdings also lent out such deposits until they discovered that only a certain proportion of deposits would be reclaimed in a particular period and so it was possible to lend by granting loans in the form of deposit receipts. This was, in effect, the beginning of the FRACTIONAL RESERVE BANKING system.

gold standard (E5)

A basis for the value of a national currency which can take the form of a GOLD BULLION STANDARD or a GOLD EXCHANGE STANDARD.

References

Gold Standard Commission (1982) *Report to Congress of the Commission on the Role of Gold in the Domestic and International Monetary System*, Washington, DC: US Government Printing Office.

good (D0)

1 A tangible output rather than a SERVICE.
2 Something which bestows UTILITY on the person possessing it.

See also: bad; brown good; consumer durable; illth; wealth; white good

Goodhart's law (E5)

This states that any measure of the MONEY SUPPLY behaves differently when it becomes an official target by the very act of targeting it. Named after Charles Goodhart, formerly chief monetary adviser at the Bank of England, who reached this conclusion after studying the monetary events of the period 1971–3 in the UK.

goodwill (M2)

An intangible asset of a firm adding to its worth. A major example is 'a good reputation' resulting from a firm having established good relations with customers or suppliers. Goodwill causes the market

value of a firm to be in excess of its BOOK VALUE.

Goodwin growth cycle (E3)

A model relating employment, profits and wages in order to explain economic CYCLES. Cycles occur because at a time of high employment and low unemployment there is a rise in wages that causes profits to fall. As a consequence investment declines and in turn employment and wages fall. With low wages, profits and investment rise causing an upswing. The theory owes much to theories advanced by RICARDO and MARX.

References

Goodwin, R.M. (1972) 'A growth cycle', in C.H. Feinstein (ed.) *Socialism, capitalism and economic growth*, Cambridge: Cambridge University Press.

Gordon model (G1)

A model of stock market prices:

$$P_t = D_t(r - g)$$

where P_t is price in time t, D_t is dividend in period t, r is the constant rate of return and g is the constant dividend growth rate.

Gosplan (P3)

The Soviet central planning organization which had the task of collecting economic data from all the republics of the USSR and their subordinate organizations to draw up medium five-year plans and annual operational plans. Its well-known five-year plans began with a plan for industry covering the years 1923–4 to 1927–8. It also had to audit enterprises to check that plans had been followed. It had the important task of material balancing, i.e. matching expected demand with expected supply.

Gossen, Hermann Heinrich, 1810–58 (B3)

An early MARGINALIST educated in law and government in the Universities of Bonn and Berlin. After a spell as an indolent civil servant from 1834 to 1847, he worked in the insurance industry. His short work of 1854 expounded the law of DIMINISHING MARGINAL UTILITY, analysed market exchange, examined the nature of RENT and provided the basis for a theory of LABOUR SUPPLY. JEVONS and MARSHALL acknowledged their debt to him.

Gossnab (P3)
The central supplies committee of the USSR which had the task of allocating materials to enterprises. In the 1990s, its role was to change to being a wholesaler of capital goods.

government bond (E5, G1)
A long-term stock market security issued by a central, state or local government which is either irredeemable or to be repaid after a stated number of years.

See also: gilts

government broker (G1)
The stockbroker dealing in financial markets on behalf of a government. In London, the senior partner of Mullens & Co. participated in gilts for the Bank of England.

government intervention (H1, H2, L5)
A series of measures undertaken by a government to achieve goals not guaranteed by a market system, i.e. fairer income and wealth distribution, PUBLIC GOODS, MERIT GOODS, improved SOCIAL WELFARE, appropriate infrastructure investment and a full equilibrium for the economy. Intervention can avoid chaos by establishing PROPERTY RIGHTS, controlling access to economic activities and regulating monetary operations. But intervention has its shortcomings: the use of price controls and the limiting of competition have often distorted markets.

See also: fine-tuning; fiscal policy; incomes policy; monetary policy; prices policy

Government National Mortgage Association (G2)
US association responsible for issuing guarantees of the securities backed by a pool of Federal Housing Administration and Veterans Administration mortgage loans; known as 'Ginny Mae'.

government procurement practice (F1, L3)
The purchasing method a governmental organization or agency uses to choose its suppliers of goods and services. Preference for a domestic supplier is a type of NON-TARIFF BARRIER.

government role (H1)
The economic functions carried out by governmental organizations, together with the range of policies affecting the economic behaviour of firms and households. Under LAISSEZ-FAIRE principles, a government's role will be minimal – not much more than defence and law and order – so that market forces will not be curbed. The earliest lists of the functions of government in the works of PETTY, SMITH and John Stuart MILL were slightly longer. Petty approved of state financing for clergy and doctors, Smith of the building of bridges and the provision of schools, Mill of some government participation in the running of industry. In the nineteenth and twentieth centuries, the growth of trade unions and socialist parties together with the theory of ECONOMIC PLANNING have persuaded many governments to extend their functions and to influence the pattern of production and the distribution of incomes. Only in the SOVIET ECONOMY before the 1960s was there an attempt to give governments so large a role as to leave little decision-making power in the hands of other economic agents.

government security (G1)
A BILL or BOND issued by a local, regional or central government. Lower levels of government tend to borrow for shorter periods than central governments. The ultimate guarantor of the payment of interest and the repayment of the sum borrowed is usually the central government.

grace (G0) *see* days of grace

gradualist monetarism (E3)
A form of MONETARISM that accepts that the association between money supply increases and price increases is a long-term phenomenon. Thus, in the short run, there is a limited role for the stimulation of aggregate demand through the use of fiscal and monetary policies. However, monetarists of this kind would prefer there to be no DEMAND MANAGEMENT because of their belief that, as an economy is basically self-adjusting, manipulation of aggregate demand would cause fluctuations. FRIEDMAN (USA) and Laidler (UK) have adhered to this view; the NEW CLASSICAL ECONOMICS writers are instant monetarists.

See also: instant monetarism

graduated income tax (H2)
A tax on income with a different rate for different bands of income.

See also: bracket creep; progressive tax

graduate tax (H2)
A tax on the earnings of graduates imposed to recover the public expenditure incurred in financing college or university education. The tax is related to future earnings but there can be a 'tax holiday' covering the first few years of employment or until a threshold level of income has been reached. Proponents of the tax argue that it makes possible a greater expansion in the number of students; opponents assert that this increase in taxation will discourage participation in higher education.

Gramm–Rudman–Hollings Act (H6)
The Balanced Budget and Emergency Deficit Control Act 1985 (US federal statute). This set a legal target for the federal budget deficit of $171.9 billion in 1986, with the contradictory requirement that automatic spending cuts should be limited to $11.7 billion, making the deficit target unattainable without an increase in tax revenues. After 1986, the deficit target was $144 billion in 1987, falling to zero in 1991. But at the beginning of 1991, a projected deficit of $318 billion was announced. This draconian measure has given questionable powers to the OFFICE OF MANAGEMENT AND BUDGET and CONGRESSIONAL BUDGET OFFICE as well as necessitating unpopular spending cuts in successive years. In 1986, the US Supreme Court ruled the automatic SEQUESTRATION provision of the Act unconstitutional.

grandfather clause (F1, K2)
An item in an agreement permitting the retention of laws in conflict with the essence of the agreement. GATT contained such clauses.

grandfathering (Q0)
Distributing tradable permits to pollute according to countries' existing levels of emissions of pollutants.

Granger causality (C1)
A statistical technique which uses phase correlations between two variables to predict future values of one of the variables. A popular use of this has been in correlating GDP and stock market prices.

grant-back clause (O0)
The right in a contract granting the owner of a patent the right to all improvements and modifications in the technology discovered by the licensee. In the European Union the licensee grants back the right to the licensor of the use of these modifications in another place. In some countries the licensor owns the modifications as intellectual property.

grant in aid (H7)
US federal grant to state or local governments. It can be a flat grant (equal to the sum raised by a state government), a proportionate grant (proportional to the contribution of the recipient government) or a percentage grant (percentage of the cost to the recipient government for maintaining a particular programme). The purpose of these grants is to ensure that a desired level of public service is reached in all the states whatever the ability or willingness of individual states to finance it.

grants economics (H3)

A type of economics examining both two-way transfers (exchanges) and one-way transfers (grants). To understand grants is to be able to comprehend the nature of much of fiscal policy, as it is concerned with providing TRANSFER INCOMES for persons who exchange nothing for them, and of expenditure programmes which create social goods. This type of economics is also useful in the analysis of international aid.

References

Boulding, K.E. (1973) *The Economy of Love and Fear: A Preface to Grants Economics*, Belmont, CA: Praeger.

gravity model (R1)

A method of predicting the amount of interaction between two places. It asserts that interaction is directly related to the product of the two populations and inversely to the distance between the places concerned. A familiar version of these models takes the form $M_{ij} = P_i P_j / d_{ij}^2$ where M_{ij} is the amount of movement between i and j, P_i is the population of place i, P_j is the population of place j and d_{ij} is the distance between places i and j. The interaction M_{ij} can be the number of migrants, the volume of goods transported, the number of letters and telephone calls, etc. Distance can be measured in various ways, including route miles or kilometers and transport cost. More sophisticated models include the characteristics of the populations, weighting them accordingly.

References

Carrothers, G.A.P. (1956) 'An historical review of the gravity and potential concepts of human interaction', *Journal of the American Institute of Planners* 22: 94–102.

Great Depression (N1)

1 The period 1873–96 in the English economy when agriculture was especially depressed.
2 The period 1929–36 when world trade,

partly through PROTECTION and the cautious FISCAL POLICIES of national economies, suppressed the level of economic activity.

See also: beggar-my-neighbour policy; depression; recession; slump

References

Bernstein, M.A. (1988) *The Great Depression*, New York and Cambridge: Cambridge University Press.
Friedman, M. and Schwartz, A.I. (1966) *The Great Contraction*, Princeton, NJ: Princeton University Press.
Kindleberger, C.P. (1986) *The World in Depression, 1929–39*, London: Allen Lane (reprinted Harmondsworth: Penguin, 1987).
Saul, S.B. (1969) *The Myth of the Great Depression*, London and Basingstoke: Macmillan.
Temin, P. (1976) *Did Monetary Forces Cause the Great Depression?*, New York: W.W. Norton.

Great Leap Forward (N1, P2)

China's attempt in its Second Five-Year Plan of 1958–62 to replace Soviet-type planning with its own over-ambitious development schemes. A system of large-scale rural communes in the agricultural sector and the use of labour-intensive methods and decentralization of productive activities were introduced. A symbol of this change was the installation of a small steel furnace in each village. Continued economic failure, natural disasters and the withdrawal of Soviet technical assistance brought the experiment to an end in 1960.

Great Society (I3)

The visionary programme of President Lyndon B. Johnson announced in 1964 to move beyond the goals of a rising GROSS NATIONAL PRODUCT and FULL EMPLOYMENT to a more moral and spiritual society. In practice, it meant a set of complex federal programmes, in many respects similar to the New Deal, which included action on poverty, education, housing, Medicare and equal opportunities. President Nixon announced its demise in 1973.

Greenbury Code (G3, J3)
Recommendations of The Study Group on Directors' Remuneration (also known as the Greenbury Committee) in 1995 on pay for executive directors. This UK group proposed that independent outsiders would constitute a compensation committee with the task of preventing excessive executive pay, instituting employment contracts lasting more than a year, creating new long-term incentive plans in place of existing stock option plans and reporting annually on all aspects of pay, including pensions.

See also: corporate governance

green conditionality (Q2)
The rule that lending and expenditure are subject to the condition that the environment is not harmed.

green currency (F3)
The exchange rate for converting the agricultural prices of the EUROPEAN COMMUNITY into the domestic prices of a particular member country, originally expressed in EUROPEAN UNIT OF ACCOUNTS.

greenfield (Q2)
Land previously used only for agriculture or a wilderness with the potential for housing or other building.

See also: brownfield

greenhouse effect (Q0)
The entrapment of the sun's energy near the earth's surface by the atmosphere. This natural phenomenon becomes hazardous when pollutants, especially carbon dioxide, enter the atmosphere.

greenmail (G3)
A method of preventing the takeover of one's company by the purchase of holdings made by possible predators and ARBITRAGE.

green pound (G3)
The GREEN CURRENCY used by the UK.

green revolution (Q1)
The transformation of agriculture in Third World countries since 1945 by irrigation, the use of fertilizers and better seeds. It was hoped that substantial increases in the yields of wheat and rice would reduce many world food shortages as well as hunger in the less developed countries. Radical critics of the green revolution assert that the technology used is often monopolized by large commercial farmers who come to dominate agriculture and create a landless proletariat.

References
Cleaver, H.M. (1972) 'The contradictions of the Green Revolution', *American Economic Review* 62: 176–86.
Poleman, T.T. and Freebairn, D.K. (eds) (1973) *Food, Population, and Employment. The Impact of the Green Revolution*, New York: Praeger.

green stripe price (G1)
A stock market price on a visual display unit of the STOCK EXCHANGE AUTOMATED QUOTATION SYSTEM showing the best price quoted by any market-maker for small transactions in a particular stock.

Gresham's law (E4)
'Bad money drives out good.' A maxim of Sir Thomas Gresham (1519–79), the founder of the Royal Exchange, London, who asserted it in 1560 with reference to base silver coin. The contemporary experience of coinage being debased through CLIPPING prompted this observation. The law operates because of the public's propensity to hoard more valuable currency, thereby withdrawing it from circulation.

grey area (R5)
Part of a country in declining prosperity.

grey belt (J1)
An area with a high proportion of retired people in its population. In many countries, the grey belt is situated on the coastline with the best climate.

See also: ageing population

grey good (D2)
A woven or knitted fabric before it is bleached or dyed.

See also: brown good; white good

grey knight (G3)
A second bidder who enters uninvited into a takeover battle and is able to benefit from knowing the outcome of the first round of the battle.

grey market (G1)
Unofficial market in newly issued shares prior to official dealings in them. It exists in European financial centres but not in the USA. Only the orders of large institutions are handled.

Grey Monday (G1)
The date 16 October 1989 when the Financial Times Stock Exchange 100 share index dropped by 70.5 points on the London market. This was less drastic than BLACK MONDAY's fall of 500.

grey society (J1)
A society whose population has a high proportion of elderly persons. The decline in the birth rate and increased life expectancy experienced by many industrialized countries have produced increasingly ageing populations. The principal economic problems for an economy arising from this change in the age distribution are the financing of pensions and the reduction in the size of its labour force with the consequence of a declining or stationary NATIONAL INCOME.

See also: ageism

gross dividend yield (G1)
The return to, or income from, a stock market investment before the deduction of any tax.

See also: dividend net

gross domestic fixed capital formation (E2)
National expenditure in a given time period on physical productive assets, e.g. buildings, civil engineering works, machinery, equipment and vehicles. It consists of both NET INVESTMENT and REPLACEMENT INVESTMENT to maintain the capital stock intact. This form of investment is to be distinguished from investment in inventories and in financial assets.

gross domestic product (E0)
The total output of goods and services produced within a given country in a particular time period. It is equal to the sum of the VALUE ADDED by each industry, net of all inputs, including imported INTERMEDIATE GOODS: this is equal to the FACTOR INCOMES of all persons engaged in domestic production. Gross domestic product together with net property income from abroad constitute gross national product.

See also: national income

gross federal debt (H6)
The broadest definition of the US federal debt. It includes the borrowings of the US Treasury and of various federal agencies.

See also: total public debt

gross national product (E0)
The total value of the economic activity of a country in a given time period, including replacement investment, valued at factor cost or market prices. It is used as a crude measure of ECONOMIC WELFARE. Its growth can be divided into real growth and growth due to inflation.

See also: growth domestic product; measure of economic welfare; national income

gross social product (E0, P2)
Gross national product of a centrally planned socialist economy.

gross state product (H7)
The GROSS DOMESTIC PRODUCT of the labour and property located in a particular state of the USA.

Group of Five (F3)
The finance ministers of the USA, UK, France, Germany and Japan who meet informally to discuss international monetary problems and to set the agenda for the Group of Ten.

Group of Seven (F3)
A grouping of finance ministers and CENTRAL BANK governors of the leading

Western economies – Canada, France, Germany, Italy, Japan, the UK and the USA. They signed the LOUVRE ACCORD and in December 1987 continued with their search for international monetary stability by recommending the elimination of large international payments deficits through a clarification of national economic objectives, especially for fiscal policy. Since November 1975 they have held annual ECONOMIC SUMMITS attended by heads of government and finance ministers.

Group of Seventy-seven (F1)

The group of LESS DEVELOPED COUNTRIES at the United Nations: all of these countries attended the first meeting of the UNITED NATIONS CONFERENCE ON TRADE AND DEVELOPMENT in 1964.

Group of Ten (F3)

A group of leading capitalist countries founded informally as the 'Paris Club' in 1956 and formally in 1982. It consists of the USA, the UK, West Germany, France, Belgium, the Netherlands, Italy, Sweden, Canada and Japan, together with Switzerland in an honorary capacity. It agreed in 1962 to lend its currencies to the INTERNATIONAL MONETARY FUND under the GENERAL AGREEMENT TO BORROW. The group also discusses international monetary arrangements, usually at the BANK FOR INTERNATIONAL SETTLEMENTS.

Group of Thirty (F3)

The Consultative Group on International Economic and Monetary Affairs Incorporated set up in 1978 with the aim of studying in depth the international dimensions of economics and finance. The group's distinguished individual members are joined in six-monthly meetings by invited outsiders. It was originally financed by the Rockefeller Foundation, now by banks and corporations.

Group of Twenty-four (F3)

The inner circle of the GROUP OF SEVENTY-SEVEN. It conducts many negotiations on behalf of LESS DEVELOPED COUNTRIES at the United Nations.

growth (O4) *see* economic growth

growth accounting (M4, O4)

1 The decomposition of economic growth into the consequences of changes in factor inputs and the SOLOW RESIDUAL. This accounting is used to explain differences in the GDP growth rates of various countries.

2 The analysis of NATIONAL INCOME figures to ascertain the relative contribution to growth made by increased quantities of factor inputs, increased PRODUCTIVITY and TECHNICAL PROGRESS.

References

Denison, E. (1967) *Why Growth Rates Differ*, Washington, DC: Brookings Institution.

growth pole (R1)

1 The massing of a population in a great urban concentration of 10 million or more to achieve external ECONOMIES OF SCALE, with the object of reviving a depressed region.

2 The establishment of a group of industries in a cluster around an expanding industry.

Although this was a new approach to regional policy in Western Europe in the 1960s, it can be traced back to PETTY who wanted the English economy to reach the levels of Dutch productivity by the relocation of population into a confined area of England.

growth recession (E3)

A downturn in an economic CYCLE when an ECONOMY is still enjoying modest economic growth.

growth theory of the firm (L1)

A hypothesis stating that a firm attempts to maximize its growth, subject to a takeover restraint. Marris and PENROSE advanced this theory as a plausible explanation of managerial behaviour. Penrose argues that there is an internal process of development in firms which leads to cumulative movements of growth or decline: this argument is then expanded to take into account mergers and acquisitions. It is essentially an optimistic account that regards large DISECONOMIES OF SCALE as unlikely.

See also: managerial models of the firm

References

Marris, R. (1964) *The Economic Theory of Managerial Capitalism*, London: Macmillan.

Penrose, E.T. (1959) *The Theory of the Growth of the Firm*, Oxford: Basil Blackwell.

guestworker (F2)

A foreign worker with a short-term work permit and fewer employment rights than resident workers. Countries such as Germany and Switzerland with severe labour shortages in the 1960s recruited many workers from Turkey and other less developed countries.

guild socialism (P2)

A UK movement of the 1920s and 1930s which emphasized WORKERS' PARTICIPATION. It was proposed that each industry should be run by its own national guild and that these guilds should be co-ordinated by a supreme council. S.G. Hobson in *The National Guilds – An Inquiry into the Wage System and the Way Out* (1914) was a leading thinker of the movement, as were G.D.H. Cole and other early members of the Fabian Society. Guild socialists rejected market systems of allocation in favour of ECONOMIC PLANNING. However, the movement's lack of policy towards the

depression of the 1930s contributed to its demise.

References

Cole, G.D.H. (1972) *Self Government in Industry*, London: Hutchinson.

Glass, S.T. (1966) *The Responsible Society: The Ideas of the English Guild Socialist*, London: Longman.

guinea (E5)

UK gold coin first minted in 1663 from gold shipped by the Royal African Company from the Guinea Coast to England. It was not used as a unit of account, despite many prices being quoted in guineas. The pound sterling remained the unit.

Gulf Co-operation Council (F0)

A council consisting of representatives from six countries of the Persian Gulf – Bahrain, Kuwait, Oman, Qatar, Saudi Arabia and the United Arab Emirates.

Gulf Plus (Q4)

The basis for pricing crude or refined oil secretly agreed in 1928 between the major oil companies. Wherever oil was exported from, it would be priced as if it had travelled from the Gulf of Mexico. This anti-competitive price was intended to equalize the prices of all oil available to a particular consumer.

See also: basing-point pricing; posted price

gunslinger (G1)

A fund manager seeking high returns by investing in high-risk stocks.

H

Haavelmo, Trygve, 1911– (B3)
A major founder of ECONOMETRICS who was awarded the NOBEL PRIZE FOR ECONOMICS in 1989. He was educated at the University of Oslo where he was professor of economics from 1948 to 1979. In 1946–7 he was at the COWLES COMMISSION. His important contributions to quantitative economics include the formulation of economic theories in probabilistic terms and the study of interdependence problems.

Habakkuk thesis (N0, O3)
The proposal that technological progress in the USA in the nineteenth century in manufacturing making use of interchangeable parts was stimulated by high wages and labour scarcity.

References
Habakkuk, J. (1962) *American and British technology in the nineteenth century*, Cambridge: Cambridge University Press.

Haberler, Gottfried, 1900–1995 (B3)
An Austro-American economist, educated at the University of Vienna, and lecturer and later professor of economics and statistics there from 1928 to 1936. He worked at the Finance Division of the League of Nations in 1934–6, crowning his career as Professor of International Trade at Harvard from 1936 to 1971. His books of the mid-1930s are his principal monument. In one, he brilliantly restated the classical doctrine of COMPARATIVE ADVANTAGE in terms of GENERAL EQUILIBRIUM theory; in the other, he synthesized business cycle theories, providing a basis for the empirical testing of hypotheses about economic fluctuations. Later in his career he made many proposals for the reform of the INTERNATIONAL MONETARY SYSTEM, discussing the conditions under which a DEVALUATION of a currency in a pegged exchange rate regime improves a country's balance of payments.

References
Bhagwati, J.N. and Chipman, J.S. (1980) 'Salute to Gottfried Haberler on the occasion of his 80th birthday', *Journal of International Economics* 10: 313–18.
Haberler, G. (1936) *Theory of International Trade, with its Application to Commercial Policy*, London: William Hodge.
—— (1937) *Prosperity and Depression*, 5th edn, London: Allen & Unwin.

Hahn, Frank Horace, 1925– (B3)
Born in Berlin, the son of a celebrated German philosopher and mathematician, he came to the UK as a teenager and graduated from the London School of Economics. Subsequently, he taught at the universities in Birmingham from 1948 to 1960 and Cambridge from 1960 to 1967 before holding chairs at the London School of Economics in 1967–72 and at Cambridge in 1972–92. The leading theme of his works has been MATHEMATICAL ECONOMICS, particularly in its applications to GENERAL EQUILI-

BRIUM theory. His first interest was in income distribution; then his concerns were to build on the foundations of HICKS's *Value and Capital* and to study stability. Also, his joint work with ARROW, *General Competitive Analysis* (1971), is a landmark in modern economics. In his works, Hahn has rigorously set out the conditions for order in a competitive market, a line of enquiry justified in his Cambridge Inaugural Lecture, 'On the Notion of Equilibrium in Economics' (1972).

References

Hahn, F. (1985) *Money, Growth and Stability*, Cambridge: Cambridge University Press.

Haig–Simons definition of income (D3)
Personal income regarded as the sum of the market values of rights expressed in consumption and the change in the value of assets in a given time period.

References

Simons, H.C. (1938) *Personal Income Taxation: the Definition of Income as a Problem of Fiscal Policy*, Chicago: University of Chicago Press.

Hansen, Alvin Harvey, 1887–1975 (B3)
US economist, educated at Yankton College, Dakota, and the University of Wisconsin; professor at Harvard University from 1937 to 1962; previously Director of Research for President Roosevelt's Committee of Inquiry on National Policy in International Relations, 1933–4. For forty years he was a leading US exponent of Keynesian theory and of FISCAL POLICY. His frequent use of IS-LM CURVES, a synthesis of classical and Keynesian economics, led to the diagram being named after both him and HICKS. Although he originally had a negative reaction to KEYNES'S GENERAL THEORY, by the age of 52 he had become an avid Keynesian.

References

Barber, W.J. (1987) 'The career of Alvin H. Hansen in the 1920s and 1930s: a study

in intellectual transformation', *History of Political Economy* 19: 191–205.

hansom cab economy (P0)
An ECONOMY that strives to keep its traditional industries in production, regardless of market demand.

hard commodity (D0, L7)
A mineral such as copper or iron ore.

hard currency (E5, F3)
A currency that retains a high value against others for long periods of time, usually because of a favourable BALANCE OF PAYMENTS year after year. Such currencies are very popular as RESERVE CURRENCIES. Major hard currencies of the world have included the yen, the Deutschmark and the Swiss franc.

See also: soft currency

hard ecu (F3)
A version of the ecu proposed by the UK initially as a COMMON CURRENCY to be used in the EUROPEAN COMMUNITY for all monetary transactions alongside existing national currencies. The hope was that this ecu would become a single currency.

hard landing (E6)
A major downward adjustment in a national economy or in a stock market. Prices, incomes and employment sharply move towards a state of RECESSION.

See also: soft landing

harmonic mean (C1)
This is calculated for a set of values by taking the ratio of the number of values to the sum of the reciprocals of each value. The harmonic mean of 5, 12 and 16 is 3 divided by $1/5 + 1/12 + 1/16$.

See also: arithmetic mean; geometric mean

harmonization (E6, F0)
The process of aligning government regulations or practices to eliminate differences between parties to an agreement. A major example is the attempt to harmonize taxation within the EUROPEAN UNION.

harmonized index of consumer prices (E3)

A chain price index required by the MAAS-TRICHT TREATY and used by the EUROPEAN COMMISSION and EUROPEAN CENTRAL BANK for comparisons of the economic performance of EUROPEAN UNION member states. It has a base of 1996 = 100 and is calculated by EU countries, apart from Luxemburg, Norway and Iceland. As consumption patterns differ from state to state, a smaller range of consumer items is represented in these indices than in national consumer price indices.

Harrod–Domar model (O4)

A major model of economic growth independently asserted by both HARROD and Domar in 1948. It uses the concepts of the NATURAL RATE OF GROWTH and the WARRANTED RATE OF GROWTH.

References

Domar, E.D. (1957) *Essays in the Theory of Economic Growth*, pp. 70–82, New York: Oxford University Press.

Harrod neutral (O3)

A type of technical change which relatively increases the amount of labour input.

See also: Hicks neutral; Solow neutral

Harrod, Sir Roy Forbes, 1900–78 (B3)

Oxford economist from 1922 to 1967, as well as philosopher, biographer and prolific economic journalist. In his training at Oxford he was greatly influenced by EDGE-WORTH but subsequently he learned much from KEYNES, becoming a leading disciple and expositor, as well as his official biographer.

As an economist, he was best known for his contributions to the debates leading to Keynes's *General Theory*, for his works on the TRADE CYCLE which introduced the novelty of combining the multiplier with the accelerator, for his path-breaking growth theory in his London School of Economics lectures of 1948 and for his work on international economics, for which he was awarded a readership at Oxford. He participated in most of the major price theory debates of his time, both at Cambridge on IMPERFECT COMPETITION and at Oxford on FULL-COST PRICING. He was a close adviser to Churchill in the Second World War.

References

Harrod, R.F. (1936) *The Trade Cycle*, Oxford: Clarendon Press (reprinted New York: Augustus M. Kelly, 1965).
—— (1948) *Towards a Dynamic Economics: Recent Developments of Economic theory and their Application to Policy*, London: Macmillan.
Phelps-Brown, E.H. (1980) 'Sir Roy Harrod: a biographical memoir', *Economic Journal* 90: 1–33.

Harsanyi, John Charles, 1920–2000 (B3)

Educated at Budapest, Sydney and Stanford Universities. After teaching at Budapest, Queensland, Stanford and Wayne State Universities, he became professor of business administration at the University of California at Berkeley from 1964 to 1990. He examined what it means for rational persons to make ethical judgements, and the games theory problem of establishing appropriate behaviour for rational persons, companies and nations in conflict with each other. His major works include *Rational Behaviour and Bargaining Equilibrium* (1977) and *A General Theory of Equilibrium Selection in Games* (1988, with Reinhard Selten). He shared the NOBEL PRIZE FOR ECONOMICS in 1994 with NASH and SELTEN.

Havana Charter (F1)

The written agreement to set up the INTERNATIONAL TRADE ORGANIZATION in 1947–8 agreed by most Western countries. It sought to promote balanced growth by the abolition of EXCHANGE CONTROLS, trade barriers (with the exception of protection for INFANT INDUSTRIES) and discrimination. It advocated FULL EMPLOYMENT throughout the world. All signatories had to grant MOST FAVOURED NATION treatment to the others. The Havana Charter is doctrinally connected with the INTERNATIONAL MONE-

TARY FUND in its opposition to trade restrictions and to monopoly.

See also: General Agreement on Tariffs and Trade; World Trade Organization

hawala (G2) *see* underground banking

Hawtrey, Sir Ralph, 1879–1971 (B3)

UK civil servant and monetary theorist. After graduating in mathematics from Trinity College, Cambridge, he was a Treasury civil servant from 1904 to 1945 and then professor of international economics at Chatham House, London, from 1947 to 1952. He learned his economics in the course of his work, not at university.

He was a leading monetary theorist of the first half of the twentieth century using an income approach to integrate monetary theory with general economics. His theory of the TRADE CYCLE attributed fluctuations to the instability of bank credit: he argued that short-term, not long-term, interest rates should be used to regulate credit. His traditional attitude to running the economy meant that he agreed to PUBLIC WORKS being used to revive a depressed economy. His most important works were *Currency and Credit* (1919), *Capital and Employment* (1937) and *The Art of Central Banking* (1930).

References

Davis, E.G. (1981) 'R.G. Hawtrey', in D.P. O'Brien and J.R. Presley (eds) *Pioneers of Modern Economics in Britain*, London: Macmillan.

Hayek, Friedrich A. von, 1899–1992 (B3)

Libertarian moral philosopher and economist born and educated in Vienna, where he graduated with doctorates in jurisprudence and economics. His long academic career, culminating in the NOBEL PRIZE FOR ECONOMICS shared with MYRDAL in 1974, began as Director of the Austrian Institute for Business Cycle Research in 1927 and privatdozent at the University of Vienna in 1929. His guest lectures at the London School of Economics, published as *Prices*

and Production in 1931, took the unpopular view of the TRADE CYCLE that high levels of consumption would cause falling investment and depression. As professor at the London School of Economics from 1932 to 1950, he wrote on capital theory in *Profits, Interest and Investment* (1939) and in *The Pure Theory of Capital* (1941); his respect for John Stuart MILL is evident in *John Stuart Mill and Harriet Taylor* (1951). Subsequently, he became a professor at Chicago from 1950 to 1962 and at Freiburg from 1962 to 1965.

He argued that information can always be used more efficiently in a decentralized economy than in a centralized planning system. This stance was based on his observation that the competitive market system generates information on demand and supply by changes in product prices and consequently factor prices, providing incentives for factors to move to the best uses. In his macro-theory Hayek went beyond a simple QUANTITY THEORY OF MONEY in aggregate terms to considering the effects on relative prices of monetary disturbances. Combining that approach with the Austrian theory of the trade cycle, he demonstrated that credit affects prices and production. He long opposed Keynesian-style macroeconomic management as it relies on economic omniscience: a free market can generate better information.

Parallel to his economics writing was a series of works on psychology and libertarian political philosophy. A central theme of his attack on SOCIALISM was his exposition of the role of information in economic decision making.

References

Barry, N.P. (1979) *Hayek's Social and Economic Philosophy*, London: Macmillan.

Butler, E. (1983) *Hayek: His Contribution to Political and Economic Thought*, London: Temple Smith.

Hayek, F.A. (1944) *The Road to Serfdom*, London: Routledge.

—— (1963) *The Sensory Order: An Inquiry into the Foundations of Theoretical*

Psychology, Chicago: University of Chicago Press.

—— (1976) *The Constitution of Liberty*, London: Routledge & Kegan Paul.

—— (1982) *Law, Legislation and Liberty: A New Station of Liberal Principles*, London: Routledge & Kegan Paul.

Wood, I.C. and Woods, R. (1991) *Friedrich A. Hayek. Critical Assessments*, London: Routledge.

hazard (D0, Q0)

1 A venture.
2 A risk or what is risked.
3 In environmental economics, the probability of a potentially destructive natural phenomenon occurring in a given place at a given time.

headline rate of inflation (E4)

The rate of UK price inflation as stated by the RETAIL PRICE INDEX which includes mortgage interest, value-added tax, local taxation and excise duties. It is the most publicized inflation rate.

See also: underlying inflation rate

head tax (H2) *see* poll tax

health care indicators (I1)

The World Health Organisation ranks health care in each major country by five indicators. These are overall level of health (number of years of healthy life a person can expect), child mortality rates, levels of patient satisfaction, how well persons with different economic status are served by their country's health care arrangements, and the distribution of the health system's financial burden measured by a household's capacity to spend on health care directly or through the state and private insurance.

health economics (I1)

Evaluation of the effectiveness of health care, particularly by examining the social OPPORTUNITY COSTS of alternative forms of treatment. The peculiar nature of the market for health care – that doctors have a major influence on both demand and supply – has attracted attention, as has the study of the options available for financing such services.

See also: quality-adjusted life years

References

Drummond, M.F. (1980) *Principles of Economic Appraisal in Health Care*, Oxford: Oxford University Press.

Folland, S., Goodman, A.C. and Stano, M. (2001) *The economics of health and health care*, 3rd edn, Upper Saddle River, NJ: Prentice Hall.

McGuire, A., Henderson, J. and Mooney, G. (1987) *The Economics of Health Care*, London: Routledge.

Smith, G.T. (1987) *Health Economics: Prospects for the Future*, London: Croom Helm.

Zweifel, P. and Breyer, F. (1997) *Health economics*, New York and Oxford: Oxford University Press.

heavy industry (L6)

An industry using raw materials heavy in weight, and a great amount of fixed capital, e.g. shipbuilding. The decline of such industries in the twentieth century has produced DE-INDUSTRIALIZATION in many Western countries.

See also: light industry

heavy share (G1)

UK company share whose price is high relative to the average for similar companies. As a consequence, companies sometimes issue bonus shares to their shareholders to reduce the share price.

See also: penny share

Heckman, James Joseph 1944– (B3)

Born in Chicago and educated at Colorado College and Princeton University. His professorial career at the University of Chicago began in 1974. He has developed statistical methods for handling selective samples and applied the methods to the evaluation of public sector labour market and educational programmes. For this work on micro-data he was awarded the NOBEL PRIZE FOR ECONOMICS with Daniel MCFADDEN in 2000.

Heckscher, Eli Filip, 1879–1952 (B3)
Swedish economist and economic historian who was professor at the Stockholm
Business School from 1909 to 1929. His
monumental historical works on MERCANTI-
LISM and population are as famous as his
contribution to international trade theory,
now known as the HECKSCHER–OHLIN TRADE
THEOREM.

Heckscher–Ohlin trade theorem (F1)
An explanation of international trade in
terms of the relative FACTOR ENDOWMENTS of
different countries. A country, for example, with an abundance of labour would
export goods produced by labour-intensive
methods more than capital-intensive
goods. In the absence of transport costs
and specialization, trade would eventually
bring about factor price equalization. Empirical examination of this theory has not
awarded it very high marks – hence the
LEONTIEF PARADOX.

References

Heckscher, E. (1949) 'The effect of foreign
trade on the distribution of income', in
H.S. Ellis and L.A. Metzler (eds) *Read-
ings in the Theory of International Trade*,
Philadelphia: Blakiston.
Ohlin, B. (1967) *Interregional and Interna-
tional Trade*, Cambridge, MA: Harvard
University Press.

hedge ratio (G1)
The ratio of the number of OPTION contracts to the position in the underlying
instrument being hedged against.

hedging (G1)
Dealings in FUTURE MARKETS to cover spot
positions to reduce the risk of price movements, especially in commodity and currency markets. Hedging permits producers
to stabilize their incomes because selling
futures protects a producer against a price
fall.

See also: spot market

hedonic output (D2)
Output measured in terms of both quantity and quality.

References

Spady, R. and Friedlaender, A.F. (1978)
'Hedonic cost functions for the regu-
lated trucking industry', *Bell Journal of
Economics* 9 (Spring): 59–79.

hedonic price (D0)
The shadow price of the characteristic of a
commodity, e.g. the value of a good view
from a house. The concept is much used in
COST–BENEFIT ANALYSIS and in environmental
economics, e.g. for valuing the level of
amenities such as good air quality.

References

Rosen, S. (1974) 'Hedonic prices and implicit
markets: product differentiation in pure
competition', *Journal of Political Economy* 82: 34–55.

hedonic pricing method (D4)
This relates the price of a marketed good
to its characteristics by establishing how
much a consumer is willing to pay for each
characteristic. This is used extensively as
an evaluation method in environmental
economics, especially to discover the effect
of environmental features on house prices.
It is a cheaper method than CONTINGENT
VALUATION.

See also: characteristics theory of demand

hedonic wages (J3)
The factor payment offered by an employer for a bundle of job characteristics,
including status, training opportunities
and working conditions. This wage is
determined by the interaction between the
demand of and supply for both worker
characteristics and job characteristics.

References

Lucas, R.E.B. (1977) 'Hedonic wage equations and psychic wages in the returns
to schooling', *American Economic Review* 67: 549–58.

hegemonic cycle (E3, N0)
A systematic shift in economic activity
between a period dominated by one power
and a period unstable because of rivalry
between world powers. These cycles last
about 100 years.

See also: Kondratieff cycle; logistic cycle

References

Arrighi, G. (1994) *The Long Twentieth Century*, London: Verso.

helicopter money (E4)
An unanticipated increase in the nominal stock of money leading to an increase in demand for goods and a rise in the general price level of an economy.

Herfindahl–Hirschman index (L1)
A measure of market CONCENTRATION. In an industry with *i* firms, the index is calculated as follows:

$$H = \sum_i s_i^2$$

where s_i is the market share of the *i*th firm. The index reflects both the number of firms and their relative size. The value of the index will be 1 if there is only one firm in the industry and tend towards unity if there are only a few firms or some firms of much greater size than others.

heterogeneous agent model (O3)
Used by SCHUMPETER in his account of innovation. Individual decision rules influence each other.

heteroscedasticity (C1)
The property of a LINEAR REGRESSION model with a changing VARIANCE of its disturbances.

See also: homoscedasticity

heuristic (C1)
Using a process of discovery, of trial and error, to discover the truth. This approach is central to the use of computation in economics.

H-form (L2)
A type of enterprise organized as a holding company: each of its divisions will be affiliated with the parent company as a subsidiary company. Corporate staff of a holding company are principally concerned with financial evaluation, using

similar criteria to those employed by stock market analysts.

See also: M-form; U-form; X-form

Hicks charts (E1) *see* IS–LM curves

Hicksian demand function (D1)
Consumer demand as a function of price assuming consumer utility is held constant. Also known as a compensated demand curve as a price change does not change a consumer's utility.

References

Hicks, J. (1956) *A Revision of Demand Theory*, Oxford: Clarendon Press.

Hicksian income measure (D3)
'The maximum value which [a man] can consume during a week, and still expect to be as well off at the end of the week as he was at the beginning.' This measure, suggested in Hicks's *Value and Capital* (1939, ch. 14), relies on the concept of EXPECTATIONS. It can be contrasted with the approach of MEADE and STONE who defined money income as the sum of the money value of consumption plus the increase in the money value of one's capital assets.

Hicks neutral (O3)
TECHNICAL CHANGE which does not affect the MARGINAL RATE OF SUBSTITUTION between two inputs.

Hicks, Sir John Richard, 1904–89 (B3)
The greatest Oxford economist of the twentieth century. His Oxford education in mathematics and philosophy, politics and economics led to a lectureship at the London School of Economics from 1926 to 1935 where he contributed to an alternative to contemporary Cambridge economics by joining with ROBBINS and HAYEK to build on WICKSELL's ideas, although an increasing interest in Keynesian ideas drove him to Cambridge, 1935–8, at the height of the *General Theory* debate. Much of the rest of his life, as a professor at Manchester from 1938 to 1946, as a fellow of Nuffield

College, Oxford, from 1946 to 1952 and in the senior Oxford chair as Drummond Professor of Political Economy from 1952 to 1965, he was to be a major extender and clarifier of Keynesian ideas.

The breadth of Hicks's gigantic contribution to economics, much of it now the bread and butter of economics teaching in the West, is evident in his long series of books and articles since 1932, recognized in the award of a NOBEL PRIZE FOR ECONOMICS, shared with ARROW, in 1972 for his early work on WELFARE ECONOMICS. His first work, *A Theory of Wages* (1932), went beyond traditional labour economics to consider the ELASTICITY OF SUBSTITUTION and the relative income shares of labour and capital. His *Value and Capital* (1939) expounded consumer theory by using INDIFFERENCE CURVES. His careful reaction to Keynes's *General Theory* was in his celebrated article of 1937 in *Econometrica* ('Mr Keynes and the Classics') which introduced IS–LM analysis into macroeconomics, clarifying the contrast between goods and money markets and between what was old and new in Keynesian theory. Subsequently, Hicks, seeing the overuse of the apparatus, regarded it as an albatross. His *Social Framework* (1942), unusually for an introductory economics textbook, used NATIONAL INCOME accounting as a starting point. In the post-war period, his range was considerable: economic dynamics in *A Contribution to the Trade Cycle* (1950), a development of revealed preference theory in *A Revision of Demand Theory* (1956), growth theory in *Capital and Growth* (1965) and in *Capital and Time: a Neo-Austrian Theory* (1973) and historical development in *A Theory of Economic History* (1969). With his wife Ursula, he was co-author of works on PUBLIC FINANCE. Throughout his long academic career his many applications of GENERAL EQUILIBRIUM theory enabled him to provide a powerful synthesis of microeconomics and macroeconomics.

References

Baumol, W.J. (1972) 'John R. Hicks's contribution to economics', *Swedish Journal of Economics* 74: 503–27.

Hahn, F. (1990) 'John Hicks the theorist', *Economic Journal* 100: 539–49.

Helm, D. (1984) *The Economics of John Hicks*, Oxford: Basil Blackwell.

Hicks, J.R. (1979) 'The formation of an economist', *Banca Nazionale del Lavoro Quarterly Review* 130: 195–204.

Hicks, Sir J. (1991) *The Status of Economics*, Oxford: Basil Blackwell.

hidden reserves (G2)

Bank reserves allowed by law to be kept off a bank's published balance sheet to increase its perceived strength. All UK CLEARING BANKS prior to 1968 had this privilege; after then only UK MERCHANT BANKS.

hidden unemployment (J6)

1 Underemployed labour. A comparison of PRODUCTIVITY or wage levels of different sectors of an economy indicates how much employed labour is working below its capacity. SOVIET-TYPE ECONOMIES were noted for their low wages and low productivity: the state's FULL-EMPLOYMENT policy and willingness to pay the wage bill gave managers no incentive to economize in the use of labour. Although the Soviet labour force enjoyed easy, secure employment, the economy suffered from chronic labour shortages and poor product quality. PERESTROIKA sought to reduce this problem. East European economies still have considerable labour reserves in their agricultural sectors.

2 Part of a population excluded from a measure of unemployment because of the definition of unemployment used.

hiding hand (D0, E0)

An economic mechanism allowing underestimated difficulties to be offset by the unestimated creative response to them.

hierarchical decomposition principle (L2)
An analysis of an organization into a vertical slice of operating activities and a horizontal slice of strategic planning corresponding to the lower and higher parts of the hierarchy.

References
Simon, H.A. (1962) 'The architecture of complexity', *Proceedings of the American Philosophical Society* 106 (December): 467–82.
—— (1973) 'Applying information technology to organization design', *Public Administration Review* 33 (May–June): 268–78.

hierarchy theory (J3)
An attempt to explain the wage structure through taking into account the fact that managers are arranged in hierarchies according to their relative decision-making power. An application of the THEORY OF THE FIRM.

high-consumption society (P0, P1)
A country with an AVERAGE PROPENSITY TO CONSUME approaching one. It has a low rate of household saving and high level of consumer debt. The USA is cited as a major example.

high employment surplus (H6)
An estimate of the excess of tax revenues over government expenditures at a FULL-EMPLOYMENT level of NATIONAL INCOME. This is used as a yardstick of a government's FISCAL STANCE.

See also: structural deficit

high-leveraged takeover (G3)
A takeover mainly financed by fixed interest finance, e.g. borrowing from banks.

high net worth individual (J3)
A rich person.

See also: fat cat

high-powered money (E5, G2)
Currency, bankers' balances at a CENTRAL BANK and other eligible reserve assets of deposit banks. An increase in the supply of this money permits a multiple expansion of bank deposits because of the operation of the MONEY MULTIPLIER, e.g. a central bank in an open market operation buys bonds from the public thereby increasing the amount of cash available to banks.

See also: fractional reserve banking

high-technology industry (L6, O3)
An INDUSTRY, usually CAPITAL INTENSIVE, requiring a high level of RESEARCH AND DEVELOPMENT to maintain its international standing. Leading examples are the aerospace, pharmaceutical and computer industries.

high-yield financing (G1, M2)
A type of financing based on JUNK BONDS.

hire purchase (G2)
The hiring of a good, especially a CONSUMER DURABLE, by a customer who, on the completion of paying instalments equal to the full price of the good plus interest, owns it.

Hirschman, Albert Otto, 1915– (B3)
A leading development economist. Born in Berlin and educated at the Sorbonne, the London School of Economics and Trieste, before emigrating to the USA in 1941. He was financial adviser at Columbia University from 1952 to 1956, and subsequently professor at Yale from 1956 to 1958, Columbia from 1958 to 1964 and Harvard from 1964 to 1974. His work as a development economist took the unusual path of advocating unbalanced economic development, based on key industries producing intermediate products. His EXIT-VOICE analysis provided a new method of examining the organizational response to a decline of firms, suggesting that a firm changes rather than go out of business.

References
Hirschman, A.O. (1958) *The Strategy of Economic Development*, New Haven, CT: Yale University Press.
—— (1970) *Exit, Voice and Loyalty: Responses to Decline in Firms, Organizations and States*, Cambridge, MA: Harvard University Press.

—— (1981) *Essays in Trespassing: Economics to Politics and Beyond*, Cambridge: Cambridge University Press.

histogram (C1)

A method of presenting a FREQUENCY DISTRIBUTION graphically in a number of rectangles varying in size according to the number of observations in each class; see the figure.

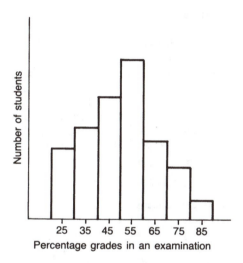

Percentage grades in an examination

historic cost (M4)

The original valuation of an asset. This measure is respected by accountants because of its objectivity and verifiability. However, in periods of INFLATION, this value must be adjusted to take into account specific price changes for the asset if an accurate current valuation is to be obtained.

See also: inflation accounting; replacement cost

hog cycle (E3, Q1)

An alternation between excess demand and excess supply in the pig market in the USA. The cycle inspired the COBWEB theorem.

holding company (L2)

A company consisting of a parent company and a number of subsidiary companies of which it is the majority owner.

See also: bank holding company; H-form; pyramiding

holding gain (M2)

The gain to a business arising from the current market value of its assets being more than their historical cost. This gain is realized when the asset is sold or, in the case of raw materials, when they are embodied in a sold finished good.

hold-out (J3)

The time period between the expiry of an old labour contract and the signing of a new contract. During this period work continues under the old contract but a union may adopt a work-to-rule to strengthen its bargaining position. There are often hold-outs in US collective bargaining.

hold-up (D0)

A form of economic opportunism occurring when assets and investments have a value specific to an exchange, e.g. an employee with SPECIFIC TRAINING can use that HUMAN CAPITAL investment as the basis for demanding higher remuneration.

References

Goldberg, V.P. (1976) 'Regulation and administered contracts', *Bell Journal of Economics* 7: 426–48.

hold-up problem (C7)

A problem of contracting arising from the making of investments prior to concluding a transaction and the unknown form of an optimal transaction. To reduce UNCERTAINTY the possibility of making contracts rigid is considered.

References

Rogerson, W.P. (1992) 'Contractual solutions to the hold-up problem', *Review of Economic Studies* 59: 777–93.

holism (P4)

1 A theory of the universe as an interacting whole.
2 The opposite of atomism.
3 The simultaneous consideration of all parts of a system.

home banking (G2)

The use of banking facilities at home by means of a computer linked to the main computer of a particular bank. Each home, in a sense, becomes a personalized branch of the single bank. Home banking was first offered by the Nottingham Building Society (UK) in November 1983, and then by Australia's Commonwealth Banking Corporation. By September 1984, seventy-one US banks and other financial institutions offered such a facility. In France, fifty banks offer the limited service of transmission of bank statements to home television sets. This service is attractive to banks for it is a cheaper method of expansion for a geographically concentrated bank than the opening of new branches.

home economics (D1)

The practical study of nutrition and hygiene; the examination of the science underlying household production.

See also: new home economics

homeless (R2)

The condition of being without any housing. This occurs because of insufficient income to pay the market rates for purchasing or renting a home or because of an insufficient housing supply. Rent controls by reducing the supply of private sector housing and insufficient repairs to the national housing stock magnify this problem. Geographical mobility from poorer to richer parts of a country, especially a capital city, produces hordes of homeless people who often in desperation have to use discarded cardboard boxes as shelter.

home production (D2)

Non-market production of goods and services in households Allocation of time by home producers will depend on the relative values placed on each good or service produced. Much of this work is carried out by married women outside the labour force; it often involves as many weekly hours as average employment in the labour market. In less developed countries it is a common form of production.

References

Gronau, R. (1980) 'Home production - a forgotten industry', *Review of Economic Statistics* 62: 408–16.
Havrylyshyn, O. (1976) 'The value of household services: a survey of empirical estimates', *Review of Income and Wealth* 22: 101–31.

homework (J2)

Working as a subcontractor at home doing LABOUR-INTENSIVE work, e.g. addressing envelopes or tailoring. This type of labour has often been cited as most subject to EXPLOITATION. Both trade unions and wages councils have found it difficult to protect workers. As computers have made it possible to do sophisticated work at home, the wage levels of these workers might rise.

See also: networking economy

homo economicus (D0)

'ECONOMIC MAN' – the self-interested economic agent. In CLASSICAL and NEOCLASSICAL ECONOMICS the UTILITY-MAXIMIZING objectives of individual economic agents were taken to be the basis of economic activity.

See also: altruism

homogeneous function (C6)

For a function to be homogeneous all the variables must be of the same degree, e.g. to the power 3. Homogeneity is a cardinal property. These functions are used in economics to explain production, demand, cost and utility.

homogeneous good (D0)

A good whose units are regarded as identical by consumers. Thus purchasers express, for example, indifference between one bag of homogeneous rice and another. Although there may be differences analysable by chemists and others, consumers regard the differing aspects of several units as irrelevant to their purchasing decisions. Under PERFECT COMPETITION, it is essential that goods are homogeneous so that individual firms have no MONOPOLY POWER.

See also: branding; product differentiation

homoscedasticity (C1)
The property of a LINEAR REGRESSION model which has disturbances with constant VARIANCE.

See also: heteroscedasticity

homo sovieticus (D0)
An altruistic economic agent who will produce without economic incentives. This agent is prepared to work for the sake of the common good, including overall production. At the beginning of the twenty-first century this type of person is more mythical than real: *homo economicus* is a more common species.

See also: economic man; Soviet-type economy

homothetic function (C6)
A function which can be decomposed into an inner function monotonically increasing and an outer function homogeneous of degree 1. Homotheticity is an ordinal property.

horizontal discrimination (J7)
The unfair treatment of persons in the same category. In the labour market, for example, men and women in the same occupational group can have unequal pay, despite doing the same work. A great deal of legislation in the 1960s and 1970s, e.g. the UK's EQUAL PAY ACT and US civil rights legislation, attempted to remove discrimination of this kind.

See also: discrimination; vertical discrimination

horizontal equity (D6)
The identical treatment of individuals or groups with the same amount of a relevant characteristic, e.g. income. Following this principle, families of the same size and income pay the same amount in direct taxes.

See also: vertical equity

horizontal integration (L1)
The merger of firms in the same industry, usually to reduce competition and to obtain ECONOMIES OF SCALE. Mergers of this kind are viewed with great suspicion in COMPETITION POLICY as they are expected to increase AGGREGATE CONCENTRATION.

See also: vertical integration

host region (R5)
That part of a national economy receiving inward investment from a governmental agency or a private firm.

hot money (F2)
Short-term international capital flows induced by differences in interest rates, and the relative appreciation and depreciation of national currencies. These flows add to the volatility of a BALANCE OF PAYMENTS.

See also: capital flight

household behaviour (D1)
The behaviour of members of a household, individually or collectively, in product and factor markets. An examination of their motivations and aims explains consumer behaviour, as well as LABOUR SUPPLY and the supply of savings. A comprehensive analysis of such behaviour includes an examination of personal spending patterns and of all factor markets.

household decision making (D1)
Choices reflecting individual tastes and influenced by taxation which determine behaviour in product and factor markets. The major decisions made are the choices between work and leisure, and between saving and spending, as well as about gifts and the composition of assets. Such analysis is crucial to an understanding of LABOUR FORCE PARTICIPATION and the CONSUMPTION FUNCTION, as well as being the basis of much of neoclassical theorizing.

See also: labour force participation rate; neoclassical economics

household work (D1, J2)
The production of services and some goods by members of a family for the

other members. Cleaning, cooking, nursing and some education are the principal examples of these activities. This production is not marketed so the producers are unpaid.

H share (G1)

A company share floated and listed on the Hong Kong Stock Exchange.

See also: red chip

human capital (I2)

The education and training embodied in a human person that gives rise to increased future income. Human capital measures should include an estimate of formal and informal training, as well as income forgone during the period of training, but in practice the measurement of human capital is often restricted to measuring the cost of formal training only. Human capital can be 'general', i.e. useful in many occupations such as reading and writing, or 'specific', i.e. useful only to employment in a particular firm or job, such as a knowledge of the internal accounting procedures of a TRANSNATIONAL CORPORATION. Although estimates of human capital were attempted as early as PETTY and the concept was clearly explained by SMITH, it was not until the 1960s, through BECKER and SCHULTZ, that the concept was extensively applied in economics.

Critics of this approach have argued that calculations of the rate of return to human capital investments ignore social returns. Also it is difficult to separate human capital investment from personal consumption as all personal expenditure, including expenditure on health care, clothing and social life, has a possible effect on future earnings. However, there have been useful applications of the concept to the study of job search in labour markets, wage differentials and MIGRATION.

References

Becker, G.S. (1964) *Human Capital: A Theoretical and Empirical Analysis with Special Reference to Education*, New York: Columbia University Press.

—— (1981) *A Treatise on the Family*, New Haven, CT: Harvard University Press.

Blaug, M. (1975) 'The empirical status of human capital theory', *Journal of Economic Literature* 14: 827–55.

Mincer, J. (1974) *Schooling, Experience and Earnings*, New York: National Bureau of Economic Research.

OECD Centre for Educational Research and Innovation (1998) *Human capital investment: an international comparison*, Paris and Washington, DC: OECD.

Psacharopoulos, G. (1981) 'Returns to education: an updated international comparison', *Comparative Education* 17: 321–41.

humaneness indicators (D6)

These quality of life measures include GDP per capita, education (net primary enrolment), mortality (infant mortality, life expectancy), health (access to safe water, sanitation, number of doctors per 1,000 people), proportion of public expenditure on social services and private consumption per capita.

human scale economics (A1)

An economic philosophy based on need not money. As there is a concentration on simple food and housing needs, it is possible to use BARTER as the means of exchange.

Hume, David, 1711–76 (B3)

Scottish philosopher, historian and economist who, within the scope of only nine essays of his *Political Discourses* (first published 1752), provided an important rejection of MERCANTILIST ideas, heralding the new dawn in economics of which Adam SMITH was to be principal luminary. His account of the price SPECIE-FLOW MECHANISM refuted much of previous mercantilist thought; his praise of manufacturing exposed the narrowness of PHYSIOCRACY; his discussion of taxation showed an early awareness of TAX INCIDENCE problems. Although his *History of England* was immensely successful in his day, his philosophical and economic ideas now command more attention.

References

Rotwein, E. (ed.) (1955) *David Hume: Writings on Economics*, London: Nelson.

Humphrey–Hawkins Act 1978 (E6)

US federal statute, formally known as the Full Employment and Balanced Growth Act, which extended the EMPLOYMENT ACT 1946 by stating the priorities for the economic goals set for the US president. It also established procedures to improve the co-ordination between the president, Congress and the Federal Reserve System with the hope of improving the formulation of economic policy.

Hunt Commission (G2, K2)

The body which investigated the US securities industry. It recommended more freedom for financial firms to respond to new technology and the emergence of new types of financial firm.

See also: Big Bang; Mayday

References

Report of the President's Commission on Financial Structure and Regulation, Washington, DC: US Government Printing Office, 1971.

hurdle rate of return (M2)

The minimum rate of return to an investment project to justify it being undertaken.

hybrid auction (D4)

A method of selling government bonds used in Japan. Most of an issue is allocated conventionally through a syndicate but the remainder is auctioned. Bidders make a quantity bid, rather than a price bid, committing themselves to taking a certain amount of an issue. The price will be fixed by the subsequent price negotiated by the syndicate.

See also: auction

hybrid income tax (H2)

A combination of a comprehensive INCOME TAX and an EXPENDITURE TAX. It was gradually introduced in Japan to encourage savings, e.g. in the form of tax-exempt savings and flat rate capital gains tax.

See also: double taxation of savings

hyperinflation (E3)

A rise in product prices of more than 50 per cent per month. In extreme cases, prices can double in one day. The best known examples have been Germany in 1923, Hungary in 1946 and some Latin American countries in the 1980s. Germany's inflation rose from a mark valued in the summer of 1914 at 4.2 to the US dollar to 4,200,000,000,000 on 15 November 1923. This type of inflation forces people to abandon the use of money in favour of BARTER and INDEXATION. SAVING is discouraged and fixed income groups with little bargaining power, including the RENTIER class, suffer a massive fall in income. Governments, finding it difficult to collect taxes, often resort to increasing the money supply as a source of income in such circumstances.

References

Siklos, R.K. (1990) *War Finance, Hyperinflation and Stabilization in Hungary 1938–48*, London and New York: Macmillan and St Martin's Press.

hypothecation (G1, H2)

1 Pledging a security without delivering it.
2 Relating a particular tax revenue to a particular public expenditure.

See also: dedicated budget; earmarking; mortgage; ringfencing

hysteresis (J6)

The hypothesis, applied to the study of UNEMPLOYMENT, which states that a level of unemployment does not have a tendency to return to an equilibrium rate and certainly not the NATURAL RATE OF UNEMPLOYMENT. (Originally a term used by James Ewing in the 1880s to describe the properties of ferric metals.) In the UK, hysteresis has been used as an explanation of persisting unemployment throughout the 1980s. It has been noted that when an economy expands, the increased demand leads to higher wages for workers at present employed rather than to employment for the jobless. Also, a long duration of unemployment de-skills workers, making it less likely that they will be re-employed.

References

Cross, R. (1988) *Unemployment, Hysteresis and the Natural Rate Hypothesis,* Oxford: Basil Blackwell.

ideal limit (R1)
The maximum distance a consumer will travel to purchase goods.

See also: central place theory

identification problem (C1)
The ECONOMETRIC problem of discovering from data which equation is being estimated. A major example of this is the problem of separating demand from supply curves when attempting to construct a demand curve from raw data. If, over a period of time, there are shifts in a demand curve, different observations A, B, C and D will be on different demand curves X_1X_1–X_4X_4 and so a supply curve (line YY) rather than a demand curve has been identified. As this problem arises because the CETERIS PARIBUS conditions do not hold, only by collecting data on such back-

Quantity demanded and supplied

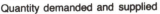

ground variables is it possible to identify a demand curve.

identity theft (K4)
Stealing the identity of a creditworthy person in order to acquire credit fraudulently.

Ifo Business Climate Index (E6)
A monthly index published by the Ifo-Institute for Economic Research, Munich, which surveys 7,000 businesses to appraise the business situation as good, satisfactory or poor and to ascertain whether business expectations for the next six months are the same, better or worse. There are separate indexes for West Germany and East Germany calculated as the geometric mean of survey results.

ill-being (D6)
A state of deprivation evident in low income, poor health and few opportunities for betterment. The opposite of WELL-BEING.

References

Srinivasan, T.N. (1994) 'Destitution: a discourse', *Journal of Economic Literature* 32: 1842–55.

illiquid (G1)
The state of an asset inconvertible into cash.

illth (D6)
Goods and services giving negative satisfaction; the opposite of wealth. Many

goods can be regarded as both wealth and illth, e.g. tobacco. A term coined by John Ruskin in the nineteenth century.

See also: bad; wealth

References

Ruskin, J. (1985) *Unto this Last*, essay 4, London: Penguin; New York: Viking Penguin.

immigration (F2, J1)
The permanent settling of people from other countries. Immigrants take up a new residence to escape the poverty or persecution of their original countries, to increase their personal and ECONOMIC WEL-FARE in a new country or to join relatives who have already migrated. The effects of immigration on a country include, at the macro level, impacts on inflation, technical progress and public expenditure and, at the micro level, a change in the pattern of demand for goods and services and extra labour supply to particular labour markets. Immigrants are absorbed into an economy in different ways: as ENTREPRE-NEURS, as members of the SECONDARY LA-BOUR MARKET or into enclaves.

See also: enclave economy; migration

References

Piore, M.I. (1979) *Birds of Passage: Migrant Labor and Industrial Societies*, New York: Cambridge University Press.

immiseration (P1)
The increasing poverty of the working class under CAPITALISM. MARX did not equate this simply with a fall in real wages as immiseration has also psychological and spiritual dimensions.

See also: alienation; division of labour

References

Plamenatz, J. (1975) *Karl Marx's Philosophy of Man*, Oxford: Clarendon Press.

immiserizing growth (O4)
A decline in the ECONOMIC WELFARE of a country, despite an expansion of its pro-

duction and exports, brought about by a deterioration in its TERMS OF TRADE.

References

Bhagwati, J.N. (1958) 'Immiserizing growth: a geometrical note', *Review of Economic Studies* 25: 201–5.
Johnson, H.G. (1967) 'The possibility of income losses from increased efficiency or factor accumulation in the presence of tariffs', *Economic Journal* 77: 151–4.

impact multiplier (E0)
The impact on a national economy in a given year of the EXOGENOUS VARIABLES for that year and the ENDOGENOUS VARIABLES for prior years.

References

Goldberger, A.S. (1959) *Impact Multipliers and the Dynamic Properties of the Klein-Goldberger Model*, Amsterdam: North-Holland.

imperfect competition (L1)
The state of a market, similar to MONOPOLIS-TIC COMPETITION, first identified by Joan ROBINSON. The term is also used in the broad sense to refer to all markets without all the characteristics of PERFECT COMPETITION.

References

Robinson, J. (1933) *The Economics of Imperfect Competition*, London: Macmillan.

imperialism (P1) *see* capitalist imperialism

implementation lag (E6)
The time it takes to institute a discretionary change in policy. These lags are usually shorter for MONETARY POLICY than for FISCAL POLICY as in the former case a sudden announcement of a change in interest rates can be made, whereas fiscal changes often need legislation.

See also: recognition lag

implicit contract theory (J4)
A labour market theory which asserts that labour contracts can be successfully based on EXPECTATIONS, e.g. of promotion or stable employment, instead of on legally binding terms. The theory recognizes that

in many employment relationships there is a deficiency of information. Typically, an employment contract is incomplete because it omits reference to work effort and so an employer has to monitor the contract to achieve the exchange of a 'fair day's pay' for a 'fair day's work'. However, it has been argued that some contracts are more explicit than originally thought, as evidenced by union resistance to unfavourable revisions of them. Implicit contracting explains short-term temporary unemployment. The theory assumes that wages are sticky and that employees will accept such contracts because of their aversion to risk.

References

Akerlof, G.A. and Miyazaki, H. (1980) 'The implicit contract theory of unemployment meets the wage bill argument', *Review of Economic Studies* 47: 321–38.

Okun, A.M. (1981) *Prices and Quantities*, Washington, DC: Brookings Institution.

Rosen, S. (1985) 'Implicit contracts: a survey', *Journal of Economic Literature* 23: 1144–75.

implicit cost (D0, M2)
A cost of production which is not included in the accounts of a business but nevertheless is incurred. This often happens when firms are owned by sole proprietors who underestimate the cost of their labour.

See also: explicit cost

implicit marginal income (H2)
The size of the fall in the amount of a subsidy when income rises. This typically occurs when welfare benefits are stopped because income has reached a threshold level.

See also: poverty trap

implicit price deflator (E3)
The ratio of the GROSS NATIONAL INCOME at current prices to the gross national product at constant prices × 100. This deflator is produced as a by-product of NATIONAL INCOME accounting.

implied price index (C1, E3) *see* implicit price deflator

import (F1)
The purchase of a good or a service that has been produced by another country. Exports net of imports are included in a country's GROSS DOMESTIC PRODUCT. An ECONOMY at the beginning of an expansionary phase will often increase its imports of raw materials and semi-finished goods. An OPEN ECONOMY will have a high volume of imports: the smaller or more specialized an economy is, the more it will have to import to satisfy consumers' demand for a wide range of goods and services.

See also: export; inter-industry trade; intra-industry trade; marginal propensity to import

import penetration ratio (E2, F1)
The ratio of imports to domestic consumption for a class of goods of a particular country. This measure reflects non-tariff trade restrictions at a particular time but does not separate these effects from other reasons for importation (e.g. a lack of domestic product substitutes) and is not adjusted for overvaluation or undervaluation of a currency.

import substitution (F4, O2)
A development policy encouraging domestic production. This is achieved in various ways including the imposition of TARIFFS to keep out foreign-produced goods and the reduction in the prices of home-produced goods through subsidization or a change in their quality.

See also: infant industry

impossibility theorem (D7)
Arrow's assertion that under democracy majority choice produces a stalemate, as an unambiguous social choice cannot be achieved if there are more than two options facing voters. Assume individuals A, B and C and options x, y and z. A prefers x to y and y to z; B prefers y to z and z to x; C prefers z to x and x to y. Each option is thus ranked first by one of

the three individuals, second by another. Since there is no overall favourite, there is a stalemate.

References

Arrow, K.J. (1966) *Social Choice and Individual Values*, 2nd edn, New York: Wiley.

impost (H2)
A tax or duty.

impulse response function (C6)
An equation or graph indicating the response of a system to a shock, e.g. changes in output or consumption resulting from an increase in the stock of money.

impure public good (H4) *see* mixed good

imputed income (D3, H2)
The benefit received from a service not measured by a monetary transaction. Some forms of this income are estimated to obtain a fuller measure of the GROSS NATIONAL PRODUCT. In the USA, national income accounting imputes an income to food grown and consumed by farmers. Also, to raise more revenue from an income tax the imputed income from owner-occupied houses can be added to income actually received by taxpayers.

in-bond manufacturing (L6)
The manufacturing of duty-free imported raw materials that are processed and assembled for re-export. In some cases, the VALUE-ADDED TAX of the country ultimately purchasing them is levied. This arrangement between Mexico and the USA has flourished since the 1960s.

See also: freeport

incentive compatible (D0)
A state of affairs under which an individual has no incentive to change, e.g. under PERFECT COMPETITION when a buyer or seller accepts market determination of prices and cannot benefit by attempting to influence them.

incentive contract (H5)
A type of contract often made between governmental bodies and private firms which consists of a fixed part (which is a function of the expected cost) and another part (which is proportional to the difference between the expected cost and the actual *ex post* cost). A private contractor has the greatest incentive to keep costs down if he or she expects to lose most of the difference between the *ex ante* and *ex post* costs.

See also: *ex ante, ex post*

incentive effect (H2)
The encouraging effect of a tax on the supply of an activity, especially work. A progressive income tax can have incentive effects if individuals want to achieve a target post-tax income and can only do this by working harder in the face of steep tax progression.

See also: disincentive effect; impact multiplier; progressive tax

incentive pay scheme (J3)
A wage or salary system that relates all or part of employment earnings to the output of a worker. Manual (blue-collar) workers have often had the opportunity to participate in PRODUCTIVITY schemes, including being paid by the number of 'pieces' produced rather than by the amount of time supplied. Many sales staff have a high proportion of their pay in the form of commission. Managerial staff in many organizations are offered a profit-sharing scheme. Workers are most likely to increase their productivity when a new scheme is introduced – hence the suggestion that incentive schemes should be periodically replaced.

incidence (H2) *see* tax incidence

income (D0, E0)
The flow of value, expressed in money or in goods and services, accruing to a government, a firm or an individual over a specified time period.

See also: Haig–Simons definition of income; Hicksian income measure; money income; psychic income; real income; stock and flow concepts; wealth

References

Parker, R.H., Harcourt, G.C. and Whittington, G. (eds) (1986) *Readings in the Concept and Measurement of Income*, 2nd edn, Oxford: Philip Allan.

income and substitution effects (D0)
The effects of a price change. The income effect occurs because a fall in price raises real income (or lowers it if the price rises); the substitution effect encourages more consumption of the good which has become relatively cheaper (the opposite if the price has increased). Thus, in the figure, when the price of good B falls, this consumer moves from combination x to combination y and chooses OQ of B instead of combination OP. An extra BUD-GET LINE is inserted to separate the price effect into income and substitution effects and another combination z is discovered. The price effect is the movement x to y (PQ on the horizontal axis); the income effect is the movement from z to y (RQ on the horizontal axis). The substitution effect is the movement from x to z (PR on the horizontal axis).

These effects are analysed in the study of consumer behaviour to determine the effect of a price change on quantity demanded, in the study of TAX INCIDENCE as prices are affected and in the study of LABOUR SUPPLY to discover the particular TRADE-OFF between work and leisure chosen by a worker.

See also: Slutsky effect; Slutsky equation

income–consumption curve (D0)
A graphical representation of the relationship between changing amounts of consumption of alternative goods as real income changes, using INDIFFERENCE CURVES and BUDGET LINES. The parallel budget lines show real income increases as one moves away from the origin. The income–consumption curve joins together the points of tangency between indifference curves I_1, I_2, I_3 and I_4 and budget lines representing different income levels. The curve can be used to demonstrate which of two goods is the INFERIOR GOOD.

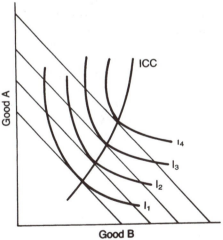

See also: Engel's law; price–consumption curve

income differential (D3, J3)
The ratio of the average income of one group of persons to another. Persons can

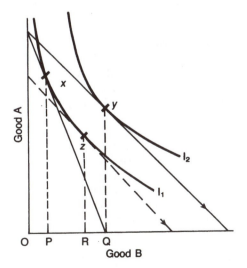

be grouped according to occupation, location, industry or type of income giving rise to occupational, industrial and regional wage differentials in the labour market. In capitalist societies, differences between employment and investment incomes are also of concern to researchers. In idealistic societies, there is an aversion to large differentials as EGALITARIANISM is often a major goal, e.g. PLATO believed that the richest member of society should not be more than four times better off than the poorest member of society.

See also: wage differentials

income distribution (D3)
A classification of personal incomes according to the FACTOR OF PRODUCTION (land, labour or capital) that has produced it, or according to its size.

income drawdown scheme (J3)
Taking income from a pension fund instead of buying an annuity.

income elasticity of demand (D0)
The ratio of the percentage increase in demand for a good or service to a percentage increase in income. Thus, if an increase in income of 4 per cent is associated with an increase in demand for food of 2 per cent, the income elasticity will be 0.5. Income elasticities for foodstuffs and agricultural raw materials are often less than one, with the consequence that the

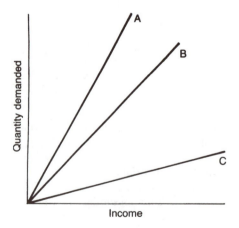

Income

divergence in economic prosperity between primary producing countries and industrialized countries increases in periods of world economic growth. Income elasticities are positive for NORMAL GOODS and negative for INFERIOR GOODS. In the figure, A is a luxury good as more of it is demanded at higher incomes, B is a normal good and C is an inferior good as less of it is demanded at higher incomes.

See also: Engel's law; price elasticity of demand

income multiple (G2)
The amount of a loan divided by the borrower's annual income. In times of inflation multiples rise helping to sustain rising property prices. UK house loans as a multiple of incomes were on average 1.67 in 1980 and rose to 6.0 in 2000.

income–offer curve (D0)
Another name for the INCOME-CONSUMPTION CURVE.

income-splitting system (H2)
A method of taxing the income of married couples. The aggregated income of the couple is halved and then the income tax is levied on each half. The couple pay double the amount on the notional equal incomes. There are several variants of this system.

incomes policy (E6)
A macroeconomic policy directly controlling factor incomes. Many Western countries since 1945 have used it as an alternative to FISCAL and MONETARY POLICIES with the hope that, by controlling wage fixing in the labour market, the rate of increase of product prices would be reduced. The most extreme form is a wages freeze, e.g. the UK's in 1966. Milder forms include setting a norm for wage increases in line with the rise in PRODUCTIVITY, allowing for exceptional increases (e.g. to help low-paid workers, to alleviate a labour shortage or to preserve comparable pay for different occupational groups), or an

exhortation to pay smaller increases (MORAL SUASION).

Many countries, including the UK and the USA, have only used incomes policies intermittently, but the Netherlands is exceptional in achieving the implementation of a long-term policy from 1948 to the 1960s. Some incomes policies have included restrictions on increases in company dividends in order to restrain all types of personal incomes: however, this approach has produced distortions in capital markets.

There were many US experiments in incomes policies in the period 1962–71, some of them inspiring the shape of UK incomes policies. In January 1962 the US COUNCIL OF ECONOMIC ADVISERS published *Guideposts for Non-inflationary Wage and Price Behavior* in which the trend in productivity was used as the general guidepost for non-inflationary wage settlements. Specific guideposts were abandoned in 1967 but in 1970 a National Commission on Productivity was set up; inflation alerts were published when there were significant wage and price increases. In 1971 there was a ninety-day wage–price freeze: its sequel was the setting up of a tripartite Pay Board and a Price Commission. The effectiveness of this policy has long been debated: it is difficult to establish that the guideposts reduced wage inflation.

The UK had statutory incomes policies for the periods 1966–70 and 1972–74, compulsory policies 1975–7 and voluntary policies 1948–50, 1961–2 and 1977–9. There was a tendency to impose an incomes policy in a crisis in the most severe form – a wage freeze for up to one year – and then to relax the policy by permitting exceptions to the principle that wage increases should be in line with general productivity increases. An innovation of the 1970s was to choose as a wage norm a flat rate cash increase; this helped the lower paid but reduced wage differentials, opening the door to a flood of subsequent wage claims.

Some observers of incomes policies are more sympathetic towards them. ROSTOW, for example, has noted that in 1984 Japan, West Germany and Switzerland were able by means of incomes policies to have lower prime interest rates, lower unemployment, lower inflation and large balance of payments surpluses. In sum, to be successful an incomes policy should provide more helpful economic and financial information and education in its use to wage bargainers, as well as an element of real wage increases.

See also: collective bargaining

References

Claudon, M.P. and Cornwall, R.R. *An Incomes Policy for the United States: New Approaches*, Boston: Nijhoff.
Holden, K., Peel, D.A. and Tompson, L.L. (1987) *The Economics of Wage Control*, Basingstoke: Macmillan.
Urquidi, V.L. (ed.) (1989) *Incomes Policies*, Basingstoke: Macmillan.

income statement (M4) *see* profit and loss account

income support (H2)
A welfare payment in cash. This alternative to in-kind benefits gives welfare recipients more freedom in their spending.

income tax (H2)
A tax levied on taxable income. It is a complex tax because of different rates for different types of income, exemption of some types of income (particularly fringe benefits) and allowances/deductions for various categories of expenditure (e.g. expenses related to employment, charitable covenants). It was first used in England in 1435, 1450 and 1798–1805 to finance the Napoleonic Wars; from 1842, it has been a permanent feature of the UK tax system. In the USA it was used to finance the Civil War in 1861–72 but an attempt to reintroduce it in 1894 failed as it was declared unconstitutional, making necessary the 16th Amendment to the US Constitution in 1913 to legitimize it. The

principal theoretical justification advanced for the tax is the SACRIFICE THEORY.

In all countries, income tax is invariably paid on employment income, dividends, net business income, income from immovable property and the income of farmers and small traders. Sometimes it is paid on some types of fringe benefit, IMPUTED INCOME from home ownership, pensions, unemployment benefit and sickness benefits.

See also: direct and indirect taxation; tax evasion

References

Atkinson, A.B. (1995) *Public economics in action: the basic income/flat tax proposal*, Oxford and New York: Oxford University Press.

income terms of trade (F1)
A measure of the purchasing power of exports in terms of imports. The formula used for calculating it is

$$I = \frac{P_x}{P_m} \times Q_x$$

where Q_x is the volume of exports (I is income, P is price, Q is quantity, x is exports and m is imports). This is a more useful indication of the effect of international trade on a country's national economy than the NET BARTER TERMS OF TRADE because income terms take into account both the prices and volumes of trade but net barter terms ignore volume changes.

See also: terms of trade

incomplete contract (D0, K0)
An agreement with insufficient clauses to anticipate all possible relationships between the contracting parties. To overcome the shortage of contingency clauses residual rights are often assigned to one of the parties.

References

Hart, O. and Moore, J. (1999) 'Foundations of incomplete contracts', *Review of Economic Studies* 66: 115–38.

incomplete market (D4, G1)
A real or financial market with an incomplete structure. Difficulties arise from the conflicting objectives of firms, time and uncertainty. A common example of such markets is an insurance market in which not all individuals are insured against the risk of losing income.

References

Hart, O. (1975) 'On the optimality of equilibrium when the market structure is incomplete', *Journal of Economic Theory* 11: 418–43.

increasing opportunity costs law (D2)
The TRADE-OFF between an increasing amount of one good and an increasing amount of another in an economy with FULL EMPLOYMENT. The opportunity cost of having more of one good is the increasing cost of losing quantities of the other good. This is the principle underlying a PRODUCTION POSSIBILITY FRONTIER.

increasing returns to scale (D2)
An increase in output at a faster rate than the increase in factor inputs. From SMITH onwards, theorists of ECONOMIC GROWTH have been interested in investigating the circumstances in which there can be increasing returns to particular industries or a national economy as a whole. CLASSICAL ECONOMISTS asserted that agriculture was subject to diminishing returns and increasing returns were only possible in manufacturing.

See also: Kaldor's laws; returns to scale; Verdoorn's law

References

Young, A. (1928) 'Increasing returns and economic progress', *Economic Journal* 38: 527–42.

incremental capital–output ratio (E0)
The extra amount of capital needed to produce one more unit of output. In the simplest of ACCELERATOR models, the accelerator coefficient is equivalent to the incremental capital–output ratio. Changes in efficiency, rather than in technology,

can change the ratio. It is always difficult to measure because of the problems of measuring capital.

incremental cost (D0) *see* marginal cost

indecomposability (P0)
The interrelatedness of an economic system such that the product of each industry is used as an INTERMEDIATE GOOD of at least one more industry. If every industry, including itself, uses it as an intermediate product, then there is perfect indecomposability.

See also: input–output analysis

indexation (M2)
An adjustment clause in contracts to maintain the real value of the items central to the contract. Clauses of this kind are much used in building contracts, labour contracts (often used in the USA and Israel) and for government bonds (e.g. in France and the UK in the 1980s to attract savers). As indexation accepts and institutionalizes inflation, it has attracted much criticism.

See also: cost of living adjustment; escalator clause

References
Dombusch, R., Sinionsen, M.H. and Vargas, F.G. (1983) *Inflation, Debt and Indexation*, Cambridge, MA: MIT Press.

indexing (G1)
An investment strategy based on choosing a portfolio of stocks likely to achieve the total return to the stocks in a stock market index.

See also: enhanced indexing

index-linked gilt (E5, G2)
A government bond with a link between a price index and the bond's capital value and yield. These GILTS, popular in times of inflation, are attractive to unadventurous investors desirous of a low-risk portfolio and steady real income. Finland introduced these gilts in 1947, France in the 1950s and the UK in 1975.

index number (C1)
A device for measuring changes in an economic variable, especially NATIONAL INCOME or prices, over a period of time. The value of the variable in the initial year (the 'base' year) is set equal to 100 and the value for each subsequent year is calculated as a percentage of it. To calculate quantity changes, e.g. in the GROSS DOMESTIC PRODUCT, the components of the GDP are weighted by the prices of each item; to calculate price changes, quantity weights reflecting the relative amounts consumed or produced are used. The best known indices are those of Laspeyres and Paasche. Before JEVONS and others constructed index numbers in the 1860s, there was little accurate knowledge of the precise degree of inflation in industrialized economies, and there was often a confusion between the causes and amount of INFLATION.

References
Allen, R.G.D. (1975) *Index Numbers in Theory and Practice*, London: Macmillan.
Stuvel, G. (1989) *The Index-Number Problem and its Solution*, London: Macmillan.

index-tracking fund (G2)
An investment fund investing in the specific securities which are included in a major STOCK MARKET PRICE INDEX. Although the value of units of the fund rise and fall with the index, the upward trend in these indices gives investors long-term growth.

indicative planning (P4)
Central ECONOMIC PLANNING based on influential forecasts that indicate the future direction of a national ECONOMY. Fiscal inducements, rather than governmental direction as in the traditional SOVIET-TYPE ECONOMY, are used to encourage private sector firms to carry out sufficient investment. Although ROBERTSON argued as early as 1915 that business fluctuations could be reduced by the joint forecasting of business investment, the major implementation of indicative planning has been in France since 1946 under the original Monnet Plan and its many successors. In the UK, the

NATIONAL PLAN attempted to introduce this type of planning for nine months in 1965–6.

indicators (E3, E6) *see* coincident indicators; economic indicators

indicator variable (E6)
An economic statistic which describes the current state of an economy and guides a policy-maker in his or her actions, particularly whether to deflate or reflate the economy.

See also: coincident indicators; economic indicators

indifference curve (D0)
A curve representing many combinations of two goods, all of which give the consumer the same level of UTILITY. As

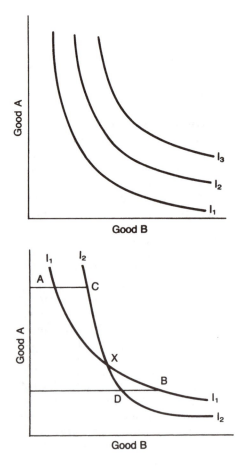

Good A / Good B

each combination renders the same utility, the consumer is 'indifferent' as to which bundle of goods to choose. The curves further from the origin represent higher levels of utility. Indifference curves must not intersect for otherwise two different levels of utility are represented at the point of intersection (X in the figure). Also there is inconsistency as combination C is preferred to combination A and combination B to combination D.

indirect cost (D0)
Overhead and other costs not directly attributable to the cost of producing one unit of output; a fixed cost.

See also: direct cost

indirect cost recovery (D4, M2)
Pricing a service or activity so that OVERHEAD COSTS are covered.

indirect factor content (D2)
The total amount of the FACTORS OF PRODUCTION used in all stages of production prior to the last to achieve a particular output.

indirect tax (H2) *see* direct and indirect taxation

indirect utility function (D3)
The total utility of a consumer related to the prices of consumption goods and the consumer's income.

See also: direct utility function

individual income tax (H2)
US INCOME TAX introduced in 1913 and now the major source of federal government revenue. It is a progressive tax with a countercyclical impact.

individualism (D1, P4)
Seeking to maximize the utility of an individual person rather than a collective entity such as society at large or a corporate body. Individualism is often equated with SELF-INTEREST or even selfishness. The individualist values economic and political freedom but prizes personal responsibility highly. Individualists respond to incentive

mechanisms and contribute to the dynamism of an economy.

See also: altruism

indivisibility (D0)
The nature of a FACTOR OF PRODUCTION or commodity supplied only in discrete amounts, not increasing or decreasing in quantity continuously. Energy or liquid raw materials, for example, are divisible, but a piece of capital equipment or a skilled employee will be available only in a minimum-sized quantity. Indivisibilities are responsible for many FIXED COSTS in the short run and give rise to production economies of scale at high levels of output.

induced technical progress (O3)
The effect on productivity of changes in relative factor prices.

inducement good (D0)
A consumer good expected to stimulate producers to make other goods in exchange for it. Such goods are of great importance in developing countries. David Hume argued in support of manufacturing that it would induce higher agricultural productivity.

inducement mechanism (O3)
The means of effecting economic change, especially a shock to an economy which brings about technical progress. INVENTIONS and their application to production have been induced by major wars as well as by more minor events such as industrial strikes. Development economists have often referred to this mechanism.

industrial action (J5)
1 STRIKES, go-slows, working-to-rule.
2 Seizing control of a factory, according to the principles of SYNDICALISM.
3 The donation of a day's work, in the USSR, to celebrate Lenin's birthday.

Industrial and Commercial Finance Corporation (G2)
A UK financial organization founded in 1945 jointly by the BANK OF ENGLAND and the London and Scottish CLEARING BANKS to provide long-term capital for small and medium-sized businesses. The corporation was thought to be necessary because of the so-called 'MACMILLAN GAP'.

industrial capitalism (P1)
The phase of CAPITALISM beginning with the INDUSTRIAL REVOLUTION; the stage of economic development following MERCHANT CAPITALISM.

industrial concentration (L1) *see* concentration

industrial democracy (L2)
Participation by employees in the management and/or ownership of their firms. Varied schemes range from the distribution of shares (popular in the UK in the 1950s and 1980s to prevent renationalization), works councils to disseminate management proposals, and producer co-operatives. Later there were proposals to have workers' representation on company boards. Germany's two-tier company structure since 1950 (the upper tier with 50 per cent worker representatives but the lower with executive directors alone) partially inspired the BULLOCK COMMITTEE's recommendations of 1977. The short-lived experiments of British Steel and the Post Office have been the major UK attempts at worker democracy to date. Some of the co-operatives in older UK small-scale industries such as clothing and footwear have had a continuous history in the English Midlands since the 1890s. More ambitious, larger unit co-operatives have flourished at Mondragon, Spain.

See also: workers' participation

References
Thimm, A. (1980) *The False Promise of Codetermination: The Changing Nature of Europe in Workers' Participation*, Lexington, MA: Lexington Books.
Thomas, H. and Logan, C. (1982) *Mondragon*, London: Unwin Hyman.
Variek, J. (1970) *The General Theory of Labor Managed Economies*, Ithaca, NY: Cornell University Press.
Witte, L.F. (1980) *Democracy, Authority*

and Alienation in Work: Workers' Participation in an American Corporation, Chicago: University of Chicago Press.

industrial dispute (J5)

1 A breakdown in labour–management relations usually resulting in the partial or total withdrawal of labour on the instructions of a TRADE UNION.
2 STRIKE.

industrialization (O1)

A stage in DEVELOPMENT consisting of shifting resources from agriculture into manufacturing. It is variously measured by manufacturing's percentage share of GROSS DOMESTIC PRODUCT, gross industrial output per capita, energy consumption per capita or industrial exports as a percentage of total exports. To finance industrialization, extra real resources are necessary; these can be found by obtaining foreign exchange through increasing agricultural and manufactured exports or by increasing the domestic rate of savings. Although this is still an issue in Third World countries, the countries of the ORGANIZATION FOR ECONOMIC CO-OPERATION AND DEVELOPMENT are more concerned with DEINDUSTRIALIZATION and the switch of resources into the service sector.

industrial muscle (J5)

The ability of a group of workers to press a demand for increased wages or improved working conditions because they are in an industry producing essential goods or services. Workers in energy and transport industries have usually been more powerful in COLLECTIVE BARGAINING because the withdrawal of their labour creates a crisis in a national economy.

See also: strike

industrial organization (L0)

Also known as industrial economics, this applied branch of microeconomics was partly founded to provide theoretical support for the analysis of ANTITRUST but now includes the examination of all the functions of management. A major aspect of the subject is the study of market structures and an examination of the implications of those structures for pricing, investment and company performance. In a sense, industrial organization was started by MARSHALL in his *Economics of Industry* and *Principles of Economics* (Book IV).

See also: structure–conduct–performance model; theory of the firm

References

Mason, E.S. (1957) *Economic Concentration and the Monopoly Problem*, Cambridge, MA: Harvard University Press.
Stigler, G.J. (1968) *The Organization of Industry*, Homewood, IL: Richard D. Irwin.

industrial policy (L5)

Measures attempting to speed the process of resource allocation among or within industrial sectors with the aim of correcting market distortions. Much of industrial policy is concerned to prevent a complete international specialization of labour and is often PROTECTIONIST in character, unless the policy is part of an international agreement. As the alternative to chauvinistic industrial policies, it has been suggested that the OECD might produce an overall industrial policy for a number of countries: the specific national industry marked out for expansion would develop with the help, not the competition, of other advanced countries. The mercantilists were among the first to advocate industrial policies.

In Japan, industrial policy attempts to anticipate and accelerate response to market signals. Subsidization of research and development and guidance are offered to growth sectors. The MINISTRY OF INTERNATIONAL TRADE AND INDUSTRY offers differential help to sectors and firms, including tax incentives, export–import measures and technology subsidies. In France, industrial policy measures are part of the national and sectoral plans. France's largest bank, the Caisse des Dépôts et des Désignations, finances the largest industrial projects. In

Germany, the three major banks, themselves with substantial industrial investments, collaborate with the BUNDESBANK in implementing industrial policy. The German Ministry of Economy supports research and development and training. The industrial policies of the NEWLY INDUSTRIALIZED COUNTRIES attempt to save expenditure on imports and the pursuit of regional and industrial balance. In the USA industrial policy is conducted at the level of states: popular policies have been the encouragement of 'silicon valleys' and other concentrations of high-technology industries. The establishment of the EUROPEAN COMMUNITY's single market threatens the existence of West European national industrial policies.

References

Adams, R.G. and Klein, L.R. (eds) (1983) *Industrial Policies for Growth and Competitiveness*, Lexington, MA: D.C. Heath.
Behrman, J.N. (1984) *Industrial Policies: International Restructuring and Transnationals*, Lexington, MA: D.C. Heath.
Bingham, R.D. (1998) *Industrial policy American style: from Hamilton to HDTV*, Armonk, NY, and London: Sharpe
Foreman-Peck, J. and Federico, G. (eds) (1999) *European industrial policy: the twentieth century experience*, Oxford and New York: Oxford University Press.

industrial relations (J5)
1 A study of the rules governing the relationships between employers and TRADE (LABOR) UNIONS at national, industry or firm level.
2 An examination of the procedures for fixing wages, co-operating in production and deciding workplace discipline.

Industrial relations systems are examined with respect to the 'actors' participating in the system, i.e. employers, unions and governments, to the levels at which relations take place, i.e. national, industrial or company, and to the legislative framework within which the actors are allowed to perform. These systems are usually classified according to the degree of their centralization and the extent to which they are co-operative (as when there is WORKER'S PARTICIPATION in management) or adversarial (in the sense that employers and unions oppose each other until a compromise settlement can be reached).

See also: industrial democracy; strike

References

Clegg, H.A. (1976) *The System of Industrial Relations in Great Britain*, 3rd edn, Oxford: Basil Blackwell.

Industrial Reorganization Corporation (L5)
The UK state-financed financial institution in existence from 1967 to 1971 with the aim of restructuring UK industry. It provided finance to bring about desirable mergers between firms so as to make them more internationally competitive, British Leyland being one of its more famous cases. Also, it invested directly in several high-technology firms. The subsequent Conservative government abolished it because of its belief that government-financed bodies should not be engaged in risky investment activities.

See also: National Enterprise Board

References

Hague, D.C. and Wilkinson, G.C.G. (1983) *The IRC – An Experiment in Industrial Intervention: A History of the Industrial Reorganization Corporation*, London: Allen & Unwin.

industrial revolution (N6)
A discontinuity in the growth of an economy, taking the form of a rapid rate of technical progress leading to a sustained increase in per capita real incomes. This revolution is usually accompanied by a change in the occupational structure as factory replaces handicraft production, and urbanization of the population. Rostow mentions four industrial revolutions. The first was in the 1780s associated with the textile industry, the second the railway

boom of the 1830s and 1840s, the third, based on steel, machine tools and motor vehicles, which came to an end in the 1970s and the fourth, which is now taking place, based on electronics and biology. A disruptive feature of the fourth is the use of robots to replace workers in manufacturing, creating unpredictable and undesired employment effects.

See also: Kondratieff cycle; take-off

References

Deane, P. (1979) *The First Industrial Revolution*, 2nd edn, Cambridge: Cambridge University Press.
Rostow, W.W. (1971) *The Stages of Economic Growth: A non-communist manifesto*, Cambridge: Cambridge University Press.

industrial share (G0)
An EQUITY forming part of the financial capital of an industrial company or corporation.

industrial society (P0)
A term developed by Marxists in Europe and the USA in the 1950s to describe a society with large-scale industrial production. A capitalist or a non-capitalist society can take this form. The advent of Keynesianism and improved techniques of industrial management, it was hoped, would produce a stability in society, particularly in the relationship between capital and labour.

References

Kerr, C. (1962) *Industrialism and Industrial Man: The Problems of Labor and Management*, London: Heinemann.

industrial training grant (I2, J2)
A payment made by central government or by a fund financed by the firms of an industry to pay for vocational training. Without such grants it would be difficult for many small firms to finance adequate training and there would be a tendency for firms undertaking little training to attempt to acquire trained workers by paying above-market wage rates. In a period of

great technological change, industrial training has become central to the survival and successful future of many firms.

See also: general training

industrial union (J5)
A TRADE (LABOR) UNION which is the sole organizer of labour in a particular industry. Germany has sixteen industrial unions to organize its labour force. Many have suggested a similar structure for UK unions (who had recommended industrial unionism to the Federal Republic of West Germany) but have stumbled on the major obstacle to such change – the dismemberment of powerful GENERAL UNIONS.

See also: craft union; enterprise union

industry (L0)
A group of firms producing the same principal product. In a broad classification of industries, all industrial activity of an economy can be divided into only ten or a hundred industries but narrower classifications make possible a division into as many as a thousand or more. Types of industry are contrasted as HEAVY or LIGHT, mature or high-tech, smokestack or sunrise.

See also: Standard Industrial Classification; three-digit industry; two-digit industry

industry cluster (L0, R1)
A group of interlinked industries based on COMPARATIVE ADVANTAGE.

industry supply curve (D2) *see* supply curve

inefficient equilibrium (D4)
A market balance that excludes some TRADES which could have been executed.

inelasticity (D0)
1 The unresponsiveness of one economic variable to another.
2 Demand or supply ELASTICITY less than unity in value. In product markets, demand is inelastic for essential goods and services, including goods that produce addiction. In labour markets, the

short-term inelastic supply reflects the lengthy nature of training.

inequality (D3)

The character of a particular income or wealth distribution with different rather than equal shares for members of a population. In developed countries, inequality arises from WAGE DIFFERENTIALS, the regional distribution of economic activity and accumulations of income-earning assets. Inequality is more severe in less developed countries because UNEMPLOYMENT is much greater, unemployment benefits are rare, much labour is immobile and often a few families have a disproportionate share of wealth.

The effects of inequality have long been debated. Some argue that it leads to inefficiency as many in a population, seeing little chance of economic advancement, are unwilling to sacrifice present consumption to make possible economic development and are likely to underinvest in their children's education; others point to the devastating effects on PRODUCTIVITY and ECONOMIC GROWTH of the lack of incentives in an EGALITARIAN society.

See also: Gini coefficient; Lorenz curve

References

Atkinson, A.B. (1982) *The Economics of Inequality*, 2nd edn, Oxford: Clarendon Press.
Sen, A. (1997) *On economic inequalilty*, 2nd edn, Oxford and New York: Clarendon Press.
Silber, J. (ed.) (1999) *Handbook of income inequality measurement*, Boston, Dordrecht and London: Kluwer Academic.
Townsend, P. (1979) *Poverty in the United Kingdom*, Harmondsworth: Penguin.

inertial effect (E6)

A government's passive acceptance of an economic condition inherited from a previous government, e.g. acceptance of wage increases previously negotiated.

inertial inflation (E3)

The expected rate of INFLATION built into an economy. This rate is based on historical experience and assumed in contracts.

infant industry (L0)

A new industry with a low output and high average cost. As it is usually uncompetitive relative to producers in other countries, it often attracts assistance under an INDUSTRIAL POLICY or through PROTECTION.

See also: tariff

infant industry argument (F1)

The case for tariff PROTECTION for a new industry with high unit costs (often because its labour force is untrained, its fixed capital is expensive or it lacks production experience) to enable it to increase its output and reduce its unit costs until it is internationally competitive. This has often been regarded as the most justifiable of reasons for a tariff as the social benefits of setting up a new industry outweigh the private cost of being denied lower priced imports. However, experience has shown that many of these 'infants' have not reached adulthood.

References

Baldwin, R.E. (1969) 'The case against infant industry tariff protection', *Journal of Political Economy* 77: 295–305.

inferior good (D0)

1 A good demanded less as consumers' incomes rise.
2 A good with an INCOME ELASTICITY OF DEMAND of less than one. Some foodstuffs, e.g. potatoes, rice and margarine, are in this category. An inferior good can be distinguished from a normal good in an income demand curve.

See also: Giffen paradox

infession (E3)

World inflation caused by a breakdown in the world monetary system leading to world RECESSION. This concept was introduced to provide a better explanation of the STAGFLATION of the 1970s.

inflation (E3)

A general sustained rise in the price level

that reduces the purchasing power of that country's currency. It has been ascribed to increases in the money supply, excess demand, rises in public expenditure (particularly in times of war), the behaviour of the labour market and changes in costs – in the case of the 1970s, oil-price increases.

See also: core inflation rate; cost-push inflation; hyperinflation; inertial inflation; inflation accounting; menu costs of inflation; pure inflation; shock inflation; shoe leather costs of inflation; structural inflation; wage-push inflation

References

Brown, A.J. (1985) *World Inflation since 1950*, Cambridge: Cambridge University Press.

Fleming, J.S. (1976) *Inflation*, Oxford: Oxford University Press.

inflation accounting (E3, M4)

Accounts measuring costs, revenue, profit and loss at constant prices. Major professional bodies of accountants have produced conventions to deal with the effects of inflation so that a true and accurate description of the financial state of an enterprise is achieved. The current cost approach is used in the UK, Australia, Canada and New Zealand. In the USA, the SECURITIES AND EXCHANGE COMMISSION requires large corporations to use the replacement cost approach, stating both specific price changes and movements in the general price index.

See also: current cost accounting; Sandilands Report

References

Tweedie, D.P. and Whittington, G. (1984) *The Debate on Inflation Accounting*, Cambridge: Cambridge University Press.

inflation-adjusted deficit (H6)

That part of a government's fiscal deficit deflated by a price index.

inflationary gap (E0)

The excess of AGGREGATE DEMAND over AG-GREGATE SUPPLY. This gap is the cause of DEMAND-PULL INFLATION and is usually illustrated as in the figure.

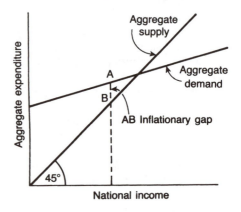

inflation illusion (E3) *see* money illusion

inflationist (E3)

A person advocating inflation as a means of stimulating an economy. This is recommended because gross profit margins increase in a period of inflation, making possible increased net investment and employment.

inflation targeting (E5)

Setting as the goal for a CENTRAL BANK the achievement of price inflation at or below a prescribed rate. New Zealand in 1990 was the first to adopt this policy; Canada, the UK, Sweden and Australia were next to adopt targeting. In the USA the FEDERAL RESERVE under the EMPLOYMENT ACT 1946 has a broader remit which includes both economic growth and the control of inflation.

See also: Monetary Policy Committee (UK)

inflation tax (H2)

1 A tax that fines employers and/or workers who permit wages to rise faster than desired by a government. Its aim is to make labour more competitive through bringing about a reduction in unemployment.

2 A reduction in the resources of house-

holds and firms because a government has sanctioned an increase in the money supply and caused inflation.

See also: forced saving; marginal employment subsidy; seignorage; tax-based incomes policy

informal economy (P0)

Part of an economy consisting of unrecorded and often illegal economic activities. In developing economies the informal sector is the subsistence agricultural sector, in developed economies subcontracting activities such as tailoring. The dynamic of this sector, springing from the avoidance of governmental regulation, produces well-known consequences – long hours, a disregard for safety, do-it-yourself activities and barter. Also known as the unofficial economy.

See also: black economy; time budget survey

References

Alessandrini, S. and Dallago, B. (eds) (1987) *The Unofficial Economy: Consequences and Perspectives in Different Economic Systems*, Aldershot: Gower.

Thomas, J.J. (1989) *Informal Economic Activity*, Hemel Hempstead: Philip Allan; Cambridge, MA: MIT Press.

informal ownership (K0) *see* extralegal property

information agreement (L1, L4)

A RESTRICTIVE PRACTICE consisting of the circulation of prices and/or costs to members of a business association with a view to encouraging them to restrict competition by setting similar product prices. In the UK such agreements, some of which have existed throughout the twentieth century, have been within the scope of restrictive trade practices legislation since 1968.

See also: competition policy

information cost (M2)

The cost to an organization of obtaining knowledge of its business environment.

information disclosure (K2)

The publication of facts about the state and activities of an organization. For a company, much disclosure is a legal requirement, but there is also voluntary release of information to appease inquisitive shareholders, attract more investment, achieve political acceptability and the general approval of society.

information externality (D8)

The supply of a PUBLIC GOOD by a private individual; for example, the activity of a pioneer that indicates to successors whether a venture is worthwhile.

information technology (O3)

Methods of generating, processing and communicating information, especially using computer hardware and software. EXPERT SYSTEMS, data networks and electronic mail have revolutionized many functions of management and made possible the globalization of financial markets. In modern economies it has become central to the working of most firms and could be responsible for the beginning of a new LONG WAVE.

References

Zorkoczy, P. (1982) *Information Technology. An Introduction*, London and Marshfield, MA: Pitman.

information theory (D8)

The principles underlying the criteria used to select summary statistics which describe empirical distributions. Information is used to revise previous probabilities.

References

Kullback, S. (1959) *Information Theory and Statistics*, New York: Wiley.

information trap (D4)

An equilibrium state in which prices fail to reveal all the information in the market. Mistaken beliefs about the information possessed by other market participants produce this trap.

infraco (L2)

An INFRASTRUCTURE company such as an operator of railways.

infrastructure (H4)

The basic services or SOCIAL CAPITAL of a

country, or part of it, which make economic and social activities possible by providing transportation, public health and education services and buildings for community activities. Railways, airports, hospitals, schools, roads, sewerage systems and reservoirs constitute the major types of social capital. Although in the nineteenth century many of these were financed privately (e.g. the railways), after 1945 in many countries most infrastructure investment has been the responsibility of the public sector. Countries with the poorest infrastructures are either those with low per capita incomes, i.e. the less developed countries, or those with governments practising LAISSEZ-FAIRE policies which seek to minimize the role of the state.

inheritance tax (H2)

A tax on WEALTH transferred after the decease of an individual person. This tax aims to raise revenue and bring about an intergenerational shift in wealth distribution. Inheritance taxes have long had their advocates, e.g. John Stuart MILL, as a major method of reducing INEQUALITY in society.

in-home banking (G2) *see* home banking

initial public offering (G1)

The first sale of shares of a company to the public when it decides to offer a stake in its ownership to outside investors. Usually an investment bank advises a company on coming to market and might guarantee the sale through a firm commitment to buy all the shares and then resell to other investors.

See also: primary offering

injection (E0)

A stimulus to AGGREGATE DEMAND, e.g. net investment or exports, which raises the level of the NATIONAL INCOME by causing a MULTIPLIER expansion of incomes. Injections are exogenous in character.

See also: exogenous variable; leakage; withdrawal

in-kind transfer (H2)

Provision of a good or service by a government, often freely or at less than market prices, to low-income individuals and families. The aim of these 'gifts' is to increase the welfare of persons with low incomes and few resources to obtain food, housing and medical care. The transfers can take various forms including food stamps, housing vouchers and free access to medical services or subsidized medical insurance.

See also: transfer income

innovation (O3)

The application of an INVENTION to a process of production or the introduction of a new product. A method of measuring an innovation is by estimating the extent to which an industry uses the new process or product. Innovations occur more in concentrated industries as PRODUCT DIFFERENTIATION, necessitating frequent product changes, is a major market strategy of OLIGOPOLIES.

See also: diffusion rate; invention; research and development

References

Freeman, C. (1982) *The Economics of Industrial Innovation*, 2nd edn, London: Pinter.

innovation possibility frontier (O3)

A line showing the trade-off between

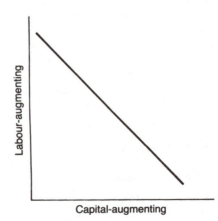

labour-augmenting and *capital-augmenting* technical progress. It is assumed that firms seek to maximize the instantaneous rate of unit cost reduction.

input—output analysis (C1, L0)

A tabular summary of the flows of goods and services between industries and the final demand of an economy with the output of each sector being the inputs of other sectors (see typical table below). The technology of the economy determines the ratios (or coefficients) of each input to the output it helps to produce. In the case of inter-industry trade, institutional factors, including custom, will determine the input—output ratios for the household sector. The static version of input—output analysis can be solved by ordinary linear equations; the dynamic version (which includes, as well as flows, stocks of goods and fixed capital) uses linear difference equations for its solution. The pioneer of the technique, LEONTIEF, first produced an input—output table for the US economy in 1936, although QUESNAY produced a flow table for the French economy in 1758.

In its static form, this analysis shows how much the *n* industries of an economy have to produce to satisfy the total demand for each particular product. It is assumed that in each industry there are constant returns to scale, a fixed input—output ratio and a homogeneous product. The model is 'open' if there are both *n* industries and a sector, e.g. households, which exogenously determines final demand; it is closed if the model shows relationships only between the *n* industries. Simultaneous equations are used to determine the inputs required for final demand to be satisfied. Dynamic versions of input—output analysis can take into account time lags in production, the adjustment of output to excess demand and the accumulation of inventories and fixed capital.

Sales	Ind. 1	Ind. 2	Ind. 3	Purchases etc.	A	B	C	D	E	F
Industry 1										
Industry 2										
Industry 3										
etc.										
Imports										
Total goods and services										

A total intermediate output of industries
B final buyers – current expenditure
C final buyers – gross domestic capital formation
D final buyers – exports
E total final output B + C + D
F total output A + E

References

Leontief, W.W. (1951) *The Structure of the American Economy*, 2nd edn, New York: Oxford University Press.

—— (1986) *Input-Output Economics*, 2nd edn, New York: Oxford University Press.

input trade (F1)

International trade in labour and other FACTORS OF PRODUCTION.

References

Jones, R.W. (2001) *Globalization and the theory of input trade*, Cambridge, MA: MIT Press.

inside lag (E6)

A time lag occurring either because it takes time to recognize the state of an economy or because it takes time to take action to remedy an undesired state of affairs. A lag of this kind is either a RE-COGNITION LAG or an IMPLEMENTATION LAG. Such lags can be reduced by AUTOMATIC STABILIZERS which, by their nature, operate without any decision- making response to a change in an economy.

See also: outside lag

inside money (E4)

A type of money arising from private sector debt. The principal modern example of this is the commercial bank deposit matched by a loan to another person in the private sector.

See also: outside lag

References

Gurley, J.G. and Shaw, E.S. (1960) *Money in a Theory of Finance*, Washington, DC: Brookings Institution.

Johnson, H.G. (1969) 'Inside money, outside money, income, wealth and welfare in contemporary monetary theory', *Journal of Money, Credit and Banking* 1 (February): 30–45.

insider trading (G2)

Stock market trading based on financial information gained improperly from inside a firm. A typical situation is that of an employee of the mergers and acquisitions department of a MERCHANT/INVESTMENT BANK trading in the stock of the client company using the veil of a NOMINEE ACCOUNT or even a company set up for such transactions in a country noted for its secrecy, e.g. Liechtenstein. A large stockholding is built up by carefully timed transactions of a magnitude not to attract attention and then sold well before a bid is announced. Insider trading is investigated in the USA by the SECURITIES AND EXCHANGE COMMISSION and in the UK by the Department of Trade and Industry, with a view to the prosecution of offenders. In the UK, it was made an offence subject to criminal proceedings under the Companies Act 1980 and subsequently under the Company Securities (Insider Dealing) Act 1985.

References

Rider, B.A.K. (1983) *Insider Trading*, Bristol: Jordan.

insider wage setting (J3)

Wage determination within a firm resulting in the gain from increased PRODUCTIVITY being passed on as increased wages for the existing labour force. If the 'insiders' were concerned with the labour force as a whole they would be willing to accept a lower rate of pay which their employers would be able to offer also to persons outside the firm, thereby expanding employment.

See also: outsider wage setting

References

Lindbeck, A. and Snower, D.J. (1989) *The Insider-Outsider Theory of Employment and Unemployment*, Cambridge, MA, and London: MIT Press.

Solow, R.M. (1985) 'Insiders and outsiders in wage determination', *Scandinavian Journal of Economics* 87: 411–28.

insolvency (K0, M2)

The condition of a legal person with liabilities in excess of assets. This inability to meet the demands of creditors usually leads to BANKRUPTCY.

instant monetarism (B2)

The school of thought, usually identified as the New Classical, which believes that wage and price adjustment are almost instantaneous as the wages and prices set are expected to be at the equilibrium level.

See also: gradualist monetarism

Institute for Fiscal Studies (H0)

An independent, privately financed, London-based institute founded in 1971 which prepares regular assessments of UK fiscal policy and also undertakes many detailed studies of particular aspects of public finance.

Institute for International Economics (F0)

Founded in 1981 and based in Washington, DC. It studies international economics in the widest sense to include trade policies, exchange rates, Japan's role in the world and the Third World debt.

Institute for International Finance (F0)

Founded in 1984 and based in Washington, DC. COMMERCIAL BANKS set it up to collect information on developing countries and their debts. Although its main role is still data collection, it has co-ordinated debt rescheduling.

Institute of Economic Affairs (A1)

An independent educational trust founded in 1957 and situated in London. Academic economists, as well as major politicians, have produced hundreds of pamphlets, and some books, on policy issues, especially in its Hobart Papers series. It has consistently advocated the application of market principles to the major economic problems of the day. It was founded by Anthony Fisher and Ralph Harris; Arthur Seldon was its most famous director.

See also: Adam Smith Institute; David Hume Institute

institution (A1) *see* economic institution

institutional economics (A1)

An approach developed by a succession of US economists, beginning with VEBLEN, who have used a variety of social science disciplines to analyse the structure of economies, the process of economic change and the nature of economic decision making. Prominent contributors to this approach include John COMMONS and AYRES. GALBRAITH is the last major figure of the school.

References

Samuels, W.J. (1988) *Institutional Economics*, 3 vols, Aldershot: Edward Elgar.

institutional investor (G2)

A pension fund, insurance company, bank or other institution with a large portfolio of securities. After 1950, these investors diversified their portfolios by increasingly purchasing equities.

instrument variable (E6)

An economic variable directly controllable by a governmental authority responsible for an economic policy. These variables include bank reserve ratios and short-term interest rates.

See also: goal variable; target variable

References

Tinbergen, J. (1970) *On the Theory of Economic Policy*, Amsterdam: North-Holland.

insurance (D0)

A method of sharing risks. Originally it was chiefly concerned with insuring shipping, the riskiest of business ventures in earlier centuries, but the principle was extended to cover all types of risk, including damage to property, personal injury and death. The fairest type of insurance is where the cost to the insured of premiums and the cost to insurers of administration do not exceed the total payout on risks which have occurred. However, the MONOPOLY POWER of many insurers permits them to make excessive profits. The government insures some risks in the public sector and should, it is argued, underwrite personal injury compensation in the private sector. Insurance against risk is not universal. Its absence can be explained on the grounds of MORAL HAZARD as insurance induces recklessness and of adverse selection as only the worst risks apply for insurance.

References

Borch, K. (1988) *Economics of Insurance*, Amsterdam: North-Holland.

insurance market (G2)

A market that arranges the sharing of a large risk amongst many individuals. The best example is LLOYD'S of London, noted for marine and aviation insurance but prepared to consider any risks except standard life cover.

Insurance Ombudsman Bureau (G2)

A regulatory body for the UK insurance industry covering the insurance groups and companies who have volunteered to come under its jurisdiction.

See also: self-regulatory organization

intangible wealth (D0)

An asset generating income because of its owner's legal rights or trading reputation. This wealth includes patents, trademarks, copyrights, FRANCHISES and goodwill.

See also: tangible wealth

integrated fare (D4, R4)

A charge enabling a passenger to use one ticket for several forms of transport.

integrated pollution control (Q2)

A system of pollution licences covering a wide range of industries intended to control the overall levels of air and water pollution in a particular area.

See also: Environmental Protection Agency; pollution control

intellectual property (D0, O3)

Intangible property resulting from inventive activity, e.g. patents, trademarks and copyrights.

References

Rushing, F.W. and Brown, C.G. (eds) (1990)

Intellectual Property. Rights in Science, Technology and Economic Performance, Boulder, CO: Westview Press.

Inter-American Development Bank (G2)

Founded in 1960 by the USA and nineteen Latin American countries to provide finance for development projects in South America largely from private sources. Originally only the countries of the Organization of American States were members. In 1983 it established the Intermediate Financing Facility to defray up 5 per cent per annum of interest charges paid by borrowers on certain loans from the bank.

See also: development bank

inter-dealer broker (G1)

A London broker who enables market-makers in GILTS to record anonymously on an electronic noticeboard their requests to buy or sell blocks of government stocks.

interdependent economy (P0)

An ECONOMY with close trading links with another economy.

See also: open economy

interest (E4)

1 The income paid to the owner of capital for its use.
2 A legal title to property.

See also: rate of interest

interest-bearing eligible liabilities (G2)

Customer's interest-bearing deposits with UK CLEARING BANKS.

See also: eligible liability

interest elasticity of savings (E2)

The responsiveness of SAVINGS to a change in the RATE OF INTEREST. As in many empirical studies savings appear to be interest INELASTIC, other savings theories have been advanced, especially the LIFE-CYCLE approach.

interest equalization tax (H2)

US federal tax introduced in July 1963 which increased the cost of foreign portfolio borrowing on the US market by 1 per cent. This fiscal measure was designed to reduce the capital outflow from the USA.

interest rate (E4) *see* rate of interest

interest rate agreement (E4, G2)
An agreement for one party to pay an initial premium to another party in return for receiving at specified time intervals the difference between a reference market interest rate and a predetermined level of interest. If the difference is specified to be greater, the agreement is an interest rate cap; if smaller, an interest rate floor. These agreements are used in asset-liability management to reduce the risk arising from interest rate movements.

interest rate cartel (G2)
An agreement between London CLEARING BANKS to prevent competition in interest rates of both borrowers and lenders; abolished in 1971.

interest rate risk (G1)
The RISK to a borrower of the lender increasing the interest rate on a loan.

interest rate smoothing (E5)
Small changes in interest rates in the same direction, either up or down, carried out by a CENTRAL BANK often by using OPEN MARKET OPERATIONS. This attempt to stabilize output and control inflation has often been criticized for making too modest a response to macroeconomic changes.

interest rate swap (G2)
An exchange of a fixed for a variable interest rate arrangement. Despite the high risk of these swaps, in practice the return on the deal can be as low as one-twentieth of 1 per cent. This form of rescheduling debts was used in the 1980s by UK local authorities and led to great losses when interest rates rose.

interest risk (D0, E4)
A risk arising from unexpected changes in the rate of interest. A business, for example, which is financed by bank loans rather

than EQUITY will face greater financial charges when interest rates suddenly rise.

See also: exchange risk

intergenerational distribution of income (D3)
1 The relationship between the incomes of persons alive today and their descendants. One way of effecting an intergenerational transfer is for a generation to increase the income of its successors through abstaining from consumption now and undertaking long-term investments. If individuals are reluctant to make such sacrifices, governments can raise taxation to effect long-term improvements in economic welfare; this is often cited as a major justification for state educational expenditure.
2 The relationship between the incomes of workers currently in the labour force and those retired from it.

See also: overlapping generations model

intergenerational equity (H2)
Fairness, particularly in public finance, between this and future generations. According to the BENEFIT APPROACH TO TAXATION each generation should pay its own expenses, but in practice capital projects are often financed, as are wars, by public debt which burdens future generations.

References
Ferguson, J.M. (ed.) (1964) *Public Debt and Future Generations*, Chapel Hill, NC: University of North Carolina Press.

intergenerational loan (G2, R2)
A means of financing house purchase over a period as long as 100 years. The children of the original mortgagor continue to service their parents' mortgage. In times of high property prices property becomes affordable as annual payments are lower than under conventional mortgage arrangements.

See also: equity release scheme

interim management (M1)
Short-term management often to deal with

a specific problem, or to cover before a more permanent member of staff is recruited or to cope with a seasonal upsurge in demand. As these stop-gap managers are often self-employed, the companies using their services can save many employment costs.

inter-industry trade (F1)

Trade in different goods and services between different industries, e.g. the exchange of agricultural products for machines. Trade of this kind occurs most often between ECONOMIES at different stages of development, especially between countries of the FIRST and THIRD WORLDS. Increasingly trade between developed countries, e.g. within the OECD, has become INTRA-INDUSTRY TRADE. Within a national economy, inter-industry trade flows are shown in an INPUT–OUTPUT ANALYSIS.

INTERLINK (C5)

An economic forecasting model of the twenty-three OECD countries plus eight regions with 7,000 equations based on a Keynesian expenditure approach, providing short- and medium-term forecasts for the world economy. It enables policymakers to examine the relationship between national MONETARY and FISCAL policies by considering international feedback effects. Only broad macroeconomic factors are taken into account.

See also: linkage models

References

OECD (1982) *OECD Interlink System: Structure and Operation, Vol. 1*, Paris: OECD.

interlinked transaction (L1)

The tying of a purchase in one market with one in another, e.g. the purchase of equipment and raw materials or the servicing of it. In developing countries, it is common to find the provision of credit tied to a tenancy or to the provision of agricultural labour. Interlinking reduces transactions costs but has long been a method of monopoly exploitation.

See also: bundling; tying contract; upselling

References

Bardhan, D.K. and Rudra, A. (1978) 'Interlinkage of land, labour and credit relations: an analysis of village survey data in East India', *Economic and Political Weekly* 13: 367–84.

interlocking directorship (L4, M1)

A directorship held by a person who is also on the board of other companies or corporations. The holding of the financial stock of several firms by one person can lead to collusive behaviour. Sections 7 and 8 of the CLAYTON ACT forbid such directorships if competition is lessened substantially or another antitrust provision is violated as a consequence.

Intermarket Trading System (G2)

The US electronic stock market which links US regional stock exchanges with the two New York exchanges and the National Association of Securities Dealers Automated Quotation System. The Intermarket Trading System's display terminals state the current prices of that trader's market, together with the best price available elsewhere. Despite the convenience of the system, it is not a threat to the New York Stock Exchange.

intermediate good (D0)

A good used in the production of another, e.g. steel used in electrical goods industries. Intermediate goods can be identified by an INPUT–OUTPUT ANALYSIS.

See also: final good

intermediate target (E6)

A guide to the policy strategy needed to reach an ultimate policy goal, e.g. a rate of growth of the money supply designed to achieve inflationless economic growth.

intermediate technology (D2)

Production methods using simple tools and LABOUR-INTENSIVE techniques. This approach was a reaction to large-scale development schemes which attempted to convert traditional societies rapidly into modern industrialized societies, with all the consequential unemployment and environmental problems.

See also: appropriate technology; Schumacher

intermediation (G2)

The bringing together of lenders and borrowers (savers and investors) by a bank or other financial institution. This activity attempts to reduce market imperfections which have arisen from uneven amounts of information in the market and ECONOMIES OF SCALE, provides insurance against risk and responds to the different preferences of lenders and savers for holding a financial asset.

See also: disintermediation

internal balance (E0, F4)

The FULL-EMPLOYMENT level of AGGREGATE DEMAND for a country, assuming that there is complete mobility of labour and constant money wage rates. This is contrasted with EXTERNAL BALANCE. It is the task of macroeconomic policy-makers to achieve internal and external balances simultaneously. (See the figure.)

References

Meade, J.E. (1951) *The Theory of International Economic Policy, Vol. 1, The*

Balance of Payments, ch. 10, Oxford: Oxford University Press.

internal capital (M2)

Capital accumulated within a firm from past earnings. A firm should charge itself the market rate of interest to ensure it uses its resources well.

internal debt (H6)

The debt a government owes to the firms and households of the country it rules. This is the result of a government spending more than it taxes.

See also: external debt

internal economics of the firm (J4, M2)

see internalization theory; internal labour market

internal economy of scale (D0)

An ECONOMY OF SCALE occurring within a firm or other organization and benefiting it alone. An example is the fall in unit costs brought about by spreading the initial tooling costs for a production line. In a SOVIET-TYPE ECONOMY, most economies are internal as all enterprises, agencies and industrial ministries are linked together into a monolithic organization.

See also: external economy of scale

internalization theory (L2)

A theory of the firm attempting to explain why companies prefer internal markets within themselves to the external market. Inspired by COASE, this has been used to explain the existence and growth of multinational companies. Trading costs are reduced.

internalizing an externality (D0) *see* externality

internal labour market (J4)

A labour market existing within a large firm. In such markets, most recruitment is of young workers as most senior positions are filled through the internal promotion of employees trained by the firm. There is a proliferation of job grades and a salary system based on seniority to encourage workers to remain within the firm. Most examples of these markets are within monopolistic and oligopolistic firms. The phenomenon was noted by Clark Kerr when he discussed the 'balkanization' of labour markets.

See also: external labour market

References

Kerr, C. (1959) 'The balkanization of labor markets', in E.W. Bakke (ed.) *Labor Mobility and Economic Opportunity*, Boston: MIT Press; New York: Wiley.
—— (1969) *Marshall, Marx and Modern Times: The Multidimensional Society*, London: Cambridge University Press.

internal labour market contracting (J4)
see employment contract

internal market (F0, L2)

1 The market gradually created in the EUROPEAN UNION from 1992 with no barriers to trade or economic mobility. Some would like this increased degree of integration to lead to the creation of a single European bank, issuing a single currency for all member countries.
2 The trading relationships between the parts of a large firm. MULTINATIONAL CORPORATIONS are noted for such markets.

See also: Delors Plan; Eurofed; single market

internal rate of return (E2, M2)
The DISCOUNT RATE making the NET PRESENT VALUE of an investment project equal to zero. This is a widely used method of investment appraisal as it takes into account the timing of cash flows. In COST–BENEFIT ANALYSIS it is measured by the formula

$$\sum_{j=0}^{n} \frac{B_j - C_j}{(1+i)^j}$$

where i is the internal rate of return.

Internal Revenue Service (H1)
The principal office for collecting US tax revenues established in 1862. It has sixty-two district offices and 60,000 tax agents. It enforces all internal revenue laws except for alcohol, tobacco, firearms and explosives. Its cost-effectiveness is high as its costs are only 1 per cent of the total tax revenue it raises.

internal search (J6)
The job search by an employer limited to his/her own labour force. This method of recruitment operates either by inducing existing workers to switch from their present to different jobs or by getting their present employees to pass on to friends and relatives notice of internal vacancies. This approach to hiring has become more common through the growth of INTERNAL LABOUR MARKETS.

International Accounting Standards Committee (M4)
A private organization independent of government founded in 1973 to harmonize accounting standards and financial reporting throughout the world. By 2000 it had 153 professional accounting bodies from 112 countries as members and had devised 41 International Accounting Standards (IAS1, IAS2, . . .). Core accounting standards for matters as diverse as depreciation accounting, events after balance sheet date, the effects of changes in foreign exchange rates and intangible assets have been agreed.

International Air Travel Association (L9)
Founded in 1945 in Havana, covering most scheduled airlines, whose aims include promoting safe, regular and economical air transport. In practice, it has been a major example of an international cartel that has kept fares high on many international routes by licensing few operators. Licences were awarded for operating lucrative routes, especially across the Atlantic, if the same airline undertook to fly on loss-making routes. State-owned airlines have been avid to maintain such protection. However, such a restriction on competition

is increasingly challenged in the case of flights between the countries of the EUR-OPEAN COMMUNITY.

International Bank for Economic Co-operation (P3)

A COMECON organization founded in 1964 to help the non-capitalist world in a way similar to the WORLD BANK's financing of the development of other countries.

International Bank for Reconstruction and Development (F3) *see* World Bank

International Banking Act 1978 (G2, K2)

US federal statute, the first after 1945 to deal with the overseas activities of banks. It gave EDGE ACT CORPORATIONS authority to engage in a wider range of activities. The Federal Reserve was allowed to authorize the creation of international banking facilities in the form of loan accounts for non-US purposes to be used by US overseas affiliates or foreign parties. Parity of treatment was given to foreign and domestic banks, especially in interstate operations: thus the same rules on bank branching applied. Under the Act, foreign banks are required to have federal deposit insurance on deposits over $100,000.

International Clearing Union (F3)

A set of international institutions proposed by KEYNES at BRETTON WOODS. The ICU was to be the world's banker by setting up a World Bank which would be able to make adjustments of exchange rates, as well as providing a Board for International Investment, a scheme of commodity controls and an International Economic Board. Keynes hoped that this new set of institutions would combat the evils of the TRADE CYCLE. Exchange rate stabilization was to be achieved by fixing each exchange rate in terms of a new international bank money, BANCOR, which would itself be fixed in terms of gold. CENTRAL BANKS would keep their accounts with the ICU to settle outstanding balances at the par value of their currencies expressed in bancor. Ban-cor credit balances, with the approval of central banks in credit, would be used to finance debtor countries. Overdraft facilities would give countries time for adjustment. Each country would have a 'quota', i.e. a maximum debit balance, equal to the sum of the country's exports and imports on the average of the three pre-war years. If the quota was exceeded by more than one-quarter, then the country would be entitled to devalue up to 5 per cent without the consent of the ICU. If the quota was exceeded by more than one-half, then the ICU would require a stated devaluation, control of outward capital transactions and the surrender of a suitable percentage of gold or other liquid reserve assets. If the quota was exceeded by more than three-quarters, then a country could be declared in default and no longer entitled to draw on its account without the approval of the governing body of the ICU. Thus, this proposal was a step towards a world central bank operating in an international currency.

See also: International Monetary Fund; World Bank

international comparisons (E6, F0)

Assessment of the relative performance of different national economies. Since 1945 the advent of NATIONAL INCOME accounting has led to GROSS DOMESTIC PRODUCT and GROSS NATIONAL PRODUCT measures being frequently used for this purpose. Micro-economic institutions are also compared with a view to remodelling them in the light of foreign experience. Before the systematic and regular collection of economic statistics, international comparisons in the form of travellers' accounts of foreign countries were often used by economists, e.g. PETTY, SMITH and MALTHUS.

international comparisons of the cost of living (D6, F0)

The cost of purchasing the same representative bundle of goods and services in different countries of the world. Regular surveys are carried out to ascertain the proper levels of remuneration for executives employed by international firms and organizations. Japan is relatively expensive and Spain quite inexpensive.

international competitiveness (F0)

A comparison of the prices of goods of different countries, or of unit labour costs, expressed in the same currency. To avoid the problems of translating one currency into another, sometimes the comparison is made in terms of the amount of labour time needed to produce a particular good, e.g. a car with a 2-litre engine.

International Development Association (F3)

Formed in 1960 as an affiliate of the International Bank for Reconstruction and Development (WORLD BANK) to provide SOFT LOANS to developing countries which are unable to borrow because of their low credit standing.

International Energy Agency (Q4)

Vienna-based organization of the OECD countries (with the exception of Finland, France and Ireland) founded in 1974 to develop policies for the conservation of energy and the production of energy alternatives to oil.

International Finance Corporation (F3)

Affiliate of the WORLD BANK founded in 1956 and based in Washington, DC. It seeks to further the economic growth of less developed countries by supplementing the investment of private capital in private enterprises.

international illiquidity (F4)

The state of a particular country's financial system in which its short-term foreign currency obligations are less than its short-term access to foreign currency.

International Investment Bank (P3)

A bank set up by COMECON in 1971 to finance long-term capital projects.

See also: development bank

International Labour Organization (J0)

Founded in 1919 with its constitution derived from Part XIII of the Versailles Peace Treaty after demands from an international meeting of trade unions at Berne. Its General Conference works on the principle of tripartite representation from each country – of two government delegates, one workers' delegate and one employers' delegate. The worker and employer representatives on the governing body are elected internationally. It collects statistics on working conditions, passes conventions and receives annual reports on whether they have been implemented. Member states have a duty to enact domestic legislation to make effective a convention or recommendation within twelve months of its enactment. The ILO's constitution was rewritten by the Philadelphia Charter of 1946 to take into account its twenty-five years of experience and to make it part of the United Nations Organization. Its basic principles were stated as follows:

1 labour is not a commodity;
2 freedom of expression and association for all;
3 redistribution of international income to poorer countries;
4 war against want within countries by the promotion of common welfare;
5 lasting peace in the world through justice.

Member states play a lesser role in the ILO than in many other international organizations because of the workers and employers representatives. National Ministries of Labour have been accorded an enhanced and international importance through the existence of the ILO. The Nobel Peace Prize was awarded to it in 1969 in recognition of its efforts. By 1988, it had 150 members.

international liquidity (F3)

Internationally acceptable means of paying for the goods and services supplied by any country in the world. Under the GOLD BUL-

LION STANDARD, gold was used for the purposes of international settlement. Now, in addition to gold, the major currencies of the world, particularly the US dollar, the euro the yen and the pound sterling, are used as well as SPECIAL DRAWING RIGHTS of the INTERNATIONAL MONETARY FUND. The growth of EUROCURRENCY MARKETS has also increased liquidity.

References

Williamson, J. (1973) 'Surveys in applied economics: international liquidity', *Economic Journal* 83: 685–746.

International Miners' Organization (J5)

Paris-based federation of national miners' trade unions.

International Monetary Fund (F3)

International agency founded at Bretton Woods in 1945 and now located in Washington, DC, with 151 member countries providing a pool of currencies, gold and SPECIAL DRAWING RIGHTS to stabilize currencies. The only major countries outside it have been the USSR and Switzerland. It was set up to end the BEGGAR-MY-NEIGHBOUR policies of the 1930s by establishing an exchange rate regime. KEYNES had wanted an INTERNATIONAL CLEARING UNION providing automatic credit to countries in difficulties, but the US view that it should be a small, tightly controlled fund, obeying the rules of US capitalism, prevailed. Originally, under Article 1 of its Charter, the IMF's broad objectives included facilitating the balanced growth of free international trade according to the principle of COMPARATIVE ADVANTAGE. In practice, it has been principally concerned with broad macroeconomic policies designed to reduce the BALANCE OF PAYMENTS deficits and currency difficulties of member countries. Criticisms of its policies include the view that it forces adjustment on the countries in difficulty, rather than on those who have caused balance of payments deficits, e.g. by contributing to a change in the TERMS OF TRADE. The departments of the IMF cover the major areas of the world, stabilization programmes, research on international monetary economics and the provision of advice on public finance and central banking.

See also: additional facilities

International Monetary Market (G1)

A Chicago-based market established in 1982 for dealing in money futures.

international monetary system (F3)

The financial arrangements between sovereign states in force at a particular time. These consist largely of agreements for the fixing of exchange rates and the settlement of debts, particularly balance of payments deficits. Countries have a choice between market mechanisms under FLOATING EXCHANGE RATES or an order managed by an international body. The most famous international monetary systems have been the GOLD STANDARD, BRETTON WOODS and the EUROPEAN MONETARY SYSTEM.

References

Solmon, R. (1977) *The International Monetary System, 1945–76: An Insider's View*, New York and London: Harper & Row.

Tew, B. (1982) *The Evolution of the International Monetary System, 1945 to 1981*, London: Hutchinson.

international reserves (E5)

A CENTRAL BANK's holdings of foreign currencies, gold and SPECIAL DRAWING RIGHTS which can be used in foreign exchange markets to change the value of a currency.

International Securities Regulatory Organization (G1)

The partner of the INTERNATIONAL STOCK EXCHANGE since 1986 in regulating the market activities of UK stock exchanges.

International Standard Classification of Occupations (J2)

The INTERNATIONAL LABOUR OFFICE's standardized description of occupations based on the type of work performed, the degree of specialization and the skills required to perform particular jobs. This is a hierarchical classification with four layers. It has inspired a number of national occupational classifications.

References

International Labour Office (1990) *ISCO International Standard Classification of Occupations*, Geneva: ILO.

International Trade Commission (F1)
An independent, quasi-judicial US federal agency which advises the US Congress and Executive on trade matters and directs actions against unfair trade practices.

International Trade Organization (F1)
An international organization recommended by the HAVANA CHARTER but never established. The UNITED NATIONS CONFERENCE ON TRADE AND DEVELOPMENT, founded in 1964, achieved what was intended to be the role of the International Trade Organization.

See also: General Agreement on Tariffs and Trade; World Trade Organization

international trade theory (F1)
A succession of attempts to explain why nations trade particular goods with each other. The best-known early theories are of ABSOLUTE ADVANTAGE and COMPARATIVE ADVANTAGE; later theories include the HECKSCHER-OHLIN factor endowment theory. Many of these theories assume that commodities are mobile but factors of production are not.

References

Jones, R.W. and Kenen, P.B. (1984) *Handbook of International Economics, Vol. 1*, Amsterdam: North-Holland.

international union (J5)
An association of US LOCAL UNIONS and their affiliates abroad. The largest is the famous Teamsters union, which organizes a considerable range of occupations from truck drivers to nurses. The majority of internationals are affiliated to the AFL–CIO.

international union federation (J5)
An association of national TRADE (LABOR) UNIONS concerned with all the issues affecting the labour of one industry world-wide. Statistics on wages, bargaining and work conditions are collected and, occasionally, industrial action is undertaken to help the bargaining of trade unions, especially in their dealings with MULTINATIONAL CORPORATIONS. The industries with these federations include coal, chemicals, motor manufacturing and printing.

international wage levels (J3)
Comparisons of the average earnings of workers of the major industrial countries. These are used in conjunction with PRODUCTIVITY figures to calculate unit labour costs as a guide to the international competitiveness of national economies.

inter-nation equity (F1, H2)
1 Fairness in the world-wide distribution of tax revenues by attempting to ensure that each national treasury receives the tax yield it deserves. A crude method of achieving this is by international treaties which reciprocally agree that all income is taxed at source. The considerable growth of TRANSNATIONAL CORPORATIONS has made this a major policy issue.
2 The equal economic treatment of different nations, e.g. by free trade.

See also: transfer pricing

interpersonal utility comparisons (D0)
Comparisons of the amount of UTILITY (or satisfaction) acquired by different persons. The consequence of the difficulty of making such comparisons is that schemes of redistribution which are proposed as a means to increasing economic welfare can in many cases be justified only on political grounds. In the twentieth century WELFARE ECONOMICS has attempted to validate comparisons of this kind.

intersection price (D4)
The unique price where demand and supply price schedules cross.

See also: equilibrium price

Interstate Commerce Commission (L5)
US federal commission set up in 1887 by the Interstate Commerce Act to regulate rail traffic across state boundaries. This was one of the earliest US attempts to control monopoly and achieve fair prices, together with an adequate standard of service across the nation. This Washington-based commission today also regulates trucks, buses, oil pipelines and inland water transportation.

interval estimate (C1)
An estimate in a range between two numbers of a population PARAMETER.

See also: point estimate

intervention currency (E5, F3)
A currency, often a RESERVE CURRENCY, used by CENTRAL BANKS for intervening in exchange markets to affect the price of a currency.

intervention price (Q1)
The price of an agricultural commodity at which a governmental agency begins to purchase that commodity in order to maintain its price at that level and to stabilize farmers' incomes. In the EUROPEAN COMMUNITY, under the COMMON AGRICULTURAL POLICY, intervention prices are guaranteed minimum prices that attempt to stabilize individual commodity markets.

See also: Common Agricultural Policy

in-the-money (G1)
Referring to an OPTION where the UNDERLIER is above the STRIKE PRICE for a CALL OPTION or below that price for a PUT OPTION.

intra-household economics (D1)
A new microeconomics, pioneered by BECKER, which examines the determinants of production of goods and services within the household.

See also: new home economics

intra-industry trade (F1)
International trade between countries in the same type of good with both countries being exporters and importers. This has happened increasingly in the EUROPEAN COMMUNITY, e.g. in the car industry. The growth of TRANSNATIONAL CORPORATIONS and the consequent increased international specialization of production have made this type of trade flourish. The greatest degree of intra-industry trade is when there is an equal amount of exports and imports in that good; the lowest is when a country predominantly imports primary products and exports manufactures. The formula used to measure this type of trade is

$$B_i = (X_i + M_i) - \frac{|X_i - M_i|}{X_i - M_i}$$

It shows the extent to which the absolute amount of the commodity exports (X) in a particular industry or a commodity grouping is offset by imports (M) in the same grouping.

See also: border trade; cyclical trade

References

Greenaway, D. and Milner, C. (1986) *Economics of Intra-Industry Trade*, Oxford: Basil Blackwell.

intrapreneur (L2)
A company employee who is financed by his/her employer to set up an independent company and become a subcontractor. This financial arrangement gives talented persons greater independence than regular work in a large organization would provide.

References

Lessen, R. (1987) *Intrapreneurship: How to be an Enterprising Individual in a Successful Business*, Aldershot: Wildwood House.

intra-product specialization (D2) *see* fragmentation

intrinsic value (D0) *see* value in use

invention (O3)
A discovery of a new product or process of production which is often crudely measured by PATENT statistics. Economists have analysed the rate of invention as a function of the business cycle, the type of market or the organization of scientific research.

See also: innovation; research and development

inventory (M2)
The stocks of goods held by a firm for the purposes of production or final sale. An increase (or decrease) in an inventory will be a form of investment (disinvestment). Because of fluctuations in final demand, unintended investment (or disinvestment) often occurs and is frequently the most volatile component of national output.

See also: Kitchin cycle

inventory cycle (E3)
Fluctuations in the stocks of raw materials, semi-finished goods and goods available for sale within an ECONOMY. Changes in inventories occur more frequently than fluctuations in fixed investment. Anticipated and unanticipated changes in final demand, changes in the cost of financing stockholdings and errors in the planning of production all generate inventory cycles.

See also: Kitchin cycle

inverse demand function (D4, M3)
This indicates market price as a function of the quantity demanded, reversing the usual sequence of causality. Often, for marketing reasons, a firm chooses an output level before a product price.

inverse elasticity rule (D0)
This states that the PRICE ELASTICITY OF DEMAND for a good is inversely proportional to price minus marginal cost divided by

price (if all CROSS PRICE ELASTICITIES OF DEMAND are ignored). Thus the margin between price and cost is large when elasticity is small: under MONOPOLY, there will be a very INELASTIC demand and the ability to make SUPERNORMAL PROFITS.

See also: Lerner index

investment (E2, G0)
1 An addition to the stock of capital goods in the public or private sector over a given time period. Gross investment includes both this net investment and the replacement investment to keep the stock intact. Theories of the determination of the volume of investment include the ACCELERATOR PRINCIPLE and MARGINAL EFFICIENCY OF CAPITAL APPROACHES.
2 The purchase of a FINANCIAL asset.

See also: capital theory; financial investment; human capital

References
Junanker, P.N. (1972) *Investment: Theories and Evidence*, London: Macmillan.

investment appraisal (M2)
The calculation of the prospective return to an investment project with a view to ascertaining whether it is worthwhile. The different methods used by firms include calculating the RATE OF RETURN, THE DISCOUNTED CASH FLOW and the NET PRESENT VALUE. Large-scale investments in the public sector often make use of COST-BENEFIT ANALYSIS.

References
Lumby, S. (1982) *Investment Appraisal and Related Decisions*, Wokingham: Van Nostrand Reinhold.
Merrett, A.J. and Sykes, A. (1986) *Capital Budgeting and Company Finance*, London and Harlow: Longman.

investment banking (G2)
A specialist type of US banking concerned with CORPORATE FINANCE, ARBITRAGE in secondary markets and the underwriting of

and dealing in securities. It consists of either executing the orders of other investors or proprietary trading when a bank deals on its own account. The GLASS-STEAGALL ACT ordered the separation of investment from deposit-taking banking, thereby preventing the growth of FINANCIAL CONGLOMERATES to the extent which has subsequently become possible in the UK. In the USA the TOP 'BULGE-BRACKET' FIRMS are virtually an oligopoly, having 80 per cent of the business in debt and other securities markets.

See also: merchant bank

investment climate (E6)
The mood or level of business confidence. This will affect the rate of investment in an economy.

See also: animal spirits; economic climate

investment dollar pool system (F3)
A method of exchange control. Under this system the people of a non-dollar country wishing to purchase US securities are only allowed to acquire them by buying them from another local resident or by borrowing them. A tougher version of this system used in the UK prior to 1979 required 25 per cent of foreign currency proceeds from the sale of assets to be sold in the official market; also dividends on dollar investments had to be repatriated through the official exchange market.

investment fundamentals (E2, M2)
Cash flow; cash stock.

investment reserve system (E3, E6)
A method of encouraging countercyclical private sector investment. In prosperous times, tax incentives encourage firms to accumulate reserves that are in later years spent on capital projects when the economy is heading for recession.

Since 1938 in Sweden there has been a policy of influencing the timing of capital expenditures by fiscal incentives to reduce fluctuations in the national economy. Companies can set aside up to 50 per cent

of pre-tax profits in non-interest-bearing Bank of Sweden accounts in return for tax reductions: after five years, 30 per cent of a deposit can be used at the request of the company tax-free and at other times, in recessions, the government can authorize the release of these funds tax-free to stimulate the economy. In addition, since the mid-1960s, these funds can be used to help depressed regions whatever the state of the national economy.

See also: countercyclical policy

investment trust (G2)
A company whose capital is invested in the stocks and shares of other companies. It offers the investor the opportunity of benefiting from a spread of different investments. This type of trust was invented by Foreign and Colonial in 1886 (still a market leader). Compared with UNIT TRUSTS, they have the advantages of GEARING in that loan capital can be used for the benefit of shareholders, of lower costs and of being able to retain their underlying shares during a stock market panic.

See also: mutual fund

investor sentiment (G1)
The psychological biases of investors causing them to value securities at prices other than their FUNDAMENTAL VALUES. These investors are also known as noise traders.

invisible foot (D3)
A reduction in redistribution caused by political competition. Invisibility comes about because of the difficulties of observation, quantification and measurement. An example of an invisible foot would be the movement of people between locations to obtain a better mix of taxes and public expenditure, thereby invisibly creating an efficient resource allocation.

See also: fiscal mobility; Tiebout hypothesis

invisible hand (D0)
The underlying mechanism of a MARKET

ECONOMY that causes self-interested economic agents through exchange to promote the general good of society. The idea originated in the discussion of natural law by the English philosopher John LOCKE but is usually associated with Adam SMITH who, in his *Theory of Moral Sentiments* and less so in his *Wealth of Nations*, developed this PHYSIOCRATIC notion. Smith's use of the principle was less sensational than MANDEVILLE's that described how private vices promote public virtue. Ahmad has identified four functions of the 'invisible hand': to limit the size of the landlord's stomach, to curb the residual selfishness of a landlord, to optimize production and to preserve the natural order.

References

Ahmad, S. (1990) 'Adam Smith's four invisible hands', *History of Political Economy* 22: 137–43.

invisible handshake (J5)
An informal understanding between an employer and workers, or between a firm and its customers, whose terms are not legally binding because of their implicit nature. Employers make such tacit agreements as part of their pursuit of long-term profitability. This concept was inspired by OKUN's study of STAGFLATION in the 1970s.

See also: implicit contract theory

invisible trade (F1)
International trade in services, particularly banking, insurance, shipping, tourism and professional advice. This is the principal economic activity of the City of London and other leading financial centres.

See also: balance of payments

involuntary unemployment (J2, J6)
1 Not wanting to work at a given wage but still doing so.
2 Lack of jobs.
3 Being unable to obtain employment at a given wage rate.
4 A case of DISEQUILIBRIUM in the labour market. KEYNES was particularly noted

for identifying this type of UNEMPLOYMENT, partly because he prescribed an increase in AGGREGATE DEMAND to eliminate it.

See also: voluntary unemployment

IOU money (E4)
Money in the form of a promise to pay based on the debt of a firm or an individual. Much of this money is in the form of bank deposits.

See also: bill of exchange; commercial paper

iron law of wages (B1, J3)
The SUBSISTENCE theory of wages used by many CLASSICAL ECONOMISTS. It was argued that if workers are paid more than subsistence there will be an increase in population which, with a short time lag given that child labour was used, will increase the labour force, in turn pushing wages back to the subsistence level. Conversely, wages below the subsistence rate will reduce the population, cause excess demand for labour and push wage rates back up to subsistence. The law, in essence, described a long-run equilibrium wage rate. Adam SMITH challenged the law on the empirical grounds that food prices and wages often move in different directions. Growing real wages in the nineteenth century also refuted the law.

IS (E1, F1)
1 The equilibrium of investment and savings, usually expressed as one of the curves in the IS-LM diagram. An increase in government expenditure, through its MULTIPLIER effects, will cause the IS curve to shift outwards from the origin.
2 IMPORT SUBSTITUTION.

Isard, Walter, 1919– (B3)
US authority on regional science, of German descent, who was educated at Temple and Harvard Universities and taught at Harvard, Philadelphia (1956–79) and Cornell Universities. His revival of LOCATION THEORY led to his founding regional science

which placed location theory in the wider economic context of GENERAL EQUILIBRIUM theory by using INPUT–OUTPUT ANALYSIS and REGIONAL MULTIPLIERS and linked it to other social sciences.

See also: regional economics

References

Isard, W. (1956) *Location and Space Economy*, Cambridge, MA: MIT Press.
—— (1971) *Methods of Regional Analysis*, Cambridge, MA: MIT Press.
Isard, W. and Langford, T.W. (1971) *Regional Input-Output Study: Recollections, Reflections and Diverse Notes on the Philadelphia Experience*, Cambridge, MA: MIT Press.

Islamic banking (G2)

A distinctive type of banking which attempts to avoid the Koranic prohibitions concerning *riba* (usury). Usury was objected to both for exploiting the poor who needed to borrow and for giving a reward unrelated to productive effort. Later medieval Islamic thinkers devised intricate *hiyal* (stratagems) to circumvent this problem. Today, Islamic banks impose service charges, instead of interest, on bank loans; these charges, based on a percentage of the value of the loan, resemble interest. Also, money lenders often lend in kind, e.g. purchasing a piece of equipment and then leasing it to the borrower who pays instalments which, in total, are in excess of the original purchase price.

There have been Arab-owned banks since the 1920s, the period in which the Banque Misr of Egypt and the Arab Bank of Palestine were founded. After the oil-price rise of 1973–4, new banks operating according to strict Islamic principles have been established. The largest are in Saudi Arabia: the Islamic Development Bank founded in 1975 as a specialist development assistance agency not dealing with the general public, the Al-Baraka Group founded in 1982 and the Al-Rajhi Company founded in 1985. To allow *riba*-free participation in Western markets, Dar al-

Maal al-Islami, the House of Islamic Funds, was founded in Geneva in 1981: although it has some short-term funds in cash and commodities, it invests chiefly in property and equities.

The expansion of Islamic banks into competition with traditional banking is difficult as they cannot be accepted as commercial banks in Western countries until they have Western government securities as part of their assets; their lack of official status prevents them from soliciting for deposits from the public. Although Islamic banks are often regarded as a new development in banking, Islamic authors argue that many banking principles, including the use of bank deposits and cheques, have been practised from the early days of Islam.

References

Abdeen, A.N. and Shook, D.N. (1984) *The Saudi Financial System in the Context of Western and Islamic Finance*, Chichester: Wiley.
Mills, P.S. and Presley, J.R. (1999) *Islamic finance: theory and practice*, New York: St Martin's Press; London: Macmillan.
Rodinson, M. (1974) *Islam and Capitalism*, London: Allen Lane.
Saleh, N.A. (1986) *Unlawful Gain and Legitimate Profit in Islamic Law: Riba, Gharar and Islamic Bartering*, Cambridge: Cambridge University Press.
Wilson, R. (1983) *Banking and Finance in the Arab Middle East*, London: Macmillan.

Islamic economics (B0)

A study of the economic teachings of Islam and an Islamic critique of modern Western economic theory and policy. Its central themes include the idea that property is to be held in trust for God, that economic activity should have social objectives, that the return to capital should only be a reward for risk taking and that the quality aspects of economic growth should be considered. There is a distinctive Islamic contribution to taxation, comparative economic systems, co-operatives, income distribution, business cycles, business finance and poverty. Although much of Islamic economics is capitalistic in tone, there is also some overlap with socialism. This literature is published in Arabic, Urdu and the major European languages.

References

Rahman, A. (1975, 1976) *Economic doctrines of Islam*, Lahore: Islamic Publications.

Islamic fiscal policy (H2)

The application of the principles of the Koran, particularly the avoidance of usury, to the financing of a government's expenditure. Islamic governments aim to balance their budgets to avoid borrowing; if borrowing is needed, government securities can be issued at less than their redemption value as a means of disguising an interest payment. Also, there are severe problems in raising revenue as purchase tax exploits the needy and incomes are too low to have a broad-based income tax. Even the special tax under Islamic law, the 'zakat', which is an annual wealth tax, can only be used to finance social purposes, mainly at the local level.

island (J2, J4)

A location of jobs or employers such that at a point in time firms cannot move but workers can. On each island, the competitive labour market there sets wages equal to the MARGINAL PRODUCT OF LABOUR on that island; as productivity differs from island to island, so do wage offers. Workers engage in job search to find islands with better wages.

See also: job search

References

Lucas, R.E., Jr and Prescott, E.C. (1974) 'Equilibrium search and unemployment', *Journal of Economic Theory* 7: 188–209.

IS–LM–BP model (E1)

The IS-LM MODEL with the addition of a balance of payments curve to indicate both internal and external equilibrium for

an economy. A version of the MUNDELL-FLEMING MODEL.

IS–LM curves (E1)

Investment–savings and liquidity–money curves. An apparatus invented by HICKS (who originally called them IS and LL curves) and HANSEN to synthesize the Keynesian macroeconomic system; Hicks was to regret its excessive use by other economists. The IS curve, plotting the rate of interest i against national income Y, joins together all combinations of i and Y for which $I = S$, shows equilibrium in the goods market; the LM curve, plotted on the same axes, shows equilibrium in the money market as at each point on the curve the demand for money is equal to its supply. KEYNESIANS believe that the IS curve is steep, with the consequence that fiscal policy is more powerful than MONETARY POLICY; MONETARISTS suggest a steep LM curve with CROWDING OUT the consequence of fiscal expansion (i increases; Y is unchanged).

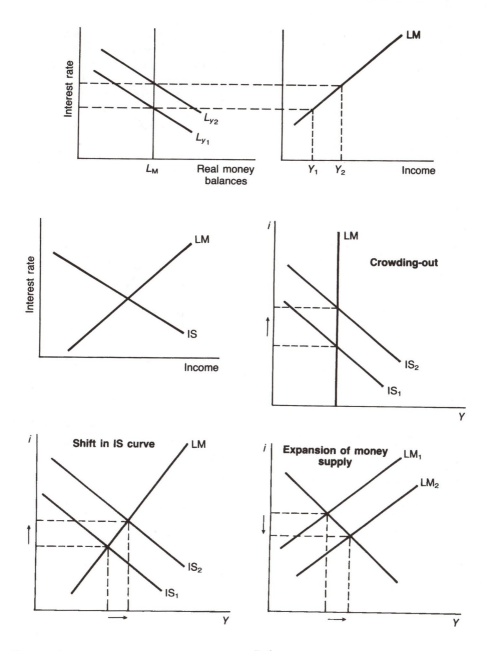

Changes in government expenditure shift the IS curve and raise or lower national income and the interest rate; an expansion of the money supply effects a shift in the LM curve (from LM_1 to LM_2 say) and reduces interest rates but increases income.

References

Hicks, J.R. (1937) 'Mr Keynes and the "Classics": a suggested interpretation', *Econometrica* 5: 147–59.
Young, W. (1987) *Interpreting Mr Keynes*, Cambridge: Polity Press.

isocost (D0)
A straight line showing different combinations of two factors of production for the same cost. The slope of the line will alter if the relative prices of the factors change.

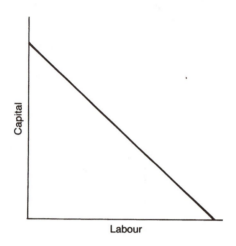

isolated market equilibrium (D0)
A market for one good or one service in which the quantity demanded equals the quantity supplied.

See also: general market equilibrium

isolated state (R1)
Von THUNEN's model of a closed economy which showed optimum locations for agricultural activities.

See also: location theory

isoproduct (D0) *see* isoquant

isoquant (D2)
A curve showing different minimum combinations of two factors of production producing the same level of output; also known as an isoproduct curve. In the figure each isoquant shows the output which results from different combinations of two inputs, capital and labour: C is the isoquant for complements; S is the isoquant for substitutes; P is the isoquant for perfect substitutes.

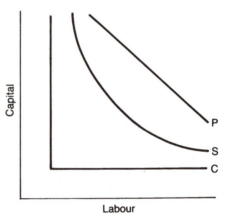

Israel–US Trade Free Trade Area (F1)
Founded in 1985 to create free trade between the two countries.

issuing house (G2)
A financial institution concerned with arranging the issue of new shares in accordance with the current regulations of the International Stock Exchange.

See also: underwriter

J

Jackson Amendment (F1)
An amendment to US trade law proposed in 1975 by Senator Jackson: it denies MOST FAVOURED NATION status to countries not permitting free emigration.

Jamaica Agreement (F3)
An agreement made by members of the INTERNATIONAL MONETARY FUND in 1974 whereby the IMF sold one-third of its gold stock, making the profits of the sale the basis of a special trust fund which provides balance of payments assistance on soft terms to the poorest countries.

See also: soft loan

Japanese auction (D0)
An ENGLISH AUCTION that does not accept any new bidders after the bidding starts. The bidders must indicate whether they want to continue to bid, or drop out.

Japanese capitalism (P1)
A set of economic institutions founded during the US occupation of the late 1940s. There are also a strong amount of government intervention in industry, paternalism in the labour market and high levels of personal savings.

Japanese socialism (P2)
A managed form of CAPITALISM with regulations to restrict new entrants to industries and to protect weak firms and industries. Also there is a welfare state promoting social equity, a financial sector under the control of the Ministry of Finance, and employment practices based on the socialist principles of lifetime employment and seniority systems.

References
Takeuchi, Y. (1998) 'Japan's transition from socialism to capitalism', *The Japanese Economy* 26: 3–24.

Japanese tax system (H2)
A tax system after 1945 with many of the characteristics of the US tax system, i.e. the use of income tax as a major source of revenue, no VALUE-ADDED TAX and with most collection of taxes by central government with local government reliant on central government grants. Japan's income tax was first introduced in 1887, assuming its modern form in 1940. The present system was to a large extent designed by the SHOUP MISSION.

References
Ishi, H. (1989) *The Japanese Tax System*, Oxford: Clarendon Press.
Tax Advisory Commission (1960 onwards) *Proposals* (in Japanese).

jawbone (E6)
Attempting to achieve voluntarily by persuasion the goals of MONETARY or INCOMES POLICIES as an alternative to statutory controls. Also known as MORAL SUASION.

J-curve (F3)
A curve showing the effects of the

DEVALUATION of a currency with a fixed exchange rate on the BALANCE OF PAYMENTS current account. It is based on the observation that initially after devaluation, before there can be responses to the changed import and export prices, the total cost of imports will be higher and the total value of exports lower. An appreciation of a currency, conversely, will produce an inverted J-curve. The curve plots the balance of payments current account balance against time (in the figure, t_d is the date at which devaluation occurs).

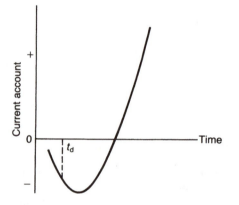

Jevons, William Stanley, 1835–82 (B3)

A leader of the MARGINALIST School who was educated at the Mechanics Institute High School, Liverpool, and University College, London. His university studies began with chemistry and mathematics and were interrupted by four years in Australia as assayer to the Sydney Mint before he returned to study political economy and logic. In Australia, his first researches were into climate and the effects of railways on land values and rent; also there he acquired the habit of 'pricking off curves' on squared paper to study fluctuations in economic time series. He held academic posts at Owen's College, Manchester, and Queen's College, Liverpool, before becoming professor of political economy at University College, London from 1876 to 1881. He drowned in 1882.

His principal works were *A Serious Fall in the Value of Gold Ascertained and its Social Effects Set Forth* (1863) which introduced a new method of measuring price changes, *The Coal Question: An Inquiry Concerning the Progress of the Nation and the Probable Exhaustion of the Coalmines* (1865) which caused a national scare and his *Theory of Political Economy* (1871) which was regarded by Keynes as 'the first modern book on economics'. Jevons's theory of exchange was the focal point of his *Theory*: by switching from cost to subjective UTILITY as the basis of value he was able to begin the precise theorizing which constitutes NEOCLASSICAL microeconomics. His theory of the RATE OF INTEREST made a contribution to the development of marginal productivity theory. His influence on the development of economics in England was profound.

See also: marginalism; Menger; Walras

References

Collison Black, R.D. and Konckamp, R. (eds) (1972) *Papers and Correspondence of William Stanley Jevons*, Vols 1–7, London and Basingstoke: Macmillan.
Schabas, M. (1990) *A World Ruled by Number: William Stanley Jevons and the Rise of Mathematical Economics*, Princeton, NJ: Princeton University Press.
Stigler, G.J. (1946) *Theories of Production and Distribution: The Formative Period*, ch. 11, New York: Macmillan.

job acceptance schedule (J6)

The relationship between a real wage rate and the number of persons prepared to accept jobs. Changes in the ratio of real wages to unemployment benefit can cause shifts in this schedule.

See also: voluntary unemployment

jobber (G1)

A specialized dealer on UK stock exchanges who, from 1908 until 1986, bought and sold stocks and shares from stockbrokers, but not from the general investing public. This system of separating functions was peculiar to the UK and was supported on the grounds that it separated the risk of unsold stock (jobber's risk) from the risk of unpaid accounts (broker's risk). This distinctive arrangement of the London market was replaced by a system of MARKET-MAKERS.

See also: Big Bang

job centre (J6)
UK advice centre provided by the government to assist in job search by providing information on vacancies. Originally they were intended to separate the two principal functions of the former employment exchanges: the payment of unemployment benefit and the placement of the unemployed with employers notifying vacancies. It was hoped that an improved public employment service would make it more attractive to employers and would reduce the amount of frictional unemployment in the economy. Re-merger of them with benefit offices occurred in 1987.

job cluster (J4)
The occupations of an INTERNAL LABOUR MARKET which are subject to the same wage determination process because of custom, technology or an administrative process. For each cluster, there is a key rate.

job control unionism (J5)
A form of TRADE (LABOR) UNIONISM which insists on strict DEMARCATION for each job and a particular wage rate being linked to a highly defined job. There are examples of this in both the US and UK labour markets.

See also: featherbedding

job destruction (J6)
Reduction in the labour force of a firm, industry, region or country. Declining markets and technical change are the principal determinants of these job losses.

job displacement (J6)
An individual person's loss of a job as the result of the closure of the whole or part of a firm.

job evaluation (J2)
A hierarchical ordering of a set of jobs according to their characteristics or content.

job generation (J6)
The expansion of employment in either the public or private sector. In the former, regional and other policies are used to create jobs; in the latter, new jobs are preceded by an expansion in a market.

job hopping (J5)
Movement from job to job to acquire employment information, e.g. about the characteristics of employers, of other workers, of working conditions. This is a common practice of young workers in times of low unemployment.

See also: search unemployment

job lock (J3)
Being kept in a particular employment because the alternative employment does not have the same range of benefits, especially health insurance.

See also: golden handcuffs

jobs-based analysis (J0)
A mixed approach to the study of work, wages and labour markets using a cluster of theories, including TOURNAMENT MODELS, hierarchies, HEDONIC WAGE analysis, job investment, insurance and work sharing.

References
Lazear, E.P. (1995) 'A jobs-based analysis of labor markets', *American Economic Review* 85: 260–5.

job search (J6)
All the activities by employers and workers to fill vacant jobs. Advertisements, informal recommendations, head-hunting by specialized personnel agencies and publicly financed employment agencies are the principal channels used.

See also: search cost; search unemployment

job security (J2)
Guaranteed tenure of a job. This TRADE (LABOR) UNION goal is realizable in only certain types of employment, particularly public sector white-collar jobs and employment in major oligopolistic firms. The Japanese system of PERMANENT EMPLOYMENT was a leading case, although even that was less prevalent than imagined by foreign observers.

See also: flexible labour market; white-collar worker

job seeker's allowance (J6)
A welfare payment to an unemployed person. It can be related to income and savings, or to accumulated contributions. This was introduced in the UK in October 1996 in succession to unemployment benefit and income support. It is so called because the qualification for being an unemployed member of the labour force, rather than a non-participant, is job search activity.

job separation (J6)
A voluntary or involuntary termination of a person's employment.

job sharing (J2)
The splitting of full-time jobs so that each job is performed by two persons. This type of scheme is primarily proposed as a means of reducing unemployment by converting full-time jobs into part-time jobs. The occupations for which this has been tried include teaching and social work. It is always feared that sharing will lead to an increase in total labour costs, especially social security contributions, recruitment and training costs. However, shorter hours raise productivity as the division of jobs reduces the boredom which comes from long hours spent on the same task.

Johnson, Harry Gordon, 1923–79 (B3)
A prolific Canadian economist, who in his bustling life wrote 41 books and pamphlets and 526 learned articles and edited 5 leading journals, covering the whole range of economics. He was educated at the Universities of Toronto, Cambridge and Harvard. In his industrious career, he was a fellow of King's College, Cambridge, from 1949 to 1956, professor of economics at Manchester from 1956 to 1959, and professor at Chicago from 1959 to 1977, combining that chair with other academic posts, particularly one at the London School of Economics from 1966 to 1974 which he relinquished, in a blaze of publicity, because of UK taxation. A central interest of his career was international economics, to which he often returned, as well as monetary theory, development economics and the major economic policy issues of the day. His much-used pen attacked vulgar applications of Keynesianism and collectivism.

References
Johnson, H.G. (1958) *International Trade and Economic Growth: Studies in Pure Theory*, London: Allen & Unwin.
—— (1967) *Economic Policies towards Less Developed Countries*, London: Allen & Unwin.
—— (1969) *Essays in Monetary Economics*, 2nd edn, London: Allen & Unwin.
—— (1971) *Aspects of the Theory of Tariffs*, London: Gray-Mills.
—— (1972) *Macroeconomics and Monetary Theory*, London: Allen & Unwin.

joint cost (D0)
The cost of producing two or more goods or services which arise from the same inputs. Joint costs are not divisible into the separate costs for each good or service. Many managerial and research costs are of this nature. John Stuart MILL in his *Principles of Political Economy*, Book III, ch. 16, laid down the rule that the sum of the prices of joint products must equal their joint cost. Today, joint costs are often arbitrarily allocated between products

using an indirect measure, e.g. an analysis of the time of a manager.

See also: indivisibility

joint demand (D1)
The demand for COMPLEMENTS, e.g. for computers and software, which is such that an increase in the demand for one leads to an increase in the demand for the dependent complement. There is often an inverse relationship between the price of one good and the demand for its complement, e.g. cheaper cameras encourage an increase in the demand for photographic supplies, because consumers allocate so much of their incomes to a particular activity which requires several related goods to pursue it.

See also: cross price elasticity of demand

joint equity venture company (L2)
A firm jointly owned by a public authority or government and a private company. This is a popular way for foreign companies to invest in countries with substantial public sectors or state planning. Sometimes the company only exists as long as it takes to undertake a major project, e.g. the building of a bridge.

See also: venture capital

joint products (D2)
Products which are the inseparable consequence of a single production process, e.g. cattle farming yields milk, meat and hides, coal mining produces coal, coke, gas and a variety of chemicals. In many cases, the rate of production for each of the products is the same.

joint stock company (L2)
A firm permitted under company legislation to be a distinct legal personality with its members subscribing shares of the capital and having limited liability. By the mid-nineteenth century in the UK the need for large amounts of capital led to

such companies gradually replacing partnerships in many industries,

joint venture (L2)
The creation of a new firm by at least two private or public enterprises for the purpose of carrying out a particular project. This type of organization made possible the gradual introduction of private capital into communist countries, e.g. Yugoslavia and China.

See also: joint equity venture company

References
Morris, R.M. (1987) *Joint Ventures: An Accounting Tax and Administrative Guide*, New York: Wiley.

Jones Act 1920 (L5, R4)
US federal CABOTAGE statute, 'The Maritime Marine Act', which required sea transportation of cargo and passengers between US ports to be in ships US built, US owned and US crewed. Although there is some political support for this form of protectionism, the Act is increasingly obsolete as so many goods are shipped under foreign flags.

See also: Navigation Acts

J-shaped frequency curve (C1)
A frequency curve with a positive slope.

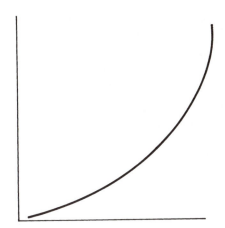

Jubilee 2000 (F3, O0)

An international movement in sixty-five countries to cancel by the end of 2000 the unpayable debts of developing countries who jointly had a population of one billion. The purpose of this crusade was to allow poor countries to divert expenditure on servicing debts into spending on health and education. This crusade was inspired by the ancient Jewish idea of 'jubilee', a year of emancipation and restoration occurring every fifty years. It started with a resolution in 1990 of the All African Council of Churches to cancel Africa's debts.

Juglar cycle (E3)

A cycle in economic activity lasting seven to eleven years. It was first identified by Clement Juglar (1819–1905) in 1862. He noticed such cycles in prices, interest rates and central bank balances.

See also: Kitchin cycle; Kondratieff cycle; Kuznets cycle

References

Juglar, C. (1862) *Les Crises Commerciales et leur Retour Périodique en France, en Angleterre et aux Etats Unis*, English trans. by W. Thorn from the 3rd edn, 1916 (reprinted Farnborough: Gregg Press, 1968).

jump (G1)

A sudden and unexpected fall, or even crash, in a financial market which cannot be hedged against.

junior debt (G0)

A loan of lower rank than SENIOR DEBT in the event of a company defaulting.

junk bond (G0)

High-yielding, high-risk bonds rated below the investment grades assigned by the top US bond CREDIT RATING agencies Standard & Poor and Moody's. Although the risk of default is great, their high yield has made them very popular. Also, they have provided a vehicle for entrepreneurs to take over slumbering corporations. Junk bonds first made their appearance in the USA in the 1920s; by 1990 over $200 billion in 1,000 issues of these securities were outstanding. Such bonds have enabled non-blue-chip US corporations to raise very large sums of money, originally through the principal broker Drexel Burnham Lambert, which handled half of such new issues until its collapse in 1990. Investors willing to buy them included specialized MUTUAL FUNDS, the US government, insurance companies and SAVINGS AND LOANS ASSOCIATIONS. An effect of the junk bond has been to draw to the attention of COMMERCIAL BANKS the need for more finance for small firms.

See also: blue chip

References

Rubin, S.M. (1990) *Junk Bonds: After the Crises*, London: Euromoney.

Yago, G. (1991) *Junk Bonds: How High Securities Restructured Corporate Finance*, New York: Oxford University Press.

junk of junk status (G1)

Low grade of a bond.

Jurgensen Report (E5, F3)

A report to the World Economic Summit in Williamsburg, Virginia, in 1983 on central bank intervention in currency markets.

just-in-time production (D2)

A method of reducing stocks by producing goods only when they are wanted. This approach to the scheduling of production reduces the costs of holding inventories/stocks and increases the pace of production. It is extensively used in Japan and is increasingly being followed by UK manufacturers.

just price (D0)

The price giving labourers a just recompense and in the estimation of buyers and sellers, or of magistrates with price-fixing powers, is fair. This approach to price theory was central to the economic thinking of AQUINAS and his contemporaries. It contains elements of both the LABOUR THEORY OF VALUE and the concept of UTILITY.

References

Demant, V.A. (ed.) (1930) *The Just Price: An Outline of the Mediaeval Doctrine and an Examination of its Possible Equivalent Today*, London: Student Christian Movement.

Hollander, S. (1965) 'On the interpretation of the just price', *Kyklos* 18: 615–34.

just wage (J3)

The wage which reflects a worker's contribution to society. AQUINAS and his scholastic contemporaries expounded this ethical view of wages. Today, Islamic scholars argue that the just wage is unrelated to time spent as time is valueless. Also, modern writers on WAGE DIFFERENTIALS and INCOMES POLICIES have implicitly used concepts of fairness and justice.

References

Fogarty, M. (1961) *The Just Wage*, London: G. Chapman.

K

Kahn, Richard Ferdinand, 1905–89 (B3)
Famous in the development of Keynesian economics for his influential article on the employment MULTIPLIER. Educated at King's College, Cambridge, where he remained a fellow from 1929 to his death; professor of economics from 1951 to 1972. His *Making of Keynes' General Theory* (1984) illuminated the development of Keynes's thought from 1923 to 1936. He was opposed to modern NEOCLASSICAL ECONOMICS in the USA and MONETARISM.

Kaldor–Hicks compensation principle (D6)
A compensation test of WELFARE ECONOMICS stating that there will be a net gain in SOCIAL WELFARE if those who have welfare gains can both compensate losers and still have a net gain for themselves.

References
Hicks, J.R. (1939) 'Foundations of welfare economics', *Economic Journal* 49: 696–712.
Kaldor, N. (1939) 'Welfare propositions of economics and interpersonal comparisons of utility', *Economic Journal* 49: 549–52.

Kaldor, Nicholas, 1908–86 (B3)
A Hungarian economist, at school in Budapest and at university in Berlin and at the London School of Economics where he was subsequently a lecturer and reader from 1932 to 1947. He served as Director of the Research and Planning Division of the UN Economic Commission for Europe from 1947 to 1949, after which he was a fellow of King's College, Cambridge until 1986, rising to a chair of economics which he held from 1966 to 1975. He was awarded a peerage in 1974.

He wrote prolifically on taxation, growth and distribution. He was a precocious Keynesian who turned to growth theory and the study of increasing returns, emphasizing the importance of the manufacturing sector as the impetus to the expansion of the economy. His long career as a tax adviser to the UK, Indian and various Third World governments produced a range of tax proposals, including the SELECTIVE EMPLOYMENT TAX which was in force in the UK from 1966 to 1970. He served as Special Adviser to the UK Chancellor of the Exchequer in 1964-8 and 1974-6. His clear disapproval of the policies of THATCHERISM was evident in his *The Scourge of Monetarism* (1982).

References
Kaldor, N. (1978–80) *Collected Economic Essays*, London: Duckworth.
Thirlwall, A.P. (1987) *Nicholas Kaldor*, Brighton: Wheatsheaf.

Kaldor's laws (L6, O4)
The laws relating to economic growth set out by KALDOR in his Cambridge inaugural lecture of 1966. These three laws state that there is a strong relationship between the growth of manufacturing output and the

growth of total output, that the growth of manufacturing output is a powerful cause of the growth of the productivity of manufacturing industry and that a faster rate of growth of manufacturing output is positively related to the rate of industrial labour mobility from non-manufacturing to manufacturing industry.

See also: Verdoorn's law

References

Thirlwall, A.P. (1987) *Nicholas Kaldor*, ch. 7, Brighton: Wheatsheaf.

Kalecki, Michal, 1899–1970 (B3)

A Polish economist who independently discovered many of the key concepts of Keynesian theory. After studying engineering at the Polytechnics of Warsaw and Gdansk, he became a freelance economic journalist and analyst at the Polish Research Institute for Business Cycles and Prices from 1929 to 1937. At the Oxford Institute of Statistics, from 1940 to 1955, he worked on wartime rationing schemes and refined his study of economic dynamics and cycles. From 1955 to 1970 he was economic adviser to the Polish government and then Polish representative at the United Nations. His major contribution to macroeconomics was late in being acknowledged (the translation from Polish was delayed) despite Joan ROBINSON's frequent praise. With MARX as his starting point, he developed a long-run model of equilibrium growth integrating it with his business cycle theory. He believed that FULL EMPLOYMENT was a short-lived phenomenon. He has been a great inspiration for the POST-KEYNESIANS. He provided an account of the microfoundations for macroeconomics in his theory of MARK-UP pricing (the mark-up reflecting the relative power of an oligopolistic firm in an industry). This pricing theory is then applied to both the distribution and level of the national income as the prices of oligopolists will have a crucial effect on cyclical movements of national output. His model of the economy combines

Marx's scheme of REPRODUCTION and the MULTIPLIER.

References

Feiwel, G.R. (1975) *The Intellectual Capital of Michal Kalecki*, Knoxville, TN: University of Tennessee Press.

Kalecki, M. (1954) *Theory of Economic Dynamics: An Essay on Cyclical and Long-run Changes in the Capitalist Economy*, London: Allen & Unwin.

—— (1969) *Introduction to the Theory of Growth in a Socialist Economy*, trans. from 2nd Polish edn by Z. Sadowski, Oxford: Basil Blackwell.

—— (1987) *Selected Essays on Economic Planning*, Cambridge: Cambridge University Press.

Osiatinsky, J. (1990 onwards) *The Collected Works of M. Kalecki*, Oxford: Oxford University Press.

Sawyer, M.C. (1985) *The Economics of Michal Kalecki*, Basingstoke: Macmillan.

Kalman filter (C1)

A recursive procedure used for calculating the least squares method.

Kantorovich, Leonid Vitalievich, 1912– (B3)

Russian mathematician and economist, the principal originator of LINEAR PROGRAMMING. After graduating in mathematics from Leningrad University in 1930, he taught in Leningrad before becoming professor at the University of Leningrad in 1934. From 1939 he concerned himself with major applications of mathematics to economics. His many achievements merited the Lenin Prize in 1965 and, with KOOPMANS, the NOBEL PRIZE FOR ECONOMICS in 1975. Much of his work was concerned with improving socialist economic planning, recommending decentralization and the use of shadow pricing; he has lived to see many of his recommendations incorporated into Soviet planning reforms.

References

Kantorovich, L.V. (1960) 'Mathematical methods of organizing and planning production', *Management Science* 6: 363–422.

—— (1965) *The Best Use of Economic Resources*, trans. P.F. Knightsfield, Oxford and New York: Pergamon.

Ward, B. (1960) 'Kantorovich on economic calculation', *Journal of Political Economy* 68: 545–56.

kappa (G1)
The ratio of the change in the price of an OPTION to a 1 per cent change in the expected price volatility.

Katona effect (E2)
The effect of creeping inflation on saving. Katona argued that in such inflationary times there would still be expectations of rising real incomes so individuals would continue to invest in fixed interest securities: the rate of inflation would be sufficiently low for money still to be regarded as 'safe'. In times of runaway inflation, there would be scare buying and hoarding of goods.

References

Katona, G. (1960) *The Powerful Consumer: Psychological Studies of the American Economy*, ch. 12, New York: McGraw-Hill.

Keidanven (J5)
Federation of Economic Organizations (Japan).

keiretsu (L1)
A confederation of loosely related Japanese companies based on having a common banker or supply network.

See also: zaibatsu

Kemp–Wan theorem (F1)
A study of the welfare gains from the formation of CUSTOMS UNIONS. These unions are not harmful to any country if there is a costless redistribution of trade between partners of a union after its formation. Also the COMMON EXTERNAL TARIFF has to be at an appropriate level.

References

Richardson, M. (1995) 'On the interpretation of the Kemp-Wan theorem', *Oxford Economic Papers* 47: 696–703.

Kennedy Round (F1)
A set of tariff reductions arranged under the auspices of the GATT conducted from 1964 to 1967. This sixth round of multilateral trade negotiations reduced tariff rates by up to 50 per cent across the board, except for items such as steel, textiles, clothing and footwear where there were considerable employment implications. President J.F. Kennedy was authorized to make this reduction under the US Trade Expansion Act of 1962.

See also: Dillon Round; Tokyo Round; Uruguay Round

kerb market (G1)
The unofficial trading of a stock market outside the building after the exchange has closed for the day.

See also: after-hours dealing

key currency (E5, F3)
A major international medium of exchange. A country whose currency is in great demand because of being a key currency has the advantage of being able to finance its balance of payments deficits easily, as the USA has found since 1951.

See also: sterling area

Keynes effect (E3)
The indirect effect on the demand for commodities resulting from a change in the general price level. This price level will affect the price of bonds and hence interest rates, the level of net investment and so the demand for commodities. A shift in the LM curve shows that this effect is in operation.

References

Ackley, G. (1951) 'The wealth-saving relationship', *Journal of Political Economy* 59: 154–61.

Keynes expectations (E0)
Expectations in the short term about the price a producer expects to get for his or her product and in the long term about the returns to extra capital expenditure. The latter, crucial to his concept of the

MARGINAL EFFICIENCY OF CAPITAL, was regarded by Keynes as a central innovation of his *General Theory*. Unlike other theories of expectations, the concept is not used as a central element in a theory of inflation.

Keynesian cross diagram (E1)

A simple macroeconomic model of the national ECONOMY derived from Keynes's *General Theory* which can be used to expound the theory of aggregate demand and demonstrate the effects of fiscal policy and the MULTIPLIER. Planned expenditure is plotted against national output to indicate various levels of national output for which the economy can be in equilibrium or disequilibrium. It cannot cope with the problems of inflation and monetary policy, unlike IS–LM curves.

See also: equilibrium

Keynesian economics (E0)

A distillation of the ideas in Keynes's *General Theory* into a macroeconomic theory and policy consisting principally of a model of aggregate income and expenditure using IS–LM curves, an emphasis on the importance of the investment MULTIPLIER, an assertion that the LIQUIDITY preference schedule is stable in the long run and unaffected by the actions of CENTRAL BANKS, and an insistence on the major importance of fiscal policy so that money and the rate of interest are of little importance to the management of the economy. Keynesian policy is most popularly regarded as the use of national budget deficits to maintain full employment. Although it was frequently praised in the 1950s and 1960s, it is doubtful whether many Western governments have pursued such policies for sustained periods of time. Heller cites the 1964 US tax cut of the Johnson Administration that he claims created 7 million jobs, doubled profits and increased gross domestic product by one-third. Other popular examples, e.g. the New Deal, have subsequently been challenged as only ephemeral exercises in applied Keynesianism. The Major government in the UK, 1992–7, is a more recent case of deficit spending. Just as MARX is reputed to have said 'Je ne suis pas une marxiste', Keynes would have been an uneasy member of the Keynesian School.

References

Coddington, A. (1976) 'Keynesian economics: the search for first principles', *Journal of Economic Literature* 14: 1258–73.

Hall, P.A. (ed.) (1989) *The Political Power of Economic Ideas: Keynesianism across Nations*, Princeton, NJ: Princeton University Press.

Hamond, O.F. and Smithin, J.N. (eds) (1988) *Keynes and Public Policy After Fifty Years*, Aldershot: Edward Elgar; New York: New York University Press.

Hicks, J. (1974) *The Crisis in Keynesian Economics*, Oxford: Basil Blackwell.

Hutton, W. (1986) *The Revolution that Never Was: An Assessment of Keynesian Economics*, London: Longman.

Leijonhufvud, A. (1968) *On Keynesian Economics and the Economics of Keynes*, New York: Oxford University Press.

Patinkin, D. and Clarke Leith, J. (1977) *Keynes, Cambridge and the General Theory*, London: Macmillan.

Wattel, H.L. (ed.) (1986) *The Policy Consequences of John Maynard Keynes*, Basingstoke and London: Macmillan.

Keynesian equilibrium (E0)

A short-term equilibrium in a static model of an economy which is not necessarily a FULL-EMPLOYMENT equilibrium.

Keynes, John Maynard, 1883–1946 (B3)

The most influential Western economist of the twentieth century. With the benefit of an academic background (his father John Neville Keynes wrote an important book on economic methodology before becoming a university administrator), a brilliant degree in mathematics and tuition from MARSHALL in economics, he passed second in the Civil Service examinations. He worked in the India Office from 1906 to 1908, before returning to lecture in economics at Cambridge from 1908 to 1920, and was a fellow of King's College, Cambridge, until his death. Despite his major economic writing and editorship of the *Economic Journal* (1911–45), the leading UK economics journal, he had time to advise the Treasury in two world wars, serve on the Royal Commission on Indian Finance and Currency (1913–14), the Macmillan Committee on Finance and Industry (1929–31) and the Economic Advisory Council (1930–39), chair an insurance company, be a patron of the arts, be a leading bibliophile and write extensively and entertainingly on many aspects of public affairs.

His early works were not confined to economic theory, although he wrote a monograph on Indian currency. His attack on the Versailles Peace Treaty in *The Economic Consequences of the Peace* (1919) showed great skill for attacking the core of bad policy; his *A Treatise on Probability* (1921) indicated that, like his Bloomsbury Group friends, he was capable of tackling a tough philosophical issue.

In a series of three books, he groped towards a theory which was to dominate Western macroeconomics for over thirty years. His trilogy *A Tract on Monetary Reform* (1923), *Treatise on Money* (1930) and supremely *The General Theory of Employment, Interest and Money* (1936) contain the major Keynesian contribution to economics. Connected together are theories of the CONSUMPTION FUNCTION, AGGREGATE DEMAND, the MULTIPLIER, the MARGINAL EFFICIENCY OF CAPITAL, LIQUIDITY PREFERENCE and EXPECTATIONS. Keynes had, he believed, dealt a mortal blow to the complacent depression-inducing economics of CLASSICAL ECONOMICS. Soon after his 1936 triumph his health deteriorated; but he was able to advise on the financing of the war and the setting up of a new international economic order (BRETTON WOODS) to avoid the crises of the interwar period. Although he was a member of the Liberal Party and described by Lenin as 'a bourgeois of the first water', he recommended the extinction of the RENTIER class and the socialization of investment. His parents attended his funeral.

See also: Cambridge Circus

References

Harrod, R.F. (1951) *The Life of John Maynard Keynes*, London: Macmillan.

Johnson, E. and Moggridge, D. (eds) (1971–87) *The Collected Writings of John Maynard Keynes*, 30 vols, London and New York: Macmillan.

Keynes, M. (ed.) (1975) *Essays on John Maynard Keynes*, London and New York: Cambridge University Press.

Lawson, T. and Pesaran, H. (eds) (1985) *Keynes's Economics: Methodological Issues*, London: Croom Helm.

Skidelsky, R. (1983, 1990, 2000) *John Maynard Keynes*, 3 vols, London: Macmillan.

Wood, J.C. (1963) *Critical Assessments of John Maynard Keynes*, London: Croom Helm.

Keynes Plan (F3) *see* International Clearing Union

Keynes's *General Theory* (E0)
The General Theory of Employment, Interest and Money, first published in 1936, is often regarded as the most influential economics book to have been written in the twentieth century. It begins with an attack on the postulates of CLASSICAL ECONOMICS and an assertion of the principle of EFFECTIVE DEMAND, lists definitions and ideas, and then discusses the propensity to consume, the inducement to invest, money wages and prices before an epilogue relating the *General Theory* to the TRADE CYCLE, MERCANTILISM and future social philosophy. Keynes accepted the summary of the *General Theory* made by Harrod in a letter of 30 August 1935: 'Your view, as I understand it is broadly this: – Volume of investment determined by marginal efficiency of capital schedule and the rate of interest. Rate of interest determined by the liquidity preference schedule and the quantity of money. Volume of employment determined by the

volume of investment and the multiplier. Value of the multiplier determined by the propensity to save.'

Admirers of Keynes have seen a development of the theory of the rate of interest and the crucial use of expectations in this grand theory, but critics, including LUCAS, have disliked the tone of the book and the decision of Keynes to work in units of money and labour alone to discuss economic aggregates; also, it has often been stated that the theory is not as 'general' as Keynes declared, that it is crippled by the use of the COMPARATIVE STATICS method and that it needed later growth theory to complement it.

References

Clarke, P. (1988) *The Keynesian Revolution in the Making, 1924–36*, Oxford: Clarendon Press.
Keynes, J.M. (1936) *The General Theory of Employment, Interest and Money*, London: Macmillan.
Vicarelli, F. (ed.) (1985) *Keynes's Relevance Today*, London: Macmillan.

key rate (J3)
A wage rate set by an INTERNAL LABOUR MARKET linking it to the EXTERNAL LABOUR MARKET. A key rate is associated with each JOB CLUSTER of a particular firm's internal market.

kibbutz (P3)
A type of egalitarian community set up in Israel. These largely agricultural societies were strictly controlled by oppressive rules to stamp out INDIVIDUALISM and pay was according to need. Kibbutzim were abandoned by many of their members towards the end of the twentieth century.

See also: utopia

kickback (J3) *see* sweetener

kinked demand curve (L1)
A curve shaped like a mansard roof describing the behaviour of non-collusive oligopolists. It is based on the idea that these oligopolists will follow each other in cases of price decreases but not when one

of them raises prices. Thus a demand curve results which consists of the joining together of two demand curves – the demand curve of the firm which raises its prices and the industry demand curve. The theory, although suspect empirically, has been used to account for price rigidity in oligopolistic markets. In the figure the demand curve *D* up to output OK is ELASTIC and so, if a firm raises its price, total revenue will fall; beyond output OK the demand curve of the firm, which is also the industry's demand curve, is inelastic and so a decrease in price will lower total revenue also (AR is average revenue, MR is marginal revenue and MC is marginal cost).

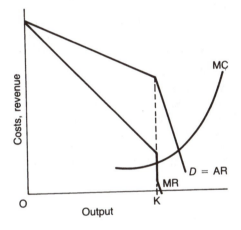

References

Hall, R.L. and Hitch, C.L (1939) 'Price theory and business behaviour', *Oxford Economic Papers* 2: 12–45.
Reid, G.C. (1975) *The Kinked Demand Curve Analysis of Oligopoly: Theory and Evidence*, Edinburgh: Edinburgh University Press.
Sweezy, P.M. (1939) 'Demand under conditions of oligopoly', *Journal of Political Economy* 47: 568–73.

kinked supply curve (D4)
A conjectural supply curve reflecting supply rigidities that arise from a discontinuity in the underlying cost function. A labour supply curve often begins with a horizontal

portion from the vertical axis and then rises sharply, especially if a MINIMUM WAGE law is in force. Kinks have also been observed in supply curves for regulated markets such as for rented property and in the long-run Keynesian aggregate supply curve.

Kitchin cycle (E3)

A cycle in general economic activity of three to five years' duration, mostly caused by changes in inventories (stocks). Kitchin first identified this type of fluctuation in 1923. When economists refer to the 'business cycle' they often mean this cycle.

See also: Juglar cycle; Kondratieff cycle; Kuznets cycle

References

Kitchin, J. (1923) 'Cycles and trends in economic factors', *Review of Economics and Statistics* 5: 10–16.

Klein, Lawrence R., 1920– (B3)

A celebrated US econometrician noted for his leadership of the research groups that produced influential large-scale econometric models of the UK and US economies in the period 1955–75. He is also well known as an interpreter of KEYNES. After a university education at Berkeley, California, and the Massachusetts Institute of Technology, he was at the Oxford Institute of Statistics from 1954 to 1958 and then professor at the University of Pennsylvania from 1958 to 1968. He was awarded the NOBEL PRIZE FOR ECONOMICS in 1980.

References

Klein, L.R. (1968) *The Keynesian Revolution*, 2nd edn, London: Macmillan.
—— (1983) *The Economics of Supply and Demand*, Oxford: Basil Blackwell.

Knight, Frank Hyneman, 1885–1973 (B3)

A founder of the Chicago School, being professor at Chicago from 1927 to 1955 after an education at Tennessee and Cornell Universities. His doctoral thesis, published as *Risk, Uncertainty and Profit*

(1921), is a classic of twentieth-century economics. It stated that profit 'arises out of the inherent, absolute unpredictability of things, out of the sheer brute fact that the results of human activity cannot be anticipated'. His social philosophy is expounded in *The Ethics of Competition* (1935). His other contributions include an onslaught on the Austrian measurement of capital in terms of a period of production, PIGOU's notion of SOCIAL COST and post-war social engineering.

Kondratieff cycle (E3)

A long wave in economic activity identified in 1926 from index numbers of commodity prices by N.D. Kondratieff, who was born in 1892 and died sometime after his arrest in 1930. This wave lasts forty-five to sixty years and is associated with cycles in investment in basic capital goods, e.g. transportation systems. Commodity prices rise in the upswing and fall in the downswing. For England, he noted troughs in 1789, 1849 and 1896 and peaks for 1814, 1873 and 1920; for France, peaks in 1873 and 1920 with a trough in 1896; for the USA, peaks in 1814, 1866 and 1920 with troughs in 1849 and 1896. (Each cycle is measured from peak to peak or trough to trough.) It is difficult to justify the use of price data in the manner of Kondratieff for later in the twentieth century as the ending of the GOLD STANDARD, the growth of OLIGOPOLY, major changes in AGGREGATE DEMAND and INDEXATION of wage contracts have changed the relationship between prices and general economic activity.

References

Kondratieff, N.D. (1935) 'The long waves in economic life', *Review of Economics and Statistics* 17: 105–15.
Mager, N.H. (1986) *The Kondratieff Waves*, New York and London: Praeger.
Solomou, S. (1987) *Phases of Economic Growth, 1850–1973: Kondratieff Waves and Kuznets Swings*, Cambridge: Cambridge University Press.

Koopmans, Tjalling Charles, 1910–84 (B3)

Dutch econometrician and economist who shared the NOBEL PRIZE FOR ECONOMICS with KANTOROVICH in 1975 for his work on LINEAR PROGRAMMING. Although educated in mathematics and physics at the Universities of Utrecht and Leiden, he turned to econometrics and economics when he worked at the League of Nations in Geneva from 1936 to 1940. Subsequently, he was at the COWLES COMMISSION, University of Chicago, from 1944 to 1955 and a professor at Chicago from 1946 to 1955 and then Yale from 1955 to 1984. His major contributions to activity analysis (operations research) were used to solve transport problems in the Second World War and during the 1948 Berlin airlift.

References

Koopmans, T.C. (1937) *Linear Regression of Economic Time Series*, Haarlem: De Aerren F. Bohn.
—— (1957) *Three Essays on the State of Economic Science*, New York: McGraw-Hill.

Kornai, Janos, 1928– (B3)

Hungarian mathematical economist, educated in science at the Hungarian Academy of Science and in economics at the Karl Marx University of Economics, Budapest. He has been professor of economics at the Hungarian Academy from 1955 and at Harvard from 1986. Apart from his mathematical modelling of the planning process, he has been famous for his attack on Walrasian GENERAL EQUILIBRIUM theory and for his demonstration of how quantity, not price, balances supply and demand. Later he considered the similarities between communist and capitalist economies. His ideas have had considerable influence in the West.

References

Kornai, J. (1959) *Overcentralization in Economic Administration: A Critical Analysis Based on Experience in Hungarian Light Industry*, London: Oxford University Press.

—— (1967) *Mathematical Planning of Structural Decisions*, Amsterdam: North-Holland.
—— (1971) *Anti-Equilibrium on Economic Systems Theory and the Tastes of Research*, Amsterdam: North-Holland.
—— (1980) *The Economics of Shortage*, Amsterdam: North-Holland.
—— (1982) *Growth, Shortage and Efficiency: A Microdynamic Model of the Socialist Economy*, Oxford: Basil Blackwell.

Krueger, Anne Osborn, 1934– (B3)

Educated at Oberlin College and the University of Wisconsin. After teaching economics in the Universities of Wisconsin and Minnesota from 1955 to 1982, she became Vice-President, Economic Research, of the WORLD BANK from 1982 to 1986; subsequently professor at Duke and Stanford Universities. Her contributions to international trade theory include an examination of the relationship between income differentials and factor endowments and applications of RENT SEEKING. Her applied work includes trade studies of Turkey, India and Korea.

krugerrand (E5)

South African gold coin weighing one troy ounce (31.1 g).

kursmakler (G1) *see* specialist

kurtosis (C1)

The extent to which a distribution is peaked relative to a NORMAL DISTRIBUTION. A highly peaked distribution is leptokurtic, a flat-topped distribution platykurtic

Leptokurtic: with a high peak

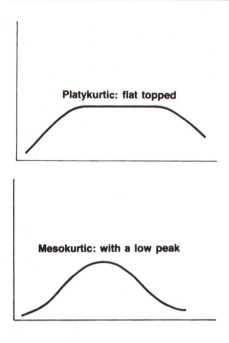

and a low-peaked distribution mesokurtic (see figures).

Kuznets curve (D3, O4)
This shows the relationship between ECONOMIC GROWTH and INCOME DISTRIBUTION, plotting income per capita against percentile or decile shares of different income groups. The share of top income groups is constant but income inequality falls for other income groups as per capita income rises.

References
Kuznets, S.S. (1955) 'Economic growth and income inequality', *American Economic Review* 45: 1–28.

Kuznets cycle (E3)
A cycle in economic activity lasting fifteen to twenty-five years first identified by KUZNETS in 1930. Changes in residential and other types of construction, particularly brought about by large-scale immigration, create these cycles. Each cycle consists of three phases: the rebound from DEPRESSION taking three to see years; steady growth at FULL EMPLOYMENT lasting seven to eleven years; depression or stagnation of four to

seven years with high unemployment in most years. In the case of the USA, immigration stimulated the steady growth phase. The cycle has been less pronounced since 1945.

See also: Juglar cycle; Kitchin cycle; Kondratieff cycle

References
Kuznets, S.S. (1967) *Secular Movements in Production and Prices: Their Nature and Their Bearing on Cyclical Fluctuations*, Boston and New York: A.M. Kelly.

Kuznets, Simon S., 1901–85 (B3)
US economist and statistician of Russian origin. After emigration to the USA in 1922, he was educated at Columbia University and began his distinguished career in a project with Wesley MITCHELL on national income at the US NATIONAL BUREAU OF ECONOMIC RESEARCH. He was professor at the Universities of Pennsylvania (1930–54), Johns Hopkins (1954–60) and Harvard (1960–71). His work on statistical data earned him the NOBEL PRIZE FOR ECONOMICS in 1971.

His major contributions to economics include a reconstruction of US NATIONAL INCOME accounts from 1869, discovering cycles of fifteen to twenty years in the economy, which he described in *Secular Movements in Production and Prices* (1930), and investigating the relationship between growth and income distribution. In his long, 929-page book *National Income and its Composition, 1919–38* (1940), he showed his great care in the use of accounting concepts and the refining of raw data.

His approach to the study of economic growth led him to examine productivity and SOCIAL COSTS and to formulate the thesis that the dominating factor in economic growth is the proportion of labour and capital of a country devoted to its growth industries. He noted that income inequality increased with economic growth in poor countries and the reverse in rich countries. Although regarded as the father of NATIONAL INCOME analysis, he has been the most wary critic of its use as an indicator of ECONOMIC WELFARE.

See also: Stone, John Richard Nicholas

References

Lundberg, E. (1971) 'Simon Kuznets' contribution to economics', *Scandinavian Journal of Economics* 73: 444–61.

Kyoto Summit (Q0)

A summit meeting held in Japan in 1997 on climate change which elaborated the UNITED NATIONS FRAMEWORK CONVENTION ON CLIMATE CHANGE. It committed the signatories to cutting 1990 levels of greenhouse gas emissions, mainly carbon dioxide, by on average 5.2 per cent by 2012. Although the treaty covers developing countries, they are excluded from meeting the targets for economic reasons.

L

L (E4)

A measure of the US money supply consisting of M3 + non-bank public holdings of US savings bonds + short-term treasury securities + commercial paper + bankers' acceptances (net of money mutual market fund holdings of these assets).

Labor Management Relations Act 1947 (J5) *see* Taft–Hartley Act

Labor Management Reporting and Disclosure Act 1959 (J5) *see* Landrum–Griffin Act 1959

labor union (J5) *see* trade union; US labor union

labour (J0)

A FACTOR OF PRODUCTION consisting of the effort and time of human beings engaged in the production of goods or services. The notions of HUMAN CAPITAL and ECONOMIC RENT blur the distinction between this factor and the others, CAPITAL and LAND.

See also: forced labour; labour supply

labour-augmenting technical progress (O3)

Technical progress which raises output with the same number of hours of labour input as at full employment.

See also: capital-augmenting technical progress

labour compact (J0)

The unwritten implicit agreement between government, employers and labour concerning labour market rules, working conditions and pay. This is more evident in European countries than in the USA.

labour cost (J2)

All the costs of employing a person. In addition to wages or salaries, FRINGE BENEFITS and group facilities are often financed by an employer. In countries such as the USA where COLLECTIVE BARGAINING covers a wide range of issues, total labour costs can be considerably greater than the total wage and salary bill.

labour disutility theory (D0)

A LABOUR THEORY OF VALUE expounded by SMITH. It asserts that value is proportional to the 'toil and trouble', or DISUTILITY, of producing a good.

See also: labour theory of value

labour force (J2)

All the persons of a country who are employed for a minimum number of hours per week, e.g. twelve, or are self-employed or are unemployed. The most difficult problems of labour force measurement arise from counting the unemployed and those engaged in economic activity within households. Some countries, including the USA, use JOB SEARCH as an indicator of an unemployed person's attachment to the labour force. The size of a national labour force will be determined by permanent international IMMIGRATION and a combination of natural increase and LABOUR FORCE PARTICIPATION RATES.

See also: homework; unemployment

labour force participation rate (J2)
The proportion of the population or a section of the population belonging to the labour force. If a country has 20 million women aged 25 to 44 years of whom 15 million are in the labour force, the labour force participation rate for those women is 75 per cent. In many advanced countries, most of labour force growth is attributable to changes in labour force participation rates.

Labour force participation has been studied as a product of the decision making of a household and regarded as being determined by wages, unemployment, education and attitudes to work. In the twentieth century, the most noticeable change in labour force participation in industrialized countries has been the increasing participation by married women. This has occurred because a reduction in SEXUAL DISCRIMINATION has opened higher education and most occupations to women, and the reduction in the birth rate, changing attitudes to women's abilities and the rise in real wages have increased the OPPORTUNITY COST of not working. There has been a slight decline in male labour force participation. In the UK, labour force participation rates are usually referred to as 'activity rates'.

See also: additional worker hypothesis; discouraged worker hypothesis

References

Bowen, W.G. and Finegan, T.A. (1969) *The Economics of Labor Force Participation*, Princeton, NJ: Princeton University Press.

labour intensive (D2)
A method of production employing a greater amount of labour than capital compared with other methods. Typically, only simple machines are used so that most production costs are labour costs. In

countries short of capital, especially in the Third World, such methods are widespread in many sectors. But in advanced countries goods made by craft workers and personal services, e.g. hairdressing, are always labour intensive.

See also: appropriate technology; capital intensive

labour-managed firm (L2) *see* industrial democracy

labour market (J0, J4)
A factor market consisting of firms as buyers and workers as sellers which exists to match job vacancies with job applicants and to set wages. It is linked to the product market because the demand for labour is derived from the demand for goods and services. Much of the notion of the demand for labour is derived from MARGINAL PRODUCTIVITY THEORY; the determinants of LABOUR SUPPLY have attracted more attention. It is often difficult to analyse labour markets because it is not clear who is participating in a particular market, especially one international in scope, e.g. a market for financial dealers.

See also: dual market; external market; internal labour market; local labour market; search cost

References

Addison, J.T. and Siebert, W.S. (1979) *The Market for Labor: An Analytical Treatment*, Santa Monica, CA: Goodyear.

labour market intermittency (J2)
Interrupting a career before retirement as happens with many female workers who take time off to rear children.

labour market policy (J6)
Attempts to improve the clearing of labour markets. Central to the policy is the role of governmental agencies in reducing the SEARCH COSTS of employers and workers by providing free information. Many countries, e.g. Sweden and the UK, offer the services of employment agencies freely. However, the roles of private agencies and

press advertising have always been important. A successful labour market policy will remove the coexistence of unemployment and unfilled vacancies (i.e. DISEQUILIBRIUM) as well as contributing to the reduction of wage inflation.

See also: job centre

labour market rigidities (J6)
Barriers to the free fixing of wages by each firm and region of a country and to the free movement of workers between occupations, regions and industries. Rigidities are particularly caused by national wage fixing, APPRENTICESHIP schemes and housing policies that make it very costly to change residence. Divergent regional unemployment rates and high wage inflation are symptoms of such rigidities.

See also: European Social Charter; mobility trap

labour mobility (J6) *see* mobility of labour

labour power (J0)
1 The capacity of a worker to work for a given period of time.
2 Potential labour services, according to MARX, regarded by capitalists as commodities with both use and exchange values.

See also: human capital

labour process theory (J0)
Marxist theory which shows the changing forms of the submission of labour to capital by analysing social relationships between workers and capitalists to indicate how SURPLUS VALUE is created and values are transformed into prices.

labour's share of national income (E0, J2)
The ratio of total wages and salaries of an economy to NATIONAL INCOME. In the twentieth century, there were increases in some Western countries in labour's share, possibly because of growth in the HUMAN CAPITAL stock, and PRICES AND INCOME POLICIES responsible for a squeeze in profits.

See also: functional income distribution

References

Phelps Brown, E.H. and Browne, M.H. (1968) *A Century of Pay: The Course of Pay and Production in France, Germany, Sweden, the United Kingdom and the United States of America 1860–1960*, ch. 4, London: Macmillan; New York: St Martin's Press.

labour standard (E4)
The value of money in terms of labour. HICKS asserted that after the abandonment of the GOLD STANDARD in 1931, which had determined wages within a given monetary framework, MONETARY POLICY adjusts the equilibrium level of wages to the actual level. Thus the value of money is the consequence of the behaviour of the wage-fixing institutions of a state. The labour standard is a national standard, unlike the international GOLD STANDARD. Hicks's long interest in LABOUR ECONOMICS ensured that he took into account both economic and social determinants of wages.

See also: commodity reserve currency

References

Hicks, J.R. (1955) 'The economic foundations of wage policy', *Economic Journal* 65: 389–404.

labour supply (J2)
The supply of persons, hours or effort for the production of goods and services. The labour supply includes both those employed and those not employed but desirous of being so. More persons are supplied through increases in the population (NATURAL INCREASE or by IMMIGRATION) and through increases in LABOUR FORCE PARTICIPATION RATES; more hours are typically supplied through overtime working; more effort is encouraged by productivity-based bonus schemes.

See also: labour force

labour theory of value (D0)
One of the oldest VALUE theories, suggested even by ARISTOTLE, but not clearly ex-

pounded until the CLASSICAL ECONOMISTS made it a central feature of their theory. Both SMITH and RICARDO attempted to relate long-term equilibrium value to the labour input of production but MARX is best known as an adherent of this view. Labour theories have a variety of forms. Smith's three versions were labour quantity (the value of a good is proportional to the amount of labour needed to make it), labour command (the value of a good is proportional to the amount of labour of others obtained in exchange) and labour disutility theory (value is proportional to the toil and trouble incurred in production). Neoclassical economists firmly dismissed such theories in favour of a MARGINAL UTILITY approach. JEVONS stated that once labour is expended in production it no longer enters into value but is lost and gone for ever.

References

Meek, R. (1973) *Studies in the Labour Theory of Value*, London: Allen & Unwin.

Lachmann, Ludwig, 1906–90 (B3)

Educated at the University of Berlin. He fled in 1933 from Germany to work at the London School of Economics where contact with HAYEK allowed him to develop his economics in the tradition of the AUSTRIAN SCHOOL; in 1948 he became professor of economics and economic history at Witwatersrand University, South Africa, where he taught a wide range of economics and encouraged the study of major economics texts. In his *Capital and Its Structure* (1956) he viewed capital as being in a ceaseless state of mutation. His work on knowledge and expectations anticipated SHACKLE.

lacking (E2, E3)

ROBERTSON's term for SAVINGS.

Laffer curve (H2)

A graphical representation of the relationship between AVERAGE TAX RATES and total tax revenues which asserts that above a certain average rate of tax, total tax revenue will decline. The curve is named

after Professor Arthur Laffer, a prominent economic adviser to US President Reagan in the 1980s and a popular leader of the SUPPLY-SIDE school of economics. Although Laffer's supporters are eager to specify more clearly the shape of the curve, it still has the curious feature of associating each tax revenue with two tax rates, one high and the other low, except at point X where government revenue is at a maximum (t_m is the tax rate which maximizes tax revenues). The curve implies that, as there is a ceiling to the amount a government can raise, there is a limit to the level of public goods which can be provided. DUPUIT in 1844 stated the same principle.

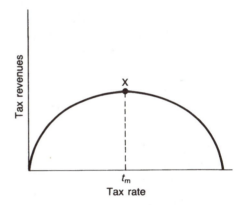

lag (E6)

The period of time elapsing between the change in value of an economic variable and the appearances of the effects of that change, e.g. the time lag between an income tax cut and an increase in consumer spending. These lags can be technological, psychological or institutional. They are a common feature of most economic relationships, especially relating to FISCAL POLICY, because a lapse of time is necessary before legislation and institutional behaviour can be adjusted: it takes time to change tax law, to pay out incomes and to spend money.

See also: administration lag; implementation lag; inside lag; Lundberg lag; outside lag; Robertsonian lag

lagged variable (C1)
A dependent variable in an equation referring to a period previous to the time associated with the independent variable.

lagging indicator (E3)
A series of economic statistics registering a change after the turning point of a reference cycle. The principal indicators of this kind are consumer income and spending, and interest rates.

See also: coincident indicators; economic indicators; leading indicators

laissez-faire (H0)
The doctrine, first propounded by the PHYSIOCRATS, that economic activities should follow their natural course, being subjected to few, if any, governmental regulations in order to encourage production and give consumers complete freedom. Thomas Carlyle described it as 'anarchy plus the constable'. As new roles for the state have been widely acknowledged, there are few adherents of the doctrine in its purest form.

See also: minimal state

References
Viner, J. (1960) 'The intellectual history of laissez-faire', *Journal of Law and Economics* 3: 45–69.

Lamfalussy Report (F0, G2)
A set of proposals for creating a free market in financial services in the EUROPEAN UNION produced in 2001. It recommended an EU Securities Regulators Committee.

land (D2, Q3)
1 The fixed FACTOR OF PRODUCTION described by RICARDO as 'the original and indestructible powers of soil'.
2 All natural resources.
3 A source of VALUE. PETTY and CANTILLON both regarded it as the basis, with labour, of value, the latter asserting a par between land and labour as a particular quantity of land is necessary to provide subsistence to a worker, e.g. 1 worker = X acres.

In practice it is difficult conceptually to separate land from other factors of production: its return is merged with that of the return to the capital expended upon it and other factors of production can be as fixed in supply for long periods of time.

See also: differential theory of rent; economic rent; rent

References
Barlowe, R. (1978) *Land Resource Economics and the Economics of Real Estate*, Englewood Cliffs, NJ: Prentice Hall.

land bank (G2)
A commercial bank that lends on the security of the landholding of the borrower. In countries short of gold and silver this form of banking enabled an expansion of credit. The Scottish financier John LAW was an early advocate of land banks. Today these banks exist in many countries, including the USA and Egypt.

land economy (Q0)
The study of property valuation and the economic factors determining the capital costs of land and buildings within an ECONOMY. This study comprehends the examination of the development of bare land to meet the market demands of the economy for accommodation, supply and property investments, ranging from those of agricultural land through to the optimal development of urban properties, e.g. offices and retail developments. Land economy matches demand for accommodation with the needs of the property investor and the restrictions of planners.

landownership (Q0)
The distribution of the land of a country, a product of its land tenure system, much of which is based on custom enshrined in a country's property laws. Countries that have undergone a socialist revolution often have transferred much land to the state or to small peasant proprietors. The pattern of landownership is a crucial determinant of agricultural efficiency: too much divi-

sion of land into small farming units affects the productivity of most types of agricultural production.

Landrum–Griffin Act 1959 (J5)

US federal labour statute which responded to cases of corruption in several labour unions by giving union members a Bill of Rights which guaranteed participation in the determination of dues and initiation fees, protection of freedom of speech and information on the financial status of their union. Rules for the filing of union constitutions and union committee decisions and election of union officials and the exclusion of Communist Party members were also features of the Act.

See also: Norris–La Guardia Act 1932; Taft–Hartley Act 1947; Wagner Act 1935

large-scale models (C5)

An econometric model of a national ECONOMY that uses hundreds of equations to estimate the relationship between key economic variables. These try to simulate different government policies and are the basis of major economic forecasts.

See also: linkage models

laser banking (G2)

Banking specializing in the financial needs of a particular region or type of customer, or with a narrow range of functions.

See also: niche bank

Laspeyres index (C1, E3)

A price or output index which uses the weights of the original year. The price index will be

$$\frac{\sum p_1 q_0}{\sum p_0 q_0}$$

where p_1 are the prices of the later year, p_0 are the prices of the base year and q_0 are the 'weights' of the base year. The output index will be

$$\frac{\sum p_0 q_1}{\sum p_0 q_0}$$

where q_1 are the quantities produced in the later year, q_0 are the quantities produced in the base year and p_0 are the prices of the base year being used throughout to value quantities.

Lassalle's law of wages (J3)

The view of the socialist Ferdinand Lassalle (1825–64) that wages under capitalism would tend to fluctuate around the subsistence level providing bare physiological existence. He proposed that the state should give capital to workers to enable them to found producers' co-operatives.

last-in, first-out (J2, M2)

1 A principle for the rotation of inventories/physical stocks. In UK NATIONAL INCOME accounting conventions it enables all items to be valued at current prices; a firm using this principle is able to finance the replacement of stocks in inflationary periods.
2 The employment policy of firms which lay off first the workers who have been recruited most recently.

See also: first-in, first-out

late capitalism (P1)

The LONG BOOM in Western capitalist economies after the Second World War regarded by Mandel and other Marxist writers not as a new epoch in capitalist development but as a further development of MONOPOLY CAPITALISM. It could be analysed according to the laws of capitalist development set out by MARX in *Das Kapital*.

References

Mandel, E. (1972) *Late Capitalism*, trans. Joris De Bres, rev. edn 1975, London: Verso; New York: Routledge, Chapman and Hall.

latent entrepreneurship (M1)

The unfulfilled desire to set up one's own business.

Latin American Free Trade Association (F1)
An association of Argentina, Brazil, Chile, Mexico, Paraguay, Peru and Uruguay created by the Montevideo Treaty in 1960 (Colombia, Bolivia and Venezuela subsequently joined) with the aim of creating completely free trade between these countries by 1980. Failing to achieve its objective, LAFTA was superseded by the Latin American Integration Association in 1980.

Lauderdale (James Maitland), Eighth Earl of, 1759–1830 (B3)
British political economist and politician educated at Edinburgh and Oxford Universities. He was Member of Parliament for Newport from 1780 until he succeeded to his father's peerage in 1789. He is noted for being one of the first economic writers to consider macroeconomic issues. In his important work, *Inquiry into the Nature and Origin of Public Wealth and into the Means and Causes of its Increase* (1804), he praised extra spending as a means of increasing public wealth and attacked both saving and sinking funds as ways of diminishing it. He also provided the first integrated theory of PROFIT and CAPITAL and proposed UTILITY in place of labour as the basis of value.

References

Paglin, M. (1961) *Malthus and Lauderdale: The Anti-Ricardian Tradition*, New York: Augustus M. Kelly.

laundering money (K4)
The transfer of cash or bank deposits through several banks in order to disguise the ownership of it and its place of origin. This technique, long used by criminals to disguise ill-gotten gains, is extensively used by the world's drug barons today.

See also: drug economy

Lausanne School (B1)
A group of economists of the MARGINALIST School who worked in Switzerland in the late nineteenth century. With WALRAS and PARETO as its leaders it developed GENERAL EQUILIBRIUM analysis and set out the criteria for welfare optima. There are many prominent descendants of this school, including HICKS, SAMUELSON, ARROW and HAHN.

Lautro (G2)
Life Assurance and Unit Trusts Regulatory Organization, a London-based SELF-REGULATORY ORGANIZATION. One of its earliest policies, in 1987, was to recommend a cut in the commission of independent agents on the sale of life bonds from 5.2 per cent to 3 per cent over a four-year period, harmonizing the commission with the rate for the sale of UNIT TRUSTS.

See also: Financial Services Act 1986

law and economics (K0) *see* economics of law

Law, John, 1671–1729 (B3)
Born in Edinburgh, Scotland. After imprisonment in London for murder, he escaped to France where he soon became its leading banker. He proposed the establishment of a Bank of France to issue paper money on the security of land. He set up his General Bank in 1716 and founded companies in Louisiana and Mississippi whose stock was used to redeem the French national debt. After his scheme collapsed at a time of wild stock market speculation he fled to Venice. His principal work was *Money and Trade Considered: With a Proposal for Supplying the Nation With Money* (1705).

law of diminishing marginal utility (D0) *see* diminishing marginal utility law

law of diminishing returns (D2) *see* diminishing returns law

law of one price (D4) *see* one-price law

law of reciprocal demand (F1) *see* reciprocal demand law

law of reflux (E5)
A banking 'law' expounded by SMITH and later by the BANKING SCHOOL that there could not be a permanent over-issue of notes as any excess would return to the issuing bank, being of no use.

See also: real bills doctrine

law of satiable wants (D0)
The general tendency for people to derive UTILITY from only a limited quantity of a good or service.

See also: diminishing marginal utility law

law of value (D0, P1)
The mechanism in a CAPITALIST SOCIETY for distributing total LABOUR POWER between branches of production via the prices of products. A consequence of the law is that the pattern of investment is determined according to the deviation of specific rates of profit from the average rate of profit.

law of variable proportions (D2)
The DIMINISHING RETURNS LAW.

See also: returns to scale

Lawson boom (E3, N0, N1)
The period of high inflation in the UK in the late 1980s when Nigel Lawson was Chancellor of the Exchequer. It occurred in the upswing of an economic cycle when the economy was also suffering the effects of the COMMUNITY CHARGE.

leading firms ratio (C1, L1) *see* N-firm concentration ratio

leading indicators (E3)
A series of economic statistics that changes prior to a change in the REFERENCE CYCLE of an ECONOMY. The principal leading indicators are the index for the construction industry, the index for industrial materials prices, new orders for industrial durable goods, profits, business failures and common stock prices.

See also: economic indicators; lagging indicator

leads and tags (F4)
The advancing (leading) of payments and the delaying (lagging) of receipts, particularly in international trade. If the view is taken that a country's currency is about to depreciate, or to be devalued, then traders of that country, in order to protect themselves against losses, will pay earlier for imports and will delay converting export receipts into the depreciating currency. It has been argued that in the past DEVALUATIONS of currencies were precipitated by a change in the timing of payments, e.g. the devaluation of the pound sterling in 1967.

leakage (E0)
A withdrawal from the circular flow of NATIONAL INCOME, especially savings, imports or taxation. The MULTIPLIER effect of leakages is to reduce the level of the national income.

See also: injection

leaky bucket (H2)
The partial failure to redistribute the entire yield from taxes on the rich through TRANSFER INCOMES to the poor. OKUN, who invented the term, ascribed leakages to administrative and COMPLIANCE COSTS and distortions in working, investing and saving behaviour. Anti-poverty programmes often suffer from this problem.

learning-by-doing (O3)
The increase in PRODUCTIVITY resulting from repeated performance of a particular activity. SMITH recognized this in his discussion of the DIVISION OF LABOUR principle. Modern theorists of growth and international trade have considered this form of learning as an explanation of technical progress independent of the scale of production.

References

Arrow, K.J. (1962) 'The economic implications of learning by doing', *Review of Economic Studies* 29: 155–73.

learning-by-helping (J2)
The process of mentoring in an organization which enables the transfer of firm-specific human capital. By a sponsor connecting protégés to a network and acquiring fuller information on them, the promotion of newer members of a firm is enhanced.

learning curve (O3)
A graphical representation of the relationship between cumulative productivity and cumulative output. The relationship, observed in several manufacturing industries, states that productivity increases through the experience of production.

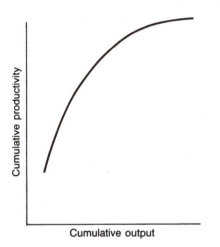

See also: Kaldor's laws; Verdoorn's law

least squares method (C1)
A method of obtaining the best-fitting line to a set of observations by minimizing the squares of the deviations of the values plotted from a line going through the values. The line can be described by the equation $Y = a + bX$, where a and b are constants, Y is the dependent variable and X is the independent variable and is the regression curve of Y on X.

See also: scatter diagram

legal tender (E5)
The money decreed by a central bank or a currency commission that must be accepted for the discharge of any debt in that country. This makes token money acceptable. Bank of England notes are legal tender in England and Wales but not in Scotland and Northern Ireland, but £1 and £2 coins are acceptable for unlimited amounts. In the USA the Coinage Act 1965 made all US notes and coins legal tender.

leisure (J2)
The alternative to work. LABOUR FORCE PARTICIPATION decisions are determined by the trade-off between work and leisure. Leisure confers UTILITY.

leisure class (P0)
VEBLEN's term for the wealthy classes who live off investment income and use sport and socializing as a substitute for labour market activity.

References

Veblen, T. (1905) *The theory of the leisure class: an economic study of institutions*, New York: Macmillan.

Leibenstein, Harvey, 1922–92 (B3)
US economist educated at Northwestern and Princeton Universities. In his career he was professor at Berkeley from 1951 to 1967 and then Professor of the Economics of Population at Harvard from 1967 to 1992. His studies of business decision making inspired him to invent the concept of X-EFFICIENCY.

References

Leibenstein, H. (1966) 'Allocative efficiency versus X-efficiency', *American Economic Review* 56: 392–415.

lemonade stand capitalism (P1)
An ideal type of CAPITALISM consisting of small one-person businesses operating under PERFECT COMPETITION.

lemons market (D8)
The market for used cars of less than

average quality: the famous example used by AKERLOF to illustrate ASYMMETRIC INFORMATION. As sellers have more information than buyers, quality uncertainty about the cars will have the effect, in the manner of GRESHAM'S LAW, that good cars leave the market so that only lemons are traded. This principle is applicable to insurance, the employment of minorities, the costs of dishonesty and credit markets in underdeveloped countries. Guarantees, brand names and the licensing of professionals can be used to protect against such uncertainty.

References

Akerlof, G. (1970) 'The market for lemons: quality uncertainty and the market mechanism', *Quarterly Journal of Economics* 84: 488–500.

lender of last resort (E5)
The chief function of a CENTRAL BANK – to guarantee the LIQUIDITY of a banking system by always being the ultimate source of credit. Thus in the UK, the BANK OF ENGLAND is always prepared to lend to the money market by discounting the bills held by the discount houses; in the USA, the twelve FEDERAL RESERVE BANKS will discount the bills of member banks.

lender's risk (G0)
The chance of financial harm plus the chance that a borrower will renege owing to MORAL HAZARD.

lending rate (E4)
The RATE OF INTEREST on bank loans. It varies according to the type of customer. In the UK, major quoted companies are charged base rate plus 1 per cent, small companies base rate plus 2 per cent and personal borrowers base rate plus 5 per cent.

Leontief paradox (F1)
An empirical contradiction of HECKSCHER–OHLIN international trade theory that international trade is based on the relative factor endowments of different countries. It was found that US exports are LABOUR

INTENSIVE and its imports CAPITAL INTENSIVE, despite the capital abundance of the US economy.

References

Leontief, W.M. (1956) 'Factor proportions and the structure of American trade: further theoretical and empirical analysis', *Review of Economics and Statistics* 38: 386–407.

Leontief technology (O3)
A technology employing factor inputs as fixed proportions of outputs so that no substitution between inputs is possible in the PRODUCTION FUNCTION.

Leontief, Wassily W., 1906–99 (B3)
The pioneer of INPUT–OUTPUT ANALYSIS. He was born in St Petersburg, Russia, where his father was a professor of labour economics at the city's university from which he himself graduated before further study in Berlin. After a period as economic adviser to the government of China, he emigrated to the USA, spending 1931 to 1932 at the NATIONAL BUREAU OF ECONOMIC RESEARCH, Washington, before beginning his long tenure of a Harvard professorship, from 1932 to 1975. He was awarded the NOBEL PRIZE FOR ECONOMICS in 1973.

His work on input–output analysis started with a paper and input–output table for the US economy in 1925. Later he developed his model by incorporating the effects of excess capacity, price changes and technical progress. In 1973, he ambitiously began the modelling of the world economy using input–output methods. His studies led him to advocate five-year planning for the USA as a means of reducing the costs of labour and capital being unemployed in phases of the BUSINESS CYCLE. Another celebrated study in applied economics was his attack on the HECKSCHER–OHLIN theorem of international trade in 1954. Leontief objected to many aspects of KEYNESIAN ECONOMICS, particularly its methodology which, because it relies so much on the definitions used, produces inevitable conclusions and policy prescriptions.

References

Leontief, W.W. (1951) *The Structure of the American Economy, 1919–39*, 2nd edn, New York: Oxford University Press.
—— (1966) *Input-Output Economics*, New York: Oxford University Press.
—— (1966, 1977) *Essays in Economics: Theories, Facts and Policies*, Oxford: Basil Blackwell.

leptokurtic (C1) *see* kurtosis

Lerner, Abba Ptachya, 1903–82 (B3)
Anglo-American economist, born in Bessarabia (Romania), who emigrated as a child to the UK. After working as a businessman, he studied and taught at the London School of Economics from 1929 to 1939. In 1939 he emigrated to the USA, where he was to teach in nine universities, including Berkeley from which he retired in 1979. His measure of monopoly power published in 1934 helped to found the MARGINAL COST PRICING rule of applied WELFARE ECONOMICS. His London School of Economics doctoral thesis was published as *The Economics of Control* in 1944: it sets out the basic principles to be followed by an economic policy-maker, including PARETO OPTIMALITY, equal distribution of income and budgeting with reference to employment and price effects. He was an early convert to KEYNESIANISM which he enhanced by his work after 1945 on the problem of controlling inflation, including the construction of his anti-inflation plan.

See also: market anti-inflation plan

References

Colander, D.C. (ed.) (1983) *Selected Economic Writings of Abba P. Lerner*, New York: New York University Press.
Scitovsky, T. (1984) 'Lerner's contribution to economics', *Journal of Economic Literature* 22: 1547–71.

Lerner effect (E2)
An upward shift in the CONSUMPTION FUNCTION caused by an increase in the level of money or public debt claims, leading to a FULL-EMPLOYMENT equilibrium level of public debt.

References

Lerner, A.P. (1948) 'The burden of the national debt', in *Income, Employment and Public Policy – Essays in Honour of Alvin H. Ransen*, New York: W.W. Norton.

Lerner index (L2)
The measure of the degree of MONOPOLY using the formula [(price minus marginal cost) divided by price]. This measure follows directly from the standard treatment of monopoly with an INELASTIC demand curve showing a divergence between PRICE and MARGINAL COST at the profit-maximizing level of output. Under PERFECT COMPETITION, this index will be zero for firms in a state of long-run equilibrium.

See also: concentration; Herfindahl–Hirschman index

less developed country (O0)
A country with a low per capita income, a large agricultural sector and often little industrialization, high population growth, low life expectancy and able to export only a few products. Previously called 'an underdeveloped country'.

See also: economic development; poverty

letter of credit (G2)
A document issued by a bank to guarantee payment of sums due under BILLS OF EXCHANGE and cheques. In most cases, these letters are requested by importers to make them sufficiently creditworthy to be able to order goods from foreign exporters.

letter stock (G2)
Common or preferred stock sold through an investment letter obliging the purchaser not to sell until there is a public sale. Their prices are lower than those of registered stock.

level of significance (C1)
The maximum probability at which a Type I error is risked. Usually the levels chosen are 0.01 (1 per cent) or 0.05 (5 per cent).

leverage (E0, G0)

1 The ratio between a company's long-term debt and the total capital it employs.

2 GEARING.

3 The difference between the actual level of GROSS DOMESTIC PRODUCT and the hypothetical level which would result in the absence of receipts and expenditures of the public sector. The Musgraves measured it as

$$L = \frac{1}{1-c+m} \times [(1-g)P - (c-m)(R-\text{Tr})]$$

where P is government purchases, R is its receipts, Tr are transfers, g is the government's propensity to consume, c is the private propensity to consume and m is the private propensity to consume imports.

References

Musgrave, R.A. and Musgrave, P.B. (1968) 'Fiscal policy', in R.E. Caves and associates (eds) *Britain's Economic Prospects*, ch. 1, Washington, DC: Brookings Institution; London: Allen & Unwin.

leveraged management buyout (G3)

The purchase of a company by its management using fixed interest loans, which increases the leverage of the newly constituted company. The need to service the loans often makes managers more cost conscious, thereby increasing the profitability of the company.

See also: management buyout

Lewis–Fei–Ranis model (O2)

A model of economic development for a two-sector closed ECONOMY. The growth of the industrial sector increases demand for the agricultural sector's produce and attracts labour from the low-productivity agricultural sector, thus raising overall output and productivity of the economy as a whole. As there are few developing economies which are isolated from the effects of international trade, the application of the model is limited.

References

Fei, J.C.H. and Ranis, G. (1965) *Development of the Labor Surplus Economy*, Homewood, IL: Richard D. Irwin.

Lewis, W.A. (1954) 'Economic development with unlimited supplies of labour', *Manchester School* 22: 139–91.

Lewis, William Arthur (Sir Arthur), 1915–91 (B3)

A West Indian economist educated at the London School of Economics and Manchester University where he was professor of economics from 1948 to 1958 before becoming Principal and Vice-Chancellor of the University of the West Indies from 1958 to 1963, President of the Caribbean Development Bank from 1970 to 1973, and professor at Princeton University from 1963 to 1970 and 1973 to 91. With SCHULTZ, he was awarded the NOBEL PRIZE FOR ECONOMICS in 1979 for his work in DEVELOPMENT ECONOMICS. His early work was on price theory and PUBLIC UTILITIES but his fame was established by a celebrated article, published in the *Manchester School* in May 1954, which inspired the study of developing countries as DUAL ECONOMIES.

References

Datta, A. (1986) *Growth and Equity: A Critique of the Lewis-Kuznets Tradition with Special Reference to India*, Calcutta and New York: Oxford University Press.

Lewis, W.A. (1955) *Theory of Economic Growth*, London: Allen & Unwin.

—— (1966) *Development Planning: The Essentials of Economic Planning*, London: Allen & Unwin.

—— (1978) *Growth and Fluctuations, 1870–1913*, London: Allen & Unwin.

—— (1978) *The Evolution of the International Economic Order*, Princeton, NJ: Princeton University Press.

liability management (G0)

Using interest rate changes to attract deposits.

liberal collectivism (P4) *see* social liberalism

Liberman, Yevsei, 1912– (B3)

Soviet economist and professor at the Institute of Engineering and Economics, Kharkov University, whose proposals for reforming the planning system, published as *Plan, Profit and Premium* in 1962, led to major changes in the running of Soviet enterprises set out in the Enterprise Statute of 1965. He criticized the use of gross output as the key performance target and suggested that some notion of 'profit' acceptable to socialist theory should be employed. It was hoped that this change would lead to more efficient use of factor inputs and would make possible the setting up of incentive funds in each enterprise to reward more productive managers and workers.

libertarian economics (B2)

A school of economics which emphasizes the importance of markets and the limited role of governments. Although the PHYSIO-CRATS and some CLASSICAL ECONOMISTS preached this *laissez-faire* approach, it is particularly associated with the AUSTRIAN, CHICAGO and NEOCLASSICAL SCHOOLS, making HAYEK and FRIEDMAN its gurus.

lifeboat operation (E5, G2)

The rescue of UK SECONDARY BANKS in 1973–4 by the BANK OF ENGLAND, assisted by London and Scottish CLEARING BANKS. Imprudent lending by non-clearing banks during the property boom caused many of these minor banks to have an increased number of bad debts. The nature of the Bank of England's help was compared with a rescue of the shipwrecked.

life-cycle hypothesis (E2)

Ando and Modigliani's theory of saving and the CONSUMPTION FUNCTION which recognizes that for each age group there is an associated AVERAGE PROPENSITY TO CONSUME with the consequence that a change in a country's age distribution will affect aggregate saving and consumption. This hypothesis has been applied to the financing of pensions as during a person's

working life saving is accumulated which is spent in retirement. A reverse life-cycle hypothesis asserts that at the beginning of one's working life there is DISSAVING to finance education, house purchase or consumer durables: expenditure precedes saving in these cases.

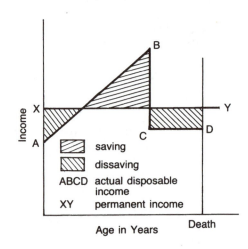

References

Ando, A. and Modigliani, F. (1963) 'The life cycle hypothesis of saving: aggregate implications and tests', *American Economic Review* 53: 55–84.

lifetime averaging (H2) *see* long-term income averaging

lifetime client value (M3)

The benefit to a firm from retaining the loyalty of a client. Marketing costs including advertising will be lower and the market will be more stable.

light industry (L6)

An industry using raw materials and components light in weight and noted for a great amount of VALUE ADDED, e.g. the computer assembly industry.

See also: heavy industry; industry

limited arbitrage (G0)

Market activity that is too weak to bring security prices back to their efficient levels because of the arbitrageurs having limited capital, short investment horizons and an aversion to risk.

limited company (L2)
A firm owned by shareholders whose liability is limited to the amount of capital subscribed. Since the mid-nineteenth century this has been a powerful means of financing large firms. The extent to which this form of organization is used varies from country to country. In Germany, for example, as it is viewed with suspicion, very few companies are limited liability and public. The development of SECONDARY MARKETS in unlisted securities has encouraged the movement to limited liability.

See also: joint stock company; Unlisted Securities Market

limited general competitive bidding (D4)
A form of competition limited to those who have stated qualifications.

limited market liberalization (P0)
A partial transition from a planned to a MARKET ECONOMY. Goods allocated under the plan cannot be resold and scheduled deliveries cannot be purchased on the market. Without these priorities, there would be full market liberalization.

limited partnership (K2, M1)
A partnership consisting of limited, or sleeping, partners who provide finance rather than contribute to management and general partners who manage the firm. Limited partners have no personal liability; general partners have unlimited liability.

limit order (G1)
An order to buy a SECURITY at or below a specified price or to sell it for at least a particular price.

See also: market order

limit order book (G1)
A list for a SECURITY of LIMIT ORDERS ranked by price and then chronologically according to the time entry that is kept by a SPECIALIST. Priority is given to stocks that

have been longest on the book. Increasingly there are movements towards the creation of a computerized central book for each stock exchange.

limit price (D4)
The highest common price set by a group of sellers colluding together that they believe they can charge without new firms seeking to enter that industry in search of high profits.

Lindahl equilibrium (H4)
A set of 'Lindahl prices' such that at those prices everyone demands the same level of each PUBLIC GOOD. These prices are individuals' shares of the tax burden. This equilibrium is the equivalent of a competitive equilibrium for an economy with public goods. When in equilibrium, the tax rate for an individual will equal his or her marginal utility from that public good. All markets for private goods are perfectly competitive and the government provides public goods. PARETO OPTIMALITY is achieved by an appropriate redistribution of income.

References
Milleron, J.C. (1972) 'Theory of value with public goods: a survey article', *Journal of Economic Theory* 5: 419–77.

Lindahl price (H2, H4)
The share of total tax revenue paid by an individual that is the basis for his or her 'demanding' PUBLIC GOODS. This price is equal to the MARGINAL UTILITY from a public good. The sum of Lindahl prices for an economy is equal to the cost of supplying public goods.

linear correlation (C1) *see* linear regression

linear programming (C1, I3, R4)
An optimization technique originally applied to two problems: the transportation problem of determining the cheapest pattern of routes to supply a number of markets from a number of sources, and the diet problem of determining the cheapest diet which will provide a minimum

nutritional intake. Since the first use of this technique in the 1940s, it has come to be used extensively in the public and private sectors.

References

Baumol, W.J. (1958) 'Activity analysis in one lesson', *American Economic Review* 48: 837–73.

Dorfman, R., Samuelson, P.A. and Solow, R.M. (1958) *Linear Programming and Economic Analysis*, New York: McGraw-Hill.

Gass, S.I. (1969) *Linear Programming Methods and Applications*, 3rd edn, New York: McGraw-Hill.

Luenberger, D.E. (1984) *Introduction to Linear and Non-Linear Programming*, 2nd edn, Wokingham and Reading, MA: Addison-Wesley.

linear regression (C1)
The relationship between two variables which approximates graphically to a straight line.

See also: least squares method

line item veto (H6)
The power to veto part of a budget whilst approving the rest. In the USA, forty-three governors can veto parts of state budgets but the US president has no such power over the federal budget.

linkage (D2)
The forward or backward connection between industries at different stages of production. The measurement of the increases in employment and value added brought about by the expansion of one part of an ECONOMY uses the linkage idea. Most aspects of an economy – prices, taxes, public expenditure, technology and information – are considered. Some enthusiasts, who have emphasized linkages as the key to ECONOMIC GROWTH, have ignored the existence of resource constraints.

See also: backward linkage; forward linkage

linkage models (C5)
Large-scale econometric models that link together national macroeconomic models to show the relationships between major national economies, especially trade and monetary flows and exchange rates.

See also: COMET; INTERLINK

Lipsey, Richard George, 1928– (B3)
Canadian economist educated at the University of British Columbia, Toronto, and the London School of Economics, where he was later lecturer and professor from 1955 to 1964. He was professor at Essex University from 1964 to 1970 and subsequently at Queen's University in Kingston, Ontario, from 1970 to 1985.

He is famous to hundreds of thousands of students in the Western world for his textbooks: *An Introduction to Positive Economics*, first published in 1963, which is, as its name suggests, strongly empirical in tone and hence has been frequently revised; and *Economics*, which was first published in 1966 in the USA. He first made his mark as an economist with his joint article with Lancaster, 'The general theory of the second best' (*Review of Economic Studies* June 1956), which made a major contribution to welfare economics. Subsequently, in a series of articles on inflation, he provided the microeconomic explanations for the PHILLIPS CURVE. His numerous other works include articles on CUSTOMS UNIONS, LOCATION THEORY and monetary theory.

References

Lipsey, R.G. (1991) *The Collected Essays of Richard G. Lipsey*, 3 vols, Aldershot: Edward Elgar.

liquid assets (E5, G2)
Cash plus short-term assets (loans and bills of exchange soon to mature) which can be quickly converted into cash without a capital loss to the asset holder.

liquid assets ratio (E5)
A reserve assets ratio which takes into account both cash and monetary assets soon to mature and hence convertible into cash with small risk of capital loss. At

various times from 1971 the UK banks, for example, were asked to have different liquidity ratios, the required percentage changing with the redefinition of liquid assets.

liquidity (E4, G0)

The characteristic of assets immediately available for the discharge of financial obligations: the most liquid of assets is CASH. For there to be pure liquidity, it is necessary that the asset market is perfect with the consequence that the sale of an asset does not affect its price. Also the asset is riskless because its price is constant. Securities are only liquid if there is an organized market for them.

liquidity preference (E4)

Reasons for holding money classified by KEYNES according to motive. He identified the TRANSACTIONS, PRECAUTIONARY and SPECULATIVE DEMAND FOR MONEY.

See also: IS–LM curves

liquidity trap (E4)

The minimum floor to the rate of interest. Keynes expounded the view that the SPECULATIVE DEMAND FOR MONEY would introduce this factor price rigidity because security prices would rise to a level that investors consider a maximum and consequently interest rates would reach a minimum. This 'trap' challenges the classical view that complete flexibility in factor prices brings about a full-employment equilibrium.

liquid market (G1)

A market where buying and selling are easy and low cost with the consequence that prices tend to their underlying values.

List, Friedrich, 1789–1846 (B3)

German economist and leading defender of PROTECTIONISM who was professor of economics at the University of Tubingen from 1817 to 1819, a journalist in the USA from 1825 to 1832 and subsequently US Consul in Leipzig and then Baden. He campaigned vigorously for the creation of a German railway system and Zollverein, or CUSTOMS UNION. He committed suicide. His most celebrated work was *The National System of Political Economy*, originally published in 1841. In it he is very critical of SMITH's 'cosmopolitan', or FREE-TRADE, economics for assuming that there was the universal peace which free trade requires and for ignoring the fact that Great Britain had grown strong through protectionism. List argued that free trade was to the benefit of merchants rather than to the advantage of a nation as a whole, for the basis of national economic power is the encouragement of 'productive powers', especially manufacturing, through protection.

See also: mercantilism

listed bank (G2) *see* clearing bank; commercial bank

listed company (L2)

A company whose securities are quoted in the list of a stock exchange's traded stocks. This listing increases the marketability of a company.

listed security (G1)

A stock or share whose price is published on the official list of a stock exchange. The INTERNATIONAL STOCK EXCHANGE insists that for a company's securities to be listed it must agree to publish regularly many types of financial information, in addition to what is required under company legislation.

list price (D4)

A price announced in a catalogue or other list of a producer or retailer. This is not necessarily a TRANSACTION PRICE as many list prices are subject to discounts and negotiation.

little dragons (P0)

South Korea, Taiwan, Hong Kong, Singapore.

See also: newly industrialized country

living wage (J3)

A MINIMUM WAGE sufficient to cover

expenditure on food, fuel, clothing and relaxation.

Lloyd's (G2)

London insurance market founded in the coffee house of Edward Lloyd in 1688. It consists of underwriting members with unlimited liability for the risks they have underwritten and non-underwriting members. Syndicates of underwriters are responsible for most of the risk. Originally, Lloyd's was concerned with marine insurance but it has diversified its interests to fire, accident, motor and aviation insurance. Lloyd's Agents throughout the world and the Lloyd's List provide crucial information for the insurance industry. Although based in the UK, Lloyd's has long done most of its business with US insurance companies.

References

Hodgson, G. (1984) *Lloyd's of London. A Reputation at Risk*, London: Allen Lane and Viking Press.

Lloyd's name (G2)

An underwriting member of Lloyd's insurance market who accepts unlimited liability. The tax advantages associated with membership have always attracted wealthy investors. Mismanagement, alleged fraud and billions of claims over asbestos and oil spillages in the 1980s caused the bankruptcy of many names. In 1993 Lloyd's rules were changed to allow corporate investors to join. The number of names fell from 34,000 at its peak to about 3,000 in 2000.

LM curve (E1) *see* IS–LM curves

load fund (G2)

A MUTUAL FUND charging disproportionately large commissions on smaller investments.

See also: no-load fund

loanable funds theory (E4)

A popular theory of the determination of the rate of interest dominant in economics before Keynes's *General Theory*. Under the theory, the investment demand for funds and the supply of loanable funds through savings would in equilibrium bring about a unique rate of interest.

loanshark (G2, K4)

A person lending money at exorbitant rates of interest usually to borrowers with no collateral and no access to conventional lenders such as banks. This form of lending has long been a major activity of organized crime.

loan stock (G1)

A stock exchange security with a fixed rate of interest and, usually, prior entitlement to payment out of any available earnings.

See also: debenture

Local Enterprise Agency (R5)

An agency in the UK financed by private sector firms to help potential entrepreneurs to set up in business. This aid chiefly takes the form of free specialist services.

local expectations theory (G1)

The assertion that over a short-term investment horizon the yields of bonds of different maturities will be the same.

local government finance (H7)

The financing of the government of a region, city or district by local taxation, charges and grants from central government. At the local level property taxes, local sales taxes and local income taxes are the principal forms of taxation used. In order to maintain the same standards of service throughout a country, a national government often provides grants to cover part of local costs, e.g. educational expenditures. Major problems arise if the local revenue is too small to meet local needs, e.g. if there is a large non-resident population, as in New York City or Glasgow, using facilities without paying full local taxes. Also, if there is not a clear separation of powers between the levels of government, a local government might pursue macroeconomic policies, e.g. employment policies, which are too expensive for it to finance, as has happened in the

UK. Although property taxes are often a major source of local revenue and provide an additional tax base, they have been criticized for their regressive nature over some ranges of incomes.

See also: community charge; federal finance; fiscal mobility; rates

local labour market (J4)

A geographical market which brings together buyers and sellers within a given area, often defined as a journey-to-work area in which employers and workers are in close contact with each other. CLASSICAL ECONOMISTS, following SMITH's celebrated discussion of WAGE DIFFERENTIALS, believed that the free movement of workers in response to wage differentials would bring about an equalization of the net advantages of employment. Labour economists believe that there are fewer market imperfections, especially of an informational kind, in these local markets than in other labour markets. However, the conflict between INTERNAL and EXTERNAL LABOUR MARKETS has made it more difficult to see local markets of this kind functioning in a classical manner. Also, the concept applies mostly to markets for less skilled workers. Managerial and professional workers consider themselves participants in the wider national and international labour markets.

See also: labour market; labour mobility

References

Robinson, D. (ed.) (1970) *Local Labour Markets and Wage Structures*, London: Gower.
Smith, A. (1776) *The Wealth of Nations*, ed. R.H. Campbell and A.S. Skinner, Book 1, ch. 10, Oxford: Clarendon Press, 1976.

local monopoly (L1) *see* spatial monopoly

local public good (H4)

A public good locally provided for the benefit of a local community and financed largely out of local taxation; a spatially limited public good.

See also: Tiebout hypothesis

local union (J5)

US LABOR UNION which organizes workers in one establishment, company or craft and hence is the smallest part of a US labor union. In 1982, the average local union had only 200 members. Locals play a significant role in collective bargaining, especially the negotiation of labour contracts between labour and management, and are combined into federations known as INTERNATIONAL UNIONS. A US labor union member has direct contact with the local, and not the international, union.

See also: company union; enterprise union

location theory (R1, R3)

A study of the determinants of the geographical distribution of agriculture, industry and other economic activities. An early influential model was von Thünen's which viewed the location of activities in terms of concentric rings around a central urban market with land uses and land values being reduced the further they were from the centre. Later theorists, including Losch, sought to explain how industrial activity would be located at the point of minimum transport cost and maximum profitability, given the dispersion of raw material sources and consumers. As the theory of the firm was expanded to consider aims other than PROFIT MAXIMIZATION, location theory took into account the possibility that a location could be chosen to satisfice rather than maximize the benefit to a firm and that sales rather than profits were of dominant concern. Much of location theory is now incorporated into URBAN ECONOMICS and REGIONAL ECONOMICS as location theorists have increasingly studied urban settlements.

References

Beckman, M. (1968) *Location Theory*, New York: Random House.
Hall, P. (ed.) (1966) *Von Thunen's Isolated State (1826)*, Oxford and New York: Pergamon.

Isard, W. (1956) *Location and the Space Economy*, Cambridge, MA: MIT Press.

Losch, A. (1954) *The Economics of Location*, New Haven, CT: Yale University Press.

locked-in effect (E4, H2)

1 The effect of rising interest rates on the holding of government bonds. Holders of long-term government securities in times of rising interest rates (and hence falling bond prices) are reluctant to sell because of the consequent capital losses.

2 The effect of capital gains taxes being greater than inheritance taxes so that shareholders can benefit from refraining from selling stocks that have appreciated in value and passing them untaxed to their heirs.

locked-in industry (L0)

An industry which cannot easily move because some locations are more expensive than others.

See also: footloose industry

locked-in knowledge (O3)

Technical knowledge specific to a particular production process and not transferable to other processes; also known as 'tacit' knowledge.

See also: footloose knowledge

locomotive effect (O4)

The expansionary effect of the economic growth of a large country on smaller countries which experience an increase in demand for their exports.

lockout (J5)

Industrial action by an employer to prevent employees from working until they agree to the terms and conditions of employment proposed.

See also: strike

logistic cycle (E3, N0)

A cycle in economic activity of 150–300 years' duration which, when plotted as a graph of industrial production against time, approximates to the statistical logistic curve of an expansion phase followed by a stagnation phase. The first cycle was from 1100 to 1450, the second from 1450 to 1750 and the third has not been completed.

See also: Kondratieff cycle; long wave

References

Cameron, R. (1973) 'The logistics of European economic growth: a note on historical periodization', *Journal of European Economic History* 2: 145–58.

logit model (C5)

An econometric model comparing the odds of the occurrence of an event or state of affairs with the non-occurrence of that event or state. To obtain a linear model the logarithm of the odds ratio is used – hence the term logit.

See also: probit model; Tobin model

logrolling (H0)

The political practice, extensively practised in the USA, of legislators trading votes. A vote is given for a particular proposal in return for voting for another proposal. Thus, projects with only minority support can be approved because their proposers have given their votes on other issues. The concept is essential to understanding how US federal public expenditure is approved.

Lombard rate (E4)

The rate of interest usually 1/2 per cent above the discount rate charged by the BUNDESBANK when acting in its capacity as LENDER OF LAST RESORT. Banks can borrow for up to three months against the collateral of certain high-quality securities, which include treasury bills and federal bonds.

Lomé Convention (F0)

An agreement, originally signed in 1975 and subsequently extended in 1980 and 1985, which is unique in north–south relations. It was between the members of the EUROPEAN COMMUNITY and forty-six developing countries of Africa, the Caribbean and the Pacific. It has exempted these less developed countries from all industrial and 96 per cent of agricultural tariffs of the European Community and is established through European Development Fund technical and financial assistance. Although another seventeen less developed countries have become beneficiaries, Asian countries are still excluded. The granting of aid under this scheme is now subject to human rights being respected in the recipient country. The amount of aid per capita provided is only a few US dollars per head.

References

Alting von Geusau, E.A.M. (ed.) (1977) *The Lomé Convention and a New International Economic Order*, Leyden: Sijthoff.

London Discount Market Association (G1)

London's nine DISCOUNT houses that constitute the UK's short-term money market.

London Inter-Bank Offered Rate (E4)

The interest rate on dollar deposits lent between first-class banks in London. Its principal use is as the base interest rate on which the prices of EURODOLLAR and other EUROCURRENCY loans are calculated. The INTERNATIONAL MONETARY FUND uses it as a benchmark for calculating the interest rate on most of its lending. These loans specify an agreed spread above a LIBOR three- or six-month rate, usually of ½–2 per cent. There is no set procedure or set time for changing LIBOR. Other financial centres, including Paris, Singapore and Tokyo, have offered rates.

London International Financial Futures Exchange (F1)

A market founded in 1982 to deal in a wide range of FUTURES in financial securities, including gilts, US Treasury bonds and Eurodollars; founded in 1982. It is smaller than the leading Chicago market, founded in 1972. New York, Canada and Australia have similar markets.

London Traded Options Market (F1)

A market associated with the INTERNATIONAL STOCK EXCHANGE, founded in 1978.

In 1991, it merged with the LONDON INTERNATIONAL FINANCIAL FUTURES EXCHANGE.

long (F3)

A foreign exchange surplus. A foreign exchange dealer is 'in long' when his or her bank has a surplus of a particular currency.

See also: short

Long Boom (N1, O4)

The period from the 1940s to 1960s (or 1990 some assert) which was characterized by historically high economic growth rates, low unemployment and fairly stable prices. Cheap oil prices helped to sustain the boom.

long fraud (G0, K4)

A method of luring a supplier into advancing TRADE CREDIT through a borrower acquiring a reputation for settling accounts. The fraudster reliably pays all debts when due and, after establishing such trustworthiness, incurs a large debt, especially on a major order, and then disappears.

longitudinal data (C8)

Statistical information on changes to a cohort through time, e.g. the career of persons.

See also: time series

long period (D0)

1 The period in which all adjustments have been made to a price change.
2 The period in which supply is very ELASTIC as a great expansion in the quantities of factors of production is possible.

See also: Marshallian long period

long-term credit bank (G2)

A bank that makes long-term loans to finance industry and arranges the issue of securities. Major examples of these banks are three state-owned Japanese banks, the Industrial Bank of Japan, the Long-Term Credit Bank of Japan and Nippon Credit Bank. Exposure to domestic declining industries in which they have long invested and increasing competition from other banks have forced them to diversify into new markets, including the international syndicated loan market.

long-term income averaging (H2)

A method of calculating income to produce fairer progressive taxation of persons with fluctuating incomes. Without averaging, a person with only occasional years of high income would be taxed much more heavily in those years than is fair when the years of low income are also taken into consideration. The principal method suggested is to tax cumulative average income in order to avoid long-term taxation unduly reflecting the few years of high income. However, there are critics of this system as the stabilization effects of progressive taxation are reduced. Australia has repeatedly attempted to deal with this problem. In the USA, the TAX REFORM ACT 1986 eliminated income averaging but reduced tax burdens by cutting top marginal tax rates.

References

Musgrave, R.A. and Shoup, C.S. (eds) (1959) *Readings in the Economics of Taxation*, pp. 77–92, London: Macmillan.

long wave (E3)

A cycle in economic activity of about fifty years' duration, usually referred to as the KONDRATIEFF CYCLE. This cycle in time series data was noted as early as 1847 by Hyde Clarke. A variety of explanations have been suggested for these waves, including a cluster of major INNOVATIONS, wars, major changes in transportation systems and major changes in primary product markets.

See also: logistic cycle

References

Reijnders, J. (1990) *Long Waves in Economic Development*, Aldershot: Edward Elgar.
van Duijn, J.J. (1983) *The Long Wave in Economic Life*, London: Allen & Unwin.

Lorenz curve (C1, D6)

A graphical representation of INEQUALITY first proposed in 1905 by US-born statistician Max Otto Lorenz. On the vertical and horizontal axes are measured accumulated percentage distributions, e.g. of firms and their sales. This is used in the study of income distribution and of industrial CONCENTRATION.

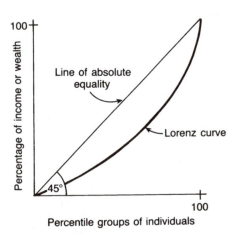

Percentile groups of individuals

loss function (C1)

This shows the deviation of a data point from a least squares fitted line through a scatter of points measured on the vertical axis as a function of the deviation measured on the horizontal axis. This has been applied to DISUTILITY to indicate what has to be minimized.

See also: least squares method

loss leader (M3)

A good or service sold at less than the cost of producing it as an inducement to consumers to use a particular retail outlet. Supermarkets have made much use of this marketing device.

Lotharingian axis (R1) *see* Rhinelands hourglass

lottery (C7)

A game of chance to obtain prizes funded by the sale of tickets; a set of pay-offs each with its own probability. In Italian 'lotto' means destiny or fate. Lotteries are as ancient as Moses' in the Book of Numbers, chapter 26, and Julius Caesar's to fund repairs to Rome. Several major US universities and the British Library used lotteries to raise initial funding. Today many US states have their own lotteries. A national lottery was reintroduced in the UK in 1994. Within three years 70 per cent of the population were regularly playing the game and 13 per cent of the gaming market had been secured by the lottery. A private consortium, Camelot, has run the lottery for a fee of 1 per cent of the sales revenue. It has distributed 50 per cent of the take in prize money and 28 per cent has been devoted to 'good causes' not otherwise funded by the government, especially sport and the arts. Lottery fever has always provoked concern as the gullible poor can ruin themselves through buying tickets. The odds of winning the jackpot in the UK lottery, 14 million to 1, illustrate the view of Adam Smith: 'the chance of gain is naturally overvalued, we may learn from the universal success of lotteries' (*Wealth of Nations*, Book I, ch. X, Part I).

Louvre Accord (F3)

An agreement of February 1987 between the leading industrialized nations of the OECD to stabilize exchange rates between major currencies by maintaining the value of the US dollar in a period with a large US balance of payments deficit. The USA promised to use fiscal measures to reduce demand for imports and Japan and West Germany promised to employ monetary and fiscal means to expand their economies, with the hope the demand for US exports would increase. In order to keep the dollar's value high, higher US interest rates and a fall in stock market values were inevitable. The accord provided a useful forum for the discussion of the economic policies of leading economies and their international implications.

lower quartile (C1)

A value in a set of numbers such that three-quarters of the numbers are greater in value; the seventy-fifth percentile. This value is a benchmark to measure LOW PAY.

See also: median; upper quartile

low pay (J3)

The pay of workers in the bottom part of the earnings structure. Various measures of low pay include being paid less than the lower quartile of earnings (bottom 25 per cent), less than the level of social security benefit or less than is paid to comparable workers. Increasingly low pay is regarded as relative deprivation rather than being below the subsistence level – even SMITH and RICARDO recognized that the notion of subsistence varies with time and place, being not only sufficient for food, housing and clothing but enough to participate fully in a particular society. The low-pay problem is narrower than the poverty problem as it concerns only employed persons who either regard it as a problem because they are paid less than their marginal products, or regard it as unjust to receive little for working normal hours. Suggestions for removing this labour market problem include MINIMUM WAGE legislation, a narrowing of WAGE DIFFERENTIALS and INCOMES POLICIES biased towards the low paid.

loyalty bonus (G0)

The extra shares awarded to the original shareholders of a company for retaining their investment for a stipulated period. Bonuses of this kind have been a feature of UK PRIVATIZATION issues.

Loyd, Samuel Jones, 1796–1883 (B3)

English banker and leading monetary theorist of the CURRENCY SCHOOL. Educated at Cambridge University; Baron Overstone from 1850. As a Member of Parliament and subsequently adviser to the BANK OF ENGLAND, he opposed many of the banking innovations of his day, including joint stock banking. His recommendations formed the basis for the BANK CHARTER ACT 1844.

References

McCulloch, J.R. (ed.) (1858) *Tracts and Other Publications on Metallic and Paper Currency*, London: Longman.
O'Brien, D.P. (ed.) (1971) *The Correspondence of Lord Overstone*, 3 vols, Cambridge: Cambridge University Press.

L share (G1)

A share of a Chinese company listed on the London Stock Exchange.

Lucas, Robert E., Jr, 1937– (B3)

US economist, originally trained as a historian at Chicago University, where he has been John Dewey Distinguished Service Professor of Economics since 1980. As a vigorous advocate of the theory of RATIONAL EXPECTATIONS, he has become a leader of the NEW CLASSICAL ECONOMICS School.

References

Lucas, R.E. (1981) *Studies in Business-Cycle Theory*, Oxford: Basil Blackwell.
Lucas, R.E. and Sargent, T.E. (1981) *Rational Expectations and Econometric Practice*, London: Allen & Unwin.

Lucas supply function (E1)

This states that output is the function of growth in technical progress, population, output in the previous period and errors in expectations of the price level:

$$y_t = k_t + \gamma(p_t - p_t^*) + \lambda Y_{t-1}$$

in which y is real output, p_t is the price level, p_t^* is the expected price level, γ and λ are parameters and k_t is the growth term. This function introduced a different notion of expectations from ADAPTIVE EXPECTATIONS.

Luddite (J5, N3)

1 A member of a gang of English craft workers led by Ned Ludd in the period 1811–13 who showed opposition to the introduction of textile machines in Nottingham, England, and surrounding places and the consequent loss of employment by smashing the machines at night.

2 A person who takes INDUSTRIAL ACTION in an attempt to prevent the implementation of technical change.

lump of labour fallacy (J2)

The view that in at least the short run there is a fixed demand for labour. Employment can only be increased by job sharing and by reducing the hours worked by the existing labour force. This opinion suggests that macroeconomic policy is limited in its ability to stimulate an economy.

lump-sum tax (H2)

A tax of the same amount whatever the activity or circumstances of the taxpayer, e.g. a POLL TAX. A lump-sum tax on a firm increases its fixed costs but leaves MARGINAL COST the same, and thus the output and price of a profit-maximizing firm are unaffected in the short run. In the long run, however, when all costs are variable, a high lump-sum tax would shut down some firms.

Lundberg, Erik Filip, 1907–89 (B3)

Leading Swedish specialist on the theory and policy of the TRADE CYCLE. He was educated at Stockholm University and subsequently was professor of economics there from 1946 to 1965. From 1937 to 1955 he was Director of the Economic Research Institute. His exposition of trade cycle analysis has been applied to Swedish stabilization policy.

References

Lundberg, E. (1937) *Studies in the Theory of Economic Expansion*, London: P.S. King.

Lundberg lag (E2)

The slow adjustment of production to changes in income causing investment or disinvestment in stocks as sales respond more rapidly than output. When incomes are rising, sales are more than output and so stocks are run down, causing unintended disinvestment; when incomes are falling, there is an unintended investment in stocks.

Luxemburg effect (F2)

The causal relationship between the flow of money capital and the flow of capital goods from a metropolis to colonies or other satellites. Rosa LUXEMBURG asserted that this could assume different forms including loans between states, PORTFOLIO INVESTMENT in foreign-owned enterprises and direct investment in overseas subsidiaries. The metropolis benefits from this in that the money flows generate a demand for its capital goods and the repayment of loans by satellites forces them into economic dependence.

Luxemburg, Rosa, 1870–1919 (B3)

Prominent socialist writer who was born in Zamose, Poland, the daughter of a Jewish businessman. Educated at the Russian Second Gymnasium for Girls, Warsaw, and Zurich University where she graduated with a doctorate in law and political science in 1897 (her thesis on *The Industrial Development of Poland* was an original work of economic history arguing against the formation of a nation state of all Polish nationals). She spent much of her life as a political journalist in Germany and as organizer of the Social Democratic Parties of Germany and Poland. As early as 1904, despite following many of MARX's ideas, she criticized LENIN for his autocratic centralist views. Many aspects of the Bolshevik Revolution of 1917 in Russia upset her, including the methods used and the signing of the Treaty of Brest-Litovsk with Germany. In her greatest work, *The Accumulation of Capital* (1913), she developed the Marxian idea of capital accumulation, predicting that, as further capital accumulation is impossible in a closed economy, imperialist expansion into foreign markets and less developed countries would occur so that capitalists would be able to obtain further SURPLUS VALUE. Like her other economic writings, it was notable for its powerful historical illustrations. She was assassinated by a soldier outside a hotel in Berlin and her body was thrown into the River Spree, later to be recovered and buried.

References

Luxemburg, R. (1951) *The Accumulation of Capital*, London: Routledge & Kegan Paul.

Nettl, J.P. (1966) *Rosa Luxemburg*, London: Oxford University Press.

luxury (D0)

A superior good or service affordable and increasingly demanded at higher income levels. The poor cannot buy luxuries; the rich, having been able to satisfy basic needs, have a choice between purchasing luxuries or saving. The concept of INCOME ELASTICITY OF DEMAND is used to identify luxuries: if that elasticity is greater than one, then the good or service is a luxury. Luxuries are often purchased to show the high-ranking status of a person.

See also: Giffen paradox; income and substitution effects; inferior good; Veblen good

M

M0 (E4)

The narrowest definition of the money supply consisting only of notes and coin in circulation plus bankers' deposits with the Banking Department of the BANK OF ENGLAND. This measure was introduced into the UK in October 1983 and given increasing prominence in Treasury statements from October 1985. So many payments are made by the transfer of bank deposits that M0 is only a partial picture of economic activity in a modern economy. Also changes in the method of wage payment from cash to cheque change the extent to which M0 is representative. However, it has recently been regarded as a useful guide to the size of the BLACK ECONOMY that is dominated by cash transactions. Changes in M0 can lead or lag NOMINAL GROSS DOMESTIC PRODUCT.

M1 (E4)

Non-interest-bearing components of the wide monetary base plus private sector non-interest-bearing sterling sight bank deposits (UK). Currency outside the Treasury, Federal Reserve Banks and vaults of depository institutions plus travellers' checks of non-bank issuers plus demand deposits of all commercial banks plus OTHER CHECKABLE DEPOSITS (USA).

M2 (E4)

A measure of the money supply created in 1982 in the USA to provide a good transactions measure of money. In the USA, it consists of M1 plus overnight and continuing contract repurchase agreements and overnight Eurodollars issued to US residents plus MONEY MARKET DEPOSIT ACCOUNTS plus savings and time deposits of less than $100,000 plus balances in general purpose and broker–dealer MONEY MARKET MUTUAL FUNDS. In the UK, it consists of M1 plus private sector interest-bearing sterling bank deposits plus private sector holdings of retail building society shares and deposits and national savings bank ordinary deposits.

M3 (E4)

In the USA this is defined as M2 plus large denomination time deposits and term repurchase liabilities plus term Eurodollars held by US residents at foreign branches of US banks and the banks of the UK and Canada plus institution-only MONEY MARKET MUTUAL FUNDS.

M3c (E4)

STERLING M3 plus private sector holdings of foreign currency bank deposits ('c' refers to the currency assets included).

M4 (E4)

Sterling M3 plus private sector holdings of BUILDING SOCIETY shares and deposits and sterling certificates of deposit minus building society holdings of bank deposits and bank certificates of deposit, and notes and coin.

M5 (E4)
M4 plus holdings by the private sector, other than building societies, of money market instruments (bank bills, treasury bills, local authority deposits), certificates of tax deposit and national savings instruments (excluding savings certificates, SAYE and other long-term deposits).

Maastricht Treaty (F0)
A treaty of the EUROPEAN UNION amending the TREATY OF ROME signed in December 1991 which established the Economic and Monetary Union, a common defence and foreign policy and the Economic and Social Cohesion Fund.

macaroni defence (G3)
A tactic employed by a company resisting a takeover bid. It issues many bonds subject to the condition that they be redeemed at a high price after a takeover.

See also: poison pill

machinery question (O3)
The effect on unemployment of the introduction of machinery. CLASSICAL ECONOMISTS, especially RICARDO, took the view that an increase in FIXED CAPITAL would reduce the size of the WAGES FUND and be injurious to workers, whereas John Stuart MILL presented a more subtle analysis of the variety of effects of increasing CAPITAL–LABOUR RATIOS. This issue of technological unemployment is still pertinent to many discussions in DEVELOPMENT ECONOMICS.

References
Berg, M. (1980) *The Machinery Question and the Making of Political Economy 1815–48*, Cambridge: Cambridge University Press.
Mill, J.S. (1848) *Principles of Political Economy: With Some of their Applications to Social Philosophy*, Book I, ch. 6, ed. by J. M. Robson, Toronto: University of Toronto Press, 1965, Vol. 1.
Nicholson, J.S. (1892) *The Effects of Machinery on Wages*, rev. edn, London: Sonnenschein.

Ricardo, D. (1817) *Principles of Political Economy and Taxation*, ch. 31, ed. by R.M. Hartwell, Harmondsworth: Penguin, 1971.

Machlup, Fritz, 1928–83 (B3)
An Austro-American economist born near Vienna and educated at the University of Vienna, where he was taught by Ludwig von MISES, the supervisor of his doctoral thesis on the GOLD STANDARD. In 1933 he emigrated to the USA and held chairs at the Universities of Buffalo (1933–47), Johns Hopkins (1947–60), Princeton (1960–71) and New York for the remainder of his life. He was a leading authority on international monetary co-operation, as is evident in his seventeen books and almost a hundred articles (e.g. *Remaking the International Monetary System* (1968) on that subject). His other interests in economics included the THEORY OF THE FIRM, THE PATENT SYSTEM and ECONOMIC METHODOLOGY.

References
Dreyer, J.S. (1978) *Breadth and Depth in Economics: Fritz Machlup: The Man and His Ideas*, Lexington, MA: Lexington Books.

Macmillan Gap (G2)
An institutional gap in the range of financial institutions observed by the Macmillan Committee on Finance and Industry (UK) of 1931. Small and medium-sized firms found it difficult to raise finance as they were too small to issue shares but reluctant to use expensive bank advances. It was thought that the performance of many companies, especially in export markets, was adversely affected by their shortage of capital. Since 1931, many new financial institutions, including the INDUSTRIAL AND COMMERCIAL FINANCE CORPORATION, have been set up to deal with this problem. Also, the availability of VENTURE CAPITAL and the growth of the UNLISTED SECURITIES MARKET have provided more finance for such firms.

macroeconomic demand schedule (E0)
The schedule showing different combinations of the price level and real income to

equate planned spending with actual output, assuming that interest rates maintain the money market in equilibrium.

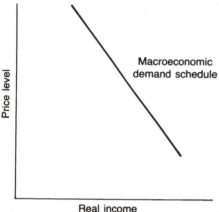

Macroeconomic demand schedule

Price level

Real income

macroeconomic policy (E6)

Measures used by governments to influence major economic aggregates, especially GROSS NATIONAL PRODUCT, UNEMPLOYMENT, INFLATION and the MONEY SUPPLY. Macro-policies have been possible since 1945 through the availability of NATIONAL INCOME accounting, other increases in economic data collection and the theoretical framework provided by KEYNES, his successors and rivals. Increasingly it has been difficult to separate macro-policies from micro-policies, particularly in the labour market.

See also: Employment Act 1946; full employment

macroeconomics (E0)

The study of the relationship between economic aggregates, particularly national income, total consumption, investment and the money supply. Although ROBERTSON in his *A Study of the Trade Cycle* in 1915 was perhaps the first economist to emphasize the importance of considering output in aggregate terms, the Keynesian revolution made this new approach a concern of economics; the associated advent of NATIONAL INCOME accounting provided data to measure the relationships.

Since macroeconomics is used to analyse governments' economic policies, it is inevitably surrounded by controversy.

References

Blanchard, O.I. and Fischer, S. (1989) *Lectures on Macroeconomics*, Cambridge, MA, and London: MIT Press.

Phelps, E.S. (1990) *Seven Schools of Macroeconomic Thought*, Oxford: Clarendon Press.

magic quadrilateral (E0)

Joan ROBINSON's description of an ECONOMY simultaneous with FULL EMPLOYMENT, fast ECONOMIC GROWTH, stable prices and a balance of payments equilibrium.

Mahalanobis model (O2)

The basis of the second Indian five-year plan of the 1950s which propounded the view that a shift to investing in machines to make capital goods, i.e. heavy industry, instead of investment in light industry would eventually produce a higher level and faster growth rate of consumption. In some senses this was a repetition of the philosophy of the early Soviet five-year plans. The model has been criticized for neglecting supply constraints, other than a shortage of capital, and for ignoring the fact that many industries supply both intermediate and final goods. The model is named after Prasanta Mahalanobis (1893–1972) who was a world-renowned authority on statistical sampling and a member of the Indian Planning Commission from 1955 to 1967.

Main Street (G1)

A collective expression for investment analysts and brokers.

Malinvaud, Edmond, 1923– (B3)

Leading Western econometrician and economic theorist who has been a major influence on the construction of economic models. He was born in Limoges, France, and educated in law at the Ecole Polytechnique, Paris, before turning to statistics. He was Professor-Director at the Ecole National de la Statistique et de l'Administration Economique from 1957 to 66 and Director General of INSEE. His researches have included the normative theory of optimal resource allocation and the proper rules for the definitions fundamental to economic statistics and national accounts.

References

Malinvaud, E. (1972) *Lectures on Microeconomic Theory*, trans. A. Silvey, Amsterdam: North-Holland.

—— (1980) *Statistical Methods of Econometrics*, 3rd edn, Amsterdam: North-Holland.

—— (1980) *Profitability and Unemployment*, Cambridge: Cambridge University Press.

—— (1985) *The Theory of Unemployment Reconsidered*, 2nd edn, Oxford: Basil Blackwell.

malleable capital (E0, O4)

Physical capital capable of being instantly and costlessly changed into another form. A term much used in neoclassical growth theory to dispense with the problem of expectations.

Malthus, Thomas Robert, 1766–1834 (B3)

A leading classical economist who played a major part in founding modern DEMO-GRAPHY. After Cambridge, where he was a student and fellow of Jesus College (1784–1805), for the rest of his career he was professor of modern history and political economy at Haileybury College, Hertfordshire, training clerks for the East India Company.

The optimism of William Godwin's *Enquiry Concerning Political Justice* (1793) prompted him to write *An Essay on the Principle of Population* (1798) which asserted that population grows in a GEOMETRICAL PROGRESSION but that the means of subsistence increases in only an ARITHMETIC PROGRESSION. Unless population growth is subject to a preventive check (e.g. abortion) or a positive check (war, famine, pestilence) there will be misery and vice. In subsequent editions he included more

analysis of population statistics and another check ('moral restraint'). Despite contemporary criticism, it became a pillar of the Ricardian system. Later, socialists and other critics attacked such pessimistic predictions for ignoring the beneficial effects of technical progress. Nevertheless Malthus's *Essay* was an inspiration to Charles Darwin when he was formulating his theory of evolution. Malthus's *Principles of Political Economy* (1820) provided a fuller analysis of value and price theory than RICARDO and discussed the problem of a deficiency in 'EFFECTUAL DEMAND' (a general glut), causing KEYNES to rank Malthus as one of his major predecessors as a macroeconomic theorist.

References

Cunningham Wood, J. (1986) *Thomas Robert Malthus: Critical Assessments*, London: Croom Helm.

James, P. (1979) *Population Malthus: His Life and Times*, London: Routledge & Kegan Paul.

Wrigley, E.A. and Souden, D. (eds) (1986) *The Works of Thomas Robert Malthus*, 8 vols, London: Pickering & Chatto.

managed currency fund (F3, G2)

An investment fund with its assets in several currencies which creates profits for investors by buying and selling foreign currencies in anticipation of fluctuations in their value and from earnings arising from deposit holdings and interest on short-term bonds.

managed floating system (F3)

The post BRETTON WOODS exchange rate regime in which the extent to which exchange rates could freely move to establish their market values was limited by the intervention of CENTRAL BANKS.

See also: dirty float

managed trade (F1)

The abandonment of a free market and FREE TRADE for government intervention. This form of protectionism is often undertaken to help particular industries. In the USA in the 1980s there was managed trade for the automobile, steel and semi-conductor industries especially to cope with Japanese imports.

See also: infant industry argument

management accounting (M4)
The financial appraisal of the past, present and future activities of a firm. It includes CASH BUDGETING (a prediction of future cash inflows and outflows which indicates what further finance is required), CAPITAL BUDGETING (appraisal of investment plans) and TRANSFER PRICING. Management accountants are also concerned to monitor the design of present accounting systems to prevent fraud and to meet the growing needs of management for information. It developed from cost accounting in response to the increasing complexity of large firms.

See also: accounting; financial accounting

management buyout (G3)
A management's purchase of a company from its shareholders. Buyouts have become increasingly popular in the UK and the USA since the 1960s as many managers fear the dismemberment of their company by a receiver. Often managers finance the acquisition by fixed interest borrowing using the collateral of the company's assets in a leveraged buyout.

See also: asset stripping

management by objectives (M1)
The setting of specific targets for subordinate managers relating to each of their tasks so that the individual efficiency of each unit of an organization can be monitored regularly.

managerial models of the firm (L2)
Explanations of the behaviour of a FIRM according to its dominant aims. The various aims assumed include sales maximization, PROFIT MAXIMIZATION, MANAGERIAL UTILITY FUNCTION MAXIMIZATION and maximization, of the rate of growth of the firm. It has been argued that the passing of the control of firms from shareholders to

managers has been responsible for a change of aims. However, some Marxists argue that the aims of firms essentially remain the same as shareholders and managers have similar socioeconomic backgrounds.

References

Marris, R. (1964) *The Economic Theory of Managerial Capitalism*, London: Macmillan.

managerial revolution (M1)
James Burnham's theory that after 1914 there was a transition from a capitalist to a managerial society with the class of managers dominant, operating most effectively where the state owns the means of production. Because managers became the ruling class, they exploited workers just as individual capitalists had done before, ensuring that there would be an unequal distribution of income. As managers without capital will not be guided by a profit motive, the economy they run will be less subject to cyclical fluctuations and crises and can be successfully planned; this planning will take a long-term view to encourage invention and innovation. Much of Burnham's argument is couched in Marxist terms as in his career as professor of philosophy at New York University (1932–54) his dominant concern was a socialist critique of contemporary society. GALBRAITH and others have viewed this revolution more loosely as a recognition of the transfer of power in corporations from shareholders to hired managers.

References

Burnham, J. (1945) *The Managerial Revolution*, Harmondsworth: Penguin.

managerial utility function maximization (L2)
Maximization of the satisfaction of the managers of a FIRM. The utility of managers will be increased if their status improves by an enlargement of staff expenditures, as this shows ability to manage, or if managerial salaries and profits

are higher than an acceptable minimum level.

References

Williamson, O.E. (1964) *The Economics of Discretionary Behavior: Managerial Objectives in a Theory of the Firm*, Englewood Cliffs, NJ: Prentice Hall.

Manchester School (B1)
Benjamin Disraeli's term in 1848 for the nineteenth-century Lancashire cotton manufacturers and politicians who strenuously advocated FREE TRADE, buying in the cheapest and selling in the dearest market. The original centre of the school was the Anti-Corn Law League (founded in 1838 by Richard Cobden and John Bright) but it expanded its LAISSEZ-FAIRE principles over other policy issues. It was more of an action group than a school of economics; contemporary German PROTECTIONISTS contemptuously called it 'Manchestertum'.

See also: Corn Laws

References

Grampp, W.D. (1960) *The Manchester School*, Stanford, CA: Stanford University Press.

Mandeville, Bernard, 1670–1733 (B3)
Dutch doctor of medicine and essayist who, after acquiring a doctorate in medicine at the University of Leiden in 1691, settled in London. In a series of poems and essays compiled as *The Fable of the Bees* (1714, 1724) he demonstrated that private vices such as vanity, fraud and theft promote the public good by providing much employment. In a sense he anticipated the INVISIBLE HAND principle of SMITH and the LAISSEZ-FAIRE views of some classical economists.

References

Hayek, F. A. (1966) 'Mandeville', *Proceedings of the British Academy* 52: 125–41.
Mandeville, B. (1970) *The Fable of the Bees*, ed. P. Harth, Harmondsworth: Penguin.

manpower forecasting (J2)
Estimating the future demand for and supply of labour. These forecasts can be made for a nation, a region or a firm. They consist of deriving a demand for labour forecast from an output forecast using fixed labour–output coefficients (sometimes revised by informed management opinion) and a supply of labour forecast based on population projections, LABOUR FORCE PARTICIPATION RATES and estimations of labour migration.

manpower policy (J2)
Various measures to train the LABOUR FORCE, increase LABOUR FORCE PARTICIPATION RATES, improve the allocation of the existing labour force and bring about a close match between labour demand and supply in the future. The first step in the operation of this policy is to prepare a manpower forecast, often by applying fixed labour–output coefficients to output forecasts. From these forecasts it is possible to see which instruments of manpower policy should be chosen, e.g. training measures to eliminate an expected shortage of skilled workers. Although many countries had active manpower policies during the Second World War as the demands of the armed forces for personnel created labour shortages elsewhere in most economies, it was not until the 1950s and 1960s that the UK and the USA pursued active policies.

See also: labour market policy

maple leaf (E5)
Canadian gold coin weighing one troy ounce (31.1 g).

Maquiladora (F1)
A trade programme established in 1965 and expanded in 1989 to allow duty-free imports into Mexico for transformation into Mexican exports.

Marcet, Jane, 1769–1858 (B3)
Wife of a distinguished physician and daughter of a Swiss merchant; very famous in her day as a writer on economics. Her *Conversations on Political Economy, in which the Elements of that Science are Familiarly Explained* (1816), published ten

years after her successful *Conversations on Chemistry*, anticipated some of RICARDO's ideas and was praised by both him and SAY. Her stern summary of CLASSICAL ECONOMICS takes the form of conversations between Mrs B and Caroline on twenty-one topics, including property, division of labour, capital, wages, population, the condition of the poor, revenue from factors of production, value, money, foreign trade and expenditure. Caroline is encouraged to study economics as 'you will seldom hear a conversation amongst liberal-minded people without some reference to it'.

See also: female economists

marginal cost (D0)
The cost of producing another unit of output. Whether marginal cost falls, rises or is constant depends on whether there are increasing, decreasing or constant RETURNS TO SCALE.

See also: average incremental cost

marginal cost of abatement (Q0)
The cost of removing the last unit of a nuisance, e.g. a noise or some form of physical pollution. This measure can be used to see whether it is worthwhile to reduce the external costs of an activity, e.g. to calculate the expense of reducing a noise by a decibel at a time until an acceptable level has been reached.

marginal cost pricing (D4)
Setting a price so that it is equal to the marginal cost of producing that good or service. It is justified on the grounds of maximizing social efficiency. In practice, there are difficulties in following this rule.

   Deficits can arise for a firm with declining average total costs, and consequently falling marginal costs, as prices, if set equal to marginal costs, would fail to cover fixed costs. However, these can be covered separately – by government subsidy or by a TWO-PART TARIFF, part of which would be the 'price of entry' to the market, e.g. a telephone rental can cover fixed costs and the charge for calls marginal costs. Com-

putational experience in applying this principle has increasingly dealt with the problems of fixed costs, complex production and distribution systems and changes in demand and technology. Critics of this type of pricing remain concerned about its MONOPOLY and INCOME DISTRIBUTION effects.

References

Rees, R. (1984) *Public Enterprise Economics*, ch. 5, London: Weidenfeld & Nicolson.

marginal efficiency of capital (E2)
The rate of discount which will make the present value of a stream of annual incomes from an investment in fixed capital

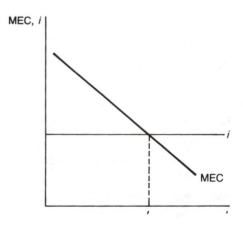

equal to the current supply price of that asset. The concept can be expressed in a diagram: net investment *I* will expand until it reaches I_1, where the marginal efficiency of capital MEC is equal to the rate of interest *i*.

References

Keynes, J.M. (1936) *The General Theory of Employment, Interest and Money*, Book IV, ch. 2, London: Macmillan; New York: St Martin's Press.

marginal efficiency of investment (E2)
The INTERNAL RATE OF RETURN on capital, net of the rate of interest.

marginal employment subsidy (H2, J3)
A government subsidy given to firms for the creation of every additional job above a stated reference level of employment. This scheme can be more effective than a general employment subsidy as it targets pockets of severe unemployment.

marginal firm (L2)
An established firm of an industry only earning NORMAL PROFITS. It would leave that industry if its net earnings were less. This concept is crucial to PERFECT COMPETITION.

marginalism (B4)
An economic method, central to NEOCLAS-SICAL ECONOMICS, much used since 1870 in economics. In most cases, it compares an incremental change in one variable with a similar change in another, e.g. an addition to total costs compared with an addition to total revenue. It assumes automatic movement to EQUILIBRIUM and ignores institutional impediments.

marginalists (B1)
A group of economists of the 1870s who powerfully used differential calculus to examine the effects of small changes in economic quantities and were amongst the founders of the school of NEOCLASSICAL ECONOMY. Simultaneously, JEVONS in Manchester, MENGER in Vienna and WALRAS in Lausanne emphasized the notion of MAR-GINAL UTILITY as central to value theory, thereby abandoning the LABOUR THEORY OF

VALUE popular with many of the CLASSICAL ECONOMISTS. Although many have viewed their work as a revolution in economics, they had many predecessors who share their glory, particularly COURNOT, THÜNEN, DUPUIT and GOSSEN.

See also: continuity thesis

References

Black, R.D., Coats, A.W. and Goodwin, C.D.W. (1973) *The Marginal Revolution in Economics*, Durham, NC: Duke University Press.

marginal physical product (D2)
The extra physical amount of output from employing another unit of a factor of production, e.g. labour or capital.

See also: marginal revenue product; returns to scale

marginal private cost (D0)
The cost to a household or firm of producing an extra unit of output.

See also: marginal social cost

marginal private damage (Q0)
The cost to a firm of producing another unit of a good or service generating externalities, e.g. a chemical works will have to bear the costs of corroded pipes.

See also: marginal social damage

marginal productivity theory (D2, D3, J3)
A theory of the demand for a FACTOR OF PRODUCTION by a profit-maximizing firm. It is asserted that labour or capital will be demanded until the MARGINAL REVENUE from employing it is equal to its MARGINAL COST. The theory, first expounded by John Bates CLARK, has been used to explain wage determination but, as it says nothing about supply, is only useful in explaining wages in the short run when labour supply is completely INELASTIC.

marginal product of labour (D0, J2)
The extra output from one more unit of labour input. It is difficult to measure for large sectors and so, as a proxy, what is

measured is the extra product resulting, on average, from an extra labour input.

See also: average incremental cost

marginal propensity to consume (E2)
The change in consumption resulting from increasing income by one unit. For example, if all the additional income is consumed, the marginal propensity to consume (MPC) is 1; if only one-half, the MPC is 0.5. This measure is essential in CONSUMPTION FUNCTION and MULTIPLIER analysis. Consumer research shows that MPCs are usually lower for higher income groups.

marginal propensity to import (F1)
The change in the value of imports brought about by income increasing by one unit. If all extra income is spent on imports, the marginal propensity to import (MPM) is 1; if only 10 per cent is spent on imports, the MPM is 0.1. Calculation of the MPM is essential to a measurement of the FOREIGN TRADE MULTIPLIER.

marginal propensity to save (E2)
The change in saving resulting from income increasing by one unit. In a simple economy described by the equation national income = consumption + saving, the MARGINAL PROPENSITY TO CONSUME plus the marginal propensity to save is equal to unity. An economy with a high marginal propensity to save will have little scope for MULTIPLIER expansion of its national income as saving is a withdrawal from the CIRCULAR FLOW of income.

marginal rate of substitution (D1)
The amount of one good which a consumer receives as compensation for giving up one unit of another good. It is equal to the ratio of the MARGINAL UTILITIES of two goods and is represented by the slope of an INDIFFERENCE CURVE.

References

Hicks, J.R. (1939) *Value and Capital*, ch. 1, Oxford: Oxford University Press.

marginal rate of transformation (D2)
The reduction in the amount of output of good X as a consequence of an additional unit of a related good Y being produced; the slope of the PRODUCTION POSSIBILITY FRONTIER. This marginal rate is equal to the marginal cost of Y divided by the marginal cost of X.

marginal revenue (D0)
The increase in total revenue resulting from output increasing by one unit. Under PERFECT COMPETITION, a firm's marginal revenue will equal the price of its product as its demand curve is horizontal. For a firm to maximize its profits, it must choose the output level where its marginal revenue is equal to marginal cost.

marginal revenue product (D0)
A MARGINAL physical PRODUCT (MPP) multiplied by the MARGINAL REVENUE obtained from that unit. Under PERFECT COMPETITION, as price is equal to MARGINAL REVENUE, the marginal revenue product (MRP) is equal to the product of the marginal physical product and the price. The MRP shows the addition to the TOTAL REVENUE of a firm of producing another unit.

marginal social cost (D0, Q0)
The extra cost to society of one unit of output.

See also: externality; marginal private cost

marginal social damage (Q0)
The total cost, private and non-private, to society of producing another unit of a good or service injurious to people and the environment, e.g. a chemical works with pollutant by-products will increase the private costs of its owner and also any member of society coming into contact with the pollution. There is no incentive to abate pollution if the marginal cost of abatement is greater than the marginal social damage.

See also: marginal cost of abatement; marginal private damage

marginal tax rate (H2)
The amount of tax paid on an extra unit of money income. In the study of labour supply, marginal tax rates are often calculated to see whether high marginal rates have an incentive or disincentive effect on labour supply. An incentive effect occurs if a taxpayer has a target post-tax income achievable only by working more after a rise in the marginal rate of tax; a disincentive effect occurs if a higher marginal tax rate makes the taxpayer opt for leisure instead of work.

See also: average tax rate

marginal utility (D0)
The amount of satisfaction obtained from consumption of the last unit of a good or service. Although there were hints of such an analytical tool in economics before 1870, particularly in BENTHAM's writings, it was the MARGINALISTS who were first to make extensive use of the concept, employing differential calculus. The LAW OF DIMINISHING MARGINAL UTILITY was enunciated simultaneously.

See also: cardinal utility; util; utility

margin call (G1)
A broker's demand for additional cash. This request insures a broker against a price fall as an investor deposits an amount of cash with his or her broker proportionate to the value of share purchases.

margin of safety (M2)
Total sales revenue minus breakeven point sales revenue.

See also: breakeven level of income

margin requirements (E5)
The banking rule imposed by the FEDERAL RESERVE SYSTEM on its member banks which determines the minimum amount which has to be paid in advance for the purchase of stock market securities.

margins (J3)
Additions to the Australian BASIC WAGE to reward different skills and create OCCUPATIONAL WAGE DIFFERENTIALS.

margin trading (G1)
Purchases of securities only requiring payment for a portion of the transaction, with interest being charged on the debit balance. If the margin were 20 per cent only $20,000 of a purchase costing $100,000 would be requested by a broker. In the USA , the practice has long been common, contributing to the financial panic of 1929 as then small investors with few resources used loans to purchase stock; when the loans were recalled, the demand for and prices of stocks collapsed.

See also: margin requirements

market (D4)
A medium for exchanges between buyers and sellers. Some markets are physically located in one place; others connect buyers and sellers by telephone, fax and e-mail, especially in the case of financial markets. Markets for goods and services are termed 'product' markets; for labour and capital, 'factor markets'. There is a linkage between factor and product markets in that the demand for a factor is derived from the demand for its product. Dealers in a market seek to create an EQUILIBRIUM between demand and supply at a particular price. However, the existence of many market imperfections, e.g. MONOPOLY and ASYMMETRIC INFORMATION, distorts markets. A full set of markets must include markets for FUTURES and for risk taking. Markets have also been classified according to whether they are FIXPRICE or FLEXPRICE.

See also: black market; buyer's market; capital market; clearing market; common market; contingent market; controlled market; currency market; discount market; dual labour market; efficient market; Eurobond market; Eurodollar market; external labour market; factor market;

federal funds market; forward market; free market; futures market; gold market; grey market; insurance market; internal labour market; internal market; International Monetary Market; labour market; lemons market; local labour market; London Traded Options Market; missing market; over-the-counter market; primary labour market; primary market; secondary labour market; secondary market; second market; securities market; seller's market; shallow market; short-term money market; spot market; swap market; third market; UK gilts market; Unlisted Securities Market; US Treasury bond market; white market; wholesale money market

marketable discharge permit (Q0)

A permit to discharge air and water pollutants up to a standard level of environmental quality which can be sold to another firm. This is a modified pollution offset system.

References

Krupnick, A., Oates, W. and Van De Verg, E. (1983) 'On marketable air pollution permits: the case for a system of pollution offsets', *Journal of Environmental Economics and Management* 10: 233–47.
McGartland, A.M. and Oates, W.X. (1985) 'Marketable permits for the prevention of environmental deterioration', *Journal of Environmental Economics and Management* 12: 207–28.

market adjustment (D0)

The changes in prices and quantities arising from changes in demand and supply of a market.

market anti-inflation plan (E3)

A proposal to keep the general price level stable but individual prices flexible by a system created by legislation which would issue sales rights to firms. These rights would equal current net sales at pre-existing prices, corrected for changes in a firm's capital and labour inputs and the average growth in national productivity. Relative prices could change by a firm buying sales rights unused by other firms.

See also: incomes policy; Lerner; prices policy

References

Lerner, A.P. and Colander, D.C. (1980) *MAP: A Market Anti-inflation Plan*, New York: Harcourt Brace Jovanovich.

market balance of payments (F4)

The balance of demand for and supply of a country's currency in the exchange market at a given exchange rate.

See also: balance of payments

market capitalization (G1, M2)

The EQUITY value of a company equal to the total number of its shares multiplied by their market price.

market clearing (D0)

Adjusting demand and supply to each other until an EQUILIBRIUM is established. To clear, either price or quantity changes can be used.

market clearing price (D0)

The ruling price in a particular period for which there is sufficient demand to equal the amount supplied, even if there are simultaneous shocks to the economy. Some markets rarely appear to produce clearing prices as they are in DISEQUILIBRIUM for long periods of time, e.g. the labour market where involuntary unemployment and vacancies coexist for long periods of time.

market concentration (L1)

The concentration of sales of an industry or a market accounted for by the largest firms, e.g. the proportion of electrical goods sold by the largest four firms.

See also: aggregate concentration

market-conforming chain of causation (O1)

A market-friendly economic development strategy which attempts to increase ECONOMIC GROWTH through greater competition and improvements in the educational system. Freedom of entry and exit of firms are crucial to this strategy.

market demand (D0)
The total demand for a good or service by all the consumers who pay for it.

See also: sponsor demand

market discrimination coefficient (J7)
BECKER'S measure of pure DISCRIMINATION which is the residual after differentials produced by variations in education, skills and job experience have been removed. It is measured by the formula

$$\text{MDC} = \frac{Y(W)}{Y(N)} - \frac{Y_0(W)}{Y_0(N)}$$

where $Y(W)$ and $Y(N)$ are the actual incomes of the dominant group W and the oppressed group N respectively and the incomes Y_0 are those in the absence of discrimination.

See also: discrimination

market distortion (D0)
A market allocation that fails to reach a social optimum. Sometimes this occurs because of government intervention.

market economy (P1)
An economy with extensive private ownership of capital and with allocation of goods and services by the price mechanism in the absence of government intervention. The PHYSIOCRATS and CLASSICAL ECONOMISTS praised this form of economy; NEOCLASSICAL ECONOMISTS have analysed it in detail, e.g. by showing how a system of COMPETITIVE TRADING is used for the exchange of all commodities. For a market economy to flourish, goods must be available in competitive markets at prices which reflect their long-run scarcities and businesses must be motivated by profit.

market equilibrium (D0)
A state of rest for a market with the quantity of a good or service traded constant and prices not moving up or down, with the consequence that there is no incentive for buyers or sellers to modify their behaviour. In the simplest case of a market relationship, only the relationship between price and quantity is analysed. If anything else which could affect the quantities demanded and supplied changes, the EQUILIBRIUM is disturbed, e.g. if consumers' incomes or tastes change, the weather is poor, there is a change of government or a war.

See also: disequilibrium; equilibrium

market failure (D0, H4, Q0)
1 The malfunctioning of a market because of the imperfections in it.
2 EXTERNALITIES because a market is producing social costs.
3 The lack of a market for a particular good or service, as in the case of PUBLIC GOODS.

The most familiar of failures are UNEMPLOYMENT, persistent shortages of particular skills, balance of payments disequilibria, the production of PRIVATE GOODS at considerable external cost, regional problems and unanticipated inflation.

See also: market distortion; missing market

market forces (L1)
1 Demand for and supply of FACTORS OF PRODUCTION and the goods and services produced by them.
2 The determinants of prices, investment and output in competitive markets.
3 The system of allocation which is the alternative to ECONOMIC PLANNING.

market form (D4, L1) *see* market structure

market-maker (G1)
A stockbroker who both carries out clients' orders to buy or sell and trades on his or her own account. By being prepared to buy and sell at all times, he or she creates a market in stocks and shares. The London STOCK EXCHANGE copied this system from the NATIONAL ASSOCIATION OF SECURITIES DEALERS AUTOMATED QUOTATION SYSTEM when the jobbing system peculiar to the UK was abandoned in 1986. But London did not

follow the narrow New York rule of having a single market-maker per stock. In 1987, there were forty in London, a much larger number than thought necessary.

See also: jobber; primary dealer

market order (G1)
An order to buy or sell a SECURITY at the current market price.

See also: limit order

market power (D0)
A buyer's or seller's ability to influence a market price. For a seller, this power, the consequence of the INELASTICITY of the demand curve facing it, often results in high profits.

See also: concentration

market prices (E3)
A valuation of the NATIONAL INCOME that includes indirect taxes net of subsidies.

See also: factor cost; gross national product

market rate of interest (E4)
The RATE OF INTEREST set by a particular financial market.

See also: natural rate of interest; Wicksell

market risk (D0)
The possible losses caused by a volatile market subject to frequent price changes. Also known as 'price risk'.

market segmentation (D4, J4)
The division of a market into sub-markets separated by barriers. John Stuart MILL described the sub-markets as non-competing groups. DISCRIMINATION has caused many labour markets to be segmented. To increase total revenue firms use PRICE DISCRIMINATION to separate one part of a market from another.

market share (L1, M3)
The proportion of the sales of an industry sold by a particular firm or group of firms. This share is the basis of the concept of an AGGREGATE CONCENTRATION ratio and is often used as a major managerial goal.

market socialism (L2, P4)
1 A planned economy which attempts to improve allocation by using markets. This type of ECONOMY experienced many economic problems; for example, the most famous case, the former Yugoslavia, experienced high inflation, low economic growth and rising unemployment.
2 Various forms of workers' control and self-management.

See also: industrial democracy; workers' participation

References

Devine, P.J. (1988) *Democracy, and Economic Planning*, Cambridge: Polity Press.
Prout, C. (1985) *Market Socialism in Yugoslavia*, Oxford: Clarendon Press.

market space (M3)
The total amount of customer spending with a particular company. It depends on the proportion of a customer's income available to the company and on the range of products the customer is willing to buy.

See also: market share

market structure (L1)
1 The organizational form of a market.
2 The number of firms, buyers and products related to each other.

The principal structures are competitive, oligopolistic and monopolistic. The structure has a major effect on the freedom of a firm to make economic decisions and also affects the level of product prices. Such structures form a continuum differing from each other by the degree of CONCENTRATION in that market.

See also: duopoly; monopolistic competition; oligopoly; perfect competition

marking (D0, G1)
1 The valuation of assets or income.
2 A recorded sale or purchase of securities.

See also: historic cost

Markov chain model (C1, F2)

A probabilistic analysis showing how each state in an evolutionary process produces the next state in a finite chain. This has been applied to the study of reproduction and migration, e.g. migration between two countries depends on past movements of population.

References

Bartholomew, D.J. (1982) *Stochastic Models for Social Processes*, 3rd edn, New York and Chichester: Wiley.

Markovitz efficient portfolio (G1)

A portfolio of securities with the highest expected return for a given level of risk. Sometimes called a mean–variance efficient portfolio.

Markovitz, Harry Max, 1927– (B3)

Educated at the University of Chicago and professor at Rutgers University since 1980. He has been principally concerned in his works with the theory of rational behaviour under uncertainty and portfolio theory. He has contributed to production theory and the creation of software to aid business decision making. In 1990, he shared the NOBEL PRIZE FOR ECONOMICS with SHARPE and MILLER for his contribution to portfolio theory.

mark-up (D4)

The margin for profits added to average cost when pricing products according to a formula.

mark-up pricing (D4)

The formation of a product price by adding a percentage for profit to unit average cost. A gross mark-up includes a contribution to overhead costs; a net mark-up does not, as the unit cost includes a contribution to overheads, assuming a particular output. The theory was designed as a realistic alternative to using marginal measures to calculate prices. It has been asserted that this pricing method is a major cause of COST-PUSH INFLATION.

See also: Kalecki

marriage allowance (H2)

The additional tax relief given to married people to enable a spouse to be more easily supported; also known as marriage deduction.

See also: income-splitting system

Marshall, Alfred, 1842–1924 (B3)

The Cambridge economist who dominated economics in the UK from the late nineteenth century to the 1930s. After graduating in mathematics from Cambridge in 1865 and becoming a fellow of St John's College, Cambridge, he turned to the study of ethics and psychology. It was his passionate interest in social issues that led him to economics, beginning with a translation of classical economics into mathematics and some papers on international trade theory. In 1877 he married a pupil, Mary Paley (with whom he wrote his first book, *The Economics of Industry* (1879)), and was appointed Principal and Professor of Political Economy at the new University College, Bristol. From 1885 to 1908 he was professor of political economy at Cambridge, retiring early to concentrate on his writing.

It was the publication of his *Principles of Economics* in 1890 that established his leadership of the economics profession. This beautifully written book, which relegates difficult points to footnotes and appendices, was intended to build on the theories of the CLASSICAL and MARGINALIST Schools an integrated analytical framework for the subject. His vast knowledge of economic history and the industrial and labour conditions of his day is evident throughout. He achieved an exposition of price theory still basic to modern microeconomics. ELASTICITY OF DEMAND, the distinction between short and long periods, the concept of ECONOMIC RENT, CONSUMER'S SURPLUS and internal and external ECONOMIES OF SCALE are all carefully explained. Some innovations, e.g. the REPRESENTATIVE FIRM, were less successful. His sympathy for much of classical economics and his reading of psychology gave him an organic view of the development of firms. He intended to publish a second volume to cover industrial fluctuations, money and international trade but it was not until 1923 that he was able to do so in his *Money, Credit and Commerce*, when it was too late for him to write with the force he had achieved in his *Principles* or to refine his analysis. By achieving the separation of the teaching of economics from the other 'moral sciences' he soon made Cambridge the centre of UK economics. His star pupils PIGOU and KEYNES used many of his analytical tools and continued the veneration of him and his works.

See also: continuity thesis

References

Groenewegen, P. (1995) *A Soaring Eagle: Alfred Marshall 1842–1924*, Aldershot: Edward Elgar.
Guillebaud, C.W. (ed.) (1965) *Marshall's Principles of Economics*, variorum edn, London: Macmillan.
O'Brien, D.P. and Presley, J.R. (eds) (1965) *Pioneers of Modern Economics in Britain*, ch. 2, London: Macmillan.
Pigou, A.C. (ed.) (1925) *Memorials of Alfred Marshall*, London: Macmillan.

Marshallian demand curve (D0)
MARSHALL's graphical representation of a demand schedule showing the relationship between two variables, price and quantity demanded, assuming that any other determinants of demand remain the same as prices change. FRIEDMAN and others have discussed the implications of the *ceteris paribus* assumptions, especially the difficulty of keeping real income constant as prices change.

References

Friedman, M. (1953) *Essays in Positive Economics*, pp. 47–99, Chicago and London: University of Chicago Press.
Marshall, A. (1920) *Principles of Economics*, 8th edn, Book 3, ch. 3 and Mathematical Appendix, London: Macmillan

Marshallian long period (D2)
A period of several years in which normal

prices are established, the FACTORS OF PRODUCTION are adjusted to demand and the supply of these factors is changed – a stationary state similar to that assumed in RICARDO's theory of value. MARSHALL distinguished it from the period of secular change in which there is a 'gradual growth of knowledge, of population, and of capital, and the changing conditions of demand and supply from one generation to another'.

References

Marshall, A. (1920) *Principles of Economics. An Introductory Volume*, 8th edn, Book 5, ch. 5, London: Macmillan.

Marshallian methodology (B4)
The PARTIAL EQUILIBRIUM ANALYSIS central to NEOCLASSICAL ECONOMICS. Marshall, fond of the motto *natura non facit saltum* (nature does not make a jump), was concerned to demonstrate the continuous nature of economic change, examining economic phenomena 'a bit at a time' so that the forces which bring about EQUILIBRIUM could be adequately examined. He forged new tools to achieve his analytical goals: these included substitution, the ELASTICITY coefficient, the REPRESENTATIVE FIRM, CONSUMER'S SURPLUS, QUASI-RENT, internal and external ECONOMIES OF SCALE, PRIME AND SUPPLEMENTARY COST, the short run and the long run.

Marshallian short period (D2)
The period of time in which output can only be increased by using existing factor supplies more intensively.

Marshallian stability (D0)
Market stability brought about by the adjustment of quantity to differences between demand price and supply price. A new EQUILIBRIUM is not achieved if price or quantity moves in the wrong direction or if there is overadjustment of price or quantity.

See also: cobweb

Marshall–Lerner condition (F4)
The values of PRICE ELASTICITIES OF DEMAND for imports and exports required for a

DEVALUATION of a currency to succeed in improving a country's BALANCE OF PAYMENTS. The condition states that the sum of the price elasticities of demand for imports and exports, measured in the same currency, must be more than unity and ELASTICITIES OF SUPPLY must be high. Thus if the demand for imports is not elastic enough to discourage consumption of them when import prices have risen consequent on devaluation, the demand for exports can be so elastic that the increased value of imports induced by devaluation will compensate. This is a PARTIAL EQUILIBRIUM approach as only import and export markets are considered.

See also: J-curve

Marshall Plan (N1, O2)

US AID to sixteen countries of Western Europe proposed by General George Marshall, US Secretary of State, which, in the form of economic and military grants and loans, amounted to $16.4 billion in the period 1948–52. Western Europe's loss of overseas investments, the ending of much of its trade with Eastern Europe and the decline in its TERMS OF TRADE necessitated outside help. In 1946, large European balance of payments deficits required immediate US assistance consisting of shipments of goods and finance for reconstruction. It was given to these countries, members of the ORGANIZATION FOR ECONOMIC CO-OPERATION AND DEVELOPMENT, as part of the European Recovery Programme and was administered by the European Co-operation Administration.

The recipient countries were expected to follow orthodox economic policies to control inflation, get their exchange rates at the right level and adjust their domestic policies to achieve an external balance. It was hoped that Marshall Aid would avoid a major world depression after the Second World War. The gift of US dollars to Europe enabled European countries to finance imports from the USA, but the dollar gap was slow to disappear and the amount of Marshall Plan assistance far

from generous: more was given after the plan than during the period of its operation. The Marshall Plan hoped to create a new international order by linking Europe, North America and the Third World. The USA would purchase raw materials from less developed countries which would then be able to buy exports from Western Europe. The economic plight of East European countries after 1989 has prompted demands for a similar major aid initiative.

See also: European Bank for Reconstruction and Development

References

Hogan, M.I. (1987) *The Marshall Plan: America, Britain and the Reconstruction of Western Europe, 1947–52*, Cambridge and New York: Cambridge University Press.

Wexler, I. (1983) *The Marshall Plan Revisited: The European Recovery Program in Economic Perspective*, Westport, CO: Greenwood.

Martineau, Harriet, 1802–76 (B3)

Leading popularizer of economics in England in the mid-nineteenth century. Born in Norwich, the daughter of a Unitarian cloth manufacturer, she studied SMITH, RICARDO and MALTHUS from the age of 14 and was inspired to write on political economy by MARCET's popular works. Severe deafness forced her to adopt a literary career, which she successfully did with her twenty-four part *Illustrations of Political Economy, Fables with Morals*, beginning with an account of life in the wilds of South Africa. This work followed the typical classical division of the subject into production, distribution, exchange and consumption, and gained her a reputation as a female Malthusian. She said that the research materials she used were 'the standard works on the subject of what I then took to be a science'.

See also: female economists; Malthus

References

Fox, C. (1883) *Harriet Martineau's Autobiography*, 2 vols, London: Virago Press.

Martineau, H. (1859) *Illustrations of Political Economy*, 9 vols, London: Routledge, Warner & Routledge.

martingale (C7)

Originally a French betting system in which the stakes are doubled after each loss to assure a favourable outcome with a high probability of success. This mathematical model of a fair game, a stochastic process, has been applied to the analysis of asset prices, particularly to see whether the rates of return to assets are such that asset prices and cumulated dividends at their present values are equal to the discounted value of a mutual fund.

References

Hall, P. and Heyde, C.C. (1980) *Martingale Limit Theory and its Applications*, New York: Academic Press.

Le Roy, S.T. (1989) 'Efficient capital markets and martingales', *Journal of Economic Literature* 27 (December): 1583–621.

Marxian economics (E6, P2)

The application of MARX's theories of VALUE and EXPLOITATION to price theory, COMPETITION and the working of modern CAPITALIST economies. In recent years Marxian economists have attempted to provide an alternative to NEOCLASSICAL analysis of most areas of economic theory and policy, including monetary and general macroeconomic theory as well as a study of TRANSNATIONAL CORPORATIONS, income distribution and the business cycle. Prominent Marxian economists in the twentieth century have included Paul BARAN, Maurice Dobb and Ronald Meek.

References

Roemer, J.E. (1981) *Analytical Foundations of Marxian Economic Theory*, Cambridge: Cambridge University Press.

Marx, Karl Heinrich, 1818–83 (B3)

German-born philosopher, sociologist, journalist and leading classical economist. Born in Trier, the son of a prosperous lawyer, he was educated at the University of Bonn (briefly) and at the University of Berlin where he received a doctorate in

1841 for his research into post-Aristotelian Greek philosophy. His interest in socialism was first aroused by conversations with Baron von Westphalen, whose daughter Jenny he was later to marry; his taste for metaphysics was stimulated by involvement in the Young Hegelian Group from 1837. His career as a journalist began with his editing of the liberal paper *Rheinsche Zeitung* from October 1842; his interest in economics dates from his residence in Paris in 1844 where he had migrated to study contemporary French socialism. It was to SMITH, RICARDO and JAMES MILL that he turned to obtain an analytical training to tackle what was to be his life-long research project, CAPITALISM. Fortunately, in Paris he met Friedrich ENGELS who was to be until death his collaborator and, on many occasions, financial supporter. After a three-year sojourn in Brussels he visited England to see at first hand the most advanced industrial country. Apart from short periods in Paris and Cologne in 1848–9 to participate in the socialist movements which sprang up at the time of the 1848 European revolutions, he spent the rest of his life in London financially precarious and incessantly acquiring in the British Museum Reading Room the masses of knowledge which fuelled his analysis of history and society.

His contribution to economics appears in *Grundrisse* (1857–8), *Das Kapital* (1867, 1885 and 1894) and *Theories of Surplus Value* (1905–10). Although many of the ideas in his works had long been discussed by classical economists, e.g. value in use and value in exchange, the decline in the rate of profit and labour as a basis of value, he was able to form them into a powerful new synthesis. This consisted of the TURGOT-SMITH stages theory, an analysis of the circulation of money and of commodities and his examination of the determinants of SURPLUS VALUE to expose the defects of capitalism in a way unparalleled in economics. But he has not been without his critics, particularly because many of his prophecies were unfulfilled with respect to the collapse of capitalism and the increasing IMMISERATION of the working class. Marx realized that the TRANSFORMATION PROBLEM was a major challenge to his value and price theories: devotees since his death have tried to solve it but their proposed solutions usually require so many restrictive assumptions as to make their results trivial. Whatever may have been his defects as an economic theorist, his influence has been massive with thousands of academic disciples throughout the world determined to study economics in a sociological and ideological context.

References

Elster, J. (ed.) (1986) *Karl Marx: A Reader*, Cambridge: Cambridge University Press.
Freedman, R. (ed.) (1962) *Marx on Economics*, Harmondsworth: Penguin.
Junankar, P.N. (1982) *Marx's Economics*, Oxford: Philip Allan.
McLellan, D. (1973) *Karl Marx: His Life and Thought*, London: Macmillan.
Wheen, F. (2000) *Karl Marx*, London: Fourth Estate.

marzipan layer (G2, M1)
The managers below the level of director or partner who are responsible for the operations of a financial institution such as a bank or brokerage house,

matching (J6)
Connecting a job vacancy to a person willing to fill it. This is the central task of a labour market but public employment offices often provide a free service.

See also: market clearing

matching function (D4, M4)
1 The number of contacts recurring at any moment of time as a function of the number of searchers on both sides of a market.
2 A statement in accounts of all costs associated with a stream of income.

material balance (E1)
The balance of demand and supply for a particular class of commodities. This balancing was a central feature of planning techniques in the Soviet-type economy. If there is excess demand when expected supply has been calculated, the planners can recommend the importation of extra quantities of the scarce resource or cut down the amounts requested by subordinate organizations.

material good (D0)
A good which has the widest availability because access to it is a function of absolute, not relative, real income.

See also: positional good

mathematical economics (C6)
'Economics, if it is to be a science at all, must be a mathematical science' (W.S. Jevons). Although the use of mathematics was to characterize the MARGINALIST School, it was not until after 1950 that mathematical models, with increasing momentum, became so central to the formulation and exposition of economic theory. SAMUELSON's *Foundations of Economic Analysis* (1948) did much to show the power of mathematical tools and subsequent mathematical economists were to develop equilibrium and maximizing models. The mathematical techniques most frequently employed include calculus, differential equations, matrix algebra and LINEAR PROGRAMMING. MARSHALL, according to KEYNES, was slightly contemptuous of 'the rather "potty" scraps of elementary algebra, geometry and differential calculus which make up mathematical economics'.

References

Arrow, K.J. and Intriligator, M.D. (eds) (1981–4) *Handbook of Mathematical Economics*, Amsterdam: North-Holland.
Chiang, A.C. (1984) *Fundamental Methods of Mathematical Economics*, 3rd edn, Tokyo: McGraw-Hill.
Nicola, P.C. (2000) *Mainstream mathematical economics in the twentieth century*, Heidelberg and New York: Springer Verlag.

mature economy (N0, O3)
A stagnant advanced economy; an economy

at its peak making full use of available technology.

maturity (G0)
The terminal date at which a BOND, BILL or debt is due to be paid.

See also: term structure of interest rates

maturity mismatch (G2)
A difference between the maturities of the assets and liabilities of a financial institution. Banks, such as UK banks in the past, avoided this problem through a policy of lending only short term; Germany and other European banks have traditionally permitted long-term lending, increasing the possibility of a mismatch.

maturity structure of debt (G0)
An analysis of government debt according to the number of years to redemption of each government-issued security. The percentage of the total government debt in each category of years to maturity is stated, e.g. *X* per cent to mature within five years, *Y* per cent to mature in six to ten years. This analysis of the national debt is essential to debt management.

maturity transformation (G0)
The activity of banks and building societies of borrowing short and lending long. This practice is possible because of the slow changing habits of borrowers and the general law of averages which ensures little variation in the total amount deposited.

maximin (C7)
Maximizing the gains to the worst off.

See also: Rawlsian justice

maximum likelihood estimator (C1)
The value of a sample statistic which minimizes the squares of the differences between a regression line and actual data.

See also: least squares method

Mayday (G2)
The deregulation of the Wall Street securities industry on 1 May 1975. Price competition was increased by abolishing minimum commissions, a system that had existed on the New York Stock Exchange since 1792. A major effect of this change was a reduction in the number of securities firms.

See also: Big Bang

McFadden Branch Banking Act 1927 (G2)
US federal statute which helped national banks to compete with state-chartered banks by allowing them the same power to open branches as the state banks in that area. An aim of the Act was to encourage banks to stay in the FEDERAL RESERVE SYSTEM.

McFadden, Daniel L., 1937– (B3)
Born in Raleigh, North Carolina, and educated in physics and economics at Minnesota University. Since 1963 he has been a professor at the University of California, Berkeley, apart from a period at the Massachusetts Institute of Technology from 1978 to 1991. He has also been Director of the Econometrics Laboratory at Berkeley since 1991. In the 1970s he developed statistical methods based on the economic theory of discrete choice and applied them widely, even to traffic planning. He shared the NOBEL PRIZE FOR ECONOMICS in 2000 with James HECKMAN for developing new methods of consumer demand analysis.

MCM (C5)
The multicountry econometric model used by the US Federal Reserve Board, covering the USA, Canada, Japan, the UK, Germany and the rest of the world.

See also: linkage models

References
Howe, H.E., Hernandez-Cata, E., Stevens, G., Berner, R., Clark, P. and Kwack, S.Y. (1981) 'Assessing international interdependence with a multi-country model', *Journal of Econometrics* 15: 65–92.

Meade, James E., 1907–96 (B3)
UK economist educated at Cambridge and Oxford Universities. As Economics Fellow of Hertford College, Oxford, from 1930 to

1938 he contributed to the emerging macroeconomics of KEYNES by participating in the CAMBRIDGE CIRCUS. His subsequent career was spent at the League of Nations (1940–7), as professor of commerce at the London School of Economics (1947–57) and at Cambridge as professor of political economy (1957–67). He was awarded the NOBEL PRIZE FOR ECONOMICS in 1977, with OHLIN, for his work on international trade. In wartime, with Richard STONE, he produced *National Income and Expenditure* (1944), a book which influenced much of post-war NATIONAL INCOME accounting. Subsequent books on international economics, especially *Theory of International Policy* (1951, 1955), clearly expounded the leading aspects of the subject, e.g. his examination of the relationship between a country's INTERNAL AND EXTERNAL BALANCES which has become a standard tool of macroeconomic analysis. Like the leading economists of the nineteenth century, he produced his *Principles of Political Economy* (four volumes, 1965–76). Numerous other works include those on CAPITAL THEORY, wealth distribution and INCOMES POLICY. In 1978 he chaired the Meade Commission on 'The Structure and Reform of Direct Taxation'.

References

Howson, S. and Moggeridge, D. (eds) (1988–90) *The Collected Papers of James Meade*, Vols I–IV, London: Unwin Hyman.

Johnson, H.G. (1978) 'James Meade's contribution to economics', *Scandinavian Journal of Economics* 80: 64–85.

mean (C1)

A measure of the central tendency of a POPULATION or SAMPLE.

See also: arithmetic mean; geometric mean; harmonic mean

mean deviation (C1)

The sum of the differences between the numbers of a set and the ARITHMETIC MEAN of the set, divided by the number of numbers in that set, e.g. for the set 3, 4, 5, 6, 7 whose arithmetic mean is 5, the mean deviation is [(3 − 5) + (4 − 5) + (5 − 5) + (6 − 5) + (7 − 5)] divided by 5, i.e. 1.2, ignoring signs after the differences have been calculated.

means of payment (E4)

A general function of money enabling it to be an immediate way of making a payment.

See also: medium of exchange

measure of economic welfare (D6)

GROSS NATIONAL PRODUCT adjusted by the subtraction of 'bads' (which include pollution and services such as law and order) and the addition of 'goods' (which include household activities such as do-it-yourself (DIY) work) which are not conventionally measured in NATIONAL INCOME accounting. Nordhaus and TOBIN introduced the term.

median (C1)

The middle value (or ARITHMETIC MEAN of the two middle values when there is an even number of values) of numbers arranged in order of magnitude, e.g. the median of 10, 15, 20, 25, 30 is 20.

See also: mean; mode

median voter theorem (H0)

The proposition that the MEDIAN voter determines the outcome of an election in a majority vote, assuming that the distribution of preferences has a single peak.

medium of account (E4)

A NUMÉRAIRE used for quoting prices and valuing the quantities used in accounts. It is usually, but not necessarily, a circulating currency, as in the case of guineas.

See also: unit of account

medium of exchange (E4, G0)

1 A means of making a payment in the future.
2 A form of credit which allows a transaction to proceed.

See also: means of payment

medium of redemption (E4)
Cash, or another type of money, into which banknotes are convertible.

Medium-term Financial Strategy (E6, H5)
The UK policy for public borrowing and monetary growth first announced in May 1979 for the period 1979–84. Originally, it was argued that announcing the government's strategy gave everyone in the economy a firm basis for expectations. However, increasingly in the 1970s, the strategy became a looser statement of intent. It continued to be published annually in the UK budget report as a set of targets for public borrowing and monetary growth

See also: Red Book

megacorp (L2)
A large global corporation controlled by its executives, not its shareholders. These corporations have been able to replace smaller competitive firms because technological change made possible production ECONOMIES OF SCALE and national and international markets. Also, the modernization of financial markets enabled the raising of capital to finance mergers and the expansion of existing firms and advances in accounting and management science removed managerial DISECONOMIES as a barrier to growth. But continued expansion of megacorps is always threatened by the powers of tough governmental COMPETITION POLICIES to break up firms that have acquired too much monopoly power.

Menger, Carl, 1840–1921 (B3)
The founder of AUSTRIAN ECONOMICS who, with JEVONS in Manchester and WALRAS in Lausanne, is also credited with founding MARGINALISM in the 1870s by using the idea of DIMINISHING MARGINAL UTILITY as the foundation of a theory of VALUE.

He was educated at the Universities of Vienna, Prague and Cracow before becoming a journalist and civil servant. In 1871 he published his principal work, *Principles of Economics*; he became professor at the University of Vienna in 1879. He was also tutor to Crown Prince Rudolf.

Menger set the tone for much of later Austrian economics in that he objected to the use of mathematics (unlike Jevons) because it dealt with quantities, not essences, and led to arbitrary statements. He sought to enunciate laws based on simple elements, e.g. needs, satisfaction, goods, which were not influenced by time and space. Like many of his successors he had a libertarian attitude to economic policy.

See also: Hayek; Mises; Wieser.

References
Alter, M. (1990) *Carl Menger and the Origins of Austrian Economics*, Boulder, CO: Westview Press.
Hicks, J.R. and Weber, W. (eds) (1973) *Carl Menger and the Austrian School of Economics*, Oxford: Clarendon Press.

menu costs of inflation (E3)
The costs of changing the prices on goods in an inflationary period, i.e. new price tags, catalogues and price lists.

See also: shoe leather costs of inflation

References
Caplin, A. and Spulber, D. (1987) 'Menu costs and the neutrality of money', *Quarterly Journal of Economics* 102: 703–25.

mercantilism (B1)
A system of ideas and government policies advanced by a series of writers of economic pamphlets, many of them merchants (hence the term), who in the period 1550–1750 advanced theories of international trade, money, prices and employment. The major writers of this school include HALES, MALYNES, NORTH, MUN and CHILD. The earlier writers emphasized the importance of keeping the balance of payments in surplus so that bullion could be accumulated. Money was not seen, initially, as being a factor of production, except to finance wars. TARIFFS, EXCHANGE CONTROLS and monopoly trading companies were advocated to achieve these ends.

Later writers developed more subtle theories looking at the balance of payments as a whole. Since the East India Company exported silver bullion to India to pay for imports from India, writers had to provide a more complex theory of international economics, moving from particular to general balances. In a sense, mercantilism was an elaborate theoretical justification for tariffs, then a major source of government revenue. This school of economics can be viewed more sympathetically as promoters of policies which would create national strength and growth. They were worried about unemployment, especially in England which was adjusting to the problem of provision for the poor after the dissolution of the monasteries and the decline in the wool industry. Unemployment prevented a nation from achieving its full output potential so they advocated public works and regional policies not dissimilar from many which have been used in Western countries in the twentieth century. The critiques of HUME and SMITH – particularly Hume's assault in his SPECIE-FLOW MODEL and Smith's discussion of the nature of money and of the desirability of free trade – relegated mercantilist doctrines to the sidelines of economics. But some nineteenth-century writers, including LIST, had ideas with a mercantilist tinge. The recent school of NEO-MERCANTILISM has kept these writers' ideas firmly on the agenda of economic policy discussions.

References

Heckscher, E.F. (1935) *Mercantilism*, trans. M. Shapiro, ed. E. F. Soderlund, London: Allen & Unwin.

Magnusson, L. (1994) *Mercantilism: the shaping of an economic language*, London and New York: Routledge.

McCulloch, J.R. (1954) *Early English Tracts on Commerce*, Cambridge: Cambridge University Press.

Viner, J. (1937) *Studies in the Theory of International Trade*, chs 1 and 2, London: Allen & Unwin.

merchandise balance of trade (F4)
Visible balance of trade.

See also: balance of payments

merchant bank (G2)
A SECONDARY BANK specializing in the finance of trade, portfolio management, CORPORATE FINANCE and MERGERS. As it does not receive deposits directly from the public, it obtains finance for lending from WHOLESALE MONEY MARKETS. It has the exclusive right under the Companies Acts to transfer undisclosed sums from its profit and loss account to its hidden reserves. The more famous merchant banks have included Morgan and Grenfell, Hill Samuel, Kleinwort Benson, Rothschilds, Hambros and Lazards. Increasingly, in the USA 'merchant banking' refers to a high-risk form of investment banking which has extended the range of its services to include the provision of BRIDGING finance and EQUITY investment in firms purchased through a LEVERAGED MANAGEMENT BUYOUT.

See also: investment banking

merchant capitalism (N0, P1)
An economic system consisting of wholesalers who advance funds to manufacturing workers to produce goods for the merchants' market. This stage of economic development was succeeded by INDUSTRIAL CAPITALISM.

merger (G3)
An amalgamation of two or more firms into a new firm. A vertical merger occurs when firms in industries at different stages of bringing a good to the final consumer, i.e. extractive, manufacturing or distribution, join together. If the firms are in the same industry, there is a horizontal merger. A CONGLOMERATE MERGER is an amalgamation of firms with dissimilar activities. Mergers often come in waves, particularly in times of general economic depression as a way of reducing costs, e.g. in the USA in 1901–3 and in the UK in the 1920s. As a high proportion of conglomerate mergers fail to make efficiency gains in RESEARCH AND DEVELOPMENT, production or marketing, it is argued that they are without

industrial logic; horizontal mergers have a better reputation for improving profitability and efficiency; vertical mergers make no significant difference. In the USA, e.g. in 1982 and 1984, guidelines for what are acceptable mergers have been published by the Antitrust Division of the Department of Justice.

See also: horizontal integration; vertical integration

References

Mussati, G. (eds) (1995) *Mergers, markets and public policy*, Dordrecht, Boston and London: Kluwer Academic.

merger arbitrage (G3)
Tactical use of the accumulated stocks of companies in takeovers, often practised by US investment banks. Arbitrageurs can determine the outcome of takeover bids, and often precipitate them.

See also: greenmail

merit bad (H4)
A good or service disapproved of by a government because of research into its bad effects. Drugs, tobacco and various unauthorized medical practices are major examples. Taxation and prohibition under the criminal law have been used as ways of preventing consumption of them.

merit good (H4)
A good provided by a government because of the belief that its general consumption is desirable. Thus education and libraries are often freely provided. It is argued that the superior wisdom of governments based on detailed research justifies them in assuming this paternalist role.

merit want (H4)
A demand for a good or service encouraged by the state so supplied free, e.g. education, health care. Public expenditure is necessary to satisfy these wants.

See also: merit bad; merit good

Merton, Robert C., 1944– (B3)
Born in New York City, the son of a sociology professor. At Columbia University and the California Institute of Technology he studied mathematics. At the Massachusetts Institute of Technology he learned economics from SAMUELSON's *Foundations of Economic Analysis* and was soon to become his research assistant. From the age of 10 he had invested in the stock market so naturally turned to mathematical finance theory, working on the pricing of WARRANTS and applying the notion of EXPECTED UTILITY to optimal portfolio selection. Subsequently he emphasized in his work the dynamics of institutional change as a guide to understanding the financial system and developed a formula for valuing stock OPTIONS. His academic career began in 1970 at the Sloan School of MIT; in 1988 he migrated to the Harvard Business School for the rest of his career. In 1997 he shared the NOBEL PRIZE FOR ECONOMICS with Myron SCHOLES. He has served on the boards of several MUTUAL FUNDS and been involved in long-term capital management.

mesoeconomy (P0)
That part of the ECONOMY run by big business. It is intermediate between households or small firms and national governments.

References

Holland, S. (1987) *The Market Economy from Micro to Mesoeconomics*, London: Weidenfeld & Nicolson.

metallist (E4)
Someone who believes that the value of a currency depends on the intrinsic value of the gold, silver or copper it is made of, or which backs a note issue.

See also: bimetallism; cartalist; Currency School

Metropolitan Statistical Area (J1, R1)
A large population centre of the USA including the adjoining communities socially and economically integrated with it. In rural areas, except New England, MSAs refer to counties. This term re-

placed the 'Standard Metropolitan Statistical Area' after June 1963.

See also: Consolidated Metropolitan Statistical Area; Primary Metropolitan Statistical Area

Metzler paradox (F1)

Despite a tariff imposing a charge, it can lead to a lower post-tariff price if the world price is forced down through an inelastic foreign demand for the importing country's export good.

References

Metzler, L.A. (1949) 'Tariffs, international demand, and domestic prices', *Journal of Political Economy*, 57:345–51.

Mexican peso crisis (F3)

The devaluation of the peso in December 1994 and its aftermath in 1995. Dramatic political events, including an armed insurrection, the killing of leading politicians, terrorism and the kidnapping of leading businessmen preceded a speculative attack on the currency and subsequent financial crisis. Mexico's fixed exchange rate regime made its currency vulnerable.

mezzanine finance (G2, M2)

An unsecured loan, often used to finance a MANAGEMENT BUYOUT, which ranks after secured loans but before equity in the event of a liquidation of a company. The interest charged on these loans is higher than for secured loans and linked equity is often given to the lender. This form of finance is used to supplement other sources to effect management buyouts.

M-form (L2)

A multidivisional type of enterprise organized with its operating divisions separated from its strategic decision-making divisions. This structure, arranged as profit centres for different products, brands and geographical markets, was pioneered by Du Pont and General Motors.

See also: H-form; U-form; X-form

References

Armour, H.O. and Teece, D.J. (1978) 'Organization, structure and economic performance: a test of the multidivisional hypothesis', *Bell Journal of Economics* 9: 106–22.

microcredit (G2, O1)

Small loans used to encourage small businesses in developing countries such as Bangladesh.

microeconomics (D0)

The study of the economic behaviour of part(s) of an economic system, especially a household or a firm. To make this possible, PARTIAL EQUILIBRIUM ANALYSIS, inaugurated by MARSHALL, and GENERAL EQUILIBRIUM analysis, largely founded by WALRAS, are used. The major issues discussed are matters of pricing, distribution, investment, WELFARE ECONOMICS, demand and supply. The school of NEOCLASSICAL ECONOMICS was to emphasize the microeconomic character of much of economics; KEYNESIANISM had the opposite effect as its construction of macroeconomic models returned economics to the wider concerns which had been prominent in CLASSICAL, and other, schools of economics. Increasingly economists have found it difficult in their construction of models to separate microeconomics from macroeconomics.

See also: macroeconomics

Microproduction function (D2)

A firm's production function showing the maximum output which can be produced by its physical inputs, given the constraint of its technology.

See also: production function

microsimulation model (C8)

An attempt to reproduce the complex micro reactions to an external stimulus within a household or a firm. Micro data sets detailing household labour market behaviour, income, expenditure and demographic characteristics have been analysed to consider, for example, the micro consequences of a tax and benefit system.

References

Sutherland, H. (1995) 'Static microsimulation models in Europe. A survey', University of Cambridge, Microsimulation Unit Discussion Paper, MU 9503.

middle price (G1)

The average of the buying and selling prices of securities on London's STOCK EXCHANGE which are quoted in the Stock Exchange Daily Official List. Prices quoted in the financial press usually approximate to the middle price.

middle product (D2)

A semi-finished good requiring further processing before being suitable for final consumption. It is both an output of a productive process and an input to another. Much of the trade between subsidiaries of a MULTINATIONAL company is of this kind.

See also: intermediate good

References

Sanyal, K. and Jones, R.W. (1982) 'The theory of trade in middle products', *American Economic Review*, 72: 16–31.

migrant labour (F2, J2)

Foreign labour available in an economy for short periods of time, i.e. several months or a few years. This labour provides a national economy with a secondary labour force. It is popular with employers as it increases the ELASTICITY of labour supply and, being rarely unionized, can often be obtained at lower wage rates.

See also: guestworker; reserve army of labour; secondary labour market

migration (F2, J1)

Movement of population, labour or capital between countries or between regions. The most studied form of migration has been the international migration of labour, especially the large westward migrations of the nineteenth century to the USA. As part of the process of economic development of a country, there is rural–urban migration within it: this has happened in developed economies such as the USA and increasingly in less developed countries. Also, since 1960 attention has been paid to the movement of workers from the Mediterranean regions to more northern regions of EUROPEAN COMMUNITY countries, of highly skilled workers to the USA, and of New Commonwealth (i.e. the Indian subcontinent and Caribbean) workers to the UK.

Many explanations of migration are in terms of an analysis of factors pushing workers out of a country (unemployment, low incomes) and of factors pulling workers into a country (high growth, high pay and career advancement). The increasing provision of social services in advanced countries has contributed to demands for immigration controls. Ravenstein (1834–1913) distilled from UK population censuses of 1861, 1871 and 1881 'laws' of migration which concluded that migration is largely caused by economic circumstances and is typically a step-by-step process of short movements from rural to urban areas.

See also: brain drain; gravity model; hot money

References

Grigg, D.B. (1977) 'E.G. Ravenstein on the laws of migration', *Journal of Historical Geography* 3: 41–54.

Shaw, R.P. (1975) *Migration Theory and Fact: A Review and Bibliography of Current Literature*, Philadelphia, PA: Regional Science Research Institute.

migration-fed unemployment (J6)

A type of unemployment common to many Third World countries. Migration initially occurs because the urban wage rate is more than the SUPPLY PRICE of rural workers and continues until deterred by urban unemployment. This type of unemployment seems near insoluble because any policy measures to create urban jobs will stimulate migration, causing labour supply to grow faster than demand and thus creating further unemployment.

military–industrial complex (P0)
The set of relationships between a defence ministry and the industries supplying weapons and other goods and services for the armed forces. It is argued that this complex is crucial to the functioning of many major capitalist economies as industrial output is to a large extent determined by defence requirements. GALBRAITH and several radical economists have discussed the role of this complex in their analysis of modern Western economic systems. However, within the USSR there was also for a long time a close link between defence industries and the armed forces.

military Keynesianism (E6)
The maintenance of a high level of AGGREGATE DEMAND by huge government expenditures on defence. This has been used as a description of the US economy post-1945.

Miller, Merton, 1923–2000 (B3)
Educated at Harvard and Johns Hopkins Universities and professor at the University of Chicago from 1981. Along with MODIGLIANI, from 1958 he established that in corporate finance a firm's value is determined by its investment decisions, not its dividend policy. His interests broadened to include the regulation of financial services through his directorships of the Chicago Board of Trade and Chicago Mercantile Exchange. In 1990, he shared the NOBEL PRIZE FOR ECONOMICS with MARKOVITZ and SHARPE for pioneering work in the theory of financial economics.

Mill, James, 1773–1836 (B3)
Born in Montrose, Scotland, the son of a cobbler and educated at Montrose Academy and Edinburgh University where he studied divinity and learned economics from Dugald Stewart. Licensed in 1797 to preach in the Church of Scotland and an itinerant preacher until he went to London in 1802 and took to journalism becoming editor of *The Literary Journal* and *St James's Chronicle*. His first work on economics was *Essay of the Impolicy of Bounty on the Exportation of Grain* (1804)

and he acquired more fame with *Commerce Defended* (1807). He became an ardent disciple of BENTHAM who gave him much financial support necessary in his early years to bring up nine children. He personally tutored his eldest son JOHN STUART MILL. James Mill's *History of British India* (1817) helped him to gain an assistant examinership at the East India Company: he rose to the top post of Chief Examiner and was succeeded by his illustrious son. He encouraged RICARDO in his writing of his *Principles of Political Economy* (1817).

Mill, John Stuart, 1806–73 (B3)
English philosopher, political theorist and major classical economist. His father, James MILL, a close friend of BENTHAM, educated him at home in a rigorous programme which started with Greek at the age of 3 and reached political economy ten years later. John learned economics by making notes on RICARDO's *Principles* which his father then published as *Elements of Political Economy* (1821). He followed his father into a clerkship in the East India Company where he was employed until 1858 and engaged in the political reform movements of the day being Member of Parliament for Westminster from 1865 to 1868. John turned his attention to a range of philosophical and political issues, writing on women's rights, representative government, logic, UTILITARIANISM and liberty. But he made an outstanding contribution to economics, being more than he modestly claimed – a clarifier of SMITH's and RICARDO's ideas.

In his brilliant *Essays on Some Unsettled Questions of Political Economy*, written when he was only 23 but not published until 1844, he developed the theory of RECIPROCAL DEMAND to explain the ratios at which nations would trade if they followed the principle of COMPARATIVE ADVANTAGE. Also he introduced the idea of a demand schedule, refined SAY'S LAW and expounded one of the earliest theories of the TRADE CYCLE which he attributed to price delusion. He returned to economics in his large *Principles of Political Economy with Some of their Applications to Social Philosophy*, first published in 1848, republished seven times in his lifetime and the standard textbook on the subject in the UK until MARSHALL's *Principles* superseded it in 1890. Many features of the work were novel. He introduced a discussion of idealist SOCIALISM (ST SIMON and FOURIER) – partly under the influence of Harriet Taylor, later to be his wife – and clearly expounded what have become key economic concepts. In the *Principles*, OPPORTUNITY COST, ECONOMIES OF SCALE, the problem of JOINT COSTS and SEXUAL DISCRIMINATION in the labour market are some of his numerous innovations. His self-confident claim that he had finally sorted out the theory of value invited the ridicule of later writers, particularly JEVONS, but MARSHALL can in many respects be regarded as a follower.

References

Hollander, S. (1985) *The Economics of John Stuart Mill*, Oxford: Basil Blackwell.

Mill, J.S. (1963) *The Collected Works of John Stuart Mill*, Toronto: University of Toronto Press; London: Routledge & Kegan Paul.

Ryan, A. (1974) *J. S. Mill*, London: Routledge.

mineral-based economy (N0, P0)
An industrial economy using large machinery driven by a plentiful supply of energy, especially coal. This economy, less reliant on agricultural products, can sustain a higher POPULATION DENSITY than its predecessor, the ADVANCED ORGANIC ECONOMY.

References

Wrigley, E.A. (1988) *Continuity, Chance and Change*, ch. 3, Cambridge: Cambridge University Press.

minimal state (H1)
A state limited to a few functions, usually only protection against force, theft, fraud and the enforcement of contracts. It is argued that as the price of promoting

fairness is inefficiency and governments are fallible, it is undesirable to give governments an extensive role. This notion of LAISSEZ-FAIRE in modern clothes is attributable to NOZICK.

References

Nozick, R. (1975) *Anarchy, State and Utopia*, Oxford: Basil Blackwell.

minimax (C7)
Minimizing the maximum disadvantage; a GAMES THEORY principle for choosing a course of action.

minimum efficient scale (D2)
The level of output of a firm at which the L-shaped AVERAGE COST curve becomes a plateau of many minimum cost outputs. It is used to show the significance of ECONOMIES OF SCALE, e.g. by seeing the effect on costs of reducing the level of output to half the minimum efficient size or by comparing this level of production with the entire domestic demand for the products of that industry.

See also: optimum firm

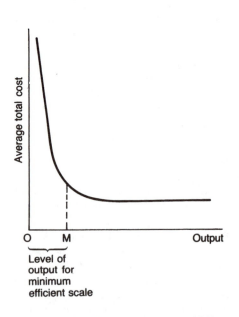

Level of output for minimum efficient scale

minimum funding requirement (G2)
A financial rule compulsory for UK pro-

viders of final salary pension schemes which insists on a stated proportion of the liabilities of the scheme being covered by assets.

minimum lending rate (E4)

The UK's successor to the BANK RATE used from October 1971 to August 1981 by the Bank of England for financing the money market when acting as LENDER OF LAST RESORT. Unlike the bank rate, the minimum lending rate was usually tied to short-term money market interest rates, with the possibility of it being changed on the occasions when monetary policy demanded an administrative change.

See also: federal funds rate; Lombard rate; prime rate of interest

minimum list heading (L0)

Title of an industry or industrial group in UK production statistics.

minimum reserve requirements (F3)

A form of exchange control that aims to reduce the impact on domestic liquidity of a foreign currency inflow.

minimum supply price of labour (J3)

The lowest wage a worker will accept. Rather than accept less, a person will prefer to be either unemployed or out of the labour force.

See also: reservation wage; voluntary unemployment

minimum wage (J3)

The minimum rate of employee remuneration fixed by a government for an hour's work in a particular industry, region or whole economy. Many countries, including France and Australia, have long used this policy response to the problem of LOW PAY. Minimum wage legislation was passed in the UK in 1998. It is often argued that the imposition of a new minimum wage, or an increase in existing levels, will have an unemployment effect and will fuel inflation by increasing the entire WAGE CONTOUR; in the figure, setting a minimum wage W_m above the equilibrium wage W_e reduces

employment by $Q_e - Q_m$. There are many countries where this has happened but detailed labour market analysis, especially where MONOPSONY is present, is needed before such policies are wholly abandoned.

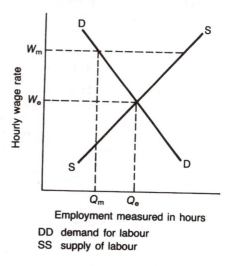

Employment measured in hours

DD   demand for labour
SS   supply of labour

References

Starr, G. (1981) *Minimum Wage Fixing: An International Review of Practices and Problems*, Geneva: ILO.

Ministry of International Trade and Industry (L5)

The key Japanese ministry for administering INDUSTRIAL POLICY. It acts primarily through giving administrative guidance rather than through controls and subsidization. It helps firms plan long term, giving advice on the appropriate level of investment to meet future demand and exporting. Its other tasks include the implementation of policies on the encouragement of small businesses, consumer protection and environmental policy. In the 1950s it took a major role in developing the steel and shipbuilding industries, in the 1960s electronics and heavy construction and in the 1980s advanced technologies.

Minsky, Hyman Philip, 1919–96 (B3)

A prominent US POST-KEYNESIAN economist who was educated at Chicago and Harvard Universities and has been professor of economics at Washington University in St Louis. He studied the flaws of capitalism, acknowledging the influence of SCHUMPETER. His POST-KEYNESIAN views were crucially influenced by meeting Joan ROBINSON and her circle in a visit to Cambridge, England, in 1968–9.

References

Minsky, H.P. (1975) *John Maynard Keynes*, New York: Columbia University Press.

Mirrlees, James A., 1936– (B3)

Born in Galloway, Scotland, and educated in mathematics at Edinburgh and Cambridge Universities. He was supervised at Cambridge for a PhD on INDICATIVE PLANNING by Richard STONE. A trip to India initiated his interest in economic development: his *Project Appraisal and Planning* (1994) has been extensively used by investors in less developed countries. Edgeworth Professor of Economics at Oxford from 1968 to 1995 and then subsequently professor at Cambridge. He shared with William VICKREY the NOBEL PRIZE FOR ECONOMICS in 1996 for his work on optimal taxation when there is competition between tax rates and labour has little substitutability. His research has also included a study of MORAL HAZARD, incentive structures in tax systems, insurance markets and credit allocation.

misaligned rate of exchange (F3)

An exchange rate which persistently departs from its FUNDAMENTAL EQUILIBRIUM level.

Mises, Ludwig Edler von, 1881–1973 (B3)

A leading Viennese economist whose influential seminar conducted when he was professor of the University of Vienna (1913–36) included many famous economists, such as MACHLUP and HAYEK. He taught at the Graduate Institute of International Studies, Geneva, from 1934 to 1940 and was professor of economics at New York University from 1945 to 1969. As an economic liberal, he was a leading member of the AUSTRIAN SCHOOL, which

seemed to be eclipsed by KEYNESIANISM until its powerful revival in the 1970s. Like his Austrian contemporaries, Mises began with UTILITY theory and a study of BUSINESS CYCLES but after the First World War attacked the nature of allocation in socialist societies and then investigated economic philosophy in great detail. In his *The Theory of Money and Credit* (1912) he was one of the first economists to integrate MICROECONOMICS and MACROECONOMICS by founding his theory of money and credit on the individualism of Austrian microeconomics. He also used a cash balance and EXPECTATIONS APPROACH to money. His novel approach to the trade cycle based on the SPECIE-FLOW MECHANISM with bank credit being crucial to the generation of booms and slumps was to be a major inspiration to HAYEK.

References

Butler, E. (1988) *Ludwig von Mises*, Aldershot: Gower.

von Mises, L.E. (1912) *The Theory of Money and Credit*, trans. H. E. Batson, London: Jonathan Cape.

—— (1937) *Socialism: An Economic and Sociological Analysis*, 2nd edn, trans. J. Kahane, New York: Macmillan.

—— (1949) *Human Action, A Treatise on Economics*, New Haven, CT: Yale University Press.

—— (1962) *The Ultimate Foundation of Economic Science*, Princeton, NJ: Van Nostrand.

Moss, L.S. (ed.) (1976) *The Economics of Ludwig von Mises*, Kansas City, KS: Sheed and Ward.

misintermediation (G0)

Mismatching the maturities of assets and liabilities by banks and other financial intermediaries who borrow short and lend long. The consequences of this are financial instability and the possibility of increased fluctuations in an economy.

See also: disintermediation; intermediation; maturity mismatch; term structure of interest rates

References

McCulloch, J.H. (1981) 'Misintermediation and macroeconomic fluctuations',
Journal of Monetary Economics 8(July):
103–15.

missing market (D0)

A market not existing now but a possibility in the future to cope with an EXTERN-
ALITY. The creation of these new markets is
undertaken with the aim of reaching a
social optimum. Often there is an absence
of markets for RISK, information and
future goods and HOME PRODUCTION.

References

Hahn, F. (ed.) (1989) *The Economics of
Missing Markets, Information and Games*,
Oxford: Clarendon Press.

Mitchell, Wesley Clair, 1874–1948 (B3)

A leading US INSTITUTIONAL ECONOMIST who
laid the foundations for modern studies of
the BUSINESS CYCLE. Educated at Chicago
University, professor at the Universities of
California (1903–13) and Columbia (1913–
19 and 1922–44) and director of the New
School of Social Research (1919–31). His
work *Business Cycles* (1927) began a long
and dedicated investigation into economic
fluctuations. Together with Arthur BURNS
he set up the NATIONAL BUREAU OF ECONOMIC
RESEARCH's method of measuring of business cycles.

References

Burns, A.F. (ed.) (1952) *Wesley Clair
Mitchell: the Economic Scientist*, New
York: National Bureau for Economic
Research.

mixed bundling (M3)

The sale of two or more goods or services
either jointly in a package deal or separately.

See also: bundling; pure bundling

mixed credit (F3, G0)

A mixture of a loan supplied by a financial institution at a commercial rate of
interest and a SOFT LOAN. With a more
generous form of credit, the volume of

international trade and Third World development would have grown faster.

mixed economy (P4)

An ECONOMY combining the methods and
goals of CAPITALISM and SOCIALISM, particularly by encouraging the growth of the
public sector. Partly under the influence of
KEYNES, there has been in many Western
countries a commitment to FULL EMPLOY-
MENT which encouraged the growth of the
public sector and, hence, the mixed economy. In this type of economy, the basic
capitalist model is augmented in a number
of ways. To market principles are added
some income redistribution through taxation and welfare benefits; to private sector
firms, state-owned bodies; to pricing, a
planning system, usually of no more than
an INDICATIVE kind. Many West European
economies, particularly Germany and
Sweden, are of this kind. The UK economy until 1979 was often described as
being mixed, but in the 1980s with the
abandonment of INCOMES POLICIES, the PRI-
VATIZATION of several NATIONALIZED INDUS-
TRIES and the attempt to apply
MONETARISM, the term is less applicable.

References

Lord Roll of Ipsden (ed.) (1982) 'The
mixed economy', *Proceedings of Section
F (Economics) of the British Association
for the Advancement of Science Meeting*,
London: Macmillan.

mixed good (D0)

A good with the characteristics of both
PRIVATE and PUBLIC GOODS.

See also: club good

mobility of labour (J6)

Movements of members of the LABOUR
FORCE between areas (geographical mobility), between industries (industrial mobility) or between occupations (OCCUPATIONAL
MOBILITY). In the classical account of the
labour market, mobility would continue
until the net advantages of jobs were
equalized (see SMITH's *Wealth of Nations*,
Book 1, ch. 10). However, increasingly

labour economists became aware of the imperfections of the labour market splitting it up into NON-COMPETING GROUPS. Later, the cost of information and job search were emphasized as barriers to movement. The measurement of labour mobility depends greatly on the classification of areas, industries and occupations used: the broader the classification, the lower the amount of mobility. The right of labour to move freely within the EUROPEAN COMMUNITY is granted by Article 48 of the TREATY OF ROME and enforced by Article 49; the Council of Ministers by Regulation 1612 in 1968 gave effect to this principle.

See also: motility; search cost

mobility status (J6)
A classification of the US population which compares the place of residence of an individual person at different dates.

mobility trap (R2)
An area of low house prices whose residents are prevented from moving to an urban area with higher property prices, e.g. from North East England which has lower property prices than London.

mode (C1)
The value of a set of numbers which most frequently occurs, e.g. 7 is the mode of 2, 3, 3, 4, 5, 6, 6, 7, 7, 7, 11, 11. Some distributions are without modes.

See also: mean; median; unimodal distribution

model (C0) *see* economic model

model company management (G3)
The recommendations of the MYNERS COMMITTEE concerning the presentation of annual information to shareholders, shareholder meetings and the need to follow best practice in disclosure.

model institutional investor (G3)
The ideal conduct of large investors according to the MYNERS COMMITTEE. These investors should communicate to manage-

ment an evaluation of the particular corporation, active participation in CORPORATE GOVERNANCE and a clear policy for executive remuneration.

Model Tax Convention (H2)
The OECD's consensual rules for taxing income and capital to avoid double taxation and the consequential discouragement to investment. This guide, first published in 1992 and regularly updated, has been the basis for over 1,500 tax treaties throughout the world.

modern economy (N0, P4)
An ECONOMY which has reached an advanced stage of DEVELOPMENT with high per capita incomes, a full range of political and financial institutions, industries using the latest available technology and a large service sector. The shorthand measure of modernity, real GROSS NATIONAL PRODUCT per head, is misleading because countries with different ranges of economic activity have been put on a par, e.g. China with India, Haiti with Mali, France with Libya. Increasingly, the overall level of technological diffusion has been chosen as a better indicator.

Modigliani, Franco, 1918– (B3)
Italian-born US economist who was educated at the University of Rome and the New School for Social Research. In his early career, he taught at the University of Illinois, Carnegie Institute of Technology and Northwestern University. From 1962 he has been a professor at the Massachusetts Institute of Technology. A major aspect of his work has been to relate CORPORATE FINANCE to MACROECONOMICS, making it possible to see the impact of business finance on real variables. All students of economics are aware of his life-cycle approach to the CONSUMPTION FUNCTION. He was awarded the NOBEL PRIZE FOR ECONOMICS in 1985.

References
Modigliani, F. (1980–9) *The Collected Works of Franco Modigliani*, 3 vols, Cambridge, MA, and London: MIT Press.

moments (C1)
The sum of the deviations of the values of a variable from a point in a distribution divided by the number of values (first moment); for the second moment, the squares of the deviations have to be calculated; for the third moment, the cubes of the deviations, etc.

monetarism (B0, E4)
A modern revival of the QUANTITY THEORY OF MONEY, making use of modern NEOCLASSICAL ECONOMICS. It regards the money supply as the most important determinant of aggregate money income and reasserts the relevance of price theory to macroeconomics. Central to monetarism are the concepts of a TRANSMISSION MECHANISM to allow money to influence output, via relative prices, of normal output (employment) instead of FULL EMPLOYMENT, of the NATURAL RATE OF UNEMPLOYMENT, of monetary impulses between transitory and more permanent components of movements in price level and output, and of a POLITICAL ECONOMY of society which analyses the role of government non-sociologically. FRIEDMAN's works from the 1950s are the most famous writings on this subject. Popularly, monetarism is thought of as a tough FISCAL STANCE and careful attention to monetary variables when targeting the economy. In practice, most monetarists use the gradualist approach of aiming for a rate of monetary expansion likely to achieve long-term price stability. DEMAND MANAGEMENT is avoided because of the belief that an economy will always tend to the NATURAL RATE OF UNEMPLOYMENT. It made headlines in the USA when the 1968 tax increase failed to curb inflation and when the monetarists at the Federal Reserve Bank of St Louis made striking predictions for 1969. In the USA from 1979 to 1981 and in the UK from the mid-1970s to mid-1980s, with varying degrees of enthusiasm, governments attempted to apply monetarist principles to their macroeconomic policy making.

References
Friedman, M. (ed.) (1956) *Studies in the Quantity Theory of Money*, Chicago: Chicago University Press.
—— (1969) *The Optimum Quantity of Money and other Essays*, London: Macmillan.
Laidler, D., Tobin, J., Matthews, R.C.O. and Meade, J.E. (1981) 'Conference papers on monetarism – an appraisal', *Economic Journal* 91: 1–57.
Stein, J.L. (ed.) (1976) *Monetarism*, Amsterdam: North-Holland.

monetarist approach to the balance of payments (F4)
The view that BALANCE OF PAYMENTS adjustments are made through capital movements and interest rate changes in capital markets. This is the alternative to the KEYNESIAN approach of adjusting expenditure to achieve a balance of payments equilibrium.

monetary accommodation (E5)
A discretionary change in the nominal money supply by central monetary authorities in response to a price change which has changed the real money supply.

monetary base (E5)
Cash, banker's deposits with a CENTRAL BANK and short-term monetary assets which form the basis of bank credit; also known as HIGH-POWERED MONEY. MONETARY POLICY sometimes takes the form of controlling the size of the monetary base as a means of restricting the growth of the money supply, but it cannot simply hope that a change in the monetary base will ensure a corresponding change in total bank credit as there may be many portfolio adjustments, existing high-powered

money in excess of reserve requirements and DISINTERMEDIATION.

Monetary Control Act 1980 (G2)

The popular shortened title of the DEPOSITORY INSTITUTIONS DEREGULATION AND MONETARY CONTROL ACT 1980.

monetary inflation (E3)

INFLATION brought about by an increase in the MONEY SUPPLY.

monetary overhang (E2, E3)

Accumulated savings which could cause future inflation. This overhang has long been a feature of East European economies because shortages have meant that individuals could not spend as much of their incomes as they desired. This extra purchasing power when released pushes up prices.

monetary policy (E5)

A governmental policy, for the most part implemented by a CENTRAL BANK, which influences AGGREGATE DEMAND by a variety of methods, including the changing of interest rates, OPEN MARKET OPERATIONS and the setting of targets for the MONEY SUPPLY. The least active of monetary policies is a long-term linkage between money supply growth and real GROSS DOMESTIC PRODUCT (see FRIEDMAN); the most active, frequent changes to fine-tune the economy. The earliest of monetary policies used interest rates as a means of controlling an economy, especially under the GOLD STANDARD, and then a range of methods to control the volume of bank deposits through required cash and reserve asset ratios was used. In the 1970s and 1980s in the USA and the UK, it was fashionable to adopt MONETARISM. However, limiting monetary policy chiefly to setting targets for the rate of growth of key monetary aggregates was difficult so monetary policy reverted to using a variety of former methods.

See also: cheap money; monetarism; rules versus discretion

References

Bain, A. (1980) *The Control of the Money Supply*, Harmondsworth: Penguin.

Chick, V. (1977) *The Theory of Monetary Policy*, Oxford: Basil Blackwell.

Dow, I.C.R. and Saville, I.D. (1988) *A Critique of Monetary Policy: Theory and British Experience*, Oxford: Oxford University Press.

Goodhart, C. (1989) *Money, Information and Uncertainty*, 2nd edn, London: Macmillan.

Great Britain Treasury (1980) *Monetary Control; A Consultation Paper*, London: HMSO, Cmnd 7858.

Kuroda, I. (ed.) (1997) *Towards more effective monetary policy*, New York: St Martin's Press; London: Macmillan.

Monetary Policy Committee (UK) (E5)

The committee set up in 1997 to set interest rates independently of the Treasury. It has the single task of maintaining a target rate of inflation set by the CHANCELLOR OF THE EXCHEQUER. It has been noted for increasing the volatility of interest rates. Its narrow remit resembles New Zealand's rather than the US's comparable committee.

monetary veil (E4)

Money regarded as a veil that distracts attention from the real activities of the economy.

See also: classical dichotomy

monetization (H6)

The financing of government debt by increasing the MONEY SUPPLY. This occurs when, at existing interest rates, it is difficult for a government to borrow by issuing bonds and has to resort to borrowing directly from the commercial banks and the money market, which in turn can expand their deposits and, hence, the money supply. The aim of monetization is to keep down interest rates and prevent CROWDING OUT. The extent of monetization in an economy is sometimes used as an indicator of economic DEVELOPMENT.

See also: securitization

money (E4)

1 Anything which is immediately and generally acceptable for the discharge of a debt or in exchange for a good or service.
2 In most cases, a liability of a government introduced into an economy by making transfer payments to firms and households or by purchasing assets.

To be used as a measure of value, money must be expressible in units and stable in value. It makes the DIVISION OF LABOUR possible, saving the time that would have to be spent on barter. As early as ARISTOTLE, it was recognized that money serves as a medium of exchange, a unit of account and a store of value. What serves as money has varied from society to society and from time to time. In primitive societies commodities are used (even today tobacco is widely used in prisons), in societies of medium development coins and then BANKNOTES, in modern economies the deposits of the leading COMMERCIAL BANKS.

See also: call money; coinage; credit money; fiat money; high-powered money; inside money; IOU money; near money; outside money; paper money; plastic money; token money

References

Friedman, B.M. and Halm, F.H. (eds) (1990) *Handbook of Monetary Economics*, Amsterdam: North-Holland.
Galbraith, J.K. (1975) *Money. Whence it Came, Where it Went*, Boston: Houghton Mifflin.
Harrod, R.F. (1969) *Money*, London: Macmillan; New York: St Martin's Press.
Jones, R.A. (1976) 'The origin and development of media of exchange', *Journal of Political Economy* 84: 757–75.
Laidler, D. (1969) 'The definition of money. Theoretical and empirical problems', *Journal of Money, Credit and Banking* 1: 508–25.
Newlyn, W.T. (1978) *The Theory of Money*, 3rd edn, Oxford: Clarendon Press.

money at call (E4, G1)
The most liquid of banks' assets after cash. This money can be immediately recalled from the money market to which it is lent.

See also: overnight money

money centre bank (G2)
In terms of assets, one of the largest US banks. There are about eight or nine, mostly based in New York.

money gross domestic product (E0)
The nominal value of all of the incomes arising from the economic activities within a country in a given period. This has often been a popular central target in macroeconomic policy making.

money illusion (E4)
Confusing money values with real values, a phenomenon of inflationary periods. Workers and consumers may be prepared to accept inferior bargains because they have not fully taken inflation into account. In collective bargaining, too much attention to money wage rates can lead to workers not being compensated sufficiently for price changes; frequent product price changes make it difficult for consumers to be aware of the extent of inflation. Also known as inflation illusion.

See also: price perception

money income (D0, M4)
Receipts expressed in money at the prices current when that income was paid; 'nominal income'.

See also: real income

money laundering (K4) *see* laundering money

money market certificate (G1)
A six-month US money market security, much used by THRIFTS for investing in US federal funds.

money market deposit account (G2)
US RETAIL BANK deposit based on holdings of money market assets introduced in 1982.

money market mutual fund (G2)
US UNIT TRUST consisting of money market securities. THRIFTS have provided this means of allowing small investors to participate in short-term money markets; corporations find the funds useful for liquid investments.

money multiplier (E4)
The change in the stock of money resulting from a change in the MONETARY BASE by one unit, e.g. by one pound or one dollar. Thus if there is a change in a reserve asset of $1 million and the total volume of bank deposits increases by $5 million, the money multiplier has the value of 5. Any alteration in the desired LIQUID ASSETS RATIO of the banking system will change the value of the money multiplier. The importance of this multiplier has been exaggerated as monetary authorities may make the level of interest rates a more important monetary target. Also, changes in the methods of monetary control and in the public's demand for currency require changes in reserve ratios.

moneyness (E4, G1)
1 Being near enough to CASH to be suitable as a MEDIUM OF EXCHANGE.
2 The degree to which an OPTION is IN-THE-MONEY.

money-order economy (O1, P0)
A poor national ECONOMY which receives much of its income in the form of remittances from relatives of its population living abroad.

money-purchase pension (G2)
A pension with fixed contributions but benefits related to the state of the financial markets in which the fund's assets are invested.

money supply (E4)
The total amount of money available within a country. It is variously measured in a narrow or broad way depending on which types of bank deposit are included and on whether bank deposits in other currencies are included.

See also: M0; M1; M2; M3; M3c; M4; M5; sterling M3

References
Bank of England (1990) 'Monetary aggregates in a changing environment: a statistical discussion paper', 47.

monkey (E4)
Five hundred units of a currency, e.g. of the dollar or pound sterling.

Monnet's law (D0)
People only accept change when they are faced with necessity and only recognize necessity when a crisis is upon them. This was first enunciated by Jean Monnet (1888–1979), the father of French INDICATIVE PLANNING.

monobank (G2)
The single state-owned bank of a Soviet-type economy which functions both as a CENTRAL BANK and as a RETAIL BANK throughout the economy. Although most capitalist economies have separate banking institutions which specialize in different banking functions, in the nineteenth century in several European countries there were banks with united functions.

mono-economics (A1)
The type of economic theory regarded as applicable to every type of economic system and country, irrespective of its stage of development and economic conditions. CLASSICAL and MARXIST ECONOMICS emphasize the theoretical implications of different stages of development.

See also: stages theory

Monopolies and Mergers Commission (L4)
The UK body which investigated proposed mergers, monopoly situations and anti-competitive practices referred to it by the Director-General for Fair Trading or the Secretary of State for Trade and Industry. Its predecessors were the Monopolies and Restrictive Practices Commission (1948 to 1956) and the Monopolies Commission (1956 to 1965): a change of name was

necessary when the extra task of considering mergers was added to its remit. Its lack of power has often been noted: it cannot initiate its own inquiries, nor take action to remedy the situations it criticizes. It was succeeded by the COMPETITION COMMISSION in 1998.

See also: antitrust; competition policy

monopolistic competition (L1)

A market structure first discussed by Edward CHAMBERLIN in 1932. It is similar to PERFECT COMPETITION, apart from the crucial assumption of PRODUCT DIFFERENTIATION which has the effect of introducing selling costs. These costs create a BARRIER TO ENTRY with the effects of reducing the number of firms in the industry and creating a small amount of monopoly power for each producer. Since monopolistically competitive firms produce, in equilibrium, at a point of the AVERAGE COST curve above the minimum, monopolistic competition is criticized for resulting in lower output and higher product prices than under perfect competition.

See also: excess capacity theorem

References

Chamberlin, E.H. (1933) *The Theory of Monopolistic Competition*, Cambridge, MA: Harvard University Press.

monopoly (L1)

The sole producer of the entire output of goods and services of an industry. A monopoly usually has INELASTIC demand for its products, unless the industry is so narrowly defined that there are some near substitutes produced by other industries. Under monopoly, the demand curve for the firm is also the demand curve for the industry. If the monopoly follows the rule of profit maximization, i.e. it equates the MARGINAL REVENUE and MARGINAL COST of production, it has an opportunity to earn SUPERNORMAL PROFITS. In the past, major examples of monopolies were chartered trading companies such as the East India Company; today, PUBLIC ENTERPRISES are the

best examples as in the private sector COMPETITION POLICY has opposed monopolization.

supernormal profits
D demand
AR average revenue   AC average cost
MR marginal revenue   MC marginal cost

See also: concentration;
Herfindahl–Hirschman index;
Lerner index

monopoly capitalism (L2, P1, P2)

1 An ECONOMY whose economic activities are dominated by OLIGOPOLISTIC industries so that a surplus, or SUPERNORMAL PROFITS, can be earned.

2 A CENTRALLY PLANNED ECONOMY whose industry is run by huge state monopolies to facilitate the co-ordination of economic activities.

3 TRANSNATIONAL CORPORATIONS who have behaved, according to Marxian economists, as economic imperialists.

References

Baran, P. and Sweezy, P. (1966) *Monopoly Capital*, New York: Monthly Review Press.

monopoly power (L1)

The power of a dominant firm or firms over a particular market or economy. Proxy measures of this take the form of CONCENTRATION RATIOS.

See also: Herfindahl–Hirschman index; Lerner index

monopoly profit (D3) *see* supernormal profit

monopoly zoning (H7)
A local government strategy to create a fiscal surplus based on maximizing fiscal revenue and minimizing the cost of service provision by a careful drawing of local boundaries.

monopsony (D0)
The sole buyer in a particular market. In product markets, public authorities are the major examples, e.g. the UK's National Health Service; in labour markets, any large firm employing a large proportion of the industry's workforce. As a monopsonist faces an upward-sloping factor supply curve, its MARGINAL COST curve is above its average cost curve. Monopsonistic firms employ fewer workers at lower wages than competitive firms, if they are PROFIT MAXIMIZERS.

p_m	price under monopsony
p_c	price under perfect competition
q_m	quantity under monopsony
q_c	quantity under perfect competition
MC	marginal cost
MRP	marginal revenue product
D	demand
S	supply

Monte Carlo methods (C9)
Computer simulation experiments used to estimate the values of parameters by random sampling and regressing the results of successive experiments to establish that least squares estimators are unbiased.

Mont Pelerin Society (P4)
A group of liberals who first met in April 1947 at Mont Pelerin, near Montreux, Switzerland, to discuss liberalism, its decline and possible revival. Its original membership, dominated by HAYEK, Karl Popper, Michael POLYANI, Lionel ROBBINS and MISES, was later extended to include FRIEDMAN and STIGLER. Its powerful political associates have included in Germany Konrad Adenauer, in the USA Arthur BURNS, and in the UK Enoch Powell, Sir Keith Joseph and Sir Geoffrey Howe.

moonlight economy (K4, P0)
Part of a national economy noted for extensively using cash for transactions to avoid records being kept which could be available to tax authorities.

See also: cash economy

moonlighting (J2)
The unauthorised holding of another job in addition to one's principal employment. One job provides the main source of employment income and the other a supplement. This practice is widespread in low-wage economies or underpaid sectors of a national economy.

moral hazard (D0)
A problem of INSURANCE: by insuring property or one's life, the insured may indulge in more risky behaviour increasing the probability of the undesired event occurring. Thus an insurance system can cause MARGINAL SOCIAL COST to be in excess of MARGINAL PRIVATE COST, a suboptimal situation. This encourages post-contractual optimism.

See also: risk

moral suasion (E5)
A method the BANK OF ENGLAND uses to

control commercial banks by negotiation, rather than by OPEN MARKET OPERATIONS.

See also: jawbone

Morgan Stanley Capital International World Index (G1)

An index of stock market prices gathered from the world's leading stock exchanges covering about 60 per cent of their market capitalization.

Morgenstern, Oskar, 1902–77 (B3)

A German-American mathematical economist, born in Silesia, Germany, but educated at the University of Vienna. In his early career he was Director of the Austrian Institute for Business Cycle Research from 1931 to 1938 and professor of Vienna University from 1931 to 1938, when he was also a member of the Vienna Circle of philosophers and mathematicians. In 1938, the Nazi occupation of Austria led to his dismissal from the university and emigration to the USA. At Princeton University, he fruitfully collaborated with NEUMANN, persuading him to apply GAME THEORY to economics: their collaboration resulted in *The Theory of Games and Economic Behaviour* (1944). His later work included books on economic prediction and aspects of US defence.

References

Morgenstern, O. (1965) *On the Accuracy of Economic Observations*, 2nd edn, Princeton, NJ: Princeton University Press.
—— (1970) *The Predictability of Stock Market Prices*, Lexington, MA: Lexington Books.

Morishima, Michio, 1923– (B3)

Japanese-born UK professor of economics. He was born in Osaka, Japan, and graduated from Kyoto University. After teaching at Kyoto and Osaka and visiting Oxford and Yale, in 1968 he permanently emigrated to the UK where he was professor at Essex University from 1968 to 1970 and subsequently at the London School of Economics. He is a mathematical economist of note who has synthesized GENERAL EQUILIBRIUM theory, INPUT–OUTPUT ANALYSIS and economic dynamics in his *Theory of Economic Growth* (1969). Also he has fruitfully applied mathematical economics to the study of MARX's ideas in *Marx's Economics: A Dual Theory of Value and Growth* (1973) and in *Value, Exploitation and Growth* (1978). His *Economic Theory of Modern Society* (1975) has popularized many results of mathematical economics previously inaccessible to the non-mathematician.

References

Morishima, M. (1971) *Walras' Economics: A Pure Theory of Capital and Money*, Cambridge: Cambridge University Press.
—— (1976) *The Economic Theory of Modern Society*, trans. D. W. Anthony, Cambridge: Cambridge University Press.

mortgage (G0)

Literally a 'dead pledge'; in practice a charge over property given to a lender so that a borrower can raise finance either to effect the original purchase of it or to acquire funds for other purposes. This centuries' old legal device has made possible the financing of mass house ownership throughout non-socialist economies.

See also: adjustable rate mortgage; building society; collateralized mortgage obligation; equity-linked mortgage; mortgage bond; mortgage strip; thrift

mortgage bond (G0)

A securitized form of a loan backed by a mortgage. These bonds have been created by investment institutions selling off their outstanding home loans to another company which finances the purchase by a bond issue (often a Eurobond). The borrower continues to pay interest to the original lender who then passes on the interest to service the coupon on the bonds which have been issued. SECURITIZATION increases the amount of mortgage lending, without the original lenders having to increase their capital. Also, BUILDING SOCIETIES and housing loan associations become more competitive in the loans market, through securitization, as they are able to lend at lower interest rates. There are more examples of these bond issues in the USA than in the UK, despite more elaborate regulation of them. Mortgage bonds in sterling were first issued in 1987.

mortgage credit association (G2)
An association owned by its members which raises finance by issuing bonds on a stock exchange. The interest payable on loans fixed over a five-year period is kept low by the relatively small costs of administration. This type of association has flourished in Denmark.

See also: building society; savings and loan association

mortgage equity withdrawal (G2)
A remortgaging of a house to obtain finance for consumer expenditure.

mortgage pass-through security (G2)
A share or a participating certificate in a pool of mortgages.

mortgage strip (G2)
The division of a mortgage into an interest-only part and a principal-only part to increase its marketability and to dispose of the assets of a THRIFT or other financial institution.

most favoured nation (F1)
The status that accords a country the same trading privileges, e.g. exemptions from tariffs, as the other signatories to a commercial treaty or agreement. Under the rules of the GENERAL AGREEMENT ON TARIFFS AND TRADE, all parties to the agreement are usually expected to accord this privilege to their fellow trading partners.

mothballing (D2)
The preservation of unused productive capacity in working order in case a change in demand or costs makes resumption of production viable.

motility (J6)
The tendency of a worker to be mobile in a labour market. This can be measured by a questionnaire concerning a worker's intentions. Determinants of motility include a person's level of education, type of occupation and financial ability to obtain housing in another area.

See also: mobility of labour

Motor of Europe (E6)
Germany, the largest and key ECONOMY.

moving averages (C1, E3)
A method of smoothing the fluctuations in a time series by calculating a series of ARITHMETIC MEANS. This is regularly used to eliminate seasonal fluctuations, e.g. a twelve-month moving average is calculated for January by dividing the sum of the values for January to December by 12, for February by dividing the sum of the values for the twelve months from February to the following January by 12, and so forth.

multicollinearity (C1)
The state of an econometric relation such that some or all of the explanatory variables are highly correlated with each other.

See also: autocorrelation

Multi-Fibre Arrangement (F1)
A trade agreement covering textiles and clothing negotiated in 1973 between twenty-seven developing countries and sixteen developed countries which is a major exception to the GENERAL AGREEMENT ON TARIFFS AND TRADE. It has been renewed several times and is scheduled to be phased out in 2005. This quota scheme for producers was originally designed to provide gradual adjustment to international shifts in COMPARATIVE ADVANTAGE and to liberalize world trade gradually. In practice, it restricts the exports of fibres to consumer countries, e.g. the UK and USA. In 1986, the MFA was extended to more fibres (sisal, jute and ramie – a flax-like substance). A production limit is assigned to a country which then shares it out among individual producers: if one manufacturer wants to expand production then it can buy an enlarged quota on the open market. The GATT believes that the

MFA distorts the pattern of world trade as it impedes the expansion of low-cost producers. The MFA's effects have been to raise the cost of clothing and the profits of domestic producers in developed countries. It has curbed the exports of developing countries but has encouraged a shift to higher quality products amongst the established Third World producers. In the URU-GUAY ROUND it was agreed to phase out MFA quotas over ten years.

References

Choi, Y.-R., Chung, H.S. and Marian, N. (1985) *The Multi-Fibre Arrangement in Theory and Practice*, London: Pinter.

multilateral aid (F3, O0)

FOREIGN AID which consists of the distribution to developing countries by an international agency, e.g. the WORLD BANK, of the grants given by wealthier countries. Although it is argued that aid in this form is fairer than BILATERAL AID, it is still possible for there to be biases in the distribution policy of a major agency.

Multilateral Investment Guarantee Agency (F3)

An offshoot of the WORLD BANK created in 1988 to promote foreign investment by guaranteeing against many risks, including expropriation and currency transfer. It also offers advice to developing countries wanting to make their economies more attractive to the potential foreign investor.

multilevel marketing (M3) *see* pyramid selling

multimarket contact (L4)

Meetings between two large CONGLOMER-ATES in several markets. As this can lead to tacit co-operation to stabilize prices and market shares, it has attracted the attention of ANTITRUST regulators.

multimodal frequency curve (C1)

A FREQUENCY CURVE with more than two maxima.

Variable observed

multinational corporation (F2, L2)

An international firm that produces goods or services in several countries, without being concentrated in a single country, Although the term first became popular in the 1960s, by the late nineteenth century several US, UK and Dutch firms had acquired such characteristics.

The advantages of production abroad, rather than exporting from the original country of operation, include a saving in transport costs, the adjustment of product design to make products more acceptable to local markets, a reduction, in many cases, in corporate taxation and access to local labour and capital which may be more abundant than at home. The immense success of this form of organization, prominent in many industries, including motor cars, computers, pharmaceuticals, food processing, oil and soap, has attracted envy and criticism: envy from national governments with less economic power and competence; criticism from Marxists who see the growth of multinationals as a sinister international expansion of CAPITALISM. TRADE UNIONS complain about competition from cheap labour countries; science graduates lament the increased concentration of research and development activities in the USA to the detriment of other countries; national governments object to the loss of tax revenue and the difficulties of operating industrial and employment policies when much of their industrial sector is controlled by foreign-owned entities.

Many controls have been suggested to reduce what are seen to be the less attractive effects of multinationals: governments and trade unions lay down strict conditions for foreign countries wishing to invest, fiscal devices are used to maintain tax revenues and domestically owned multinationals are monitored. In extreme cases, exasperated national governments have nationalized the assets of foreign-owned subsidiaries, but in many cases this has been as sensible as cutting the hands off a worker and expecting the severed hands to do the same work as before – a subsidiary, unsupported by the services of the rest of the corporation, is a poor shadow of its former self. Despite so many attempts to curb the activities of multinationals, they continue to grow, enjoying all the benefits of ECONOMIES OF SCALE and retaining their status as major world economic institutions.

References

Caves, R.E. (1982) *Multinational Enterprise and Economic Analysis*, Cambridge: Cambridge University Press.

multiple correlation (C1)
The extent to which there is a relationship between three or more variables, measured by the COEFFICIENT OF MULTIPLE CORRELATION.

See also: linear correlation

multiple equilibria (D5)
1 The state of market in which balances in several parts occur simultaneously. This is represented by a diagram with several points of intersection between, for example, when an aggregate supply curve is linear but the aggregate demand curve is S-shaped.
2 The coexistence in a national ECONOMY of a low-efficiency, low-output equilibrium and a high-efficiency, high-output equilibrium.

multiple exchange rate (F3)
An exchange rate with different values according to the nature of the international transaction. Often, BALANCE OF PAYMENTS current account transactions are at a different rate from capital account transactions. Central banks allow these different rates because of the different pressures on parts of their balance of payments, e.g. needing imports of capital but not imports of luxury goods. Common examples of multiple rates are the existence of official and BLACK MARKET exchange rates in operation simultaneously and an official rate together with more favourable rates for industries being helped under an industrial policy.

See also: dual exchange rate

multiple unit auction (D0)
A sale of identical units of a good in which the buyers can bid for only one, or less than the total number. There is no reserve price or minimum bid.

multiplier (E0)
The relationship between an increment in income and a change in AGGREGATE DEMAND; in particular, the ratio of extra expenditure to extra investment. There were hints of a multiplier concept as early as the seventeenth century in PETTY's works but it was not until KAHN postulated an employment multiplier in 1930 that formal attempts were made to measure it, particularly by Colin CLARK. It has become a central idea in macroeconomics. For a simple closed economy described by the equation

$$Y = C + I$$

where Y is national income, C is aggregate consumption and I is net investment, the multiplier is $1/(1 - MPC)$, with MPC the marginal propensity to consume; for an open economy described by the equation

$$Y = C + I + (X - M)$$

where X is exports and M is imports, the multiplier is $1/[1 - (MPC + MPM)]$, with MPM the marginal propensity to import.

See also: balanced budget; employment; foreign trade multiplier; money multiplier; regional multiplier; super multiplier

References

Hansen, A.H. (1948) *Income, Employment and Public Policy: Essays in Honor of Alvin H. Hansen*, New York: Norton.

multiplier–accelerator model (E3)

An economic model attempting to explain business cycles: the MULTIPLIER makes income respond to investment and the ACCELERATOR ensures that changes in income will generate net investment. Given certain values in the basic equations, fluctuations will be generated, but it is usual for there to be ceilings and floors to economic activity to cause turning points in the aggregate activity of a national economy.

References

Goodwin, R.M. (1948) 'Secular and cyclical aspects of the multiplier and the accelerator', in *Income, Employment and Public Policy: Essays in Honor of Alvin H. Hansen*, New York: Norton.

Hicks, J.R. (1950) *A Contribution to the Theory of the Trade Cycle*, Oxford: Oxford University Press.

Samuelson, P.A. (1939) 'Interactions between the multiplier analysis and the principle of acceleration', *Review of Economic Statistics* 21: 75–8.

multistage tax (H2)

A tax raised at each stage of production; a VALUE-ADDED or TURNOVER TAX.

multivariate analysis (C1)

The examination of the relationship between several variables, usually a dependent variable and several independent variables. An example of this would be a study of the determinants of the unemployment rate (the dependent variable) and educational qualifications, age and previous work experience (independent variables).

See also: regression

Mun, Thomas, 1571–1641 (B3)

Director of the East India Company and leading MERCANTILIST whose formulation of economic theory in *England's Treasure by Forraign Trade* (first published posthumously in 1664) represented the finest flowering of late mercantilist ideas. To justify the export of silver bullion by the company, he extended the current idea of the balance of payments as being a particular balance between two countries to the concept of a general balance between one country and the rest of the world, permitting some individual balances to be in deficit. Adam SMITH's view of mercantilism was heavily influenced by Mun.

References

Appleby, J.O. (1978) *Economic Thought and Ideology in Seventeenth Century England*, Princeton, NJ: Princeton University Press.

Mundell–Fleming model (E1)

An open economy model extending the IS–LM model on which an FF curve is imposed to show that the economy is in equilibrium when there are equilibria in its money and goods markets and its imports equal its exports. The TERMS OF TRADE affect the positions of both the IS and FF curves.

See also: IS–LM curves

References

Mundell, R.A. (1968) *International Economics*, New York: Macmillan.

Mundell, Robert A., 1932– (B3)

Born in Kingston, Ontario, and educated at the University of British Columbia and MIT. He was on the staff of the International Monetary Fund from 1961 to 1966 and held chairs at Chicago from 1966 to 1971 and at Columbia from 1974. He has written extensively on international economics and is an authority on optimum currency areas. He has advised many international organisations, including the United Nations and the EEC whom he advised on a single currency. In 1999 he was awarded the NOBEL PRIZE IN ECONOMICS for 'his analysis of monetary and fiscal policy under different exchange rate regimes and his analysis of optimum currency areas'.

Mundell–Tobin effect (E3, E4)
The effect on interest rates of price inflation. Nominal interest rates rise at a slower rate than inflation because the public holds less in money balances in inflationary times thereby driving down interest rates.

muni (H7)
US municipal bond.

Muth–Mills model (R4)
A study of the relationship between the differential costs of commuting in an urban area and the differences in house prices. This model is used to explain the internal structure of cities. Lower house prices in the suburbs are sufficient to justify high commuting costs to the central business district.

References

Mills, E.S. (1967) 'An aggregative model of resource allocation in a metropolitan area', *American Economic Review* 57: 197–210.
Muth, R.F. (1969) *Cities and Housing*, Chicago: Chicago University Press.

mutual fund (G2)
US UNIT TRUST. There are many types. General equity funds invest in a range of equities with the aim of outperforming the market as measured by, for example, STANDARD & POOR'S 500 index. Index funds are invested in the leading stocks which comprise the principal stock market price indices. Strategic funds are very diversified as they invest in all markets, including currency and futures markets. Sector funds specialize in one sector of the stock market. Overseas funds consist of the stocks of a foreign country or a group of them, e.g. Japan or Europe. Precious metal funds invest in gold, silver and other high-

value metals. Tax-free funds invest in tax-exempt bonds of, for example, US states. Funds of funds spread risk by investing in several mutual funds. Social conscience funds avoid investments in industries or countries subject to moral criticism.

See also: investment trust

mutual insurance company (G2)
An insurance company owned by its members. Increasingly these have changed their status and been quoted on the stock market.

Myners Committee (G3)
A working group chaired by Paul Myners and set up by the UK Department of Trade and Industry in 1995. In its report, *Developing a Winning Partnership: How Companies and Institutional Investors are Working Together*, it set out the broad criteria for being a MODEL COMPANY MANAGEMENT or MODEL INSTITUTIONAL INVESTOR.

Myrdal, Gunnar, 1898–1987 (B3)
A leading Swedish economist and sociologist. He studied at Stockholm University under WICKSELL, CASSEL and HECKSCHER in preparation for his notable academic and public career. In his varied life he was professor at Geneva (1931–2) and at Stockholm (1933–9 and 1961–5) Universities, as well as being a Senator of the Swedish Parliament from 1934 to 1936 and 1942 to 1946, Minister for Trade and Commerce from 1945 to 1947 and Executive Secretary of the UN Economic Commission for Europe from 1947 to 1957. He was awarded the NOBEL PRIZE FOR ECONOMICS, with HAYEK, in 1974; his wife, whom he married in 1924, gained the Nobel Peace Prize in 1982.

His major contribution to economics has been his work *Monetary Equilibrium*, a central work of the STOCKHOLM SCHOOL, in which he developed his 1927 doctoral thesis on price formation and change to show the importance of the *ex ante, ex post* distinction in macroeconomics. He is also famous for his contributions to methodological debates, particularly in his work *The Political Element in the Development of Economic Theory and Objectivity in Social Research* in which he advanced the idea of a value-free economics. His commitment to development economics is evident in his *Asian Drama*, as is his sociological ability in *American Dilemma*.

References

Kindleberger, C.P. (1987) 'Gunnar Myrdal, 1898–1987', *Scandinavian Journal of Economics* 87: 393–403.

Myrdal, G. (1939) *Monetary Equilibrium*, London: W. M. Hodge.
—— (1944) *American Dilemma: The Negro Problem and Modern Democracy*, New York: Harper.
—— (Swedish edn 1930, English edn 1953) *The Political Element in the Development of Economic Theory*, trans. P. Streeton, London: Routledge & Kegan Paul.
—— (1968) *Asian Drama: An Inquiry into the Poverty of Nations*, London and New York: Twentieth Century Fund.
—— (1970) *Objectivity in Social Research*, London: Duckworth.

N

nanny state (I3)
An ECONOMY which is a WELFARE STATE providing so many benefits as to take away much personal responsibility and create a DEPENDENCY CULTURE.

narcodollars (F3, K4)
Dollars used to launder the money of drug barons of the world.

See also: laundering money

Nash bargaining (C7)
A two-person economic game in which there is collusion between the players. Equilibrium is such that an individual's MARGINAL RATE OF SUBSTITUTION = the MARGINAL RATE OF TRANSFORMATION. This equilibrium is inefficient because the price facing the consumer is equal to the price of the PUBLIC GOOD, with some of the benefit accruing to others. This has been applied to oligopoly to show how a firm makes the best response to the decisions of its rivals.

Nash equilibrium (C7)
In a game with two players an equilibrium occurs when each strategy of a pair is the best response to the other. Each player uses the highest possible pay-off, given the other player's strategy. This was invented in 1950.

Nash, John Forbes, 1928– (B3)
Born at Bluefield, West Virginia, he was educated at Carnegie and Princeton Universities. He taught in the 1950s at the Massachusetts Institute of Technology until mental illness caused his retiral; later he was a visiting scholar at the Institute for Advanced Study, Princeton University. An economist and mathematician who is famous for distinguishing co-operative from non-co-operative games and formulating the Nash equilibrium. In 1994 he shared the NOBEL PRIZE FOR ECONOMICS with HARSANYI and SELTEN for his contribution to games theory.

References

Nasar, S. (1998) *A Beautiful Mind*, London: Faber and Faber.
Nash, J.F. (1951) 'Non-cooperative games', *Annals of Mathematics* 54: 286–95.

National Association of Securities Dealers and Investment Managers (G2)
UK association of insurance brokers and investment advisers, some of whom deal in over-the-counter shares.

See also: over-the-counter market

National Association of Securities Dealers Automated Quotation System (G2)
US securities market founded in 1938 which lists over-the-counter securities not listed on regular exchanges. By the end of the 1980s, it became the second largest securities market in the USA and the third largest in the world, making it the strongest stock market in competition to the

New York Stock Exchange, particularly because of its innovations in technology and market making. The price quotations of its MARKET-MAKERS are the basis of competition in this electronic market; each stock has a minimum of two market-makers. From 1982, only stocks with at least 100,000 shares worth at least $5 each have been included, i.e. 2,500 stocks. It is also linked to the INTERNATIONAL STOCK EXCHANGE to provide a TRANSATLANTIC MARKET in 600 securities.

See also: over-the-counter market

National Banking Act 1863 (G2)
US federal statute whose provisions included the setting up of the COMPTROLLER OF THE CURRENCY to increase the supervision and, therefore, the solvency of COMMERCIAL BANKS. It restricted nationally chartered banks to operating only one branch.

See also: branch banking; McFadden Branch Banking Act 1927

National Board for Prices and Incomes (E3, J3)
The UK public board which administered a national prices and incomes policy in 1965–72. Of its 170 reports, some were on whether particular price or wage increases were justified and others were concerned to relate these two aspects of inflation. The board produced much applied microeconomic analysis noted for having a greater depth than the publications of many other public authorities of the day; the subsequent Pay Board produced less profound reports.

See also: incomes policy; prices policy

References

Fels, A. (1972) *The British Prices and Incomes Board*, Cambridge: Cambridge University Press.

Mitchell, J. (1972) *The National Board for Prices and Incomes*, London: Secker & Warburg.

National Bureau of Economic Research (E6)
An independent economics institute founded in 1920 and based in Washington, DC. Its famous research series includes the seminal work of KUZNETS on NATIONAL INCOME and the studies by MITCHELL and BURNS of the business cycle. Its dominant concerns have been macroeconomic.

national debt (H6)
The total indebtedness of the central and local governments of a country at a particular time to its own public and foreign creditors taking the form of short-term BILLS and long-term BONDS. In most cases, such debt has accumulated because the country's public expenditure is more than its tax revenue. The burden of a national debt is usually measured by the ratio of national debt to gross national product. Long-term debt can be regarded as a burden to subsequent generations.

See also: overlapping generations model

National Economic Development Council (E6)
A tripartite council set up in the UK in 1962 consisting of representatives of the government, trade unions and employers. Its original aim was to introduce INDICATIVE PLANNING into the UK. Although some general economic forecasts were published, it soon, with the use of Economic Development Councils for particular industries, concentrated on producing detailed recommendations for improving sectors of the UK economy. Until its abolition in 1992, it was valued as a forum by all participants apart from in the 1980s when trade unions were in dispute with the government over de-unionization of workers in intelligence establishments. In the 1980s, it moved from INDUSTRIAL POLICY measures to SUPPLY-SIDE ECONOMICS. It was abolished in 1992.

National Enterprise Board (L5)
A UK public corporation created by the Industry Act 1975 to encourage industrial investment and restructuring; in a sense a successor to the INDUSTRIAL REORGANIZATION CORPORATION. It used its funds to invest in private sector firms to effect mergers. Also

it had the task of managing existing government shareholdings in major firms, especially British Leyland and Rolls Royce, helping small firms and allocating grants under REGIONAL POLICY. In 1980, the Conservative government considerably reduced its role by selling off many of its investments and by cutting its annual funds.

national income (E0)

1 The money value of the goods and services resulting from the economic activities of the residents of a country over a time period, usually of a quarter or whole year.

2 A monetary flow showing net additions to wealth.

3 The sum of FACTOR INCOMES.

4 The net national product (gross national product less depreciation) because income is a FLOW CONCEPT showing net additions to wealth over a time period.

Different countries have varying views on what constitutes 'an economic activity' so differ in what they include in their national income accounts. However, there is conceptual accord that national income, national product and national expenditure are identical because there is in every economy a CIRCULAR FLOW of income: an economic activity produces an output which, when sold, constitutes expenditure and creates incomes for the factors of production that have made it. The national income at market prices includes in the valuation of economic activities indirect taxes net of subsidies; the valuation at factor cost does not.

Rough estimates of the national income were made as early as the seventeenth century by PETTY and Gregory King, but fairly accurate national income accounting is a product of the macroeconomic revolution in economic thinking in the 1930s: CLARK and STONE in the UK and KUZNETS in the USA laid the foundations for today's national accounting. International comparisons of different countries' national

incomes should be treated with caution. Apart from different statistical conventions from country to country, there is also the problem of translating income estimates in one currency into those of another, often the US dollar. In general, measures of the national income usually exclude non-market activities, leisure and environmental social costs, making them inaccurate as measures of ECONOMIC WELFARE.

See also: accounts; European system of accounts; measure of economic welfare; National Income and Product Accounts; net economic welfare; physical quality of life; purchasing power parity; System of National Accounts

References

Beckerman, W. (1966) *International Comparisons of Real Income*, Paris: OECD.
—— (1980) *An Introduction to National Income Analysis*, 3rd edn, London: Weidenfeld & Nicolson.
Kravis, I.B. (1978) *International Comparisons of Real Product and Purchasing Power*, Baltimore, MD: published for the World Bank by Johns Hopkins University Press.
Shaikh, A.M. and Tonak, E.A. (1994) *Measuring the wealth of nations: the political economy of national accounts*, Cambridge, New York and Melbourne: Cambridge University Press.
United Nations International Comparison Project (1978) *Phase II*.

National Income and Product Accounts (E0)

The national income accounts of the USA which began in 1947; earlier estimates had been produced by the US Department of Commerce with the advice of KUZNETS but they lacked an expenditure breakdown of the national product. The need for better economic information in the Second World War prompted the creation of this new accounting framework. The new accounts had the aims of providing a consistent and interrelated system, improving statistical procedures for estimating all series using the latest data and incorporating changes in basic aggregates to make the definitions used more useful.

The basic table is

gross national
product =

personal consumption expenditures
+
gross private domestic investment
+ net exports of goods and services
+ government purchases

Further tables present disaggregated statistics of the principal components.

See also: European System of Accounts; national income; System of National Accounts

References

Eisner, R. (1988) 'Extended accounts for national income and product', *Journal of Economic Literature* 26 (December): 1611–84.
Foss, M.F. (1983) *The US National Income and Product Accounts. NBER Studies in Income and Wealth*, Vol. 47, Chicago: University of Chicago Press.
US Bureau of Economic Analysis, *The National Income and Product Accounts of the United States, 1929–82. Survey of Current Business*, July issues.

National Industrial Recovery Act 1933 (N6)

A major US federal statute of the New Deal which sought to promote industrial recovery. Under section 7, the codes of competition (statements of price and output policies) had to recognize the right of workers to organize collectively making this statute an important forerunner of the WAGNER ACT.

National Institute for Economic and Social Research (E6)

UK independent economics institute founded in 1938 to research into economic and social conditions. Apart from occasional pamphlets, it publishes an influential quarterly review and undertakes its own economic forecasting.

national insurance contribution (H2, I3)

UK employment tax created in 1948. The contributions from employers, employees and the self-employed are kept in a separate fund to finance a range of benefits, including those for the unemployed, the sick and the retired. BEVERIDGE, when devising this system, was inspired by the older social security system of Germany introduced by Bismarck.

nationalization (L5)

The acquisition of privately owned enterprises by a government, with or without compensation.

See also: nationalized industry; public enterprise

nationalized industry (L5)

A publicly owned firm engaged in the production of goods and services. Although governments have been involved in the ownership of industrial concerns as early as the MERCANTILISTS and post offices have long been state owned in many countries, it is in the twentieth century that large basic industries have been state owned, e.g. in France and in the UK. In the latter, most of these were established by the Labour government of 1945 to 1950 as an implementation of clause 4 of the Labour Party Constitution; private sector firms in the basic industries of transport, energy and steel, as well as the Bank of England, were purchased. The extension of public ownership gave the UK the character of a MIXED ECONOMY. Other countries, particularly France, greatly extended public ownership in the 1930s; in the USA, the creation of AMTRAK was a rare US example of this organizational form. But in the 1980s, it became UK government policy to 'privatize' the more profitable nationalized industries, including telecommunications, water, gas and electricity.

The trading position of a nationalized industry is affected by its monopoly position and the lack of market discipline, both by having public finance to supplement borrowings from capital markets and by being kept in existence when virtually bankrupt. As a consequence, a high proportion of government grants has been to subsidize wage bills, rather than to finance long-term investment. In September 1981 President Mitterrand of France, one of the last to argue the case for nationalization, gave as reasons for taking large industrial groups and banks into state ownership, the elimination of monopoly and quasi-monopoly situations which provide a basis for political influence in France, safeguarding national sovereignty and the provision of tools for industrial development in the future.

See also: privatization; public enterprise

References

Chester, N. (1975) *The Nationalisation of British Industry*, 1945–51, London: HMSO.
Pryke, R. (1971) *Public Enterprise in Practice: The British Experience of Nationalisation over Two Decades*, London: MacGibbon & Kee.
—— (1981) *The Nationalised Industries: Policies and Performance since 1968*, Oxford: Robertson.

National Labor Relations Act 1935 (J5)
see Wagner Act 1935

National Labor Relations Board (J5)
US federal board created in 1933 and subsequently authorized by the WAGNER ACT. It attempts to prevent and remedy unfair labour practices, to promote COLLECTIVE BARGAINING by conducting secret ballots to establish whether a labour organization can represent a group of workers.

National Plan (UK) (E6)
An exercise in INDICATIVE PLANNING which

began in 1965 but, instead of lasting until 1970, terminated nine months later when the seamen's strike exacerbated a balance of payments problem necessitating deflation in place of the growth aims of the plan. It was hoped that the UK national income would increase by 25 per cent over five years. This was unlikely as many of the assumptions, e.g. those for export growth and labour mobility, were regarded as too generous; the industrial inquiry which provided a database for the planners was regarded as highly inaccurate. The essence of indicative planning – that government forecasts are sufficiently influential to encourage investment – was lacking: few believed in the ambitious schemes of these planners.

References

The National Plan, London: HMSO, Cmnd 2764, (1965).

national wealth (E0)
The total assets owned by the residents of a country on a particular day. The most reliable estimates are for firms as they have to keep balance sheets. Many household assets are only valued on death so the sample of wealth statistics produced from probate sources is non-random. It could be argued that HUMAN CAPITAL estimates should be included in the national wealth as trained labour is a major national asset. But few countries are statistically ambitious enough to attempt such a measure, although it is possible to produce an estimate if a POPULATION CENSUS asks questions about educational qualifications and training.

See also: balance sheet; stock and flow concepts; wealth

References

Goldsmith, R.W. (1985) *Comparative National Balance Sheets. A Study of Twenty Countries 1688–1978*, Chicago and London: University of Chicago Press.
Revell, L.L. (1967) *The Wealth of the Nation: The National Balance Sheet of*

the United Kingdom, 1957–61, Cambridge: Cambridge University Press.

natural economy (Q0)

1 The means of producing goods and services based on Nature.
2 Environmentally provided assets – soil, water, atmosphere, wildlife, forests.
3 An ECONOMY free of government intervention following its natural course.

natural increase (J1)

The increase in a human population resulting from an excess of live births over deaths. Natural increase rates are higher in the THIRD and FOURTH WORLDS than in the FIRST WORLD.

natural monopoly (L0)

An INDUSTRY which, it is argued, should be run as a MONOPOLY, usually to achieve the maximum amount of ECONOMIES OF SCALE. If a natural monopoly brought about by the technology of an industry were replaced by COMPETITION, there would be an increase in unit costs, as happens when a natural monopoly in energy distribution is split up, losing the advantages of technical scale economies. Another case for monopolies of this kind is that a good or service is not supplied by any private concern and can only be supplied by the government, e.g. national defence.

References

Di Lorenzo, T.J. (1996) 'The myth of natural monopoly', *Review of Austrian Economics*, 9: 43–58.
Shaked, A. and Sutton, J. (1983) 'Natural oligopolies', *Econometrica* 51: 1469–84.
Sharkey, W.W. (1982) *The Theory of Natural Monopoly*, New York and Cambridge: Cambridge University Press.

natural price (D0)

The central long-run equilibrium product price around which market prices fluctuate. Adam SMITH, in introducing this concept, said that the natural price would be the sum of the natural prices of land, labour and capital.

natural rate of growth (O4)

The maximum long-term rate of ECONOMIC GROWTH. In the HARROD–DOMAR growth model it is measured as the sum of the rate of population growth and the rate of TECHNICAL PROGRESS reflected in labour PRODUCTIVITY: $G = n + t$, where G is the natural rate of growth, n is the rate of population growth and t is the rate of technical progress. Population growth leads to a growth of the LABOUR FORCE; technical progress increases labour productivity.

See also: warranted rate of growth

natural rate of interest (E4)

Marginal product of capital.

See also: market rate of interest; Wicksell

natural rate of unemployment (J6)

1 The single rate of unemployment compatible with a constant rate of inflation.
2 The long-term rate of unemployment around which an economy fluctuates as EXPECTATIONS of wage and price changes are fully realized by the associated rate of inflation. Attempts to move the economy to a lower rate of unemployment by fiscal and monetary stimulation are unsuccessful as expectations increase leading to inflationary increases in prices and wages which push the unemployment rate back to the natural rate. The natural rate changes in response to changes in the composition of the labour force as flows in and out of the stock of the unemployed are affected. The natural rate is usually illustrated by a vertical PHILLIPS CURVE.

References

Friedman, M. (1968) 'The role of monetary policy', *American Economic Review* 58 (March): 1–17.

natural resources (Q0)

LAND, including soil, air, water, minerals, animal and plant life. Environmental resources supporting life and health and providing amenities and energy resources are included; human resources and physical capital are excluded.

See also: externality; pollution control

References

Johnson, R.L. and Johnson, G.V. (eds) (1990) *Economic Valuation of Natural Resources. Issues, Theory, and Applications*, Boulder, CO: Westview Press.

Pearce, D. and Turner, K. (eds) (1989) *Economics of Natural Resources and Environment*, Brighton: Harvester Wheatsheaf.

natural trade (F1)

FREE TRADE that follows its natural course and is not distorted by government subsidies. Strongly advocated by Adam SMITH.

Navigation Acts (F1, L5, N4)

Legislation which insisted that all outward and homeward trade must be in the shipping of that country. England's first Navigation Act was in 1381; Scotland also had such Acts. Apart from being a protective device for maintaining the income of and employment in the shipping industry, these Acts also ensured that there were sufficient ships to provide a naval reserve. Adam SMITH approved of this exception to FREE TRADE. The UK repealed these acts in 1850.

See also: Jones Act

near money (E4)

TIME DEPOSITS with financial institutions which, on notice, can be converted into money, e.g. BUILDING SOCIETY deposits, CDs. These lack the essential characteristic of money – being immediately usable as a MEDIUM OF EXCHANGE – but readily can be converted into money.

near rationality (D0)

The tendency to take a decision differing from an optimal decision by the amount Δ because of inertia, adjustment, menu costs or errors in implementation.

References

Akerlof, G. and Yellen, J. (1985) 'Can small deviations from rationality make significant differences in economic equilibria?', *American Economic Review* 75: 708–20.

needs of trade (B1)

A banking doctrine, advanced by the BANKING SCHOOL, that demand, rather than the amount of specie held by a bank, should determine the amount of banknotes in circulation.

needs standard (D3, D6)

A principle of DISTRIBUTION based on Louis Blanc's notion 'From each according to ability, to each according to needs'. It is difficult to implement this approach to income distribution as the concept of 'need' is subjective and it has the disincentive effect of discouraging more industrious and talented workers whose reward is diminished by the extra income given to the poor.

negative equity (G0)

The amount by which the value of an asset, such as a house or a consumer durable, falls short of the amount borrowed to finance its purchase. Negative equity often occurs in falling property markets.

negative externality (D0)

An action adversely affecting the production or consumption of a third party.

See also: externality

negative feedback (O4)

The unfavourable effects of fast economic growth which make further growth difficult, e.g. because of the LAW OF DIMINISHING RETURNS in an agrarian economy.

negative income tax (H2)

An income maintenance scheme which makes cash payments to persons with less than an arbitrary level of income (which is notionally related to SUBSISTENCE). Advocates of such schemes argue that the POVERTY TRAP is eliminated, there is a reduction in administration costs and the labour supply from low-income households is increased because they would no longer be caught by high MARGINAL TAX RATES when moving from welfare benefits to employment incomes under a discontinuous benefit tax scale. Short-run US experiments of this kind have included urban schemes in New Jersey and rural projects in Iowa.

See also: social dividend scheme

References

Parker, H. (1989) *Instead of the Dole: An Inquiry into the Integration of the Tax and Benefit Systems*, London: Routledge.

Pechman, L.A. and Timpane, R.M. (eds) (1975) *Work Incentives and Income Guarantees*, Washington, DC: Brookings Institution.

negative saving (E2) *see* dissaving

negotiable order of withdrawal (G2) *see* NOW account

negotiated co-ordination (E0, P4)
A form of democratic national planning, resembling French INDICATIVE PLANNING, in which interest groups nationally, and within each sector of an economy, reach agreement before their conclusions are reviewed by a national representative assembly. The principal issues in negotiations are investment and labour.

References

Marquand, D. (1988) *The Unprincipled Society: New Demands and Old Politics*, London: Jonathan Cape.

neighbourhood effect (Q0)
An EXTERNALITY, or spillover effect, which has a spatial impact. Industrial pollution provides many examples of costly effects; beautiful buildings and gardens increase the welfare of nearby residents.

neoclassical economics (B1)
The school of economics emerging in the UK and the USA in the late nineteenth century, after 'the Marginal Revolution', MARSHALL, EDGEWORTH, PARETO, WICKSELL and WALRAS being its most prominent founders. Building on marginal analysis, it dominates much of US economics today,

especially at Chicago University. It takes the view that an economy's equilibrium will occur after a disturbance because of a *tâtonnement* process with flexible wages and prices. As prices disseminate information and provide incentives for economic agents, economic plans and activities are co-ordinated.

This school of economics, emphasizing the roles of consumers, producers and savers, has shifted from a study of market allocation to the science of individual and institutional choices about resources in markets and other economic institutions. It provides little macroeconomic analysis, except in its aggregation of individuals' choices. HICKS and SAMUELSON have been the most brilliant theorists of the school in the twentieth century. Critics of neoclassicism reject the view of economic agents as being concerned with maximization of utility, profit or net income and want to dethrone the central principles of diminishing MARGINAL UTILITY and diminishing MARGINAL RATES OF SUBSTITUTION. However, the neoclassicals continue to show the usefulness of the principles of maximization, equilibrium and substitution at the margin in their study of a host of modern problems, including job search, crime, time, marriage and housing, and the elegance of their theorizing.

See also: continuity thesis; marginalists

References

Boland, L. (1982) *Foundations of Economic Method*, London: Allen & Unwin.

Henry, L.E. (1990) *The Making of Neoclassical Economics*, London: Unwin Hyman.

neoclassical synthesis (D0, E0)
An approach to economic theory combining the price theory created by CLASSICAL ECONOMICS and KEYNESIAN macroeconomics. SAMUELSON popularized this concept in his bestselling textbook *Economics*.

neo-Keynesians (B2)
A modern refinement of KEYNESIAN macroeconomics, particularly associated with

HICKS and MEADE in the UK and with TOBIN, KLEIN, MODIGLIANI and Blinder in the USA. To undertake this enhancement of Keynes's ideas, the IS–LM framework and the PHILLIPS CURVE have been extensively used. This theoretical approach often refers to the failures of markets, particularly the labour market that does not clear because money wages are often inflexible downwards. A major policy prescription of this school of economics is DEMAND MANAGEMENT to keep an economy in equilibrium.

References

Benassi, C., Chirco, A. and Colombo, C. (1994) *The new Keynesian economics*, Oxford and Cambridge, MA: Blackwell.

neo-Malthusians (B1)

Followers of MALTHUS who in the nineteenth century advocated birth control as a means of checking population growth; in the twentieth century they have been more concerned to emphasize the conservation of natural resources, given limited technical progress.

See also: Club of Rome

References

Soloway, R.A. (1982) *Birth Control and the Population Question in England, 1877–1930*, London and Chapel Hill, NC: University of North Carolina Press.

neo-Marxists (B2)

A group of economists, especially Mandel and Sweezy, who have tried to reinterpret MARX in the light of more recent economic thought, including KEYNES's.

References

Mandel, E. (1968) *Marxist economic theory*, London: Merlin Press.
Sweezy, P.M. (1968) *Theory of capitalist development: Principles of Marxian political economy*, New York and London: Modern Reader Paperbacks.

neo-mercantilism (B2, F1)

The modern advocacy of PROTECTIONISM as a means of encouraging employment growth.

See also: alternative economic strategy; infant industry argument; mercantilism; Smoot–Hawley Tariff Act

References

Johnson, H.G. (ed.) (1974) *The New Mercantilism: Some Problems in International Trade, Money and Investment*, Oxford: Basil Blackwell.

neo-Ricardian theory (B2, D0)

A return to the LABOUR THEORY OF VALUE of RICARDO, based on SRAFFA's seminal work of 1960 which attempted to solve problems such as the formulation of a satisfactory theory of a surplus-producing economy. A class analysis, rather than a NEOCLASSICAL approach, is used to show how the surplus produced is divided into PROFITS, INTEREST and RENT. Prices are not explained by labour time values but by a cost of production theory, stating the socially necessary conditions of production. Thus prices = physical quantities of machines and raw materials employed + wages paid to the workforce + a mark-up on those costs. The theory develops Marxian theory, discarding the view that the tendency of the rate of profit is to fall and the development tendencies of the capitalist mode of production. Neo-Ricardian analysis has been applied to specific aspects of twentieth-century capitalism, especially oligopoly.

References

Fine, B. and Harris, L. (1979) *Rereading Capital*, New York: Columbia University Press.
Steedman, I. (1977) *Marx after Sraffa*, London: New Left Books.

net acquisition of financial assets (E1)

A set of sectoral balances used to analyse the overall state of an economy. These balances can be individually in deficit or surplus. The CAMBRIDGE ECONOMIC POLICY GROUP frequently used this approach in its analysis of the PUBLIC SECTOR borrowing requirement.

net asset value (G0)

The value of the total assets of a company after deduction of all debts. It is expressed as X pence, or dollars, per share.

net barter terms of trade (F1)

The ratio of an index of export prices to an index of import prices; the most commonly used measurement of the TERMS OF TRADE.

net economic welfare (D6)

GROSS NATIONAL PRODUCT adjusted by subtracting from it 'bads' such as pollution and by adding the value of beneficial non-market activities, including leisure.

See also: measure of economic welfare

net investment (E2)

An addition to the stock of capital in a given time period. Net investment plus REPLACEMENT INVESTMENT constitute gross investment.

See also: accelerator principle

net present value (M2)

The discounted value of future income from a particular investment less the discounted value of expected costs. A positive net present value indicates that an investment project is worthwhile.

See also: marginal efficiency of capital

net property income from abroad (F4)

The receipts of rents, profits and interest arising from ownership of foreign assets, less the payments of the same to non-residents. Net property income from abroad is added to the GROSS DOMESTIC PRODUCT to calculate the GROSS NATIONAL PRODUCT.

See also: balance of payments

netput (D2)

Net output.

netting (G0)

The reduction of offsetting obligations to create a single 'net' obligation.

networker (J2)

A person who works at home or at a local network office providing the head office of a firm with various services, e.g. marketing, research, training, financial analysis. These workers use computers linked by telephone to a main office. An obvious advantage of this system is a reduction in office accommodation costs, but the social implications of isolated work and the effect on industrial relations of the geographical fragmentation of the labour force could be considerable in the long run.

See also: homework

network externality (D1)

The effect on a user of a product or services of other people using compatible products or services. Major sources of these are the Internet and telephone services.

networking economy (P0)

An ECONOMY consisting of many small specialist firms, or NETWORKERS, linked together by an information system, a POST-INDUSTRIAL SOCIETY.

network theory (D0)

An account of how a network establishes trust leading to a reduction in costs.

net worth (M2, M4)

1 Total assets minus total liabilities.
2 The capital a proprietor employs in a business.

neural network model (C8) *see* automatic neural network modelling

neutral budget (G0, H5)

1 A national financial budget with the FISCAL STANCE of seeking to avoid stimulation or contraction of a national economy.
2 A national STRUCTURAL DEFICIT equal to zero.

neutrality of money (E4)

A money supply able to affect the price level but not real output and employment. This view of money is challenged by NEO-KEYNESIAN economists, who argue that an increase in the money supply, by causing a shift in the LM curve, will bring down interest rates and increase real output.

See also: classical dichotomy

neutral real rate of interest (E4)
That level of interest at which MONETARY POLICY neither expands nor contracts the economy.

neutral technical progress (O3)
INVENTIONS or INNOVATIONS which do not affect the relative PRODUCTIVITIES of the FACTORS OF PRODUCTION used. HICKS, more precisely, defined this type of economic growth as raising the marginal productivities of capital and labour in the same proportions for unchanged factor inputs, whereas HARROD sought to describe it as progress which does not change the CAPITAL-OUTPUT RATIO when there is a constant rate of interest and rate of profit on capital.

New Cambridge economics (B2)
The analytical approach of the CAMBRIDGE ECONOMIC POLICY group led by Wynne Godley who offered an ALTERNATIVE ECONOMIC STRATEGY for the UK economy in the 1970s. The group believed that inflation can be caused by trade union power, an increase in world commodity prices and devaluation. Its policy recommendations included an expansionary fiscal policy, import quotas to correct balance of payments problems and the setting of tax rates at a level likely to bring about full employment and a balance of payments equilibrium.

References

Cuthbertson, K. (1979) *Macroeconomic Policy. The New Cambridge, Keynesian and Monetarist Controversies*, London and Basingstoke: Macmillan.

new classical economics (B2)
A modern US and UK school of economics combining the use of the RATIONAL EXPECTATIONS hypothesis with MONETARISM and a LAISSEZ-FAIRE approach to economic policy. All markets are assumed to be perfectly competitive in their behaviour and all unemployment is voluntary because it arises only when employers and employees

make mistakes. Central to this technically sophisticated theory is the belief that markets clear. The principal proponents of these views in the USA are LUCAS and Thomas Sargent; in the UK, Patrick Minford and Michael Beenstock.

See also: perfect competition

References

Buiter, W.H. (1980) 'The macroeconomics of Dr Pangloss: a critical survey of the new classical macroeconomics', *Economic Journal* 90: 34–50.
Hoover, K.D. (1988) *The New Classical Economics*, Oxford: Basil Blackwell.

New Deal (J2, N1)
1 The US policies used by President Franklin D. Roosevelt to revive the depressed US economy of 1933–7. Loosely called 'KEYNESIAN', these policies included the creation of budget deficits. Financial stability was sought through DEPOSIT INSURANCE, the setting up of the SECURITIES AND EXCHANGE COMMISSION and the extension of the powers to regulate banks. COLLECTIVE BARGAINING was extended through the Wagner Act and through the codes of the National Recovery Administration. There was a new partnership between business and government that, in a sense, created a MIXED ECONOMY.
2 The training programme introduced in the UK in 1997 and financed initially out of a windfall tax on the profits of public utilities.

References

Lippman, W. (1938) *The Good Society*, London: Allen & Unwin.

New Earnings Survey (J3)
An annual survey of UK earnings published by the Department of Employment in 1968 and every year from 1970. It provides detailed statistics on the occupational, industrial and regional distributions of employment incomes.

new economic geography (R1)
The study of the determinants of the

geographical distribution of economic activity. With its roots in MARSHALL's notion of EXTERNAL ECONOMIES and DISECONOMIES OF SCALE, as well as CENTRAL PLACE THEORY, this subject has expanded to include regional science and trade theory.

new economic history (N0)

A study of the differences in and evolution of institutions over time. This approach takes into account property rights, the role of ideology and bargaining power. Social efficiency is sacrificed to the interests of rulers.

References

North, D. (1990) *Institutions, Institutional Change and Economic Performance*, Cambridge: Cambridge University Press.

New Economic Mechanism (P4)

1 Hungarian economic reforms of 1968. Under this mechanism, the planning system was modified by replacing plan directives to a large extent by direct relationships between firms; price determination was more influenced by market forces through the linkage of domestic prices of exports and imports to world market prices and most investment decisions were decentralized.
2 Soviet economic reforms announced in 1987: changes to prices and wages were proposed in order to increase economic efficiency and improve economic incentives.

See also: perestroika

New Economic Policy (P2)

The second phase of LENIN's economic policy for the USSR in the 1920s which, in an attempt to increase production, replaced war communism with decentralization of industry and a measure of privately owned small-scale trade.

References

Krugman, P. (1991) *Geography and Trade*, Cambridge, MA: MIT Press.

new economy (P0)

1 A structurally modern economy using the latest technology, exposed to GLOBALIZATION based on knowledge and employing highly skilled workers. It is noted for risk, uncertainty and constant change. An early indication of an economy becoming 'new' is the development of a large services sector. Fast electronic communications have made possible swifter transactions and trading in goods and services over the Internet. This type of economy has high employment, low inflation and rapid growth in productivity, with the expectation of unending expansion.
2 The 'Neue Economie' is the German government's attempt to create a 'third way'.

new federalism (H7)

A view of the relationship between US federal and state governments announced by President Nixon in 1971 and revived by President Reagan in the 1980s, that there should be devolution of many federal activities to the states, including education and welfare programmes.

See also: dual federalism

new fiscal federalism (H7)

US system of FEDERAL FINANCE proposed by President Ronald Reagan and agreed by the US Congress in 1996 which instituted block grants to states in place of categorical grants usually based on entitlements for eligible families and persons. This new system was intended to reduce federal spending and to give states more discretion in spending.

References

Hosek, J. and Levine, R. (1986) *The New Fiscal Federalism and the Social Safety Net. A View from California*, Santa Monica, CA: RAND Corporation.

new home economics (D1)

The study of the reasons for the creation of families. It is argued that people's behaviour is a function of their needs and propensities.

See also: home economics

References

Becker, G. (1991) *A Treatise on the Family*, Cambridge, MA: Harvard University Press.

new industrial state (P0)

GALBRAITH's term for the modern economy which is dominated by a 'technostructure' of large firms dedicated to stable production and the creation of wants so that there is no deficiency of demand for their products. He argues that the planning system used can be practised by both CAPITALIST and SOCIALIST ECONOMIES.

References

Galbraith, L.K. (1967) *The New Industrial State*, London: Hamish Hamilton; Boston, MA: Houghton Mifflin.

new institutional economics (G0, H0, L0, O0, P0)

An interdisciplinary study approach to economics employing AGENCY THEORY, PROPERTY RIGHTS and TRANSACTION COSTS economics to analyse economic institutions and provide an alternative to NEOCLASSICAL ECONOMICS. Its many applications include industrial organization, corporate governance, public choice, the economics of development and the transformation of post-socialist economies.

References

Samuels, W. (1995) 'The present state of institutional economics', *Cambridge Journal of Economics* 19: 569–90.

new international division of labour (F0)

Specialization, particularly by Third World countries, in a narrow range of exports, either because of the historical development of their industries or because of the global production planning practised by MULTINATIONAL CORPORATIONS.

New International Economic Order (F0)

A proposal, popular amongst Marxian economists, to alleviate the problems of the THIRD WORLD by changes in international trading arrangements and a writing-off of Third World countries' debts. Originally proposed in a resolution of the General Assembly of the United Nations in May 1974, this order was intended to reduce, by international co-operation, the widening inequality between rich and poor countries. Marketing boards, similar to the ORGANIZATION OF PETROLEUM EXPORTING COUNTRIES, were suggested for many PRIMARY PRODUCTS so that income would be redistributed to poorer countries in the form of monopoly profits. Also, it was suggested that preferential treatment should be given for developing countries' exports to developed countries to enhance poorer countries' foreign trade earnings. This order overall hoped to raise living standards by a different approach to economic DEVELOPMENT.

See also: Brandt Commission; world debt problem

new issue (G2)

The shares offered by a company when it is marketing its securities on a stock market for the first time or raising additional capital. The shares can be issued by TENDER or by prospectus.

See also: placing; rights issue; stag

new Keynesian (B2) *see* neo-Keynesians

New Left (B2) *see* radical economics

newly industrialized country (O0)

Spain, Brazil, Mexico, South Korea, Taiwan, Hong Kong and Singapore. These countries have acquired their status either because of the absolute size of their manufacturing sectors or through the rate of growth of their manufacturing industries. Some of these countries have used TARIFFS to protect their INFANT INDUSTRIES.

new macroeconomics (B2)

An examination of the microeconomic foundations of macroeconomics, particularly theories of INFLATION and the NATURAL RATE OF UNEMPLOYMENT. The school also incorporates some of the ideas of the POST-KEYNESIANS.

References

Phelps, E.S. *et al.* (1970) *The Microeconomic Foundations of Employment and Inflation Theory*, New York and London: Macmillan.

new political economy (D0, E0)

A school of economics which attempts to demonstrate that actual economic policies are determined by a political mechanism. Income distribution and the nature of political institutions are especially emphasized. GAME THEORY, PRINCIPAL–AGENT, TRANSACTIONS COSTS and the POLITICAL BUSINESS CYCLE are all used as tools of analysis.

References

Drazan, A. (2000) *Political economy in macroeconomics*, Princeton, NJ: Princeton University Press.

Persson, T. and Tabellini, G. (2000) *Political Economy: Explaining Economic Policy*, Cambridge, MA: MIT Press.

new protectionism (F1) *see* neo-mercantilism

new regionalism (F1)

The formation of new trading blocs in the world because of the shortcomings of multilateral agreements such as GATT, e.g. NAFTA. These new blocs often have deep integration and can consist of smaller countries making concessions to a larger one – as in the case of Mexico being subordinate to the USA. This development makes moderate trade concessions and creates deep links between national economies.

New Right (B2)

Political and economic thinkers who came to prominence in the 1980s in the USA and Western Europe through advocating LIBERTARIAN ECONOMICS. Their proposals include a minimal role for the state, little government intervention in the running of national economies, a market approach to production and distribution and PRIVATIZATION.

See also: economic devolution; laissez-faire

References

Thompson, G. (1990) *The Political Economy of the New Right*, London: Pinter.

'news' (G0)

Information about fundamental macroeconomic variables, e.g. unanticipated movements in interest rates, NATIONAL INCOME or a BALANCE OF PAYMENTS current account which causes unanticipated changes in exchange rates.

References

Frenkel, L.A. (1981) 'Flexible exchange rates, prices and the role of 'news'. Lessons from the 1970s', *Journal of Political Economy* 89: 665–705.

new town (R5)

Government-financed urban developments in the UK designed to reduce the population of the larger cities, especially London and Glasgow. The establishment of new towns occurred in two waves: in the late 1940s and the 1960s. All of these twenty-six towns were originally run by separate corporations charged with the tasks of building sufficient housing and attracting industrial and commercial investment. Although the planners of these towns hoped to integrate residential and industrial areas to reduce COMMUTING, this has not happened as much as expected, partly because of a mismatch of jobs and workers. Increasingly these towns have found it difficult to grow as they have suffered, like the major old cities, from the decline of the UK manufacturing sector. The utopian hopes for these towns have been dashed by rising unemployment and crime.

new trade theory (F1)

Models of international trade which have built on earlier models which assumed PERFECT COMPETITION to incorporate IMPERFECT COMPETITION and INCREASING RETURNS.

References

Krugman, P.R. (1979) 'Increasing returns, monopolistic competition and international trade', *Journal of International Economics* 9: 469–79.

New York Mercantile Exchange (G1)
The biggest market for energy futures and options; usually referred to as NYMEX.

New York Stock Exchange (G1)
Established in 1792 when twenty-four brokers signed an agreement in Wall Street. It moved indoors in 1793 and took its present name in 1863. Every stock traded is assigned to a specialist who also acts as a broker. All of the exchange's transactions are published daily. By 1987, the NYSE had 1,366 members. In 1980, its subsidiary, the NEW YORK FUTURES EXCHANGE, was opened.

See also: American Stock Exchange

N-firm concentration ratio (L1)
The ratio of the sales of a group of firms of an industry to the sales of that industry as a whole. The number of firms most commonly chosen for industrial censuses is three, four, five, eight or sixteen and hence the ratios are sometimes called three-firm, four-firm, eight-firm or sixteen-firm ratios. Also known as the leading firms ratio.

See also: concentration; monopoly power

niche bank (G2)
1 A specialist bank with a particular place in the financial sector. The consequence of this concentration on particular types of customer or financial service gives it higher profitability but the greater risk of not being diversified in its activities.
2 A LASER BANK.

niche trading (G1)
Specializing in a particular form of trading, which is a characteristic of many securities markets.

Nikkeiren (J5)
Japanese Federation of Employers' Associations.

See also: shunto

Nobel Prize for Economics (B3)
The 'Nobel Memorial Prize in Economic Sciences' awarded to distinguished economists and econometricians since 1969. Prominent in the list of prize winners are persons from the USA, France, Scandinavia, the USSR and the UK:

1969	Ragnar Frisch; Jan Tinbergen
1970	Paul Samuelson
1971	Simon Kuznets
1972	Kenneth Arrow; John Hicks
1973	Wassily Leontief
1974	Friedrich von Hayek; Gunnar Myrdal
1975	Leonid Kantorovich; Tjalling C. Koopmans
1976	Milton Friedman
1977	James Meade; Bertil Ohlin
1978	Herbert Simon
1979	W. Arthur Lewis; Theodore Schultz
1980	Lawrence Klein
1981	James Tobin
1982	George Stigler
1983	Gerard Debreu
1984	Richard Stone
1985	Franco Modigliani
1986	James M. Buchanan
1987	Robert M. Solow
1988	Maurice Allais
1989	Trygve Haavelmo
1990	Harry Markovitz; Merton Miller; William Sharpe
1991	Ronald H. Coase
1992	Gary S. Becker
1993	Robert W. Fogel; Douglass C. North
1994	John Harsanyi; John F. Nash; Reinhard Selten
1995	Robert Lucas
1996	James A. Mirrlees; William Vickrey
1997	Robert C. Merton; Myron S. Scholes
1998	Amartya Sen
1999	Robert A. Mundell
2000	James J. Heckman; Daniel L. McFadden
2001	George A. Akerlof; Andrew M. Spence; Joseph E. Stiglitz

References

Breit, W. and Spencer, R.W. (1986) *Lives of the Laureates*, Cambridge, MA, and London: MIT Press.

Lindbeck, A. (1985) 'The prize in economic science in memory of Alfred Nobel', *Journal of Economic Literature* 23 (March): 37–56.

nodal pricing (D4, Q4)

A set of prices related to each node of a system such as electricity transmission. The opposite of ZONAL PRICING.

noise (C1)

Random disturbances which distort a signal. The probability distribution of what is received depends on what is sent.

See also: white noise

noise trader (G1) *see* investor sentiment

no-load fund (G1)

A MUTUAL FUND not charging sales commission.

See also: load fund

nomenklatura (P2)

Members of the political elite of the former East European countries appointed by the Communist Party. Social and economic privileges were given to members of committees ranging from the Central Party Committee to district committees. Although out of power in the 1990s, the nomenklatura continued to exercise power in many TRANSITION ECONOMIES.

nominal (D0, E0)

The current money value unadjusted for inflationary change of an economic variable, e.g. EXCHANGE RATE, RATE OF INTEREST, rate of protection or tariff.

nominal gross domestic product (E0)

GROSS DOMESTIC PRODUCT at current prices. This is regarded as a suitable reference target for regulating public expenditure. In the UK and the USA, GDP figures are published quarterly.

nominal income (D0) *see* money income

nominal tax rate (H2)

The published rate of tax on a good, income or capital. The whole burden of such taxes is often reduced by tax allowances or credits.

nominee account (G2)

An arrangement for hiding the beneficial ownership of shares. Banks and other financial institutions buy shares in the name of a nominee account for persons or companies wishing to be anonymous. This is most useful to a company which is accumulating another company's shares with a view to making a takeover bid. This system is chiefly supported for its administrative convenience.

non-accelerating inflation rate of unemployment (E3) *see* natural rate of unemployment

non-bank activities (G2) *see* Bank Holding Company Act 1956

non-basic commodity (D0)

A commodity affecting the production of some, but not all, other commodities.

See also: basic commodity

non-basic industry (L0)

An industry providing services to a complex of basic industries.

non-competing group (J4)

An occupational group of the labour market separated from other groups by BARRIERS TO ENTRY. John Stuart MILL, who first noted this market imperfection, likened the labour market to a hereditary caste system. Restricted access to education, union rules and discrimination separate the labour force into these groups, giving rise to occupational WAGE DIFFERENTIALS.

non-employment (J1, J6)

Being without a job. The unemployed, retired, sick, the rich living on investment income alone and carers for dependants make up this population category. Some of this underutilization of labour is associated with a lack of opportunity for, or restricted access to, paid employment.

See also: labour force

non-goal equilibrium (E0)
An EQUILIBRIUM state that is the consequence of the interaction of economic forces, not the conscious pursuit of a particular agent. A major case is NATIONAL INCOME in a MARKET ECONOMY.

See also: goal equilibrium

non-interest-bearing MI (E4)
A component of M1, introduced because some banks changed the character of CURRENT DEPOSITS (SIGHT DEPOSITS) by paying interest on them.

non-linear correlation (C1)
The relationship between two variables which approximates in a diagram to a curve.

See also: least squares method; linear regression; scatter diagram

non-linear pricing (D4) *see* second-degree price discrimination

non-market sector (P0)
The part of an economy which does not sell its goods and services. The output of governments, households and farms (in the case of less developed economies) makes up much of the activity of this sector.

non-parametric model (C5)
An econometric model that attempts to use statistical inference and economic data to explore the relationship between economic variables without using a given functional relationship.

non-pecuniary returns (J3)
The reward to a worker other than wages, salaries and fringe benefits. Personal satisfaction, power, status and continual happiness are amongst these returns.

non-profit enterprise (L3)
An organization, other than a firm, whose members have no private PROPERTY RIGHTS

associated with it and, hence, no entitlement to profits. These enterprises, usually financed by donations, endowments or government grants, aim to maximize the quantity and quality of the service provided and to break even. In the public sector, most governmental institutions are NPEs; in the private sector, households, charitable foundations, mutual insurance companies and a variety of clubs are the major examples. The motives for establishing NPEs are various, including the provision of MERIT GOODS, the subsidization of religion and the arts and the commemoration of a major benefactor. A dislike of market mechanisms and altruistic attitudes have been fundamental to the growth of NPEs.

References
Gassler, R.S. (1986) *The Economics of Non-profit Enterprise: A Study in Applied Economic Theory*, New York and London: University Press of America.
Holtman, A.G. (1988) 'Theories of non-profit institutions', *Journal of Economic Surveys* 2: 30–45.
Rose-Ackerman, S. (ed.) (1986) *The Non-Profit Sector: Economic Theory and Public Policy*, Oxford: Oxford University Press.

non-renewable resources (Q3)
Fossil fuels or metals which are exhaustible deposits of the earth's surface.

non-standard tax relief (H2)
A reduction in the taxable income of a person on account of actual expenses incurred. These expenses are recognized by a tax authority as deductible.

non-tariff barrier (F1)
A barrier to imports, other than an import tax. The non-tariff methods used include the imposition of rigid safety standards, strict administrative standards, global and bilateral quotas, orderly marketing arrangements and VOLUNTARY EXPORT RESTRAINTS. Examples include the MULTI-FIBRE ARRANGEMENT, the USA's orderly marketing arrangement with Korea and Taiwan on

non-rubber footwear, safety measures on colour TVs and CB radios, and the EUROPEAN COMMUNITY's import restrictions in 1981 on steel from Korea. The GENERAL AGREEMENT ON TARIFFS AND TRADE approximately measures the extent of the application of restrictive measures as the ratio of restricted imports/total imports. This measure is imprecise as a restriction will affect the total flow of imports. Non-tariff barriers can also be measured by calculating restricted imports as a share of the total consumption of manufactured goods, or consumption of restricted manufactured goods as a share of the total consumption of manufactured goods.

See also: protection; tariff

non-tradables (F1)
Goods and services that do not enter into international trade. Many services of a personal kind, e.g. hairdressing, can only be sold within a country, but most goods can be traded with the exception of those which cannot be preserved from perishing and those which are too heavy and fixed to remove, e.g. buildings (although there are exceptional cases of UK buildings being shipped to the USA).

non-zero-sum game (C7)
A situation in which the total amount to be distributed amongst the players is not equal to zero. The game may be a positive sum game, a negative sum game, or the sum may vary because of the strategies or decisions of the players, as in the PRISONERS' DILEMMA game.

See also: zero-sum game

normal distribution (C1)
A symmetric distribution shaped like a bell.

See also: kurtosis

normal good (D0)
A good whose demand increases as income rises. Such a good will have an INCOME ELASTICITY OF DEMAND more than one.

See also: inferior good

normal price (D4)
MARSHALL's notion of an equilibrium price.

See also: natural price

normal profit (D0)
The minimum amount of PROFIT a firm must earn to remain in existence. The normal profit rate is the OPPORTUNITY COST to the firm of employing capital in that industry. Since this profit is the minimum supply price of ENTREPRENEURSHIP, it will be included along with other costs in the total costs of a firm. When measuring MONOPOLY POWER, normal profit is used as a benchmark: if a firm has profits in excess of normal profit, it is to some extent a monopolist.

normative economics (A1)
Economics based on value judgments stating what should be the case, e.g. 'personal incomes should be equal'. The distinction between this type of economics and POSITIVE ECONOMICS includes in its ancestry HUME's 'is–ought' dichotomy. Normative issues, central to WELFARE ECONOMICS, cannot be settled by appeals to facts.

See also: economic methodology

References
Myrdal, G. (1954) *The Political Element in the Development of Economic Thought*, trans. P. Strecten, London: Routledge & Kegan Paul.

Norris–La Guardia Act 1932 (J5)
US federal statute that gave US LABOR UNIONS substantial relief from judicial interference. Under section 3 of the Act, YELLOW DOG CONTRACTS were made unenforceable; under section 5 courts were prohibited from granting injunctions on the grounds of unlawful combination or conspiracy. Similar Acts were passed by several US states.

See also: Wagner Act 1935; Taft–Hartley Act 1947

North American Free Trade Area (F1)
An extension of the US–Canada Free

Trade Agreement of 1989 to include Mexico, agreed in 1992. Over fifteen years all duties, tariffs and non-tariff barriers between the countries will be eliminated. For trade-sensitive products such as beer, footwear and maize there will be long periods of adjustment. A three-nation panel will consider trade disputes, including related employment and environmental matters.

North, Douglass Cecil, 1920– (B3)

Educated at the University of California, he taught at the University of Washington from 1950 to 1983 and was subsequently Henry R. Luce Professor of Law and Liberty at Washington University, St Louis. His celebrated work in CLIOMETRICS considers the evolution and economic effects of legal and social institutions. He is famous for *The Economic Growth of the United States, 1790–1860* (1961) and *Structure and Change in Economics* (1981). In 1993 he was awarded the NOBEL PRIZE FOR ECONOMICS with FOGEL.

north–south gap (R5)

The regional difference in prosperity in Great Britain and many other countries usually measured by GDP per capita, property prices and levels of unemployment. Some countries such as Italy have a north more prosperous than the south. The gap often represents the difference between the region with the national capital and peripheral areas. In the world as a whole there is a disparity in income between prosperous countries north of the equator and the poorer countries to the south.

note issuance facility (G2)

Promises by banks to lend money to companies when they cannot raise it in short-term securities markets. This is a form of OFF-BALANCE-SHEET FINANCING or adjusted claim. Increasingly US banks are using NIFs as an alternative to traditional medium-term credit facilities, often arranged with a syndicate of banks.

See also: revolving underwriting facility

'Not in my backyard' (R0)

A frequently made objection to an environmental change perceived to be detrimental with the recommendation that someone else suffer. This plea, nicknamed 'NIMBY', is often uttered when waste dumps and unsightly buildings are proposed.

no-trade equilibrium (D0)

An equilibrium position with domestic demand equal to domestic supply for an autarkic state.

See also: autarky

NOW account (G2)

Negotiable order of withdrawal account; a CHECKING ACCOUNT (US) which bears interest. Super-NOW accounts offer a higher rate of interest.

Nozick, Robert, 1938–2002 (B3)

US philosopher of the NEW RIGHT famous for his notion of the 'minimal state'. He was educated at Columbia College and Princeton University. He has taught at Princeton from 1962 to 1965 and been a full professor of philosophy at Harvard since 1969. His libertarian view of the limited role of government is in accord with much of the thinking of FRIEDMAN and HAYEK.

See also: forced labour

References

Nozick, R. (1974) *Anarchy, State and Utopia*, Oxford: Basil Blackwell.

N share (G1)

An AMERICAN DEPOSITORY RECEIPT issued by a Chinese company and listed on the New York Stock Exchange.

See also: A share; B share; L share

null hypothesis (C1)

In statistics, the hypothesis that there are no differences between the characteristics of a population and a sample taken from it, or between two samples of that population.

numéraire (D0, E4)

A measuring rod for stating relative prices;

WALRAS's term for a commodity used for this measurement purpose.

nutcracker theory of the business cycle
(E3)
A cycle in economic activity in which profits are squeezed like a nut from the two sides of limited demand and rising costs. This occurs because in every expansion of an economy costs rise faster than demand as a cycle reaches its peak.

References

Sherman, H.J. (1991) *The Business Cycle: Growth and Crisis under Capitalism*, Princeton, NJ: Princeton University Press.

O

Oaxaca wage decomposition (J3, J7)
A method of distinguishing wage differences due to human capital characteristics from those based on DISCRIMINATION.

References

Oaxaca, R. with Ransom, M. (1994) 'On discrimination and decomposition of wage differentials', *Journal of Econometrics*, 61: 5–21.

objective function (D0, E0)
A statement in equation form of a dependent variable which has to be maximized or minimized by independent variables attaining optimal values. In the case, e.g. of a UTILITY FUNCTION, utility is the dependent variable to be maximized and quantities of different goods are the independent variables which have to be optimally combined.

objectives of firms (L2)
What a FIRM has as its aim or target. PROFIT MAXIMIZATION is assumed in many theories of the firm to be the central aim of a firm but research since the 1930s has noted that managers have many other objectives, partly because they are not shareholders directly rewarded in proportion to a firm's profitability. Objectives replacing profit maximization include sales maximization, maintaining (or increasing) a market share and achieving a target rate of return on capital employed.

See also: managerial models of the firm; theory of the firm

occupation (J2)
The work activity of a person defined according to the education, skill, responsibility and experience demanded by an employer.

References

International Labour Organisation (1968) *The International Standard Classification of Occupations*, Geneva: ILO.

occupational licensing (J2, K2)
The regulation of types of employment or SELF-EMPLOYMENT, including the crafts and PROFESSIONS. The regulatory bodies engaged in licensing have included guilds and professional associations. They aim to maintain the quality of a particular occupational group by supervising training, punishing malpractice and limiting entry.

occupational mobility (J6)
A worker's movement between one type of job and another. The amount of mobility depends greatly on the fineness of the occupational classification chosen. Since 1945, even with the broadest classification of occupations, a great shift from manual to white-collar jobs has been apparent in many advanced countries, partly because of DE-INDUSTRIALIZATION and the expansion of the service industries.

See also: labour mobility

occupational segregation (J4)

An occupational distribution of a labour force such that men, or women, or different ethnic groups, are under-represented or over-represented in particular occupations compared with their proportions in the total labour force. An example of this would occur if overwhelmingly black males worked in domestic service. In many countries women are heavily concentrated in nursing, retailing, secretarial and domestic service jobs.

See also: crowding hypothesis; discrimination

off-balance-sheet financing (G3, M4)

Funds raised for a business not shown in its BALANCE SHEET. This type of financing is resorted to when the company has borrowed near to the limit set by its Articles of Association or when it wants to avoid increasing its GEARING and attracting an adverse stock market reaction. The appearance of a company's balance sheet can be improved by transferring liabilities to associated companies or by using particular devices, e.g. the leasing of capital equipment, the artificial sale of stock to a financial company to acquire extra funds, mortgage SECURITIZATION, FACTORING, sale and repurchase agreements and loan transfers. Increasingly, the bodies supervising the accountancy profession are demanding fuller and more open financial reporting.

See also: creative accounting

offer curve (F1)

A curve showing what a country will offer in exports for the amount it imports in a model of two goods. It is used to analyse the effects of tariffs. Also known as a reciprocal demand curve.

offer price (G1)

1 The price at which a company offers to sell its shares to the public.
2 The selling price of UNIT TRUST units.

off-exchange instrument (G2)

A financial product that is not traded on an official stock exchange but resembles officially recognized products. An example is a bank CERTIFICATE OF DEPOSIT linked to the performance of STANDARD & POOR'S 500 stock index.

Office of Fair Trading (L4)

UK organization set up in 1973 to administer COMPETITION policy. Its tasks include examining monopoly situations, monitoring ANTI-COMPETITIVE PRACTICES in the UK, regulating CONSUMER CREDIT and considering proposed mergers which might be referred to the COMPETITION COMMISSION. It maintains the register of permitted restrictive trade practices.

Office of Management and Budget (H1)

An office of the US president set up in 1970 in succession to the Bureau of the Budget (founded 1921) which is responsible for preparing the Executive's budget for presentation to Congress in January each year. After examination by House and Senate committees, a concurrent resolution on the budget is announced by 15 April to be followed by legislation by 15 May. Once the budget is passed, the OMB supervises and controls its administration and provides data on programme performance.

official development assistance (O0)

Aid granted by a national government to an international organization such as the WORLD BANK.

See also: foreign aid

official financing (F4)

An item in the balance of payments of a country which is the amount of finance which has to be raised from overseas monetary authorities, by currency borrowing and drawing on official reserves to finance a deficit in the current and capital accounts.

official reserves (E5) *see* international reserves

offshore banking (G2)

Banking activities conducted abroad to evade domestic monetary controls. UK financial institutions have resorted to small Commonwealth countries such as the Bahamas and a number of islands, including the Channel Islands and the Isle of Man. (The USA regards banking activities in every foreign country, including the UK, as 'offshore'.) The principal activities of offshore banks are the management of investment trusts and participation in Eurodollar and Eurobond markets.

off-the-job training (J2)
Formal training, usually away from the premises of one's employer, which takes the form of lectures, tutorials and practical sessions. A switch to this type of training has been necessary because of the haphazard nature of much ON-THE-JOB TRAINING and the increasing amount of technical knowledge required for many occupations.

See also: general training

Ohlin, Bertil, 1899–1979 (B3)
Swedish international trade and macroeconomic theorist and a leader of the STOCKHOLM SCHOOL, who was educated at Lund University, the Stockholm School of Business Administration, Harvard University and at the University of Stockholm where he was a doctoral student of CASSEL. He was a professor of economics from 1925 to 1930 at Copenhagen and at Stockholm from 1930 to 1965 (as successor to HECKSCHER). In a parallel political career, he was a member of the Swedish parliament (1938–70), leader of the Swedish Liberal Party (1944–67) and Minister of Trade (1944–45).

As a member of the STOCKHOLM SCHOOL, he in many ways anticipated KEYNESIAN ideas by using the concepts of the PROPENSITY TO CONSUME, LIQUIDITY PREFERENCE and the MULTIPLIER in articles of 1933 and 1934. In times of excess capacity, he argued (in 1934) that the government should undertake investment projects that would not compete with the private sector and would be deficit financed. He developed Heckscher's factor price equalization theory of international trade to produce the

HECKSCHER–OHLIN TRADE THEOREM. His most famous work is *Interregional and International Trade* (1933). His contribution to international trade theory earned him, with MEADE, the NOBEL PRIZE FOR ECONOMICS in 1977.

References
Samuelson, P.A. (1981) 'Bertil Ohlin (1899–1979)', *Scandinavian Journal of Economics* 83: 355–71.
Steiger, O. (1976) 'Bertil Ohlin and the origins of the Keynesian Revolution', *History of Political Economy* 8: 341–66.

oil-price increases (E3, Q4)
Major supply shocks in 1973–4 caused by the ORGANIZATION OF PETROLEUM EXPORTING COUNTRIES raising the price of oil and in 1979–80 by a cutback in Iranian oil production and exports after the Iranian Revolution. In 1973–4, the price rose from $1.90 to $9.76; in 1979–80 from $17.26 to $28.67; and in 1990, Iraq's invasion of Kuwait also led briefly to oil-price inflation.

Okun, Arthur M., 1928–80 (B3)
US economist and policy adviser who was educated at Columbia University and taught at Yale University from 1952 to 1963. He was a member of the COUNCIL OF ECONOMIC ADVISERS from 1964 to 1968, the year in which he was chairman. His most influential work was with the BROOKINGS INSTITUTION as its senior fellow from 1969, contributing to *Brookings Papers on Economic Activity* as joint editor. His fame largely rests on his *The Political Economy of Prosperity* (1970), *Equality and Efficiency – The Big Trade-off* (1975) and his posthumous classic *Prices and Quantities – A Macroeconomic Analysis* (1981). His work as a macroeconomist had the major concern of attaining economic growth without inflation; the trade-off between equality and efficiency also interested him.

See also: discomfort index; invisible handshake; leaky bucket; Okun's law

References
Gordon, R.J. and Hall, R.E. (1980)

'Arthur M. Okun: 1928–80', *Brookings Papers on Economic Activity* 1: 1–5.

Okun's law (E0)

A rule of thumb, applicable to the US economy in 1960–80, which states that when the ratio of actual to potential annual GROSS NATIONAL PRODUCT changes by 3 per cent (more recent estimates state 2 per cent), the observed unemployment rate changes in the opposite direction by 1 per cent. The potential gross national product is measured by extrapolating the US gross national product of 1950 (when there was full employment and full capacity) and adding to it the long-run trend of productivity improvements. A relationship noted by the US economist, Arthur OKUN.

References

Okun, A.M. (1970) *The Political Economy of Prosperity*, Washington, DC: Brookings Institution.

Old Age, Survivors, Disability and Health Insurance (I3)

The largest social insurance programme in the USA established by the Social Security Act 1935. It covers over 90 per cent of retired US citizens, although eligibility is based on age, not retired status. Employers, employees and self-employed persons finance it on a 'pay-as-you-go' principle through payroll taxes. The benefits granted are a percentage of average earnings, over the period when a person could expect to have been in employment covered by the scheme. Since the Revenue Act 1942, it has been US federal policy to encourage the expansion of private pension plans.

See also: payroll tax; Social Security Act 1935

old economy (P0)

That national ECONOMY, or part of it, which makes little use of information technology organizing the production of goods and services in factories, offices and shops.

See also: new economy

Old Lady of Threadneedle Street (E5)

see Bank of England

old staples (L5, L6)

The heavy industries once the basic industries of industrialized economies: coal, iron and steel and shipbuilding are the principal examples. They were concentrated in areas with major rivers and large mineral deposits.

See also: commanding heights; heavy industry

oligopoly (L1)

A MARKET or INDUSTRY consisting of a small group of sellers, often five or less. This term was originally coined by Sir Thomas More in his *Utopia* (1518). An oligopolistic type of market structure is usual in modern science-based industries, e.g. computer hardware, pharmaceuticals. Oligopolies can be collusive (firms make joint-pricing and output decisions) or non-collusive. However, collusive oligopoly is less common because of competition laws that have outlawed it in many countries. Oligopoly price theory tries to explain the interaction of the decision making of firms in non-collusive situations: the KINKED DEMAND CURVE is a major example of this approach, as are PRICE LEADERSHIP models. The most recent developments in oligopoly analysis have included the STRUCTURE-CONDUCT-PERFORMANCE, strategic entry deterrence and CONTESTABLE MARKETS approaches.

See also: kinked demand curve

References

Friedman, J.W. (1983) *Oligopoly Theory*, Cambridge and New York: Cambridge University Press.

oligopsony (L1)

A market controlled by a few dominant buyers.

See also: monopsony

Omnibus Budget Reconciliation Act (H6)

US federal statute which includes both

changes in tax laws and appropriations to various government spending programmes. An Act of this kind removes the legislative work of passing several appropriation and revenue bills.

one-bank holding company (G2)
US corporation with only one banking subsidiary other subsidiaries which can be engaged in activities prohibited to banks.

one-club policy (E6)
MACROECONOMIC POLICY which chiefly uses one policy instrument, e.g. interest rates, to the exclusion of others.

one country, two systems (P4)
A CENTRALLY PLANNED ECONOMY which permits CAPITALISM to operate in part of it. This arrangement was designed for Hong Kong when it ceased to be a British colony in 1997 so that capitalism could survive in the planned Chinese economy.

one-crop economy (O0)
An ECONOMY whose production is largely concentrated on one PRIMARY PRODUCT and hence is vulnerable to fluctuations in its TERMS OF TRADE and major threats to production, e.g. bad weather. Economies producing copper, ground nuts, sugar and coffee have often been of this type.

one hundred per cent reserve banking (G2)
A form of banking which maintains a bank's total volume of deposits (liabilities) equal to reserve assets. Under this system, a bank is unable to make advances through credit creation. Although such banking can resist RUNS ON A BANK, it makes little profit through not holding illiquid bills, bonds and loans.

See also: Fisher; fractional reserve banking

one-price law (D0)
The market rule that only one price is produced by a market in equilibrium. The PHYSIOCRATS were early exponents of the view that internationally traded goods should be sold in the domestic market at the world equilibrium price.

See also: multiple equilibria

one-shot game (C7)
A game with the initial decisions on price, output and advertising expenditure maintained throughout the game.

one-tailed test (C1)
A statistical significance test which is only concerned with the upper or the lower part of a distribution of a variable.

See also: two-tailed test

One two three bank (G2)
A fringe bank licensed by the UK Board of Trade under the Companies Act 1967, section 123. As there was lax control over these new banks and no supervision by the Bank of England, the banks were shown to be unstable during the BARBER BOOM of the 1970s and the consequent SECONDARY BANKING CRISIS.

on-the-job training (J2)
The acquisition of skills through copying the example of experienced workers who are continuously present to supervise the work attempts of the trainee. Most APPRENTICESHIP schemes are of this nature. BECKER included this type of training in his concept of HUMAN CAPITAL.

See also: off-the-job training

open bidding system (D0) *see* general competitive bidding

open economy (F1, P0)
An economy engaged in international trade. The degree of openness of an economy can be measured by its imports or exports as a proportion of gross domestic product: for the most open of economies this can be over 60 per cent. The smaller an economy, the more open it usually is, as it is unlikely to produce a full range of goods and services. Open economies such as the UK, Holland and Belgium are, therefore, much affected by fluctuations in world trade.

See also: autarky; closed economy

open-ended fund (G2)
A UNIT TRUST or MUTUAL FUND whose size is determined by the amount of units sold and hence is 'open'.

open market operations (E5)
Purchases and sales of bills and government bonds by a CENTRAL BANK in order to change their prices and hence interest rates and the quantity of reserve assets held by the banking system. If a fall in interest rates is desired, the central bank will buy bonds to increase their prices and hence lower their yields. This is a principal tool of MONETARY POLICY that can be used any day that markets are open and does not need legislative approval.

open population (J1)
A population subject to emigration of its residents and/or immigration from other areas.

See also: economic refugee

open shop (J5)
A workplace where workers are employed whether or not they have TRADE UNION membership.

See also: closed shop; union shop

Operation Twist (E5)
Manipulation of the US TERM STRUCTURE OF INTEREST RATES in 1961 by the Kennedy Administration raising short-term rates and holding, or allowing to fall, long-term rates. The effects of this policy were hoped to be an improvement in the balance of payments through HOT MONEY flows attracted by higher short-term interest rates and some stimulus to investment by not raising the long-term rates.

References
Modigliani, F. and Sutch, R. (1966) 'Innovations in interest rate policy', *American Economic Review* 56 (May) (Papers and Proceedings): 178–97.

opportunistic behaviour (C7, D0)
The actions of a partner to an exchange

who has an informational (or other) advantage, e.g. exclusive knowledge of the true quality of a good offered for sale.

See also: asymmetric information; lemons market

opportunity cost (D0)
The value of the alternative forgone by choosing a particular activity. A major example is the choice of work rather than leisure, where the opportunity cost of working is the amount of leisure sacrificed. Such a cost arises from the scarce nature of resources. The economist uses opportunity cost as the central meaning of cost. The much-used expression 'there's no such thing as a free lunch' reflects the fact that all goods and services have their opportunity costs.

See also: accounting costs; Wieser

optimal control (C6)
The use of mathematical techniques to choose among several policies in order to regulate or control a system. This approach is used increasingly to select a mixture of FISCAL and MONETARY POLICIES, as well as to manage a portfolio of securities.

References
Pindyck, R.S. (1973) *Optimal Planning for Economic Stabilization: The Application of Control Theory to Stabilization Policy*, Amsterdam: North-Holland.

optimal peg (F3)
A currency peg intended to stabilize the prices of traded goods or the BALANCE OF TRADE or the TERMS OF TRADE or the rate of INFLATION of a particular economy by attaching that economy's currency to a basket of other currencies in order to reflect the pattern of a country's trade. Pegging attempts to achieve an external balance continuously for that country.

References
Williamson, J.H. (1982) 'A survey on the literature on the optimal peg', *Journal of Development Economics* II: 39–61.

optimal rate of pollution (Q2)
The rate of pollution at which the marginal

social benefit of pollution control and marginal social cost of pollution are equal.

optimal taxation (H2)

A tax structure maximizing SOCIAL WELFARE. As a taxation system uses a variety of taxes, optimal income taxes and optimal commodity taxes have to be determined simultaneously. Optimality is obtained by a correct TRADE-OFF between economic efficiency and distributional objectives.

See also: Ramsey rule

optimal work effort (J2)

The amount of work which equates the MARGINAL UTILITY of an hour's work with the marginal utility of another hour's leisure.

optimization problem (D0)

The task of maximizing or minimizing an OBJECTIVE FUNCTION. Major cases of optimization in economics include a consumer with a fixed income buying a combination of goods and services which will maximize his/her utility, the maximization of the wealth of equity shareholders by finding the best growth policy for a firm and minimizing the cost of producing a particular output by choosing the appropriate combination of factors of production. Different forms of programming are used to solve these problems.

References

Baumol, W.J. (1965) *Economic Theory and Operations Analysis*, 2nd edn, Englewood Cliffs, NJ: Prentice Hall.
Vajda, S. (1961) *Mathematical Programming*, Reading, MA: Addison-Wesley.

optimum city (R1)

A large settlement which maximizes the SOCIAL WELFARE function of the households residing there.

References

Mirrlees, J. (1972) 'The optimum town', *Swedish Journal of Economics* 74: 114–35.

optimum currency area (F3)

The group of countries ideally covered by one currency or by a number of linked currencies, e.g. the EUROPEAN MONETARY SYSTEM. The necessary conditions for an optimum area include wage and price flexibility and mobility of capital and labour. The social and political unity of the area is more important than its size. Setting up an area with a COMMON CURRENCY brings about the adjustment costs of extra unemployment, reductions in residents' income and wealth and migration, which can be financed out of a joint FISCAL POLICY for the area.

See also: European Monetary System

References

Ishiyama, Y. (1975) 'The theory of optimum currency areas: a survey', *International Monetary Fund Staff Papers* 22: 344–83.
Mundell, R.A. (1961) 'A theory of optimum currency areas', *American Economic Review* 51: 657–65.

optimum firm (L2)

A firm whose output is produced at minimum average cost. A unique optimum is only possible for firms with U-shaped average costs and only likely to exist in the short run.

See also: minimum efficient scale

optimum income tax (H2)

That rate of income tax that maximizes economic welfare within the production possibilities available. This tax rate depends on the skill distribution within the population and the population's labour–consumption preferences.

References

Mirrlees, J. (1971) 'An exploration in the theory of optimal income taxation', *Review of Economic Studies* 38: 175–208.

optimum population (J1)

An ideal-sized population that maximizes output per head. As this is not the maximum-sized population that a country can support, the population can exceed such an optimum. Critics of this concept have noted that there is no consensus supporting the view that output per head should be maximized; for example, for military reasons a larger population may be preferred.

optimum quantity of money (E4)

The quantity of money associated with a nominal rate of interest of zero and maximum consumer welfare. This can only be adopted as a policy if there is a model of how money is used in a national economy.

References

Bewley, T. (1983) 'A difficulty with the optimum quantity of money', *Econometrica* 51: 1485–1504.

Friedman, M. (1969) *The Optimum Quantity of Money and Other Essays*, Chicago: Aldine.

optimum tariff (F1, F3)

1 The tariff that will maximize the economic welfare of a country. Providing it is a large economy and the elasticity of supply is less than infinite, through changing the TERMS OF TRADE by imposing a tariff it is possible to have increased revenue from trade despite its lower volume.

2 A TARIFF that increases a country's welfare by maximizing the return to its potential MONOPOLY or MONOPSONY power. This tariff must be set at that rate which equalizes the social benefit and social cost of the marginal import. Optimum tariffs have been recommended for less developed countries with a substantial monopoly in their export trade. If the optimum tariff is zero, then there is a strong case for FREE TRADE. Corden refers to an 'orthodox optimum tariff' as an export tax which changes the TERMS OF TRADE as the tax restricts exports and raises their prices.

References

Corden, W.M. (1974) *Trade Policy and Economic Welfare*, Oxford: Clarendon Press.

option (G2)

The right to buy or sell a currency, commodity or financial asset at a specified price in a stated time period.

See also: call option; put option

option demand (D0)

Demand for a good or service which is usually not consumed by the person regarding it as desirable, e.g. private car users may desire there to be a public transportation service not for themselves but for those who cannot afford private transportation. A high option demand can reduce the price of the good or service in question: demand for insurance is of this kind – the more entering an insurance scheme, the lower the premiums for insuring against a particular risk.

See also: sponsor demand

options exchanges (G1)

OPTIONS were first traded in 1973 with the opening of the Chicago Board Options Exchange (CBOE). Now option trading is offered by more than a dozen US exchanges and on the major European exchanges. On some exchanges more than 1 million contracts are traded daily in many products. Apart from equities and bonds, option trading is also available for precious metals, oil, agricultural commodities, foreign currencies and market indexes.

orderly market agreement (F1, L1)

1 A restrictive trading agreement between the firms of an industry which is experiencing a decline in the total demand for its output. In response to this decline, voluntary quotas are agreed between firms to allow a more orderly adjustment to a lower level of sales, avoiding cut-throat price competition so that each firm can at least maintain its individual sales level. But there is limited scope for introducing these agreements as, if they are made by a group of firms without the approval of government, they are likely to violate national COMPETITION POLICIES.

2 An agreement between countries to

restrict exports to a country with trade deficits as a means of protecting its industries.

ordinalist revolution (D6)

The major advance in welfare economics in the 1930s, particularly wrought by HICKS, which founded welfare theorems on the ordering of persons' utilities, not on the actual units of UTILITY derived from consumption. The INDIFFERENCE CURVE was a major new tool of this analysis.

See also: revealed preference

References

Cooter, R. and Rappoport, P. (1984) 'Were the ordinalists wrong about welfare economics?', *Journal of Economic Literature* 22 (June): 507–30.

Hicks, J.R. (1939) *Value and Capital*, ch. 1, Oxford: Clarendon Press.

ordinal utility (D0)

Subjective satisfaction expressed as ordered preferences. This makes possible the ranking of satisfactions as first, second, third and so forth without having to state the amount by which one satisfaction is greater or less than another.

See also: cardinal utility; util; utility

ordinary share (G1)

An EQUITY of a company which usually constitutes a major part of its issued capital. These shares will be paid a dividend if priority capital holders of debentures or preference shares have been paid and the directors decide to distribute the remaining earnings.

See also: common stock

organic composition of capital (D0, E0)

A Marxian term for the ratio of constant to variable capital. Constant capital is regarded as the dead labour embodied in the means of production and variable capital the live labour, i.e. the labour required at that stage of production. It can be regarded as a CAPITAL–LABOUR RATIO.

organic premium (Q0)

The higher prices consumers are prepared to pay to obtain food which has been produced by an 'organic' farmer, i.e. someone using traditional agricultural methods and not artificial fertilizers and additives. The higher costs associated with this small-scale farming partially justify the higher product prices.

organizational economics (A1)

A branch of microeconomics which has made use of psychology, sociology, political science, biology, ecology and anthropology to study the nature of organizations and the phenomena associated with them. From early studies of power within organizations and the consequences of being dependent on outside resources, this form of economics has changed to using transaction cost, TEAM THEORY, business strategy, AGENCY THEORY and the EVOLUTIONARY THEORY OF THE FIRM.

See also: Williamson

References

Barney, J.B. and Ouchi, W.G. (eds) (1986) *Organizational Economics*, San Francisco and London: Jossey-Bass.

Organization for Economic Co-operation and Development (F0)

The group of rich industrialized countries founded in 1961 and consisting of the eighteen European countries of the ORGANIZATION FOR EUROPEAN ECONOMIC CO-OPERATION, the USA and Canada. Later to join were Japan (1964), Finland (1969), Australia (1971) and New Zealand (1973), with the result that it now produces about two-thirds of the world's output with only one-sixth of its population. This Paris-based organization provides a forum for the discussion of policies for promoting ECONOMIC GROWTH, FREE TRADE and FOREIGN AID to less developed countries and has an independent secretariat which produces tables of standardized economic data of member countries and economic forecasts (more accurate than many national forecasts because of the joint forecasting of linked economies). Its influential economic policy committee meets two or three times a year and is chaired by the chairman of the US President's Council of Economic Advisers.

See also: INTERLINK

Organization for European Economic Co-operation (F0)

An international organization founded in 1948 to administer US aid to the eighteen West European countries benefiting under the Marshall Plan. Its principal achievements were the creation of the European Monetary Agreement in 1956, its organization of the negotiations which established the EUROPEAN COMMUNITY and its contribution to trade liberalization. The ORGANIZATION FOR ECONOMIC CO-OPERATION AND DEVELOPMENT succeeded it in 1961.

Organization of Petroleum Exporting Countries (F0, Q4)

The major world oil producers' forum established by the Baghdad Conference of 1960, on the initiative of Venezuela. It has aimed to restore oil prices to their pre-September 1960 levels, to keep oil companies' prices stable and to oblige countries not to agree to increase production if another country failed to reach an agreement with an oil company. The five founder members – Iraq, Iran, Kuwait, Saudi Arabia and Venezuela – were joined by Qatar in 1961, Libya and Indonesia in 1962, Abu Dhabi in 1967, Algeria in 1969, Nigeria in 1971, Ecuador in 1973 and Gabon in 1975. Its affairs were conducted in six-monthly regular and further extraordinary meetings. Following years of turbulent negotiations with oil companies that failed to raise the incomes of the oil countries as much as they desired, the six Gulf oil producers in October 1973 unilaterally increased their oil price by 70 per cent and cut production by 5 per cent; in December 1973, there was a further price increase of 13 per cent. OPEC was able to agree on common prices and quotas until dual pricing was introduced in 1976. Thus frustration with the oil companies made OPEC assume the role of price fixing. However, the 1981 price increase was too great: Saudi Arabia dissented from the subsequent cut, leading to a price war and the weakening of the joint power of OPEC.

See also: oil-price increases

References

Ghanem, S. (1986) *OPEC: The Rise and Fall of an Exclusive Club*, London: KPI.

organization theory (L2)

A modern THEORY OF THE FIRM that asserts that the goals and behaviour of a firm are the consequences of its organizational structure. This theory challenges earlier theories based on PROFIT MAXIMIZATION. A major example of this new approach is the assertion that managers are satisficiers, not maximizers.

See also: managerial models of the firm

original issue discount bond (G1)

A type of JUNK BOND issued at a large discount below its par value with COUPON rates below the market yields at the time of issue. After an initial period, the coupon rate is raised.

orphan assets (G2)

Money unclaimed from maturing life assurance and pension schemes.

other checkable deposits (G2)

NOW ACCOUNTS + ATS accounts (USA).

'other things being equal' (D0)

see ceteris paribus

out of the money (G2)

For a CALL OPTION where the UNDERLIER is below the STRIKE PRICE; for a PUT OPTION where the underlier is above that price.

outlier (C1)

A data point which is more than an arbitrary distance from a regression line.

outplacement agency (J6)

An employment agency specializing in placing redundant executives. Financial sector DEREGULATION in New York and London caused these agencies to flourish.

output budgeting (H6, M2)
The division of an organization's budget into sub-budgets so that expenditures and output can be compared. Although this disaggregation is often arbitrary, it is a conscious attempt to improve the effectiveness of expenditure, particularly in the US public sector. Also known as the PLANNING, PROGRAMMING, BUDGETING system.

output capacity (D2)
Performance from a machine or a productive mechanism available to a consumer. A concept especially applicable to the oil industry.

output floor regulation (L5)
An alternative to PRICE CAP REGULATION. This requires a regulated firm to produce a minimum output. Under this form of regulation profit is usually lower than under price regulation. The two forms of regulation coincide under a monopoly.

References
Weitzmann, M.L. (1974) 'Prices vs. quantities', *Review of Economic Studies* 41: 477–91.

output gap (E1)
The difference between the actual level of output of an economy and its potential or capacity output level, usually based on econometric modelling. A positive output gap reflects labour and other shortages threatening inflation; a negative gap restrains inflation.

See also: inflationary gap

output–inflation trade off (E3) *see* Phillips curve

outside lag (E6)
The time between the implementation of an economic policy and the realization of all of the effects of the use of that policy instrument. As these instruments, e.g. tax rates, affect economic behaviour, it is unlikely that economic agents can or will

change their decisions to buy, sell, invest, save, work or engage in leisure immediately.

See also: inside lag

outside money (E4)
A monetary asset of the private sector that is a liability of a government, assuming government demand does not fall as its total debt rises in real terms. Gold coins under the GOLD STANDARD, currency and bank reserves under a FIAT MONEY system and HIGH-POWERED MONEY are the major examples.

See also: inside money

outsider wage setting (J3)
The fixing of wages by the forces of an EXTERNAL LABOUR MARKET rather than by the personnel and labour policies of a particular firm.

See also: insider wage setting

outsourcing (D2)
Subcontracting a productive activity to another firm in the same or another country.

overaccumulation (E2)
Investing too much so that current consumption has to be reduced; investing in projects with low rates of return.

over-award payment (J3)
An addition to the Australian BASIC WAGE and MARGINS awarded by the Arbitration Commission. It is the cause of WAGE DRIFT in the Australian labour market.

overdraft (G2) *see* advance

overfunding (E5, H6)
The issue of more government bills and bonds than is necessary to finance government expenditure. A phenomenon of the UK in the 1980s.

See also: Public Sector Debt Repayment

overhead capital (E2) *see* social capital

overhead costs (D0)
1 FIXED COSTS to pay for administration of an organization.
2 Costs that do not vary with the level of output.

overheating (E6)
An excessive expansion in the level of economic activity of an economy, often as a result of the using of DEMAND MANAGEMENT to expand demand at a faster rate than the output potential of the economy permits. In some cases, a simplistic application of KEYNESIANISM which poorly estimates sustainable growth and the amount of excess capacity in an economy is responsible.

See also: Medium-term Financial Strategy

overlapping generations model (D9)
A GENERAL EQUILIBRIUM model which examines the consequences of an economy being demographically structured such that each generation overlaps in time with its successor. This model has been used in the study of the rate of interest, business cycles, national debt and tax incidence.

References

Diamond, P.A. (1965) 'National debt in a neoclassical growth model', *American Economic Review* 55: 1126–50.
Kareken, J.M. and Wallace, N. (eds) (1980) *Models of Monetary Economics*, Proceedings and Contributions from Participants of a December 1978 Conference, Federal Reserve Bank of Minneapolis.
Samuelson, P.A. (1958) 'An exact consumption loan model of interest with or without the social contrivance of money', *Journal of Political Economy* 66: 467–82.
Wilson, C.A. (1981) 'Equilibrium in dynamic models with an infinity of agents', *Journal of Economic Theory* 24: 95–111.

overnight money (E4)
Short loans of one to three days' duration by banks to the money market. In London this is the major source of finance of the DISCOUNT HOUSES.

overseas assets (F3)
The holdings by a country's government and residents of financial and other assets of other countries. The income from them, less payments overseas of the same nature,

constitutes the NET PROPERTY INCOME FROM ABROAD item of the balance of payments. Short-term assets often accumulate through a difference in interest rates; long-term assets by the direct investment of MULTINATIONAL CORPORATIONS.

overseas sterling area (F0)
A group of countries connected with the UK that used sterling for international transactions as a principal currency reserve and linked the value of their currencies to the pound. It consisted principally of Commonwealth countries (except Canada), South Africa, Iceland, Ireland, Kuwait and Jordan and existed in its full form until June 1972, only Ireland and Gibraltar remaining until final abolition in October 1979 when UK EXCHANGE CONTROLS ended. These countries acquired their sterling balances in several ways: by having a favourable current account surplus with the UK or by UK direct investment in them or by deposit in the UK of foreign currencies and gold earned by trade with countries outside the sterling area.

See also: sterling; sterling area

overshooting (E6)
A short-term reaction to a shock greater than the response in the long run.

overshooting price (D0)
A price which in the short run over-adjusts to changing market conditions and thereby overshoots the long-run price.

Overstone, Lord (B3) *see* Loyd, Samuel Jones

over-the-counter market (G1)
Trading in shares outside of a stock exchange by licensed brokers. This type of stock market has existed in the USA since the 1870s.

overtime (J2)
Work outside normal daily or weekly contractual hours, e.g. working longer than 8 hours per day or 40 hours per week. A COLLECTIVELY BARGAINED agreement or a

labour contract will clearly state what is normal and what is overtime working.

This work attracts a higher hourly rate of pay than normal hours' working but can still be attractive to an employer when a temporary increase in production is necessary or when the non-wage labour costs are so high as to inhibit the recruitment of further workers. Despite the recessions of many countries in the 1970s and 1980s, since the 1960s much overtime working still occurs.

See also: working hours

overtrading (M2)

Operating a firm with a low CURRENT RATIO, a shortage of working capital so that a shortage of cash makes payment of wages, taxes and sums due to trade creditors impossible on the date due.

See also: undertrading

over-urbanization (R1)

The growth of a city at a higher rate than its creation of high-wage employment, often brought about by the unrealistic expectations of persons in rural areas. There are many examples of such growth in less developed countries, especially in Africa.

References

Mills, E. and Becker, C. (1986) *Studies in Indian Urban Development*, New York: Oxford University Press.

overvalued currency (F3)

A currency with a value above its sustainable market rate.

Owen, Robert, 1771–1858 (B3)

Born in Newtown, Montgomeryshire, Wales, the son of a saddler, ironmonger and postmaster. He started his career as a draper at the age of 10 in London and by the age of 19 became a partner in a Manchester cotton mill. The partnership acquired the New Lanark Mills in 1800: by 1810 the mills employed 2,000 and were famed for their enlightened labour practices. In 1817 he published a plan to change the whole of society by the establishment of villages where the inhabitants held their property in common and combined rural and industrial occupations to avoid the division of labour. He used up his own capital in founding ideal communities at New Harmony, Indiana, in 1825 and at Queenwood, Hampshire, in 1839. They both failed but many Owenite organizations flourished, including the London Co-operative Society. In his final years he turned to spiritualism.

References

Owen, R. (1813–16) *A New View of Society*.
—— (1820) *Report to the County of Lanark* (1820)

owner occupation (R2)

Housing occupied by the owner. In the UK, in 1914, 10.6 per cent of its housing stock was owner occupied; in 1950, 29.5 per cent but in 1985, 61.9 per cent. In the USA, 55 per cent of housing units were owner occupied in 1950 and 64 per cent in 1987. Tax relief on mortgage interest and the disappearance of much private sector housing available for renting have encouraged this growth.

ownership structure (K2, Q0)

1 A classification of the business sector by sole proprietor, partnership, corporation or limited liability company.
2 An analysis of the beneficial ownership of a firm distinguishing private individuals from investment institutions and the government.
3 Types of property tenure.

own rate of interest (E4)

SRAFFA's notion, used by KEYNES, that for every durable commodity there is a rate of interest for it in terms of itself, e.g. a wheat rate of interest, a steel rate of interest. A steel rate of interest of 10 per cent means that 110 tonnes of steel in a year's time exchanges for 100 tonnes now. The money rate of interest is based on the same principle. The difference between market and spot prices is the basis for calculating own rates for particular commodities. Own rates show the relationship between the value of the future services of an asset and its present cost, expressed as a YIELD or A RATE OF RETURN.

References

Keynes, J.M. (1936) *The General Theory of Employment, Interest and Money*, ch. 17, London: Macmillan.

P

Paasche index (E3)

An index of output or prices which uses weights of the current year. The Paasche price index is

$$\frac{\sum p_i q_i}{\sum p_0 q_1}$$

where p_1, are the prices of the current year, p_0 are the prices of the base year and q_1 are the weights of the current year. The Paasche output index is

$$\frac{\sum p_i q_i}{\sum p_1 q_0}$$

where q_1 are the quantities of the current year, q_0 are the quantities of the base year and p_1 are the prices of the current year and p_0 are the prices of the base year.

Pacific Rim (O0)

The thirty-four countries and twenty-three islands around the Pacific covering 70 million square miles (180 square kilometres) and consisting of 2.4 billion people (more than a half of the world's population). Since 1979 this world region has achieved more than half of the world's economic growth. Future prospects for growth around the Pacific are considerable as the combination of Japanese production, innovation and marketing methods harnessed to Chinese resources is formidable.

References

Daly, M.T. and Logan, M.I. (1989) *The Brittle Rim*, Harmondsworth: Penguin.

package deal (D0, L1) *see* interlinked transaction

panel bank (G2)

A bank in the Euribor market with a high volume of business in the EUROZONE money markets. When that market was set up there were forty-seven banks from the first European Union countries to adopt the euro, four banks from other EU countries and six large international banks of the USA and Japan.

panel data (C8)

Data collected regularly over a period time from a randomly selected number of individuals. Many types of economic behaviour, including consumption, have been observed by this method.

Panglossian economics (A1)

A complacent optimism about the future. Dr Pangloss, a fictional character in Voltaire's *Candide*, asserted that every effect has a cause and everything is for the best.

paper gold (F3) *see* special drawing rights

paperless entry (G2)

Electronic banking pioneered by the System Committee on Paperless Entry set up by the bank clearing houses of San Francisco and Los Angeles and the Federal

Reserve in 1968. By 1978 a national network was set up.

See also: dematerialization

paper money (E4)

BANKNOTES generally acceptable in payment of a debt. Originally this paper derived its status from being convertible into gold or silver because of their intrinsic value. Since 1931, banknotes have usually been inconvertible so paper money can act as a MEDIUM OF EXCHANGE because of the financially sound character of the banking system issuing it. The status of paper money is recognized by making it 'LEGAL TENDER'.

See also: Banking School; gold standard; Thornton

paper profit (M4)

An increase in the BOOK VALUE of an asset yet to be realized. This profit is expressed in nominal terms and does not take into account INFLATION.

paradox of costs (E0)

A case of higher wages being associated with higher macro profits. This occurs because higher wages cause higher household incomes in turn leading to higher demand and profits.

paradox of debt (G3)

The impossibility of a particular company reducing its debt (leverage) ratio because other companies are following the same strategy. If debt ratio reduction becomes widespread, capital accumulation and profits fall with the consequence that the rate of growth of internal funds based on profits is less than the rate of growth of borrowing.

References

Steindl, J. (1952) *Maturity and Stagnation in American Capitalism*, Oxford: Blackwell.

paradox of lending (G2)

Banks are most willing to lend to people with least need to borrow. People with high incomes and little debt are the most creditworthy and hence attractive as bank customers but in less need of bank finance.

paradox of liquidity (G0)

The attempt to obtain cash by selling non-liquid assets which fails if done on a large scale. When many owners liquidate assets, asset prices fall and it is more difficult to obtain purchasers. Thus the strong desire to increase liquidity has made the fulfilment of the desire less achievable.

paradox of thrift (E2)

The contradictory effects of saving as it is both beneficial in providing funds for investment but detrimental to an underemployed economy. SMITH and other CLASSICAL ECONOMISTS believed that what is saved is invested so there cannot be excessive saving. However, KEYNES and leading Swedish economists of the 1930s believed that there could be an imbalance between EX ANTE saving and investment. Hoarding savings instead of investing them contributes to a reduction in AGGREGATE DEMAND and the making of a recession. The new millennium began with low personal sector savings in many industrialized countries.

See also: savings ratio; Stockholm School

paradox of value (D0)

This states that goods with great usefulness, e.g. water, command a low price but those with little usefulness, e.g. diamonds, are expensive. Although this so-called paradox was known to the Greeks, especially PLATO, it was SMITH's citing it in *The Wealth of Nations* which made it popular as a justification for cost of production, especially labour, theories of value. Despite his resolution of the paradox in his *Lectures on Jurisprudence* of 1762–63 in terms of dearness being caused by scarcity, it was not until the MARGINALISTS clearly set out the DIMINISHING MARGINAL UTILITY LAW and distinguished total from marginal utility that the 'paradox' was put to rest. They asserted that water has a high total, but low marginal, utility and diamonds the reverse; price is proportional to marginal, not total, utility in NEOCLASSICAL ECONOMICS.

paradox of voting (D7) *see* impossibility theorem

parallel currency strategy (F3)
The simultaneous use of a COMMON CURRENCY, e.g. the ecu, and national currencies.

See also: hard ecu

parallel importing (F1)
The importation of two versions of the same product, e.g. a branded pharmaceutical and a cheaper substitute. To avoid this competition dual pricing of the branded product is practised.

parallel loan (F3)
A two-way currency loan between two firms in different countries to protect them against exchange rate fluctuations, e.g. a UK firm and an Italian firm may lend each other their own currency for six months after which time they repay that currency.

parallel market economy (P4) *see* second economy

parallel plants (J5, L1)
Manufacturing plants or factories producing the same product for the same employer but at different locations so that if a strike occurs in one, production can be switched to another, reducing the power of a TRADE (LABOR) UNION.

parallel pricing (D4) *see* price leadership

parameter (C1)
A quantified characteristic of a statistical population, e.g. MEAN, STANDARD DEVIATION.

parametric pricing (D4)
A method of pricing based on the costs and prices of the previous year adjusted for learning, affordability and changing levels of risk. This estimating technique uses a price function.

parasitic city (R1)
A city which impoverishes the surrounding region by drawing into it capital and better quality labour. There are many cities in the THIRD WORLD of this kind.

See also: generative city

parasitic industry or trade (J3, L0)
A group of firms noted for paying wages so low that workers have to be subsidized by welfare payments or by relatives. Unequal bargaining power is often the cause of low wages and poor health the result.

References
Webb, S. and Webb, B. (1920) *Industrial Democracy*, London: Longman, Green.

parastatal (I3)
A company at least 50 per cent owned by the state. As the state is responsible for any deficits made there is a tendency for such firms to have poor financial discipline and excessive labour forces. In Latin American countries parastatals have only been maintained by increases in the money supply with inevitable inflationary consequences for the national economy.

See also: joint equity venture company; nationalized industry

Pareto efficiency (D2)
The efficiency of a system which cannot produce more of any product from the same level of inputs without reducing the output of another product by switching inputs between products or by changing techniques. This view of efficiency has been challenged because of the difficulties of valuing outputs and comparing them, its ambiguity in referring to many alternative allocations and the possibility that present allocations may produce different outputs in the future.

Pareto improvement (D6)
Making at least one person in a community better off without anyone else being made worse off.

See also: Pareto optimum

Pareto optimum (D6)
An allocation of resources such that no one can be made better off without someone else being made worse off; the most famous notion of optimality in WELFARE ECONOMICS.

Pareto, Vilfredo, 1848–1923 (B3)
French-born Italian sociologist and economist who made a leading contribution to
WELFARE ECONOMICS by setting out the conditions for a welfare optimum, always
known now as the 'Pareto optimum'. In
his *Cours d'Economie Politique* (1896) he
attempted a synthesis of economics, sociology and Marxist thought: economic
UTILITY was examined in a psychological
and sociological context and Marxian
class analysis was extended to a study of
the nature of conflict between interest
groups. Realizing the consequences for
society of political democracy, he was
reluctant to retain a socialist approach to
conflict in his work *Les Systèmes Socia-
listes* of 1902. Like WALRAS, he was a
member of the LAUSANNE SCHOOL.

References

Borkenau, F. (1936) *Pareto*, New York:
  Wiley.
Bucolo, P. (ed.) (1979) *The Economics of
  Vilfredo Pareto*, London and Totowa,
  NJ: Cass.

Paris Club (F0) *see* Group of Ten

Parkinson's law (M1)
'Work expands so as to fill the time
available for its completion.' C. Northcote
Parkinson postulated the law in 1955 after
his observation of Admiralty staffing in
the UK.

partial equilibrium analysis (D0)
A technique of microeconomic analysis
pioneered principally by COURNOT and MAR-
SHALL to analyse a market or other part of
an economy by itself. Usually the relationship between only two variables is considered, with the assumption that anything
which can influence that relationship remains unchanged. In demand analysis, the
relationship between price and quantity
demanded is analysed, assuming that
'other things being equal', i.e. that tastes,
incomes, other prices, or anything which
could influence the quantity demanded do
not change.

See also: *ceteris paribus*; general equilibrium

partial unemployment (J6) *see* work
sharing

participating security (G1)
A security entitling the holder both to a
fixed amount of interest or dividends and
to extra earnings above a pre-set level.

partnership (L2)
A business jointly owned by two or more
persons who are personally responsible for
its debts and each share in its profits. This
form of business has long been popular
with professional persons, e.g. lawyers and
accountants; banking often was organized
in partnerships before the coming of joint
stock companies.

See also: limited company

par value (F3, G1)
1 The nominal value of a share printed
  on a stock certificate at the time of
  issue.
2 The value of a currency under a fixed
  exchange rate regime.

See also: Bretton Woods Agreement

patent (O3)
An official document conferring exclusive
privileges on an invention for a period of
years. Patents create a formidable technological barrier to entry, establishing and
maintaining MONOPOLY POWER. Since patents
allow monopoly profits to accrue to their
inventors, they are a major private incentive to research and development. Non-
patent-holders can only use patented technical knowledge by licence. Although the
patent system may encourage inventors, it
has been criticized on the grounds that all
scientific knowledge should be a free good
and that the considerable legal costs of
registering and protecting a patent exclude
the poor inventor from using the system.

See also: invention; product cycle

path dependent (D0)
The dependence of a network or a system

on previous decisions made by producers and consumers. A current price of a good or service, for example, is dependent on past sales.

Patinkin, Don, 1922–97 (B3)

A major Israeli monetary economist and interpreter of KEYNES who was born in Chicago where he attended and taught at the University of Chicago. Since 1949 he was a lecturer and (from 1956) professor at the Eliezer Kaplan School of Economics and Social Sciences, Hebrew University of Jerusalem. From 1969, he was Director of Research at the Maurice Falk Institute for Economic Research in Israel.

In *Money, Interest and Prices* (1956) he applied Hicksian general EQUILIBRIUM analysis to Keynesian macroeconomics, brilliantly integrating the real and monetary economies by treating money as a commodity which renders services. However, in his other numerous writings he had sharp words of criticism for central elements of Keynes's *General Theory*, particularly the notion of 'INVOLUNTARY UNEMPLOYMENT' and the absence of a supply function in Keynes's macro model.

patriarchal monopoly (D1)

The state of a household in which the wife does no market work, cannot exit through divorce and has ECONOMIC RENT extracted by her husband. The husband buys goods at market prices and sells them to his wife at a higher, indirectly measured, price thus obtaining the rent.

patrimonial industry (L0, O2)

An industry in which the original country retains a controlling interest so that foreign ownership is limited to 49 per cent. This rule is applied in the Mexican economy to the industries constituting its basic infrastructure.

See also: joint equity venture company; parastatal

pattern model (C5)

An empirical economic model based on case studies rather than on a priori assumptions such as those of rational choice theory. By a process of induction themes emerge to reveal the unity of part of the economic system. These models aim to produce interconnected patterns which approximate to the real economic system.

References

Wilber, C.K. and Harrison, R.S. (1978) 'The methodological basis of institutional economics: pattern model, storytelling, and holism', *Journal of Economic Issues* 12: 61–89.

pattern settlement (J3)

A wage agreement which follows the pay deal of a dominant bargaining group. Sweden and Japan both have co-ordinated bargaining of this kind, often with the bargain of the metal industries setting a pattern for other bargaining groups of TRADE UNIONS and EMPLOYERS' ASSOCIATIONS. Lower inflation and higher levels of employment are associated with centralized collective bargaining of this kind.

See also: wage round

payback method (M2)

A method of INVESTMENT APPRAISAL that assesses a project by the length of time needed to repay that investment by its earnings. As a method, it has been criticized for bias against some projects which necessarily will yield earnings only in the long run.

PAYE (H2)

Pay as you earn. A method of paying income tax or contributing to a social security fund. The UK introduced this system in 1944, partly on the advice of KEYNES. In the USA, this is known as income tax withholding.

pay freeze (E3, E6)

A phase of an INCOMES POLICY in which no increase in wages and salaries is permitted. This can be used as an extreme measure by a national government in times of inflation or by an employer in serious financial difficulties. It is difficult to enforce a pay freeze for long as it usually makes workers suffer a fall in real incomes and prevents the labour market from using wage rates to clear the labour market.

payment by results (J3) *see* incentive pay scheme

payment-in-kind bond (G1)
A JUNK BOND such that the issuer can issue more debt in lieu of a cash COUPON payment over the early part of the bond's life.

See also: original issue discount bond

pay-off (C7, D0)
1 In GAME THEORY the expected values assigned to different combinations of strategy and counter-strategy.
2 The benefit derived from a course of action, net of cost.

See also: minimax; regret

pay performance sensitivity (G1, J3)
The link between executive remuneration and the value of stock OPTIONS. If the executive performs well then the market value of the firm will increase and also the value of any stock options.

pay policy (E6) *see* incomes policy

payroll tax (H2)
A tax on labour usually equal to a fixed proportion of the wage bill or of an individual employee's remuneration. In the USA, this tax became part of the federal revenue system by the Social Security Act 1935 when it was introduced to finance social security programmes. National insurance in the UK is based on this principle.

peace dividend (H5)
The extra amount of revenue governments hope to have available for public expenditure or tax cuts because of a reduction in defence expenditures resulting from the ending of the 'Cold War' in 1989. However, the scope for turning guns into butter is limited by the political instability of several regions of the world.

peak-load pricing (D4, L1)
The charging of higher prices to consumers at times of peak demand to reflect the higher costs of supplying them then. There are many examples of this in the supply of energy and passenger transport, e.g. charging less for the electricity consumed by night storage heaters and lower rail fares on days with less traffic. Industries needing this type of pricing face demand conditions which fluctuate over the cycle of a day or a year and by a supply with high fixed costs and low variable costs. The higher prices charged to pay for extra capacity cannot be too great, otherwise consumers will shift their demand to other times which will make it increasingly difficult to raise sufficient revenue to cover the costs of peak-load special capacity.

See also: two-part tariff

References

Crew, M.A. and Kleindorfer, P.R. (1986) *The Economics of Public Utility Regulation*, Cambridge, MA: MIT Press.
Williamson, O.E. (1966) 'Peak load pricing and optimal capacity under indivisibility constraints', *American Economic Review* 56: 810–27.

Pearson Report (O0)
The Report in 1969 of the Commission on International Development headed by Lester Pearson, a former prime minister of Canada. It recommended that developing countries should encourage DIRECT FOREIGN INVESTMENT, that all developed countries should by 1975 devote at least 1 per cent of GROSS DOMESTIC PRODUCT to FOREIGN AID and that aid should not be tied to procuring goods in the donor's country.

References

World Bank Commission on International Development (1969) *Partners in Development: Report of the Commission on International Development*, New York and London: Pall Mall Press.

pecking-order theory (G3, M2)
An explanation of a firm's financial capital structure. It asserts that a firm first uses internal funds, then marketable securities,

then new debt and finally new common stock (ordinary shares).

pecuniary economy of scale (D0, G0)
A reduction in the cost of purchasing inputs or obtaining investment finance as a result of operating at a higher output.

See also: economy of scale

pecuniary external economy (D0)
A reduction in the average costs of a firm brought about by the financial actions of other firms. A major example of this is the simultaneous undertaking of several investment projects that reduce costs by reducing the risk of one of the projects failing.

See also: economy of scale

pecuniary returns (D3)
Rewards to a FACTOR OF PRODUCTION in the form of money.

See also: non-pecuniary returns

pegged exchange rate (F3)
An exchange rate kept in the same relationship to another currency, or to gold, through using that country's central bank reserves or through borrowing from the INTERNATIONAL MONETARY FUND or other central banks. This is done to avoid unnecessary exchange rate fluctuations and because of the belief that central banks are more astute than private parties in setting exchange rates. Most pegging is done against the dollar. There are many examples of pegging. For almost 100 years, until 1934, the US dollar was 20.67 per fine ounce of gold. The UK pound was pegged at US$2.80 in the period 1948–67; Haiti pegged the gourde at 5 gourdes to the dollar from 1907 onwards.

See also: Exchange Rate Mechanism; gold standard

pendulum arbitration (J5)
A system of arbitration under which the arbitrator has to choose either management or union proposals. As no compromise is possible, both sides are moderate in their stances. Although this was practised in the UK coal industry as early as the period 1893–14, it has been revived as a method of wage dispute settlement, e.g. in Japanese companies to avoid strikes. Arbitration is compulsory in twenty US states for public sector industrial disputes, eight using only pendulum arbitration and two using it to some extent. Perhaps such arbitration is most suitable when there is a general principle at stake, e.g. wage cuts or wage increases. Also known as flip-flop, final offer or straight-choice arbitration.

References

Davis, D. (1989) *The Power of the Pendulum*, London: Institute of Economic Affairs.

Treble, J.G. (1990) 'The pit and the pendulum: arbitration in the British Coal Industry, 1893–1914', *Economic Journal* 100: 1095–108.

penny share (G1)
A share in a UK company worth less than 50p. The potential for capital growth is considerable for many of these securities.

See also: heavy share

Penrose, Edith Tilton, 1914–96 (B3)
After an education at Johns Hopkins University and various academic posts, including one in Baghdad, Penrose was Professor of Economics at the School of Oriental and African Studies, University of London, from 1964 to 1979. Her most famous contribution to economics is her theory of the growth of the firm. It had the optimistic theme that the human and material resources managed by a firm can be used to achieve its limitless expansion through product and market diversification and the recruitment of additional high-level managers. Her other works included books on the international PATENT system, the international petroleum industry and Middle East oil.

References

Penrose, E.T. (1959) *The Theory of the Growth of the Firm*, Oxford: Basil Blackwell.

pension (H2, J3)

1 A replacement of employment earnings for retired persons. It can take the form of a flat rate benefit or be related to previous earnings and be arranged by a government or firm or financial institution. Pensions can be financed from an insurance fund or on a 'pay-as-you-go' principle with contributions and government grants financing the payout of benefits.

2 A regular payment by a government to a person for distinguished service or achievements, e.g. to a soldier or a writer.

pension fund (G2)

The accumulated contributions of an employer and employees of a firm, or other employing organization, which are used to finance the future payment of retirement pensions. In the UK, the largest funds are those of the long-established public corporations, major private sector firms and local governments. Pension funds since 1945 have become major INSTITUTIONAL INVESTORS with the potential to have a great influence on the movement of share prices.

pension mis-selling (G2)

The sale of complicated pension schemes without explaining the full nature of the pension scheme. In the UK this led in the 1990s to many retired people having lower than expected incomes.

pension scheme (G2)

An arrangement to pay a regular income to a person too old or too ill to work. By the late nineteenth century, many governments realized that some provision for the elderly was needed; in the twentieth century, the spread of COLLECTIVE BARGAINING brought a proliferation of private pension plans.

See also: Old Age, Survivors and Disability Insurance; State Earnings Related Pensions Scheme

percentage grant (H7) *see* grant in aid

percentile (C1)

A value obtained by dividing data arranged in order of magnitude into 100 equal parts. The first percentile, for example, shows that value below which 1 per cent of the values of a variable lie. The LOWER QUARTILE is the 25th percentile; the MEDIAN is the 50th percentile; the UPPER QUARTILE is the 75th percentile.

See also: decile; median

perestroika (P4)

The reconstruction of the Soviet economy proposed in detail in 1987 consisting of granting greater independence from many planning directives to enterprises, even to the extent of being able to go bankrupt. As part of economic democratization, the rewards of all workers would depend on their contribution to the success of an enterprise. To improve economic efficiency, a more realistic structure of prices was proposed. The price structure in the 1980s was much in need of reform as rents had last been fixed in 1928, communal charges in 1946 and many food items, including bread, in 1954. This price rigidity prevented demand and supply reaching equilibrium in particular markets. The principal limitation on the freedom of enterprises was giving priority to state orders. This change was not popular with unskilled workers as many faced unemployment for the first time in their lives.

See also: Liberman

References

Gorbachev, M.S. (1987) *Perestroika: New Thinking for our Country and the World*, London: Collins.

Rapoport, V. (1989) *Perestroika: A Selection of Articles*, London: Overseas Publications Interchange.

perfect competition (L1)

A market which has a large number of buyers and sellers engaged in the trading of a HOMOGENEOUS GOOD, with freedom of entry and exit for firms, no government intervention, no transport costs and a perfectly elastic supply of factors of production. Although few markets, apart from some securities and commodities markets, even approach such a state of affairs, perfect competition is very important conceptually as an extreme case in the classification of markets. Many economic theories do not advance beyond the assumption of perfect competition.

Short run

Long run

	supernormal profits
AR	average revenue
ATC	average total cost
D	demand
MC	marginal cost
MR	marginal revenue

References

Knight, F.H. (1921) *Risk, Uncertainty and Profit*, Part II, Boston and New York: Houghton Mifflin.

Stigler, G.J. (1965) *Essays in the History of Economics*, ch. 8, Chicago and London: University of Chicago Press.

perfect price discrimination (D0) *see* first-degree price discrimination

performance-related pay (J3)

An INCENTIVE PAY SCHEME which attempts to link all or part of an employee's remuneration to the achievement of output and output-related goals instead of to the amount of time supplied by an employee to a firm. It is hoped by firms with performance-related pay (PRP) schemes that turnover, profits, loyalty to the firm and quality of work done will increase and that industrial unrest and ABSENTEEISM will diminish.

See also: profit-related pay

peripheral capitalism (P1)

The dependent CAPITALISM of THIRD WORLD countries. The gradual INDUSTRIALIZATION of less developed countries at the periphery raises their productivity and labour incomes and creates a surplus that is transferred to advanced countries at the 'centre'. The centre thus has a faster rate of capital accumulation and income growth than the periphery. Also, the centre is assumed to have greater technological progress than the periphery, as well as different income and price ELASTICITIES of demand for manufactures and primary products. The income and wealth disparities between centre and periphery which result have prompted the demand by PREBISCH and others for a range of socialist policies to appropriate the surplus created at the periphery, to limit imports and to increase industrialization.

periphery firm (L1)

A small or medium-sized firm in a largely OLIGOPOLISTIC industry which is dominated by core firms.

perks (J3) *see* fringe benefits

permanent arms economy (P0)

An ECONOMY able to continue its accumulation beyond the limit set by a fall in the rate of profit because permanent value is increasingly diverted into unproductive consumption. A term coined by a UK Marxist, Kidron, to describe Western economies, despite being as applicable to many SOVIET-TYPE ECONOMIES.

See also: military–industrial complex; military Keynesianism

References

Kidron, M. (1968) *Western Capitalism since the War*, London: Weidenfeld & Nicolson.

Melman, S. (1974) *The Permanent War Economy*, New York: Simon & Schuster.

permanent employment (J2)

A Japanese practice of offering lifetime employment to workers, when they join a firm from school or university. This became popular with firms short of labour in the 1950s and anxious about labour turnover. The system has rarely been applied to small firms and less to women than to men. Under this system, all employees, except senior management, retire at 55. Increasing pressures in the Japanese economy in the 1990s threatened the existence of the system.

References

Taira, K. (1970) *Economic Development and the Labor Market in Japan*, New York: Columbia University Press.

permanent income hypothesis (E2)

A theory of the CONSUMPTION FUNCTION that income can be divided into permanent income (expected lifetime income) and transitory income (e.g. WINDFALL GAINS) so that permanent consumption is a function of permanent income and transitory consumption a function of transitory income. Before FRIEDMAN, the theory was suggested by several writers.

See also: absolute income hypothesis; lifecycle hypothesis; relative income hypothesis

References

Friedman, M. (1957) *A Theory of the*

Consumption Function, Princeton, NJ: Princeton University Press.

perpetuity (G0)

A fixed interest bond with no redemption date.

See also: consol

personal bank (G2)

A bank with deposits from individual men and women and no commercial clients. Many savings banks were of this nature until extensive financial deregulation encouraged diversification.

personal capitalism (P1)

Ownership of industry by the families of the founders of major firms.

See also: capitalism; merchant capitalism

personal equity plan (G0)

UK fiscal arrangement introduced in 1987 that originally permitted individuals to invest up to £200 per month, or £2,400 per year, in EQUITIES, with the incentive of not having to pay income tax on dividends received from these investments. Plans can only be arranged by a 'registered manager', i.e. a bank, building society, stockbroker or licensed dealer in securities.

personal income (D3)

The amount of income a person receives from being engaged in productive activity or owning income-producing assets. It is determined by an individual's endowments (including abilities and HUMAN CAPITAL), tastes (for work, leisure, saving and risk taking), and luck (windfall gains and losses). A person's income takes the form of wages, salaries, interest, dividends, gifts and rents. As all countries levy taxation, for most persons DISPOSABLE INCOME is less than personal income.

personal income distribution (D3)

The distribution of income between individuals; the SIZE DISTRIBUTION OF INCOME. Statistics on this indicate what proportion of total household income is received by individuals in each income band, e.g. the top 5 per cent. Most studies show the stability of this distribution over time and considerable inequality.

References

Atkinson, A.B. (1983) *The Economics of Inequality*, 2nd edn, Oxford: Clarendon Press.
Phelps Brown, E.H. (1977) *The Inequality of Pay*, Oxford and New York: Oxford University Press.

personal sector liquid assets (G0)

Savings deposits of persons with banks, building societies and state savings institutions. These deposits can be converted into cash at short notice.

personnel economics (J2)

The study of the business aspects of human resources based on microeconomic principles, especially the notions of maximizing agents, equilibrium and efficiency.

References

Lazear, E.P. (2000) 'The future of personnel economics', *Economic Journal* 110: 611–39.

per-unit tax (H2)

A tax which increases the cost of producing a unit of a good by the amount of the tax;

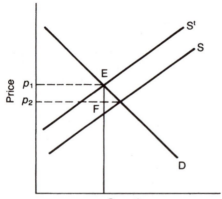

Quantity

EF   tax
p_1 price paid to producers
p_2 price paid by consumers
D   demand
S   supply before imposition of an indirect tax
S^t supply after the indirect tax has been imposed

import TARIFFS, taxes on FACTORS OF PRODUCTION (e.g. the SELECTIVE EMPLOYMENT TAX), employer contributions to social security schemes and VALUE-ADDED TAXES. Diagrammatically, such a tax is shown by an upward shift of the MARGINAL COST curve by the amount of the tax. The extent to which producers and consumers pay the tax will depend on the ELASTICITY of the demand and supply curves. A tax of this kind is usually contrasted with a LUMP-SUM TAX.

perverse price (D0)

A price which falls as a consequence of an increase in demand.

See also: Giffen paradox

References

Broome, J. (1978) 'Perverse prices', *Economic Journal* 88: 778–87.

Peter principle (M1)

The hypothesis that in a hierarchical organization each person rises to the level of his or her incompetence and stays there. Poor information within INTERNAL LABOUR MARKETS is largely responsible for this. Professor Lawrence J. Peter (1920–90) of the University of Southern California sadly formulated this principle after extensively studying many organizations.

References

Peter, L. and Hull, R. (1969) *The Peter Principle: Why Things Always Go Wrong*, London: Souvenir Press.

petrocurrency (E4)

A currency whose value is influenced by the large part oil plays in that country's balance of payments.

petrodollars (F3)

The surplus receipts of oil-producing countries which were invested abroad rather than spent on imports. Surpluses invested in Japan were termed petroyens, in Switzerland, petrofrancs.

petroleum revenue tax (H2)

UK tax levied on the proceeds from selling oil and gas above a certain sales levy. Operating costs and royalties are deducted from sales revenue before the tax is charged. The exploitation of North Sea oil reserves brought about this tax which enabled UK governments to share in the oil industry's prosperity.

Petty, Sir William, 1623–87 (B3)

Described by MARX as the 'founder of political economy' and by KEYNES as 'the father of modern economics'. He had an eventful life rising from being a cabin boy of humble origins to a chair of anatomy at Oxford, a chair of music at Gresham's College, London, Physician-General to Cromwell's army in Ireland, a founder of the Royal Society and an original thinker in economics, far surpassing most of his MERCANTILIST contemporaries. His principal mentor was Thomas Hobbes, particularly in matters of taxation.

Most of his economic writings, dictated at night to his secretaries as he paced up and down his study munching raisins, were attempts to solve the policy problems posed by the Restoration of Charles II. His most comprehensive work was the first economic work on public finance, *A Treatise of Taxes* (1662); his posthumous *Political Arithmetick* (written 1671, published 1690) introduced the quantification of economic variables to political economy. He is credited with the first clear enunciation of many economic ideas, including HUMAN CAPITAL, the LABOUR THEORY OF VALUE, EXPENDITURE TAXES, PUBLIC WORKS as a cure for UNEMPLOYMENT, the DIFFERENTIAL THEORY OF RENT, the TRADE CYCLE, THE CIRCULAR FLOW of income, the bank creation of credit and the VELOCITY OF CIRCULATION.

References

Hull, C.H. (ed.) (1899) *The Economic Writings of Sir William Petty*, Cambridge: Cambridge University Press (reprinted New York: A.M. Kelley, 1964–5).

Roncaglia, A. (1985) *Petty: The Origins of Political Economy*, Cardiff: University College Cardiff Press.

Petty's law (O4)

The tendency as an economy develops for the proportion of the labour force engaged in SERVICES to increase.

Phillips, Alban William Housego, 1914–75 (B3)

New-Zealand-born economist who invented in 1958 a major tool of macroeconomics, the 'Phillips curve', which originally showed the trade-off between wage inflation and unemployment and was subsequently applied to changes in the general price level. Also, in a series of articles he examined multiplier–accelerator relationships and did much to introduce the optimal control approach to stabilization policy.

In 1938, at the beginning of his career, he graduated as an electrical engineer, and then ran a cinema and hunted crocodiles in Queensland before acquiring a BA in sociology and economics (1949) and a PhD (1952) at the London School of Economics. As an undergraduate, he saw scope for applying his engineering knowledge to economics. He was able to construct an analogue machine which applied dynamic control theory to a CIRCULAR FLOW model of the economy; this met with the approval of leading economists such as MEADE and HICKS and led to his first academic appointment. He was soon appointed to the Tooke Chair of Economic Science at the London School of Economics, which he held from 1954 to 1967. As a professor at the Australian National University (1968–70), he pursued his interest in the Chinese economy.

See also: multiplier–accelerator model

References

Blyth, C.A. (1975) 'A.W.H. Phillips, MBE', *Economic Record* 51: 303–7.

Phillips, A.W. (1950) 'Mechanical models in economic dynamics', *Economica* New Series, 17 (August): 283–99.

—— (1958) 'The relation between unemployment and the rate of change of money wage rates in the United Kingdom, 1861–1957', *Economica* New Series, 25: 283–300.

Phillips curve (E3)

The relationship between unemployment and inflation so named by SAMUELSON and SOLOW after Phillips attempted to identify it in 1958 by plotting data on changes in UK money wage rates for 1861–1957 against the national unemployment rates (a measure of overall demand in the UK economy). Later work on the Phillips curve sought to take into account INCOMES POLICIES and inflationary expectations. The long-run Phillips curve is vertical at the NATURAL RATE OF UNEMPLOYMENT. From the mid-1980s in the USA and UK this curve has been almost horizontal so economic policy can effect changes in unemployment without increasing inflation.

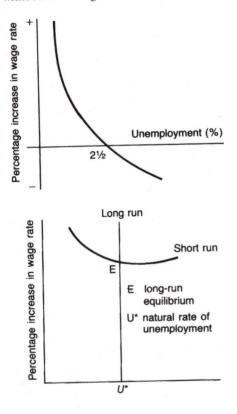

References

Phillips, A.W. (1958) 'The relationship between unemployment and the rate of change of money wage rates in the United Kingdom, 1861–1957', *Economica* New Series, 25: 283–99.

Santomero, A.N. and Seater, J.J. (eds) (1978) 'The inflation-unemployment trade-off: a critique of the literature', *Journal of Economic Literature* 15: 499–544.

Sawyer, M.C. (1991) *The Political Economy of the Phillips Curve*, Aldershot: Edward Elgar.

physical quality of life index (D6)

A measure of ECONOMIC WELFARE more sophisticated than GROSS NATIONAL PRODUCT per capita. This index, pioneered by the Overseas Development Council of Washington, DC, is based on the percentage of literacy in a population, infant mortality and life expectancy after age 1 (to avoid double counting of infant deaths). Some countries rank much lower by this index than by per capita gross national product, e.g. oil-producing countries. Critics of the index are concerned about its narrowness as there are so many other physical indicators of welfare.

References

Morris, M.D. and Alpin, M.B. (1980) *Measuring the Condition of the World's Poor: The Physical Quality of Life Index*, New Delhi: Promilla.

Physiocrats (B1)

The leading French school of economic thought which was active in the 1760s and 1770s and whose members were the first to be called 'économistes'. QUESNAY, Mirabeau, Dupont de Nemours and TURGOT used the name Physiocrats to mean 'Lords of Nature' as they took the view that the economy should pursue its natural course. There should be no interference by government and agriculture should be accorded a unique status as it produces a surplus through plants and animals reproducing themselves unlike machines, the product of sterile manufacture. Apart from presenting one of the earliest models of the economy (in Quesnay's *Tableau Economique*), they also advocated an *impot unique* (single tax) based on agricultural rents and laid the foundations for classical price theory. Much of their work had been more clearly set out by CANTILLON. But the high praise accorded to them by SMITH and MARX ensures that they will never be forgotten.

References

Meek, R.L. (1962) *The Economics of Physiocracy: Essays and Translations*, London: Allen & Unwin.

picketing (J5)

Verbal or physical persuasion of workers not to enter the premises of a firm where there is an INDUSTRIAL DISPUTE. In the UK, only peaceful picketing to convey information by no more than six pickets assembled is legal.

piece rate (J3)

A specific wage rate per unit of output. Piece rates were a major method of paying workers and now are useful in incentive pay schemes.

See also: time rate

piecework system (J3)

A wage system that rewards workers according to the number of pieces/units of a product they produce. This is the alternative to remunerating workers according to the time a worker contracts to offer an employer. Piecework was introduced to relate work to productivity. However, it has often been criticized for causing unstable earnings and causing stress to workers who overexert themselves.

Pigou, Arthur Cecil, 1877–1959 (B3)

The Cambridge economist who was a fellow of King's College from 1902 to 1959 and professor of economics, in succession to MARSHALL, from 1908 to 1943. In *Wealth and Welfare* (1912), which was expanded into *The Economics of Welfare* (1920), he built upon Marshallian foundations a study of the size and distribution of national income and the case for government intervention. His other major works included *Industrial Fluctuations* (1927), *Public Finance* (1928) and *Employ-*

ment and Equilibrium (1941). Although he was initially critical of KEYNES'S GENERAL THEORY, by 1949 he was prepared to concede that it was an original contribution to economic analysis.

References

Casson, M. (1983) *Economics of Unemployment*, Oxford: Martin Robertson.
O'Brien, D.P. and Presley, J.R. (eds) (1981) *Pioneers of Modern Economics in Britain*, ch. 4, London: Macmillan.

Pigou effect (E2)

The effect on consumption of a change in the real value of cash balances brought about by a change in the money supply, e.g. an increase in the money supply which causes a rise in prices, a reduction in the purchasing power of cash balances which results in lower consumption. Diagrammatically, this effect can be shown as a shift in the IS curve. Also known as the 'real balance effect'.

See also: IS–LM curves

Pigovian subsidy (H2)

A SUBSIDY encouraging the production of goods and services which provide external benefits.

See also: externality; Pigou

Pigovian tax (H2)

A tax charging firms for the external costs which arise from their productive activities.

See also: externality; Pigou

Pink Book (F0)

UK BALANCE OF PAYMENTS accounts.

pink economy (L1)

The business sector with a range of goods and services for consumption by homosexuals often run by the same. These include bars, restaurants, hotels, clothes shops and bookshops. Since so many homosexuals have no dependants, they have high disposal incomes available for consumption in this sector.

See also: economy

Pippy (J1)

Person inheriting parents' property: usually a middle-aged person living in an area with high property prices. The increased wealth of the person helps maintain the price level.

See also: grey belt

pit committee (G1)

An exchange committee charged with the task of fixing the daily settlement prices of futures contracts.

Pittsburgh-plus (D4) *see* basing point pricing

placing (G1)

A method of selling shares by which a seller and buyer privately arrange the transaction, instead of trading on a stock exchange.

planning, programming, budgeting (H6, M2)

A budgetary system evaluating expenditure programmes in their entirety by taking into account the total effects of them, using COST-BENEFIT ANALYSIS. This system, introduced into the US Department of Defense in the early 1960s, was extended to other US Departments in 1965.

See also: cost-effectiveness analysis

References

Harberger, A.C. (1982) *Project Evaluation: Collected Papers*, London: Macmillan.

plastic money (E4)

CREDIT CARDS and DEBIT CARDS made with plastic and used instead of BANKNOTES, COINS and bank CHEQUES to pay for consumer goods and services.

Plato, 428/7–348/7 BC (B3)

Ancient Greek philosopher who was one of the first to discuss fundamental economic concepts, particularly in his *Republic* and *Laws* (Book V). He advocated a DIVISION OF LABOUR based on different natural abilities, discussed the role of money and advocated EXCHANGE CONTROLS and common property amongst the guardians of his ideal republic.

See also: Ancient Greeks; Aristotle

platykurtic (C1) *see* kurtosis

Plaza Agreement (F3)

The agreement of the GROUP OF FIVE meeting at the Plaza Hotel, New York, in September 1985 to intervene in exchange markets to bring down the value of the US dollar. $12 billion was spent by central banks in the first few weeks of the agreement. Within a year the US dollar was devalued by 22 per cent. However, the US trade deficit continued to be large.

Plaza Two (F3)

An agreement of the GROUP OF FIVE in Paris in February 1987 to support the US dollar by attempting to increase Japanese and West German imports and to stabilize leading currency rates at the same levels.

Plowden Committee (H5) *see* Public Expenditure Survey Committee

point elasticity (C1, D0)

The responsiveness of quantity demanded or supplied to an infinitely small price change. It is calculated, using differential calculus, as the product of two ratios. In the case of price elasticity of demand, it is given by

$$\text{point elasticity} = \frac{(\Delta Q_i | Q_i) \times 100}{\Delta P_i | P_i) \times 100}$$

$$= \frac{\Delta Q_i P_i}{Q_i \Delta P_i}$$

See also: arc elasticity; elasticity

point estimate (C1)

An estimate of a PARAMETER of a population which is given by one number.

See also: interval estimate

point-input, point-output model (E1)

An economic model based on the assumption that the output from a labour input takes one period to be produced.

poison pill (G3)

A way of resisting a company takeover consisting of making the equity capital less attractive to a predator.

See also: macaroni defense

Polanyi, Karl, 1886–1964 (B3)

Hungarian socialist who migrated from Budapest to Vienna in 1919 and then to England in 1933. He lectured for the Workers' Educational Association before moving in 1947 to Columbia University where he conducted seminars on comparative economic institutions and ECONOMIC ANTHROPOLOGY. He is noted for his analysis of exchange systems and examination of socialist planning. In his *The Great Transformation* (1944) he argued that under CAPITALISM, labour and land had been turned into commodities so that human society had become subordinated to the economic system.

polarization (G2)

The rule of the Securities and Investment Board (UK) that banks and building societies must choose either to give independent advice on all life and UNIT TRUST products available on the market or to sell the products of only one company. Although the aim of the rule is to give consumers independent advice, it has resulted in less advice being offered in retail outlets.

polarization effect (F0)

The cumulative and dynamic consequence to a country in an economic union of ECONOMIC INTEGRATION. This can result in growing or diminishing prosperity. The countries more attractive are those whose production centres grow at the expense of the others.

policy credibility (E6)

A characteristic of a policy conducted by rational agents who have used the correct economic model and all available information when forming their expectations.

See also: new classical economics

policy harmonization (E6, H2)

1 The alignment of the economic policies of one country with those of another. This form of economic integration can remove barriers to the movement of goods and services and factors of production. In the EUROPEAN COMMUNITY, there have been many attempts to do this, especially between countries belonging to the EUROPEAN MONETARY SYSTEM.

2 Taxation treaties between countries which establish the rules for the taxation of incomes of individuals who receive incomes from countries of which they are not residents.

policy lag (E6) *see* inside lag; outside lag

policy smoothing (E6)

Reducing the amplitude in swings in a policy from one limit to another often by using independent non-political boards of experts to formulate policy changes. Monetary policy is often conducted by an independent central bank.

See also: European Central Bank; Federal Reserve System; Monetary Policy Committee

policy variable (E0) *see* choice variable

political business cycle (E3)

Fluctuations in economic activity brought about by democratically elected governments seeking to win successive elections. It has been argued that political parties have a choice between unemployment and inflation so that in the period before an election they will stimulate a boom to reduce unemployment at the expense of price rises but after the election will deflate when returned to power. This discretionary use of fiscal policy destabilizes an economy. The theory appears to be more applicable to some ORGANIZATION FOR ECONOMIC CO-OPERATION AND DEVELOPMENT economies, e.g. the USA and Germany, than others. In 2001 in the UK large accumulated tax revenues were released to coincide with the General Election.

See also: Phillips curve

References

Lachler, U. (1982) 'On political business cycles with endogenous election dates', *Journal of Public Economics* 17: 111–17.

MacRae, C.D. (1977) 'A political model of the business cycle', *Journal of Political Economy* 85: 239–63.

Minford, P. and Peel, D. (1982) 'The political theory of the business cycle', *European Economic Review* 10: 253–70.

Nordhaus, W.D. (1975) 'The political business cycle', *Review of Economic Studies* 42: 169–90.

political economy (A1)

The term used for economics in the eighteenth and nineteenth centuries and revived in recent years to reflect a policy-oriented view of the subject. Liberal political economy was founded by Adam SMITH and was concerned then with the art of managing public finances and the advising of statesmen on revenue maximization. SCHUMPETER, in his *History of Economic Analysis*, defined it as 'an exposition of a comprehensive set of economic policies that its author advocates on the strength of certain unifying normative principles, such as the principles of economic liberalism [or] … Socialism'. ROBBINS asserted that political economy is concerned with policy prescriptions. Today, this applied view of economics rejects the world of PERFECT COMPETITION, criticizes the uncertainties of free enterprise and makes use of PUBLIC CHOICE theory.

See also: Post-Keynesians

References

Lange, O. (1963 and 1971) *Political Economy*, 2 vols, New York and Oxford: Pergamon.

poll tax (H2, H7)

A tax of a fixed monetary amount levied on every member of a population. In feudal societies, the amount depended on rank so the same amount per head would be charged within a certain class but a different amount from class to class. The regressive nature of many poll taxes has often led to them being criticized. In the USA, poll taxes have been used by state and local governments. Until the 24th Amendment of the US Constitution of 1964 outlawed it, the payment of a poll tax was required of voters in some southern states, thus excluding the poor, many of whom were black. In the UK, a 'COMMUNITY CHARGE' which has some of the characteristics of a poll tax was introduced in 1989–90 to replace 'rates', the local property tax.

pollution charge (H2, Q2)

1 An EFFLUENT FEE.
2 A USER CHARGE.

pollution control (Q2)

Measures to reduce emissions of noxious gases and other wastes into the air, rivers and sea. Legislation, e.g. the US Clean Air Acts of 1970, 1977 and 1990 and the 1972 Amendments to the Federal Water Pollution Control Act, together with private actions and the orders of regulatory agencies are used to curb polluting activity and fine or sue the perpetrators of it. Pollution control programmes vary in effectiveness: often the control of the first and major emissions has a higher return to anti-pollution expenditure than further marginal expenditures. Increasingly it has been noted that pollution control measures reduce economic growth and profits.

References

Baumol, W.J. and Oates, W. E. (1975) *The Theory of Environmental Policy*, Englewood Cliffs, NJ: Prentice Hall.

pollution tax (H2, Q2)

A tax on firms responsible for emissions that should be equal to the marginal value of the damage caused. The aim of such a tax is to induce firms to follow optimal production techniques.

See also: effluent fee

poop (G1)

A person with insider information capable

of affecting the value of a stock market security.

Poor Laws (I3, N4)

The succession of English statutes beginning with those of 1597 and 1601 which aimed to relieve poverty by providing welfare benefits or work within workhouses. This welfare programme was financed by levying a 'poor rate' on the landowners of each parish. The poor were confined to the parish of birth and separated into the able-bodied and 'impotent', i.e. infants, elderly persons, invalids and lunatics. Under an Act of 1722, the first 200 workhouses were erected for the aged and infirm; the able-bodied were given outdoor relief.

Growing rural poverty in the late eighteenth century prompted many economists of the day, including MALTHUS, to argue that the Poor Laws encouraged population growth and a magnification of the problem of poverty. SMITH was opposed to arrangements restricting GEOGRAPHICAL MOBILITY by keeping the poor in the parishes of birth. A Royal Commission, which included Nassau SENIOR, was set up to investigate the administration of the Poor Laws. In its report of 1834, it recommended that relief should be confined to the 'indigent', i.e. the able-bodied pauper, the aged and the sick, and available only within workhouses. Poor Laws, the Royal Commission argued, should not be available for the poor in general as that would include help to low-paid workers. Other proposals in the period of CLASSICAL ECONOMICS included BENTHAM's idea of profit-making industry houses into which the poor would be confined (*Pauper Management Improved*, 1798) and G. Poulett Scrope's insurance scheme financed by employers' contributions (*Principles of Political Economy*, 1832, ch. 12).

See also: poverty; subsistence

References

Boyer, G.R. (1990) *An Economic History of the English Poor Law*, Cambridge: Cambridge University Press.

Himmelfarb, G. (1984) *The Idea of Poverty: England in the Early Industrial Age*, New York: Alfred A. Knopf., London: Faber & Faber.

popular capitalism (P1)

An ECONOMY which allows a large proportion of the population to share in the profits arising from private ownership under CAPITALISM, usually through WIDER SHARE OWNERSHIP.

population (J1)

1 All of the finite number of items from which a statistical sample is taken.
2 The total number of residents of a country or area within it. World population is dominated by China's population that constitutes about a quarter of the total. The major determinants of population growth are the birth rate, the death rate and international MIGRATION.

See also: Malthus; statistics

population census (J1)

The counting of the number of persons within a country, or part of it, and the measurement of their characteristics. Most modern national censuses take place every five or ten years, the oldest continuous census being the USA's which started in 1790 (England and Wales has had a continuous census since 1801, apart from 1941). Earlier limited censuses were conducted in several countries, e.g. Iceland's in 1703, but these were only occasional. The United Nations has played a major role in standardizing the categories of information sought by enumerators and in encouraging the universality of national censuses, which was achieved by 1983. Common to most censuses are data on age, sex, place of birth, marital status, normal residence and occupation. Increasingly planners have used the population census as a means of obtaining a broad range of socioeconomic data. This has met with some resistance as people are sensitive about revealing many personal characteristics with the consequence that there can be under-enumeration as the average person may suspect that the purpose of a census is to provide a statistical basis for conscription or increased taxation.

See also: de facto population; de jure population; demographic accounting; demography

References

Benjamin, B. (1970) The Population Census, London: Heinemann.

Casley, D.J. and Lury, D.A. (1987) Data Collection in Developing Countries, 2nd edn, Oxford: Clarendon Press.

United Nations (1980) Principles and Recommendations for Population and Housing Censuses, New York: United Nations.

population density (J1)

The number of persons per unit of land area. This is a major determinant of property prices, of much public expenditure, of many social costs and of productivity. Population densities vary greatly from country to country. Some less developed countries appear to have low population densities because a high proportion of their land areas is uninhabitable mountains, deserts or swamps. PETTY and others have argued that higher population densities increase PRODUCTIVITY.

See also: growth pole

population explosion (J1)

The acceleration of the rate of population growth, especially after 1800 in industrialized countries, and in less developed countries in the twentieth century. A fall in the death rate as a consequence of the increased availability of public health measures and the slow spread of contraception in poorer countries have brought about this population growth. The major curb to growth is often, regrettably, famine.

See also: Malthus; neo-Malthusians

population policy (J1)

Co-ordinated government measures to achieve a desired size, structure and rate

of growth of population. Many population policies regard the birth rate as the key control variable as it is the major cause of rapid population growth or decline. If population growth is outstripping a country's economic development, as in China, birth control and rules on the maximum family size are introduced. If population decline is of concern to a country, e.g. because of a shortage of young men to maintain the size of a national army, fiscal inducements including lower taxes are offered to increase average family size. Whatever the rate of growth of population, there are often policies to change the geographical distribution of population in order to equalize population density between regions, e.g. the creation of NEW TOWNS in the UK.

See also: regional policy

References

United Nations (1982) World Population Trends and Policies: 1981 Monitoring Report, Vols 1 and II, New York: United Nations.

populist interest rate (E4)

A RATE OF INTEREST chosen by at least two governments.

pork barrel legislation (H5)

US federal legislation that grants federal money to projects non-essential in character and of benefit to small areas in the hope of maintaining voters' loyalty. As most of the taxpayers financing this expenditure do not benefit because of its connections with specific localities, it is usually only possible to pass such legislation by including it in wider bills of national appeal and by LOGROLLING.

portfolio balance (G0)

The distribution of a person's or a society's wealth among different assets according to the preferences of the portfolio holder. TOBIN has, following KEYNES'S GENERAL THEORY, used this approach to monetary theory. As yields vary from asset to asset, this approach has been used as an explanation of the structure of interest rates.

See also: term structure of interest rates

portfolio investment (G0)
Investment in securities.

See also: foreign direct investment

portfolio optimization (G1)
Seeking the best trade-off between RISK and reward. A technique used to strike this balance is the mean variance optimization approach to diversification.

portfolio selection (G0)
The choice of a mixture of financial assets to constitute the holdings of wealth of an individual or an institution. Available information, attitude towards risk and the income aims of the holder of the portfolio will all determine the selection. The resultant portfolio will often be a mixture of risky and safe assets.

References

Tobin, J. (1958) 'Liquidity preference as behaviour towards risk', *Review of Economic Studies* 25: 65–86.

portfolio trade (G0)
The sale of the whole portfolio of a fund or other financial institution. The firm bidding for it knows the quality of the components of the portfolio but not the details of which securities are included.

positional good (D0)
A GOOD whose access is determined by an individual's income relative to others'. Many goods are positional because they are fixed in amount, as is land available for leisure purposes. When an ECONOMY is growing, positional goods assume more importance. There is an increased demand for them but as their supply is fixed economic growth becomes of limited benefit.

See also: material good

References

Hirsh, F. (1977) *Social Limits to Growth*, London: Routledge & Kegan Paul.

position-risk capital (G2)
That capital of a securities house used to guard against sudden downturns in markets. The past price volatility of a particular type of SECURITY will determine how much position-risk capital is needed to insure against a fall in stock market prices.

positive discrimination (J7)
Granting the minorities of society enhanced access to education and jobs in an attempt to reduce overall discrimination against them. This approach to helping the disadvantaged is deeply resented by the well-qualified applicants who are rejected and by minority groups who believe they are being patronized.

See also: affirmative action; discrimination; reverse discrimination

positive economics (A1)
Empirical, scientific economics based on a quantitative analysis of economic data. Although contrasted with NORMATIVE ECONOMICS, the distinction is often blurred, particularly because of the controversial nature of much of economic data. Positive economics has been criticized for the positivist philosophy from which it derives its methodology.

See also: economic methodology

positive feedback (O4)
The favourable consequences of economic growth in generating further growth, e.g. because the first phase of growth includes the improvement of the infrastructure.

See also: negative feedback

POS machine (G2)
Point of service register in a shop communicating directly with the customer's bank.

See also: debit card

postcode lottery (H4, I1)
Rationing of goods and services, especially health care, in the UK according to the place of residence, described by a postcode.

post-contractual optimism (D0) *see* moral hazard

posted price (Q4)
The price at which an oil company is willing to sell its crude oil. This term reflects the practice of early oil producers posting on their rigs their selling prices.

See also: Gulf Plus

post-entry discrimination (J7)
Setting the pay or promotion prospects of employed persons lower than could be expected on the basis of productivity and job performance. Workers who are female, non-white or old often suffer in this way.

See also: pre-entry discrimination

post-industrial society (P0)
An economically advanced society with a declining manufacturing activity and expanding service sector. This inter-sectoral switch has coincided with the shrinking of the size of the working class, the growth of education and the growth of new industries based on INFORMATION TECHNOLOGY. With declining manufacturing activity, an economy becomes more decentralized as, increasingly, productive activities move from factories and offices back to the home, in some senses resembling the pattern of economic activity before the Industrial Revolution.

See also: de-industrialization; new economy

References
Bell, D. (1973) *The Coming of Post-Industrial Society*, Cambridge, MA: Harvard University Press.
Shelp, R.K. (1981) *Beyond Industrialization*, New York: Praeger.

post-Keynesians (B2)
Economists, including Sidney WEINTRAUB, Joan ROBINSON, Paul DAVIDSON, Al Eichner and Hyman MINSKY, who tried to synthesize RICARDO, MARX, KALECKI and KEYNES to incorporate a theory of income distribution into macroeconomics. This school believes that in goods, labour and money markets, demand determines supply, whatever the price level: this overthrows the entire classical theory of competition and price determination. The school has a stronger interest in macroeconomic relationships than in macroeconomic quantities, prefers to regard firms as using MARK-UP rather than market determination of prices, and in its monetary theory believes that money creates speculative excesses which destabilize the economy. Empirical realities are preferred to the notion of equilibrium. The principal policy recommendations of this school are INCOMES POLICIES, a new international monetary system and INDICATIVE PLANNING.

See also: political economy

References
Eichner, A.S. (ed.) (1979) *A Guide to Post-Keynesian Economics*, London and New York: Macmillan.
Kregel, J.A. (1972) *The Reconstruction of Political Economy: An Introduction to Post-Keynesian Economics*, London and Basingstoke: Macmillan.
Pheby, J. (1988) *New Directions in Post-Keynesian Economics*, Aldershot: Edward Elgar.

postmodern economics (A1)
An epistemological critique of modern economic theory that takes into account the community producing such knowledge. It attacks the use of a deterministic 'scientific' methodology economics and a GENERAL EQUILIBRIUM approach in favour of recognizing indeterminacy, uncertainty, the randomness and multiplicity of possible causes. In its analysis of LATE CAPITALISM it recognizes the fragmented nature of modern life and the many motivations inspiring economic conduct.

References
Cullenberg, S., Amariglio, J. and Ruccio, D.F. (2001) *Postmodernism, Economics and Knowledge*, London and New York: Routledge.

post-neoclassical endogenous growth theory (O4)
The hypothesis that ECONOMIC GROWTH depends on changes in technology and hu-

man capital previously regarded as exogenous in neoclassical theory. This theory has been used to explain long-term convergence in per capita incomes and outputs between countries. Also it has been applied to regional development.

References

Romer, Paul M. (1994) 'The origins of endogenous growth', *Journal of Economic Perspectives* 8: 3–22.

potential output (D2)

The maximum achievable output of an economy if all of its FACTORS OF PRODUCTION are fully employed. Actual output is often much less.

See also: full employment

References

Okun, A.M. (1983) 'Potential GNP: its measurement and significance', in J. Pechman (ed.) *Economics for Policymaking*, Cambridge, MA: MIT Press.

potential surprise function (E0)

SHACKLE'S view of EXPECTATIONS that the degree of surprise caused to us by the non-occurrence of a given outcome, assuming there has been no change in our relevant knowledge, is a function of the values of a continuous variable. The function is $y = y(x)$ where y is the degree of potential surprise and x is a continuous variable. Intensities of surprise lie between zero and the maximum intensity when what was believed impossible occurs. One of two hypotheses is more attractive if the potential surprise is nil and has a more desirable content than the other.

References

Shackle, G.L.S. (1949) *Expectations in Economics*, Cambridge: Cambridge University Press.

poverty (I3)

1 Low income per person.
2 The state of being below an arbitrary income level and regarded as poor by a particular society. When a society upgrades what it regards as minimal subsistence, it immediately statistically enlarges the poor sector of its population. In less developed countries, with large agricultural sectors, income and earnings figures are not always available so indirect measures, e.g. the rates of change of unemployment and food consumption, and the lack of technical progress are used as poverty indicators.

References

Schiller, B.R. (1989) *Economics of Poverty and Discrimination*, 5th edn, Englewood Cliffs, NJ: Prentice Hall.
Sen, A. (1981) *Poverty and Famines: An Essay on Entitlement and Deprivation*, New York: Oxford University Press.
—— (1983) *On Economic Inequality*, Oxford: Clarendon Press.
Townsend, P. (1979) *Poverty in the United Kingdom*, Harmondsworth: Penguin.
Zheng, B. (1997) 'Aggregate poverty measures', *Journal of Economic Surveys* 11:123–62.

poverty line (I3)

The level of INCOME just sufficient to provide minimum subsistence for an individual or family. The social security legislation of a country usually defines it for the purposes of paying out benefits. There is always much controversy over the appropriate minimum. Even SMITH and RICARDO were reluctant to define it in terms of physical survival alone.

See also: low pay; poverty; poverty trap

poverty trap (H2, I3)

1 Keeping low-income groups at the same level of disposable incomes because the rules of a country's tax and benefit system penalize the shift from welfare to employment incomes.
2 Having no incentive to move from being a welfare recipient to an employed person. These people pay high MARGINAL TAX RATES on their incomes because when they have an increase in income they both lose their cash welfare benefits and begin to pay income tax. The trap is calculated as the ratio of income tax + NATIONAL INSURANCE CONTRIBUTIONS +

cash benefits lost/an extra increment of income.

power law (C0)
A straight line on a logarithmic scale. This is the fingerprint of a critical system showing how small events effect great changes.

praxeology (D0)
A general theory of successful action showing what can be deduced from the self-evident axiom that human beings act purposively. MISES used praxeology as the basis for explaining markets.

Prebisch, Raúl D., 1901–86 (B3)
Argentinian economist, who virtually founded UNCTAD, being its first secretary-general from 1962 to 1969. He was a graduate and professor of political economy of the University of Buenos Aires. After employment in the Ministry of Finance, he was appointed the first director-general of the Latin American Institute for Economic and Social Planning in 1948, a recognition of his status as a leading authority on Latin American economic problems. On the restoration of democracy to Argentina in 1984, he became an adviser to the new president. His policy proposals have influenced thinking on a NEW INTERNATIONAL ECONOMIC ORDER.

Prebisch–Singer thesis (F1)
A thesis arguing that as the TERMS OF TRADE have moved against developing countries, protection and import substitution should be used to promote industrialization in such countries. This approach was advocated as a means of reducing income inequalities between nations.

References

Prebisch, R. (1950) *The Economic Development of Latin America and its Principal Problems*, New York: United Nations.
Singer, H.W. (1950) 'The distribution of gains between investing and borrowing countries', *American Economic Review* 40: 473–85.

precautionary demand for money (E4)
The CASH needed to meet unforeseen expenditures. The expansion of credit facilities has reduced this demand.

See also: speculative demand for money; transactions demand for money

predator–prey model (E3)
A biological explanation of trade CYCLES suggested by Goodwin. Initially there are few predators but many prey, but the abundance of prey causes predators to increase. This leads to a fall in the number of prey and then consequently of predators. With fewer predators prey flourish and the cycle starts up again. This cycle is analogous to MARX's model of the relationship between capital and labour, and between wages and profits.

References

Goodwin, R.M. (1967) 'A growth cycle', in C.H. Feinstein (ed.) *Socialism, Capitalism and Economic Growth*, Cambridge: Cambridge University Press.

predatory pricing (D4)
Reductions in the prices of products below cost, usually in OLIGOPOLISTIC industries, to drive rival firms out of business. The increased output that usually results, with consequential ECONOMIES OF SCALE, makes it even more difficult for new firms to enter. To stop this practice, the charging of prices below short-run marginal cost is declared illegal, as has happened in several US ANTITRUST cases, e.g. the Standard Oil case of 1911.

References

Areeda, P.E. and Turner, D.F. (1975) 'Predatory pricing and related practices under section 2 of the Sherman Act', *Harvard Law Review* 88: 697–733.
McGee, J.S. (1958) 'Predatory pricing: the Standard Oil (NJ) case', *Journal of Law and Economics* 1: 137–69.

pre-emption right (G0)
The right of existing shareholders, under company law and stock exchange listing

requirements, to subscribe for new shares in proportion to their existing holdings.

pre-entry discrimination (J7)

1 Discrimination in the educational system.
2 A refusal to hire because of the applicant's age, race or sex.

See also: closed shop; discrimination; post-entry discrimination

preference falsification (D0)

The expression in public of preferences different from private preferences.

References

Kuran, T. (1995) *Private Truths. Public Lies. The Social Consequences of Preference Falsification*, Cambridge, MA: Harvard University Press.

preference share (G0)

Fixed interest shares with first entitlement to a company's earnings after the payment of interest on DEBENTURES. Cumulative preference shares accumulate unpaid interest for payment at a later date.

preferential trading arrangement (F3)

An agreement between countries to lower or eliminate import tariffs among a group of countries to less than those charged to the rest of the world. It can take the form of a CUSTOMS UNION or COMMON MARKET.

preferred habitat theory (E4)

A theory of the TERM STRUCTURE OF INTEREST RATES which asserts that the structure is governed by the desire of traders to equalize expected returns, adjusted for risk premiums, taking into account that the trader will have a preference for a short- or long-term investment 'habitat'.

References

Modigliani, F. and Sutch, R. (1966) 'Innovations in interest rate policy', *American Economic Review* (Papers and Proceedings) 56: 178–97.

premium (D0, G0)

1 An additional amount of money paid above a standard product or factor price.

2 The extent to which a market price of a security is in excess of its offer price (if the share is newly issued) or in excess of its asset value.
3 In insurance markets, the periodic payment, usually monthly or annually, an insured person has to make to have a risk covered.

See also: grey market; new issue; organic premium; stag

premium pay (J3)

Additional pay for working outside normal hours (overtime) or in special circumstances, e.g. at night, or at a higher rate of PRODUCTIVITY.

Premium Savings Bond (E2)

A form of national savings introduced in the UK in 1956: there are monthly prizes of up to £1 million instead of the payment of interest to all bondholders. They are redeemable on demand.

present value (D0, E0)

The value now of future incomes or costs which is calculated by using the technique of DISCOUNTING. This is central to much investment appraisal, especially when COST-BENEFIT ANALYSIS is employed. Keynes gave this approach prominence by introducing the concept of the MARGINAL EFFICIENCY OF CAPITAL.

presumptive tax (H2)

A tax based on an estimate of a taxpayer's income.

See also: forfait system

price (D0)

The amount of money, or something of value, requested, or offered, to obtain one unit of a good or service. Relative prices are not expressed in terms of money but in other goods or other services. Prices have been described as SIGNALLING devices: a price increase will indicate an excess of demand over supply encouraging producers to invest in increased productive capacity and the converse for a price fall.

See also: value

price bunching (D4)

Synchronized price setting by firms in the same or related markets.

See also: price leadership; price staggering

price cap regulation (L5)

A method of limiting the price increases of public utilities, especially telecommunications, by a formula including an X factor. The formula could take the form of 'permitted price increase = consumer price rise − X'. Such regulation aims to encourage the utilities to be more efficient. In the UK the formula is known as RPI − X, the adjusted retail price index.

price ceiling (E3)

The maximum price set under a prices policy, or under specific legislation such as Rent Acts (UK), usually to help low-income households. As the price ceiling is characteristically below the equilibrium price, there will be excess demand and a need for rationing.

Price Commission (E3)

UK public body administering PRICES POLICY in 1973–80. It applied the rules of a price code which were enforced most rigorously against the largest companies, which had to gain approval in advance of price increases, whereas the smallest merely had to keep records available for inspection to show compliance with the code. The rules included a statement of which cost increases could be passed on into product price increases and safeguards to maintain profits so that investment would not suffer. Many aspects of the code were similar to the French price policies in force in the 1950s and 1960s. The Competition Act 1980 abolished the Price Commission.

price–consumption curve (D0)

The relationship between changes in relative prices and the consumption of two goods. INDIFFERENCE CURVES (I_1, I_2, I_3 and I_4) and BUDGET LINES are used to trace the path of consumption (the price–consump-

tion curve, PCC). From this curve can be derived a DEMAND CURVE DD. The demand curve plots quantity demanded against price, which is the amount of money a consumer will give up to obtain one unit of a good. Thus at a consumption level of 1, a point on the demand curve can be obtained by measuring the distance between PCC and the top line, parallel to the horizontal axis, which encloses it. When two units of good B are demanded, a point on the demand curve is obtained by measuring half the distance between PCC and the top line, and so on.

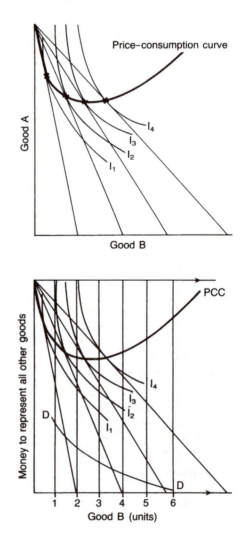

See also: income consumption curve

price controls (E3)
Governmental interference with the price mechanism to achieve prices which are not necessarily what a market would determine. These often take the form of either a PRICE CEILING or a PRICE FLOOR.

See also: prices policy

References
Galbraith, J.K. (1952) *A Theory of Price Control*, Cambridge, MA: Harvard University Press.
Rockoff, H. (1991) *Price Controls*, Aldershot: Edward Elgar.

price determination (D0)
The method used by a market or administrators to fix a price. Increasingly many economists have noted that some important prices are not determined in the market by demand and supply but by herd instinct, social contract, negotiation, domination, politics, power and speculation: major examples of non-market-determined prices are oil prices, the wage rate and the rate of interest.

See also: administered pricing

price discovery process (D4, G1)
The continual interaction between buyers and sellers to determine prices in a marketplace.

See also: Austrian School

price discrimination (D0)
1 The practice of charging different prices to different customers despite the cost of production being the same.
2 Setting different prices for different quantities of the same good.

Common ways of discriminating are according to consumers' incomes, e.g. charging students and retired workers less than others for entertainment, transport and professional services. This is possible because the ELASTICITY of the demand curve changes from point to point on most downward-sloping demand curves. For a monopolist, the incentive to discriminate arises from being able to increase profits through capturing some of the CONSUMER SURPLUS of the buyers. For the PROFIT-MAX-IMIZING monopolist, the pricing rule to follow is to set prices such that the MARGINAL REVENUE in each sub-market is equal to the marginal revenues in the others. It is essential for the monopolist to be able to prevent resale by customers in one sub-market to those in others.

See also: discriminating monopoly; first-degree price discrimination; second-degree price discrimination; third-degree price discrimination

price–earnings ratio (G1)
The ratio of the market buying price of a share to its earnings per share. The *Financial Times* calculates this net of corporation tax and unrelieved advance corporation tax. A ratio for a company higher than that of other companies in the same sector reflects the market's belief that its earnings are expected .to grow more rapidly, and conversely if this ratio is low. It is difficult to use this ratio to make international comparisons of the value of companies as earnings are measured differently from country to country, e.g. more conservatively in Germany and Japan for taxation reasons.

See also: cash–price–earnings ratio

price effect (D0)
The effect on quantity demanded of a change in price. As changes in prices affect the relative ability to purchase particular goods and services and consumers' real incomes, the price effect can be analysed into INCOME AND SUBSTITUTION EFFECTS.

price elasticity of demand (D0)
The responsiveness of quantity demanded to a change in price. It is measured crudely as the ratio of the percentage change in quantity demanded to the percentage change in price; more accurately as ARC or POINT ELASTICITY. This basic tool of microeconomic analysis owes its

precise formulation to MARSHALL, although the idea was present in the works of MUN and John Stuart MILL.

price flexibility (D0)

Complete freedom of prices to move up and down in response to changes in demand and supply. Only in unregulated markets is this possible.

See also: flexprice

price floor (L5)

A minimum price usually set by a governmental order. The major examples of these are MINIMUM WAGES and supported agricultural prices. The purpose of such intervention in markets is usually to maintain the income of certain groups, particularly of non-unionized workers or farmers.

price gap (D4)

A difference between two prices, especially between a current price and an equilibrium price.

price incentive (D0)

An inducement arising from goods and services having different prices. These incentives were regarded as crucial to generating ECONOMIC GROWTH by SMITH and his successors as they determine choices between work and leisure, between goods and labour, between present and future consumption (via the interest rate) and among goods.

price leadership (D4)

The pricing practice of many OLIGOPOLISTIC industries which consists of the largest firm publishing its price list ahead of its competitors who closely follow the prices already announced. This anti-competitive practice has often been used as a substitute for COLLUSION. Also known as parallel pricing.

price level (E0)

The average of the prices of all the goods and services sold in an economy. This key macroeconomic concept is used in many models of an economy, e.g. AGGREGATE DEMAND and AGGREGATE SUPPLY curves plot real income against the price level. Changes in the price level are measured by price indices, e.g. in the UK the RETAIL PRICE INDEX and in the USA the CONSUMER PRICE INDEX and GROSS DOMESTIC PRODUCT deflator.

price-maker (D4, G1)

1 A MONOPOLIST who can dictate the market price.
2 A member of a stock exchange who sets the initial prices for securities.

See also: seller's market

price–offer curve (D0)

Another name for the PRICE-CONSUMPTION CURVE.

price perception (D0)

Awareness of an actual price relative to other prices. When units of a currency are changed, e.g. through DECIMALIZATION or through many price changes in a period of general INFLATION, consumers are often unable to understand what price is being stated.

See also: money illusion

price rigidity (D0)

The characteristic of ADMINISTERED PRICES that are constant over longish periods of time. Many OLIGOPOLISTIC industries provide examples of this.

See also: fixprice

price risk (D0) *see* market risk

price-sensitive information (G0)

Unpublished knowledge about a company, especially its current profitability and any takeover offers it has received, which can affect its share price. Dealing in such information is a major form of INSIDER TRADING.

prices policy (E3)

An anti-inflation policy often used in conjunction with an INCOMES POLICY to set rules for the determination of product prices. There has been a variety of such policies in France: price freezes, target average prices with freedom to vary individual prices in a product group, price fixing according to a formula stating which costs can be passed on into product prices. In the UK, there were such policies in the 1960s and the 1970s under the NATIONAL BOARD FOR PRICES AND INCOMES and the PRICES COMMISSION, whose rules were partially inspired by the prices policy of the Nixon Administration in the USA. The main problems of such policies are that they can cause a shrinkage of profit margins and net investment, and reduce the responsiveness of price structures to changing market conditions.

price stabilization (L5)

A scheme to maintain product prices at a constant price level in order to stabilize producer incomes. This is a method extensively used for PRIMARY PRODUCTS. Under such schemes, a BUFFER STOCK is established to adjust supply to fluctuations in demand and a price is set which, it is hoped, will avoid excessive accumulation or decline in the stocks held. Attempts by KEYNES in 1942 to establish a global scheme were frustrated by governments opposed to state intervention in markets. Some schemes instituted by UNCTAD have survived only a few years.

References

Newbery, D.M.G. and Stiglitz, J.E. (1981) *The Theory of Commodity Price Stabilization: A Study in the Economics of Risk*, Oxford: Clarendon Press.

price staggering (D4)

Price setting which responds slowly to the other price decisions made in that market. An advantage of staggering is that a more carefully determined price is more sustainable.

See also: price bunching

References

Blanchard, O. (1987) 'Individual and aggregate price adjustment', *Brookings Papers on Economic Activity* 1: 57–109.

price system (D0, P1)

A method of allocating goods and services or factors of production by the free movement of prices. The characteristics of this system are its economy in the amount of information needed for decision making and its ability to bring about swift adjustments of supply to demand. Excess DEMAND automatically pushes up prices, giving a direct signal to producers to increase their labour forces and capital stocks. However, the price system is criticized on the grounds that it ignores many SOCIAL COSTS as these are rarely evaluated and charged to those responsible and can create income inequalities.

See also: central planning

price taking (L2)

A firm's acceptance of market prices as its own prices because it has no influence over market price determination. This occurs in markets in which each firm has only a small proportion of the total output or sales. Under PERFECT COMPETITION, all firms are price-takers.

price twist (L1, L5)

The raising of one type of price relative to another, e.g. of non-farm prices relative to farm prices.

See also: Operation Twist

price war (L1)

A ruthless campaign to drive rival firms from a market by repeatedly cutting prices. The only way an existing firm can escape the effects of such a conflict is to have some kind of price agreement with other firms, or to become the lowest cost firm.

See also: destructive competition

primary capital (G2)

The most secure form of BANK CAPITAL. According to current US and UK definitions, it includes COMMON STOCK or EQUITY, retained earnings and minority interests in subsidiaries and excludes INTANGIBLE WEALTH and investments in unconsolidated subsidiaries.

See also: secondary capital

primary care trust (I1)
A statutory National Health Service body in the UK responsible to a Health Authority. It provides a full range of medical and related services or can commission them. It can, for example, employ general practitioners or offer contracts to self-employed doctors.

primary commodity prices (Q0)
World market prices of agricultural produce and minerals. As several Third World countries are greatly dependent on one or a few primary products for a very high proportion of their export earnings, they attempt to use international agreements to maintain price levels or, at least, prevent secular declines in prices. The most powerful international agreement is cartelization of production. Price stability will be always threatened by climate changes and the consequential variation in harvests.

See also: commodity agreement; one-crop economy; primary product

primary dealer (G1)
A MARKET-MAKER in UK gilt-edged securities.

primary deficit (H6)
The excess of a government's expenditure (excluding interest payments) over its income. Sometimes called the 'actual deficit'.

primary employment (E0) *see* employment multiplier

primary labour market (J4)
That part of a national labour market consisting of large firms whose workers have good pay, job security and training.

See also: dual labour market; internal labour market; secondary labour market

primary market (G1)
A financial market concerned with new issues of a particular bond, stock or other financial asset. Many markets combine primary and secondary functions.

See also: secondary market

Primary Metropolitan Statistical Area (J1)
An individual component of a CONSOLIDATED METROPOLITAN STATISTICAL AREA.

primary mortgage market (G2)
The market for real estate and property loans. Banks, BUILDING SOCIETIES, THRIFTS and insurance companies offer these loans in return for a MORTGAGE.

See also: secondary mortgage market

primary offering (G1)
An issue of shares to the investing public other than the INITIAL PUBLIC OFFERING.

primary product (Q1)
An unprocessed agricultural product, particularly crops grown for food and textile manufacturing, as well as fossil fuels and metals. The production of primary products is the principal economic activity of many Third World countries – hence changes in primary product prices cause fluctuations in their national incomes. Changes in the TERMS OF TRADE have often been to the disadvantage of less developed economies.

See also: one-crop economy

primary ratio (M4)
The ratio of operating profit to capital employed.

primary standard (Q2)
The legal limit permitted for pollutants in the air: beyond this limit, there is a danger to human health.

See also: ambient standard; secondary standard

Prime-1 (G0)
The top rating of creditworthiness of COMMERCIAL PAPER made by Moody's Investors Service.

See also: AAA

prime age worker (J2)
In developed economies, a man or woman aged 25 to 55. This age classification is often used in studies of LABOUR FORCE PARTICIPATION as prime workers regard the la-

bour market differently from other age groups with the consequence that their participation rates are higher than those of younger or older workers.

prime bank (G2)
A large bank with a high volume of deposits operating in the major money centres.

prime bank scam (G2)
An investment scheme by a financial institution giving itself the exalted title of 'prime bank' in order to attract funds from unsophisticated, often older, investors, who are tempted by promises of rates of return of over 100 per cent.

prime cost (D0)
The direct cost of running a business, particularly labour, energy and raw material costs; VARIABLE COSTS. A term used by MARSHALL.

See also: supplementary cost

prime rate of interest (E4)
The rate of interest that US commercial banks charge small and medium-sized firms for borrowing. Historically, this was the interest rate the most creditworthy customers of banks were charged but with the development of the COMMERCIAL PAPER market, the largest customers borrow below the prime rate.

See also: base rate

primitive economy (N0)
A pre-agricultural society. It obtains its food through hunting animals and the gathering of berries and other wild crops. Human needs are few and little work is required to obtain a simple subsistence livelihood. As there is no scarcity, economic problems do not arise. Adam SMITH called this economy the 'rude society' and stated, with an example of the trading of deer for beavers, that VALUE in this society would be determined by relative labour quantities.

principal (G0)
A capital sum lent at a fixed rate of interest.

principal–agent (D0)
A contractual relationship much discussed in economics as it is at the heart of so many transactions. The principal increases RISK by delegating to another person the performance of an economic transaction. The advent of limited liability divorced the shareholder owners from the manager agents. Principals can be more effective through agents but have to design an incentive scheme to make their agents follow their preferences.

principalship (G0)
Part of a bond or mortgage entitling the owner to receive payment of the amount originally lent.

prisoners' dilemma (C7)
The most famous of economic games. Two prisoners have a choice between confessing or not confessing to a crime. If both

Prisoners' dilemma

Tom \ John	Not confess	Confess
Not confess	2 years / 2 years	20 years / 1 year
Confess	1 year / 20 years	10 years / 10 years

confess, they are sentenced to ten years; if both do not, they are sentenced to two years for being present at the scene of the crime; if one confesses and the other does not, the former will get a one-year sentence and the other twenty years. The matrix of alternatives is used to illustrate the principle that the pursuit of individual self-interest does not lead to a socially optimal result.

See also: game theory

private cost (D0)
The cost to an individual person, or a firm, of the resource(s) used, measured at market prices. In many cases, private cost approximates to the OPPORTUNITY COST of employing such inputs.

See also: social cost

private cost of unemployment (J6)
Loss of employment income and unquantifiable personal stress.

See also: social cost of unemployment

private enterprise (L2)
1 The principal type of industrial or commercial firm in a capitalist or mixed economy.
2 The private sector of an economy.

Under private enterprise, the capital is owned principally by individual persons or non-governmental organizations and its major decisions, particularly on investment, the scale of production and prices, are chosen by the firm itself, with government providing a framework for the activity of the enterprise rather than participating in the firm's decision making. Increasingly, even in SOVIET-TYPE ECONOMIES, private enterprises operated alongside state-owned and state-run firms. In the late 1980s, increasingly in Eastern Europe and other communist countries private enterprise re-emerged: for example, from 1987, in the USSR, simple service industries, including taxi driving, could be run as private concerns.

See also: public enterprise

private enterprise system (P1)
A decentralized CAPITALIST economy which permits private ownership of business, much freedom of decision making and the absence of most government direction except the regulation of MONOPOLY and PUBLIC UTILITIES and corporate taxation.

See also: economic devolution

Private Finance Initiative (H3)
A method of financing public sector projects introduced by the UK government in 1992. It sought to separate the ownership of public sector facilities from the provision of services. Hospital buildings, roads, train networks and computer systems have been financed in this way. A private consortium does the building and then lets it back on a long lease to a public body such as a hospital trust. Although this can be an expensive way to finance public sector projects, it does reduce Treasury borrowing.

private good (D0)
A good which when consumed by one person cannot be consumed by another and whose supply can be restricted to one consumer. These properties of being 'rival' and 'exclusive' separate goods such as food from PUBLIC GOODS.

See also: club good

private marginal benefit (D0) *see* marginal utility

private placement (G0)
A direct method by which a firm can issue its shares by using the services of a financial institution to sell large blocks of the issue to institutional investors (pension funds, banks, insurance companies, etc.). The growth of EQUITY investment by these institutions since 1945 has made large private placements possible.

See also: institutional investor; underwriter

private rate of discount (D0) *see* discount rate

private sector (P1)

That part of the economy consisting of firms owned by legal persons other than the state. In a MARKET ECONOMY the private sector encompasses most economic activity

private sector liquidity (UK) (E4)

This broad measure of the money supply was much used in the 1980s and took two forms:

PSL1 =   private component of sterling M3 excluding deposits of over two years' original maturity
+ private sector holdings of money market instruments
+ certificates of tax deposit

PSL2 =   PSL1
+ more liquid building society shares and deposits and other similar forms of liquid savings instruments
+ SAYE deposits
+ bank deposits with an original term longer than two years

See also: M5

privatization (L5)

The sale of publicly owned assets, especially industrial capital, to private investors. Many countries in the 1980s undertook this kind of reduction of the public sector to achieve a variety of aims: to improve industry by freeing it from bureaucratic state control, to augment public revenue, to widen share ownership, and to increase competition to benefit consumers. One example is the sale of several UK NATIONALIZED INDUSTRIES to the public, notably gas, steel, oil, water, electricity, telecommunications, the state airline, and airports. Examples in other countries include France's sale of St Gobain, Paribas and Suez, Japan's sale of its railways and Hungary's sale of state firms to companies and individuals. Privatization has also taken the form of

the sale of state and local authority housing.

In practice, the programme has not met all of its aims. Competition has not increased as much as was hoped because state monopolies in many cases have become private monopolies, instead of being split into competing companies. Also, some of the assets were sold at less than their market value thus reducing the amount of public revenue received from their sale.

See also: economic devolution

References

Gayle, D.J. and Goodrich, J.N. (eds) (1991) *Privatisation and Deregulation in Global Perspective*, London: Pinter.

Swann, D. (1988) *The Retreat of the State: Deregulation and Privatisation in the UK and USA*, Brighton: Harvester Wheatsheaf.

Thompson, D., Kay, I. A. and Mayer, C. (eds) (1986) *Privatisation: The UK Experience*, Oxford: Clarendon Press.

probability (C1)

The likelihood of an event occurring which is calculated as the total number of actual occurrences divided by the total number of possible occurrences. The value of a probability lies between 0 and 1.

probable error (C1)

A quantity equal to 0.6745 STANDARD DEVIATIONS of the estimate of a population PARAMETER.

probit model (C5)

Similar to the LOGIT model but producing a different estimate of parameters. Grouped data are used to estimate the rate of change of a probability. Also known as the normit model.

See also: Tobit model

producer price index (E3)

US price index of commodities calculated by the Bureau of Labor Statistics; published since 1890. It uses sellers' prices by direct sale, or through an organized market, of the first considerable large-volume commercial transactions of each commodity. It is based on over 10,000 commodity price series.

See also: consumer price index

producer's surplus (D2)
The gain to a producer arising from selling some of its goods and services at more than the market price.

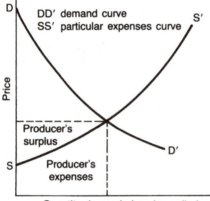

DD' demand curve
SS' particular expenses curve

Price

Producer's surplus

Producer's expenses

S

Quantity demanded and supplied

See also: consumer's surplus

References

Marshall, A. (1920) *Principles of Economics*, 8th edn, appendix H, London: Macmillan; New York: St Martin's Press.

producer subsidy equivalent (Q1)
A method of agricultural support devised by the OECD to convert different types of farm aid into this single measure which is calculated as the ratio of the cash value of government support to the value of agricultural produce.

product compatibility (L1)
Tying a product to another in order to reduce competition, e.g. through producing computer software usable only on a particular type of personal computer.

See also: tying contract

product differentiation (L1, M3)
A change in the appearance or presentation of a product to entice consumers to believe that it is different from similar products. This differentiation is undertaken to give the producer to some extent the power of a monopolist with a unique product. The concept is at the heart of the theory of MONOPOLISTIC COMPETITION but in practice occurs most frequently in OLIGOPOLISTIC industries.

production asymmetry (P4)
A characteristic of a DUAL ECONOMY resulting from the traditional agricultural sector using a different combination of factors of production from the modern industrialized sector.

production function (E1)
The statistical relationship between output and the factor inputs needed to produce it which reflects the technology of a process of production. The most famous of these functions are the COBB–DOUGLAS and CES functions.

See also: microproduction function

References

Heathfield, D.F. (1971) Production Functions, London: Macmillan.

production possibility frontier (D0)
A curve showing the maximum possible combinations of two goods that can be

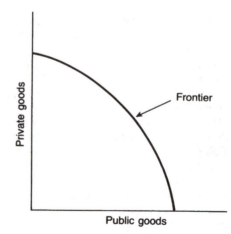

Private goods

Frontier

Public goods

efficiently produced given a nation's resources. Each point on this curve shows
the TRADE-OFF between the output of the
two goods, or the OPPORTUNITY COST of
producing more of one good.

production quota (D2)
The limit to the permitted output of a
particular product.

productive capital (H4)
That portion of SOCIAL CAPITAL invested in
those sectors of the economy in which
SURPLUS VALUE is created.

productive labour (J0)
A classification of labour first introduced
by SMITH and later to be prominent in
MARXIAN ECONOMICS. Smith regarded labour
as productive if it added value to the raw
materials used, provided maintenance for
the labourer and profits for the employer
and produced a vendible commodity; MARX
regarded this type of labour as that which
produces SURPLUS VALUE. The distinction
between productive and unproductive labour has influenced the measurement of
NATIONAL INCOME.

productive potential (O4)
The maximum growth rate of a country
extrapolated from past trends. It is measured by considering both the growth rates
of the supply of factors of production
(labour and capital) and the PRODUCTIVITY
of those factors.

See also: natural rate of growth; potential
output

productivity (O4)
The amount of real output produced by
one unit of a factor input. Labour and
capital productivities have been extensively
studied to understand the process of
economic growth and the international
trade performance of individual countries.
US studies show that productivity is
higher in more CAPITAL-INTENSIVE industries,
which are also unionized and where the
cost of turnover and supervision is lower
and there is more industrial harmony.

Labour productivity is measured as output
per person, assuming that the quantities of
other factors employed are constant (a
difficult assumption in the case of capital).
In general, labour productivity can be
regarded as a function of investment and
the business cycle, as well as the degree of
supervision of the workforce and of salary
differentials and incentives.

References

Barrell, R., Mason, G. and O'Mahony, M.
(eds) (2000) *Productivity, innovation and
economic performance*, Cambridge, New
York and Melbourne: Cambridge University Press.
Davies, S.W. and Caves, R.E. (1987) *Britain's Productivity Gap – A Study Based
on British and American Industries,
1968–77*, Cambridge: Cambridge University Press.
Denison, E.E. (1967) *Why Growth Rates
Differ*, Washington, DC: Brookings Institution.
Kravis, I.B. (1976) 'A survey of international comparisons of productivity',
Economic Journal 86 (March): 1–44.

productivity bargaining (J3)
1 Wage bargaining which rewards workers
for consenting to new working arrangements so that output can be increased.
It was very popular in the UK in the
1960s under an INCOMES POLICY which
allowed supernorm increases if there
was a genuine increase in productivity.
Many difficulties arose, including the
difficulty of separating labour from
capital productivity, the resentment that
workers who had long held back productivity growth by their RESTRICTIVE
PRACTICES were disproportionately rewarded and the difficulty of applying
the principle to some sectors of the
labour market, particularly the service
industries. There was much less productivity bargaining in the USA in that
period. Passing on productivity gains in
higher wages, rather than in lower
prices and higher output, it is argued,
threatens the long-term employment
prospects of workers.

2 COLLECTIVE BARGAINING that uses productivity measures as a major determinant of increases in pay.

References

McKersic, R.B. and Hunter, L.C. (1973) *Pay, Productivity and Collective Bargaining*, London: Macmillan.

productivity shock (J6)
A change in unemployment brought about by a labour-saving innovation or a general fluctuation in PRODUCTIVITY levels.

product life cycle (D2)
The life cycle of a product from when it is an innovation, often protected by PATENTS and hence earning monopoly profits for its producer, through the stage when it is competing with substitutes to its final stage of maturity when its profitability is for the most part due to the ECONOMICS OF SCALE arising from a large output. This has been used to explain trade patterns and the behaviour of MULTINATIONAL CORPORATIONS.

References

Vernon, R. (1971) *Sovereignty at Bay*, ch. 2, Harmondsworth: Penguin.

product market (D0, M3)
A set of relationships between buyers and sellers to retail goods or services.

product moment formula (C1)
For a LINEAR CORRELATION coefficient, this measure of the symmetry between X, the independent variable, and Y, the dependent variable, is calculated as the ratio of the sum of the products of the values of X and Y divided by the square root of the product of the sum of the squares of X values and the sum of the squares of Y values.

profession (J2)
An occupation requiring a considerable period of education and training. The original professions were in medicine, the law, the church, the army and the universities. In the nineteenth century many occupations acquired the status of a profession by the founding of institutes to arrange examinations, certify competence and regulate behaviour. After 1900 in many countries the expansion of universities increased the supply of entrants to professions and eroded their pay differential with other occupations reducing the private rate of return to HUMAN CAPITAL. Also professional pay has lagged behind other salaries as much professional employment is in the public sector.

professional trader (G1) *see* specialist

profit (D3)
A surplus of revenue over cost. Economists, unlike accountants, include in total costs imputed OPPORTUNITY COST. Until the ENTREPRENEUR was recognized as a factor of production, there was little debate about why profits were paid: reasons subsequently suggested by CLASSICAL ECONOMISTS and later economists include that it is either a payment for supervising and co-ordinating land, labour and capital or a recompense for risk taking.

References

Knight, F.H. (1921) *Risk, Uncertainty and Profits*, Boston and New York: Houghton Mifflin.

profitability (M2)
The rate of return to capital achieved by a firm. It is a function of managerial ability, resources available, the state of markets and the behaviour of trade unions (which can have a negative effect on the price/cost margin and on return to capital employed). Business analysts argue that 'profitability' is a vague concept as the data on profits are entirely dependent on accounting conventions and the nature of revenue/taxation law.

profit and loss account (M4)
A financial statement of the revenue and expenditure of a firm and its consequential profit or loss. Unlike a balance sheet, it refers to a period of time, not a state of affairs at a point in time.

profit centre (M4)
A part of a firm or other organization

with separate accounts so that costs and revenues can be attributed to it and its contribution to the total profits of that organization calculated. In MULTINATIONAL CORPORATIONS, this form of decentralized accounting is essential to maintain efficiency.

profit maximization (L2)

A possible goal for a firm implemented by setting prices so that MARGINAL REVENUE equals MARGINAL COST. When, at the margin, revenue is greater than cost, total profits could be increased by further output; when costs are greater than revenue, total profits decline. In the diagram the total profits curve is plotted by calculating the vertical distances between the total costs and total revenue curves. Up to output OM total profits are increasing as marginal revenue is greater than marginal cost; after output OM marginal cost is greater than marginal revenue and so total profits decline. At OM, where total profits are at a maximum, marginal revenue is equal to marginal cost. Traditionally regarded as the central aim of the capitalist firm.

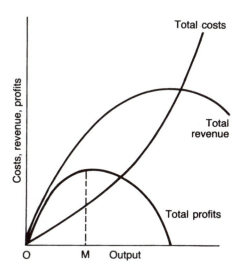

See also: managerial models of the firm

profit motive (D0, P1)

The desire for personal gain which is the reason for a person engaging in an economic activity. This is regarded as the basic force driving CAPITALISM.

See also: altruism; economic man; non-profit enterprise

profit-related pay (J3)

Employee remuneration consisting of, or based on, PROFITS as well as wages and salaries. This form of pay has the advantages of fluctuating with profits, so that a firm's wage bill falls in bad times and rises only in times of prosperity, and possibly influencing worker behaviour as the divide between ownership and employment is bridged by giving employees two types of factor income. There are long-established examples of this approach, e.g. granting Scottish fishermen shares of the proceeds from each catch of fish, and profit distributions to Japanese workers. With fiscal encouragement and a managerial desire to reward increased performance without raising labour costs, there are likely to be more pay schemes related to profits. One disadvantage of this type of pay is that employees may resist further recruitment of staff as more employees will reduce per capita entitlements to profit.

profit squeeze (D3, E0)

A steady reduction in profits caused by the costs of labour or other factor inputs rising at a faster rate than product prices. This can occur at the level of the firm, the industry or the national ECONOMY. Squeezes often occur when prices are more severely controlled than wages, as in the UK in 1974–9.

See also: prices policy

profit taking (G0)

A sale of shares that have risen in price. This practice, often by short-term speculators, can cause temporary downturns in stock market price indexes. Taking profits can also be done to avoid capital gains taxation.

programme deal (G1)

Block portfolio switching by which a fund

manager of an investment bank or stock-broking firm exchanges a bundle of unwanted securities for a portfolio with different characteristics. This popular US practice has spread to the London stock market. In most cases, the deals are based on the mid-price of the stocks on a particular day; the expected marketability of the stocks will determine the cost of the transaction.

program trading (US) (G1)
Wall Street, New York, method of computer trading conducted by watching the relationship between the trend and fluctuations of stock market prices. In favour of this system it is claimed that INSTITUTIONAL INVESTORS benefit as they can tolerate large short-term losses but few individuals are rich enough to participate in this type of trading. However, the system can cause a high volume of sell orders to occur simultaneously bringing about massive declines in stock prices as took place in October 1987. As a result of the BRADY COMMISSION, the program trading of the NEW YORK STOCK EXCHANGE is prohibited whenever stocks fall by more than 50 points in any one trading day. A similar method is used in the UK.

See also: circuit breaker mechanism

progressive tax (H2)
A tax whose rate rises as income or expenditure rises. The principal examples of these are taxes on personal and corporate incomes. Some INDIRECT TAXES, e.g. VALUE-ADDED TAX, are progressive if they exempt goods which constitute a higher proportion of the budget of lower income groups so that the tax falls more on higher income groups.

Progressive taxes aim to achieve a more equal distribution of income post-tax than pre-tax: this goal is central to the economic philosophies of some countries, particularly those with SOCIAL MARKET ECONOMIES (e.g. Sweden). However, critics of tax progression are concerned about the impact of such tax structures on the supply of labour and the encouragement of a BRAIN DRAIN. Much of present-day TAX REFORM severely challenges the progressive principle, despite its long ancestry. In the USA, for example, the Tax Reform Act 1981 reduced tax progression but the TAX REFORM ACT 1986 increased it again. Rousseau argued that the wealthy, because of having more property, need more protection from the state so should pay more tax. SMITH in his *Wealth of Nations* argued that tax contributions should be in proportion to ability to pay but did not indicate whether there should be an absolute or equal sacrifice. John Stuart MILL rejected the idea that taxation should be based on benefits received from the state as that would make taxation regressive. Vito di Marco justified progression in terms of the MARGINAL UTILITY of income being lower for a rich man than for a poor man, as BENTHAM had before him.

See also: benefit tax; canons of taxation; fiscal mobility; income tax; regressive tax

References
Boes, D. and Felderer, B. (1989) *The Political Economy of Progressive Taxation*, Berlin: Springer Verlag.

prohibitive tariff (F3)
A TARIFF sufficiently high to exclude all imports.

project appraisal (E2)
The calculation of the total effects of an investment project on an economy, using both market prices and SHADOW PRICES.

See also: cost–benefit analysis

References
Hansen, J.R. (1978) *Guide to Practical Project Appraisal: Social Benefit-Cost Analysis in Developing Countries*, Vienna: UNIDO.
Little, I.M.D. and Mirrlees, J.A. (1974) *Project Appraisal and Planning for Developing Countries*, London: Heinemann Educational.

proletariat (J0)
The underprivileged class of society that

has to sell its labour because it does not own the means of production. Marx regarded this class as exploited because SURPLUS VALUE from its output was appropriated by capitalists. He predicted that by social revolution the proletariat would achieve the economic justice the BOURGEOISIE denied it.

promissory note (G0)

A signed promise in a document to pay a sum of money on demand or at a future specified date. These notes are often negotiable.

propensity to consume (E2)

Either AVERAGE or MARGINAL PROPENSITY TO CONSUME.

propensity to save (E2)

Either AVERAGE or MARGINAL PROPENSITY TO SAVE.

property rights (P0)

1 The exclusive rights to use, transform and transfer particular assets, goods and services.
2 A privilege, power or immunity.

An analysis of property rights has enabled economists to develop a more realistic THEORY OF THE FIRM, rejecting the basic assumption of PROFIT MAXIMIZATION, taking into account TRANSACTIONS COSTS and recognizing diverse patterns of property ownership. The behaviour of individuals, motivated by self-interest, within organizations is central to this new approach to microeconomics.

See also: Coase

References

Carter, A. (1989) *The Philosophical Foundations of Property Rights*, New York and London: Harvester Wheatsheaf.
De Soto, H. (2000) *The mystery of capital: why capitalism triumphs in the West and fails everywhere else*, New York: Basic Books.
Furubotn, E.G. and Pejovich, S. (1972) 'Property rights and economic theory: a survey of recent literature', *Journal of Economic Literature* 10: 1137–62.

property tax (H2)

A tax based on the value of property. The revenue from this tax is often the major source of local government finance.

See also: rates; Tiebout hypothesis

property tax capitalization (H2, R2)

An effect on house values of a property tax. Full capitalization occurs when differences in house prices are equal to the present value of variations in expected tax liabilities, after taking into account housing characteristics such as structure, neighbourhood and public services.

References

Oates, W.E. (1969) 'The effects of property taxes and local public spending on property values: an empirical study of tax capitalization and the Tiebout hypothesis', *Journal of Political Economy* 77: 457–71.

proportional accounting (G2)

A term in insurance for checking the total insurance cover to ascertain what percentage of claims and premiums are assigned to a particular insurance company.

proportional tax (H2)

A tax which is fixed as a proportion of a tax base, e.g. income or expenditure generally or on a particular good or service. Although the revenue from the tax grows as the tax base expands, the marginal rate of tax continues to be equal to the average rate of tax. The US PAYROLL TAX is a proportional tax up to the ceiling on the tax.

See also: flat rate tax; progressive tax; regressive tax

proportionate grant (H2) *see* grant in aid

Proposition 13 (H2)

A proposition made binding on the State of California (USA) in 1978 to reduce the amount of taxation on residential property. It was believed that residential property owners were paying an unfair amount of taxation compared with business. The proposition reduced the assessed values of property and limited future increases of those assessments to 2 per cent per annum and rate increases to 1 per cent per annum.

proprietors' income (E0, M2)
The net income of individual proprietorships and partnerships; an item in US NATIONAL INCOME accounts which separates income of these types of firms on the grounds of their non-incorporation.

prospect theory (D8)
An account of decision making under uncertainty. It states that the value of an alternative or option is the sum of the products of specified outcomes. Each product is calculated by multiplying the utility from x by the weight attached to the objective probability of obtaining x.

See also: expected utility

References

Kahneman, D. and Tversky, A. (1979) 'Prospect theory. An analysis of decision-making under risk', *Econometrica* XX: 263–91.

prospectus (G1)
The document published by a company inviting the public to subscribe to a new issue of shares. It details the financial history, current trading, future prospects and multifarious activities of the company. A shrewd assessment of a prospectus enables an investor to judge whether the shares when marketed will sell at a PREMIUM.

See also: grey market; stag

prosperity indicators (D6)
1 Changes in real income or wealth.
2 Increased consumption of superior goods and services.

More specific measures of these include the level of consumption of CONSUMER DURABLE goods, migration rates to suburbia, a rate of increase in enrolments in higher education greater than the rate of increase of real income and disproportionate increases in outlays for medical care.

protean economy (P0)
1 A changing ECONOMY which is moving from one pattern of economic activities and production methods to another.
2 An economy in which ENTREPRENEURS are constantly transforming inputs, outputs, their relationships with each other and the nature of industries.

protection (F1)
Barriers to the international flow of goods and services. The protectionist measures available include TARIFFS, import quotas and trade regulations (e.g. concerning quality). Because protection is a departure from FREE TRADE, after the MERCANTILISTS advocated it, it was attacked by economists for its effect on the allocation of goods and services, but temporary protection has been conceded by many economists to be useful as a means of encouraging INFANT INDUSTRIES.

An analysis of the effects of protection on a national economy includes the changes in domestic production and consumption patterns and switches between foreign and domestic markets, with the consequence that employment increases at the cost to consumers of having to spend more to purchase higher priced domestically produced goods. Developing countries with small export industries and thus fewer ECONOMIES OF SCALE, sometimes have lower GROSS NATIONAL PRODUCTS as a consequence of protection.

It is measured by either the gross or net rate of protection, the latter taking into account both exports and imports. The cost of increasing employment through increasing domestic production can be measured as the 'cost per job', which is the increase in the amount of consumer expenditure to obtain the same amount of goods divided by the increased number of jobs in protected industries.

Although in times of recession, protectionist policies are popular, most lead to a reduction in world income. Despite many nations adhering to liberal trade policies, a variety of covert practices and agreements are used to protect domestic industries.

See also: effective rate of protection; Multi-Fibre Arrangement; non-tariff barrier; Smoot–Hawley Tariff Act; tariff; voluntary export restraint

References

Belassa, B. and associates (1971) *The Structure of Protection in Developing Countries*, Baltimore, MD: Johns Hopkins University Press.
Corden, W.M. (1971) *The Theory of Protection*, Oxford: Clarendon Press.
Kierzkowski, H. (ed.) (1987) *Protection and Competition in International Trade: Essays in Honor of W.M. Corden*, Oxford: Basil Blackwell.
Shutt, H. (1985) *The Myth of Free Trade: Patterns of Protectionism since 1945*, Oxford: Basil Blackwell.

protective labour legislation (J5)
Laws attempting to ensure that a worker does not suffer financially, physically or mentally from injury or unemployment.

See also: Social Charter

proto-industrialization (N6)
Domestic manufacture controlled by intermediaries who use manufacturers as homeworkers, taking away their independence as sole proprietors.

See also: homework

References

Mendels, F.E. (1972) 'Proto-industrialization: the first phase of the industrialization process', *Journal of Economic History* 32: 241–61.

proto-proletariat (I3)
The very poor who scrape a living in the informal TERTIARY SECTOR. In a sense, they live like refugees.

See also: low pay; poverty

Provisional Collection of Taxes Act (H2)
UK statute permitting changes in INDIRECT TAXES to be made before that year's Finance Act has been passed. This Act

reduces IMPLEMENTATION LAGS in UK fiscal policy.

proxy (G0)
An agent of an absent voter empowered to cast his/her vote, e.g. a person attending a company meeting who votes on behalf of an absent shareholder.

pseudo production function (E1)
Joan ROBINSON's term for a PRODUCTION FUNCTION based on imaginary equilibrium positions which ignores the idea of production as a long-term accumulation process.

P-star model (E3)
A model based on the QUANTITY THEORY OF MONEY and the belief that a price level tends to its equilibrium level. It is used to forecast inflation by calculating the gap between the current price and the equilibrium price (P-star, P^*). This equilibrium price is determined by potential output, the quantity of money in the ECONOMY and the equilibrium VELOCITY OF MONEY. If the equilibrium price is more than the current price, there is the possibility of inflation.

psychic income (D3)
The subjective pleasures flowing to an individual person in a specified period. This can be the consequence of the receipt of money or of non-pecuniary rewards to employment (e.g. job satisfaction). BENTHAM and later JEVONS and BöHM-BAWERK were to base much of economic theory on subjective sensations and experiences.

See also: utility

psychological economy (P1)
A capitalist ECONOMY that produces and administers the needs demanded by the system. This major view of the German-born US philosopher and social theorist Herbert Marcuse (1898–1979) influenced New Left writers in the 1960s.

See also: capitalism; needs standard; radical economics

References

Marcuse, H. (1964) *One Dimensional Man*, London: Sphere.

psychology (D0) *see* economics and psychology

public choice theory (E6)
Explanation of policy making in the public sector by analysis of the nature of policy selection. There are two approaches: the spatial analysis of political parties and their response to vote pressures (Downs) and the institutional approach (Brennan and BUCHANAN) which predicts the consequences of voters' choices in a specific institutional context. It is a form of applied WELFARE ECONOMICS with libertarian assumptions.

References

Brennan, G. and Buchanan, J.M. (1980) *The Power to Tax*, Cambridge: Cambridge University Press.
Downs, A. (1957) *An Economic Theory of Democracy*, New York: Harper.
McLean, I. (1987) *Public Choice*, Oxford: Basil Blackwell.
Mueller, D.C. (1989) *Public Choice II*, Cambridge: Cambridge University Press.

public commodities problem (H4)
Deciding how much of a public commodity to have when it is not clear whether the commodity is a GOOD at all in the sense of conferring a net benefit on a society.

See also: public good

public debt (H6)
The total volume of government BONDS, BILLS and other SECURITIES outstanding at a particular date. A large public debt accumulates by public borrowing over a number of years, especially to finance wars, infrastructure investments and welfare programmes. The burden of this debt can be measured as the ratio of the cost of servicing it to that country's GROSS DOMESTIC PRODUCT. The OECD provides information on government debt interest payments as a percentage of gross domestic product. The ratio rises when inflation and growth are low and real rates of interest are high and positive. OECD figures record currently high ratios for Greece and Italy and a lower ratio for the UK.

See also: debt service indicators; maturity; overlapping generations model; Third World debt problem

public economics (H0)
A study of the economic decisions of government – taxation, public expenditure, PUBLIC GOODS and public sector pricing.

See also: public finance

References

Atkinson, A.B. and Stiglitz, L.E. (1980) *Lectures on Public Economics*, Maidenhead, London and New York: McGraw-Hill.

public enterprise (L3)
An independent business organization owned by a government and subject to some political control. The name for these enterprises varies between countries, e.g. in the UK they are called NATIONALIZED INDUSTRIES or PUBLIC CORPORATIONS. The motives for taking firms into the public sector include the desire to achieve a better allocation of goods and services than the market can produce, to alter the distribution of income, to aid macroeconomic policy by having direct control over basic industries, to exploit for the country as a whole the benefits of NATURAL MONOPOLY and to advance socialism. In order to encourage public enterprises to be efficient, various goals are set for them, the most common being the requirement to achieve a minimum rate of return to capital employed and to price according to the MARGINAL COST of producing their goods and services.

See also: private enterprise

References

Borcherding, T.E., Pommerehne, W.W and Schneider, F. (1982) 'Comparing the efficiency of private and public production: the evidence from five countries', *Zeitschrift für Nationalökonomie* 42: 127–56.
Bos, D. (1986) *Public Enterprise Economics:*

Theory and Application, Amsterdam: North-Holland.

Rees, R. (1984) *Public Enterprise*, 2nd edn, London: Weidenfeld & Nicolson.

Rosenau, P.V. (ed.) (2000) *Public-private partnerships*, Cambridge, MA, and London: MIT Press.

public expenditure (H5)

The expenditure of central, regional and local governmental organizations on intermediate and final goods and services. This is undertaken to achieve a variety of goals including the redistribution of benefits in kind, the provision of PUBLIC GOODS, the correction of disequilibria in markets and the regulation of industry. In several countries, the increasing ratio of public expenditure to the national income has excited political debate. The ratio has, of course, increased when a collectivist ideology has influenced policy-makers or special interest groups have succeeded in obtaining public subsidization. But in many types of national economy the increase can be attributed to an expanding or ageing population, to public sector output being relatively more costly than production in the private sector, or to a greater use of bureaucratic methods.

public expenditure control (H5)

A variety of administrative controls to keep the total of public expenditure within a certain limit, or to keep its rate of growth within a predetermined percentage of its present level. Before KEYNES, the principal mechanisms for ensuring that public expenditure did not get out of hand were the GOLD STANDARD and the practice of balancing budgets. Since 1945, more direct methods have been employed in the periods when FISCAL POLICY was used to reduce aggregate demand which had increased through the accumulation of large government deficits. In Great Britain in 1790, the total expenditure of the public authorities was about 12 per cent of GROSS NATIONAL PRODUCT and reached a peak of 60 per cent in 1975–6 and started rising again in the 1980s. The volume of public expenditure is determined by many factors: the growth in per capita income (which increases the demand for both private and public goods), technical change (the advent of the motor car led to a demand for more and better roads), population growth and change (more schools, hospitals and senior citizens' facilities), the relative cost of PUBLIC GOODS and urbanization (the cause of congestion which requires an improved infrastructure to remedy it). As modern electorates expect governments to respond to all these changes, controlling public expenditure can be very difficult.

See also: cash limit; Medium-term Financial Strategy

References

Buchanan, J.M. and Wagner, R. (1977) *Democracy in Deficit: The Political Legacy of Lord Keynes*, New York and London: Academic Press.

Public Expenditure Survey Committee (H5)

The UK committee of officials from the Treasury and spending departments charged with the task of updating public expenditure programmes. It was created as a result of the Plowden Committee's 1961 report that recommended annual and five-year plans of public expenditure and the resources to finance it. This medium-term method of control included figures for spending according to the functions of government.

References

Lord Plowden (1961) *The Control of Public Expenditure*, London: HMSO, Cmnd 1432.

public finance (H0)

The study of the taxing and spending decisions of governments. Taxation is used instead of charging for government services or borrowing. Public expenditure is incurred because governments attempt to improve the distribution of income, to maintain FULL EMPLOYMENT and to produce goods and services which the market would not produce (or not produce at low enough prices). At the macro level, public finance examines the effectiveness of governmental attempts to achieve a tax-spending mix intended to achieve simultaneously desired levels of employment, inflation and balance of payments surplus (deficit); at the micro level, it examines the effects of public expenditure and taxation on allocation and economic behaviour (e.g. labour supply and saving). Although public finance has commanded the attention of writers as early as XENOPHON, HOBBES, PETTY and SMITH, the subject has now expanded into a broad analysis of the public sector.

See also: debt policy

References

Atkinson, A.B. and Stiglitz, J.E. (1980) *Lectures on Public Economics*, Maidenhead, London and New York: McGraw-Hill.

Cullis, J. and Jones, P. (1998) *Public finance and public choice*, 2nd edn, Oxford and New York: Oxford University Press.

Musgrave, R.A. (1959) *The Theory of Public Finance: A Study in Public Economy*, New York: McGraw-Hill.

—— (1969) *Fiscal Systems*, New Haven, CT: Yale University Press.

public good (H4)

A commodity or service which is available to everyone in a particular catchment area, cannot be withheld from non-payers and is 'non-rival', i.e. one person's consumption does not diminish that of others. The main examples are national defence, sewerage, street lighting, lighthouses, public health measures such as mass vaccination, and scientific research. As individuals cannot be charged according to consumption for goods and services collectively provided, it is usual to finance their production by taxation. Although the provision of public goods was small until the twentieth century, writers as early as PETTY, SMITH and John Stuart MILL argued for their existence. It is not always easy to distinguish between a public and a private good as some private goods gratuitously benefit third parties, e.g. maintaining a garden in a beautiful condition confers pleasure on many people in the vicinity.

See also: club good; local public good; mixed good; private good

public interest company (L3)

A proposed type of UK PUBLIC ENTERPRISE (e.g. telecommunications or gas) substantially owned by private shareholders who have no ultimate control as their shares are without voting rights. The public interest is chiefly represented by regulatory bodies, e.g. Oftel, which have the task of monitoring and controlling pricing, investment and standard of service. This form of public enterprise was proposed in the UK by the Labour Party in 1988 as a vehicle for reconverting privatized firms into public sector undertakings, without the expense of renationalization.

See also: nationalized industry

public interest theory (D6, K2)

An analysis of the net economic welfare resulting from REGULATION or DEREGULATION often employing the notions of CONSUMER SURPLUS and PRODUCER SURPLUS.

public pricing (L3)

The pricing of the goods and services produced by PUBLIC ENTERPRISES, or the governmental regulation of private sector pricing. Such government intervention is undertaken to prevent the MONOPOLY exploitation of consumers, to stabilize COBWEB markets (especially in agriculture), to provide MERIT GOODS, to prevent MERIT BADS and to achieve a better distribution of incomes and benefits. The methods used include the setting of formulae to determine the prices of public enterprises and REGULATED PUBLIC UTILITIES, the setting of maximum prices (e.g. rent controls), the provision of free services (e.g. libraries and museums) and the establishment of financial rules (e.g. the interest rates and reserve requirements to be followed by banks).

See also: prices policy

public sector (H1, L3)

All organizations at central and lower levels of government possibly together with firms subject to majority ownership by state or municipal bodies. The measurement of the size of the public sector is debatable. One method is to add up the number of activities undertaken by governmental organizations; another is to calculate the total volume of its output. Measuring output is a difficult and crude task in the case of non-marketed outputs, e.g. defence. For such it is usual to calculate output by measuring the sum of the value of inputs used: this, by ignoring factor PRODUCTIVITY, makes the bold assertion that an input increase leads to an output increase. Analysts of public policy increasingly demand more direct measures of output; for example, in the case of health services, output can be measured directly using the number of patients treated rather than indirectly using the number of staff employed.

public sector balance sheet (H0)

This consists of a range of ASSETS (social overhead capital (non-marketable) + equity in public enterprises (partially marketable) + land and mineral assets + net foreign exchange reserves + present value of future tax programme + imputed net value of the government's cash monopoly) and balancing LIABILITIES (net interest-bearing debts in domestic and foreign currencies + stock of high-powered money + present value of social insurance and other entitlements + public sector net worth).

public sector borrowing requirement (H6)

The excess of expenditure over receipts of central and local government. In more detail, it can be regarded as finance provided to the public sector by borrowing to provide for current and capital expenditure and for lending to the private sector and overseas. The public sector borrowing requirement (PSBR) is reduced by either cuts in public expenditure plans or more stringent controls of existing spending programmes. The concept only became important to UK economic policy making in the 1970s, a period when the PSBR relatively increased: in 1975 it was 19 per cent of total government expenditure and 10 per cent of gross domestic product. Despite the central importance given to the PSBR by many Treasury ministers, it is difficult to achieve a target for it as there can be many changes in the components constituting both revenue and expenditure. UK government saving in the 1980s caused the concept to be replaced by PUBLIC SECTOR DEBT REPAYMENT.

References

Peacock, A.T. and Shaw, G.K. (1981) *The Public Sector Borrowing Requirement*, Buckingham: University College at Buckingham.

public sector debt repayment (H6)

UK budget surplus; a negative PUBLIC SECTOR BORROWING REQUIREMENT. A term coined by Chancellor of the Exchequer Nigel Lawson in his UK budget speech in March 1988.

public service employment (J2)

Jobs provided by national, state, regional or local governments to reduce the amount of unemployment. Some are of short duration, a temporary expedient to cope with a recession or to reintroduce to work long-term unemployed persons whose skills have diminished or become obsolete. But the increased role of the state in many countries has expanded the number of publicly financed jobs.

See also: public works; workfare

public spending ratio (H5)

Total governmental expenditure as a proportion of the GROSS DOMESTIC PRODUCT.

See also: public sector

public utility (L2, L3)

An industry or enterprise providing basic services to the public, such as energy, water, postal services or telephones, which is sometimes owned by the state but even if privately owned (as is often the case in the USA) is usually subject to public REGULATION. It is argued that because these industries are NATURAL MONOPOLIES (at least in a local area), a special policy towards them is essential if the public is not to be exploited. Regulatory bodies pay great attention to the prices charged, safety standards and the quality of service of these utilities.

See also: regulatory capture

public works (E6, J2)
Schemes financed by central or local government to create employment. Although such recommendations have long been associated with KEYNES, they have a longer history: the MERCANTILISTS were in favour of them and the French government set up national workshops as early as 1848.

See also: crowding out; Treasury view

pump priming (E6) *see* deficit financing

purchase tax (H2)
A tax levied on a particular sale, often at different rates for different types of goods and services. Persons with a preference for the higher taxed goods suffer discrimination. In the UK, it was replaced by the VALUE-ADDED TAX in 1973.

See also: expenditure tax

purchasing power parity (F3)
An equilibrium exchange rate such that two currencies purchase the same amount of goods and services in the two economies. This theory, first suggested by the MERCANTILISTS, then eloquently expressed by CASSEL in 1916, asserts that monetary flows would affect domestic prices until parity is achieved. This approach has been criticized for being unrealistic: many goods and services do not enter into international trade and there are many non-market determinants of exchange rates. However, PPP is a more useful way of comparing international living standards

than market exchange rates which are more volatile.

References

Kravis, I.B., Heston, A. and Summers, R. (1978) *A System of International Comparisons of Gross Product and Purchasing Power*, Baltimore, MD: Johns Hopkins University Press.

pure bundling (M3)
The sale of goods or services only as part of a joint package deal.

See also: bundling; mixed bundling

pure competition (L1)
PERFECT COMPETITION without the assumptions of perfect knowledge and an absence of friction.

pure credit economy (P1)
An economy that finances all of its transactions with bank loans. An idea attributed to Wicksell.

References

Wicksell, K. (1935) *Lectures on Political Economy*, Vol. 2, trans. E. Classen, London: Routledge & Kegan Paul.

pure discretion (E6)
The conduct of an economic policy without following any policy rule.

See also: rules versus discretion

pure economic rent (D3)
The permanent return to a factor of production in excess of its TRANSFER EARNINGS. This arises from the unique nature of that factor which causes its supply to be INELASTIC. Examples of such factors include land, works of art exhibited at a charge to the public and exceptionally talented persons.

pure inflation (E3)
An extreme case of INFLATION such that the prices of all products and FACTORS OF PRODUCTION are increasing at the same rate.

pure interest rate (E4)
The RATE OF INTEREST on a riskless investment.

pure monopoly (L1)
A MONOPOLY with a demand for its products equal to the whole of consumer expenditure.

pure profit (D3)
Profit earned from the sale of a good or service after the full OPPORTUNITY COST of employing all FACTORS OF PRODUCTION, including NORMAL PROFIT for the ENTREPRENEUR, is subtracted from sales revenue.

pure public good (H4)
A good or service which is both non-excludable and non-exhaustible.

put option (G1)
A right to sell a financial instrument or commodity at the current price within a specified period, normally of three months.

See also: call option

put price (G1)
The price at which a PUT OPTION is sold. Also known as an exercise price and strike price.

put-through (G1)
The simultaneous purchase and sale of a block of SECURITIES. This is a cheaper method of dealing for INSTITUTIONAL INVESTORS as there is a smaller margin between buying and selling prices and a lower rate of broker's commission: the broker is prepared to carry out the transaction on more favourable terms because the risk of unsold stock is eliminated. Sometimes it is called a 'block trade'.

putty-clay (E2)
According to CAPITAL THEORY, a technology that in the short run allows little substitution between capital and labour. The consequence is that changes in capacity and in employment and output are closely linked.

putty-putty (E2)
The complementary character of inputs in an economic model. Capital is subject to adjustment costs in its slow response to prices.

pyramiding (G3, L1)
Acquiring many small companies to build them into a large HOLDING COMPANY.

pyramid selling (M3)
The sale by companies of goods and services to individuals who then act as retailers, often in their own homes. Goods such as cosmetics and kitchen utensils have been sold in this way. This marketing method, which first appeared in the USA in the late 1940s and in the UK in the 1960s, has often been criticized because of the pressure applied by firms to persuade their agents to buy the goods themselves and to recruit others. Also known as multilevel marketing.

Q

Q ratio (M2)
See TOBIN'S Q.

quadriad (H1)
The Treasury, the COUNCIL OF ECONOMIC ADVISERS, the OFFICE OF MANAGEMENT AND BUDGET and the FEDERAL RESERVE: the key formulators of the USA's economic policy.

quality-adjusted life years (I1)
A year of life adjusted by expected health or illness. A year of healthy life expectancy = 1, of unhealthy life expectancy < 1. Health care is beneficial if it generates positive QALYs; efficient health care activity occurs where cost per QALY is as low as possible. As low cost per QALY health care is prioritized, this approach to allocating health resources is criticized for its bias against the old and very sick.

See also: health economics

References

Harris, J. (1987) 'Qualifying the value of life', *Journal of Medical Ethics* 13: 117–23.

quality circle (J5)
An alternative approach to INDUSTRIAL RELATIONS, enabling workers to participate more in the management of their enterprises.

quantitative restrictions (F1, F3)
QUOTAS, especially on imports and foreign exchange, imposed to reduce a BALANCE OF PAYMENTS deficit.

See also: protection; tariff

quantity theory of money (E4)
A macroeconomic theory relating the stock of money to the price level. Although discussions of this theory are evident in MERCANTILIST writings (especially in LOCKE), it is to Irving FISHER, PIGOU and Milton FRIEDMAN one looks for twentieth-century expositions. The Fisher or Yale equation is

$$MV = P\text{y}T$$

where T is the total volume of transactions, V is the weighted average velocity of circulation, P_Y is an index representing the weighted average of prices of the commodities transacted and M is the total quantity of money.

The Cambridge equation, attributed to MARSHALL and PIGOU, is

$$M = kP\text{c}R$$

where M is the total quantity of money, R is the total resources enjoyed by the community, k is the proportion of those resources which the public desires to hold in the form of money and P_C is an index number which values resources in terms of consumption goods.

FRIEDMAN revived interest in the theory by expounding it as a theory of demand for real balances.

See also: monetarism

References

Fisher, I. (1911) *The Purchasing Power of Money*, New York: Macmillan.

Keynes, J.M. (1923) *A Tract on Monetary Reform*, London: Macmillan.

Laidler, D. (1991) *The Golden Age of the Quantity Theory. The Development of Neoclassical Monetary Economics 1870– 1914*, Oxford: Philip Alan.

Locke, J. (1823) *Some Considerations of the Lowering of Interest and Raising the Value of Money. Collected Works*, Vol. V, London (originally published in 1691).

quartile deviation (C1) *see* semi-interquartile range

quasi-autonomous non-governmental organization (L3)
A UK non-elected agency set up by a government department to act as a task force or to undertake activities contracted out by government. These 'quangos' have been criticized for having their members appointed under ministerial patronage and usurping many of the functions of local government. By 2000 there were hundreds of these.

quasi-fixed factor (J3)
A factor of production, especially labour, whose price has almost become a fixed cost to firms. Statutory protection of employment and changes in employment contracts have made it more difficult to vary the amount of labour employed in the short run.

References

Oi, W.Y. (1962) 'Labor as a quasi-fixed factor', *Journal of Political Economy* 70: 538–55.

quasi-market (L3)
An attempt in the public sector to introduce market discipline. In the UK in the 1980s this principle was applied to the contracting out of catering and cleaning and through the INTERNAL MARKET in the National Health Service, and in the universities where they had to bid for funds from funding councils. This market is different from a conventional market in that consumers effect their purchases using vouchers or by agents. Also non-profit-making public organizations compete with traditional profit-making firms.

References

Le Grand, J. (1991) 'Quasi-markets and social policy', *Economic Journal* 101: 1256–67.

quasi-rent (D3)
MARSHALL described this as the income an owner receives from allowing others to use machines and other productive appliances made by man. This return is in excess of the OPPORTUNITY COST of using that piece of FIXED CAPITAL. Marshall proposed the concept as part of his explanation of profits.

Quebec Declaration (F1)
The accord of thirty-four American countries, apart from Cuba, agreed in 2001 to create a FREE TRADE AREA OF THE AMERICAS by 2005.

Quesnay, François, 1694–1774 (B3)
French physician-cum-economist who founded the PHYSIOCRATIC school of economics, the first French school of economics. His position as a court physician to Louis XV made him an influential person, but it was not until his sixties that he wrote on economics. He did so in *Encyclopédie* articles on 'Fermiers' (1756) and 'Grains' (1757) and in subsequent articles on 'Hommes' and 'Impot'. But his *Tableau Economique* (first edition 1758), showing the CIRCULAR FLOW between landlords, farmers and manufacturers, anticipated IN-PUT–OUTPUT ANALYSIS and was to be much admired by Adam SMITH and MARX. Quesnay made economics a major talking point of the day: the salons were fascinated by 'les zigzags', their nickname for the *Tableau*.

References

Barna, T. (1975) 'Quesnay's Tableau in modern guise', *Economic Journal* 85: 485–96.

Meek, R.L. (1962) *The Economics of Physiocracy*, London: Allen & Unwin.

Vaggi, G. (1987) *The Economics of François Quesnay*, London and Basingstoke: Macmillan.

queuing system (D0, P4)

A method of resource allocation which distributes resources on the principle of 'first come, first served'. It is used to avoid congestion in many European bond markets and is an alternative to control by a central monetary authority. Potential issuers of bonds are placed in the queue according to their financial need, their current creditworthiness and current monetary policy. Countries with this system include Germany and France. In general, queuing can be used as a method of allocation in any market.

See also: price system

quick assets ratio (M4)

Liquid assets divided by current liabilities; also known as the 'ACID TEST RATIO'. It should be at least 1.

quit rate (J6)

The proportion of workers leaving their jobs in a particular time period. This rate is used as a measure of labour turnover.

See also: exit–voice

quota (D2, F1)

A restricted supply of a good or service. Import quotas are used to protect domestic industries; export quotas, to stabilize export earnings. Under any system of rationing, a quota will be the amount allocated to a particular person or organization.

See also: non-tariff barrier; protection; tariff; voluntary export restraint

quoted company (K2) *see* listed company

R

racial discrimination (J7)

Treating persons of another race un-equally, especially with regard to wages and employment opportunities.

See also: discrimination

Radcliffe Report (E5, G2)

A Royal Commission report, published in 1959, on the working of the UK monetary system. It promulgated the view that money is only one ASSET in the spectrum of LIQUIDITY and that, as its VELOCITY OF CIRCULATION is unstable, the control of it is incidental to interest rate policy. Although opposed to the control of the money supply, given the sophistication of the post-war UK financial system, from day to day it recommended that interest rates should be used rather than credit controls as instruments of MONETARY POLICY: this was difficult to achieve given the need for stable interest rates to maintain an orderly gilts market. It also suggested changes in monetary statistics.

References

Committee on the Working of the Mone-tary System (1959) *Report*, London: HMSO, Cmnd 827.

radical economics (A1)

An application of Marxist and socialist theories to the analysis of the problems of advanced CAPITALIST countries. The major concerns of radical economists are income inequality, international capitalism in the form of MULTINATIONAL CORPORATIONS, DE-IN-DUSTRIALIZATION, UNEMPLOYMENT, MARKET FAILURE, defence expenditure and the low provision of many PUBLIC GOODS. The hu-mane concerns of these writers have influ-enced a great deal of policy making but have yet to form the basis of a new society and economy in any major country.

References

Linder, M. (1977) *The Anti-Samuelson*, Vols I and II, New York: Urizen Books.
Sawyer, M. (1989) *The Challenge of Poli-tical Economy: Radical Alternatives to Neo-Classical Economics*, Hemel Hemp-stead: Harvester Wheatsheaf.

Rambouillet Summit (F3)

Economic summit held in France in 1975 at which it was agreed that CENTRAL BANKS would co-ordinate their policies to stabi-lize currencies. This was the first interna-tional monetary agreement after the collapse of the BRETTON WOODS system.

Ramsey prices (D0)

PARETO-optimal prices which achieve a required level of profits. These prices maximize the sum of an industry's prices and its PRODUCER'S SURPLUS. The pricing rule Ramsey asserted was that, for a regulated firm (e.g. a PUBLIC UTILITY such as electri-city), the excess of price over MARGINAL COST will be highest for those goods which have low ELASTICITIES of demand. This is second-best pricing when first best is not available. It was adopted as a pricing rule by the INTERSTATE COMMERCE COMMISSION in 1985.

References

Baumol, W.J. and Bradford, D.F. (1970) 'Optimal departures from marginal cost pricing', *American Economic Review* 60: 265–83.

Ramsey saving rule (E2)

The rate of saving multiplied by the MARGINAL UTILITY of money should always be equal to the amount by which the total net rate of enjoyment of utility falls short of the maximum possible rate of enjoyment.

References

Ramsey, F.P. (1928) 'A mathematical theory of saving', *Economic Journal* 38: 543–59.

Ramsey taxes (H2)

Taxes which raise a given revenue from proportionate taxes on commodities with the decrease in utility being kept to a minimum. Ramsey suggested that the solution to this problem posed by PIGOU was to increase tax revenue in the same proportion as the production of the taxed commodities.

References

Ramsey, F.P. (1927) 'A contribution to the theory of taxation', *Economic Journal* 37: 47–61.

Randall Commission (N7)

US commission which reported on foreign economic policy in 1954. It took the view that the policy of the USA should be to guide the world economy back to the liberal policies holding before 1914 – if not in trade, certainly in the movement of private long-term capital and in the convertibility of currencies. The main type of aid proposed by the commission was technical assistance.

random variations (C1)

Irregular movements in time series calculated by dividing the original data by the TREND, seasonal variations and CYCLICAL VARIATIONS.

random walk theory (G1)

A theory concerning successive prices independent of each other in SECURITY or commodity markets which asserts that there are no trends in prices with the consequence that today's prices cannot be used to predict future prices. Bachelier was the first to note this, in 1900, in a study of French commodity markets.

See also: chartism

References

Cootner, P.H. (ed.) (1964) *The Random Character of Stock Market Prices*, Cambridge, MA: MIT Press.

Randstad (R1)

A continuous urban area of the Netherlands from Amsterdam to Rotterdam. For centuries, it has been noted for its high population density.

range (C1)

The difference between the largest and smallest numbers in a set, e.g. 5 is the range of 2, 3, 4, 5, 6, 7.

See also: semi-interquartile range

rank correlation (C1)

The correlation between variables represented by the ranks they have in an ordered list, e.g. the relationship between cities ranked by population size and by average per capita income to see if the larger a city ranks, the greater the average income per capita.

See also: Spearman's rank correlation formula

rank-order tournament (C7)

An economic game in which the participants compete according to what is judged their rank.

rank size rule (J1, R1)

This states that the population of a city or town in an urban hierarchy of a country is approximately the population of the largest city divided by the rank of the place concerned. For example, if the largest city has a population of 2 million, then the fourth-largest city will have 500,000 inhabitants.

References

Madden, C.A. (1956) 'On some indicators of stability in the growth of cities in the United States', *Economic Development and Cultural Change* 4: 236–52.

ratchet effect (E2)

An upward shift in aggregate demand. This higher level of consumption and investment is permanent, preventing an economy in recession from reverting to a level of output lower than at the beginning of the previous expansion. The RELATIVE INCOME HYPOTHESIS asserts that when incomes are failing, consumption will not fall by the same amount as it will be difficult for households to make a swift adjustment to a new standard of living.

rate of exploitation (D3) *see* surplus value

rate of interest (E4)

1 The charge for borrowing money, usually measured as the percentage ratio between the sum payable to the lender and the amount borrowed, at an annual rate.
2 The bridge between income and capital.
3 The amount of money contractually promised at certain specified future dates as a proportion of the principal borrowed.
4 The rate of capitalization.

Theories of the rate of interest have explained this factor price as being determined by either real forces (productivity and thrift) or monetary forces (the demand for and supply of money). KEYNES took the latter approach, as did some writers as early as the MERCANTILISTS. The Judaic, Islamic and Christian religions have often condemned interest charges for exploiting persons who borrow out of necessity. However, interest has been justified on the grounds that, as the lender has to abstain from current consumption to

make the loan, he or she should be compensated.

See also: Islamic banking; loanable funds theory; Senior; usury

rate of return (G0, M2)

The ratio of the earnings from an asset to the value of that asset, usually expressed as a percentage. Companies calculate this as the ratio of pre-tax profit to the capital employed. Private and social rates of return of HUMAN CAPITAL and of major public investments are often calculated. An alternative measure is the INTERNAL RATE OF RETURN which takes into account the timing of earnings.

rate of return regulation (L3, L5)

Regulation of a PUBLIC UTILITY by insisting that product prices should be set to obtain a desired rate of return to capital employed.

rates (H7)

A tax on non-agricultural property long used in the UK to finance local government expenditure. Periodically, property was revalued on the basis of the expected rental income from property of that type to calculate its rateable value. Each local authority decided, knowing the total rateable value of all properties in its area, what rate in the pound must be levied to obtain a desired level of revenue. Each property owner paid an amount equal to the rateable value of the property times the rate in the pound. As such local taxation has long been condemned for being full of anomalies, many proposals for reforming it have been made. In 1989 in Scotland and in 1990 in England and Wales, the domestic rate was replaced by the COMMUNITY CHARGE (nicknamed 'the poll tax'); in 1990, the UNIFORM BUSINESS RATE replaced business rates.

References

Foster, C.D., Jackman, R.A. and Perlman, M. (1980) *Local Government Finance in a Unitary State*, London: Allen & Unwin.
Layfield Committee (1976) *Local Govern-*

ment Finance. Report on the Committee of Inquiry, London: HMSO, Cmnd 6453.

rate support grant (H7)
An expenditure subsidy previously paid by the UK government to local authorities which resulted in less having to be raised by rates (local property tax). This grant on average was equal to about one-half of total local government expenditure. Central government, in order to ensure that minimum standards of services, e.g. in education, are maintained, has to provide this subsidy. After the domestic rates were replaced by the COMMUNITY CHARGE, the rate support grant was replaced by a REVENUE SUPPORT GRANT.

rating agency (G2) *see* bond rating agency

ratio analysis (M4)
Percentages calculated in financial analysis to discover solvency, OVERTRADING and PROFITABILITY. Financial ratios, using balance sheet data, include quick, current, stock and capital (or earnings) ratios; operating ratios include TURNOVER (or sales) ratios and cost ratios. The most important measure of overall profitability is the ratio of profit before tax to operating assets.

rational decision (D0)
A choice that best serves a decision-maker in pursuit of a particular objective.

rational expectations (E0)
A view of how individuals form their EXPECTATIONS of the future values of economic variables first advanced by Muth in 1961 and now a central pillar of NEW CLASSICAL ECONOMICS. Individuals, when making decisions, it is assumed, have all relevant information, including knowledge of the structure of the economic system, and any errors in the analysis of that information are attributable to random forces. This approach has been used to analyse asset markets, the business cycle and the NATURAL RATE OF UNEMPLOYMENT.

There have been many criticisms of rational expectations, including questions about the assumption of rationality, the recurrence of economic processes and the adequacy of information.

References
Attfield, C.L.F., Demery, D. and Duck, N.W (1985) *Rational Expectations in Macroeconomics*, Oxford: Basil Blackwell.
Begg, D.K.H. (1982) *The Rational Expectations Revolution in Macroeconomics: Theories and Evidence*, Oxford: Philip Alan.
Muth, J.F. (1961) 'Rational expectations and the theory of price movements', *Econometrica* 29: 315–35.
Pesaran, M.H. (1987) *The Limits to Rational Expectations*, Oxford: Basil Blackwell.
Sheffrin, S.M. (1996) *Rational expectations*, 2nd edn, Cambridge, New York and Melbourne: Cambridge University Press.

rationing (D0)
A method of allocating a limited supply. The person or organization in control of the supply of a factor of production, good or service distributes it to individual consumers according to set criteria or a QUEUING SYSTEM. Although the price system will ensure that a supply is assigned to the highest bidders, governments are reluctant to use such a method for essential goods. In socialist economies (and in other economies under the strain of conducting a war) extensive use is always made of rationing by the issue of vouchers and coupons which must be exchanged to obtain goods and services.

raw data (C8)
Data not yet arranged in numerical order.

See also: frequency distribution

Rawlsian difference principle (D3, D6)
The toleration of inequalities only if it is to the advantage of the worse off through making that person as well off as possible in terms of rights, freedoms, opportunities, income and wealth. Also, inequalities must

provide economic incentives to work harder and increase production.

See also: egalitarianism; Rawlsian justice

References

Rawls, J. (1999) *A Theory of Justice*, rev. edn, Oxford : Oxford University Press.

Rawlsian justice (D3)

1 A revival of social contract theory with general application to basic social and political institutions.
2 Anti-meritocratic EGALITARIANISM.
3 A non-utilitarian approach to justice.

The view that justice is 'fairness' is based on two principles. Firstly, that each person is entitled to the most extensive amount of liberty compatible with the liberty of others. Secondly, that the arrangement of social and economic inequalities is such that they are reasonably expected to be to everyone's advantage and attached to positions and offices open to all.

See also: utilitarianism

References

Daniels, N. (ed.) (1975) *Critical Studies on Rawls' 'A Theory of Justice'*, Oxford: Basil Blackwell.

reaction curve (D0)

A diagram indicating a firm's price and output as a function of the price or output set by another firm.

reaction function (C7, E6, L1)

This shows the preferences of decision-makers as revealed by an analysis of their actions. These functions have been used to study both economic policy making by governments and the behaviour of non-collusive oligopolists.

References

Theil, H. (1964) *Optimal Decision Rules for Government and Industry*, Amsterdam: North-Holland; Chicago: Rand McNally.

Reaganomics (B2, E6)

An application of SUPPLY-SIDE ECONOMICS to the running of the US economy in the

1980s that attempted to stimulate the economy. The policies it advocated included the reduction of taxes, of governmental regulation of business, of governmental interference in the market and a switch in federal expenditure so that more was spent on defence and less on social programmes. Reaganomics were forcefully expounded by the US COUNCIL OF ECONOMIC ADVISERS in the *Economic Report of the President to the Congress* of February 1982.

See also: Thatcherism

References

Boskin, M. (1989) *Reagan and the Economy*, San Francisco: Institute for Contemporary Studies.
Niskanen, W.A. (1988) *Reaganomics: An Insider's Account of the Policies and the People*, New York: Oxford University Press.

real assets (L2, Q0)

LAND and reproducible tangible assets in the form of inventories, business fixed capital stock and dwellings.

real balance effect (E0)

A change in the aggregate demand for goods resulting from a change in the quantity of real money balances. This effect was noted by both PIGOU and PATINKIN. The effect asserts that unemployment causes a fall in prices, a rise in the real value of people's money holdings, a rise in aggregate demand and thus full employment. As this effect takes years to operate, the Keynesian 'unemployment equilibrium' is most of the time a case of DISEQUILIBRIUM. It should be contrasted with the KEYNES EFFECT.

References

Patinkin, D. (1956) *Money, Interest and Prices: An Integration of Monetary and Value Theory*, New York: Oxford University Press.

real bills doctrine (B1)

Adam SMITH's doctrine that there can never be an inflationary excess issue of

COMMERCIAL BILLS and other paper money because each bill represents a real transaction. Henry THORNTON, in his *Paper Credit* (1802), criticized the doctrine for ignoring the fact that the same sum of money can support many bills.

See also: Banking School; law of reflux

real business-cycle theory (E3)

An account of BUSINESS CYCLES generated by technological or monetary shocks, or by changes in expectations.

References

King, R. and Plosser, C. (1984) 'Money, credit and prices in a real business cycle model', *American Economic Review* 74: 363–80.

Kydland, F.E. and Prescott, E.C. (1982) 'Time to build and aggregate fluctuations', *Econometrica* 50: 1345–70.

Long, J.B. and Plosser, C.J. (1983) 'Real business cycles', *Journal of Political Economy* 91: 39–69.

real estate investment trust (G2)

A trust which manages real estate assets in the form of equities and mortgages and is financed by stock, bond and bill issues and loans from financial institutions. The high leverage of these trusts led to many of them going bankrupt in the 1970s.

real exchange rate (F3)

A currency's value in terms of its real purchasing power. A basket of goods and services representative of an average consumer's purchasing is valued in the two currencies. This calculation is often made to show the relative cost of living for executives moving between the major cities of the world or to establish the real value of investment projects.

See also: purchasing power parity

real growth (O4)

An increase in the output of goods and services measured at constant prices, i.e. after price changes have been eliminated.

real income (E3)

1 Money income adjusted by the amount of inflation over a given period. A PRICE INDEX is used to deflate money income. If, for example, prices have risen by 10 per cent and money incomes by the same amount, real income will remain constant.

2 The amount of goods and services which can be purchased with a given money income.

real interest rate (E4)

1 The money RATE OF INTEREST adjusted by the rate of inflation. When there is a positive real interest rate, increased savings will be encouraged and investment discouraged; negative real rates will make borrowing more attractive. Real interest rates are zero when the money rate of interest is equal to the rate of inflation. The high real interest rates of the UK and US economies in the 1980s were regarded as a major cause of low industrial investment in some years. Because of their effect on profit margins, high real interest rates are, in a sense, equivalent to administered price controls.

The real rate is calculated by the formula

$$\frac{100 + x}{100 \times y} \times 100 - 100$$

where x is the nominal rate of interest and y is the percentage rate of inflation.

2 The interest rate measured in goods.

See also: own rate of interest

real option theory (G2)

An extension of financial option theory to the study of real, non-financial, options. Real options are embedded in investments rather than being contractual terms. This theory is used to value private companies.

References

Amram, M. and Kulatilaka, N. (1999) *Real Options*, Cambridge, MA: Harvard Business School Press.

real price (D0)

1 The nominal price of a good adjusted by a price index.

2 A relative price showing how much of one good exchanges for other goods. These prices show economic scarcity as they make possible a comparison between the price increases of particular commodities and of all commodities in general.

real property tax (H2)

A tax based on the value of buildings and land. Such taxes are known as RATES in the UK.

real rate of return (G0)

The rate of return to capital assets after allowing for inflation. This rate, used as a target for UK nationalized industries in a White Paper of 1978, was intended to be related to the real rate of return on private sector assets, taking into account the cost of finance, SOCIAL TIME PREFERENCE and the social objectives set for that particular industry.

real-wage hypothesis (E0)

The view that real wages are inflexible downwards. This is a considerable expansion of KEYNES's assumption that money wages are inflexible downwards.

real wages (J3)

1 Money wages adjusted for inflation. Real wages can only increase if money wages rise faster than inflation.

2 The amount of goods and services a money wage can purchase.

recession (E3)

1 A phase of the business cycle which succeeds a boom and precedes a trough.

2 A six-month fall in GROSS DOMESTIC PRODUCT according to the NATIONAL BUREAU OF ECONOMIC RESEARCH of Washington, DC.

The principal indicators of this are falling output and rising UNEMPLOYMENT.

recessionary gap (E0) *see* deflationary gap

recession exposure scoring system (E3, E6)

Assigning a value in a range of +3 to −3 to show the effects of a recession in another economy with +3 being the greatest effect. Taking the USA as an example, income from US-based assets, capital flows from the USA, commodity price declines, US dollar weakness and asset price effects have been used as relevant indicators. This is more sophisticated than regarding the exposure of one country to another in terms of the proportion of exports sent to the other country.

RECHAR (Q4)

'Reconversion charbon': a EUROPEAN COMMUNITY scheme introduced in 1990 to help the revitalization of areas hit by coalpit closures.

reciprocal demand law (F1)

A refinement of the law of COMPARATIVE ADVANTAGE used to determine the TERMS OF TRADE between countries according to the relative demand measured in the amount of goods offered for the goods of another country. John Stuart MILL, in his first essay of his collection *Essays on Some Unsettled Questions of Political Economy* (1844), and TORRENS refined RICARDIAN international trade theory in this way.

Reciprocal Trade Agreements Act 1934 (F1)

US federal trade statute of the Roosevelt Administration that attempted to undo the PROTECTIONISM of the SMOOT–HAWLEY TARIFF ACT by authorizing the president to negotiate bilateral, reciprocal trade agreements to reduce the tariffs introduced in 1930. The US Congress repeatedly voted three-year extensions of the powers under this Act.

recognition lag (E6)

The length of time elapsing before an economic decision-maker is aware of a change in economic circumstances. This can occur because economic statistics take time to collect and are published less frequently than a decision-maker needs.

See also: implementation lag

recognized professional body (K2)
An institution regulating part of the UK
financial sector that has received recognition by the FINANCIAL SERVICES ACT 1986.
These are institutions, such as the Institute
of Chartered Accountants, which are not
involved in trading but in other investment
services.

See also: self-regulatory organization

reconciliation bill (H6) *see* appropriation
bill

recontract (D0)
EDGEWORTH's notion that buyers and sellers
initially make provisional contracts at DIS-
EQUILIBRIUM PRICES and then subsequently,
as a result of their exchange, make a new
contract at, or approaching, an equilibrium price.

See also: *tâtonnement*

References

Walker, D.A. (1973) 'Edgeworth's theory
of recontract', *Economic Journal* 83:
138–49.

recovery (E3)
The phase in a business cycle, after a SLUMP
and before a BOOM, in which output is
rising and, often, unemployment is falling.

rectification (E6)
Cuba's campaign for greater efficiency.
Comparable to the USSR's PERESTROIKA.

recurrent spot contracting (G0) *see*
employment contract

recursive system (C3)
A system of econometric equations such
that if we know the values of variables up
to the time $t - 1$ we can obtain their
values at time t. Systems of this kind
demonstrate unilateral causal dependence.

recycling (F3, Q3)
1 The reuse of scarce raw materials, especially paper, glass and metals.
2 The redistribution of financial reserves
from creditor to debtor countries. After

OPEC's price increases of 1973–4, the
surpluses of the oil producers were lent
on Euromarkets to poor countries, particularly of the Third World, helping to
accelerate the world debt problem

Red Book (H6) *see* Financial Statement
and Budget Report

red chip (G1)
A share in a Chinese state enterprise that
has been partially privatized. The company can be either a Mainland Chinese
company with Hong Kong subsidiaries, or
a Hong Kong company whose business is
mainly in Mainland China.

redemption date (G0)
The date by which a fixed-term stock must
be repaid by the government, company or
corporation which has issued it.

redemption yield (G0)
The yield on a stock repayable by a fixed
date which includes both the interest on
that stock and the capital gain if the
current price is less than the redemption
price. A net redemption yield adjusts the
yield for income and capital gains taxes
payable.

redlining (G2, R2)
1 Giving an area the status of a slum by
making it ineligible for mortgage finance. Once this status has been given,
redlining accelerates the decline of such
areas. This has occurred in several US
urban areas, including parts of New
York City.
2 Refusing to grant credit because the
lender cannot obtain a required return
at any rate of interest. There can be
passive redlining when a credit institution avoids contact with some categories of lender.

red tape (L5)
Regulations on business which incur high
COMPLIANCE COSTS.

reduced form equation (C1)
An equation which has been manipulated
to show each endogenous variable as the

function of the set of exogenous and, if present, error terms.

reference cycle (E3)
The basic series of economic statistics, e.g. GROSS NATIONAL PRODUCT or industrial output, which is chosen to indicate fluctuations in an economy.

See also: coincident indicators; economic indicators; lagging indicator; leading indicator

refugee capital (F2, G0) *see* capital flight; hot money

refunding (E5, H6)
Issuing new government securities to replace bonds or other securities which have matured.

See also: overfunding

regional banking pacts (G2)
US banking agreements used to overcome the restrictive banking legislation that banned interstate commercial banking to create, in effect, interstate banks. The first pacts were between neighbouring states, e.g. in New England, excluding MONEY CENTRE BANKS.

regional economics (R1, R3)
The analysis of firms' location decisions and the causes of regional growth. Economists, with geographers, have the same analytical foundations in the works of von THUNEN and Losch. It is mainly in times of high national growth that regional imbalances attract much interest.

See also: economic geography

References

Armstrong, H. and Taylor, J. (1985) *Regional Economics and Policy*, Oxford: Philip Allan.
Isard, W. (1965) *Methods of Regional Analyses: An Introduction to Regional Science*, Cambridge, MA: MIT Press; New York: Wiley.
Nijkamp, P. and Mills, E.S. (1986–7) *Handbook of Regional and Urban Economics*, 2 vols, Amsterdam and New York: North-Holland.

Temple, M. (1994) *Regional economics*, New York: St Martin's Press; London: Macmillan.

regional employment premium (H2, J2)
UK wage subsidy to firms in depressed regions in force from 1967 to 1977. Initially, it was a subsidy of £1.50 per man per week, with lower rates for women and juveniles.

regional multiplier (R1)
The number of times the income or employment of a region will multiply as a consequence of an increase in AUTONOMOUS EXPENDITURES.

Two approaches are often used: the economic base multiplier and the modified KEYNESIAN approach. The economic base approach assumes that regional income can be divided into two parts – what arises from the BASIC INDUSTRIES of the region and what springs from other regional industries. This multiplier is then calculated as $1/(1 - s)$ with s the ratio of income earned in the non-basic sector to total regional income, i.e. the regional multiplier is

$$\frac{1}{1 - (1 - t)(c - m)}$$

with t the income tax rate, c the marginal propensity to consume and m the marginal propensity to import. There are many problems in calculating this multiplier, including the fact that basic industries may vary greatly in the extent to which they export to other regions. The KEYNESIAN approach merely applies a national multiplier formula to a region. A multiplier for a particular region is usually smaller than that for the national economy of which it is part as regions are more open, thus suffering from leakages of expenditures to other regions.

See also: multiplier

regional policy (R5)

1 Measures to reduce the imbalance in prosperity between the regions of a

particular country, particularly between the region around the capital city and peripheral provinces.

2 Government aid to especially deprived cities, inner cities and other relatively small parts of a country.

Many countries have used incentives to encourage the location of expanding industries in the depressed regions and to reduce the POPULATION DENSITY of major cities. In the UK a succession of measures since 1929 to subsidize the GEOGRAPHICAL MOBILITY OF LABOUR, the building of factories, the training of workers and the payment of RATES have been used. Regional policies are measured by the number of jobs created in depressed regions and by the extent of convergence in interregional incomes, unemployment rates and rates of output growth. Regional policy is most active in times of fast national economic growth as it is then easier to finance assistance to regions.

See also: enterprise zone; growth pole

References

Diamond, D.R. and Spence, N.A. (1983) *Regional Policy Evaluation: A Methodological Review and the Scottish Example*, Aldershot: Gower Press.

Folmer, H. (1986) *Regional Economic Policy. The Measurement of its Effect*, Dordrecht and Lancaster: Nijhoff.

Vanhove, N. (1999) *Regional policy: A European approach*, 3rd edn, Aldershot, Brookfield, VT and Sydney: Ashgate.

regional selective assistance (R5)
UK government subsidization of capital and training costs of projects under the Industrial Development Act 1984, which aimed to create or maintain employment in designated depressed areas. As many projects were of a capital-intensive nature with little impact on local employment, this programme has been managed increasingly carefully.

regional trading bloc (F0)
A group of states with adjoining borders

enjoying free trade within the bloc and fixing a COMMON EXTERNAL TARIFF against other countries. Prominent examples are the EUROPEAN ECONOMIC COMMUNITY and the NORTH AMERICAN FREE TRADE AREA.

See also: new regionalism

regional wage bargaining (J3)
Wage negotiations for an industrial or occupational group covering workers in part of a country. This departure from national wage bargaining is popular with many employers. It enables pay to reflect more closely LOCAL LABOUR MARKET conditions; unions have often objected to this as it gives rise to regional wage differentials thus departing from the hallowed union tradition of setting the same pay for all workers of the same occupation or industry.

regrating (L1)
Large purchasing of goods in order to sell them nearby at a profit.

regression (C1) *see* least squares method; linear regression

regression curve (C1) *see* least squares method

regressive expectations (E0)
EXPECTATIONS that the value of an economic variable, e.g. the PRICE LEVEL, will be a weighted average of its present and past values.

See also: adaptive expectations; rational expectations

regressive tax (H2)
A tax falling disproportionately on lower income groups. If there is regression as INCOME decreases, the AVERAGE RATE OF TAX increases. Many INDIRECT TAXES, e.g. EXCISE DUTIES and sales taxes, are regarded as regressive, but the extent to which they are depends on the consumption patterns of different income groups. POLL TAXES are the simplest case of regression.

regret (C7, D8)
The difference between an actual pay-off and the pay-off that would have resulted

from choosing the correct strategy when making decisions under UNCERTAINTY. Under a MINIMAX strategy, the aim is to minimize the maximum regrets.

References

Loomes, G. and Sugden, R. (1982) 'Regret theory: an alternative theory of rational choice under uncertainty', *Economic Journal* 92: 805–24.

regrettable (D0)

A good or service not producing UTILITY directly for a consumer, e.g. health care or transport to work.

regular economy (D0, P0)

An ECONOMY with a typical set of equilibrium prices linked to characteristic data.

regular labour (J3)

Employment bound by labour contracts which is expected to last a fixed period or until usual retirement age.

See also: casualization

regulated firm (L5)

A firm subject to detailed government regulation of its pricing and investment decisions. PUBLIC UTILITIES are often controlled in this way because the goods and services they provide constitute a major part of the costs of all firms and a high percentage of the consumption expenditure of households.

regulation (L5)

Partial or complete intervention in the economic decision making of a firm or other economic institution by the government or one of its agencies. The usual justification for this departure from free market principles is MARKET FAILURE. The major forms of intervention include CONSUMER PROTECTION, the creation of PUBLIC ENTERPRISES to run industries that are natural monopolies and the fixing of prices.

See also: regulatory capture

References

Bailey, E.E. (ed.) (1987) *Public Regulation:* *New Perspectives on Institutions and Policies*, Cambridge, MA: MIT Press.

Kahn, A. E. (1988) *The Economics of Regulation: Principles and Institutions*, 2 vols, New York: Wiley.

Stigler, G.J. (1971) 'The theory of economic regulation', *Bell Journal of Economics and Management Science* 2: 3–21.

Utton, M.A. (1986) *The Economics of Regulating Industry*, Oxford: Basil Blackwell.

Regulation D (E5, G2)

An arbitrary rule of the US FEDERAL RESERVE SYSTEM that classified bank deposits held for less than thirty days as DEMAND DEPOSITS. This regulation was modified in 1980 when this classification of demand deposits conflicted with the new type of TIME DEPOSIT that has a minimum maturity of fourteen days. The regulation is subject to the requirement that banks keep to a required reserve ratio.

Regulation K (E5, G2)

A regulation of the US FEDERAL RESERVE SYSTEM governing the international banking operations of US commercial banks. It is reviewed every five years to ensure that these banks remain internationally competitive.

Regulation Q (E4, E5)

The ceiling to the rate of interest US COMMERCIAL BANKS could pay on deposits of less than thirty days' maturity in the period 1933–85. This maximum rate was fixed from time to time by the US FEDERAL RESERVE SYSTEM. One of the aims of the regulation was to reduce the cost of housing finance as THRIFTS would be able to operate with low interest rates. As the regulation was evaded by bankers borrowing abroad to replace domestic deposits, the growth of the EURODOLLAR market was encouraged and much DISINTERMEDIATION occurred. In 1980, it was decided to phase out the regulation over a five-year period.

Regulation School (B2)

A group of French economic thinkers founded in the 1970s and centred on Paris and Grenoble consisting of Michel Aglietta,

Robert Boyer and Alain Lipietz. It derives its inspiration from the French philosopher Louis Althusser. Recognizing the success of FORDISM, it advocates local government economic strategies to promote employment and revive industry.

References

Grahl, J. and Teague, P. (2000) 'The Regulation School, the employment relation and financialization', *Economy and Society*, 29: 160–78.

Regulation U (E5, G2)

US banking regulation issued by the US FEDERAL RESERVE SYSTEM under the Securities Exchange Act 1934 to limit the amount a commercial bank can lend to its customers for the purchase or holding of securities. The aim of this regulation was to reduce speculation in stock markets.

regulatory agency (L5)

A governmental organization at national/federal or state/local level with the task of supervising the decision making of firms in a particular industry. These agencies approve price increases, as well as monitoring the quality of service and other matters of concern to consumers. There are many in the USA, especially for energy, water and transportation industries; in the UK, several ministries have the task of regulating PUBLIC ENTERPRISES, e.g. the Home Office has powers over the British Broadcasting Corporation.

regulatory capture (L5)

The perversion of the aims of a regulatory agency by one of the organizations it is supposed to control. An organization can acquire power over the agency supposed to supervise it by its political influence, superior technical knowledge or by an interchange of personnel. This has occurred often to evade ANTITRUST policy.

References

Stigler, G.J. (1971) 'The theory of economic regulation', *Bell Journal of Economics* 2: 3–21.

Reid, Margaret, 1896–1991 (B3)

Born in Cardale, Manitoba, and educated at the Universities of Manitoba, Winnipeg and Chicago where she was awarded a PhD in 1931 for a thesis on 'The economics of household production'. She taught consumer economics at Iowa State College as a colleague of SCHULTZ, and was employed by the federal government from 1943 to 1948 rising to be head of the Family Economics Division of the Department of Agriculture. She measured food expenditures to produce the consumption standards reported in her *Food for People* (1943). Professor at the Universities of Illinois from 1948 to 1951 and Chicago from 1951 to 1961. She was an inspiration for MODIGLIANI, BECKER and FRIEDMAN who acknowledged her pioneering work on the PERMANENT INCOME HYPOTHESIS of 1950. The first female economist to be chosen by the American Economic Association as a Distinguished Fellow.

References

Yi, Yun-Ae (1996) 'Margaret G. Reid: life and achievements', *Feminist Economics*, 2(3): 17–36.

reinsurance (G2)

Spreading an insurance risk by making a treaty with other insurance companies to accept part of the risk in return for a share of premium income – hence this has been described as 'insuring the insurer'. Large assets such as ships and aircraft could not be insured if reinsurance were not available.

reintermediation (G2)

The return to the use of banks and other financial intermediaries after a period in which individuals and companies directly financed each other.

See also: disintermediation

relational capital (J0)

A form of HUMAN CAPITAL consisting of the information obtained through contact with clients. Lawyers, management and financial consultants, bankers and accountants particularly possess this capital. Part of remuneration, especially to older members of staff, can be considered a return to relational capital. Unlike most types of human capital, it is transferable.

relational wealth (Q0)
Non-material WEALTH based on service to the community and other people, a healthy environment and the time to develop and maintain personal relationships, rather than on consumer goods produced by the market. This concept has been suggested as a foundation for economic policy making.

References

Diwan, R. (2000) 'Relational wealth and the quality of life', *Journal of Socio-economics* 29: 305–40.

relative concentration (L1)
A measure of the distribution of economic activity, or of values of an economic variable, using Lorenz curves and Gini coefficients. This is used to examine the distribution of the size of firms and the size of individual incomes.

relative income hypothesis (E2)
Duesenberry's theory of the CONSUMPTION FUNCTION that consumption is a function of current income relative to income in preceding time periods and relative to the income of households which are regarded as models to follow. The theory was used to reconcile a conflict between time series and cross-section evidence.

References

Duesenberry, J. (1949) *Income, Saving and the Theory of Consumer Behavior*, Cambridge, MA: Harvard University Press.

relative price (D0)
The price of one good expressed in terms of another, rather than money. The relative price of apples can be expressed in terms of oranges if a consumer has a choice between consuming either apples or oranges from a given income. Relative prices can be expressed by the slope of a BUDGET LINE.

See also: opportunity cost; price

relative surplus value (D0) *see* surplus value

religion (Z1) *see* economics of religion; Christian socialism; Islamic economics

remittance (E4, F3)
A sum of money transferred to another person. A major type is a transfer to a relative or friend, often by a migrant worker to his or her family. For poor countries and poor agricultural regions, remittances can be a major source of income.

remuneration committee (G3, J3)
A subcommittee of a board of directors charged with the task of independently fixing the pay and other benefits of directors and senior executives. It is expected to link directors' rewards to shareholder value.

See also: Greenbury Code

renewable resource (Q2)
A NATURAL RESOURCE that, because of its biological nature, is self-renewing, e.g. game, fish, woodland. A greater yield can be obtained from it by growing it in an artificial environment as, for example, in a fish farm.

See also: non-renewable resource

Rengo (J5)
Japanese labour union federation created in November 1987 through the merger of DOMEI and CHURITSUROREN. By 1989, it had 5.4 million members of whom 2.8 million were in manufacturing and 1 million were in transport.

See also: enterprise union; Sohyo

rent (D3, Q0)
The charge made by the owner of property to another person wishing to use it. From PETTY onwards, it was recognized that the amount of rent would vary according to the location and fertility of land: ANDERSON and RICARDO refined this view into a DIFFERENTIAL THEORY OF RENT. Without the private ownership of property, rent would

not be paid – although in the public sector an imputed rent for the use of land and buildings is often charged in order to take into account the full cost of using factors of production.

See also: economic rent

rental payment (D3)

The payment for the use of a FACTOR OF PRODUCTION. Such payments are common in the hire of capital equipment but, in a sense, the concept applies to labour as wages are paid for labour services, not for the purchase of the worker as would be the case in slavery.

renter illusion (H2)

A form of FISCAL ILLUSION which assumes that only property owners will correctly perceive the property taxes levied by local governments with the consequence that renters of property will not correctly match the valuation of publicly provided local services with the tax passed on in rents. Because of this illusion voters who rent property will be willing to approve of higher local public expenditure.

See also: debt illusion

rentier (D3)

A person whose income is entirely derived from the ownership of FINANCIAL CAPITAL or other property. KEYNES in his GENERAL THEORY forecast the disappearance of this class of persons through an abundance of capital reducing its return to zero.

rent seeking (D0, L1)

Monopolizing activity. This is much criticized as it produces a social waste rather than a social surplus.

reoffering yield (G1)

The yield based on the price a syndicate offers a government bond to the public after its original acquisition from the issuer. It takes into account the premium or discount since the launch of the bond.

repackaging (G2)

Selling a portion of a BOND issue by reissuing it as a different type of security which will appeal to another part of the market, e.g. reissuing a fixed rate bond as a FLOATING RATE NOTE.

repeated game (C7)

A game with a modified strategy from period to period which recognizes the rival's strategy.

replacement cost (M4)

The current value of an asset measured by how much it would cost to be replaced. This is a more accurate measure of the value of an asset than HISTORIC COST.

replacement investment (E2)

Investment undertaken to keep a capital stock intact which is equal to the amount of capital which has depreciated. In NATIONAL INCOME accounting, net investment + replacement investment = gross investment.

See also: depreciation; net investment

replacement labour force (J2)

The use of migrant labour to fill job vacancies created by the movement of indigenous workers from areas of decline to the more prosperous regions of a country. In the UK, for example, immigrant labour in the 1950s took up employment in declining areas, especially northern England and the West Midlands, where inferior jobs existed as a consequence of the shift of UK workers to the south east of England.

replacement ratio (I3)

1 The ratio of welfare benefits paid to the unemployed to the average after-tax earnings of people in work.
2 The ratio of a pensioner's social security benefits and other TRANSFER INCOMES to pre-retirement income. These ratios can indicate that welfare payments are so generous as to discourage work effort or too low to prevent pensioners suffering a very large income loss.

representative firm (I2)

A term coined by MARSHALL to denote that a firm is characteristic of a particular industry or sector. It is the average firm, with 'a fairly long life, and fair success, which is managed with normal ability, and which has normal access to the economies, external and internal, which belong to that aggregate volume of production'. It is not to be equated simply with the OPTIMUM FIRM except, perhaps, in the sense of being the firm most likely to survive.

See also: economy of scale

reproduction (E2)
A new cycle of production created by a given amount of capital. Simple accumulation is a cycle with no accumulation; expanded reproduction, when accumulation is more than zero; contracted reproduction when accumulation is less than zero. This is a term popular in MARXIAN ECONOMICS.

repurchase agreement (E5)
A finance method used by the BANK OF ENGLAND and the FEDERAL RESERVE BANKS of the USA to give banks and other financial institutions extra liquidity by buying government securities for a short period, usually a day, the borrower agreeing to repurchase at a stated price. It is very popular with financial institutions as a means of maintaining their inventories of securities at a low cost.

reputational equilibrium (E3)
That rate of price INFLATION at which the benefit to a monetary authority from reneging from a monetary policy rule equals the cost of reneging, measured by future loss of reputation.

References

Backus, D. and Driffill, J. (1985) 'Inflation and reputation', *American Economic Review* 75: 530–8.
Barro, R.J. and Gordon, D.B. (1983) 'Rules, discretion and reputation in a model of monetary policy', *Journal of Monetary Economics* 12: 101–21.

reputation capital (M2)
An intangible asset of a firm created by the making of implicit promises, e.g. to maintain a particular level of product quality or to give its workers permanent employment. A firm gains from not making such promises explicit in the terms of its contracts: it can abandon its undertakings in extreme circumstances and keep employees from monitoring its assurances.

See also: goodwill; intangible wealth

References

MaCaulay, S. (1963) 'Non-contractual relations in business', *American Sociological Review* 28: 55–69.

required rental on capital (M2)
That rental equal to the OPPORTUNITY COST of owning the capital.

required reserve ratio (E5)
Ratio of reserve assets to the total deposits of a bank or other regulated financial institution set by a central bank. For UK CLEARING BANKS the ratio was set at 12½ per cent in the period 1971–81, after which the proportion of reserves they hold is at their own discretion.

resale price maintenance (L1)
A RESTRICTIVE PRACTICE of manufacturers who insist on supplying goods subject to the condition that the goods are sold at recommended prices. By 1938 in the UK at least a third of consumer expenditure was on goods subject to this rule. In 1956, collective enforcement of RPM was outlawed by the Restrictive Trade Practices Act; in 1964, the Resale Prices Act made individual enforcement illegal, unless the class of goods was exempted by the Restrictive Practices Court. Sale of books was subject to RPM under the Net Book Agreement until 1996. As there was so much evasion of RPM before 1964 through discounting, stamp schemes and violation of manufacturers' recommendations by the large supermarket chains, it was difficult to measure the effects of abolishing RPM on retail distribution. In the USA, since 1940 it has been outlawed at the federal level as a violation of the SHERMAN and FEDERAL TRADE COMMISSION

ACTS and also under state fair trade laws. The most that manufacturers legally can do is to 'suggest' to retailers an appropriate retail price and reinforce that suggestion by printing it on the packaging.

See also: competition policy

rescheduling of debt (F3)

The conversion of short-term debt into long-term debt negotiated by countries or companies finding it difficult to repay debt when payment is due. Countries reschedule their debt by applying to the Paris Club.

See also: Group of Ten; world debt problem

research and development (O3)

The activity of inventing new processes and products and applying them in industry, especially those which are science based and dependent for their survival and long-term growth on imaginative change. The study of this is often termed 'the economics of science'. Globally, much of R&D is concentrated in the USA because of large space and defence expenditures contracted out by federal agencies to private corporations and universities. Since 1890 larger industrial corporations, e.g. in the electrical industry, have conducted research in their own laboratories. Research based in Europe is on a much smaller scale, although many schemes have been introduced to increase Europe's R&D activity. In the EUROPEAN COMMUNITY, to encourage R&D reciprocal arrangements are negotiated with the USA: these aim to open public purchasing to European co-operation; joint ventures are established and national government research grants are refused to non-European high-technology companies in competition with European enterprises.

References

HMSO (annual) *Annual Review of Government Funded Research and Development*, London.

Rosenberg, N. (ed.) (1971) *The Economics of Technological Change: Selected Readings*, Harmondsworth: Penguin.

research programme (B4)

A cluster of interconnected theories constituting the principal ideas of a group of economists who have agreed on certain basic assumptions, e.g. NEW CLASSICAL ECONOMICS. Lakatos is particularly associated with this approach to economic methodology.

See also: economic methodology

References

Lakatos, I. and Musgrave, A. (eds) (1972) *Criticism and the Growth of Knowledge*, Cambridge: Cambridge University Press.

reservation price (D0)

The minimum price a seller will accept; the maximum a buyer will offer. Reservation prices commonly occur in AUCTIONS.

reservation wage (J3)

The minimum wage a worker is prepared to accept. The magnitude of this wage will depend on a worker's previous wages. In job search, a worker will continue to seek job offers until a job at or above the reservation wage is offered.

See also: minimum supply price of labour

reserve army of labour (J6)

The Marxian description of the unemployed portion of the labour force. It was MARX's view that, under CAPITALISM, CAPITAL–LABOUR RATIOS would increase and that capitalists would need an excess supply of labour to keep down money wage rates. However, it is the experience of some countries, e.g. the UK, for both REAL WAGES and unemployment to rise.

reserve assets (E5, G2)

Cash and highly liquid monetary assets required to be held by financial institutions, especially banks, under the rules of a CENTRAL BANK. In the UK these have been defined as balances with the BANK OF ENGLAND (other than SPECIAL DEPOSITS), TREASURY BILLS, company tax reserve certificates, some local authority and commercial bills and UK government stocks with less than one year to maturity. In the USA required reserves take the form of vault cash and deposits with Federal Reserve Banks. From 1971 to 1981 in the UK, under the rules set out in the COMPETITION AND CREDIT CONTROL statement of 1971, banks, and several other financial institutions, were required to observe a ratio of reserve assets of 12½ per cent. The Board of Governors of the FEDERAL RESERVE SYSTEM can impose reserve requirements.

See also: reserve requirements

reserve base (G2)
The high-powered money of the banking system. A CENTRAL BANK requires a certain proportion of cash or near-cash assets to be held: this forms the basis for the creation of bank deposits.

See also: monetary base; money multiplier

reserve currency (F3)
A currency widely used for the financing of international trade and held as an alternative to gold or SPECIAL DRAWING RIGHTS of the INTERNATIONAL MONETARY FUND. The most popular currency is the dollar. As a percentage of official holdings of foreign exchange of all countries in 1988, the US dollar accounted for 54.5 per cent, compared with sterling 15 per cent, the yen 6.7 per cent and the DM 1.6 per cent. In the past, the greater role of sterling as a reserve currency put a tremendous strain on the UK economy as the volatility of sterling balances made it more difficult to keep the pound at its fixed parity.

References

Group of Thirty (1982) *Reserve Currencies in Transition*, New York: Group of Thirty.

Grubel, H. (1984) *International Monetary System*, 4th edn, Harmondsworth: Penguin.

reserve ratio (E5) *see* cash–deposits ratio; required reserve ratio

reserve requirements (E5)
The proportion of the total assets of a COMMERCIAL BANK, or other deposit-taking institution, which a CENTRAL BANK insists should be kept in cash or short-term securities, usually with less than two years to maturity. Altering reserve requirements is a means of expanding or contracting the total money supply of an economy. In the USA, reserve requirements were instituted as early as the First Bank of the United States, founded 1791, in the twentieth century they were in force from 1913 to 1980. Reserves could be held in vault cash, a balance kept at a reserve bank or at a member bank which keeps reserves at the FEDERAL RESERVE.

In the USA after the implementation of the MONETARY CONTROL ACT 1980 various reserve requirements have been set: for net transaction accounts, 3 per cent of deposits (12 per cent for deposits over $40.4 million); for non-personal time deposits, 3 per cent if maturity of less than 1½ years (zero if greater maturity) and 3 per cent on Eurocurrency liabilities.

resident population (J1) *see de jure* population

residualization (I3)
Downgrading the status of a public asset or part of a population so that only the poorest members of society can benefit. This can happen if health care and public sector housing are offered only to the lowest income groups of a nation. MARSHALL discussed the 'residuum', a class of persons physically, mentally and morally incapable of doing a good day's work and attracting good wages: exceptional treatment, especially in education, was recommended.

Resolution Trust Corporation (G2)
US federal government's liquidation agency set up in 1989 with the task of winding up hundreds of bankrupt THRIFTS. It is supervised by the FEDERAL DEPOSIT INSURANCE CORPORATION and funded by federal government grants and bond issues.

resource economics (Q2, Q3)
The economic analysis of environmental

issues, especially exhaustible resources, energy and pollution. As early as 1866 JEVONS, in writing of an impending coal shortage, applied economic reasoning to the study of resources. However, it was particularly PIGOU's discussion of the costs of pollution in his pioneering work on WELFARE ECONOMICS and HOTELLING's seminal article on the principles concerning exhaustible resources that provided the analytical stimulus which set this subject going. Today, this branch of economics relies on the concept of externalities and COST–BENEFIT ANALYSIS and provides recommendations for many forms of economic regulation.

References

Conrad, J.M. (1999) *Resource economics*, Cambridge, New York and Melbourne: Cambridge University Press.

Hotelling, H. (1931) 'The economics of exhaustible resources', *Journal of Political Economy* 39 (April): 137–75.

Norton, G.A. (1984) *Resource Economics*, London: Edward Arnold.

Perman, R. *et al.* (1999) *Natural resource and environmental economics*, 2nd edn, New York and Harlow: Pearson Education.

Peterson, F.M. and Fisher, A.C. (1977) 'The exploitation of extractive resources: a survey', *Economic Journal* 87: 681–721.

resource monotonicity (Q0)

The rule that as a common resource grows, each agent should not lose thereby remaining at least as well off as before.

restoration cost (Q2)

The cost of returning a polluted or damaged environment to its original state rather than compensating for the loss. Costs include current market costs of equipment, materials and labour.

restrictive practice (L1, L2)

An anti-competitive practice of a firm, a group of firms or a TRADE (LABOR) UNION usually to restrict supply with a view to increasing that organization's income. Firms can do this in many ways, e.g. by practising RESALE PRICE MAINTENANCE, by collusion to fix common prices and share out a market or by PRICE LEADERSHIP. TRADE UNIONS, particularly of the craft type, can restrict LABOUR SUPPLY in the long term by agreeing with employers to limit the numbers of apprenticeships and in the short term by STRIKES. Labour restrictive practices can also take the form of minimum staffing levels which, although increasing the number of hours of labour supplied, increase wages at the expense of profits. The COMPETITION POLICY of many industrialized countries has attacked firms carrying out these practices; trade union and industrial relations legislation has played a smaller role than employers in eliminating them.

See also: craft union; demarcation

re-switching (D2)

Returning to the use of a production technique previously abandoned when its rate of return was too low because now the rate of return to the technique subsequently used has fallen lower. SRAFFA, in his *Production of Commodities by Means of Commodities* (1960), identified this as a problem for capital theory arising from the heterogeneity of capital.

retail bank (G2)

A bank attracting deposits from the general public and offering a wide range of services, including transfer of funds, personal loans, investment advice, insurance and foreign exchange. It is to be contrasted with a WHOLESALE BANK.

retail price index (E3)

The UK index of consumer prices, previously known as the cost of living index. By a monthly repricing of a bundle of goods and services representative of an average consumer's expenditure, it shows how much the price level has increased. The prices of more than 600 goods and services on sale in 180 towns are collected; data from the FAMILY EXPENDITURE SURVEY are also used. The weights used are 17.5 per cent for housing, 15.4 per cent for food and 4.2 per cent for local domestic taxation. Its emphasis on consumer prices makes it a crucial indicator of the welfare effects of inflation and is of central importance to wage negotiators. In the UK, there were changes of the base in 1974 and 1987. The inclusion of mortgage payments and local taxation is unusual by international standards.

See also: consumer price index; headline rate of inflation; Laspeyres index; Paasche index

retained earnings (M2)
The ACCOUNTING PROFITS of a firm after tax and other charges which, instead of being distributed to shareholders or its other owners, are kept as an asset available for investment in working and fixed capital. When these earnings are used, the cost of using this form of finance is the rate of interest forgone by not employing them outside the firm.

retirement age (J2)
The age when a person finally leaves the labour force. This is mainly determined by the employment and pensions legislation of a country. In developed countries it is between 60 and 65; in socialist countries 60 for males and 55 for females; in developing countries between 50 and 60 years. Uruguay has the most generous scheme: men can retire after thirty years of work and women after twenty-five, receiving a pension equal to 100 per cent of the wage rate received in the five years since reaching the age of 50. Equal opportunities legislation has led to a convergence between male and female retirement ages. Before 1900, the retirement age of workers was less of an issue as life expectancy was much lower and the provision of pensions rare.

retrophobia (J2)
Fear of going back to work and coping with the changes, including recently installed technology, which have occurred during one's absence. This problem particularly afflicts women after a mid-career break.

returns to scale (D2)
The change in output resulting from an increase in the quantities of factor inputs employed. Returns to scale can be shown by their effect on long-run average costs (LRAC). They can be increasing (output growing faster than inputs), constant (inputs and output increasing at the same rate) or decreasing (output growing at a slower rate than inputs). The returns which are most characteristic of a particular economy will determine whether it is growing, stationary or in decline. Central to CLASSICAL ECONOMICS was the assertion that there are diminishing returns to land. Allyn YOUNG, SRAFFA and Joan ROBINSON in their post-Marshallian study of the firm examined the implications of increasing returns.

References

Young, A. (1928) 'Increasing returns and economic progress', *Economic Journal* 38: 527–42.

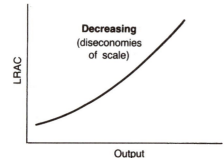

revalorization (E3, H2)
Changing prices or tax rates, e.g. periodic increases in excise duties in line with IN-FLATION so that these INDIRECT TAXES are constant in real terms.

revaluation (F3) *see* currency revaluation

revealed preference (D1)
An approach to consumer theory pio-neered by SAMUELSON in place of CARDINAL UTILITY or INDIFFERENCE CURVE methods; an empirical utility theory. It does not require complete information about a consumer's tastes but only knowledge of the combina-tions of goods actually purchased out of a consumer's total income. It is assumed that the consumer is consistent in never choosing a combination more expensive than that previously preferred.

References

Houthakker, H.S. (1950) 'Revealed prefer-ence and the utility function', *Econom-ica* New Series, 27: 159–74.
Samuelson, P.A. (1938) 'A note on the pure theory of consumers' behaviour', *Economica* New Series, 5: 61–71, 353–4.
—— (1948): 'Consumption theory in terms of revealed preference', *Economica* New Series, 15: 243–53.

revenue (H2, M2)
1 The proceeds obtained by a firm during a given time period from the sale of its output of goods and services.
2 The amount raised by a government from taxation and trading activities.

revenue economy (P4)
A non-market economy that extracts a surplus from the agricultural sector to provide sustenance for public servants. The PHYSIOCRATS in eighteenth-century France provided an early theory of it. In the twentieth century, many socialist economies have been of this type.

revenue maximization (L2) *see* sales maximization

revenue neutral (H2)
The characteristic of a tax reform which does not alter total tax revenue.

revenue seeking (F1)
Attempting to gain part of the revenue from protective tariffs.

References

Bhagwati, J.N. and Srinivasan, T.N. (1980) 'Revenue-seeking: a generalisation of the theory of tariffs', *Journal of Political Economy* 88: 1069–87.

revenue sharing (H7)
The transfer of the revenue from federal or central government taxes to state, county or local governments. In countries with federal constitutions, e.g. Australia, Canada, Ger-many or the USA, the principles for allocat-ing revenues are set out in fundamental national constitutional documents. In the UK, revenue sharing in the form of the RATE SUPPORT GRANT and, later, the REVENUE SUP-PORT GRANT, has been decided within the framework of local government law.

See also: federal finance

References

Hunter, J.S.H. (1977) *Federalism and Fiscal Balance*, Canberra: Australian National University Press and the Centre for Re-search on Federal Financial Relations.

revenue support grant (H7)
UK central government grant to local auth-orities. It consists of a needs grant reflect-ing the needs of individual authorities and a standard grant on a per capita basis.

reverse auction (D0)
An auction in which there are many sellers but only a single buyer.

reverse causation hypothesis (E4)
The view that the level of national income determines the size of the money stock, i.e. money has a passive role. This view, which was fervently advanced by KALDOR and Joan ROBINSON, is a frontal attack on the QUANTITY THEORY OF MONEY and the use of the TRANSMISSION MECHANISM in modern MONETARIST theory which asserts that money has an effect on real variables, particularly output and employment.

reverse discrimination (J7)
Favouring a disadvantaged group by giving it better education or employment or wages to correct its social status and income rather than to reward its merit. This form of discrimination is evident if workers with different levels of productivity are paid the same wages.

See also: affirmative action; discrimination; positive discrimination

reverse income tax (H2) *see* negative income tax

reverse J-shaped frequency curve (C1)
A FREQUENCY CURVE with a negative slope.

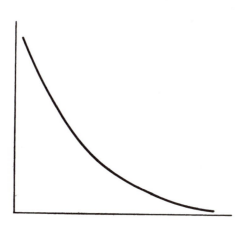

reverse takeover (G3, L1)
A takeover of the firm that was originally the bidding company. A case of this would be if Alpha Products bids for Beta Products unsuccessfully and is then taken over by Beta Products.

See also: merger; takeover

reverse yield gap (G1) *see* yield gap

reversionary bonus (G2)
A bonus given by an insurance company to a policyholder for every year the policy is in force. It is paid out at the termination of the policy or on the death of the insured.

See also: terminal bonus

revolving credit (G2)
Credit available for an indefinite term for the same amount because the credit used is matched by regular payments from the debtor. An example is permitting credit card holders to use the card up to a particular limit, $10,000: when that limit has been reached and the amount due paid, the credit is available again.

revolving underwriting facility (G2)
An extended NOTE ISSUANCE FACILITY in the form of a conventional bank loan at low short-term interest rates offered because a money market has not purchased all of the short-term commercial paper offered.

rhetoric (A1) *see* economics as rhetoric

Rhinelands hourglass (R1)
The belt of prosperous EUROPEAN COMMUNITY cities stretching from the Benelux countries and Germany to Northern Italy, with Paris as an offshoot. Also known as the Lotharingian axis.

Ricardian equivalence theorem (D9, H2, H6)
This states that deficit finance has exactly the same economic impact as current taxation. This is because individuals take into account future taxes, e.g. the bonds created to finance a deficit can be given to one's children who can use them to pay future taxes. Thus, individuals increase their savings by an amount equal to tax cuts or the increases in government spending with the consequence that deficit finance does not stimulate the national economy. This form of CROWDING OUT is named after RICARDO but formally explained by Barro.

See also: overlapping generations model

References

Barro, R. (1974) 'Are Government bonds net wealth?', *Journal of Political Economy* 82: 1095–175.

Ricardian theory of value (D0) *see* Ricardo

Ricardo, David, 1772–1823 (B3)

A leading English CLASSICAL ECONOMIST who came to economic study after a rigorous Talmudic education at the Portuguese Synagogue of Amsterdam, a lucrative career as a London stock jobber and a chance reading of SMITH's *Wealth of Nations* at Bath in 1799. The great inflation of the Napoleonic Wars period brought him to write a pamphlet on monetary economics, *The High Price of Bullion*, in 1811. The CORN LAWS controversy inspired *An Essay on the Influence of a Low Price of Corn on the Profits of Stock*, his first attempt to create a model of the economy using the DIFFERENTIAL THEORY OF RENT, the law of DIMINISHING RETURNS and the inverse relationship between wages and profits. James MILL encouraged him to expand it into the larger, and very influential, *Principles of Political Economy and Taxation*, first published in 1817. What originally had been a theory to show that restricting corn imports would lead to an extension of cultivation to marginal land and a fall in the rate of profit became an integrated theory of value, distribution, international trade and taxation. The most controversial aspect of it was, perhaps, his theory of value. This was narrower than SMITH's in that it emphasized labour quantities as an explanation of relative values at all stages of society and was more concerned with the quest for an invariable standard of value, seen by contemporaries as important at a time when INDEX NUMBERS were not available to show the extent of inflation. Although many of his key theories were not original (e.g. DIFFERENTIAL THEORY OF RENT, the law of COMPARATIVE ADVANTAGE) his central model dominated the thinking

of his day and was to be an important starting point for John Stuart MILL, MARX and MARSHALL. As a Member of Parliament from 1819 for Portarlington, a rotten borough, he was to be an influential debater on central issues, especially on monetary questions, later being a major inspiration for the Currency School. His home at Gatcombe Park, Gloucestershire (later the home of HRH The Princess Royal), was used as the venue of the Political Economy Club, the only forum for the leading economists of the time to discuss economics. He died, much admired, leaving the immense fortune of £775,000, including agricultural estates, despite having created an economic theory so despised by the landed interest.

See also: neo-Ricardians; Sraffa

References

Blaug, M. (1958) *Ricardian Economics: A Historical Study*, New Haven, CT: Yale University Press.
Hollander, S. (1979) *The Economics of David Ricardo*, Toronto: University of Toronto; London: Heinemann Educational Books.
Morishima, M. (1989) *Ricardo's Economics*, Cambridge: Cambridge University Press.
Sraffa, P. and Dobb, M.H. (eds) (1951–73) *The Works and Correspondence of David Ricardo*, Cambridge: Cambridge University Press.

Ricardo effect (D2, O3)

The substitution of machinery for labour as a consequence of a rise in wages. This occurs because the ratio of wages to product prices changes, affecting the profitability of an industry.

References

Hayek, F.A. von (1942) 'The Ricardo effect', *Economica* New Series, 9: 127–52.

rights issue (G1)

An issue of shares which existing shareholders of a company have the right to buy: this can be either exercised or sold.

The issue of these extra shares will bring about a fall in the existing share price.

See also: bonus issue; scrip issue

right-to-work state (J5)
US state which has made it illegal to require a worker to join a US LABOR UNION. Most of these twenty states are in the South.

ringfencing (H5) *see* earmarking

risk (D0)
The chance of an event occurring in accordance with a known probability. Actuarial calculations based on past experience make it possible to insure against the occurrence of such event. A person who is risk averse would require very favourable odds to make a bet; a RISK LOVER would take a gamble even when the odds are unfavourable; a risk-neutral person will be concerned not about the likelihood of particular bets being successful but on average with making a profit.

References
Bernstein, P. (1996) *Against the gods: the remarkable story of risk*, New York, Chichester and Toronto: Wiley.
Dembo, R.S. and Freeman, A. (1998) *Seeing tomorrow: rewriting the rules of risk*, New York, Chichester and Toronto: Wiley.

risk-adjusted discount rate (G0)
A risk-free discount rate augmented to take into account the risk factor.

risk asset system (G2)
A method of assessing the amount of RISK a bank is taking which weights bank assets according to the length of time banks could lose profits on them. The FEDERAL RESERVE SYSTEM recommends the adaptation of this system now in use in the EUROPEAN COMMUNITY countries and suggests weights of 0 per cent for cash (and its equivalents), 30 per cent for money market assets, 60 per cent for moderate risk assets (e.g. local authority bonds) and 100 per cent for standard bank loans. Weighting the riski-ness of bank assets makes it possible to ascertain the level of capitalization suitable for a particular bank. US and European adoption of this system is a step towards the international harmonization of banking standards.

risk aversion (D0)
Choosing assets with little risk of either capital loss or an uncertain return. Risk aversion can be expressed in different ways, including the choice of only very safe assets, e.g. government BONDS, or the diversification of an investment portfolio. Many investors associate high risk with a high return.

References
Tobin, J. (1958) 'Liquidity as behaviour towards risk', *Review of Economic Studies* 25 (February): 65–86.

risk-based banking standards (G2) *see* risk asset system

risk-based premium (G2)
An insurance premium that varies according to the riskiness of the subject of the insurance. The past record of the party insured and of persons with similar characteristics is the main determinant of the premium.

risk capital (G0)
1 Ordinary shares.
2 Common stock.
3 VENTURE CAPITAL.

These constitute the part of long-term financial capital without a claim on the assets of a firm and which will be lost if the enterprise goes bankrupt.

risk-free asset (G0)
An asset with a known return unlikely to default.

risk lover (D0)
A person who will gamble even when a mathematical calculation shows the odds are unfavourable. Risk lovers will accept a lower expected income in the hope of obtaining a greater capital gain.

risk management (M2)
The calculation of the probability of an unfortunate event occurring and the devising of strategies to minimize its impact through the use of insurance, reinsurance, DERIVATIVES, the avoidance of particular activities and the removal of hazards.

risk neutral (D0)
Indifference between certain and uncertain outcomes with the same expected return.

risk package (G2)
The mixture of types of finance used to provide credit for a particular project, e.g. a fixed interest loan and an issue of ordinary shares.

risk pooling (G2)
The adding together of the risks of many persons to reduce the cost of RISK; a basic principle of INSURANCE. Those who face the same risk are charged the same insurance premium. A major example of this is the underwriting system of Lloyd's insurance market in London.

See also: reinsurance

risk premium (D0)
The amount of income given up to leave a person indifferent between a risky choice and a certain one.

risky asset (G0)
An asset with an uncertain rate of return. Assessments of riskiness depend on consumption plans and the nature of other assets held by investors.

rival good (D0)
A GOOD which can only be consumed by one individual so his or her consumption prevents rivals from benefiting from it.

See also: club good; private good; public good

Robbins, Lionel (Lord), 1898–1984 (B3)
UK economist who was educated at the London School of Economics where he subsequently became lecturer from 1925 to 1927, professor from 1929 to 1961 and the Director and Chairman of the Court of

the Board of Governors from 1968 to 1974. Before the Second World War he established his fame as an economic theorist through articles on Marshall's REPRESENTATIVE FIRM, the ELASTICITY of demand for income in terms of effort and the stationary equilibrium. His famous *Essay on the Nature and Significance of Economic Science* (1935) firmly separated NORMATIVE from POSITIVE ECONOMICS and asserted that economics was concerned with means and not ends: this greatly influenced the course of economics throughout the Western world. By bringing HAYEK, with his knowledge of AUSTRIAN ECONOMICS, to the London School of Economics in 1931 he was able to provide an alternative to the Marshallian economics of Cambridge. In his methodological works, Robbins asserted that the propositions of economics are deductions from indisputable facts of experience, particularly the scarce nature of resources. The Austrian influence made him a strong opponent of KEYNESIANISM in the 1930s but his work with the War Cabinet (he was Director of the Economic Section) led him to make peace with his academic enemies. After 1950, he wrote a series of elegant works on the history of economic thought, including studies of Robert TORRENS and the classical theories of economic development and LAISSEZ-FAIRE. The Robbins Report of 1963 on higher education in the UK helped to bring about a decade of university expansion.

References

Lord Robbins (1952) *The Theory of Economic Policy in English Classical Political Economy*, London: Macmillan.
—— (1958) *Robert Torrens and the Evolution of Classical Economics*, London: Macmillan; New York: St Martin's Press.
—— (1971) *Autobiography of an Economist*, London: Macmillan.

Robertson, Dennis Holme, 1890–1963 (B3)
Major UK economist of the twentieth

century. He was educated at Trinity College, Cambridge, where he held a fellowship almost continuously from 1916, interrupted by a chair at the London School of Economics from 1939 to 1944. He succeeded PIGOU as professor of economics at Cambridge from 1944 to 1957. His most famous works are *A Study in Industrial Fluctuations* (1915), *Money* (1922) and *Banking and the Price Level* (1926).

Until 1929 he worked closely with KEYNES but the rupture of their friendship led to Robertson's severe criticisms of him after 1936. Robertson disputed the use made of the MULTIPLIER concept and favoured a dynamic method, rather than Keynesian COMPARATIVE STATICS. In the post-war period he championed traditional monetary policy and was suspicious of the use of fiscal policy to maintain FULL EMPLOYMENT. He was one of the trio constituting the Cohen Council on Productivity Prices and Incomes (1957–9), a body which attempted to restrain INFLATION by exhortation. Keynes was his supervisor.

He was a literary economist with an excellent writing style: not surprisingly he won the Chancellor's Medal for English Verse three times. He rarely used mathematics. *Banking and the Price Level* was his turning point, changing from the QUANTITY THEORY OF MONEY approach to saving and investment, on the road to Keynes's EFFECTIVE DEMAND. His wartime work for the Civil Service on the balance of payments led to collaboration with Keynes at BRETTON WOODS. Robertson thought that in the post-war world KEYNESIANISM would be as rigid as the earlier tradition. The difference between Robertson and Keynes was, according to HICKS, 'a difference in point of view'; Robertson was interested in stabilizing the cycle and so wanted judicious encouragement at the right time. Hicks, assessing Robertson's life for the *Dictionary of National Biography*, concluded: 'what Robertson feared was that Keynes's teaching would lead, in practice, to the over-use of encouragement and, in order to make that possible, at the same time to the over-use of restraint – an outcome which many people have felt that he was right to fear.'

References

Presley, J.R. (1979) *Robertsonian Economics: An Examination of the Work of Sir D.H. Robertson on Industrial Fluctuation*, London: Macmillan.

Robertsonian lag (E0, E2)

A LAG lasting one period, e.g. a year or a quarter. ROBERTSON applied this type of lag in his savings function: savings in one period were regarded as a function of the income of the previous period.

References

Robertson, D.H. (1926) *Banking Policy and the Price Level*, London: P.S. King (reprinted New York: Augustus M. Kelly, 1949).

Robinson Crusoe economy (E1)

An abstract model ECONOMY, based on Daniel Defoe's 1719 novel, which engages in simple capital accumulation. Although he has an initial capital endowment through salvaging goods from the shipwreck, he establishes himself as a farmer on a desert island through using ROUNDABOUT METHODS OF PRODUCTION. He learns that production is only possible when he has first attended to his security and that money is useless in an isolated economy without exchange. Robinson Crusoe has long been used as an example of an optimizing economic man who abandons AUTARKY for EXCHANGE and as the embodiment of bourgeois values, the independent modern economic man.

References

Grapard, V. (1995) 'Robinson Crusoe: the quintessential economic man?' *Feminist Economics* 1: 33–52.

Robinson, Joan Violet, 1903–83 (B3)

UK economist, educated at Cambridge University where she met her husband Austin Robinson and taught in the

Economics Faculty from 1929 to 1971, being appointed a professor in 1965.

A passionate theorist and socialist, she made major contributions to economics through her *Economics of Imperfect Competition* (1933) which influenced the teaching of microeconomics thereafter by producing independently of CHAMBERLIN a theory of the firm for markets both competitive and monopolistic. Her long guardianship of the KEYNESIAN heritage began with *Introduction to the Theory of Employment* (1937). However, the influence of SRAFFA and KALECKI led her to develop Keynesian theory from comparative statics to a dynamic growth theory, particularly in her *The Accumulation of Capital* (1956). Many of her works, especially *An Essay on Marxian Economics* (1942), attempted a synthesis of socialist and Keynesian economics.

Although trained in Marshallian analysis she became increasingly opposed to his time analysis: she moved from studying perfect competition to oligopoly, selling costs and product differentiation. In doing so, she provided a new box of tools in her theory of imperfect competition. Increasingly she saw her role as a developer of Keynesian theory but her attempt to do so in her *Accumulation of Capital* was not broad enough to achieve a satisfactory model of long-term development. Her interest in development was long-standing, dating back to her first visits to India in the 1920s and later including an on-the-spot study of Mao's China.

For the last thirty years of her life she was engaged in controversies with SOLOW and SAMUELSON about CAPITAL THEORY. The ferocity of her polemical and entertaining pen is evident in her *Collected Papers* (1951–79). In a supplementary obituary notice in *The Times*, her lodger of ten years' standing, Dr Carmen Blacker, wrote of 'her spartan way of life': 'A strict vegetarian, she slept all the year round in a small creeper-covered hut at the bottom of the garden. It was entirely unheated, and open on one side to all weathers, but

no storm, deluge or frost could persuade her to sleep in the house. ... In the early spring she was often woken by tits pecking at her hair for material for their nests.'

See also: bastard Keynesianism; Cambridge controversies

References

Gram, H. and Walsh, V. (1983) 'Joan Robinson's economics in retrospect', *Journal of Economic Literature* 21: 518–50.

Feiwel, G.R. (ed.) (1989) *Joan Robinson and Modern Economic Theory*, New York: New York University Press; London: Macmillan.

—— (1989) *The Economics of Imperfect Competition and Employment. Joan Robinson and Beyond*, London: Macmillan.

Harcourt, G.C. (1988) *Joan Robinson*, Brighton: Wheatsheaf.

Robinson, J. (1951–80) *Collected Economic Papers*, Oxford: Basil Blackwell.

—— (1969) *The Accumulation of Capital*, 2nd edn, London: Macmillan.

—— (1969) *The Economics of Imperfect Competition*, 2nd edn, London: Macmillan.

Robinson–Patman Act 1936 (L4)

US federal statute outlawing particular forms of PRICE DISCRIMINATION which were in favour of large purchasers. A discount to a larger buyer has to be either based on differences in cost or justified as a price to meet the low price of a competitor.

See also: antitrust

rolling settlement (G1)

A system allowing investors to pay a few days after the sale or purchase of securities, e.g. in the USA, five days. This method of settling accounts has been adopted by the INTERNATIONAL STOCK EXCHANGE (UK) as a successor to its long-established method of dividing the trading year into two- or three-week periods with accounts payable on settlement day.

rollover ratio (F3)

The reciprocal of the value of the average MATURITY of a country's external debt which is used as a measure of a country's creditworthiness.

See also: debt service indicators

Rooker–Wise Amendment (H2)

An amendment to the UK's 1975 Finance Bill requiring the government to raise tax allowances by the rate of increase of retail prices every March, unless parliament decided otherwise. In 1981 this principle was ignored. This attempted to reduce the depressing effect of FISCAL DRAG.

Rostow, Walt Whitman, 1916– (B3)

US economic historian and development economist, educated at Yale and Oxford, where he was a Rhodes Scholar. He has been professor of economic history at the Massachusetts Institute of Technology since 1951 apart from an interlude at the University of Texas in 1961-9. His celebrated non-Marxian account of the process of industrialization in *The Stages of Economic Growth* (1960) was further developed in several works, including *The Economics of Take-off into Sustained Growth* (1963), *The World Economy: History and Prospect* (1978) and *Why the Poor Get Richer and the Rich Slow Down* (1980). His NEOCLASSICAL approach to economic history was to inspire much of the later econometric analysis of long time series.

See also: industrial revolution; stages theory; take-off

References

Rostow, W.W. (1971) *The Stages of Economic Growth: A Neo-communist Manifesto*, 2nd edn, Cambridge: Cambridge University Press.

rotten kid theorem (J2)

In a household in which its head transfers resources to all members of the family each member, however selfish, will maximize the family income. A selfish child can only have extra consumption by increasing the family income. According to this theorem, there are no FREE RIDERS and

a need for incentive mechanisms. It is assumed that there is transferable utility within the family.

See also: invisible hand

References

Becker, G. (1974) 'A theory of social interactions', *Journal of Political Economy* 82: 1063-94.

Bergstorm, T. (1989) 'A fresh look at the rotten kid theorem – and other household mysteries', *Journal of Political Economy* 97: 1138-59.

roundabout method of production (D2)

A method of production using CAPITAL goods to increase the future PRODUCTIVITY of factors of production. In a simple case such as fishing, the roundabout method would be used if labour were first expended on producing rods and nets, rather than attempting to catch fish with one's bare hands, so that fish can be caught in greater numbers in a given time period. This concept was central to BÖHM-BAWERK'S capital theory.

See also: capitalism

roundtripping (G1)

Purchasing and reselling the same lot of securities or commodities or money when market prices are rising. An example would be if £X were borrowed for three months and interest rates rose before the end of that period; then the sum borrowed could be relent at a profit. This type of ARBITRAGE is made possible by market distortions.

Royal Economic Society (A1)

The leading UK association of economists founded in 1890 and known for its publication of the *Economic Journal*, which has always been edited by leading economists including EDGEWORTH and KEYNES.

References

Hey, J.B. and Winch, D. (eds) (1990) *A Century of Economics: 100 Years of the Royal Economic Society and the Economic Journal*, Oxford: Basil Blackwell.

RPI – X (E3)

UK retail price index excluding mortgage interest payments.

RPI – Y (E3)

UK retail price index excluding the effects of indirect taxes on final consumption, mortgage interest payments and local authority taxation.

rules versus discretion (E5)

Alternative approaches to economic policy, especially monetary policy. Rules necessitate predetermined responses to events; discretion, a response decided in the light of each economic situation and requiring specific governmental action. There is a continuum of policy stances between, in the case of MONETARY POLICY, rigid rules such as the CURRENCY SCHOOL's principle for the expansion of the note issue and FRIEDMAN's idea of an OPTIMUM QUANTITY OF MONEY, and, on the other hand, the repeated discretionary use of OPEN MARKET OPERATIONS, THE DISCOUNT RATE, RESERVE REQUIREMENTS and MARGIN REQUIREMENTS as practised on many occasions by the FEDERAL RESERVE SYSTEM. TOBIN regarded it as an overworked dichotomy because if we incorporate new information for the determination of policy, the policy is bound to become discretionary. Other economists argue that rules are used in theoretical models, rather than in policy making, as politicians and others are quick to deviate from their own rules.

References

Van Lear, W. (2000) 'A review of the rules versus discretion debate in monetary policy', *Eastern Economic Journal* 26: 29–39.

runaway industry (L0)

An industry which moves from its original location, often to benefit from reductions in costs, especially the lower costs of using non-unionized labour. Many US MULTINATIONAL CORPORATIONS have chosen foreign countries for manufacturing as a means of avoiding the use of expensive labour.

runaway inflation (E3) *see* hyperinflation

runaway shop (J5)

A workplace relocated from an area of high UNIONIZATION to one of low unionization. This relocation is inspired by a desire to reduce labour costs and the incidence of industrial disputes.

running broker (F1)

A London money market broker who 'runs a book' recording sales and purchases of short-term monetary assets.

run on a bank (G2)

The simultaneous demands of the deposit holders of a retail bank for their deposits to be paid. As it is difficult for banks to be sufficiently liquid to meet such concerted action against them without sacrificing the more profitable business of making loans, in the nineteenth and twentieth centuries CENTRAL BANKS emerged. They acted as the LENDER OF LAST RESORT to maintain the liquidity of DOMESTIC BANKING SYSTEMS as a whole and increasingly to supervise the operations of commercial banks. DEPOSIT INSURANCE is also a device to reduce bank runs as there is less point in the public demanding the return of its deposits in cash if there is a guarantee that the deposits will not be lost in a bank collapse.

See also: financial crisis; financial panic; lifeboat operation

rustbelt (R1)

US geographical area where the older manufacturing industries are located, especially Ohio, Michigan, Indiana and Illinois. As the labour forces of firms in that area are high cost and UNIONIZED, there are many incentives for relocation of plants to the US South or to Mexico.

See also: snowbelt; sunbelt

Rybczynski theorem (F1)

The effect on production, consumption and the TERMS OF TRADE of an increase in the quantity of one factor of production. As the same rates of substitution in production hold, when the quantity of the factor is increased there is an expansion in the production of the commodity using relatively more of it so that there is a deterioration in the relative price, or terms of trade, of that commodity.

See also: Heckscher–Ohlin trade theory

References

Rybczynski, T.M. (1955) 'Factor endowments and relative commodity prices', *Economica* New Series, 22: 336–41.

S

sacrifice ratio (E3)
The fall in the number of percentage points of annual output associated with a reduction in price inflation by one percentage point.

sacrifice theory (H2)
The assertion that taxation should be based on ABILITY TO PAY. This approach to taxation can be traced back to Adam SMITH and John Stuart MILL. It has been criticized for assuming that INTERPERSONAL UTILITY COMPARISONS are possible and for ignoring DISINCENTIVE EFFECTS of taxation.

See also: canons of taxation

saddle point (C7)
The determinate solution, in some games, in which all players follow a MAXIMIN STRATEGY.

See also: game theory

safe asset (G0)
An asset with a fixed and certain rate of return, e.g. a bond of a reputable government.

Saint-Simon, Claude-Henri de Rouvroy de, 1760–1825 (B3)
French aristocrat educated by tutors. He fought in the American War of Independence and then in the French Revolutionary Wars when he took the name of Bonhomme. His commercial speculations reduced him to poverty but he nevertheless studied physics and attempted to formulate a theory of society. In *Letters from an Inhabitant of Geneva to his Contemporaries* (1803), *Du Systeme Industriel* (1821) and *Catechisme des Industriels* (1823–26) he argued for a new industrial system of military and industrial associations ruled by scientists but administered by bankers to establish full employment and equality.

saitori (G1) *see* specialist

sales maximization (L2)
An aim of a firm to maximize its TOTAL REVENUE. Managers of large firms having this goal will continue to expand output to increase sales revenue, even if there is a reduction in total profits, provided that profits do not fall below a minimum level. This goal is thought to be attractive as sales revenue is more quickly and easily known than profits; also a larger volume of sales indicates greater market power.

See also: managerial models of the firm

References
Baumol, W.J (1967) *Business Behavior, Value and Growth*, rev. edn, New York: Harcourt, Brace & World.

sales ratios (M4)
Sales as a proportion of stock, debtors, fixed assets, share capital or working capital.

sales tax (H2)
A tax on a good or a service at the point of sale. Some of these taxes are levied on specific goods, as is the case with excise

duties; others are related to general categories of expenditure, e.g. the VALUE-ADDED TAX.

See also: expenditure tax

Samaritan's dilemma (D0)

The vulnerability of the compassionate person who suffers predatory attacks from those helped. Excessive encouragement of parasites can lead to self-destruction. This is a modern interpretation of the parable of the Good Samaritan in St Luke's Gospel 10: 30–37.

References

Buchanan, J.M. (1975) 'The Samaritan's dilemma', in E.S. Phelps *Altruism, Morality and Economic Theory*, New York: Russell Sage Foundation.

sample (C1)

A part of a POPULATION which is examined in order to ascertain the characteristics of the whole of that population. Random sampling (or probability sampling) is used to obtain unbiased estimates. Sampling can produce better evaluations by increasing the size of a sample or by stratification of the sampled population.

References

Kish, L. (1965) *Survey Sampling*, New York: Wiley.

Samuelson, Paul Anthony, 1915– (B3)

The leading post-war US economist who graduated from the Universities of Chicago and Harvard. He was fortunate in having as mentors men as distinguished as KNIGHT, SCHUMPETER, VINER, LEONTIEF and HANSEN. Throughout his academic career he has been at the Massachusetts Institute of Technology where he became a full professor in 1947. He was awarded the NOBEL PRIZE FOR ECONOMICS in 1970.

His vigorous rewriting of the theory of many branches of economics began with his paper on CONSUMER'S SURPLUS in 1938, deriving a demand curve from the revealed preferences of consumers. He published his doctoral dissertation as *Foundations of Economic Analysis* (1947), surveying economic theory in an attempt to move the subject towards comparative dynamics and showing how essential a mathematical approach is to economics. To the majority of economics students his fame rests on his highly successful textbook *Economics*, first published in 1948 and now jointly written with Nordhaus: to date it has sold over 10 million copies. It introduces students to a wide range of economic theory and its applications – over its twelve editions it has broadened its approach from an emphasis on the determinants of aggregate demand to a consideration of supply factors also. He is known to the economics profession as a theoretician of exceptional brilliance, with hundreds of technical papers attesting it. In many outstanding technical contributions he has provided a MULTIPLIER–ACCELERATOR theory of the TRADE CYCLE, a simplification of GENERAL EQUILIBRIUM theory to make it applicable to concrete problems, a REVEALED PREFERENCES theory for WELFARE ECONOMICS, a pure theory of public expenditure which takes into account both PRIVATE AND PUBLIC GOODS and a rigorous factor–price equalization theorem. His eminence has made some describe this as 'the age of Samuelson'. But his NEOCLASSICAL approach has aroused much opposition. His articulate expositions of current economic policy have long been available to the readers of *Newsweek* and the *New York Times*. His long distinguished career has done much to deal with the conclusion to his *Foundations*: 'Economics is a growing subject in which very much is left to be done.'

References

Brown, E.C. and Solow, R.M. (eds) (1983) *Paul Samuelson and Modern Economic Theory*, New York: McGraw-Hill.
Feiwel, G.R. (ed.) (1982) *Samuelson and Neo-Classical Economics*, Boston: Kluwer.
Samuelson, P.A. (1965) *Foundations of Economic Analysis*, New York: Atheneum.
—— (1960, 1972, 1977) *The Collected Scientific Papers of Paul A. Samuelson*, Vols I–IV, Cambridge, MA, and London: Harvard University Press.

samurai bond (G0)

A bond issued in yen in Japan by a foreign concern and purchasable by non-residents of Japan.

Sandilands Report (E3)

UK report of 1975 of a committee on inflation accounting which recommended CURRENT COST ACCOUNTING. It asserted that assets should be revalued at either their replacement or their economic value, as representative of their value to the business at the time; items in PROFIT AND LOSS ACCOUNTS should be valued at their current cost at the time of the sale of the output. The main income measure used was CURRENT OPERATING PROFIT.

satisficing (L2)

Aiming to reach a satisfactory level of performance, rather than to maximize, for example, sales or profits. Modern theories, recognizing the complexity of managerial objectives, have noted that satisficing is a common aim.

See also: managerial models of the firm; revenue maximization; sales maximization

Saudi Arabian Monetary Agency (E5)

An Arab banking organization founded in 1952 to perform the functions of a CENTRAL BANK but called an agency because of the association between 'a bank' and payments for interest which is condemned by Islamic law. SAMA is now responsible for the coinage and note issue of Saudi Arabia, the supervision of commercial banks and the fiscal operations of the government.

See also: Islamic banking; usury

References

Abdeen, A.M. and Shook, D.W. (1984) *The Saudi Financial System in the Context of Western and Islamic Finance*, Chichester: Wiley.

Saudi-ization (L5)

A method of taking foreign businesses into national ownership, not by NATIONALIZATION but by demanding the sale of the majority of shares to private citizens.

Saudi Arabia in 1977 used this approach to change the ownership of foreign-owned commercial banks.

See also: multinational corporation; public enterprise

savings (E2)

The residue of INCOME of a government, a firm or a household after all their expenditures have been incurred. There are many motives for saving. A government may do so to deflate the national economy, a firm to provide self-financing of investment, a household to provide for illness, retirement and the needs of descendants and favourite charities. In the long debate on the determinants of saving, it has been considered too simplistic to regard the rate of interest as the sole determinant because the level of prices is important too. Also, it has been noted that a strong personal motivation to save is independent of most macroeconomic variables. The AVERAGE PROPENSITY TO SAVE of households varies from country to country.

See also: lacking; life-cycle hypothesis; relative income hypothesis

savings and loan association (G2) *see* thrift

savings function (E2)

The relationship between a nation's aggre-

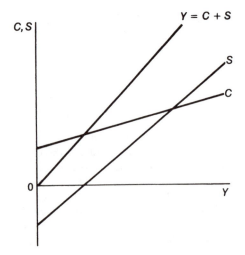

gate savings and its total disposable income. In the simplest models of an economy, in which national income (Y) is equal to consumption (C) plus savings (S), the savings function is, diagrammatically, the inverse of the CONSUMPTION FUNCTION.

savings ratio (E2)

1 The AVERAGE PROPENSITY TO SAVE.
2 Household savings as a proportion of its disposable income.
3 The proportion of a government's or firm's income retained.

In the UK the savings ratio, in the case of households, fell from 14 per cent in 1980 to 4 per cent in 1987, much lower than Japan's 18 per cent and West Germany's 13 per cent. The fall in the UK ratio in the 1980s and 1990s is not entirely caused by the greater availability of consumer credit as the fall in the rate of inflation has reduced the incentive to save as a means of retaining the real value of assets. Also, the life-cycle effect of an ageing population has been to reduce savings. The extent to which low household saving is a problem has been exaggerated as there has been compensating increased saving in the corporate and governmental sectors. Movements in the savings ratio are always imprecise if there are deficiencies in NATIONAL INCOME statistics, e.g. non-recording of BLACK ECONOMY activities (the black economy understates incomes but not consumer expenditure so official savings figures are depressed).

Say, Jean Baptiste, 1767–1832 (B3)

Born in Lyons and trained in insurance in Croydon (London) and France, in the course of which his proprietor, Clavière, encouraged him to read SMITH'S WEALTH OF NATIONS, the beginning of his interest in economics. During the French Revolution he was a journalist and secretary to Clavière, then rose to be Finance Minister and editor from 1794 to 1800 of *La Décade Philosophique, Litéraire et Politique* which expounded Smithian doctrines. In 1803 he produced his major work *Traité d'économie politique*. Opposing Napoleon's policies he resigned his post as tribune and established a cotton mill. In 1814 he returned to England to report on its economic condition for the French government, publishing a pamphlet, *De l'Angleterre et des Anglais*. In 1819 he was appointed to a new chair of industrial economy at the Conservatoire des Arts et Metiers and in 1831 to the chair of political economy at the Collège de France. His *Traité* was expanded into *Cours complèt d'économie politique pratique* (1829), a larger work with many practical applications. KEYNES revived the fame of Say by referring to 'Say's law', a law which ruled out permanent unemployment and had been largely accepted by RICARDO and many major classical writers, although MALTHUS and John Stuart MILL disputed aspects of it. Say's supply and demand analysis, incorporating the concepts of UTILITY and SCARCITY, make him one of the forerunners of NEOCLASSICAL ECONOMICS. Much of his economics was, in the French style, very abstract – as Malthus was quick to note.

Say's law (E1)

A law of markets often summarized as 'supply creates its own demand'. This view of macroeconomics was based on the idea that production creates factor incomes which bring about a demand for the goods produced elsewhere in the economy. The consequence of this 'law' for CLASSICAL ECONOMICS was that there could never be a general and permanent 'glut', i.e. a deficiency in AGGREGATE DEMAND. Although this view is particularly attributed to Say by KEYNES and his followers, many CLASSICAL ECONOMISTS, e.g. James MILL, held to the same theory. The classical conclusion derived from this law is that through price flexibility an economy will always reach a FULL-EMPLOYMENT equilibrium in the long run.

References

Mill, J.S. (1877) *Essays on Some Unsettled Questions of Political Economy*, 3rd edn, No. 2, London: Longmans & Green.

Sowell, T. (1972) *Say's Law: An Historical Analysis*, Princeton, NJ: Princeton University Press.

scalar principle (M1)

Within organizations, this principle dictates that managerial authority and responsibility should flow continuously from the highest person to the lowest in the hierarchy.

scarcity (D0, D2)

1 The limited quantity of a resource, FACTOR OF PRODUCTION or output.
2 Insufficient means to satisfy all of society's demands for resources.

As population increased and there was competition for a fixed supply of natural resources, scarcity was viewed by many economists, including ROBBINS, as the principal economic problem: it raises all the major issues of allocation and pricing and is the reason why rent is paid. Because of scarcity, if goods or services are offered freely, a non-price method of allocation must be used, e.g. RATIONING. The importance of scarcity as a concept is challenged by Marxists who identify other concepts as central.

See also: absolute scarcity

References

Robbins, L. (1935) *An Essay on the Nature and Significance of Economic Science*, London: Macmillan.

scarcity index (D0)

The real cost of capital and labour inputs per unit of an extractive output which is expressed as an index of the prices of extractive outputs relative to non-extractive outputs.

References

Barnett, H.J. and Morse, C. (1963) *Scarcity and Growth: The Economics of Natural Resource Availability*, Baltimore, MD: Johns Hopkins University Press.

scarcity pricing (D4)

Setting prices equal to MARGINAL SOCIAL COST. An approach often used in transport economics.

scarring (J6)

The psychological impact of past unemployment. It is measured by subjective well-being.

References

Clark, A.E., Georgellis, Y. and Sanfey, P. (2001) 'Scarring: the psychological impact of past unemployment', *Economica* 68: 221–41.

scatter diagram (C1)

A scatter of points with X, Y values to which a curve is fitted as a means of making a preliminary study of the relationship between the variables X and Y.

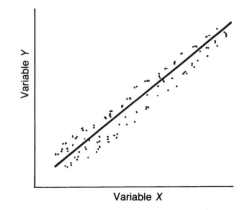

Variable *X*

See also: least squares method

schedular tax (H2)

1 A tax with different rates published in a schedule, especially a progressive tax on incomes.
2 A tax which is related to a particular schedule devised for that type of income rather than a global income tax on all types of income.

Scholes, Myron S., 1941– (B3)

Born in Timmins, Ontario, and educated at McMaster and Chicago Universities. An early passion for mathematics led to an interest in computer programming and then financial economics. For his PhD he wrote a dissertation on constructing a demand curve for securities. After teaching at the Sloan School of Management, MIT and Chicago University, he has held a chair at Stanford since 1972. In several collaborations with Robert Merton and Fischer Black he has produced definitive work on asset pricing and derivative pricing models. He shared the Nobel Prize in Economics with Merton in 1997 for producing a new method to determine the value of derivatives.

Schultz, Theodore William, 1902– (B3)
Leading US authority on HUMAN CAPITAL theory. Educated in agricultural economics at South Dakota State College and the University of Wisconsin. Since 1943, he has been professor at the University of Chicago. His NOBEL PRIZE FOR ECONOMICS, jointly awarded in 1980 with Arthur LEWIS, was for his work in agricultural economics. Although he published a major work on this topic, *The Economic Organization of Agriculture* (1953), his major contribution to mainstream economics has been in leading the modern human capital movement, especially with his *The Economic Value of Education* (1963) and *Investment in Human Capital: The Role of Education and Research* (1971).

Schumacher, Ernst Friedrich, 1911–77 (B3)
UK economist and prophet who was born in Bonn and educated at Berlin, Bonn, Oxford and Columbia Universities. When he was interned in the UK in 1940–5, he worked first as an agricultural labourer and then at the Oxford Institute of Statistics on the problem of a new INTERNATIONAL MONETARY SYSTEM, which he discussed with KEYNES. He was naturalized British at the end of the war so that he could become a member (1946–50) of the British section of the Control Commission in Germany. From 1950 to 1970 he was economic adviser and subsequently Director of Statistics to the National Coal Board. His increasing interest in Buddhism gave his economics a distinctively ecological character and prompted his appointment as economic adviser to the government of Burma. He was the principal proponent of INTERMEDIATE TECHNOLOGY and of self-help to solve the rural poverty problems of less developed countries. His famous attack on materialism and consumerism was in his immensely popular set of essays *Small is Beautiful*; as its subtitle *A Study of Economics as if People Mattered* claimed, there can be an economics based on humanitarian considerations.

References

Schumacher, E. F. (1973) *Small is Beautiful: A Study of Economics as if People Mattered*, London: Blond & Briggs.
Wood, B. (1984) *Alias Papa: A Life of Fritz Schumacher*, London: Jonathan Cape.

Schumpeter, Joseph Alois, 1883–1950 (B3)
A leading US economist who was educated at Vienna University where he was a pupil of BÖHM-BAWERK, without becoming a wholehearted convert to the AUSTRIAN SCHOOL. He held chairs at the Universities of Czernowitz and Graz from 1911 to 1918, was briefly Austrian Minister of Finance in 1920 and president of the Biederman Bank before moving to Bonn where he was professor from 1925 to 1932, completing his career as professor at Harvard from 1932 to 1950. His major contributions to economics were the study of capitalist development and industrial fluctuations and the analysis of a vast economics literature that produced an unsurpassed history of economic theory. He emphasized the role of ENTREPRENEURS and INNOVATION in a number of works: *Capitalism, Socialism and Democracy* (1942), *The Theory of Economic Development* (1951; original German edition, 1912); and his monumental *Business Cycles* (1939). His wife posthumously completed his colossal *History of Economic Analysis* (1954), a work which in a schoolmasterly fashion separated economists of many centuries into the sheep and the goats.

References

Frisch, H. (ed.) (1981) *Schumpeterian Economics*, New York: Praeger.

Schwartz, Anna Jacobson, 1915– (B3)
Leading US monetary historian and economist. Educated at Barnard College, New
York, and Columbia University. Apart from
some academic posts, she has been a research associate of the NATIONAL BUREAU OF
ECONOMIC RESEARCH since 1941. Her collaboration with Milton FRIEDMAN in the analysis of long time series to examine monetary
changes and their effects is very well known.

References
Schwartz, A. and Bordo, M.D. (1980) *A
    Retrospective on the Classical Gold Stan-
    dard*, Chicago: University of Chicago
    Press.
Schwartz, A. and Friedman, M. (1963) *A
    Monetary History of the United States
    1867–1960*, Princeton, NJ: Princeton
    University Press.
—— (1970) *Monetary Statistics of the
    United States*, New York: Columbia
    University Press.

scissors diagram (D4)
The standard diagram of a market showing normal demand and supply curves
intersecting at an EQUILIBRIUM. MARSHALL
suggested this analogy.

Scitovsky reversal test (D6)
An enlargement of the KALDOR–HICKS compensation test with the extra condition
that there is no increase in social welfare
through a return to the original situation
on the part of losers. Scitovsky's consideration of changes in real income took
into account its distribution.

See also: welfare economics

References
Scitovsky, T. (1941) 'A note on welfare
    propositions in economics', *Review of
    Economic Studies* 9: 77–88.

Scitovsky, Tibor, 1910– (B3)
Hungarian, educated at Budapest and the
London School of Economics where he also
taught before emigrating to the USA in
1946. From 1958 to 1968 he worked at the
ORGANIZATION FOR ECONOMIC CO-OPERATION
AND DEVELOPMENT, at Yale from 1968 to

1970, at Stanford from 1970 to 1976 and
back at the London School of Economics
from 1976 to 1978. He is particularly
famous for his WELFARE ECONOMICS, principally set out in his *Welfare and Competition* (1951). His numerous other interests
include international economics, e.g. *Economic Theory and Western European Integration* (1958), and an interesting work
which uses behavioural psychology to
challenge consumer sovereignty theory:
The Joyless Economy (1976).

screening (J2, J3)
An explanation of the higher pay of more
educated workers used as an alternative to
HUMAN CAPITAL theory. It is asserted that
firms choose graduates on the basis of
their qualifications as these indicate natural abilities and training potential rather
than particular skills. Also applied to the
study of UNEMPLOYMENT.

scrip issue (G1)
SHARES offered as an alternative to dividends.

See also: bonus issue; rights issue

scriptural currency (F3)
A currency without issued notes and coins.
The euro was originally issued in this form
in 1999.

S-curve (O4)
The path of long-term ECONOMIC GROWTH.

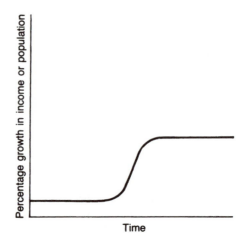

sealed bid auction (D0)
Bids are submitted in sealed envelopes. The highest bidder wins. Also known as the YANKEE BID.

search cost (D0, J0)
The costs to a buyer or seller of acquiring information about prices and quantities available in a market. Some markets, particularly the LABOUR MARKET, have suffered for a long time from imperfections such as ASYMMETRIC INFORMATION. Both employers and workers have to incur many costs (e.g. of advertising, travel, time taken from other activities) to come into contact with each other. Search costs are a form of investment by a worker, with higher wages being the return to such expenditure. If buyers and sellers are rational profit maximizers in their search activities, they will continue seeking for what they desire until the marginal cost of search equals the marginal benefit derived from it. STIGLER was a pioneer in his application of search theory to labour markets.

References
Lippman, S. and McCall, J.J. (1976) 'The economics of job search: a survey', *Economic Inquiry* 14: 115–89 , 347–68.
Pissarides, C.A. (1976) *Labour Market Adjustment*, Cambridge: Cambridge University Press.
Stigler, G.J. (1962) 'Information in the labor market', *Journal of Political Economy* 70 (October Supplement): 94 –105.

search good (D0)
A good infrequently purchased, e.g. a major consumer durable, legal services; hence the consumer has to search for information about its quality.

See also: experience good

search unemployment (J6)
FRICTIONAL UNEMPLOYMENT; being without a job during a period of looking for another one. Many workers will endure lower incomes during periods of unemployment in the hope of increasing lifetime earnings.

See also: unemployment spell

References
Fitzgerald, T.J. (1998) 'An introduction to the search theory of unemployment', *Federal Reserve Bank of Cleveland Economic Review*, 34: 2–15.

seasonal adjustment (C1)
The elimination of seasonal fluctuations from a TIME SERIES, often by the method of MOVING AVERAGES.

seasonal unemployment (J6)
The state of being without a job for a few months of a year because of month-to-month fluctuations in demand for labour of a particular industry. In the hotel and agricultural industries, especially, there is this type of unemployment.

secondary action (J5)
INDUSTRIAL DISPUTES organized by a TRADE (LABOR) UNION against an employer or employers not in dispute with the union with the aim of making the original industrial action more effective. This form of action can take the form of STRIKES and BOYCOTTS of goods of related firms. Both US and UK union law restricts the range of these actions.

secondary bank (G2)
A wholesale bank obtaining its funds from other banks and not from the general public, as is the case with RETAIL or COMMERCIAL BANKS.

See also: investment bank; merchant bank

secondary banking crisis (G2)
A crisis in 1973–4 amongst UK MERCHANT BANKS which had lent to property companies fuelling speculation in the early 1970s and then suffered from many bad debts when the property market collapsed. Some of these banks survived by being rescued in a 'lifeboat operation' mounted jointly by the BANK OF ENGLAND and leading CLEARING BANKS.

secondary capital (G2)
Bank capital consisting of LIMITED-LIFE PRE-

FERRED STOCK, BANK-SUBORDINATED NOTES and DEBENTURES, and unsecured long-term debt of the parent company and its non-bank subsidiaries.

See also: primary capital

secondary employment (E0) *see* employment multiplier

secondary labour market (J4)
That part of a national labour market consisting of small firms employing workers at low wages and offering them little training.

See also: external labour market; primary labour market

secondary market (G1)
A financial market for trading in SECURITIES already in existence, which usually takes the form of a stock exchange. The growth of the number of types of tradable financial asset has led to the creation of new markets.

See also: primary market

secondary mortgage market (G2)
The sale and purchase among banks and other investors of first mortgages made to obtain loans.

See also: primary mortgage market

secondary standard (Q2)
A standard for pollution levels necessary to protect vegetation, buildings and visibility. It is assumed that pollution control is already sufficient to protect human health.

See also: ambient standard; primary standard

second best (D0)
An allocation falling short of being PARETO-EFFICIENT by not fulfilling all of Pareto's conditions for optimality.

References
Lipsey, R.G. and Lancaster, K. (1956) 'The general theory of the second best', *Review of Economic Studies* 24: 11–32.

second-degree price discrimination (L2, M3)
Setting different prices for different quantities, e.g. offering discounts for purchasing larger quantities, but subjecting all customers to the same price schedule.

See also: price discrimination

second economy (P4)
The market-oriented part of a socialist economy run by private persons. It can be legal or illegal; increasingly, private enterprise has been permitted in the service sector in Eastern Europe.

See also: first economy

References
Grossman, G. (1977) 'The second economy of the USSR', *Problems of Communism* 26: 25–40.

second-generation product (M3)
A product in many respects similar to an existing product capturing its market from it. In science-based industries such as pharmaceuticals, a new drug is often supplanted by a related compound. The cost and riskiness of industrial research has increased because of the need to extend a product range to replace supplanted products.

second market (G1)
UNLISTED SECURITIES MARKET (UK). In France, a second market was established in 1983 to allow smaller companies to go public with lower costs and small share issues.

second-price auction (D4)
A method of selling consisting of potential buyers submitting sealed written bids for an item with the item being sold to the highest bidder at the second-highest price offered. The London stamp auctions are conducted in this way.

See also: auction

Second World (P2)
CENTRALLY PLANNED ECONOMIES of the SOVIET

TYPE. These were chiefly the economies of Eastern Europe from 1948 to 1990.

See also: First World; Fourth World; Third World

Section 20 subsidiary (L4)

A subsidiary of a US bank holding company or a bank foreign to the USA permitted by the FEDERAL RESERVE on a case-by-case basis to engage in underwriting and security dealing. The section is part of the Bank Holding Act.

sector adjustment lending (H2)

An aid-assisted loan given to improve the performance of a specific sector of an economy. As such targeting neglects other sectors of an economy, it reduces the number of linked benefits of providing finance more generally, e.g. the advanced sectors by receiving finance could bring about a general improvement through SPILLOVER EFFECTS.

See also: soft loan

Securities and Exchange Commission (G2)

US regulatory body set up in 1933 with the task of regulating US SECURITIES markets, the offer of securities to the public, mutual funds, investment companies, public utility securities and investment advisers.

See also: blue-sky laws

Securities Association (G1)

The UK body regulating stock market and related securities firms, having taken over from the Stock Exchange its regulatory function. This is the largest of the SELF-REGULATORY ORGANIZATIONS set up by the FINANCIAL SERVICES ACT. It covers more financial firms than did the Stock Exchange Council and vets both member firms and staff who have dealings with the public.

Securities Exchange Act 1934 (G1)

Basic US federal statute which regulates securities exchanges and OVER-THE-COUNTER trading, set up the SECURITIES AND EX-CHANGE COMMISSION and sets out the information which corporations have to provide to have their securities listed on an exchange.

securities market (G1)

A market where new or existing stocks and shares are sold. PRIMARY MARKETS are concerned with new issues, SECONDARY MARKETS with maintaining a market in bills, bonds, stocks and shares already issued: securities markets often combine both functions. In recent years, the principal developments in these markets have been a movement from the use of specialist trading to FINANCIAL CONGLOMERATES and the devising of methods of REGULATION appropriate to markets which have been transformed by internationalization and rapid electronic communication.

securitization (G1)

The conversion of bank loans into tradable securities. Borrowers, instead of raising loans, request merchant or investment banks to raise money for them by the issue of shares. The collapse of stock markets in 1987 made it more difficult to raise finance by new issues.

See also: monetization

References

Bonsall, D.C. (1990) *Securitisation*, London: Butterworth.

Henderson, J. and Scott, J. (1988) *Securitisation*, Cambridge: Woodhead Faulkner.

security (G1)

A financial instrument in bearer form or registered form, i.e. its owner is the bearer or the person listed in a register for that security. Securities take many forms, including bonds, stocks and shares.

See also: bearer bond; bearer shares

seed capital (G0)

A form of VENTURE CAPITAL used to finance entrepreneurs attempting to set up businesses. In the EUROPEAN COMMUNITY, the European Seed Capital Fund Network co-ordinates the provision of this capital in several European Community countries.

segmented labour market theory (J4)

The supposition that the LABOUR MARKET is divided into a number of subgroups with little mobility between them and different rules for determining wages and allocating labour within them. The best example is DUAL LABOUR MARKET theory.

seignorage (E4)

1 The levy charged by states for converting precious metals into coins (the UK abolished that charge in 1666).
2 The net earnings received by a country with a RESERVE CURRENCY from the assets it acquires through other countries holding its currency.
3 The revenue, net of the cost of production, gained from issuing banknotes or another form of currency. Seignorage is a major source of government revenue in high-inflation economies as a government can finance its deficits by creating more money.

See also: free banking

selection bias (C1)

A deviation from the random selection method of sampling. Although selections which depart from the random method of selection fail to provide an accurate description of the population sampled, models of self-selection have often been used in economics, e.g. to study occupational choice, the returns to training and the returns to schooling.

References

Roy, A.D. (1951) 'Some thoughts on the distribution of earnings', *Oxford Economic Papers, New Series* 3: 135–46.

Selective Employment Tax (H2, O4)

A tax designed by KALDOR and in force in the UK from 1966 to 1973 which sought to encourage the movement of workers from service industries to manufacturing industries by imposing a PAYROLL TAX on

the former. It led to a decline in service sector employment but did not revive manufacturing industry whose problems were more severe than a shortage of labour.

References

Reddaway, W.B. (1970) *Effects of the Selective Employment Tax. First Report. The Distributive Trades*, London: HMSO.

self-employment (J2)

Being engaged in work for pay or profit and not under the direction of another. The self-employed are part of the labour force and are present in every sector. The peasant farmer, the professional lawyer, the actor and the small shopkeeper are leading cases of self-employment. Inability to gain employment may force a person to attempt to gain an income through self-employment. Often self-employed businesses are undercapitalized because of the poor availability and higher cost of small-scale finance. Self-employment produces a hybrid income of wages and profits. An estimate of residual profits can be extracted from total income by applying a market wage rate to the number of hours worked; an estimate of wages, by applying the market rate of interest to the amount of capital employed to see how much of total income remains.

self-insurance (G0)

The absorption of unusual losses by an organization itself, without resort to insurance companies and markets. Many governmental organizations follow this principle.

self-interest (D0)

Private interest. This desire for personal gain prompts productive activity. It is not to be equated with selfishness as co-operative behaviour yields private returns. The idea was central to Adam Smith's *WEALTH OF NATIONS*.

References

Meyers, M.L. (1983) *The Soul of Modern Economic Man: Ideas of Self-Interest, Thomas Hobbes to Adam Smith*, Chicago: Chicago University Press.

self-regulation (K2, L5)

Control of a profession or a market by the members of it, rather than by the government. In the UK, the Stock Exchange has the INTERNATIONAL SECURITIES REGULATORY ORGANIZATION, IMRO, LAUTRO, Fimbra and AFBD; in the USA, the American Medical Association is a prominent example of self-regulation. If such a form of regulation is unsuccessful in preventing and prosecuting offenders, there is usually a call for governmental control.

self-regulatory organization (K2, L5)

An organization set up by a profession or group of specialist financial traders to regulate the conduct of its members instead of being subject to direct governmental control. In the UK, examples of these organizations include LLOYD'S, the SECURITIES ASSOCIATION, AFBD, Fimbra, IMRO and LAUTRO.

See also: Financial Services Act; regulation

self-sufficient economy (P4)

An ECONOMY in which the domestic supply and domestic demand are equal for all goods and services. Some US policy-makers regard this notional state as an optimal goal for the US economy.

See also: autarky

sellers' market (D4)

A market where sellers have a dominant influence on price because of EXCESS DEMAND.

See also: buyers' market

selling short (G1) *see* short selling

Selten, Reinhard, 1930– B3

Born in Breslau, then in Germany. His early interest in mathematics developed into the study of game theory at Frankfurt University. His first research was in co-operative GAME THEORY and his first paper on an oligopoly experiment before beginning a long study of bounded rationality. He introduced experimental economics into Germany. Professor at the Free University, West Berlin, from 1969 to 1972, Bielefeld from 1972 to 1984 and at Bonn since 1984. He shared the NOBEL PRIZE FOR ECONOMICS in 1994 with NASH and HARSANYI.

semi-colonial country (P1)

A politically independent country whose economy, according to MARXIAN ECONOMICS, is dominated by international imperialist CAPITALISTS.

semi-interquartile range (C1)

The UPPER QUARTILE minus the LOWER QUARTILE divided by 2, for a particular data set.

Sen, Amartya K., 1933– (B3)

Leading social choice theorist, born in Bengal and educated at the Presidency College, Calcutta, and Trinity College, Cambridge. His academic posts have been professor at the Jadavpur University, Calcutta, fellow of Trinity College, Cambridge(1957–63), professor at Delhi (1963–71), professor at the London School of Economics (1971–7), professor of economics then Drummond Professor of Political Economy at Oxford (1977–86), professor at Harvard (1987–98) and subsequently Master of Trinity College, Cambridge. Awarded the NOBEL PRIZE FOR ECONOMICS in 1998. His distinguished career has embraced SOCIAL CHOICE THEORY and DEVELOPMENT ECONOMICS. His rigorous works *Collective Choice and Social Welfare* (1971) and *On Economic Equality* (1973) show his ability to wrestle with the IMPOSSIBILITY THEOREM and to cast doubt on PARETO OPTIMALITY. As a noted contributor to development economics, he has offered practical advice in *Choice of Techniques* (1960) and *Employment, Technology and Development* (1975) as well as illuminating the poverty problem in *Poverty and Famines: An Essay on Entitlement and Deprivation* (1981) which looked at poverty in terms of a lack of income, not of food supply.

senior debt (G0)
A debt secured by collateral which has to be repaid before any other stockholders or creditors in the event of liquidation.

See also: junior debt

seniority principle (J3)
A feature of the structure of pay, benefits, promotion and redundancy procedures. Although in the USA this 'wage for age' principle has its strongest effects on the pay of non-unionized workers and on the FRINGE BENEFITS of unionized workers, in general it is most visible as the underlying principle of pay determination under TRADE (LABOR) UNIONS. In Japan, ENTERPRISE UNIONS used seniority as the basis for sharing out increases to the total wage bill. As an economic justification for this approach to wages and salary policy, it is argued that experience should be rewarded. Also, a worker aware that this principle underlies the pay structure will be more reluctant to move to another employer, thus increasing the private return to the employer of any investment in training.

See also: human capital

Senior, Nassau William, 1790–1864 (B3)
Leading CLASSICAL ECONOMIST educated at Magdalen College, Oxford, and Lincoln's Inn where he was called to the Bar in 1819. His first literary work as a reviewer for the *Quarterly Review* included commenting on the usage of key economic terms and the CORN LAWS. As Drummond Professor of Political Economy at Oxford University from 1826 to 1830 and from 1847 to 1851 he published lectures on precious metals, population, money and wages. His views on the POOR LAWS and the Factory Acts made him a prominent adviser to governments. His ABSTINENCE theory of savings and his inclusion of MARGINAL UTILITY as a cause of value estab-

lished his originality as an economic theorist.

References
Levy, S.L. (1970) *Nassau W. Senior 1790 – 1864*, Newton Abbot: David & Charles.
Senior, N.W. (1831) *Three Lectures on the Rate of Wages*, London: Murray (reprinted Thoemmes Press, Bristol, 1998, ed. Ronald Sutherland).
—— (1836) *An Outline of the Science of Political Economy*, London (reprinted New York: Augustus M. Kelley, 1965).
—— (1966) *Selected Writings on Economics: A Volume of Pamphlets 1827–1852*, New York: Augustus M. Kelley.

sequential externality (D0, Q0)
An economic activity affecting the productivity of another activity in a later time period, e.g. chemical production which reduces the effectiveness of fishing through pollution.

See also: contemporaneous externality

sequential game (C7)
An ordered game in which the move by one firm is followed by the reaction of its rival.

sequestration (H6, K0)
1 Spending cuts in the US Federal Budget imposed under the GRAMM-RUDMAN-HOLLINGS ACT.
2 Temporary seizure of assets under a court order, e.g. of union funds under UK employment legislation.

serial correlation (C1) *see* autocorrelation

service industry (L8)
An industry not producing goods but performing various tasks, including transportation, distribution, professional advice, finance. This sector has expanded rapidly in Western countries since 1950, partly as the result of firms becoming more specialized and buying in services which were previously provided in-house and partly through increased consumers' real incomes making possible the purchase of others' labour.

See also: productive labour

services (D2)

The non-physical output flowing from the employment of a FACTOR OF PRODUCTION. The major example is labour services. These can be as menial as cleaning, or as demanding as the provision of professional advice. As an ECONOMY reaches an advanced stage of development its activities are increasingly of this nature.

See also: Petty's law

servicing a debt (G0)

Repaying the interest due on a debt.

See also: debt service indicators; world debt problem

set aside (Q1)

A payment to farmers to take land out of agricultural production. The success of farmers in increasing productivity in Europe in recent decades has made necessary this approach to reducing mountains of stored produce.

severe correction (G1)

A sharp fall in stock market prices leading to widespread losses.

Sex Discrimination Acts 1975, 1986 (J7)

UK legislation requiring equal treatment of men and women.

sexual discrimination (J7)

The unfavourable treatment of one sex in matters of wages, recruitment or promotion. In the USA federal legislation first addressed itself to this in civil rights legislation of the 1960s; in the UK under the EQUAL PAY ACT 1970 and SEX DISCRIMINATION ACTS 1975, 1986; in the EUROPEAN COMMUNITY under Article 119 of the TREATY OF ROME. The economic analysis of discrimination dates back to John Stuart MILL's writings on the wages of women in his *Principles*.

See also: crowding hypothesis; occupational segregation

sexual division of labour (J2, J7)

The division of occupations into two groups: those predominantly carried out by men and those where women are in the majority. As early as John Stuart MILL it was recognized that female employment was crowded into comparatively few occupations. This concentration arose from the belief that women are only capable of doing jobs similar to their household tasks, i.e. cleaning, cooking, nursing, bringing up young children and secretarial tasks. BARRIERS TO ENTRY created by male-dominated TRADE UNIONS, e.g. in printing, perpetuated this concentration. Legislation such as the UK's SEX DISCRIMINATION ACT 1975 has earnestly sought a higher proportion of women in each occupational group.

See also: crowding hypothesis; occupational segregation

References

Mill, J.S. (1948) *Principles of Political Economy*, Book II, ch. XIV, section 5.

Shackle, George Lennox Sharman, 1903–92 (B3)

UK economist noted for his works on EXPECTATIONS. After an education at New College, Oxford, and the London School of Economics, he worked at the Oxford Institute of Statistics and, during the war, in the Economic Section of the Cabinet Secretariat before being appointed Reader in Economic Theory at Leeds University from 1950 to 1951 and Brunner Professor of Economic Science at the University of Liverpool from 1951 to 1969. He delved deeply into the central issues of KEYNES'S GENERAL THEORY, EXPECTATIONS and UNCERTAINTY, e.g. in his *Expectations, Investment and Income* (1938) and *Expectations in Economics* (1949). A lively account of the renaissance of economics in the 1930s is detailed in *The Years of High Theory* (1967). The principal questions he examined were the significance of time, the meaning and process of human choosing and the role of information in choosing.

See also: potential surprise function

References

Ford, J.L. (ed.) (1990) *Time, Expectations and Uncertainty. Selected Essays of G.L.S. Shackle*, Aldershot: Edward Elgar.

shadow director (G3)

A person who has a considerable influence over a company without being a registered director.

shadow economy (K4, L0)

The activities of the BLACK ECONOMY and of households and voluntary organizations. The value of all the goods and services produced in this way does not enter into the official NATIONAL INCOME accounts.

References

Brezinsti, H. (1991) *The Shadow Economy*, Boulder, CO: Westview Press.

Smith, S. (1986) *Britain's Shadow Economy*, Oxford: Basil Blackwell.

shadow price (D0)

An imputed price used where a market price does not exist. These prices are used by large firms for their internal transactions, by central planners for accounting purposes and in COST–BENEFIT ANALYSIS to measure the effects of a particular investment. There are shadow rates of interest, shadow exchange rates and shadow wage rates. The purpose of such pricing is to correct distortions introduced by monopoly, taxes and unemployment. The concept has many applications in both developed and less developed countries (because they tend to overvalue their labour and undervalue their foreign exchange).

References

Little, I.M.D. and Scott, M.F.G. (eds) (1976) *Using Shadow Prices*, London: Heinemann Educational.

shallow market (D0)

A market with little trading with the consequence that an individual transaction can have a great influence on the market price.

sham trading (D0, G0)

Buying or selling not backed by goods.

This type of trading is central to the idea of a FUTURES market.

Shapley value (C7)

The UTILITY that a participant in an *n*-person game with an uncertain outcome, e.g. a LOTTERY, expects to obtain. The game assumes that utility is transferable between the players and that it is a zero-sum game. Shapley values have been used in models of taxation, the allocation of joint costs and the study of voting systems.

References

Shapley, L.S. (1953) 'A value for n-person games', in H.W. Kulin and A.W. Tucker (eds) *Contributions to the Theory of Games*, Princeton, NJ: Princeton University Press.

share (G1)

A portion of the financial capital of a limited company which gives the holder an entitlement, in the case of ordinary shares, to a variable dividend decided by the board of directors, or in the case of preference shares, to a fixed return. Ordinary shares are also known as EQUITIES.

share borrowing (G1)

The borrowing of shares, usually from the holdings of large INSTITUTIONAL INVESTORS, by MARKET-MAKERS in order to effect delivery of shares more speedily. This enables payment to be received immediately, at the low fee of about 2 per cent of the value of the borrowed shares. This practice was previously permitted for JOBBERS who wanted to sell short, i.e. sell shares they did not own and then borrow to effect delivery. In the UK, the Stock Exchange restricts the practice now to MARKET-MAKERS to encourage more firms to undertake that role. Stock borrowing has long been permitted in US markets.

share buy-back (G1)

Purchase by a company of its own shares, if permitted by its Articles of Association. This practice, which aims to enhance the earnings per share of a company, is more prevalent in the USA than in the UK.

sharecropper (Q1)

A tenant farmer who pays the rent in kind as a percentage of his or her crops. In return the landlord provides seed, fertilizers, implements and other non-labour inputs. This type of JOINT VENTURE is a common feature of agriculture in less developed countries and regions. The relative shares of landlord and tenant will depend on the scarcity of labour relative to capital and local culture. The landlord's share is much larger in Middle Eastern countries than in southern Europe. In developed countries, unlike Third World countries, sharecroppers will be compensated for permanent land improvements and will be granted longer leases to encourage the development of agriculture.

References

Byres, T.J. (ed.) (1983) *Sharecropping and Sharecroppers*, London: Cass.

shared monopoly (L1) *see* oligopoly

share economy (G1, J3, P4)

1 An ECONOMY whose industry is widely owned through the distribution of EQUITY shares to employees and other small shareholders.

2 The sharing of the revenues of a firm with its employees.

See also: wider share ownership

share fisherman (Q1)

A fisherman whose remuneration is a proportion of the profits from each catch. This method of pay has long been used in Scotland.

share support operation (G3)

The purchase of the shares of a company by its directors and their associates that is intended to boost the share price, especially during a takeover.

See also: share buy-back

Sharpe, William, 1934– (B3)

Educated at the University of California, Los Angeles, and professor of economics at Stanford University since 1970. He has developed the CAPITAL ASSET PRICING MODEL to examine portfolio risk into its systematic and unsystematic elements. In 1990 he shared the NOBEL PRIZE FOR ECONOMICS with MARKOVITZ and MILLER.

See also: beta

shelf registration (G0)

A company or government bond approved prior to issue. When the market is favourable, this provisional bond is issued at short notice. This method of issue was introduced in the USA in 1982.

shell company (L2)

A company which has ceased to engage in its original activities, has few assets and earnings but usually has a stock market quotation. Some former plantation companies are of this kind. These companies provide an easy way for a new company to acquire a stock market quotation by a 'shell operation'.

shell operation (G3)

Acquisition of a shell company as a means of obtaining a stock market quotation.

sheltered employment (J2)

Employment specially provided for disabled persons. In the UK, the firm Remploy was set up in 1945 to implement the Disabled Persons (Employment) Act, but other firms were expected to offer at least 3 per cent of their jobs to the disabled. Remploy by using a fine subdivision of labour is capable of providing more technically simple jobs than other employers.

Sherman Act 1890 (L4)

The founding statute of the US federal ANTITRUST legislation. This Act prohibits 'all contracts, combinations and conspiracies in restraint of trade' (section 1) and monopolization in interstate and foreign trade (section 2). The Act was followed by further federal legislation and similar statutes for individual states.

See also: antitrust; Celler–Kefauver Antimerger Act; Clayton Act; Federal Trade Commission Act; Robinson–Patman Act

References
Bork, R.H. (1978) *The Antitrust Paradox*, New York: Basic Books.

shifting of taxes (H2)

Passing the burden of a tax from the person originally paying it to another. A principal example is the shifting of a tax on commodities from producers to consumers (forward shifting); there can also be backward shifting, e.g. when an AD VALOREM TAX has to be paid by a producer because the final prices are the same pre- and post-tax.

See also: tax incidence

shift share analysis (R1)

A technique in regional analysis for analysing the effects on a region's growth of its share of national industrial activity, usually measured by employment, being structurally different from that of the country as a whole. Thus, for example, if region X were growing faster than the country of which it was part, this analysis would indicate how much of that regional growth could be attributed to it having a higher proportion of rapidly growing industries than the country as a whole. The shift can be split into a proportional shift, reflecting differences in the mix of industrial sectors at national and regional levels, and a differential shift caused by different employment growth rates in a region and the nation of which it is part.

shifts in demand or supply curves (D0)

An upward or downward movement of a whole demand or supply curve because a variable, other than price, has changed. A change in consumer tastes, in consumer incomes or in the prices of other goods can move a demand curve; a change in technology or governmental regulation can move a supply curve. These shifts are always the result of a failure of the CETERIS PARIBUS condition.

See also: identification problem

Shinsanbetsu (J5)

National Federation of Industrial Organizations: this Japanese national-level trade union federation had a membership of 56,000 persons in October 1988 at the time of its dissolution.

See also: Rengo

shirking model (J3)

A model of wage determination that asserts a wage is fixed at a high enough level to ensure that workers do not shirk because they fear that if they were caught they would lose their high incomes. This model takes into account the MORAL HAZARD problem arising from a firm only periodically observing worker effort.

References
Shapiro, C. and Stiglitz, J.E. (1984) 'Equilibrium unemployment as a worker discipline device', *American Economic Review* 74: 433–44.

shock inflation (E3)

A once-and-for-all change in the price level which may be caused by a change in INDIRECT TAX rates or import prices or a major change in the supply of a major commodity, e.g. oil.

See also: oil-price increases

shoe leather costs of inflation (E3)

Costs in time and effort to carry out economic transactions because the falling value of money in times of inflation brings about a reduction in money holdings.

See also: menu costs of inflation; transactions cost

shop steward (J5)

An elected official of a TRADE UNION who represents a group of workers within an establishment or factory. He or she participates in local bargaining on pay, conditions of work and disciplinary procedures. It was argued in the 1960s by the DONOVAN COMMISSION that in the UK they were central actors in an informal system of factory-level industrial relations.

short (F3)

A deficit: a foreign exchange dealer is 'in

short' when he or she has a deficit in a particular currency.

See also: long

shortage economy (P4)
An economy characterized by EXCESS DE-MAND for many goods and services for substantial periods of time. This often happens because prices of basic necessities are kept below their market clearing levels for welfare reasons. In a CENTRALLY PLANNED ECONOMY, there is a tendency to adhere to the same set of prices for many years, not raising them as demand rises. Also, if the prices set by a government reflect its priorities and not those of consumers excess demand can easily develop.

See also: Soviet-type economy

short selling (G1)
Selling a SECURITY not owned by the seller who subsequently buys sufficient volume of that security to effect delivery. Such behaviour, the activity of a bear, is popular when markets are falling in price.

See also: share borrowing

short-termism (E6)
Preferring the short to the long term in economic decision making, particularly preferring to spend current income rather than invest long term. This attitude is manifest in the low proportion of total expenditure on research and development, inadequate investment in technology and poor control over the total wages bill. UK Chancellor of the Exchequer Nigel Lawson coined the term in 1986 to characterize much of the thinking of industrialists and financiers. Also, it has been argued that major INSTITUTIONAL INVESTORS, e.g. pension funds, despite their ability to make long-term investments, are too interested in capital gains from short-term market movements.

short-term money market (G1)
A market in financial securities with a life of several months at most based in a major financial centre. Since 1970, many

new markets of this kind have been established in the City of London, New York and European financial capitals. The items traded include CERTIFICATES OF DE-POSIT, TREASURY BILLS, COMMERCIAL BILLS, local authority bills, discount house deposits, local authority deposits, ECUS and SPECIAL DRAWING RIGHTS.

See also: discount market

short-time working (J2)
Working fewer hours than the standard working week, as defined by a collectively bargained agreement or an individual employment contract. This is a method of making a short-term adjustment to a fall in demand for labour; it often precedes redundancies.

See also: working hours; overtime

Shoup Mission (H2)
A mission of inquiry headed by the US economist Carl S. Shoup who recommended in 1949 a complete overhaul of the Japanese taxation system, bringing it closer to the US system than to Western Europe's.

References
Bronfenbrenner, M. and Kogiku, K. (1957) 'The aftermath of the Shoup tax reforms', *National Tax Journal* 10: 236–54.
Shoup Mission (1949) *The Report on Japanese Taxation*, Tokyo: General Headquarters, Supreme Commander for the Allied Powers.

shunto (J3)
The Japanese Spring Wage Offensive. Since 1955, the union federations have presented simultaneous wage claims to employers with one union being chosen to advance the first wage and conditions claim to act as a pacemaker for other unions. The system gives more power to a trade union movement which is characterized by 34,000 small unions mostly at the enterprise level and provides macroeconomic guidelines for enterprise bargaining.

See also: enterprise union; pattern settlement; wage round

shutdown price (D0)
A minimum price equal to the short-run average VARIABLE COST. Below this price, firms would prefer to shut down rather than accept a lower price and incur losses, including payments needed to cover FIXED COSTS.

siege economy (P4)
A national ECONOMY cut off from economic relationships with the rest of the world, usually through war or ECONOMIC SANCTIONS. To maintain the availability of a wide range of goods, such economies have to diversify into activities new to them. It has been argued in favour of tariffs that some high-cost industries should be protected from international competition in case a country is under siege in the future and needs the output from those industries.

See also: autarky; open economy

sight deposit (G2)
A bank deposit immediately payable on demand.

See also: current account; time deposit

signal extraction (C1)
The statistical removal of the trend, seasonal and irregular components in a TIME SERIES, especially using an ARIMA model.

signal jamming (L1)
A type of BARRIER TO ENTRY that 'jams', or prevents, a potential entrant from gaining information about the profitability of the existing firms of an industry.

References
Fudenberg, D. and Tirole, J. (1986) 'A "signal jamming" theory of predation', *Rand Journal of Economics* 18: 211–31.

signalling (D8)
Providing information for economic decision making, particularly by the price mechanism. Changes in prices 'signal' to producers and potential producers a change in the relationship between demand and supply in that market. If prices rise, producers will be aware of a supply deficiency and encouraged to increase their output and, if necessary, their capital stock. Similarly in labour markets an increase in occupational pay will encourage persons to acquire the appropriate training and to apply for jobs of that kind.

See also: Hayek

significance test (C1)
A procedure that calculates a statistic to ascertain whether an observed deviation from the NULL HYPOTHESIS is real or the product of chance.

See also: chi-squared distribution; *F* test; Student's *t* distribution

silver ring (G2)
The two or three City of London DISCOUNT HOUSES that principally run the books which determine the discount market.

Simon, Herbert Alexander, 1916– (B3)
US theorist of corporate behaviour who was educated at Chicago University. He taught at the Illinois Institute of Technology from 1942 to 1949, at the Carnegie Institute of Technology from 1949 to 1955 and subsequently at Carnegie-Mellon University. His eclectic knowledge of psychology, computer science and economics has enabled him to write extensively on administrative behaviour and corporate decision making. His famous textbook *Administrative Behavior* was first published in 1947. His celebrated contribution to economics has been the concept of BOUNDED RATIONALITY. He was awarded the NOBEL PRIZE FOR ECONOMICS in 1978.

Simons, Henry Calvert, 1899–1946 (B3)
Educated at the University of Michigan and professor successively at Iowa, from 1920 to 1927, and Chicago from 1927 to 1946. He was a founder of the CHICAGO SCHOOL, a prominent tax theorist whose ideas underlie the US federal INDIVIDUAL INCOME TAX and a noted libertarian in his attitude to economic policy.

References

Simons, H.C. (1938) *Personal Income Taxation: The Definition of Income as a Problem of Fiscal Policy*, Chicago: University of Chicago Press.

—— (1948) *Economic Policy for a Free Society*, Chicago: University of Chicago Press.

—— (1950) *Federal Tax Reform*, Chicago: University of Chicago Press.

simulation model (C9)

A model of economic reality concentrating on the main and crucial features of an ECONOMY and attempting to estimate the relationships between those features with a view to estimating the effects of changing the values of those variables. Such models have been used in the study of cyclical fluctuations, in corporate decision making and national ECONOMIC PLANNING.

References

Bonini, C.P. (1963) *Simulation of Information and Decision Systems in the Firm*, Englewood Cliffs, NJ: Prentice Hall.

Duesenberry, J.S., Eckstein, O. and Fromm, G. (1960) 'A simulation model of the United States economy in recession', *Econometrica* 28: 749–809.

simultaneous ascending auction (D0)

An auction for multiple items. Bidding occurs in rounds with each bidder making a sealed bid. At the end of each round there is a standing high bid which goes on to the next round. This method was used for the sale of radio spectrum licences in the USA.

single-capacity trading (G1)

The method of trading which separated jobbers from brokers on the London Stock Exchange in force from 1908 to 1986. London's deregulation, usually termed BIG BANG, gave stock exchange members the right to combine both functions and be MARKET-MAKERS.

single currency (E4)

The only currency acceptable as LEGAL TENDER in a particular country or countries, different from a COMMON CURRENCY.

Single European Act 1986 (F0)

An amendment to the TREATY OF ROME that has changed the nature of decision making in the EUROPEAN COMMUNITY by permitting majority voting instead of unanimity. It also limited the harmonization of policies to essential standards, granted the European Parliament a greater role in the creation of legislation, reaffirmed the need to increase the European Community's economic and social cohesion in labour and scientific matters and added to the treaty a recognition of organizations, such as the EUROPEAN MONETARY SYSTEM, created since 1958. The features of the Act were derived from Lord Cockfield's report *Completing the Internal Market* (1985) which listed 300 changes essential by 1992 to remove barriers to movement and trade.

single factorial terms of trade (F1)

NET BARTER TERMS OF TRADE multiplied by a PRODUCTIVITY change index for the export trades. This enables a nation to calculate what its factors of production earn in foreign goods.

See also: terms of trade

single market (F1)

The INTERNAL MARKET of the EUROPEAN COMMUNITY created by 1992 as a consequence of the Single European Act of 1986. It was hoped that the European Community market would be unified by the removal of all barriers to movement and trade, as well as unifying the financial market. Member countries were expected to gain an extra 4.25–6.5 per cent of GROSS DOMESTIC PRODUCT through the internal market leading to an exploitation of ECONOMIES OF SCALE and the efficiency which arises from increased competition and COMPARATIVE ADVANTAGE. This stage of removing the final barriers to trade in the European Community concerns the removal of remaining differences in the technical regulations of member countries, waiting at frontiers to conform with customs regulations, the restriction of competition for public contracts to the nationals of one country and the limits to competition in financial, transport and some other service industries. These gains were expected to be realized in a period of five or six years.

References

Emerson, M., Anjean, M., Catinat, M., Goybet, P. and Jacqueman, A. (1988) *The Economics of 1992*, Oxford: Oxford University Press.

single-tax movement (H2)
The campaign in the USA by Henry GEORGE for existing taxes to be replaced by a single tax on land, which would absorb all pure rents. This view was based on the observation that landlords have an unearned income arising from land as it rises in value through being fixed in supply but increasingly demanded as the population grows. A century before, the PHYSIO-CRATS, too, proposed a single tax on land. For such a change in taxation to be fair to all factors of production, ECONOMIC RENT wherever it occurs, including a portion of the earnings of talented performers, would have to be taxed.

See also: Turgot

References

George, H. (1918) *Single Tax – What It Is and Why We Urge It*, Los Angeles: Golden Press.

single-union deal (J5)
An agreement between an employer and a TRADE UNION which excludes other unions from organizing workers in that firm or its workplaces. This simplification of INDUS-TRIAL RELATIONS has increasingly been requested by firms setting up new plants and is accepted by trade unions who fear that the alternative is a non-union plant. Japanese-owned companies have been major pioneers of this approach in the UK where it was deeply resented by the trade unions who often were rejected as recognized representatives of workers. Countries with INDUSTRIAL UNIONS, e.g. Germany, or ENTER-PRISE UNIONS, e.g. Japan, have long accepted the principle of one union in charge of worker representation.

References

Bassett, P. (1986) *Strike Free: New Industrial Relations in Britain*, London: Macmillan.

sin tax (H2)
An indirect tax on a good regarded as a minor vice such as tobacco or alcohol.

size distribution (C1)
A frequency distribution classifying an economic entity according to size classes. Personal incomes can be classified to show what proportion falls into each range of income; likewise, data on firms can be presented in this way. Endowments of human and non-human capital are major determinants of the size distribution of income.

See also: personal income distribution

References

Champernowne, D.G. (1953) 'A model of income distribution', *Economic Journal* 63: 318–51.
Meade, J.E. (1964) *Efficiency, Equality, and the Ownership of Property*, London: Allen & Unwin.

size of an economy (E0)
A national ECONOMY'S GROSS DOMESTIC PRO-DUCT. This is used as a measure because NATIONAL INCOME accounting attempts to measure all the output from all economic activities in a given time period. Land areas and populations are used to measure the size of a country.

skewed frequency curve (C1)
A FREQUENCY CURVE whose maximum is near the beginning (skewed to the right, positively skewed) or near the end (skewed to the left, negatively skewed) of the range of values of a variable (see the figures).

skewness (C1)
The degree of asymmetry of a distribution. This is measured as the ARITHMETIC MEAN minus the MODE divided by the STANDARD DEVIATION. (See the figure.)

skill differential (J3) *see* wage differentials

skimming (M2, M3)
A pricing policy for new products which sets prices at a high level to 'skim' the expenditure of higher income customers. These high prices are intended to cover the costs of RESEARCH AND DEVELOPMENT.

sleeping beauty (G3)
A company worthy of takeover which is yet to receive a bid.

sleeping economy (G2)
Forgotten bank deposits and savings certificates.

See also: monetary overhang; orphan assets

sliding parity (F3)
A fixed exchange rate whose central value changes frequently by small amounts.

sliding scale (F1, J3)
A variable schedule of wages, payments or tariffs.

slump (E3)
A long period of low national output and high unemployment, e.g. the early 1930s.

See also: depression; recession

slumpflation (E3)
FRIEDMAN'S assertion that rising levels of UNEMPLOYMENT and rising rates of price INFLATION occur simultaneously. Diagrammatically this is shown by a positively sloped PHILLIPS CURVE.

See also: stagflation

Slutsky effect (D0)
A consumer's reaction to a change in price. This fundamental equation of price theory splits the effect of a price change into an INCOME EFFECT and a SUBSTITUTION EFFECT. The effect can also be applied to the effect on the labour supply of a LUMP-SUM TAX. HICKS in *Value and Capital* attributed this to the Russian mathematician and statistician SLUTSKY who contributed suggestions about consumer theory to economics.

Slutsky, Evgeny Evgenievich, 1880–1948 (B3)
Born in Russia. Educated in mathematics and political economics at Kiev University and Munich Polytechnikum. He taught at the Kiev Institute of Commerce and Moscow University, as well as being a government statistician and later working at the Institute of Mathematics of the USSR Academy of Sciences from 1938. His wide-ranging work on statistical methods included a study of stochastic processes and price theory.

References
Allen, R.G.D. (1950) 'The work of Eugen Slutsky', *Econometrica* 18: 209–16.

small firm (L2)
A FIRM often defined as having less than 200 employees and managed by its owner. Despite the growth in the size of firms in the twentieth century, there is still a role for small businesses where the market is

limited in size, ECONOMICS OF SCALE do not exist (e.g. in craft industries) or larger firms prefer to subcontract out many operations (e.g. in Japanese shipbuilding). In the UK many incentives are offered to small firms as there is the belief that they are a major source of INNOVATION and will be tomorrow's large employers.

References

Bannock, G. (1981) *The Economics of Small Firms*, Oxford: Basil Blackwell.

Curran, I., Stanworth, J. and Watkins, D. (eds) (1986) *The Survival of the Small Firm*, Vols I and II, Aldershot: Gower.

smart card (G2)

A CREDIT CARD with a built-in store of information about the holder and his or her financial state. The information is stored in a wafer-like microchip embedded in the plastic. These were pioneered in France where 3 million had been issued by the end of 1986. Banks and credit companies are prepared to pay the greater production cost of these as they are less likely than earlier types of card to be fraudulently misused. They could be the dominant card for financial transactions in the USA and many OECD countries in the near future.

See also: carte à memoire

smart money (F3)

The short-term volatile deposits of very rich persons which in times of national crisis are moved to safer havens overseas.

See also: capital flight

Smith, Adam, 1723–90 (B3)

Scottish economist and philosopher who was the founder and leader of the classical school of economics. He was born in Kirkcaldy, a Fife town to the north of Edinburgh, the only son of a Customs Commissioner who died before his birth, leaving his mother to be a major influence throughout 61 years of his life. He was educated at the local burgh school and at Glasgow University from 1737 to 1740 under Francis Hutcheson, professor of

moral philosophy, whose utilitarian ideas were to influence the early stage of Smith's economic theorizing. An unhappy period as Snell Exhibitioner at Balliol College, Oxford, from 1740 to 1746 enabled him to spend long solitary hours in acquiring the basis of his erudition. Returning to Scotland, he was successively professor of logic, from 1751 to 1752, and professor of moral philosophy, from 1752 to 1764, at Glasgow University. His wide duties as a professor included lecturing on jurisprudence which he broadly interpreted to include economics, as the police in France had the task of regulating markets. In his extant *Lectures on Jurisprudence* for the winter of 1762–3 there is an early sketch of the ideas which were to appear in THE WEALTH OF NATIONS: the DIVISION OF LABOUR, the distinction between VALUE IN USE and VALUE IN EXCHANGE, the importance of FREE TRADE and the stages of economic development are discussed. More importantly for his career, he produced in that period his *Theory of Moral Sentiments* (1759; republished five times in his lifetime) which was based on the Stoics' view of the natural order and provided an exposition of his concept of the INVISIBLE HAND which was to play an important role in the theoretical framework of *The Wealth of Nations*. A leading government minister, Charles Townsend, was so impressed by the *Theory* that he persuaded Smith to abandon his Glasgow professorship and become travelling tutor to his stepson, the young Duke of Buccleuch. This Grand Tour to France and Switzerland in the years 1764–6 enabled Smith to meet QUESNAY and TURGOT, the prominent PHYSIOCRATS who were perhaps the most important economists of the day: not surprisingly, their influence is evident in *The Wealth of Nations*.

The Grand Tour, cut short by the death of the Duke's brother, brought Smith back to Kirkcaldy where, supported by his continued stipend of £300 per annum from the Duke, he spent six years preparing his great work on economics. In London, in 1773–6, he completed it, as well as giving government ministers advice on major policy issues, including the problem of the American colonies. His highly acclaimed *Wealth of Nations* (1776 and four more editions in his lifetime) provided a powerful theory of economic growth. This was built upon the division of labour principle and the consequence of man's desire for betterment that leads to savings which are productively invested. Also theories of value, distribution, international trade and public finance were presented. Although sharing much with LAISSEZ-FAIRE economists, he allowed many exceptions to complete economic liberty: for example, on the grounds of national defence he praised the NAVIGATION ACTS which excluded foreign ships from carrying British trade. From 1778 to his death he resided as a Commissioner of Customs in Edinburgh – perhaps a strange occupation for the apostle of free trade but a useful £600 per annum addition to his income. Also, this appointment was a major mark of government approval and an opportunity to undertake empirical research into the mercantile system he so forcefully attacked. Any reader of his works is soon impressed by their breadth, humanity and fundamental arguments. Justifiably, he was then and is now regarded as one of the world's greatest thinkers and economic theorists.

See also: Adam Smith Institute; classical economics; mercantilism; *Wealth of Nations*

References

Hollander, A. (1973) *The Economics of Adam Smith*, Toronto: University of Toronto Press.
Ross, I.S. (1995) *The Life of Adam Smith*, Oxford: Oxford University Press.
Skinner, A.S. and Wilson, T. (eds) (1975) *Essays on Adam Smith*, Oxford: Oxford University Press.
Smith, A. (1976–7) *Collected Works*, ed. A.S. Skinner and T. Wilson, Oxford: Oxford University Press.

Smithsonian Agreement (F3)

A realignment of major world currencies by the GROUP OF TEN in December 1971 at the Smithsonian Institute, Washington, DC. This agreement was forced on the international financial community by US President Nixon when he ordered the US Treasury to suspend its gold sales in August 1971. Wider fluctuations of 4.5 per cent against the US dollar were permitted, the US dollar was devalued against gold by 7.9 per cent and the official gold price was raised from $35 to $38 per fine ounce. The subsequent floating of currencies, e.g. of STERLING in June 1972, quickly abrogated the principal terms of the agreement.

See also: Bretton Woods Agreement

smokestack American stocks (G1)

The COMMON STOCK of basic US industries.

Smoot–Hawley Tariff Act 1930 (F1)

The major US federal statute to establish PROTECTIONISM in the twentieth century. It included TARIFF schedules for over 20,000 products, proposing increases in many cases. It led to BEGGAR-MY-NEIGHBOUR policies which some economists claim was a major cause of the world-wide depression in the 1930s.

See also: Reciprocal Trade Agreements Act

snake in the tunnel (F3)

The exchange rate regime constituting part of the SMITHSONIAN AGREEMENT and existing December 1971 to March 1973. The 'tunnel' was the permitted range of 4.5 per cent fluctuations around the dollar; the 'snake', the band of 2.25 per cent to which the participating currencies were confined at a particular time. It also applies to the EUROPEAN MONETARY SYSTEM's currency movements since 1979.

snugging (E5)

The tightening of US MONETARY POLICY by pushing up interest rates and thereby lowering bond prices. An expression introduced by Paul Volcker when he was Chairman of the FEDERAL RESERVE SYSTEM in the 1980s.

social accounting (E0, M4) *see* national income

social adjustment cost (D0)
The social production cost, a welfare loss to a producer, brought about by increased competition from imports. A major cost of this kind is the unemployment caused by imports replacing domestic production.

See also: Trade Act

social capital (E2, H4)
1 Assets collectively owned for the benefit of the community at large.
2 The benefits resulting from feelings of sympathy and obligation. These feelings underlie terms of trade, the provision of health and education, and access to goods and services.

See also: infrastructure

Social Charter (J2) *see* European Social Charter

social choice theory (D7)
An attempt to provide a normative rationale for social decisions in societies where individuals have different preferences about the options available. BERNOULLI was the first to discuss individual decision making systematically. This theory is based on utilitarian WELFARE ECONOMICS and assumes that full information is available to a decision-maker who is then in a position to maximize SOCIAL WELFARE. As there are so many methodological problems in aggregating individual preferences, social choice theory has made an extensive examination of VOTING PROCEDURES as a means of creating aggregated social preferences. This complex theory is criticized for its unrealistic assumption of full information and for the dictatorial method of decision making it proposes. A major application of it is the study of the appropriate extent of the public sector and the mechanism for controlling it.

References

Arrow, K. (1966) *Social Choice and Individual Values*, 2nd edn, New York: Wiley.

Arrow, K.J., Sen, A. and Suzumura, K. (eds.) (1997) *Social choice theory re-examined*, New York: St Martin's Press; London: Macmillan.

Hoag, G.C. and Hallett, G. (1940) *Proportional Representation: The Key to Democracy*, New York: National Municipal League.

Rothenberg, J. (1961) *The Measurement of Social Welfare*, Englewood Cliffs, NJ: Prentice Hall.

social compact (J5) *see* social contract

social conscience fund (G2)
A MUTUAL FUND whose portfolio excludes investments in morally dubious corporations and companies. Tobacco, alcohol, arms and South African investments in the days of apartheid have all been candidates for exclusion.

social contract (J5)
An agreement, also known as the 'social compact', lasting from March 1974 to July 1975 between the UK Labour government and TRADE UNIONS to grant various social benefits, pro-labour union laws, price controls and higher public expenditure in return for the trade-unions-organized restraint of wages. The government kept its promises; the unions failed to restrain pay rising in twelve months by 32 per cent. Rather different from Rousseau's celebrated philosophy of that name.

social cost (D0)
The OPPORTUNITY COST to society of the resources it uses. This is equal to all the costs incurred by a society in producing a good or service. In most cases of production there is a divergence between private and social costs.

See also: private cost

References

Pearce, D.W. (ed.) (1978) *The Valuation of Social Cost*, London: Allen & Unwin.

social cost of monopoly (D6)
The welfare losses resulting from the restriction of output and higher prices under monopolistic production. There is

also the social cost that occurs through striving to attain a monopoly position.

See also: externality

social cost of unemployment (D6, J6)

The reduction in national output resulting from an economy operating at a production level less than FULL EMPLOYMENT.

See also: private cost of unemployment

social credit (H3)

A scheme advanced by Major C.H. Douglas in the 1920s to advance discounts to retailers, and dividends to citizens, to solve the problem of underconsumption. This attempt to cure unemployment in the interwar years (based on a theory of the TRADE CYCLE) was partially implemented in Alberta, Canada, in 1935 when a scheme to distribute to all citizens social dividends based on the real wealth of the country was introduced.

References

Douglas, C.H. (1933) *Social Credit*, 3rd edn, London: Eyre & Spottiswoode.

social dividend scheme (H3)

An integration of income maintenance with income taxation. The state fixes an income maintenance payment related to household size in order to prevent dire poverty. Income above this payment is subject to progressive taxation but income below it is supplemented by 'dividends' in the form of a cash sum. Although long advocated by many political parties, such schemes are difficult to implement.

See also: negative income tax; poverty trap

social good (H4) *see* public good

socialism (P2)

A way of organizing an economy so that the society owns productive capital and distributes the NATIONAL INCOME for the benefit of all. It is the alternative to uncontrolled CAPITALISM and to some extent a rejection of market mechanisms. Early idealistic forms of socialism, often

based on the idea of producers' CO-OPERATIVES, were suggested by OWEN, FOURIER and ST SIMON and were soon analysed in John Stuart MILL's *Principles of Political Economy* (1848). Later socialist writings departed from the co-operative principle and based their theories on wider premises. MARX, ENGELS and their followers were more ambitious in their theorizing, and provided a long-term analysis of the emergence of capitalism (mythically described by TURGOT and SMITH) and late classical theories of value and distribution.

Today, socialism for a whole economy is often associated with PLANNING (as in SOVIET-TYPE ECONOMIES). Some economies modified central planning by combining planning with market mechanisms, e.g. Hungary and Yugoslavia, to create MARKET SOCIALISM. As socialism coincided with the rise of TRADE UNIONS in the countries first to industrialize, it is not surprising that there has often been an intimate association between labour and socialist parties. The remaining idealists who desire to live in societies following strict EGALITARIAN principles would be best to choose sub-economies such as the Israeli KIBBUTZIM or the US Hutterite communities.

See also: egalitarianism; guild socialism; industrial democracy

social liberalism (P4)

The political philosophy that advocates that collective action increases individual welfare and liberty. It is argued that this type of MIXED ECONOMY preserves markets and political freedom, as well as giving a greater role to government. KEYNES and BEVERIDGE were the chief proponents of this view.

socially necessary labour time (J0)

The amount of time a worker devotes to the production of a particular good under normal conditions of production at the current standard of labour PRODUCTIVITY. MARX found it necessary to refine the notion of labour quantity in this way to avoid the implication of his theory – that laziness increases value.

social market economy (P4)
An ECONOMY combining private ownership of industry and market methods of allocation with high welfare expenditures and industrial policies. Germany has been a major example of this type of economy since the late nineteenth century.

social opportunity cost of foreign exchange (F3)
The effective local currency cost to a country of the foreign exchange it spends plus the effective local currency yield to it of the foreign exchange it generates by exporting and by IMPORT SUBSTITUTION.

social overhead capital (H4) *see* social capital

social ownership (L3)
A form of public ownership similar to NATIONALIZATION. It is different from the type of UK nationalization introduced in the 1940s in that members of the public hold non-voting shares and there is a greater degree of WORKERS' PARTICIPATION in management.

See also: co-operative; industrial democracy

social political economy (P4)
A diffuse set of normative economic theories based on the idea that the individual cannot be separated from the community. All economics is regarded as the product of social values. Early practitioners of this form of POLITICAL ECONOMY were associated with the Catholic Economic Association.

social product (E0)
The national product of a particular country or community.

See also: national income

social profit (E2)
The total return to an economy of an investment project which includes both money profit and the achievement of other

aims, including, for example, a fairer income distribution.

See also: cost–benefit analysis

social rate of discount (D9)
1 The rate at which society transfers resources between time periods.
2 The rate at which a government makes an intertemporal transfer as representing the wishes of society. The concept is central to COST-BENEFIT ANALYSIS

See also: private rate of discount

social responsiveness of corporations (G3)
Expenditures and programmes in response to social problems. This takes the form of expenditure on training, educational scholarships, disaster relief, contributions to charities, the improvement of employment and living standards and the protection of the global environment.

social security (H2)
TRANSFER INCOMES, especially retirement pensions and unemployment benefits. The provision of such benefits varies greatly from country to country, being particularly generous in Scandinavian countries and Germany. The ratio of employer and employee contributions (used to finance social security) to wages is high in countries such as the Netherlands but much lower in countries such as Japan and the USA. Many studies show that an increase in social security charges is shifted to the wage earner if he or she regards the corresponding benefits as part of his or her wage. Social security schemes increase distortions in the LABOUR MARKET by increasing the cost of labour to the firm without increasing it to wage earners who do not regard the benefits as a full addition to their incomes. Social security can be financed in two ways. It can be fully funded so that investments are accumulated to produce an income for future recipients of social security grants, or it can be financed on a 'pay-as-you-go' basis,

i.e. by current contributions, mainly by present members of the labour force.

References

Gramlich, E.M. (1998) *Is it time to reform social security?*, Ann Arbor, MI: University of Michigan Press.

Hicks, A. (1999) *Social democracy and welfare capitalism: a century of income security politics*, Ithaca, NY, and London: Cornell University Press.

Social Security Act 1935 (H2)
US federal legislation establishing a system of welfare payments financed by the contributions of employers and employees. Initially it was set up to finance retirement and survivor benefits but subsequently it has been extended to cover disability benefits and the cost of medical care.

social spending (H5)
Public expenditure on health, education and the provision of welfare benefits. After excluding expenditure on defence and grants to industry, most of a nation's public expenditure is now of this type.

See also: peace dividend

social time preference rate (D9)
The rate at which society trades consumption of one time period with consumption of another. A positive rate means that the present is preferred to the future. Although the market rate of interest has been used as a proxy for this rate, it is not in all cases suitable. There is a variety of markets and rates according to the term and the purpose of the loan. The preferences of persons, including children, who neither borrow nor lend at interest are ignored. Market rates can be pushed up by the monopoly power of banks and by the risk of non-repayment. The shorter life expectancies and time horizons of the poor, especially in less developed countries, limit the usefulness of this concept.

social wants (H4)
The collective demand by a community to increase its welfare. Individuals do not desire these solely for their own consump-

tion and as they are indivisibly supplied they cannot be charged to individuals. Prominent examples of such wants include POLLUTION CONTROL and expenditure on law and order.

See also: merit want

social welfare (H0)
The economic well-being of a society as a whole, often measured by the total volume of goods and services becoming available to it over a given period, i.e. real income. An appropriate measure of welfare is disputable as NATIONAL INCOME accounting does not cover all GOODS and BADS of an economy and total income measure ignores income distribution. As changes in social welfare are used to judge the efficacy of economic policies, a variety of tests have been used to see whether there has been an unambiguous increase in welfare. The stark PARETO approach has been challenged and replaced by other approaches, notably by SCITOVSKY and Rawls, to deal with the problem of the extent to which losers' reduction in welfare is more than compensated for by gainers' increase, after redistribution of real income. Much of WELFARE ECONOMICS is concerned with this difficult problem which, as Little has shown, reflects the value-loaded nature of many welfare discussions.

See also: measure of economic welfare; Rawlsian difference principle

References

Little, I.M.D. (1957) *Critique of Welfare Economics*, 2nd edn, Oxford: Oxford University Press.

social welfare function (H0)
The total well-being of a society as a function of its resource allocation. Originally this was regarded as the sum of individual utilities but ARROW showed the impossibility of this when individuals have divergent opinions. The four conditions of collective rationality – the PARETO principle, non-dictatorship and independence of any alternative in an environment other

than where the social choice is made – cannot simultaneously be satisfied.

See also: Arrow; Bergson; impossibility theorem

Society for Worldwide Interbank Financial Telecommunications (G2)

A private network established in 1973 in Brussels and operational from 1977 by European banks for the transfer of funds; by 1988 this financial information service had been extended to Asia, Australia and Latin America.

sociological utility theory (D1)

This states that utilities are systematically interdependent as wants are formed by observing the consumption of other individuals.

References

Duesenberry, J.S. (1949) *Income, Saving and the Theory of Consumer Behavior*, Cambridge, MA: Harvard University Press.

soft budget (H6)

A budget with a flexible limit. In CEN-TRALLY PLANNED ECONOMIES, the budgets of many firms were 'soft' because loss-making firms are kept in business by subsidies, tax concessions and credits.

soft commission (G2)

Commission for a stockbroker's services based on actual services supplied, and thus lower than a standard commission.

soft commodity (Q1)

An agricultural product such as coffee, cotton or sugar.

See also: primary product

soft currency (F3)

A currency few people want to hold as it is continuously depreciating, except in the periods when the inducement of high interest rates encourages foreigners to hold deposits of it. The currencies of Italy, Iceland and Mexico were of this kind for many years.

See also: hard currency

soft dollar services (G2)

Investment research and related services offered by brokers without any charge added to dealing fees.

soft landing (E6)

Reaching a desired macroeconomic position for a country painlessly. Usually a landing of this kind makes possible the reduction of inflation without causing a recession.

soft loan (G0)

A loan on easy terms, i.e. at a lower than market rate of interest and repaid over a longer period of time than is customary. This easing of the terms of credit has often been used to encourage the development of Third World countries and the depressed regions of industrialized countries.

soft modelling (C5)

A form of factor analysis with as few PARAMETERS as possible. This approach is used to build socioeconomic models where there is little information on the place of each variable in a causal chain.

References

Joreskog, K. and Wold, H. (1982) *Systems under Indirect Observation*, Amsterdam: North-Holland.

sogo bank (G2)

A Japanese mutual bank set up after the Second World War to finance small and medium-sized local firms with a minimum capital of 400 million yen (compared with 1 billion yen for commercial banks). When faced with the competition of deregulated COMMERCIAL BANKS and of local CREDIT UN-IONS, many sogos have turned to very risky lending; others have converted into commercial banks.

sogo shosha (L2)

Japanese transnational trading company.

Sohyo (J5)

General Council of Trade Unions of Japan: this national federation of trade unions had a membership of 3.9 million by 1989, of whom 1.2 million worked in the government sector, 1.1 million in services, 0.84 million in transport and communications and 0.52 million in manufacturing.

See also: enterprise union; Rengo

sole proprietor (L2)
A person who is both the sole owner and manager of a firm, receiving all its post-tax profits and entirely responsible for its liabilities. The growth of SELF-EMPLOYMENT is some indication of the increasing popularity of this form of enterprise.

See also: partnership; small firm

Solow neutral (O3)
TECHNICAL PROGRESS which increases capital but does not affect the distribution of GNP between labour earnings and capital yield.

References

Solow, R.M. (1956) 'A contribution to the theory of economic growth', *Quarterly Journal of Economics* 70: 65–94.

Solow residual (O4)
That part of economic growth that cannot be explained by the growth of the labour force or the stock of capital.

References

Solow, R.M. (1957) 'Technical change and the aggregate production function', *Review of Economic Studies* 39: 312–20.

Solow, Robert M., 1924– (B3)
A leading US capital and growth theorist, at SAMUELSON's side in the CAMBRIDGE CONTROVERSIES. After a university education at Harvard, since 1950 he has spent his entire academic career at the Massachusetts Institute of Technology. Some of his contributions to growth theory are evident in his text *Growth Theory: An Exposition* (1969). His NEOCLASSICAL position in capital theory emerges in his *Capital Theory and the Rate of Return* (1963). Later works included research into the economics of non-renewable resources. His major contributions to MACROECONOMICS earned him the NOBEL PRIZE FOR ECONOMICS in 1987.

sophisticated leader (L1)
A firm that employs a strategy to obtain the best profit level consistent with the reaction curve of its rivals.

South African Customs Union (F0)
A customs union of Botswana, Lesotho, Swaziland and the Republic of South Africa set up in 1969.

South African Development Co-ordination Committee (O0)
An organization formed in April 1980 to co-ordinate the transport, trade and development of Angola, Botswana, Lesotho, Malawi, Mozambique, Swaziland, Tanzania, Zambia and Zimbabwe.

sovereign loan (G0)
A commercial loan to a sovereign state. Collateral is not offered with such loans and so there is little redress in the case of default. Much of the large foreign debts of Third World countries today are of this nature. The only way of enforcing repayment of capital and interest is by negotiation and by refusing further credit facilities.

See also: senior debt; world debt problem

sovereign risk (G1)
The rating given to an issue of government bonds by Standard & Poor or another rating agency. The grades are AAA, AA, A, BBB, BB and B.

Soviet Material Product System (E0, P3)
The distinctive system of NATIONAL INCOME accounting used in the USSR. Government services and many private services were excluded. This attitude to national income accounting, so different from that used by Western countries, is founded on the distinction between PRODUCTIVE and UNPRODUCTIVE LABOUR used by CLASSICAL ECONOMISTS.

Soviet-type economy (P2)
A CENTRALLY PLANNED ECONOMY of the kind set up under the five-year plans of the 1920s and 1930s which was adopted by most East European economies after 1948 and increasingly abandoned after 1989.

This economy was based on a one-party state, largely organized in state-owned enterprises reporting in vertical hierarchies to industrial ministries which handed down detailed orders on every aspect of production within the framework of five-year and annual operational plans. TRADE UNIONS, also organs of the state, were given the tasks of overseeing the welfare of workers and contributing to the audit of individual enterprises. When the system failed to be efficient and supply the needs of consumers, reforms were attempted. These included devolving more decision making to individual enterprises, allowing them to trade directly with each other and with foreign enterprises, allowing more incentives to managers and workers to encourage better use of resources, and more flexible pricing including MARGINAL COST PRICING.

References

Ellman, M. (1979) *Socialist Planning*, Cambridge and New York: Cambridge University Press.

spaceman economy (P4)

An economy which aims to minimize the amounts of inputs needed to produce a stable stock of goods, consistent with a stability of life-supporting environmental systems. BOULDING devised this notion in keeping with the idea of a 'Spaceship Earth' with finite resources and fragile biological life-support mechanisms.

See also: cowboy economy

Spanish customs/practices (J2)

Restrictive labour practices, often unauthorized, which result in a worker being paid for doing little work, e.g. the ways of avoiding work which were for a long time rife amongst Fleet Street, London, printers, merchant seamen and television technicians in the UK. These customs are 'Spanish' in the sense of making possible a siesta-like existence.

See also: featherbedding; restrictive practice

spatial benefit limitation (H4)

The benefits derived from LOCAL PUBLIC GOODS.

See also: Tiebout hypothesis

spatial duopoly (R1)

Two firms located at different places competing for the same group of dispersed customers.

spatial equalization (R1)

The reduction in interregional inequalities in incomes or another economic variable.

See also: regional policy

spatial monopoly (R1)

A dominant firm controlling a market because of its remote distance from others. The growth of transport systems in the twentieth century has caused the disappearance of most monopolies of this type.

spatial oligopoly (R1)

Several firms of the same industry located at different places competing for the same group of dispersed customers.

Spearman's rank correlation coefficient (C1)

This measures the interrelatedness of the ranks of two variables. The coefficient is given by

$$r_s = 1 - \frac{6\sum_{i=1}^{N}(X_i - Y_i)^2}{N(N^2 - 1)}$$

where X and Y are the two variables and N is the number of pairs of values of X and Y.

special bracket firm (G2)

An INVESTMENT BANK or similar financial institution at the top of a list of a syndicate of UNDERWRITERS on a TOMBSTONE.

special deposit (E5)

An additional cash deposit by COMMERCIAL BANKS required on occasions by the BANK OF ENGLAND. The purpose of these deposits has been to reduce the total volume of bank deposits and hence the MONEY SUPPLY by a shrinkage of the LIQUID ASSETS of banks. This UK technique of credit control was first used in 1958; in 1971 it was also applied to the larger finance houses.

See also: 'corset'

special drawing rights (F3)

International reserve assets under the control of the INTERNATIONAL MONETARY FUND available for settling intercountry indebtedness since 1968. This 'paper gold' was created after the Washington Communiqué of March 1968 closed the Gold Pool because leading countries saw no need for more official holdings of official gold. Special drawing rights have a gold guarantee and carry a small amount of interest; they are 70 per cent wholly owned and 30 per cent credit. Over a five-year period each participant country must keep, on average, 30 per cent of its reserves in special drawing rights to avoid a few countries having all. On 1 January 1970, $3,500 million were distributed, followed by $3,000 million on 1 January 1971 and $3,000 million on 1 January 1972. A country can use its special drawing rights to finance a BALANCE OF PAYMENTS deficit or to support its exchange rate. When drawing on them, a country informs the managing director of the IMF who finds a partner to swap special drawing rights for currency. Special drawing rights grew to about one-twentieth of world reserves within twenty years of their creation. Without the large US balance of payments deficit and the resources of the EURODOLLAR market, a larger volume of special drawing rights would be needed.

special employment measures (J2)

A variety of UK schemes to reduce unemployment of particular types. The Job Release Scheme aims to cut labour supply; the Community Programme and Enterprise Allowance aim to create jobs, especially for the long-term unemployed; and the Youth Training Scheme and Young Workers Scheme aim to cut youth unemployment.

specialist (G1)

A stockbroker who creates a continuous market in stocks assigned to him or her by a particular stock exchange and corrects imbalances in supply and demand. This system is used by both the New York and Toronto Stock Exchanges (in the latter, the specialist is called a 'professional trader' or 'pro'). Also, on these exchanges, the specialists are permitted to deal on their own account. On other exchanges there are similar but government-appointed stockbrokers, e.g. at Frankfurt the *Kursmakler* and at Paris *l'agent de change*; similarly, on the Tokyo exchange, the *saitori*.

specialization (D2, L0)

1 Subdivision or DIVISION OF LABOUR.

2 A reduction in the number of economic activities of a country with a view to reducing costs and maximizing output. One of the major examples of specialization is in international trade, first justified by the doctrine of absolute advantage and subsequently by COMPARATIVE advantage. Advocates of specialization always point out the general increase of real incomes which results from factors of production being employed in their best uses.

specie (E4)

Gold or silver coins.

specie-flow mechanism (F4)

The automatic means under the GOLD BULLION STANDARD that brought about a balance of payments equilibrium. An outflow of gold lowered the prices of domestic production, thereby improving that country's BALANCE OF TRADE and inducing an inflow of BULLION (the reverse would happen when there is an inflow). David HUME, one of the earliest proponents of this view, used this argument to refute the early MERCANTILIST view that a country should, and can, have a permanent balance of payments surplus. Although this approach is appropriate to fixed exchange rate systems, it has inspired modern theories of the balance of payments which concentrate on the supply of, and demand for, money.

specification (C1)

An initial stage in REGRESSION analysis in which an econometrician obtains assumptions by making inferences from data. These assumptions can be selected by examining the data or by repeated attempts using one assumption after another to ascertain what inferences follow.

See also: identification problem

References

Leamer, E.E. (1978) *Specification Searches*, New York: Wiley.

specific duty (H2)

An INDIRECT TAX of the same amount whatever the value of the good or service taxed. Taxes on spirits and tobacco are often taxed in this way so that the duty levied does not change with producers' prices. Many import duties are specific in nature. The opposite of a specific duty is an AD VALOREM TAX.

specific egalitarianism (H5)

The assignment of particular goods to groups regarded as being most in need to ensure equal distribution of them. A major example is RATIONING in wartime.

See also: egalitarianism

specific risk (G1)

The RISK uniquely associated with an individual asset.

specific training (J2)

Training of use to only one employer because of its specialized nature, e.g. knowledge of a particular production process. Employers are encouraged to invest in training of this kind as they, and not others, will receive the return from it.

See also: Becker; general training; human capital

speculation (G1)

Buying and selling in commodity or financial markets which are subject to many price fluctuations in order to make a capital gain. It has been described as 'arbitrage through time'. Although much condemned as an unreal activity for private gain, it does contribute to price stability.

speculative attack model (F3)

A balance of payments model describing the nature of the speculation which attacks a currency. The first-generation models indicated how declining reserves effected the collapse of a fixed exchange rate system. The second-generation version demonstrated that declining economic fundamentals and inconsistent government policies make fixed exchange rates unsustainable.

References

Flood, R.P. and Garber, R.M. (1984) 'Gold monetization and gold discipline', *Journal of Political Economy* 92: 90–107.
Krugman, P. (1979) 'A model of balance of payments crises', *Journal of Money, Credit and Banking* 11: 311–25.

speculative demand for money (E4)

The DEMAND FOR MONEY arising from stock market speculators leaving the market because of their expectation that no further capital gain can be obtained from investing their cash holdings. As bond prices and interest rates are inversely related, when bond prices are thought to have reached a peak, interest rates will be at their minimum – the LIQUIDITY TRAP. There is thus an inverse relationship between the rate of interest and the speculative demand for money.

speculative price data (C8, F0, G0)

Numerical information on stock market prices, DERIVATIVES, exchange rates and interest rates.

Spence, Andrew Michael, 1943– (B3)

Born in Montclair, New Jersey, and educated at Princeton, Oxford and Harvard Universities. He has held chairs at Harvard (1973–90) and subsequently at Stanford. John Bates Clark medal 1981; NOBEL PRIZE FOR ECONOMICS with AKERLOF and STIGLITZ in 2001. An authority on competition policy and the market signalling aspects of information economics.

spiders (G1)
Standard & Poor's Depository Receipts which are units in the unit investment trust that tracks the prices and dividend yields of the S&P 500 index.

spillover effect (J3, J5)
The indirect effect on another person(s) of a gain or loss to the original person(s). In UK COLLECTIVE BARGAINING in which an increase in wages granted to UNIONIZED workers is given to non-unionized workers, this effect is commonplace. Other spillover effects in the labour market include unemployment amongst unionized workers because of pay increases and a shrinkage of WAGE DIFFERENTIALS when there is an increased supply of less skilled workers (e.g. through mass immigration). In some markets injurious spillover effects can be compensated for by actions in tort/delict. But in the labour market the extent to which those responsible pay for the indirect effects of their actions is often restricted under labour relations legislation.

See also: externality; insider wage setting; secondary action; social cost

sponsor demand (D0)
A demand for a good or service paid for by a person other than the consumer, e.g. the commercial financing of sporting events.

See also: market demand; option demand

spot market (F3)
A market where currencies or commodities are traded for immediate delivery. In currency markets, the spot market is linked to a FORWARD MARKET by interest rate differences between countries, by SPECULATION and by HEDGING.

spot price/rate (F0, G0)
The present price of an asset, currency or commodity for immediate delivery.

See also: future; option

spread (G1)
The range of a share price between its buying and selling prices. Spreads are lower the more LIQUID and efficient a stock market.

spread effect (O4)
The transmission of ECONOMIC GROWTH in one region to another.

See also: backwash effect

spreading (F3)
Price ARBITRAGE over time, often practised in commodity markets. It involves the purchase of a contract in one delivery month and the selling of a contract for a related commodity in a different delivery month. In option markets, 'spreading' is buying a CALL OPTION at one striking price and selling it at another.

Sraffa, Piero, 1898–1983 (B3)
Born in Turin, the son of a law professor, and educated at Turin University. He was a professor at the Universities of Perugia and Cagliari from 1924 to 1926 before his long and influential Cambridge, UK, career successively at King's and Trinity Colleges from 1927 to his death. His move to Cambridge was made possible by an article attacking the Marshallian THEORY OF THE FIRM published by the *Economic Journal* (1926), the first indication of his theoretical brilliance. His greatest contribution to economics was his edition of the works of RICARDO (1951–73) and his most controversial a short book, *Production of Commodities by Means of Commodities* (1960), which began a critique of economics that founded the NEO-RICARDIAN School. LEONTIEF and Pasinetti saw his work more as another example of linear production theory.

References

Roncaglia, A. (1977) 'The Sraffian revolution', in S. Weintraub (ed.) *Modern Economic Thought*, Oxford: Basil Blackwell.
Steedman, I. (1988) *Piero Sraffa*, Brighton: Wheatsheaf.
—— (ed.) (1989) *Sraffian Economics*, Vols I and II (Schools of Thought in Economics No. 4), Aldershot: Edward Elgar.

stabex system (F3)
A scheme that assists African, Caribbean and Pacific countries to make up the shortfalls in their agricultural export earnings.

Stability and Growth Pact (F0)
An agreement of the EUROPEAN UNION on fiscal policy agreed in Dublin in 1996. Although it attempts to produce a stable long-term fiscal policy, it allows some budgetary flexibility in times of economic weakness. A decline in real GDP of more than 0.75 per cent over a year is regarded as a serious setback. When a fiscal deficit is more than 3 per cent of GDP, reasons for the shortfall have to made in writing to the European Commission for decision by the Council of Ministers. Sanctions can be imposed by the EU countries in the EUROPEAN MONETARY SYSTEM. These include an interest-free deposit of 0.2 per cent of GDP in the first year and then in subsequent years 0.1 per cent of GDP for every percentage point of an excess deficit up to 0.5 per cent of GDP. If the deficit is still excessive after two years, the deposit becomes a fine.

stabilization policy (E3) *see*
countercyclical policy

stable equilibrium (D0, E0)
An EQUILIBRIUM state maintained by the rules of the system concerned.

Stackelberg duopoly model (D4)
A model of DUOPOLY in which one firm is the price leader and the other the price follower. Market equilibrium is reached only if one firm is the leader and one the follower; there is DISEQUILIBRIUM if both want to be price leaders or price followers.

Stackelberg model (L1)
A model of DUOPOLY devised by Heinrich von Stackelberg in his 1934 book *Marktform unter Gleichgewicht*. This describes the relationship between a leading firm and a follower in their output decisions. A follower chooses the profit-maximizing output. Each firm desires to act as a follower knowing the other will do so also.

stag (F1)
A speculator who attempts to make a profit from subscribing to new issues of shares and selling them immediately they are marketable. For the stag to be successful, the offer price has to be lower than the market price. Stagging is encouraged by financial press reports that attempt to assess the true value of the issuing company and predict the market price when trading starts.

See also: grey market

stages theory (O0)
A theory of economic development showing the transition of an economy from its most primitive state to modern CAPITALISM. TURGOT and SMITH independently advanced such views in 1750 but the late classical use of it in the hands of MARX immortalized it. Smith divided history into four ages – hunters, shepherds, agriculture and commerce. More recently ROSTOW has suggested a five-stage theory which is as ambitious as Marx's but without a theory of class conflict incorporated into it. Rostow's theory has been regarded as being essentially an account of a WALRASIAN moving equilibrium.

stagflation (E3)
An unhappy combination of high price INFLATION, high unemployment and low economic growth. Although the phenomenon was first extensively discussed in the 1960s, it was present in Western economies before the First World War. It was regarded as an indication of the failure of KEYNESIAN-style demand management and led to a call for INCOMES POLICIES, including a TAX-BASED INCOMES POLICY.

See also: infession

References

Cornwall, J. (ed.) (1984) *After Stagflation: Alternatives to Economic Decline*, Oxford: Martin Robertson.
Helliwell, J.F. (1988) 'Comparative macro-

economics of stagflation', *Journal of Economic Literature* 26 (March): 1–28.

Okun, A. M. (1981) *Prices and Quantities*, Washington, DC: Brookings Institution; Oxford: Basil Blackwell.

Weitzman, M.L. (1984) *The Share Economy*, Cambridge, MA: Harvard University Press.

staggered wage contract (J3)

Contracts made at different times with the consequence that the later contracts are influenced by the terms of the previously concluded contracts.

See also: wage round

stakeholder (G0, M1)

1 A person with an interest in a business, a fund or a community. The interest can arise from financial investment, employment or citizenship.
2 A member of society aware of collective obligations and freedoms.
3 A trustee of society balancing the interests of one group against another.
4 A person relying on shared values and co-operative behaviour opposed to INDIVIDUALISM.

References

Plender, J. (1997) *A Stake in the Future. The Stakeholding Solution*, London: Nicholas Brealey.

stamp duty (H2)

An indirect tax or duty collected by affixing a stamp on the article or document representing a transaction to be taxed. Sales of property and stock market securities attract this form of taxation. The British Stamp Act of 1765 on goods bound for the American colonies caused agitation for American independence.

stand-alone cost (D0)

The cost of production equal to a simulated market price that is the maximum which can be charged without buyers going to a rival firm.

See also: constrained market pricing

Standard & Poor 100 (G1)

A stock market index derived from the Standard & Poor 500 stock index: it covers about 60 per cent of the value of stocks traded on the New York Stock Exchange on most days. Its base date is 1976.

Standard & Poor 500 (G1)

This stock index represents 80 per cent of the value of stocks traded on the New York Stock Exchange and is one of the twelve leading indicators used by the US Department of Commerce to gauge economic performance. The index, with a base date of 1941–3, consists of 400 company stocks, 40 financial stocks, 20 transportation stocks and 40 public utility stocks, each weighted in the index by the number of shares issued.

standard commodity (D0)

COMPOSITE COMMODITY whose price does not change when there is a change in the distribution of income. The components of the standard commodity are in the same proportions as in aggregate production. This concept was introduced by SRAFFA to solve RICARDO's search for an invariant standard of value.

References

Sraffa, P. (1960) *Production of Commodities by Means of Commodities: Prelude to a Critique of Economic Theory*, Cambridge: Cambridge University Press.

standard deviation (C1)

A measure of the dispersion of values of a variable about its ARITHMETIC MEAN that is calculated as the square root of the sum of the differences between each of those values and the arithmetic mean divided by the number of values minus one.

See also: mean deviation; variance

standard error of estimate (C1)

A measure of the scatter of values about a regression line of Y on X which is measured by the square root of the sum of deviations of Y values from the estimated value of Y divided by the number of values.

See also: linear regression

Standard Industrial Classification (L0)
A way of arranging economic data according to the major divisions of a country's industrial structure, using industry codes. In the USA, the classification used eleven divisions:

A   agriculture, forestry and fishing
B   mining
C   construction
D   manufacturing
E   transportation, communication, electric, gas and sanitary services
F   wholesale trade
G   retail trade
H   finance, insurance and real estate
I   services
J   public administration
K   non-classifiable establishments

Each division is divided into major groups and each industry is assigned a four-digit classification. In the UK, the revised 1980 classification also has a divisional structure:

0   agriculture, forestry and fishing
1   energy and water supply industries
2   extraction of minerals and ores other than fuels, manufacture of metals, mineral products and chemicals
3   metal goods, engineering and vehicles industries
4   other manufacturing industries
5   construction
6   distribution, hotels and catering, repairs
7   transport and communication
8   banking, finance, insurance, business services and leasing
9   other services

References

CSO (1979) *Standard Industrial Classification*, London: HMSO (revised 1980).
Executive Office of the President, Office of Management and Budget (1987) *Standard Industrial Classification Manual 1987*.

Standard International Trade Classification (F1)
A classification of commodities and manufactured goods almost universally employed to describe imports and exports. The ten principal sections are as follows:

0   food and live animals
1   beverages and tobacco
2   crude materials, inedible, except fuels
3   mineral fuels, lubricants and related materials
4   animal and vegetable oils, fats and waxes
5   chemical and related products not elsewhere specified
6   manufactured goods, classified chiefly by material
7   machinery and transport equipment
8   miscellaneous manufactured articles
9   commodities and transactions not classified in the previous sections

These sections are further subdivided into two-digit sections and subsequently into three-, four- and five-digit sections.

Standard Metropolitan Statistical Area (J4)
A term used in the wage statistics of the Bureau of Labor Statistics (USA). This concept was introduced into the US census in 1950 to describe a metropolitan labour market in which COMMUTING connected cities and the surrounding areas.

See also: local labour market

Standard Statistical Metropolitan Area (J4)
An urban area of the USA. This concept was used until June 1963 when it was replaced by the METROPOLITAN STATISTICAL AREA.

staple export (F1)
A product internationally traded which is based on the exploitation of natural resources; a PRIMARY PRODUCT. In some developing countries, the performance of this

sector has a crucial effect on the development of the economy as a whole.

See also: one-crop economy

staple theory of growth (O4)

An explanation of the growth of newly settled regions in terms of their interactions with the international economy, the purchaser of exported staple products. It is a version of export-led growth.

References

Pomfret, R. (1981) 'The staple theory as an approach to Canadian and Australian economic development', *Australian Economic History Review* 21: 133–46.

Star Chamber (H1)

Popular name for the UK governmental committee chaired by the Deputy Prime Minister. It considers the public expenditure proposals of the spending ministers with a view to reducing their aggregate to the planning total. The name derives from an English court of justice, abolished in 1640, noted for its arbitrary procedure.

state capitalism (P2)

A transitional stage to COMMUNISM, as typified by the original Soviet economic system. The state owns almost 100 per cent of industrial capital and agricultural land, using a hierarchy of industrial ministries, agencies and enterprises to run the productive sector of the economy.

See also: Soviet-type economy

State Earnings-Related Pension Scheme (I3)

UK state PENSIONS SCHEME introduced in 1975 and intended to be fully implemented by 1998. It originally entitled employees to 25 per cent of indexed qualifying earnings during the best twenty years of indexed earnings in a working life. The size of the pension would be within the range of a flat rate for a single person to an upper limit of 6.5–7.5 times the minimum level. Contracting out was permitted, provided that a guaranteed minimum pension was paid.

When reviewed in 1985, SERPS was criticized for its costs, for not targeting on the needy, for giving too large a role to the state and for discouraging private schemes. It was initially proposed then to replace the scheme with the requirement that at least 4 per cent of earnings be contributed to an occupational or private scheme to purchase an ANNUITY; subsequently this was modified to the recommendation to reduce contributions by setting pension levels lower so that they would only replace 20 per cent of employment earnings.

See also: Old Age, Survivors, Disability and Health Insurance

state enterprise (I3, P3)

A firm owned by the state. These have often been founded because of the lack of private initiative and capital to establish them, e.g. Dutch state mines in Holland around 1900 and various enterprises in Turkey in 1923. It was John Stuart MILL who argued that there should be state enterprises where an undertaking was necessary but no private concern would establish or run it.

There are various ways of organizing state enterprises, e.g. the UK method of creating separate public corporations and the Italian method of creating holding companies (IRI and ENI). In Germany, the government has major or majority stakes in 900 businesses, including Lufthansa and Volkswagen. As many state enterprises make trading losses, it is unlikely that they would be able to raise capital without government help. Since 1978, China has allowed a variety of enterprises, e.g. collective, individual (two helpers can be employed plus five apprentices) and joint ventures between state-owned and individual enterprises with profits distributed as dividends.

See also: privatization; public enterprise

Statements of Standard Accounting Practice (M4)

Accounting standards issued by the Accounting Standards Committee for the UK and Irish institutes of chartered accountants in 1975 and subsequently revised. The goal of these statements is to ensure that accounts provide a TRUE AND FAIR VIEW of the financial position of the organization described in a set of accounts.

The standards cover the treatment of accounting policies, the results of associated companies, earnings per share, government grants, extraordinary items and prior year adjustments, changes in the purchasing power of money, taxation under the imputation system, stocks and work in progress, source and application of funds, deferred taxation, depreciation, current cost accounting, post-balance-sheet events, contingencies, investment properties, foreign currency translation, leases and hire purchase contracts, goodwill, acquisitions and mergers, and research and development.

state monopoly capitalism (P2)

A type of economic system, particularly the SOVIET-TYPE ECONOMY, in which the state owns all the means of production (except for a few minor services and agricultural enterprises) and exploits scale economies by running each branch of production as a state-owned monopoly. MARX regarded such a stage of economic development as the prelude to full communism when the state itself would wither away.

See also: monopoly capitalism

References

Cowling, K. (1982) *Monopoly Capitalism*, London: Macmillan.
Fine, B. and Marfin, A. (1984) *Macroeconomics and Monopoly Capitalism*, Brighton: Wheatsheaf.

state preference theory (D8)

An approach to uncertainty pioneered by Arrow and Debreu. It asserts that choices under uncertainty by agents maximizing their utility functions are between commodities differentiated by their contextual states.

state regulation (L5)

The monitoring of the conduct of business by government departments and their appointed agencies. This occurs not only when industry is extensively owned by the state. Even in countries with a large private sector this form of regulation is preferred to SELF-REGULATION because of the hope that it is more impartial, has more sanctions to employ and is less risky.

state theories (D7)

Explanations of government behaviour in terms of voting systems, the goals of bureaucrats and class interests. All these involve conflict – between different voters' wishes or between bureaucrats and legislators or between labour and capital. The relative power of each group will be influenced by the amount of information possessed.

state trading organization (P4)

An agency of an East European economic ministry under communism which had the task of importing and exporting on behalf of domestic industrial enterprises. Gradually reform came in countries such as Hungary and Russia where enterprises were given a limited power to engage directly in international trade.

static gains from trade (F1)

The immediate benefits to a country and to factors of production of engaging in international trade. The gains include an improved TRADE BALANCE and higher profits through more specialization.

See also: dynamic gains from trade

static model (E1)

An equation, or equations, describing economic relationship(s) with all the constituent variables measured at the same time.

See also: comparative statics; dynamic economics

stationary state (E0)

The position of an economy with zero output growth, the rate of profit at a minimum and only subsistence wages. CLASSICAL ECONOMISTS, with economic DEVELOPMENT as one of their central concerns, feared the movement of an economy towards this state, with the major exception of John Stuart MILL who welcomed an economy not concerned with ruthless expansion that could instead pay attention to income distribution and the quality of life.

See also: steady state economy

References

Mill, J. S. (1965) *Principles of Political Economy: With Some of Their Applications to Social Philosophy*, ed. J.M. Robson, Book IV, ch. VI, Toronto: University of Toronto Press.

statistical population (C1)
A group, finite or infinite in size, of persons or things with at least one common characteristic. Statisticians attempt to learn about the nature of a population by taking samples.

statistics (C1)
A set of methods for the collection, presentation, summary and analysis of data with a view to the drawing of valid conclusions.

References

Hughes, A.J. (1971) *Statistics: A Foundation for Analysis*, Reading, MA: Addison-Wesley.

statutory incidence (H2) *see* tax incidence

statutory minimum wage rate (J3)
The minimum wage set in the UK by a WAGES COUNCIL for the group of workers covered by that council. Trade union and employer representatives sit with independent members of a council to make the recommendation of a new minimum wage rate to the Secretary of State for Employment. The reduction in the number of such councils in the 1980s reduced the number of these wage rates. The new UK government introduced a national minimum wage in 1998.

See also: minimum wage; wages council

Statutory Reserve Deposit (G2)
An account of an Australian trading bank at the Reserve Bank which must be equal to 7 per cent of the bank's total deposits.

steady state economy (E0)
An economy with a constant size of population and stock of capital goods. The number of births and immigrants is equal to the number of deaths and emigrants; investment is only undertaken to maintain the existing capital stock.

See also: stationary state

steady state equilibrium (D0)
An EQUILIBRIUM whose stability is such that the market to which it refers returns to its original state after a temporary change in an EXOGENOUS VARIABLE, or moves to a new equilibrium after a permanent change in an exogenous variable.

steady state growth (O4)
Growth such that capital, labour, total consumption and output change at the same rate. As the rate of growth of capital depends upon savings, steady state growth requires the savings function to have stable characteristics: debt policy can promote stability by keeping the rate of interest constant. Steady state growth does not entail FULL EMPLOYMENT as it is compatible with various levels of unemployment.

stealth tax (H2)
An indirect tax hardly noticed by the taxpaying public. Usually, as in the UK in the late 1990s, these taxes are gradually increased as part of complex tax legislation to avoid much public reaction.

step cost (M2)
A cost which is fixed over a range of output and then rises to a new level, or plateau, over a range of larger output. Fixed costs have to be paid when output is zero. (See the figure.)

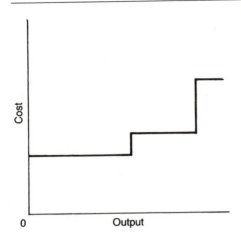

0   Output

stepped bond (G0)
A bond with an interest rate increasing over its lifetime. This method of financing a company pushes up the company's rate of profit in the short term as it reduces its interest charges.

sterilization (E5)
Isolating the domestic money supply from the effects of BALANCE OF PAYMENTS deficits and surpluses. This is achieved by a central bank's OPEN MARKET OPERATIONS; for example, in the case of a balance of payments deficit it will buy bonds from domestic bond-holders to increase the amount of cash available. Under the GOLD STANDARD, sterilization required preventing an inflow of gold from increasing the quantity of money domestically in circulation.

sterling (E4)
The UK's domestic currency which is extensively used internationally as a UNIT OF ACCOUNT (e.g. in the invoicing of trade), as a MEANS OF PAYMENT (e.g. an intervention currency) and as a STORE OF VALUE (especially as a reserve currency).

See also: sterling area

sterling area (F0)
The group of countries, mainly of the Commonwealth, defined in the Exchange Control Act 1947 of the UK, which pegged their currencies to sterling and held their foreign exchange balances in sterling. It

arose out of the dominance of the UK economy before 1914 but declined in the 1950s when many of these countries diversified their reserves, much to the relief of the UK which was often threatened with the sale of such sterling holdings and a consequential attack on the pound. To cope with these sterling balances, UK governments successively negotiated dollar guarantees in Basle in 1968 and 1977. Today, few countries can be said to be in the sterling area.

See also: overseas sterling area

References
Strange, S. (1971) *Sterling and British Policy: A Political Study of an International Currency in Decline*, Oxford: Oxford University Press.

sterling commercial paper (G1)
Commercial bills of exchange denominated in sterling which are short term and negotiable. These are popular with firms seeking an additional source of finance for WORKING CAPITAL and with institutional investors wanting a short-term investment.

sterling M3 (E4)
Broad definition of the MONEY SUPPLY now known as M3. It is measured as M1 plus private sector sterling time bank deposits plus private sector holdings of sterling bank CERTIFICATES OF DEPOSIT. It was used to target the UK money supply in 1979–85. Overshooting of targets for its growth has made it less useful for policy making.

See also: M3c

sterling warrant into gilt-edged stock (G1)
An OPTION to buy or sell a specific gilt stock which was introduced in July 1987 in London. They have a life of up to twelve months. They are popular with securities houses as a hedging device. Gilt options are also traded by the LONDON INTERNATIONAL FINANCIAL FUTURES EXCHANGE and the INTERNATIONAL STOCK EXCHANGE.

sticky price (D0)
A price with limited flexibility. The princi-

pal examples of these are money wage rates inflexible downwards and interest rates with a minimum level. Prices of this kind are fundamental to the KEYNESIAN macroeconomic model.

See also: fixprice; liquidity trap

References

Barro, R. and Grossman, H. (1976) *Money, Employment and Inflation*, Cambridge and New York: Cambridge University Press.

Stigler, George Joseph, 1911–91 (B3)
A leading twentieth-century US microeconomist. After an education at Washington, Northwestern and Chicago Universities, he became a professor at Brown University in 1946 and then was professor at Columbia from 1947 to 1958 and subsequently at Chicago from 1958 to 1981. Also, he worked for the NATIONAL BUREAU OF ECONOMIC RESEARCH from 1943 to 1959. He was awarded the NOBEL PRIZE FOR ECONOMICS in 1982 for his theory of economic regulation. His PhD thesis, supervised by Frank KNIGHT and published as *Production and Distribution Theories* (1941), began his extensive writings on the history of economic thought, as is evident in his *Essays in the History of Economics* (1965). But his eminence is derived from a lifetime of work on microeconomics, beginning with *The Theory of Price* (1942) and continuing with more specialized topics, e.g. his empirical refutation of the KINKED DEMAND CURVE (*Journal of Political Economy* October, 1947) which challenged many writers on the subject. An article on information in labour markets (*Journal of Political Economy, Supplement* October, 1962) inspired much work on search models of unemployment. His contribution to the economics of regulation is notable: controversially, he has held that regulatory agencies act in the producer's, and not the consumer's, interest.

Stiglitz, Joseph Eugene 1943– (B3)
Born in Gary, Indiana and educated at Amherst College. He has held chairs at Yale (1967–74), Stanford (1974–76, 1976–79) and Princeton (1979–88) Universities. Chairman of the Council of Economic Advisers from 1995 to 1997. John Bates Clark Medal 1979; NOBEL PRIZE FOR ECONOMICS, with AKERLOF and SPENCE, in 2001. A central theme of his work has been incomplete information and uncertainty and their applications to labour, credit and agricultural markets. Also noted for his work on public finance; his *Lectures in Public Economics* written with A.B. Atkinson (1980) quickly became a leading textbook. Through his work at the World Bank since 1997 he has become a trenchant critic of the free market philosophy of the World Bank and the IMF.

stochastic process (C1)
A distribution with random probability that can be analysed statistically.

stochastic term (C1)
A random variable.

See also: disturbance term

stock adjustment principle (E2)
The adjustment made to the ACCELERATOR PRINCIPLE to allow for unused capacity. The accelerator equation would produce too high a prediction of the required level of net investment if the amount of excess capacity were not subtracted.

stock and flow concepts (E0, M4)
A stock (e.g. wealth) is measured at a point in time; a flow (e.g. income) is measured over a period. A BALANCE SHEET uses stock concepts; a PROFIT AND LOSS ACCOUNT, flow concepts. This distinction, crucial to MACROECONOMICS, is increasingly used in the analysis of UNEMPLOYMENT.

stock borrowing (G1) *see* share borrowing

stock buy-back (G3) *see* stock repurchase

stock exchange (G1)
A physical and electronic market in which government BONDS and the SECURITIES of companies are regularly traded. The world's leading exchanges are usually com-

pared in terms of the volume and dollar value of stocks traded, the range of financial products marketed and the number of members entitled to trade.

See also: International Stock Exchange; National Association of Securities Dealers Automated Quotation System

References

Goldenberg, S. (1986) *Trading inside the World's Leading Stock Exchanges*, London: Sedgwick & Jackson.

Stock Exchange Automated Quotation System (G1)

A screen-based dealing system which allows all MARKET-MAKERS in a particular security to display their buying and selling prices to all users simultaneously. For a screen price quotation, there must be a minimum of 1,000 shares; the system is open from 9 a.m. to 5 p.m., Monday to Friday. This system had to be introduced in London in 1986 after DEREGULATION of the Stock Exchange.

stock externality (Q0)

SOCIAL COSTS resulting from the stock rather than the flow of pollution; for example, as the consequence of the decay of a stock.

stockholder diffusion (G1, L2)

The extent to which ownership of a company/corporation is spread amongst several investors.

See also: wider share ownership

Stockholm School (B1, B2)

A group of Swedish economists, particularly MYRDAL, OHLIN, LINDAHL and HAMMERSKOLD, who developed their own macroeconomic theory and policy in the 1920s and 1930s. Although there are certain similarities with the work of KEYNES, this school was particularly noted for its use of the dynamic method, introducing the distinction between EX ANTE and EX POST values of variables. Its principal recommendation was the use of FISCAL POLICY as a means of reducing unemployment. These economists were the lineal descendants of WICKSELL.

See also: *ex ante* variables; *ex post* variables

References

Hansson, B.A. (1982) *The Stockholm School and the Development of the Dynamic Method*, London: Routledge.

Sandelin, B. (ed.) (1991) *The History of Swedish Economic Thought*, London and New York: Routledge.

stock index arbitrage (G1)

An investment strategy to gain from the difference between the prices included in stock indices on the futures market and the underlying cash value of stocks.

stock index futures market (G1)

US market for HEDGING and ARBITRAGE to minimize risks and maximize returns in the stock market. This Chicago-based market, inspired by Chicago commodity futures, started in 1980; New York now has a similar market. The item traded, stock indices, can be regarded as baskets of shares. Institutions and corporations have found them attractive as portfolio insurance.

stock market correction (G1)

A small fall in the stock price index of a leading stock market.

stock market crash (G1)

A fall of 20 per cent or more in the index of a leading stock market.

stock market indices (G1) *see* world stock market indices (Appendix B)

stock market price index (G1)

An indicator of the change in value of the stocks and shares traded on a particular stock exchange. This is calculated by adding together the price changes in the leading stocks. See Appendix B.

stock–output ratio (M4)

The ratio of stocks of raw materials, components and semi-finished goods to the output of a firm. Stocks are held during the period of production to safeguard against late delivery of supplies able to hold up production schedules.

stock ratios (M4)

1 Raw material stock divided by total turnover.
2 Work in progress divided by total turnover.
3 Raw material stock divided by purchases.
4 Finished stock divided by total turnover.

stock repurchase (G3)

The purchase by a company of the stocks or shares it has already issued to the investing public. A repurchase is popular with existing shareholders as the value of their investment is increased. It is regarded as a good practice when a company's shares have a low price–earnings ratio.

stocks (D0, G0)

1 Fixed interest securities issued by governments or companies.
2 Accumulated raw materials, semi-finished goods and unsold finished goods.

Changes in such stocks can be very volatile, being responsible for much of the annual change in the NATIONAL INCOME and the BALANCE OF PAYMENTS.

See also: common stock

Stolper–Samuelson theorem (F1)

An international trade theorem which states that, when the relative price of one of two commodities increases, the factor of production used more intensively in its production has an increased real rate of return and the factor less intensively used has a lower rate of return. Sometimes called 'a magnification effect'.

References

Stolper, W. and Samuelson, P.A. (1941) 'Protection and real wages', *Review of Economic Studies* 9: 58–73.

Stone, John Richard Nicholas, 1913–1991 (B3)

Cambridge economist and statistician who pioneered much of NATIONAL INCOME analysis. He was educated at Cambridge University and a member of the Central Statistical Office of the UK War Cabinet from 1940 to 1945 before returning to Cambridge to be Director of the Department of Applied Economics, from 1945 to 1955, and Professor of Financial Accounting, from 1955 to 1980. His first work, an article on costs, appeared in *Econometrica* as early as 1936. Not only national income accounting but demand analysis, INPUT-OUTPUT ANALYSIS and aggregate consumption and savings functions have been central to his research. He was awarded the NOBEL PRIZE FOR ECONOMICS in 1984.

References

Deaton, A. (ed.) (1981) *Essays in the Theory and Measurement of Consumer Behaviour in Honour of Sir Richard Stone*, Cambridge: Cambridge University Press.
Stone, R. (1954–66) *The Measurement of Consumers' Expenditure and Behaviour in the United Kingdom, 1920–38*, Cambridge: Cambridge University Press.
—— (1959) *Social Accounting and Economic Models*, London: Bowes & Bowes.

stop–go (E3)

UK macroeconomic policies of the 1950s and 1960s that alternately deflated and stimulated the economy. The expansion was often with a view to winning an imminent General Election; the retrenchment, a recognition that the economy had become so overheated that the balance of payments was suffering. When FINE-TUNING became increasingly unsuccessful, stop–go policies disappeared.

See also: Butskellism; political business cycle

store of value (E4)

A function of money making it possible to defer the use of income received. In times of high INFLATION money ceases to have this use and non-monetary assets are preferred to money.

storming (P2)

Leaving most of a required amount of work to the weeks or days immediately preceding a production deadline. This was a common practice under Soviet central planning.

St Petersburg paradox (C7)

A paradox of game theory identified by BERNOULLI and so called because of its first being stated in the *Commentarii* of the St Petersburg Academy. This paradox in a game of chance is that the mathematical expectation of gain is infinite but the fair price to the player is finite. Bernoulli's approach to this problem was to replace mathematical expectation (probabilities of winning multiplied by monetary prices) by moral expectation (probabilities of winning multiplied by personal utilities).

References

Samuelson, P.A. (1977) 'St Petersburg paradoxes: defanged, dissected and historically described', *Journal of Economic Literature* 15: 24–55.

straddle (G1)

Buying a futures contract in one market and simultaneously selling it in another.

straight bond (G0)

A bond carrying a set rate of interest, redeemable over a set period at the price on the bond.

straight-choice arbitration (J3, J5) *see* pendulum arbitration

strategic bequest motive (D1)

A calculated reason for making a bequest: the wealth is bestowed in a manner likely to influence conduct rather than express ALTRUISM.

References

Bornheim, B.D., Shleifer, A. and Summers, L.H. (1985) 'The strategic bequest motive', *Journal of Political Economy* 93: 1045–76.

strategic tax planning (H2)

The use of TAX AVOIDANCE schemes to reduce tax liability.

strategic trade theory (F1)

A theory of international trade which aims to show that some forms of PROTECTION, including price controls on exports and export subsidies, can make an efficiency gain.

References

Meza, D. de (1989) 'Not even strategic trade theory justifies export subsidies', *Oxford Economic Papers* 41: 720–36.

streaker (G1) *see* zero coupon bond

stress test (G2)

A test of CAPITAL ADEQUACY related to an optimal debt–equity funding mix. For a bank this shows the capacity of the bank's capital to absorb potentially large losses. As a result of the test, there is an estimate of the amount of risk-free collateral required.

strike (J5)

A work stoppage by a group of workers undertaken to enforce a particular demand, in most cases a wage increase. The legalization of TRADE UNIONS and, in some countries, the protection of them by making them immune from actions in tort/delict for the losses caused by the strike have increased the incidence of strikes in the twentieth century. International comparisons of strikes are difficult because of different definitions of strikes, especially whether to include political strikes and very small stoppages. It does seem that some countries, e.g. Switzerland and Norway, have few strikes, but others, e.g. Australia and Italy, have recorded a high level of strike activity in many years. Determinants of strike activity include a country's industrial structure as some industries (e.g. mining and transport) are particularly strike-prone, the COLLECTIVE BARGAINING system, the phase of the TRADE CYCLE and the extent of industrial CONCENTRATION in large organizations. In the UK in the 1960s and 1970s there were many strikes in General Election years as these invariably coincided with the breakdown of an incomes policy. The effects of strikes are difficult to calculate. There has to be a comparison between output on a 'normal day', which may be rare, and output on a day that there was a stoppage; also the allocation of fixed costs may be too arbitrary to identify the extent of losses caused by strikes. Some would view strikes as an inevitable frictional cost of a collective bargaining system. Certainly, in a few industries it is a well-tried tool in wage bargaining. Strikes can be PARETO OPTIMAL *ex ante* in that not striking would make the employer or trade union worse off, despite the strike being suboptimal *ex post*.

See also: *ex ante, ex post*

References

Hayes, B. (1984) 'Unions and strikes with asymmetric information', *Journal of Labor Economics* 2: 57–83.

Hyman, R. (1972) *Strikes*, London: Fontana Collins.

Jackson, M.P. (1988) *Strikes: Industrial Conflict in Britain, USA and Australia*, Hemel Hempstead: Harvester Wheatsheaf.

Knowles, K.G.J.C. (1952) *Strikes: A Study in Industrial Conflict*, Oxford: Basil Blackwell.

strike-free deal (J5)
A legally enforceable employment contract under which a TRADE UNION promises to refrain from striking for a period of time. This can take the form of a COLLECTIVE BARGAIN explicitly stated as being enforceable under section 18 of the TRADE UNIONS AND LABOUR RELATIONS ACT or an individual contract with an employee.

See also: strike

strike price (G1)
A pre-fixed price to buy or sell an OPTION.

See also: put price

strike replacement legislation (J5)
Laws preventing an employer from hiring new workers during a STRIKE. These measures attempt to increase job security and prevent dismissal but can reduce employment. Canadian provinces including Quebec, Ontario and British Columbia have such legislation.

stripped security (G1)
A mortgage-backed SECURITY which is separated into two securities – the principal and the interest. These have the attractions of being guaranteed by the US federal government and having a higher yield than treasury bonds. Changes in the rate of prepayments causes a fluctuation in their value.

See also: mortgage strip

strong efficiency (G1)
The pricing of a security to take into account all publicly and privately available information.

See also: weak efficiency

strong equilibrium (C7)
An EQUILIBRIUM such that there is no coalition of players which can gain by a simultaneous deviation from it.

structural adjustment policy (O4)
An attempt to effect a major change to an economy, often after an external shock. This policy aims to get the economy back to its pre-shock growth path, improving its BALANCE OF PAYMENTS over the medium term, i.e. about five years. The main policy instruments used are incentives to increase production, saving and investment in the public and private sectors, together with supporting monetary and budgetary policies. Also, there are often specific policies for energy and agriculture. The oil-price increases of 1973 made policies of this kind an urgent priority in many economies.

structural deficit (H6)
The excess of a government's expenditure over its income when that economy is at FULL EMPLOYMENT.

structural inflation (E3)
INFLATION caused by supply shortages especially in the agricultural and exporting sectors of an economy. This type of inflation was thought to be the main cause of inflation in several Latin American economies.

References

Seers, D. (1962) 'A theory of inflation and growth in underdeveloped economies based on the experience of Latin America', *Oxford Economic Papers, New Series* 14: 173–95.

structural model (E1)

A set of equations based on an economic theory showing endogenous variables as equal to a mixture of exogenous variables and constants. For example, if one of the equations is a CONSUMPTION FUNCTION, then $C = a + cY$, i.e. aggregate consumption C is equal to a constant a plus national income Y multiplied by the marginal propensity to consume c.

structural unemployment (J6)

UNEMPLOYMENT caused by a difference between the structure of employment vacancies and the structure of unemployment, usually brought about by technological change. Unemployed persons have different skills from those being demanded by employers or are located in a different place from a potential employer. Critics of this concept regard it as only a case of extreme FRICTIONAL UNEMPLOYMENT.

structure–conduct–performance model (L0)

An approach to industrial economics, often applied to the study of OLIGOPOLY, showing how tastes, technology and institutions produce market structures which dictate a firm's conduct and subsequent performance. The aspects of 'structure' considered include CONCENTRATION, BRANDING and BARRIERS TO ENTRY; 'conduct' includes deciding what to produce and at what prices and carrying out all the functions of a firm; 'performance' is measured by efficiency, profitability, technical progress and employment creation. A policy conclusion of this model has been the demand for tougher ANTITRUST policy.

References

Mason, E.S. (1939) 'Price and production policies of large-scale enterprises', *American Economic Review, Papers and Proceedings* 29: 61–74.
Reid, G.C. (1987) *Theories of Industrial Organization*, Oxford: Basil Blackwell.

stub equity (G1)

That part of the equity of a company retained by the vendor of that company when it is sold. A stake of this kind expresses confidence in the new management.

See also: vendor finance

Student's *t* distribution (C1)

A statistical distribution (named after W.S. Gosset, 1876–1937, a chemist working at the Guinness brewery in Dublin who used the pseudonym 'Student') which is calculated as follows:

$$t = \frac{X - \mu}{s} \sqrt{(N - 1)}$$

where X is the sample mean, μ is the population mean, s is the sample standard deviation and N is the sample size. These t statistics are calculated for the testing of hypotheses.

See also: chi-squared distribution; null hypothesis

stylized fact (E0)

A fact of the real world simplified and made more abstract to be usable in an economic model. Each school of economics has its favourite stylized facts, e.g. that there are steady long-term capital–output ratios and KUZNETS' view that the AVERAGE PROPENSITY TO CONSUME is relatively constant over long periods.

References

Kaldor, N. (1961) 'Capital accumulation and economic growth', in F. Lutz (ed.) *The Theory of Capital. Proceedings of a Conference held by the IEA*, London: Macmillan.

subordinate debt (G0)

A loan with less claim to earnings or assets than SENIOR DEBT.

subsidiarity (H1)
The principle of limiting the powers of the higher levels of government and devolving economic decision making as far as possible downwards so that those affected by governmental actions have the maximum amount of control over them. Subsidiarity is constantly mentioned as a goal for the EUROPEAN COMMUNITY.

See also: economic devolution

subsidiary (L2)
A subordinate part of a firm or other organization. MULTINATIONAL ENTERPRISES in particular have many subsidiaries which can specialize in marketing or production, or concentrate on a single activity different from the rest of the firm or pioneer new products and activities.

subsidy (H2)
A negative tax, a payment by the government to a firm or household. In most cases these are payments to a firm to reduce the cost of the labour or capital it employs. Subsidies can distort the pattern of production and, if used for a long period of time, will become increasingly expensive as the economy's output will diverge more and more from the pattern of demand. Households can also be subsidized to reduce the cost of goods and services they purchase: many countries have subsidized food to increase the welfare of lower income households. The SOVIET-TYPE ECONOMY made extensive use of subsidies.

See also: corrective subsidy; export subsidy; Pigovian subsidy; wage subsidy

subsistence (I3)
The minimum amount of resources, particularly food, that a worker needs to survive. By the time of Adam SMITH, the idea of subsistence in physiological terms had been replaced by psychological subsistence, which takes into account differences in custom, the nature of societies and time periods. Social-policy-makers emphasize today that subsistence must include sufficient income to function in that society.

See also: iron law of wages; poverty

References
Townsend, P. (1979) *Poverty in the UK*, Harmondsworth: Penguin.

subsistence theory of wages (J3) *see* iron law of wages

substitute (D0)
A good or service that a consumer regards as providing as much utility as its alternative. The character of being a substitute can be established by measuring the CROSS PRICE ELASTICITY OF DEMAND between the two goods (services). If that elasticity measure is positive, then the goods (services) are substitutes.

substitution effect (D0) *see* income and substitution effects

sunbelt (L6, R3)
An area of a country with new growing industries, e.g. California or the UK belt from Cambridge through Berkshire and Hampshire to Bristol. The expansion of such an area often poses a threat to the prosperity of an older industrial area.

sunk cost (D0)
Costs incurred by a firm which remain even if it leaves that industry.

sunk cost fallacy (D2)
The mistaken view that a firm should take into account the fixed costs it has incurred when deciding whether to continue with production. Concern for sunk costs rejects the marginal approach to decision making and ignores the notion of SHUTDOWN PRICE.

sunrise industry (L6, R3)
An industry based on new technology, e.g. a computer software industry. In the USA, these industries are concentrated in California and around Boston; in the UK, around Cambridge and in the Thames Valley.

See also: sunbelt

sunset clause (L5)
A statement in a regulation of the date on which it expires.

sunspot theory (D6, E3)
1 A TRADE CYCLE theory first enunciated by JEVONS which asserted that fluctuations in an economy are caused by periodic spots over the sun which cause bad weather, poor harvests, output decline and commercial crises.
2 Random phenomena, an extrinsic uncertainty without an effect on tastes, endowments or production possibilities.

References

Cass, D. and Shell, K. (1983) 'Do sunspots matter?', *Journal of Political Economy* 91: 193–227.
Jevons, W.S. (1884) *Investigations in Currency and Finance*, London: Macmillan.

super-multiplier (E2)
The double effect of investment as investment increases income and the level of investment raises the equilibrium level of income.

References

Hicks, J.R. (1950) *The Trade Cycle*, Oxford: Oxford University Press.

superneutrality (E6)
Economic policies with no real effects as they only bring about nominal changes in an economy.

supernormal profit (D0)
Profits in excess of NORMAL PROFIT. This can occur under PERFECT COMPETITION in the short run but is often a permanent feature of many MONOPOLISTIC and OLIGOPOLISTIC firms.

supplementary cost (D0)
The general expenses of running a firm which are incurred even if output is zero; a term used by MARSHALL.

See also: fixed cost; prime cost

Supplementary Financing Facility (F3)
The provision by the INTERNATIONAL MONETARY FUND in February 1979 of $7.8 billion of special drawing rights to add further

financial help when a country is suffering from a structural problem with its balance of payments.

supplementary special deposits scheme (E5) *see* 'corset'

supplier-induced demand (D0)
Demand for a good or service determined by the producer because of the consumer's ignorance of the need for it. The best example is medical services where consumers lack the knowledge required to diagnose a condition and prescribe a treatment.

supply control (D2, Q1)
A reduction in production undertaken to maintain or increase prices and producers' incomes. This policy, much used in the agricultural sectors of a number of economies, has been criticized for its effects on efficiency and land values.

See also: Common Agricultural Policy; set aside

supply curve (D0)
1 The relationship between product prices and quantities supplied in a product market, holding all other factors constant.
2 The relationship between amounts of a FACTOR OF PRODUCTION and its peculiar factor price – wage rate, RENT or RATE OF INTEREST. It shows how much is supplied at each price.

Under PERFECT COMPETITION there is a supply curve that is independent of the demand curve because price is equal to marginal cost and the market supply curve is the aggregation of individual firms' MARGINAL COST curves. Under MONOPOLY, demand and supply are interdependent because when a monopolist decides how much to produce, both marginal revenue and MARGINAL COST have to be considered as both are affected by output. This usually upward-sloping curve was first devised by MARSHALL.

supply function (D0)

The relationship between the amount of a good or service produced and its price.

See also: aggregate supply

supply price (D0)

The minimum price at which a FACTOR OF PRODUCTION, especially labour, is willing to be employed.

See also: reservation wage

supply-side economics (B2)

A major US school of economics which inspired the economic policies of the USA under President Reagan and of the UK under Prime Minister Thatcher. Opposing the KEYNESIAN view that AGGREGATE DEMAND is central to determining the level of economic activity, supply-siders place emphasis on aggregate supply. Thus there has been a revival in the respectability of Say's law and a concern for the DISINCENTIVE EFFECTS of taxation. The LAFFER CURVE has been a major innovation of the school. The adherents of supply-side economics and MONETARISM often coincide. The NEW CLASSICAL ECONOMISTS have formalized many of their insights.

See also: Reaganomics; Thatcherism

References

Bartlett, B. and Roth, T.P. (1984) *The Supply-side Solution*, Manhattan Institute for Policy Research; London and Basingstoke: Macmillan.

Minford, P. (1991) *The Supply Side Revolution in Britain*, Aldershot: Edward Elgar.

supply-side shocks (F4)

Events external to an economy affecting its production of goods and services. Major recent shocks have been the KENNEDY ROUND of tariff reductions in 1968–70, the oil-price increases of 1973 and 1979 and the INFORMATION TECHNOLOGY revolution.

supply-side socialism (P2)

The economic policy stance of the UK government headed by Clement Attlee, 1945–51, which used planning and severe rationing in order to release resources for the export industries.

suppressed inflation (E3)

Inflation restrained by price controls. Although this ECONOMY has EXCESS DEMAND, it has not yet experienced factor and product price increases.

surplus approach (D0)

The view of classical theories of VALUE and DISTRIBUTION that they are dependent on there being a surplus above the necessary inputs required for production. This approach was most emphasized in MARX's analysis of capitalist economies.

See also: Physiocrats; surplus value

References

Marx, K. (1969–72) *Theories of Surplus Value*, trans. E. Burns, London: Lawrence & Wishart.

surplus economy (E0)

An economy producing a surplus product in excess of the amount needed to maintain that society. QUESNAY in his *Tableau économique* postulated that the agricultural sector had the unique characteristic of producing a *produit net* (surplus). Classical economists, especially SMITH and RICARDO in their use of the concept of profit in their DISTRIBUTION theory, extended the notion of 'a surplus' to all sectors of a national economy.

See also: surplus value

surplus value (J0)
The value produced by labour in excess of the amount needed to maintain it. This concept is used as a measure of the extent of EXPLOITATION of workers in MARXIAN ECONOMICS.

Absolute surplus value arises from the lengthening of the working day or the increased speed of the production process so that a worker works more hours than required to provide SUBSISTENCE. Relative surplus value is the result of decreasing the amount of labour needed to produce subsistence for the worker, i.e. increasing labour productivity. In early stages of capitalist development, surplus value is absolute in nature but it is largely relative in later stages. The rate of surplus value, also known as the rate of EXPLOITATION, is measured by the ratio of surplus value to VARIABLE CAPITAL.

survival process (D4)
An application of Darwinism to the price system. ALCHIAN asserted that the price system selects firms as fit to survive according to their ability to make greater profits than their competitors.

References
Alchian, A. A. (1950) 'Uncertainty, evolution and economic theory', *Journal of Political Economy* 58: 211–21.

survivor firm (L2)
A firm of a particular size which is the modal firm over a long period of time. For example, in a series of censuses of production, if most firms have 51 to 100 employees then a firm of that size is the survivor firm.

sustainability (W0)
Meeting the needs of both the present and future generations by choosing a particular range of economic activities.

sustainable development (O2)
Long-term development including the establishment of the basic social and economic institutions necessary for continuing economic growth. The conservation of plant and animal species is recommended for the sake of future generations. Sustainable development is more difficult if there are trade-offs to be considered between different economic activities.

See also: Brundtland Report

sustainable economic growth rate (O4)
The annual rate of growth of real GROSS DOMESTIC PRODUCT which is in line with the growth of productivity and the present level of capacity utilization. A growth rate in excess of this leads to inflation and/or an increase in a balance of payments current account deficit.

swap market (G1)
The market for the exchange of debt obligations that aims to take advantage of conditions in different financial markets.

swap network (E5)
An arrangement in the USA between the FEDERAL RESERVE SYSTEM and fourteen foreign central banks, together with the BANK FOR INTERNATIONAL SETTLEMENTS, which permits short-term currency swaps between the Federal Reserve System and other central banks.

swaption (G1)
An OPTION to enter an interest rate swap agreement by a certain date.

sweated trade (J2)
An arduous set of occupations with long hours, tedious work and low pay. Most common examples are in the clothing industry. Often the trade is characterized by small firms and a lack of UNIONIZATION.

sweat equity (G1)
An asset in a company created by the hard work of the owner.

Swedish budget (H6)
A budget balanced not annually but over a period of years. This principle was originally followed by UK NATIONALIZED INDUSTRIES.

Swedish School (B2) *see* Stockholm School

sweetener (D0, G3)
An amount of cash given to encourage an economic agent to agree to an economic transaction, e.g. the purchase of a state-owned company. Also known as a 'kickback'.

sweetheart contract (J2)
An employment contract whose terms are fixed by management.

See also: company union

swing producer (L1)
A producer who agrees with the other producers of an industry to absorb the fluctuations in demand for the industry's products by producing whatever is required above the output level set for the other producers. Saudi Arabia agreed to assume this role for the ORGANIZATION OF PETROLEUM EXPORTING COUNTRIES in the 1980s.

symmetallism (F3)
MARSHALL's plan for an international currency based on gold and silver. This BIMETALLIC version of RICARDO's plan was proposed by Marshall to the Gold and Silver Commission, 1888. The international currency was based on a gold bar of 100 grams and a silver bar of 2,000 grams.

References
Marshall, A. (1923) *Money, Credit and Commerce*, Book I, ch. VI, London: Macmillan.

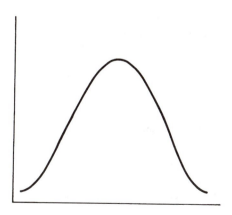

symmetrical frequency curve (C1)
A FREQUENCY CURVE with the shape of a bell with one-half the mirror image of the other. This symmetrical curve is also called 'bell shaped'. (See figure.)

sympathetic impartial observer (D6)
Sympathy and the impartial observer are crucial to the moral philosophy expounded by Adam SMITH in his *Theory of Moral Sentiments*. Economists have made use of this notion to show that INTERPERSONAL UTILITY COMPARISONS are possible.

syndicalism (P4)
Co-operative worker control of industry brought about by direct strike action. This extreme form of trade unionism has attracted more support in France than elsewhere.

See also: industrial democracy; workers' participation

References
Sorel, G. (1941) *Reflections on Violence*, trans. T.E. Hulme, New York: P. Smith.

syndicated loan (G2)
A loan underwritten or managed by a syndicate of financial institutions. Since 1970, there have been many cases of these in Euromarkets and through the recycling of the revenues of OPEC.

synergy (L1)
The extra dynamic caused by the merging of two or more organizations together. The new larger structure is more effective than the sum of the two previous firms, particularly because of a variety of types of ECONOMY OF SCALE. This principle has often been appealed to as a justification for mergers.

systematic risk (G1)
1 The RISK of holding a set of stocks representative of a particular stock market constituting a stock market index.
2 An insurance risk affecting the whole class of the insured, e.g. householders in a given city.

See also: specific risk

systemic risk (G2)

A system-wide failure because of the interconnectedness of economic agents. Shocks are communicated through a chain, especially in a banking system which is highly interconnected by nature: banks are in frequent contact with each other through borrowing and lending. A local event or shock is transmitted rapidly to affect a whole market.

systemism (P4)

Understanding a system as a comprehensive set of functional relations. This is an approach between INDIVIDUALISM and HOLISM.

System of Material Product Balances (P2)

The framework for the national income statistics of centrally planned economies used by the United Nations. It uses as basic sectors the socialist sector and the private sector. The principal tables of these statistics are as follows:

1 Net material product by use
2 Net material product by kind of activity
3 Primary incomes by kind of activity in the material sphere
4 Primary incomes from net material product
5 Supply and disposition of goods and material services
6 Capital formation
7 Final consumption
8 Personal consumption
9 Total consumption of the population

The differences between this national income accounting system and the SYSTEM OF NATIONAL ACCOUNTS include different methods of treating depreciation, different definitions of residents for the purposes of recording external transactions and the exclusion of non-material services.

References

Standing Statistical Commission, Council of Mutual Economic Assistance (1969) *Basic Methodological Rules for the Com-* *pilation of the Statistical Balance of the National Economy*, Moscow.

System of National Accounts (E0)

A set of accounting conventions drawn up by the United Nations. This provides a framework for the systematic recording of transaction flows in a national economy. The sectors in the accounts are as follows:

- General government
- Corporate and quasi-corporate enterprises
- Households and private unincorporated enterprises
- Non-profit institutions serving households
- Rest of the world.

For each country, the flows are defined as follows:

1 Total supply of goods and services

    Gross output of goods and services
    Imports of goods and services

2 Disposition of total supply: intermediate and final uses

    Intermediate consumption
    Government final consumption expenditure
    Private final consumption expenditure
    Gross capital formation
    Exports of goods and services

3 Cost components and income shares

    Value added and gross domestic product
    Compensation of employees
    Operating surplus
    Consumption of fixed capital
    Indirect taxes
    Subsidies
    Withdrawals from quasi-corporations
    Property income

4 Taxes and unrequited transfers

    Casualty insurance transactions
    Taxes and other government receipts
    Household transfer receipts
    Transfers received by private non-profit

institutions
Other current transfers

5 Finance of gross accumulation

Net saving
Surplus of the nation on current trans-
actions
Purchases of land, net
Purchases of intangible assets, net
Capital transfers
Net lending

6 Financial assets and liabilities

7 Other assets

Reproducible tangible assets
Non-reproducible tangible assets
Non-financial intangible assets.

These flows are recorded in tables divided
into four parts:

1 Summary information
2 Final expenditures on gross domestic
product: detailed breakdowns and supporting tables
3 Institutional sector accounts: detailed
flow accounts
4 Production by kind of activity: detailed
breakdowns and supporting tables.

This accounting framework is used for all
national income statistics of United Nations countries except for CENTRALLY
PLANNED ECONOMIES which use the SYSTEM
OF MATERIAL PRODUCT BALANCES.

References

A *System of National Accounts, Studies in
Methods*, Series F, No. 2, New York:
United Nations, 1968.

T

Tableau économique (B2) *see* Quesnay

tacit knowledge (O3) *see* locked-in knowledge

Taft–Hartley Act 1947 (J5)
'The Labor–Management Relations Act', a major US federal labour statute amending the WAGNER ACT particularly by attempting to balance the rights and responsibilities of labour and management. Section 8(c) listed six unfair labour practices by unions: (1) restraining/coercing employees in their rights to engage in or refrain from collective bargaining; (2) causing an employer to discriminate against non-union workers; (3) refusing to bargain with an employer despite being the representative of its workers; (4) engagement in or inducement of workers to engage in strikes, refusals to work and boycotts when, for example, union recognition has not been certified by the NATIONAL LABOR RELATIONS BOARD; (5) charging an excessive or discriminatory fee to enter a union under a union shop clause; and (6) extorting a payment from an employer for services not performed or about to be performed.

Taft–Hartley also banned the closed shop, authorized states to have right-to-work laws, gave the US President the power to direct the Attorney-General to petition for an eighty-day injunction against a strike or lockout which constituted a national emergency, attacked communist infiltration of US labor unions by requiring union officials to swear anti-communist affidavits before they could use the National Labor Relations Board, and banning unions and corporations from political expenditures. Many of these new prohibitions could be enforced under the criminal law. For years, the labour movement attacked Taft–Hartley for creating 'slave labor' as organizing labour became more difficult.

See also: Norris–La Guardia Act; right-to-work state; US labor union

References

Getman, J.G. and Blackburn, J.D. (1983) *Labor Relations: Law, Practice and Policy*, Mineola, NY: Foundation Press.
Morris, C.J. (ed.) (1983) *The Developing Labor Law*, Vols 1 and 2, Washington, DC: Bureau of National Affairs.

take-off (N0, O0)
The crucial stage of economic DEVELOPMENT when an economy 'takes off' into steady growth because its capital–output and savings ratios rise to at least 10 per cent of national income. This first occurred in the older industrialized countries – in Great Britain in the 1780s, in the USA in the 1820s, in France and Germany in the 1850s. Critics of this approach to development have asserted that it ignores the interplay between economic, social and technological determinants. However, the

proponent of this theory, ROSTOW, argued from an examination of economic trends that there are five stages of growth: the traditional society, preconditions for take-off (e.g. INVENTIONS, the rise of ENTREPRE-NEURS), take-off, the drive to maturity and the age of mass consumption.

References

Rostow, W.W. (1960) *Process of Economic Growth*, 2nd edn, Oxford: Clarendon Press.

—— (1971) *The Stages of Economic Growth: A Non-communist Manifesto*, 2nd edn, Cambridge: Cambridge University Press.

takeover (G3, L1)
A method of merging two firms by which one firm bids for another and, if successful, acquires it. Acquisition by the stealthy purchase of shares in public companies is now outlawed under the strict rules of major stock exchanges.

See also: merger

takeover panel (G1)
UK non-statutory committee founded in 1968 and supervised by the Bank of England. It regulates the code of takeovers in the UK having the power to suspend access by a company to securities markets temporarily or permanently. In its work it attempts to achieve fair play.

take-up rate (I3)
The proportion of those eligible for a particular benefit who claim it. Pecuniary and psychic costs (including embarrassment) cause the rate always to be less than 100 per cent. Many voluntary organizations attempt to publicize benefits available to claimants, thereby increasing the take-up rate and making it more difficult to maintain the present rate of benefit.

tangible net worth (G1, M4)
Shareholders' EQUITY minus intangible assets.

tangible wealth (M4)
The FIXED CAPITAL and INVENTORIES of firms.

See also: intangible wealth

tap stock (G1)
A government bond issued, e.g. in the UK or USA, at a fixed price but not sold in its entirety as some of it is held back 'on tap' to be released gradually when market conditions are favourable. Other government stocks are sold by tender.

targeting (E6)
The use of specific policy instruments to reach particular targets, e.g. a low rate of inflation. This principle of macroeconomic policy making is suboptimal if there are side effects from targeting which create distortions in allocation.

target price (Q1)
The price of an agricultural product of the EUROPEAN COMMUNITY which is annually fixed by the agricultural ministers of member countries. This is higher than an INTERVENTION PRICE.

See also: Common Agricultural Policy

target variable (E6)
A quantified policy goal, e.g. 5 per cent unemployment.

tariff (D0, F1)
1 A PRICE. A CHARGE.
2 An import tax. The superiority of a tariff to import licensing arises from its lower administrative costs and the production of revenue; few tariffs succeed in excluding all imports and so they earn revenue. As a form of taxation, tariffs have been used from earliest recorded history as in primitive economies they had the advantage of involving fewer valuation problems than taxes on income or on capital. In the post-war period, tariff reductions aimed to reduce the protectionism of the 1930s; most of these had withered away before the DILLON, KENNEDY, TOKYO and URUGUAY ROUNDS.

In the figure, DD is the demand curve, SS is the supply curve, $p_1 - p$ is the tariff and $p_2 - p$ is a prohibitive tariff which excludes all imports. QQ_1 is the protective effect, i.e. an increase in domestic production, Q_2Q_3 is the consumption effect, i.e. the reduction in total consumption, and QQ_3 are the imports at price p before a tariff is imposed. a is the redistribution effect, i.e. additional economic rent to domestic producers continuing in production and economic rent to new domestic producers, b and d are deadweight losses of the tariff and c is the revenue effect, i.e. the tax revenue obtained by the government by imposing the tariff $p_1 - p$.

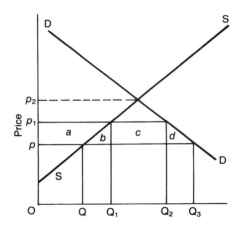

See also: free trade; protection

References

Ratner, S. (1972) *The Tariff in American History*, New York: Van Nostrand.

Scott, M.F., Corden, W.M. and Little, I.M.D. (1980) *The Case Against General Import Restrictions*, London: Trade Policy Research Centre.

tariffication (D4)

The introduction of charges for services which were previously free. A recent example has been the introduction of bank charges for many client transactions.

tariff jumping (F1)

A response to PROTECTION. International companies avoid import taxes and restrictions by investing in the protected countries so that a local market can be supplied

by local production rather than through international trade.

taste (D0)

The view of an individual of the relative merits of several things or possibilities. Assumptions about tastes are crucial to the analysis of choice in economics and are usually represented by INDIFFERENCE CURVES. In the study of consumer behaviour, tastes are depicted as a choice between goods with different UTILITIES; in labour market analysis as a choice between work and leisure; in the analysis of risk as a choice between outcomes with different probabilities. Assumptions about tastes are central to NEOCLASSICAL ECONOMICS.

tâtonnement (D0, D5)

A process of market clearing in which, by bargaining, an EQUILIBRIUM is reached between buyers and sellers. WALRAS introduced this term, meaning 'groping', into economics with his example of bidding.

taxable capacity (H2)

The extent to which households and firms can pay a tax and a fiscal authority can collect it.

taxable income (H2)

Income subject to DIRECT TAXATION. Personal and other allowances are deducted from total pre-tax income to ascertain what is taxable.

taxation (H2)

A method of raising revenue for a government by levies on persons and firms. Taxes can be direct or indirect and can be raised centrally or locally. A government will choose its taxation policy with reference to its effects on income distribution post-tax, on incentives and on investment and economic growth. Also, the taxation raised will be decided as part of its FISCAL STANCE. Instead of taxation, a government can finance its activities by charging for the services it offers or by borrowing.

See also: canons of taxation

References

Blinder, A.S., Solow, R.M., Break, G.F., Steiner, P.O. and Netzer, D. (1974) *The Economics of Public Finance*, Washington, DC: Brookings Institution.

Kay, J.A. and King, M.A. (1990) *The British Tax System*, 5th edn, Oxford: Oxford University Press.

Pechman, J. (1977) *Federal Tax Policy*, 3rd edn, Washington, DC: Brookings Institution.

tax avoidance (H2)

Taxpayers' careful arrangement of their activities and business affairs to minimize liability to taxation.

See also: tax evasion

tax base (H2)

That which is taxed, especially income, wealth, property, expenditure or consumption. A government can raise its total tax revenue by using several tax bases. If the country has a federal structure, then a different tax base can be used for each level of government. Originally little was taxed because of problems of valuation and collection; gradually, there has been a movement from INDIRECT TAXES on imports and various types of consumption to IN-COME TAX and PROPERTY TAX.

See also: federal finance; taxable capacity

tax-based incomes policy (E3)

A method of controlling the growth of wages and salaries by increasing the taxation of firms which have paid more than the prescribed maximum for pay increases. Firms would be liable for taxation on the unauthorized addition to their average wage bills. In the USA, this policy has frequently been advocated on the grounds of its supposed administrative simplicity. The version of this policy suggested by OKUN was to offer an anti-inflationary tax credit of 1½ per cent of salary (on salaries up to $20,000 per annum) in return for the employer not increasing pay by more than 6 per cent.

See also: market anti-inflation plan

References

Seidman, L.S. (1978) 'Tax-based incomes policies', *Brookings Papers* 2: 301–48.

tax bracket creep (H2) *see* bracket creep

tax buoyancy (H2)

The growth of total tax revenue at the same, or a greater, rate of the growth of income or output.

See also: tax elasticity

tax burden (H2)

1 The ratio of the total tax revenues of a country to its GROSS DOMESTIC PRODUCT.

2 The total effects of a country's taxes on all its residents or on certain sectors or types of taxpayer, e.g. firms or households.

Although objectively this burden is the transfer to government of part of taxpayers' resources, many taxpayers would subjectively regard the burden as greater. Governments impose taxes primarily to finance expenditure, but they can unintentionally inhibit the growth of incomes and the capital stock. A guide to tax burdens in OECD countries is published annually in the May issue of *Economic Trends* (UK). The tax burden is high in industrialized Europe but low in less industrialized Europe, e.g. Portugal and Turkey. An approximate measure of the tax burden often used is the AVERAGE RATE OF TAX. More elaborate assessments of a tax burden take into account collection costs, the effect on productivity of a tax structure, the extent to which taxpayers can plan because the tax system is stable, and the degree of horizontal and vertical equity.

References

Pechman, I.A. and Okner, B.A. (1974) *Who Bears the Tax Burden?*, Washington DC: Brookings Institution.

tax capitalization (H2)

The effects on the price of a taxed good, e.g. a house, of the discounted present value of future tax payments. Thus if a house is expected to be liable to high property taxes in the future, a present valuation of it will take that into account. As high local property taxes lower property values, residents are encouraged by this capitalization effect to move to other areas.

See also: fiscal mobility; Tiebout hypothesis

tax competition (H3)
The fiscal rivalry of national governments who attempt to have lower taxes than their competitors in order to attract investors.

See also: fiscal union

tax credit (H2)
An amount subtracted from the taxes owed to a government to lower tax liability.

tax effort (H2)
The extent of success in collecting a tax from a tax base.

See also: taxable capacity

tax elasticity (H2)
The responsiveness of tax revenue to an increase in income or output. If tax revenue grows faster than the TAX BASE, the tax is elastic.

See also: tax buoyancy

tax erosion (H2)
The reduction in tax revenues brought about by exemptions from the comprehensive taxation of income, e.g. capital gains allowances and the tax exemption of fringe benefits.

tax evasion (H2)
Reduction of one's tax burden by inaccurate statements of income and other circumstances relevant to tax liability. The amount of evasion depends on the probability of being detected in such conduct and the penalties for such offences.

See also: income tax; tax avoidance

References

Allingham, M.G. and Sandmo, A. (1972) 'Income tax evasion: a theoretical ana-

lysis', *Journal of Public Economics* 1: 323–38.
Ehrlich, I. (1973) 'Participation in illegitimate activities: a theoretical and empirical investigation', *Journal of Political Economy* 81: 521–65.

Tax Exempt Special Savings Account (H2)
The savings incentive scheme, known as 'Tessa', introduced by the UK government in 1990 and effective from January 1991. Tax on interest was exempt provided that capital is not withdrawn for five years and no more than £9,000 was accumulated. If interest were withdrawn it was taxed at the basic rate of income tax. Savings were accumulated in either bank or BUILDING SOCIETY accounts.

tax expenditure (H2)
A tax incentive or tax subsidy, a departure from the normal tax structure, e.g. TAX CREDIT, deductions and deferrals of tax liabilities. This loss of a government tax revenue is intended to further social goals, e.g. raising the post-tax income of the lower paid, encouraging education or promoting residential investment. This concept was introduced in the USA by the Treasury in 1968 and is now a spending programme of the US Internal Revenue Service.

References

Surrey, S.S. and McDaniel, P.R. (1985) *Tax Expenditures*, Cambridge, MA, and London: Harvard University Press.

tax farming (H2)
Delegation of the right to collect taxes to private tax collectors who then have the freedom to raise more than the quota requested by government. This ancient system is open to much exploitation of taxpayers.

See also: goal system

taxflation (E3) *see* wage–tax spiral

Tax Freedom Day (H2)
The day in the year when people in effect stop working to pay taxes. This is deter-

mined by calculating the average tax rate for the population and applying that percentage to the number of days in the year. For national economies with an average tax rate around 40 per cent the day occurs in May or June.

tax harmonization (H2)

The standardization of tax rates, tax rules and tax definitions throughout a number of countries. Usually, in a harmonization exercise the most common existing practice is adopted as the standard. Sometimes harmonization is necessary to achieve other policy goals, e.g. in the EUROPEAN COMMUNITY the harmonization of INDIRECT TAXATION is necessary if the goal of unimpeded movement of goods is to be achieved.

References

European Parliament (1990) *The Economic Consequence of Fiscal Harmonization in Europe*, Luxemburg: Office for Publications of the European Communities.

Shibata, H. (1969) *Fiscal Harmonization under Freer Trade: Principles and their Applications to a Canada-US Free Trade Area*, Toronto: University of Toronto Press.

tax haven (H2)

A country with very low rates of taxation that attracts companies and individuals wishing to minimize tax liability. The countries benefit from the influx of currency and the consequential commercial activity. Most of these havens are small islands or countries off the USA, e.g. the Bahamas and the Virgin Islands, or on the perimeter of Europe, e.g. Monaco and the Channel Islands. Larger countries would find it difficult to finance public expenditure if they adopted such a low-tax policy.

tax incidence (H2)

Reduction of personal or corporate income caused by the imposition of a tax. Incidence is classified according to the group or sector on which a tax falls. These groups can be producers or consumers, those with a particular size of income,

regions, industries, countries or generations.

The incidence is shifted forward to the consumer if the price of the final good rises because of the tax; backward, if there is a decline in demand for final goods and the price of intermediate goods falls. The incidence is shifted to future generations if current public expenditure is debt financed. Tax incidence can be analysed through a PARTIAL EQUILIBRIUM approach as is the case when taxes on goods are analysed and the demand and supply elasticities are calculated, or with a GENERAL EQUILIBRIUM approach when, e.g. with a CORPORATION TAX, the effects on output and on CAPITAL-LABOUR RATIOS are examined. Statutory incidence shows liability under tax laws. Economic incidence shows how taxation affects economic behaviour, e.g. the number of hours worked or the amount saved: such incidence traditionally concentrated on the effect of taxation on the FUNCTIONAL INCOME DISTRIBUTION. Increasingly it has been examined in the context of the SIZE DISTRIBUTION OF INCOME. Tax incidence was discussed as early as the eighteenth century by the PHYSIOCRATS.

See also: absolute tax incidence; differential tax incidence

References

Harberger, A.C. (1962) 'The incidence of the corporation income tax', *Journal of Political Economy* 70: 215–40.

Pechman, I.A. (1985) *Who Paid the Taxes, 1966–85?*, Washington, DC: Brookings Institution.

—— (1989) *Tax Reform: The Rich and the Poor*, Brighton: Harvester Wheatsheaf.

Shoven, J.B. (1976) 'The incidence and efficiency effects of taxes on income from capital', *Journal of Political Economy* 84: 1261–84.

tax reform (H2)

A change in a tax system attempting to improve allocation, efficiency and EQUITY. Tax reform usually takes the form of reducing the number of separate rates of tax and abolishing many tax allowances.

Because tax reform is motivated by a desire to reduce administrative costs, as well as to reduce TAX AVOIDANCE, there have to be fewer tax allowances, a simpler progression of tax and the abolition of certain types of tax, e.g. on capital.

Tax reform is high on the political agenda of many countries, including the UK, Canada, New Zealand, France, Japan and Sweden. Common to many of these proposals is a switch from income to expenditure taxes and a reduction of the top marginal income tax rates. Indexation of personal allowances is often removed, thus increasing tax yields in times of inflation. In the UK, the top marginal rate of income tax was reduced in 1979 from 83 per cent to 60 per cent and value-added tax was raised from two rates of 8 per cent and 12.5 per cent to a single rate of 15 per cent; in stages, corporation tax has been reduced from 52 per cent to 35 per cent. But in the Budget of 1988 income tax was simplified by the reduction in the number of bands to two – at 25 per cent and 40 per cent. In the USA, the Reagan Administration quickly reduced the top marginal rate of income tax from 70 per cent to 50 per cent and in 1986 the top rate was cut to 28 per cent. Japan reduced the top income tax rate from 85 per cent to 65 per cent; great reductions in corporate tax rates are envisaged and to maintain tax revenue a value-added tax at 5 per cent and a withholding tax of 20 per cent on postal savings and bank accounts are to be introduced. West Germany also cut income tax and corporation tax rates: the top income tax rate from 56 per cent to 53 per cent, minimum rates from 22 per cent to 19 per cent and corporation tax from 56 per cent to 50 per cent with cuts in many allowances. Australia proposed cutting top income tax rates from 60 per cent to 49 per cent in harness with an incomes policy. Tax cuts to a top rate of 50 per cent have no redistributive effect but a cut below 50 per cent does. Curiously some countries, e.g. Japan, have known both high economic growth and high marginal tax rates.

The transition to a new system can produce undesired effects, e.g. a decline in the capital value of assets. To implement a tax reform, either a gradualist approach of dealing with a particular tax at a time or a package approach of widespread change can be adopted. Civil servants prefer the former but it leads to more confrontation with lobbies; there is likely to be support for the package approach only if there is widespread discontent with the current system.

See also: US tax reform

References

Aaron, H.J. and Galper, H. (1985) *Assessing Tax Reform*, Washington, DC: Brookings Institution.

Ballantine, J.G. (1986) *Tax Reform in Japan and the United States – A Stimulus to New Economic Vitality?*, New York: Japan Society.

Boskin, M.J. (1996) *Frontiers of tax reform*, Stanford, CA: Hoover Institution Press.

Feldstein, M.S. (1976) 'On the theory of tax reform', *Journal of Public Economics* 6: 77–104.

Kay, J.A. (1990) 'Tax policy: a survey', *Economic Journal* 100: 18–75.

Pechman, J. (1989) *Tax Reform: The Rich and the Poor*, London: Harvester Wheatsheaf.

Tax Reform Act 1986 (H2)

US federal statute that undertook the sweeping reform of the US tax system from January 1987. It simplified the structure of taxation by introducing two rates of individual tax at 28 per cent and 15 per cent instead of the fifteen rates previously in force; given the loss of previous allowances, in practice the top MARGINAL TAX RATE became 33 per cent. The corporate rate was cut from 46 per cent to 34 per cent with a minimum rate of 21 per cent. To compensate for the loss of revenue from cutting tax rates, many tax deductions have been phased out. Consumer interest on debt (except for housing), lower tax rates for capital gains, pension plans, real estate investments and business meals and entertainment ceased to attract concessions.

See also: tax reform

References

Davies, D.G. (1986) *United States Taxes and Tax Policy*, Cambridge: Cambridge University Press.

tax revenue (H2)
The yield from a particular tax, or of the tax system as a whole. The amount of revenue depends on the TAX BASE chosen, the tax rates set and the amount of compliance with tax legislation. In some countries, there is a heavy reliance on one particular tax, e.g. the USA uses an INDIVI-DUAL INCOME TAX to raise a high proportion of federal government revenues. The growth in tax revenue can be measured by INCOME ELASTICITY OF DEMAND.

See also: Laffer curve

tax smoothing (H2)
1 The linear relationship between a fore-cast of future government expenditure and the current value of a variable consisting of the fiscal deficit, private saving and the average tax rate.
2 A fiscal policy minimizing the economic costs of raising taxes to finance varying amounts of public expenditure. It sets an average tax rate over a period to yield budget surpluses followed by bud-get deficits when expenditure rises.

tax structure (H2)
The set of tax rates applying to a particular tax base, e.g. different rates of income tax or different rates of VALUE-ADDED TAX. For income taxes, the simplest tax structure is based on the principle of a constant average tax rate: this is rare as so many tax structures are regressive or progressive. In a diagram the tax structure is apparent by plotting post-tax income against pre-tax income (OC is changes in income in the absence of an income tax, OA is income exempt from tax, OBD shows the course of income when there is a constant

marginal tax rate on incomes above OA and OBEFG shows the course of income under a progressive income tax with higher marginal rates on higher income bands).

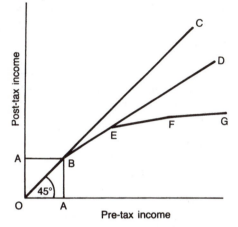

See also: direct–indirect taxes ratio

tax threshold (H2)
The income level where income becomes liable to taxation.

tax unit (H2)
The person or group subjected to taxation, e.g. a single person, a married couple or a household.

tax wedge (H2)
1 The difference between the marginal cost of producing a good and the marginal benefit from consumption in the case of indirect taxes.
2 The difference between the marginal value of leisure sacrificed by a worker and the marginal value to society of another hour of work in the case of personal income taxes.
3 The difference between gross and net, after tax, rates of return in the case of investors.
4 The difference between the total cost of employing a worker and the money wages the worker receives.

Tax wedges produce a distortion in eco-nomic welfare.

Taylorism (M1)

The US creed of scientific management suggested by F.W. Taylor (1856–1915) who applied at the Bethlehem Steel Company the principle of work study and a greater subdivision of labour as a means of achieving increased efficiency.

References

Merkle, J.A. (1980) *Management and Ideology: The Legacy of the International Scientific Management Movement*, Berkeley, CA: University of California Press.

Taylor, F.W. (1911) *The Principles of Scientific Management*, New York: Harper.

Taylor's rule (E5)

A suggested REACTION FUNCTION for the FEDERAL RESERVE named after John B. Taylor concerning the appropriate FEDERAL FUNDS RATE to achieve FULL EMPLOYMENT and price stability. The nominal federal funds rate should equal the targeted real funds rate + actual inflation. The real funds rate is to equal the potential growth rate + (actual − targeted inflation)/2 + (% actual − % potential GDP)/2.

References

Taylor, J.B. (1993) 'Discretion versus policy rules in practice', *Carnegie-Rochester Conference Series on Public Policy* 39: 195–214.

team briefing (J5)

Direct communication between managers and employees as an alternative to indirect contact with workers via trade unions. Although it reduces the role of trade unions, it sometimes exists in unionized firms.

team theory (D7)

A study of the efficient joint choices of several persons. A team has common interests and beliefs and performs various tasks. The theory is concerned with the optimal allocation of tasks and information within the team.

References

Marshak, J. and Radner, R. (1972) *Economic Theory of Teams*, New Haven, CT: Yale University Press.

team work (D2)

A method of organizing production which rejects a hierarchical organization in favour of collaboration.

TechMARK (G1)

Part of the London Stock Exchange which provides a market in the shares of innovative technology companies. This 'market within a market' began in November 1999 with over 100 companies quoted.

technical change (O3)

The process which begins with INVENTION and then proceeds to INNOVATION.

technical efficiency (D2)

Production using a method that maximizes production from given quantities of factor inputs.

See also: allocative efficiency

technical progress (Q3)

The use of new techniques; the introduction of new products. Historically technical progress has taken the form of the saving of labour and of raw materials, mechanization and the application of inventions. In most cases, changes in the capital stock are necessary to achieve it. Technical progress can be measured by examining changes in the proportion of output using a particular technique, by increases in speed or by improvements in product quality. Technical progress is a major determinant of ECONOMIC GROWTH.

See also: diffusion rate; disembodied technical progress; embodied technical progress; innovation; invention; labour-augmenting technical progress; research and development

References

Heertje, A. (1977) *Economics and Techni-*

cal Change, trans. Z. St-Gallay, London: Weidenfeld & Nicolson.

technological rent (D0, O3)
That part of monopoly profits created by TECHNICAL PROGRESS.

telecommuting (J2)
Working for a firm at home, connected by telephone lines to supply work from a personal computer. This is a major development in the small-firm sector.

See also: homework; networker

temporary equilibrium (D0, E0)
HICKS's idea that over a short period of a 'week' variations in prices can be neglected. During this period both current prices and expected prices are allowed to influence plans for consumption and production. The stability of this equilibrium depends on the ELASTICITY of price expectations. This concept of equilibrium is crucial to Hicksian dynamic analysis.

References

Hicks, J.R. (1939) *Value and Capital*, chs 10, 11, 12, Oxford: Oxford University Press.

tender (D4, G1)
1 A method of selling shares by which prospective buyers specify the price at which they are willing to buy.
2 Direct sale of government securities.
3 A method of fixing the price of a contract often used in the construction and heavy engineering industries.

See also: tap stock

1040 ('ten forty') (H2)
1 The basic tax form used in the USA for individuals and families to report their personal incomes. A taxpayer first calculates his or her adjusted gross income, subtracts a standard deduction (personal exemptions) and then deducts TAX CREDITS. Persons with lower incomes and no deductions against tax use a simplified version of this form.
2 A US government bond redeemable at the option of the government after ten

years but only has to be paid up after forty years.

Tennessee Valley Authority (L3)
A public corporation established in 1933 and owned by the US federal government. Its tasks include flood control, wholesale power supply to parts of seven states, economic development of tourism and natural resources, and job training. It receives appropriations from the US Congress to finance its activities, apart from its self-financing power programme.

tenure profile (J2)
A description of a firm's labour force showing the proportions of it with different lengths of service.

terminal bonus (G2)
A bonus given by an insurance company to the policyholder at the time when an insurance policy matures.

See also: reversionary bonus

term premium (G0)
The difference between the yields of fixed income securities of different maturities not attributable to current or anticipated future levels of short-term interest rates. Expected returns on exogenous securities, the quantity of extant securities, the distribution of asset holdings and the flows of new wealth across different classes of investors, classified according to their attitude to risk, have all been suggested as determinants of these premiums.

terms of trade (F1)
1 The ratio of the values of the goods and services traded between countries.
2 The weighted or unweighted ratio of export price indices to import price indices.

As changes in the terms of trade have so great an effect on the GROSS NATIONAL PRODUCT of OPEN ECONOMIES there are many policy responses to deteriorating terms. These include changing the underlying bargaining relations in international trade, the collective self-reliance of less developed countries in trade and investment, import substitution and changes in types of export. Some studies suggest that the deterioration in the terms of trade has been more the result of the characteristics of countries than of commodities.

The best measures of the terms of trade have been the INTERNATIONAL MONETARY FUND's index of thirty primary commodities exported by less developed countries deflated by the United Nations' index and the WORLD BANK's indicators of market prices divided by a unit value index of total manufactures exported from developed market economies to less developed countries.

See also: commodity terms of trade; double factorial terms of trade; factorial terms of trade; income terms of trade; net barter terms of trade; single factorial terms of trade

terms of trade argument (F1)
A reason for PROTECTION. A large country by imposing a TARIFF, quota, or export tax can obtain imports at lower relative prices

term spread (E4)
The difference between a long-term and a short-term interest rate.

term structure of interest rates (E4)
The relationship between interest rates on SECURITIES of different maturities, particularly the relationship between short- and long-term interest rates. Economists, in-

cluding HICKS, have attempted to explain this structure in terms of EXPECTATIONS; others have attributed the structure to the attitudes of borrowers and lenders to LIQUIDITY and RISK or to market segmentation that prevents funds being shifted from short-term to long-term markets. Long-term interest rates are often more than short-term rates as many investors cannot lend long term and so have to be paid a premium to be encouraged to lend.

References
Meiselman, D. (1962) *The Term Structure of Interest Rates*, Englewood Cliffs, NJ: Prentice Hall.
Nelson, C.R. (1972) *The Term Structure of Interest Rates*, New York: Basic Books.

tertiary sector (L8, P0)
That part of an economy producing SERVICES. The formal part of this sector is dominated by schools, hospitals, retailing, banks and insurance; the informal part is dominated by self-employed persons in the BLACK ECONOMY. In the USA and the UK, as a consequence of DE-INDUSTRIALIZATION, it has become, as measured by employment, the major sector of the economy.

test rate of discount (E2, L3)
The real rate of return that UK public sector investments are expected to achieve at the margin. The UK government, in its continuing attempts to improve investment appraisal in NATIONALIZED INDUSTRIES, proposed this rate in a White Paper of 1967. It was originally set at 8 per cent, to represent 'the minimum rate of return to be expected in a marginal low-risk project undertaken for commercial reasons' with the hope that there would be greater consistency in the granting of approval for projects. It has subsequently been changed to reflect market changes in interest rates.

References
The Chancellor of Exchequer (1967) *Nationalized Industries: A Review of Economic and Financial Objectives*, London: HMSO, Cmnd 3437.

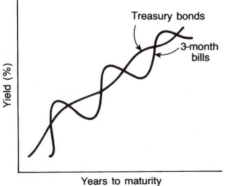

Treasury bonds

3-month bills

Yield (%)

Years to maturity

test statistic (C1)

The distribution of a standardized variable, also known as a z score. For a normal distribution the z score is the statistic minus the mean of the sample all divided by the STANDARD DEVIATION of the sample.

Thatcherism (E6)

An attitude of frugality towards public expenditure and a belief in the supremacy of market forces. Mrs Margaret Thatcher in 1970 as UK Secretary of State for Education, by abolishing free school milk, gained the former reputation; as Prime Minister of the UK from 1979 to 1990, her emphasis on monetary control (instead of extensive government intervention backed by public funds), on the PRIVATIZATION of nationalized industries and on the removal of LABOUR MARKET RIGIDITIES expressed her desire to unleash free market forces. She frequently used the analogy of good household management for such policies and is thus the contemporary expounder of Gladstonian finance. Sir Geoffrey Howe in his first Budget speech of 1979 outlined the programme of Thatcherism in his four principles: the strengthening of economic incentives, the reduction of the burden of financing the public sector, the reduction in the role of the state to increase freedom of individual choice and increased responsibility in collective bargaining. In practice MONETARISM was short-lived and public spending prodigal in many years.

References

Johnson, C. (1991) *The Economy under Mrs Thatcher, 1979–90*, Harmondsworth: Penguin.
Thompson, G. (1986) *The Conservatives' Economic Policy*, London: Croom Helm.
Walters, A.A. (1986) *Britain's Economic Renaissance: Margaret Thatcher's Reforms, 1979–84*, Oxford and New York: Oxford University Press.

theonomy (B2)

1 The application of biblical theology, especially the Law of Moses set out in the Old Testament.

2 A form of Christian reconstruction especially applied to the economy.

References

Rushdoony, R.S. (1973) *The Institutes of Biblical Law*, Nutley, NJ: Craig Press.

theory of clubs (H4)

An explanation of the nature of CLUB GOODS sharing some of the characteristics of PUBLIC GOODS without non-excludability. This theory can be traced back to PIGOU and KNIGHT; recent writers on this subject include BUCHANAN and Tiebout.

References

Buchanan, I.M. (1965) 'An economic theory of clubs', *Economica New Series*, 32: 1–14.
Sandler, T. and Tschirhart, J. (1980) 'The economic theory of clubs: an evaluative survey', *Journal of Economic Literature* 18: 1481–521.

theory of the firm (L2)

An explanation of how the aims of a firm are related to its decision making. Since MARSHALL, economists have studied the rationale for managerial decisions on pricing, product mix, output, advertising and investment. Earlier theories were built on the assumption of PROFIT MAXIMIZATION; later theories have attempted to incorporate wider theories of managerial behaviour and to recognize different organizational forms. The theory of the firm constitutes a major part of microeconomics.

See also: Coase; structure–conduct–performance model

References

Baumol, W.J. (1967) *Business Behavior, Value and Growth*, New York: Harcourt, Brace & World.
Clarke, R. and McGuinness, T. (eds) (1987) *The Economics of the Firm*, Oxford: Basil Blackwell.
Marshall, A. (1920) *Principles of Economics*, 8th edn, London: Macmillan.
Ricketts, M. (1994) *The economics of business enterprise: an introduction to economic organisation and the theory of the firm*, 2nd edn, New York, London

and Toronto: Simon and Schuster; Harvester Wheatsheaf.

Stigler, G.I. (1952) *The Theory of the Firm*, rev. edn, New York: Macmillan.

Williamson, O.E. (1963) *Economics of Discretionary Behavior: Managerial Objectives in a Theory of the Firm*, Englewood Cliffs, NJ: Prentice Hall.

theta (G1)

The ratio of the change in the price of option to the decrease in time to expiration. Also known as time decay.

thin trading (G1)

Little trading of a SECURITY or other marketable item. A low turnover of a security, or of the market as a whole, indicates thinness. A consequence will be a divergence between the observed and true values of BETA.

third age (J1)

The period of a person's life from the age of 50 years. This age group has a dominant role in many consumer markets of industrialized countries in the late twentieth century.

See also: grey society

third-degree price discrimination (D4, M3)

Charging different prices to different customers. This is the most common form of price discrimination. Discrimination is often on the basis of the income, age, student or unemployed status of the consumer.

See also: price discrimination

third market (G1)

The UK stock exchange founded in January 1987 to allow the trading of small companies' SECURITIES. The first and second markets consist of the main list of the INTERNATIONAL STOCK EXCHANGE and the UNLISTED SECURITIES MARKET. As the companies using this market are small, and often new, investment in their shares is very risky. Nevertheless, it is a market with great growth potential, partly because of the

companies promoted by the BUSINESS EXPANSION SCHEME.

third-party effect (D0, Q0) *see* externality; spillover effect

third way (P4) *see* market socialism

Third World (O0)

Developing economies apart from oil producers, with low per capita incomes, large agricultural sectors and a shortage of most kinds of capital. Some have defined the Third World as those countries in receipt of FOREIGN AID.

See also: First World; Second World

References

Reitsma, H.A. and Kleinpenning, I.M.G. (1985) *The Third World in Perspective*, Assen and Maastricht: Van Gorcgum.

Reynolds, L.G. (1985) *Economic Growth in the Third World, 1850–1980*, New Haven, CT, and London: Yale University Press.

Worsley, P. (1967) *The Third World*, 2nd edn, London: Weidenfeld & Nicolson.

Third World debt problem (F3, O0) *see* world debt problem

Thirty Share Index (G1) *see* Financial Times Industrial Ordinary Share Index

Thomson Report (R5)

Report on the Regional Problems in the Enlarged Community, a report of a EUROPEAN COMMUNITY Commissioner in 1973 which surveyed the economic and social problems of the member countries on the eve of the first oil crisis.

Thornton, Henry, 1760–1815 (B3)

London banker and leading monetary theorist of the early nineteenth century who was a member of the Clapham Sect, a group of Evangelical social reformers who succeeded in abolishing British participation in the slave trade. Member of Parliament for Southwark from 1782 to 1815. His famous book *Paper Credit* (1802), much praised by SCHUMPETER, HAYEK and HICKS, defended the issue of inconvertible banknotes, showed the relationship between interest rates and international gold flows, analysed the market for loanable funds, defined the nature of inflation and presented a definition of FULL EMPLOYMENT.

References

Hicks, J.R. (1967) *Critical Essays in Monetary Theory*, ch. 10, Oxford: Clarendon Press.

Thornton, H. (1939) *An Enquiry into the Nature and Effects of the Paper Credit of Great Britain*, ed. F. von Hayek, London and New York: George Allen & Unwin.

threat effect (J3, J5)
Effect on the wages of a non-unionized labour force of the threat of a TRADE (LABOR) UNION organizing to raise wages. A non-unionized employer wanting to prevent unionization raises wages to the union level. Threat effects contribute to the spread of wage inflation.

three-digit industry (L0)
An INDUSTRY defined according to a fine classification such that the economy's industrial structure is broken down into as many as 999 industries.

See also: two-digit industry

three-stage least squares (C1)
A rewriting of TWO-STAGE LEAST SQUARES estimators and the application of generalized least squares to all the relations in the model to obtain a simultaneous estimate of all parameters.

References

Zellner, A. and Theil, H. (1962) 'Three-stage least squares: simultaneous estimation of simultaneous equations', *Econometrica* 30: 54–78.

threshold population (J1, R1)
The minimum size a population must be to carry out the functions of a town or city. A major determinant of this size will be AGGLOMERATION ECONOMICS.

See also: central place theory

thrift (E2, G2)
1 Excessive saving. In KEYNESIAN econom-

ics thrift is attacked because a hoarding of income lowers aggregate demand.
2 A mutual savings bank or SAVINGS AND LOAN ASSOCIATION (USA), similar to a UK BUILDING SOCIETY through providing MORTGAGES. In the 1980s, the US thrifts went further into insolvency as a consequence of financial deregulation, including the ending of REGULATION Q and the diversification of their investments; lax supervision and the guaranteeing of deposits contributed to poor financial control.
3 Careful management of resources.

See also: paradox of thrift; Resolution Trust Corporation

Thünen, Johann Heinrich von, 1783–1850 (B3)
A Prussian landlord who can be credited with creating MARGINALISM and managerial economics and presenting one of the first general equilibrium models and models of locations.

References

Samuelson, P.A. (1983) 'Thünen at two hundred', *Journal of Economic Literature* 21 (December): 1469–88.

tick (G1)
One thirty-secondth of a percentage point, especially of the interest rate of UK gilts.

Tiebout hypothesis (H7, R1)
The view that there should be small local government areas in order to increase the amount of citizen choice between different combinations of facilities and local taxes. Individuals would be able to obtain the combination closest to their preferences by moving between these small areas.

See also: fiscal mobility

References

Mieszkowski, P. and Zodrow, G.R. (1989) 'Taxation and the Tiebout model: the differential effects of head taxes, taxes on land rents, and property taxes', *Journal of Economic Literature* 27 (September): 1098–1146.
Oates, W.Y. (1969) 'The effect of property

taxes and local public spending on property values: an empirical study of tax capitalization and the Tiebout hypothesis', *Journal of Political Economy* 77: 957–71.

Tiebout, C. (1956) 'A pure theory of local government expenditures', *Journal of Political Economy* 64: 416–24.

tied aid (F3, O2)

FOREIGN AID given on condition that the recipient purchases the exports of the donor country. This has been called 'devalued aid' as the recipient may have to purchase goods higher in price and lower in quality than are available on international markets; in extreme cases the aid is supplied in physical amounts, e.g. food and medicines. However, many donor countries with their own BALANCE OF PAYMENTS problems would give little aid at all if it were not in this form.

See also: bilateral aid; multilateral aid

tied cottage (Q1, R2)

A house provided to a worker holding a particular job, especially in the agricultural sector. When the worker ceases to hold that job, he or she has to seek alternative accommodation.

tied house (L8)

In the UK brewery industry, a public house (inn) which can only sell the products of the brewery to which it is connected, usually by ownership.

tight fiscal policy (H3)

Low government expenditure, high taxation or both.

tight monetary policy (E5)

A strict MONETARY POLICY attempting to curb the growth of the money supply and raising interest rates. This policy is often employed by economies with an unacceptable rate of inflation and/or balance of payments problems. These goals are sought by reducing aggregate demand and inducing capital inflows from other countries.

till money (G2)

The cash that UK clearing banks have on their premises for payments to customers. Until 1971 it could be included in the RESERVE ASSETS of these banks: it was excluded then as cash needed for transactions purposes could not be regarded as a reserve.

time budget survey (C8, J2)

An investigation into the allocation of time between paid work, unpaid work (e.g. household cleaning) and leisure which aims to discover the range of a person's activities. Data are collected from the diary entries of volunteers. Surveys of this kind have been used to assess the extent of the INFORMAL ECONOMY and to measure LABOUR FORCE PARTICIPATION RATES.

References

Birdsall, N. (1980) 'Measuring time use and nonmarket exchange', in W.P. McGreevy (ed.) *Third World Poverty: New Strategies for Measuring Development Progress*, Lexington, MA: Lexington Books.

Stafford, F.P. (1985) *Time, Goods and Well Being*, Ann Arbor, MI: Survey Research Center, Institute for Social Research, University of Michigan.

time decay (G1) *see* theta

time deposit (G2)

A sum of money that the depositor does not have the right to withdraw within six days of making the deposit, unless the deposit is subject to an early withdrawal penalty of at least seven days' simple interest.

time rate (J3)

A wage rate per unit of time, often an hour.

See also: piece rate

time series (C1, C8)

A collection of data showing the values of an economic variable at different dates, e.g. expenditure on clothing for each year of a decade. Movements of time series can be divided into secular (long term), cyclical, seasonal and random changes.

See also: cyclical variations; random variations; seasonal adjustment trend

References

Box, G.E.P. and Jenkins, G.M. (1970) *Time Series Analysis: Forecasting and Control*, San Francisco: Holden-Day.

timeshare (R2)
The property right to use a house or apartment, usually for holiday purposes, for specified weeks of a year, either over a fixed term of years or in perpetuity. The right can be bought and sold. Timesharers often have to pay an annual maintenance charge to the firm organizing these properties.

time span (J3)
The amount of time an employee can work without reporting to his or her immediate superior. These spans have been used as a proxy measure of all the attributes of a job giving rise to occupational pay differentials. Elliott Jaques extensively applied this to the rationalization of organizations' pay structures, e.g. at Glacier Metals (UK) and Honeywell Computers (USA).

See also: wage differentials

References

Jaques, E. (1956) *Measurement of Responsibility*, Cambridge, MA: Harvard University Press.
—— (1964) *Time-span Handbook*, London: Heinemann.

time value of money (E4)
The enhanced value of money arising from it being invested at interest over a time period.

Tinbergen, Jan, 1903–94 (B3)
Prominent Dutch econometrician who, after studying physics at Leiden University and gaining a PhD for a thesis on extremum problems in economics and physics, conducted business cycle research from 1929 to 1945 at the Dutch Central Bureau of Statistics. He was Director of the Netherlands Central Planning Bureau from 1945 to 1955, Professor of Development Planning at Erasmus University,

Rotterdam, from 1955 to 1973, and Professor of International Co-operation at Leiden from 1973 to 1975. With FRISCH, he won the first NOBEL PRIZE FOR ECONOMICS in 1969; four years later his brother shared the Nobel Prize for Medicine. His skills as an econometrician yielded many books, directly arising from the jobs he held. His first works were on business cycles but his experience with the Central Planning Bureau produced renowned works on economic policy that asserted that government policy must have the same number of instruments as it has quantified targets. Later he turned to DEVELOPMENT ECONOMICS and the study of income distribution.

References

Tinbergen, J. (1952) *On the Theory of Economic Policy*, Amsterdam: North-Holland.
—— (1956) *Economic Policy: Principles and Design*, Amsterdam: North-Holland.
—— (1968) *Statistical Testing of Business Cycle Theories*, New York: Agathon Press.

tit-for-tat strategy (L1)
The behaviour of a firm which deliberately imitates the initial strategy of its rivals.

Tobin, James, 1918–2002 (B3)
US economist educated at Harvard University and an economics professor at Yale University since 1947; in 1981 he was awarded the NOBEL PRIZE FOR ECONOMICS. A prominent KEYNESIAN who has attacked the narrowness of MONETARISM with his wider PORTFOLIO SELECTION theory. In a paper on LIQUIDITY PREFERENCE in 1958, he extended Keynesian analysis by asserting that liquidity preference is a response to the risk associated with the probability distribution of interest rate expectations. In many papers, he has repeatedly used a GENERAL EQUILIBRIUM approach to a study of financial INTERMEDIATION and flow of funds analysis. In 1961–2 he served on President Kennedy's COUNCIL OF ECONOMIC ADVISERS. His wide-ranging interests include STABILI-

ZATION POLICIES, growth policies and the poverty problem. He originated the TOBIT MODEL method.

See also: flow of funds account

References

Purvis, D. and Myhrman, J. (1982) 'James Tobin's contribution to economics', *Scandinavian Journal of Economics* 84: 61–88.

Tobin, J. (1974 and 1975) *Essays in Economics*, Vols I and II, Cambridge, MA: MIT Press.

—— (1974) *The New Economics: One Decade Older*, Princeton, NJ: Princeton University Press.

Tobin's Q (M2)

The ratio of the market value of a firm's assets to their replacement value. This is the driving force of investment decisions according to Professor James Tobin of Yale University.

Tobin tax (F3, H2)

A proposed uniform tax levied by all countries of the world on all foreign exchange transactions with the aim of making short-term HOT MONEY movements unprofitable.

Tobit model (C5)

An econometric model which copes with the problem of missing data in the form of a shortage of observations beyond a limit point, e.g. zero, so that there are no negative values. TOBIN was the first to tackle this problem in his analysis of household expenditure on a durable good.

References

Amemiya, T. (1984) 'Tobit models: a survey', *Journal of Econometrics* 24: 3–61.

Tobin, J. (1958) 'Estimation of relationships for limited dependent variables', *Econometrica* 26: 24–36.

token money (E4)

Anything accepted as money, not because of its intrinsic value, but because of custom or legal enactment. Thus banknotes are token money and gold coins are not. Token money costs less to produce

than its face value, e.g. a pound note in the UK costs only several pence.

See also: fiat money

Tokyo Round (F1)

A series of tariff cuts arranged under the auspices of the GENERAL AGREEMENT ON TARIFFS AND TRADE in the period 1973–9. Tariff reductions were to be implemented in equal annual amounts from 1980 to 1987. A duty of 20 per cent was reduced by 59 per cent, a 10 per cent duty by 42 per cent and a 5 per cent duty by 26 per cent. The EUROPEAN COMMUNITY and Japan made advance reductions; other countries by 1990. It was the intention that in this round tariff averages weighted by total imports of manufactured goods would decline by 30 per cent in the USA, 28 per cent in the European Community and 46 per cent in Japan. Smaller reductions in tariffs of goods from developing countries (as in the KENNEDY ROUND) were agreed as they are sensitive products, e.g. textiles. At the end of the round, tariffs on manufactured goods, weighted by total imports, were to be cut by 4.9 per cent in the USA, 6 per cent in the European Community and 5.4 per cent in Japan.

See also: General Agreement on Tariffs and Trade; Uruguay Round

toll (D0)

The charge for the use of a service; in some cases an excessive charge. Major examples of tolls are those for the use of highways and a telephone system to make long-distance calls.

toll model (J4)

OKUN's model of a LABOUR MARKET in which a firm hiring a worker has to pay a 'toll' to cover the costs of training and initiation. This model is used to explain cyclical variations in employment and unemployment.

References

Okun, A.M. (1981) *Prices and Quantities: A Macroeconomic Analysis*, ch. 2, Washington, DC: Brookings Institution; Oxford: Basil Blackwell.

tombstone (G1)

A press advertisement recording the details of a new issue or loan. The names on the tombstone are the managers and underwriters (or syndicate members) to the issue. The amount of the loan and the listing terms are also given.

tontine (G2)

A scheme, invented by Lorenzo Tonti, a Neapolitan banker, in 1653, consisting of several subscribers advancing the same amount to a borrower who pays the same amount of interest in total to all the subscribers until the survivor receives all the interest on the amount advanced. Thus if there are 100 subscribers receiving £50 each in interest, when there are only 50 left each subscriber will obtain £100 each and the survivor will receive £5,000 per annum. This popular method of raising funds in the eighteenth and nineteenth centuries was last used by the British government to raise a loan in 1789. One of the most amusing accounts of a tontine is given in Robert Louis Stevenson's short novel.

References

Jennings, R.M. and Trout, A.P. (1976) 'The tontine: fact and fiction', *Journal of European Economic History*, 5: 663–70.

Stevenson, R.L. and Osbourne, L. (1889) *The Wrong Box*, London: Longman.

top-down linkage model (C5, R5)

A regional model showing the local reaction to national economic change, e.g. cyclical fluctuations in NATIONAL INCOME. It usually ignores the upward feedback of economic activity from the region.

References

Klein, L.R. (1969) 'The specification of regional econometric models', *Papers of the Regional Science Association* 23: 105–15.

top-level efficiency (D0, D6)

An increase in the total collection of goods available to a society that makes everyone better off. This type of efficiency combines both production and exchange efficiencies.

See also: Pareto optimum

top-sided federalism (H7)

A description of US federalism of the 1968–78 period in which federal aid and state spending grew faster than local spending. One way in which this occurred was through the COMPREHENSIVE EMPLOYMENT AND TRAINING ACT 1973 which replaced thirteen separate manpower training programmes to channel additional federal aid to local governments.

See also: fiscal federalism

Torrens, Robert, 1780–1864 (B3)

A prolific English classical economist who served in the Royal Marines from 1797 to 1835 and was a Member of Parliament from 1831 to 1835. In a long series of publications from 1808, he participated in the major economic debates of the day, particularly on monetary questions, switching from being an anti-bullionist in the 1820s to membership of the CURRENCY SCHOOL. He also formulated the law of comparative advantage independently of Ricardo and the law of reciprocal demand independently of John Stuart MILL.

References

Fetter, F.W. (1962) 'Robert Torrens: Colonel of Marines and political economist', *Economica New Series*, 29: 152–65.

Robbins, L. (1958) *Robert Torrens and the Evolution of Classical Economics*, London: Macmillan.

total costs (D0)

All the costs of producing a good or service. In the short run the total is divisible into fixed and variable costs, but in the long run all costs are variable.

total fertility rate (J1)

A measure of the average number of live births throughout a woman's child-bearing period. It is calculated by adding the average number of live births of all age-specific groups (15–44 years) together.

total public debt (H6)
All the bonds and bills issued by the central and local governments of a country outstanding at a particular time. In the USA this consists only of borrowings by the US Treasury. It is limited in size by the GRAMM–RUDMAN–HOLLINGS ACT.

See also: gross federal debt; public sector borrowing requirement

total revenue (D0, M2)
1 All the proceeds from selling a particular amount of output.
2 The total quantity sold multiplied by price.

Maximizing total revenue is a practical objective of some firms.

See also: managerial models of the firm

total shareholder return (G1)
Dividends + bonus share issues + capital gain.

tournament model (D0)
A model of contracting in which the winner receives a carrot and the loser a stick. This reduces the MORAL HAZARD problem posed by the cost of monitoring performance. The model is applicable to all compensation schemes which base pay on relative performance, especially those for sportsmen or women and top executives. Ever larger prizes are needed to motivate the players. The size of the top prize should increase with the number of contestants.

References

McLaughlin, K.J. (1988) 'Aspects of tournament models', *Research in Labor Economics* 9: 225–56.

town clearing (G2)
Same-day clearing of a cheque with a value of more than £10,000 within a specified central area of the City of London after over-the-counter trading has closed for the day.

tracker fund (G1)
A unit trust investing in the companies which are included in a stock market index, e.g. the FTSE 100. Its aims are a combination of income and capital growth.

tracking stock (G1)
A stock issued by a public company which tracks the value of one part of the company. This permits different valuations of divisions of a firm. The stock can be issued to the market or to existing shareholders. If the new stock has a high price–earnings ratio, the cost of raising capital is reduced.

tradable discharge permit (Q0)
A permit allowing the holder to discharge a specified amount of a pollutant. As this permit can be sold to another person, the permission can be transferred.

tradable emission permit (Q0) *see* marketable discharge permit, tradable discharge permit

trade (D0, F1, G1)
1 The sale of goods and services.
2 Exporting and importing.
3 A transaction in a financial market.

Trade Act 1974 (F1)
US federal statute regulating the foreign trade of the USA. Under an escape clause, industries can apply for TARIFFS and other trade restrictions to be erected in their favour if it can be proved that the industry concerned has suffered from foreign competition as seen in a fall in employment, output or profits. Under the Act, workers unemployed or threatened with unemployment as a consequence of imports can be given income support, relocation allowances, job search allowances and training.

trade balance (F1)
A sub-balance of a country's BALANCE OF PAYMENTS showing the relationship between total exports and total imports. It is usually divided into a visible balance, referring to goods, and an invisible balance, referring to services. The balance is in surplus if exports exceed imports; in deficit if imports are in excess of exports.

See also: current account

trade bill (G2)
A BILL OF EXCHANGE payable in one, two, three or six months.

trade creation (F1)
The effect of a CUSTOMS UNION increasing the volume of trade through the elimination of previous trade barriers between members.

See also: trade diversion

trade credit (G2)
1 Loans between non-financial firms, e.g. a wholesaler's financing of a new retailer by allowing payment months after the delivery of supplies.
2 Credit offered by a firm to its customers.

In times of monetary stringency caused by a TIGHT MONETARY POLICY, trade credit often replaces bank credit.

trade cycle (E3)
Fluctuations in the level of national economic activity over a period of years. Although first observed by PETTY, it was not until MALTHUS, John Stuart MILL and MARX that there were serious attempts to explain such oscillations. As most trade cycle theories explain fluctuations in terms of changes in investment, the length of the cycle depends on the durability of the capital good: the shortest are inventory cycles, the longest are infrastructure investment cycles, e.g. in transport systems.

See also: business cycle; Juglar cycle; Kitchin cycle; Kondratieff cycle; Kuznets cycle

References
Haberler, G. (1964) *Prosperity and Depression*, 5th edn, London: Allen & Unwin.
Matthews, R.C.O. (1959) *The Trade Cycle*, Cambridge: Cambridge University Press.

trade deficit (F1)
An excess of imports over exports.

See also: trade balance

trade diversion (F1)
The effect of a CUSTOMS UNION in changing the flows of goods and services between countries with increasing volumes going to other members of the union.

See also: trade creation

traded option (G2)
An OPTION that can be bought and sold until its expiry date; at expiry, the last holder can exercise the option.

Trade Expansion Act 1962 (F1)
US federal trade statute concerned with the liberalization of trade.

See also: Kennedy Round

trade-off (D0)
The relationship between two inversely connected variables such that more of one means less of another. Trade-offs occur in many parts of both microeconomics and macroeconomics, e.g. the trade-off between work and leisure, between consumption of one good and of another of a consumer with a fixed income, between high wages and high employment, between efficiency and equity. Famous trade-offs include RICARDO's between wages and profits and PHILLIPS's between unemployment and inflation. The conflicting aims of individuals and of governments make trade-offs inevitable; scarcity necessitates choice between competing alternatives.

See also: opportunity cost

trade policy (F1) *see* commercial policy

trade regime (F1, P0)
A country, or countries, following a particular trade policy of PROTECTION or FREE TRADE. Within the policy there can be different rules for various industries and products, e.g. import substitution for some and export promotion for others.

trade strategy (F1)
The balance between production for domestic and foreign markets. An outward-oriented strategy would leave to domestic producers only those goods that cannot be

more cheaply produced abroad; an inward-oriented strategy follows the principles of IMPORT SUBSTITUTION and PROTECTION. As PROTECTION invites retaliation, a country that is inward looking is unlikely to enjoy many ECONOMIES OF SCALE and to be more monopolistic. Outward-oriented economies, e.g. Singapore, Hong Kong and South Korea, have experienced higher rates of growth in real national income per head than inward-oriented countries.

trade surplus (F1) *see* trade balance

trade threat (F1)
A trade restriction designed to change non-trade policies of a government, e.g. concerning human rights or the cleanliness of the environment. A BOYCOTT is the most common form of threat.

See also: economic sanctions

trade union (J5)
An association of workers or employers, especially the former. Trade unions have always been concerned with both the short- and the long-term welfare of their members – with varying degrees of success. These unions have been analysed as monopolists in the labour market, creating market imperfections. Unions are often criticized for opposing technical change but they can raise PRODUCTIVITY by encouraging co-operation between management and labour. Many models of wage bargaining assume that the employer unilaterally selects the level of employment and that the union can only influence the wage level, but there are models assuming that unions can bargain about both employment and wages.

See also: closed shop; right-to-work state; strike; union shop; US labor union; yellow dog contract

References

Booth, A.L. (1995) *The economics of the trade union*, Cambridge, New York and Melbourne: Cambridge University Press.
Hirsch, B.T. and Addison, I.T. (1986) *The Economic Analysis of Unions: New Ap-*proaches and Evidence, Boston: Allen & Unwin.
MacDonald, I.M. and Solow, R.M. (1981) 'Wage bargaining and employment', *American Economic Review* 71: 896–908.

Trade Union Act 1984 (J5)
UK industrial relations statute that imposed a duty on unions to hold secret ballots of their memberships for the election of the officers of the principal executive committee every five years. Also, ballots are required every ten years for the setting up of union political funds. Political dues cannot be collected from union members who are certified as exempt from contributing or object to doing so.

See also: Employment Act 1980

Trade Union Reform and Employment Rights Act 1993 (J5)
A UK statute which extended the rules for the balloting of union members, reinforced the union members' rights, including the right, in most cases, not to be excluded or expelled from a union, further clarified employment rights and abolished the setting of statutory minimum wages by wages councils.

Trade Unions and Labour Relations Act 1974 (J5)
A UK statute which repealed the Industrial Relations Act 1971 but retained its provisions on the right not to be unfairly dismissed and industrial tribunals. It asserted trade unions' immunity from actions in tort and permitted peaceful picketing.

trade-weighted exchange rate (F3)
The exchange rate of one country's currency for another's adjusted to reflect the composition of the exports of each country.

trading on the equity (M2)
The effect on the earnings of high GEARING of a company with PREFERENCE SHARES and DEBENTURES as well as ORDINARY SHARES. A disproportionate amount of an increase in

earnings will be available for distribution to holders of ordinary shares.

trading potential (F1)
An estimate of the possible volume of exports from one country to another. The greater the NATIONAL INCOME of the countries, the higher the potential; the greater the cultural and geographical distance between them, the less likely there will be exporting. GRAVITY MODELS have been used to make this calculation.

trading price (D0)
A price that emerges as the consequence of a trading activity.

See also: list price; transaction price

Tragedy of the Commons (Q0)
The overgrazing of common land through each family ignoring the EXTERNALITY of grazing its own sheep. As each family ignores the impact of its own land use, the quality of the land available to other families declines. The problem could be solved by a local government regulation of the number of graziers or by an AUCTION of a fixed number of permits giving access to the land.

See also: common property resources

transaction bonus (J3)
A reward to a senior executive for the successful completion of a TAKEOVER deal.

transaction cost (D0, F3)
1 The running costs of an economic system.
2 The cost of effecting an exchange or other economic transaction.

These costs, which vary in magnitude from one economic system to another, include those of negotiating and drafting contracts and the subsequent costs of adjusting for misalignments. This concept is fundamental to the analysis of economic REGULATION, labour market hiring, VERTICAL INTEGRATION and competition in the capital market.

See also: Commons

References

Coase, R. (1937) 'The nature of the firm', *Economica New Series*, 4: 386–405.
Commons, J.R. (1934) *Institutional Economics: Its Place in Political Economy*, Madison, WI: University of Wisconsin Press.
Demsetz, H. (1968) 'The cost of transacting', *Quarterly Journal of Economics* 82: 33–53.
Williamson, O.E. (1975) *Markets and Hierarchies: Analysis and Antitrust Implications*, New York: Free Press.

transaction cost economics (B2)
A branch of economics using 'the transaction' as the fundamental concept of economics and analysing economic problems as contracting problems. This approach to economics considers institutional alternatives and uses as its assumptions BOUNDED RATIONALITY, opportunism and asset specificity. One of the first economists to emphasize the importance of transactions was COMMONS.

References

Groenewegen, J. (ed.) (1996) *Transaction cost economics and beyond*, Boston, Dordrecht and London: Kluwer Academic.
Williamson, O.E. (1985) *The Economic Institutions of Capitalism*, New York: Free Press; London: Collier Macmillan.

transaction price (D4)
The price actually paid to obtain a unit of a good or service. This is often different from the LIST PRICE.

transactions demand for money (E4)
The amount of money an individual wishes to hold in order to finance current purchases of goods and services. No monetary theorist disputes that such a demand exists.

See also: demand for money

transferable discharge permit (Q0) *see* marketable discharge permit, tradable discharge permit

transfer earnings (D3)
The minimum income of a FACTOR OF PRO-

DUCTION that will keep it in that employment rather than another, measured by the earnings of that factor in the best alternative employment. Any part of a factor's earnings in excess of transfer earnings is ECONOMIC RENT.

See also: opportunity cost

transfer income (D0)

The income of a person or a firm not arising from productive activity but, often, from a governmental grant. The principal examples of these are retirement pensions, student maintenance grants and subsidies to farmers. If such transfer incomes were included in the NATIONAL INCOME there would be double counting of FACTOR INCOMES – when originally received and when redistributed as a transfer.

transfer pricing (D4, L2)

The pricing of the goods and services transferred within large organizations, especially within MULTINATIONAL CORPORATIONS. As many of these goods and services are not marketed outside that organization, arbitrary pricing rules, often of a cost-plus type, are used. It is argued that transfer pricing can be unfair and used as a device to avoid corporation taxation in high-tax countries. Increasingly tax codes have insisted on corporations following set rules to produce fair prices. Transfer pricing also has a major impact on the value of international trade as a high proportion of it consists of trade between subsidiaries of large international enterprises.

transfer problem (F2, F3)

The difficulty of transferring capital in large quantities from one country to another, e.g. the reparation payments Germany had to make after the First World War. The imposition of a second burden on countries having to make the transfer raises the possibility of transfers changing the TERMS OF TRADE. Whether this happens depends on the relative size of the MARGINAL PROPENSITIES TO CONSUME of the recipient and donor countries for a particular product.

transformation curve (D0) *see* production possibility frontier

transformation problem (D0)

The problem stated in MARX's *Das Kapital* of deriving prices from values and of deriving profits from SURPLUS VALUE. Solutions offered by mathematical economists have attracted criticism on account of their restrictive assumptions.

References

Böhm-Bawerk, E. von (1949) *Karl Marx and the Close of his System*, New York: Augustus M. Kelly.
Junankar, P.N. (1982) *Marx's Economics*, ch. 3, Oxford: Philip Alan.
Roemer, J. (1981) *Analytical Foundations of Marxian Economic Theory*, Cambridge: Cambridge University Press.

transition economy (P4)

A national ECONOMY in the process of abandoning a CENTRALLY PLANNED ECONOMY for market mechanisms. After 1989 many of the East European and Soviet economies are of this kind. In Central Europe the transition economies are the Czech Republic, Hungary, Poland, Croatia, the Slovak Republic and Slovenia; in South Eastern Europe, Albania, Bulgaria, FYR, Macedonia and Romania; in the Baltic states, Estonia, Latvia and Lithuania.

References

European Bank for Reconstruction and Development, *Transition Report 1999*, London.
Lavigne, M. (1999) *The Economics of Transition*, 2nd edn, New York: St Martin's Press.

transitory income (D0)

Unexpected income in addition to permanent income. Legacies and wins from gambling are prominent examples.

transmission mechanism (E4)

The means by which changes in the money supply have an effect on output, employment and prices. The change in the money supply leads to a change in interest rates in different markets which, in turn, brings about a change in expenditures and output. However, the speed of reaction to monetary changes depends on the nature of LAGS in the economy. This mechanism can be regarded as portfolio adjustment as a growth in the money supply faster than the growth in output will push up prices of non-monetary assets, e.g. property and durable goods, and stimulate output of them. There has always been controversy about the mechanism because of the two-way causality between money supply and expenditure changes.

See also: Friedman; monetarism

transnational corporation (L2)
A firm with substantial operations in many countries but controlled from its original home base. This location of activities in many countries is a response to the world-wide distribution of resources, governmental constraints, market opportunities and technology. A firm with this wide geographical BASE is able to benefit from increased economies of scale, full utilization of its management and greater returns to its RESEARCH AND DEVELOPMENT expenditures. The first examples of transnationals are probably the large overseas trading monopolies advocated by the MERCANTILISTS, e.g. the East India Company.

See also: multinational corporation

transport economics (R4)
The study of the demand for transport and the relative merits of different systems for carrying persons and goods. This requires applications of consumer theory to determine demand for what is both an intermediate and a final service, and an analysis of transport industries to understand supply problems. Early transport economists attempted to set out the rules for optimal pricing, investment and cost allocation; later there was more interest in the impact of government regulation on resource allocation and distribution, congestion and the multiproduct nature of transportation firms. Increasing use has been made of COST–BENEFIT ANALYSIS and

there has been close collaboration with URBAN ECONOMICS.

References
Glaister, S. (1981) *Fundamentals of Transport Economics*, Oxford: Basil Blackwell.
Winston, C. (1985) 'Conceptual developments in the economics of transportation: an interpretive survey', *Journal of Economic Literature* 23: 57–94.

traveller's cheque (G2)
A cheque denominated in a major currency and widely accepted throughout the world for the purchase of local goods and services and for exchange into local currencies. American Express invented this financial instrument in 1891.

traverse (E0)
The route an economic system takes as it moves from one EQUILIBRIUM to another. In a sense, an economy is in DISEQUILIBRIUM as it proceeds along the traverse.

References
Hicks, J.R. (1965) *Capital and Growth*, ch. 16, Oxford: Oxford University Press.

treasury (H1, M1)
A department in charge of finance in a government or corporation.

treasury bill (G1, H6)
A short-term means of government borrowing modelled on a commercial BILL OF EXCHANGE; invented by BAGEHOT in 1877. In the UK treasury bills effect borrowing for ninety-one days, in the USA for three, six, nine or twelve months.

Treasury model (C5)
The economic forecasting model used by the UK Treasury introduced in the 1970s and relating 200 variables to each other; by 2001 in a series of experiments 357 were used.

References
'Forecasting in the Treasury', *Economic Progress Report*, June 1981.

Treasury view (N1)
The attitude towards the management of

the UK economy in the 1920s and 1930s attacked by KEYNES. The Treasury believed in balanced national budgets and attacked PUBLIC WORKS schemes on the grounds that they would not stimulate aggregate economic activity because of 'CROWDING OUT'. This view was abandoned in 1937 when the Treasury at last conceded the role of public works as part of a COUNTERCYCLICAL POLICY.

References

Middleton, R. (1985) *Towards the Managed Economy: Keynes, the Treasury and the Fiscal Policy Debate of the 1930s*, London: Methuen.

Peden, G.C. (1984) 'The "Treasury View" on public works and employment in the inter-war period', *Economic History Review* 37: 167–81.

treat effect (J3)

A deliberate increase in the wages of non-union employees of a firm undertaken by a management to show that UNIONS confer no benefit on workers. This tactic has been used as a means of reducing the UNIONIZATION of a firm's labour force.

See also: threat effect

Treaty of Rome (F0)

The treaty that set up the EUROPEAN ECONOMIC COMMUNITY in 1958. The signatories were France, West Germany, Italy, the Netherlands, Belgium and Luxemburg. Subsequent treaties have enlarged the EEC: in 1973 the UK, Ireland and Denmark joined, in 1981 Greece and in 1986 Spain and Portugal. The treaty establishes the EEC as a CUSTOMS UNION with mobility of capital and labour within it.

See also: Maastricht Treaty

trembling-hand perfect equilibrium (C7)

In GAME THEORY a co-operative equilibrium, e.g. when a player defects for a number of rounds from a game and then returns to co-operation. There can be trembling-hand perfection through NASH EQUILIBRIA

being immune to small probabilities of error when players make their choices.

trend (C1)

The general movement of a time series in the long term; the secular change. This is often measured by the LEAST SQUARES METHOD where the variable examined is the dependent variable and time is the independent variable.

trending price (D0)

A price which follows a trend.

trend periods (E3) *see* Kondratieff cycle

trickle-down theory (O1)

A theory of economic DEVELOPMENT asserting that development should follow traditional growth patterns with prosperity gradually coming to the least deprived members of society. This theory has also been applied to advanced free market economies in which the richer members of society through their spending raise the real incomes of the poor. The extent of trickling down is usually measured by an increase in the real incomes of the poor, rather than by the removal of all income inequality which would need a 'flood'.

See also: dual economy; Mandeville

Triffin paradox (F3, N2)

Although extra US dollars were needed after 1945 throughout the world to increase foreign currency reserves, the extra dollars accelerated inflation causing the extra dollars to be devalued thereby reducing the value of reserves. This problem seriously undermined the BRETTON WOODS system.

trigger mechanism (G2)

A method of PROGRAM TRADING. This method of mathematical analysis uses as key market indicators a cash index to indicate present values and a futures index to indicate future values.

truck (J3)

A wage payment in goods or in vouchers to obtain goods at the shops of the employer. In the UK, the Truck Acts of

1831, 1887 and 1896 made the truck system illegal, replacing it with wage payments in the current coin of the realm.

See also: Wages Act 1986

true and fair view (M4)

An auditor's opinion that a set of accounts are both devoid of fraud and in conformity with measurement conventions regarded by professional accounting institutes as accurate for portraying the current state of a business. A major concern since 1970 has been to ensure that the values used in statements of accounts have been adjusted to eliminate the effects of inflation.

See also: current cost accounting; statements of Standard Accounting Practice

trust fund (G2, H5)

1 A fund managed by a group of trustees for the benefit of others.
2 The US federal government fund which receives the revenue from a particular tax in order to finance a particular welfare payment. The best known is the OLD AGE, SURVIVORS, DISABILITY AND HEALTH INSURANCE (founded in 1935 and extended to cover disabled persons in 1956) which is financed out of the revenue from the payroll tax. Other trust funds include the Hospital Insurance Fund and the Unemployment Insurance Fund. In the USA the balance of a trust fund is either held as a cash balance with the US Treasury or invested in US securities.

Truth in Lending Act 1968 (G2, R2)

US CONSUMER PROTECTION LEGISLATION requiring lenders of money to inform borrowers of the true rate of interest on their loans. The UK parallel is the Consumer Credit Act.

Turgot, Anne-Robert Jacques, 1727–81 (B3)

French PHYSIOCRAT. Educated at a Paris seminary and the Sorbonne, he abandoned careers in the church and the law to become a tax administrator as intendant of Limoges, from 1761 to 1774, and

Controleur General of France, from 1774 to 1776. His celebrated *Réflexions sur la Formation et la Distribution des Richesses* (1776) anticipated many of the central themes of SMITH's *Wealth of Nations* in that it discussed FREE TRADE, a LAISSEZ-FAIRE approach to industry, the effects of the DIVISION OF LABOUR, VALUE and price theory, a STAGES THEORY and the determinants of factor prices.

References

Groenewegen, P.D. (1977) *The Economics of A.R.J. Turgot*, Dordrecht and Lancaster: Martinus Nijhoff.

turnkey contract (M2)

A construction and engineering contract to build and equip a factory, a power station or other large capital project so that it is completely ready for use. The purchaser merely has to turn the key in the front door to start using the capital asset. Contracts of this kind are popular in Third World countries.

turnover ratios (M4) *see* sales ratios

turnover tax (H2)

A tax levied on the value of the sales revenue of a firm. It is distortionary in that the total tax paid will be higher for goods passing through several firms to their final sale than for those which do not.

turnpike theorem (O4)

A proposition in the theory of ECONOMIC GROWTH for providing an optimal programme over a finite horizon to reach a particular objective. These theorems make different assumptions about the quantities and relative prices of factor inputs required to follow a particular growth path.

References

Dorfman, R., Samuelson, R.A. and Solow, R.M. (1958) *Linear Programming and Economic Analysis*, New York: McGraw-Hill.

tweenies/tweenagers (J1, M3)

Persons aged 10 to 14 years in the transition period from being children to being teenagers. Their formidable spending power has been noted by marketing analysts.

twenty-four-hour trading (G2)
Trading at any time of day on the world's stock exchanges because of their being located in different time zones and often allowing AFTER-HOURS DEALINGS.

two-digit industry (L0)
An INDUSTRY defined according to a broad classification such that an economy's industrial structure is divided into no more than ninety-nine industries. This is usually contrasted with a THREE-DIGIT INDUSTRY.

two-dollar broker (G2)
An independent broker on the NEW YORK STOCK EXCHANGE who executes orders to buy and sell on behalf of commission brokers.

two-gap development model (O2)
A planning model which takes into account a savings gap (savings needed to reach a growth target less actual domestic savings) and a foreign exchange gap (between expenditure needed on imports to achieve target growth and earnings from exports).

References
Chenery, H.B. and Bruno, M. (1962) 'Development alternatives in an open economy: the case of Israel', *Economic Journal* 72: 79–103.

two-part pricing (D4)
The separate pricing of the products of a fixed input and a variable input in order to maximize profit. The prices usually consist of a fixed fee and a variable charge. This has long been used for pricing in the energy and telecommunications industries.

two-part tariff (D0)
A price consisting of two parts. One part pays for fixed costs, the other for VARIABLE COSTS. A major example of this is the charging of a telephone rental to cover fixed costs and the separate charging for calls to pay for variable costs.

See also: price discrimination

References
Feldstein, M. (1972) 'Equity and efficiency in public sector pricing: the optimal two part tariff', *Quarterly Journal of Economics* 86: 175–87.

two-speed economy (E6, P0)
A modern national ECONOMY with one sector in recession and the other booming. Often it is manufacturing that is in decline and the services flourishing.

two-stage least squares (C1)
An econometric method which makes use of all predetermined variables in an econometric model so that the parameters of a single relation can be estimated. The independent variable is replaced by a matrix of least squares regressions of that variable on all the predetermined variables. The final stage is to apply least squares again to the variables of the equation.

See also: three-stage least squares

two-tailed test (C1)
A statistical test to show that a NULL HYPOTHESIS lies between a plus and minus range of a statistic. If a 95 per cent CONFIDENCE INTERVAL is used, then the null hypothesis is rejected if it lies in the +2.5 or −2.5 per cent tails.

See also: one-tailed test

tying (L4)
A restrictive trade practice by which a supplier requires a customer to buy with one product associated products; for example, with soap, soap dispensers.

tying contract (L4, M3)
A sales contract which specifies that a particular good or service will only be supplied if an associated one is purchased, e.g. that oxygen will only be supplied if ancillary equipment is ordered. Under US and UK law this RESTRICTIVE PRACTICE is outlawed.

See also: upselling

Type I error (C1)
The rejection of a NULL HYPOTHESIS which should be accepted.

Type II error (C1)
The acceptance of a NULL HYPOTHESIS which should be rejected.

U

U-form (L2)

The unitary form of business enterprise organized in the traditional way of dividing it up according to function. This is an appropriate structure for smaller enterprises; for larger organizations, a U-form imposes high communication costs.

See also: H-form; M-form; X-form

U hypothesis (O4)

A view of the income distribution of less developed countries advanced by KUZNETS and others that the share of NATIONAL INCOME going to the poorest part of the population declines at the start of economic development and rises only in the later stages of development, often because of a change in government policies to help the poor. The income distribution often changes over time in this way because development has taken the form of industrialization of benefit to only a small part of the economy.

See also: Kuznets curve

References

Adelman, I. and Marris, C.T. (1973) *Economic Growth and Social Equity in Developing Countries*, Stanford CA: Stanford University Press.
Kuznets, S. (1966) *Modern Economic Growth: Rate, Structure and Spread*, New Haven, CT: Yale University Press.

UK economic forecasting (E6)

The work of organizations that regularly produce detailed independent forecasts of the UK economy. Apart from the Treasury and the BANK OF ENGLAND, forecasting is also undertaken by Henley Forecasting, the NATIONAL INSTITUTE OF ECONOMIC AND SOCIAL RESEARCH, London Business School, Liverpool University, Oxford Economic Forecasting, the CONFEDERATION OF BRITISH INDUSTRY, Goldman Sachs and the OECD.

See also: economic forecasting; linkage models

References

HMSO, *Economic Trends*, monthly.
Laury, J.S.E., Lewis, G.R. and Ormerod, P.A. (1978) 'Properties of macroeconomic models of the UK economy: a comparative study', *National Institute Economic Review* 83: 52–72.

UK gilts market (G1)

Market in UK government bonds. About 150 government securities are traded in this market. After the London market was deregulated twenty-nine PRIMARY DEALERS established themselves in the market, using the USA as a model: with this number of dealers no firm will have a vital proportion of the market. The Central Gilts Office acts as the clearing house for transactions in gilts.

UK stock exchanges (G1) *see* International Stock Exchange

UK taxation (H2)

A mixture of taxation on households

(income tax and national insurance contributions), on firms (corporation tax), on wealth (capital gains and capital transfer taxes) and on goods and services (VAT and excise duties) with offsetting allowances at the national level. Local government currently has the revenue from the COUNCIL TAX and UNIFORM BUSINESS RATE. Recent statistics indicate both the relative yield of these taxes and the switch from direct to indirect taxation since 1979.

References

Kay, J.A. and King, M.A. (1990) *The British Tax System*, 5th edn, Oxford: Oxford University Press.

umbrella fund (G2)

A fund set up abroad to evade restrictions on investment imposed by a domestic government.

Umbrella Group (O2, Q0)

The negotiating group of non-EU developed countries at climate conferences consisting of Norway, Russia, the USA, Canada, Japan, Australia, New Zealand and Switzerland.

unbiased estimator (C1)

A PARAMETER of a population that is the same as the corresponding statistic for a sample taken from it, e.g. the ARITHMETIC MEANS are the same.

unbundling (G2, G3)

1 The separate charging for the services provided by a bank or other financial institution.
2 A de-merger which involves the selling off of the component parts of a firm.

uncertainty (D8)

A state of affairs with an unknown outcome not subject to a probability distribution. In economics, there are many states of uncertainty, e.g. of demand, of returns to investment. Uncertainty imposes many costs, e.g. the holding of higher inventories to safeguard against an irregular supply of raw materials and components. The forms of uncertainty are as various as its determinants – competition, technological

change, the business cycle and change of government or governmental policies.

See also: risk

References

Borch, K.H. (1968) *The Economics of Uncertainty*, Princeton, NJ: Princeton University Press.

unconditional grant (H7)

Australian federal grant to an individual state which is a means of sharing tax revenues to provide public services at the same level throughout Australia. As the use of these grants is not stipulated, it is possible for them to be used to reduce taxes rather than to maintain services.

See also: Commonwealth Grants Commission; federal finance

uncovered interest parity (E4)

The assertion that domestic interest rates will equal foreign interest rates when converted into the domestic currency, given that investors are risk neutral and capital controls are absent.

UNCTAD Liner Code (L9)

The set of rules of UNCTAD allowing shipping conferences to fix cargo rates and to share out routes between the ports of UNCTAD members.

undepletable externality (D0, Q0)

An EXTERNALITY with collective effects so that if one person is affected by it the effect on others will not be diminished, e.g. smog.

See also: pollution control

underemployment (J2)

Work with a low PRODUCTIVITY, e.g. agricultural labour on small farms; part-time employment of workers who want full-time jobs. The extent of underemployment is reflected in low wages and in a lower output per person than that of workers in the most efficient enterprises of that industry. Much underemployment occurs in the secondary sector of the labour market.

underground banking (G2)

A way of transferring money that disguises the transaction; often used for LAUNDERING MONEY. To effect a secret transfer from X to Y, X deposits the money with a banker who then asks a third party to give that amount of money to Y. This type of banking has been practised for centuries in the Middle East and Asia, especially in India where it is known as *hawala*. It requires much trust in the banker.

underground economy (K4, P0)

The economic activities of a nation not officially recorded and sometimes illegal.

See also: black economy; informal economy

References

Geige, E.L. (ed.) (1989) *The Underground Economies*, Cambridge: Cambridge University Press.

underlier (G1)

The asset delivered under a DERIVATIVE instrument contract. For example, for a wheat futures contract, wheat is the underlier. Also an underlier can be a market variable (such as an interest rate or security price) for derivatives settled in cash.

underlying inflation rate (E3)

The adjusted RETAIL PRICE INDEX with seasonal food prices, the COUNCIL TAX and mortgage interest payments removed.

See also: core inflation; headline rate

undertrading (M2)

Operating a firm with excess capacity because of a low demand for its products.

See also: overtrading; X-efficiency

underwater stock option (G1)

An OPTION whose exercise price is more than the current market price.

underweight on a share (G1)

Possessing a holding of a stock market security below the desired amount.

underwriter (G2)

1 A financial institution promising to take up the unsold shares of a new issue.
2 An insurance company or LLOYD'S syndicate which accepts an insurance risk.

unemployment (J6)

1 The state of being part of a LABOUR FORCE, wanting to work, but without a job.
2 A DISEQUILIBRIUM phenomenon arising from inflexible prices.

Unemployment can take many forms – VOLUNTARY, INVOLUNTARY, FRICTIONAL, STRUCTURAL. It has been measured both as a STOCK and as a FLOW, using as statistical sources registers of persons declaring themselves to be unemployed and household surveys. In CLASSICAL ECONOMICS, unemployment is viewed as a temporary phenomenon until price flexibility restores an economy to full employment. KEYNES challenged the classical view and later economists have been sceptical about the clearing of markets.

See also: natural rate of unemployment

References

Layard, R. (1986) *How to Beat Unemployment*, Oxford: Oxford University Press.
Minford, P. (1983) *Unemployment: Cause and Cure*, Oxford: Basil Blackwell.
Sinclair, P. (1987) *Unemployment: Economic Theory and Evidence*, Oxford: Basil Blackwell.

unemployment causes (J6)

A method of classifying the types of UNEMPLOYMENT, based on the theory of employment held by a particular labour economist. CLASSICAL ECONOMISTS, with their belief that all markets ultimately clear, believed that unemployment was a short-term phenomenon of a FRICTIONAL type; if it was longer it could be attributed to a change in the structure of industry. KEYNES insisted that unemployment could be INVOLUNTARY, as a consequence of a deficiency in demand. Thus, it became popular to classify unemployment as FRICTIONAL or STRUCTURAL. The rapid pace of technological change and the growth of welfarism in many countries in the post-1945 period suggested new causes of unemployment. Changes in the relative cost of capital and labour and the relationship between the level of unemployment benefits and the pay of jobs at the bottom of the earnings league have also been noted as causing unemployment.

References

Sachs, J.D. (1983) 'Real wages and employment in the OECD countries', *Brookings Paper on Economic Activity.*

unemployment compensation (J6)

A welfare payment to unemployed people often based on an insurance scheme. This benefit is a usual provision in developed countries, but it is as rare in developing countries as it was in the Soviet-type economies. In those countries offering this form of compensation, payments have become more generous over time: after 1973, the unemployment benefit rate reached 75 per cent of after-tax incomes in major European countries.

unemployment spell (J6)

A completed period of UNEMPLOYMENT. Spells are likely to be longer at higher levels of benefit, when workers have savings and when the overall rate of unemployment is high. The number of spells has been increasing in both the US and UK labour markets.

References

Akerlof, G.A. and Main, B.G.M. (1980) 'Unemployment spells and unemployment experience', *American Economic Review* 70: 885–93.

unemployment statistics (J6)

Data on the total numbers within a country's labour force without a job but seeking employment. It is customary to subdivide this information by sex, age, industry, occupation and duration of unemployment. European unemployment statistics are regularly published in the Eurostats Labour Force Survey; US statistics are published by the Bureau of Labor Statistics (USA); and UK statistics by the Department for Education and Employment (UK). Governmental bodies charged with the task of collecting these data constantly attempt to refine their definition of unemployment to obtain a more accurate measure: by doing so, they invite the accusation that they are distorting the figures. In the UK, for example, there were fifteen changes in the statistical conventions used in the period 1979–86 which some critics have claimed illegitimately reduced the numbers unemployed by 400,000.

unemployment trap (J6)

The barrier to employment caused by unemployment benefits. If these benefits are greater than the wages of low-paid workers, job search and accepting jobs are often discouraged. The extent of this trap is measured by the ratio of benefits to income, the REPLACEMENT RATIO.

See also: poverty trap

unequal exchange (D0, F1)

Trading which is systematically biased against one party because of a movement in the NET BARTER TERMS OF TRADE or because of an unequal distribution of productive assets.

unfair labour practice (J2)

Conduct of an employer or an employee attracting penalties under labour relations legislation. It was possible for employers to commit such practices under the National Labor Relations Act (WAGNER ACT) of 1935 in the USA; in 1947, the TAFT–HARTLEY ACT extended this to US labor unions also. The short-lived Industrial Relations Act of 1971 in the UK made use of this concept.

uniform business rate (H7)

UK property tax on businesses levied at the same rate throughout England from April 1990, with separate Scottish and Welsh business rates, to replace business RATES previously fixed by local authorities. By making this form of local taxation uniform, rates rose in the more prosperous south of England and fell in the less prosperous north. Transitional arrangements over a five-year period cushioned the effects of the change.

See also: community charge; rates

Uniform Commercial Code (K2)
A legal code enacted in 1952 in Pennsylvania and then copied, with some variations, by all other US states and territories except Louisiana and Puerto Rico. It provides a flexible approach to the formation and performance of contracts.

uniformity assumption (D4)
CHAMBERLIN's assumption that under MONOPOLISTIC COMPETITION each firm of an industry has identical cost and demand curves.

uniform price (D0)
A price that is the same for all groups of consumers because no PRICE DISCRIMINATION is being practised.

unimodal distribution (C1)
A distribution of numbers with only one MODE.

unintended investment (E3)
Investment that occurs despite not having been planned. It chiefly takes the form of an accumulation of stocks (inventories) because sales are less than predicted.

union (J5) *see* international union; local union; trade union; US labor union

union density (J5) *see* unionization

Union Douaniére et Economique de l'Afrique Centrale (F0)
A CUSTOMS UNION with a common central bank set up in 1966 between Cameroon, the Central African Republic, the Congo and Gabon.

unionization (J5)
The proportion of a LABOUR FORCE in membership of TRADE (LABOR) UNIONS. Unionization varies greatly from country to country, being very high in Scandinavia,

Israel and Eastern Europe but low in the USA. Between regions of a country it varies because of differences in the industrial structure and in state laws if the country has a federal constitution (e.g. in the USA, southern states with 'RIGHT-TO-WORK' legislation have lower levels of unionization). Unionization is higher in most large and OLIGOPOLISTIC firms as the MARGINAL COST of recruiting an extra member is lower there than in scattered small firms. Before the growth of WHITE-COLLAR trade unions it was thought that technical change would reduce unionization and also that increases in female LABOUR FORCE PARTICIPATION would reduce overall participation. These fears have not been entirely fulfilled. However, the pattern of increasing unemployment, particularly the decline of heavy industries with many manual jobs, has reduced overall unionization. Unionization is also known as union density.

Union of National Economic Associations in Japan (J5)
Founded in 1950 as the only nation-wide Japanese federation of associations of scholarly economics, commerce and business administration organizations. Its thirty-five groups include societies for accounting, agricultural economics, economic sociology, economic geography, the history of economic thought, planning, public utility economics and socialist economies. It is based at Waseda University, Tokyo.

union shop (J5)
A firm which requires all employees within a short specified time of taking up employment to be members of a US LABOR UNION recognized as having COLLECTIVE BARGAINING rights in that firm,. The US equivalent of the UK post-entry CLOSED SHOP. The looser meaning of a union shop is a workplace with unionized workers.

See also: agency shop; right-to-work state

union threat model (J5)
An economic model which shows that

employers pay above the market rate to discourage unions from recruiting workers into membership.

See also: bargaining theory of wages

union wage effect (J5)

The difference between the wages of unionized and non-unionized workers. In the figure, the union raises wages from W_0 to W_1 by restricting employment to N_1. As the principal concern of unions is wage negotiations, this effect is an indicator of their success. US studies suggest that the effect is about 30–40 per cent when union and non-union wages are compared. The effect is larger for young than for older workers, for non-whites than for whites. It is greater in industries with MONOPOLY POWER and in sector-wide bargaining. It was greater in the interwar depression, and in the late 1970s, because the unionized sector could fight wage cuts. In the UK, the effect is measured by comparing wages under COLLECTIVE BARGAINING agreements with those elsewhere in the economy: the effect can vary from 10 to 25 per cent. Pure union wage effects are difficult to measure as there may be a difference in the quality of unionized and non-unionized workers.

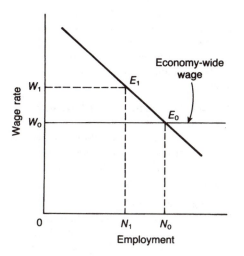

References

Lewis, H.G. (1963) *Unionism and Relative Wages in the United States*, Chicago: University of Chicago Press.
—— (1983) 'Union relative wage effects: a survey of macro estimates', *Journal of Labor Economics* 1: 1–27.
Mulvey, C. (1978) *The Economic Analysis of Trade Unions*, Oxford: Martin Robertson.

union wage policy (J3, J5)

The course of action of US LABOR or TRADE UNIONS in wage negotiations, usually with the aims of obtaining the same pay for the same job within an establishment and the equalization of pay for similar workers across establishments. DUNLOP treated the union as a firm with the overall aim of maximizing the total wage bill of its members – a view regarded as too simplistic by Ross who encouraged labour economists to examine more facets of union behaviour in COLLECTIVE BARGAINING. The greatest achievement of union wage policy is the standardization of wage rates for workers in the same occupational group, thus preventing labour from competing against itself.

References

Dunlop, J.T. (1950) *Wage Determination under Trade Unions*, 2nd edn, New York: Augustus M. Kelly; Oxford: Basil Blackwell.
Ross, A.M. (1948) *Trade Union Wage Policy*, Berkeley, CA: University of California Press.

unipolar concentration (R1)

The build-up of the principal economic activities of a country in one centre, as, for example, in the Tokyo area. This concentration takes advantage of ECONOMIES OF SCALE, ECONOMIES OF SCOPE and of regional specialization.

unitary elastic (D0)

ELASTICITY equal to +1. If a demand curve is of this elasticity throughout, then it will take the shape of a rectangular hyperbola. Over the part, or whole, of a demand curve of unitary elasticity, there will be constant TOTAL REVENUE associated with each point on the curve because the percentage change in quantity demanded will be matched by a percentage change in price of the same magnitude in the opposite direction.

unit banking (G2)
A domestic banking system with single banks each operating from only one location. US retail banking was originally of this form but gradually in the twentieth century BRANCH BANKING throughout a county or a state was permitted and BANK HOLDING COMPANIES were permitted.

See also: correspondent bank; McFadden Branch Banking Act 1927

unit cost (D2)
The cost of producing one unit of a product. This is calculated as the AVERAGE COST of producing a batch or a standard unit for that type of production, e.g. a book or a barrel of beer, or the MARGINAL COST of producing the last unit.

United Nations Conference on Trade and Development (F1, O0)
An organ of the General Assembly of the United Nations with the aim of improving the trade of less developed countries, particularly through international commodity agreements. After its first meeting

in 1964, it has met subsequently in 1968, 1972, 1976, 1979, 1983 and 1987; all members of the United Nations and its specialized agencies belong to it.

Its efforts have been less than successful: in the 1980s, international agreements on rubber, coffee, cocoa and tin were incapable of protecting Third World countries from falls in prices and the great increase in their foreign debts. The tin agreement failed in 1985 with the bankruptcy of the buffer stock; coffee producers found it increasingly difficult to come to an agreement. Success is unlikely until developed countries reflate their economies to provide bigger markets for primary products and less developed countries diversify their economies.

United Nations Development Programme (O2)
A United Nations organization formed in 1965 to render technical assistance to developing countries. It undertakes the work previously done by the UN Expanded Programme of Technical Assistance and the UN Special Fund. It offers soft loans for development.

United Nations Framework Convention on Climate Change (Q0)
A set of principles formulated at the Earth Summit in Brazil in 1992. It concentrated on climate change attributable to human activity and recommended precautionary measures to anticipate this change. The parties to the agreement were expected to promote sustainable development, especially by reducing carbon dioxide emissions.

United Nations Industrial Development Organization (O2)
A Vienna-based organization created in 1967 to promote Third World industrialization by advising on industrial strategy and evaluating projects.

unitization (G2, R1)
The division of real property into tradable portions to provide a new form of investment. Thus a large building can be sold in

portions which are regularly traded like shares in companies.

See also: timeshare

unit of account (E4)
A MEDIUM OF ACCOUNT used as a measure or standard of value because of the stability of its value. Hard currencies are particularly used for this purpose.

See also: medium of account; numéraire

unit pricing (D0)
Quoting prices per unit of weight, e.g. *X* cents per ounce (or gram), so that goods produced in different standard sizes can be compared.

unit tax (H2)
A tax per unit sold usually taking the form of a SALES or PURCHASE TAX.

unit trust (G2)
A trust that purchases stock exchange SECURITIES and sells unit portions of the portfolio acquired to the general public. Many unit trusts have specialized portfolios, concentrating on property shares or securities of a particular country, on the yield of a portfolio or the rate of growth of its capital value. The trust managers charge the unit holders for their investment management. This investment device, introduced in the UK from the USA in 1931, is attractive to the small investor as a means of diversifying RISK.

See also: investment trust; mutual fund

unit value index (D0)
A price index calculated by dividing the total value of a good by the total quantity of it. Since technical progress involves the substitution of light goods for heavy goods, unit value indices underestimate the magnitude of price changes.

universal banking (G2)
1 World-wide provision of financial services by one bank.
2 Provision of banking facilities for a whole population.
3 A large bank, or a post office, with an extensive branch network.
4 A bank offering a broad range of financial services, including retail banking, corporate banking and treasury operations.

Unlisted Securities Market (G1)
The second tier of the London Stock Exchange, created in November 1980, to enable directors unwilling to apply for a full listing on the exchange to deal in their company's shares. For a listing on the USM a company needs a three-year record of successful business and the directors must sell at least 10 per cent of the company, whereas for a full listing the company needs a five-year record and a minimum sale of 25 per cent. In 1980 thirty-five companies were given a listing on the USM; in 1985 ninety-eight companies joined; about 350 companies were listed by 1987. The attraction of a listing on this market is the lower cost compared with being listed on the exchange. In the first five years of its existence, the USM raised £882.6 million. It was succeeded by the Alternative Investment Market in 1995.

References

Bannock, G. and Doran, A. (1987) *Going Public: A Report on Unlisted Securities*, London: Economist Intelligence Unit.

unpaid work (D1, J3)
Productive employment without remuneration that occurs within households and family-owned businesses. Such work is broadly defined as any activity which is perceived to produce utility, satisfying either market or non-market needs. It is measured by its OPPORTUNITY COST and is usually excluded from national accounts calculations of output, excepting in the case of work on family farms. Children are often ordered to do this kind of work; adults out of moral obligation often become unpaid CARERS.

unproductive labour (J0) *see* productive labour

unreported sector (K4, P0)
That part of a national economy that evades government statisticians and is largely untaxed.

See also: black economy

upcoding (M2)
A device to obtain higher medical or other professional fees by exaggerating the seriousness of the condition being addressed.

upper quartile (C1)
The value of a set of numbers such that three-quarters of the numbers are lower in value. This is often used in the study of income distributions. The seventy-fifth PERCENTILE.

See also: lower quartile; median

upselling (M3)
Selling an extra item allied to the original purchase, e.g. selling a side dish to a main course in a restaurant.

upstream firm (L2)
A firm engaged in an early stage of production; for example in the case of the oil industry, before refining is done.

urban economics (R0)
The study of land use, location decisions and the growth of cities and towns. This broad subject encompasses the economic dimension of all activities in urban areas, including industry, housing, crime and poverty.

See also: land economy

References

Alonso, W. (1964) *Location and Land Use: Toward a General Theory of Land Rent*, Cambridge, MA: Harvard University Press.
Evans, A.W. (1985) *Urban Economics: An Introduction*, Oxford: Basil Blackwell.
Fujita, M. (1989) *Urban Economic Theory*, New York and Cambridge: Cambridge University Press.
Maki, W.R. and Lichty, R.W. (2000) *Urban regional economics: concepts, tools, applications*, Ames, IA: Iowa State University Press.
Mieszkowski, P. and Straszheim, M. (eds)

(1979) *Current Issues in Urban Economics*, Baltimore, MD, and London: Johns Hopkins University Press.

Uruguay Round (F1)
The GATT negotiations of 1986–91 with 92 participant countries. The principal features of this round were an attempt to reduce the protectionism of developed countries, without full reciprocity from less developed countries, and to reduce US and EUROPEAN COMMUNITY subsidies to agriculture thereby cutting surpluses and making world agricultural markets work more smoothly. This is the first time a policy to deal with agricultural products has been the subject of GATT negotiations – even reductions in agricultural sanitary regulations have been proposed as they can act as a barrier to trade. Trade-related investment, INTELLECTUAL PROPERTY rights and trade services were also covered.

See also: Dillon Round; Kennedy Round; Tokyo Round

user charge (D0, H0)
1 A charge per quantity of an emission discharged into a sewerage system.
2 A charge for a service provided by a central or local government or by a public enterprise, e.g. a ticket for admission to a swimming pool. These charges are based on the AVERAGE COST or MARGINAL COST of providing the service.

user cost (M2, M4)
1 The cost of capital depreciation attributable to one unit of output.
2 The price a firm should pay for using its own capital stock.

use value (D0) *see* value in use

US federal finance (H7)
Finance raised by taxes and borrowing to finance the activities of the federal government of the USA. The power to tax is derived from Article 1, section 8, of the US Constitution that gives the Congress power to levy and collect taxes and duties in order to pay debts and provide for common defence and the general welfare

of the USA. This article also requires that the rates of taxation should be uniform throughout the states of the union. Most of tax revenue at the federal level comes from the individual income tax and is used both to finance federal expenditures and to give grants to state governments.

See also: federal finance

U-shaped frequency curve (C1)
A frequency curve in the shape of the letter 'U' with maxima at both ends of it.

US labor union (J5)
A voluntary association of employees with the major aim of COLLECTIVE BARGAINING for improvements in wages and other conditions. These are either LOCAL UNIONS (restricting membership to a local area) or INTERNATIONAL UNIONS (covering the whole of the USA). Although unions have existed in the USA for 200 years, they have not achieved the same levels of UNIONIZATION as in many other countries, including the UK, partly because of the anti-union legislation in some of the southern states.

See also: right-to-work state

References

Freeman, R.B. and Medoff, J.L. (1984) *What Do Unions Do?*, New York: Basic Books.

US tax reform (H2) *see* Tax Reform Act 1986

US Trade Representative (H1)
An office set up in 1963 as part of the Executive Office of the US President to direct trade negotiations and formulate trade policy. It now operates under the authority of the Omnibus Trade and Competitiveness Act 1988.

US Treasury bond market (G1)
US bond market consisting until 1986 of only thirty-five PRIMARY DEALERS. Its daily dealings of $100 billion or more make it one of the most influential financial markets in the world, as do the prices it sets of US Treasury bonds which influence the cost of capital throughout the world be-

cause of the importance of the dollar. Entry to the market is difficult. As a dealer must have 0.75 per cent of daily turnover, excluding trades among dealers, to qualify, entry means either attracting business away from existing dealers or purchasing an existing dealer, as some UK and other banks are now attempting. The margins have to be very small, sometimes as low as 1/64 of a point, to be competitive.

US Treasury market (G1)
US securities market in which 35,000 different bonds, bills and notes issued by governmental agencies are traded. Dominant in the market is the Federal Reserve Bank of New York that does 25 per cent of the clearing.

usury (E4)
An exploitative rate of interest; formerly the term for 'the rate of interest' as the Judaic, Islamic and Christian religions condemned any rate of interest as wrong. Usury laws were common either to outlaw the charging of interest or to impose a ceiling rate. Economists as far back as the MERCANTILISTS realized that a maximum rate of interest is often unenforceable. There are still laws in the UK and USA governing the maximum rate of interest that money lenders can charge. Usury is a major issue in ISLAMIC BANKING today.

util (D0)
One unit of satisfaction. If it were possible to measure CARDINAL UTILITY then the amount of satisfaction would be expressed in utils. Most economists have regarded it as impossible to count utils as UTILITY is a subjective valuation.

See also: ordinal utility; revealed preference

utilitarianism (B1)
An approach to moral philosophy popularized by BENTHAM and originally devised by Beccaria and Helvetius and later used by Godwin and John Stuart MILL. It is concerned to show that the rightness of an action is to be judged by its consequences

in terms of pain and pleasure, using a 'balance sheet' approach to see whether there is a net advantage. The goal of utilitarians is to achieve 'the greatest happiness for the greatest number'. Critics of utilitarianism have pointed out the difficulties of reducing values to utilities and of aggregating the happiness of individual persons.

See also: cardinal utility; felicific calculus; Hutcheson

References

Halevy, E. (1934) *The Growth of Philosophic Radicalism*, trans. M. Morris, London: Faber & Faber.
Lyons, D. (1965) *Forms and Limits of Utilitarianism*, Oxford: Oxford University Press.
Smart, J.J.C. and Williams, B. (1974) *Utilitarianism: Pro and Con*, Cambridge: Cambridge University Press.

utility (D0)
The satisfaction derived from an activity, particularly consumption. The total amount of such satisfaction is total utility; the satisfaction from the last unit is MAR-GINAL UTILITY. BENTHAM in his suggested calculus of pleasure and pain was influential in introducing this notion into economics but the MARGINALISTS were the first economists to make it the central concept of economic theory. The measurement of utility has provoked long debates between cardinal utility (utility measured in units) and ordinal utility (utility revealed through preferences). Without this concept, much of NEOCLASSICAL economic theory would not be possible. Earlier economic writers, especially those of the CLASSICAL SCHOOL, used 'utility' in the objective sense of the inherent worth of something.

References

Majumdar, T. (1961) *The Measurement of Utility*, London: Macmillan.
Page, A.N. (ed.) (1968) *Utility Theory: A Book of Readings*, New York: Wiley.

Robertson, Sir D., (1956) *Economic Commentaries*, ch. II, London: Staples Press.

utility function (D0)
This is generally expressed in the form $U = f(x_1, x_2, x_3, x_4, x_5, \ldots)$. It shows a consumer's UTILITY as a function of the quantities of goods and services 1, 2, 3, 4, 5, ... he or she consumes.

References

Green, H.A.J. (1972) *Consumer Theory*, Harmondsworth: Penguin.

utility possibility frontier (D0)
This connects the PARETO-EFFICIENT combinations of the UTILITIES of two individuals. A movement from B to A is Pareto efficient as both Adam and Eve are better off; a movement from A to C increases Eve's utility but reduces Adam's.

utopia (P4)
An ideal state suggested in Plato's *Republic* and Thomas More's *Utopia*. In subsequent centuries many socialists, including OWEN and FOURIER, devised utopian community schemes. Many utopias attempt to minimize the amount of work and division of labour in favour of an egalitarian existence conforming to a regimented lifestyle.

See also: dystopia

valorization (D0)

The process by which capital increases its own value. In MARXIAN economics, it is asserted that this occurs because capital increases its own value by the production of SURPLUS VALUE.

value (D0)

Intrinsic worth or price of a good or service. Earlier economic writers from ARISTOTLE made the distinction between VALUE IN USE and VALUE IN EXCHANGE (prices) with, in many cases, the objective use value being measured by the cost of production of that article. CANTILLON, SMITH, RICARDO and John Stuart MILL agonized over the determinants and measure of different types of value, often using the so-called 'water and diamonds paradox': the PARADOX OF VALUE. Apart from Marx and his disciples, interest in the concept of INTRINSIC VALUE waned and attention was concentrated on prices, except inasmuch as intrinsic value can be equated with long-term equilibrium prices.

value added (D0, D2)

1 The contribution to total production made by an industry, a firm or a worker. In the case of a firm, it is calculated by subtracting from its sales its purchases from other firms. It is used to measure the NATIONAL INCOME by the output method and is a frequently used base for indirect taxation.

2 An amount equal to the sum of factor incomes at one stage of production.

value-added network service (L8)

A service electronically produced, e.g. electronic mail and computerized information. The provider of the service adds value to the transmission and switching provided by the telephone company.

See also: networker

value-added tax (H2)

A tax levied on the value added by a firm. As 'value added' can be variously measured, different tax bases are possible. The tax can be a percentage of the income of a firm (its wage payments and return to capital net of depreciation). Secondly it might be the value of what it produces (its income not allowing depreciation). Thirdly it could be the value of what is consumed by its customers minus the firm's purchases of inputs and expenditure on capital goods.

The sales of small firms and the sale of basic goods, e.g. food and children's clothing, are often excluded from the tax – as are export sales (unlike import purchases). The principal method of tax collection is the invoice method of examining the sales invoices of all taxable traders, thus checking the accuracy of both intermediate and final sales simultaneously. It is argued that taxing most goods is more equitable than a more selective tax but the regressive effects of value-added tax on all goods and services at a single rate have long been debated. As a proportion of the revenue from value-added taxes in member countries of the EUROPEAN COMMUNITY constitutes the major source of European Community revenue, there are pressures for higher and standard rates through the European Community.

References

Aaron, H.J. (ed.) (1981) *The Value-Added Tax: Lessons from Europe*, Washington, DC: Brookings Institution.

value at risk (G1)

The maximum loss that occurs with the certain probability P in a certain time interval. This measure is used to estimate the amount one can lose from one's portfolio in a specified period.

value discrepancy hypothesis (G3)

The theory that a firm will only bid for another firm if it values it higher than its present owners do. This attempt to explain mergers is based on there being imperfect information and UNCERTAINTY in the private industrial sector.

References

Gort, M. (1969) 'An economic disturbance theory of mergers', *Quarterly Journal of Economics* 82: 624–42.

value driver (M2)

The creator of VALUE ADDED in an organization. Both the principal productive and ancillary parts of a firm can be creative.

value in exchange (D0)

The price of a good or service. Classical economists contrasted this with VALUE IN USE.

value in use (B1, D4)

The intrinsic value, or usefulness, of a good. CLASSICAL ECONOMISTS contrasted this with VALUE IN EXCHANGE.

value share (M2)

The expenditure on a particular commodity or FACTOR OF PRODUCTION divided by total expenditure.

value subtractor (L0, F3)

An enterprise with negative VALUE ADDED as a result of its activities. Such a firm has such high labour and capital costs that it cannot even cover the cost of the raw materials it uses: thus the value of the inputs it uses is greater than the revenue it obtains from its sales. Many SOVIET-TYPE ECONOMIES were discovered to have a substantial number of value subtractors at the end of the 1980s.

Vanek, Jaroslav, 1930– (B3)

A Czech who obtained degrees in statistics, mathematics and economics at the Sorbonne (1952) and at Geneva (1954). He emigrated to the USA in 1955, gaining a PhD at the Massachusetts Institute of Technology in 1957 and spending most of his academic career as a professor at Cornell University. He is a leading theorist of labour-managed enterprises. His major work, *The General Theory of Labor-Managed Market Economies* (1970), was modified by the concessions to consumers in his *The Participatory Economy: An Evolutionary Hypothesis and a Development Strategy* (1971). The development of his ideas is apparent in his *The Labor-Managed Economy: Essays by Jaroslav Vanek* (1977).

variable capital (J3)

The MARXIAN term for the WAGES FUND.

See also: organic composition of capital

variable cost (D0)

A cost varying with the level of output. In the short run, it is distinct from a fixed cost (the same at all levels of output); in the long run all costs are variable. Labour, the favourite example of such a cost, has become more fixed in nature in recent years as a result of employment legislation and a change in labour contracts.

See also: quasi-factor fixed cost

variable-sum game (C7)

A game in which gains are not offset by corresponding losses.

See also: zero-sum game

variance (C1)
The average of the sum of the squares of deviations of data from their MEAN, calculated for a STATISTICAL POPULATION or a sample taken from it; the square of a STANDARD DEVIATION.

vault cash (G2)
Money kept by US COMMERCIAL BANKS on their premises which is included in the banks' reserves.

Veblen good (D0)
A good for which there will be a fall in demand if the price falls because of the belief that the quality has fallen.

See also: conspicuous consumption; Giffen good

Veblen, Thorstein Bunde, 1857–1929 (B3)
A leading US INSTITUTIONALIST ECONOMIST, famous for his analysis of CONSPICUOUS CONSUMPTION. He was educated at Carleton College and Yale University, subsequently teaching economics at Chicago, Stanford, Missouri and New York. Inspired by a Darwinian evolutionary approach to the social sciences, he took a multidisciplinary view of economics, linking it to anthropology and sociology. His biting analysis of modern industrialism in *The Theory of the Leisure Class* (1899), *The Theory of Business Enterprise* (1904), *The Higher Learning in America* (1918) and *Absentee Ownership* (1923) provided a non-Marxist critique of contemporary CAPITALISM. In some senses he was an inspiration for GALBRAITH.

References

Diggins, J.P. (1978) *The Bard of Savagery: Thorstein Veblen and Modern Social Theory*, Brighton: Harvester Press.

vector autoregression (C5)
An econometric methodology used as the alternative to large structural models of national economies which forecasts the joint movements of principal macroeconomic variables, ignoring their microeconomic determinants. An application of vector autoregression has been the study of the independence of real macroeconomic variables from nominal variables. Critics have noted that the economic hypotheses used are very broad.

References

Sims, C.A. (1980) 'Macroeconomics and reality', *Econometrica* 48: 1–45.

vector autoregressive model (C5)
An econometric model using a vector of two or more variables and a lagged value of the dependent variable to be autoregressive. It does not make an a priori distinction between endogenous and exogenous variables.

vega risk (G1)
The risk arising from fluctuations in implied VOLATILITY. This risk should be considered when examining portfolios containing options.

References

Dumas, B., Fleming, J. and Whaley, R.E. (1998) 'Implied volatility functions: empirical tests', *Journal of Finance* 53: 2059–106.

vegetative control (D2)
A mechanism for organizing economic activity in a modern ECONOMY with much DIVISION OF LABOUR using quantity adjustments rather than price signals. It is characterized by simple behavioural rules, e.g. the rule that production is increased if output stocks fall or the sales of other firms increase and the rule that more inputs are purchased if production increases. This control is exercised bilaterally between single pairs of buyers and sellers; price signals have no influence on the level of production. A major user of this mechanism was the West German economy in 1946–8.

References

Kornai, J. (1980) *The Economics of Shortage*, Vols A and B, Amsterdam: North-Holland.

vehicle bias (D0)
A difference in willingness to pay arising from the vehicle or payment instrument chosen, e.g. local taxes, entrance fees, higher prices.

velocity of circulation (E4)
The number of times a stock of money circulates to finance a level of expenditure or income or output. Thus if the money supply is £100 million and national expenditure or NATIONAL INCOME is £500 million, the velocity of circulation will be 5. Erratic changes in the money supply since 1970 have made velocities unstable and the relationship between changes in the money supply and changes in output more difficult to predict.

See also: monetarism

velocity of money (E4) *see* velocity of circulation

vendor finance (G3, M2)
1 Finance provided by the seller of a company in the form of deferred payment for it or retained equity in the company.
2 Credit provided by retailers rather than a financial institution, especially for the purchase of consumer durables.

See also: stub equity

vent for surplus (F1)
An explanation for international trade. Adam SMITH asserted that trade arises because the domestic market is too small to purchase all of an economy's output and so trade is necessary. This reflected his view that the DIVISION OF LABOUR is limited by the extent of the market. The view was challenged by John Stuart MILL who wondered why a surplus was initially created. But more recently it has been applied to the study of economic development, e.g. by Myint in the 1950s.

References

Myint, H. (1958) 'The "Classical theory" of international trade and the under-developed countries', *Economic Journal* 68: 317–37.

venture capital (G2)
Finance for new high-risk companies. There are large venture capital industries in the USA, the UK and Canada. INVESTMENT BANKS, MERCHANT BANKS and governmental agencies all supply this capital in the hope that new businesses have a potential for long-term growth.

See also: seed capital

Verdoorn's law (O4)
The dynamic relationship between the rate of growth of output and the growth of PRODUCTIVITY arising from INCREASING RETURNS. This is named after the Dutch economist who first noted the relationship in 1948. It was applied to the UK economy by KALDOR in the 1960s and 1970s. Also it was the theoretical justification for his recommendation of the SELECTIVE EMPLOYMENT TAX in 1966 which was designed to shift the labour force increasingly into manufacturing (which was alleged to have labour shortages); a higher rate of growth of employment was expected to stimulate manufacturing productivity.

vertical discrimination (L1)
The different treatment of persons at different levels of an employing organization, e.g. new entrants and persons holding the top jobs. A much quoted example is the easy entry of women and minority races to less skilled and lower paid jobs and their difficulties in gaining promotion. Vertical discrimination is less susceptible to legislative treatment than HORIZONTAL DISCRIMINATION as there are fewer records of promotion processes than there are of earnings.

See also: discrimination; horizontal discrimination

vertical equity (H2)
The treatment of persons in different income groups according to the ABILITY TO PAY principle. This principle is used to justify a progressive tax system.

See also: horizontal equity; progressive tax

vertical expansion (L1)
The expansion of a firm's activities into another stage of production, e.g. by undertaking retailing as well as manufacturing. This form of internal expansion usually takes the form of the creation of new subsidiaries; not a VERTICAL MERGER.

vertical formation (L2)
The creation of a firm with several stages of production.

vertical integration (L1)
The joining together of two or more stages of production either through a VERTICAL MERGER or VERTICAL EXPANSION.

vertical merger (L1)
A merger of firms at different stages of production, e.g. a merger between a manufacturer and a retailer. The search for economies in marketing, production and finance motivates such integration.

Vickrey auction (D0)
Bids are sealed and the item is sold to the highest bidder at the price of the second-highest bid. Bidders revise their bids upwards knowing that they will not have to pay too high a price. This auction has been used for foreign exchange in some African countries.

References

Vickrey, W. (1967) 'Counterspeculation, auctions and competitive sealed tenders', *Journal of Finance* 16: 8–37.

Vickrey, William Spencer, 1914–96 (B3)
Born in Victoria, British Columbia, and educated at Yale in mathematics and then at Columbia University, New York, where he was awarded a PhD for a thesis on progressive taxation and taught for fifty years. During the Second World War he was a conscientious objector working in the US Treasury designing a new inheritance tax for Puerto Rico. He pioneered PEAK-LOAD PRICING and was a prominent POST-KEYNESIAN. In 1996 he was awarded the NOBEL PRIZE FOR ECONOMICS with James MIRRLEES and died three days later.

villa economy (P0)
An economy consisting of an extended household, as in Ancient Rome and Ancient Greece. The villa was the centre of the economic activities of a rural area, receiving and processing raw produce, including the milling of corn and the pressing of grapes.

See also: agricultural household; Ancient Greeks; economics

Viner, Jacob, 1892–1970 (B3)
Canadian economist, born in Montreal and educated at McGill and Harvard Universities. He was a professor at Chicago University from 1925 to 46 (also editor of the *Journal of Political Economy* from 1928 to 1946) and at Princeton from 1946 to 1960. His career began in international economics as a postgraduate student of Frank W. TAUSSIG: he published his doctoral thesis *Dumping. A Problem in International Trade* in 1923. Then he tested the classical theory of balance of payments adjustments in *Canada's Balance of International Indebtedness, 1900–13* (1924). Before KEYNES published his *General Theory*, Viner was an advocate of budget deficits and increased public spending to stimulate the economy. Also, he anticipated many of the ideas of MONOPOLISTIC COMPETITION. He made many outstanding contributions to the history of economic thought, e.g. his critique of MERCANTILISM in *Studies in the Theory of International Trade* (1937) and his detailed biographical essay on Adam SMITH which formed the introduction to the reprint of John Rae's *Life of Adam Smith* (1965).

vintage effect (E2)
The effect on PRODUCTIVITY of a capital stock being old.

visible hand (D0)
A non-market method of allocation, e.g. as happens in the US economy through the activities of dominant large corporations.

References

Chandler, A. D., Jr (1977) *The Visible Hand: The Managerial Revolution in American Business*, Cambridge, MA: Belknap Press.

vital revolution (J1) *see* demographic transition

voice (H0, J0) *see* exit voice

volatility (D0, E4)

Fluctuations in the value of a variable, especially a price. It can be historic, implied (based on a model) or forecast. It can be cyclical, persistent or reverting to the mean. It is measured by the average range (high – low) of a price for a given time period.

'volatility industry' (G2)

The part of the financial services sector which derives its income from fluctuations in interest rates and financial instability.

volume ratio (J2)

Actual hours worked divided by budgeted hours for that productive activity all multiplied by 100.

voluntary export restraint (F1)

A non-TARIFF form of PROTECTIONISM. A country whose domestic industry is suffering from high levels of imports negotiates with the principal supplying country/countries the maximum amount traded. Western countries have entered into such agreements with Japan, particularly to limit car imports.

See also: Multi-Fibre Arrangement

voluntary unemployment (J6)

UNEMPLOYMENT, at a given wage rate, caused by members of the labour force refusing to take jobs offered.

See also: involuntary unemployment

von Neumann, John, 1903–57 (B3)

A leading mathematical economist who pioneered GAMES THEORY and made major contributions to cybernetics. After an education at Budapest, Zurich and Berlin Universities, he emigrated to the USA and became a professor at Princeton University in 1933. His famous collaboration with the economist Oskar MORGENSTERN resulted in *Theory of Games and Economic Behavior* (1944).

References

Morgenstern, O. (1958) 'Obituary. John von Neumann, 1903–57', *Economic Journal* 68: 170–4.
Taub, A. H. (1961) *Collected Works of John von Neumann*, New York and Oxford: Pergamon.

von Neumann–Morgenstern stable set (C7)

A set of outcomes of a game not dominated by one of its outcomes. This concept has been applied to the analysis of parliaments and cartels.

References

von Neumann, J. and Morgenstern, O. (1944) *Theory of Games and Economic Behavior*, Princeton, NJ: Princeton University Press.

voting procedures (H0)

A democratic method of choosing between different persons or policies in an election. The simplest method is the majority principle of choosing whoever or whatever gains 50 per cent of the votes plus one. Other systems include the plurality rule in which a candidate is chosen for receiving the largest number of votes of all the other candidates. More complicated systems include using the CONDORCET CRITERION.

References

Mueller, D.C. (1989) *Public Choice II*, chs 4–11, Cambridge and New York: Cambridge University Press.

voucher privatization (L0)

A method of transferring assets from public to private ownership. Russia used this approach to privatization from 1992 to transfer 75 per cent of state assets. This allowed the state to give away its assets to a public unable to pay for shares.

voucher system (H0)

A method for consumers of government-provided goods and services to choose between alternatives. Instead of a government agency deciding who gets what, individuals are given vouchers entitling them to purchase up to a particular cash amount. This has been used in the USA under the food stamp scheme. In both the USA and the UK vouchers have been suggested as a means of parental choice between schools, tenants' choice between various forms of rented accommodation and adults' choice in health care. As these schemes can be expensive to administer, they have not flourished as much as expected.

See also: Lindahl price

Vredeling directive (J2)
The 'Draft Directive on Procedures for Informing and Consulting Employees' proposed by the Dutch Commissioner Vredeling of the EUROPEAN COMMUNITY in 1980. It proposed that companies with more than 1,000 employees should keep their workers fully informed about all the activities of the company concerned, except for secret and confidential matters. At least annually a report would be given to workers' representatives about the structure of the company and plans for employment and investment. Workers in subsidiary companies would be informed about changes in activities, output and working methods with thirty days to express an opinion before a change was made. Trade unions welcomed the directive but there was much opposition from employers' organizations, including the CONFEDERATION OF BRITISH INDUSTRY.

See also: industrial democracy; workers' participation

vulgar economists (B0)
Marxian term for economists who are concerned with appearances and not real relationships as were the PHYSIOCRATS and classical economists such as SMITH.

vulture fund (G1)
A MUTUAL FUND practising GREENMAIL. It targets underperforming companies.

W

wage (J3) *see* wages

wage contour (J3)
The connected wage rates offered by firms with INTERNAL LABOUR MARKETS to persons in the EXTERNAL LABOUR MARKET. These are the 'key rates' for the few jobs at which a person can enter a firm; they are connected into a contour because competing firms in the external labour market cannot get out of line with other employers' wage offers.

References

Dunlop, J. J. (1957) 'The task of contemporary wage theory', in G.M. Taylor and F.C. Pierson (eds) *New Concepts in Wage Determination*, pp. 117–39, New York: McGraw-Hill.

wage curve (J3)
The relationship between the level of wages and unemployment. Wages in many countries are lower in the presence of higher unemployment. This negative correlation is noticeable in LOCAL LABOUR MARKETS.

See also: Phillip's curve

References

Blanchflower, D.G. and Oswald, A.J. (1994) *The Wage Curve*, Cambridge, MA, and London: MIT Press.
Card, D. (1995) 'The wage curve; a review', *Journal of Economic Literature* 33: 785–799.

wage differentials (J3)
Differences in employment income reflecting the segmented nature of the LABOUR MARKET. The labour force has several structures – geographical, industrial, occupational, sexual and racial – which create corresponding wage differentials. Regional wage differentials exist because of the relative prosperity of capital regions and peripheral areas as well as a traditional ranking of regions in terms of pay. In the USA, the most famous regional difference is between northern and southern states. Industrial differentials reflect the degree of concentration and productivity of particular industries. Occupational differentials arise from differences in bargaining ability and the amounts of education necessary to enter each occupation. Many differentials have been stable for long periods of time because of the forces of custom. The skill differential (the ratio of the pay of skilled to unskilled workers in the same trade), which was constant for many centuries prior to 1914 in many capitalist countries, has subsequently shrunk because of an increasing amount of publicly financed education and a declining supply of unskilled labour. Sexual and racial differentials reflect different levels of investment in HUMAN CAPITAL and DISCRIMINATION.

References

Phelps Brown, E. H. (1977) *The Inequality*

of Pay, Oxford and New York: Oxford University Press.

wage diffusion (J3)

The transmission of wage increases in the leading sector of a national labour market, or major bargaining group, to other workers in a national economy. This can occur because of the established wage leadership of an industrial or occupational group, or because of traditional wage DIFFERENTIALS in a national wage structure.

See also: pattern settlement; shunto; wage round

wage drift (J3)

The difference between the percentage increase in earnings and the percentage increase in basic wage rates agreed under a COLLECTIVE BARGAINING procedure. An example would be an annual growth of earnings by 10 per cent and basic wage rates by 6 per cent creating wage drift of 4 per cent. This major labour market phenomenon of the UK in the 1950s and 1960s was largely attributed to a two-tier COLLECTIVE BARGAINING system with the national level determining basic wages and the local level responsible for supplements to basic pay. Wage drift often occurs under piecework systems.

See also: Donovan Commission

wage flexibility (J3)

A policy advocated by classical and new classical economists to restore an economy to FULL EMPLOYMENT. KEYNES challenged wage flexibility as a feasible policy as he believed that money wages are inflexible downwards. Later economists argue in favour of flexibility because workers have 'priced themselves out of a job'; opponents of flexibility assert that the free movement of wages contributes to the problem of low pay.

wage gap (J3)

The relative wage differential between UNIONIZED and non-unionized labour brought about by a trade union exercising its bargaining rights.

References

Mincer, J. (1983) 'Union effects: wages, turnover, and job training', in I. D. Reid, Jr (ed.) *New Approaches to Labor Economics: A Research*, Annual Supplement 2, Greenwich, CT: JAI Press.

wage insurance (J3)

The nature of a labour contract which pays a worker more than productivity at the beginning of employment and less later when the worker's productivity declines.

wage mobility (J3)

The movement of workers from one part of the wage distribution to another. A matrix showing transition from one decile to another measures it.

wage–price spiral (E3)

A self-sustaining inflationary process: higher wages lead to increased product prices which lead to more wage claims and higher wages. Wage INDEXATION is a major cause of such spirals.

wage-push inflation (E3)

Price inflation initiated by increases in wages brought about by powerful trade unions and not by an EXCESS DEMAND for labour. This is a type of COST-PUSH INFLATION.

wage-rental ratio (D0)

The ratio of the wage cost to the rental cost of using a particular technique of production, which is dependent on the capital–labour ratio chosen, which is in turn dependent on the relationship between wages and rental costs.

wage rigidity (J3)

The phenomenon of wages remaining at the same level absolutely or relative to other rates of pay in the same wage structure. At the national level wage rigidity occurs if LABOUR'S SHARE OF THE NATIONAL INCOME is constant, as it has been in some countries for long periods of time.

See also: labour market rigidities

wage round (J3)

An annual set of pay negotiations by the

major bargaining groups, usually with one industry (often engineering) making a settlement which becomes a pace-setter for other groups. Particularly true of the UK in the 1950s and 1960s and, even more so, in Japan under SHUNTO.

See also: pattern settlement; wage diffusion

wages (J3)

Payment to workers for supplying their services for a particular amount of time, or for producing a defined amount of output. To avoid the abuse known as the TRUCK system, UK wages by law were paid in cash unless workers consent to direct payment into a banking account. The Wages Act 1986 has removed the right to payment in cash unless that is already the method of payment.

See also: wage differentials; wage theory

Wages Act 1986 (J3)

UK statute repealing the Truck Acts of 1831–1940, abolishing the requirement for wages to be paid in the coin of the realm. The Act also limited the powers of remaining wages councils.

wages council (J5)

A tripartite council with union, employer and independent representatives (appointed by government) given the task of recommending (in the case of the UK, to the Employment Secretary) minimum wage rates and hours for the low-paid workers covered by a particular council. This innovation of the state of Victoria, Australia, was introduced into the UK in 1909; wages councils still deal with about a tenth of the UK labour force, particularly in agriculture and catering. Their popularity with TRADE UNIONS arises from the difficulty unions experience in organizing workers in sectors with many small firms and from their approval of the inspectorate set up to monitor the wages actually paid by employers. In the 1980s, the UK government opposed the existence of these councils as it was believed that the mini-

mum wage rates set were too high, especially for young workers, thus contributing to unemployment.

wages fund theory (B1)

The classical theory of the demand for labour. Each employer needs a fund of CIRCULATING CAPITAL to finance the period until products are sold; an economy will have a wages fund which is the aggregate of each firm's fund and will be the maximum amount which can be paid out nationally in wages. The average wage rate of the economy is simply the wages fund divided by the employed labour force. The rigid adherents of this theory used it as a justification for resisting union demands for higher remuneration, pointing out that a higher average wage rate would cause unemployment. The idea of the wage fund ignores other methods of financing production, exaggerates the degree to which the total fund is fixed and does not consider how a capitalist will allocate income between different types of investment and consumption.

References

Taussig, F.W. (1896) *Wages and Capital: An Examination of Wages Fund Doctrine*, London: Macmillan.

wage subsidy (H2, J3)

A payment to a firm of a grant equal to a proportion of its wage bill or of its wage rates to encourage higher levels of employment in a particular sector, e.g. manufacturing, or throughout the economy. In the 1960s in the UK, the labour cost of employing workers in manufacturing was subsidized and service sector employers more heavily taxed under the SELECTIVE EMPLOYMENT TAX. Wage subsidies are often paid only for employing additional staff as the aim of wage subsidization is usually to increase employment.

See also: regional employment premium

wage–tax spiral (E3)

An explanation of INFLATION in terms of the effects of government taxation and social security charges on the labour market. It is argued that a widening gap between pre-tax and post-tax employment incomes (i.e. an increase in AVERAGE TAX RATES) encourages TRADE UNIONS to ask for higher money wages which in turn leads to general inflation. Also known as 'taxflation'.

References

Jackson, D., Turner, H.A. and Wilkinson, F. (1972) *Do Trade Unions Cause Inflation?*, Cambridge: Cambridge University Press.

wage–tenure profile (J3)
A description of a wage distribution showing the relationship between pay and length of service.

wage theory (J3)
Explanations of the determination of wages at the macro and micro levels. The earliest theories, of the JUST WAGE, were normative in character. In the eighteenth century, CANTILLON and SMITH discussed the determinants of WAGE DIFFERENTIALS, and the idea of a WAGES FUND was used to explain the average level of wages in an economy. In NEOCLASSICAL ECONOMICS, the concept of MARGINAL PRODUCTIVITY was used to explain wage rates. With the growth of COLLECTIVE BARGAINING, wage theory paid more attention to institutional influences on wages, especially UNION WAGE EFFECTS: HICKS, PIGOU and DUNLOP all made early contributions to bargaining theories. The exploration of the distinction between INTERNAL and EXTERNAL LABOUR MARKETS constituted a further attempt to make wage theory more realistic, as has the discussion of INSIDER and OUTSIDE WAGE SETTING.

wage unit (J3)
The money wage of a unit of labour, i.e. the wages and salaries bill divided by the quantity of employment. KEYNES relied greatly on this method of measurement in his *GENERAL THEORY*, by measuring NATIONAL INCOME in wage units.

Wagner Act 1935 (J5)
US federal labour statute (also known as

the Wagner–Connery Act) which sought to establish collective bargaining in inter-state commerce through dealing with the problems of union recognition, of employers who refuse to bargain and of COMPANY UNIONISM. The NATIONAL LABOR RELATIONS BOARD was established as an independent administrative agency to enforce the provisions of the Act. It succeeded the National Labor Board set up in 1933 to hear complaints against employers who refused to bargain.

Unfair labour practices which could be committed by management were listed in section 8 of the Wagner Act. These were (1) interfering with the rights of employees to organize themselves; (2) interfering in the affairs of a labor union; (3) discriminating in the hiring of workers to affect union membership; (4) discriminating against or discharging workers who had complained under the Act; and (5) refusing to bargain with chosen representatives of employees.

The Act was criticized for being too pro-union. It was a major cause of the great expansion in US labor union membership from 3.7 million members in 1935 to 14.8 million in 1945.

See also: Taft–Hartley Act

Wagner's law (H5)
Adolph Wagner's assertion in 1883 that public expenditures would expand as industrial society developed. He prophesied that pressures for social progress would entail a continuous growth of the public sector and an expanding share of public expenditure in the national income. The assertion of this law reflected the foundation of a WELFARE STATE in the Germany of his day.

References

Musgrave, R.A. and Peacock, A. (eds) (1958) *Classics in the Theory of Public Finance*, pp. 1–16, London and New York: Macmillan.

waiting period (G1)
The twenty-day period required by the US

Securities and Exchange Commission between the registration and offering of new securities.

wallpaper (G1)
The worthless stock market security of a failed company.

Walras exchange economy (D5, P0)
A market ECONOMY with a finite number of traders and commodities.

Walrasian stability (D5)
The dynamic stability of a market or the economy as a whole: this is possible because prices respond with infinite velocity to DISEQUILIBRIUM situations. Positive excess DEMAND (demand greater than supply) causes price rises; negative excess demand (demand less than supply) causes price falls.

Walras, Marie Esprit Léon, 1834–1910 (B3)
French-born economist who, with MENGER and JEVONS, was a founder of the MARGINALIST School and the first to use GENERAL EQUILIBRIUM analysis. His father, Auguste Walras, had already made use of the concept of marginal utility (or *rareté*, as he termed it) to explain the basis of value. His son, with the mathematical help of a professor of mechanics, was to extend its application powerfully. From 1870 to 1892, Léon Walras was professor of economics at the University of Lausanne, Switzerland (to be succeeded by PARETO). In an ambitious writing career he sought to expound political economy in a threefold manner – as pure, applied and social. The first branch of his theory was published as *Eléments d'Economie Politique Pure* (1874–7; English translation, 1953): it is his chief claim to be regarded as one of the world's greatest economic theoreticians. In the *Eléments* he uses GENERAL EQUILIBRIUM analysis to present an integrated theory of exchange, production, capital and money.

References

Hicks, J.R. (1934) 'Léon Walras', *Econometrica* 2: 338–48.
Morishima, M. (1977) *Walras' Economics.*

A Pure Theory of Capital and Money, Cambridge: Cambridge University Press.
Walker, D.A. (ed.) (1983) *William Jaffe's Essays on Walras*, Cambridge: Cambridge University Press.
Walras, L. (1954) *Elements of Pure Economics or The Theory of Social Wealth*, trans. W. Jaffe, London: Allen & Unwin.

Walras's law (D5)
A GENERAL EQUILIBRIUM law that if the first $n - 1$ markets are in equilibrium then the last market is also in equilibrium. This is so because the AGGREGATE DEMAND for goods, including money, must equal their AGGREGATE SUPPLY.

Walsh–Healy Act 1936 (K2)
US federal statute insisting on the observance of MINIMUM WAGE standards in all government contracts worth over $10,000.

See also: Fair Wages Resolution

war babies/brides (G1)
Popular names for the US common stock of defence contractors.

war dividend (O4)
The favourable economic consequences of a nation engaging in war usually taking the form of increased output and technical advance.

See also: peace dividend

warehouse economy (F1, P4)
An ECONOMY importing most of the manufactured goods it consumes, rather than making them itself. A description applied to the UK economy during the 1980s.

See also: autarky

warehouse receipt (G2)
The receipt issued to the depositor of inventories with a warehouse company. This receipt can be a negotiable security and act as collateral for a loan. This arrangement is a popular method of finance in the US agricultural sector.

warrant (G1)
A document authorizing the payment of a DIVIDEND or SHARE.

warranted rate of growth (O4)
The rate of growth of national income that maintains the equality of planned saving and planned investment. In the HARROD–DOMAR growth model it is measured as $G_w = s/v$, where G_w is the warranted rate of growth, s is the MARGINAL PROPENSITY TO SAVE and v is the INCREMENTAL CAPITAL–OUTPUT RATIO. HARROD called it a fruitful tautology.

See also: natural rate of growth

warranty (K0)
The right of a buyer to get a seller to rectify or compensate for the failure of a product to meet its stated level of performance. The US Magnuson–Moss Warranty – Federal Trade Commission Improvement Act 1975 requires explicit warranties for all products selling for more than $15. A warranty is different from a service contract (which is not related to the product's performance). Products carrying warranties are more attractive to consumers as the risk to buyers of non-performance is eliminated.

Warsaw Convention (L9)
The Air Warsaw Convention of 1929 standardizing passenger tickets, luggage tickets and carrier liability. All members of the INTERNATIONAL AIR TRAVEL ASSOCIATION are bound by it.

waste (D0)
1 The undesired costs resulting from a particular economic activity; a major EXTERNALITY.
2 Transactions which do not create WEALTH, e.g. RENT-SEEKING behaviour.
3 Costs arising from the inherent inefficiency of some types of economic organization. For example, BARTER economies waste time through the need of buyers and sellers to search for each other; competitive economies are wasteful in needing advertising and other selling expenditures.

water and diamonds paradox (D0) *see* paradox of value

wave train (O3)
The long wave in the growth of average labour productivity that oscillates between bunches of innovations. It was inspired by SCHUMPETER's notions of technological diffusion and innovation. Wave trains are linked to the life cycles of techniques.

References
Iwai, K. (1984) 'Schumpeterian dynamics. Part II. Technological progress, firm growth and "economic selection"', *Journal of Economic Behavior and Organization* 5: 321–51.

weak efficiency (G1)
The pricing of a security to take into account its past price and trading history.

See also: strong efficiency

wealth (E0, E0)
The stock of assets held by a person, a firm or a country. Wealth is measured at a particular date, e.g. 31 December, and not over a period as is the case with INCOME. Wealth statistics are subject to much error because of valuation problems and owners' concealment, especially if wealth and inheritance taxes are in force. Many forms of income, e.g. rent and profits, are a return to the wealth a person holds.

See also: human capital; national wealth

wealth creation (E2)
The process of increasing the net worth of a person or a firm. Often this requires innovation, a high rate of saving and a framework of economic incentives. Critics of accumulating wealth emphasize the importance of income distribution rather than increasing individual prosperity.

See also: economic growth

wealth distribution (D3)
The interpersonal distribution of asset holdings, often stated as the proportion of national wealth held by the top 5 per

cent, or some other portion, of the population.

References

Atkinson, A.B. and Harrison, A.J. (1978) *The Distribution of Personal Wealth in Britain*, Cambridge: Cambridge University Press.

Wolff, E.N. (ed.) (1987) *International Comparisons of the Distribution of Household Wealth*, Oxford: Clarendon Press.

wealth effect (E2)

The effect of a change in interest rates and the price level on aggregate demand, particularly consumption.

See also: Pigou effect

Wealth of Nations (B1)

Adam SMITH's masterly treatise on economics first published in 1776. Although CANTILLON had previously produced a general work on economics as a whole, it was Smith's which was to provide a comprehensive statement of the subject and to found the school of CLASSICAL ECONOMICS. The unity of this work, divided into five parts, is provided by his central concern – an enquiry of the causes of wealth, i.e. ECONOMIC GROWTH. The two important determinants of growth were declared to be the DIVISION OF LABOUR and the ratio between PRODUCTIVE and unproductive labour (a less important cause of the growth process). As a leader of the Scottish Enlightenment, he saw the growth process as being founded on the desire for betterment leading to saving, which is then invested making possible the division of labour. As the specialization of economic activity inherent in the division of labour principle requires large markets, he fervently supported FREE TRADE. Like the PHYSIOCRATS before him, the government was to be limited to a few basic functions and taxation was to be levied according to strict principles. Just as Cantillon had given a perceptive account of international finance because of his experience as a banker, Smith, acutely aware of the great advances in banking in his native Scot-

land, could set out many of the issues for the subsequent classical debate on monetary theory.

See also: absolute advantage; canons of taxation; economic growth

wealth tax (H2)

A tax levied on the amount of CAPITAL a person owns. Although there are different schemes from country to country, the tax is usually levied on the net value of assets. It should be distinguished from a tax on capital income.

See also: capital gains tax; capital tax

weight (C1)

An amount by which the values of an economic variable are multiplied so that the relative significance of each variable in an index, particularly a price index, is taken into account.

See also: Laspeyres index; Paasche index

weightless economy (P0)

A national economy heavily reliant on service industries and often conducting much of its business electronically. A FOOTLOOSE economy.

welfare economics (D6)

The branch of economics setting out the rules for maximizing the welfare of society by considering both the size of SOCIAL WELFARE and its distribution. As normative issues are its concern this is one of the most abstract and theoretical branches of economic science. The subject has advanced much from PIGOU's *Economics of Welfare* (1919) that defined economic welfare as 'that part of social welfare that can be brought directly or indirectly into relation with the measuring-rod of money' and then examined the relationship between private and social products, discussed PARETO OPTIMALITY and considered in detail welfare problems raised by monopoly and wages. As so many attempts are made to increase social welfare through income redistribution, it was inevitable that the principles for compensation were rigorously discussed – particularly in the KALDOR-HICKS compensation principle, the SCITOVSKY reversal test and in Rawls's MAXIMIN principle. Other approaches include the attempt to devise a SOCIAL WELFARE FUNCTION, seemingly sunk by ARROW'S IMPOSSIBILITY THEOREM and the general theory of the SECOND BEST. Despite so many false theoretical starts, welfare economics has inspired a great number of empirical studies, some using cost–benefit analysis, in matters as diverse as health, transport and energy economics.

See also: normative economics

References

Just, R.E., Hueth, D.L. and Schmitz, A. (1982) *Applied Welfare Economics and Public Policy*, Englewood Cliffs, NJ, and London: Prentice Hall.
Little, I.M.D. (1957) *A Critique of Welfare Economics*, 2nd edn, Oxford: Oxford University Press.
Sugden, R. (1981) *The Political Economy of Public Choice: An Introduction to Welfare Economics*, Oxford: Martin Robertson.

welfare state (I3)
A nation that provides for basic needs by using taxation to finance benefits for low-income groups and to deliver free personal services, especially health care. Germany provides one of the earliest examples of a welfare state; Sweden, one of the most comprehensive amongst MIXED ECONOMIES. Since 1945 it was thought that a mixed economy with a welfare state was the natural way for Western industrialized economies to evolve but the problems of controlling inflation in the 1970s brought many to criticize the extent of state welfare provision. Welfare states are becoming increasingly expensive because of the ageing of the populations of advanced countries and rising expectations of increased welfare benefits and improved health care. Inevitably, there are vigorous debates on means testing and alternative methods of finance and a crusade in favour of greater ECONOMIC EFFICIENCY.

References

Barr, N. (1987) *The Economics of the Welfare State*, London: Weidenfeld & Nicolson.
Barry, N. (1990) *Welfare*, Milton Keynes: Open University Press.
Hills, J. (ed.) (1990) *The State of Welfare. The Welfare State in Britain since 1974*, Oxford: Oxford University Press.
Marsh, D. (1970) *The Welfare State*, London: Longman.
Ringen, S. (1988) *The Possibility of Politics. A Study in the Political Economy of the Welfare State*, Oxford: Clarendon Press.

welfare trap (I3) *see* poverty trap

well-being (D6)
Having a high income, much education, good health mentally and physically and many opportunities for personal advancement.

Werner Report (E5)
EUROPEAN COMMUNITY report of 1970 setting out the conditions for monetary union as (1) total and irreversible convertibility of currencies, (2) complete liberalization of capital transactions and a complete integration of banking and other financial markets, and (3) the irrevocable locking of exchange rate parities to end margins of fluctuation.

See also: Delors Plan

Wharton model (E6)
A quarterly model of the US economy that has been used for forecasting purposes since 1963. Originally it was based on KEYNESIAN principles of income determination, but increasingly in the 1980s it had a monetary content.

References

Klein, L.P., Friedman, E. and Able, S. (1983) 'Money in the Wharton quarterly model', *Journal of Money, Credit and Banking* 15: 237–59.

whistleblower (M1)
A person in an organization who reveals a

bad state of affairs, e.g. incompetence, deceit and fraud.

white-collar worker (J2)

A non-manual worker employed in an office, laboratory or shop; a manager, professional worker, clerk, technician or sales assistant. There have been proportionately more of these workers in the labour force because of technological change, the growth of the public sector and the increasing bureaucratization of firms in oligopolistic industries. It was feared in the 1950s that this shift in the occupational structure would lead to the demise of TRADE UNIONS but instead new trade unions specializing in the organization of white-collar workers have emerged, especially in the public sector. This upgrading of the labour force has contributed to rising labour costs.

white good (D0, L6)

1 A consumer durable, such as a washing machine, cooker or refrigerator, which is usually painted white.
2 Household linen (the original meaning of the term).

See also: brown good; consumer durable

white knight (G3)

A friendly bidder for a company already facing a hostile takeover bid.

white market (D4)

A legal market not in contravention of any governmental regulation; the opposite of a BLACK MARKET.

white noise (C1)

A completely random time series, all lagged correlations being zero; its spectrum density is constant.

white revolution (Q1)

An agricultural revolution, particularly promoted in India, which encouraged the growth of herds of dairy cattle.

white squire (G3)

A company or several companies acting jointly in support of a WHITE KNIGHT in the fight against a predatory company participating in a TAKEOVER battle.

whole life insurance (G2)

Insurance which both promises to pay a stated amount on the death of the insured and has an accumulated cash value available as collateral for a loan.

wholesale bank (G2)

A bank acquiring its deposits from corporations and the interbank market.

See also: retail bank

wholesale money market (G1)

An interbank market in which banks offer or obtain large deposits from each other. This is an important way for MERCHANT, INVESTMENT and other SECONDARY BANKS to obtain deposits as they do not receive deposits directly from the public.

wholesale price index (E3)

UK index of the group of commodities bought and sold by wholesalers. Changes in this index precede and indicate likely changes in the RETAIL PRICE INDEX.

See also: coincident indicators

Wicksell, Knut, 1861–1926 (B3)

Leading Swedish economist whose ideas were to inspire the STOCKHOLM SCHOOL and form a basis for a macroeconomic theory alternative to KEYNESIANISM. Educated at Uppsala University in mathematics, Wicksell soon showed himself to be a courageous liberal, especially in propagating NEO-MALTHUSIAN views – like John Stuart MILL he was arrested for doing so. Income from journalism and various grants enabled him to undertake independent study in 1885–1900; he came under the influence of BÖHM-BAWERK and acquired a great admiration for his theory of capital. This influence was clear in his celebrated *Value, Capital and Rent* (1893, original German edition) and *Interest and Prices* (1898, original German edition). A major theme of his work was the relationship between NATURAL RATES and MARKET RATES OF INTEREST which, he believed, are at the heart of cumulative processes of expansion and contraction in the economy. His work, as indicated by his lectures at Lund University (where he was a professor from 1901), shows that he was eager to synthesize the capital theory of the AUSTRIAN SCHOOL with Walrasian GENERAL EQUILIBRIUM notions and other NEOCLASSICAL insights.

See also: pure credit economy

References

Gardlund, T. (1958) *The Life of Knut Wicksell*, Stockholm: Almqvist & Wiksell.
Uhr, G.C. (1960) *The Economic Doctrines of Knut Wicksell*, Berkeley, CA: California University Press.

wide monetary base (E4)
Notes and coins in circulation with the public plus banks' till money plus bankers' balances with the Bank of England (UK).

wider share ownership (G0)
Widespread ownership of the shares of public companies throughout the population. It is argued that encouragement of this, as in the UK, makes private capitalism more acceptable throughout the country and that companies are less vulnerable to TAKEOVER as private shareholders retain their shares longer than INSTITUTIONAL INVESTORS do. In the UK, PRIVATIZATION has increased the number of persons holding shares.

widget (D0)
A convenient term for a non-specified product or service used in discussions of the principles of costing or industrial processes.

widow's cruse (E0)
1 The Cambridge expression, used by KAHN and Joan ROBINSON, to refer to an economy which continues at the same level of output, neither expanding nor contracting as any spending of entrepreneurs' profits leads to an equal creation of other profits elsewhere in the economy.
2 The money-creating process of continually increasing money through bank lending.

Williamson, Oliver Eaton, 1932– (B3)
Educated at MIT, Stanford and Carnegie Mellon Universities. Apart from a time as assistant professor at Berkeley, University of California, in 1963–5, he has been a professor at the University of Pennsylvania from 1965. His work on TRANSACTION COSTS, organizational hierarchies and ANTITRUST policy have made him a leader of the revived school of INSTITUTIONAL ECONOMICS.

References

Williamson, O.E. (1970) *Corporate Control and Business Behavior*, Englewood Cliffs, NJ: Prentice Hall.
—— (1975) *Markets and Hierarchies*, New York: Free Press.
—— (1986) *Economic Organization: Firms, Markets and Policy Control*, Brighton: Harvester Wheatsheaf.

windfall gain or loss (E0)
An unexpected increase or decrease in *ex post* income; if it had been expected, it would have been included in *ex ante* income. These windfalls are part of TRANSITORY INCOME but not of PERMANENT INCOME.

windfall profit (D0, E0)
An unexpected PROFIT arising from a circumstance not controlled by a firm or an individual. These profits constitute TRANSITORY INCOME and can give rise to unusual consumer behaviour.

window dressing (G2)
Interbank borrowing to improve the appearance of a bank's balance sheet. This was abandoned by UK CLEARING BANKS in 1946 but is still practised in some banking systems, e.g. in France.

winner's curse (C7)
Paying more for an item than its value. This is measured by the difference between a winner's bid and the next lower bid in a single unit auction.

withdrawal (E0)
Not spending income on domestically produced goods and services but using it to buy imports, pay taxes or make savings

with the consequence that the value of the MULTIPLIER is reduced. The CIRCULAR FLOW OF INCOME distinguishes withdrawals from INJECTIONS. Also known as a leakage.

withholding tax (H2)
A tax on earnings, interest or dividend payments deducted at source. This tax is designed to simplify the collection of tax and to ensure that tax is not evaded. By taxing dividends due for repatriation, it is hoped that foreign-owned companies will be encouraged to invest in the country where their subsidiaries are located.

women economists (B3) *see* female economists

Wootton, Barbara, 1897–1988 (B3)
Economist and social scientist noted for her works on INCOMES POLICY, PLANNING and criminology. She was educated at Girton College, Cambridge, where she originally read classics before a reading of MARSHALL's *Principles of Economics* caused her to specialize in economics. Although being awarded first-class honours with distinction, university regulations prevented her, as a woman, from taking her degree. Soon she was made a fellow of Girton and Director of Studies in Economics. In 1922, she became a research officer of the Trades Union Congress. From 1926 to 1928 she was Principal of Morley College for Working Men and Women, then Director of Studies for Tutorial Classes in the University of London (1928–45), Professor of Social Studies (1945–52) and at the end of her career a Nuffield research fellow.

Her achievements were recognized by the award of many honorary degrees, a life peerage and being made a Companion of Honour. Throughout her works there is a practical utilitarian concern to relate problems to reality. Her attack on Lionel ROBBINS's definition of economics in her *Lament for Economics* and her approach to planning and wage policy all indicated her desire to influence policy-makers by using an empirical approach. Much of her knowledge of economy and society came

from membership of many committees and commissions on leading public issues covering topics ranging from criminal statistics, hallucinogens and broadcasting to taxation, shop hours and the Civil Service. She married John Wesley Wootton when she was 20; he was killed five weeks later in the First World War. She was married a second time in 1934 to a student, George Wright.

References

Bean, P. and Whynes, D. (eds) (1986) *Barbara Wootton. Social Science and Public Policy. Essays in her Honour*, London and New York: Tavistock.
Wootton, B. (1934) *Plan or No Plan*, London: Gollancz.
—— (1938) *Lament for Economics*, London: Allen & Unwin.
—— (1945) *Freedom under Planning*, London: Allen & Unwin.
—— (1959) *Social Science and Social Pathology*, London: Allen & Unwin.
—— (1964) *The Social Foundations of Wage Policy: A Study of Contemporary British Wage and Salary Structure*, 2nd edn, London: Allen & Unwin.
—— (1967) *In a World I Never Made: Autobiographical Reflections*, London: Allen & Unwin.

workable competition (D4, L1)
Competition meeting only some of the conditions for PERFECT COMPETITION; an absence of ANTI-COMPETITIVE PRACTICES. It is a SECOND-BEST situation. The criteria for an industry being in a state of workable competition are its level of profits relative to normal profits, its costs relative to those of the most efficient scale, the extent of its product variation and selling costs and its rate of technical progress relative to what is considered satisfactory. These conditions indicate how NORMATIVE the concept is. The notion is central to the implementation of US ANTITRUST policy and increasingly used in UK COMPETITION POLICY.

References

Clark, J.M. (1961) *Competition as a Dynamic Process*, Washington, DC: Brookings Institution.

Sosnick, S.H. (1958) 'A critique of concepts of workable competition', *Quarterly Journal of Economics* 72: 380–423.

Utton, M.A. (1986) *The Economics of Regulating Industry*, Oxford: Basil Blackwell.

work classification (J2)

A method of classifying work requirements which is an alternative to job description. The elements in the classification are the work range, the work structure (how changeable work goals are), work control (how much discretion is involved) and the cognitive effort required. This classification has been applied to knowledge-intensive WHITE-COLLAR work.

worker compensation insurance (I3)

Sickness and accident benefits financed by employers' premiums. In the USA the amount of such insurance varies from state to state and according to the accident record of the firm.

workers' participation (L2)

The participation of employees in the management of their firms. In Europe, a major example since 1950 has been Germany. There, two basic laws govern such schemes: the works constitution law (*Betriebsverfassungsgesetz*) and co-determination law (*Mitbestimmungsgesetz*). Under the former, works councils, which can determine several matters including working hours and vacations, can be formed if more than five workers are regularly employed. Co-determination law deals with the structure of the supervisory board that exists in addition to an executive board and has worker representatives. The law, originally applied only to the iron, steel and coal industries, stipulated an equal number of employee and shareholder representatives on supervisory boards. Gradually, this type of workers' participation has spread to private sector firms. In 1976, the law was extended to all companies with over 2,000 employees, an extension to smaller companies being strongly resisted by employers. The chairman, a shareholders' representative, has a second (cast-ing) vote and the representation of senior staff on the supervisory board has, it is argued, weighted the composition in favour of the management.

See also: industrial democracy

workfare (J2, J6)

US schemes of community work qualifying the unemployed for social security benefits. The idea was first used by the Roosevelt Administration in the 1930s. The US Federal Act of 1981, the Omnibus Budget Reconciliation Act, forced all recipients of federal or state aid to register for work or job training and gave the states the powers to require such persons to participate in work incentive, job search or work experience programmes. These schemes have been criticized for creating slave labour, for displacing existing workers, for adding to administrative costs and for reducing the chance of the unemployed seeking good jobs. The most enthusiastic implementation of the scheme has been in West Virginia. Other countries, e.g. Sweden, have versions of such schemes to keep down the level of unemployment.

References

Ravallion, M. (1999) 'Appraising Workfare', *World Bank Research Observer* 14: 31–48.

working capital (M2)

Current assets minus current liabilities; capital available to provide short-term financing for a firm. CLASSICAL ECONOMISTS regarded this as mainly the raw materials and the WAGES FUND. Today it is often regarded as a measure of the LIQUIDITY of a firm.

working capital ratio (M4) *see* current ratio

working hours (J2)

The total number of hours a person works per day or per week. The view that reduced hours increases workers' welfare and chances of employment is based on too simplistic an analysis: a reduction in hours often raises unit labour costs which, in turn, reduces international competitiveness and profit margins on traded goods leading to lower economic growth and employment. If reduced working hours raise PRODUCTIVITY, no extra demand for labour results. In France, working hours were reduced from forty to thirty-nine per week, with full compensation, in January 1982; in West Germany, the Metalworkers Union demanded in 1984 a reduction from forty to thirty-five hours with partial compensation.

MARX made the length of the working day a key issue: he argued that working hours longer than those spent in producing subsistence for workers created SURPLUS VALUE. Paradoxically, working hours have been longer in socialist countries, being forty-two to forty-five hours per week. But in the developing countries of Africa and Asia weekly working hours are often as much as fifty or fifty-five. Japan, which has industrialized only recently, still has long average working hours, about forty-eight per week (three-quarters of the labour force works a six-day week).

working population (J2) *see* labour force

working-time regime (J2)
The rules set down in the EUROPEAN SOCIAL CHAPTER stating the maximum length of the working week and working day and the dispersion of hours. Full-time and part-time work are both covered.

See also: annualized-hours system; flexible working-time schemes

work sharing (J6)
A method of reducing unemployment by splitting a full-time job into two part-time jobs. Parents sometimes do this in order to share in domestic duties and child rearing. Occupations introducing this form of sharing include school teaching and social work.

See also: job sharing

World Bank (F3, G2)
Popular name for the International Bank for Reconstruction and Development which was conceived at BRETTON WOODS in 1944 and started business in 1947; it was intended that it should be linked to the INTERNATIONAL MONETARY FUND by member countries belonging to both. It aims to encourage the provision of private, rather than public, investment. Of its initial authorized capital of $10 million, one-tenth was paid in dollars and gold. Federal and state bonds of the bank issued in the USA raised a substantial amount of the original capital. At different phases of its life, it has been a bank of reconstruction, a development bank and a policy reformer.

Current aims suggested for the bank include the major provision of funds and technical advice to Third World borrowers, the co-ordination of aid to less developed countries and theoretical leadership in development policy. Some people in the USA regard the World Bank as a means of spreading US political philosophy and monetarism, but the financial rise of Japan as the world's major lender increasingly diminished US influence. In recent years, the bank has lent about 90 per cent of its advances for infrastructure projects, e.g. education, health, irrigation and telecommunications. Currently, recipient countries are being asked to adopt price reforms and market-related trading reforms.

world debt problem (F3)
The consequences of the large debts of less developed countries accumulated since 1970. The magnitude of this indebtedness has given rise to problems of debt servicing and the stability of the banking system. The significance of the debts has often been measured by the ratios of debt to gross national product or of debt to service, but it has been asserted that a better measure is the comparison of the rate of growth of export earnings with the rate of interest. Several approaches have been suggested to reduce this indebtedness, e.g. in 1986 the World Bank suggested SECTOR ADJUSTMENT LENDING as a means of reducing the indebtedness of

certain THIRD WORLD countries. Some countries have reduced their indebtedness by a policy of exchanging debt for equity but there are limits to such conversions as many national governments are alarmed to see more foreign ownership of domestic companies. Major Western banks have gradually written off these loans as bad debts.

See also: debt service indicators; Jubilee 2000

References

Griffith-Jones, S. (ed.) (1988) *Managing World Debt*, Brighton: Harvester Wheatsheaf.
Holley, H.A. (1987) *Developing Country Debt: The Role of the Commercial Banks*, London: Routledge.

World Economic Forum (F0)

An annual meeting of leading politicians and bankers at Davos, Switzerland, to discuss strategies to keep the world economy on an even course. In 1970 Professor Klaus Schwab convened an informal gathering of Europe's chief executives at Davos under the patronage of the Commission of European Communities and the following year created a non-profit-making foundation, the European Management Forum, subsequently renamed the World Economic Forum in 1987. It has expanded its activities to organize meetings for all major world regions and brought together heads of states and governments too. Increasingly it has been lobbied at its meetings by protestors against global capitalism.

world inflation (E3)

The rates of inflation country by country around the world, measured by annual rates of increase of consumer or producer prices. Countries with high post-war inflation records include Argentina, Brazil, Israel, Mexico and Yugoslavia; countries with low post-war inflation records include Japan, Switzerland, the USA, and West Germany before reunification.

References

Brown, A.L. (1985) *World Inflation since 1950*, Cambridge: Cambridge University Press.
Horsman, G. (1988) *Inflation in the Twentieth Century*, Brighton: Harvester Wheatsheaf.

World Intellectual Property Organization (O3)

A Geneva-based body concerned with upholding international conventions on protected ideas and with harmonizing national laws concerning such property.

See also: intellectual property

world monetary reserve assets (F3)

The total of the assets of all the countries of the world, in the form of special drawing rights, gold and reserve currencies.

See also: reserve assets

world monetary system (F3)

The institutional mechanism for settling intercountry indebtedness and for providing loans to increase the liquidity of countries in need. After the GOLD STANDARD, there was a world institutional gap until the BRETTON WOODS system was devised. Although the arrangements for pegging exchange rates ended in 1971, the INTERNATIONAL MONETARY FUND and the WORLD BANK remain as pillars of a world system.

See also: European Monetary System

world stock market indices (G1) *see* Appendix B

world systems perspective (O0)

A method of analysing economic development which uses a structural approach to put FOREIGN AID in the context of being part of the world economy and measures that country's relationship with the rest of the world economy.

world trade (F1)

The sum total volume of exports or imports of every national ECONOMY. The growth of trading within MULTINATIONAL CORPORATIONS, much of it measured at ARTIFICIAL TRANSFER PRICES, has made it more difficult to gain a precise idea of the value of exports of particular countries. The volume of world trade fluctuates according to the state of major economies, especially the USA, and grows at different rates within particular trading blocs and between them.

World Trade Organization (F1)

The successor to GATT inaugurated in 1995 and based in Geneva, Switzerland. It administers the global rules of trade of a multilateral trading system to facilitate and to encourage world trade. It has over 140 member countries and covers more than 90 per cent of world trade. Decisions on trade disputes are settled consensually. The WTO also administers trade agreements and reviews national trade policies.

worst case consequence analysis (Q2)

A form of risk management in which controlled experiments provide an awareness of the consequences of an extreme event. This is used as part of environmental controls.

writer (G1)

A CALL seller in an option market who sells OPTIONS against shares he or she already owns in order to improve their performance.

X

X-efficiency (D4)

LEIBENSTEIN's concept of efficiency that rejects the technical efficiency notion of profit maximizing and cost minimizing. He argued that individual workers are free to choose their effort level and interpret their own jobs. The equilibrium position for a firm will be when every individual is in his or her 'inert area', an effort point which, if moved away from, would reduce utility. This level of 'efficiency' and associated cost is comfortable for a firm's individuals. Prices are fixed using conventional formulae.

References

Leibenstein, H. (1976) *Beyond Economic Man: A New Foundation for Macroeconomics*, Cambridge, MA: Harvard University Press.

—— (1978) *General X-Efficiency Theory and Economic Development*, New York and London: Oxford University Press.

—— (1980) *Inflation, Income Distribution and X-Efficiency Theory*, London: Croom Helm; New York: Barnes & Noble.

Xenophon, 430–354 BC (B3)

A follower of Socrates before embarking on military campaigns, including the expedition of Cyrus. The three works attributed to him most relevant to economics are *Ways and Means to Increase the Revenues of Athens*, perhaps the first work on PUBLIC FINANCE in which he argued for state intervention to expand silver mining, *Oeconomicus* which included a discussion of the nature of wealth and income differentials and *Cyropaedia* which explains that the DIVISION OF LABOUR is limited by the extent of the market.

See also: Ancient Greeks; Aristotle; Plato

Xetra (G1)

The electronic cash market trading system for securities of the Frankfurt exchange. Both auctions and continuous trading are used for dealing in over 5,000 equities and over 10,000 warrants. Safety mechanisms such as volatility interruptions are in force. The trading platform of the iX international exchanges.

X-form (L2)

A hybrid type of business enterprise that is a mixture of the H- and M-FORMS.

See also: U-form

References

Williamson, O.E. (1986) *Economic Organization: Firms, Markets and Policy Control*, ch. 4, Brighton: Harvester Wheatsheaf.

Y

Yankee bid (D0) *see* sealed bid auction

Yankee bond (G1)
A bond issued in the US securities market by a non-US concern.

yearling (G1)
A UK local government stock maturing in a year.

See also: government bond

yellow dog contract (J5)
An individual employment contract whereby a worker promises not to join a TRADE (LABOR) UNION. This standard practice of many US firms in the 1920s was used to impede the growth of union membership. It was outlawed by the NORRIS–LA GUARDIA ACT.

yellow stripe price (G1)
A stock market price shown on a screen of the STOCK EXCHANGE AUTOMATED QUOTATION SYSTEM which refers to large BARGAINS of a particular stock.

yield (D2, G0)
1 Return to an investment measured by dividend or interest receivable divided by price of that security.
2 The annual produce from cultivating a piece of land.

See also: redemption yield

yield curve (G0)
The relationship between the percentage yield of a bond and the number of years to its maturity. An inverse yield curve is downward sloping, a positive yield curve upward sloping and a flat yield curve horizontal. In most cases the yield, determined in a secondary market, is for a previously issued bond. The yield is also a guide to the pricing of new bond issues. The TERM STRUCTURE OF INTEREST RATES

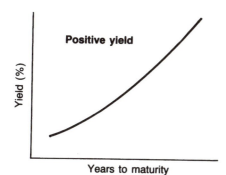

Positive yield

Yield (%)

Years to maturity

determines the curve, e.g. if short-term rates are higher than long-term, there will be an inverse yield curve.

See also: term structure of interest rates

yield gap (G0)
The YIELD on equities minus the yield on bonds. Inflation after 1959 depressed the capital values of bonds, raising their yields in both the UK and the USA: this created a reverse yield that has fluctuated between about 1 per cent and 9 per cent.

Young, Allyn Abbott, 1876–1929 (B3)
Educated at Hiram College, Ohio, and the University of Wisconsin. His many academic appointments included professorships at Stanford and, from 1913, at Cornell. His wide-ranging articles included demography and many aspects of applied economics, public finance and antitrust policy. He will long be remembered for his immensely influential article on IN-CREASING RETURNS TO SCALE that both advanced the theory of ECONOMIC GROWTH and challenged the Marshallian THEORY OF THE FIRM. Tragically, he died relatively young of influenza in London.

References

Young, A.A. (1928) 'Increasing returns and economic progress', *Economic Journal* 38: 527–42.

yuppie, yuppy (J1)
A young urban professional. Most of these aggressive young graduates are employed in financial centres such as New York and London. These health-conscious workaholics firmly believe in free market economics. Their high salaries have made it possible for them to contribute to the GENTRIFICATION of inner city areas.

Z

zaibatsu (L2)
A Japanese group of large companies owned by a family-controlled holding company.

See also: chaebol

zai teku (G0, M1)
Financial management (Japanese).

zakat (H2)
Under Islamic law, a tax on surplus wealth, e.g. on buried treasure acquired through little labour, or on a herd above a certain size. The tax is levied to help the poor and needy.

zero base budgeting (H6)
A method of governmental budgeting which begins with an appraisal of all spending projects on their merits and then, by aggregation, produces a budget total. It was intended, when it was introduced by the Carter Administration in the USA in the 1970s, to replace the traditional budget method of deciding first on an expenditure total and then allocating that sum among different programmes. In practice, it is questionable whether this method can be implemented as project analysis is long, costly and difficult – and not applicable to all parts of a budget.

References
Sarant, P.C. (1978) *Zero-base Budgeting in the Public Sector: A Pragmatic Approach*, Reading, MA: Addison-Wesley.

zero coupon bond (G1)
A bond bearing no interest. As the bond is issued at a discount, it has a REDEMPTION YIELD.

See also: junk bond

zero growth (E0, O4)
The characteristic of an economy in a STATIONARY STATE. CLASSICAL ECONOMISTS feared the movement of the economy to stationarity, excepting John Stuart MILL who was willing to approve of no growth, providing that there was a satisfactory income distribution. In modern advanced economies this has been suggested as a goal on the grounds that growth of the GROSS NATIONAL PRODUCT generates SOCIAL COSTS in the form of pollution, congestion and more arduous work, as well as running down non-renewable resources too rapidly. Zero growth is often expressed as a condemnation of all growth rather than an attack on particular undesirable economic activities. However, changes to more environmentally-friendly production techniques make economic growth more acceptable.

See also: Club of Rome

zero–infinity dilemma (Q2)
A problem in environmental economics when the probability of damage is small but the impact of a pollutant is potentially large.

zero population growth (J1)
The goal of many twentieth-century disciples of MALTHUS usually taking the form of advocating birth control. In many West European countries the use of contraceptive pills since the 1960s has brought the natural rate of increase below the replacement level.

See also: neo-Malthusians

zero priced (D0)
Free. This term enables the prices of everything to be placed on a continuum from zero to a considerable sum. Many goods and services provided by the public sector are given freely to consumers, e.g. most of the health care provided by the UK's National Health Service. Although goods can be free to a consumer, they are not costless because of the scarcity of factor inputs.

zero profit (D0)
The absence of SUPERNORMAL PROFITS in the long run, under conditions of PERFECT COMPETITION, as firms earn only NORMAL PROFITS which are included in average costs.

zero-rated good (H2)
A good not subject to VALUE-ADDED TAX. Exemptions from value-added tax vary from country to country but the principal items excluded in some countries have been food, clothing and educational materials.

zero real interest (E4)
A nominal rate of interest equal to the rate of inflation of that country.

zero-sum game (C7)
Economic activities in which gains to the winners equal losses to the losers. There are many examples of these games, e.g. the attempt of all major trading countries to have export surpluses.

Zeuthen, Frederik Ludvig Baug, 1888–1959 (B3)
Danish mathematical economist who graduated from Copenhagen University in 1912 and was employed by the Danish social security system from 1912 to 1930 before beginning his academic career. He developed a theory of COLLECTIVE BARGAINING based upon the possible outcomes of expected conflict, as perceived by management and labour, and developed the theory of DUOPOLY by expanding the notion of PRODUCT DIFFERENTIATION.

References
Zeuthen, F.L.B. (1930) *Problems of Monopoly and Economic Welfare*, London: G. Routledge & Sons.
—— (1959) *Economic Theory and Method*, Cambridge, MA: Harvard University Press.

Zipf's law (R1)
A linear relationship between the logarithm of the largest cities and the logarithm of those cities' populations after ranking the cities by size starting with the largest. It is claimed to be universally true and to reflect constant RETURNS TO SCALE in cities.

See also: Gibrat's law

References
Zipf, G. (1949) *Human behaviour and the principle of last effort*, Cambridge, MA: Addison-Wesley.

zombie (G3)
A company insolvent but continuing to operate.

See also: overtrading

zonal pricing (D4, Q4)
The aggregation of NODAL PRICES to produce the same prices over part of a system such as electricity transmission.

zone of freedom (D0, L9)
A price range of the tariffs set by major airlines. The 'zone' is the range below and above a single reference level within which an air tariff must be set.

zoning (Q3)
A local government method of regulating land use. By the prohibition of certain types of building in particular areas, land

values and the nature of economic activity are affected.

Z-score (G0, M2)

A measure of the overall performance of a company which takes the form of a weighted index. The index is $a + b \times$ profitability $- c \times$ gearing. In this expression, a is a constant and b and c are coefficients reflecting the relative importance of each ratio. The score for an individual company is compared with a test score to judge whether the company is a financial failure or a success.

Appendix A
Currencies of the world (F3)

Afghani: Afghanistan
A/Guilder: Netherlands Antilles
Australian dollar: Australia, Kiribati, Nauru Islands, Tuvalu
Bahama dollar: Bahamas
Baht: Thailand
Balboa: Panama
Barbados dollar: Barbados
Belgian franc: Belgium*
Belize dollar: Belize
Bermuda: Bermudian dollar
Bolivar: Venezuela
Boliviana: Bolivia
Brunei dollar: Brunei
Burundi franc: Burundi
Canadian dollar: Canada
Cedi: Ghana
CFA franc: Benin, Burkina Faso, Cameroon, Central African Republic, Chad, Congo, Côte d'Ivoire, Equatorial Guinea, French Community/Africa, Gabon, Guinea-Bissau, Mali Republic, Niger Republic, Senegal, Togo Republic
CFP franc: French Pacific Islands
Chilean peso: Chile
CI dollar: Cayman Islands
Colombian peso: Colombia
Colon: Costa Rica, El Salvador
Comoros franc: Comoros
Congo franc: Congo Democratic Republic
Cuban peso: Cuba
CV escudo: Cape Verde
Cyprus pound: Cyprus
Dalasi: Gambia

Danish krone: Denmark, Faroe Islands, Greenland
Denar: Macedonia
Deutschmark: Germany*
Dinar: Algeria, Bahrain, Sudan Republic, Tunisia
Dirham: Morocco, United Arab Emirates
Djibouti franc: Djibouti
Dobra: São Tomé
Dominican peso: Dominican Republic
Dong: Vietnam
Drachma: Greece*
Dram: Armenia
East Caribbean dollar: Antigua, Dominica, Grenada, Montserrat, St Christopher, St Lucia, St Vincent
Egyptian pound: Egypt
Escudo: Azores, Madeira, Portugal*
Ethiopian birr: Ethiopia
Falkland pound: Falkland Islands
Fiji dollar: Fiji Islands
Florin: Aruba
Forint: Hungary
French franc: Andorra, France*, Guadeloupe, Monaco, Réunion Island, St Pierre & Miquelon
Gibraltar pound: Gibraltar
Gold cordoba: Nicaragua
Gourde: Haiti
Guarani: Paraguay
Guilder: Netherlands*
Guinea franc: Guinea
Guyanese dollar: Guyana
Hong Kong dollar: Hong Kong

Hryvna: Ukraine
Icelandic krona: Iceland
Indian rupee: India
Iraqi dinar: Iraq
Jamaican dollar: Jamaica
Jordanian dinar: Jordan
Kenya shilling: Kenya
Kina: Papua New Guinea
Koruna: Czech Republic, Slovakia
Krona: Sweden
Kroon: Estonia
Kuna: Croatia
Kuwaiti dinar: Kuwait
Kwacha: Malawi, Zambia
Kyat: Burma
Lari: Georgia
Lats: Latvia
Lebanese pound: Lebanon
Lek: Albania
Lempira: Honduras
Leone: Sierra Leone
Leu: Moldavia, Romania
Lev: Bulgaria
Liberian dollar: Liberia
Libyan dinar: Libya
Lilangeni: Swaziland
Lira: Italy*, San Marino, Turkey, Vatican
Litas: Lithuania
Local franc: French Guiana, Martinique
Luxemburg franc: Luxemburg*
Maltese lira: Malta
Maluti: Lesotho
Manat: Azerbaijan
Marka: Bosnia Herzegovina
Markka: Finland*
Mauritius rupee: Mauritius
Metical: Mozambique
Mexican peso: Mexico
MG franc: Madagascar
Naira: Nigeria
Namibian dollar: Namibia
Nepalese rupee: Nepal
New dinar: Yugoslavia
New kip: Laos
New shilling: Uganda
New sol: Peru
New Zealand dollar: New Zealand, Pitcairn Islands
Ngultrum: Bhutan

Norwegian krone: Norway
Ouguiya: Mauritania
Pa'anga: Tongo Islands
Pakistan rupee: Pakistan
Pataca: Macao
Peso: Argentina, Philippines
Peso Uruguayo: Uruguay
Pound: St Helena, United Kingdom
Pound sterling: Pitcairn Islands
Pula: Botswana
Punt: Irish Republic*
Quetzal: Guatemala
Rand: South Africa
Readj kwanza: Angola
Real: Brazil
Renminbi: China
Rial: Iran, Yemen Republic
Rial Omani: Oman
Riel: Cambodia
Ringgit: Malaysia
Riyal: Qatar, Saudi Arabia
Rouble: Belarus, Russia
Rufiya: Maldive Islands
Rupiah: Indonesia
Rwanda franc: Rwanda
Schilling: Austria*
SDR: Special Drawing Right (IMF)
Seychelles rupee: Seychelles
Shekel: Israel
Shilling: Somali Republic, Tanzania
Singapore dollar: Singapore
Solomon Islands dollar: Solomon Islands
Som: Kyrgyzstan
Spanish peseta: Andorra, Balearic Islands, Canary Islands, Spain*, Spanish ports in North Africa
Sri Lanka rupee: Sri Lanka
Sum: Uzbekistan
Surinam guilder: Surinam
Swiss franc: Liechtenstein, Switzerland
Syrian pound: Syria
Taiwanese dollar: Taiwan
Taka: Bangladesh
Tala: Western Samoa
Tenge: Kazakhstan
Tolar: Slovenia
Trinidadian dollar: Trinidad & Tobago
Tugrik: Mongolia
US dollar: Ecuador, Guam, Puerto Rico,

Turks and Caicos, United States of America, Virgin Islands
Vatu: Vanuatu
Won: North Korea, South Korea
Yen: Japan
Zimbabwian dollar: Zimbabwe
Zloty: Poland

Notes:

*Currency officially replaced by the euro on 1 January 2002.

Some currencies with the same name have different values.

Appendix B
World stock market indices (G1)

The principal indices are:

Argentina: General
Australia: All Ordinaries
Austria: ATX
Belgium: BEL 20
Brazil: Bovespa
Canada: TSE 100
Chile: ICPA General
China: Shanghai A and B; Shengzhen A
  and B
Colombia: CSE
Czech Republic: PX 50
Denmark: KFX
Egypt: SE General
Estonia: Tallinn General
Finland: HEX General
France: CAC 40
Germany: XETRA Dax
Greece: Athens Gen
Hong Kong: Hang Seng
Hungary: Bux
India: BSE Sens.
Indonesia: Jakarta Comp.
Ireland: ISEQ Overall
Israel: Tel Aviv 100
Italy: Mibtel General
Japan: Nikkei
Jordan: Amman SE
Latvia: Riga SE

Lithuania: General
Malaysia: KLSE Comp.
Mexico: IPC
Morocco: CASA
Netherlands: AEX
New Zealand: Cap. 40
Nigeria: SE All-Share
Norway: Total All-Share
Pakistan: KSE 100
Peru: Lima Gen
Philippines: Manila Comp.
Poland: Wig
Portugal: BVL 30
Romania: BET
Russia: RTS
Singapore: Straits Times
Slovakia: SAX
South Africa: JSE All Share
South Korea: KoreaCmpEx
Spain: Madrid SE
Sri Lanka: CSE All Share
Sweden: AffarsvardnGen
Switzerland: SMI
Taiwan: Weighted Price
Thailand: Bangkok SET
Turkey: IMKB Nat 100
UK: FTSE 100; FTSE all-share
USA: Dow Jones; NASDAQ comp.
Venezuela: IBC
Zimbabwe: ZSE Industrial

Subject classifications

These classifications are as used in *The Economic Journal* (the journal of The Royal Economic Society) and the *Journal of Economic Literature.*

A General economics and teaching

- A1 General economics
- A2 Teaching of economics

B Methodology and history of economic thought

- B0 General
- B1 History of economic thought to 1925
- B2 History of economic thought since 1925
- B3 History of economic thought: individuals
- B4 Economic methodology

C Mathematical and quantitative methods

- C0 General
- C1 Econometric and statistical methods: general
- C2 Econometric methods: single equation models
- C3 Econometric methods: multiple equation models
- C5 Econometric modelling
- C6 Mathematical methods and programming
- C7 Game theory and bargaining theory
- C8 Data collection and data estimation methodology; computer programmes
- C9 Design of experiments

D Microeconomics

- D0 General
- D1 Household behaviour and family economics
- D2 Production and organisations
- D3 Distribution
- D4 Market structure and pricing
- D5 General equilibrium and disequilibrium
- D6 Economic welfare
- D7 Analysis of collective decision-making
- D8 Information and uncertainty
- D9 Intertemporal choice and growth

E Macroeconomics and monetary economics

- E0 General
- E1 General aggregative models
- E2 Consumption, saving, production, employment and investment
- E3 Prices, business fluctuations and cycles
- E4 Money and interest rates
- E5 Monetary policy, central banking, and the supply of money and credit
- E6 Macroeconomic aspects of public finance, macroeconomic policy and general outlook

F International economics

- F0 General

F1 Trade
F2 International factor movements
F3 International finance
F4 Macroeconomic aspects of international trade and finance

G Financial economics

G0 General
G1 General financial markets
G2 Financial institutions and services
G3 Corporate finance and governance

H Public economics

H0 General
H1 Structure and scope of government
H2 Taxation and subsidies
H3 Fiscal policies and the behaviour of economic agents
H4 Publicly provided goods
H5 National government expenditures and related policies
H6 National budget, deficit and debt
H7 State and local government: intergovernmental relations

I Health, education and welfare

I1 Health
I2 Education
I3 Welfare and poverty

J Labour and demographic economics

J0 General
J1 Demographic economics
J2 Time allocation, work behaviour and employment determination
J3 Wages, compensation and labour costs
J4 Particular labour markets
J5 Labour management relations: trade unions and collective bargaining
J6 Mobility, unemployment and vacancies
J7 Discrimination

K Law and economics

K0 General
K2 Regulation and business law
K4 Legal procedure, the legal system and illegal behaviour

L Industrial organisation

L0 General
L1 Market structure, firm strategy and market performance
L2 Firm objectives, organisation and behaviour
L3 Non-profit organisations and public enterprise
L4 Anti-trust policy
L5 Regulation and industrial policy
L6 Industry studies: manufacturing
L7 Industry studies: primary products and construction
L8 Industry studies: services
L9 Industry studies: utilities and transport

M Business administration and business economics; marketing; accounting

M0 General
M1 Business administration
M2 Business economics
M3 Marketing and advertising
M4 Accounting

N Economic history

N0 General
N1 Macroeconomics: growth and fluctuations
N2 Financial markets and institutions
N3 Labour, demography, education, income and wealth
N4 Government, law and regulation
N5 Agriculture, natural resources and extractive industries
N6 Manufacturing and construction
N7 Transport, trade, energy and other services

O Economic development

O0 General
O1 Economic development
O2 Development, planning and policy
O3 Technological change
O4 Economic growth and aggregate productivity
O5 Economy-wide country studies

P Economic systems

P0 General
P1 Capitalist systems
P2 Socialist systems
P3 Socialist institutions

P4 Other economic institutions
P5 Comparative economic systems

Q Agricultural and natural resource economics

Q0 General
Q1 Agriculture
Q2 Renewable resources and conservation: environmental management
Q3 Non-renewable resources and conservation
Q4 Energy

R Urban, rural and regional economics

R0 General
R1 General spatial economics
R2 Household analysis
R3 Production analysis and firm location
R4 Transport
R5 Regional government analysis

Z Other topics

Z1 Cultural economics

A General economics and teaching

A1 General economics

American Economic Association
'dismal science'
economic anthropology
economic journals
economics
economic specificity
economyth
endowment
human scale economics
Institute of Economic Affairs
institutional economics
mono-economics
normative economics
organizational economics
Panglossian economics
political economy
positive economics
postmodern economics
radical economics
Royal Economic Society

A2 Teaching of economics

economics

B Methodology and history of economic thought

B0 General

anarchism
Islamic economics
monetarism
vulgar economists

B1 History of economic thought to 1925

Ancient Greeks

Austrian School
Cambridge School
central place theory
classical dichotomy
classical economics
continuity thesis
Currency School
female economists
Free Banking School
French Circuit School
German Historical School
iron law of wages
Lausanne School
Manchester School
marginalists
mercantilism
needs of trade
neoclassical economics
neo-Malthusians
Physiocrats
real bills doctrine
Stockholm School
utilitarianism
value in use
wages fund theory
Wealth of Nations

B2 History of economic thought since 1925

African–American economists
Austrian School
Cambridge Circus
Cambridge Economic Policy Group
Cambridge School
Chicago School
Cowles Commission
female economists
French Circuit School
Gandhian economics

German Historical School
instant monetarism
libertarian economics
neo-Keynesians
neo-Marxists
neo-mercantilism
neo-Ricardian theory
New Cambridge economics
new classical economics
new macroeconomics
New Right
post-Keynesians
Reaganomics
Regulation School
Stockholm School
supply-side economics
theonomy
transaction cost economics

B3   History of economic thought: individuals

Abramovitz, Moses, 1912–
Akerlof, George Arthur, 1940–
Allais, Maurice, 1911–
Anderson, James, 1739–1808
Aquinas, St Thomas, 1225–74
Aristotle, 384–22 BC
Arrow, Kenneth Joseph, 1921–
Ayres, Clarence Edwin, 1891–1972
Bagehot, Walter, 1826–77
Bailey, Samuel, 1791–1870
Bain, Joe Staten, 1912–
Baran, Paul, 1910–64
Barbon, Nicholas, c.1640–98
Bauer, Peter Thomas, 1915–
Baumol, William Jack, 1922–
Bayes, Thomas, 1702–61
Becker, Gary Stanley, 1930–
Bentham, Jeremy, 1748–1832
Bergson, Abram, 1914–
Beveridge, William Henry, 1879–1963
Blaug, Mark, 1927–
Böhm–Bawerk, Eugen von, 1851–1914
Boisguilbert, Pierre Le Pesant de, 1646–1714
Boulding, Kenneth Ewart, 1910–92
Buchanan, James McGill, 1919–
Burns, Arthur Frank, 1904–87
Cantillon, Richard, c.1680–c.1734
Cassel, Karl Gustav, 1866–1945
Chamberlin, Edward Hastings, 1899–1967
Chenery, Hollis Burnley, 1918–
Child, Sir Francis, 1684?–1740
Clark, Colin Grant, 1905–89

Clark, John Bates, 1847–1938
Coase, Ronald Harry 1910–
Commons, John Rogers, 1862–1945
Cournot, Antoine Augustin, 1801–77
Deane, Phyllis Mary, 1918–
Debreu, Gerard, 1921–
Dobb, Maurice Herbert, 1900–76
Domar, Evsey David, 1914–
Douglas, Paul Howard, 1892–1976
Dunlop, John Thomas, 1914–
Dupuit, Arsène Jules Etienne Juvénal, 1804–66
Edgeworth, Francis Ysidro, 1845–1926
Engel, Ernst, 1821–96
Engels, Friedrich, 1820–95
Feldstein, Martin, 1939–
Fisher, Irving, 1867–1947
Fogel, Robert William, 1926–
Fourier, Charles, 1772–1837
Friedman, Milton, 1912–
Frisch, Ragnar Anton Kittil, 1895–1973
Galbraith, John Kenneth, 1908–
George, Henry, 1839–97
Giffen, Sir Robert, 1837–1910
Gossen, Hermann Heinrich, 1810–58
Haavelmo, Trygve, 1911–
Haberler, Gottfried, 1900–1995
Hahn, Frank Horace, 1925–
Hansen, Alvin Harvey, 1887–1975
Harrod, Sir Roy Forbes, 1900–78
Harsanyi, John Charles, 1920–2000
Hawtrey, Sir Ralph, 1879–1971
Hayek, Friedrich A. von, 1899–1992
Heckman, James Joseph 1944–
Heckscher, Eli Filip, 1879–1952
Hicks, Sir John Richard, 1904–89
Hirschman, Albert Otto, 1915–
Hume, David, 1711–76
Isard, Walter, 1919–
Jevons, William Stanley, 1835–82
Johnson, Harry Gordon, 1923–79
Kahn, Richard Ferdinand, 1905–89
Kaldor, Nicholas 1908–86
Kalecki, Michal, 1899–1970
Kantorovich, Leonid Vitalievich, 1912–
Keynes, John Maynard 1883–1946
Klein, Lawrence R., 1920–
Knight, Frank Hyneman, 1885–1973
Koopmans, Tjalling Charles 1910–84
Kornai, Janos, 1928–
Krueger, Anne Osborn, 1934–
Kuznets, Simon S., 1901–85
Lachmann, Ludwig, 1906–90

Zeuthen, Frederik Ludvig Baug, 1888–1959

B4 *Economic methodology*

economic methodology
economic paradigm
economics as rhetoric
marginalism
Marshallian methodology
research programme

C   Mathematical and quantitative methods

C0 *General*

butterfly effect
Cowles Commission
power law

C1 *Econometric and statistical methods: general*

analysis of variance
arc elasticity
arithmetic mean
autocorrelation
average
backtesting
Bayesian method
bimodal frequency curve
boundary constraint
Box–Jenkins
breakeven analysis
breakeven pricing
bunch map
catastrophe theory
central limit theorem
chi-squared distribution
choice variable
classical econometrics
coefficient of correlation
coefficient of determination
coefficient of multiple correlation
coefficient of multiple determination
coefficient of variation
confidence interval
confidence level
confluence analysis
contingency table
corner solution
correlation
cost–benefit analysis
critical value
cross price elasticity of demand
current prices
cyclical variations
data-mining

decile
degrees of freedom
diffusion index
distributional/social weights
disturbance term
dummy variable
Durbin–Watson statistic
econometrics
efficient estimator
error
exogenous variable
extremum
F test
frequency curve
frequency distribution
frequency polygon
generalized least squares
geometric mean
Gerschenkron effect
Gini coefficient
Granger causality
harmonic mean
heteroscedasticity
heuristic
histogram
homoscedasticity
identification problem
index number
input–output analysis
interval estimate
J-shaped frequency curve
Kalman filter
kurtosis
lagged variable
Laspeyres index
least squares method
level of significance
linear programming
linear regression
Lorenz curve
loss function
lower quartile
Markov chain model
maximum likelihood estimator
mean
mean deviation
median
mode
moments
moving averages
multicollinearity
multimodal frequency curve
multiple correlation
multivariate analysis
noise

non-linear correlation
normal distribution
null hypothesis
one-tailed test
outlier
parameter
percentile
point elasticity
point estimate
probability
probable error
product moment formula
random variations
range
rank correlation
reduced form equation
reverse J-shaped frequency curve
sample
scatter diagram
seasonal adjustment
selection bias
semi-interquartile range
signal extraction
significance test
size distribution
skewed frequency curve
skewness
Spearman's rank correlation
    coefficient
specification
standard deviation
standard error of estimate
statistical population
statistics
stochastic process
stochastic term
Student's t distribution
symmetrical frequency curve
test statistic
three-stage least squares
time series
trend
two-stage least squares
two-tailed test
Type I error
Type II error
unbiased estimator
unimodal distribution
upper quartile
U-shaped frequency curve
variance
weight
white noise

C2 *Econometric methods: single equation models*

econometrics

C3 *Econometric methods: multiple equation models*

aggregation problem
econometrics
recursive system

C5 *Econometric modelling*

ARMA
Bayesian econometrics
change point analysis
Cobb–Douglas production function
cobweb
constant elasticity of substitution
    production function
economic forecasting
EPA
error-correction model
event study
INTERLINK
large-scale models
linkage models
logit model
MCM
non-parametric model
pattern model
probit model
soft modelling
Tobit model
top-down linkage model
Treasury model
vector autoregression
vector autoregressive model

C6 *Mathematical methods and programming*

arithmetic progression
continuous variable
derivative
difference equation
differentiation
discrete variable
domain
exogenous variable
extremum
fractal Brownian motion
geometric progression
homogeneous function
homothetic function
impulse response function
mathematical economics
optimal control

contingent commodity
contingent valuation
contract curve
contracting
core
cross price elasticity of demand
decision cycle
demand
demand curve
depletable externality
derived demand
devalorization
differentiated good
direct cost
direct utility function
disappointment aversion
discounting
discount rate
disequilibrium
disequilibrium economics
disutility
economic agent
economic devolution
economic efficiency
economic good
economic man
economic model
economism
Edgeworth box
eigenprices
elasticity
elasticity of a factor of production
elasticity of demand
elasticity of expectations
elasticity of substitution
elasticity of supply
employment
endogenous variable
envelope curve
equilibrium
equilibrium price
excess capacity
excess demand
excess supply
exchange
exclusion principle
exit–voice
expectations
expected utility
experience good
explicit contract
explicit cost
external economy of scale
externality
extrapolative expectations

factor cost
factor of production
felicific calculus
final good
fixed cost
fixprice
flexprice
free good
fungible asset
future
future goods
Giffen good
Giffen paradox
goal equilibrium
good
hard commodity
hazard
hedonic price
hiding hand
hold-up
homo economicus
homogeneous good
homo sovieticus
implicit cost
incentive compatible
income
income and substitution effects
income–consumption curve
income elasticity of demand
income–offer curve
incomplete contract
indifference curve
indirect cost
indivisibility
inducement good
inelasticity
inferior good
insurance
intangible wealth
intellectual property
interest risk
intermediate good
internal economy of scale
interpersonal utility comparisons
inverse elasticity rule
invisible hand
isocost
isolated market equilibrium
Japanese auction
joint cost
just price
labour disutility theory
labour theory of value
law of satiable wants
law of value

long period
luxury
marginal cost
marginal private cost
marginal product of labour
marginal revenue
marginal revenue product
marginal social cost
marginal utility
market adjustment
market clearing
market clearing price
market demand
market distortion
market equilibrium
market failure
market power
market risk
marking
Marshallian demand curve
Marshallian stability
material good
microeconomics
missing market
mixed good
money income
Monnet's law
monopsony
moral hazard
multiple unit auction
natural price
near rationality
negative externality
neoclassical synthesis
neo-Ricardian theory
network theory
new political economy
nominal
non-basic commodity
normal good
normal profit
no-trade equilibrium
numéraire
objective function
one-price law
opportunistic behaviour
opportunity cost
optimization problem
option demand
ordinal utility
organic composition of capital
overhead costs
overshooting price
paradox of value
partial equilibrium analysis

path dependent
pay-off
pecuniary economy of scale
pecuniary external economy
perverse price
point elasticity
positional good
praxeology
preference falsification
premium
present value
price
price–consumption curve
price determination
price discrimination
price effect
price elasticity of demand
price flexibility
price incentive
price–offer curve
price perception
price rigidity
price system
prime cost
principal–agent
private cost
private good
production possibility frontier
product market
profit motive
queuing system
Ramsey prices
rational decision
rationing
reaction curve
real price
recontract
regrettable
regular economy
relative price
rent seeking
reservation price
reverse auction
risk
risk aversion
risk lover
risk neutral
risk premium
rival good
Samaritan's dilemma
scarcity
scarcity index
sealed bid auction
search cost
search good

second best
self-interest
sequential externality
shadow price
shallow market
sham trading
shifts in demand or supply curves
shutdown price
simultaneous ascending auction
Slutsky effect
social adjustment cost
social cost
sponsor demand
stable equilibrium
stand-alone cost
standard commodity
steady state equilibrium
sticky price
stocks
substitute
sunk cost
supernormal profit
supplementary cost
supplier-induced demand
supply curve
supply function
supply price
surplus approach
sweetener
tariff
taste
tâtonnement
technological rent
temporary equilibrium
toll
top-level efficiency
total costs
total revenue
tournament model
trade
trade-off
trading price
transaction cost
transfer income
transformation problem
transitory income
trending price
two-part tariff
undepletable externality
unequal exchange
uniform price
unitary elastic
unit pricing
unit value index
user charge

util
utility
utility function
utility possibility frontier
valorization
value
value added
value in exchange
variable cost
Veblen good
vehicle bias
Vickrey auction
visible hand
volatility
wage-rental ratio
waste
white good
widget
windfall profit
zero priced
zero profit
zone of freedom

D1 Household behaviour and family economics

aggregate demand
axioms of preference
behavioural economics
brand loyalty
characteristics theory of consumer
   demand
compensated demand curve
consumer equilibrium
consumerism
consumer protection legislation
consumer society
consumer sovereignty
consumer's surplus
cornucopia
diminishing marginal rate of substitution
diminishing marginal utility law
economics and psychology
fad
Family Expenditure Survey
feminist economics
football pool
free rider
Hicksian demand function
home economics
household behaviour
household decision making
household work
individualism
intra-household economics

joint demand
marginal rate of substitution
network externality
new home economics
patriarchal monopoly
revealed preference
sociological utility theory
strategic bequest motive
unpaid work

D2 *Production and organisations*

bottleneck
brown good
capacity
capital intensive
capital–labour ratio
capital–output ratio
capital re-switching
capital theory
capital utilization
chain index method
Cobb–Douglas production function
cobweb
commodity fetishism
concrete labour
constant capital
constant elasticity of substitution
    production function
diminishing returns law
diseconomy of scale
diversification
division of labour
division of thought
domestic resource cost
domestic system
economic calculation
economic methods
economic planning
economy of scale
economy of scope
economy of size
Engel coefficient
factor productivity
filière concept
fragmentation
grey good
hedonic output
home production
increasing opportunity costs law
increasing returns to scale
indirect factor content
intermediate technology
isoquant
joint products
just-in-time production

labour intensive
land
law of variable proportions
linkage
marginal physical product
marginal productivity theory
marginal rate of transformation
Marshallian long period
Marshallian short period
Microproduction function
middle product
minimum efficient scale
mothballing
netput
output capacity
outsourcing
Pareto efficiency
potential output
producer's surplus
production quota
product life cycle
quota
re-switching
returns to scale
Ricardo effect
roundabout method of production
scarcity
services
specialization
sunk cost fallacy
supply control
team work
technical efficiency
unit cost
value added
vegetative control
yield

D3 *Distribution*

abstinence
adding-up controversy
Cambridge controversies
class savings theory
contribution standard
differential theory of rent
disposable income
distribution
earnings
economic profit
economic rent
egalitarianism
Euler's theorem
factor income
falling rate of profit
free cash flow

functional income distribution
Gini coefficient
Haig–Simons definition of income
Hicksian income measure
imputed income
income differential
income distribution
indirect utility function
inequality
intergenerational distribution of income
invisible foot
Kuznets curve
marginal productivity theory
needs standard
pecuniary returns
personal income
personal income distribution
profit
profit squeeze
psychic income
pure economic rent
pure profit
quasi-rent
Rawlsian difference principle
Rawlsian justice
rent
rental payment
rentier
transfer earnings
wealth distribution

D4 *Market structure and pricing*

administered pricing
anticipatory pricing
auction
bargain
barter
binomial charge
black market
Black–Scholes option pricing model
breakeven analysis
breakeven pricing
bubble
buyers' market
capacity charge
catallactics
ceiling price
competitive trading
constrained market pricing
contingent fee
contingent market
continuous double auction
controlled market
costing margin

Cournot's duopoly model
cross-trading
discriminating auction
disequilibrium price
dual pricing
Dutch auction
ecodevelopment valuation
efficient market
English auction
exchange standpoint epistemology
factor market
fair price
false trading
first-degree price discrimination
first-price auction
flawed marketplace
floor price
free market
full-cost pricing
hedonic pricing method
hybrid auction
incomplete market
indirect cost recovery
inefficient equilibrium
information trap
integrated fare
intersection price
inverse demand function
kinked supply curve
limited general competitive bidding
limit price
list price
marginal cost pricing
market
market segmentation
mark-up
mark-up pricing
matching function
nodal pricing
normal price
parametric pricing
peak-load pricing
predatory pricing
price bunching
price discovery process
price gap
price leadership
price-maker
price staggering
scarcity pricing
scissors diagram
second-price auction
sellers' market
Stackelberg duopoly model
survival process

tariffication
tender
third-degree price discrimination
transaction price
transfer pricing
two-part pricing
uniformity assumption
value in use
white market
workable competition
X-efficiency
zonal pricing

D5 *General equilibrium and disequilibrium*

approximate equilibrium
Arrow–Debreu model
extended equilibrium
general equilibrium
general market equilibrium
multiple equilibria
tâtonnement
Walras exchange economy
Walrasian stability
Walras's law

D6 *Economic welfare*

bad
Bergson social welfare function
bliss point
bourgeoisie
Coase theorem
compensation principle
consumption externality
contemporaneous externality
corrective subsidy
cost–benefit analysis
deadweight loss
dependency culture
distortion
ecfare
economic justice
economic welfare
equality
equality of opportunity
equality standard
equivalent variation
exchange efficiency
First Welfare Theorem
horizontal equity
humaneness indicators
ill-being
illth
international comparisons of the cost
   of living
Kaldor–Hicks compensation principle

Lorenz curve
measure of economic welfare
needs standard
net economic welfare
ordinalist revolution
Pareto improvement
Pareto optimum
physical quality of life index
prosperity indicators
public interest theory
Rawlsian difference principle
Scitovsky reversal test
social cost of monopoly
social cost of unemployment
sunspot theory
sympathetic impartial observer
top-level efficiency
welfare economics
well-being

D7 *Analysis of collective decision-making*

bargaining
impossibility theorem
social choice theory
state theories
team theory

D8 *Information and uncertainty*

economics of information
framing effects
information externality
information theory
lemons market
prospect theory
regret
signalling
state preference theory
uncertainty

D9 *Intertemporal choice and growth*

overlapping generations model
Ricardian equivalence theorem
social rate of discount
social time preference rate

E   **Macroeconomics and monetary economics**

E0 *General*

accounting identity
adaptive expectations
adverse supply shock
bad equilibrium
butterfly effect
Cambridge controversies

capacity utilization
capital
corridor
cultivated capital
disequilibrium economics
effective demand
effectual demand
employment multiplier
employment rate
equilibrium
equilibrium GNP
European system of accounts
ex ante, ex post
ex ante variables
exogenous expectations
expectations
ex post variables
extrapolative expectations
full employment
GDP deflator
gross domestic product
gross national product
gross social product
hiding hand
impact multiplier
income
incremental capital–output ratio
inflationary gap
injection
internal balance
Keynes expectations
Keynesian economics
Keynesian equilibrium
Keynes's *General Theory*
labour's share of national income
leakage
leverage
macroeconomic demand schedule
macroeconomics
magic quadrilateral
malleable capital
money gross domestic product
multiplier
national income
National Income and Product
    Accounts
national wealth
negotiated co-ordination
neoclassical synthesis
new political economy
nominal
nominal gross domestic product
non-goal equilibrium
objective function
Okun's law

organic composition of capital
paradox of costs
potential surprise function
present value
price level
profit squeeze
proprietors' income
rational expectations
real balance effect
real-wage hypothesis
regressive expectations
Robertsonian lag
size of an economy
social product
Soviet Material Product System
stable equilibrium
stationary state
steady state economy
stock and flow concepts
stylized fact
surplus economy
System of National Accounts
temporary equilibrium
traverse
wealth
widow's cruse
windfall gain or loss
windfall profit
withdrawal
zero growth

E1 *General aggregative models*

circular flow
classical model
coconut model
COMET
comparative statics
dynamic economics
economic model
endogenizing the exogenous
endogenous variable
flow of funds account
IS
IS–LM–BP model
IS–LM curves
Keynesian cross diagram
Lucas supply function
material balance
Mundell–Fleming model
net acquisition of financial assets
output gap
point-input, point-output model
production function
pseudo production function
Robinson Crusoe economy

Say's law
static model
structural model

E2 Consumption, saving, production, employment and investment

absolute income hypothesis
absorptive capacity
accelerator principle
accumulation
aggregate demand
aggregate output
aggregate supply
animal spirits
augmented GNP
autonomous consumption
autonomous expenditure
autonomous investment
average propensity to consume
average propensity to save
balanced budget multiplier
C
capital accumulation
capital deepening
capital reversing
capital theory
capital utilization
capital value
capital widening
conspicuous consumption
constant capital
consumption function
contractual savings
corn model
crowding in
crowding out
Denison's law
dissaving
domestic absorption
Engel's law
expenditure function
final income
fixed capital
forced saving
gestation period
gross domestic fixed capital formation
import penetration ratio
interest elasticity of savings
internal rate of return
investment
investment fundamentals
Katona effect
lacking
Lerner effect
life-cycle hypothesis

Lundberg lag
marginal efficiency of capital
marginal efficiency of investment
marginal propensity to consume
marginal propensity to save
monetary overhang
net investment
overaccumulation
paradox of thrift
permanent income hypothesis
Pigou effect
Premium Savings Bond
project appraisal
propensity to consume
propensity to save
putty-clay
putty-putty
Ramsey saving rule
ratchet effect
relative income hypothesis
replacement investment
reproduction
Robertsonian lag
savings
savings function
savings ratio
social capital
social profit
stock adjustment principle
super-multiplier
test rate of discount
thrift
vintage effect
wealth creation
wealth effect

E3 Prices, business fluctuations and cycles

acyclical
administered inflation
automatic stabilizer
Barber boom
bell-wether of the economy
boom
boom and bust
business cycle
ceiling
coincident indicators
conflicting claims approach to
    inflation
constant prices
consumer price index
core inflation rate
cost-push inflation
countercyclical policy
CPI-U

CPI-W
crisis
critical economy
deflation
demand-pull inflation
demand-shift inflation
depression
diffusion index
discomfort index
disequilibrium
disequilibrium economics
disinflation
disinflation cost
East Asian economic crisis
economic indicators
floor
glut
gnomes of Zurich
Goodwin growth cycle
gradualist monetarism
growth recession
harmonized index of consumer prices
hegemonic cycle
hog cycle
hyperinflation
implicit price deflator
inertial inflation
infession
inflation
inflation accounting
inflationist
inventory cycle
investment reserve system
Juglar cycle
Keynes effect
Kitchin cycle
Kondratieff cycle
Kuznets cycle
lacking
lagging indicator
Laspeyres index
Lawson boom
leading indicators
logistic cycle
long wave
market anti-inflation plan
market prices
menu costs of inflation
monetary inflation
monetary overhang
moving averages
multiplier–accelerator model
Mundell–Tobin effect
National Board for Prices and
    Incomes

nutcracker theory of the business cycle
oil-price increases
Paasche index
pay freeze
Phillips curve
political business cycle
predator–prey model
price ceiling
Price Commission
price controls
prices policy
producer price index
P-star model
pure inflation
real business-cycle theory
real income
recession
recession exposure scoring system
recovery
reference cycle
reputational equilibrium
retail price index
revalorization
RPI $-$ X
RPI $-$ Y
sacrifice ratio
Sandilands Report
shock inflation
shoe leather costs of inflation
slump
slumpflation
stagflation
stop–go
structural inflation
sunspot theory
suppressed inflation
tax-based incomes policy
trade cycle
underlying inflation rate
unintended investment
wage–price spiral
wage-push inflation
wage–tax spiral
wholesale price index
world inflation

E4 *Money and interest rates*

agio theory of interest
annual percentage rate (of interest)
asset motive
broad money
buffer stock
bullion
call money
Cantillon effect

cap
capacity
cartalist
cash
cash-in-advance constraint
cash nexus
cheap money
classical dichotomy
coinage
collar
commodification
compound interest
coupon
credit money
cycles
demand for money
denationalized money
deposit base
discount rate
disequilibrium money
Divisia money index
ecu
equilibrium velocity
European Unit of Account
expected monetary value
expensive easy money
flight from money
floor
generalized medium
Gresham's law
headline rate of inflation
helicopter money
inside money
interest
interest rate agreement
interest risk
IOU money
L
labour standard
lending rate
liquidity
liquidity preference
liquidity trap
loanable funds theory
locked-in effect
Lombard rate
London Inter-Bank Offered Rate
M0
M1
M2
M3
M3c
M4
M5
market rate of interest

means of payment
medium of account
medium of exchange
medium of redemption
metallist
minimum lending rate
monetarism
monetary veil
money
money at call
money illusion
money multiplier
moneyness
money supply
monkey
Mundell–Tobin effect
natural rate of interest
near money
neutrality of money
neutral real rate of interest
non-interest-bearing M1
numéraire
optimum quantity of money
outside money
overnight money
own rate of interest
paper money
petrocurrency
plastic money
populist interest rate
precautionary demand for money
preferred habitat theory
prime rate of interest
private sector liquidity (UK)
pure interest rate
quantity theory of money
rate of interest
real interest rate
Regulation Q
remittance
reverse causation hypothesis
seignorage
single currency
specie
speculative demand for money
sterling
sterling M3
store of value
term spread
term structure of interest rates
time value of money
token money
transactions demand for money
transmission mechanism
uncovered interest parity

unit of account
usury
velocity of circulation
volatility
wide monetary base
zero real interest

E5 Monetary policy, central banking, and the supply of money and credit

Bank Charter Act 1844
Bank Holding Company Act 1956
Banking Act 1979
Banking Act 1987
Bank of Canada
Bank of England
Bank of Italy (BOI)
Bank of Japan (BOJ)
bank rate
Banque de France
base rate
bimetallism
Bradbury
Britannia
Bundesbank
Cash Management Bill
central bank
central bank independence
Chapter 17
clipping
Competition and Credit Control
'corset'
credit crunch
credit rationing
decimalization
demand management
discount window
disinflation cost
domestic credit expansion
earmarked gold
easy money policy
eligible liability
European Central Bank
Eurosystem
Exchange Equalization Account
Exchequer
Exchequer White
federal funds
federal funds rate
Federal Open Market Committee
Federal Reserve Note
Federal Reserve System
fiat money
fiduciary issue
Fisher effect
Fisher equation of exchange

foreign exchange
forex
fountain pen money
General Agreement to Borrow
gilts
gold coinage
gold reserves
gold standard
Goodhart's law
government bond
guinea
hard currency
high-powered money
index-linked gilt
inflation targeting
interest rate smoothing
international reserves
intervention currency
Jurgensen Report
key currency
krugerrand
law of reflux
legal tender
lender of fast resort
lifeboat operation
liquid assets
liquid assets ratio
maple leaf
margin requirements
monetary accommodation
monetary base
monetary policy
Monetary Policy Committee (UK)
moral suasion
open market operations
Operation Twist
overfunding
Radcliffe Report
refunding
Regulation D
Regulation K
Regulation Q
Regulation U
repurchase agreement
required reserve ratio
reserve assets
reserve requirements
rules versus discretion
Saudi Arabian Monetary Agency
snugging
special deposit
sterilization
swap network
Taylor's rule
tight monetary policy

Werner Report

E6 Macroeconomic aspects of public finance, macroeconomic policy and general outlook

activist
Adam Smith Institute
announcement effect
balanced budget multiplier
bastard Keynesianism
Beige Book
Blairism
Blue Book
Brookings Institution
Butskellism
catalytic policy mix
Centre for Policy Studies
Collor Plan
decision cycle
deflation
deflationary gap
dual-decision hypothesis
dynamically inconsistent policy
economic climate
economic summits
economic weather
Employment Act 1946
external shock
fine-tuning
foreign trade multiplier
fundamentals
goal variable
hard landing
harmonization
Humphrey–Hawkins Act 1978
Ifo Business Climate Index
implementation lag
incomes policy
indicator variable
inertial effect
inside lag
instrument variable
intermediate target
international comparisons
investment climate
investment reserve system
jawbone
lag
macroeconomic policy
Marxian economics
Medium-term Financial Strategy
military Keynesianism
Motor of Europe
National Bureau of Economic Research

National Economic Development Council
National Institute for Economic and Social Research
National Plan (UK)
one-club policy
outside lag
overheating
overshooting
pay freeze
policy credibility
policy harmonization
policy smoothing
public choice theory
public works
pure discretion
reaction function
Reaganomics
recession exposure scoring system
recognition lag
rectification
short-termism
soft landing
superneutrality
targeting
target variable
Thatcherism
two-speed economy
UK economic forecasting
Wharton model

F International economics

F0 General

Andean Common Market
Arab Common Market
Arab Maghreb Union
arbitrage
Association of South East Asian Nations
Benelux
butterfly effect
Cairn's Group
Caribbean Basin Initiative
Caribbean Community
Center for International Studies
centre–periphery system
common market
Communauté Economique de L'Afrique de l'Ouest
Council for Mutual Economic Aid
customs union
Davos man
Delors Plan
dependent economy

F1 Trade

Group of Seventy-seven
Havana Charter
Heckscher–Ohlin trade theorem
import
import penetration ratio
income terms of trade
infant industry argument
input trade
inter-industry trade
International Trade Commission
International Trade Organization
international trade theory
inter-nation equity
intra-industry trade
invisible trade
IS
Israel–US Trade Free Trade Area
Jackson Amendment
Kemp–Wan theorem
Kennedy Round
Latin American Free Trade
    Association
Leontief paradox
London International Financial
    Futures Exchange
London Traded Options Market
managed trade
Maquiladora
marginal propensity to import
Metzler paradox
most favoured nation
Multi-Fibre Arrangement
natural trade
Navigation Acts
neo-mercantilism
net barter terms of trade
new regionalism
new trade theory
non-tariff barrier
non-tradables
North American Free Trade Area
offer curve
open economy
optimum tariff
orderly market agreement
parallel importing
Prebisch–Singer thesis
protection
quantitative restrictions
Quebec Declaration
quota
reciprocal demand law
Reciprocal Trade Agreements Act
    1934
revenue seeking

running broker
Rybczynski theorem
single factorial terms of trade
single market
sliding scale
Smoot–Hawley Tariff Act 1930
stag
Standard International Trade
    Classification
staple export
static gains from trade
Stolper–Samuelson theorem
strategic trade theory
tariff
tariff jumping
terms of trade
terms of trade argument
Tokyo Round
trade
Trade Act 1974
trade balance
trade creation
trade deficit
trade diversion
Trade Expansion Act 1962
trade regime
trade strategy
trade threat
trading potential
unequal exchange
United Nations Conference on Trade
    and Development
Uruguay Round
vent for surplus
voluntary export restraint
warehouse economy
world trade
World Trade Organization

F2 International factor movements

brain drain
capital controls
capital flight
capital mobility
chain migration
direct foreign investment
eclectic theory
economic refugee
export requirement
foreign direct investment
Gastarbeiter
Gerschenkron effect
guestworker
hot money
immigration

Luxemburg effect
Markov chain model
migrant labour
migration
multinational corporation
transfer problem

F3 *International finance*

accommodating credit
additional facilities
adjustable peg
artificial currency
Baker plan
bancor
Bank for International Settlements
base currency
BigMac index
Brandt Commission
Bretton Woods Agreement
buffer stock
bull
chart point
clean float
Committee of Twenty
commodity reserve currency
common currency
compensatory financial facility
competitiveness index
conditionality
convergence criteria
convertible currency
cost, insurance and freight
counterpurchase
countertrade
crawling peg
credit reserves
credit tranche facility
currency
currency appreciation
currency basket
currency cocktail
currency depreciation
currency devaluation
currency reform
currency revaluation
currency risk
currency stabilization scheme
currency swap
debasing a currency
debt–equity swap
depreciation
dirty float
divergence indicator
divergence threshold
dollar

dollarization
dollar overhang
dollar standard
dual exchange rate
dual pricing
effective exchange rate
end of geography
euro
Eurocheque
Eurodollar
Eurodollar market
euro interbank offered rate
Euro overnight index average
European Investment Bank
European monetary co-operation
European Monetary Co-operation
    Funds
European Monetary System
European Monetary Union
eurozone
exchange controls
exchange cross-rate
exchange rate
exchange rate agreement
Exchange Rate Mechanism
exchange rate premium
exchange rate regime
exchange rate target zone
exchange risk
export
export promotion
extended fund facility
financial architecture
fixed exchange rate
floating exchange rate
forfaiting
franchise financing
General Agreement to Borrow
global deregulation
global monetarism
gold bullion standard
gold demonetization
gold exchange standard
gold franc
green currency
Group of Five
Group of Seven
Group of Ten
Group of Thirty
Group of Twenty-four
hard currency
hard ecu
International Clearing Union
International Development
    Association

International Finance Corporation
international liquidity
International Monetary Fund
international monetary system
intervention currency
investment dollar pool system
Jamaica Agreement
J-curve
Jubilee 2000
Jurgensen Report
key currency
long
Louvre Accord
managed currency fund
managed floating system
Mexican peso crisis
minimum reserve requirements
misaligned rate of exchange
mixed credit
multilateral aid
Multilateral Investment Guarantee
   Agency
multiple exchange rate
narcodollars
optimal peg
optimum currency area
optimum tariff
overseas assets
overvalued currency
par value
parallel currency strategy
parallel loan
pegged exchange rate
petrodollars
Plaza Agreement
Plaza Two
preferential trading arrangement
prohibitive tariff
purchasing power parity
quantitative restrictions
Rambouillet Summit
real exchange rate
recycling
remittance
rescheduling of debt
reserve currency
rollover ratio
scriptural currency
short
sliding parity
smart money
Smithsonian Agreement
snake in the tunnel
social opportunity cost of foreign
   exchange

soft currency
special drawing rights
speculative attack model
spot market
spreading
stabex system
Supplementary Financing Facility
symmetallism
tied aid
Tobin tax
trade-weighted exchange rate
transaction cost
transfer problem
Triffin paradox
value subtractor
World Bank
world debt problem
world monetary reserve assets
world monetary system

F4 Macroeconomic aspects of international trade and finance

absorption approach
accounting balance of payments
Balance for Official Financing
balance of payments
balance of payments equilibrium
balancing item
below the line
bilateral aid
branch economy
cable
capital account
current account
debt sustainability
deficit financing
external account
external balance
external credit ratings
external debt
FF curve
fundamental equilibrium
import substitution
internal balance
international illiquidity
leads and tags
market balance of payments
Marshall–Lerner condition
merchandise balance of trade
monetarist approach to the balance of
   payments
net property income from abroad
official financing
specie-flow mechanism
supply-side shocks

G Financial economics

G0 General

acceleration clause
accrual interest rate
advance
amortization
annual percentage rate (of interest)
annuity
arbitrage
ask price
asset
asset specificity
auto-economy
balloon payment
basis point
borrower's curse
capital adequacy
credit rating
days of grace
debt
debt contract
debt neutrality
debt restructuring
debt security
debt service indicator
debt trap
demandable debt instruments
event study
fad
financial journalism
gearing
goldbug
industrial share
investment
junior debt
junk bond
lender's risk
leverage
liability management
limited arbitrage
liquidity
long fraud
loyalty bonus
maturity
maturity structure of debt
maturity transformation
medium of exchange
misintermediation
mixed credit
mortgage
mortgage bond
negative equity
net asset value

netting
neutral budget
new institutional economics
'news'
paradox of liquidity
pecuniary economy of scale
perpetuity
personal equity plan
personal sector liquid assets
portfolio balance
portfolio investment
portfolio selection
portfolio trade
pre-emption right
preference share
premium
price-sensitive information
Prime-1
principal
principalship
private placement
profit taking
promissory note
proxy
rate of return
real rate of return
redemption date
redemption yield
risk-adjusted discount rate
risk capital
risk-free asset
risky asset
safe asset
samurai bond
seed capital
self-insurance
senior debt
servicing a debt
sham trading
shelf registration
soft loan
sovereign loan
speculative price data
spot price/rate
stakeholder
stepped bond
stocks
straight bond
subordinate debt
term premium
wider share ownership
yield
yield curve
yield gap
zai teku

Z-score

G1 *General financial markets*

AAA
accretion of a discount
American option
arb
Arrow–Debreu security
A share
Asian option
asset card
at the money
Automated Real-time Investment
    Exchange
backtesting
backwardation
barbell
barrier option
bear
bearer bond
bearer share
bed and breakfast
behavioural finance
bell-wether stock
beta
beta stock
bid price
Big Bang
'Big Board'
bill
bill of exchange
blackboard trading
black chip
Black Monday
Black–Scholes option pricing model
block of shares
blue chip
blue-sky laws
bogey
bond
bond fund
bond market
bond rating agency
bonus issue
boomernomics
bootstrap
borrower's risk
bottom fisher
bought deal
bourse
Brady Commission
British depository receipt
brokered deposit
broker loan rate
B share

bubble
bull
bulldog bond
bulldog issue
bullet strategy
bunny bond
call
call option
cap
capital asset pricing model
capitalization
capital market
capping an interest rate
Cash Management Bill
cash price–earnings ratio
cats and dogs
chaos theory
chart point
Chicago Board Options Exchange
churning
circuit breaker mechanism
closed-end fund
collateralized mortgage obligation
collectivized investment
commercial bill
commercial paper
Commodity Exchange of New York
common stock
consideration
consol
contango
contingent market
contrarian investment strategy
conversion
coupon
cover
crashometrics
credit enhancement
credit spread
C share
cumulative security
D
dawn raid
day trade
DDD
dead cat bounce
debenture
deep discount bond
delta stock
dematerialization
derivative
disappointment aversion
discount bond
discount market
discounted share price

diversification
dividend
dividend discount model
dividend yield
dogs of the Dow
East Asian economic crisis
elephant
end of geography
equity
equity comovement
equity premium
Eurobond
Eurobond market
Euromarket
Euronext
European option
fair value
falling knife
federal funds market
financial asset
financial capital
financial crisis
financial investment
Financial Times Actuaries All-Share
    Index
Financial Times Industrial Ordinary
    Share Index
Financial Times Stock Exchange 100
    Share Index
fix
floating rate note
flotation
Footsie
foreign exchange market
forex trading
forward market
franchise gap
fundamental value
future
futures market
gamma stock
gap analysis
gilts
global depository receipt
golden share
gold market
Gordon model
government bond
government broker
government security
green stripe price
grey market
Grey Monday
gross dividend yield
gunslinger

heavy share
hedge ratio
hedging
high-yield financing
H share
hypothecation
illiquid
incomplete market
indexing
initial public offering
inter-dealer broker
interest rate risk
International Monetary Market
International Securities Regulatory
    Organization
in-the-money
investor sentiment
jobber
jump
junk of junk status
kappa
kerb market
limit order
limit order book
liquid market
listed security
loan stock
local expectations theory
London Discount Market Association
L share
Main Street
margin call
margin trading
market capitalization
market-maker
market order
marking
Markovitz efficient portfolio
middle price
money at call
money market certificate
moneyness
Morgan Stanley Capital International
    World Index
New York Mercantile Exchange
New York Stock Exchange
niche trading
no-load fund
N share
offer price
options exchanges
ordinary share
original issue discount bond
over-the-counter market
participating security

par value
payment-in-kind bond
pay performance sensitivity
penny share
pit committee
placing
poop
portfolio optimization
price discovery process
price–earnings ratio
price-maker
primary dealer
primary market
primary offering
programme deal
program trading (US)
prospectus
put option
put price
put-through
random walk theory
red chip
reoffering yield
rights issue
rolling settlement
roundtripping
scrip issue
secondary market
second market
Securities Association
Securities Exchange Act 1934
securities market
securitization
security
severe correction
share
share borrowing
share buy-back
share economy
short selling
short-term money market
single-capacity trading
smokestack American stocks
sovereign risk
specialist
specific risk
speculation
spiders
spread
Standard & Poor 100
Standard & Poor 500
sterling commercial paper
sterling warrant into gilt-edged stock
stock exchange

Stock Exchange Automated Quotation
    System
stockholder diffusion
stock index arbitrage
stock index futures market
stock market correction
stock market crash
stock market price index
straddle
strike price
stripped security
strong efficiency
stub equity
swap market
swaption
sweat equity
systematic risk
takeover panel
tangible net worth
tap stock
TechMARK
tender
theta
thin trading
third market
tick
tombstone
total shareholder return
tracker fund
tracking stock
trade
treasury bill
UK gilts market
underlier
underwater stock option
underweight on a share
Unlisted Securities Market
US Treasury bond market
US Treasury market
value at risk
vega risk
vulture fund
waiting period
wallpaper
war babies/brides
warrant
weak efficiency
wholesale money market
writer
Xetra
Yankee bond
yearling
yellow stripe price
zero coupon bond

G2 *Financial institutions and services*

accepting house
account
account days
adverse selection
affinity card
African Development Bank
after-hours dealings
aftermarket
agency broker
agency pass-through
agent bank
agreement corporation
allotment letter
alpha stock
American Depository Receipt
American Stock Exchange
A share
Asian Development Bank
Association of International Bond
    Dealers
automated clearing house
automated teller machine
bank capital
bank charges
bank deposits
bank efficiency
banker's turn
bank holding company
Bank Holding Company Act 1956
banking
Banking Act 1979
Banking Act 1987
bank margin
banknote
bank settlement system
bank underwriting
bargain
Barings Bank collapse
base capital
base rate
Basle Concordat on Banking
    Supervision
BB
BBB
branch banking
bridging
brokered deposit
building and loan association
Building Societies Act 1986
Building Societies Association
building society
bulge-bracket firm
Business Expansion Scheme

C
call money
captive insurance
Caribbean Development Bank
carte à mémoire
cash–deposits ratio
cash dispenser
cash economy
cashless society
cash management account
certificate of deposit
chain bank
charge
charge card
chartism
checking account
cheque
cheque card
'Chinese Wall'
clearing
clearing bank
clearing house
Clearing House Interbank Payments
    System
closed-end credit
closed pension fund
collar
collecting bank
commercial bank
Commodity Futures Trading Commis-
    sion
Competitive Equality Banking Act
    1987
composite insurance company
Comptroller of the Currency
Computer-assisted Trading System
consolidation loan
consortium bank
consumer credit
Consumer Credit Act 1974
contractual savings
correspondent bank
counterparty capital
country fund
credit
credit card
credit scoring
credit union
cum dividend
currency run
current account
current deposit
debit card
debt–equity swap
debt finance

demand deposit
deposit account
deposit base
deposit insurance
Depository Institutions Deregulation and Monetary Control Act 1980
deposit-taking business
development bank
discount house
disintermediation
dividend net
domestic banking system
Douglas Amendment 1965
Dow Jones Industrial Average
Du Pont formula
earnings per share
earnings ratio
earnings yield
Edge Act Corporation
eftpos
eligible liability
endowment effect
endowment insurance
equipment trust bond
equity-linked mortgage
equity release scheme
equity-style management
equity taxation
equity warrant
ethical unit trust
Eurobank
Eurocheque
Euroclear
Eurocurrency market
Eurodollar market
Euroequity
Eurofranc
Euromoney deposit
European Bank for Reconstruction and Development
European Investment Bank
ex dividend
executive leasing
expedited funds availability
expensive easy money
Export Import Bank
external account
external credit ratings
factoring
Federal Deposit Insurance Corporation
Federal Home Loan Board
Federal Savings and Loan Insurance Corporation
financial centre

financial conglomerate
financial contagion
financial crisis
financial deepening
'financial engineering'
financial intermediary
financial leverage ratio
financial liberalization
financial panic
financial regime
financial repression
Financial Services Act 1986
financial system
five-star mutual fund
floor planning
fractional reserve banking
free banking
front-end loading
fronting loan
full employment
full insurance
Garn St Germain Depository Institutions Act 1982
Glass–Steagall Act 1933
goldsmith banking system
Government National Mortgage Association
hidden reserves
high-powered money
hire purchase
home banking
Hunt Commission
income multiple
index-linked gilt
index-tracking fund
Industrial and Commercial Finance Corporation
insider trading
institutional investor
insurance market
Insurance Ombudsman Bureau
Inter-American Development Bank
interest-bearing eligible liabilities
interest rate agreement
interest rate cartel
interest rate swap
intergenerational loan
Intermarket Trading System
intermediation
International Banking Act 1978
investment banking
investment trust
Islamic banking
issuing house
Lamfalussy Report

land bank
laser banking
Lautro
letter of credit
letter stock
lifeboat operation
liquid assets
Lloyd's
Lloyd's name
load fund
loanshark
long-term credit bank
Macmillan Gap
managed currency fund
marzipan layer
maturity mismatch
Mayday
McFadden Branch Banking Act 1927
merchant bank
mezzanine finance
microcredit
minimum funding requirement
Monetary Control Act 1980
money centre bank
money market deposit account
money market mutual fund
money-purchase pension
monobank
mortgage credit association
mortgage equity withdrawal
mortgage pass-through security
mortgage strip
mutual fund
mutual insurance company
National Association of Securities
    Dealers and Investment Managers
National Association of Securities
    Dealers Automated Quotation
    System
National Banking Act 1863
new issue
niche bank
nominee account
non-bank activities
note issuance facility
NOW account
off-exchange instrument
offshore banking
one-bank holding company
one hundred per cent reserve banking
One two three bank
open-ended fund
option
orphan assets
other checkable deposits

out of the money
panel bank
paperless entry
paradox of lending
pension fund
pension mis-selling
pension scheme
personal bank
polarization
position-risk capital
POS machine
primary capital
primary mortgage market
prime bank
prime bank scam
proportional accounting
Radcliffe Report
real estate investment trust
real option theory
redlining
regional banking pacts
Regulation D
Regulation K
Regulation U
reinsurance
reintermediation
repackaging
reserve assets
reserve base
Resolution Trust Corporation
retail bank
reversionary bonus
revolving credit
revolving underwriting facility
risk asset system
risk-based premium
risk package
risk pooling
run on a bank
secondary bank
secondary banking crisis
secondary capital
secondary mortgage market
Securities and Exchange Commission
sight deposit
silver ring
sleeping economy
smart card
social conscience fund
Society for Worldwide Interbank
    Financial Telecommunications
soft commission
soft dollar services
sogo bank
special bracket firm

Statutory Reserve Deposit
stress test
syndicated loan
systemic risk
terminal bonus
thrift
till money
time deposit
tontine
town clearing
trade bill
trade credit
traded option
traveller's cheque
trigger mechanism
trust fund
Truth in Lending Act 1968
twenty-four-hour trading
two-dollar broker
umbrella fund
unbundling
underground banking
underwriter
unit banking
unitization
unit trust
universal banking
vault cash
venture capital
'volatility industry'
warehouse receipt
whole life insurance
wholesale bank
window dressing
World Bank

G3 *Corporate finance and governance*

adjustable rate mortgage
black knight
Cadbury code of corporate governance
corporate finance
corporate governance
endowment mortgage
'financial engineering'
financial leverage ratio
financial policy
fronting loan
giro
green pound
Greenbury Code
greenmail
grey knight
high-leveraged takeover
leveraged management buyout
macaroni defence

management buyout
merger
merger arbitrage
model company management
model institutional investor
Myners Committee
off-balance-sheet financing
paradox of debt
pecking-order theory
poison pill
pyramiding
remuneration committee
reverse takeover
shadow director
share support operation
shell operation
sleeping beauty
social responsiveness of corporations
stock repurchase
sweetener
takeover
unbundling
value discrepancy hypothesis
vendor finance
white knight
white squire
zombie

H Public economics

H0 *General*

contract compliance
credit rating
David Hume Institute
debt illusion
Institute for Fiscal Studies
laissez-faire
logrolling
median voter theorem
new institutional economics
public economics
public finance
public sector balance sheet
social welfare
social welfare function
voting procedures
voucher system
user charge

H1 *Structure and scope of government*

administrative costs of regulation
Bureau of Economic Analysis
Bureau of the Budget
Chancellor of the Exchequer

Commodity Futures Trading
   Commission
Comptroller of the Currency
Consolidated Fund
Council of Economic Advisers
crisis management
European Co-operation
   Administration
General Accounting Office
General Household Survey
government intervention
government role
Internal Revenue Service
minimal state
Office of Management and Budget
public sector
quadrid
Star Chamber
subsidiarity
treasury
US Trade Representative

H2 *Taxation and subsidies*

ability to pay
abortive benefits
absolute tax incidence
Accelerated Cost Recovery System
accelerated depreciation
additionality
administrative cost
advance corporation tax
ad valorem tax
announcement burden of a tax
assistance-in-kind
average tax rate
basic relief
benefit approach to taxation
benefit tax
blue return
bracket creep
budgetary policy
budget incidence
buoyant tax
cadastral survey
canons of taxation
capital gains tax
capital income tax
capital tax
capitalization effect of a tax
capital transfer tax
carbon tax
carry-back, carry-forward system
cash transfer
categorical grant
clear income

Colbertism
commodity tax
community charge
consumption tax
corporate income tax
corporation income tax
corporation tax
corrective subsidy
corrective tax
council tax
cumulative multistage cascade system
daisy-chain scheme
Dalton improving tax reform
deemed tax
deficiency payment
dependency culture
differential tax incidence
direct and indirect taxation
direct–indirect taxes ratio
disconnective taxation
disincentive effect
disposable income
distortionary tax
double taxation of savings
double-taxation relief
effective tax rate
excess burden of a tax
excise duty
expenditure tax
export subsidy
factor tax
Farm Credit System
fiscal approximation
fiscal crisis
fiscal dividend
fiscal union
flat rate tax
forced labour
foreign aid
forfait system
formal indexation
general sales tax
gifts tax
goal system
government intervention
graduated income tax
graduate tax
hybrid income tax
hypothecation
implicit marginal income
impost
imputed income
incentive effect
income support
income-splitting system

income tax
individual income tax
inflation tax
inheritance tax
in-kind transfer
interest equalization tax
intergenerational equity
inter-nation equity
Islamic fiscal policy
Japanese tax system
Laffer curve
leaky bucket
Lindahl price
locked-in effect
long-term income averaging
lump-sum tax
marginal employment subsidy
marginal tax rate
marriage allowance
Model Tax Convention
multistage tax
national insurance contribution
negative income tax
nominal tax rate
non-standard tax relief
optimal taxation
optimum income tax
PAYE
payroll tax
pension
per-unit tax
petroleum revenue tax
Pigovian subsidy
Pigovian tax
policy harmonization
poll tax
pollution charge
pollution tax
poverty trap
presumptive tax
progressive tax
property tax
property tax capitalization
proportional tax
Proposition 13
Provisional Collection of Taxes Act
purchase tax
Ramsey taxes
real property tax
regional employment premium
regressive tax
renter illusion
revalorization
revenue
revenue neutral

Ricardian equivalence theorem
Rooker–Wise Amendment
sacrifice theory
sales tax
schedular tax
sector adjustment lending
Selective Employment Tax
shifting of taxes
Shoup Mission
single-tax movement
sin tax
social security
Social Security Act 1935
specific duty
stamp duty
stealth tax
strategic tax planning
subsidy
taxable capacity
taxable income
taxation
tax avoidance
tax base
tax buoyancy
tax burden
tax capitalization
tax credit
tax effort
tax elasticity
tax erosion
tax evasion
Tax Exempt Special Savings Account
tax expenditure
tax farming
Tax Freedom Day
tax harmonization
tax haven
tax incidence
tax reform
Tax Reform Act 1986
tax revenue
tax smoothing
tax structure
tax threshold
tax unit
tax wedge
1040 ('ten forty')
Tobin tax
turnover tax
UK taxation
unit tax
value-added tax
vertical equity
wage subsidy
wealth tax

withholding tax
zakat
zero-rated good

H3 *Fiscal policies and the behaviour of economic agents*

active fiscal policy
automatic stabilizer
Cambridge Economic Policy Group
decelerator
demand management
disincentive effect
fiscal crisis
fiscal drag
fiscal illusion
fiscal indicators
fiscalist
fiscal mobility
fiscal neutrality
fiscal policy
fiscal rectitude
fiscal stance
fiscal year
forced saving
grants economics
Private Finance Initiative
social credit
social dividend scheme
tax competition
tight fiscal policy

H4 *Publicly provided goods*

club good
collective good
infrastructure
Lindahl equilibrium
Lindahl price
local public good
market failure
merit bad
merit good
merit want
postcode lottery
productive capital
public commodities problem
public good
pure public good
social capital
social wants
spatial benefit limitation
theory of clubs

H5 *National government expenditures and related policies*

above the line

Aid and Trade Provisions
Appropriation Bill
Australian Loan Council
Autumn Statement
budget cutting
budget incidence
Budget Resolution
budget year
cash limit
compensatory finance
cost-effectiveness analysis
earmarking
functional financing
incentive contract
Medium-term Financial Strategy
neutral budget
peace dividend
pork barrel legislation
public expenditure
public expenditure control
Public Expenditure Survey Committee
public spending ratio
social spending
specific egalitarianism
trust fund
Wagner's law

H6 *National budget, deficit and debt*

actual budget
aggregate demand
balanced budget
below the line
Congressional Budget and Impound-
    ment Control Act 1974
Consolidated Fund standing services
dedicated budget
deficit financing
external debt
Financial Statement and Budget
    Report
full-employment budget
funding
funding gap
general fund
general government net worth
generational accounting
Gramm–Rudman–Hollings Act
gross federal debt
high employment surplus
inflation-adjusted deficit
internal debt
line item veto
monetization
national debt
Omnibus Budget Reconciliation Act

labour
labour compact
labour market
labour power
labour process theory
productive labour
proletariat
relational capital
search cost
socially necessary labour time
surplus value

J1 Demographic economics

ageing population
baby-boom period
baby-bust generation
carrying capacity
chain migration
circular migration
closed population
Consolidated Metropolitan Statistical
  Area
crude population rate
de facto population
de jure population
demographic accounting
demographic transition
demography
demometrics
dependency ratio
Dinks
economic refugee
empty nester
GLAM
grey belt
grey society
immigration
Metropolitan Statistical Area
migration
natural increase
non-employment
open population
optimum population
Pippy
population
population census
population density
population explosion
population policy
Primary Metropolitan Statistical Area
rank size rule
third age
threshold population
total fertility rate
tweenies/tweenagers

yuppie, yuppy
zero population growth

J2 Time allocation, work behaviour and employment determination

absenteeism
activity rate
additional-worker hypothesis
alienated work
annualized-hours system
apprenticeship
blue-collar worker
casualization
central occupation
community programme
Comprehensive Employment and
  Training Act 1973
crowding hypothesis
current population survey
demarcation
discouraged workers hypothesis
early retirement scheme
employee ratios
employment
employment contract
employment function
employment rate
ergonomics
featherbedding
flexible working-time schemes
gender division of labour
general training
homework
household work
industrial training grant
International Standard Classification
  of Occupations
involuntary employment
island
job evaluation
job security
job sharing
labour cost
labour force
labour force participation rate
labour market intermittency
labour's share of national income
labour supply
last-in, first-out
learning-by-helping
leisure
lump of labour fallacy
manpower forecasting
manpower policy
marginal product of labour

migrant labour
moonlighting
networker
New Deal
occupation
occupational licensing
off-the-job training
on-the-job training
optimal work effort
overtime
permanent employment
personnel economics
prime age worker
profession
public service employment
public works
regional employment premium
replacement labour force
retirement age
retrophobia
rotten kid theorem
screening
self-employment
sexual division of labour
sheltered employment
short-time working
Spanish customs/practices
special employment measures
specific training
sweated trade
sweetheart contract
telecommuting
tenure profile
time budget survey
underemployment
unfair labour practice
volume ratio
Vredeling directive
white-collar worker
work classification
workfare
working hours
working-time regime

J3 *Wages, compensation and labour costs*

access differential
age–earnings profile
annualized-hours system
backward-bending labour supply curve
bargaining theory of wages
basic wage
check-off provision
classical classical fallacy
comparable worth
compensating wage differential

cost of living adjustment
cost of living index
earnings
efficiency wage
Employee Stock Ownership Plan
employment contract
equalizing wage differential
Equal Pay Act 1963 (USA)
Equal Pay Act 1970 (UK)
Equal Pay Directive
executive stock option
Fair Wages Resolution
fat cat
final salary pension
fringe benefits
going rate
golden handcuffs
golden handshake
golden hello
golden parachute
golden rate
Greenbury Code
hedonic wages
hierarchy theory
high net worth individual
hold-out
incentive pay scheme
income differential
income drawdown scheme
insider wage setting
international wage levels
iron law of wages
job lock
just wage
key rate
Lassalle's law of wages
living wage
low pay
marginal employment subsidy
marginal productivity theory
margins
minimum supply price of labour
minimum wage
National Board for Prices and Incomes
New Earnings Survey
non-pecuniary returns
Oaxaca wage decomposition
outsider wage setting
over-award payment
parasitic industry or trade
pattern settlement
pay performance sensitivity
pension
performance-related pay

piece rate
piecework system
premium pay
productivity bargaining
profit-related pay
quasi-fixed factor
real wages
regional wage bargaining
regular labour
remuneration committee
reservation wage
screening
seniority principle
share economy
shirking model
shunto
sliding scale
spillover effect
staggered wage contract
statutory minimum wage rate
threat effect
time rate
time span
transaction bonus
treat effect
truck
union wage policy
unpaid work
variable capital
wage contour
wage curve
wage differentials
wage diffusion
wage drift
wage flexibility
wage gap
wage insurance
wage mobility
wage rigidity
wage round
wages
Wages Act 1986
wage subsidy
wage–tenure profile
wage theory
wage unit

J4 *Particular labour markets*

cab rank rule
domestic labour
dual labour market
external labour market
football transfer system
implicit contract theory

internal labour market
island
job cluster
labour market
local labour market
market segmentation
non-competing group
Occupational segregation
primary labour market
secondary labour market
segmented labour market theory
Standard Metropolitan Statistical
    Area
Standard Statistical Metropolitan
    Area
toll model

J5 *Labour management relations: trade unions and collective bargaining*

Advisory, Conciliation and
    Arbitration Service
AFL–CIO
agency shop
arbitration
at-will employment contract
autogestion
bargaining
bargaining unit
BDI
blackleg
Blue Book
Boulwareism
boycott
Bridlington rules
Bullock Committee
Central Arbitration Committee
Certification Officer
Churitsuroren
closed shop
collective bargaining
Combination Acts
company union
countervailing power
craft union
demarcation
Domei
Donovan Commission (UK)
economic specificity
employer–employee bargaining
employers' association
Employment Act 1980
Employment Act 1982
Employment Act 1988
Employment Appeal Tribunal

Employment Relations Act 1999
English disease
enterprise union
free rider
general strike
general union
industrial action
industrial dispute
industrial muscle
industrial relations
industrial union
International Miners' Organization
international union
international union federation
invisible handshake
job control unionism
job hopping
Keidanven
Landrum–Griffin Act 1959
local union
lockout
Luddite
National Labor Relations Board
Nikkeiren
Norris–La Guardia Act 1932
open shop
parallel plants
pendulum arbitration
picketing
protective labour legislation
quality circle
Rengo
right-to-work state
runaway shop
secondary action
Shinsanbetsu
shop steward
single-union deal
social contract
Sohyo
spillover effect
strike
strike-free deal
strike replacement legislation
Taft–Hartley Act 1947
team briefing
threat effect
trade union
Trade Union Act 1984
Trade Union Reform and Employment
    Rights Act 1993
Trade Unions and Labour Relations
    Act 1974
unionization

Union of National Economic
    Associations in Japan
union shop
union threat model
union wage effect
union wage policy
US labor union
wages council
Wagner Act 1935
yellow dog contract

J6 Mobility, unemployment and vacancies

cyclical unemployment
discomfort index
discouraged workers hypothesis
disguised unemployment
dole bludger
downsizing
early retirement scheme
efficient job mobility
frictional unemployment
hidden unemployment
hysteresis
internal search
involuntary employment
job acceptance schedule
job centre
job destruction
job displacement
job generation
job search
job seeker's allowance
job separation
labour market policy
labour market rigidities
matching
migration-fed unemployment
mobility of labour
mobility status
motility
natural rate of unemployment
non-employment
occupational mobility
outplacement agency
private cost of unemployment
productivity shock
quit rate
reserve army of labour
scarring
search unemployment
seasonal unemployment
social cost of unemployment
structural unemployment
unemployment
unemployment causes

unemployment compensation
unemployment spell
unemployment statistics
unemployment trap
voluntary unemployment
workfare
work sharing

J7 *Discrimination*

affirmative action
ageism
Civil Rights Act 1964
contract compliance
crowding hypothesis
discrimination
equality of opportunity
Equal Opportunities Commission
Equal Pay Act 1963 (USA)
Equal Pay Act 1970 (UK)
Equal Pay Directive
exploitation
horizontal discrimination
market discrimination coefficient
Oaxaca wage decomposition
positive discrimination
post-entry discrimination
pre-entry discrimination
racial discrimination
reverse discrimination
Sex Discrimination Acts 1975, 1986
sexual discrimination
sexual division of labour

K   Law and economics

K0 *General*

aleatory contract
consideration
contracting
economics of law
incomplete contract
insolvency
sequestration
warranty

K2 *Regulation and business law*

bankruptcy
blue-sky laws
Brady Commission
Building Societies Act 1986
Competitive Equality Banking Act
   1987
Consumer Credit Act 1974
consumer protection legislation

Depository Institutions Deregulation
   and Monetary Control Act 1980
deregulation
droit de suite
Financial Services Act 1986
floor price
freezing assets/an account
Garn St Germain Depository Institutions Act 1982
Glass–Steagall Act 1993
gold plating
grandfather clause
Hunt Commission
information disclosure
International Banking Act 1978
limited partnership
occupational licensing
ownership structure
public interest theory
recognized professional body
self-regulation
self-regulatory organization
Uniform Commercial Code
Walsh–Healy Act 1936

K4 *Legal procedure, the legal system and illegal behaviour*

corruption
economic crime
economics of crime
fraud
identity theft
laundering money
loanshark
long fraud
moonlight economy
narcodollars
shadow economy
underground economy
unreported sector

L   Industrial organisation

L0 *General*

basic industry
chaebol
commanding heights
Confederation of British Industry
cottage industry
diversification
Dutch disease
filière concept
footloose industry
Fortune 500
industrial organization

industry
industry cluster
infant industry
input–output analysis
locked-in industry
minimum list heading
natural monopoly
new institutional economics
non-basic industry
parasitic industry or trade
patrimonial industry
runaway industry
shadow economy
specialization
Standard Industrial Classification
structure–conduct–performance model
three-digit industry
two-digit industry
value subtractor
voucher privatization

L1 Market structure, firm strategy and market performance

aggregate concentration
anticipatory pricing
artificial barrier to entry
asymmetric information
atomistic competition
barometric firm leadership
barrier to entry
barrier to exit
Bertrand duopoly model
bilateral monopoly
branding
cartel
competition
competitive fringe
competitive process
concentration
concentration ratio
conglomerate merger
contestable markets thesis
cookie jar accounting
core firm
cost leader
countervailing power
Cournot's duopoly model
cross-subsidization
deconcentration
destructive competition
differentiation
divestment
dominant firm
dominant strategy
duopoly

economic planning
evolutionary theory of the firm
excess capacity theorem
forward integration
full-set industrial structure
growth theory of the firm
Herfindahl–Hirschman index
horizontal integration
imperfect competition
information agreement
interlinked transaction
keiretsu
kinked demand curve
market concentration
market forces
market share
market structure
monopolistic competition
monopoly
monopoly power
N-firm concentration ratio
oligopoly
oligopsony
orderly market agreement
parallel plants
peak-load pricing
perfect competition
periphery firm
pink economy
price twist
price war
product compatibility
product differentiation
pure competition
pure monopoly
pyramiding
reaction function
regrating
relative concentration
rent seeking
resale price maintenance
restrictive practice
reverse takeover
signal jamming
sophisticated leader
Stackelberg model
swing producer
synergy
takeover
tit-for-tat strategy
vertical discrimination
vertical expansion
vertical integration
vertical merger
workable competition

L2 *Firm objectives, organisation and behaviour*

agency theory
basing point pricing
behavioural economics
bucket shop
Bullock Committee
call centre
capitalist imperialism
closely held corporation
collaborative production
collusion
contracting out
co-operative
corporatism
corporate veil
crisis management
customize
dot com company
downstream firm
firm
firm consumption
firm-specific asset
flexible firm
Gibrat's law
H-form
hierarchical decomposition principle
holding company
industrial democracy
infraco
internalization theory
internal market
intrapreneur
joint equity venture company
joint stock company
joint venture
Lerner index
limited company
listed company
managerial models of the firm
managerial utility function
    maximization
marginal firm
market socialism
megacorp
M-form
monopoly capitalism
multinational corporation
objectives of firms
optimum firm
organization theory
partnership
price taking
private enterprise

profit maximization
public utility
real assets
restrictive practice
sales maximization
satisficing
second-degree price discrimination
shell company
small firm
sogo shosha
sole proprietor
stockholder diffusion
subsidiary
survivor firm
theory of the firm
transfer pricing
transnational corporation
U-form
upstream firm
vertical formation
workers' participation
X-form
zaibatsu

L3 *Non-profit organisations and public enterprise*

altruism
com-dev company
contracting out
cross-subsidization
direct labour organization
directly unproductive profit-seeking
    activities
economics of religion
Employment Institute
government procurement practice
non-profit enterprise
public enterprise
public interest company
public pricing
public sector
public utility
quasi-autonomous non-governmental
    organization
quasi-market
rate of return regulation
social ownership
Tennessee Valley Authority
test rate of discount

L4 *Anti-trust policy*

anti-competitive practices
antitrust
Australian Industries Preservation
    Acts 1906–50

Celler–Kefauver Antimerger Act 1950
Clayton Act 1914
Competition Commission
competition policy
Consumer Advisory Council
deconcentration
exclusive dealing
Federal Cartel Office
information agreement
interlocking directorship
Monopolies and Mergers Commission
multimarket contact
Office of Fair Trading
Robinson–Patman Act 1936
Section 20 subsidiary
Sherman Act 1890
tying
tying contract

L5 *Regulation and industrial policy*

administrative costs of regulation
Averch–Johnson effect
CAT standard
ceiling price
Colbertism
constrained market pricing
controlled market
Davignon Plan
deregulation
dirigisme
evolutionary theory of the firm
Federal Trade Commission
Federal Trade Commission Act 1914
government intervention
industrial policy
Industrial Reorganization Corporation
Interstate Commerce Commission
Jones Act 1920
Ministry of International Trade and
    Industry
National Enterprise Board
nationalization
nationalized industry
Navigation Acts
old staples
output floor regulation
price cap regulation
price floor
price stabilization
price twist
privatization
rate of return regulation
red tape
regulated firm
regulation

regulatory agency
regulatory capture
Saudi-ization
self-regulation
self-regulatory organization
state regulation
sunset clause

L6 *Industry studies: manufacturing*

badge engineering
batch production
brown good
Census of Manufactures
de-industrialization
Fordism
heavy industry
high-technology industry
in-bond manufacturing
Kaldor's laws
light industry
old staples
sunbelt
sunrise industry
white good

L7 *Industry studies: primary products and construction*

hard commodity

L8 *Industry studies: services*

bed and breakfast
bucket shop
Census of Retail Trade
distribution
e-commerce
e-tail company
service industry
tertiary sector
tied house
value-added network service

L9 *Industry studies: utilities and transport*

cabotage
International Air Travel Association
UNCTAD Liner Code
Warsaw Convention
zone of freedom

M Business administration and business economics; marketing; accounting

M0 *General*

business studies
corporate morality
cowboy economy

direct factor content
economic agent

M1 Business administration

business organization
chaebol
chartered company
chief executive officer
company
compulsory competitive tendering
conglomerate
corporation
cowboy
department
Edge Act Corporation
entrepreneur
equity joint venture
establishment
executive stock option
expense preference
expert system
fat cat
going concern
golden share
interim management
interlocking directorship
latent entrepreneurship
limited partnership
management by objectives
managerial revolution
marzipan layer
Parkinson's law
Peter principle
scalar principle
stakeholder
Taylorism
treasury
whistleblower
zai teku

M2 Business economics

accounting profit
acid-test ratio
activity ratio
administered pricing
administrative cost
allocative efficiency
angel
asset stripping
asset sweating
bill
bond
bonding cost
bottom-line accounting
breakeven level of income

capacity charge
capital budgeting
capital consumption
capital value
cash budgeting
cash flow
circulating capital
commercial paper
cost gradient
costing margin
cost ratio
current assets
current liabilities
current operating profit
current purchasing power
current ratio
daisy-chain scheme
debt
Delphi method
designated competitive bidding
disintermediation
diversification discount
earnings
economy of size
escalator clause
funding gap
general competitive bidding
general fund
goodwill
high-yield financing
holding gain
hurdle rate of return
implicit cost
indexation
indirect cost recovery
information cost
insolvency
internal capital
internal rate of return
inventory
investment appraisal
investment fundamentals
last-in, first-out
margin of safety
market capitalization
mezzanine finance
net present value
net worth
output budgeting
overtrading
payback method
pecking-order theory
planning, programming, budgeting
profitability
proprietors' income

Q ratio
rate of return
reputation capital
required rental on capital
retained earnings
revenue
risk management
skimming
step cost
Tobin's Q
total revenue
trading on the equity
turnkey contract
undertrading
upcoding
user cost
value driver
value share
vendor finance
working capital
Z-score

M3 Marketing and advertising

above the line
advertising
below the line
branding
brand loyalty
brand stretching
cash positive
consumer sovereignty
countervailing power
differentiated good
differentiated marketing
direct sale
droit de suite
fair trading
franchise
inverse demand function
lifetime client value
loss leader
market share
market space
mixed bundling
product differentiation
product market
pure bundling
pyramid selling
second-degree price discrimination
second-generation product
skimming
third-degree price discrimination
tweenies/tweenagers
tying contract
upselling

M4 Accounting

account
accounting
accounting costs
accounting cycle
accounting identity
accounting profit
accrual accounting
accrued expense
accrued income
acid-test ratio
activity ratio
audit market
balance sheet
book value
cash accounting
cash flow accounting
clean opinion
creative accounting
current cost accounting
current purchasing power
depreciation
deprival value
direct product profitability
discounted cash flow
discounting
double counting
double discounting
economic life
economic profit
environmental accounting
financial accounting
Financial Reporting Council
first-in, first-out
fraud
free cash flow
free depreciation
growth accounting
historic cost
inflation accounting
International Accounting Standards
    Committee
management accounting
matching function
money income
net worth
off-balance-sheet financing
paper profit
primary ratio
profit and loss account
profit centre
quick assets ratio
ratio analysis
replacement cost

sales ratios
Statements of Standard Accounting
    Practice
stock and flow concepts
stock–output ratio
stock ratios
tangible net worth
tangible wealth
true and fair view
user cost

N   Economic history

N0 General

agricultural household
chartism
climacteric
cliometrics
Cultural Revolution
Gerschenkron effect
goldilocks economy
Habakkuk thesis
hegemonic cycle
logistic cycle
mature economy
merchant capitalism
mineral-based economy
modern economy
new economic history
primitive economy
take-off

N1 Macroeconomics: growth and fluctuations

Barber boom
Chinese modernization drive
East Asian economic crisis
First Industrial Revolution
Lawson boom
Long Boom

N2 Financial markets and institutions

Bank Charter Act 1844
Banking School
bimetallism
Bullionist controversy
catching-up hypothesis
Currency School
gold shortage
Great Depression
Great Leap Forward
Marshall Plan
New Deal
Treasury view
Triffin paradox

N3 Labour, demography, education, income and wealth

bourgeoisie
Luddite

N4 Government, law and regulation

Colbertism
Corn Laws
feudalism
Navigation Acts
Poor Laws

N5 Agriculture, natural resources and extractive industries

collectivization of agriculture
Corn Laws

N6 Manufacturing and construction

Colbertism
industrial revolution
National Industrial Recovery Act 1933
proto-industrialization

N7 Transport, trade, energy and other services

Canal Age
Randall Commission

O   Economic development

O0 General

Aid and Trade Provisions
Brandt Commission
capitalist imperialism
Cohesion Fund
foreign aid
Fourth World
Gang of Four
grant-back clause
Jubilee 2000
less developed country
multilateral aid
new institutional economics
newly industrialized country
official development assistance
one-crop economy
Pacific Rim
Pearson Report
South African Development
    Co-ordination Committee
stages theory
take-off
Third World
United Nations Conference on Trade
    and Development

world systems perspective

O1 *Economic development*

bilateral aid
blocked development
dependency theory
development
development economics
falling rate of profit
First Development Decade
industrialization
market-conforming chain of causation
microcredit
money-order economy
trickle-down theory

O2 *Development, planning and policy*

alleviation
development planning
do-able
economic planning
factor-augmenting technical progress
import substitution
Lewis–Fei–Ranis model
Mahalanobis model
Marshall Plan
patrimonial industry
sustainable development
tied aid
two-gap development model
Umbrella Group
United Nations Development
    Programme
United Nations Industrial
    Development Organization

O3 *Technological change*

appropriate technology
best available technology
breakthrough
capital-augmenting technical progress
creative destruction
diffusion rate
disembodied technical progress
epidemic model
footloose knowledge
Habakkuk thesis
Harrod neutral
heterogeneous agent model
Hicks neutral
high-technology industry
induced technical progress
inducement mechanism
information technology
innovation

innovation possibility frontier
intellectual property
invention
labour-augmenting technical progress
learning curve
learning-by-doing
Leontief technology
locked-in knowledge
machinery question
mature economy
neutral technical progress
patent
research and development
Ricardo effect
Solow neutral
technical change
technological rent
wave train
World Intellectual Property
    Organization

O4 *Economic growth and aggregate productivity*

antagonistic growth
balanced growth
big push
Buddhist economics
capital deepening
catching-up hypothesis
Club of Rome
debt-led growth
Denison residual
development
disequilibrium growth theory
economic growth
embodied technical progress
endogenous growth theory
engine of growth
exogenous growth model
golden age
golden rule
growth accounting
Harrod–Domar model
immiserizing growth
Kaldor's laws
Kuznets curve
locomotive effect
Long Boom
malleable capital
natural rate of growth
negative feedback
Petty's law
positive feedback
post-neoclassical endogenous growth
    theory

productive potential
productivity
real growth
S-curve
Selective Employment Tax
Solow residual
spread effect
staple theory of growth
steady state growth
structural adjustment policy
sustainable economic growth rate
turnpike theorem
U hypothesis
Verdoorn's law
war dividend
warranted rate of growth
zero growth

P   Economic systems

P0   *General*

advanced organic economy
altruism
anarchism
Asiatic mode of production
autarky
barter economy
binary economy
bioeconomics
black economy
blue economy
bootblack economy
branch economy
cash economy
cashless society
cash nexus
Celtic tiger
centre–periphery system
closed economy
common ownership
communal economy
commune
community
consumer society
convergence hypothesis
core economy
cornucopia
corporate state
corporatism
countervailing power
critical economy
decentralized market economy
dependent economy
disembedded economy
drug economy

dual economy
dystopia
East Asian economic crisis
economic devolution
economic institution
economic system
economic transition
economic underpinning
economy
enclave economy
enterprise culture
extralegal property
first best economy
fiscal military state
formal economy
forms of integration
goldilocks economy
hansom cab economy
high-consumption society
indecomposability
industrial society
informal economy
interdependent economy
leisure class
limited market liberalization
little dragons
mesoeconomy
military–industrial complex
mineral-based economy
money-order economy
moonlight economy
networking economy
new economy
new industrial state
new institutional economics
non-market sector
old economy
open economy
permanent arms economy
post-industrial society
property rights
protean economy
regular economy
tertiary sector
trade regime
two-speed economy
underground economy
unreported sector
villa economy
Walras exchange economy
weightless economy

P1   *Capitalist systems*

Anglo-Saxon capitalism
bubble economy

capitalism
creative destruction
department
economic programming
financial economy
First World
Fordism
German capitalism
high-consumption society
immiseration
industrial capitalism
Japanese capitalism
late capitalism
law of value
lemonade stand capitalism
market economy
merchant capitalism
monopoly capitalism
peripheral capitalism
personal capitalism
popular capitalism
price system
private enterprise system
private sector
profit motive
psychological economy
pure credit economy
semi-colonial country

P2 *Socialist systems*

accession tax
centrally planned economy
Christian socialism
communism
economic calculation
economic methods
economic planning
Fabian Society
first economy
Great Leap Forward
gross social product
guild socialism
Japanese socialism
Marxian economics
monopoly capitalism
New Economic Policy
nomenklatura
Second World
socialism
Soviet-type economy
state capitalism
state monopoly capitalism
storming
supply-side socialism
System of Material Product Balances

P3 *Socialist institutions*

command economy
five-year plan
foreign trade organization
Gosplan
Gossnab
International Bank for Economic
    Co-operation
International Investment Bank
kibbutz
Soviet Material Product System
state enterprise

P4 *Other economic institutions*

communitarianism
estate economy
Euroland
Gandhian economics
gang system economy
holism
indicative planning
individualism
market socialism
mixed economy
modern economy
Mont Pelerin Society
negotiated co-ordination
New Economic Mechanism
one country, two systems
perestroika
production asymmetry
queuing system
revenue economy
second economy
self-sufficient economy
share economy
shortage economy
siege economy
social liberalism
social market economy
social political economy
spaceman economy
state trading organization
syndicalism
systemism
transition economy
utopia
warehouse economy

Q Agricultural and natural resource economics

Q0 *General*

anthropogenic climate impact
bioeconomics

Brundtland Report
choke price
common access resources
common pool resources
common property resources
common resource problem
contemporaneous externality
contingent valuation
cultivated capital
dose–response function
ecodevelopment valuation
ecological capital
ecological footprint
environmental determinism
environmental issues
externality
factor endowment
grandfathering
greenhouse effect
hazard
Kyoto Summit
land economy
landownership
marginal cost of abatement
marginal private damage
marginal social cost
marginal social damage
marketable discharge permit
market failure
natural economy
natural resources
neighbourhood effect
organic premium
ownership structure
primary commodity prices
real assets
relational wealth
rent
resource monotonicity
sequential externality
stock externality
tradable discharge permit
Tragedy of the Commons
Umbrella Group
undepletable externality
United Nations Framework
    Convention on Climate Change

Q1 *Agriculture*

adjustment gap
agribusiness
Agricultural Adjustment Act 1933
agricultural policy
cash crop
Commodity Credit Corporation

Common Agricultural Policy
deficiency payment
Farm Credit System
Food and Agriculture Organization
food chain
green revolution
hog cycle
intervention price
primary product
producer subsidy equivalent
set aside
share fisherman
sharecropper
soft commodity
supply control
target price
tied cottage
white revolution

Q2 *Renewable resources and conservation: environmental management*

abundance
ambient standard
bid rent
bid vehicle
bioeconomics
bubble policy
carbon sequestration
carbon sink
carbon tax
Clean Air Act Amendments 1970
Coase theorem
command and control regulation
crisis management
effluent fee
emission charge
emission fee
emission reductions banking
Environmental Protection Agency
environmental tax
exploitation
flex mex
green conditionality
greenfield
integrated pollution control
optimal rate of pollution
pollution charge
pollution control
pollution tax
primary standard
renewable resource
resource economics
restoration cost
secondary standard
sustainability

R5 ***Regional government analysis***

assisted area
backwash effect
enterprise zone
European Regional Development Fund
grey area
host region
Local Enterprise Agency
new town
north–south gap

regional policy
regional selective assistance
Thomson Report
top-down linkage model

Z Other topics

Z1 ***Cultural economics***

cultural economics